# Ellicott's

## COMMENTARY
## ON THE
## WHOLE BIBLE

A VERSE BY VERSE
EXPLANATION

EDITED BY
CHARLES JOHN ELLICOTT

VOLUME III

I Kings —— Esther

WIPF & STOCK · Eugene, Oregon

Wipf and Stock Publishers
199 W 8th Ave, Suite 3
Eugene, OR 97401

Ellicott's Commentary on the Whole Bible Volume III
I Kings - Esther
By Ellicott, Charles J.
ISBN 13: 978-1-4982-0138-4
Publication date 7/28/2016
Previously published by Cassell, 1897

This is a reprint of the 1959 Zondervan edition. Originally published in 1897 by Cassell as A Bible Commentary for English Readers.

## I. Kings
BY
THE RIGHT REV. ALFRED BARRY, D.D.

## II. Kings
BY
THE REV. C. J. BALL, M.A.,
*Late Chaplain of Lincoln's Inn.*

## I. Chronicles
BY
THE REV. C. J. BALL, M.A.

## II. Chronicles
BY
THE REV. C. J. BALL, M.A.

## Ezra
BY
THE REV. W. B. POPE, D.D.

## Nehemiah
BY
THE REV. W. B. POPE, D.D.

## Esther
BY
THE REV. R. SINKER, B.D.

# CONTENTS

| | PAGE |
|---|---|
| INTRODUCTION TO THE BOOKS OF THE KINGS | 1 |
| I. KINGS | 8 |
| II. KINGS | 101 |
| INTRODUCTION TO THE BOOKS OF THE CHRONICLES | 209 |
| I. CHRONICLES | 215 |
| II. CHRONICLES | 337 |
| GENERAL INTRODUCTION TO EZRA AND NEHEMIAH | 457 |
| INTRODUCTION TO EZRA | 460 |
| EZRA | 461 |
| INTRODUCTION TO NEHEMIAH | 483 |
| NEHEMIAH | 484 |
| INTRODUCTION TO ESTHER | 511 |
| ESTHER | 514 |

# THE FIRST BOOK OF THE KINGS

# INTRODUCTION
## TO
# THE BOOKS OF THE KINGS*

**I. Unity of the Book, and Relation to the Earlier Books.**—The history of the kings (*Sépher Melachim*) is really but one book. The division into two books, which has no existence in the old Hebrew canon, and has been borrowed by us from the LXX. and Vulgate, is a purely arbitrary division, not even corresponding to any marked epoch in the history. It may have been made merely for convenience of use and reference. It may have been simply artificial; for there is a curious note in St. Jerome's account of the arrangement of the Hebrew Canon in twenty-two books, according with the letters of the Hebrew alphabet, in which he remarks that to the five double letters corresponded five double books, of which the Book of Kings is one. In any case it is to be disregarded, and the two books treated as having a perfect unity of idea and authorship.

In the LXX., followed in this by the Vulgate, the Books of Samuel are called the "First and Second Books of the Kings," and our Books of Kings are made the Third and Fourth. It has been supposed that this ancient alteration of the Hebrew titles is intended to point to a common authorship. Some have gone so far as to make the whole history from Judges to Kings one unbroken compilation, in which the present divisions are but accidental; and in confirmation of this view it has been noticed that all the successive books open with the simple conjunction "And" (in our version, "Now"), that the various books contain common phrases and terms of expression, and that even in the Book of Judges (chaps. xvii. 6, xviii. 1, xix. 1) we find allusions to the future monarchy of Israel. Now these indications certainly show that the successive books were regarded as forming part of one history, and that the compilers had probably much the same ancient sources of information before them. Possibly they may also imply the agency of what we should call an editor, at the time of the inclusion of the books in the Canon. But they cannot argue anything as to contemporaneous compilation. The connection in particular of the Books of Samuel and Kings is easily accounted for without any such supposition, by the consideration that, in actual fact, these books do include the whole history of the Israelitish monarchy. Against the notion of common authorship we must set the marked difference of language and character, which can hardly escape the most careless reader. Even in respect of the language of the books, there seems little doubt that the Hebrew of the Books of Samuel belongs to an earlier and purer age. But looking to the whole style and narrative, we observe that the Books of Kings have far more of an official and annalistic character; they mark dates and epochs, and quote authorities; they include the story of some 430 years in the same space which in the earlier books is devoted to about a century. Except in the sections which deal with the lives of Elijah and Elisha, and include descriptions of the characters of Ahab and Jezebel, they have far less freedom of style, less graphic vividness and beauty, and less of moral and spiritual force than the earlier books. There is (for example) no character in them which stands out with the living personality of David, or even of Saul; unless perhaps the characters of the two great prophets may be excepted. The successive kings are viewed as kings, rather than as men. Many of them are to us little more than names marking epochs. Even where they are drawn in some detail, as in the case of Solomon, Jehoshaphat, Jehu, Hezekiah, Josiah, the kingly character mostly predominates over the human individuality. It is impossible not to see that each of the two works has a marked internal unity of peculiar style and character, in which it differs from the other. By whomsoever they were compiled, they must be referred to different hands, and to different periods.

**II. Sources from which it was Drawn.**— While, however, the Books of Kings have been brought by one hand into their present form, they are manifestly a compilation from more ancient sources. This is, indeed, avowed in their constant appeal to extant documents. But it would be obvious, even without such appeal, from internal evidence—from the alternate accordance and discordance with them of the independent record contained in the Books of Chronicles; from the occurrence of expressions (as "unto this day," in 1 Kings viii. 8 and elsewhere) which could not belong to the time of compilation; and from the marked variety of style and treatment in the various parts of the history itself. The only sources to which they actually refer are "the book of the Acts of Solomon" (1 Kings xi. 41), and the "books of the Chronicles of the kings of Israel and of Judah." The former is expressly ascribed, in 2 Chron. ix. 29, to the authorship of Nathan the prophet, Ahijah the Shilonite, and Iddo the seer. The latter may have been most frequently drawn up by "the recorder" or chronicler, whom we find mentioned as a court official in the successive reigns (see 2 Sam. viii. 16; 1 Kings iv. 3; 2 Kings xviii. 18). But in many cases the office of annalist was undoubtedly discharged by the prophets; as, for example, by Shemaiah and Iddo for Rehoboam (2 Chron. xii. 15), by Iddo for Abijah (2 Chron. xiii., 22), by Jehu son of Hanani, for Jehoshaphat (2 Chron. xx. 34), by Isaiah for Uzziah (2 Chron. xxvi. 22). In the record of the reign of Hezekiah, the compiler of the Books of Kings has embodied, almost *verbatim*, the historical chapters appended to the earlier part of the Book of Isaiah (Isa. xxxvi.—xxxix.). It is, indeed, thought that the later

---

* While I alone am answerable for this Introduction, I have to acknowledge with gratitude some valuable criticisms and suggestions from my colleague in the work, the Rev. C. J. Ball, A.B.

name for Seer (*Chözeh*), which is altogether distinct from the earlier title (*Rôeh*) applied to Samuel (1 Sam. ix. 9, 11, &c.), was an official title, indicating a position of authority and service in the court. Among the duties of his office the work of the historian may have been sometimes included. Probably it is not by mere technical arrangement that the historical books were included among "the Prophets" in the Jewish division of the Old Testament.

But although these sources alone are distinctly indicated, we can hardly doubt that others were actually available. There were Temple archives, from which so much of the record of the Book of Chronicles appears to be drawn; and it is difficult not to suppose that from these much is taken of the almost technical account of the building and furniture of the Temple, and of the full and detailed history of its consecration. The records, again, of the careers of the prophets, especially of the great prophets Elijah and Elisha, bear the impress of a character wholly different from that of the more official parts of the history. The beauty and vividness of the style, and the spiritual force of the narrative, appear to indicate that they are taken from some personal biographies, probably produced in the Schools of the Prophets, and possibly handed down by oral tradition, before they were committed to writing. The story of Elijah at Carmel and at Horeb, and on the great day of his translation, the picture of Elisha in his intercourse with Naaman, in the house of the Shunammite, amidst the angel guards at Dothan, or in the prophetic foresight of his dying hour, could have come from no official records. In the Books of the Chronicles (see *Introduction* to Chronicles) we find repeated references to prophetic annals. It is hardly likely that a prophetic School of History would have omitted to dwell on the glorious history of the prophetic order. The supposition entertained by some critics, and enunciated with an almost intolerant positiveness, that the story of the great prophets is a half-imaginative composition of later growth, is contradicted by the very characteristics of the story itself—the unity and vividness of the characters depicted, the graphic touches of detail, and the solid realism of the whole narrative. Probably it would never have been entertained, except on the ground of *a priori* objection to all record of miracle.

III. **Date of its Compilation.**—While, however, these older materials of various kinds were employed, it is clear, from the general coherency of the narrative, the recurrence of fixed phrases and methods of treatment, and the characteristics of the style and language, that the books, as we at present have them, were put into form by one author. They may previously have passed through many hands, each compiler leaving his work to be dealt with by his successor. There may be a germ of truth in the confident assertions of the Biblical critics who describe the "old prophetic Book of Kings" as confidently as if they had collated it, and distinguish the contributions of the "Deuteronomist editor" as if they had seen him at work. But, as the book now stands, it is acknowledged by all that the style, the language, and some of the expressions used, refer it very plainly to the era of the Captivity. The curious notice, in the closing verses of the Second Book, of the release of Jehoiachin from prison by Evil-Merodach, the king of Babylon, in the thirty-seventh year of his captivity (unless, indeed, it be supposed, somewhat arbitrarily, to be an addition), may be taken, like the abrupt conclusion of the Acts of the Apostles, to indicate the actual date of the final composition of the books themselves.

**Tradition of Authorship.**—The old Jewish tradition, embodied in the Talmud, ascribing the book to the prophet Jeremiah, at least points unmistakably to its composition in this era. On the accuracy of this ascription itself the most careful criticism is still divided. The traditions of the Talmud vary very greatly in antiquity and value; and the strange character of some of the ascriptions of authorship of Scriptural books obliges us to receive all with reservation. Still they must have some *primâ facie* force of testimony, unless they be plainly contradicted by internal evidence. In this case, moreover, it cannot be doubted that the tradition has in its favour considerable probability, when we remember the great honour in which Jeremiah was held by the Chaldæan conquerors (see Jer. xxxix. 11—14, xl. 2—6), and the consequent facilities which he might have enjoyed for saving some of the records of the Temple before its destruction (illustrated by the curious legend of his preservation of the Ark and the Tabernacle in 2 Macc. ii. 1—6); when we consider how naturally he, the last of the prophets of the era of Israel's independence, would be led to preserve the record of its long probation; and when we trace his actual devotion to the work of the historian, as shown in the many historical chapters interwoven with his prophecy. To these considerations many critics add some notable similarities which they believe that they trace between these books and the Book of Jeremiah, not only in detailed points of the history, but in style and diction;* they note also the coincidence, with variations of detail, of Jer. lii. with the last chapter of the Second Book of Kings (which, however, would in itself only show that the compiler of the latter book had knowledge of the Book of Jeremiah); and dwell on the remarkable omission of all notice in the Book of Kings of the prophet Jeremiah, who played so important a part in the history, and who is expressly noticed more than once in the far briefer account in the Chronicles. (See 2 Chron. xxxv. 25, xxxvi. 12.)† These evidences are not conclusive; but, when we take them in conjunction with the old Jewish tradition, and the probabilities of the case, we cannot but conclude that there is at least some considerable ground for the theory of the authorship of Jeremiah, or perhaps of Baruch the scribe, to whom the written form of some part at least of the Book of Jeremiah (see Jer. xxxvi. 4, 32, xlv.) must be traced.

IV. **Its General Character and Purpose.**—The compiler, whoever he was, was evidently much more than a mere copyist. The very character of his work shows that he had in view throughout the great purpose which pervades the whole prophetic utterances—to bring out the Divine government over the covenanted people; to trace their sins and their repentance, God's punishments and His forgiveness; to draw forth, for the learning of the servants of God in all ages, the spiritual lessons taught by the voice of "God in history." To suppose that the carrying out of this didactic purpose is in the slightest degree incompatible with faithful accuracy in narration of facts, is to misunderstand the main principles of true historical composition, which alone make history something higher than the "old almanac" of the shallow epigrammatist. To study the

---

* See Canon Rawlinson's Introduction in the *Speaker's Commentary*, § 4.
† See, for example, Keil's Introduction, the article "KINGS" (by Bishop Lord A. Hervey), in the *Dictionary of the Bible*, and Canon Rawlinson's Introduction in the *Speaker's Commentary*.

# KINGS.

books themselves without discovering in them, again and again, evidences of historical and geographical accuracy, even in points of detail—traces of the incorporation of official documents and of the narratives of eye-witnesses—curious signs of independence, and yet of coincidence, in respect of the glimpses into Tyrian, Egyptian, Assyrian, Babylonian, and even Moabite history, which recent discoveries have given us—marks of a lofty and austere candour, not only disregarding the prejudices of patriotic vainglory, but even bringing out the better features of character in those whom it condemns—examples of a simple profoundness of insight into the causes underlying external history—might well seem to be impossible; unless we bring to the study some foregone conclusions as to the impossibility of the miraculous, in fact or in foresight, which are destructive of the historical character of the whole of Scripture. Still that the historian is a true prophet, teaching by examples, is obvious in every line of his history.

The evidence of this purpose is not to be found only or chiefly in the passages of grave reflection scattered through the books. Such are, for example, the constant references to the prohibited "high places," showing that in these he, by the light of subsequent events, saw a danger which escaped even the most earnest reformers of earlier times. (See 1 Kings iii. 3, xv. 14, xxii. 43, &c.) Such, again, is the significant notice (in 1 Kings xii. 15) of the judicial blindness of Rehoboam, as carrying out the appointed vengeance of the Lord on the apostasy of Solomon; the reflections on the sentences pronounced on the houses of Jeroboam and Baasha, and on the special sin of Ahab, which drew down similar destruction on the house of Omri (1 Kings xii. 30, xiii. 33, 34, xvi. 7, xxi. 25, 26); the emphatic reference to the mercy of God, giving to the kingdom of Israel a last deliverance and probation in the revival of power under Joash and Jeroboam II. (2 Kings xiii. 5, 6); above all, the solemn chapter of sad confession of God's righteous judgment, in the fall of that kingdom after many warnings and many acts of forgiveness (2 Kings xvii. 7—23), and the corresponding reference in the case of Judah to the unpardonable and ineradicable corruptions introduced by Manasseh, which even Josiah's reformation could not take away (2 Kings xxi. 10—15, xxiii. 26, 27, xxiv. 3, 4, 20). In all these there is a deep prophetic insight into the ways of God, not untinged by the sadness so characteristic of all the prophets (especially of Hosea and Jeremiah, the prophets of woe to Israel and to Judah), but yet convinced that the Judge of the whole earth must do right, and even resting with satisfaction on His righteous judgment.

But the whole tenor and construction of the history tell this story with even greater emphasis. On attentive study it will be seen to be not so much a continuous narrative, as a series of records of great epochs of historical significance, strung on a thin thread of mere annalistic sequence. Thus, (a) the First Book opens with a section of comparatively detailed narrative, full of lessons of practical instruction, describing the great reign of Solomon, and the revolution which avenged its apostasy and destroyed its glory (chaps. i.—xiv.). After this, (b) a period of at least forty years is dismissed in two chapters (chaps. xv., xvi.) with the briefest possible notice, only just sufficient to give connection to the general narrative. To this succeeds (c) the most magnificent section of the whole book (1 Kings xvii.—2 Kings xi.), unsurpassed in power in the historical books of the Old Testament, which, in the lives of the great prophets Elijah and Elisha, represents to us the great crisis of the Baal apostasy, the victorious struggle against it by the prophetic inspiration, supported by a special outburst of miraculous power, and the final vengeance which extirpated it, alike in Israel and in Judah. After this comes (d) an epoch of important historical events—first, of a marvellous revival of prosperity and power to Israel under Joash and Jeroboam II., to Judah under Joash, Amaziah, Uzziah; next, of a period of revolution, anarchy, and bloodshed, which ushered in the final destruction of the northern kingdom. But it was (as the prophetic writings of Amos and Hosea show us) an epoch in which no spiritual vitality showed itself through national prosperity or national disaster; and therefore it is compressed within six chapters (2 Kings xii.—xvii.) in which, moreover, whole reigns, like the long and prosperous reign of Jeroboam II., are all but a blank. (e) Similarly in the last epoch, when the kingdom of Judah alone survived, the two reigns of religious reformation—those of Hezekiah and Josiah—are given in graphic and detailed narrative, occupying five chapters (chaps. xviii.—xx., xxii., xxiii.), while the long reign of Manasseh, which, in its apostasy and corruption, filled up hopelessly the measure of national iniquity, is dismissed in a few verses (chap. xxi. 1—18), and the whole history of the last agony of Judah, after the death of Josiah, occupies little more than two chapters (chaps. xxiv., xxv.). It is clear from the very method of the historical narrative that the purpose of the book is mainly didactic. The writer dwells rather on the lessons of history than the mere record of facts; on typical characters of good and evil, which appeal to the humanity of all times, rather than on the social and political conditions of the nation which belonged only to his own age; on the solemn march of the righteous providence of God, rather than on the confused and multitudinous struggles of human wills. In other words, he discharges what is virtually the prophetic office—only that he declares the works, instead of the direct word, of God. In this lies the spiritual value of the book for us. In this characteristic view of all events, far more than of the miraculous element of the record, we find the distinctive characteristic of what we call "Sacred history."

V. **Illustrations from other Books.**—The study of the books, moreover, from this point of view is greatly helped by the illustration which they derive from comparison with other books of Holy Scripture, belonging to the same period of Jewish history.

**The Chronicles.**—It is, of course, obvious to compare them with the parallel record given in the Second Book of Chronicles. That record is of far later date. We cannot doubt that the Chronicler had the Books of Kings before him; for there are places in which he seems deliberately to pass over, or merely to glance at, what had been fully recorded there. But it is also clear that his work is, on the whole, independent; he evidently had and used the same ancient materials, and, besides these, other materials, especially the Temple records, and the prophetic annals, which he frequently cites; in passages of general coincidence there are constantly touches of variation, sometimes of apparent discrepancy; and in the history of the kingdom of Judah, to which he confines himself, there are many epochs in which he fills up generally what in our book is but a bare outline, or supplies special incidents which are there omitted. (See *Introduction to Chronicles*.) Considering the date and character of the two works, it is probably well to take the Book of Kings as the standard account, and so far accept the significance of the title of Παραλειπομένων ("things omitted"), given in the LXX. to the Chronicles, as to make them a commentary, an illustration, and a supplement of the older work. But each has its independent character and value. The Book of Kings has been called the prophetic record, the Book of Chronicles the priestly record, of the time. This would be a misleading antithesis, if it was taken to convey the notion of antagonism or even marked diversity of idea between the books, which any attentive study of both must dissipate. But it is so far true as this—that the Book of Kings, dealing so largely with the kingdom of Israel, naturally gives special prominence to the office and work of the older prophets, who ministered chiefly to that kingdom; while the Book of Chronicles, being almost exclusively the history of Judah, brings out the power of the priesthood and the royalty of David, which played so great a part—sometimes in union, sometimes in antagonism—in the spiritual history of the southern kingdom.

But besides this direct comparison of the two historical records, there is illustration no less valuable of the idea and purpose of the Books of Kings to be derived from other Scriptural books not properly historical, which, indeed, its narrative binds together in one continuous order of development.

**The Psalms.**—The illustration to be derived from the Psalms would be far more instructive, if we were not driven to rely mainly on internal evidence as to their date and occasion, and were not accordingly, in most cases, unable to fix these points with any certainty. But even with this drawback, the illustration is invaluable, as painting to us the inner life of Israel during the period of our history; for to this period a large portion of the Psalter must certainly be referred. There seems much probability that the first division of the Psalter (Pss. i.—xli.) took shape in the time of Solomon, for use in the Temple worship. In the later divisions many psalms are, with more or less authority, ascribed to Asaph, to Heman (and the sons of Korah), and to Ethan, the three chief musicians of David, and probably of Solomon also. Of these subsequent divisions it is at least not unlikely that some mark and illustrate the religious revivals of Jehoshaphat, Hezekiah, and Josiah. Nor is more particular reference altogether wanting. Two psalms (lxxii., cxxvii.) are ascribed to Solomon—the one, a picture of the glory and majesty of his kingdom; the other (one of "the Songs of Degrees"), ascribing to the Lord alone the blessings of earthly prosperity and happiness. Other psalms, especially among those ascribed to the sons of Korah, are of a national character—crying to God in national disaster (Ps. xliv.), thanking Him in the hour of triumph and deliverance (Pss. xlvi.—xlviii., lxxxv.), singing hymns at the marriage of the king (Ps. xlv.), or proclaiming the loveliness and gladness of the dwellings of the Lord of Hosts (Ps. lxxxiv.). One group (Pss. xci.—c.) has been thought by some to belong to the golden age of Hezekiah's glory and Isaiah's prophecy. The "great Hallel" (Pss. cxiii.—cxviii.), though found in the divisions of the Psalter belonging to the era after the Captivity, yet illustrates the festal worship of the people in the Temple of God: such psalms as Ps. cxxxvii. mark the sorrows of the Captivity by "the waters of Babylon." In all cases, the Psalms are the lyric expression of the inner life of the chosen people, and of the individual servants of God, underlying the simple narrative which our books supply. We must study them if we would catch the spirit which animates the letter of the historic record itself.

**The Sapiential Books.**—But plainer illustration is gained from books which can be more certainly referred to distinct periods in the history. Thus the golden age of the glory of Solomon is illustrated by consideration of the various books which may be called "Sapiential." The great Book of PROVERBS, both in its poetical and gnomic portions, tracing itself to him as the chief master of wisdom—perhaps much as the Psalter bears the name of David—is in its representation of wisdom the key at once to the true nature of the culture and glory of his age, and to the tendencies which, gaining the mastery, brought on its fall. The SONG OF SOLOMON—now by all the best authorities referred unhesitatingly to his age, probably to his hand—is full of the passion for beauty, the delight in nature, the sensibility to pure love, the knowledge of humanity marking both the character of the great king, and the culture of his time; yet is not without the tendency to rest on the visible and the sensual, in which was the germ of his voluptuous polygamy. The Book of JOB—which, whatever be the date of its original materials, is commonly referred to his time—certainly opens the great questions of Natural Religion, concerning man as man, which belong to an age searching after wisdom, and having contact with the thought and inquiry of races outside the covenant. The wonderful Book of ECCLESIASTES, to whatever period it is to be referred, in its depiction of a soul's tragedy shows no little insight into the character of him in whose person it speaks, as wearied out with the search after happiness in wisdom and in pleasure, in contemplation and in action, and coming back at last in despair to the simple command, "Fear God, and keep His commandments," which was the first teaching of childhood. Only when studied in connection with the history can these books be rightly understood; so studied they give, on the other hand, an infinite life and colour to the bare massive outline drawn in the historical books.

**The Prophetic Books.**—Again, the later history of the Second Book borrows even greater illustration from the prophetic writings—much as the earlier part of the record derives its chief interest from the action of the elder prophets of unwritten prophecy from Ahijah to Elisha. Thus, the period of national revival in Israel under Jeroboam II., and the unhappy period of decline and fall which succeeded it—so briefly and coldly narrated in our books—live in the pages of AMOS, the prophet of the day of hollow and licentious prosperity, and HOSEA, the prophet of the well-merited doom of judgment. There we discover the evils which lurked under a material prosperity and an outward semblance of religion; there we see how they burst out, rending the very bonds of society, as soon as that prosperity began to wane. So, again, the character of the reckless and cruel greatness of the Assyrian Empire, shown so terribly in the destruction of Israel and in the imminent danger of Judah, is marvellously illustrated by NAHUM, in his grand patriotic hymn of triumph over the foreseen fall of Nineveh. To the days of prosperity of Uzziah, who "loved husbandry," belong (it seems) the utterances of JOEL, picturing physical disasters as God's judgment, calling to repentance, promising temporal and spiritual blessing, and beginning the series of Apocalyptic visions of the vain struggle of the enemies against the people of God. Once more, the great epoch of Hezekiah's religious revival is marked by the writings of the prophet MICAH, who, indeed, gave the signal for it (see Jer. xxvi. 8), and in whom first Messianic prophecy becomes clear and definite. The two grand crises of that reign —the danger under Ahaz from Syria and Israel, and the invasion of Sennacherib—form two chief themes of the supreme prophecy of ISAIAH, out of which the Messianic hope rises almost to actual vision. To the interval between Hezekiah and Josiah, when the Chaldean power begins to come into prominence, we may perhaps refer the magnificent brevity of the prophecy of HABAKKUK. Certainly the pathetic interest of the reign of Josiah is illustrated by the foreboding utterances of ZEPHANIAH. The bitterness of the captivity of Judah—probably the great Captivity—is brought out in the denunciation of Edomite triumph and cruelty in the hour of Judah's disaster by OBADIAH. Nor is it too much to say that the whole history of the last agony of the kingdom of Judah can be read adequately only in the historical and prophetical chapters of the great Book of JEREMIAH. The Books of Kings supply the thread of connection, which binds the prophetic books together, enabling us rightly to understand the substance of each, and the method of prophetic development running through them all. The prophecies, on the other hand, supply constantly the key to the true sense of the history, drawing out explicitly the lesson which it teaches by implication, and giving us a living picture of the ages which it sketches only in outline.

**VI. Illustrations from Profane History.**— To these all-important illustrations must be added, as subsidiary, the light thrown upon the narrative by the study of the various heathen records, whether found in the works of ancient historians, or read in the monumental history of nations which came in contact with Israel, discovered and deciphered in modern times. This kind of illustration, hardly known in the case of the earlier books, begins substantially in the Book of Kings.

The account of Josephus, with all its acknowledged defects, is of very great value, both as a gloss on the Scriptural account, and an occasional supplement to it. The variations found in the LXX. version, in the way of transposition, addition, and omission, are not, indeed, of great importance; for the only substantial addition in the history of Jeroboam (see Note at the end of 1 Kings xi.) is obviously legendary. But they are of considerable interest, and occasionally indicate the existence of independent traditions. The authors quoted by Josephus or early Christian historians (such as Berosus, Manetho, Ptolemy), the monuments of Egypt, Assyria, and Babylon, even the Moabitic stone, all throw light again and again on the Book of Kings; and, though not without occasional difficulties and discrepancies of detail, have unquestionably furnished the strongest confirmation of its historic truth, and have cleared up some obscurities in its brief record. The history, it will be observed, comes in contact with the history of Tyre in the reigns of Hiram and Ethbaal, father of Jezebel; with the history of Egypt in the reign of the Pharaoh father-in-law of Solomon, of Shishak, of "Zerah the Ethiopian," of Sabaco (the *So* or *Seveh* of 2 Kings xvii. 3), of Tirhakah, and of Pharaoh-necho; with the history of Assyria under the "Pul" of 2 Kings xv. 19, Tiglath-pileser, Shalmaneser, Sargon, Sennacherib, Esarhaddon; with the history of Babylon under Nebuchadnezzar; even with our one glimpse of the history of Moab under Mesha in the reign of Jehoram of Israel. Most of our knowledge of these histories is comparatively new. When it is read through the extraordinary monumental records of Egypt, Assyria, and Babylon—the discovery and deciphering of which form some of the most wonderful chapters in historical study—it not only brings out facts, determines dates, confirms or corrects our interpretations, but it gives us a vivid picture of the very life and character of the great Empires, which often explains the different views taken of them in Scripture, and always gives force and colour to our conceptions of the Scripture history itself. The treasure-house is far from being exhausted. Future generations may rival or excel the advance made in this generation and the last, and every advance will be of no inconsiderable value to the student of Scripture history.

The effect of all this study and illustration of the book is to bring out more and more both its historical authenticity and its didactic value. The substance of the history, and even the text, have but few obscurities, and these are generally elucidated by comparison with the ancient versions.

**VII. The Numbers given in the Book.**—The one difficulty in the interpretation of the book lies in the numbers, chronological and other, which occur in it. These are now always written in full; but there is every reason to believe that in the original manuscripts they were, as usual, indicated by Hebrew letters —a method of indication which, as is well known, gives the greatest facility to accidental or intentional corruption. Thus, in our book, and still more in the Chronicles, it is difficult not to suppose that the large numbers given in the history (as, for example, 1 Kings xx. 29, 30; 2 Chron. xiv. 8, 9, xvii. 12—18, xxv. 5, 6, xxvi. 12, &c.) are without authority, due to careless transcription, or to corruption of the original document by the exaggeration of Jewish scribes.

**The Chronology.**—It is possible that this facility of corruption in numbers may bear upon what is the chief critical difficulty of the book, the determination of its chronology. In this book, unlike the earlier historical books, the calculations of dates are given in the text with great exactness, whether by the hand of the historian or by that of some later chronologer.

The first remarkable date is that mentioned in 1 Kings vi. 1, fixing the commencement of the Temple in the 480th year after the Exodus. With regard to this date, which has presented much difficulty to chronologers, see Note on the passage. By whomsoever given, it deserves very careful consideration in the calculation of Biblical chronology.

Next we have the reign of Solomon given at forty years (1 Kings xi. 43); against which the statement of Josephus that he reigned eighty years (*Ant.* viii. 7. 8) can hardly be held to be of serious moment.

From the time of the disruption, we have, marked with great precision, first, the duration of the successive reigns of the kings of Israel; next, the duration of the reigns of the kings of Judah; lastly, statements of the synchronism of accessions in each line with certain years in the reigns of the kings of the other line. Now, in the present condition of the text, these three lines of calculation present occasional discrepancies; and this is especially the case with the synchronistic notices, which are, indeed, believed by many to have been added by a later hand, both because of their rather formal artificiality, and of the evident confusion which they introduce. Setting these last aside, the discrepancies are slight. In any case they are not great and may be easily exhibited.

The whole history (after the reign of Solomon) can be divided into three periods—(a) from the contemporaneous accession of Jeroboam and Rehoboam to the contemporaneous deaths of Jehoram of Israel and Ahaziah of Judah by the hand of Jehu; (b) from the contemporaneous accession of Jehu and Athaliah to the fall of Samaria in the sixth year of Hezekiah; (c) from the sixth year of Hezekiah to the capture of Jerusalem. Now, (a) in the first period there is no difficulty. The united reigns in Israel amount to 98 years,[*] in Judah to 95; and, remembering that the dates are always given in round numbers, reckoning, after the Hebrew manner, any part of a year as a year, there is here no real discrepancy, even in the synchronistic notices. We may accept the lower calculation, or perhaps something even less than this, as the true period. In the second period (b) the discrepancy begins. The united reigns in Israel amount to 143 years, in Judah to 165; and the synchronistic notices in the later part of the period are not only disturbed by this discrepancy, but are occasionally self-contradictory.[†] Of this discrepancy there must be some account to be given; for it is too patent to have escaped the notice of the historian himself, or even of a later chronologer. It is, of course, possible to refer it to corruption of the text; but of such corruption we have no indication in any variations of the ancient versions. If this be set aside, there are but two ways of accounting for it. There may have been (as Archbishop Ussher supposed) periods of interregnum in Israel—one of eleven years after the death of Jeroboam II., and before the accession of Zachariah, the other of about the same period between Pekah and Hoshea. But of these the former is most unlikely, for the period of anarchy had not yet set in; the latter, more probable in itself, is apparently inconsistent with the actual words of the historian (2 Kings xv. 30); of neither is there any trace in the history. The only other possible supposition is, that in Judah some kings may, after common Oriental custom, have acceded to power during their fathers' reigns, as co-adjutors or substitutes. It happens that this is specially likely during this period in two cases. If, as has been thought by some critics, Amaziah after his defeat by Joash was kept in captivity till his conqueror's death, it would be natural that his son should be placed on the throne; and, when Uzziah had been smitten with leprosy, we actually know that Jotham acted as king before his father's death (2 Kings xv. 5). This supposition is, on the whole, most probable. It will not correct the confusion of the synchronistic notices, but it will account for the discrepancy in the collective duration of the reigns in the two lines. In this case it is perhaps, therefore, best again to take the lower calculation. In the third period (c), amounting to 133 years, Judah exists alone, and no difficulty can arise.

The general result, therefore, is that, taking the shorter calculation, we have, from the division of the kingdom to the fall of Samaria, a period of 238 years, and from the same point to the fall of Jerusalem a period of 371 years. If the longer calculation be taken, twenty-two years must be added to each of these periods.

Now, we are able to test these calculations by independent chronological data, found in ancient historians and chronologers, and in the Egyptian and Assyrian monuments. By such comparison their general accuracy is very remarkably illustrated, although some discrepancies in detail occur.

(a) Thus the capture of Samaria is fixed by Ptolemy's Canon in B.C. 721; the capture of Jerusalem is determined by undoubted authorities in B.C. 586. The interval between these dates corresponds almost exactly with the time assigned in our text to the sole existence of the kingdom of Judah.

(b) Starting from either of these dates, the calculation in the text, taking the shorter reckoning, would place the accession of Rehoboam at 957 or 959 B.C. Now, the Egyptian records fix the accession of Shishak at about 985 B.C. His invasion took place in his twentieth year, B.C. 963, and as this coincided with the fifth year of Rehoboam, this would fix the accession of Rehoboam at B.C. 968—about half-way between the dates determined by the longer and shorter calculations of the chronology of our book.

(c) The invasion of Pharaoh-necho is placed in our history about twenty-three years before the final capture of Jerusalem, i.e., about B.C. 609. But the Egyptian chronology fixes his reign from 610 to 594, and makes his expedition against Assyria take place early in his reign.

(d) The accession of Sabaco II. (the So or Seveh of 2 Kings xvii. 4) is fixed by the Egyptian records in B.C. 723; the Hebrew text notes the intercourse between him and Hoshea about three years before the capture of Samaria, i.e., 723 or 724. In all these cases there is a very close coincidence between the two chronologies.

(e) The Assyrian chronology agrees less closely. Thus our text makes Menahem's reign end about thirty years before the fall of Samaria, i.e., B.C. 751. The Assyrian records make Tiglath-pileser receive tribute for him in 741. In our text the expedition of Sennacherib is fixed to about eight years after the fall of Samaria, i.e., B.C. 713. The Assyrian monuments place it about B.C. 701; and this later date seems to be confirmed by the Canon of Ptolemy. These discrepancies cannot be removed, except by alteration of our text, unless there be some error in the data of our Assyrian calculations. It will be observed that they are simply in detail.

(f) The chronological notices in Josephus, which by their minute accuracy suggest some independent sources of information, do not enable us to pronounce decisively between the two reckonings of the text. Thus (α) he has placed Josiah's fulfilment of the prophecy against the altar at Bethel 361 years after its utterance, immediately after the division of the kingdom (Ant. x. 1. 4). Now the eighteenth year of Josiah would be according to the shorter reckoning about 336 years, according to the longer reckoning about 352 years, after the division of the kingdom; and the incident recorded took place not earlier, though it may have been later, than the 18th year. (β) In Ant. x. 8. 4 he remarks that the kings of David's race reigned on the whole 514 years, "during twenty of which " (he adds, oddly enough) " Saul reigned, who was not the same tribe." Allowing forty years for David and eighty (according to Josephus' calculation) for Solomon, and (it would seem) twenty for Saul, the period for the division of the kingdom to the fall of Jerusalem would be 370 years, which agrees with the shorter reckoning. (γ) The Temple is said (Ant. x. 8. 5) to have fallen "in the tenth day of the sixth month of the 470th year" after its dedication; but since this was in the eleventh year of Solomon, or (according to Josephus) sixty-nine years before the disruption, this would give 401 years for the same period,

---

[*] If the civil war of four years (see 1 Kings xvi. 15—23) between Omri and Tibri be not included in the reign of Omri, then the period is 102 years.

[†] See (for example) 2 Kings xv. 27, 30, 32, xvi.

which is in excess even of the longer reckoning. (3) In *Ant.* ix. 14. 1, he gives the period from the disruption to the fall of Samaria as "240 years, 7 months, and 7 days," which agrees almost exactly with the 238 years of the shorter reckoning.

Hence the effect of this comparison, assuming the general correctness of the non-Scriptural records, is to bring out more clearly—what the condition of the chronology itself would suggest—the existence of some confusions in detail, but an undoubted general correctness even in this, which is acknowledged to be the point of the greatest difficulty. The books thus stand out as true history in the highest sense of the word, uniting clear historical accuracy, even of detail, with vivid depiction of character, and high prophetic insight into the laws of the Providence of God.

[In respect both of the *Introduction* and the Notes on the First Book of Kings, the author has to express his obligation to the Commentaries of Keil and Thenius; to Ewald's *History of Israel*, and (in less degree) to Stanley's *Lectures on the Jewish Church*; to Canon Rawlinson's valuable Introduction and Notes in the *Speaker's Commentary*, and his *Bampton Lectures*; to many articles in Smith's *Dictionary of the Bible*, and Winer's *Realwörterbuch*, and to Prof. Robertson Smith's article ("KINGS") in the *Encyclopædia Britannica*. For the study of the text, the *Variorum Bible* of Messrs. Eyre and Spottiswoode is invaluable. The comparison of the text with the ancient versions, and the study of Josephus' history, which is, in the main, virtually a paraphrase, are matters of course.]

# THE FIRST BOOK OF THE KINGS

COMMONLY CALLED

## THE THIRD BOOK OF THE KINGS

CHAPTER I.—<sup>(1)</sup> Now king David was old *and* ¹stricken in years; and they covered him with clothes, but he gat no heat. <sup>(2)</sup> Wherefore his servants said unto him, ²Let there be sought for my lord the king ³a young virgin: and let her stand before the king, and let her ⁴cherish him, and let her lie in thy bosom, that my lord the king may get heat. <sup>(3)</sup> So they sought for a fair damsel throughout all the coast of Israel, and found Abishag a Shunammite, and brought her to the king. <sup>(4)</sup> And the damsel *was* very fair, and cherished the king, and ministered to him: but the king knew her not. <sup>(5)</sup> Then Adonijah the son of Haggith exalted himself, saying, I will ⁵be king:

B.C. 1015.

1 Heb., *entered into days.*
2 Heb., *Let them seek.*
3 Heb., *a damsel, a virgin.*
4 Heb., *be a cherisher unto him.*
5 Heb., *reign.*

---

**General Summary of the Book.**—The narrative of this book falls naturally into three sections: First, (*a*) in chaps. i.—xiv. we have a comparatively detailed record of the accession and reign of Solomon, and of the revolution which produced the disruption both of the kingdom and of the worship of Israel. This record itself varies greatly, both in style and in fulness. In some parts it is graphic and full of spiritual interest; in some it is clearly marked by official, and almost technical, detail; while in others it is brief and summary in style, more like a series of historical notes than a regular narrative. But although it covers only about forty years, it occupies more than half of the entire book. Secondly, (*b*) in chaps. xv. and xvi. we find only short annalistic accounts of the succession in the two kingdoms, and the chief events of each reign, from Jeroboam to Ahab, and from Rehoboam to Jehoshaphat. Thirdly, (*c*) in chaps. xvii.—xxii., with the appearance of Elijah the whole style of the narrative changes to increased fulness, great vividness of description, and expressive spiritual significance, and so continues to the end of the book, and through that portion of the second Book which contains the close of the history of Elijah and the history of Elisha.

In this variety of character we see clear evidence of compilation from older sources—the annals of the kings, the official records of the Temple, and the biographies of the prophets. In it we find, moreover, distinct evidence of the historical accuracy of a record, which is full, where it can draw from detailed records, and contents itself with brief summary, where such materials are wanting. (On the chronology, see *Introduction*.)

The opening narrative of the beginning of Solomon's reign, in chaps. i.—iii., and especially of the accession to the throne, in chap. i., is given with remarkable vividness and unusual fulness of detail. When we read in 2 Chron. ix. 29, that the acts of Solomon were written partly " in the book of Nathan the prophet," it is impossible not to conjecture that the record of these early days is drawn from this book of one who had been a prominent actor in the whole.

<sup>(1)</sup> **Now king David.**—" Now " is the simple illative conjunction " and," found at the beginning of all the historical books (Exodus, Numbers, Joshua, Judges, Ruth, 1 Samuel, &c.). It marks the general conception of the unity of the whole history, but implies nothing of special connection of time or authorship with the books of Samuel. In fact, although these books are in some sense the continuation of the former, yet the narrative is hardly continuous. The history passes at once to the closing scene of David's life, leaving a comparative blank in the period succeeding the restoration after the defeat of Absalom—a blank which is partly filled up in the later books (1 Chron. xxii.—xxix.).

**Stricken in years**—about seventy years old. Since " clothes " mean " bed-clothes," the meaning is that the King was now too feeble to rise from his bed. His life began its responsibilities early; it had been hard and trying; and, as the history shows, not wholly free from self-indulgence. Hence, at no excessive age, its complete decrepitude.

<sup>(3)</sup> **A Shunammite.**—Shunem is in the territory of Issachar (Josh. xix. 18), and in the plain of Jezreel (1 Sam. xxviii. 4), near Mount Gilboa. As Eusebius, describing its position carefully, calls it " Sulem," and as this variation of name is confirmed by its ready identification with the modern village of *Solam*, it has been conjectured (see Smith's *Dictionary of the Bible*, SHULAMITE), ingeniously and not improbably, that Abishag is the " fair Shulamite " of the Song of Solomon (chap. vi. 13). The conjecture certainly throws some light on the occurrences of chap. ii. 13—25. Probably the whole notice of Abishag is only introduced on account of her subsequent connection with the fate of Adonijah.

<sup>(5)</sup> **Adonijah** (*my Lord is Jehovah*), David's fourth son, born in Hebron (2 Sam. iii. 4), at least thirty-three years before. From the words of Solomon in chap. ii. 22, we may gather that he claimed the throne as being now the eldest son. Hence it is probable that Chileab (or Daniel, see 2 Sam. iii. 3; 1 Chron. iii. 1), the second son, was dead, as well as Amnon and Absalom. The similarity between Adonijah and Absalom, in respect of personal beauty, favour with a too-indulgent father, ambition and trust in popularity, is evidently suggested by the narrative, which places them in close connection, although born of different

*Adonijah usurps*        I. KINGS, I.        *the Kingdom.*

and he prepared him chariots and horsemen, and fifty men to run before him. <sup>(6)</sup> And his father had not displeased him <sup>1</sup>at any time in saying, Why hast thou done so? and he also *was a very goodly man*; and *his mother* bare him after Absalom. <sup>(7)</sup> And <sup>2</sup>he conferred with Joab the son of Zeruiah, and with Abiathar the priest: and they <sup>3</sup>following Adonijah helped *him*. <sup>(8)</sup> But Zadok the priest, and Benaiah the son of Jehoiada, and Nathan the prophet, and Shimei, and Rei, and the mighty men which *belonged* to David, were not with Adonijah. <sup>(9)</sup> And Adonijah slew sheep and oxen and fat cattle by the stone of Zoheleth, which *is* by <sup>4</sup>En-rogel, and called all his brethren the king's sons, and all the men of Judah the king's servants: <sup>(10)</sup> but Nathan the prophet, and Benaiah, and the mighty men, and Solomon his brother, he called not.

<sup>(11)</sup> Wherefore Nathan spake unto Bath-sheba the mother of Solomon, say-

*Marginal notes:*
1 Heb., *from his days.*
2 Heb., *his words were with Joab.*
3 Heb., *helped after Adonijah.*
4 Or, *the well Rogel.*

---

mothers. The means, moreover, which Adonijah employed, the body-guard of fifty men, and the maintenance of "chariots and horsemen," are exactly imitated from the example of Absalom (2 Sam. xv. 1); and we note that the festal sacrifice, with the support of two important leaders in peace and war, recalls the same model. But Adonijah hardly shows the craft and ruthless determination of the elder rebel. His attempt on the crown seems crude and ill-planned in conception, and wanting in promptitude of action.

<sup>(7)</sup> **Joab.**—The books of Samuel have brought out clearly the career and character of Joab, as being (in some degree like Abner) a professed soldier, raised to a formidable and half-independent power by the incessant wars of Saul and David. He stands out in consistent portraiture throughout, as a bold, hard, and unscrupulous man; in his relations to the king often imperious and disobedient; but nevertheless an absolutely loyal servant, to whom, in great degree, the establishment of David's throne was due, and who, moreover (as is shown by his remonstrance against the numbering of the people, recorded in 2 Sam. xxiv. 3; 1 Chron. xxi. 3, 6), was not without some right instincts of policy and of duty to God.

**Abiathar the priest.**—Of Abiathar we also know that he had been the companion of all David's adversity, and of his reign at Hebron (1 Sam. xxii. 20, xxiii. 6, 9, xxx. 7; 2 Sam. ii. 1—4); that he was installed (with Zadok) as high priest at Jerusalem, and remained faithful to David in the rebellion of Absalom (2 Sam. viii. 17, xv. 24—29).

The adhesion of these two faithful servants of David, as also of "the king's sons," and "the men of Judah, the king's servants," to the rash usurpation of Adonijah, seems strange at first sight. Probably Joab had never recovered his position in the king's favour since the death of Absalom; and it is possible that the evident growth of despotic power and state in David's latter years may have alienated from him the trusty friends of earlier and simpler days. But the true explanation would seem to be, that the attempt of Adonijah was not viewed as an actual rebellion. Solomon was young; David's designation of him for the succession might be represented as the favouritism of dotage; and the assumption of the crown by the eldest son, a man in the prime of life and of popular qualities, might seem not only justifiable, but even right and expedient.

<sup>(8)</sup> **Zadok the priest** (son of Ahitub) was the representative of the family of Eleazar, elder son of Aaron, as Abiathar of the family of Ithamar, the younger son (1 Chron. xxiv. 3). As a "young man of valour," under "Jehoiada, leader of the Aaronites," he joined David at Hebron with 3,700 men (1 Chron. xii. 28), and had been left in charge of the Tabernacle at Gibeon (1 Chron. xvi. 39) after the removal of the Ark to Jerusalem. On his relation to Abiathar, see chap. ii. 35.

**Benaiah**, the son of "Jehoiada, a chief priest," and therefore of Levitical origin. (See 2 Sam. viii. 18, xxiii. 20—23; 1 Chron. xxvii. 5, 6.) His rank is given in 2 Sam. xxiii. 23, as intermediate between the "three mighty men" and "the thirty," and in 1 Chron. xxvii. 5, as "the third captain of the host for the third month"; but his command of the bodyguard gave him special importance, second only to that of Joab (2 Sam. xx. 23), and perhaps of even greater importance for immediate action. (It is notable that there is no mention of Abishai, who is named as prior to Benaiah among "the mighty men" in 2 Sam. xxiii. 18—22. It may be inferred that he was dead; otherwise he could hardly have been omitted here.)

**Nathan the prophet.**—See 2 Sam. vii. 2, xii. 1, 25. In the whole chapter he appears rather as a chief officer and counsellor of David, than in the loftier aspect of the prophetic character. He was also the royal chronicler of the reigns of David and Solomon (1 Chr. xxix. 29; 2 Chr. ix. 29).

**Shimei, and Rei.**—Ewald conjectures that these were two brothers of David, called Shimma and Raddai in 1 Chron. ii. 13, 14. These, however, being older than David, would now be in extreme old age. Of Rei, we have no mention elsewhere; but there is a Shimei (in 1 Kings iv. 18), a high officer of Solomon; a "Shimea," brother of Solomon (in 1 Chron. iii. 5), and a "Shammah," one of the "mighty men" (in 2 Sam. xxiii. 11).

**The mighty men.**—See 2 Sam. xxiii. 8—39. The name *Gibbôrim* is a technical name, and is thought to designate a picked body of troops, the standing nucleus of the armies of Israel. It is commonly inferred that they were the successors of the six hundred men of David's band during his life of wandering and exile, and that "the three" and "the thirty" (2 Sam. xxiii.) were their officers. They are mentioned as attached to the person of David in 2 Sam. x. 7; xvi. 6; xx. 7.

<sup>(9)</sup> **The stone of Zoheleth.**—The meaning is uncertain. The derivation seems to be from a root, meaning to "crawl," or "steal on." Some interpreters render, the "stone of the serpents;" the Targums make it "the rolling stone;" other authorities "the stone of the conduit," which would suit well its position as here described.

**En-rogel.**—"The spring of the fuller." (See Joshua xv. 7, xviii. 16; 2 Sam. xvii. 17.) Its proximity would be useful for the purposes of sacrifice; for it appears to be the only natural spring near Jerusalem, situated not far from Siloam.

<sup>(11)</sup> **Wherefore Nathan.**—The initiative taken by Nathan is especially natural, since he had been the

ing, Hast thou not heard that Adonijah the son of ᵃHaggith doth reign, and David our lord knoweth *it* not? ⁽¹²⁾ Now therefore come, let me, I pray thee, give thee counsel, that thou mayest save thine own life, and the life of thy son Solomon. ⁽¹³⁾ Go and get thee in unto king David, and say unto him, Didst not thou, my lord, O king, swear unto thine handmaid, saying, Assuredly Solomon thy son shall reign after me, and he shall sit upon my throne? why then doth Adonijah reign? ⁽¹⁴⁾ Behold, while thou yet talkest there with the king, I also will come in after thee, and ¹confirm thy words.

⁽¹⁵⁾ And Bath-sheba went in unto the king into the chamber: and the king was very old; and Abishag the Shunammite ministered unto the king. ⁽¹⁶⁾ And Bath-sheba bowed, and did obeisance unto the king. And the king said, ²What wouldest thou? ⁽¹⁷⁾ And she said unto him, My lord, thou swarest by the LORD thy God unto thine handmaid, *saying*, Assuredly Solomon thy son shall reign after me, and he shall sit upon my throne. ⁽¹⁸⁾ And now, behold, Adonijah reigneth; and now, my lord the king, thou knowest *it* not: ⁽¹⁹⁾ and he hath slain oxen and fat cattle and sheep in abundance, and hath called all the sons of the king, and Abiathar the priest, and Joab the captain of the host: but Solomon thy servant hath he not called. ⁽²⁰⁾ And thou, my lord, O king, the eyes of all Israel *are* upon thee, that thou shouldest tell them who shall sit on the throne of my lord the king after him. ⁽²¹⁾ Otherwise it shall come to pass, when my lord the king shall sleep with his fathers, that I and my son Solomon shall be counted ³offenders.

⁽²²⁾ And, lo, while she yet talked with the king, Nathan the prophet also came in. ⁽²³⁾ And they told the king, saying, Behold Nathan the prophet. And when he was come in before the king, he bowed himself before the king with his face to the ground. ⁽²⁴⁾ And Nathan said, My lord, O king, hast thou said, Adonijah shall reign after me, and he shall sit upon my throne? ⁽²⁵⁾ For he is gone down this day, and hath slain oxen and fat cattle and sheep in abundance, and hath called all the king's

---

*a* 2 Sam. 3. 4.

1 Heb., *fill up*.

2 Heb., *What to thee?*

3 Heb., *sinners*.

---

medium both of the prophecy to David of the son who should build the Lord's house (2 Sam. vii. 12—15), and also of the blessing on Solomon, embodied in the name Jedidiah ("beloved of Jehovah," 2 Sam. xii. 25). Perhaps for this very reason the conspirators had altogether held aloof from him.

⁽¹²⁾ **The life of . . . Solomon.**—The usurpation of Adonijah would, as a matter of course, be sealed by the blood of his rival Solomon. (Comp. 2 Chron. xxi. 4.) Bath-sheba herself need hardly have been sacrificed; but her position of favour with David would excite jealousy, and Solomon, being still young, might well be thought only an instrument in her hands.

⁽¹³⁾ **Didst not thou . . . swear.**—Of this oath we have no mention elsewhere. It may have belonged to the time of Solomon's birth (2 Sam. xii. 24, 25). In 1 Chron. xxii. 6—13, we find a designation of Solomon for succession, apparently earlier than this time—it being clearly understood (see verse 20), according to Oriental custom, that such designation, without strict regard to priority of birth, lay in the prerogative of the reigning king.

⁽¹⁴⁾ **While thou yet talkest.**—The whole history seems to indicate a growth of royal state and Oriental reverence for the king's person since the defeat of Absalom, contrasted with the comparative simplicity of intercourse with him in earlier days, and preparatory to the still greater development of majesty and despotism under Solomon. Bath-sheba's entrance into the bedchamber seems to be looked upon as an intrusion, to be ventured upon only in the humble attitude of a suppliant. Nathan does not presume to approach the king with remonstrance, till the maternal anxiety of Bath-sheba has paved the way. (Comp. in Esther iv. 10—16, the picture of the still more unapproachable royalty of Persia.)

⁽²¹⁾ **Shall sleep with his fathers.**—Here this phrase, so constantly used in the record of the death of the kings, occurs in these books for the first time. (It is also found in the message of promise by Nathan, 2 Sam. vii. 12, relating to the succession of the son who should build the Temple.) We find corresponding expressions in Gen. xv. 15; Deut. xxxi. 16. Without connecting with the use of this phrase anything like the fulness of meaning which in the New Testament attaches to "the sleep" of the departed servants of God (as known to be a "sleep in Jesus"), it seems not unreasonable to recognise in it, at least, a rudimentary belief in death as rest and not extinction. The addition, "with his fathers," has probably a reference to "the tombs of the kings;" especially as we find that it is not adopted in the cases of Jehoram (2 Chron. xxi. 20) and Joash (2 Chron. xxiv. 25), who were not buried therein.

⁽²⁴⁾ **Hast thou said.**—The question here and in verse 27 is, of course, merely intended to draw out denial; but it is singularly true to nature that it does so by the assumption (natural in court language) that nothing of such a kind could be even conceived as done without the king's will. There is something striking in the contrast of the deference of Nathan as a counsellor on state business with the bold superiority of his tone in the discharge of his true prophetic office (as in 2 Sam. vii. 2—17, xii. 1—14).

⁽²⁵⁾ **God save king Adonijah.**—Literally (as in 1 Sam. x. 24; 2 Sam. xvi. 16, &c.), "May the king live;" like the "Let the king live for ever" of verse 31, and of Neh. ii. 3; Dan. ii. 4, iii. 9, &c.

*David renews his*     I. KINGS, I.     *Oath to Bath-sheba.*

sons, and the captains of the host, and Abiathar the priest; and, behold, they eat and drink before him, and say, ¹God save king Adonijah. ⁽²⁶⁾ But me, *even* me thy servant, and Zadok the priest, and Benaiah the son of Jehoiada, and thy servant Solomon, hath he not called. ⁽²⁷⁾ Is this thing done by my lord the king, and thou hast not shewed *it* unto thy servant, who should sit on the throne of my lord the king after him? ⁽²⁸⁾ Then king David answered and said, Call me Bath-sheba. And she came ²into the king's presence, and stood before the king. ⁽²⁹⁾ And the king sware, and said, *As* the LORD liveth, that hath redeemed my soul out of all distress, ⁽³⁰⁾ even as I sware unto thee by the LORD God of Israel, saying, Assuredly Solomon thy son shall reign after me, and he shall sit upon my throne in my stead; even so will I certainly do this day. ⁽³¹⁾ Then Bath-sheba bowed with *her* face to the earth, and did reverence to the king, and said, Let my lord king David live for ever.

⁽³²⁾ And king David said, Call me Zadok the priest, and Nathan the prophet, and Benaiah the son of Jehoiada. And they came before the king. ⁽³³⁾ The king also said unto them, Take with you the servants of your lord, and cause Solomon my son to ride upon ³mine own mule, and bring him down to Gihon: ⁽³⁴⁾ and let Zadok the priest and Nathan the prophet anoint him there king over Israel: and blow ye with the trumpet, and say, God save king Solomon. ⁽³⁵⁾ Then ye shall come up after him, that he may come and sit upon my throne; for he shall be king in my stead: and I have appointed him to be ruler over Israel and over Judah. ⁽³⁶⁾ And Benaiah the son of Jehoiada answered the king, and said, Amen: the LORD God of my lord the king say so too. ⁽³⁷⁾ As the LORD hath been with my lord the king, even so be he with Solomon, and make his throne greater than the throne of my lord king David.

⁽³⁸⁾ So Zadok the priest, and Nathan the prophet, and Benaiah the son of

1 Heb., *Let king Adonijah live.*
2 Heb., *before the king.*
3 Heb., *which belongeth to me.*

---

⁽²⁹⁾ **As the Lord liveth, that hath redeemed my soul.**—A characteristic adjuration of David, found also in 2 Sam. iv. 9; but now peculiarly appropriate in the old man, who was so near the haven of rest, after all the storms of life. "O Lord, my strength and my Redeemer," is the climax of his address to God, as the Creator of all things and the ruler of all men, in Ps. xix. 14.

⁽³²⁾ **Call me Zadok.**—This sudden flash of the old energy in David, and the clear, terse directions which he gives for carrying out all the necessary parts of the inauguration of Solomon's royalty, striking enough in themselves, are still more striking in contrast with the timidity and despondency with which, when far younger, he had received the news of Absalom's rebellion. For then he felt the coming of God's threatened chastisement; now he knows that this is passed, and that God is on his side.

⁽³³⁾ **Gihon** ("breaking forth") is clearly a place in the valley, under the walls of Jerusalem, mentioned as having a watercourse, or torrent, diverted by Hezekiah in his preparation of the city for siege (2 Chron. xxxii. 30), and as forming one end of a new wall "up to the fish gate," built by Manasseh; but whether it is on the west of the city, near the present Jaffa gate, or (as seems more probable) on the south, at the end of the valley called the *Tyropœon*, running through the city, has been doubted. The Targums here read *Siloam*; and this agrees with the latter supposition, which is also supported by the proximity to Adonijah's feast at En-rogel, implied in the narrative.

⁽³⁴⁾ **Anoint him . . . king.**—It is notable that of this solemn inauguration of royalty, marked emphatically as a religious consecration by the common phrase "the Lord's anointed"—then especially in use (1 Sam. xvi. 6, xxiv. 6, xxvi. 9; 2 Sam. i. 14, xix. 21), though found also occasionally in the later books (Lam. iv. 20)—there is no mention of the tumultuous usurpation of Adonijah. Probably, as in the appointment of Saul and David himself, the right to anoint was recognised as belonging to the prophetic order (see chap. xix. 16), inasmuch as it signified the outpouring of the Holy Spirit of the Lord. (Comp. Acts x. 38.) Hence, in the absence of Nathan, it could not be attempted. In the case of David, such anointing had marked (1 Sam. xvi. 13) his first private designation for the kingdom by Samuel, and his public accession to royalty, first over Judah (2 Sam. ii. 4), then over all Israel (2 Sam. v. 3).

The completeness of the old King's provision is especially to be noticed. The "riding on the King's mule," attended by the body-guard, marked the royal sanction; the anointing, the sanction of priest and prophet; and the acclamation the adhesion of the people. Then are to follow the enthronement and homage.

⁽³⁵⁾ **Over Israel and over Judah.**—The phrase clearly refers to the distinction, already tending to become a division, between Israel and Judah in relation to the monarchy. In the case of David himself, it may be observed that the record of his accession to royalty over Israel contains the notice of "a league" made by him with the elders of Israel (2 Sam. v. 3), to which there is nothing to correspond in the account of his becoming king over Judah (2 Sam. ii. 4). This perhaps indicates from the beginning a less absolute rule over the other tribes. Certainly the history of the rebellion of Absalom (2 Sam. xv. 10, 13, xviii. 6, 7), the disputes about the restoration of David (2 Sam. xix. 41–43), and the attempt of Sheba to take advantage of them (2 Sam. xx. 1, 2), show a looser allegiance of Israel than of Judah to the house of David.

⁽³⁸⁾ **The Cherethites, and the Pelethites.**—See 2 Sam. viii. 18, xv. 28, xx. 7, 23. The body-guard—per-

Jehoiada, and the Cherethites, and the Pelethites, went down, and caused Solomon to ride upon king David's mule, and brought him to Gihon. <sup>(39)</sup> And Zadok the priest took an horn of oil out of the tabernacle, and anointed Solomon. And they blew the trumpet; and all the people said, God save king Solomon. <sup>(40)</sup> And all the people came up after him, and the people piped with ¹pipes, and rejoiced with great joy, so that the earth rent with the sound of them.

<sup>(41)</sup> And Adonijah and all the guests that were with him heard it as they had made an end of eating. And when Joab heard the sound of the trumpet, he said, Wherefore is this noise of the city being in an uproar? <sup>(42)</sup> And while he yet spake, behold, Jonathan the son of Abiathar the priest came: and Adonijah said unto him, Come in; for thou art a valiant man, and bringest good tidings. <sup>(43)</sup> And Jonathan answered and said to Adonijah, Verily our lord king David hath made Solomon king. <sup>(44)</sup> And the king hath sent with him Zadok the priest, and Nathan the prophet, and Benaiah the son of Jehoiada, and the Cherethites, and the Pelethites, and they have caused him to ride upon the king's mule: <sup>(45)</sup> and Zadok the priest and Nathan the prophet have anointed him king in Gihon: and they are come up from thence rejoicing, so that the city rang again. This is the noise that ye have heard. <sup>(46)</sup> And also Solomon sitteth on the throne of the kingdom. <sup>(47)</sup> And moreover the king's servants came to bless our lord king David, saying, God make the name of Solomon better than thy name, and make his throne greater than thy throne. And the king bowed himself upon the bed. <sup>(48)</sup> And also thus said the king, Blessed be the LORD God of Israel, which hath given one to sit on my throne this day, mine eyes even seeing it.

<sup>(49)</sup> And all the guests that were with Adonijah were afraid, and rose up, and went every man his way. <sup>(50)</sup> And Adonijah feared because of Solomon, and arose, and went, and caught hold on the horns of the altar. <sup>(51)</sup> And it was told Solomon, saying, Behold, Adonijah feareth king Solomon: for, lo, he hath caught hold on the horns of the altar.

¹ Or, flutes.

---

haps of foreign troops—"the executioners and runners" (as some render them) to carry out the King's commands.

<sup>(39)</sup> **An horn of oil out of the tabernacle.**—The sacred oil, the making of which is described in Exod. xxx. 22—30, was to be used for anointing the Tabernacle itself, and the altars and vessels. as well as the priests. It was this oil, no doubt, which was used in this case. The Tabernacle proper was still at Gibeon (see 2 Chron. i. 3); but a tent or tabernacle had been set up in Zion over the ark (2 Chron. i. 4), and the haste with which all was done would necessitate the taking the oil from the nearer source, in spite of the fact that Abiathar presided in Zion, and Zadok only in Gibeon.

<sup>(40)</sup> **Piped with pipes.**—The Greek Version has "danced in dances," by a slight variation of reading. The graphic description of the acclamation of the people indicates something more than conventional loyalty. The attempt of Adonijah relied on the support only of the great men, and perhaps the army, but had no popular following.

<sup>(41)</sup> **When Joab heard.**—It is one of the many lifelike touches of the narrative that it is the old warrior Joab who, amidst the revelry of his companions, notices the sound of the trumpet, and the acclamation following. Adonijah affects to disregard it.

<sup>(42)</sup> **Jonathan the son of Abiathar.**—See 2 Sam. xv. 27, xvii. 17—21, where he is named, with Ahimaaz, as a swift runner, fit to be a messenger. It is curious that a similar greeting to his companion Ahimaaz is used by David in 2 Sam. xviii. 27—possibly as a kind of omen of good fortune.

<sup>(46)</sup> **And also Solomon sitteth.**—Jonathan's announcement here takes up the narrative of events after verse 40. The public enthronement in the palace (ordered by David in verse 35) follows the anointing and acceptance by the acclamations of the people, as an integral part of the inauguration of royalty.

<sup>(47)</sup> **The king bowed himself,** that is, in worship (comp. Gen. xlvii. 31), at once joining in the prayer of his servants, and thanking God for the fulfilment of His promise.

<sup>(49)</sup> **And all the guests.**—Nothing is more striking than the sudden and humiliating collapse of the attempt of Adonijah, strongly supported as it was by Joab and Abiathar, in contrast with the formidable character of the rebellion of Absalom. This is another indication that the royal power had been greatly consolidated during the last peaceful years of David's reign. Perhaps, moreover, the usurpation of Adonijah, not being viewed as a rebellion against David, but only a presumption on his favour, was accordingly crushed at once by the expression of his will. It is strange that of all the conspirators Adonijah alone seems to have feared punishment at this time; his accomplices, the other conspirators, are apparently allowed to disperse in safety, and their rebellion is ignored.

<sup>(50)</sup> **The horns of the altar.**—The horns were projections from the altar, to which (see Ps. cxviii. 27) the victims were fastened, and on which the blood was sprinkled (Exod. xxix. 12). To take hold of them was, of course, to claim the right of sanctuary—a right, however, which the Law, ruled as usual by moral considerations, formally denied to wilful murder (Exod. xxi. 14), and which accordingly (see chap. ii. 30, 31) was refused hereafter to Joab. Adonijah, by the acknowledgment of "King Solomon," seems to represent his usurpation as one of those acts of haste and inadvertency, to which alone sanctuary was conceded.

*Adonijah is Spared.*     I. KINGS, II.     *David counsels Solomon.*

saying, Let king Solomon swear unto me to day that he will not slay his servant with the sword. <sup>(52)</sup> And Solomon said, If he will shew himself a worthy man, there shall not an hair of him fall to the earth: but if wickedness shall be found in him, he shall die. <sup>(53)</sup> So king Solomon sent, and they brought him down from the altar. And he came and bowed himself to king Solomon: and Solomon said unto him, Go to thine house.

CHAPTER II.—<sup>(1)</sup> Now the days of David drew nigh that he should die; and he charged Solomon his son, saying, <sup>(2)</sup> I go the way of all the earth: be thou strong therefore, and shew thyself a man; <sup>(3)</sup> and keep the charge of the LORD thy God, to walk in his ways, to keep his statutes, and his commandments, and his judgments, and his testi-

*a* Deut. 29. 9; Josh. 1. 7.

1 Or, *do wisely.*

*b* 2 Sam. 7. 12.

2 Heb., *be cut off from thee from the throne.*

*c* 2 Sam. 3. 27.

*d* 2 Sam. 20. 10.

3 Heb., *put.*

monies, as it is written in the law of Moses, that thou mayest <sup>a 1</sup>prosper in all that thou doest, and whithersoever thou turnest thyself: <sup>(4)</sup> that the LORD may continue his word which he spake concerning me, saying, If thy children take heed to their way, to walk before me in truth with all their heart and with all their soul, <sup>b</sup>there shall not <sup>2</sup>fail thee (said he) a man on the throne of Israel. <sup>(5)</sup> Moreover thou knowest also what Joab the son of Zeruiah did to me, *and* what he did to the two captains of the hosts of Israel, unto <sup>c</sup>Abner the son of Ner, and unto <sup>d</sup>Amasa the son of Jether, whom he slew, and <sup>3</sup>shed the blood of war in peace, and put the blood of war upon his girdle that *was* about his loins, and in his shoes that *were* on his feet. <sup>(6)</sup> Do therefore according to thy wisdom, and let not his hoar head go down to the grave in

---

<sup>(52)</sup> **There shall not a hair of him fall.**—Solomon's pardon, though, according to Oriental ideas, an act of extraordinary grace, was yet characteristically cautious and conditional, to be withdrawn accordingly on the first symptom of any renewal of Adonijah's pretensions.

II.

The narrative in this chapter still continues much in the same graphic style and detail as in the previous chapter. During the interval between the two chapters we have in 1 Chron. xxviii., xxix. the record of a great assembly of the "princes of Israel" and the whole realm—a solemn farewell of David to the people, with charge to aid in building the Temple, followed by offerings for it, and the making of "Solomon king the second time" (chap. xxix. 22). This possibly represented his accession to the royalty not only over Judah, but over the rest of Israel, with formal acceptance by the representatives of all the tribes. (Comp. xii. 1, in respect of the accession of Rehoboam.) In this detailed record it is specially noticed (1 Chron. xxviii. 2) that the old king "stood up on his feet," as though the excitement of the great occasion had renewed for a time his strength, and enabled him to rise from his bed. It is also recorded that "all the sons of David," who had apparently favoured Adonijah, submitted themselves to Solomon the king (chap. xxix. 24).

<sup>(2)</sup> **I go the way of all the earth.**—Comp. Josh. xxiii. 14.

<sup>(3)</sup> **Keep the charge.**—The main charge to Solomon is noble enough. He is to "show himself a man," in spite of his youth; he is to take heed in all things to follow the Law of the Lord; he is to trust both in the general promise of God to obedience, and in the special promise made to the house of David (2 Sam. vii. 12—16). It is remarkably in harmony with the beautiful Psalm, "the last words of David," preserved in 2 Sam. xxiii. 3—5, telling how "he that ruleth over men must be just, ruling in the fear of God," and, in spite of consciousness of shortcomings from this high ideal,

trusting in the "everlasting covenant of God" with him, "ordered in all things, and sure." Nor does it accord less with the equally beautiful prayer of 1 Chron. xxix. 18, 19, for Solomon and for the people. In all this David speaks in the spirit of a true servant and saint of God. But in the special charges that follow we see the worldly prudence of the old statesman, and in one case some trace of long-remembered grudge, singularly true to imperfect human nature, although utterly unworthy of an ideal picture of a hero-king.

<sup>(5)</sup> **What Joab . . . did.**—The charge as to Joab has a certain righteousness in it. David could not—probably since Joab's knowledge of his great crime, he dared not—punish him as he deserved. There is a graphic vividness in the description of the blood of his victims, shed as "the blood of war in peace," spirting over the girdle and sandals of the murderer, which shows how the horror of the crimes had dwelt on David's imagination. The murder of Abner, treacherous as it was, probably had some show of justification in the rough justice wrought out by the duty laid in ancient law on the "avenger of blood." David disclaims it (2 Sam. iii. 28, 29, 37—39), without actually condemning it as inexcusable. The more recent and shameful murder of Amasa was simply one of revenge and ambition, because Amasa had been put in Joab's place; yet David, broken in spirit, does not dare to blame it, and quietly acquiesces in the resumption by Joab of the dignity conferred on the murdered man. That these crimes should be punished by a king whose hands were clean, and who owed Joab nothing, was perhaps just, certainly within the letter of the law; though clemency might have spared the old and now fallen warrior, who had at least served David ably with long and faithful service. It is singularly true to nature, that the old King makes no mention of the act for which nevertheless, in all probability, he most bore grudge against Joab—the reckless slaughter of Absalom against his own express commands and entreaties—and does not deign to allude to his recent treason, which probably had already embittered Solomon against him.

13

peace. (7) But shew kindness unto the sons of *Barzillai the Gileadite, and let them be of those that eat at thy table: for so they came to me when I fled because of Absalom thy brother. (8) And, behold, *thou hast* with thee *b*Shimei the son of Gera, a Benjamite of Bahurim, which cursed me with a ¹grievous curse in the day when I went to Mahanaim: but he came down to meet me at Jordan, and I sware to him by the LORD, saying, *c*I will not put thee to death with the sword. (9) Now therefore hold him not guiltless: for thou *art* a wise man, and knowest what thou oughtest to do unto him; but his hoar head bring thou down to the grave with blood.

(10) So *d*David slept with his fathers, and was buried in the city of David. (11) And the days that David *e*reigned over Israel *were* forty years: seven years reigned he in Hebron, and thirty and three years reigned he in Jerusalem.

(12) *f*Then sat Solomon upon the throne of David his father; and his kingdom was established greatly. (13) And Adonijah the son of Haggith came to Bath-sheba the mother of Solomon. And she

*a* 2 Sam. 19. 31.

*b* 2 Sam. 16. 5.

1 Heb., *strong*.

*c* 2 Sam. 19. 23.

*d* Acts 2. 29 & 13. 36.

*e* 2 Sam. 5. 4; 1 Chron. 29. 26, 27.

*f* 2 Chron. 29. 23.

² Heb., *turn not away my face*.

said, Comest thou peaceably? And he said, Peaceably. (14) He said moreover, I have somewhat to say unto thee. And she said, Say on. (15) And he said, Thou knowest that the kingdom was mine, and *that* all Israel set their faces on me, that I should reign: howbeit the kingdom is turned about, and is become my brother's: for it was his from the LORD. (16) And now I ask one petition of thee, ²deny me not. And she said unto him, Say on. (17) And he said, Speak, I pray thee, unto Solomon the king, (for he will not say thee nay,) that he give me Abishag the Shunammite to wife. (18) And Bath-sheba said, Well; I will speak for thee unto the king.

(19) Bath-sheba therefore went unto king Solomon, to speak unto him for Adonijah. And the king rose up to meet her, and bowed himself unto her, and sat down on his throne, and caused a seat to be set for the king's mother; and she sat on his right hand. (20) Then she said, I desire one small petition of thee; *I pray thee,* say me not nay. And the king said unto her, Ask on, my mother: for I will not say thee nay. (21) And she said, Let Abishag the Shu-

---

(7) **Shew kindness.**—The charge of favour to the sons of Barzillai (see 2 Sam. xix. 37—40) stands out in pleasant contrast. It has been noted that in Jer. xli. 17 there is a reference to "the habitation of Chimham," as being "by Bethlehem," David's own birthplace; as if David had given him inheritance there, out of what was especially his own.

(8) **Thou hast with thee Shimei.**—The most ungenerous charge is the virtual withdrawal of the pardon, freely granted to Shimei long before (2 Sam. xix. 18—23). It is, perhaps, partly dictated by policy; for the notice of Shimei (2 Sam. xvi. 5—8, xix. 17) shows that he was powerful, and that he assumed a dangerous championship of the fallen house of Saul. But there are unmistakable traces of the old grudge rankling in David's heart, reminding us of the bitterness of such psalms as Ps. lxix.

(10) **Buried in the city of David**—that is, evidently in Mount Sion. In Neh. iii. 16 the "sepulchres of David" are noticed, and they are plainly alluded to in Ezek. xliii. 7, 9. They became the regular tombs of the kings, with some exceptions particularly noticed. It was in token of special honour that the high priest Jehoiada, the preserver of the royal dynasty, was buried therein (See 2 Chron. xxiv. 16).

(12) **His kingdom was established greatly.**—From the notice in the closing verse of the chapter, that after the deaths of Adonijah, Joab, and Shimei, and the degradation of Abiathar, "the kingdom was established in the hand of Solomon," it would seem that, under the smooth surface of apparent loyalty, there lurked some elements of disaffection and danger—perhaps aggravated by enmity from without; for we gather from chap. xi. 14—25 that the death of David was the signal for some attempts at rebellion in the conquered nations. But these are apparently crushed without the slightest effort, though with no little fierceness and severity; and the royalty of Solomon rises at once to a colossal greatness.

(13) **And Adonijah . . . came.**—The application of Adonijah to Bath-sheba, and the signs of honour paid to her by the king—of which there is no trace in her approach to the presence of David (chap. i. 15, 16, 28, 31)—illustrate the universal custom of Eastern monarchies; by which, while the wives of the king, being many, are seldom held to be of any great political account, the mother of the reigning king is a person of great dignity and influence. We may notice how constantly the name of each king's mother is recorded in the history.

(15) **Thou knowest.**—Adonijah's words show craft, flattering Bath-sheba by extolling her influence, and making merit of his surrender to Solomon, in obedience to the Lord's decree, of a kingdom which, in evident contradiction to fact, he asserts to have been destined to him by popular desire. The petition, however, apparently harmless, and (since Abishag was concubine of David only in name) involving nothing unnatural, had perhaps a covert design: for, by universal Eastern custom, to take a king's wives was the known privilege or duty of his successor. Hence the counsel, most unseemly but still probably politic, given by Ahithophel to Absalom (2 Sam. xvi. 21). If, therefore, Adonijah had publicly espoused Abishag, it might have seemed a virtual renewal of his claim to the crown. This Solomon sees at once, though Bath-sheba, strangely enough, does not see it.

*Adonijah is Slain.*  I. KINGS, II.  *Joab flies to the Altar*

nammite be given to Adonijah thy brother to wife. <sup>(22)</sup> And King Solomon answered and said unto his mother, And why dost thou ask Abishag the Shunammite for Adonijah? ask for him the kingdom also; for he *is* mine elder brother; even for him, and for Abiathar the priest, and for Joab the son of Zeruiah. <sup>(23)</sup> Then King Solomon sware by the LORD, saying, God do so to me, and more also, if Adonijah have not spoken this word against his own life. <sup>(24)</sup> Now therefore, *as* the LORD liveth, which hath established me, and set me on the throne of David my father, and who hath made me an house, as he <sup>a</sup>promised, Adonijah shall be put to death this day. <sup>(25)</sup> And King Solomon sent by the hand of Benaiah the son of Jehoiada; and he fell upon him that he died.

<sup>(26)</sup> And unto Abiathar the priest said the king, Get thee to Anathoth, unto thine own fields; for thou *art* <sup>1</sup>worthy of death: but I will not at this time put thee to death, because thou barest the ark of the Lord GOD before David my father, and because thou hast been afflicted in all wherein my father was afflicted. <sup>(27)</sup> So Solomon thrust out Abiathar from being priest unto the LORD; that he might <sup>b</sup>fulfil the word of the LORD, which he spake concerning the house of Eli in Shiloh.

<sup>(28)</sup> Then tidings came to Joab: for Joab had turned after Adonijah, though he turned not after Absalom. And Joab fled unto the tabernacle of the LORD, and caught hold on the horns of the altar. <sup>(29)</sup> And it was told king Solomon that Joab was fled unto the tabernacle of the LORD; and, behold, *he is* by the altar. Then Solomon sent

*a* 2 Sam. 7. 12, 13.
<sup>1</sup> Heb., *a man of death.*
*b* 1 Sam. 2. 31, 35.
B.C. 1014.

---

<sup>(22)</sup> **And why dost thou ask?**—In Solomon's answer there is a certain bitterness, venting itself in irony, which seems to argue the mingling with kingly dignity and policy of some passionate feeling, not unlike the bursts of passion in his father, as in the case of Nabal (1 Sam. xxv. 21, 22). It certainly gives some probability to the conjecture (see Note on i. 3) that Abishag was the "fair Shulamite" of the Song of Solomon, already loved by the youthful king. In his wrath he infers, rightly or wrongly, that the hand of the conspirators is seen in this petition, and executes vengeance accordingly, summarily and without giving them any trial or opportunity of excusing themselves.

<sup>(23)</sup> **God do so to me, and more also.**—See Ruth i. 17; 1 Sam. iii. 17, xiv. 44, xx. 13, xxv. 22, 2 Sam. xi. 14, &c. This well-known formula of imprecation—which the LXX. renders, "May God do these things to me and add these things also"—was probably accompanied with some gesture signifying utter destruction.

<sup>(24)</sup> **As the Lord liveth, which hath...**—There is something characteristic in this adjuration, as compared with that of David in chap. i. 29. In David we always see the living man, whose soul longs after God with a vivid personal devotion. Solomon is emphatically the king, sitting on the throne of David, with his house established for ever. In the majesty of his royalty his individual character is to us almost entirely merged.

<sup>(25)</sup> **Sent by the hand of Benaiah.**—The chief of the body-guard is the chief of "the executioners" (see chap. i. 38), apparently, in the case of great criminals, carrying out the sentence of condemnation with his own hand. (Comp. Judges viii. 20, 21.)

<sup>(26)</sup> **Anathoth** is noted, in Josh. xxi. 18; 1 Chron. vi. 60, as a city of the priests in the territory of Benjamin, but a few miles from Jerusalem, and is best known to us as the birthplace of Jeremiah (Jer. i. 1, xxxii. 7).

It is notable that it is not Abiathar's priestly character which protects him, but the remembrance of his long friendship to David in adversity, and probably of that special promise which David made to him, perhaps not without remorse, when he found that his deceit to Ahimelech had drawn down Saul's bloody vengeance upon him and his family (1 Sam. xxii. 20—23).

<sup>(27)</sup> **That he might fulfil.**—In these words is described, not the purpose, but the effect of Solomon's action. The prophecy referred to is, of course, that of 1 Sam. ii. 30—35, iii. 11—14, fulfilled by the degradation, in Abiathar's person, of the house of Ithamar, and the exaltation, or restoration, in Zadok, of the house of Eleazar, to whom, as the elder son of Aaron, the primacy would have seemed naturally to belong. It seems clear from verse 35 that Abiathar had hitherto had some superiority, although in the various notices of the two, Zadok's name stands first; but whether of actual authority, or only of priority of dignity, cannot be determined. While the Tabernacle remained at Gibeon under Zadok's charge, and the Ark was in Mount Zion under Abiathar, there might, indeed, be something like co-ordination between the two. This, in any case, must have disappeared at the building of the Temple; and the disgrace of Abiathar determined that the undivided dignity should pass to Zadok.

<sup>(28)</sup> **Joab had turned.**—It is strange that Joab should have been in no danger or anxiety immediately after the actual failure of the conspiracy; and it is also notable that, although the real motive for putting him to death was to punish his support of Adonijah, now renewed, yet Solomon's words in pronouncing sentence on him refrain from mention of any thing except the old crimes dwelt upon in the dying charge of David. Possibly this was done to bring Joab's case within the emphatic declaration of the Law, that no sanctuary should protect the wilful and treacherous murderer, and that innocent blood, so shed and left unavenged, would pollute the land (Exod. xxi. 14; Num. xxxv. 33). It is significant, moreover, of the increased power of the monarchy, even in hands young and yet untried, that the old captain of the host, who had been "too hard" for David, even before David's great sin, should now fall, as it would seem, without a single act of resistance or word of remon-

15

Benaiah the son of Jehoiada, saying, Go, fall upon him. (30) And Benaiah came to the tabernacle of the LORD, and said unto him, Thus saith the king, Come forth. And he said, Nay; but I will die here. And Benaiah brought the king word again, saying, Thus said Joab, and thus he answered me. (31) And the king said unto him, Do as he hath said, and fall upon him, and bury him; that thou mayest take away the innocent blood, which Joab shed, from me, and from the house of my father. (32) And the LORD shall return his blood upon his own head, who fell upon two men more righteous and better than he, and slew them with the sword, my father David not knowing thereof, to wit, *a* Abner the son of Ner, captain of the host of Israel, and *b* Amasa the son of Jether, captain of the host of Judah. (33) Their blood shall therefore return upon the head of Joab, and upon the head of his seed for ever: but upon David, and upon his seed, and upon his house, and upon his throne, shall there be peace for ever from the LORD. (34) So Benaiah the son of Jehoiada went up, and fell upon him, and slew him: and he was buried in his own house in the wilderness. (35) And the king put Benaiah the son of Jehoiada in his room over the host: and Zadok the priest did the king put in the room of Abiathar.

(36) And the king sent and called for Shimei, and said unto him, Build thee an house in Jerusalem, and dwell there, and go not forth thence any whither. (37) For it shall be, *that* on the day thou goest out, and passest over the brook Kidron, thou shalt know for certain that thou shalt surely die: thy blood shall be upon thine own head. (38) And Shimei said unto the king, The saying *is* good: as my lord the king hath said, so will thy servant do. And Shimei dwelt in Jerusalem many days. (39) And it came to pass at the end of three years, that two of the servants of Shimei ran away unto Achish son of Maachah king of Gath. And they told Shimei, saying, Behold, thy servants *be* in Gath. (40) And Shimei arose, and saddled his ass, and went to Gath to Achish to seek his servants: and Shimei went, and brought his servants from Gath. (41) And it was told Solomon that Shimei had gone from Jerusalem to Gath, and was come again. (42) And the king sent and called for Shimei, and said unto him, Did I not make thee to swear by the LORD, and protested unto thee, saying, Know for a certain, on the day thou goest out, and walkest abroad any whither, that thou shalt surely die? and thou saidst unto me, The word *that* I have heard *is* good. (43) Why then hast thou not kept the oath of the LORD, and the commandment that I have charged thee with? (44) The king said moreover to Shimei, Thou knowest all the wickedness which thine heart is privy to, that thou didst to David my father: therefore the LORD shall return thy wickedness upon thine own head; (45) and king Solomon *shall be* blessed, and the throne of David shall be established before the LORD for ever. (46) So the king commanded Benaiah the son of Jehoiada; which went out, and fell upon him, that he died, and the *c* kingdom was established in the hand of Solomon.

*a* 2 Sam. 3. 27.

B.C. 1011.

*b* 2 Sam. 20. 10.

*c* 2 Chr. 1. 1.

---

strance on his behalf, after a long career of faithful service, only once tarnished by disloyalty. It has been noticed that if (as is probable) the "Tabernacle of the Lord" at Gibeon is meant, Joab falls close to the scene of his murder of Amasa, "at the great stone in Gibeon" (2 Sam. xx. 18).

(35) **And the king put.**—Benaiah succeeds to Joab's command over the host: but it is notable that in the Hebrew text of chap. iv. 2—6, there is no mention of any successor to his command over the body-guard.

(36) **Called for Shimei.**—The command given to Shimei is in itself a reasonable precaution against treason, in one already powerful and of doubtful fidelity; and the reference to crossing the Kedron shows that it was designed to prevent his resorting to his native place, Bahurim. But it is difficult, in face of David's charge, to doubt that it was in some degree intended as a snare; and this view is confirmed by Solomon's words in verse 44, which refer back to the old offence of Shimei against David. The narrative gives no hint that Shimei's expedition to Gath was not made in good faith, simply to regain his slaves; and a command, which had its justification in the danger likely to result from his residence in Bahurim, among his own people, could hardly be disobeyed in spirit by a temporary journey to a foreign country. Legally the execution was justifiable, and it may have been politic; but it cannot stand examination on the ground of equity or generosity. It is here probably related by anticipation.

(39) **Achish son of Maachah.**—In 1 Sam. xxvii. 2 we read of Achish son of Maoch, king of Gath; but chronology makes it most unlikely that the same person should here be referred to. The name may have been hereditary.

## I. KINGS, III.

**CHAPTER III.**—(1) And ᵃSolomon made affinity with Pharaoh king of Egypt, and took Pharaoh's daughter, and brought her into the city of David, until he had made an end of building his own house, and the house of the Lord, and the wall of Jerusalem round about.

(2) Only the people sacrificed in high places, because there was no house built unto the name of the Lord, until those days. (3) And Solomon loved the Lord, walking in the statutes of David his father: only he sacrificed and burnt incense in high places.

(4) And the king went to Gibeon to sacrifice there; for that *was* the great high place: a thousand burnt offerings did Solomon offer upon that altar. (5) In Gibeon the Lord appeared to Solomon in a dream by night: and God said, Ask what I shall give thee. (6) And

B.C. 1014.

ᵃ ch. 7. 8.

---

III.

This chapter completes, in a narrative singularly beautiful and instructive, the detailed record of the early days of Solomon's reign—a record which bears such marks of continuity as argue derivation from a single source.

(1) **Pharaoh king of Egypt.**—At this time it would appear, from the Egyptian records and traditions, that Egypt was weak and divided, and that what is called the twenty-first dynasty of the Tanite kings was ruling in Lower Egypt. This, and a corresponding abeyance (judging from the monuments) of Assyrian power, gave scope for the rise to sudden greatness and wealth of the Israelite kingdom under Solomon, and probably induced the Egyptian king of those days to consent to an alliance which, at other times, the greatness of the Pharaohs might have spurned. No fault is found with the alliance by the sacred historian, for the Egyptians were never looked upon with the same aversion as the strange women of the Canaanite races. As, moreover, it is not in any way connected with Solomon's subsequent declension into idolatry, noticed in chap. xi. 1—8, it is not unlikely that the new queen literally acted on the call of the Psalmist (Ps. xlv. 10) to "*forget her own people and her father's house.*"

(2) **In high places.**—The historian, writing from the point of view of his own time, when, after the solemn consecration of the Temple, the worship at "the high places," which form natural sanctuaries, was forbidden, explains that "because there was no house built unto the name of the Lord," the people, and Solomon himself, sacrificed and burnt incense in the high places. It is clear that these high places were of two kinds—places of sacrifice to false gods, and unauthorised sanctuaries of the Lord, probably associating His worship with visible representations of Deity. The former class were, of course, absolute abominations, like the high places of the Canaanite races, so sternly denounced in Deut. xii. 2, 3. The prohibition of the other class of high places—constantly disobeyed by some even of the better kings—appears to have had two distinct objects—(*a*) to guard against all local corruptions of God's service, and all idolatry, worshipping Him (as at Bethel) under visible forms; (*b*) to prevent the breach of national unity, by the congregation of the separate tribes round local sanctuaries. But besides these objects, it served (*c*), as a very remarkable spiritual education for the worship of the invisible God, without the aid of local and visible emblems of His presence, in accordance with the higher prophetic teaching, and preparatory for the perfect spirituality of the future. It is, indeed, hardly to be conceived that there should not have been before the Captivity some places of non-sacrificial worship, in some degree like the synagogues of the period after the exile, although not as yet developed into a fully organised system. Unless we refer Ps. lxxiv. 8 to the Maccabæan times, it must be supposed to describe the Chaldæan invasion, as destroying not only the Temple, but also "all the houses of God"—properly "assemblies," and in our Bible version actually translated "synagogues"—"in the land." But these places of prayer and praise and instruction would be different in their whole idea from the "high places" rivalling the Temple. Up to this time it is clear that, even under Samuel and David, sacrificial worship elsewhere than in the Tabernacle was used without scruple, though certainly alien from the spirit of the Mosaic Law as to the supreme sacredness of the "place which God should choose to place his name there." (See, for example, 1 Sam. vii. 10, xiii. 9, xiv. 35, xvi. 5; 1 Chron. xxi. 26.) After the solemn consecration of the Temple, the circumstances and the character of such worship were altogether changed.

(4) **Gibeon.**—The name itself, signifying "belonging to a hill," indicates its position on the central plateau of Israel, in the land of Benjamin, whence rise several round hills, on one of which the town stood. There was now reared the Tabernacle, with the brazen altar of sacrifice, to which the descendants of the old Gibeonites were attached as "hewers of wood and drawers of water" (Joshua ix. 23). It was therefore naturally "the great high place."

(5) **The Lord appeared.**—This direct communication to Solomon by a dream—standing in contrast with the indirect knowledge of the Lord's will by David through the prophets Nathan and Gad (2 Sam. vii. 2—17, xii. 1—14, xxiv. 11—14), and by "enquiring of the Lord" through the priest (1 Sam. xxiii. 9—12, xxx. 7; 2 Sam. ii. 1)—is perhaps the first indication of some temporary abeyance of the prophetic office, and (as appears still more clearly from the history of the consecration of the Temple), of a loss of leadership in the priesthood. At the same time it is to be noted that the vision of the Lord through dreams, being of a lower type than the waking vision, is mostly recorded as given to those outside the Covenant, as Abimelech (Gen. xx. 3—7), Laban (Gen. xxxi. 24), Pharaoh and his servants (Gen. xl. 5, xli. 1—8), the Midianite (Judges vii. 13), and Nebuchadnezzar (Dan. ii. 1, iv. 10—18); as belonging to the early stages of revelation, to Abraham (Gen. xv. 12), Jacob (Gen. xxviii. 12—15), and Joseph (Gen. xxxvii. 5—10); and as marking the time of cessation of the regular succession of the prophets during the Captivity (Dan. ii. 19, vii. 1).

(6) **And Solomon said.**—On Solomon's "wisdom," see Note on chap. iv. 29. Here it is clear that the wisdom which he asks is that of the ruler, involving

Solomon said, Thou hast shewed unto thy servant David my father great ¹mercy, according as he walked before thee in truth, and in righteousness, and in uprightness of heart with thee; and thou hast kept for him this great kindness, that thou hast given him a son to sit on his throne, as *it is* this day. ⁽⁷⁾ And now, O LORD my God, thou hast made thy servant king instead of David my father: and I *am but* a little child: I know not *how* to go out or come in. ⁽⁸⁾ And thy servant *is* in the midst of thy people which thou hast chosen, a great people, that cannot be numbered nor counted for multitude. ⁽⁹⁾ ᵃGive therefore thy servant an ²understanding heart to judge thy people, that I may discern between good and bad: for who is able to judge this thy so great a people? ⁽¹⁰⁾ And the speech pleased the Lord, that Solomon had asked this thing. ⁽¹¹⁾ And God said unto him, Because thou hast asked this thing, and hast not asked for thyself ³long life; neither hast asked riches for thyself, nor hast asked the life of thine enemies; but hast asked for thyself understanding ⁴to discern judgment; ⁽¹²⁾ Behold, I have done according to thy words: lo, I have given thee a wise and an understanding heart; so that there was none like thee before thee, neither after thee shall any arise like unto thee. ⁽¹³⁾ And I have also ᵇgiven thee that which thou hast not asked, both riches, and honour: so that there shall not be any among the kings like unto thee all thy days. ⁽¹⁴⁾ And if thou wilt walk in my ways, to keep my statutes and my commandments, as ᶜthy father David did walk, then I will lengthen thy days. ⁽¹⁵⁾ And Solomon awoke; and, behold, *it was* a dream. And he came to Jerusalem, and stood before the ark of the covenant of the LORD, and offered up burnt offerings, and offered peace offerings, and made a feast to all his servants.

⁽¹⁶⁾ Then came there two women, *that were* harlots, unto the king, and stood before him. ⁽¹⁷⁾ And the one woman said, O my lord, I and this woman dwell in one house; and I was delivered of a child with her in the house. ⁽¹⁸⁾ And it came to pass the third day after that I was delivered, that this woman was delivered also: and we *were* together; *there was* no stranger with us in the house, save we two in the house. ⁽¹⁹⁾ And this woman's child died in the night; because she overlaid it. ⁽²⁰⁾ And she arose at midnight, and took my son from beside

---

1 Or, *bounty.*
a 2 Chron. 1. 10.
2 Heb., *hearing.*
3 Heb., *many days.*
4 Heb., *to hear.*
b Wisd. 7. 11; Matt. 6. 33.
5 Or, *hath not been*
c ch. 15. 5.

---

elements both moral and intellectual—the wisdom to discern and do true justice between man and man. He calls himself "a little child"—his age is variously estimated from twelve to twenty at this time—and trembles at the responsibility of ruling over "so great a people." But, in the characteristic spirit of the true godliness of the Old Testament, he looks for wisdom, not as the mere result of human teaching and experience, but as an inspiration of God, and prays for it accordingly, in a prayer of singular beauty and humility, pleading simply God's promise to his father, and its fulfilment in his own accession to the throne.

⁽¹¹⁾ **Because thou hast asked.**—It is obvious to note this verse as a fulfilment of the Divine law, "Seek first the kingdom of God and his righteousness, and all these things shall be added unto you" (Matt. vi. 33). All these secondary blessings are good, just so far as they conduce to the supreme good, which is the growth of the human nature, by the knowledge of God and by faithfully doing His work on earth, to the perfection designed for it in His wisdom. So long as Solomon used them in subordination to true wisdom, they were a blessing to him; when he made them idols, they became a curse. The connection of these lower gifts with the moral and intellectual gifts of wisdom, is the result of the natural law of God's Providence, so far as that law overcomes the resistance of evil and folly, still allowed to strive against it.

⁽¹⁴⁾ **I will lengthen.**—In this promise only one point, "length of days," is conditional; and it was not fulfilled. For though Solomon's age at the time of death is not given, yet, as his reign is given as lasting forty years, it could hardly have exceeded sixty. (Josephus, indeed, with his usual tendency to amplification, extends the reign to eighty years, and makes Solomon die in extreme old age.) The rest received an extraordinary fulfilment. The greatness of Solomon's kingdom stands out remarkable in its sudden and unique development, the fruit of David's long career of conquest and improvement, destined to wither at once at Solomon's death. Then, for the first and last time, did the monarchy assume something of the character of an empire, unequalled in peaceful prosperity of wealth and power, and in splendour of civilisation.

⁽¹⁵⁾ **Stood before the ark of the covenant,** in its Tabernacle on Mount Sion, which now constituted a second, and probably still more sacred, place of worship. The great sacrifice—now distinctly a thank-offering, followed as usual by a sacred feast—is naturally repeated there.

⁽¹⁶⁾ **Then came there.**—The celebrated "judgment of Solomon," given here as a specimen of his wisdom, is simply an instance of intuitive sagacity, cutting the Gordian knot of hopeless difficulty by the appeal to maternal instinct—an appeal which might, of course, fail, but which was, under the exceptional circumstances, the only appeal possible. It is in the knowledge how to risk failure rather than be reduced to impotence, and how to go straight to the heart of a difficulty

*Solomon judges between*       I. KINGS, IV.       *the two Women.*

me, while thine handmaid slept, and laid it in her bosom, and laid her dead child in my bosom. (21) And when I rose in the morning to give my child suck, behold, it was dead: but when I had considered it in the morning, behold, it was not my son, which I did bear. (22) And the other woman said, Nay; but the living *is* my son, and the dead *is* thy son. And this said, No; but the dead *is* thy son, and the living *is* my son. Thus they spake before the king.

(23) Then said the king, The one saith, This *is* my son that liveth, and thy son *is* the dead: and the other saith, Nay; but thy son *is* the dead, and my son *is* the living. (24) And the king said, Bring me a sword. And they brought a sword before the king. (25) And the king said, Divide the living child in two, and give half to the one, and half to the other. (26) Then spake the woman whose the living child *was* unto the king, for her bowels [1]yearned upon her son, and she said, O my lord, give her the living child, and in no wise slay it. But the other said, Let it be neither mine nor thine, *but* divide *it*. (27) Then the king answered and said, Give her the living child, and in no wise slay it: she *is* the mother thereof.

(28) And all Israel heard of the judgment which the king had judged; and they feared the king: for they saw that the wisdom of God *was* [2]in him, to do judgment.

CHAPTER IV.—(1) So king Solomon was king over all Israel.

(2) And these *were* the princes which he had; Azariah the son of Zadok [3]the priest, (3) Elihoreph and Ahiah, the sons of Shisha, [4]scribes; Jehoshaphat the son of Ahilud, the [5]recorder. (4) And Benaiah the son of Jehoiada *was* over the host: and Zadok and Abiathar *were* the priests: (5) And Azariah the son of Nathan *was* over the officers: and Zabud the son of

[1] Heb., *were hot.*

[2] Heb., *in the midst of him.*

[3] Or, *the chief officer.*

[4] Or, *secretaries.*

[5] Or, *remembrancer.*

---

when the slow, regular approaches of science are impossible, that we recognise what men call "a touch of genius," and what Scripture here calls the "wisdom of God."

### IV.

The style of this and the succeeding chapter changes from the vividness and fulness of the preceding chapters to a drier and barer record, evidently drawn from the national archives.

(1) **King over all Israel.**—The emphasis laid upon "all" is characteristic of the writer, who compiled the book after the disruption of the kingdom.

(2) **And these were.**—The officers described are of two classes—those attached to Solomon's Court, and those invested with local authority.

**The princes** are evidently Solomon's high counsellors and officers, "eating at the king's table." The word is derived from a root which means to "set in order." It is significant that whereas in the lists of David's officers in 2 Sam. viii. 16—18, xx. 23—26, the captain of the host stands first, and is followed in one list by the captain of the body-guard, both are here preceded by the peaceful offices of the priests, scribes, and the recorder.

**Azariah the son of Zadok the priest.**—In 1 Chron. vi. 9, 10, we find Azariah described as the son of Ahimaaz, and so grandson of Zadok; and the note in verse 10 (which is apparently out of its right place) seems to show that he was high priest at the time when the Temple was built. The title the "priest" in this place must be given by anticipation, for it is expressly said below that "Zadok and Abiathar were now the priests." The use of the original word, *Cohen* (probably signifying "one who ministers"), appears sometimes to retain traces of the old times, when the priesthood and headship of the family were united, and to be applied accordingly to princes, to whom perhaps still attached something of the ancient privilege. Thus it is given to the sons of David in 2 Sam. viii. 18, where the parallel passage in 1 Chron. xviii. 17 has a paraphrase, "chief about the king," evidently intended to explain the sense in which it is used in the older record. We may remember that David himself on occasions wore the priestly ephod (see 2 Sam. vi. 14). Possibly in this sense it is applied in verse 5 to Zabud, the "king's friend" (where the Authorised Version renders it by "principal officer"). But in this verse there is every reason for taking it in the usual sense. Azariah was already a "prince" before he succeeded to the high priesthood. The mingling of priestly and princely functions is characteristic of the time.

(3) **Sons of Shisha.**—In 1 Chron. xviii. 16 "Shavsha," and in 2 Sam. xx. 25 "Sheva," is mentioned as the scribe of David. Probably these are variations of the same name, and the office may have become virtually hereditary. The "scribe," or (see Margin) "secretary," is constantly referred to as a high officer, issuing the king's edicts and letters, and acting in his name, like our "Secretaries of State."

**Jehoshaphat the son of Ahilud** is named in 2 Sam. viii. 16, xx. 24, and 1 Chron. xviii. 15 as having been under David also the "recorder" or "remembrancer"—probably the annalist who drew up and preserved the archives of the kingdom.

(4) **Zadok and Abiathar . . . the priests.**—Abiathar, though disgraced and practically deposed, was still regarded theoretically as priest (much as Annas is called "high priest" in the Gospels), for the priesthood was properly for life.

(5) **Son of Nathan.**—Probably Nathan, son of David, and own brother of Solomon (1 Chron. iii. 5), is here intended; for the title *Cohen*, here given to Zabud, is expressly ascribed in 2 Sam. viii. 18 to the "sons of David;" and Nathan the prophet always has his title, "the prophet," appended to his name wherever first mentioned in this book. (See chap. i. 8, 10, 22, 32, &c.)

Nathan *was* principal officer, *and* the king's friend: ⁽⁶⁾ And Ahishar *was* over the household: and ᵃAdoniram the son of Abda *was* over the ¹tribute.

⁽⁷⁾ And Solomon had twelve officers over all Israel, which provided victuals for the king and his household: each man his month in a year made provision. ⁽⁸⁾ And these *are* their names: ²The son of Hur, in mount Ephraim: ⁽⁹⁾ ³the son of Dekar, in Makaz, and in Shaalbim, and Beth-shemesh, and Elonbeth-hanan: ⁽¹⁰⁾ ⁴the son of Hesed, in Aruboth; to him *pertained* Sochoh, and all the land of Hepher: ⁽¹¹⁾ ⁵the son of Abinadab, in all the region of Dor; which had Taphath the daughter of Solomon to wife: ⁽¹²⁾ Baana the son of Ahilud; *to him pertained* Taanach and Megiddo, and all Beth-shean, which *is* by Zartanah

ᵃ ch. 5. 14.

1 Or, *levy.*

2 Or, *Ben-hur.*

3 Or, *Ben-dekar.*

4 Or, *Ben-hesed.*

5 Or, *Ben-abinadab.*

---

Azariah is the "chief of the officers"—that is, chief over the twelve officers mentioned below (verses 7—19)—living, however, at Court.

Zabud, besides the title of *Cohen*, has that of "the king's friend," previously given to Hushai (2 Sam. xv. 37, xvi. 16), and apparently indicating special intimacy and wisdom as a "privy counsellor."

⁽⁶⁾ **Over the household**,—like the "High Steward" of a modern Court. In 2 Kings xviii. 18 we have the same three officers mentioned ("Eliakim, who was over the household, and Shebna the scribe, and Joah the son of Asaph the recorder").

**Adoniram . . . over the tribute** (or "levy"),—evidently the head of Solomon's great public works. (See chap. v. 14.) The name is elsewhere given as *Adoram*. It is to be noticed that in the enumeration of David's officers in the early part of the reign (2 Sam. viii. 16—18) no such officer is found; but that in the latter part of his reign the list contains the name of Adoram (2 Sam. xx. 24). It has been thought that the numbering of the people recorded in 2 Sam. xxiv. and 1 Chron. xxi., was in preparation for such forced work, and hence was odious to Joab and others. In 1 Kings xii. 18 we read how the holder of this office, being naturally most unpopular with those who had felt the burden of Solomon's splendour, was stoned to death in the insurrection against Rehoboam.

To this list the Greek Version adds: "Eliab the son of Shaphat was over the body-guard." As the office of captain of the body-guard is found in the other lists, and is too important to be omitted, it is possible that this addition corrects some defect in the Hebrew text. Yet it is also possible that no successor to Benaiah was appointed, as experience had shown, in the crushing of the rebellion of Adonijah, how easily the captaincy of the body-guard might become a quasi-independent power.

⁽⁷⁾ **Provided victuals for the king and his household.**—This denotes the collection of revenue—mostly, no doubt, in kind—for the maintenance of the Court and household and guards of the king; and perhaps may have included also the management of the royal domain lands, such as is described under David's reign in 1 Chron. xxvi. 25—31. It is curious that in five cases only the patronymic of the officer is given, probably from some defect in the archives from which this chapter is evidently drawn. The office must have been of high importance and dignity, for in two cases (verses 11, 15) the holders of it were married into the royal house. The provinces over which they had authority—nine on the west and three on the east of Jordan—coincide only in a few cases with the lands assigned to the several tribes. It is not unlikely that by this time much of the tribal division of territory had become obsolete, although we see from 1 Chron. xxvii. 16—22, that for chieftainship over men, and for levy in war, it still remained in force.

⁽⁸⁾ **And these are their names.**—The first division, "mount Ephraim," included all the higher part of the territory of Ephraim, one of the most fertile and beautiful regions in Palestine, surrounding the city of Shechem, which lies in a rich plain between Mount Ebel and Gerizim, and including the strong site of the future Samaria. See the description of the country in the blessing of Moses (Deut. xxxiii. 13—17).

⁽⁹⁾ The second division included the territory in the maritime plain to the north-west of Judah; assigned to Dan, but in all the earlier history held, with perhaps a few exceptions, by the Philistines. The cities Shaalbim, Elon, and Beth-shemesh, or Ir-shemesh, are noted in Josh. xix. 41—43. Makaz is not mentioned elsewhere. There is here the addition to the name *Elon of beth-hanan* ("the house of Hanan") In 1 Chron. viii. 23 there is a Hanan among the chief men of Benjamin; and 1 Chron. l. 43 a Hanan among David's mighty men. The only one of these cities known in history is Beth-shemesh, the first resting-place of the Ark (1 Sam. vi. 12—21) when restored by the Philistines.

⁽¹⁰⁾ The third division was also in the land of the Philistines, being part of the territory assigned to Judah. Sochoh is mentioned in Josh. xv. 35, and is noticed in 1 Sam. xvii. 1—3 as close to the field of battle on which David slew Goliath. Hepher is an old Amorite city which was conquered by Joshua (Josh. xii. 17), still, by a curious survival, giving its name to the whole district, to which the name Aruboth (otherwise unknown) is here also given.

⁽¹¹⁾ The fourth division, "all the region of Dor," still lies along the coast, but to the north of the preceding districts, close under Mount Carmel, in the territory assigned to Manasseh. Dor is named in Josh. xi. 2, as forming a part of the confederacy of the north under Jabin, and as subsequently conquered (chap. xii. 23), and given to Manasseh (chap. xvii. 11).

⁽¹²⁾ The fifth division must have been large and important, including much of the great plain of Esdraelon or Jezreel, the garden and battle-field of Northern Palestine, and extending to the Jordan valley. Taanach, Megiddo, and Beth-shean are all named as Canaanitish cities not taken by Manasseh, but made tributary (Josh. xvii. 11; Judges i. 27). Taanach and Megiddo are referred to in the song of Deborah (Judges v. 19). Megiddo is the place of the death of Ahaziah (2 Kings ix. 27) and the fall of Josiah (2 Kings xxiii. 29). Beth-shean is the city in which the body of Saul was exposed in triumph (1 Sam. xxxi. 12). Abel-meholah, the birth-place of Elisha (1 Kings xix. 16), lies south of Beth-shean, and is mentioned in the record of the rout of the Midianites by Gideon (Judges vii. 22). Jokmeam

*Solomon's Officers.*     I. KINGS, IV.     *The Peace and Size of his Kingdom.*

beneath Jezreel, from Beth-shean to Abel-meholah, *even* unto *the place that is* beyond Jokneam: <sup>(13)</sup> ¹the son of Geber, in Ramoth-gilead; to him pertained the towns of Jair the son of Manasseh, which *are* in Gilead; to him *also* pertained the region of Argob, which *is* in Bashan, threescore great cities with walls and brasen bars: <sup>(14)</sup> Ahinadab the son of Iddo *had* ²Mahanaim: <sup>(15)</sup> Ahimaaz *was* in Naphtali; he also took Basmath the daughter of Solomon to wife: <sup>(16)</sup> Baanah the son of Hushai *was* in Asher and in Aloth: <sup>(17)</sup> Jehoshaphat the son of Paruah, in Issachar: <sup>(18)</sup> Shimei the son of Elah, in Benjamin: <sup>(19)</sup> Geber the son of Uri *was* in the country of Gilead, *in* the country of Sihon king of the Amorites, and of Og king of Bashan; and *he was* the only officer which *was* in the land.

<sup>(20)</sup> Judah and Israel *were* many, as the sand which *is* by the sea in multitude, eating and drinking, and making merry. <sup>(21)</sup> And <sup>a</sup>Solomon reigned over all kingdoms from the river unto the land of the Philistines, and unto the border of Egypt: they brought presents, and

1 Or, *Ben-geber.*
2 Or, *to Mahanaim.*
a Ecclus. 47. 13.

---

(for such is the right reading) is a Levitical city in Ephraim (1 Chron. vi. 68), apparently called Kibzaim in Josh. xxi. 22, and must have been an outlying part of this division.

<sup>(13)</sup> The sixth division, large, but probably less fertile, crosses the Jordan, and includes a great portion of the territory of Manasseh and Gad. The region of Argob, "the rocky region" (afterwards translated into the Greek name *Trachonitis*), is noticed in Deut. iii. 4, 13, 14, as the land of Og, covered with great cities, taken by Jair, son of Manasseh, and called *Havoth-Jair*—"the towns of Jair." Ramoth-gilead was a Levitical city and a city of refuge, in Gad (Deut. iv. 43; Josh. xx. 8, xxi. 38), famous afterwards in the wars with the Syrians (1 Kings xxii. 3; 2 Kings viii. 28, ix. 1).

<sup>(14)</sup> The seventh division, still on the other side of Jordan, is the region of Mahanaim, in the territory of Gad. Mahanaim ("the camps"), the scene of Jacob's angelic vision on his return to Canaan (Gen. xxxvi. 3), assigned to Dan after the Conquest (see Josh. xiii. 26, 30, xxi. 38), must have been afterwards an important place; for it was the seat of Ishbosheth's government (2 Sam. ii. 8, 12, 29), and the place where David established himself on fleeing from Absalom (2 Sam. xvii. 24, 27), and where he received large supplies from Barzillai and other chiefs.

<sup>(15)</sup> The eighth division is the upper valley of the Jordan, south of Mount Hermon, including part of the north-west coast of the sea of Gennesareth and the water of Merom. In it lie Hazor, forming the centre of the native confederacy of the north, and the Levitical city of refuge, Kedesh-Naphtali (Josh. xii. 22, xix. 37; Judg. iv. 6).

<sup>(16)</sup> The ninth division, "in Asher and Aloth," bordered on the Tyrian territory, stretching north from Mount Carmel, first along the coast, and then behind the ranges of Lebanon. In Judg. i. 31, 32, we read that the tribe of Asher did not occupy the territory assigned them (Josh. xix. 24—30), but mingled with the native inhabitants. Aloth (or in the Greek Version *Baloth*) is unknown, and Josephus places this province on the coast, near Achzib.

<sup>(17)</sup> The tenth division, the territory of Issachar, lying north of Manasseh, included part of the great plain of Esdraelon, and must have been so closely connected with the fifth division that the frontiers could hardly be discerned.

<sup>(18)</sup> The eleventh division, the territory of Benjamin (properly including Jerusalem itself), though small, is singularly strong and populous, including Jericho, Bethel, Gibeon, Ramah, extending from Judah to Ephraim, and commanding the centre of the high land of what was afterwards the kingdom of Judah.

<sup>(19)</sup> The twelfth division was on the east of Jordan, south of the seventh, including the pastoral country of Reuben and part of Gad on the borders of Moab, probably occupied by the royal flocks and herds.

In place of the reading of the text, "and *he was* the only officer in the land"—which yields very little meaning, for in each of the divisions there was but one governor—the LXX. here reads, "and Naseph (or an officer), one only in the land of Judah." The reading seems probable; for it will be noticed that in the enumeration the territory of Judah is otherwise altogether omitted. It supplies accordingly here the mention of a special governor, over and above the twelve, for the royal tribe. It has been thought that as Judah was the home province, it was under no other government than that of the king's officers at Jerusalem; but for purposes of revenue it seems hardly likely that it should have been excepted from the general system. Possibly Azariah, who was over the officers residing at the Court, may have been its territorial governor.

In some MSS. of the Greek Version, verses 27, 28 immediately follow verse 19, and (as verses 20, 21 are omitted) they form a link between verses 7—19 and verses 22, 23, in a very natural order.

<sup>(20)</sup> **Were many.**—The description of the condition of the people here and in verse 25, as multiplied in numbers, and living in festivity and peace, is evidently designed to specify not only their general prosperity and wealth, but also the fact noticed in chap. ix. 20—22, that at this time they were a dominant race, relieved from all burden of labour, and ruling over the subject races, now reduced to complete subjection and serfship. (That it was otherwise hereafter is clear from the complaints to Rehoboam in chap. xii. 4.) Now, for the first time, did Israel enter on full possession of the territory promised in the days of the Conquest (Josh. i. 4), and so into the complete fulfilment of the promise to Abraham, alluded to in the words, "many as the sand which is by the sea in multitude" (Gen. xxii. 17).

<sup>(21)</sup> **And Solomon reigned.**—His dominion is described as extending on the south to the land of the Philistines and the border of Egypt, including what we call Arabia (see Ps. lxxii. 10, and comp. chap. x. 15); on the east to "the river" Euphrates, as far north as Tiphsah (the Greek Thapsacus); on the west it would, of course, be bounded by the sea; and on the north it extended far beyond Damascus, probably

served Solomon all the days of his life. <sup>(22)</sup> And Solomon's ¹provision for one day was thirty ²measures of fine flour, and threescore measures of meal, <sup>(23)</sup> ten fat oxen, and twenty oxen out of the pastures, and an hundred sheep, beside harts, and roebucks, and fallowdeer, and fatted fowl. <sup>(24)</sup> For he had dominion over all *the region* on this side the river, from Tiphsah even to Azzah, over all the kings on this side the river: and he had peace on all sides round about him. <sup>(25)</sup> And Judah and Israel dwelt ³safely, every man under his vine and under his fig tree, from Dan even to Beer-sheba, all the days of Solomon. <sup>(26)</sup> And ªSolomon had forty thousand stalls of horses for his chariots, and twelve thousand horsemen. <sup>(27)</sup> And those officers provided victual for king Solomon, and for all that came unto king Solomon's table, every man in his month: they lacked nothing. <sup>(28)</sup> Barley also and straw for the horses and ⁴dromedaries brought they unto the place where *the officers* were, every man according to his charge.

<sup>(29)</sup> And ᵇGod gave Solomon wisdom

---

1 Heb., *bread*.
2 Heb., *cors*.
3 Heb., *confidently*.
a 2 Chron. 9. 25.
4 Or, *mules*, or, *swift beasts*.
b Ecclus. 47. 14, 15, 16.

---

up to the borders of the Assyrian Empire. It seems also clear that the Syrian Kingdoms (like the kingdom of Tyre), were allies on a footing of some dependence, though not exactly tributaries. This extension of dominion was the fruit of the warlike energy of the two preceding reigns. As in all ancient Eastern empires, it represented, not an organised monarchy, but the supremacy of a dominant kingdom over tributaries gathered round—" the kings on this side the river" who "brought presents"—apparently at that time numerous, and ruling over small territories. Such an empire would rise rapidly, and as rapidly fall to pieces; and in Solomon's case it was sustained less by military power than by the peaceful forces of wealth and policy, and was largely dependent on his own personal ascendancy.

<sup>(22)</sup> **Measures.**—The "measure" (*cor*) is variously estimated (from 86 to 42 gallons). In any case the quantity is very large, and, like the other notices of provisions supplied, indicates a vast number, probably several thousands, belonging to the royal household, court, and body-guard. The "harts, roebucks, &c.," whatever the exact meaning of each word may be, evidently denote the wild game, as distinct from the herds and flocks; the "fatted fowl" apparently signifies "dainty food" generally, as distinct from the staple of ordinary meat.

<sup>(24)</sup> **On this side the river.**—This translation, although it expresses the true reference, viz., to the country west of the Euphrates, is literally incorrect. The words mean, "on the further side of the river," considered from the point of view of Babylon (see the use in the later books, or in Ezra iv. 6, vi. 6, &c.); and accordingly indicate composition at the time of the Exile, or, at any rate, at a period when the Babylonish empire was so established in supreme sovereignty as to determine the geographical nomenclature of the East.

<sup>(24)</sup> **Azzah** is the well-known Philistine city, Gaza.

<sup>(26)</sup> **Forty thousand.**—By comparison with the parallel passage in 2 Chron. ix. 25, and with the notice in chap. x. 26 (one thousand four hundred), it seems clear that for "forty thousand" "four thousand" should be read. They were kept in various "chariot cities," as well as at Jerusalem. This multiplication of horses and horsemen—forbidden to the future king in Deut. xvii. 16, but foretold by Samuel at the inauguration of the kingdom (1 Sam. viii. 11, 12)—is significant of military conquest and an extended empire. The Israelite armies, in frequent contradistinction from their enemies, had been hitherto mainly of infantry; and in Josh. xi. 9 the chariots and horses captured were not used, but destroyed, "as the Lord bade Joshua." Such armies were powerful for defence, not for invasion. Now, as it would seem for the first time, this provision of the ancient law, like many others, was set aside, and Solomon's empire assumed the character of other great Oriental monarchies.

<sup>(28)</sup> **Dromedaries**—properly (see Margin), *swift beasts;* probably the horses of the royal messengers, as distinguished from the war horses.

<sup>(29)</sup> **Wisdom and understanding . . . and largeness of heart.**—In this passage, "understanding," which is high intellectual power, and "largeness of heart," which is clearly capacity of knowledge, boundless as "the sand on the sea-shore," are both distinguished from the higher gift of wisdom, to which they are but means—the one being the capacity of wisdom within, the other the education of that capacity from without. (*a*) Wisdom, in the true sense in which it is used in Scripture (especially in the Books of Proverbs and Ecclesiastes), is properly the attribute of God, and then, by His gifts of revelation and inspiration, reflected in man. The "wisdom of God" (see, for example, Prov. viii.) is, in relation to man, His Divine purpose in the creation and government of the world, which all things work out. The "wisdom of man" is the knowledge of the true end and object of his own being—which if he fulfil not, it were better for him not to have been born—whether that object be called happiness or perfection. For such knowledge the Book of Ecclesiastes describes a vain search. Such knowledge, as found already, is embodied in the Proverbs; sometimes in the lowest sense of knowledge of what will conduce to our own happiness; sometimes in the higher knowledge of what will best serve man; most often in the supreme knowledge, how we may best do God's will and show forth His glory. (*b*) But, since the purpose of our own being cannot be discovered, if our life be regarded as isolated from the history of the world and from its great design, this wisdom in man is regarded as possible, only when he has some glimpse of the wisdom of God, as manifested to man in His visible Providence, in His declared law, and His special revelation to the soul. Hence, "the fear of the Lord" is its "beginning;" and faith in God is the supplement of its necessary imperfection. (*c*) It will be obvious that, even so considered, this desire for wisdom is more self-contained and self-conscious than "the thirst for God, even the living God," in which the soul of the Psalmist expresses absolute dependence on God. If the sense of the need of God's

and understanding exceeding much, and largeness of heart, even as the sand that *is* on the sea shore. (30) And Solomon's wisdom excelled the wisdom of all the children of the east country, and all the wisdom of Egypt. (31) For he was wiser than all men; than Ethan the Ezrahite, and Heman, and Chalcol, and Darda, the sons of Mahol: and his fame was in all nations round about. (32) And he spake three thousand proverbs: and his songs were a thousand and five. (33) And he spake of trees, from the cedar tree that *is* in Lebanon even unto the hyssop that springeth out of the wall: he spake also of beasts, and of fowl, and of creeping

revelation and of the necessity of faith beyond knowledge be lost, then this consciousness of wisdom may well become a self-idolatry, in which the mind prides itself on having pierced to the secret of being, holds that by such knowledge it becomes superior to ordinary law and duty, and delights in philosophical contemplation, rather than in active energy and religious devotion.

(30—34) The whole passage implies a general growth of wisdom, a largeness of knowledge, and an outburst of literature, of which, as usual with great men, Solomon is at once the child and the leader.

(30) **The wisdom of all the children of the east.**—The phrase "children of the east" is apparently used (see Gen. xxix. 1; Judg. vi. 3, 33, vii. 12, viii. 10) for the tribes of the country lying between the country of Israel and Mesopotamia. Of these "men of the east," Job is expressly said to be one, and among the chief (Job i. 3). What their wisdom was, the utterances of Job and his friends may testify, showing as they do large knowledge of nature and of man, speculating on the deepest moral questions, and throughout resting, though with an awe greater than was felt within the circle of the Abrahamic covenant, upon the consciousness of the one God. The Book of Job also shows that this wisdom was not unconnected with the proverbial "wisdom of Egypt," with which it is here joined. The Egyptian wisdom (as the monuments show) was a part of a more advanced and elaborate civilisation, enriched by learning and culture, and manifesting itself in art and science, but perhaps less free and vigorous than the simpler patriarchal wisdom of the children of the east.

(31) **He was wiser.**—The wisdom of "Heman, Ethan, Chalcol, and Darda," then rivals of Solomon's fame, is now only known to us from this passage. In the genealogy of 1 Chron. ii. 6, "Ethan, Heman, Chalcol, and Dara" (or "Darda") are found as sons of Zerah, the son of Judah; and the coincidence is remarkable enough to suggest identification. But this identification can scarcely hold. This passage evidently implies that these rivals of Solomon were contemporary with him, not belonging, therefore, to a family many generations earlier. Now it happens that we know of a Heman and an Ethan (see 1 Chron. vi. 33, 44) set by David over the service of song in the Tabernacle, and called "Ezrahites" in the titles of Pss. lxxxviii., lxxxix. ascribed to them. Heman is, moreover, designated as "the king's seer in the words of the Lord" (1 Chron. xxv. 5); and his Psalm (Ps. lxxxviii.) is singularly full of thought, moral speculation, and sense of mystery in life and death. Chalcol and Darda are described as sons of Machol. The word *Machol* may be a proper name. But it is curious that it signifies "dance," or "music"; and it is at least possible that they also, like Heman and Ethan, may have been thus designated, as connected with the music of the Temple. However this may be, it can hardly be wrong, in spite of the repetition of the group of names, to refer this passage to this Heman and this Ethan, and hold Chalcol and Darda to be, like them, contemporaries with Solomon.

(32) **Proverbs.**—The word "proverb" (*mashal*), from a root signifying "comparison," has the various meanings of (*a*) parable or allegory, (*b*) proverb in the modern sense, (*c*) riddle or enigmatical poem, (*d*) figurative and antithetical poetry, like the "parable" of Balaam. The Book of Proverbs belongs mainly, but not exclusively, to the second class. Its main part consists of two series of "Proverbs of Solomon" (Prov. x.—xxiv., xxv.—xxix.), composed or collected by him; falling, however, far short of the number given in this verse. The earlier portion (see especially chaps. i. 20—33, ii., viii.) partakes more of the character of the first and fourth classes; and in Eccl. xii. 3—6, and perhaps Prov. xxx. 15, 16, 24—31, we have specimens of the third. If the "three thousand" of the text be intended to be taken literally, it is obvious that only a small part of Solomon's proverbs has been preserved. His declension into idolatry might induce care in selection, by such prophetic compilers as "the men of Hezekiah" (Prov. xxv.).

**His songs.**—We have still ascribed to Solomon the "Song of Songs" and two Psalms (lxxii. and cxxvii.); but nothing else is, even by tradition, preserved to us. This passage is singularly interesting, as showing that the Old Testament Canon is not a collection of chance fragments of a scanty literature, but that out of a literature, which at this time, at any rate, was large and copious, deliberate selections by prophetic authority were made. (The "men of Hezekiah," named in Prov. xxv. 1, are by Jewish tradition Isaiah and his companions.) In the case of Solomon some special caution would be natural, and much of his poetry may have been purely secular. The "Psalter of Solomon" (including eighteen psalms) is a Greek apocryphal book, of the time of the Maccabees or later.

(33) **He spake of trees.**—Of this verse there have been many interpretations. Josephus (*Ant.* viii. c. 2, § 5) supposes Solomon's utterances on these natural products to have been allegorical and symbolic, although he declares that he described them and their properties "like a philosopher." Rabbinical and Oriental legends, eagerly accepted in mediæval times, ascribed to him mystic knowledge and magical use of their occult properties. Modern writers have seen in this utterance the first dawn of a scientific natural history and idyllic poetry. In all these suppositions there is some truth, though each in its literal meaning evidently interprets the work of Solomon by the ideas of its own time. An examination of the Song of Songs, and even of the Book of Proverbs—to say nothing of Ecclesiastes and several of the Psalms, and of the Book of Job, which has been thought to belong to the age of Solomon—shows in them repeated exemplifications of a deep sense of the wonder and the beauty of Nature, and also a keen observation of Natural history in detail.

things, and of fishes. (34) And there came of all people to hear the wisdom of Solomon, from all kings of the earth, which had heard of his wisdom.

CHAPTER V.—And Hiram king of Tyre sent his servants unto Solomon; for he had heard that they had anointed him king in the room of his father: for Hiram was ever a lover of David. (2) And <sup>a</sup> Solomon sent to Hiram, saying, (3) Thou knowest how that David my father could not build an house unto the name of the LORD his God for the wars which were about him on every side, until the LORD put them under the soles of his feet. (4) But now the LORD my God hath given me rest on every side, *so that there is* neither adversary nor evil occurrent. (5) And, behold, I <sup>1</sup> purpose to build an house unto the name of the LORD my God, <sup>b</sup> as the LORD spake unto David my father, saying, Thy son, whom I will set upon thy throne in thy room, he shall build an house unto my name.

*a* 2 Chron. 2. 3.

1 Heb., *say.*

*b* 2 Sam. 7. 13; 1 Chr. 22. 10.

2 Heb., *say.*

3 Heb., *heard.*

4 Heb., *send.*

(6) Now therefore command thou that they hew me cedar trees out of Lebanon; and my servants shall be with thy servants: and unto thee will I give hire for thy servants according to all that thou shalt <sup>2</sup> appoint: for thou knowest that *there is* not among us any that can skill to hew timber like unto the Sidonians.

(7) And it came to pass, when Hiram heard the words of Solomon, that he rejoiced greatly, and said, Blessed *be* the LORD this day, which hath given unto David a wise son over this great people. (8) And Hiram sent to Solomon, saying, I have <sup>3</sup> considered the things which thou sentest to me for: *and* I will do all thy desire concerning timber of cedar, and concerning timber of fir. (9) My servants shall bring *them* down from Lebanon unto the sea: and I will convey them by sea in floats unto the place that thou shalt <sup>4</sup> appoint me, and will cause them to be discharged there, and thou shalt receive *them*: and thou

---

But it also shows, as might have been expected, a constant contemplation of God in and over Nature (much as in Ps. civ.), a desire to know the secret of His dispensation therein, a conception of a unity in His law over all being, and as a necessary consequence of this, a tendency to mystic interpretation and parable. If in the works here referred to, and now lost to us, there were (as Ewald supposes) "the rudiments of a complete natural history," it would be an anachronism to doubt that they were marked by these leading characteristics.

V.

In contrast with the brief notes of the previous chapter, the fifth chapter begins another section of the fuller history (chaps. v.—ix. 9), describing in great detail the building and consecration of the Temple, and evidently drawn from contemporary documents.

(1) **Hiram** is first mentioned in 2 Sam. v. 11 (and the parallel, 1 Chron. xiv. 1) as having sent workmen and materials to David for the building of his house. He is described as a "lover of David." Ancient tradition makes him a tributary or dependent monarch; and his attitude, as described in Scripture, towards both David and Solomon agrees with this. Josephus (*c. Apion*, i. 17, § 18) cites from Dios, a Phœnician historian, and Menander of Ephesus, a description of Hiram's parentage, of his prosperous reign and skill in building; and quotes, as from the Tyrian archives (*Ant.* viii. 11, §§ 6, 7), letters passing between him and Solomon. The embassy here noticed from Hiram is clearly one of congratulation, perhaps of renewal of fealty. (In 2 Chron. ii. 14, 15 occur the phrases, " my lord, my lord David thy father.")

(3) **Thou knowest.**—In the description (1 Chron. xxii. 4) of David's collection of materials for the Temple, it is noted that "the Zidonians and they of Tyre brought much cedar wood to David." Hence Hiram knew well his desire of building the Temple, and the care with which, when disappointed of it, he prepared for the happier experience of his successor.

(6) **Cedar trees out of Lebanon.**—The central range of Lebanon is bare; but in the lower ranges there is still—probably in old times there was to a far greater extent—a rich abundance of timber, specially precious to the comparatively treeless country of Palestine. The forest of Lebanon was proverbial for its beauty and fragrance (Cant. iv. 11; Hosea xiv. 6, 7), watered by the streams from the snowy heights (Jer. xviii. 14), when all Palestine was parched up. The cedars which now remain—a mere group, at a height of about six thousand feet—are but a remnant of the once magnificent forest which "the Lord had planted" (Ps. civ. 16). Solomon's request—couched almost in the language of command—is simply for cedar wood, or rather, for skilled labour in felling and working it, for which the Tyrians were proverbially famed in all ancient records. For this labour he offers to pay; while he seems to take for granted a right for his own servants to come and bring away the timber itself. Hiram's answer (verse 8) mentions " timber of fir" also, which agrees exactly with the fuller account of Solomon's request given in 2 Chron. ii. 8. The pine still grows abundantly in the sandstone regions of Lebanon; but it is almost certain that "the fir" here named is the cypress.

(7) **Blessed be the Lord.**—Hiram's answer is one of deference, still more clearly marked in 2 Chron. ii. 12—16. His acknowledgment of Jehovah the God of Israel is a token rather of such deference to Israel, than of any acceptance of Him as the one true God.

(9) **Shall bring them.** — The timber was to be carried down, or, perhaps, let down on slides along the face of the mountain towards the sea, and brought round by rafts to Joppa (2 Chron. ii. 16), to save the

shalt accomplish my desire, in giving food for my household.

(10) So Hiram gave Solomon cedar trees and fir trees *according to* all his desire. (11) And Solomon gave Hiram twenty thousand ¹measures of wheat *for* food to his household, and twenty measures of pure oil: thus gave Solomon to Hiram year by year. (12) And the LORD gave Solomon wisdom, *ᵃas he promised him: and there was peace between Hiram and Solomon; and they two made a league together.

(13) And king Solomon raised a ²levy out of all Israel; and the levy was thirty thousand men. (14) And he sent them to Lebanon, ten thousand a month by courses: a month they were in Lebanon, *and* two months at home: and *ᵇ*Adoni-ram *was* over the levy. (15) And Solomon had threescore and ten thousand that bare burdens, and fourscore thousand hewers in the mountains; (16) beside the chief of Solomon's officers which *were* over the work, three thousand and three hundred, which ruled over the people that wrought in the work. (17) And the king commanded, and they brought great stones, costly stones, *and* hewed stones, to lay the foundation of the house. (18) And Solomon's builders and Hiram's builders did hew *them*, and the ³stone-squarers: so they prepared timber and stones to build the house.

CHAPTER VI.—(1) And *ᶜ*it came to pass in the four hundred and eightieth year after the children of Israel were

---

1 Heb., *cors.*

*ᵃ* ch. 3. 12.

2 Heb., *tribute of men.*

*ᵇ* ch. 4. 6.

3 Or, *Giblites*: as Ezek. 27. 9.

*ᶜ* 2 Chron. 3. 1.

B.C. 1012.

---

enormous cost and difficulty of land carriage. The grant of "food for his household" in return (instead of "hire") brings out that which is recorded so many ages afterwards in Acts xii. 20—that the country of the Tyrians was "nourished" by Palestine. The commerce and wealth of the Tyrians collected a large population; the narrow slip of land along the coast, backed by Lebanon, must have been, in any case, insufficient to maintain them; and, moreover, all their energies were turned, not to agriculture, but to seamanship. In the grand description in Ezek. xxvii. of the imports of Tyre from all parts of the world, Judah and Israel are named as supplying "wheat, and honey, and oil, and balm."

(11) **Twenty thousand measures of wheat.**—This agrees well enough with the calculation in chap. iv. 22 of ninety measures a day—something over 32,000 a year—for Solomon's Court, presumably greater than that of Hiram. But the "twenty measures of oil"—even of the pure refined oil—is so insignificant in comparison, that it seems best to adopt the Greek reading here (agreeing with 2 Chron. ii. 10, and with Josephus) of 20,000 *baths*, or 2,000 *cors*, of oil.

(13) **Levy out of all Israel.**—This, though far from being onerous, appears to have been at this time exceptional. For in chap. ix. 22 we read that "of the children of Israel did Solomon make no bondmen: but they were men of war, and his servants, and his princes, and his captains." Thus exceptionally introduced at first for the special service of God, it may have been the beginning of what was hereafter an oppressive despotism over the Israelites themselves. Probably even now the Israelite labourers were (under the chief officers) put in authority over the great mass of 150,000 bondmen, evidently drawn from the native races. (See 2 Chron. ii. 17.) But the whole description suggests to us—what the history of Exodus, the monuments of Egypt, and the description by Herodotus of the building of the Pyramids confirm—the vast sacrifice of human labour and life, at which (in the absence of machinery to spare labour) the great monuments of ancient splendour were reared.

(16) **The chief of Solomon's officers** we should certainly have supposed to have been taken from the Israelites (as clearly were the 550 named in chap. ix. 23). But the passage in Chronicles (2 Chron. ii. 18)—reckoning them at 3,600—seems to imply that they were, like the overseers of Israel in the Egyptian bondage (Exod. v. 14, 15), taken from the subject races.

(17) **Great stones.**—The stones, so emphatically described as "great stones, costly stones, and hewed stones," were necessary, not so much for "the foundation" of the Temple itself, which was small, but for the substructure of the area, formed into a square on the irregular summit of Mount Moriah. In this substructure vast stones are still to be seen, and are referred by many authorities to the age of Solomon. The labour of transport must have been enormous, especially as all were worked beforehand. (See chap. vi. 7.)

(18) **The stone-squarers.**—This rendering is a curious gloss on the proper name, "*Giblites*" (see margin)—the inhabitants of Gebal (mentioned in Ezek. xxvii. 9 in connection with Tyre, and probably in Ps. lxxxiii. 7), a city on the coast of Phœnicia—simply because the context shows that they were clever in stone-squaring. As they are distinguished from Hiram's builders, it is possible that they were serfs under them, like the Canaanites under Solomon's builders.

VI.

Chapters vi. and vii. form a section almost technically descriptive of the Temple and other building works of Solomon. (*a*) The general account of the building of the Temple occupies chap. vi.; (*b*) to this succeeds a briefer description of the other works of Solomon (chap. vii. 1—12); (*c*) lastly, we have a full and detailed description of the work of Hiram for the ornaments and furniture of the Temple (chap. vii. 13—51). The whole may be compared with 2 Chron. iii., iv., with the account in Josephus (*Antt.*, viii. 3), and with the descriptions (in Exod. xxv.—xxvii., xxxv.—xxxviii.) of the Tabernacle, which determined the construction of the Temple in many points. With some variations, depending on the nature of the prophetic vision, it may also be illustrated from Ezek. xl.—xlvi. On the details of these chapters there has been much learned discussion; but most light has been thrown on it by the articles in the *Dictionary of the Bible* (TEMPLE, PALACE, JERUSALEM), written by Mr. Fergusson, who

come out of the land of Egypt, in the fourth year of Solomon's reign over Israel, in the month Zif, which *is* the second month, that he ¹began to build the house of the LORD.

⁽²⁾ And the house which king Solomon built for the LORD, the length thereof *was* threescore cubits, and the breadth thereof twenty *cubits*, and the height thereof thirty cubits. ⁽³⁾ And the porch before the temple of the house, twenty cubits *was* the length thereof, according to the breadth of the house; *and* ten cubits *was* the breadth thereof before the house. ⁽⁴⁾ And for the house he made ² windows of narrow lights. ⁽⁵⁾ And ³against the wall of the house he built ⁴chambers round about, *against* the walls

1 Heb., *built.*

2 Or, *windows broad within, and narrow without: or, skewed and closed.*

3 Or, *upon, or, joining to.*

4 Heb., *floors.*

unites with antiquarian learning extensive acquaintance with the history and the details of architecture.

⁽¹⁾ **In the fourth year.**—This date, given with marked precision, forms a most important epoch in the history of Israel, on which, indeed, much of the received chronology is based. In the LXX., 440 is read for 480, possibly by an interchange of two similar Hebrew letters, or, perhaps, by reckoning from the completion of Exodus at the death of Moses instead of its beginning. The Vulgate agrees with the Hebrew text. Josephus, on the other hand, without any hint of any other reckoning in the Scriptural record, gives 592 years. The date itself, involving some apparent chronological difficulties, has been supposed to be an interpolation; but without any sufficient ground, except Josephus's seeming ignorance of its existence, and some early quotations of the passage by Origen and others without it; and in neglect of the important fact that, disagreeing *prima facie* with earlier chronological indications in Scripture, it is infinitely unlikely to have been thus interpolated by any mere scribe.

These indications are, however, vague. The period includes the conquest and rule of Joshua, the era of the Judges down to Samuel, the reigns of Saul and David, and the three years of Solomon's reign already elapsed. Now, of these divisions, only the last three can be ascertained with any definiteness, at about 83 years. The time occupied by the conquest and rule of Joshua, cannot be gathered with any certainty from Scripture. The same is the case with the duration of some of the subsequent Judgeships. Even the numerous chronological notices given in the Book of Judges are inconclusive. We cannot tell whether they are literally accurate, or, as the recurrence of round numbers may seem to suggest, indefinite expressions for long periods; nor can we determine how far the various Judgeships were contemporaneous or successive. The tradition followed by St. Paul (Acts xiii 19—21), assigning to the whole a period of 450 years, agrees generally with the latter idea. The genealogies given (as, for example, of David, in Ruth iv. 18—22; 1 Chron. ii. 3—15, and elsewhere) agree with the former. Hence, these vague chronological statistics cannot constitute a sufficient ground for setting aside a date so formally and unhesitatingly given at an important epoch of the history, corresponding to the equally formal determination of the date of the Exodus in Exod. xii. 40, 41. The omission of the date in quotations, again, proves little. The different date given by Josephus, without any notice of that which we now have, presents the only real difficulty. But it is possible that he may have been inclined tacitly to harmonise his chronology with some other reckoning known in his time among the heathen; and in any case it is doubtful whether his authority can outweigh that of our present text and the ancient versions. On the whole, therefore, the grounds assigned for rejection of the chronological notice of this verse, are insufficient.

⁽²⁾ **The length.**—By comparison with Exod. xxvi. 16—23, we find that the Temple itself was in all its proportions an exact copy of the Tabernacle, each dimension being doubled, and the whole, therefore, in cubical contents, eight times the size. It was, therefore—whatever measure we take for the cubit—a small building. Taking the usual calculation of eighteen inches for the cubit, the whole would be ninety feet long, thirty feet wide, and forty-five feet high—not larger than a good-sized parish church, and in proportion not unlike a church of Gothic construction. It is, indeed, curious to note that this likeness is carried out in the existence of the porch (which is even represented in 2 Chron. iii. 4 as rising into a lofty entrance tower), the division of the house into two parts, like a nave and chancel, the provision of something like aisles (though opening outwards) and of clerestory windows, and the high pitch of the roof. This resemblance is probably not mere coincidence; for in the old Freemasonry, which had a great influence on mediæval architecture, the plan of Solomon's Temple was taken in all its details as a sacred guide. The "Oracle," or Most Holy place, was lower than the rest, forming an exact cube of thirty feet; the height of the Holy place (sixty feet long and thirty feet wide) is not given, but was probably the same, so that there would be an upper chamber over the whole under the roof—which, like that of the Tabernacle, appears to have been a high-pitched roof—fifteen feet high along the central beam, with sloping sides. This is apparently alluded to in 2 Chron. iii, 9, and possibly in 2 Kings xxiii. 12, and in the remark of Josephus, "There was another building erected over it, equal in its measures." The Temple was, in fact, only a shrine for the ministering priests—the outer court, or courts, being the place for the great assembly of the congregation—and it relied for magnificence not on size, but on costliness of material and wealth of decoration.

⁽³⁾ **The porch** was thirty feet wide and fifteen feet deep. The height is not here given; but in the present text of 2 Chron. iii. 4 (followed by some MSS. of the LXX., and by Josephus) it is made 120 cubits, or 180 feet. This height is hardly in accordance with anything else known on ancient architecture. It is, however, not at all unlike the western tower of a Gothic church.

⁽⁴⁾ **Windows of narrow lights.**—The marginal reading, "windows broad within and narrow without"—splayed as in ordinary Gothic architecture—is supported by very good authorities; but the most probable meaning is "windows with fixed beams"—that is, with fixed lattices, like jalousies, useful for ventilation, but immovable, so that no one could look out or in.

⁽⁵⁻¹⁰⁾ The general meaning of these verses is clear, though some of the words are doubtful. Round three sides of the Temple was built a kind of aisle, opening,

*The Building*          I. KINGS. VI.          *of the Temple.*

of the house round about, *both* of the temple and of the oracle : and he made ¹chambers round about :  ⁽⁶⁾ the nethermost chamber *was* five cubits broad, and the middle *was* six cubits broad, and the third *was* seven cubits broad : for without *in the wall* of the house he made ²narrowed rests round about, that *the beams* should not be fastened in the walls of the house. ⁽⁷⁾ And the house, when it was in building, was built of stone made ready before it was brought thither : so that there was neither hammer nor ax *nor* any tool of iron heard in the house, while it was in building. ⁽⁸⁾ The door for the middle chamber *was* in the right ³side of the house : and they went up with winding stairs into the middle *chamber*, and out of the middle into the third. ⁽⁹⁾ So he built the house, and finished it ; and covered the house ⁴with beams and boards of cedar. ⁽¹⁰⁾ And *then* he built chambers against all the house, five cubits high : and they rested on the house with timber of cedar.

⁽¹¹⁾ And the word of the LORD came to Solomon, saying. ⁽¹²⁾ *Concerning* this house which thou art in building, if thou wilt walk in my statutes, and execute my judgments, and keep all my commandments to walk in them ; then will I perform my word with thee, *a* which I spake unto David thy father : ⁽¹³⁾ and I will dwell among the children of Israel, and will not not forsake my people Israel.

⁽¹⁴⁾ So Solomon built the house, and finished it. ⁽¹⁵⁾ And he built the walls of the house within with boards of cedar, ⁵both the floor of the house, and the walls of the cieling : *and* he covered *them* on the inside with wood, and covered the floor of the house with planks of fir. ⁽¹⁶⁾ And he built twenty cubits on the sides of the house, both the floor and the walls with boards of cedar : he even built *them* for it within, *even* for the oracle, *even* for the most holy *place*. ⁽¹⁷⁾ And the house, that *is*, the temple before it, was forty cubits *long*. ⁽¹⁸⁾ And the cedar of the house within *was* carved

*Marginal notes:*
1 Heb., *ribs*.
2 Heb., *narrowings, or, rebatements*.
3 Heb., *shoulder*.
4 Or, *the vault-beams and the cielings with cedar*.
*a* 2 Sam. 7. 13 ; 1 Chron. 22. 10.
B.C. 1005.
5 Or, *from the floor of the house unto the walls, &c., and so ver. 16*.

---

however, outwards and not into the Temple, having three storeys of low chambers (each only five cubits high), so arranged that the beams of their roofs were supported on rests on the outside of the wall (each rest being a cubit wide), leaving the wall itself intact. Thus the chambers of the lowest storey were narrowest—five cubits broad ; the second storey six cubits, and the highest storey seven cubits broad. The higher storeys (see verse 8), in which the chambers no doubt opened into one another, were approached by a staircase, having an external entrance on the right side of the building ; the chambers of the lowest storey probably had external doors of their own. Above the highest storey were still five cubits of wall, which would give room for the windows (like clerestory windows) previously mentioned. Nothing is said of the use of these chambers ; but they would be, no doubt, for residence of the priests, stores for the Temple, and furniture.

The word rendered "chambers" in the former part of verse 5 is a singular noun, signifying the whole of this aisle or side building ; the "chambers" in the latter part of the verse—properly, "side pieces," or "ribs"—denote the separate apartments, or perhaps each of the storeys of the building.

⁽⁷⁾ **Neither hammer nor ax . . . heard.**—This striking provision, involving much labour, and requiring no little skill, was one of reverence. It may have been suggested by the prohibition (see Exod. xx. 25 ; Deut. xxvii. 5) of the use of tools on the altar of the Lord. But the idea implied in this prohibition was rather different —viz., the use for the altar of stones in their simple, natural condition, without "pollution" by the art of man. It has been chronicled in Heber's well-known lines :—

"No workmen's steel, no ponderous axes rung ;
Like some tall palm the noiseless fabric sprung."

⁽⁹⁾ **And covered**—that is, roofed the house with a roof of cedar beams and boarding thereon. Some have supposed that he "covered" the outside walls with cedar, so that the whole should still look like a wooden tabernacle ; but this is not necessarily implied, and is in itself unlikely.

⁽¹¹⁻¹³⁾ In the midst of this architectural description is inserted a brief notice of the Lord's promise concerning the Temple ; which may be compared, and in some degree contrasted, with the fuller utterance given (see ix. 3—9) after the consecration was over. Unlike this latter, it is one of simple promise of blessing, with no note of warning. But it is to be observed that, in accordance with the general principle laid down in Jer. xviii. 5—10, the promise—repeating the promises already made to David in 2 Sam. vii. 10—15, and to Moses in Exod. xxv. 8, but with special application to the newly-built Temple—is made strictly conditional on obedience. In its main points, indeed, as working out the great covenant with Abraham for the blessing of all families of the earth, it was to be in any case fulfilled. But for each generation the enjoyment of the blessings promised was contingent on faith and obedience, and for the whole nation it was from time to time forfeited, until the final destruction of Israel as a nation. Yet even now, St. Paul (Rom. xi. 29) teaches that for Israel there is still some hope of the ancient promise of blessing.

⁽¹⁵⁾ **Both the floor.**—The true reading is that of the margin, agreeing generally with the LXX. and the Vulgate : that "from the floor to the walls of the ceiling" (including in this phrase the surface of the ceiling itself) "he covered all with cedar, and laid the floor with planks of cypress."

⁽¹⁶, ¹⁷⁾ These verses describe the division of the Temple, by a partition from floor to ceiling of cedar wood, into "the Oracle," or Holy of Holies, occupying twenty cubits of the length, and the rest of the house, exclusive of the porch, occupying forty cubits. The

with ¹knops and ²open flowers: all *was* cedar; there was no stone seen. ⁽¹⁹⁾ And the oracle he prepared in the house within, to set there the ark of the covenant of the LORD. ⁽²⁰⁾ And the oracle in the forepart *was* twenty cubits in length, and twenty cubits in breadth, and twenty cubits in the height thereof: and he overlaid it with ³pure gold; and *so* covered the altar *which was of* cedar. ⁽²¹⁾ So Solomon overlaid the house within with pure gold: and he made a partition by the chains of gold before the oracle; and he overlaid it with gold. ⁽²²⁾ And the whole house he overlaid with gold, until he had finished all the house: also the whole altar that *was* by the oracle he overlaid with gold.

⁽²³⁾ And within the oracle he made two cherubims *of* ⁴ ⁵olive tree, *each* ten cubits high. ⁽²⁴⁾ And five cubits *was* the one wing of the cherub, and five cubits the other wing of the cherub: from the uttermost part of the one wing unto the uttermost part of the other *were* ten cubits. ⁽²⁵⁾ And the other cherub *was* ten cubits: both the cherubims *were* of one measure and one size. ⁽²⁶⁾ The height of the one cherub *was* ten cubits, and so *was* it of the other cherub. ⁽²⁷⁾ And he set the cherubims within the inner house: and *a*⁶they stretched forth the wings of the cherubims, so that the wing of the one touched the *one* wall, and the wing of the other cherub touched the other wall; and their wings touched

1 Or, *gourds.*
2 Heb., *openings of flowers.*
3 Heb., *shut up.*
4 Or, *oily.*
5 Heb., *trees of oil.*
*a* Exod. 25. 20.
6 Or, *the cherubims stretched forth their wings.*

---

cedar panelling was carved throughout with (see margin) "gourds and open flowers," probably festooned, as usual in ancient architecture. In all this the influence of the Tyrian architects was probably felt.

⁽²⁰⁾ **In the forepart.**—Although this is a literal translation of the original, the sense is clearly (as the Vulgate renders the phrase) "in the inner part." Gesenius supposes the meaning to be properly, "the wall facing the entrance;" thence the opposite, or "inner," wall or region.

**Covered the altar . . .**—Our translators have been misled by the context to anticipate what is said below (verse 22). The meaning is "he covered the altar" (presumably of stone) "with cedar."

⁽²⁰⁻²²⁾ These verses describe the overlaying with pure gold of the panelling of the house and of the Oracle, the partition dividing them, and the altar of incense. Even the floor was similarly covered. (See verse 30.)

⁽²¹⁾ **He made a partition by (the) chains of gold before the oracle.**—This phrase is difficult. The LXX. and Vulg. have wholly different readings; but our translation appears to be substantially correct, and to signify either that Solomon made a chain-work decoration on the partition, or (perhaps more probably) that he made a golden chain to go across the entrance in the partition before the Oracle, in front of the veil, so as to be an additional guard against intrusion.

⁽²²⁾ **The whole altar that was by** (or belonged to) **the oracle.**—This is the altar of incense, which, although it stood (see Exod. xxx. 6, xl. 26) before the veil, and therefore in the Holy place, was considered to belong in idea rather to the Holy of Holies; since the offering of incense on it signified the approach by worship to the unseen presence of God, symbolised in the darkness and silence of the inner shrine; and the taking of the censer from it was a condition for the actual entrance into the Holy of Holies on the great Day of Atonement. Hence in Exod. xl. 5 the altar is said to be "set before the ark of the testimony," and here to "belong to the oracle." Probably this is the explanation of the well-known passage in the Epistle to the Hebrews (chap. ix. 4), where the Holiest place is said to have "had the altar of incense" (wrongly rendered "censer" in our Authorised Version).

⁽²³⁾ **Cherubim.**—These were copied from the Tabernacle, but apparently with some differences, over and above the necessary increase of size, and the change of material from solid gold to olive-wood overlaid with gold. In Exod. xxv. 18—20, xxxvii. 7—9, they are described as having their faces towards the mercy-seat, and covering the mercy-seat with their wings. Here, from the careful description of the outstretched wings, of ten cubits in width for each cherub, meeting in the midst of the house and touching the walls, it would seem that they must have been turned so as to face the entrance. The cherubim over the ark are described only in three places in the Old Testament—in the passages in Exodus, here, and in the parallel 2 Chron. iii. 10—13, and in those great visions of the priestly prophet Ezekiel (Ezek. i. 4—25, x. 1—22) which have determined the imagery of the Apocalypse. In no case is their form distinctly mentioned, unless, by comparison of Ezek. x. 14, 15 with Ezek. i. 10, it may be inferred to have been the form of a winged bull; whence would be naturally derived the golden calves of the idolatry introduced into Israel in the time of Jeroboam. Josephus, indeed, in his description of the Temple (*Antt.* viii. c. 3, § 3), expressly says that "no one can tell, or even conjecture, of what shape the cherubim were." The tradition, therefore, must have been lost in the Second Temple, where there was no ark; and this is the more strange, because in Exodus xxvi. 1 the cherubim are said to have been represented in the embroidery of the curtains, and here (in verses 32, 35) to have been similarly carved on the walls.

But, whatever the cherubim were, it is certain that they were in no sense representations or emblems of Deity, like the winged figures of Assyria or Egypt, with which they have been often compared. They appear to symbolise the great physical forces of the universe, as guided by superhuman angelic intelligence to serve the supreme will of God. Thus, when first mentioned in Scripture (Gen. iv. 24), the cherubim are associated with "the flaming sword, turning every way, to guard the tree of life"; in Ps. xviii. 10, the Lord is said to "ride upon the cherubim," and "come flying upon the wings of the wind"; in Ezek. i. 10, the four living creatures, or cherubim, sustain the throne of God, and bear it away upon their wings; in Rev. iv. 6—8, v. 8, 9, the same living creatures unite with the elders,

one another in the midst of the house. <sup>(29)</sup> And he overlaid the cherubims with gold.

<sup>(29)</sup> And he carved all the walls of the house round about with carved figures of cherubims and palm trees and <sup>1</sup>open flowers, within and without. <sup>(30)</sup> And the floor of the house he overlaid with gold, within and without.

<sup>(31)</sup> And for the entering of the oracle he made doors *of* olive tree: the lintel *and* side posts *were* <sup>2</sup>a fifth part *of the wall*. <sup>(32)</sup> The <sup>3</sup>two doors also *were of* olive tree; and he carved upon them carvings of cherubims and palm trees and <sup>4</sup>open flowers, and overlaid *them* with gold, and spread gold upon the cherubims, and upon the palm trees. <sup>(33)</sup> So also made he for the door of the temple posts *of* olive tree, <sup>5</sup>a fourth part *of the wall*. <sup>(34)</sup> And the two doors *were of* fir tree: the two leaves of the one door *were* folding, and the two leaves of the other door *were* folding. <sup>(35)</sup> And he carved *thereon* cherubims and palm trees and open flowers: and covered *them* with gold fitted upon the carved work. <sup>(36)</sup> And he built the inner court with three rows of hewed stone, and a row of cedar beams.

<sup>(37)</sup> In the fourth year was the foundation of the house of the LORD laid, in the month Zif: <sup>(38)</sup> and in the eleventh year, in the month Bul, which *is* the

---

1 Heb., *openings of flowers*.
2 Or, *five-square*.
3 Or, *leaves of the doors*.
4 Heb., *openings of flowers*.
5 Or, *four-square*.

---

representing the Church of redeemed humanity, in worship of the Lord upon His throne. The representation, therefore, of the cherubim in the Temple simply expresses the claim for Jehovah, the God of Israel, of such lordship over all creation as is hymned in the seraphic song of Isa. vi. 3. Possibly the change of attitude of the cherubim in the Temple denoted a change of idea, characteristic of Solomon and his age. The old attitude is clearly that of worship of God: the new rather of manifestation of His glory to man.

<sup>(29)</sup> **And he carved.**—If we take this literally, we must suppose that this carving of the cherubim and the palm-trees, in addition to the general decoration of the "gourds and open flowers," was spread over all the "walls of the house." Otherwise we might have supposed it confined to the Oracle "within," and to the partition "without," which would seem more appropriate, as the cherubim belonged especially to the Oracle.

<sup>(31)</sup> **Doors.**—The two doors of olive wood, from the Holy place into the Oracle, which as a rule stood open, showing the veil and the golden chains, were of moderate size. If our version (as is probable) is correct, the outside measure of the lintel and post was a fifth part of the wall, that is, four cubits, or six feet. Each door, therefore, would be something less than six feet by three. The description of the gilding states with minute accuracy that in overlaying the whole of these doors with gold, gold was "spread," that is, made to cover the carvings in relief (the cherubim of verse 35); in the other doors the gold was fitted, probably beaten into shape, over the carved work.

<sup>(32)</sup> **The two doors.**—Those into the Holy place from the porch, of cypress wood, were naturally made larger. The posts were a fourth of the wall. Hence, according as the wall is taken to be 20 cubits square, or 30 cubits high by 20 wide, the height would be 5 cubits (7½ feet), or 7½ cubits (11¼ feet). The width is not given; possibly it is taken to be the same as that of the other doors. As these doors would be much heavier, and more frequently opened and shut, each leaf was made to fold again upon itself.

<sup>(36)</sup> **The inner court** (probably the "higher court" of Jer. xxxv. 10) is described as built round the Temple proper, evidently corresponding to the outer court of the Tabernacle. As this was (see Exod. xxvii. 9–13) 50 cubits by 100, it may be inferred, that by a duplication similar to that of all dimensions of the Temple itself, Solomon's Court was 100 cubits (or 150 feet) by 200 cubits (or 300 feet), covering a little more than an acre. The verse has been interpreted in two ways: either that the floor of the court was raised by three courses of stone, covered with a planking of cedar, or (as Josephus understands it) enclosed by a wall of three courses of stone, with a coping of cedar wood. The latter seems more probable. For in this court stood the altar of burnt offering and the laver, and all sacrifices went on, and this could hardly have been done on a wooden pavement; and besides this we observe that the whole arrangement is (chap. vii. 12) compared with that of the great outer court of the palace where the wooden pavement would be still more unsuitable. It was what was called afterwards the "Court of the Priests," and in it (see Ezek. xl. 45) appear to have been chambers for the priests.

The mention of the "inner court" suggests that there was an outer court also. We have in 2 Kings xxi. 5, xxiii. 12, a reference to the "two courts" of the Temple, and in Ezek. xl. 17, xlii. 1, 8, a mention of the "outward" or "utter court." Josephus (*Antt.* viii. 3, § 3) declares that Solomon built beyond the inner court a great quadrangle, erected for it great and broad cloisters, and closed it with golden doors, into which all could enter, "being pure and observant of the laws." Even beyond this he indicates, though in rather vague and rhetorical language, an extension of the Temple area, as made by Solomon's great substructures, forming a court less perfectly enclosed, like the Court of the Gentiles in the later Temple. Of these outer courts and cloisters the tradition remained in the assignment of the title of "Solomon's Porch" to the eastern cloister of the later Temple. It has been thought that in this outer court were planted trees (in spite of the prohibition of Deut. xvi. 21); and this may have been the case, till the association of idol worship with them made these seem to be unfit for the House of the Lord. But the passages usually quoted to support this view are from the Psalms (Pss. lii. 8, xcii. 13), of which the former certainly refers to the Tabernacle, and the latter may do so.

<sup>(37)</sup> **Zif** (the "brightness of flowers") corresponds to about May;

<sup>(38)</sup> **Bul** (the month of "rain") to about November. The whole time occupied was, therefore, seven years and a half.

eighth month, was the house finished ¹throughout all the parts thereof, and according to all the fashion of it. So was he seven years in building it.

CHAPTER VII.—⁽¹⁾ But Solomon was building his own house ᵃthirteen years, and he finished all his house.

⁽²⁾ He built also the house of the forest of Lebanon; the length thereof was an hundred cubits, and the breadth thereof fifty cubits, and the height thereof thirty cubits, upon four rows of cedar pillars, with cedar beams upon the pillars. ⁽³⁾ And it was covered with cedar above upon the ²beams, that lay on forty five pillars, fifteen in a row. ⁽⁴⁾ And there were windows in three rows, and ³light was against light in three ranks. ⁽⁵⁾ And all the ⁴doors and posts were square, with the windows: and light was against light in three ranks. ⁽⁶⁾ And he made a porch of pillars; the length thereof was fifty cubits, and the breadth thereof thirty cubits: and the porch was ⁵before them: and the other pillars and the thick beam were ⁶before them. ⁽⁷⁾ Then he made a porch for the throne where he might judge, even the porch of judgment: and it was covered with cedar ⁷from one side of the floor to the other. ⁽⁸⁾ And his house where he dwelt had another court within the porch, which was of the like work.

Solomon made also an house for Pharaoh's daughter, ᵇwhom he had taken to wife, like unto this porch.

⁽⁹⁾ All these were of costly stones, according to the measures of hewed stones, sawed with saws, within and without, even from the foundation unto the coping, and so on the outside toward the great court. ⁽¹⁰⁾ And the foundation was of costly stones, even great stones, stones of ten cubits, and stones of eight cubits. ⁽¹¹⁾ And above were costly stones, after

---

1 Or, *with all the appurtenances thereof, and with all the ordinances thereof.*
a ch. 9. 10.
B.C. 1005 till B.C. 992.
2 Heb., *ribs.*
3 Heb., *sight against sight.*
4 Or, *spaces and pillars were square in prospect.*
5 Or, *according to them.*
6 Or, *according to them.*
7 Heb., *from floor to floor.*
b ch. 3. 1.

---

VII.

The first section of this chapter (verses 1—12) describes briefly, but with some technical details (not always easy of interpretation), the building of the royal palace, including in this the hall of state, or "the house of the forest of Lebanon," with its porch (verses 2—6), the hall (or porch) of judgment (verse 7), the royal residence, and the residence of the queen (verse 8). These must have constituted a large group of buildings enclosed in a great court, situate on the Western Hill ("the city of David"), which is opposite the Temple on Mount Moriah, with a viaduct crossing the intervening valley (ordinarily called the Tyropœon), by which the king went up to the House of the Lord (see chap. x. 5; 1 Chron. xxvi. 16; 2 Chron. ix. 4). Josephus (*Antt.* viii., chap. 5) supplies a few additional details, but his account is rather vague and rhetorical.

The house of the forest of Lebanon—evidently so called from the forest of cedar pillars which supported it—was apparently a great hall of audience, 150 feet long, 75 feet wide, and 45 feet high; along it ran longitudinally rows of pillars, supporting cedar beams and walls over them, and cedar roofs. In verse 2 it is said that there were "four rows of pillars," and yet in verse 3 that the cedar beams rested on "forty-five pillars, fifteen in a row." The difficulty thus created, of course vanishes if we are content to accept the LXX. reading, which has in verse 2 "three rows" instead of "four." But this is probably a correction made to avoid the apparent contradiction, and gives no explanation of the origin of the curious reading of the Hebrew text. It is, perhaps, a better explanation of the passage to suppose that one row of pillars was built into the side wall, so that only three would bear the cedar beams. Josephus says that the hall was built after "the Corinthian manner," that is (see *Dict. of the Bible,* PALACE), with a clerestory. In this case it would be not unlike a Basilica, having a higher central aisle between two rows of pillars, with a wall and windows above each, and two lower sides, or aisles, in one of which the side row of pillars was built into the wall, in the other standing clear of the wall. It is clear from verses 4, 5, that there were three rows of windows, one, perhaps, in the clerestory, and two in the side walls.

⁽⁶⁾ **A porch of pillars**, although by some authorities it is held to be a separate building, seems by the exact agreement of dimensions—its "length" being just the breadth of the hall—to have been a propylæon, or entrance vestibule, to the hall of state (like the porch, or vestibule, of the Temple), probably corresponding in the general arrangement of its pillars, and perhaps also in height. It had also a porch of its own, with a threshold (for the last clause of the verse should be rendered, "and a porch before it with pillars, and a threshold before them,") forming a kind of plinth, or, possibly, a flight of steps.

⁽⁷⁾ **The porch** (or hall) **of judgment** was clearly a separate building, not described in the text, except as having been floored and ceiled with cedar. Mr. Fergusson, comparing it "with the remains of Assyrian and Persian examples," supposes it to have been square, supported on four pillars in the centre, between which the throne stood, and having openings on the four sides for the public, the king, and his officers.

(8—11) The residence of the king, and the separate palace for the queen, distinct from the apartments of the inferior wives and concubines, are not described; except that they lay "within the porch," that is, in the rear in another court, and were of "like work." This is further explained by saying that they had costly stones of great size in the foundation, and stones above, hewn and sawn from top to bottom, carefully finished on the outside towards the great court, as well as on the inside, and were in all cases roofed with cedar. Josephus tells us that the inner court was adorned with trees and fountains, and had colonnades round it; and

*Hiram of Tyre*         I. KINGS, VII.         *and his Work.*

the measures of hewed stones, and cedars. (12) And the great court round about *was* with three rows of hewed stones, and a row of cedar beams, both for the inner court of the house of the LORD, and for the porch of the house.

(13) And king Solomon sent and fetched Hiram out of Tyre. (14) He *was* [1] a widow's son of the tribe of Naphtali, and his father *was* a man of Tyre, a worker in brass: and he was filled with wisdom, and understanding, and cunning to work all works in brass.

And he came to king Solomon, and wrought all his work. (15) For he [3] cast two pillars of brass, of eighteen cubits high apiece: and a line of twelve cubits did compass either of them about. (16) And he made two chapiters *of* molten brass, to set upon the tops of the pillars: the height of the one chapiter *was* five cubits, and the height of the other chapiter *was* five cubits: (17) *and* nets of

[1] Heb., *the son of a widow woman.*

[2] Heb., *fashioned.*

---

he gives an enthusiastic description of the internal decoration of the rooms, panelled up to a certain height with polished marble, with a band of highly-wrought metal-work of foliage of all kinds above this, and the rest of the wall up to the ceiling plastered and painted in colours ("ceiled with cedar, and painted with vermilion." Jer. xxii. 14). This description is curiously confirmed and illustrated by some of the recent discoveries at Nineveh.

(12) **The great court.**—Finally, "the great court" round about is said to have resembled the "inner court" of the Temple, having an enclosure of three rows of stones, probably of large size, with a cedar coping. It seems evidently to have enclosed the whole palace, and may have contained quarters for the guards and the household. There must have been, of course, inner courts, round which both the more public and the more private buildings of the palace were grouped.

(13–50) The exceedingly graphic and elaborate description of the work of Hiram on the vessels and furniture of the Temple, and on the great pillars, bears on the very face of it the most evident marks of historical accuracy and of the use of contemporary documents, and it has, moreover, great antiquarian interest. Looked at in itself, it shows that the Temple (like many other buildings in the comparative infancy of architecture) depended for its effect, not so much on size or proportion, as on rich material, elaborate decoration, and costly furniture, on which all the resources both of treasure and art were lavished. But besides this, the sense of the especial sacredness attached to all the vessels of the Temple, which was hereafter to degenerate into a Pharisaic superstition (see Matt. xxiii. 16—18), suggested the most careful record of every detail, and reverently traced to "the Spirit of God" the gift of "wisdom of heart" "to devise curious works, to work in gold, and in silver, and in brass," as in Bezaleel and Aholiab for the Tabernacle (Exod. xxxv. 31, 32), so also in Hiram for the Temple. There is something especially remarkable in this broad comprehensiveness of conception which recognises the illuminating and inspiring power of the Spirit of God, not only in the moral and religious teaching of the prophet and the devotional utterances of the psalmist, but in the warlike enthusiasm of the Judge, the sagacity of the statesman, the imaginative skill of the artist, and the wisdom of the philosophic thinker. Nothing could more strikingly illustrate the Apostolic declaration: "There are diversities of gifts, but the same Spirit" (1 Cor. xii. 4).

(13) **And king Solomon sent.**—The record in the Chronicles (2 Chron. ii. 7, 13, 14) gives what is evidently a more exact description of the facts here briefly alluded to. In Solomon's first letter to King Hiram he asks for "a man cunning to work," and with the answer the artificer Hiram is sent. His mixed parentage would enable him to enter into the spirit of the Israelite worship, and yet to bring to bear upon it the practical skill of the Tyrian artificer.

(15–22) With regard to the two pillars, *Jachin* ("He shall establish") and *Boaz* ("In it is strength"), the text gives no account of their destination, except that they were set up in the porch of the Temple (verse 21). Mr. Fergusson considers that they were supports to the roof of the vestibule; and if this were thirty cubits high, the twenty-seven cubits of each pillar, allowing for the slope of the roof to the apex, would suit well enough. But the absence of all reference to their position as parts of the building, and the entire separation of the description of their fabrication from the account of the building itself, rather favoured the other supposition, that they were isolated pillars set up in front of the porch as symbolic monuments, conveying the idea of Ps. xlvi., "God is our hope and strength;" "God is in the midst of her, therefore shall she not be removed." It is particularly noticed (2 Kings xxv. 13—16; Jer. lii. 17, 20—23) that they were broken up by the Chaldæans on the capture of Jerusalem, and the brass carried away. The description is exceedingly elaborate, and, except in one or two parts, clear enough. The shaft of each pillar was twenty-seven feet high, and its diameter something less than six feet. Josephus says that it was hollow, but of considerable thickness. Above the shaft was a chapiter (or capital) of great proportionate size (seven and a half feet high), covered with a net-work and festoons of metal-work, and ornamented with two rows of pomegranates, a hundred in each row. Over these again was "lily-work" of six feet in height—probably some conventionalised foliage, technically known by that name, like the "honeysuckle ornament" in classical architecture, or the conventional "dog-tooth" or "ball-flower" of Gothic. The whole height, even if there were no base or plinth below, would be twenty-seven cubits, or forty feet and a half. In the *Dict. of the Bible* (TEMPLE) is given a drawing of a pillar at Persepolis, which bears a considerable resemblance to the general description here given, but, being executed in stone, is far less elaborate in ornamentation. The whole style of the narrative shows that these were regarded as monuments of the highest artistic skill, and well known to all, as from their position they would be constantly before the eyes both of priests and people. There was, so far as can be seen, nothing to correspond to them in the Tabernacle.

(17) **Seven for . . .**—This is probably an erroneous reading. It should be "a net-work (or lattice-work) for the one chapiter, and a net-work for the other."

checker work, and wreaths of chain work, for the chapiters which *were* upon the top of the pillars; seven for the one chapiter, and seven for the other chapiter. (18) And he made the pillars, and two rows round about upon the one network, to cover the chapiters that *were* upon the top, with pomegranates: and so did he for the other chapiter. (19) And the chapiters that *were* upon the top of the pillars *were* of lily work in the porch, four cubits. (20) And the chapiters upon the two pillars *had pomegranates* also above, over against the belly which *was* by the network: and the pomegranates *were* two hundred in rows round about upon the other chapiter. (21) *a* And he set up the pillars in the porch of the temple: and he set up the right pillar, and called the name thereof ¹Jachin: and he set up the left pillar, and called the name thereof ²Boaz. (22) And upon the top of the pillars *was* lily work: so was the work of the pillars finished.

(23) And he made a molten sea, ten cubits ³from the one brim to the other: *it was* round all about, and his height *was* five cubits: and a line of thirty cubits did compass it round about. (24) And under the brim of it round about

*a* 2 Chron. 3. 17.

1 That is, *He shall establish.*

2 That is, *In it is strength.*

3 Heb., *from his brim to his brim.*

*b* 2 Chron. 4. 3.

there were knops compassing it, ten in a cubit, *b* compassing the sea round about the knops *were* cast in two rows, when it was cast. (25) It stood upon twelve oxen, three looking toward the north, and three looking toward the west, and three looking toward the south, and three looking toward the east: and the sea *was set* above upon them, and all their hinder parts *were* inward. (26) And it *was* an hand breadth thick, and the brim thereof was wrought like the brim of a cup, with flowers of lilies: it contained two thousand baths.

(27) And he made ten bases of brass; four cubits *was* the length of one base, and four cubits the breadth thereof, and three cubits the height of it. (28) And the work of the bases *was* on this *manner*: they had borders, and the borders *were* between the ledges: (29) and on the borders that *were* between the ledges *were* lions, oxen, and cherubims: and upon the ledges *there was* a base above: and beneath the lions and oxen *were* certain additions made of thin work. (30) And every base had four brasen wheels, and plates of brass: and the four corners thereof had undersetters: under the laver *were* undersetters molten, at the side of

---

(20) **Over against** (or rather, *close to*) **the belly which was by the network.**—The "belly" here (like the "bowls" or "globes" of the chapiters in verses 41, 42) seems to signify the rounded form of the capital, where it comes down to join the shaft. At this junction the bands of pomegranate ornament ran round the shaft. In this verse it is obvious that there is an omission in the text. It should be, "were two hundred in rows round about the one chapiter, and two hundred in rows round about the other chapiter." Hence the "four hundred" of verse 42 and 2 Chron. iv. 13.

(23—26) **A molten sea**—a gigantic laver for the ablution of the priests—corresponding to the laver of brass in the Tabernacle (Exod. xxx. 18—21, xxxviii. 8). It had a diameter of 15 feet, and a height of 7½ feet; but as it held 2,000 baths, that is, 17,000 gallons (or, as in 2 Chron. iv. 3, 3,000 baths, that is, 25,500 gallons), it is clear that it could not have been a hemisphere, but must have bulged out in section. There must, however, have been first a bulging inwards, immediately under the rim: for the right translation of verse 26 declares that the rim was in "the form of a lily flower," that is, curving outwards. Under the rim ran a double row of "gourd ornaments," like those carved in the cedar-panelling of the Temple. The sea stood on twelve oxen, corresponding perhaps to the twelve tribes of Israel—the ox being possibly the same emblem which was used in the form of the cherubim—till it was taken down and placed on the pavement by Ahaz (2 Kings xvi. 17), and, like the great pillars, was broken up at last by the Chaldeans for the sake of the brass (2 Kings xxv. 13).

(27—29) The smaller lavers of brass for washing the sacrifices, and the movable bases on which they rested, are described still more elaborately. Some of the details of the description are obscure, and it is clear that our translators were very much at fault about them. Generally, however, it appears that each base was a kind of hollow chest, 6 feet square on plan, and 4½ feet high, having at the angles pilasters or fillets ("ledges" in verse 28), with panels on each side ("borders" in verse 28), ornamented with "lions, oxen, and cherubims," below which hung festoons of thin metal-work—("certain additions made of thin work," in verse 29). Each base was set on four brazen wheels with brazen axles ("plates" in verse 30) only 27 inches high, and with naves, felloes, and spokes, all cast in brass. On each base was a convex circular stand (verse 35), with a "mouth," or circular opening (apparently "the chapiter" of verse 31), upon which, or over which, the laver stood. This was nine inches high, ornamented with carvings of "cherubims, lions, and palm-trees." From the four corners of the upper surface of the base sprang "undersetters," apparently brackets helping to support the laver, which rested above the "mouth" of the convex stand, and to keep it fast in its place (verses 30, 34). The laver was 6 feet in diameter, and held 40 baths, or about 360 gallons. The whole stood high, no doubt to bring it nearly on a level with the brazen altar, which was 15 feet high. In form, perhaps, each laver was a smaller copy of the molten sea. Of the whole a conjectural description and sketch are given in the *Dictionary of the Bible*, art. LAVERS.

every addition. **(31)** And the mouth of it within the chapiter and above *was* a cubit: but the mouth thereof *was* round *after* the work of the base, a cubit and an half: and also upon the mouth of it *were* gravings with their borders, foursquare, not round. **(32)** And under the borders *were* four wheels; and the axletrees of the wheels *were* [1] joined to the base: and the height of a wheel *was* a cubit and half a cubit. **(33)** And the work of the wheels *was* like the work of a chariot wheel: their axletrees, and their naves, and their felloes, and their spokes, *were* all molten. **(34)** And *there were* four undersetters to the four corners of one base: *and* the undersetters *were* of the very base itself. **(35)** And in the top of the base *was there* a round compass of half a cubit high: and on the top of the base the ledges thereof and the borders thereof *were* of the same. **(36)** For on the plates of the ledges thereof, and on the borders thereof, he graved cherubims, lions, and palm trees, according to the [2] proportion of every one, and additions round about. **(37)** After this manner he made the ten bases: all of them had one casting, one measure, and one size.

**(38)** Then made he ten lavers of brass: one laver contained forty baths: *and* every laver was four cubits: *and* upon every one of the ten bases one laver.

1 Heb., *in the base.*
2 Heb., *nakedness.*
3 Heb., *shoulder.*
4 Heb., *upon the face of the pillars.*
5 Heb., *made bright*, or, *scoured.*
6 Heb., *in the thickness of the ground.*
7 Heb., *for the exceeding multitude.*
8 Heb., *searched.*

**(39)** And he put five bases on the right [3] side of the house, and five on the left side of the house: and he set the sea on the right side of the house eastward over against the south. **(40)** And Hiram made the lavers, and the shovels, and the basons.

So Hiram made an end of doing all the work that he made king Solomon for the house of the LORD: **(41)** the two pillars, and the *two* bowls of the chapiters that *were* on the top of the two pillars; and the two networks, to cover the two bowls of the chapiters which *were* upon the top of the pillars; **(42)** and four hundred pomegranates for the two networks, *even* two rows of pomegranates for one network, to cover the two bowls of the chapiters that *were* [4] upon the pillars; **(43)** and the ten bases, and ten lavers on the bases; **(44)** and one sea, and twelve oxen under the sea; **(45)** and the pots, and the shovels, and the basons: and all these vessels, which Hiram made to king Solomon for the house of the LORD, *were of* [5] bright brass. **(46)** In the plain of Jordan did the king cast them, [6] in the clay ground between Succoth and Zarthan. **(47)** And Solomon left all the vessels *unweighed*, [7] because they were exceeding many: neither was the weight of the brass [8] found out.

**(48)** And Solomon made all the vessels that *pertained* unto the house of the

---

**(31) And the mouth.**—This is most obscure, and in our version unintelligible. Keil renders it: "And the mouth of it (the laver) was within the chapiter, and in a cubit above it; and the mouth of it (the chapiter) was round, after the manner of a pedestal, a cubit and a half; and upon the mouth was carved work, and the panels of it (the mouth) were square, not round." But the rendering of the word "mouth," now for the laver, now for the chapiter, is arbitrary, and the whole is still obscure. As the circular stand (or chapiter) was half a cubit deep, it looks as if the lower surface of the laver was a cubit above the "mouth." If the laver were emptied by a cock near the bottom, this circular stand may have received the drippings. And as the top of this base would be square on plan, and the stand circular, there would be, of course, spaces left at each corner, which may possibly be the engraved "panels" referred to.

**(39) The sea.**—This was placed on the south-eastern side of the Temple, on one side of the great altar; the ten smaller lavers were ranged five on each side.

**(40) The lavers.**—These should be (as in verse 45) "pots." The verse describes the completion of Hiram's work by the making of the smaller vessels.

It is curious that no mention is made of the construction of the brasen altar. It has been supposed by some that the old altar reared by David (2 Sam. xxiv. 25) was retained. But in 2 Chron. iv. 1, and in Josephus's account, it is expressly said that a brasen altar was made by Hiram, 30 feet square and 15 feet high. Probably, therefore, the absence of all mention of it here is simply an omission in the record.

**(46) In the plain of Jordan did the king cast them.**—The casting was done in the Jordan valley. Succoth is on the east side of Jordan, in the territory of Gad (see Gen. xxxiii. 17; Josh. xiii. 27; Judges viii. 5)—the place of the halt of Jacob on his way from Padan-aram, and of the insult offered to Gideon and his revenge. Zarthan, or Zaretan (Josh. iii. 16), is on the western side, in the territory of Manasseh, not far from Bethshan, and nearly opposite Succoth.

**(47) Solomon left all the vessels unweighed.** —The brass for these vessels had (1 Chron. xviii. 8) been taken by David from Tibhath and Chun, cities of the territory of Zobah, and laid up with other stores for the purpose of the Temple. How these cities were so rich in brass we are not told; but there are very ancient copper-mines, once worked by the Egyptians, in the Sinaitic peninsula; and the allusions to mining of various kinds in Job xxviii. 1—11 (perhaps belonging to the time of Solomon) are very striking.

**(48) The altar of gold.**—The altar of gold (chap. vi. 20, 22) is the altar of incense. On it (see Exod. xxx. 1—10) incense was to be burnt morning and

*The Vessels of Gold.*      I. KINGS, VIII.      *Assembly of the Elders.*

LORD: the altar of gold, and the table of gold, whereupon the shewbread *was*, <sup>(49)</sup> and the candlesticks of pure gold, five on the right *side*, and five on the left, before the oracle, with the flowers, and the lamps, and the tongs *of* gold, <sup>(50)</sup> and the bowls, and the snuffers, and the basons, and the spoons, and the [1] censers *of* pure gold; and the hinges *of* gold, *both* for the doors of the inner house, the most holy *place, and* for the doors of the house, *to wit,* of the temple.

<sup>(51)</sup> So was ended all the work that king Solomon made for the house of the LORD. And Solomon brought in the [2] things [a] which David his father had dedicated; *even* the silver, and the gold, and the vessels, did he put among the treasures of the house of the LORD.

CHAPTER VIII. — <sup>(1)</sup> Then [b] Solomon assembled the elders of Israel, and all the heads of the tribes, the [3] chief of the fathers of the children of Israel, unto king Solomon in Jerusalem, that they might bring up the ark of the

[1] Heb., *ash pans.*
[2] Heb., *holy things of David.*
[a] 2 Chron. 5. 1.
[b] 2 Chron. 5. 2.
[3] Heb., *princes.*

---

evening. The horns of the altar were to be touched with the blood of the sin offering (Lev. iv. 7, 18) offered for the priests or the people; and it was to be solemnly purified by the blood of the sacrifice on the great Day of Atonement (Lev. xvi. 18, 19). The offering of incense, therefore, pre-supposed sacrifice already offered, and atonement made for sin. To the Israelites it clearly symbolised the offering of an acceptable worship by man, as restored to the love and communion of God. (See Ps. cxli. 2.) The priest, as a mediator between God and man, alone entered the Holy Place and offered the incense; the people "stood praying without" (Luke i. 10). To us it symbolises the intercession of the One Mediator, offered for us in the Most Holy Place of heaven, by whom alone our worship ascends to God. (See Heb. ix. 11, 12, 24, x. 19—22; Rev. viii. 3.)

For the table of shewbread, see Exod. xxv. 23—28, xxxvii. 10—15; for the shewbread itself, see Lev. xxiv. 5—9. The "shewbread"—properly "bread of the face" (or presence) of God, translated in the LXX. Version as "bread of offering" or "of presentation"— was clearly of the nature of an Eucharistic offering to God of His own gift of bread—a kind of first-fruits, acknowledging that the whole sustenance of life comes from Him, and possibly also implying the truth more closely symbolised by the pot of manna, that "man doth not live by bread alone, but by every word proceeding out of the mouth of God."

<sup>(49)</sup> **The candlesticks of pure gold.**—Whether these ten candlesticks were to supersede the one seven-lighted candlestick made for the Tabernacle (Exod. xxv. 31—40, xxxvii. 17—26), or were to be used in addition to it, we are not told. The latter supposition is, however, far more probable, both because it seems most unlikely that the old sacred candlestick should have been disused, and because in the second Temple only the one seven-lighted candlestick was provided, and (as the sculpture on the Arch of Titus shows) was carried in the Roman triumph after the destruction of the city. (In 2 Chron. iv. 8, 19, there is a mention of ten tables for shewbread, similarly ranged on each side of the Holy Place, probably in the same way, additional to the one proper table.) Josephus, in his rhetorical exaggeration, declares that Solomon made ten thousand candlesticks and ten thousand tables; but he distinguishes the one proper candlestick and table from the rest. The candlestick is elaborately described in the history of the construction of the Tabernacle, as of great costliness of material and workmanship. Placed in the Holy Place, opposite to the table of shewbread, and fed carefully with the sacred oil, it appears to have symbolised the gift of light to the world, as the shewbread the gift of life and sustenance, flowing from the presence of God.

**The flowers, and the lamps, and the tongs** are the parts of the candlestick (mentioned in Exod. xxv. 31, 37, 38); the "flowers" being the ornaments of the stem and branches, the "lamps" being the seven lights, and the "tongs" being used for trimming.

<sup>(50)</sup> The various articles here mentioned are also enumerated in the description of the furniture of the Tabernacle, Exod. xxv. 29—38.

**The snuffers.**—The word is derived from a root signifying "to prune," and is used for "pruning knives" in Isa. ii. 4 and Micah iv. 3. Some accordingly render it here by "knives," but the common rendering "snuffers" suits the derivation well enough.

**The spoons.**—The name signifies simply "something hollow;" and in Num. vii. 86 "the spoons" are said to have been "full of incense," and to have "weighed ten shekels apiece." The right meaning is probably "incense pans."

**The censers.**—This rendering is clearly erroneous. It should be "snuff-dishes," or "ash-pans," as in Exod. xxv. 38.

<sup>(51)</sup> **The things which David his father had dedicated.**—For the account of the dedication of various treasures, by David and by the princes of Israel, for the House of the Lord, see 1 Chron. xviii. 8, 10, 11, xxii. 3—5, 14—16, xxviii. 14—18, xxix. 2—5. The accumulation was enormous. It had evidently been the work of years to gather it out of the spoils of many victories, offered in that spirit of thankful devotion which is expressed in David's own words: "Both riches and honour come of thee . . . and of thine own have we given unto thee" (1 Chron. xxix. 12, 14). The words used in the text seem to indicate that besides the vessels of gold, silver, and brass, gold and silver, in money or in ingots, were brought into the sacred treasury.

VIII.

The exceedingly minute and graphic character of the narrative of the consecration of the Temple, the almost exact verbal coincidence with it of the account given in the Second Book of Chronicles, and the occurrence in verse 8 of the phrase, "There they are unto this day," which could not have belonged to the time of the composition of the book—all show that the compiler must have drawn from some contemporary record, probably some official document preserved in the Temple archives. The beauty and spiritual significance of this chapter—which from time immemorial has been made to yield teaching

covenant of the LORD out of the city of David, which *is* Zion. ⁽²⁾ And all the men of Israel assembled themselves unto king Solomon at the feast in the month Ethanim, which *is* the seventh month. ⁽³⁾ And all the elders of Israel came, and the priests took up the ark. ⁽⁴⁾ And they brought up the ark of the LORD, and the tabernacle of the congregation, and all the holy vessels that *were* in the tabernacle, even those did the priests and the Levites bring up. ⁽⁵⁾ And king Solomon, and all the congregation of Israel, that were assembled unto him, *were* with him before the ark, sacrificing sheep and oxen, that could not be told nor numbered for multitude. ⁽⁶⁾ And the priests brought in the ark of the covenant of the LORD unto his place, into the oracle of the house, to the most holy *place*, *even* under the wings of the cherubims.

and encouragement for the consecration of Christian churches—stand in remarkable contrast with the mere technical detail of the preceding; yet each, in its own way, bears equally strong marks of historical accuracy.

Throughout the whole history, the sole majesty of the king is conspicuous. The priests perform only the ministerial functions of ritual and sacrifice. The prophetic order is absolutely unrepresented in the narrative. Solomon, and he alone, stands forth, both as the representative of the people before God in sacrifice and prayer, and as the representative of God in blessing and exhortation of the people. He is for the time king, priest, and prophet, in one—in this a type of the true "Son of David," the true "Prince of Peace." It is not unlikely that from this unequalled concentration on his head of temporal and spiritual dignity came the temptation to self-idolatry, through which he fell; and that the comparative abeyance of the counterbalancing influences wielded by the prophet and (in less degree) by the priest gave occasion to the oppressive, though splendid, despotism under which Israel groaned in his later days.

⁽¹⁾ **The elders.**—If in this description—found also in 2 Chron. v. 2, and taken, no doubt, from the original document—"the elders of Israel," are to be distinguished from the "heads of the tribes," and not (as in the LXX.) identified with them, the former expression probably refers to the chiefs of official rank, such as the princes and the counsellors of the king, and the latter to the feudal chiefs of the great families of the various tribes. These alone were specially summoned; but as the Dedication festival (being deferred for nearly a year after the completion of the Temple) was blended with the Feast of Tabernacles, "all the men of Israel" naturally "assembled at Jerusalem" without special summons.

⁽²⁾ **The month Ethanim** (called after the Captivity *Tisri*), corresponded with the end of September and beginning of October. The name is supposed (by Thenius) to be properly, as in the LXX., *Athanim*, and to signify the "month of gifts," so called as bringing with it the gathering in of the vintage, and of the last of the crops. According to the Chaldee Targum, it was in old times the beginning of the civil, as *Abib* of the ecclesiastical year. The feast in this month was the Feast of Tabernacles—of all feasts of the year the most joyful—marking the gathering in of all the fruits of the land, commemorating the dwelling in tabernacles in the wilderness, and thanking God for settlement and blessing in the land (Lev. xxiii. 33—44). It was, perhaps, the time when the Israelites could best be absent from their lands for a prolonged festival; but there was also a peculiar appropriateness in thus giving it a higher consecration, by celebrating on it the transference of the ark from the movable tabernacle to a fixed and splendid habitation. In this instance the festival was doubled in duration, from seven to fourteen days. (See verse 65.)

⁽³⁾ **The priests took up the ark.**—To bear the ark on its journeys was properly the duty of the Levites of the family of Kohath (Num. iii. 31; iv. 5); but to bring it out of the Holy of Holies (or, as here, from whatever corresponded thereto in the tent erected for the ark on Mount Zion), and to replace it therein, was the work of the priests alone. Hence in this passage, with literal accuracy, it is said, first, that "the priests took up the ark;" then (verse 4) that the priests and Levites brought up the ark and the holy things; and, lastly (verse 6), that "the priests brought in the ark into the oracle." Josephus, indeed, declares that, as was natural on this occasion of special solemnity—just as at the passage of the Jordan, and the circuit round the walls of Jericho (Josh. iii. 6—17, vi. 6)—the priests themselves bore the ark, while the Levites bore only the vessels and furniture of the Tabernacle.

⁽⁴⁾ **The tabernacle of the congregation** (see 1 Chron. xvi. 39, 40; 2 Chron. i. 3) was still at Gibeon; and the priests and Levites had hitherto been divided between it and the lesser tabernacle over the ark on Mount Zion. Probably each section of the priests and Levites now brought up in solemn procession the sacred things entrusted to them. According to the order of the Mosaic law (Num. iii. 25—37), the Kohathites had charge on the march of the ark and the vessels, the Gershonites of the Tabernacle and its hangings, and the Merarites of the boards and pillars of the Tabernacle and the outer court. This order, no doubt, was followed, as far as possible, on this its last journey. What became of the Tabernacle and its furniture (so far as this was disused), we are not told; but all was probably deposited, as a sacred relic of antiquity, somewhere in the precincts of the Temple. This seems to be implied in the famous Jewish tradition (see 2 Macc. ii. 4—6), that Jeremiah was enabled to hide by miracle "the Tabernacle and the ark and the altar of incense" on the destruction of the Temple.

⁽⁵⁾ **Sacrificing.**—This inaugural sacrifice corresponded on a grand scale to the ceremonial of the day, when David brought up the ark to Zion. "When they that bare the ark of the Lord had gone six paces, he sacrificed oxen and fatlings," "seven bullocks and seven rams" (2 Sam. vi. 13; 1 Chr. xv. 26). It was offered "before the ark," either as it left Mount Zion, or on arrival in the Temple, before it passed out of sight into the oracle.

⁽⁶⁻⁸⁾ **And the priests brought in the ark.**—It is clear from this description that the ark was placed lengthways between the cherubim, so that the staves by which it was borne, when drawn out (though

(7) For the cherubims spread forth *their* two wings over the place of the ark, and the cherubims covered the ark and the staves thereof above. (8) And they drew out the staves, that the ¹ends of the staves were seen out in the ²holy *place* before the oracle, and they were not seen without: and there they are unto this day. (9) *There was* nothing in the ark *a* save the two tables of stone, which Moses put there at Horeb, ³when the LORD made *a covenant* with the children of Israel, when they came out of the land of Egypt.

(10) And it came to pass, when the priests were come out of the holy *place*, that the cloud *b* filled the house of the LORD, (11) so that the priests could not stand to minister because of the cloud: for the glory of the LORD had filled the house of the LORD.

(12) Then spake Solomon, The LORD

1 Heb., *heads.*
2 Or, *ark: as* 2 Chron. 5. 9.
*a* Deut. 10. 5.
3 Or, *where.*
*b* Exod. 40. 34.

---

still partly attached to the ark) were seen—probably by projections visible through the veil—in the Holy Place; although, as the narrative remarks with characteristic minuteness of accuracy, "not without" from the porch. The reason why this detail is dwelt upon is obvious. Up to this time it had been forbidden to withdraw the staves (Exod. xxv. 13—15), so that the ark might always be ready for transference; now the withdrawal marked the entrance on a new period, during which it was to rest unmoved.

**There they are unto this day.**—This phrase —not unfrequently repeated in the narrative (see ix. 21, x. 12, xii. 19, &c.)—is an interesting indication of quotation from older documents; for at the time of the compilation of the book the Temple and all that it contained had been destroyed or removed. It is remarkable that in the record of the successive spoilings of the Temple by the Chaldæans (2 Kings xxiv. 13, xxv. 13—17), while the various vessels, the brazen pillars, and the sea are mentioned in detail, nothing is said of their carrying away the ark, which would have been the choicest, as most sacred, of all the spoils. (See Notes on these passages.) About the Jewish tradition, referred to above (see Note on verse 4), setting aside the supposed miracle, there is no intrinsic improbability, considering the respect paid to Jeremiah by the Chaldæans. (See Jer. xxxix. 11—14.)

(9) **There was nothing.**—The emphasis of this (repeated in 2 Chron. v. 10) is remarkable, and seems intended to make it clear that the various things laid up "before the testimony"—the pot of manna (Exod. xvi. 33, 34), the rod of Aaron (Num. xvii. 10), the copy of the Law (Deut. xxxi. 24—26)—were not in the ark, but (as in the last case is actually stated), at "the side of the ark." Unless any change afterwards took place—which is highly improbable—this clear statement must determine the interpretation of the well-known passage in the Epistle to the Hebrews (chap. ix. 4), in which no stress need be laid on the literal accuracy of the word "wherein;" for its purpose is simply a general description of the Temple, its chief parts, and its most sacred furniture. The command to deposit the tables in the ark is recorded in Exod. xxv. 16, and the actual deposit of them there in Exod. xl. 20, immediately after the erection of the Tabernacle.

There is something singularly impressive in the especial hallowing of the granite tables of the Law of Righteousness, as the most sacred of all the revelations of the Nature of God; thus indissolubly binding together religion and morality, and showing that God is best known to man, not in His omnipotence, or even in His infinite wisdom, which man can only in slight degree imitate, but in His moral nature, as the very Truth and Righteousness, of which all that in man is called true and righteous is but the reflection. The one main object of all prophetic teaching was to bring out the truth here implied, thus writing the law on the heart and on the mind (Jer. xxxi. 33), and rebuking moral evil at least as strongly as religious error and apostasy. The very name of the Messiah for whom they prepared is "Jehovah our righteousness" (Jer. xxiii. 6).

(10) **The cloud.**—The bright Shechinah of the Divine Presence, at once cloud and fire—which had been the sign of the presence of God on Sinai (Exod. xxiv. 15—18), and had hallowed the consecration of the Tabernacle (Exod. xl. 34, 35)—now similarly descended on the Temple, as a sign of its acceptance with God. In the visions of Ezekiel the same glory is seen, first filling the house of the Lord, and then departing from it, as polluted by manifold idolatry (Ezek. x. 4, 18). Its return to the restored Temple is solemnly promised by Haggai (chap. ii. 7, 9) in distinct reference to the coming of the Messiah; and it is declared that it shall be even greater than in the magnificence of Solomon's Temple. The symbol clearly implies a revelation of Divine glory, as it is seen, not in the unveiled brightness of heaven, but in the glorious cloud of mystery; through which it must always be seen on earth, and which, indeed, is all that the eye of man can bear to contemplate. Out of that glory comes the only revelation which can be distinct to man—the voice or the word of the Lord (Deut. iv. 12).

The record of the Chronicles (2 Chron. v. 11—13)— dwelling, as usual, on the musical and ritual service of the Levites—notes here that this descent of the glory of the Lord came, as it were, in answer to a solemn burst of worship from the Levites and the people, "praising the Lord, because He is good; for His mercy endureth for ever."

(11) **The priests could not stand to minister.** —So in Exod. xl. 35, "Moses was not able to enter into the Tabernacle; for the cloud rested thereon, and the glory of the Lord filled the Tabernacle." They shrank from the glory of the Lord, whom none could see and live; just as Isaiah (vi. 5) felt "undone" when he beheld the glory of the Lord in the Temple; and as even the Apostles trembled, when they entered into "the bright cloud which overshadowed them" on the Mount of Transfiguration, and "knew not what they said" (Luke ix. 33, 34). But it was not so much from terror of the Lord, who is "a consuming fire," as simply from awe and reverence of His unspeakable glory.

(12) **The Lord said . . .**—The words of Solomon, though—as is natural in a moment of mingled awe and thankfulness—somewhat broken and abrupt, are clear enough in their general meaning and connection. He refers to the frequent declarations made in old time that the cloud is the symbol of God's indwelling presence (such as Exod. xix. 9, and Lev. xvi. 2);

*said that he would dwell in the thick darkness. <sup>(13)</sup> I have surely built thee an house to dwell in, a settled place for thee to abide in for ever.

<sup>(14)</sup> And the king turned his face about, and blessed all the congregation of Israel: (and all the congregation of Israel stood;) <sup>(15)</sup> and he said, Blessed be the LORD God of Israel, which spake with his mouth unto David my father, and hath with his hand fulfilled *it*, saying, <sup>(16)</sup> Since the day that I brought forth my people Israel out of Egypt, I chose no city out of all the tribes of Israel to build an house, that my name might be therein; but I chose <sup>b</sup> David to be over my people Israel. <sup>(17)</sup> And it was in the heart of David my father to build an house for the name of the LORD God of Israel. <sup>(18)</sup> And the LORD said unto David my father, Whereas it was in thine heart to build an house unto my name, thou didst well that it was in thine heart. <sup>(19)</sup> Nevertheless thou shalt not build the house; but thy son that shall come forth out of thy loins, he shall build the house unto my name. <sup>(20)</sup> And the LORD hath performed his word that he spake, and I am risen up in the room of David my father, and sit on the throne of Israel, as the LORD promised, and have built an house for the name of the LORD God of Israel. <sup>(21)</sup> And I have set there a place for the ark, wherein *is* the covenant of the LORD, which he made with our fathers, when he brought them out of the land of Egypt.

<sup>(22)</sup> And Solomon stood before <sup>c</sup> the altar of the LORD in the presence of all

*a* 2 Chron. 6. 1.

*b* 2 Sam. 7. 8.

*c* 2 Chron. 6. 13.

B.C. 1004.

---

he recognises in the appearance of the cloud the sign that the Divine presence is granted to the Temple; and accordingly he exults in the proof that his foreordained work is accomplished by the building of a house, a "settled habitation" for the Lord. The description of the cloud as "thick darkness," in no way contradicts the idea of the glory shining through it; for human eyes are easily "darkened by excess of light." This mingled light and darkness symbolises—perhaps more strikingly than even the literal darkness of the Most Holy Place—the mystery which veils the presence of God, known to be, and to be infinitely glorious, but in its nature incomprehensible.

Thenius, from a single Chaldee version, suggests for "thick darkness" the correction "Jerusalem;" dwelling on the closer harmony of the reading with verse 16, quoting the promise of Psalm cxxxii. 13, 14 (closely connected there with the great promise of David), and urging the likelihood of the citation of this promise by Solomon, and the greater simplicity thus given to his whole utterance. The suggestion is ingenious; but it lacks authority, both external and internal. The LXX., in the Alexandrine MS. (for the Vatican MS. omits the whole), and the Vulg. agree with the Hebrew text; and Josephus, though he gives a verbose paraphrase of the prayer, evidently had our reading before him, for he contrasts the mystery and ubiquity of the Divine presence with the material shrine. Nor is it easy to conceive how from a passage so simple and prosaic, as this would be with the reading "Jerusalem," the more difficult, but far more striking, reading of the present text could have arisen.

<sup>(14)</sup> **And the king.**—We are told in the book of Chronicles (2 Chron. vi. 13) that the king stood on a "brasen scaffold" three cubits high, in the midst of the court before the altar of sacrifice, so that he could alternately turn towards the Temple and towards the people in the outer court.

<sup>(15—21)</sup> His address to the people—apparently preceded by a silent blessing with the usual uplifting of the hands—is the counterpart and expansion of the few abrupt words which he had just uttered before God—calling them to bless God with him for the fulfilment of one part of His promise to David, in the present acceptance of the Temple. The record of that promise is given in 2 Sam. vii. 5—16; 1 Chron. xvii. 4—14. Here it is freely cited with some variation, so far as it relates to the Temple. It is remarkable that in quoting it, David twice (1 Chron. xxii. 8, xxviii. 3) adds to it the instructive reason for the prohibition, that (unlike Solomon the Peaceful) he had "shed blood abundantly, and had made great wars." With much grace of filial piety, Solomon refrains from mention of that reason, though there seems to be some allusion to it in his words to Hiram (chap. v. 3). On the other hand, he does add—what is not found in the earlier records—the declaration that, though David was not to build the Temple, "he did well that it was in his heart" to build it.

<sup>(16)</sup> **I chose no city.**—In this verse, as in some other cases, for coherence of idea, it seems necessary to correct from the fuller version in 2 Chron. vi. 5, 6, by an addition after the word "therein." It should run: "Neither chose I any man to be ruler over my people, but I have chosen Jerusalem, that my name might be there, and I have chosen David to be over my people Israel." The parallel in the two points referred to is exact. As there were temporary resting places for the ark—such as Gilgal, Shiloh, Kirjath-jearim, and Zion—so there were rulers raised up successively for a time, and then removed. Now there was to be one fixed place as the Sanctuary of God, and one royal house of David to continue for ever.

<sup>(21)</sup> **Wherein is the covenant of the Lord**—the Tables, that is, containing the "words of the covenant" (Exod. xxxiv. 28). This remarkable application of the word "covenant" illustrates strikingly the characteristics of the Divine covenants with man. Such covenants are not (like most human covenants) undertakings of reciprocal engagements between parties regarded as independent. For such a conception of the relation between God and man is monstrous. God's covenants proceed simply from His will, expressed in His call to an individual or a nation. They begin in free grace and blessing from Him; they require simply that men

the congregation of Israel, and spread forth his hands toward heaven: <sup>(23)</sup> and he said, ª Lᴏʀᴅ God of Israel, *there is* no God like thee, in heaven above, or on earth beneath, who keepest covenant and mercy with thy servants that walk before thee with all their heart: <sup>(24)</sup> who hast kept with thy servant David my father that thou promisedst him: thou spakest also with thy mouth, and hast fulfilled *it* with thine hand, as *it is* this day. <sup>(25)</sup> Therefore now, Lᴏʀᴅ God of Israel, keep with thy servant David my father that thou promisedst him, saying, <sup>*b* 1</sup> There shall not fail thee a man in my sight to sit on the throne of Israel; ²so that thy children take heed to their way, that they walk before me as thou hast walked before me. <sup>(26)</sup> And now, O God of Israel, let thy word, I pray thee, be verified, which thou spakest unto thy servant David my father.

<sup>(27)</sup> But will God indeed dwell on the earth? behold, the heaven and heaven of heavens cannot contain thee; how much less this house that I have builded? <sup>(28)</sup> Yet have thou respect unto the prayer of thy servant, and to his supplication, O Lᴏʀᴅ my God, to hearken unto the cry and to the prayer, which thy servant

*a* 2 Mac. 2. 8.

*b* 2 Sam. 7. 12; ch. 2. 4.

¹ Heb., *There shall not be cut off unto thee a man from my sight.*

² Heb., *only if.*

---

should believe and accept His call, and act in obedience to that belief. Thus the Decalogue opens with the words, "I am the Lord thy God, who brought thee out of the land of Egypt, out of the house of bondage," describing the gift of salvation from the mercy of God, which constituted Israel afresh as His peculiar people. (See Exod. iii. 7—15.) On the ground of this salvation, rather than of His Omnipotence as Creator and Sustainer of the world, He calls for their obedience to the commandments, which are thus "the words of the covenant." Similarly St. Paul, when (Rom. xii. 1) he calls Christians to absolute self-devotion, appeals to them by "the mercies of God," on which he had so fully dwelt —the larger and more spiritual covenant in Christ.

(23—53) The prayer of Solomon, uttered (see verse 54) on his knees with hands uplifted to heaven, long and detailed as it is, is yet of extreme simplicity of idea. It begins (*a*), in verses 23—25, with a thankful acknowledgment of the fulfilment of one part of the great promise to David, and a prayer for the like fulfilment of the other; next (*b*), in verses 26—30, acknowledging that God's presence can be limited to no Temple, it yet asks that His peculiar blessing may rest on prayer uttered toward the place which He has hallowed; and then (*c*), in verses 31—53, applies that petition to the various contingencies, of oath taken in His name, of rain withheld, of disaster in battle, of famine and pestilence, of captivity in a foreign land, and extends it not only to Israel, but to the stranger who shall acknowledge and invoke the Lord Jehovah. Its constantly recurring burden is, "Hear Thou from heaven thy dwelling-place, and when Thou hearest, Lord, forgive." It is plain that before Solomon's mind there are continually present in some form the blessing and the curse pronounced in the Law (see Lev. xxvi.; Deut. xxviii.); and it is most true to human nature, and especially characteristic of the thoughtfulness of his philosophic temper, that over the bright hour of exultation there seems to hover a constant foreboding of evils and trials to come.

<sup>(23)</sup> **There is no God like Thee.**—These words, often used in the Psalms (Ps. lxxi. 19, lxxxvi. 8, lxxxix. 6), and especially found in the thanksgiving of David after the great promise (2 Sam. vii. 22), are evidently suggested by more ancient utterances of devotion; as for example, in the first recorded Psalm at the Red Sea (Exod. xv. 11). In them we trace the spiritual process by which the Israelites were trained from the polytheism of their forefathers to the knowledge of the One only God. He is known to them, first, in the close personal relation of "the God of Abraham, Isaac, and Jacob," to whom "none is like" of all gods whom others worshipped; but next, in His universal relation to the universe as the "God Almighty, and the Judge of the whole earth" (Gen. xvii. 2, xviii. 25); lastly, as Jehovah, "God," indeed, "of Israel," but, by the very meaning of the name, the One Self-existent Being source of all other life. Thus, in the thanksgiving of David to the words, "none is like Thee," is added at once the higher belief, "there is no God beside Thee." In this prayer of Solomon there follows at once the striking confession that the "heaven of heavens cannot contain" His Infinity.

**Who keepest covenant and mercy.**—This phrase, again, familiar in prayer (see Deut. vii. 9; Neh. i. 5; Dan. ix. 4), is clearly traceable to the conclusion of the Second Commandment (Exod. xx. 6), and the special revelation of God to Moses in the Mount (Exod. xxxiv. 6, 7). It is notable, not merely because it describes God as manifesting Himself "most chiefly by showing mercy and pity," but also because it declares this manifestation of mercy to be pledged to man as a chief part of His covenant. So in the New Testament it is said that, to those who claim His covenant in Christ, "He is *faithful and just* to forgive sins."

<sup>(25)</sup> **Therefore now.**—The larger and grander part of the promise to David extends beyond Solomon's quotation of it. For (see 2 Sam. vii. 12—16; Ps. lxxxix. 28—37) it expressly declares that, even if the seed of David fall away, they shall indeed be chastised, but they shall not be cast off. The prophet Jeremiah (Jer. xxxi. 36; xxxiii. 20—26) as well as the Psalmist (Ps. lxxxix. 36, 37) enforce the declaration by comparing the certainty of its fulfilment with the fixity of "the ordinances of the sun and moon." Like the ordinary dispensations of His Providence, it is in itself fixed and immutable, although the actual enjoyment of its blessing by each individual, or each age, is conditional on right reception of it.

<sup>(27, 28)</sup> **Will God indeed dwell.**—The thought expressed here exemplifies a constant antithesis which runs through the Old Testament. On the one hand, there is the most profound and unvarying conception of the Infinity, eternal, invisible, incomprehensible, of the Lord, as "the High and Holy One who inhabiteth eternity," whom "the heaven of heavens"—the heaven, that is, in all its vastest extent—"cannot contain;" and the spirituality of this conception is guarded by the

prayeth before thee to day: (29) that thine eyes may be opened toward this house night and day, *even* toward the place of which thou hast said, *ᵃMy name shall be there*: that thou mayest hearken unto the prayer which thy servant shall make ¹toward this place. (30) And hearken thou to the supplication of thy servant, and of thy people Israel, when they shall pray ²toward this place: and hear thou in heaven thy dwelling place: and when thou hearest, forgive.

(31) If any man trespass against his neighbour, ³and an oath be laid upon him to cause him to swear, and the oath come before thine altar in this house: (32) then hear thou in heaven, and do, and judge thy servants, condemning the wicked, to bring his way upon his head; and justifying the righteous, to give him according to his righteousness.

(33) When thy people Israel be smitten down before the enemy, because they have sinned against thee, and shall turn again to thee, and confess thy name, and pray, and make supplication unto thee ⁴in this house: (34) then hear thou in heaven, and forgive the sin of thy people Israel, and bring them again unto the land which thou gavest unto their fathers.

(35) When heaven is shut up, and there is no rain, because they have sinned against thee; if they pray toward this place, and confess thy name, and turn from their sin, when thou afflictest them: (36) then hear thou in heaven, and forgive the sin of thy servants, and of thy people Israel, that thou teach them the good way wherein they should walk, and give rain upon thy land, which thou hast given to thy people for an inheritance.

(37) If there be in the land famine, if there be pestilence, blasting, mildew, locust, *or* if there be caterpiller; if their enemy besiege them in the land of their

---

*ᵃ* Deut. 12. 11.

1 Or, *in this place.*

2 Or, *in this place.*

3 Heb., *and he require an oath of him.*

4 Or, *towards.*

---

sternest prohibition of that idolatry which limited and degraded the idea of God, and by rebuke of the superstition which trusted in an intrinsic sacredness of the Ark or the Temple. On the other hand, there is an equally vivid conviction that the Infinite Jehovah is yet pleased to enter into a special covenant with Israel, beyond all other nations, to reveal Himself by the cloud in the midst of His people, to bless, with a peculiar blessing, "the place which He chooses to place His Name there." The two conceptions co-exist, as in the text, in complete harmony, both preparing for the perfect manifestation of a "God with us" in that kingdom of the Messiah, which was at once to perfect the covenant with Israel, and to include all peoples, nations, and languages for ever and ever. The words of Solomon in spirit anticipate the utterance of the prophet (Isa. lxvi. 1), quoted by St. Stephen against idolatry of the Temple (Acts vii. 48), and even the greater declaration of our Lord (John iv. 21—24) as to the universal presence of God to all spiritual worship. Yet he feels the reality of the consecration of the House raised by the command of God; and prays that all who recognise it by prayer "toward this house," may enter into the special unity with God which it symbolises, and be heard by Him from heaven. By an instructive contrast, the Temple is described as the place where God's "Name"—that is, His self-revelation—is made to dwell; but heaven, and it alone, as the true dwelling-place of God Himself.

(31, 32) **If any man trespass.**—These verses deal with the simplest exemplification of the sacredness of the Temple in the case of the oath of expurgation of one accused of crime (see Exod. xxii. 7). Of these oaths, and the sophistical distinctions between the various forms of them, we have Our Lord's notice in Matt. xxiii. 16—22. Such an oath has a twofold force—a force purely spiritual, inasmuch as it solemnly recognises the Presence of God, and by such recognition shames all falsehood as a kind of sacrilege; and a force which is "of the Law," inasmuch as the invocation of God's punishment in case of falsehood appeals to godly fear. Solomon prays that God will accept the oath under both aspects, and by His judgment distinguish between the innocent and the guilty.

(33, 34) **When thy people.**—From the individual, the prayer turns to those which touch the whole nation. It pictures various national calamities, and in each recognises not mere evils, but chastisements of God, who desires by them to teach, and is most ready to forgive. First it naturally dwells on disaster in battle, which, in the whole history of the Exodus, of the Conquest, of the troubled age of the Judges, and of the reigns of Saul and David, is acknowledged as a sign of unfaithfulness in Israel, either through sin or through idolatry, to the covenant of God, on which the victorious possession of the promised land depended. On that history the blessing and the curse of the Law (Lev. xxvi. 17, 32, 33; Deut. xxviii. 25) form a commentary of emphatic warning, and the Psalms again and again bring the same lesson home (Pss. xliv. 1—3, 9—17, lx. 9—11, lxxxix. 42—46). With characteristic seriousness, Solomon looks back from his peaceful prosperity on the stormy past, and from it learns to pray for the future.

(35, 36) **When heaven is shut up.**—Next, Solomon dwells on the plague of famine, from rain withheld, by which, in the striking language of the Law (Lev. xxvi. 19; Deut. xxviii. 23, 24), "the heaven should be as brass, and the earth as iron," and all vegetation perish from the parched land of Palestine, as now it seems actually to have failed in many places once fertile. In such plague he acknowledges the chastisement of God, sent to "teach Israel the right way," and then to be withdrawn in mercy. The whole history of the famine in the days of Elijah is in all parts a striking commentary on this clause of the prayer.

(37—40) **If there be pestilence.**—He then passes on to the various plagues threatened in the Law—famine, pestilence, blasting of the corn, mildew on the

¹cities; whatsoever plague, whatsoever sickness *there be;* ⁽³⁸⁾ what prayer and supplication soever be *made* by any man, *or* by all thy people Israel, which shall know every man the plague of his own heart, and spread forth his hands toward this house: ⁽³⁹⁾ then hear thou in heaven thy dwelling place, and forgive, and do, and give to every man according to his ways, whose heart thou knowest; (for thou, *even* thou only, knowest the hearts of all the children of men;) ⁽⁴⁰⁾ that they may fear thee all the days that they live in the land which thou gavest unto our fathers.

⁽⁴¹⁾ Moreover concerning a stranger, that *is* not of thy people Israel, but cometh out of a far country for thy name's sake; ⁽⁴²⁾ (for they shall hear of thy great name, and of thy strong hand, and of thy stretched out arm;) when he shall come and pray toward this house; ⁽⁴³⁾ hear thou in heaven thy dwelling place, and do according to all that the stranger calleth to thee for: that all people of the earth may know thy name, to fear thee, as *do* thy people Israel; and that they may know that ²this house, which I have builded, is called by thy name.

⁽⁴⁴⁾ If thy people go out to battle against their enemy, whithersoever thou shalt send them, and shall pray unto the LORD ³ toward the city which thou hast chosen, and *toward* the house that I have built for thy name: ⁽⁴⁵⁾ then hear thou in heaven their prayer and their supplication, and maintain their ⁴cause.

⁽⁴⁶⁾ If they sin against thee, (ᵃfor *there is* no man that sinneth not,) and thou be angry with them, and deliver them to the enemy, so that they carry them away captives unto the land of the enemy, far or near; ⁽⁴⁷⁾ *yet* if they shall ⁵ bethink themselves in the land whither they were carried captives, and repent, and make supplication unto thee in the land of them that carried them captives,

---

1 Or, *jurisdiction.*

2 Heb., *thy name is called upon this house.*

3 Heb., *the way of the city.*

4 Or, *right.*

ᵃ 2 Chron. 6. 36; Eccles. 7. 22; 1 John 1. 8, 10.

5 Heb., *bring back to their heart.*

---

fruit, locust and caterpillar (see Lev. xxvi. 25, 26; Deut. xxviii. 22—24, 38—42), the distress of siege, so terribly depicted (Deut. xxviii. 52—57), and so often terribly fulfilled (not least in the last great siege of Jerusalem), and adds, to sum up all, "whatsoever plague, whatsoever sickness there be." Through any, or all of these, he pictures each man as brought to "know the plague of his own heart"—that is, as startled into a consciousness of sin, and recognition of it as the true "plague," the cause of all outward plagues, and so drawn to prayer of penitence and of godly fear.

**Thou only, knowest the hearts ... of men.** The emphasis laid on this knowledge of the heart (as in Pss. xi. 4, cxxxix. 2—4; Jer. xvii. 9, 10) as the special attribute of Deity, though, of course, belonging to all vital religion, yet marks especially the leading thought of the Psalms and the Proverbs, which always realise the presence of God, not so much in the outer spheres of Nature and history, as in the soul of man itself. It carries with it, as here, the conviction that, under the general dealings of God's righteousness with man, there lies an individuality of judgment, making them to each exactly what his spiritual condition needs. The plague, for example, which cuts off one man unrepentant in his sins, may be to another a merciful "deliverance out of the miseries of this sinful world."

(41—43) **Moreover, concerning a stranger.**—These verses in a striking digression (perhaps suggested by the general acknowledgment in the previous verse of God's knowledge of every human heart), interpose in the series of references to Israel a prayer for the acceptance of the prayer of the "stranger" who should come from afar to confess the Lord Jehovah, and to "pray toward this house." Such recognition of the stranger, not as an enemy or even a complete alien, but as in some sense capable of communion with the true God, was especially natural in Solomon; first, because in his days many strangers came from afar, drawn by the fame of his wisdom and magnificence, so that the old exclusiveness of the Israelites must have been greatly broken down; and next, because the character of the thought and writing of his age, searching (as in the books of Job, Proverbs, and Ecclesiastes) into the great religious problems which belong to man as man, naturally led to that wider view of the kingdom of God over all nations, which is worked out so strikingly in the writings of the prophets. That the case contemplated is probably not imaginary, is shown by the examples of King Hiram and the Queen of Sheba. Admiration of the glory of Israel would lead inevitably to some belief in, and "fear" of, the God of Israel; and it might well go on to the further result, here contemplated, of a fuller acknowledgment of the Lord Jehovah, and of the sacredness of the worship of His appointed Temple, which would tell silently on all the religions of the East. It was expressly provided for in the Law (Num. xv. 14—16): and in spite of the greater exclusiveness of the ages after the Captivity, heathen princes were often allowed to offer in the Temple. This recognition of the stranger from afar is different from the frequent recognition of the resident "stranger within their gates," as being under the protection of God, and to be "loved" by those who had been "strangers in the land of Egypt" (Deut. x. 18, 19). But, like it, it nobly distinguished the Law of Israel from most ancient codes; it stood out as a striking, though often unheeded, protest against the hard exclusiveness of the Jewish temper; it was a tacit anticipation of the future gathering in of all nations to enjoy the blessing which was from the beginning expressly destined for "all families of the earth."

(44—50) **If thy people go out.**—The prayer here returns once more to invoke God's aid against earthly enemies. It is characteristic of the foreboding tone of sadness, which runs through the whole prayer, that it touches but lightly on the first petition, for God's blessing on the arms of Israel, so often granted in days gone by, and enlarges on the

saying, We have sinned, and have done perversely, we have committed wickedness; ⁽⁴⁸⁾ and so return unto thee with all their heart, and with all their soul, in the land of their enemies, which led them away captive, and pray unto thee toward their land, which thou gavest unto their fathers, the city which thou hast chosen, and the house which I have built for thy name: ⁽⁴⁹⁾ then hear thou their prayer and their supplication in heaven thy dwelling place, and maintain their ¹cause, ⁽⁵⁰⁾ and forgive thy people that have sinned against thee, and all their transgressions wherein they have transgressed against thee, and give them compassion before them who carried them captive, that they may have compassion on them: ⁽⁵¹⁾ for they be thy people, and thine inheritance, which thou broughtest forth out of Egypt, from the midst of the furnace of iron: ⁽⁵²⁾ that thine eyes may be open unto the supplication of thy servant, and unto the supplication of thy people Israel, to hearken unto them in all that they call for unto thee. ⁽⁵³⁾ For thou didst separate them from among all the people of the earth, *to be* thine inheritance, *ᵃ*as thou spakest by the hand of Moses thy servant, when thou broughtest our fathers out of Egypt, O Lord God.

⁽⁵⁴⁾ And it was *so,* that when Solomon had made an end of praying all this prayer and supplication unto the LORD, he arose from before the altar of the LORD, from kneeling on his knees with his hands spread up to heaven. ⁽⁵⁵⁾ And he stood, and blessed all the congrega-

¹ Or, *right.*

*ᵃ* Exod. 19. 6.

---

second petition, for mercy and deliverance in the event of defeat and captivity. The spirit, and in the confession of verse 47 the very words, of this prayer of Solomon are strikingly reproduced in the solemn supplication of Daniel, when the close of the Babylonish captivity drew near (Dan. ix. 4—15). There we find a confession of sin, perverseness, and wickedness, literally the same; we find also a similar pleading with God, as "keeping covenant and mercy," a similar reference to the deliverance from Egypt, and a similar emphasis on the consecration of the city and its people by God's "great name." There is a striking pathos of circumstance in the fact, that over "the sanctuary that was desolate" (Dan. ix. 17), with "his windows open towards Jerusalem," Daniel utters the same prayer, which had marked the day of its consecration in all magnificence and prosperity.

⁽⁵⁰⁾ **Forgive . . . and give them compassion.**—This prayer was singularly fulfilled at the captivity of Judah in Babylon, though we hear of no such thing in relation to the captivity of the "lost tribes" of Israel in Assyria. We see this in the exceptional favour of Nebuchadnezzar and of the Ahasuerus of the Book of Esther to the Jews in Babylon; we see it still more in the greater boon of restoration granted them by Cyrus and Darius, and the Artaxerxes of the Book of Nehemiah. Like the whole course of the fortunes of the Jews in their subsequent dispersion, these things,—however they may be accounted for—are certainly unique in history.

⁽⁵¹⁻⁵³⁾ **For they be thy people.**—This pleading with God by His deliverance of the people from Egypt, and by His promise to Moses to make them His inheritance (see Exod. xix. 5; Deut. ix. 26, 29, xiv. 2), although especially suggested by the last petition for deliverance from captivity, may be held to apply to the whole of Solomon's prayer. It implies the belief not only that the declared purpose of God cannot fail, but that, even for the manifestation of His glory to man, it must needs be visibly fulfilled before the eyes of the world. This same conviction breathes in many of the utterances of Moses for Israel (see Exod. xxxii. 12, 13; Num. xiv. 13, 14); it is expressed in the "Help us, O Lord, and deliver us for Thy name's sake," of Ps. lxxix. 9, 10, or the "Defer not for Thine own sake, O my God" of Dan. ix. 19: it is declared on the part of the Lord again and again in Ezek. xx. 9, 14, 22, "I wrought for my name's sake." It may, indeed, seem to jar upon our fuller conception of the infinite majesty of God, incapable of being augmented or lessened, and of the infinite love which does all for the sake of His creatures. Yet it is not wholly unlike our Lord's prayer (John xii. 28), "Father, glorify thy name," or the Apostolic declarations of the great purpose of redemption, as designed for "the praise of God's glory" (Ephes. i. 6, 12, 14), and of all Christian life as commanded to "do all to the glory of God" (1 Cor. x. 31). In some respects it is like the pleading with our Lord, in the Litanies of the Church in all ages, by all the various acts of His redemption, and the prayer of the old Latin hymn—

" Redemisti crucem passus ;
Tantus labor ne sit cassus."

But, indeed, all that might seem to us strange or unworthy in such prayers vanishes at once, when we consider that the knowledge of God in His self-manifestation is the highest happiness of man; on which, indeed, depend all depth and harmony of human knowledge, and all dignity and purity of human life. Hence, in the Lord's Prayer, the three petitions "for God's glory," preceding all special petitions for our own needs, are really prayers for the highest blessing of all mankind. God's care for His glory is not for His own sake, but for ours.

⁽⁵⁴⁾ **And it was so.**—At this point occurs in 2 Chron. vii. 1—3 a striking passage, describing the kindling of the sacrifice by fire from heaven, and, apparently, a second manifestation of the cloud of glory. (See Note on the passage.)

⁽⁵⁵⁾ **Blessed all the children of Israel.**—To bless the congregation was the special duty and privilege of the priests (see Num. vi. 23—27); but throughout the whole of this narrative the king, and the king alone, is conspicuous. It is, however, to be noted that Solomon's words here are not strictly of blessing, but rather of praise and prayer to God, and exhortation to the people.

*He Blesses the People.*        I. KINGS, VIII.        *The Sacrifice of Peace Offerings.*

tion of Israel with a loud voice, saying, **(56)** Blessed *be* the LORD, that hath given rest unto his people Israel, according to all that he promised : there hath not ¹failed one word of all his good promise, which he promised by the hand of Moses his servant. **(57)** The LORD our God be with us, as he was with our fathers : let him not leave us, nor forsake us : **(58)** that he may incline our hearts unto him, to walk in all his ways, and to keep his commandments, and his statutes, and his judgments, which he commanded our fathers. **(59)** And let these my words, wherewith I have made supplication before the LORD, be nigh unto the LORD our God day and night, that he maintain the cause of his servant, and the cause of his people Israel ²at all times, as the matter shall require: **(60)** that all the people of the earth may know that the LORD *is* God, *and that there is* none else. **(61)** Let your heart therefore be perfect with the LORD our God, to walk in his statutes, and to keep his commandments, as at this day.

**(62)** And *ᵃ* the king, and all Israel with him, offered sacrifice before the LORD. **(63)** And Solomon offered a sacrifice of peace offerings, which he offered unto the LORD, two and twenty thousand oxen, and an hundred and twenty thousand sheep. So the king and all the children of Israel dedicated the house of the LORD. **(64)** *ᵇ* The same day did the king hallow the middle of the court that *was* before the house of the LORD: for there he offered burnt offerings, and meat offerings, and the fat of the peace offerings : because the brasen altar that *was* before the LORD *was* too little to receive the burnt offerings, and meat

*Marginal notes:* 1 Heb., *fallen.*   2 Heb., *the thing of a day in his day.*   *a* 2 Chron. 7. 4.   *b* 2 Chron. 7. 7.

---

**(56) That hath given rest.**—Now for the first time the frequent promise of rest (Exod. xxxiii. 14; Deut. xii. 10, &c.)—partially fulfilled after the conquest of the days of Joshua (Josh. xxi. 44, 45, xxiii. 1, 14), and after the establishment of the kingdom of David (2 Sam. vii. 1)—was perfectly accomplished under Solomon the Peaceful, and the whole charter of gift of the promised land (Josh. i. 3, 4) for the first time thoroughly entered upon. Of the "rest" of Israel, the transfer of the Ark of the Lord from the shifting Tabernacle to the fixed Temple was at once a sign and a pledge. Yet Solomon's subsequent words imply that "entering into that rest" was conditional on fulfilment of Israel's part in the covenant, by "walking in the ways of the Lord." That condition, which he knew so well, he himself broke, and all Israel with him. Hence the fulfilment of the foreboding which emerges so constantly in his prayer. The glory of rest and happiness of his age was but a gleam of prosperity, soon to be swallowed up in dissension and disaster.

**(58) That he may incline . . .**—Comparing this verse with the exhortation of verse 61, we find exemplified the faith which pervades all Holy Scripture and underlies the whole idea of covenant with God. It is a faith in the true, though mysterious, co-operation of the "preventing grace" of God, which must be recognised in all adequate conceptions of Him, as the Source of all life and action, physical and spiritual, and of that free responsibility of man which is the ultimate truth of the inner human consciousness. God "inclines the heart" and yet the heart must yield itself. The conviction of this truth naturally grows deeper and plainer, in proportion as man realises better the inner life of the soul as contrasted with the outer life of event and action, and realises accordingly the dominion of God over the soul by His grace, over and above His rule over the visible world by His providence. Hence it comes out especially in the Psalms, the Proverbs, and the Prophetic books. It is instructive, for example, to observe how through the great "psalm of the Law" (Ps. cxix.) the conviction again and again expresses itself that only by His gift can the heart be enabled to obey it. (See verses 26, 27, 32, 33, 36, &c.) In the New Testament, the "covenant of the Spirit," the truth is brought out in all its fulness; perhaps most vividly in the celebrated paradox of Phil. ii. 12, 13, "Work out your own salvation . . . For it is God which worketh in you both to will and to do of His good pleasure."

**(59) And Solomon offered.**—The idea that the king on this occasion, and on others, performed the priest's ministerial office is manifestly improbable. At all times he who brought the sacrifice was said to "offer" it. (See, for example, Lev. ii. 1, iii. 2, 7, &c.) The priest accepted it in the name of the Lord, and poured the blood at the foot of the altar of sacrifice, or sprinkled it on the altar of incense. But still the absence of all mention of the priests, even as to the "hallowing" of the court for sacrifice, is characteristic of the tone of the whole narrative, in which the king alone is prominent.

**(63) And Solomon offered.**—The number here given, enormous as it is, can hardly be supposed due to any error in the text; for it is exactly reproduced in the Chronicles and by Josephus. Much explanation of it has been wasted through misunderstanding of the real difficulty involved. It is comparatively easy to conceive how such a mass of victims could be brought as offerings or consumed, when we consider the vastness of the assembled multitude from the whole of the great dominions of Solomon, dwelling in or encamped about the city. Even at the Passovers of the last days of Jerusalem the multitude of worshippers seems to have been numbered by hundreds of thousands. The real difficulty is to conceive how, even through the fourteen days of the festival, and over the whole of the hallowed portion of the court, the victims could have been offered. But it is not unlikely that on such an occasion it might be deemed sufficient actually to sacrifice only certain representative victims of each hecatomb, and simply to dedicate the rest to the Lord, leaving them to be killed and eaten elsewhere.

This profusion of sacrifices, good as expressing the natural desire of all to offer at such a time, may perhaps have involved something of the idea, so frequent in heathen sacrifice, and so emphatically condemned by the prophets, that the Lord would be "pleased with

*Feast of the Dedication.*     I. KINGS, IX.     *The Lord appears to Solomon.*

offerings, and the fat of the peace offerings. <sup>(65)</sup> And at that time Solomon held a feast, and all Israel with him, a great congregation, from the entering in of Hamath unto the river of Egypt, before the LORD our God, seven days and seven days, *even* fourteen days. <sup>(66)</sup> On the eighth day he sent the people away: and they <sup>1</sup> blessed the king, and went unto their tents joyful and glad of heart for all the goodness that the LORD had done for David his servant, and for Israel his people.

CHAPTER IX.—<sup>(1)</sup> And *a*it came to pass, when Solomon had finished the building of the house of the LORD, and the king's house, and all Solomon's desire which he was pleased to do, <sup>(2)</sup> that the Lord appeared to Solomon the second time, *b*as he had appeared unto him at Gibeon.

<sup>(3)</sup> And the LORD said unto him, I

<sup>1</sup> Or, *thanked.*

B.C. cir. 992.

*a* 2 Chron. 7. 11.

*b* ch. 3. 5.

---

thousands of rams and ten thousands of rivers of oil"—something also of that display of the magnificence of the king and his people, even in the very act of homage to God, which the history throughout seems to imply. If so, in these ideas lurked the evils which hereafter were to overthrow the prosperity of Israel, and make the Temple a heap of stones.

<sup>(65)</sup> **The entering in of Hamath,** is the significant name given to the great valley between Lebanon and Anti-Lebanon, which the Greeks called *Cœle-Syria*; for it was the main entrance to Palestine from the north, down which the hosts of Assyria and Babylon so constantly poured. Evidently it extended at this time beyond Damascus.

**The river of Egypt** is not, as might naturally be thought, the Nile, or any of its branches; for the word used signifies rather a "brook" or "torrent," and the torrent, described in Num. xxxiv. 5 and Josh. xv. 4 as the border of Israel, is identified by all authorities with the torrent falling into the sea at El-Arish.

<sup>(65, 66)</sup> **Seven days and seven days, even fourteen days. On the eighth day . . . .** —The origin of this curious phrase is singularly illustrated by the account in 2 Chron. vii. 9, 10, for it tells us that the people were dismissed on "the three and twentieth day" of the month, which was the day after the close of the Feast of Tabernacles. Hence it is clear that the festival week of the Dedication preceded the regular feast; and the day of dismissal was the "eighth day," regularly so-called, of the close of the Feast of Tabernacles.

**Unto their tents.**—The old memory of the wandering life of Israel still lingers in this expression, as in the well-known phrase "To your tents, O Israel!" (2 Sam. xx. 1; 1 Kings xii. 16.) It may have been suggested to the writer in this place by the ideas symbolised in the Feast of Tabernacles, of which he had just recorded the observance.

IX.

Of this chapter, the first portion (verses 1—9) forms the conclusion of the detailed narrative of the preceding chapter; the latter portion is wholly different in style and subject.

<sup>(1)</sup> **And it came to pass.**—The obvious *primâ facie* meaning of this verse would land us in much difficulty. By chaps. vi. 38, vii. 1, we find that, while the Temple was built in seven years, the erection of the palace and the other buildings occupied thirteen years; and from chap. v. 10 and 2 Chron. viii. 1 it appears that these works were successive, and therefore that the completion of the palace could not have taken place till thirteen years after the completion of the Temple. Hence we should have to conclude, either that the dedication was postponed for thirteen years, till all the buildings were finished—which is in itself infinitely improbable, and contradicts the express declaration of Josephus—or that a similar period intervened between Solomon's prayer and the Divine answer to it, which is even more preposterous. The variation in 2 Chron. vii. 11 probably suggests the true key to the difficulty: viz., that the notice in this verse is merely a summary of the history of chaps. vi.–viii., which records the whole of the building works of Solomon, and is not intended to fix the date of the vision of verses 2—9.

<sup>(3-9)</sup> **And the Lord said unto him.**—This vision of the Lord presents a remarkable contrast with that recorded in chap. vi. 11—13, while the Temple was in building. Then all was promise and encouragement; now, not only is warning mingled with promise, but, as in Solomon's own prayer, the sadder alternative seems in prophetic anticipation to overpower the brighter. In this there is (as has been often remarked) a striking exemplification of the austere and lofty candour of the inspired narrative, sternly contradicting that natural hopefulness in the hour of unexampled prosperity, which would have shrunk from even entertaining the idea that the blessing of God on the Temple should be frustrated, and the glory of Israel should pass away.

It is notable that, in its reference to the two parts of the promise to David, there is a subtle and instructive distinction. As for the Temple, now just built in fulfilment of that promise, it is declared without reserve that, in case of unfaithfulness in Israel, it shall be utterly destroyed, and become an astonishment and a proverb of reproach before the world. But in respect of the promise of the perpetuity of David's kingdom—the true Messianic prediction, which struck the key-note of all future prophecies—it is only said that Israel shall be "cut off from the land," and so " become a proverb and a byword" in captivity. Nothing is said to contradict the original declaration, that, even in case of sin, the mercy of God would chastise and not forsake the house of David (2 Sam. vii. 13, 14; Ps. lxxxix. 30—37). So again and again in prophecy captivity is denounced as a penalty of Israel's sin; but the hope of restoration is always held out, and thus the belief in God's unchanging promise remains unshaken. The true idea is strikingly illustrated by the prophet Amos (chap. ix. 9—11): "I will sift the house of Israel, among all nations . . . yet shall not the least grain fall upon the earth . . . I will raise up the tabernacle of David that is fallen, and close up the breaches thereof."

<sup>(3)</sup> **To put my name there for ever.**—The meaning of the words "for ever," is determined by the

*God's Covenant*        I. KINGS, IX.        *With Solomon.*

have heard thy prayer and thy supplication, that thou hast made before me: I have hallowed this house, which thou hast built, *a*to put my name there for ever; and mine eyes and mine heart shall be there perpetually. (4) And if thou wilt walk before me, as David thy father walked, in integrity of heart, and in uprightness, to do according to all that I have commanded thee, *and* wilt keep my statutes and my judgments: (5) then I will establish the throne of thy kingdom upon Israel for ever, *b*as I promised to David thy father, saying, There shall not fail thee a man upon the throne of Israel. (6) But if ye shall at all turn from following me, ye or your children, and will not keep my commandments *and* my statutes which I have set before you, but go and serve other gods, and worship them: (7) then will I cut off Israel out of the land which I have given them; and this house, which I have hallowed *c* for my name, will I cast out of my sight; and Israel shall be a proverb and a byword among all people: (8) and at this house, *which* is high, every one that passeth by it shall be astonished, and shall hiss; and they shall say, *d* Why hath the LORD done thus unto this land, and to this house? (9) And they shall answer, Because they forsook the LORD their God, who brought forth their fathers out of the land of Egypt, and have taken hold upon other gods, and have worshipped them, and served them: therefore hath the LORD brought upon them all this evil.

(10) And *e* it came to pass at the end of twenty years, when Solomon had built the two houses, the house of the LORD, and the king's house, (11) (Now Hiram the king of Tyre had furnished Solomon with cedar trees and fir trees, and with gold, according to all his desire,) that then king Solomon gave Hiram twenty cities in the land of Galilee. (12) And Hiram came out from Tyre to see the cities which Solomon had given him;

*a* ch. 8. 29.

*b* 2 Sam. 7. 12; 1 Chron. 22. 10.

*c* Jer. 7. 14.

*d* Deut. 29. 24; Jer. 22. 8.

*e* 2 Chron. 8. 1.

---

prayer which they answer. They simply mark the Temple as the "settled habitation to abide in for ever" (see chap. viii. 13), in contradistinction from the movable tabernacle. Whether they were to have a larger significance is expressly declared to depend on the faithfulness of Israel (see verses 7, 8).

**Mine eyes and mine heart.**—See viii. 29.

(5) **If thou wilt walk.**—The fall of the house of Solomon from dominion over all Israel is an emphatic comment on the conditional nature of this promise. Yet the essence of the covenant with David was kept in that preservation of the diminished kingdom to an unbroken succession of his descendants—singularly contrasted with the changes of dynasty in the greater rival kingdom—which is expressly declared to have been granted "for David's sake" (chap. xi. 12, 13).

(7) **Then will I cut off.**—These warnings were repeated with terrible force by Jeremiah on the eve of their fulfilment. (See Jer. vii. 12—14, xxiv. 9, xxv. 9.) The destruction of the Temple is by him compared with that which fell on Shiloh—no doubt, after the great defeat by the Philistines in the time of Eli (1 Sam. iv., v.), although the history gives no record of it. The continued existence of the people, as a people, to be "a proverb and a byword," through the Babylonish captivity, and through their present dispersion, is a fact to which the history of the world undoubtedly furnishes no parallel.

(8) **At this house, which is high.**—The word "which" is not in the original Hebrew here (although found in the present Hebrew text of 2 Chron. vii. 21). The true meaning is certainly "This house shall be high;" which is the reading of the LXX., while the Vulg. has a good explanatory gloss, "This house shall be for an example." Various corrections have been proposed, but there seems no necessity for them. There is evidently an allusion to the lofty position of the Temple. Generally the exaltation of "the mountain of the Lord" is made a type of its glory (as in Micah iv. 1, 2; Ps. lxviii. 15, 16, &c.); here of its destruction. Its magnificence and its ruin are equally conspicuous: for "a city set on a hill cannot be hid."

(9) **Brought . . . out of the land of Egypt.**—This is appealed to here in exactly a converse sense to the mention of it in Solomon's prayer. There it was made the ground for pleading with the Lord for His continued favour (see chap. viii. 51—53); here for His claim of the undivided allegiance of the people, for it marked His new "covenant" with the people, now become a nation (see Jer. xxxi. 32), and therefore involved (as in all covenants) reciprocal claims. Afterwards the deliverance from Babylon was to take its place, both as a proof of God's love and a motive for the loyal obedience of the people (Jer. xvi. 14, 15, xxiii. 7, 8).

(10) **And it came to pass.**—To this detailed account of the building and consecration of the Temple, ending at verse 9, succeed, first, a notice of a visit of Hiram; and then a section of wholly different character, a series of brief notes (evidently official records), of the works and the government of Solomon, which continues—broken only by the episode of the visit of the Queen of Sheba—to the end of the next chapter.

(11) **Gave Hiram . . . cities.**—This implies a debt to him for timber and gold, and probably stone also, over and above the payment in kind stipulated for in chap. v. 9. From the notice in 2 Chron. viii. 2, that, when these cities were restored by Hiram, Solomon rebuilt them, and peopled them with Israelites, it seems likely that they were previously cities of the subject races, which he would have no scruple in alienating; although, indeed, the often-quoted enactment of the Law (Lev. xxv. 23, 24), would not have been likely to be strictly observed under his self-reliant despotism.

and they ¹pleased him not. ⁽¹³⁾ And he said, What cities *are* these which thou hast given me, my brother? And he called them the land of ²Cabul unto

¹ Heb., *were not right in his eyes.*

² That is, *displeasing*, or, *dirty.*

this day. ⁽¹⁴⁾ And Hiram sent to the king sixscore talents of gold.

⁽¹⁵⁾ And this *is* the reason of the levy which king Solomon raised; for to build

---

⁽¹²⁾ The cities are said to have been in "the land of Galilee." The name *Galilee*, signifying properly a "circle" or "ring" of territory, is used twice in the Book of Joshua for a region round Kedesh-Naphtali (Josh. xx. 7, xxi. 32), lying to the north-west of the Lake of Gennesareth, and extending to the Waters of Merom. (See also 2 Kings xv. 29.) The western portion of this territory would lie nearly on the frontiers of Tyre, and so would suit well the purpose both of Hiram and of Solomon. The discontent of Hiram probably referred to the condition of the cities (which afterwards had to be rebuilt), not to their geographical position.

⁽¹³⁾ **Cabul.**—The derivation of this word is uncertain. Josephus evidently did not know it as a Hebrew word; for he expressly says, that in the Phœnician language it signifies "what is unpleasing." (*Ant.* viii. c. 5, sect. 3). A city Cabul is mentioned in Josh. xix. 27, in the territory of Asher, evidently on the Tyrian frontier, and in the neighbourhood in question. Hiram, it is thought, takes up this name, and applies it to the whole territory, and by a play of words on it signifies his discontent with Solomon's gift. Ewald supposes a Hebrew derivation for the word ("as nought"); others take it to be "like that which vanishes." Either would suit the sense indicated in the text well; but unless these derivations represent something cognate in the Tyrian language, they hardly accord with the requirements of this passage, which (as Josephus says) implies a Phœnician origin for the word.

⁽¹⁴⁾ **Hiram sent to the king sixscore talents of gold.**—The payment, on any calculation, was a large one, though little more than a sixth of Solomon's yearly revenue. (See chap. x. 14.) How it is connected with the previous verses is matter of conjecture. It may possibly be a note referring back to verse 11, and explaining the amount of gold which Hiram had sent. If this is not so, it would then seem to be a payment in acknowledgment of the cession of the cities, as being of greater value than the debt which it was meant to discharge. Hiram's depreciation of the cities need not imply that he did not care to keep them. "It is naught, it is naught, saith the buyer: but when he is gone his way, then he boasteth." (Prov. xx. 14). Josephus (*Ant.* viii. 5, 3), has a quaint story in connection with this intercourse between Hiram and Solomon (quoted from Dios), declaring that a contest in riddles took place between these kings, and that, when Hiram could not solve the riddles of Solomon, he "paid a large sum of money for his fine," but adds that he afterwards retaliated on Solomon, by aid of Abdemon of Tyre. It appears by 2 Chron. vii. 2, that the cities were afterwards restored to Israel—how, and why, we know not.

⁽¹⁵⁻²⁸⁾ The rest of the chapter consists of brief historical notes, partly referring back to the previous records. Thus, verse 15 refers back to chap. v. 13; verses 20—22 to chap. v. 15; verse 24 to chap. vii. 8; verse 25 is a note connected with the history of the dedication of the Temple. The style is markedly different from the graphic and picturesque style of the passages preceding and following it.

⁽¹⁵⁾ **The levy.**—This (see chap. v. 13, 15) was both of Israelites and of the subject races, first originated for the building of the Temple, afterwards extended to the other great building works.

The building works enumerated are, first in Jerusalem, then in various parts of the country of critical importance, either for war or for commerce.

**Millo,** or (as it always has the definite article), "the Millo." The Hebrew word seems to signify "piling up," or "heaping up," and its most simple meaning would be a "fortified mound." From the mention, however, in Judges ix. 6, 20, of the "house of Millo," in connection with the men of Shechem, it has been supposed to be a Canaanitish word; and it is possible that "the Millo" of Jerusalem may have been the name of a quarter of the old Jebusite city, especially as it is first used in connection with the narrative of its capture (2 Sam. v. 9; 1 Chron. xi. 8). That it was a part of the fortification of "the city of David" is clear by this passage, by verse 24 and chap. xi. 27, and by 2 Chron. xxxii. 5; and the LXX. invariably renders it "Acra," or "the citadel," a name always applied in the later history to the fortification on Mount Zion. Josephus, in describing the works of Solomon, merely says that he made the walls of David higher and stronger, and built towers on them. From the derivation of the word it is possible that the work was the raising a high fortification of earth crowned with a wall, where the hill of Zion slopes down unto the valley known subsequently as the *Tyropœon*.

**Hazor, Megiddo, and Gezer.**—These cities were all of important geographical positions, and all had belonged to the subject races.

**Hazor** was in the north, on high ground near the waters of Merom. It had been the city of Jabin, head of the northern confederacy (Josh. xi. 1). After the great victory over this confederacy, Joshua burnt Hazor (Josh. xi. 13), and the territory was assigned to Naphtali (chap. xix. 36). But it must have been regained by its old possessors, and rebuilt, for it appears again under another Jabin in Judges iv. It was evidently important, as commanding the great line of invasion through Hamath from the north. Hence it was fortified by Solomon, and probably the native inhabitants were dispossessed.

**Megiddo** lay in the great plain of Jezreel or Esdraelon, the battle-field of Northern Palestine, commanding some of the passes from it into the hill country of Manasseh, to which tribe it was assigned after the conquest (Josh. xvii. 11). But it was not subdued by them (Josh. xvii. 12, 13; Judges i. 27, 28), and, with Taanach, appears as a hostile city in the Song of Deborah (Judges v. 19). Now it was fortified, and is named subsequently as an Israelite city (2 Kings ix. 27, xxiii. 29). In later times the Romans seem to have occupied it, and their name for it, *Legio* (now *el-Lejjûr*), superseded the old title.

**Gezer** or **Gazer**, was near Bethlehem, close to the maritime plain. Its king was conquered by Joshua (Josh. x. 33, xii. 12), and the city was allotted to the Levites in the territory of Ephraim (Josh. xxi. 17), but it remained unsubdued (Judges i. 29). From the notice in the next verse, it must have been in rebellion

*Solomon's*        I. KINGS, IX.        *Works.*

the house of the LORD, and his own house, and Millo, and the wall of Jerusalem and Hazor, and Megiddo, and Gezer. <sup>(16)</sup> *For* Pharaoh king of Egypt had gone up and taken Gezer, and burnt it with fire, and slain the Canaanites that dwelt in the city, and given it *for* a present unto his daughter, Solomon's wife. <sup>(17)</sup> And Solomon built Gezer, and Beth-horon the nether, <sup>(18)</sup> and Baalath, and Tadmor in the wilderness, in the land, <sup>(19)</sup> and all the cities of store that Solomon had, and cities for his chariots, and cities for his horsemen, and <sup>1</sup> that which Solomon desired to build in Jerusalem, and in Lebanon, and in all the land of his dominion.

<sup>(20)</sup> *And* all the people *that were* left of the Amorites, Hittites, Perizzites, Hivites and Jebusites, which *were* not of the children of Israel, <sup>(21)</sup> their children that were left after them in the land, whom the children of Israel also were not able utterly to destroy, upon those did Solomon levy a tribute of bondservice unto this day. <sup>(22)</sup> But of the children of Israel did Solomon <sup>a</sup> make no bondmen: but they *were* men of war, and his servants, and his princes,

<sup>1</sup> Heb., *the desire of Solomon which he desired.*

B.C. cir. 1014.

*a* Lev. xx. 39.

---

against Israel, perhaps in the early and more troubled days of Solomon; and was accordingly taken by the Egyptian army (which could easily march up the plain, and attack it therefrom). The passes here were of critical importance, as appears in the Philistine wars (1 Chron. xx. 4; 2 Sam. v. 25), in relation to any advance from the plain.

<sup>(16)</sup> **A present**—that is, of course, a dowry, on her marriage with Solomon.

<sup>(17)</sup> **Beth-horon the nether.**—The name "Beth-horon" ("the house of caves,") was given to two small towns or villages (still called *Beit-ûr*), near Gezer, commanding the steep and rugged pass from the maritime plain, celebrated for three great victories of Israel—the great victory of Joshua (Josh. x.), the victory of Judas Maccabæus (1 Macc. iii. 13—24), and the last victory of the Jews over the Roman army of Cestius Gallus, before the fall of Jerusalem (Josephus, *Wars of the Jews,* ii. 19). The lower Beth-horon stands on a low eminence on the edge of the plain.

<sup>(18)</sup> **Baalath** is said by Josephus to have been in the same neighbourhood; and this agrees with the mention of it in Josh. xix. 44, as lying in the region assigned to Dan, on the edge of the Philistine country. The three, Gezer, Beth-horon, and Baalath, evidently form a group of fortified places commanding the passes from the sea-coast.

**Tadmor in the wilderness, in the land.**—The Hebrew text here has *Tamar* (with, however, *Tadmor* as a marginal reading). From this fact, and from the peculiar expression "in the land," which certainly seems to designate the land of Israel, and from the juxta-position of the name in this passage with the names of places situated in the southern part of Palestine, it has been thought that the place meant is the *Tamar* of Ezek. xlvii. 19, xlviii. 28), or, perhaps, *Hazazon-Tamar,* the old name of En-gedi; and that the marginal reading, and the reading of the old versions, have arisen from a mistaken identification of this place with the Tadmor of 2 Chron. ix. 4. But, on the whole, these considerations are not sufficient to counterbalance the invariable reference of this passage, by all the ancient versions and by the narrative of Josephus, to the celebrated *Tadmor,* the name of which is a local variety of the Hebrew name *Tamar* (or "the palm-tree,") preserved in the later name of Palmyra. If this be meant, it is indeed difficult to suppose that there is not some omission after the words "in the land."

**Tadmor,** or Palmyra, is described by Josephus as "in the desert above Syria, a day's journey from the Euphrates, and six long days' journey from Babylon the Great." Its foundation is described in 2 Chron. ix. 4, as connected with a subjugation of Hamath-zobah, and it may have had a military purpose. But situated on a well-watered oasis, in the midst of the desert, south-west of Tiphsah or Thapsacus on the Euphrates, also occupied by Solomon (see chap. iv. 24), and about 120 miles from Damascus, it would be eminently fitted for trade both with Damascus and with Babylon and the north. Its importance is indicated by its long existence as a great city, and by its splendour (still traceable in its ruins), in Greek and Roman times, down to, at least, the age of Diocletian.

<sup>(19)</sup> **That which Solomon desired to build.**—See, in Eccl. ii. 4—10, the description of the vineyards, and gardens, and orchards, in Jerusalem, with trees of all manner of fruits and pools of water, "whatsoever mine eyes desired;" and in Cant. ii. 10—13, iv. 8, vii. 11—13, the vivid pictures of the pleasure-gardens of Lebanon. The text seems evidently to refer to these, in contradistinction from the cities of commercial and military importance previously mentioned.

<sup>(20)</sup> **A tribute of bond service.** — This was probably not originated, but simply enforced and organised, by Solomon. It dated, in theory at least, from the Conquest. The most notable example of it is the case of the Gibeonites (Josh. ix. 21—27); but there are incidental notices of similar imposition of serfship in Judges i. 28, 30, 33, 35. Many of the dangers of the stormy age of the Judges were due to the uprising of these subject races; as in the revival of the northern confederacy at Hazor under Sisera (Judges iv.), and the usurpation of Abimelech by aid of the Shechemites (Judges ix.). Probably their subordination to Israel varied according to the strength or weakness of each age; but, when the monarchy became organised under David and Solomon, it was fixed definitely and permanently, although, like the serfship of the Middle Ages, it might vary in its severity in different times and in different regions.

<sup>(22)</sup> **No bondmen.**—This exemption, however it may have continued in theory, must virtually have been set aside in the later days of Solomon. (See chap. xii. 4.) They are here described as occupying the position of a dominant race—as warriors, servants about the person of the king, princes, and officers in the army — like the free vassals under a feudal monarchy. But as the absolute power of the king increased, and with it, perhaps, the wealth and arrogance of his favourites and greater officers, the condi-

*Solomon's Officers.*           I. KINGS, IX.           *His Navy.*

and his captains, and rulers of his chariots, and his horsemen. <sup>(23)</sup> These *were* the chief of the officers that *were* over Solomon's work, five hundred and fifty, which bare rule over the people that wrought in the work.

<sup>(24)</sup> But ᵃ Pharaoh's daughter came up out of the city of David unto her house which *Solomon* had built for her: then did he build Millo.

<sup>(25)</sup> And three times in a year did Solomon offer burnt offerings and peace offerings upon the altar which he built unto the LORD, and he burnt incense ¹ upon the altar that *was* before the LORD. So he finished the house.

<sup>(26)</sup> And king Solomon made a navy of ships in Ezion-geber, which *is* beside Eloth, on the ² shore of the Red sea, in the land of Edom. <sup>(27)</sup> And Hiram sent in the navy his servants, shipmen that had knowledge of the sea, with the servants of Solomon. <sup>(28)</sup> And they came to Ophir, and fetched from thence gold,

*a* Chron. 8. 11.

¹ Heb., *upon it.*

² Heb., *lip.*

---

tion of the Israelites at large might be removed from serfship more in name than in reality. Even the subject races might be played off against them, as against the Macedonians in the later years of Alexander the Great, when his royalty passed into something like a true Oriental despotism. Certainly, in later times we find, both from the history and the prophetical books, that there was such a thing as serfship of the poor to the princes. (Jer. xxxiv. 8—11; Neh. v. 11.)

<sup>(23)</sup> **Five hundred and fifty.**—In chap. v. 16 we read of just six times as many officers as those here mentioned over the workers for the Temple. But in that passage there would seem to be reference to the special levy then raised; here the description is apparently of a regularly established system.

<sup>(24)</sup> **Pharaoh's daughter came up . . .**—In 2 Chron. viii. 11 a reason is assigned for this removal: "My wife shall not dwell in the house of David king of Israel, because the places are holy whereunto the ark of the Lord hath come." In this passage the notice of her withdrawal is evidently connected with the building of "the Millo" described in verse 15, which perhaps trenched on her former quarters in the city of David.

<sup>(25)</sup> **And three times in a year.**—This verse seems by the last words to be a kind of note or postscript to the description of the completion and consecration of the Temple. To the record of the great inaugural sacrifice it adds a notice of the solemn renewal of the royal offering, both of victims and of incense, three times in a year—no doubt at the three great feasts, the Passover, the Feast of Weeks, and the Feast of Tabernacles. As has been already said (see Note on chap. viii. 63), there is no reason to suppose that on these occasions, or on any others, Solomon personally usurped the priest's office.

<sup>(26)</sup> **Ezion-geber.**—This place is first noticed in Num. xxxiii. 35 and Deut. ii. 8 as a station in the wanderings of the Israelites, reached not long before their entrance into Canaan. It lies at the head of the Gulf of Akabah, the nearest point of the Red Sea, on the edge of the mountain country of Edom. Its very name ("the giant's backbone") indicates the nature of the country around it, which (it has been noted) could hardly have itself supplied timber for ship-building. But from 2 Chron. viii. 18 it appears that the ships, or the materials from which they were built, were sent from Tyre.

<sup>(27)</sup> **Shipmen that had knowledge of the sea.** —The Tyrians were known far and wide as the great sailors both of the Mediterranean and the seas beyond it, till they were rivalled and superseded by their own colonists in Carthage and by the Greeks. How greatly their seamanship, their commerce, and their civilisation impressed the imagination of Israel, is shown in the magnificent chapters of Ezekiel on the fate of Tyre (Ezek. xxvi.—xxviii.). The Israelites, on the contrary, had but little care for the sea, and little knowledge of seamanship. The coast line of Palestine is but scantily furnished with harbours; and even at the height of their power they were content to use the maritime skill of the Tyrians, without encroaching upon their commerce or attempting to seize their famous ports. This was natural; for their call to be a peculiar and separate people was absolutely incompatible with maritime enterprise and commerce. Even in this attempt at maritime expedition under Tyrian guidance, Solomon's action was, as in other points, exceptional, departing from Israelite tradition; and we hear of no similar enterprise, except in the age of Ahab and Jehoshaphat, when the intermarriage of the royal houses of Israel and Phœnicia renewed the close connection with Tyre (1 Kings xxii. 48; 2 Chron. xx. 35). We observe, accordingly, that the sea is mostly regarded in the Old Testament in its terrible power of wave and storm, restrained from destroying only by the Almighty hand of God; and even the one psalm (Ps. cvii. 23—31), which describes the seafarer's experience, dwells with awe on "God's wonders in the deep." In the description of the glory of "the new heaven and earth" of the hereafter, it is declared with emphasis that "there was no more sea" (Rev. xxi. 1).

<sup>(28)</sup> **Ophir.**—All that can be certainly gathered from the mention of Ophir in the Old Testament is, first, that it was situated to the east of Palestine and approached by the Red Sea (as is clear from this passage, from chap. xxii. 48, and from 2 Chron. viii. 18, ix. 10), and next, that so famous was the gold imported from it, that the "gold of Ophir" became proverbial (Job xxii. 24, xxviii, 16; Ps. xlv. 10; Isa. xiii. 12; 1 Chron. xxix. 4). All else is matter of speculation and tradition. Setting aside merely fanciful conjectures, substantial reasons have been given for fixing it geographically in Africa, Arabia, and India; and of these three positions, evidence strongly preponderates for the second or third. Tradition is in favour of India; the LXX. renders the name as *Soufir*, or *Sofir*, which is the Coptic word for "India;" the Arabic versions actually render it "India;" and Josephus (*Ant.* viii. 6, 4) states unhesitatingly that Ophir was in his day called "The Golden Chersonesus," which is the Malay peninsula. On the other hand, it is urged that "Ophir," in the ethnological list of Gen. x. 29, is placed among the sons of Joktan, clearly indicating an Arabian position; and that the mention of Ophir (here and in chap. x. 11), stands in close connection with the visit of the Queen of Sheba and the gold brought from Arabia. But neither of these considerations is conclusive. Looking to the products described as brought from Ophir, the

four hundred and twenty talents, and brought *it* to king Solomon.

CHAPTER X.—⁽¹⁾ And when the queen of Sheba heard of the fame of Solomon concerning the name of the LORD, she came to prove him with hard questions. ⁽²⁾ And she came to Jerusalem with a very great train, with camels that bare spices, and very much gold, and precious stones: and when she was come to Solomon, she com-muned with him of all that was in her heart. ⁽³⁾ And Solomon told her all her ¹questions: there was not *any* thing hid from the king, which he told her not. ⁽⁴⁾ And when the queen of Sheba had seen all Solomon's wisdom, and the house that he had built, ⁽⁵⁾ and the meat of his table, and the sitting of his servants, and the ²attendance of his ministers, and their apparel, and his ³cupbearers, and his ascent by which he went up unto the house of the LORD;

*a* 2 Chron. 9. 1; Matt. 12. 42; Luke 11. 31.

1 Heb., *words*.

2 Heb., *standing*.

3 Or, *butlers*.

---

"gold and precious stones" would suit either, but India better than Arabia (although, indeed, so far as gold is concerned, Western Africa would have better claim than either); while the "almug," or "algum" wood is certainly the "sandal wood" found almost exclusively on the Malabar coast, and the very word "algum" appears to be a corruption of its Sanscrit name *valguka*. If the other imports mentioned in chap. x. 22 were also from Ophir, this latter argument would be greatly strengthened. (See Note there.) But putting this aside as doubtful, the preponderance of evidence still appears to be in favour of India. The Tyrians, it may be added, are known to have had trading settlements on the Persian Gulf, and to have rivalled in the trade of the East the Egyptians, to whom it would more naturally have belonged. Various places have been named conjecturally as identical with Ophir: as in Arabia, *Zaphar* or *Saphar*, *Doffir*, and *Zafari*; in Africa, *Sofala*; and in India, *Abhira*, at the mouth of the Indus, and a *Soupara* mentioned by ancient Greek geographers, not far from Goa.

### X.

In verses 1—18, the visit of the queen of Sheba is described graphically and with some detail; the remainder of the chapter returns to a series of brief notes on the government and wealth of Solomon.

⁽¹⁾ **The queen of Sheba.**—The name "Sheba" must be distinguished from *Seba*, or *Saba* (which begins with a different Hebrew letter). (*a*) The name Seba denotes a Cushite race (Gen. x. 7), connected, in Isa. xliii. 3, xlv. 14, with Egypt and Cush, and named with Sheba ("the kings of Sheba and Seba") in the Psalm of Solomon (Ps. lxxii. 10). Seba is, indeed, with great probability identified (see Jos. *Ant*. ii. 10, 2) with the Ethiopian city and island of Meroë. It is probably from confusion between Sheba and Saba that Josephus (*Ant.* viii. 6, 5) represents the queen of Sheba as a "queen of Egypt and Ethiopia." (*b*) The name "Sheba" is found in the ethnological lists of Gen. x. 7, among the descendants of Cush of the Hamite race, in Gen. x. 28, among the Semitic Joktanites, and in Gen. xxv. 3, among the Abrahamic children of Keturah. The kingdom of Sheba referred to in this passage must certainly be placed in Arabia Felix, the habitation of the Joktanite race (in which the Keturahites appear to have been merged), for the Cushite Sheba is probably to be found elsewhere on the Persian Gulf. The queen of Sheba would therefore be of Semitic race, not wholly an alien from the stock of Abraham.

**The fame of Solomon concerning the name of the Lord.**—If the reading of the text be correct, the phrase "concerning the name of the Lord" (to which there is nothing to correspond in 2 Chron. ix. 1) must refer to the constant connection of the fame of Solomon—especially in relation to his wisdom, which is here mainly referred to—with the name of Jehovah, as the God to whom, in the erection of the Temple, he devoted both his treasure and himself.

**Hard questions**—or, *riddles*. The Arabian legends preserved in the Koran enumerate a list of questions and puzzles, propounded by the queen and answered by Solomon, too puerile to be worth mention. The "hard questions" (in which Solomon is said by Josephus to have had a contest with Hiram also) must surely have been rather those enigmatic and metaphorical sayings, so familiar to Eastern philosophy, in which the results of speculation, metaphysical or religious, are tersely embodied. The writings representing the age of Solomon—Job, Proverbs, and (whatever be its actual date) Ecclesiastes—are all concerned with these great problems, moral and speculative, which belong to humanity as such, especially in its relation to God. In solving these problems, rather than the merely fantastic ingenuity of what we call riddles, the wisdom of Solomon would be worthily employed.

⁽²⁾ **Spices.**—The "spices" of Arabia were famous in all ages. Sheba is mentioned in Ezek. xxvii. 22 as trafficking with Tyre "in chief of all spices, and precious stones, and gold." The spices of "the incense-bearing sands" of Arabia are constantly dwelt upon both in Greek and Roman literature. Frankincense especially was imported from Arabia into Palestine (see Isa. lx. 6; Jer. vi. 20), although now it comes chiefly from India. Myrrh also was in ancient times drawn chiefly from Arabia. Cassia is a product of Arabia and India. Of all spices, the frankincense for sacrifice and the myrrh for embalming the dead would be most in request.

**Gold, and precious stones.**—These may have been native products of Sheba, or have been brought from the farther East. Gold is not now known to exist in Arabia, nor any precious stones except the onyx and the emerald. But in ancient times it was commonly believed to produce both gold and precious stones largely.

⁽⁴, ⁵⁾ **And when the queen of Sheba had seen.**—There is something curiously inartificial and true to nature in the accumulation of different impressions as made upon the imagination of the queen. First of all comes the primary impression of Solomon's wisdom, known by his answering all her questions, and "seen" in the various ordinances of his court and his government. Then the magnificence of the palace and all the arrangements of its service are referred to in detail, as especially likely to tell on one whose own splendour was probably of a simpler and more barbaric

there was no more spirit in her. (6) And she said to the king, It was a true ¹report that I heard in mine own land of thy ²acts and of thy wisdom. (7) Howbeit I believed not the words, until I came, and mine eyes had seen *it:* and, behold, the half was not told me: ³thy wisdom and prosperity exceedeth the fame which I heard. (8) Happy *are* thy men, happy *are* these thy servants, which stand continually before thee, *and* that hear thy wisdom. (9) Blessed be the LORD thy God, which delighted in thee, to set thee on the throne of Israel: because the LORD loved Israel for ever, therefore made he thee king, to do judgment and justice. (10) And she gave the king an hundred and twenty talents of gold, and of spices very great store, and precious stones:

1 Heb., *word.*

2 Or, *sayings.*

3 Heb., *thou hast added wisdom and goodness to the fame.*

4 Or, *rails.*

5 Heb., *a prop.*

a 2 Chron. 9.12.

6 Heb., *according to the hand of king Solomon.*

there came no more such abundance of spices as these which the queen of Sheba gave to king Solomon.

(11) And the navy also of Hiram, that brought gold from Ophir, brought in from Ophir great plenty of almug trees, and precious stones. (12) And the king made of the almug trees ⁴ ⁵pillars for the house of the LORD, and for the king's house, harps also and psalteries for singers: there came no such ᵃalmug trees, nor were seen unto this day.

(13) And king Solomon gave unto the queen of Sheba all her desire, whatsoever she asked, beside *that* which Solomon gave her ⁶of his royal bounty. So she turned and went to her own country, she and her servants.

(14) Now the weight of gold that came to Solomon in one year was six hundred

---

sort. Lastly, if our translation be correct, the record singles out the ascent or viaduct crossing the valley from the palace to Mount Moriah, and forming the royal entrance into the Temple (see 1 Chron. xxvi. 16; 2 Kings xvi. 18), evidently a unique and remarkable structure. But it must be noticed that the LXX. and Vulgate and other versions render here, "the burnt offerings, which he offered in the house of the Lord," and Josephus has the same interpretation. The magnificent scale of his sacrifices is illustrated in chap. viii. 63, and it is certainly natural that this point should not be left unmentioned in the description of the wonders of his court. This rendering, therefore, which the Hebrew will well bear, has much probability to recommend it.

(6—9) **And she said.**—These words (repeated almost word for word in 2 Chron. ix. 5—8) are clearly from some contemporary document. They breathe at once the spirit of Oriental compliment, and a certain seriousness of tone, as of a mind stirred by unusual wonder and admiration. It is worth notice that they touch but lightly on external magnificence and prosperity, and go on to dwell emphatically on the wisdom of Solomon, as a wisdom enabling him to do judgment and justice, and as a gift from Jehovah, his God. The acknowledgment of Jehovah, of course, does not imply acceptance of the religion of Israel. It expresses the belief that He, as the tutelary God of Israel, is to be held in reverence, proportionate to the extraordinary glory which He has given to His nation. (See chap. v. 7.)

(11, 12) **Gold from Ophir.**—The insertion of this notice is obviously suggested by the mention of the gold and precious stones brought from Sheba. The wood of the "almug" tree, called (apparently more properly) the "algum" tree in 2 Chron. ix. 10, is (see Note on chap. ix. 25) the red sandal-wood found in China and the Indian Archipelago, and still used for precious utensils in India. The "pillars for the house of the Lord" could not have been any of the larger supports of the Temple. They are usually supposed to have been (see margin) "rails" or "balustrades" for stairs. (See 2 Chron. ix. 11.) For the harps and the "psalteries" (which appear to have been like our guitars) the beauty and hardness of the wood would be especially appropriate. These represent the stringed instruments chiefly in use in the service of the Temple. The harp (*kinnor*) is the more ancient, traced (see Gen. iv. 21) even to antediluvian times. The psaltery (*nebel*) is first mentioned (generally with the harp) in the Psalms. Both seem to have been played either with the hand, or with a *plectrum* or quill.

(13) **All her desire.**—The terms here employed indicate a position of inferiority, although well graced and honoured, in the queen of Sheba. Her present is of the nature of tribute. Solomon gives her of "his bounty," both what she asked for (probably by praising it) and what else he would.

(14) **Talents.**—The word properly signifies a "circle," or "globe," and the talent (among the Hebrews and other Orientals, as among the Greeks) denoted properly a certain weight. (*a*) The ordinary talent of gold contained 100 "manehs," or "portions" (the Greek *mna*, or *mina*), and each maneh (as is seen by comparing verse 17 with 2 Chron. ix. 16) contained 100 shekels of gold. According to Josephus (*Ant.* xiv. 7, 1), each maneh contained 2½ Roman pounds, and the talent, therefore, 250 Roman pounds, or 1,262,500 grains; and this agrees fairly with his computation elsewhere (*Ant.* iii. 8, 10), that the gold shekel was equivalent to the *daric*, which is about 129 grains. (See *Dictionary of the Bible*: "WEIGHTS AND MEASURES.") According to this calculation, 666 talents would give a weight of gold now worth £7,780,000. (*b*) On the other hand, the talent of silver is expressly given (by comparison of Exod. xxx. 13—15 and xxxviii. 25—28) at 3,000 "shekels of the sanctuary," and such a shekel appears, by the extant Maccabæan coins, to be about 220 grains. Of such talents, 666 would give a little more than half the former weight; hence, if the talent of gold here be supposed to be in weight the same as the talent of silver, the whole would give a weight of gold now worth about £4,000,000. Considering that this is expressly stated to be independent of certain customs and tributes, the smaller sum seems more probable; in any case, the amount is surprisingly large. But it should be remembered that at certain times and places accumulations of gold have taken place, so great as practically to reduce its value, and lead to its employ-

threescore and six talents of gold, (15) beside *that he had* of the merchantmen, and of the traffick of the spice merchants, and of all the kings of Arabia, and of the ¹governors of the country. (16) And king Solomon made two hundred targets *of* beaten gold: six hundred *shekels* of gold went to one target. (17) And *he made* three hundred shields *of* beaten gold; three pound of gold went to one shield: and the king put them in the ᵃhouse of the forest of Lebanon. (18) Moreover the king made a great throne of ivory, and overlaid it with the best gold. (19) The throne had six steps, and the top of the throne *was* round ²behind: and *there were* ³stays on either side on the place of the seat, and two lions stood beside the stays. (20) And twelve lions stood there on the one side and on the other upon the six steps: there was not ⁴the like made in any kingdom. (21) And all king Solomon's drinking vessels *were of* gold, and all the vessels of the house of the forest of Lebanon *were of* pure gold; ⁵none *were of* silver: it was nothing accounted of in the days of Solomon. (22) For the king had at sea a navy of Tharshish with the navy of Hiram: once in three years came the navy of Tharshish, bringing gold, and silver, ⁶ivory, and apes, and peacocks.

¹ Or, *captains.*

ᵃ ch. 7. 2.

² Heb., *on the hinder part thereof.*

³ Heb., *hands.*

⁴ Heb., *so*

⁵ Or, *there was no silver* in them.

⁶ Or, *elephants' teeth.*

---

ment, not as a currency, but as a precious ornament. Making all allowance for exaggeration, this must have been the case among the Mexicans and Peruvians before the Spanish conquests. It is not improbable that the same may have occurred in the time of Solomon.

(15) **The governors of the country.**—The word "governor" (*pechah*) is supposed to be of foreign origin—possibly cognate to the Sanscrit word *paksha* "friend." It is used constantly of foreign officers, or satraps: as in chap. xx. 24, of the Syrian officers; in 2 Kings xviii. 24 and Isa. xxxvi. 9, of the Assyrians; in Jer. li. 23, of the Babylonians; in Esther viii. 9, Neh. v. 14, 18, xii. 26, &c., of the Persians. Hence it would seem to be used here, not for the officers in the land of Israel described in chap. iv., but for governors (Israelite or foreign) in tributary countries; and it may possibly be a word of later origin than the age of Solomon, introduced by the compiler of the book.

(16, 17) The shields overlaid with gold—the larger called "targets," and the lesser called "shields"—were evidently used for ornamenting the king's palace, and (as we may gather from the notice in 2 Chron. xii. 11, of the brazen shields which superseded them) taken down and borne before the king on solemn occasions, as "when he went to the house of the Lord." We have notices of shields of gold among the Syrians of Zobah (2 Sam. viii. 7; 1 Chron. viii. 7), and of shields hung on the walls of Tyre (Ezek. xxvii. 10, 11). The use of such ornaments argues a plethora of gold, too great to be absorbed either in currency or in personal and architectural decorations.

(17) **Pound**—that is, *maneh*, equal (see 2 Chron. x. 16) to one hundred shekels.

(18) **Ivory.**—This seems to have been brought in by the Tyrians (verse 22), and it may be noted that the only other notice of ivory in the history is in the "ivory house" of Ahab (chap. xxii. 39), who was allied with Tyre. In Ps. xlv. 8 (presumably of the age of Solomon) we find mention of "ivory palaces," or possibly "caskets." The Tyrians are described in Ezek. xxvii. 15 as receiving it through Dedan in Arabia, whither, no doubt, it came from India. But the Egyptians used ivory largely, drawing it from Africa; and there was, in later times, a port on the Red Sea which was a mart for ivory. The Tyrians may, therefore, have imported it both from India and from Africa. The throne of Solomon was probably inlaid with ivory and gold. Traces of such inlaying are found in Assyrian and Egyptian monuments. It is probable that, like his other architectural and decorative work, it was executed by Tyrian workmen, and the detailed description of it shows how greatly it impressed the imagination of Israel. The lion was the emblem of the house of Judah; the number twelve corresponded to the twelve tribes; and the exaltation of the throne—specially remarkable in a country where men sat commonly on the ground or on cushions—was the emblem of majesty. In the *Dictionary of the Bible* ("THRONE") is given a sketch of an Assyrian throne, from a Nineveh bas-relief, which has horses in the position, supporting "the stays," or arms of the throne, here ascribed to the lions.

(21) **None were of silver . . .**—See 2 Chron. ix. 27, "The king made silver in Jerusalem as stones." The importation of silver (see verse 22) was by the navy of Tarshish; and the mention of the plentifulness of silver seems the reason for noticing the existence of this navy.

(22) **A navy of Tharshish.**—There seems little doubt that the Tarshish of Scripture is properly Tartessus in Spain, which name, indeed, is drawn from an Aramaic form of Tarshish. For (*a*) Tarshish is first noted in Gen. x. 4 as among the descendants of Javan, the son of Japhet, which probably points to a European position; (*b*) in some other places (Isa. xxiii. 1, 6, 10, 14; Ezek. xxvii. 12, 13) as here, and in chap. xxiii. 48, it is closely connected with Tyre, of which Tartessus is expressly said by Arrian to have been a colony: (*c*) from Jonah i. 3, iv. 2, we gather that it was on the Mediterranean Sea; (*d*) the silver, which was evidently the chief import by this navy of Tarshish, was in ancient times found in large quantities in Spain, as also "the iron, lead, and tin," mentioned with the silver in Ezek. xxvii. 12. But the phrase "ships of Tarshish" appears to have become a technical phrase for ships of large size (see Isa. ii. 17; Jer. x. 9; Ps. xlviii. 8); hence a "navy of Tarshish" would not necessarily mean a navy going to Tarshish.

Now, the fleet of Solomon here named is not in the text identified with the navy of Ophir, starting from Ezion-geber. Its imports (except gold, which is not distinctive) are not the same, and the separate mention of it seems rather to argue its distinctness. "The

(23) So king Solomon exceeded all the kings of the earth for riches and for wisdom. (24) And all the earth ¹sought to Solomon, to hear his wisdom, which God had put in his heart. (25) And they brought every man his present, vessels of silver, and vessels of gold, and garments, and armour, and spices, horses, and mules, a rate year by year.

(26) ᵃAnd Solomon gathered together chariots and horsemen: and he had a thousand and four hundred chariots, and twelve thousand horsemen, whom he bestowed in the cities for chariots, and with the king at Jerusalem. (27) And the king ²made silver *to be* in Jerusalem as stones, and cedars made he *to be* as the sycamore trees that *are* in the vale, for abundance.

(28) ᵇ³And Solomon had horses brought out of Egypt, and linen yarn: the king's merchants received the linen yarn at a

1 Heb., *sought the face of*.
a 2 Chron. 1. 14.
2 Heb., *gave*.
b 2 Chron. 1. 16, & 9. 28.
3 Heb., *And the going forth of the horses which was Solomon's*.

sea," moreover, unless otherwise determined by the context, would most likely mean the Great, or Mediterranean Sea; and in 2 Chron. ix. 21 (as also afterwards, in 2 Chron. xx. 36) it is expressly said that the fleet "went to Tarshish." But the difficulty of this view lies in this—that the imports of the fleet, except the silver (which, indeed, is chiefly dwelt upon), point to an Eastern, and probably an Indian origin. Not only do the "peacocks" expressly indicate India, which may be called their native country; but of the names used, *koph*, for "ape," is not a Hebrew word, but closely resembles the Sanscrit *kapi*; and *tukki*, for "peacock," is similarly a foreign word, closely resembling the Tamil *tôka*. (If the ordinary reading, *shen habbim*, for "ivory," stands, this, which is an unusual word for ivory (generally simply *shen*, "a tooth"), bears resemblance again in its second member to *ibha*, the Sanscrit name for "elephant." But it is generally thought that the correction, *shen habnim*, "ivory [and] ebony," should be accepted, especially as we find those two words used together in Ezek. xxviii. 15.) The only solution of this serious difficulty seems to be the supposition of a circumnavigation of Africa by fleets from Tyre to Ezion-geber, touching in Africa and India. This view also accounts for the emphatic mention of the "three years'" voyage, which could not be necessary for going only to Tartessus and its neighbourhood. There is, indeed, something startling in the idea of so daring an enterprise in this early age. But there is a well-known passage in Herodotus (Book iv. 42) which records exactly such a voyage in the days of Pharaoh-Necho, not apparently as a new thing—to say nothing of the celebrated record of the *Periplus* of Hanno; and it seems clear that the Tyrian seamanship and maritime enterprise were at their height in the days of Solomon.

(23—25) **All the kings.**—These verses indicate the character of the empire of Solomon, as a loosely-compacted group of tributary states round the dominant kingdom of Israel, kept to their allegiance mainly by the ascendency of his personal wisdom and ability, partly by the ties of commercial intercourse and the attractions of his wealth and splendour, and to some degree (though in his case to a less extent than usual) by an imposing military force. It rose rapidly in the comparative abeyance of the great neighbouring empires of Egypt and Assyria, and fell as rapidly on the death of Solomon and the disruption of the kingdom. In the grand description of it in Ps. lxxii., we observe that while its wealth and prosperity are painted in bright colours, the chief stress is laid on its moral greatness, as a kingdom of righteousness and peace: "All kings shall fall down before him; all nations shall serve him. For he shall deliver the needy when he crieth . . . He shall judge thy people with righteousness, and thy poor with judgment." Here, with the same general idea, but with a characteristic difference of expression, the chief emphasis is laid on the wisdom of Solomon, acknowledged as the gift of God (see Note on chap. iv. 29), and being a moral and religious at least as much as an intellectual power. In this higher character it was the type of the kingdom of the true Son of David. In this, rather than in wealth and power, lay its true glory; and the falling away from this in the later days of Solomon brought at once decay and ruin.

(26) **Gathered together chariots.**—See above, chap. iv. 36. This gathering of chariots—the sign of military conquest and extended empire—is evidently noticed here in connection with the growth of commerce and wealth, as one of the powers which held Solomon's kingdom together. Josephus (*Ant.* viii. 7, 4), in mentioning them, gives a vivid description of the use of these chariots and horsemen for progresses of royal magnificence and pleasure. But their chief use was, no doubt, military. The "chariot cities" would be the fortified posts, in the various parts of Solomon's own dominions and in the tributary countries.

(27) **Made silver . . . as stones.**—This influx of wealth is specially noted as enriching Jerusalem, probably without preventing the imposition of heavy burdens on the provinces. Hence the division of interest and allegiance manifested at the accession of Rehoboam. In the earlier years of the reign its prosperity is described as extending to all "Judah and Israel" (chap. iv. 20). But the wealth gathered by tribute, and by a commerce entirely in the hands of the king, would enrich only the Court and the capital; and much Oriental history, both ancient and modern, shows that such enrichment might leave the general population impoverished and oppressed.

(28) **Linen yarn.**—The introduction of this seems to be an error. If the reading of the Hebrew text is to stand, the sense appears to be, "And Solomon's horses were brought from Egypt; a troop of the king's merchants obtained a troop (of horses) at a fixed price." The horses were brought up (that is) in caravans from the plains of Egypt, where they abounded (see Gen. xlvii. 17; Exod. ix. 3, xiv. 9; Deut. xvii. 17; Isa. xxxi. 1, xxxvi. 9), although from their not being represented on the monuments before the eighteenth dynasty it is thought they were introduced from abroad, perhaps by the *Hyksos*, or shepherd kings. But the LXX. has a remarkable various reading "and from Tekoa" (from which the Vulg. *et de Coa*, probably comes), according to which the passage runs very simply: "And Solomon's horses were brought from Egypt; and from Tekoa the king's merchants," &c. Tekoa lay on the hills to the east of Hebron, not far from Bethlehem, and might well be an emporium for caravans from

51

price. <sup>(29)</sup> And a chariot came up and went out of Egypt for six hundred *shekels* of silver, and an horse for an hundred and fifty: and so for all the kings of the Hittites, and for the kings of Syria, did they bring *them* out ¹ by their means.

CHAPTER XI.—<sup>(1)</sup> But king Solomon loved *ª* many strange women, ² together with the daughter of Pharaoh, women of the Moabites, Ammonites, Edomites, Zidonians, *and* Hittites; <sup>(2)</sup> of

¹ Heb., *by their hand.*

*ª* Deut. 17. 17; Ecclus. 47. 19.

² Or, *besides.*

*b* Exod. 34. 16.

the nations *concerning* which the LORD said unto the children of Israel, *ᵇ* Ye shall not go in to them, neither shall they come in unto you: *for* surely they will turn away your heart after their gods: Solomon clave unto these in love. <sup>(3)</sup> And he had seven hundred wives, princesses, and three hundred concubines: and his wives turned away his heart. <sup>(4)</sup> For it came to pass, when Solomon was old, *that* his wives turned away his heart after other gods: and

---

Egypt. The parallel passages of 2 Chron. i. 16, 17, ix. 28, give us no help, for the former is exactly the same as this, and the latter runs thus: "And they brought unto Solomon horses out of Egypt and out of all lands."

**<sup>(29)</sup> A chariot.**—This is the chariot and its team of two or three horses; the "horse" is the charger. The price (though so far considerable as to indicate a large expenditure on the whole) shows that the supply was large, and the commerce regular.

**The kings of the Hittites, and the kings of Syria**—evidently allies or tributaries of Solomon, who were allowed, or compelled, to purchase their horses and chariots through his merchants. Of all the earlier inhabitants of Palestine the Hittites alone are mentioned as having existed in power after the conquest (as here and in 2 Kings vii. 6); and this statement is curiously confirmed by both Egyptian and Assyrian inscriptions, describing a powerful confederacy of Hittites in the valley of the Orontes in Syria, not far from Phœnicia, with whom both empires waged war. The possession of horses and chariots by the northern confederacy round Hazor is especially noted in the history of the Conquest (Josh. xi. 4—6).

XI.

The historical order in this chapter is curiously broken. (*a*) In verses 1—13 we have a notice of the polygamy and idolatry of Solomon, and the prediction of the transference of the kingdom to his servant; (*b*) This reference to Jeroboam suggests a brief record of the rising up of "adversaries" to Solomon, Hadad and Rezon, as well as Jeroboam himself, which belongs to the earlier times of Solomon's reign (verses 14—40). (*c*) After this digression there is the formal notice of Solomon's death and burial (verses 41—43).

**(1—8)** The defection of Solomon is distinctly traced to his polygamy, contracting numerous marriages with "strange women." Polygamy is also attributed to David (see 2 Sam. iii. 2—5; xv. 16), marking perhaps the characteristic temperament of voluptuousness, which seduced him into his great sin; but it was carried out by Solomon on a scale corresponding to the magnificence of his kingdom, and probably had in his case the political object of alliance with neighbouring or tributary kings. We find it inherited by Rehoboam (2 Chron. xi. 18—21), and it probably became in different degrees the practice of succeeding kings. Hitherto, while polygamy, as everywhere in the East, had to some degree existed in Israel from patriarchal times, yet it must have been checked by the marriage regulations of the Law. Nor had there yet been the royal magnificence and wealth, under which alone it attains to full development. We have some traces of it in the households of some of the Judges: Gideon (Judg. viii. 30), Jair (Judg. x. 4), Ibzan and Abdon (Judg. xii. 9, 14). Now, however, it became, in spite of the prohibition of the Law (Deut. xvii. 17), a recognised element of royal self-indulgence—such as is described in Eccl. ii. 7, 8, and is perhaps traceable even through the beauty of the Song of Solomon. In itself, even without any incidental consequences, it must necessarily be a demoralising power, as sinning against the primeval ordinance of God, and robbing natural relations of their true purity and sacredness. But in actual fact it sinned still more by involving forbidden marriages with idolatrous races, with the often-predicted effect of declension into idolatry.

**<sup>(1)</sup> Moabites, Ammonites, Edomites, Zidonians, Hittites.**—The first three of these races were kindred to Israel and of the stock of Abraham, and were now among the subjects of Solomon; the last two were of the old Canaanitish stock, and were now inferior allies. To the last alone properly attached the prohibition of the Law (Exod. xxxiv. 12—16; Deut. vii. 3, 4); but the reason on which that prohibition was grounded was now equally applicable to the others; for they also had fallen into the worship of false gods. Hence the extension of it to them, recognised by the Jews after the captivity (Ezra ix. 2, 11, 12; Neh. xiii. 23—29).

It is to be noted that the marriage with the daughter of Pharaoh is apparently distinguished from these connections, which are so greatly censured, and that there is no mention of the introduction of any Egyptian idolatry.

**<sup>(3)</sup> Seven hundred wives and three hundred concubines.**—The harem of an Eastern king is simply an adjunct of his magnificence, and the relation of the wives to him little more than nominal. (Comp. Esth. ii. 14.) Nor does the statement here made necessarily imply that at any one time the whole number existed. Still, the numbers here given, though found also in the LXX. and in Josephus, are not only extraordinarily large, but excessive in comparison with the "threescore queens and fourscore concubines" of Cant. vi. 8, and disproportionate in the relative number of the superior and inferior wives. It is possible that, in relation to the former, at any rate, the text may be corrupt, though the corruption must be of ancient date.

**<sup>(4)</sup> When Solomon was old.**—It is clearly implied that the evil influence belonged to the time of senile feebleness, possibly the premature result of a life of indulgence; for he could not have been very old, if he was "but a child" at the time of his accession. But, as it is not at all likely that Solomon forsook the worship of God (see verses 5, 6, and ix. 25), it would seem

his heart was not perfect with the LORD his God, as *was* the heart of David his father. <sup>(5)</sup> For Solomon went after *Ashtoreth the goddess of the Zidonians, and after Milcom the abomination of the Ammonites. <sup>(6)</sup> And Solomon did

B.C. cir. 984.

*a* Judges 2. 13.

1 Heb., *fulfilled not after.*

evil in the sight of the LORD, and <sup>1</sup> went not fully after the LORD, as *did* David his father. <sup>(7)</sup> Then did Solomon build an high place for Chemosh, the abomination of Moab, in the hill that *is* before Jerusalem, and for Molech, the abomina-

---

that his idolatry was rather the inclination to an eclectic adoption of various forms of faith and worship, as simply various phases of reverence to the One Supreme Power, each having its own peculiar significance and beauty. Such a spirit, holding itself superior to the old laws and principles of the faith of Israel, was the natural fruit of an overweening confidence in his own wisdom—the philosophic spirit, "holding no creed, but contemplating" and condescending to "all." Whatever it may have owed to the baser female influence, so well known in the countries where woman is held a mere toy, it seems likely to have been, still more naturally, the demoralising effect of an absolutely despotic power, of a world-wide fame for wisdom, and of an over-luxurious magnificence. It may have even had a kind of harmony with the weary and hopeless conviction that "all things were vanity:" for there is something of kinship between the belief that all worships are true, and that all worships are false. It may also have been thought good policy to conciliate the subject races, by doing honour to their religions, much as the Roman Empire delighted to do, when faith in its own religion had died out. How absolutely incompatible such a spirit is with the faith in the One only God of Israel, and in itself even more monstrous than avowed devotion to false gods, is indignantly declared by Ezekiel (Ezek. xiv. 3, 4, xx. 39). How utter the practical incongruity, is obvious on the slightest consideration of the contrast between the impure and bloody worship of the false gods, and the lofty spiritual worship of the God of Israel.

<sup>(5)</sup> **Ashtoreth** (or, *Astarte*).—The goddess of the Zidonians, and possibly the Hittites, corresponding to Baal, the great Tyrian god, and representing the receptive and productive, as Baal the active and originative, power in Nature. As usual in all phases of Nature-worship, Ashtoreth is variously represented, sometimes by the moon, sometimes by the planet Venus (like the Assyrian *Ishtar*, which seems a form of the same name) —in either case regarded as "the queen of heaven." (See Jer. xliv. 17, 25). There seems, indeed, some reason to believe that the name itself is derived from a root which is found both in Syriac and Persian, and which became *aster* in the Greek and *astrum* in Latin, and has thence passed into modern European languages, signifying a "star," or luminary of heaven. With this agrees the ancient name, *Ashterôth-Karnaim* (or, "the horned Ashteroth") of a city in Bashan (Gen. xiv. 5; Deut. i. 4; Josh. xiii. 12). This place is the first in which the name Ashtoreth is used in the singular number, and expressly limited to the "goddess of the Zidonians." In the earlier history we hear not unfrequently of the worship of the "Ashtaroth," that is, of the "Ashtoreths," found with the like plural Baalim, as prevalent in Canaan, and adopted by Israel in evil times (see Judges ii. 13, x. 6; 1 Sam. vii. 3, xii. 10, xxxi. 10); and the worship of the *Asherah* (rendered "groves" in the Authorised version), may perhaps refer to emblems of Astarte. In these cases, however, it seems not unlikely that the phrase, "Baalim and Ashtaroth," may be used generally of the gods and goddesses of various kinds of idolatry. The worship of the Tyrian Ashtoreth, as might be supposed from the idea which she was supposed to represent, was one of chartered license and impurity.

**Milcom, the abomination of the Ammonites.** —The name *Milcom* (like the *Malcham* of Jer. xlix. 1, 3) is probably only a variety of the well-known *Molech*, which is actually used for it in verse 7. The name "Molech" (though here connected expressly with the Ammonite idolatry) is a general title, signifying only "king" (as Baal signifies "lord"), and might be applied to the supreme god of any idolatrous system. Thus the worship of "Molech," with its horrible sacrifice of children "passing through the fire," is forbidden in Lev. xviii. 21, xx. 2, evidently as prevailing among the Canaanite races (comp. Ps. cvi. 37, 38). Again, we know historically that similar sacrifice of children, by the same horrible rite, was practised by the Carthaginians in times of great national calamity—the god being in that case identified with Saturn, the star of malign influence. By comparison of Jer. vii. 31, xix. 5, 6, it is very evident that this human sacrifice to Molech is also called "a burnt-offering to Baal;" and if Molech was the "fire-god," and Baal the "sun-god," the two deities might easily be regarded as cognate, if not identical. It is notable that, in this place, while Ashtoreth is mentioned, there is no reference to any worship of the Phœnician Baal as such; possibly the Ammonite Molech-worship may have occupied its place. In any case, as the worship of Ashtoreth was stained with impurity, so the Molech-worship was marked by the other foul pollution of the sacrifice of human blood.

**Chemosh, the abomination of the Moabites.** —The name *Chemosh* probably means "the Conqueror," or "Subjugator," and indicates a god of battles. He is again and again described as the god of the Moabites who are called "the people of Chemosh" (see Num. xxi. 29; Jer. xlviii. 7, 13, 46); and the Moabite Stone speaks of the slain in war as an offering to Chemosh, and even refers to a deity, "Ashtar-Chemosh," which looks like a conjunction of Chemosh, like Baal, with Ashtoreth. In Judg. xi. 24, Jephthah refers to Chemosh as the god of the Ammonite king, an expression which may indicate a temporary supremacy of Moab over Ammon at that time, through which the name "Chemosh" superseded the name "Milcom" as descriptive of the Supreme Power. In the history, moreover, of the Moabite war against Jehoram (2 Kings iii. 26, 27) it seems that to Chemosh, as to Molech, human sacrifice was offered.

Probably, in actual practice the various worships of the Tyrians and Canaanites, the Ammonites and the Moabites might run into each other. Unlike the awful and exclusive reverence to the Lord Jehovah, the devotion of polytheistic systems readily welcomes strange gods into its Pantheon. Polytheism is also apt to pass into what has been called "Henotheism," in which, of many gods each is for the moment worshipped, as if he stood alone, and concentrated in himself the whole attributes of deity. The generality and

*God threatens him.*        I. KINGS, XI.        *Hadad the Edomite.*

tion of the children of Ammon. ⁽⁸⁾ And likewise did he for all his strange wives, which burnt incense and sacrificed unto their gods.

⁽⁹⁾ And the LORD was angry with Solomon, because his heart was turned from the LORD God of Israel, *ᵃ* which had appeared unto him twice, ⁽¹⁰⁾ and *ᵇ* had commanded him concerning this thing, that he should not go after other gods: but he kept not that which the LORD commanded. ⁽¹¹⁾ Wherefore the LORD said unto Solomon, Forasmuch as this ¹is done of thee, and thou hast not kept my covenant and my statutes, which I have commanded thee, *ᶜ*I will surely rend the kingdom from thee, and will give it to thy servant. ⁽¹²⁾ Notwithstanding in thy days I will not do it for David thy father's sake: *but* I will rend it out of the hand of thy son. ⁽¹³⁾ Howbeit I will not rend away all the kingdom; *but* will give one tribe to thy son for David my servant's sake, and for Jerusalem's sake which I have chosen.

⁽¹⁴⁾ And the LORD stirred up an adversary unto Solomon, Hadad the Edomite: he *was* of the king's seed in Edom. ⁽¹⁵⁾ *ᵈ*For it came to pass, when David was in Edom, and Joab the captain of the host was gone up to bury the slain, after he had smitten every male in Edom; ⁽¹⁶⁾ (for six months did Joab remain there with all Israel, until he had cut off every male in Edom:) ⁽¹⁷⁾ that Hadad fled, he and certain Edomites of his father's servants with him, to go into Egypt; Hadad *being* yet a little

*ᵃ* ch. 3. 5, & 9. 2.
*ᵇ* ch. 6. 12.
¹ Heb., *is with thee.*
*ᶜ* ch. 12. 15.
*ᵈ* 2 Sam. 8. 14.

---

similarity of meaning in the names, Baal ("lord"), Molech ("king"), and Chemosh ("conqueror"), seem to point in this direction. Still, these worships are described as taking, in Jerusalem, distinct forms and habitations, which continued till the days of Josiah (2 Kings xxiii. 13), no doubt disused and condemned in days of religious faithfulness, such as those of Jehoshaphat and Hezekiah, but revived, and associated with newer idolatries, in days of apostasy.

⁽⁷⁾ **On the hill that is before Jerusalem.**—evidently on the Mount of Olives (part of which still traditionally bears the name of the "Mount of Offence"), facing and rivalling the Temple on Mount Moriah. Tophet, the place of actual sacrifice to Molech, was "in the valley of the son of Hinnom" (2 Kings xxiii. 10; Jer. vii. 31), which (see Jer. xix. 2) was east or south-east of the city, and would lie not far from the foot of the mountain.

⁽⁸⁾ **Which had appeared unto him twice.**—See chap. iii. 5; ix. 2.) Stress is laid on these direct visions of the Lord to Solomon, as contrasted with the usual indirect revelation through the prophets, and so carrying with them peculiar privilege and responsibility.

⁽¹²,¹³⁾ **For David my servant's sake**—that is, evidently, in order to fulfil the promise to David. By the postponement of the chastisement, the blessing promised to his son personally would be still preserved; by the retaining of the kingdom, though shorn of its splendour, and limited to Judah, the larger and more important promise, the continuance of the family of David till the coming of the Messiah, would be fulfilled. The "one tribe" is, of course, Judah, with which Benjamin was indissolubly united by the very position of the capital on its frontier. This is curiously indicated in verses 31, 32, where "ten tribes" are given to Jeroboam, and the remainder out of the twelve is still called "one tribe."

⁽¹⁴⁻²⁵⁾ The events recorded in this section belong, at least in part, to the early years of the reign of Solomon, when the deaths of the warlike David and Joab, and the accession of a mere youth of avowedly peaceful character, may have naturally encouraged insurrection against the dominion of Israel. They are, no doubt, referred to in this place in connection with the prophecy just recorded, and the notice of Jeroboam's earlier career which it suggests. But it is implied in the case of Hadad, as it is expressly declared in the case of Rezon, that their resistance continued through all Solomon's reign. They were not, therefore, crushed, even in the days of his greatness, although then probably reduced to practical insignificance; they seem to have become formidable again during his declining years.

⁽¹⁴⁾ **Hadad the Edomite.**—The name (or rather, title) *Hadad* (with the kindred names *Hadar*, *Hadadezer* or *Hadarezer*, and *Benhadad*) is most frequently found as a designation of the kings of Syria. Here, however, as also in Gen. xxxvi. 35, 1 Chron. i. 46, 50, it is given to members of the royal family of Edom. According to ancient authorities, it is a Syriac title of the sun—in this respect like the more celebrated title *Pharaoh*—assumed by the king, either as indicating descent from the sun-god, or simply as an appellation of splendour and majesty. The Hadad here mentioned seems to have been the last scion of the royal house, escaping alone, as a child, from the slaughter of his kindred and people.

⁽¹⁵⁾ The war here described is briefly noted, with some differences of detail, in 2 Sam. viii. 12—14, 1 Chron. xviii. 11—13, and Ps. lx. (title and verse 8). It is there closely connected with the great struggle with the Syrians, and the victory is ascribed in one record to Joab, in the other to Abishai. Here David himself is described as taking part in the war—perhaps completing the conquest, as in the war with Ammon, after it had been successfully begun by Joab (2 Sam. xii. 26—31). (Instead of "David was in Edom," the LXX. and other versions read "David destroyed Edom," by a slight variation of the Hebrew text.) The war was evidently one of ruthless extermination of "every male," except those who fled the country, or found refuge in its rocky fastnesses, and was carried on by systematic ravage under the command of Joab. How it was provoked we do not know; for we have no previous notice of Edom since the time of the Exodus, except a reference to war against it in the days of Saul (1 Sam. xiv. 47).

Solomon's        I. KINGS, XI.        Adversaries.

child. <sup>(18)</sup> And they arose out of Midian, and came to Paran: and they took men with them out of Paran, and they came to Egypt, unto Pharaoh king of Egypt; which gave him an house, and appointed him victuals, and gave him land. <sup>(19)</sup> And Hadad found great favour in the sight of Pharaoh, so that he gave him to wife the sister of his own wife, the sister of Tahpenes the queen. <sup>(20)</sup> And the sister of Tahpenes bare him Genubath his son, whom Tahpenes weaned in Pharaoh's house: and Genubath was in Pharaoh's household among the sons of Pharaoh. <sup>(21)</sup> And when Hadad heard in Egypt that David slept with his fathers, and that Joab the captain of the host was dead, Hadad said to Pharaoh, [1] Let me depart, that I may go to mine own country. <sup>(22)</sup> Then Pharaoh said unto him, But what hast thou lacked with me, that, behold, thou seekest to go to thine own country? And he answered, [5] Nothing: howbeit let me go in any wise.

<sup>(23)</sup> And God stirred him up *another* adversary, Rezon the son of Eliadah, which fled from his lord Hadadezer king of Zobah: <sup>(24)</sup> and he gathered men unto him, and became captain over a band, <sup>a</sup> when David slew them *of Zobah*: and they went to Damascus, and dwelt

*Heb., send me away.*

*2 Heb., Not.*

*a 2 Sam. 8. 3, & 10. 18.*

---

<sup>(18)</sup> **They arose out of Midian.**—The expression is a curious one; for we should have expected the starting-point of the flight to have been described in Edom itself. If the reading of the text is correct, the reference must be either to some branch of the Midianitish tribes settled between Edom and the desert of Paran, or to a city Midian, not far from the Gulf of Elath, of which some ancient authorities speak, and to which the LXX. expressly refers here.

**Paran** (see Gen. xxi. 21; Num. x. 12, xii. 16, xiii. 3, 26; 1 Sam. xxv. 1) is part of the Sinaitic region, adjacent to the wilderness of Zin, and north of the range now called the *El-Tîh* mountains. It lies to the west of the Edomite territory, and was then evidently inhabited by an independent race, from which the fugitive companions of Hadad enlisted support.

**Pharaoh king of Egypt.**—The dynasty then reigning in Lower Egypt is that called the twenty-first, or Tanite, dynasty. Chronological considerations, and perhaps internal probabilities, suggest that this Pharaoh was not the same as the king who became father-in-law to Solomon. But the same policy of alliance with the occupants of Palestine and the neighbourhood is equally exemplified in both cases, though by different methods; and accords well with the apparent decadence of Egyptian power at this time, of which very little record is preserved in the monuments. Jealousy of the growing power of Israel under David and Solomon might prompt this favourable reception of Hadad, as afterwards of Jeroboam. The marriage of Solomon with the daughter of Pharaoh, and the active co-operation of Pharaoh against Gezer (chap. ix. 16), indicate an intervening variation of policy, without, however, any change in the general design of securing Egypt by alliances on the north-east. In this case the intermarriage of Hadad with the royal house, and the inclusion of his son Genubath among the children of Pharaoh, argue an unusual distinction, which could only have been due to a high estimate of the importance of influence over the strong country of Edom, and of the future chances of Hadad's recovery of the throne.

<sup>(19)</sup> **Tahpenes the queen**—a name unknown, either in history or in the Egyptian monuments.

<sup>(20)</sup> **Genubath** is similarly unknown. The weaning in the house of Pharaoh, no doubt with the customary festival (comp. Gen. xx. 18), indicated the admittance of the child into the royal family of Egypt.

<sup>(21, 22)</sup> **When Hadad heard.**—If (as the text seems to suggest) this took place on the news of the death of David and of Joab, the scourge of Edom, it belongs, of course, to the early part of the reign of Solomon, before his power was established. The courteous evasion by the Pharaoh of that time of Hadad's request for permission to return, may probably indicate the beginning of the change of attitude towards the powerful monarchy of Israel, which took effect in the subsequent close alliance of the kingdoms. As the text stands, the record here stops abruptly, and then recurs to Hadad by a curious allusion in verse 25. It can hardly be doubted that there is some omission or dislocation of the text. The LXX. (in the Vatican MS.) introduces after the words "Hadad the Edomite" in verse 14, the words "and Rezon the son of Eliadah . . . all the days of Solomon" from verses 23—25; and then, resuming the story of Hadad, adds, after the record of his request to Pharaoh, "and Hadad returned to his land. This is the mischief which Hadad did, and he abhorred Israel, and reigned over *Edom*." Josephus, on the other hand, says that at the time of the original request, Pharaoh refused permission; but that in the declining years of Solomon it was granted, and that Hadad, finding it impossible to excite rebellion in Edom, which was strongly garrisoned, joined Rezon in Syria, and with him established an independent power, and did mischief to Israel. (*Ant.* viii. 6, 6.) This account is itself probable enough; it accounts, moreover, for the close connection in the history (especially in the LXX. reading) between Hadad and Rezon, and for the insertion of the whole matter in this place; and accords also with the fact that, while Syria seems at once to become independent after the death of Solomon, we hear of no revolt of Edom till the time of Jehoshaphat (2 Chron. xx.).

<sup>(23)</sup> **Rezon the son of Eliadah.**—The name *Rezon*, which is not unlike the "Rezin" of 2 Kings xvi., appears to signify "prince," and might naturally mark the founder of a new power. In 1 Kings xv. 18 we read of a Hezion, king of Damascus, who would belong to this generation, and may be identical with Rezon. The tradition quoted by Josephus (*Ant.* vii. 5, 2) from Nicolaus of Damascus, that for ten generations from the days of David, all the kings of Syria bore the name of Hadad, probably means only that the title Hadad was the official title of the monarchy.

<sup>(24)</sup> **When David slew them of Zobah.**—The account of this war is found in 2 Sam. viii. 1—13. The kingdom of Zobah was evidently a powerful state at that time, at war with the Syrian kingdom of Hamath,

therein, and reigned in Damascus. <sup>(25)</sup> And he was an adversary to Israel all the days of Solomon, beside the mischief that Hadad *did*: and he abhorred Israel, and reigned over Syria.

<sup>(26)</sup> And <sup>a</sup>Jeroboam the son of Nebat, an Ephrathite of Zereda, Solomon's servant, whose mother's name *was* Zeruah, a widow woman, even he lifted up *his* hand against the king. <sup>(27)</sup> And this *was* the cause that he lifted up *his* hand against the king: Solomon built Millo, *and* <sup>1</sup>repaired the breaches of the city of David his father. <sup>(28)</sup> And the man Jeroboam *was* a mighty man of valour: and Solomon seeing the young man that he <sup>2</sup>was industrious, he made him ruler over all the <sup>3</sup>charge of the house of Joseph. <sup>(29)</sup> And it came to pass at that time when Jeroboam went out of Jerusalem, that the prophet Ahijah the Shilonite found him in the way; and he had clad himself with a new garment; and they two *were* alone in the field: <sup>(30)</sup> and Ahijah caught the new garment that *was* on him, and rent it *in* twelve pieces: <sup>(31)</sup> and he said to Jeroboam, Take thee ten pieces: for

*a* 2 Chron. 13. 6.

1 Heb., *closed*.

2 Heb., *did work*.

3 Heb., *burden*.

---

but holding supremacy over the Syrians of Damascus, and the "Syrians beyond the river" Euphrates; and (as the record shows) accumulating vast treasures of gold, silver, and brass. The establishment of Rezon (and Hadad?) at Damascus must have taken place later; for at the time we find that David "put governors in Damascus," and reduced its inhabitants to a tributary condition. Possibly there may have been some rising early in the reign of Solomon; for in 2 Chron. viii. 3, we find that Solomon had to "go up against Hamath-zobah," with which expedition the foundation of Tadmor seems to be connected. But it is probable that the establishment of an independent power in Damascus dated only from the later days of Solomon.

(25) **Beside the mischief that Hadad did.**—The expression, as it stands, is curiously abrupt in its recurrence to Hadad. But the text is doubtful. (See Note on verses 21, 22.) If the general reading of the LXX. be taken, the substitution of Edom for Syria (*Aram*) (it involves but slight change in the Hebrew) must be accepted; if the explanation of Josephus is correct, then the reading of the text must stand.

(26) **Jeroboam the son of Nebat.**—The life and character of Jeroboam are given in considerable detail in the history; and it is also remarkable that in some of the MSS. of the LXX. we find inserted after chap. xii. 24 an independent account of his early history (see Note at the end of the chapter), generally of inferior authority, and having several suspicious features, but perhaps preserving some genuine details. As the great rebel against the House of David, the leader of the revolution which divided Israel and destroyed its greatness, the introducer of the idolatry of the temples of Dan and Bethel, and the corrupter of the worship of Jehovah in deference to an astute worldly policy, he stands out in a vividness of portraiture unapproached, till we come to the history of Ahab at the close of the book.

**An Ephrathite of Zereda.**—The word "Ephrathite," which mostly means an inhabitant of Ephrata or Bethlehem, is here (as in 1 Sam. i. 1) simply another form of the name Ephraimite. Zereda is mostly supposed to be *Zarthan* (see vii. 46 and 2 Chron. iv. 17), a town of Ephraim in the Jordan valley. The Vatican MS. of the LXX., by a slight change in the Hebrew, reads *Sarira*, which is probably a rendering of *Zererah* or *Zererath* (Judges vii. 22), and, in the additional record noticed above, makes it a strong fortified place in Mount Ephraim.

**The son of a widow woman.**—This phrase, added to the phrase "Solomon's servant," is evidently designed to mark the utterly dependent condition from which Solomon's favour raised the future rebel.

(27) **Solomon built Millo.**—See chap. ix. 15, 24. This was apparently after he had built the Temple and the palace, some twenty years after his accession, when the delight in magnificence of building apparently grew upon him, and with it the burdens of the people.

(28) **A mighty man of valour.**—The phrase, like the "mighty valiant man," applied to the young David (1 Sam. xvi. 18), has nothing to do with war, but simply signifies "strong and capable."

**The charge** (or in margin "the burden"), is, of course, the taskwork assigned to the levy from the tribe of Ephraim (and possibly Manasseh with it). It is clear from this that the levy for the Temple—perhaps originally exceptional—had served as a precedent for future burdens, not on the subject races only, as at first (ix. 21, 22), but on the Israelites also. The LXX. addition makes Jeroboam build for Solomon "*Sarira* in Mount Ephraim" also.

**Ahijah the Shilonite.**—In the person of Ahijah, prophecy emerges from the abeyance, which seems to overshadow it during the greatness of the monarchy. Even in David's old age, the prophet Nathan himself appears chiefly as a mere counsellor and servant of the king (see chap. i.), and from the day of his coronation of Solomon we hear nothing of any prophetic action. Solomon himself receives the visions of the Lord (iii. 5, ix. 2); upon him, as the Wise Man, rests the special inspiration of God; at the consecration of the Temple he alone is prominent, as the representative and the teacher of the people. Now, however, we find in Ahijah the first of the line of prophets, who resumed a paramount influence like that of Samuel or Nathan, protecting the spirituality of the land and the worship of God, and demanding both from king and people submission to the authority of the Lord Jehovah.

(30) **Rent it in twelve pieces.**—The use of symbolical acts is frequent in subsequent prophecy (especially see Jer. xiii. 1, xix. 1, xxvii. 2; Ezek. iv., v., xii. 1—7, xxiv. 3, 15), often alternating with symbolical visions and symbolical parables or allegories. The object is, of course, to arrest attention, and call out the inquiry (Ezek. xxiv. 19): "Wilt thou not tell us what these things are to us?" Ahijah's rending of his own new garment is used, like Saul's rending of Samuel's mantle (1 Sam. xv. 27, 28), to symbolise the rending away of the kingdom. (See verses 11—13.)

(31, 39) **Take thee ten pieces.**—The message delivered by Ahijah first repeats exactly the former warning to Solomon (verses 9—13), marking, by the

thus saith the LORD, the God of Israel, Behold, I will rend the kingdom out of the hand of Solomon, and will give ten tribes to thee : <sup>(32)</sup> (but he shall have one tribe for my servant David's sake, and for Jerusalem's sake, the city which I have chosen out of all the tribes of Israel :) <sup>(33)</sup> because that they have forsaken me, and have worshipped Ashtoreth the goddess of the Zidonians, Chemosh the god of the Moabites, and Milcom the god of the children of Ammon, and have not walked in my ways, to do *that which is* right in mine eyes, and *to keep* my statutes and my judgments, as *did* David his father. <sup>(34)</sup> Howbeit I will not take the whole kingdom out of his hand: but I will make him prince all the days of his life for David my servant's sake, whom I chose, because he kept my commandments and my statutes : <sup>(35)</sup> but <sup>a</sup> I will take the kingdom out of his son's hand, and will give it unto thee, *even* ten tribes. <sup>(36)</sup> And unto his son will I give one tribe, that David my servant may have a <sup>1</sup>light alway before me in Jerusalem, the city which I have chosen me to put my name there. <sup>(37)</sup> And I will take thee, and thou shalt reign according to all that thy soul desireth, and shalt be king over Israel. <sup>(38)</sup> And it shall be, if thou wilt hearken unto all that I command thee, and wilt walk in my ways, and do *that is* right in my sight, to keep my statutes and my commandments, as David my servant did; that I will be with thee, and build thee a sure house, as I built for David, and will give Israel unto thee. <sup>(39)</sup> And I will for this afflict the seed of David, but not for ever. <sup>(40)</sup> Solomon sought therefore to kill Jeroboam. And Jeroboam arose, and fled into Egypt, unto Shishak king of Egypt, and was in Egypt until the death of Solomon.

<sup>(41)</sup> And the rest of the <sup>2</sup>acts of Solomon, and all that he did, and his wisdom,

*a* ch. 12. 15.

<sup>1</sup> Heb., *lamp*, or, *candle*.

<sup>2</sup> Or, *words*, or, *things*.

---

two reserved pieces of the garment, the duality of the "one tribe" reserved for the house of David; next, it conveys to Jeroboam a promise like that given to David (so far as it was a temporal promise), "to build thee a sure house, as I built for David," on condition of the obedience which David, with all his weakness and sin, had shown, and from which Solomon, in spite of all his wisdom, had fallen away; and lastly, declares, in accordance with the famous declaration of 2 Sam. vii. 14—16, that sin in the house of David should bring with it severe chastisement, but not final rejection. In estimating the "sin of Jeroboam," the existence of this promise of security and blessing to his kingdom must be always taken into consideration.

<sup>(40)</sup> **Solomon sought therefore to kill Jeroboam.**—The knowledge of the promise in itself would be sufficient to excite the jealousy of the old king, and incite him to endeavour to falsify it by the death of Jeroboam. But from verse 26 it may be inferred that Jeroboam, characteristically enough, had not patience to wait for its fulfilment, and that he sought in some way by overt act to clutch, or prepare to clutch, at royalty. The addition to the LXX. describes him, before his flight into Egypt, as collecting three hundred chariots, and assuming royal pretensions, taking advantage of his presidency over "the house of Joseph."

**Shishak king of Egypt.**—The Shishak of the Old Testament is certainly to be identified with the *Sheshenk* of the Egyptian monuments, the *Sesonchis* or *Sesonchosis* of the Greek historians; and the identification is an important point in the Biblical chronology, for the accession of Sheshenk is fixed by the Egyptian traditions at about B.C. 980. It is a curious proof of historical accuracy that the generic name Pharaoh is not given to Shishak here. For it appears that he was not of the old royal line, but the founder of a new dynasty (the 23rd), called the Bubastite dynasty, in which several names are believed to have a Semitic origin, arguing foreign extraction; and in one genealogical table his ancestors appear not to have been of royal rank. It seems that he united (perhaps by marriage) the lines of the two dynasties which previously ruled feebly in Upper and Lower Egypt, and so inaugurated a new era of prosperity and conquest. His invasion of Judah in the fifth year of Rehoboam (see chap. xiv. 25) is chronicled in the monuments as belonging to the twentieth year of his own reign. He was, therefore, king for the last fifteen years of Solomon's reign; and his favourable reception of the rebel Jeroboam indicates a natural change of attitude towards the Israelite power. The LXX. addition describes Jeroboam (in a passage clearly suggested by what is recorded in verses 19, 20 about Hadad) as receiving from Shishak "Ano, the elder sister of Thekemina (Tahpenes), his queen," which involves an anachronism, for Tahpenes belonged to an earlier Pharaoh. But the whole history implies a close political alliance of Shishak with Jeroboam, both as an exile and as a king.

<sup>(41)</sup> **The book of the acts of Solomon.**—In 2 Chron. ix. 29 the acts of Solomon are said to be "written in the book of Nathan the prophet, and in the prophecy of Ahijah the Shilonite, and in the visions of Iddo the seer against Jeroboam the son of Nebat." The prophets appear here in the character of annalists. The book of Nathan presumably contained only the history of the early years; that of Ahijah may have well covered most of the later reign; and the "visions of Iddo" could but have dealt incidentally with the closing acts of Solomon. The narrative as given in the Book of Kings is evidently a compilation drawn from various sources, differing in various parts, both in style and in degree of detail. Thus the account of the Temple building and dedication evidently comes from some temple record; and the references to Solomon's territory, and the arrangements of his kingdom, look like notes drawn from official archives.

*Death of Solomon.*          I. KINGS, XII.          *Rehoboam Reigns.*

*are* they not written in the book of the acts of Solomon? <sup>(42)</sup> And the ¹ time that Solomon reigned in Jerusalem over all Israel *was* ªforty years. <sup>(43)</sup> And Solomon slept with his fathers, and was buried in the city of David his father:

1 Heb., *days.*
B.C. cir. 975.
a 2 Chron. 9. 30.
b Matt. 1. 7, called *Roboam.*
c Chron. 10. 1.

and ᵇRehoboam his son reigned in his stead.

CHAPTER XII.—<sup>(1)</sup> And ᶜRehoboam went to Shechem: for all Israel were come to Shechem to make him king.

---

<sup>(42)</sup> **Forty years.**—The reign of Solomon was thus of the same length as that of his father. (See chap. ii. 11.) The coincidence is curious; but the accurate historical character of the whole narrative forbids the idea that the numbers given are merely round numbers, signifying long duration. Josephus gives eighty years—either by error in his Hebrew text, or perhaps by confusing together the duration of the two reigns.

NOTE.—The insertion in the LXX. version, found in the Vatican MS. after chap. xii. 24, runs as follows:—

"And there was a man of Mount Ephraim, a servant of Solomon, and his name was Jeroboam; and his mother's name was Sarira, a woman who was a harlot. And Solomon made him taskmaster [literally, "master of the staff," or "scourge"] over the burdens [forced labours] of the house of Joseph; and he built for Solomon Sarira, which is in Mount Ephraim; and he had three hundred chariots. He it was who built the citadel [the "Millo"], by the labours of the house of Ephraim, and completed the fortification of the city of David. And he was exalting himself to seek the kingdom. And Solomon sought to put him to death; so he feared, and stole away to Sousakim [Shishak], king of Egypt, and was with him till the death of Solomon. And Jeroboam heard in Egypt that Solomon was dead, and he spake in the ears of Sousakim, king of Egypt, saying, Send me away, and I will go back to my own land. And Sousakim said to him, Ask of me a request, and I will give it thee. And he gave to Jeroboam Ano, the elder sister of his own wife Thekemina [Tahpenes] to be his wife. She was great among the daughters of the king, and bare to Jeroboam Abias [Abijah] his son. And Jeroboam said to Sousakim, Send me really away, and I will go back. And Jeroboam went forth from Egypt, and came to the land of Sarira, in Mount Ephraim, and there gathered together to him the whole strength of Ephraim. And Jeroboam built there a fortress."

Then follows, with variations of detail, the story of the sickness of Abijah, the visit of Jeroboam's wife to Ahijah, and the message of judgment; corresponding to chap. xiv. 1—18. The narrative then continues thus:—

"And Jeroboam went his way to Shechem, in Mount Ephraim, and gathered together there the tribes of Israel; and Rehoboam, the son of Solomon, went up there. And the word of the Lord came to Shemaiah, the Enlamite, saying, Take to thyself a new garment, which has never been in water, and tear it in ten pieces; and thou shalt give them to Jeroboam, and shalt say to him, Take thee ten pieces, to clothe thyself therewith. And Jeroboam took them; and Shemaiah said, These things saith the Lord, signifying the ten tribes of Israel."

The whole concludes with an account, given with some characteristic variations, of the remonstrance with Rehoboam, the rebellion, and the prohibition by Shemaiah of the intended attack of Rehoboam, corresponding to chap. xii. 1—24.

This half-independent version of the history is interesting, but obviously far inferior in authority to the Hebrew text. The incidents fit less naturally into each other; the warning of Ahijah as to the destruction of the house of Jeroboam is obviously out of place; and by the ascription to Shemaiah of the prophecy of Jeroboam's royalty, the striking coincidence of the authorship of the two predictions of prosperity and disaster is lost. The record of Shishak's intercourse with Jeroboam is apparently imitated from the history of Hadad at the court of the earlier Pharaoh; and the circumstances of Jeroboam's assumption of royal pretensions are improbable. Josephus, moreover, ignores this version of the story altogether; nor is it found in any other version. Its origin is unknown, and its growth curious enough. But it does not seem to throw much fresh light on the history.

## XII.

The comparatively detailed style of the narrative of the reign of Solomon is continued through chaps. xii., xiii., xiv. In the section chap. xii. 1—25 the record of the Book of Chronicles (2 Chron. x. 1—xi. 4), after omitting the whole description of Solomon's idolatry, and the risings of rebellion against his empire, returns to an almost exact verbal coincidence with the Book of Kings.

The narrative of the great revolution which led to the disruption of the kingdom, illustrates very strikingly the essential characteristic of the Scriptural history, which is to be found, not principally in the miraculous events recorded from time to time as an integral part of the history, but rather in the point of view from which all events alike are regarded. (*a*) Thus it is clear that the revolution had, in the first place, personal causes—in the stolid rashness of Rehoboam, mistaking obstinacy for vigour, and not knowing how and when rightly to yield; and in the character of Jeroboam, bold and active, astute and unscrupulous, the very type of a chief of revolution. (*b*) Behind these, again, lay social and political causes. The increase of wealth, culture, and civilisation under an enlightened despotism, which by its peaceful character precluded all scope and distraction of popular energies in war, created, as usual, desire and fitness for the exercise of freedom. The division of feeling and interest between the royal tribe of Judah and the rest of the people, headed by the tribe of Ephraim (for so many generations the strongest and the most leading tribe of Israel)—already manifested from time to time, and fostered perhaps by the less absolute allegiance of Israel to the house of David—now gave occasion to rebellion, when the strong hand of Solomon was removed. Perhaps, moreover, the intrigues of Egyptian jealousy may have already began to divide the Israelite people. (*c*) But the Scriptural narrative, although it enables us to discover both these causes, dwells on neither. It looks exclusively to moral and spiritual causes: "The thing was from the Lord"—His righteous judgment on the idolatry, the pride, and the despotic self-indulgence of the Court, shared, no doubt, by the princes and people of Jerusalem, perhaps exciting a wholesome reaction of feeling elsewhere. What in other history would be, at most, in-

(2) And it came to pass, when Jeroboam the son of Nebat, who was yet in *Egypt, heard *of it*, (for he was fled from the presence of king Solomon, and Jeroboam dwelt in Egypt;) (3) that they sent and called him. And Jeroboam and all the congregation of Israel came, and spake unto Rehoboam, saying, (4) Thy father made our ᵇyoke grievous: now therefore make thou the grievous service of thy father, and his heavy yoke which he put upon us, lighter, and we will serve thee. (5) And he said unto them, Depart yet *for* three days, then come again to me. And the people departed. (6) And king Rehoboam consulted with the old men, that stood before Solomon his father while he yet lived, and said, How do ye advise that I may answer this people? (7) And they spake unto him, saying, If thou wilt be a servant unto this people this day, and wilt serve them, and answer them, and speak good words to them, then they will be thy servants for ever. (8) But he forsook the counsel of the old men, which they had given him, and consulted with the young men that were grown up with him, *and* which stood before him: (9) and he said unto them, What counsel give ye that we may answer this people, who have spoken to me, saying, Make the yoke which thy father did put upon us lighter? (10) And the young men that were grown up with him spake unto him, saying, Thus shalt thou speak unto this people that spake unto thee, saying, Thy father made our yoke heavy, but make thou *it* lighter unto us; thus shalt thou say unto them,

*a* ch. 11. 40.

*b* ch. 4. 7.

---

ferred by conjecture, as underlying more obvious causes, is here placed in the forefront as a matter of course. For the history of Israel, as a history of God's dealings with the chosen people, is the visible and supernatural type of the dealings of His natural Providence with all His creatures.

(1) **All Israel were come to Shechem to make him king.**—In the case of David, we find that, when he was made king over Israel, "he made a league" with the elders of Israel (2 Sam. v. 3), apparently implying a less absolute royalty than that to which he had been anointed, without conditions, over the house of Judah (2 Sam. ii. 4); and in his restoration after the death of Absalom, there appears to be some recognition of a right of distinct action on the part of the men of Israel in relation to the kingdom (2 Sam. xix. 9, 10, 41—43; xx. 1, 2). Even in the coronation of Solomon, we find distinction made between royalty "over all Israel and over Judah." (See chap. i. 35; and comp. chap. iv. 1.) Accordingly, Rehoboam seems to succeed without question to the throne of Judah, but to need to be "made king" by the rest of Israel, with apparently some right on their part to require conditions before acceptance. It is significant, however, that this ceremonial is fixed, not at Jerusalem, but at Shechem, the chief city of Ephraim, of ancient dignity, even from patriarchal times, as of singular beauty and fertility of position, which became, as a matter of course, the capital of the northern kingdom after the disruption. Perhaps, in this arrangement, which seems to have had no precedent, there was some omen of revolution.

(2) **For he was fled.**—In 2 Chron. x. 2, and in the LXX. version (or, rather versions, for there is variety of reading) of this passage, Jeroboam is made to return from Egypt, on hearing of the death of Solomon, to his own city, and to be "sent for" thence. This is obviously far more probable, and might be read in the Hebrew by a slight alteration of the text.

(4) **We will serve thee.**—It seems evident from the tone of the narrative, and especially from the absence of all resentment on the part of the king on the presentation of these conditions, that they were acting within their right; and whatever Jeroboam's designs may have been, there is no sign of any general predetermination of rebellion. The imposition of the burdens of heavy taxation and forced labour on the people was against old traditions, and even against the practice of Solomon's earlier years. (See chaps. iv. 20, ix. 20—22.) To demand a removal, or alleviation of these, was perfectly compatible with a loyal willingness to "serve" the new king. The demand might naturally be suggested by Jeroboam, who, by his official position, knew well the severity of the burden.

(7) **If thou wilt be a servant.**—Both the policies suggested show how corrupt and cynical the government of Israel had become. For the advice of the old counsellors has no largeness of policy or depth of wisdom. It is simply the characteristic advice of experienced and crafty politicians—who had seen the gradual development of despotic power, and had still remembrance of the comparative freedom of earlier days—understanding at once the dangerous vehemence of popular excitement, and the facility with which it may be satisfied by temporary concessions, and perhaps desiring to defeat that private ambition, which was making use for its own purposes of the natural sense of grievance. It is to give "good words," and to be for the moment "a servant to the people," with, perhaps, the intention of abolishing certain excessive grievances, but by no means of yielding up substantial power. Whether it was in itself more than superficially prudent, would depend on the seriousness of the grievances, and the social and political condition of the people.

(10) **Thus shalt thou speak.**—The advice of the young men—the spoilt children of a magnificent and luxurious despotism, of which alone they had experience—is the language of the arrogant self-confidence, which mistakes obstinacy for vigour, and, blind to all signs of the times, supposes that what once was possible, and perhaps good for the national progress, must last for ever. It is couched in needlessly and absurdly offensive language; but it is, as all history shows—perhaps not least the history of our own Stuart dynasty—a not unfrequent policy in revolutionary times; holding that to yield in one point is to endanger the whole fabric of sovereign power; relying on the prestige of an

My little *finger* shall be thicker than my father's loins. (11) And now whereas my father did lade you with a heavy yoke, I will add to your yoke: my father hath chastised you with whips, but I will chastise you with scorpions.

(12) So Jeroboam and all the people came to Rehoboam the third day, as the king had appointed, saying, Come to me again the third day. (13) And the king answered the people [1] roughly, and forsook the old men's counsel that they gave him; (14) and spake to them after the counsel of the young men, saying, My father made your yoke heavy, and I will add to your yoke: my father *also* chastised you with whips, but I will chastise you with scorpions. (15) Wherefore the king hearkened not unto the people; for the cause was from the LORD, that he might perform his saying, which the LORD *a* spake by Ahijah the Shilonite unto Jeroboam the son of Nebat.

(16) So when all Israel saw that the king hearkened not unto them, the people answered the king, saying, What portion have we in David? neither *have we* inheritance in the son of Jesse: to your tents, O Israel: now see to thine own house, David. So Israel departed unto their tents. (17) But *as for* the children of Israel which dwelt in the cities of Judah, Rehoboam reigned over them.

(18) Then king Rehoboam sent Adoram, who *was* over the tribute; and all Israel stoned him with stones, that he died. Therefore king Rehoboam [2] made speed to get him up to his chariot, to flee to Jerusalem. (19) So Israel [3] rebelled against the house of David unto this day. (20) And it came to pass, when all Israel heard that Jeroboam was come again, that

[1] Heb., *hardly*.
*a* ch. 11. 11.
[2] Heb., *strengthened himself*.
[3] Or, *fell away*.

---

authority proudly confident in itself; and trusting to cow by threats the classes long subject to despotic oppression, and despised accordingly by those who wield it. It can succeed only when the popular disaffection is superficial, or when a nation is wearied out with revolutionary fanaticism and failure.

(11) **The scorpion** is probably (like the Roman *flagellum*) a whip, the lash of which is loaded with weights and sharp points.

(15) **For the cause was from the Lord.**—The very idea of the Scriptural history, referring all things to God, necessarily brings us continually face to face with the great mystery of life—the reconcilement of God's all-foreseeing and all-ordaining Providence with the freedom, and, in consequence, with the folly and sin of man. As a rule, Holy Scripture—on this point confirming natural reason—simply recognises both powers as real, without any attempt, even by suggestion, to harmonise them together. It, of course, refers all to God's will, fulfilling or avenging itself in many ways, inspiring and guiding the good, and overruling the evil, in man. But it as invariably implies human freedom and responsibility. Rehoboam's folly and arrogance worked out the ordained judgment of God; but they were folly and arrogance still.

(16) **To your tents.**—This war-cry was not new. It had been heard once before, during the conflict between Judah and Israel after the rebellion of Absalom, when it was silenced instantly by the relentless promptitude of Joab (2 Sam. xx. 1). Only the last ironical line is added, "See to thine own house, David" (which the LXX. explains as "Feed, as a shepherd, thine own house, David"). There is perhaps a sarcastic allusion to God's promise to establish the house of David: "Be a king, but only in thine own house!"

(17) **The children of Israel which dwelt in the cities of Judah.**—The expression is doubly significant. (*a*) Historically the tribe of Judah had its semi-dependent tribes—Simeon, already absorbed into Judah; Dan, in great part transferred to the extreme north; and Benjamin, closely united to Judah by the position of Jerusalem. All these, it would seem, are here included—so that the territory of the southern kingdom would be really the *Judæa* of later times. In addition to these, we find from 2 Chron. xi. 13—16, that, at any rate after the idolatry of Jeroboam, priests and Levites and other Israelites made their way into the cities of Judah. (*b*) But, besides this, there may be a significance in the phrase "children of Israel." Although the northern kingdom henceforth inherited the proud title of the kingdom of Israel, the phrase, as here used, is perhaps intended to remind the reader that in Judah also dwelt "children of Israel"—true descendants of the "Prince of God," and inheritors of the promise.

(18) **Adoram, who was over the tribute** (or levy).—In 2 Sam. xx. 24, 1 Kings iv. 6, v. 14, we find Adoram (or Adoniram, which is a longer form of the same name) described as holding this office in the later days of David and the reign of Solomon. The Adoram here mentioned must be identical with the officer of Solomon; but, though it is possible, it is not likely that he could have held office in David's time. Probably the name and office were hereditary. The mission of Adoram shows that, too late, Rehoboam desired to deal through him with the grievance of forced labour. But the sight of the man, who had been the taskmaster of their oppression, naturally stirred the multitude to a fresh burst of fury, venting itself in his murder, and perhaps threatening his master also, had he not fled hastily at once to Jerusalem.

(19) **Unto this day.**—The phrase argues the incorporation into the narrative of an older document.

(20) **Jeroboam was come again.**—The assembly at Shechem probably broke up in disorder, carrying everywhere the news of the rebellion. It would be quite in harmony with Jeroboam's astuteness, if, after setting the revolution on foot, he himself stood aloof from leadership, and waited till "the congregation," the duly summoned assembly, sent for him and offered him the crown. The title "king over all Israel" certainly indicates a claim on the part of the ten tribes to be the true Israel, relying perhaps on the prophetic choice and

*Rehoboam Raises an Army, but*    I. KINGS, XII.    *is Forbidden by Shemaiah.*

they sent and called him unto the congregation, and made him king over all Israel: there was none that followed the house of David, but the tribe of Judah [a] only.

(21) And when Rehoboam was come to Jerusalem, he assembled all the house of Judah, with the tribe of Benjamin, an hundred and fourscore thousand chosen men, which were warriors, to fight against the house of Israel, to bring the kingdom again to Rehoboam the son of Solomon. (22) But [b] the word of God came unto Shemaiah the man of God, saying, (23) Speak unto Rehoboam, the son of Solomon, king of Judah, and unto all the house of Judah and Benjamin, and to the remnant of the people, saying, (24) Thus saith the LORD, Ye shall not go up, nor fight against your brethren the children of Israel: return every man to his house; for this thing is from me. They hearkened therefore to the word of the LORD, and returned to depart, according to the word of the LORD. (25) Then Jeroboam built Shechem in mount Ephraim, and dwelt therein; and went out from thence, and built Penuel. (26) And Jeroboam said in his heart, Now shall the kingdom return to the house of David: (27) if this people go up to do sacrifice in the house of the LORD at Jerusalem, then shall the heart of this people turn again unto their lord, *even* unto Rehoboam king of Judah, and they shall kill me, and go again to Rehoboam king of Judah. (28) Whereupon the king took counsel, and made two calves *of* gold, and said unto them, It is too much for you to go up to Jerusalem:

[a] ch. 11. 13.

[b] 2 Chron. 11. 2.

---

blessing of Jeroboam, and professing to have risen in the name of the Lord against the idolatry of Solomon and his house. Perhaps it also indicated a desire for the subjugation of Judah, which Jeroboam, with the aid of Shishak, certainly seems to have subsequently attempted.

(20, 21) In these two verses we have again the same curious juxtaposition of "the tribe of Judah only" and "the house of Judah, with the tribe of Benjamin." The army gathered would be, no doubt, drawn from Solomon's established and disciplined forces, as well as from the levy of Judah and Benjamin generally—perhaps including (as in 2 Sam. xvii. 27) contingents from the tributary races—who would be attached with a strong personal allegiance to the house of Solomon, and prepared to stamp out the rebellion, before it could thoroughly organise itself for disciplined resistance.

(22) **Shemaiah the man of God.**—From the notices in 2 Chron. xii. 5—8, 15, it would seem that, while Ahijah belonged to Shiloh in Ephraim, and continued to dwell there, Shemaiah was rather attached to Judah, and hence, that his interference to protect the new kingdom was the more striking and unexpected. In this interposition, to which probably the very preservation of Jeroboam's half-formed kingdom was due, there is a fresh indication of the great opportunity given to that kingdom to maintain itself, under the blessing of God and in devotion to His service. The phrase "your brethren, the children of Israel," marks this with much emphasis.

(25) **Jeroboam built Shechem.**—Shechem had passed through many vicissitudes of fortune. It was already a city when Abraham entered the Promised Land (Gen. xii. 6), and is from time to time mentioned in the patriarchal history (Gen. xxxiii. 18, xxxiv., xxxv. 4, xxxvii. 12, 13). At the Conquest it became a city of refuge (Josh. xx. 7, xxi. 20, 21), and the scene of the solemn recital of the blessings and curses of the Law (Josh. viii. 33—35). From its proximity to Shiloh, and to the inheritance of Joshua, it assumed something of the character of a capital (Josh. xxiv. 1, 32). Then it became the seat of the usurpation of Abimelech, which allied itself with the native inhabitants of the region; but rebelling afterwards against him, it was destroyed (Judges ix.). We then hear nothing more of it till this chapter, when the tribes assemble at Shechem, under the shadow of the famous hills of Ebal and Gerizim, to meet Rehoboam. Jeroboam is said to have "built it" anew. This may be taken literally, as indicating that it had never recovered from its destruction by Abimelech, or it may simply mean that he fortified and enlarged it as his capital. Subsequently it gave way to Tirzah and Samaria; but its almost unrivalled position preserved it in importance among the Samaritans after the Captivity, even down to our Lord's time, and under the name of Nablous (Neapolis) it has lasted to the present day, while many other cities once famous have passed away.

**Penuel.**—See Gen. xxxii. 30, 31; Judges viii. 8, 17. It lay on or near the Jabbok, on the other side of Jordan, commanding the road from the east by Succoth to the fords of Jordan and Shechem. Jeroboam rebuilt it—perhaps out of the ruin in which it had been left by Gideon—as an outpost to his new capital, and a royal stronghold among the tribes on the east of Jordan.

(27, 28) In these verses is recorded the adoption of the fatal policy which has caused Jeroboam to be handed down in the sacred record as "the son of Nebat, who made Israel to sin." Hitherto his new royalty had been inaugurated under a Divine sanction, both as receiving distinct promise of permanence and blessing (chap. xi. 37, 38), and as protected by open prophetic interference, at the critical moment when its ill-consolidated force might have been crushed. Nor is it unlikely that it may have been supported by a wholesome reaction against the idolatry, as well as against the despotism, of Solomon. Now, unsatisfied with these securities of his kingdom, and desirous to strengthen it by a bold stroke of policy, he takes the step which mars the bright promise of his accession. Yet the policy was exceedingly natural. In Israel beyond all other nations, civil and religious allegiance were indissolubly united; it was almost impossible to see how separate national existence could have been sustained without the creation, or (as it might seem)

*behold thy gods, O Israel, which brought thee up out of the land of Egypt. (29) And he set the one in Beth-el, and the other put he in Dan. (30) And this thing became a sin: for the people went to *worship* before the one, *even* unto Dan. (31) And he made an house of high places, and made priests of the lowest of the people, which were not of the sons of Levi. (32) And Jeroboam ordained a feast in the eighth month, on the fifteenth day of the month, like unto the feast that *is* in Judah, and he ¹offered upon the altar. So did he in Beth-el, ²sacrificing unto the calves that he had made: and he placed in Beth-el

*a* Exod. 32. 8.

1 Or, *went up to the altar*, &c.

2 Or, *to sacrifice*.

---

the revival, of local sanctuaries to rival the sacredness of Jerusalem. Nor was the breach of Divine law apparently a serious one. The worship at Dan and Bethel was not the bloody and sensual worship of false gods, but the worship of the Lord Jehovah under the form of a visible emblem, meant to be a substitute for the ark and the overshadowing cherubim. It might have been plausibly urged that, to wean Israel from all temptation to the abominations which Solomon had introduced, it was necessary to give their faith the visible support of these great local sanctuaries, and the lesser "high places" which would naturally follow. But the occasion was the critical moment of choice between a worldly policy—"doing evil that good might come"—and the higher and more arduous path of simple faith in God's promise, and obedience to the command designed to protect the purity and spirituality of His worship. The step, once taken, was never retraced. Eminently successful in its immediate object of making the separation irreparable, it purchased success at the price, first, of destruction of all religious unity in Israel, and next, of a natural corruption, opening the door at once to idolatry, and hereafter to the grosser apostasy, against which it professed to guard. It needed the faith of David—as shown, for example, in the patient acquiescence in the prohibition of the erection of a Temple to be the spiritual glory of his kingdom—to secure the promise of "a sure house, as for David." That promise was now forfeited for ever.

(28) **Calves of gold.**—The choice of this symbol of the Divine Nature—turning, as the Psalmist says with indignant scorn, "the glory of God into the similitude of a calf that eateth hay" (Ps. cvi. 20)—was probably due to a combination of causes. First, the very repetition of Aaron's words (Exod. xxxii. 8) indicates that it was a revival of that ancient idolatry in the wilderness. Probably, like it, it was suggested by the animal worship of Egypt, with which Jeroboam had been recently familiar, and which (as is well known) varied from mere symbolism to gross creature worship. Next, the bull, as the emblem of Ephraim, would naturally become a religious cognisance of the new kingdom. Lastly, there is some reason to believe that the figure of the cherubim was that of winged bulls, and the form of the ox was undoubtedly used in the Temple, as for example, under the brazen sea. It has been thought that the "calves" were reproductions of the sacred cherubim,—made, however, symbols, not of the natural powers obeying the Divine word, but of the Deity itself.

It is, of course, to be understood that this idolatry, against which the prohibition of many sanctuaries was meant to guard, was a breach, not of the First Commandment, but of the Second—that making of "a similitude" of the true God, so emphatically forbidden again and again in the Law. (See, for example, Deut. iv. 15—18.) Like all such veneration of images, it probably degenerated. From looking on the image as a mere symbol it would come to attach to it a local presence of the Deity and an intrinsic sacredness; and so would lead on, perhaps to a veiled polytheism, certainly to a superstitious and carnal conception of the Godhead.

(29) **Bethel and Dan,** chosen as the frontier towns of the kingdom, had, however, associations of their own, which lent themselves naturally to Jeroboam's design. Bethel—preserving in its name the memory of Jacob's vision, and of his consecration of the place as a sanctuary (Gen. xxviii. 19; xxxv. 14, 15)—had been (see Judg. xx. 18, 26, 31; xxi. 2; 1 Sam. vii. 16) a place of religious assembly; and, possibly, of occasional sojourn of the Ark. At Dan, it is not unlikely that the use of the local sanctuary, set up at the conquest of the city by the Danites, still lingered; and from the notice in Judg. xviii. 30, that the posterity of Jonathan, the grandson of Moses, were priests till "the day of the captivity of the land," it seems as if these priests of this old worship became naturally the appointed ministers of the new.

(30) **Even unto Dan.**—It has been thought that there is here a corruption of the text, and that words referring to Bethel have fallen out. But there is no sign of such variation in the LXX. (which only adds, in some MSS., "and deserted the house of the Lord") or other versions. The reason of the mention of Dan only is probably that there the old sanctuary remained, and the priesthood was ready: hence, in this case, "the people went to worship" at once. The verses which follow describe the erection of a temple and the creation of a priesthood at Bethel, necessary before the inauguration of the new worship at what naturally became the more prominent and magnificent sanctuary. This temple is called a "house of high places," partly perhaps from its actual position, partly to connect it with the use of "the high places" condemned in the Law. Indeed, as we have no notice of any time spent in building it, it is possible that some old "high place" was restored for the purpose.

(31, 32) **Of the lowest of the people.**—This is universally recognised as a mistranslation, though a natural one, of the original, "the ends of the people." The sense is "from the whole mass of the people," without care for Levitical descent—the Levites having (see 2 Chron. xi. 13, 14) generally returned into the kingdom of Judah on the establishment of this idolatry. It is hardly likely that the king would have lacked persons of the higher orders for his new priesthood. It is said that this was done "at Bethel," probably because at Dan an unauthorised Levitical priesthood was (as has been said) forthcoming.

(32) **In the eighth month, on the fifteenth day of the month . . .**—The "feast that was in Judah," to which this is said to be like, is clearly the Feast of Tabernacles, on the fifteenth day of the *seventh* month. The fixing of Jeroboam's festival of dedication for the Temple at Bethel to this special day

*The Prophecy against*     I. KINGS, XIII.     *the Altar at Bethel.*

the priests of the high places which he had made. <sup>(33)</sup> So he ¹offered upon the altar which he had made in Beth-el the fifteenth day of the eighth month, *even* in the month which he had devised of his own heart; and ordained a feast unto the children of Israel: and he offered upon the altar, ²and burnt incense.

CHAPTER XIII.—<sup>(1)</sup> And, behold, there came a man of God out of Judah by the word of the LORD unto Beth-el: and Jeroboam stood by the altar ³to burn incense. <sup>(2)</sup> And he cried against the altar in the word of the LORD, and said, O altar, altar, thus saith the LORD; Behold, a child shall be born unto the house of David, *ª*Josiah by name; and upon thee shall he offer the priests of the high places that burn incense upon thee, and men's bones shall be burnt upon thee. <sup>(3)</sup> And he gave a sign the same day, saying, This *is* the sign which the LORD hath spoken; Behold, the altar shall be rent, and the ashes that *are* upon it shall be poured out.

<sup>(4)</sup> And it came to pass, when king Jeroboam heard the saying of the man of God, which had cried against the altar in Beth-el, that he put forth his hand from the altar, saying, Lay hold

---

Margin notes: 1 Or, *went up to the altar, &c.*   2 Heb., *to burn incense.*   3 Or, *to offer.*   *a* 2 Kings 23. 17.

---

is characteristic. It at once challenged likeness to the Feast of Tabernacles, which was (see chap. viii. 2) the occasion of Solomon's dedication at Jerusalem, and yet took liberty to alter the date, and fix it in the month "which he had devised of his own heart," thus assuming the right to set aside the letter of the old law, while professing still to observe the worship of Jehovah.

**Offered**—or (see margin) *went up*—**upon the altar.**—The expression seems to imply that he ventured on a still greater innovation by taking on himself both functions of the priestly office—to offer sacrifice and (see verse 33) to burn incense. This is not, indeed, necessarily implied; for (see chap. viii. 63) the sacrificer is often said to offer, when he evidently does so only through the priests. But Jeroboam had set aside the peculiar sanctity of the Levitical priesthood already; and so was very naturally prepared to crown this process by acting as head of the unauthorised priesthood which he had created. Perhaps he had witnessed the exclusive prominence of Solomon at the great dedication festival, and desired to imitate and outdo it.

<sup>(33)</sup> **So he offered upon the altar.**—The repetition of this verse is accounted for by its belonging properly in sense to the next chapter, opening the story of the mission of the "man of God from Judah." The idea of the verse would be best conveyed by rendering the verbs of this verse in the imperfect tense: "So Jeroboam was offering," &c.

### XIII.

In this history, as in that of Elijah and Elisha, the compiler clearly draws from prophetic traditions or records. Here, accordingly, as there, the character of the narrative changes, and becomes full of graphic vividness and spiritual significance. In 2 Chron. ix. 29 we read of "the visions of Iddo the seer against Jeroboam the son of Nebat." It is natural to conjecture that from these this record is drawn.

<sup>(1)</sup> **A man of God out of Judah.**—Josephus calls him Jadon (Iddo); but from 2 Chron. xiii. 22 it appears that Iddo was the chronicler of the reign of Abijah, and must, therefore, have lived till near the close of Jeroboam's reign. Probably the tradition came from a mistaken interpretation of the "visions of Iddo against Jeroboam."

**By the word of the Lord.**—A weak rendering of the original, "in the word of the Lord." The constantly recurring prophetic phrases are, "the word of the Lord came to me," and "the Spirit of the Lord was upon me," enabling, or forcing, to declare it. The original phrase here implies both. The prophet came clothed in the inspiration of the word put into his mouth.

<sup>(2)</sup> **Thus saith the Lord.**—This is one of those rather unfrequent prophecies found in Holy Scripture, which, not content to foreshadow the future in general outline, descend to striking particularity of detail. It has been indeed suggested that the words "Josiah by name" are a marginal gloss which has crept into the text, or the insertion of the chronicler writing after the event, and not a part of the original prophetic utterance. The latter supposition is in itself not unlikely. But the mention of the name in prediction is exemplified in the well-known reference to Cyrus in Isa. xliv. 28; and in this instance, as perhaps also in that, the name is significant (for Josiah means "one healed" or "helped by Jehovah"), and is not, therefore, a mere artificial detail. The particularity of prediction, which is on all hands recognised as exceptional, will be credible or incredible to us, according to the view which we take of the nature of prophetic prediction. If we resolve it into the intuitive sagacity of an inspired mind forecasting the future, because it sees more clearly than ordinary minds the germs of that future in the present, the particularity must seem incredible. If, on the other hand, we believe it to be the supernatural gift of a power to enter, in some measure, into "the mind of God," in whose foreknowledge all the future is already seen and ordained, then it will be to us simply unusual, but in no sense incredible, that from time to time foreknowledge of details, as well as generalities, should be granted. It is beyond controversy that the latter view is the one put forward in Holy Scripture, both in the Old Testament and in the New. Prophecy is, indeed, something higher and greater than supernatural prediction; but it claims to include such prediction, both as a test of mission from God, and as a necessary part of its revelation of the dispensations of God. On the fulfilment of this prediction, see 2 Kings xxiii. 15—20.

<sup>(3, 4)</sup> **The sign.**—Both the signs, like most miraculous signs, shadow forth plainly the thing signified. The sign, announced to secure credence to the prediction, is itself a visible type of what that prediction foretold, in the shattering of the altar and the scattering of the ashes of the burnt-offering. The sign actually given includes, besides this, the sudden wither-

on him. And his hand, which he put forth against him, dried up, so that he could not pull it in again to him. ⁽⁵⁾ The altar also was rent, and the ashes poured out from the altar, according to the sign which the man of God had given by the word of the LORD. ⁽⁶⁾ And the king answered and said unto the man of God, Intreat now the face of the LORD thy God, and pray for me, that my hand may be restored me again. And the man of God besought ¹the LORD, and the king's hand was restored him again, and became as *it was* before. ⁽⁷⁾ And the king said unto the man of God, Come home with me, and refresh thyself, and I will give thee a reward. ⁽⁸⁾ And the man of God said unto the king, If thou wilt give me half thine house, I will not go in with thee, neither will I eat bread nor drink water in this place: ⁽⁹⁾ for so was it charged me by the word of the LORD, saying, Eat no bread, nor drink water, nor turn again by the same way that thou camest. ⁽¹⁰⁾ So he went another way, and returned not by the way that he came to Beth-el.

⁽¹¹⁾ Now there dwelt an old prophet in Beth-el; and his sons came and told him all the works that the man of God had done that day in Beth-el: the words which he had spoken unto the king, them they told also to their father. ⁽¹²⁾ And their father said unto them, What way went he? For his sons had seen what way the man of God went, which came from Judah. ⁽¹³⁾ And he said unto his sons, Saddle me the ass. So they saddled him the ass: and he rode thereon, ⁽¹⁴⁾ and went after the man of God, and found him sitting under an oak: and he said unto him, Art thou the man of God that camest from Judah? And he said, I *am*. ⁽¹⁵⁾ Then he said unto him, Come home with me, and eat bread. ⁽¹⁶⁾ And

¹ Heb., *the face of the Lord.*

---

ing of the king's hand, stretched out in defiance of the prophet—an equally plain symbol of the miserable failure of his strength and policy, when opposed to the Law and the judgment of God. It should be noted that the withdrawal of this last sign of wrath, on the submission of the king and the prayer of the prophet, was apparently designed to give Jeroboam one more opportunity of repentance. The last verses of the chapter (verses 33, 34) seem to imply that, but for the interposition of the old prophet of Bethel, he might still have taken that opportunity.

(7) **Come home with me . . .**—The invitation may have been in part the mark of some impression made on the king, and an impulse of gratitude for the restoration of his withered hand. Such was the request of Naaman to Elisha (2 Kings v. 15), though even this was emphatically refused. But it still savours of astute policy in Jeroboam: for the acceptance of hospitality and reward would in the eyes of the people imply a condonation of the idolatrous worship, which might well destroy or extenuate the impression made by the prophet's prediction. It indicates also—what experience of such men as "the old prophet" would have produced—a low idea of prophetic character and mission, not unlike that which is shown in Balak's treatment of Balaam. That such conceptions are perfectly compatible with a certain belief in the reality of a supernatural power in the prophet—although they, of course, derogate from its true sacredness—the monstrous request of Simon Magus (in Acts viii. 19) shows with the most startling clearness. It was evidently to provide against these things—as fatal to the effectiveness of the prophet's mission—that the prohibition of verse 9 was given; nor could its general purpose have been easily misunderstood, either by the king or by the prophet himself. It is a curious coincidence that in his refusal he uses words strangely like the reluctant refusal of Balak's offer by Balaam (Num. xxii. 18). The very strength of the language is suspicious.

(9) **Nor turn again . . .**—The significance of this command is less obvious. It may have meant that he should not suffer the way of his return (which would clearly not be the obvious way) to be known, but should vanish swiftly, like the messenger of Elisha to Jehu (2 Kings ix. 3, 10), when his work was done. If so, his neglect of the spirit of the command was the first step in the way of his destruction.

(11) **An old prophet in Beth-el.**—The narrative clearly implies—and, indeed, part of its most striking instructiveness depends on this—that this old prophet was not a mere pretender to prophetic inspiration, nor an apostate from the worship of Jehovah. Like Balaam, he united true prophetic gifts with a low worldliness of temper, capable on occasion of base subterfuge and deceit. Such union of elements, which should be utterly discordant, is only too characteristic of man's self-contradictory nature. He had thrown in his lot with Jeroboam's policy, which did not want plausible grounds of defence: in spite of this adhesion, he desired to continue still a prophet of the Lord, and to support the king's action by prophetic influence. It has been noticed that, after the maintenance of the idolatry of Beth-el, even the true prophets did not break off their ministry to the kingdom of Israel, and that, indeed, they never appeared in open hostility to that kingdom, till the introduction of Baal worship. But their case is altogether different from that of the old prophet. He deliberately supports the idolatry, and that by the worst of falsehoods—a falsehood in the name of God. They rebuke the sin (see chap. xiv. 9), but do not forsake their ministry to the sinner.

(14) **An oak.**—Properly, *the oak*, or *terebinth*; supposed to be known in that comparatively treeless country, like the oak at Shechem (Gen. xxxv. 4, 8; Josh. xxiv. 26; Judg. ix. 6), the oak at Ophrah (Judg. vi. 11), and the palm-tree of Deborah (Judg. iv. 5). This expression is an evident mark of the antiquity of the document from which the history is taken. It has been suggested that the narrative implies a needless

he said, I may not return with thee, nor go in with thee: neither will I eat bread nor drink water with thee in this place: (17) for ¹it was said to me by the word of the LORD, Thou shalt eat no bread nor drink water there, nor turn again to go by the way that thou camest. (18) He said unto him, I *am a* prophet also as thou *art;* and an angel spake unto me by the word of the LORD, saying, Bring him back with thee into thine house, that he may eat bread and drink water. *But* he lied unto him. (19) So he went back with him, and did eat bread in his house, and drank water.

(20) And it came to pass, as they sat at the table, that the word of the LORD came unto the prophet that brought him back: (21) and he cried unto the man of God that came from Judah, saying, Thus saith the LORD, Forasmuch as thou hast disobeyed the mouth of the LORD, and hast not kept the commandment which the LORD thy God commanded thee, (22) but camest back, and hast eaten bread and drunk water in the place, of the which *the* LORD did say to thee, Eat no bread, and drink no water; thy carcase shall not come unto the sepulchre of thy fathers.

(23) And it came to pass, after he had eaten bread, and after he had drunk, that he saddled for him the ass, *to wit,* for the prophet whom he had brought back. (24) And when he was gone, a lion met him by the way, and slew him: and his carcase was cast in the way, and the ass stood by it, the lion also stood by the carcase. (25) And, behold, men passed by, and saw the carcase cast in the way, and the lion standing by the carcase: and they came and told *it* in the city where the old prophet dwelt. (26) And when the prophet that brought him back from the way heard *thereof,* he said, It *is* the man of God, who was disobedient unto the word of the LORD: therefore the LORD hath delivered him unto the lion, which hath ²torn him, and slain him, according to the word of the LORD, which he spake unto him. (27) And he spake to his sons, saying, Saddle me the ass. And they saddled *him.* (28) And he went and found his carcase cast in the way, and the ass and the lion standing by the carcase: the lion had not eaten the carcase, nor ³torn the ass. (29) And the prophet took up the carcase of the man of God, and laid it upon the ass, and brought it back: and the old prophet came to the city, to mourn and to bury him. (30) And he laid his carcase in his

---

1 Heb., *a word was.*
2 Heb., *broken.*
3 Heb., *broken.*

---

loitering of the prophet of Judah on the way. Taken by itself, it would not necessarily convey this; but in relation to the temper indicated in the whole story, the thing may be not improbable.

(18) **An angel spake unto me.**—The lie was gross, and ought to have been obvious to one who had received a plain command, and must have known that "God was not a man that He should lie, or the son of man that He should repent." It was believed, no doubt, because it chimed in with some secret reluctance to obey, and, by obedience, to give up all reward and hospitality. Hence the belief was a self-deceit, and, as such, culpable. It is inexplicable that the condemnation which it drew down should have been thought strange by any who understands human nature, and knows the self-deceiving colour which our wish gives to our thought. (See the famous Sermon of Bishop Butler on "Self-deceit.")

(20) **The word of the Lord came.**—It is, perhaps, the most terrible feature in the history that the Divine sentence is spoken—no doubt, as in the case of Balaam, unwillingly—through the very lips which by falsehood had lured the prophet of Judah from the right path, and at the very table of treacherous hospitality. Josephus, with his perverse tendency to explain away all that seems startling, misses this point entirely, and assigns the revelation to the prophet of Judah himself. Striking as this incident is, it is perhaps a symbol of a general law constantly exemplifying itself, that the voice of worldly wisdom first beguiles the servants of God to disobedience by false glosses on their duty to Him, and then proclaims unsparingly their sin and its just punishment.

(24) **A lion.**—The lion is noticed in the Old Testament not unfrequently, especially in Southern Palestine: at Timnath (Judges xiv. 5); near Bethlehem (1 Sam. xvii. 34); at Kabzeel, in Judah (2 Sam. xxiii. 20); near Aphek (1 Kings xx. 36); in the thickets and forests of the Jordan valley (Jer. iv. 7, v. 6), &c. The lion of Palestine is probably of the variety still constantly found in the neighbourhood of Babylon; and the prevalence of lions is shown by the occurrence of such names as *Lebaoth,* or *Bethlebaoth,* "the house of lions" (see Josh. xv. 32), and by the many names for the lion used in Scripture, as, for example, in Job iv. 10, 11. Now that the forests have disappeared from Palestine the lions have disappeared with them.

(26) **He said, It is the man of God.**—The old prophet did not know how his prediction was to be fulfilled, but recognised at once its supernatural fulfilment. There is in his words a characteristic reticence as to his own share in the work, in respect both of the deceit and the prediction of judgment, perhaps indicating something of the strange mixture of remorse and unscrupulous policy which comes out in his later action.

(30—32) **They mourned.**—The mourning of the old prophet, and the burial of the body in his own sepulchre,

*His Burial.*            I. KINGS, XIV.            *Abijah falls sick.*

own grave; and they mourned over him, *saying*, Alas, my brother! (31) And it came to pass, after he had buried him, that he spake to his sons, saying, When I am dead, then bury me in the sepulchre wherein the man of God *is* buried; lay my bones beside his bones: (32) for the saying which he cried by the word of the LORD against the altar in Beth-el, and against all the houses of the high places which *are* in the cities of Samaria, shall surely come to pass.

(33) After this thing Jeroboam returned not from his evil way, but ¹made again of the lowest of the people priests of the high places: whosoever would, he ²consecrated him, and he became *one* of the priests of the high places. (34) And this thing became sin unto the house of Jeroboam, even to cut *it* off, and to destroy *it* from off the face of the earth.

CHAPTER XIV.—(1) At that time Abijah the son of Jeroboam fell sick.

---

1 Heb., *returned and made.*

2 Heb., *filled his hand.*

B.C. cir. 974.

a ch. 11. 31.

3 Heb., *in thine hand.*

4 Or, *cakes.*

5 Or, *bottle.*

6 Heb., *stood for his hoariness.*

---

(2) And Jeroboam said to his wife, Arise, I pray thee, and disguise thyself, that thou be not known to be the wife of Jeroboam; and get thee to Shiloh: behold, there *is* Ahijah the prophet, which told me that *ªI should be* king over this people. (3) And take ³with thee ten loaves, and ⁴cracknels, and a ⁵cruse of honey, and go to him: he shall tell thee what shall become of the child. (4) And Jeroboam's wife did so, and arose, and went to Shiloh, and came to the house of Ahijah. But Ahijah could not see; for his eyes ⁶were set by reason of his age. (5) And the LORD said unto Ahijah, Behold, the wife of Jeroboam cometh to ask a thing of thee for her son; for he *is* sick: thus and thus shalt thou say unto her: for it shall be, when she cometh in, that she shall feign herself *to be* another *woman.*

(6) And it was *so*, when Ahijah heard the sound of her feet, as she came in at the door, that he said, Come in, thou wife of Jeroboam; why feignest thou

---

probably show some touch of remorse and personal compassion for the victim of his treacherous policy, mingled with the desire of preserving the tomb, which was to be his own last resting-place, from desecration, when the prediction of the prophet of Judah should be accomplished. But, even setting aside the rather prosaic tradition of his attempts to remove any impression made on the mind of Jeroboam, which Josephus has preserved (*Ant.* viii., 9), it is evident that his policy was only too successful. The messenger of wrath had been enticed to familiar intercourse with the prophet of the new idolatry, and had been publicly proclaimed as his "brother:" probably his death had been used to discredit his warning. The result is seen in the significant notice of verse 33: "After this thing, Jeroboam returned not from his evil way." Hence the seriousness of the disobedience, which played into the hands of wickedness, and the startling severity of the penalty.

(33) **Whosoever would.**—See chap. xii. 32. The emphatic tone of the words, "whosoever would, he consecrated him," possibly indicates that, in spite of all that Jeroboam and his prophet could do, there was some difficulty in securing candidates for his unauthorised priesthood.

(34) **And this thing.**—The comment of the author of the book, evidently based on the prophetic denunciation of Ahijah in chap. xiv. 9—11, and its subsequent fulfilment. (See chap. xv. 25—30.)

XIV.

The first section of this chapter (verses 1—20) concludes the first division of the book, which gives in considerable detail the history of the reign of Solomon, and the revolution, political and religious, which marked the disruption of the kingdom. The second (verses 21—31) begins the short annalistic notices which make up the next division of the book, extending to the beginning of the reign of Ahab, and of the prophetic career of Elijah (chap. xvi. 29).

(1) **Abijah** ("whose father is Jehovah").—The coincidence of names in the sons of Jeroboam and Rehoboam is curious. Possibly it may be more than coincidence, if (as seems likely) the births of both took place about the same time, when Jeroboam was in favour with Solomon.

(2) **Shiloh**, the regular habitation of Ahijah, is hardly mentioned in Scripture after the time of Eli, and the destruction which then seems to have fallen upon it, probably after the great defeat by the Philistines (Jer. vii. 12). It is evident that the old blind prophet still remained there, and exercised his prophetic office for the benefit of Israel, though he stood aloof from, and denounced, the new idolatry of Bethel. This idolatry is always described as pre-eminently the "sin of Jeroboam," who by it "made Israel to sin." Hence, while in consequence of it the royal house is condemned, the people are still regarded as God's chosen people, to whom, even more than to the inhabitants of the kingdom of Judah, the prophets ministered, and to whom—having no longer the Temple and the consecrated royalty of David, as perpetual witnesses for God—the prophetic ministrations were of pre-eminent importance. Accordingly, the wife of Jeroboam is bidden to approach the prophet disguised as a daughter of the people.

(3) **And take.**—The presentation of this offering, designedly simple and rustic in character, accords with the custom (1 Sam. ix. 7, 8) of approaching the prophet at all times with some present, however trifling. In itself an act simply of homage, it would easily degenerate into the treatment of the prophetic function as a mere matter of merchandise. (See above, chap. xiii. 7.)

(4) **Were set.**—The same word is rendered "were dim" in 1 Sam. iv. 15. The metaphor is evidently

thyself *to be* another? for I *am* sent to thee *with* ¹*heavy tidings.* ⁽⁷⁾ Go, tell Jeroboam, Thus saith the LORD God of Israel, Forasmuch as I exalted thee from among the people, and made thee prince over my people Israel, ⁽⁸⁾ and rent the kingdom away from the house of David, and gave it thee: and *yet* thou hast not been as my servant David, who kept my commandments, and who followed me with all his heart, to do *that* only *which was* right in mine eyes; ⁽⁹⁾ but hast done evil above all that were before thee: for thou hast gone and made thee other gods, and molten images, to provoke me to anger, and hast cast me behind thy back: ⁽¹⁰⁾ therefore, behold, ᵃI will bring evil upon the house of Jeroboam, and will cut off from Jeroboam ᵇhim that pisseth against the wall, *and* him that is shut up and left in Israel, and will take away the remnant of the house of Jeroboam, as a man taketh away dung, till it be all gone. ⁽¹¹⁾ Him that dieth of Jeroboam in the city shall the dogs eat; and him that dieth in the field shall the fowls of the air eat: for the LORD hath spoken *it*. ⁽¹²⁾ Arise thou therefore, get thee to thine own house: *and* when thy feet enter into the city, the child shall die. ⁽¹³⁾ And all Israel shall mourn for him, and bury him: for he only of Jeroboam shall come to the grave, because in him there is found *some* good thing toward the LORD God of Israel in the house of Je-

1 Heb., *hard*.

*a* ch. 15. 29

*b* ch. 21. 21; 2 Kings 9. 8.

---

drawn from the solid opaque look of the iris, when affected by cataract or some similar disease.

⁽⁷, ⁸⁾ **I exalted thee.**—There is throughout a close allusion to Ahijah's prophecy (chap. xi. 31, 37, 38), which promised Jeroboam "a sure house, like that of David," on condition of the obedience of David. The sin of Jeroboam lay in this—that he had had a full probation, with unlimited opportunities, and had deliberately thrown it away, in the vain hope of making surer the kingdom which God's promise had already made sure. The lesson is, indeed, a general one. The resolution to succeed at all hazards, striking out new ways, with no respect for time-honoured laws and principles, is in all revolutions the secret of immediate success and ultimate disaster. But in the Scripture history, here as elsewhere, we are permitted to see the working of God's moral government of the world, unveiled in the inspired declarations of His prophetic messenger.

⁽⁹⁾ **But hast done evil above all that were before thee.**—The language is strong, in the face of the many instances of the worship of false gods in the days of the Judges, and the recent apostasy of Solomon—to say nothing of the idolatry of the golden calf in the wilderness, and the setting up of the idolatrous sanctuaries in olden times at Ophrah and at Dan (Judges viii. 27, xviii. 30, 31). The guilt, indeed, of Jeroboam's act was enhanced by the presumptuous contempt of the special promise of God, given on the sole condition of obedience. In respect of this, perhaps, he is said below—in an expression seldom used elsewhere —to have "cast God Himself behind his back." But probably the reference is mainly to the unprecedented effect of the sin, coming at a critical point in the history of Israel, and from that time onward poisoning the springs of national faith and worship. Other idolatries came and passed away: this continued, and at all times "made Israel to sin."

**Other gods and molten images.**—See in chap. xi. 28 the repetition of the older declaration in the wilderness, "These be thy gods, O Israel." Jeroboam would have justified the use of the calves as simply emblems of the true God; Ahijah rejects the plea, holding these molten images, expressly forbidden in the Law, to be really objects of worship—"other gods,"—as, indeed, all experience shows that such forbidden emblems eventually tend to become. Moreover, from verse 15 it appears that the foul worship of the *Asherah* ("groves") associated itself with the idolatry of Jeroboam.

⁽¹⁰⁾ **Him . . . and him.**—The first phrase is used also in 2 Sam. xxv. 22, 1 Kings xxi. 21, 2 Kings ix. 8, to signify, "every male," implying (possibly with a touch of contempt) that even the lowest should be destroyed. The words following have in the original no conjunction *and* between them. They are in antithesis to each other, signifying in some form two opposite divisions of males. The literal sense seems to be "him who is shut up, or bound, and him who is left loose;" and this phrase has been variously interpreted as "the bond and the free," "the married and the unmarried," "the child" who keeps at home, "and the man" who goes abroad. Perhaps the last of these best suits the context; it is like "the old and young" of Josh. vi. 21, Esther iii. 13, Ezek. ix. 6, &c.

**As a man taketh away dung.**—The same contemptuous tone runs on to the end of the verse. The house of Jeroboam is the filth which pollutes the sacred band of Israel; to its last relics it is to be swept away by the besom of destruction. (Comp. 2 Kings ix. 37; Ps. lxxxiii. 10.)

⁽¹¹⁾ **Him that dieth.**—The same judgment is repeated in chaps. xvi. 4, xxi. 24. (Comp. also Jer. xxxvi. 30.) The "dogs" are the half-wild dogs, the scavengers of every Eastern city; the "fowls of the air" the vultures and other birds of prey. In ancient times the natural horror of insult to the remains of the dead was often intensified by the idea, that in some way the denial of the rites of burial would inflict suffering or privation on the departed soul. Whether such ideas may have lingered in the minds of the Israelites we have no means of knowing. But certainly their whole system of law and ritual was calculated to give due honour to the body in life, as consecrated to God; and this would naturally tend to teach them that the body was a part of the true man, and therefore to deepen the repugnance, with which all reverent feeling regards outrage on the dead.

⁽¹³⁾ **Because in him there is found some good thing.**—There is something singularly pathetic in this declaration of early death, in peace and with due mourning, as the only reward which can be given to piety in the time of coming judgment. It is much like the prophetic declaration to Josiah at the time

roboam. ⁽¹⁴⁾ Moreover the LORD shall raise him up a king over Israel, who shall cut off the house of Jeroboam that day: but what? even now. ⁽¹⁵⁾ For the LORD shall smite Israel, as a reed is shaken in the water, and he shall root up Israel out of this good land, which he gave to their fathers, and shall scatter them beyond the river, because they have made their groves, provoking the LORD to anger. ⁽¹⁶⁾ And he shall give Israel up because of the sins of Jeroboam, who did sin, and who made Israel to sin.

⁽¹⁷⁾ And Jeroboam's wife arose, and departed, and came to Tirzah: *and* when she came to the threshold of the door, the child died; ⁽¹⁸⁾ and they buried him; and all Israel mourned for him, according to the word of the LORD, which he spake by the hand of his servant Ahijah the prophet.

⁽¹⁹⁾ And the rest of the acts of Jeroboam, how he warred, and how he reigned, behold, they *are* written in the book of the chronicles of the kings of Israel. ⁽²⁰⁾ And the days which Jeroboam reigned *were* two and twenty years: and he ¹slept with his fathers, and Nadab his son reigned in his stead.

⁽²¹⁾ And Rehoboam the son of Solomon reigned in Judah. *ᵃRehoboam was*

¹ Heb., *lay down.*

*a* 2 Chron. 12. 13.

---

of the approaching fall of the kingdom of Judah (2 Kings xxii. 18—20). But, at the same time, we find in the Old Testament little indication of that general view of the prevalent sorrow and burden of life, which makes Herodotus, in his celebrated story of Cleobis and Bito (Book i. c. 31), imply that at all times early death is Heaven's choicest blessing. Such a view, indeed, is expressed in such passages as Job iii. 11—22, Eccl. iv. 1—3; but these are clearly exceptional. Life is viewed —sometimes, as in Ps. lxxxviii. 10—12, Isa. xxxviii. 18, 19, even in contrast with the unseen world—as a place of God's favour and blessing, which nothing but man's wilful sin can turn to sorrow. The presence and the penalty of sin are recognised from the day of the Fall onwards, yet as only impairing, and not destroying, man's natural heritage of joy.

⁽¹⁴⁾ **Shall raise him up a king.**—Baasha. (See chap. xv. 27—30.) For, like Jeroboam, he had (see chap. xvi. 2—4) a probation before God, in which he failed, drawing down doom on his house.

**But what? even now.**—The exact meaning of these words has been much disputed. The LXX. renders "and what? even now;" the Vulgate has "in this day and in this time;" the Chaldee Targum, "what is now, and what besides shall be." Modern interpretations vary greatly. On the whole, perhaps, our version gives a not improbable rendering, and a simple and striking sense—"in that day; but what say I? the judgment is even now at hand." (Comp. our Lord's saying in Luke xii. 49: "I am come to send fire on the earth; and what will I, if it be already kindled?")

⁽¹⁵⁾ **And he shall root up Israel.**—The first prophecy of future captivity, and that "beyond the river" (Euphrates), is here pronounced against the kingdom of Israel, on account of their share in the idolatry of Jeroboam, and in the worse abominations of the "groves." Of all such utterances we must remember the express declaration of Jer. xviii. 7, 8: "At what instant I shall speak concerning a nation . . . to pluck up, and to pull down, and to destroy; if that nation . . . turn from their evil, I will repent of the evil that I thought to do unto them." The prophecy uttered does not foreclose the probation of future ages. This is, after all, only one illustration of the great truth that—however impossible it is for us to comprehend the mystery—the foreknowledge of God does not preclude the freedom and responsibility of man.

The metaphor is of the reed shaken to and fro in the river, till at last it is rooted up, swept down the stream, and cast up on some distant shore.

**Their groves.**—The word rendered "grove" is properly *Asherah*, an idol: apparently the straight stem of a tree, surmounted by an emblem of the goddess represented (whence, perhaps, the wrong translation which, from the LXX. and Vulgate, has made its way into our version). (See Exod. xxxiv. 13; Deut. vii. 5, xii. 2; Judges iii. 7, vi. 25, 28, &c.) It is thought to have been an image of some deity like Astarte; and Gesenius infers from the derivation of the name that it was dedicated to her, as the goddess of good fortune. But the worship dates from a far earlier time than the introduction of the worship of the Tyrian Astarte, and the word itself is etymologically distinct from *Ashtoreth* or *Ashtaroth*. It is notable that in 2 Kings xxiii. 15 Josiah is said not only to have destroyed the altar and high places at Bethel, but to have "burned the Asherah;" whence it may probably be concluded that (as is perhaps implied in this passage) the old worship of the Asherah, with all its superstitious and profligate accompaniments, grew up under the very shadow of the newer idolatry. From the worship of images as emblems to superstitious veneration of the images themselves, and thence to worship of many gods, the transition is unhappily only too easy.

⁽¹⁷⁾ **Tirzah.**—From this incidental notice it would seem that Jeroboam had removed his habitation, temporarily or permanently, to Tirzah, a place renowned for beauty (Cant. vi. 4), and farther from the hostile frontier than Shechem. It seems to have continued as the capital till the foundation of Samaria. Its site is generally identified with a spot now called *Tellûzah*, about nine miles north-east of Shechem, still in the high ground of Mount Ephraim.

⁽¹⁹⁾ **And the rest.**—The preceding verse closes the detailed record of Jeroboam's reign. His exaltation and the promise to him, his idolatry and its punishment, are all that the historian cares to narrate. All else is summed up in the words "how he warred" (see below, verse 30, and chap. xv. 6) and "how he reigned." It is probable that his reign was prosperous enough in peace and war, though his attempt to subdue Judah failed. (See 2 Chron. xiii.) But all this the Scriptural record passes over, and only commemorates him as "Jeroboam the son of Nebat, who made Israel to sin."

⁽²¹⁾ **And Rehoboam.**—Here begins the second series of the book—a series of brief annals, touching

*Rehoboam reigns*  I. KINGS, XIV.  *over Judah.*

forty and one years old when he began to reign, and he reigned seventeen years in Jerusalem, the city which the LORD did choose out of all the tribes of Israel, to put his name there. And his mother's name *was* Naamah an Ammonitess.

(22) And Judah did evil in the sight of the LORD, and they provoked him to jealousy with their sins which they had committed, above all that their fathers had done. (23) For they also built them high places, and [8]images, and groves, on every high hill, and under every green tree. (24) And there were also sodomites in the land : *and* they did ac-

1 Or, *standing images*, or, *statues*.

---

only the main points of the history of the kings of Israel and Judah, till the appearance of Elijah (chap. xvii. 1). In respect of the kingdom of Judah, and of Israel so far as it is connected with Judah, it is largely supplemented by the fuller record of the Chronicles (2 Chron. xi.—xvii.).

During this first epoch of the existence of the two kingdoms, including about sixty years, their relations appear to have been incessantly hostile, the aggression being on the side of the kingdom of Israel. In the reign of Rehoboam the invasion of Shishak was probably instigated, perhaps aided, by Jeroboam; subsequently the attack on Abijah, victoriously repelled, seems a direct attempt at subjugation; the same policy in substance is pursued by Baasha, and only checked by the desperate expedient of calling in the foreign power of Syria; till at last, wearied out by continual war against a superior force, Judah, even under such a king as Jehoshaphat, is forced to ally itself, apparently on a footing of something like dependence, with the kingdom of Israel.

(22) **Forty and one years old when he began to reign.**—It has been noticed that the age of forty-one assigned to Rehoboam at his accession, here and in the Chronicles (both in the Hebrew text and the ancient versions) and in the history of Josephus, presents some difficulty in relation to the youth ascribed to him and his companions at the time of his accession; and, moreover, if only forty years are given to Solomon's reign, must throw back his birth to a time when his father must have been very young. It has been accordingly proposed to read "twenty-one" (by a slight change of the Hebrew numerals); but the combined authority supporting the present reading is strong, and the difficulties above noted, though real, are not insurmountable.

**The city which the Lord did choose.**—This emphatic notice is, no doubt, intended to place Jerusalem and its worship in marked contrast with the new capitals and unauthorised sanctuaries which had sprung up. The possession of Jerusalem, with all that was associated with it, was the very life of the little kingdom of Judah, threatened by its more powerful rival and by the neighbouring nations. In Israel one capital succeeded another; Shechem, Tirzah, Samaria, Jezreel, became rival cities. In Judah no city could be for a moment placed on the level of the hallowed city of Jerusalem.

**Naamah an Ammonitess.**—The reference to the queen-mother is almost invariable in the annals of the kings, marking the importance always attaching to it in Eastern monarchies; but the mention (here and in verse 31) of Naamah as an Ammonitess is perhaps significant in relation to the description of the manifold idolatries of Rehoboam. It is curious that the succession should pass without question to the son of another and an earlier wife than Solomon's chief queen, the daughter of Pharaoh.

(22) **Judah did evil.**—From the Chronicles (2 Chron. xi. 17) we gather that, as might have been expected, the judgment which had fallen upon the house of David for idolatry, the rallying of the national feeling round the sacredness of the Temple, and the influx from Israel of the priests and Levites, produced a temporary reaction: "for three years they walked in the way of David and Solomon." With, however, the excitement, and perhaps the sense of danger (2 Chron. xii. 1), this wholesome reaction passed by, and gave way to an extraordinarily reckless plunge into abominations of the worst kind. These are ascribed not, as in the case of Solomon and most other kings, to the action of Rehoboam, but to that of the people at large; for the king himself seems to have been weak, unfit for taking the initiative either in good or evil. The apostasy of Judah was evidently the harvest of the deadly seed sown by the commanding influence of Solomon, under whose idolatry the young men had grown up. It is said to have gone beyond "all that their fathers had done," even in the darkest periods of the age of the Judges : perhaps on the ground that the sins of a more advanced state of knowledge and civilisation are, both in their guilt and in their subtlety, worse than the sins of a semi-barbarous age.

(23) **High places, and images, and groves.**—On the "high places," see chap. iii. 2, and Note there. The "images" of this passage seem undoubtedly to have been stone pillars, as the "groves" (*i.e.*, the asherahs) were wooden stumps of trees (possibly in both cases surmounted by some rude representation of the deity worshipped). The first mention of such a pillar is in Gen. xxviii. 18, xxxi. 13, xxxv. 14, there applied to the stone which Jacob raises and anoints, in order to mark the scene of the vision at Bethel; next, we find repeated commands to destroy them (with the asherahs also) as erected by the Canaanites (Exod. xxiii. 24, xxxiv. 13; Lev. xxvi. 1; Deut. vii. 5, xii. 3), and to suffer neither near the altar of the Lord (Deut. xvi. 21). Like the high places, it seems plain that both might be either unauthorised emblems of God's presence or images of false gods; and, indeed, the stone pillar appears in some cases to be associated with the worship of Baal, as the *Asherah* with that of Ashtoreth. In this passage, from the strength of the language used, and from the notice in verse 24, it seems that the grosser idolatry is referred to. It was practised "on every high hill, and every shady tree"—such trees as were notable for size and shade in the bareness of the hills of Palestine.

(24) **Sodomites.**—See chap. xv. 12; 2 Kings xxiii. 7. There is a horrible significance in the derivation of this word, which is properly "consecrated," or "devoted;" for it indicates the license, and even the sanction, of unnatural lusts in those consecrated to the abominations of Nature-worship. The appearance of such in the land, whether Canaanites or apostate Israelites, is evidently noted as the climax of the infinite corruption which had set in, rivalling—and, if rivalling, exceeding in depth of wickedness—the abominations of the old inhabitants of the land. That such horrors are

cording to all the abominations of the nations which the LORD cast out before the children of Israel.

(25) And it came to pass in the fifth year of king Rehoboam, *that* Shishak king of Egypt came up against Jerusalem: (26) and he took away the treasures of the house of the LORD, and the treasures of the king's house; he even took away all: and he took away all the shields of gold *a* which Solomon had made. (27) And king Rehoboam made in their stead brasen shields, and committed *them* unto the hands of the chief of the ¹guard, which kept the door of the king's house. (28) And it was *so*, when the king went into the house of the LORD, that the guard bare them,

*a* ch. 10. 17.

¹ Heb., *runners.*

and brought them back into the guard chamber.

(29) Now the rest of the acts of Rehoboam, and all that he did, *are* they not written in the book of the chronicles of the kings of Judah? (30) And there was war between Rehoboam and Jeroboam all *their* days. (31) And Rehoboam slept with his fathers, and was buried with his fathers in the city of David. And his mother's name *was* Naamah an Ammonitess. And Abijam his son reigned in his stead.

CHAPTER XV.—(1) Now in the eighteenth year of king Jeroboam the son of Nebat reigned Abijam over Judah. (2) Three years reigned he in Jerusalem.

---

not incompatible with advance in knowledge and material civilisation, history tells us but too plainly. To find them sanctioned under cover of religious ritual marks, however, a lower depth still.

(25) **Shishak.**—His invasion is narrated at greater length in the record of Chronicles (2 Chron. xii. 2—12), which contains a description of his army, and a notice of the preservation of Jerusalem from destruction, though not from surrender, on the repentance of the people at the call of Shemaiah. It records also the taking of "fenced cities," having noticed previously the fortifications of many such "cities of defence" by Rehoboam (2 Chron. xi. 5—10). This record is remarkably confirmed by the celebrated inscription at Karnak (see *Dict. of the Bible*: "SHISHAK") enumerating the conquests of Sheshenk (Shishak), in which names of cities, partly in Judah, partly in Israel, are traced. The latter are Levitical or Canaanitish cities; and it has been conjectured that, much as the Pharaoh of Solomon's day took Gezer and gave it to Israel (see chap. ix. 16), so the Egyptian army, coming as allies of Jeroboam, took, or helped him to take, those cities which were hostile or disloyal to him. It is not unlikely that the whole invasion was instigated by Jeroboam, in that desire to crush the kingdom of Judah which afterwards suggested his war with Abijam. (See 2 Chron. xiii.)

(26) **He even took away all.**—There is a touch of pathos in the description of the utter spoil of the treasures in which Solomon and Israel had gloried, and which now served only to buy off the victorious Egyptians. There is no notice of any sack of Jerusalem, nor, as in later cases, of any desecration of the Temple, or even of the plunder of its decorations. The record seems to imply surrender of the city and its treasures. The idea sometimes advanced, that, like the capture of Rome by the Gauls, the invasion of Shishak destroyed all ancient monuments and archives, has therefore no historical support from this passage; and with it many conclusions derived from it as to the dates of our Scriptural records must pass away.

(27) **In their stead.**—The notice of this substitution is not only a curious point of accurate detail, but perhaps intended as a symbolic representation of the change which had passed upon Judah, by which only the semblance of its old glory remained, and its "fine gold had become brass."

(28) **When the king went.**—Hence we see that Rehoboam still worshipped in the house of the Lord. If his idolatry were like that of his father, it would not have prevented this; but in 2 Chron. xii. 6—8, 12 it is implied that after the invasion he "humbled himself," and returned to the Lord.

(29) **The chronicles of the kings of Judah.** —In 2 Chron. xii. 15 the acts of Rehoboam are said to be "written in the book of Shemaiah the prophet, and of Iddo the seer concerning genealogies."

(30) **There was war . . .**—Of such war we have no record, since the day when Shemaiah forbade Rehoboam's invasion of the new kingdom; nor is there even mention of any action of Israel in aid of the Egyptian attack, although it is likely enough that such action was taken. The meaning may simply be that there was continued enmity, breaking off all peaceful relations; but in the scantiness of the record we can have no certainty that actual war did not take place, though it has found no place in the history.

XV.

The brief annals still continue, although with some details as to the important reign of Asa. It is evident that the attempt on the part of Israel to subjugate Judah continues, still (see 2 Chron. xiv. 9—15) aided by invasion from Egypt; it is checked by Abijah's victory (2 Chron. xiii. 3—20), but not baffled, till by a desperate policy, the foreign power of Syria is invoked, and a serious blow inflicted on Israel.

(1) **Abijam.**—The form of the name given in 2 Chron. xiii., "Abijah," is probably correct, as having a more distinct significance. The variation here, if not (as some think) a mere false reading, may have been made for the sake of distinction from the son of Jeroboam.

(2) **Maachah, the daughter of Abishalom.**—The *Abishalom* of this passage, called, in 2 Chron. xi. 20, *Absalom,* is in all probability the rebel son of David, whose mother (2 Sam. iii. 3) was also named Maachah. In 2 Chron. xi. 21, 22, it seems that of all the wives ("eighteen wives and threescore concubines") whom Rehoboam, following the evil traditions of his father, took, she was the favourite, and that even in his lifetime Rehoboam exalted Abijam "to be ruler among his brethren." In 2 Chron. xiii. 2 she is called Michaiah,

*And his mother's name was Maachah, the daughter of Abishalom. (3) And he walked in all the sins of his father, which he had done before him: and his heart was not perfect with the LORD his God, as the heart of David his father. (4) Nevertheless for David's sake did the LORD his God give him a ¹lamp in Jerusalem, to set up his son after him, and to establish Jerusalem: (5) because David did *that which was* right in the eyes of the LORD, and turned not aside from any *thing* that he commanded him all the days of his life, *b*save only in the matter of Uriah the Hittite. (6) And there was war between Rehoboam and Jeroboam all the days of his life. (7) Now the rest of the acts of Abijam, and all that he did, *are* they not written in the *c*book of the chronicles of the kings of Judah? And there was war between Abijam and Jeroboam. (8) And Abijam slept with his fathers; and they buried him in the city of David: and *d*Asa his son reigned in his stead.

(9) And in the twentieth year of Jeroboam king of Israel reigned Asa over Judah. (10) And forty and one years reigned he in Jerusalem. And his ²mother's name *was* Maachah, the daughter of Abishalom. (11) And Asa did *that which was* right in the eyes of the LORD, as *did* David his father. (12) And he took away the sodomites out of the land, and removed all the idols that his fathers had made. (13) And also *e*Maachah his mother, even her he removed from *being* queen, because she had made an idol in a grove; and Asa ³destroyed her idol, and burnt *it* by the brook Kidron. (14) But the high places

*a* 2 Chron. 11. 22.

B.C. 958.

1 Or, *candle*.

*b* 2 Sam. 11. 4, & 12. 9.

*c* 2 Chron. 13. 3.

*d* 2 Chron. 14. 1.

2 That is, *grandmother's*.

*e* 2 Chron. 15. 16.

3 Heb., *cut off*.

---

and said to be the daughter of "Uriel of Gibeah." This shows that, as indeed chronological considerations would suggest, she must have been the granddaughter of Absalom. She is mentioned below (verse 13) as prominent in the evil propensity to idolatry.

(3) **Walked in all the sins of his father.**—This adoption of the idolatries of Rehoboam did not prevent Abijam (see 2 Chron. xiii. 4—12) from representing himself as the champion of the Temple and the priesthood against the rival worship of Jeroboam, and dedicating treasures—perhaps the spoils of his victory—in the house of the Lord. From the qualified phrase "his heart was not perfect before God," however, it may be inferred that, like Solomon and Rehoboam, he professed to worship Jehovah only as the supreme God of his Pantheon; and it is a curious irony of circumstance that he should be recorded as inveighing against the degradation of His worship in Israel, while he himself countenanced or connived at the worse sin of the worship of rival gods in Judah.

(4) **Give him a lamp in Jerusalem.**—There is here a brief allusion to the victory recorded in the Chronicles, which obviously was the turning-point in the struggle, saving the "lamp" of the house of David from extinction, and "establishing" Jerusalem in security. "For David's sake" is, of course, for the fulfilment of the promise to David (2 Sam. vii. 12—16). In virtue of the continuity of human history, the Divine law always ordains that, in respect of consequences, the good deeds as well as the sins of fathers are "visited on their children."

(5) **Save only in the matter of Uriah.**—In this passage alone do we find this qualification of the praise of David. In the Vatican MS. and other MSS. of the LXX. it is omitted. Possibly it is a marginal note which has crept into the text, or a comment of the compiler of the book on the language of the annals from which he drew.

(6) **And there was war.**—In this verse (omitted in the Vatican MS. of the LXX.) the repetition of the notice of Rehoboam, in spite of some artificial explanations, seems inexplicable. Probably there is error in the text.

(10) **His mother's name was Maachah.**—Maachah was (see verse 2) the wife of Rehoboam, and, therefore, grandmother of Asa. She appears, however, still to have retained the place of "queen-mother," to the exclusion of the real mother of the king.

(11) **Asa did that which was right.**—This reign—happily, a long one—was a turning-point in the history of Judah. Freed from immediate pressure by the victory of Abijah over Jeroboam, Asa resolved—perhaps under the guidance of the prophets Azariah and Hanani (2 Chron. xv. 1, xvi. 7)—to renew the true strength of his kingdom by restoring the worship and trusting in the blessings of the true God, extirpating by repeated efforts the false worships introduced by Rehoboam and continued by Abijah, and solemnly renewing the covenant with the Lord, in the name of the people, and of the strangers from Ephraim, Manasseh, and Simeon, who joined them. Of all this the text here gives but brief notice: the record in the Chronicles (2 Chron. xiv., xv.) contains a detailed account. From the same record we find that he fortified his cities and strengthened his army, and that he was able to repel with great slaughter a formidable invasion from Egypt, under "Zerah the Ethiopian," in his fifteenth year.

(13) **An idol in a grove.**—The original word for "idol"—peculiar to this passage and its parallel (2 Chron. xv. 16)—appears to signify a "horrible abomination" of some monstrous kind; and instead of "in a grove," we should read "for an asherah," the wooden emblem of the Canaanitish deity (on which see chap. xiv. 22). There seems little doubt that some obscene emblem is meant, of the kind so often connected with worship of the productive powers of nature in ancient religions, substituted as a still greater abomination for the ordinary asherah. Clearly the act of Maachah was one of so flagrant a kind, that Asa took the unusual step, on which the historian here lays great stress, of degrading her in her old age from her high dignity, besides hewing down her idol, and burning it publicly under the walls of Jerusalem.

(14) **But the high places were not removed.**—The record of the Chronicles—contrasting 2 Chron. xiv. 5 with xv. 17—indicates with tolerable plainness an

were not removed: nevertheless Asa's heart was perfect with the LORD all his days. ⁽¹⁵⁾ And he brought in the ¹ things which his father had dedicated, and the things which himself had dedicated, into the house of the LORD, silver, and gold, and vessels.

⁽¹⁶⁾ And there was war between Asa and Baasha king of Israel all their days. ᵃ ⁽¹⁷⁾ And Baasha king of Israel went up against Judah, and built Ramah, that he might not suffer any to go out or come in to Asa king of Judah.

⁽¹⁸⁾ Then Asa took all the silver and the gold *that were* left in the treasures of the house of the LORD, and the treasures of the king's house, and delivered them into the hand of his servants: and king Asa sent them to ᵃBen-hadad, the son of Tabrimon, the son of Hezion, king of Syria, that dwelt at Damascus, saying, ⁽¹⁹⁾ *There is* a league between me and thee, *and* between my father and thy father: behold, I have sent unto thee a present of silver and gold; come and break thy league with Baasha king of Israel, that he may ²depart from me.

⁽²⁰⁾ So Ben-hadad hearkened unto king Asa, and sent the captains of the hosts which he had against the cities of Israel, and smote Ijon, and Dan, and Abel-beth-maachah, and all Cinneroth, with all the land of Naphtali. ⁽²¹⁾ And it came to pass, when Baasha heard *there-*

¹ Heb., *holy.*

*a* 2 Chron. 16. 2.

² Heb., *go up.*

---

attempt at this reform on Asa's part, which was not carried out successfully. In spite of all experience of the corruptions inevitably resulting from them, the craving for local and visible sanctuaries, natural at all times, and especially in generations which had been degraded by gross idolatry, proved too strong for even earnest reformers. The historian, writing under the light of later experience, dwells on this imperfection of religious reform again and again.

⁽¹⁵⁾ **Which his father had dedicated.**—These seem to be the spoils of his own victory over the Egyptian army and Abijah's victory over Jeroboam. They replenished for a time the treasury, swept bare in the reign of Rehoboam by the host of Shishak.

⁽¹⁶⁾ **There was war . . .**—According to verse 33, Baasha reigned from the third to the twenty-seventh year of Asa. The phrase, here repeated from chaps. xiv. 30, xv. 67, appears simply to mean that the old hostile relations remained, combined with, perhaps, some border war; for it is expressly said in 2 Chron. xiv. 16, that Asa's first ten years were peaceful, and the open war with Israel did not break out till after the victory over Zerah, in his fifteenth year.

⁽¹⁷⁾ **Built Ramah.**—Ramah, or properly, *the Ramah*—the word signifying only "elevation"—is mentioned in Josh. xviii. 25 as a city of Benjamin, situated (see Jos. *Ant.* viii. 12, 3) about five miles north of Jerusalem. It is mentioned in Judges iv. 5, xix. 13; Isa. x. 29; Jer. xl. 1, and is identified with the village known as *Er-Ram* at the present day.

This fortification of Ramah close to the hostile capital—like the fortification of Decelea, near Athens, in the Peloponnesian war—was a standing menace to Judah. Baasha, who was a military chief, seems to have been warned by the ill-success of former attempts to invade and subjugate Judah, and to have used this easier means of keeping the enemy in check, and provoking a conflict—if a conflict there was to be—on his own ground. The text, however, implies a further design to blockade the road between the kingdoms, perhaps explained by the statement, in 2 Chron. xv. 9, 10, of the falling away of many from Israel to Asa, now in the height of his prosperity. The new fortress was, no doubt, supported by all the military force of Israel, which Asa, in spite of his increased strength, dared not attack.

⁽¹⁸⁾ **Sent them to Ben-hadad.**—This shows that Syria, recovering its independence at the fall of Solomon's empire, was already attaining the formidable power, which so soon threatened to destroy Israel altogether. The Ben-hadad of the text is the grandson of Hezion, who must be the Rezon of chap. xi. 23. Already, as we gather from the next verse, there had been leagues between Syria and Judah in the preceding reign. Now it is clear that Baasha had attempted to supersede these by a closer league—possibly, like Pekah in later times (2 Kings xvi. 5, 6), desiring to strengthen and secure himself against invasion by the subjugation of Judah. Asa naturally resolved to bribe Ben-hadad by presents to prefer the old tie to the new; but he went beyond this, and proposed a combined attack on Israel, for the first time calling in a heathen power against his "brethren, the children of Israel." It was an expedient which, though it succeeded for its immediate purpose, yet both as a desperate policy and an unfaithfulness to the brotherhood, which, in spite of separation and corruption, still bound the two kingdoms in the covenant of God with Abraham, deserved and received prophetic rebuke. (See 2 Chron. xvi. 7—9.) Just so Isaiah, in the days of Ahaz and Hezekiah, denounced the vain trust in confederacies with the neighbouring nations and alliance with Egypt (Isa. xxx. 1—17).

⁽²⁰⁾ **Smote.**—The portion smitten now, as hereafter in the Assyrian invasion (2 Kings xv. 29), is the mountain country near the source of the Jordan, which lay most exposed to the great approach to Israel from the north by "the entering in of Hamath," through the wide valley between Lebanon and Ante-Lebanon, called by the Greeks *Cœle-Syria*.

**Ijon** is only mentioned in these two passages as belonging to the territory of Naphtali. It is supposed to have stood not far from Dan, close to the nearer, but fuller, source of the Jordan, in a position of great natural beauty and some strength, identified with the modern *Tel-Dibbin*.

**Abel-beth-Maachah** (see 2 Sam. xx. 14. 15) ("the meadow of the house of Maachah"), or (2 Chron. xvi. 4) *Abel-maim* ("the meadow upon the waters"), lay probably in the marshy ground north of the water of Merom.

**Cinneroth** or *Chinneroth*, is the name afterwards corrupted into Gennesareth, signifying evidently a region in the neighbourhood of the lake.

⁽²¹⁾ **Dwelt in Tirzah**—that is, returned to his own capital: in the first instance, of course, retiring to meet

*of*, that he left off building of Ramah, and dwelt in Tirzah.

(22) Then king Asa made a proclamation throughout all Judah; none *was* ¹exempted: and they took away the stones of Ramah, and the timber thereof, wherewith Baasha had builded; and king Asa built with them Geba of Benjamin, and Mizpah.

(23) The rest of all the acts of Asa, and all his might, and all that he did, and the cities which he built, *are* they not written in the book of the chronicles of the kings of Judah? Nevertheless in the time of his old age he was diseased in his feet. (24) And Asa slept with his fathers, and was buried with his fathers in the city of David his father: and ᵃJehoshaphat his son reigned in his stead.

(25) And Nadab the son of Jeroboam ²began to reign over Israel in the second year of Asa king of Judah, and reigned over Israel two years. (26) And he did evil in the sight of the LORD, and walked in the way of his father, and in his sin wherewith he made Israel to sin.

(27) And Baasha the son of Ahijah, of the house of Issachar, conspired against him; and Baasha smote him at Gibbethon, which *belonged* to the Philistines; for Nadab and all Israel laid siege to Gibbethon. (28) Even in the third year of Asa king of Judah did Baasha slay him, and reigned in his stead. (29) And it came to pass, when he reigned, *that* he smote all the house of Jeroboam; he left not to Jeroboam any that breathed, until he had destroyed him, according unto ᵇthe saying of the LORD, which he spake by his servant Ahijah the Shilonite: (30) because of the sins of Jeroboam which he sinned, and which he made Israel sin, by his provocation wherewith he provoked the LORD God of Israel to anger.

(31) Now the rest of the acts of Nadab, and all that he did, *are* they not written in the book of the chronicles of the kings of Israel? (32) And there was war between Asa and Baasha king of Israel all their days.

(33) In the third year of Asa king of Judah began Baasha the son of Ahijah

¹ Heb., *free.*
ᵃ Matt. 1. 8, called *Josaphat.*
² Heb., *reigned.*
ᵇ ch. 14. 10.

---

the new enemy in the north, and then obliged to give up his attempt against Asa. From chap. xx. 34, it seems as if, till the time of Ahab, Syria retained its conquests and a certain supremacy over Israel. Baasha may have had to buy peace by undertaking to leave unmolested Judah, which might be considered a tributary of Syria.

(22) **Throughout all Judah.**—Asa was not content to destroy or occupy the hostile fortress, but pushed his own fortifications further on. Geba, named in Josh. xxi. 17 as a city of the priests, in the territory of Benjamin, the scene of Jonathan's victory over a Philistine garrison in the days of Samuel (1 Sam. xiii. 3)—identified with the modern *Jeba*—lies on the edge of a valley some distance to the north. It is noted in 2 Kings xxiii. 8 as still the northern outpost of the kingdom of Judah. The Mizpah here referred to—for there were many places so called—a city of Benjamin (Josh. xviii. 26), famous in the earlier history (see 1 Sam. vii. 5—13, x. 17—25), seems to have been situated at the place afterwards called *Scopim* ("the watchtower"), on "the broad ridge which forms the continuation of the Mount of Olives to the north and east, from which the traveller gains his first view" of Jerusalem (*Dict..of the Bible*: MIZPAH).

(23) **All his might.**—This phrase, not used of Rehoboam or Abijah, is significant, indicating the increased power of Judah under Asa.

**The cities which he built.**—Fortification of cities (see 2 Chron. xi. 5—10, xiv. 6) was naturally the traditional policy of the kingdom of Judah—small in extent, menaced by more powerful neighbours, but having an exceedingly strong country and central position.

**Diseased in his feet.**—In the Chronicles it is added significantly, "in his disease he sought not to the Lord, but to the physicians" (2 Chron. xvi. 7—12); and from the same records it appears that in his last days Asa ventured to defy the prophetic authority by the imprisonment of Hanani the seer. Prosperity, it is implied, had somewhat deteriorated his character, though he still continued faithful to the worship of God. Certainly, Jehoshaphat on his accession still found much to do for the religious condition of his people.

(26) **Did evil in the sight of the Lord.**—This constantly-recurring phrase signifies (as, indeed, the context here shows) perseverance in the idolatrous system introduced by Jeroboam.

(27) **Baasha**, sprung from an obscure tribe, hardly at any time distinguished in the history, and himself, as it would seem (chap. xvi. 2), of low origin in it, is the first of the many military chiefs who by violence or assassination seized upon the throne of Israel. The constant succession of ephemeral dynasties stands in striking contrast with the unchanged royalty of the house of David, resting on the promise of God.

**Gibbethon**—a Levitical town in the territory of Dan (Josh. xix. 44, xxi. 23), probably, like other places in that region, still held by the Philistines till their subjugation by David. The text here implies a revolt of the Philistines against the enfeebled power of Israel, and the occupation of Gibbethon, commanding a pass from the plain of Sharon to the interior. The siege must have been fruitless, at least of any permanent result; for twenty-six years after we find Gibbethon still in the hands of the enemy. (See chap. xvi. 15.)

(29) **According unto the saying of the Lord.** —See chap. xiv. 10—14. There seems no reason to suppose that Baasha had any formal mission of vengeance, or that his conspiracy and assassination were due to any motive but his own ambition. The contrary,

to reign over all Israel in Tirzah, twenty and four years. (34) And he did evil in the sight of the Lord, and walked in the way of Jeroboam, and in his sin wherewith he made Israel to sin.

CHAPTER XVI.—(1) Then the word of the Lord came to Jehu the son of Hanani against Baasha, saying, (2) Forasmuch as I exalted thee out of the dust, and made thee prince over my people Israel; and thou hast walked in the way of Jeroboam, and hast made my people Israel to sin, to provoke me to anger with their sins; (3) behold, I will take away the posterity of Baasha, and the posterity of his house; and will make thy house like *a* the house of Jeroboam the son of Nebat. (4) *b* Him that dieth of Baasha in the city shall the dogs eat; and him that dieth of his in the fields shall the fowls of the air eat.

(5) Now the rest of the acts of Baasha, and what he did, and his might, *are* they not written in the *c* book of the chronicles of the kings of Israel? (6) So Baasha slept with his fathers, and was buried in Tirzah: and Elah his son reigned in his stead.

(7) And also by the hand of the prophet Jehu the son of Hanani came the word of the Lord against Baasha, and against his house, even for all the evil that he did in the sight of the Lord, in provoking him to anger with the work of his hands, in being like the house of Jeroboam; and because he killed him.

(8) In the twenty and sixth year of Asa king of Judah began Elah the son of Baasha to reign over Israel in Tirzah, two years. (9) And his servant Zimri, captain of half *his* chariots, conspired against him, as he was in Tirzah, drinking himself drunk in the house of Arza ¹steward of *his* house in Tirzah. (10) And Zimri went in and smote him, and killed him, in the twenty and seventh year of Asa king of Judah, and reigned in his stead.

(11) And it came to pass, when he began to reign, as soon as he sat on his throne, *that* he slew all the house of Baasha: he left him not one that pisseth against a wall, ²neither of his kinsfolks, nor of his friends. (12) Thus did Zimri destroy all the house of Baasha, according to the word of the Lord, which he spake against Baasha ³ by Jehu the prophet, (13) for all the sins of Baasha, and the sins of Elah his son, by which they sinned, and by which they made Israel to sin, in provoking the Lord God of Israel to anger with their vanities.

(14) Now the rest of the acts of Elah, and all that he did, *are* they not written in the book of the chronicles of the kings of Israel?

(15) In the twenty and seventh year of Asa king of Judah did Zimri reign seven

---

*a* ch. 15. 29.

*b* ch. 14. 11.

*c* 2 Chron. 16. 1.

B.C. cir. 930.

¹ Heb., *which was over.*

² Or, *both his kinsmen and his friends.*

³ Heb., *by the hand of.*

---

indeed, may be inferred from the declaration of chap. xvi. 7, that the judgment on Baasha was in part "because he killed" Nadab and his house. Sin which works out God's purpose is not the less truly sin. Of Baasha we know nothing, except his attempt on the independence of Judah, and its failure (verses 16—22).

### XVI.

The brief record continues of the troubled times of civil war and foreign danger in Israel, to which, perhaps, the tranquillity of Judah under Asa was partly due.

(1) **Jehu the son of Hanani**—probably of Hanani the seer of Judah in the reign of Asa (2 Chron. xv. 7). Jehu must have been now young, for we find him rebuking Jehoshaphat after the death of Ahab, and writing the annals of Jehoshaphat's reign (2 Chron. xix. 2, xx. 34).

(2) **Forasmuch as I exalted thee . . .**—The prophecy—closely resembling that of Ahijah against Jeroboam—clearly shows that Baasha had a probation, which he neglected; and it seems to be implied in verse 7 that his guilt was enhanced by perseverance in the very sins for which, by his hand, so terrible a vengeance had been inflicted.

(7) **And also.**—This second reference to the prophecy of Jehu seems to be a note of the historian—perhaps added chiefly for the sake of the last clause, which shows that Baasha's act, though foretold, was not thereby justified.

(9) **Drinking himself drunk.**—There seems an emphasis of half-contemptuous condemnation in the description of Elah's debauchery, evidently public, and in the house of a mere officer of his household, while war was raging at Gibbethon. On the other hand, Zimri—noted emphatically as "his servant"—was apparently the high officer left in special charge of the palace and the king's person, while the mass of the army was in the field. Hence his name passed into a proverb for unusual treachery. (See 2 Kings ix. 31.)

(13) **Vanities**—that is, *idols* (as in Deut. xxxii. 21; 1 Sam. xii. 21; Ps. xxxi. 6; Isa. xli. 29; Jer. viii. 19; &c.): not only the idols of Dan and Bethel, but the worse abominations which grew up under cover of these. In the Old Testament generally the contempt for idolatry and false worship as a gross folly, wasting faith on unrealities, is at least as strong as the condemnation of them, as outraging God's law, and connected with sensual or bloody rites. (See, for example, the utter scorn of Isa. xliv. 9—20; Ps. cxv. 4—8.)

days in Tirzah. And the people *were* encamped against Gibbethon, which belonged to the Philistines. (16) And the people *that were* encamped heard say, Zimri hath conspired, and hath also slain the king: wherefore all Israel made Omri, the captain of the host, king over Israel that day in the camp. (17) And Omri went up from Gibbethon, and all Israel with him, and they besieged Tirzah. (18) And it came to pass, when Zimri saw that the city was taken, that he went into the palace of the king's house, and burnt the king's house over him with fire, and died, (19) for his sins which he sinned in doing evil in the sight of the LORD, in walking in the way of Jeroboam, and in his sin which he did, to make Israel to sin. (20) Now the rest of the acts of Zimri, and his treason that he wrought, *are* they not written in the book of the chronicles of the kings of Israel? (21) Then were the people of Israel divided into two parts: half of the people followed Tibni the son of Ginath, to make him king; and half followed Omri. (22) But the people that followed Omri prevailed against the people that followed Tibni the son of Ginath: so Tibni died, and Omri reigned. (23) In the thirty and first year of Asa king of Judah began Omri to reign over Israel, twelve years: six years reigned he in Tirzah. (24) And he bought the hill Samaria of Shemer for two talents of silver, and built on the hill, and called the name of the city which he built, after the name of Shemer, owner of the hill, ¹Samaria. (25) But Omri

¹ Heb., *Shomeron*.

---

(16) **Made Omri . . . king.**—This exaltation of Omri, as a matter of course, shows how entirely the kingdom of Israel had become the prize of the sword. By a curious coincidence (see chap. xv. 27) the dynasty of Baasha had been founded in the camp before the same city of Gibbethon. Zimri's conspiracy appears to have been hastily planned, with no provision of adequate means of support; for Tirzah is taken at once.

(18) **The palace of the king's house.**—The same phrase is found in 2 Kings xv. 25. The word here rendered "palace" evidently means (as is clear from its derivation) "the high place," or "citadel," of the building. Some render it the "harem," with which the curious rendering (ἄντρον) of the LXX.—signifying properly a cave or "lurking-place"—may perhaps, agree. But this is not suggested by the word itself. This desperate act of Zimri, which has many parallels in Eastern history, seems to indicate that there was held to be something especially treasonable, and therefore unpardonable, in his assassination of Elah. (See verse 20, and 2 Kings ix. 31.)

(19) **In walking in the way of Jeroboam.**—The use here of this constantly-recurring phrase probably indicates only the historian's sense of the curse lying on the whole kingdom from its idolatry, which Zimri did not attempt to repudiate; unless, perhaps, his conspiracy had clothed itself under pretence of a righteous zeal for the fulfilment of the prophecy of Jehu (verses 3, 4), and had thrown off the religious pretence after the deed was done. For except in this way, he had no time for "walking in the way of Jeroboam."

(21) **Tibni.**—Of him we know nothing. No doubt he also was a military chief—possibly Zimri's colleague, under the supreme command of Omri—and the LXX. speaks of a brother, Joram, who fought and fell with him. There is an ominous significance in the terse description of the alternatives of fortune in this internecine struggle, "so Tibni died, and Omri reigned." By comparison of verse 23 with verse 15, it appears that the struggle had lasted four years.

(23) **Began Omri to reign over Israel.**—The accession of Omri after this long civil war opened a new epoch of more settled government and prosperity for about forty-eight years. Omri had (as appears from chap. xx. 34) to purchase peace with Syria by some acknowledgment of sovereignty and cession of cities. He then allied himself with the royal house of Tyre, probably both for strength against Syria, and for revival of the commercial prosperity of the days of Solomon, and proceeded to found a new capital in a strong position. That he was a warrior is indicated by the phrase, "the might that he shewed." Probably, like Jeroboam and Baasha, he also had his opportunity of restoring the spiritual strength of his people by returning to the pure worship of God, and threw it away, doing "worse than all who were before him."

(24) **Built on the hill.**—Omri only followed the usual practice of a new dynasty in the East, of which Jeroboam had set an example at Shechem, and probably Baasha at Tirzah. Possibly the seeds of disaffection may have still lurked in Tirzah, the place of Zimri's conspiracy, and (as has been conjectured) of Tibni's rival power. But the site of Samaria must have been chosen by a soldier's eye. Its Hebrew name (*Shomerôn*) means a "watch-tower," and may well have had a double derivation, from its natural position, as well as from its owner's name. Its position was one of great beauty, and, in the warfare of those days, of singular strength, as is shown by the long sieges which it withstood (1 Kings xx. 1; 2 Kings vi. 24, xvii. 5, xviii. 9, 10). It lay north-west of Shechem, on an isolated hill with precipitous sides, rising in the middle of a basin of the hills of Ephraim, not far from the edge of the maritime plain, and commanding a view of the sea. Its history vindicated the sagacity of its founder. Even after its destruction and depopulation by the Assyrians, it seems to have revived, for Alexander took it on his invasion of Palestine, and placed a Greek colony there. Again destroyed by John Hyrcanus, it was rebuilt by Herod, and called *Sebaste*, in honour of Augustus. In the Assyrian inscriptions it is known as *Beth-Khumri* ("the house of Omri").

(25) **Did worse than all that were before him.**—This phrase, used of Jeroboam in chap. xiv. 9, may indicate, in addition to the acceptance and development of the old idolatry, some anticipation of the

wrought evil in the eyes of the LORD, and did worse than all that *were* before him. ⁽²⁶⁾ For he walked in all the way of Jeroboam the son of Nebat, and in his sin wherewith he made Israel to sin, to provoke the LORD God of Israel to anger with their vanities.

⁽²⁷⁾ Now the rest of the acts of Omri which he did, and his might that he shewed, *are* they not written in the book of the chronicles of the kings of Israel? ⁽²⁸⁾ So Omri slept with his fathers, and was buried in Samaria: and Ahab his son reigned in his stead.

⁽²⁹⁾ And in the thirty and eighth year of Asa king of Judah began Ahab the son of Omri to reign over Israel: and Ahab the son of Omri reigned over Israel in Samaria twenty and two years. ⁽³⁰⁾ And Ahab the son of Omri did evil in the sight of the LORD above all that *were* before him. ⁽³¹⁾ And it came to pass, ¹as if it had been a light thing for him to walk in the sins of Jeroboam the son of Nebat, that he took to wife Jezebel the daughter of Ethbaal king of the Zidonians, and went and served Baal, and worshipped him. ⁽³²⁾ And he reared up an altar for Baal in the house of Baal, which he had built in Samaria. ⁽³³⁾ And Ahab made a grove; and Ahab did more to provoke the LORD God of Israel to anger than all the kings of Israel that were before him.

⁽³⁴⁾ In his days did Hiel the Beth-elite build Jericho: he laid the foundation thereof in Abiram his firstborn, and set up the gates thereof in his youngest *son* Segub, *ᵃaccording to the word of the LORD, which he spake by Joshua the son of Nun.

CHAPTER XVII.—⁽¹⁾ And ²Elijah the Tishbite, *who was* of the inhabitants

---

1 Heb., *was it a light thing, &c.*

a Josh. 6. 26.

2 Heb. *Elijahu*; Luke 4. 25, he is called *Elias*.

---

worse idolatry of Baal, formally introduced by Ahab. The "statutes of Omri" are referred to by Micah (chap. vi. 16) in parallelism with the "works of the house of Ahab," as the symbol of hardened and hopeless apostasy.

(31) **Ethbaal, king of the Zidonians.**—The mention of Ethbaal, clearly the *Eithobalus* of Menander (see Jos. *against Apion* i. 18), affords another comparison of Israelite with Tyrian history. He is said to have assassinated Pheles, king of Tyre, within fifty years after the death of Hiram, and to have founded a new dynasty. He was a priest of Astarte, and it is notable that he is called, not, like Hiram, "king of Tyre," but "king of the Sidonians," thus reviving the older name of "the great Zidon," which had been superseded by Tyre. His priestly origin, and possibly also this revival of the old ideas and spirit of the Phœnician race, may account for the fanatic devotion to Baal visible in Jezebel and Athaliah, which stands in marked contrast with the religious attitude of Hiram (1 Kings v. 7; 2 Chron. ii. 12). The marriage of Ahab with Jezebel was evidently the fatal turning-point in the life of a man physically brave, and possibly able as a ruler, but morally weak, impressible in turn both by good and by evil. The history shows again and again the contrast of character (which it is obvious to compare with the contrast between Shakespeare's Macbeth and Lady Macbeth), and the almost complete supremacy of the strong relentless nature of Jezebel.

2. The Baal here referred to is, of course, the Zidonian god, worshipped as the productive principle in nature, in conjunction with Astarte, the female or receptive principle. The name itself only signifies "Lord" (in which sense, indeed, it is applied, in Hosea ii. 16, to Jehovah Himself), and is marked as being a mere title, by the almost invariable prefix of the article. Being, therefore, in no sense distinctive, it may be, and is, applied to the supreme god of various mythologies. Thus we find that in Scripture the plural Baalim is first used, of "the gods many and lords many" of Canaanitish worship (see Judges ii. 11, iii. 7, x. 6; 1 Sam. vii. 4); and we have traces of the same vague use in the Baal-peor of Numbers xxv., the Baal-berith of Judges viii. 33, ix. 4, the Baal-zebub of 2 Kings i. 2, 3, and in the various geographical names having the prefix Baal. The worship of the Phœnician Baal—variously represented, sometimes as the Sun, sometimes as the planet Jupiter, sometimes half-humanised as the "Tyrian Hercules"—was now, however, introduced on a great scale, with profuse magnificence of worship, connected with the Asherah ("grove"), which in this case, no doubt, represented the Phœnician Astarte, and enforced by Jezebel with a high hand, not without persecution of the prophets of the Lord. The conflict between it and the spiritual worship of Jehovah became now a conflict of life and death.

(34) **Did Hiel . . . build Jericho.**—This marks both the growth of prosperity and power, and the neglect of the old curse of Joshua (Josh. vi. 26). The place had not, it would appear, been entirely deserted. (See Judges iii. 13; 2 Sam. x. 5.) But it was now made —what it continued to be even down to the time of Herod—an important place. Its natural advantages were great. It stood in a position well watered, and accordingly of great beauty and fruitfulness ("the city of palm trees"), and was, moreover, a city of military consequence, as commanding the pass from the valley of the Jordan to the high ground of Ai and Bethel. Having been assigned to Benjamin (Josh. xviii. 21), it should have properly belonged to the kingdom of Judah. Its being rebuilt by a Bethelite, evidently under the patronage of Ahab, is one of the indications of a half-dependent condition of the Southern kingdom at this time.

### XVII.

With this chapter begins the third section of the book, marked by a complete change in the character of the history. Drawn evidently not from official annals, but from records of the lives of the last of the elder line of prophets, Elijah and Elisha—probably preserved in the prophetic schools—it becomes detailed and graphic, full of a spiritual beauty and instructiveness,

*Elijah fed*          I. KINGS, XVII.          *by Ravens.*

of Gilead, said unto Ahab, *[a] As* the LORD God of Israel liveth, before whom I stand, there shall not be dew nor rain these years, but according to my word.

(2) And the word of the LORD came unto him, saying, (3) Get thee hence, and turn thee eastward, and hide thyself by the brook Cherith, that *is* before Jordan. (4) And it shall be, *that* thou shalt drink of the brook; and I have commanded the ravens to feed thee there. (5) So he went and did according unto the word of the LORD: for he went and dwelt by the brook Cherith, that *is* before Jordan. (6) And the ravens brought him bread and flesh in the morning, and bread and flesh in the evening; and he drank of the brook. (7) And it came to pass [1]after a while, that the brook dried up, because there had been no rain in the land.

(8) And the word of the LORD came unto him, saying, (9) Arise, get thee to *[b]* Zarephath, which *belongeth* to Zidon, and

[a] Ecclus. 48. 3; James 5. 17.
[1] Heb., *at the end of days.*
[b] Luke 4. 26, called *Sarepta.*

---

which have stamped it on the imagination of all succeeding ages. The two great prophets themselves stand out as two distinct types of the servants of God. Elijah's mission, one of narrow and striking intensity, is embodied in his name—"My God is Jehovah." Appearing at the great crisis of the conflict against the sensual and degrading Baal-worship, he is not a teacher or a law-giver, or a herald of the Messiah, but simply a warrior of God, bearing witness for Him by word and by deed, living a recluse ascetic life, and suddenly emerging from it again and again to strike some special blow. The "spirit of Elias," well expressing itself in the indignant expostulation at Mount Carmel, has become proverbial for its stern and fiery impatience of evil, wielding the sword of vengeance in the slaughter at the Kishon, and calling down fire from heaven to repel the attack of earthly force. It is high and noble, but not the highest spirit of all. It breathes the imperfection of the ancient covenant, adapted to the "hardness of men's hearts," leading to alternations of impetuosity and despondency, but doing the special work as, perhaps, no calm and well-balanced character could have done. Elisha builds on the ground which Elijah had cleared, filling a place hardly equalled since the days of Samuel, as a teacher and guide both of king and people. His very miracles, with one exception, are miracles of kindliness and mercy, helping the common life from which Elijah held aloof. It is impossible not to see in him a true, though imperfect type, of the greater than Elias, who was to come.

Chapter xvii. contains the one scene of domestic affection and rest in the stormy career of Elijah. Its abrupt beginning—though it suits well the suddenness of the appearances of Elijah—is probably due to quotation of some original document.

(1) **Elijah the Tishbite of the inhabitants of Gilead.**—The most probable rendering of this disputed passage is that of the LXX., and virtually of Josephus, "Elijah the Tishbite of Tishbe in Gilead," the last words being added to distinguish the place from a Tishbe (or Thisbe) in Naphtali, referred to, though the reading is rather doubtful, in Tobit i. 2. The word here rendered "inhabitants" (properly "sojourners") is evidently of the same derivation as the word rendered "Tishbite." The only alternative would be to render "the stranger of the strangers of Gilead," which has been adopted by some, as suggesting a startling and impressive origin of the great prophet. But it is doubtful whether the Hebrew will bear it.

**Gilead**—properly "the rocky region" that lay on the east of Jordan, between the Hieromax and the valley of Heshbon (although the name is often more widely used). Open to the desert on the east, and itself comparatively wild, with but few cities scattered through it, it suited well the recluse dweller in the wilderness.

**The Lord God of Israel before whom I stand.**—This adjuration (repeated in xviii. 15, and with some alteration by Elisha in 2 Kings iii. 14; v. 16) is characteristic. Elijah is the servant of God, standing to be sent whither He wills.

This is evidently not the first appearance of Elijah. In James v. 17, the withholding of rain, foretold again and again as a penalty on apostasy (see Lev. xxvi. 19, Deut xi. 17; and comp. 1 Kings viii. 35), is noted as an answer to the prophet's prayer, calling down judgment on the land. Evidently there had been a struggle against the Baal-worship of the time, and, no doubt, previous warnings from Elijah or from some one of the murdered prophets. This chapter introduces us suddenly to the catastrophe.

(3) **The brook Cherith**—properly "the torrent (or valley) Cherith, facing the Jordan;" evidently one of the ravines running into the Jordan valley; probably on the east from the prophet's own land of Gilead.

(4) **The ravens.**—Of the accuracy of this rendering, which is that of almost all the ancient versions and of Josephus, there can be little doubt. The singularly prosaic interpretations, substituted for this striking and significant record of miracle by some ancient and modern writers (adopting slight variations of the Hebrew vowel points) — such as "Arabs," "merchants," "inhabitants of a city Orbi or the rock Oreb"— seem to have arisen simply from a desire to get rid of what seemed a strange miracle, at the cost (be it observed) of substituting for it a gross improbability; for how can it be supposed that such regular sustenance by human hands of the persecuted prophet could have gone on in the face of the jealous vigilance of the king? But it is idle to seek to explain away one wonder in a life and an epoch teeming with miracles. It is notable, indeed, that the critical period of the great Baal apostasy, and of the struggle of Elijah and Elisha against it, is the second great epoch of recorded miracle in the Old Testament—the still more critical epoch of Moses and Joshua being the first. It is hardly less idle to determine that this or that miracle is so improbable, as to introduce any difficulty of acceptance which does not apply to miracles in general.

(9) **Zarephath**—the *Sarepta* of the LXX. and of the New Testament (Luke iv. 26). It is said by Josephus to have lain between Tyre and Sidon, and by St. Jerome to have been on the great coast-road. Hence it has been identified with a modern village, *Surafend*, in that position. The words, "which belongeth to Zidon," appear to be emphatic, marking the striking providence of God, which, when the land of Israel was

*The Meal and the Oil.*      I. KINGS, XVII.      *Raising the Widow's Son.*

dwell there: behold, I have commanded a widow woman there to sustain thee. <sup>(10)</sup> So he arose and went to Zarephath. And when he came to the gate of the city, behold, the widow woman *was* there gathering of sticks: and he called to her, and said, Fetch me, I pray thee, a little water in a vessel that I may drink. <sup>(11)</sup> And as she was going to fetch *it*, he called to her, and said, Bring me, I pray thee a morsel of bread in thine hand. <sup>(12)</sup> And she said, *As* the LORD thy God liveth, I have not a cake, but an handful of meal in a barrel, and a little oil in a cruse: and, behold, I *am* gathering two sticks, that I may go in and dress it for me and my son, that we may eat it and die. <sup>(13)</sup> And Elijah said unto her, Fear not; go *and* do as thou hast said: but make me thereof a little cake first, and bring *it* unto me, and after make for thee and for thy son. <sup>(14)</sup> For thus saith the LORD God of Israel, The barrel of meal shall not waste, neither shall the cruse of oil fail, until the day *that* the LORD <sup>1</sup>sendeth rain upon the earth. <sup>(15)</sup> And she went and did according to the saying of Elijah: and she, and he, and her house, did eat <sup>2</sup>*many* days. <sup>(16)</sup> *And* the barrel of meal wasted

B.C. cir. 910.

1 Heb., *giveth.*

2 Or, *a full year.*

3 Heb., *by the hand of.*

4 Heb., *measured.*

5 Heb., *into his inward parts.*

not, neither did the cruse of oil fail, according to the word of the LORD, which he spake <sup>3</sup> by Elijah.

<sup>(17)</sup> And it came to pass after these things, *that* the son of the woman, the mistress of the house, fell sick; and his sickness was so sore, that there was no breath left in him. <sup>(18)</sup> And she said unto Elijah, What have I to do with thee, O thou man of God? art thou come unto me to call my sin to remembrance, and to slay my son? <sup>(19)</sup> And he said unto her, Give me thy son. And he took him out of her bosom, and carried him up into a loft, where he abode, and laid him upon his own bed. <sup>(20)</sup> And he cried unto the LORD, and said, O LORD my God, hast thou also brought evil upon the widow with whom I sojourn, by slaying her son? <sup>(21)</sup> And he <sup>4</sup>stretched himself upon the child three times, and cried unto the LORD, and said, O LORD my God, I pray thee, let this child's soul come <sup>5</sup>into him again. <sup>(22)</sup> And the LORD heard the voice of Elijah; and the soul of the child came into him again, and he revived. <sup>(23)</sup> And Elijah took the child, and brought him down out of the chamber into the house, and delivered him unto his mother: and

---

apostate and unsafe, found for the prophet a refuge and a welcome in a heathen country, which was moreover the native place of his deadliest enemy.

(12) **I have not a cake.**—The famine may have already extended to Phœnicia; for there, according to Menander, it lasted for a year; or, since the country depended upon Israel for supplies, the distress may have been only the reflex effect of the famine in Israel.

**As the Lord thy God liveth.**—The phrase indicates a recognition of Elijah as a prophet of Jehovah the God of Israel, but probably (as, indeed, seems to be implied by the use of the words "thy God") no acknowledgment of Him as yet by the woman herself, such as the neighbouring heathen (as, for example, Hiram in the days of Solomon) often yielded.

(15) **The barrel of meal wasted not.**—The miracle is doubly remarkable. First, in this instance, as in the similar miracles of Elisha and of our Lord Himself, we see that God's higher laws of miracle, like the ordinary laws of His providence, admit within their scope the supply of what we should consider as homely and trivial needs—in this respect perhaps contradicting what our expectation would have suggested. Next, that it is a miracle of multiplication, which is virtual creation—not necessarily out of nothing—doing rapidly and directly what, under ordinary laws, has to be done slowly and by indirect process.

(18) **O thou man of God.**—The terms of the address (contrasted with verse 12), indicate a natural growth in the recognition of the true God by the woman, through familiar intercourse with the prophet, and experience of his wonder-working power. For it is the adoption of the regular Israelitish description of the prophet as her own. (See Judges xiii. 6; chaps. xii. 22, xiii. 1.)

**To call my sin to remembrance, and to slay my son?**—The words express the unreasonableness of natural sorrow. The underlying idea is that of the exclamation, "Depart from me, for I am a sinful man, O Lord." The better knowledge of God, gained through the presence of the prophet, had, of course, brought out in her a deeper sense of sin, and now makes her feel that her sorrow is a just punishment. With pathetic confusion of idea, she cries out against his presence, as if it were the actual cause of judgment on the sin, which it has simply brought home to her conscience.

(20) **Hast thou also brought evil.**—Elijah's complaint is characteristic of the half-presumptuous impatience seen more fully in chap. xix. He apparently implies that his own lot, as a hunted fugitive not protected by God's Almighty power, is so hard, that it must be his presence which has brought trouble even on the home that sheltered him.

(21) **He stretched himself upon the child.**—To suppose that this implies merely the use of some natural means of reviving the dead, is simply to explain the whole description away. The idea in this passage (as in 2 Kings iv. 34, xiii. 21, and, perhaps, Acts xx. 10) clearly is of a certain healing "virtue," attaching in measure to the person of the prophets, as without measure it belonged to our Lord Himself (Luke viii. 45, 46). But it is to be noted that in the case of the prophet, the power to heal or raise

Elijah said, See, thy son liveth. (24) And the woman said to Elijah, Now by this I know that thou *art* a man of God, *and* that the word of the LORD in thy mouth *is* truth.

CHAPTER XVIII.—(1) And it came to pass *after* many days, that the word of the LORD came to Elijah in the third year, saying, Go, shew thyself unto Ahab; and I will send rain upon the earth. (2) And Elijah went to shew himself unto Ahab. And *there was* a sore famine in Samaria.

(3) And Ahab called ¹Obadiah, which *was* ²the governor of *his* house. (Now Obadiah feared the LORD greatly: (4) for it was so, when ³Jezebel cut off the prophets of the LORD, that Obadiah took an hundred prophets, and hid them by fifty in a cave, and fed them with bread and water.) (5) And Ahab said unto Obadiah, Go into the land, unto all fountains of water, and unto all brooks: peradventure we may find grass to save the horses and mules alive, ⁴that we lose not all the beasts. (6) So they divided the land between them to pass throughout it: Ahab went one way by himself, and Obadiah went another way by himself.

(7) And as Obadiah was in the way, behold, Elijah met him: and he knew him, and fell on his face, and said, *Art* thou that my lord Elijah? (8) And he answered him, I *am*: go, tell thy lord, Behold, Elijah *is* here. (9) And he said, What have I sinned, that thou wouldest deliver thy servant into the hand of Ahab, to slay me? (10) *As* the LORD thy God liveth, there is no nation or kingdom, whither my lord hath not sent to seek thee: and when they said, He *is* not there; he took an oath of the kingdom

1 Heb., *Obadiahu.*
2 Heb., *over his house.*
3 Heb., *Izebel.*
4 Heb., *that we cut not off ourselves from the beasts.*

---

up is made distinctly conditional on prayer, "the Lord heard the voice of Elijah."

(24) **Now by this I know . . .**—In these words we trace the final victory of faith, brought out by the crowning mercy of the restoration of her son. First, the widow had spoken of Jehovah from without, as "the Lord thy God" (verse 14); next, had come to recognise Him as God (verse 18); now she not only believes, as she had never believed before, that His servant is "a man of God"; but, in accepting the "word of Jehovah" in his mouth as "the truth," seems undoubtedly to express conversion to Him. (Compare the stages of faith in the nobleman at Capernaum, John iv. 47, 50, 53.)

XVIII.

In this and the succeeding chapter we pass from the domestic and peaceful simplicity of the quiet refuge at Zarephath to a grand description, first, of the struggle and victory of the great warrior of God, then of his momentary failure and rebuke—brought out to our generation with fresh dramatic beauty by the glorious music in which it has been clothed by the genius of Mendelssohn. The narrative of this chapter, full of picturesque vividness and graphic touches of detail, shows in every line the record of an eye-witness of facts; yet, like all great historical scenes, it is symbolical, typifying the victorious conflict of unaided simple spiritual power against the pomp and material force of the world, of the one man who knows and feels his mission from God against the many, only half persuaded of their superstitions, and of the religion of the God of righteousness and truth against the base and sensual worship of physical power. The latter chapter, perhaps even more sublime, is in a graver and more solemn strain. It marks the reaction after triumph in a character of impulsive and vehement earnestness, looking for visible and immediate victory, and, while it foretells the continuance of his struggle through other hands, teaches the higher lesson of the subtler power of the "still small voice" of spiritual influence.

(1) **The third year.**—By the accurate tradition, preserved in Luke iv. 25, James v. 17, it would seem that the drought lasted "three years and six months." If, therefore, the expression in the text is to be taken literally, it must be reckoned from the beginning of the visit to Zarephath.

(3) **Obadiah.**—The name ("servant of Jehovah") here corresponds to the character of the man. It is curiously significant of the hesitating and temporising attitude of Ahab, that, while Jezebel is suffered to persecute, a high officer in the court is able to profess openly the service of Jehovah, and secretly to thwart the cruelty of the queen. In his heart Ahab always seems to acknowledge the true God, but is overborne by the commanding and ruthless nature of Jezebel.

(4) **Jezebel cut off the prophets.**—The persecution here referred to, in which for the first time the royal power was placed in distinct antagonism to the prophetic order, is only known by this allusion. It may probably have followed on the denunciation of judgment; and Elijah's retirement to Cherith and Zarephath may have been a means of escape from it. If Elijah's oft-repeated phrase, "I, even I, alone remain," is to be taken literally, Obadiah's merciful interposition must have availed only for a time, or have simply given opportunity of escape.

(7) **Art thou that . . .**—The sense is either (as the LXX. has it) "Is it thy very self, my lord Elijah?" or (perhaps more suitably to the context), "Thou here, my lord Elijah," when all seek thy life? The prophet's answer is still simpler in its original brevity, "Behold, Elijah!" standing in dignified contrast with the humble and almost servile address of Obadiah, which is clearly the offspring not only of reverence, but of fear.

(10) **There is no nation.**—This unremitting search —implying perhaps some supremacy or authority over neighbouring kingdoms—suits ill with the half-hearted enmity of Ahab. No doubt it was the work of Jezebel, in Ahab's name, connived at (as in the murder of Naboth) by his timidity.

and nation, that they found thee not. ⁽¹¹⁾ And now thou sayest, Go, tell thy lord, Behold, Elijah *is here*. ⁽¹²⁾ And it shall come to pass, *as soon as* I am gone from thee, that the Spirit of the LORD shall carry thee whither I know not; and *so* when I come and tell Ahab, and he cannot find thee, he shall slay me: but I thy servant fear the LORD from my youth. ⁽¹³⁾ Was it not told my lord what I did when Jezebel slew the prophets of the LORD, how I hid an hundred men of the LORD's prophets by fifty in a cave, and fed them with bread and water? ⁽¹⁴⁾ And now thou sayest, Go, tell thy lord, Behold, Elijah *is here*: and he shall slay me. ⁽¹⁵⁾ And Elijah said, *As* the LORD of hosts liveth, before whom I stand, I will surely shew myself unto him to day.

⁽¹⁶⁾ So Obadiah went to meet Ahab, and told him: and Ahab went to meet Elijah. ⁽¹⁷⁾ And it came to pass, when Ahab saw Elijah, that Ahab said unto him, *Art* thou he that troubleth Israel? ⁽¹⁸⁾ And he answered, I have not troubled Israel; but thou, and thy father's house, in that ye have forsaken the commandments of the LORD, and thou hast followed Baalim. ⁽¹⁹⁾ Now therefore send, *and* gather to me all Israel unto mount Carmel, and the prophets of Baal four hundred and fifty, and the prophets of the groves four hundred, which eat at Jezebel's table. ⁽²⁰⁾ So Ahab sent unto all the children of Israel, and gathered the prophets together unto mount Carmel.

⁽²¹⁾ And Elijah came unto all the people, and said, How long halt ye between two ¹opinions? if the LORD *be* God, follow him: but if Baal, *then* follow him. And the people answered him not a word.

⁽²²⁾ Then said Elijah unto the people, I, *even* I only, remain a prophet of the LORD; but Baal's prophets *are* four hundred and fifty men. ⁽²³⁾ Let them therefore give us two bullocks; and let them choose one bullock for themselves, and cut it in pieces, and lay *it* on wood, and put no fire *under*: and I will dress the other bullock, and lay *it* on wood, and put no fire *under*: ⁽²⁴⁾ and call ye

1 Or, *thoughts.*

---

⁽¹²⁾ **The Spirit of the Lord shall carry thee.**—In this phrase there is perhaps a survival of the original physical sense of the word "Spirit"—the whirlwind which is "the breath of the Lord." (Comp. 2 Kings ii. 16; Acts viii. 39.) To Obadiah it seemed that only by such miraculous agency could Elijah have been removed from the persecution for so long a time, and that, having emerged for a moment, he will be swept away into his hidden refuge again.

⁽¹⁷⁾ **Art thou . . .**—Probably (as in verse 7) the rendering should be, "Thou here, the troubler of Israel!"—defying vengeance (that is) in the very land which thou hast troubled.

⁽¹⁸⁾ **Baalim**—that is, as usual, "the Baalim"—the phrase being probably used contemptuously for false gods generally, the Baal, the Asherah, and perhaps other Canaanitish idols, being included.

⁽¹⁹⁾ **Carmel.**—The word signifies a "garden" or "park" (see Isa. xxix. 17, xxxii. 15, 16, &c.) and, when used for the proper name of the mountain, has commonly the article. Mount Carmel—rightly called "the park," well planted and watered, of central Palestine—is a limestone ridge, with deep ravines thickly wooded, running north-west for about twelve miles from the central hills of Manasseh, so as to form the south side of the bay of Ptolemais, and almost to reach the sea, leaving, however, a space round which the southern armies constantly poured into the plain of Jezreel. It varies from 600 feet to 1,700 feet in height. Near its higher eastern extremity there is a place still called *El Maharrakah*, "the burning," in view of the plain and city of Jezreel, and commanding from one point a glimpse of the sea, which is the traditional (and highly probable) scene of Elijah's sacrifice. Carmel is previously mentioned in Josh. xix. 26, as falling to Asher, and the existence of the altar of the Lord shows that, as was natural, it was made one of the "high places," and, indeed, it appears to have been known as such even to the heathen. In the prophetic writings it is referred to as proverbial for its luxuriant pasturage and beauty. (See Isa. xxxiii. 9; Jer. iv. 26; Amos i. 2, ix. 3; Cant. vii. 6.) No more striking scene could well be found for the great drama of this chapter.

**The prophets of the groves** (*Asherah*) . . .—These, being probably the devotees of the female deity Astarte, seem to have been especially favoured by the queen. It is, however, to be noted that, in spite of Elijah's challenge, they do not appear at all in the subsequent scene. (See verses 22, 40.)

⁽²¹⁾ **How long halt ye between two opinions?**—In this exclamation is expressed the very motto of Elijah's life. It is that of righteous impatience of the "halting" (*i.e.*, limping to and fro) "between two opinions—at all times more dangerous, because more easy, than open apostasy—which was evidently characteristic of Ahab, and probably of the mass of the people. It might have suited well the accommodating genius of such polytheism as had been brought into Israel since the days of Solomon himself, but was utterly incompatible with the sole absolute claim of the worship of Jehovah. Perhaps Jezebel would have scorned it equally for Baal. Compare the indignant expostulation of Ezekiel (Ezek. xx. 31, 39). The question, once clearly understood, is always unanswerable, and is listened to here in awestruck silence.

⁽²⁴⁾ **And call ye on the name of your gods.**—This gift of a "sign from heaven"—not unfamiliar to Israelite experience (see Lev. ix. 24; 1 Chron. xxi. 26; 2 Chron. vii. 1)—which may not, as our Lord

*Elijah and the*      I. KINGS, XVIII.      *Prophets of Baal.*

on the name of your gods, and I will call on the name of the LORD: and the God that answereth by fire, let him be God. And all the people answered and said, ¹It is well spoken. ⁽²⁵⁾ And Elijah said unto the prophets of Baal, Choose you one bullock for yourselves, and dress *it* first; for ye *are* many; and call on the name of your gods, but put no fire *under*. ⁽²⁶⁾ And they took the bullock which was given them, and they dressed *it*, and called on the name of Baal from morning even until noon, saying, O Baal, ²hear us. But *there was* no voice, nor any that ³answered. And they ⁴leaped upon the altar which was made. ⁽²⁷⁾ And it came to pass at noon, that Elijah mocked them, and said, Cry ⁵aloud: for he *is* a god; either ⁶he is talking, or he ⁷is pursuing, or he is in a journey, *or* peradventure he sleepeth, and must be awaked. ⁽²⁸⁾ And they cried aloud, and cut themselves

1 Heb., *The word is good.*
2 Or, *answer.*
3 Or, *heard.*
4 Or, *leaped up and down at the altar.*
5 Heb., *with a great voice.*
6 Or, *he meditateth.*
7 Heb., *hath a pursuit.*
8 Heb., *poured out blood upon them.*
9 Heb., *ascending.*
10 Heb., *attention.*
a Gen. 32. 28; 2 Kings 17. 34.

after their manner with knives and lancets, till ⁸the blood gushed out upon them. ⁽²⁹⁾ And it came to pass, when midday was past, and they prophesied until the *time* of the ⁹offering of the *evening* sacrifice, that *there was* neither voice, nor any to answer, nor any ¹⁰that regarded.

⁽³⁰⁾ And Elijah said unto all the people, Come near unto me. And all the people came near unto him. And he repaired the altar of the LORD *that was* broken down. ⁽³¹⁾ And Elijah took twelve stones, according to the number of the tribes of the sons of Jacob, unto whom the word of the LORD came, saying, ᵃIsrael shall be thy name: ⁽³²⁾ and with the stones he built an altar in the name of the LORD: and he made a trench about the altar, as great as would contain two measures of seed. ⁽³³⁾ And he put the wood in order, and cut the bullock in pieces, and laid *him* on the wood, and said, Fill four

---

teaches us (Matt. xii. 38, 39, xvi. 1—4), be craved for or demanded as a ground of faith, is, like all other miracles, granted unasked when it is seen by God's wisdom to be needed, in order to startle an ignorant and misguided people into serious attention to a message from heaven. In this instance the worship of Baal was a worship of the power of Nature, impersonated perhaps in the sun; and the miracle therefore entered (so to speak) on the visible sphere, especially usurped in his name, in order to claim it for the Lord Jehovah.

⁽²⁶⁾ **O Baal, hear us.**—This repeated cry—the ever-recurring burden of the prayer, uttered probably first in measured chant, afterwards in a wild excited cry—stands in an instructive contrast (which has been splendidly emphasised in Mendelssohn's music) with the simple, earnest solemnity of the prayer of Elijah. It has been obvious to see in it an illustration of our Lord's condemnation of the worship of the heathen, who "think that they shall be heard for their much speaking" (Matt. vi. 7). There is a grave irony in the notice of the blank silence which followed this frenzied cry. "There was no voice, nor any to answer, nor any that regarded."

**They leaped upon**—properly, *leaped up and down at the altar*, in one of those wild dances, at once expressing and stimulating frenzy, in which Oriental religions delight, even to this day.

⁽²⁷⁾ **Elijah mocked them.**—The mockery of Elijah —apparently even blunter and more scornful in the sense of the original—has been with over-ingenuity explained as applying to various supposed actions of Baal. It is merely the bitter irony of sheer contempt, calling Baal a god only to heap upon him ideas most ungodlike; "He is busy, or he is in retirement; he is far away, or in the noon-day heat he is asleep." Characteristic of the fierce indignation of Elijah's nature, in this crisis of conflict, it is yet not unlike the righteous scorn of the psalmists or the prophets (see Pss. cxv. 4—8, cxxxv. 15—18; Isa. xliv. 9—20, xlvi. 1—7; Jer. x. 2—10, &c.)

for the worship of "the vanities" of the heathen. There was no place for toleration of prejudice, or tender appreciation of a blind worship feeling after God, like that of St. Paul at Athens (Acts xvii. 22, 23). The conflict here was between spiritual worship and a foul, cruel idolatry; and the case was not of heathen ignorance, but of Israel's apostasy.

⁽²⁸⁾ **Lancets**—should be *lances*. This self-mutilation, common in Oriental frenzy, was possibly a portion, or a survival, of human sacrifice, in the notion that self-torture and shedding of human blood must win Divine favour—a delusion not confined to heathen religions, though excusable only in them.

⁽²⁹⁾ **They prophesied**—*raved in their frenzy*; like Saul in the hour of madness (1 Sam. xviii. 10), or of overpowering religious excitement (1 Sam. xix. 20—24). As a rule, not perhaps without some rare exceptions, the true prophetic inspiration, even if felt as overmastering the will (see Jer. xx. 7—9), gave no place to frenzy. "The spirits of the prophets are subject to the prophets."

⁽³⁰⁾ **The altar of the Lord**—evidently referred to as well known, and here accepted by Elijah as having a true sacredness. The exclusive consecration of the appointed sanctuary at Jerusalem, if ever as yet thoroughly recognised, was now obviously broken down by the religious severance of Israel.

⁽³¹⁾ **Twelve stones.**—The emphatic notice of these, as emblematical of the twelve tribes, is significant. In spite of political division, and even religious separation, the tribes were still united in the covenant of God.

⁽³²⁾ **Measures.**—The "measure," the third part of the ephah, hence also often called *shalish* (a "tierce," or "third"), was something less than three gallons. A trench to contain only six gallons seems too insignificant for the context; hence it is supposed that the sense is "large enough for the sowing (as in a furrow) of two measures of seed."

⁽³³⁾ **Fill four barrels**—or pitchers. The filling of these at the time of drought has naturally excited

*Elijah's Sacrifice.*  I. KINGS, XVIII.  *Death of the Prophets.*

barrels with water, and pour *it* on the burnt sacrifice, and on the wood. <sup>(34)</sup> And he said, Do *it* the second time. And they did *it* the second time. And he said, Do *it* the third time. And they did *it* the third time. <sup>(35)</sup> And the water <sup>1</sup>ran round about the altar; and he filled the trench also with water.

<sup>(36)</sup> And it came to pass at *the time of* the offering of the *evening* sacrifice, that Elijah the prophet came near, and said, LORD God of Abraham, Isaac, and of Israel, let it be known this day that thou *art* God in Israel, and *that* I *am* thy servant, and *that* I have done all these things at thy word. <sup>(37)</sup> Hear me, O LORD, hear me, that this people may know that thou *art* the LORD God, and *that* thou hast turned their heart back again. <sup>(38)</sup> Then the fire of the LORD fell, and consumed the burnt sacrifice,

1 Heb., *went.*

2 Or, *apprehend.*

3 Or, *a sound of a noise of rain.*

and the wood, and the stones, and the dust, and licked up the water that *was* in the trench.

<sup>(39)</sup> And when all the people saw *it*, they fell on their faces: and they said, The LORD, he *is* the God; the LORD, he *is* the God. <sup>(40)</sup> And Elijah said unto them, <sup>2</sup>Take the prophets of Baal; let not one of them escape. And they took them: and Elijah brought them down to the brook Kishon, and slew them there.

<sup>(41)</sup> And Elijah said unto Ahab, Get thee up, eat and drink; for *there is* <sup>3</sup>a sound of abundance of rain. <sup>(42)</sup> So Ahab went up to eat and to drink. And Elijah went up to the top of Carmel; and he cast himself down upon the earth, and put his face between his knees, <sup>(43)</sup> and said to his servant, Go up now, look toward the sea. And he

---

speculation. A ready surmise, by those unacquainted with the country, was that the water was taken from the sea flowing at the base of Carmel; but a glance at the position and the height of the mountain puts this not unnatural surmise out of the question, as difficult, if not impossible. Examination of the locality has discovered a perennial spring in the neighbourhood of the traditional scene of the sacrifice, which is never known to fail in the severest drought. From this, no doubt (as indeed Josephus expressly says), the water was drawn, with, of course, the object of precluding all idea of fraud or contrivance, and bringing out strikingly the consuming fierceness of the fire from heaven, so emphatically described in verse 38.

<sup>(36)</sup> **Lord God of Abraham.**—In this solemn and earnest invocation of God, as in Exod. iii. 15, vi. 2, 3, the name JEHOVAH, describing God as He is in Himself—the One eternal self-existent Being—is united with the name which shows His special covenant with "Abraham, and Isaac, and Israel." In His own nature incomprehensible to finite being, He yet reveals Himself in moral and spiritual relations with His people, through which they "know that which passeth knowledge." The prominence of the name "Jehovah," thrice repeated in this short prayer of Elijah, is significant as of the special mission, symbolised in his very name, so also of his immediate purpose. He desires to efface himself. The God of Israel is to show Himself as the true worker, not only in the outer sphere by miracle, but in the inner sphere by that conversion of the hearts of the people, which to the prophet's eye is already effected. Like his antitype in the New Testament, Elijah is but a voice calling on men "to prepare the way of the Lord."

<sup>(39)</sup> **They fell on their faces.**—Exactly as in Lev. ix. 24, at the inauguration of the sacrifices of the new Tabernacle by the fire from heaven, with the characteristic addition of the cry, "Jehovah; He, and He only, is God."

<sup>(40)</sup> **Slew them.**—This ruthless slaughter of Baal's prophets, as a judgment on their idolatry and perversion of the people, belongs alike to the fierce righteousness of the character of Elijah, and to the spirit of the old Law. (See, for example, Deut. xiii. 6—18, xvii. 2—7.) The law was adapted (as in the terrible crucial example of the slaughter of the Canaanites) to the "hardness of men's hearts." In the imperfect moral and religious education of those times, it did not recognise the difference between moral and political offences punishable by human law, and the religious sin or apostasy which we have been taught to leave to the judgment of God alone; and it enjoined an unrelenting severity in the execution of righteous vengeance, which would be morally impossible to us, who have been taught to hate the sin, and yet spare, as far as possible, the sinner. The frequent quotation of such examples by Christians—of which Luke ix. 54 is the first example —is a spiritual anachronism. In this particular case, however, it is also to be remembered that those slain were no doubt implicated in the persecution headed by Jezebel, and that the Baal-worship was a licentious and perhaps bloody system. Elijah, presiding over the slaughter which dyed the waters of the Kishon with blood, felt himself the avenger of the slaughtered prophets, as well as the instrument of the judgment of God.

<sup>(41)</sup> **Get thee up, eat and drink.**—There seems a touch of scorn in these words. Ahab, remaining passive throughout, had descended to the place of slaughter in the valley, looking on silent—if not unmoved—while the priests, whose worship he had openly or tacitly sanctioned, were slain by hundreds. Now Elijah bade him get up to his palace, taking it for granted that, fresh from that horrible sight, he is yet ready to feast, and rejoice over the approaching removal of the judgment, which alone had told on his shallow nature. The king goes to revel, the prophet to pray.

<sup>(42)</sup> **Put his face between his knees.**—The attitude is, of course, one of prayer, but is a peculiar attitude — distinct from the ordinary postures of standing and kneeling — which has been noted as existing still among the modern dervishes. Possibly it is characteristic of the vehement excitement of the moment, and of the impulsive nature of Elijah.

<sup>(43)</sup> **Go again seven times.**—From this delay of the answer to prayer Elijah's example became pro-

went up, and looked, and said, *There is nothing.* And he said, Go again seven times. ⁽⁴⁴⁾ And it came to pass at the seventh time, that he said, Behold, there ariseth a little cloud out of the sea, like a man's hand. And he said, Go up, say unto Ahab, ¹Prepare *thy chariot,* and get thee down, that the rain stop thee not. ⁽⁴⁵⁾ And it came to pass in the mean while, that the heaven was black with clouds and wind, and there was a great rain. And Ahab rode, and went to Jezreel. ⁽⁴⁶⁾ And the hand of the LORD was on Elijah; and he girded up his loins, and ran before Ahab ²to the entrance of Jezreel.

CHAPTER XIX.—⁽¹⁾ And Ahab told Jezebel all that Elijah had done, and withal how he had slain all the prophets with the sword. ⁽²⁾ Then Jezebel sent a messenger unto Elijah, saying, So let the gods do *to me,* and more also, if I make not thy life as the life of one of them by to morrow about this time. ⁽³⁾ And when he saw *that,* he arose, and went for his life, and came to Beersheba, which *belongeth* to Judah, and left his servant there.

⁽⁴⁾ But he himself went a day's journey into the wilderness, and came and sat down under a juniper tree: and he requested ³for himself that he might die; and said, It is enough; now, O LORD, take away my life; for I *am* not better than my fathers. ⁽⁵⁾ And as he lay and slept under a juniper tree, behold, then an angel touched him, and said unto

¹ Heb., *Tie, or, Bind.*
² Heb., *till thou come to Jezreel.*
³ Heb., *for his life.*

---

verbial for intensity and perseverance in supplication (James v. 17). The contrast is remarkable between the immediate answer to his earlier prayer (see verses 36, 37) and the long delay here. The one was for the sake of the people; the other for some lesson—perhaps of humility and patience—to Elijah himself. When the answer does come, it fulfils itself speedily. The "little cloud" becomes all but immediately (for so "in the mean while" should be rendered) a storm blackening the whole heavens, borne by a hurricane from the west.

⁽⁴⁵⁾ **Jezreel.**—This is the first mention of the city Jezreel, a city of Issachar (Josh. xix. 18), as a royal city. The name (signifying "Jehovah hath sown") was applied to the whole of the rich plain, the garden and battlefield of northern Palestine. (See Judges vi. 33: 1 Sam. xxix. 1; 2 Sam. ii. 9.) The city was made a royal residence by Ahab, as Samaria by Omri. It stands in a position of some strength and great beauty, supplied by unfailing springs of water, visible from Carmel, and commanding views east and west far over the plain.

⁽⁴⁶⁾ **The hand of the Lord was on Elijah**—in a striking reaction of enthusiastic thankfulness after the stern calmness of his whole attitude throughout the great controversy, and his silent earnestness of prayer. At the head of the people he brings the king, conquered, if not repentant, home in triumph. To our conception of a prophet this frenzied excitement seems strange. Nor could it have belonged to a Samuel, an Elisha, or an Isaiah. In the simple and enthusiastic warrior of God it is natural enough.

XIX.

⁽¹, ²⁾ There is a certain grandeur of fearlessness and ruthlessness in the message of Jezebel, which marks her character throughout, and places it in striking contrast with the vacillating impressibility of Ahab, whom she treats with natural scorn. (See xxi. 7.) Ahab, as before, remains passive; he has no courage, perhaps no wish, to attack Elijah, before whom he had quailed; but he cares not, or dares not, to restrain Jezebel. She disdains to strike secretly and without warning: in fact, her message seems intended to give the opportunity for a flight, which might degrade Elijah in the eyes of the people. We note that the prophet (see chap. xviii. 46) had not ventured to enter Jezreel till he should know how his deadly foe would receive the news of the great day at Carmel.

⁽³⁾ **He arose, and went for his life.**—The sudden reaction of disappointment and despondency, strange as it seems to superficial observation, is eminently characteristic of an impulsive and vehement nature. His blow had been struck, as he thought, triumphantly. Now the power of cool unrelenting antagonism makes itself felt, unshaken and only embittered by all that had passed. On Ahab and the people he knows that he cannot rely; so once more he flees for his life.

**Beer-sheba.** (See Gen. xxi. 14, 33, xxii. 19, xxviii. 10, xlvi. 1, &c.)—This frontier town of Palestine to the south is little mentioned after the patriarchal time. The note that "it belonged to Judah" is, perhaps, significant. Judah was now in half-dependent alliance with Israel; even under Jehoshaphat, Elijah might not be safe there, though his servant—traditionally the son of the widow of Zarephath—might stay without danger.

⁽⁴⁾ **Juniper tree.**—A sort of broom, found abundantly in the desert. It has been noted that its roots were much prized for charcoal, the "coal" of verse 6.

**I am not better than my fathers.**—The exclamation is characteristic. Evidently he had hoped that he himself was "better than his fathers" as a servant of God—singled out beyond all those that went before him, to be the victorious champion of a great crisis, "he, and he alone" (chaps. xviii. 22, xix. 10—14). Now he thinks his hope vain, and sees no reason why he should succeed when all who went before have failed. Why, he asks, should he live when the rest of the prophets have died?

⁽⁵⁾ **An angel touched him.**—The word may signify simply "a messenger," human or super-human; but the context suggests a miraculous ministration of some unearthly food. It is notable that, except as ministers of God in the physical sphere (as in 2 Sam. xxiv. 16, 17; 2 Kings xix. 35), the angels, whose appearances are so often recorded in earlier days, hardly appear during the prophetic period, as though the place of their spiritual ministry, as messengers of God, to the people had been supplied by the prophetic mission. Here, and in 2 Kings

*Elijah in the Wilderness,*     I. KINGS, XIX.     *and on Mount Horeb.*

him, Arise *and* eat. <sup>(6)</sup> And he looked, and, behold, *there was* a cake baken on the coals, and a cruse of water at his ¹head. And he did eat and drink, and laid him down again. <sup>(7)</sup> And the angel of the LORD came again the second time, and touched him, and said, Arise *and* eat; because the journey *is* too great for thee. <sup>(8)</sup> And he arose, and did eat and drink, and went in the strength of that meat forty days and forty nights unto Horeb the mount of God.

<sup>(9)</sup> And he came thither unto a cave, and lodged there; and, behold, the word of the LORD *came* to him, and he said unto him, What doest thou here, Elijah? <sup>(10)</sup> And he said, I have been very jealous for the LORD God of hosts: for the children of Israel have forsaken thy covenant, thrown down thine altars, and slain thy prophets with the sword; and *a*I, *even* I only, am left; and they seek

1 Heb., *bolster.*

*a* Rom. 11. 3.

my life, to take it away. <sup>(11)</sup> And he said, Go forth, and stand upon the mount before the LORD. And, behold, the LORD passed by, and a great and strong wind rent the mountains, and brake in pieces the rocks before the LORD; *but* the LORD *was* not in the wind: and after the wind an earthquake; *but* the LORD *was* not in the earthquake: <sup>(12)</sup> and after the earthquake a fire; *but* the LORD *was* not in the fire: and after the fire a still small voice. <sup>(13)</sup> And it was *so*, when Elijah heard *it*, that he wrapped his face in his mantle, and went out, and stood in the entering in of the cave. And, behold, *there came* a voice unto him, and said, What doest thou here, Elijah? <sup>(14)</sup> And he said, I have been very jealous for the LORD God of hosts: because the children of Israel have forsaken thy covenant, thrown down thine altars, and slain thy prophets

---

vi. 17, the angel is but auxiliary to the prophet, simply ministering to him in time of danger and distress, as the angel of the Agony to the Prophet of prophets.

<sup>(6)</sup> **And laid him down.**—There is a pathetic touch in the description of the prophet, wearied and disheartened, as caring not to eat sufficiently, and glad, after a morsel eaten, to forget himself again in sleep.

<sup>(8)</sup> **Forty days and forty nights.**—Unless this time includes, as has been supposed by some, the whole journey to and from Horeb, and the sojourn there, it is far in excess of what would be recorded for a journey of some two hundred miles. It may, therefore, be thought to imply an interval of retirement for rest and solitary meditation, like the sojourn of Moses in Horeb, and the sojourn of our Lord in the wilderness (Exod. xxiv. 18; Matt. iv. 2) during which the spirit of the prophet might be calmed from the alternations of triumph and despondency, to receive the spiritual lesson which awaited him. During all that time he went "in the strength" of the Divine food, that he might know that "man doth not live by bread alone, but by every word that proceedeth out of the mouth of God" (Deut. viii. 3).

<sup>(9)</sup> **A cave.**—This is properly, "the cave"—perhaps a reference to some cave already well known, as connected with the giving of the Law on Mount Sinai, or perhaps only an anticipatory reference to the cave which Elijah's sojourn was to make famous.

**The word of the Lord came to him.**—The connection suggests that this message came to him in vision or dream at night. The LXX. implies this distinctly by inserting in verse 11 the word "to-morrow," which is also found in the rather vague and prosaic paraphrase of the passage in Josephus. What Elijah replies in imagination in the vision, he repeats next day in actual words.

<sup>(10)</sup> **And he said.**—The reply to the implied reproof is one of impatient self-exculpation and even remonstrance. He himself (it says) had been very jealous for the Lord; yet the Lord had not been jealous for Himself, suffering this open rebellion of the people, the slaughter of His prophets, the persecution to death of the one solitary champion left. What use is there in further striving, if he is left unsupported and alone? The complaint is like that of Isaiah (lxiv. 1), "O that thou wouldest rend the heavens and come down!" The zeal for God's glory, as imperilled by His long-suffering, is like that of Jonah (iv. 1—3); the impatience of the mysterious permission of evil, like that rebuked in the celebrated story of Abraham and the Fire-worshipper. In the Elias of the New Testament there is something of the same despondent impatience shown in the message from prison to our Lord: 'Art Thou He that should come, or look we for another?'"

<sup>(11)</sup> **And, behold.**—In the LXX., the whole of this verse, couched in the future, is made part of the "word of the Lord." But our version is probably correct.

The whole of the vision, which is left to speak for itself, without any explanation or even allusion in the subsequent message to Elijah, is best understood by comparison with two former manifestations at Horeb, to the people and to Moses (Exod. xix. 16—18; xxxiv. 5—8). To the people the Lord had then been manifested in the signs of visible power, the whirlwind, the earthquake, and the fire—first, because these were the natural clothing of the terrors of the Law, which is the will of God visibly enforced; next, because for such visible manifestations of God, and perhaps for these alone, the hearts of Israel were then prepared. To Moses, in answer to his craving for the impossible vision of the glory of the Lord face to face, the manifestation granted was not of the Divine majesty, but of the "Name of the Lord," "the Lord God, merciful and gracious, longsuffering and abundant in goodness and truth;" for this higher conception of the majesty of God, as shown in righteousness and mercy, Moses, as being the greatest of prophets, could well understand. The vision of Elijah stands out in contrast with the one and in harmony with the other. It disclaims the visible manifestation in power and vengeance, for which he had by implication craved; it

*Elijah on Mount Horeb.*     I. KINGS, XIX.     *He meets Elisha.*

with the sword; and I, *even* I only, am left; and they seek my life, to take it away. <sup>(15)</sup> And the LORD said unto him, Go, return on thy way to the wilderness of Damascus: and when thou comest, anoint Hazael *to be* king over Syria: <sup>(16)</sup> and Jehu the son of Nimshi shalt thou anoint *to be* king over Israel: and *ª* Elisha the son of Shaphat of Abel-meholah shalt thou anoint *to be* prophet in thy room. <sup>(17)</sup> And *ᵇ* it shall come to pass, *that* him that escapeth the sword of Hazael shall Jehu slay: and him that escapeth from the sword of Jehu shall Elisha slay. <sup>(18)</sup> *ᶜ* Yet ¹I have left *me* seven thousand in Israel, all the knees which have not bowed unto Baal, and every mouth which hath not kissed him. <sup>(19)</sup> So he departed thence, and found Elisha the son of Shaphat, who *was* plowing *with* twelve yoke *of oxen* before him, and he with the twelfth: and Elijah passed by him, and cast his mantle upon him. <sup>(20)</sup> And he left the oxen, and ran after Elijah, and said, Let me, I pray thee, kiss my father and my mother, and *then* I will follow thee. And he said unto him, ²Go back again: for what have I done to thee? <sup>(21)</sup> And he returned back from him, and took a yoke of oxen, and slew them, and boiled their flesh with the instruments of the

*a* Luke 4. 27, called *Eliseus.*

*b* 2 Kings 9. 1, 3; Ecclus. 48. 8.

*c* Rom. 11. 4.

¹ Or, *I will leave.*

² Heb., *Go, return.*

---

implies in "the still small voice"—"the voice (as the LXX. has it) of a light breath"—a manifestation like that expressed plainly to Moses, of the higher power of the Spirit, penetrating to the inmost soul, which the terrors of external power cannot reach. The lesson is simply, "Not by might, nor by power, but by my Spirit saith the Lord of hosts" (Zech. iv. 6). The prophet so far reads it that he acknowledges, by veiled face of reverence, the presence of the Lord in "the still small voice," yet, with singular truth to nature, he is recorded as repeating, perhaps mechanically, his old complaint.

<sup>(15)</sup> **Go, return.**—The charge conveys indirectly a double rebuke. His cry of disappointment, "Lord . . . I am not better than my fathers," implying that he stood out beyond all others, to meet the stern requirements of the time, is met by the charge to delegate the task of vengeance for God to others; the complaint, "I, even I alone, am left," by the revelation of the faithful remnant—the seven thousand who had not bowed to Baal—unknown to him, perhaps to one another, but known and loved by God.

<sup>(16)</sup> **And Jehu.**—Of this charge Elijah fulfilled in person but one part, in the call of Elisha: for the fulfilment of the other two parts, see 2 Kings viii. 8 —13; ix. 1—6. This apparently imperfect correspondence of the event to the charge, is a strong indication of the historical character of the narrative.

The history, indeed, records no actual anointing of Elisha; and it is remarkable that in no other place is any such anointing of a prophet referred to, unless Ps. cv. 15 be an exception. The anointing, signifying the gift of grace, was first instituted for the priests (Exod. xl. 15; Num. iii. 3); next it was extended to the royal office, and became, in common parlance, especially attached to it. The prophetic office, as the third great representative of the power of Jehovah, might well be hallowed by the same ordinance, especially as the prophets dispensed it to the kings; but, whether the prophets were always consecrated with the sacred oil, or whether, as in the Prophet of prophets, the "anointing with the Holy Ghost and with power" sometimes superseded the outward sign, we do not know. Abel-meholah ("the meadow of the dance," see chap. iv. 12) lay in the rich country near the Jordan valley and the plain of Esdraelon; it was therefore on Elijah's way.

<sup>(17)</sup> **Him that escapeth the sword of Hazael.** —The vengeance wrought by Hazael and Jehu on the faithlessness of Israel speaks for itself; it is marked in bloody letters on the history (2 Kings x.). But Elisha's mission was obviously not one of such vengeance. He had to destroy enmity, but not to slay the enemies of God. The difficulty, such as it is, is one of the many marks of historic accuracy in the whole passage. Probably Elisha's mission is here described in the terms in which Elijah would best understand it. His spirit was for war; he could hardly have conceived how the completion of his mission was to be wrought out by the weapons of peace in the hand of his successor. (Comp. 2 Cor. x. 3—6.)

<sup>(18)</sup> **I have left.**—It should be "I leave, or "will leave," through all this vengeance, the seven thousand faithful; like the faithful remnant sealed in the visions of Ezekiel and St. John in the day of God's judgment (Ezek. ix. 4—6; Rev. vii. 3—8).

**Kissed him.**—(See Job xxxi. 26, 27; Hos. xiii. 2.) The passage is vividly descriptive of the worshipper on the first approach bowing the knee, on nearer access kissing the image, or the altar, or the threshold of the temple.

<sup>(19)</sup> **Twelve yoke of oxen**, or (as Ewald renders it) of land, indicate some wealth in Elisha's family, which he has to leave to follow the wandering life of Elijah. The character and mission of Elisha will appear hereafter: but the contrast between the prophets is marked in the difference of their home and origin; even the quiet simplicity of Elisha's call stands contrasted with the sudden, mysterious appearance of Elijah.

**Cast his mantle**—*i.e.*, the rough hair-mantle characteristic of the ascetic recluse. The act is said to have been a part of the form of adoption of a child; hence its spiritual significance here, which, after a moment's bewilderment, Elisha seems to read.

<sup>(20)</sup> **Let me, I pray thee.**—It is impossible not to compare this with the similar request made to our Lord (Luke ix. 61, 62) by one who declared readiness to follow Him. The comparison suggests that the answer of Elijah is one of half-ironical rebuke of what seemed hesitation—"Go back, if thou wilt; what have I done to constrain thee?" In both cases we have the stern but necessary rejection of half-hearted service, even if the heart be distracted by the most natural and sacred love. But Elijah sees that Elisha means simply farewell, and he apparently waits till it is over.

<sup>(21)</sup> **And he returned.**—Like Matthew in Luke ix. 27—29, Elisha, probably after sacrifice, makes a feast of farewell to his home, and of homage to his new master. The hasty preparation is made by the use of the

oxen, and gave unto the people, and they did eat. Then he arose, and went after Elijah, and ministered unto him.

CHAPTER XX. <sup>(1)</sup> And Ben-hadad the king of Syria gathered all his host together: and *there were* thirty and two kings with him, and horses, and chariots: and he went up and besieged Samaria, and warred against it. <sup>(2)</sup> And he sent messengers to Ahab king of Israel into the city, and said unto him, Thus saith Ben-hadad, <sup>(3)</sup> Thy silver and thy gold *is* mine; thy wives also and thy children, *even* the goodliest, *are* mine. <sup>(4)</sup> And the king of Israel answered and said, My lord, O king, according to thy saying, I *am* thine, and all that I have.

<sup>(5)</sup> And the messengers came again, and said, Thus speaketh Ben-hadad, saying, Although I have sent unto thee, saying, Thou shalt deliver me thy silver, and thy gold, and thy wives, and thy children; <sup>(6)</sup> yet I will send my servants unto thee to morrow about this time, and they shall search thine house, and the houses of thy servants; and it shall be, *that* whatsoever is [1] pleasant in thine eyes, they shall put *it* in their hand, and take *it* away. <sup>(7)</sup> Then the king of Israel called all the elders of the land, and said, Mark, I pray you, and see how this *man* seeketh mischief: for he sent unto me for my wives, and for my children, and for my silver, and for my gold; and [2] I denied him not. <sup>(8)</sup> And all the elders and all the people said unto him, Hearken not *unto him*, nor consent. <sup>(9)</sup> Wherefore he said unto the messengers of Ben-hadad, Tell my lord the king, All that thou didst send for to thy servant at the first I will do: but this thing I may not do. And the messengers departed, and brought him word again.

<sup>(10)</sup> And Ben-hadad sent unto him, and said, The gods do so unto me, and more also, if the dust of Samaria shall suffice

B.C. 901.

1 Heb., *desirable.*

2 Heb., *I kept not back from him.*

---

wooden implements for fuel, as in the sacrifice at the threshing-floor of Araunah (2 Sam. xxiv. 22). Henceforth from a master he became a servant, ministering to Elijah, and willing to be known, even when he became himself the prophet of God, as "he that poured water on the hands of Elijah" (2 Kings iii. 11).

### XX.

This chapter, evidently drawn from a different source, is interposed in the middle of the record of the prophetic career of Elijah. The history evidently belongs to the latter years of Ahab's reign, probably some time after the events of the previous chapter. The existence of the schools of the prophets, and the prophetic authority exercised, appear to indicate that for some reason Jezebel's influence on behalf of Baal had been reduced to impotence, and the worship of God restored. (Comp. xxii. 5—28.) It touches mainly on the external history of the reign, and shows it to have been one of no inconsiderable prosperity.

<sup>(1)</sup> **Ben-hadad.**—This is the inherited title of the Syrian kings. (See Amos i. 4; Jer. xlix. 27.) From the allusion in verse 34 it appears that this Benhadad was the son of a king who had been victorious against Omri—possibly pushing still further the advantage gained in the time of Baasha. It is evident that he assumed, perhaps by inheritance, a sovereignty over Israel.

**Thirty and two kings.**—All the notices of Syria show it as divided into small kingdoms, confederated from time to time under some leading power. In the days of David this leading power was that of Hadadezer of Zobah (2 Sam. viii. 3—13; x. 19), although Hamath was apparently independent. Now Damascus, under the dynasty of Hadad, assumes a most formidable predominance. Ahab cannot stand before it, but shuts himself up, probably after defeat, within the strong walls of Samaria.

(2–4) **And he sent.**—This message and the answer of Ahab ("My lord, O king") are the assertion and acceptance of Syrian sovereignty over Israel: all the possessions and the family of the vassal are acknowledged to be the property of his superior lord. Ahab surrenders, but not at discretion. Ben-hadad refuses all qualified submission.

<sup>(6)</sup> **Whatsoever is pleasant.**—The demand, which is virtually for the plunder of Samaria, probably neither expects nor desires acceptance, and is therefore a refusal of all but unconditional surrender. It is notable that in the last extremity Ahab falls back on an exceptional appeal to the patriotism of the people.

The "elders of the land" (evidently present in Samaria at this time) were the representatives in the northern kingdom of the ancient assembly of the "elders of Israel," existing from the time of Moses downwards as a senate, having power not only of advice, but of concurrence, in relation to the Judge or King. (See Exod. iii. 16, xii. 21, xxiv. 1; Deut. xxvii. 1, xxxi. 9; Josh. vii. 6; 2 Sam. v. 3; 1 Kings viii. 3). The solemn appointment of the seventy in Numb. xi. 24, 25 seems to be simply the re-constitution and consecration of the original body. Each tribe and each town had also its lesser body of elders. (See 1 Sam. xxx. 26, "the elders of Judah;" Deut. xix. 12, xxi. 3, &c., "the elders of the city.") The authority of all these assemblies must have been at all times largely overborne by the royal power (see chap. xxi. 11), and must have varied according to time and circumstance.

<sup>(10)</sup> **The dust of Samaria**—when razed to the ground. The phrase probably implies a threat of destruction, as well as a boast of overwhelming strength. Josephus (*Ant.* viii. 14, 2) has a curious explanation—that, if each of the Syrians took only a handful of dust, they could raise a mound against the city, higher than the walls of Samaria.

The historian, with a touch of patriotic scorn, paints Ben-hadad as a luxurious and insolent braggart. He

*Battle between*        I. KINGS, XX.        *Ahab and Ben-hadad.*

for handfuls for all the people that ¹follow me. (11) And the king of Israel answered and said, Tell *him*, Let not him that girdeth on *his harness* boast himself as he that putteth it off. (12) And it came to pass, when *Ben-hadad* heard this ²message, as he *was* drinking, he and the kings in the ³pavilions, that he said unto his servants, ⁴Set *yourselves in array*. And they set *themselves in array* against the city.

(13) And, behold, there ⁵came a prophet unto Ahab king of Israel, saying, Thus saith the LORD, Hast thou seen all this great multitude? behold, I will deliver it into thine hand this day; and thou shalt know that I *am* the LORD. (14) And Ahab said, By whom? And he said, Thus saith the LORD, *Even* by the ⁶young men of the princes of the provinces. Then he said, Who shall ⁷order the battle? And he answered, Thou.

(15) Then he numbered the young men of the princes of the provinces, and they were two hundred and thirty two: and after them he numbered all the people, *even* all the children of Israel, *being* seven thousand. (16) And they went out at noon. But Ben-hadad *was* drinking himself drunk in the pavilions, he and the kings, the thirty and two kings that helped him. (17) And the young men of the princes of the provinces went out first; and Ben-hadad sent out, and they told him, saying, There are men come out of Samaria. (18) And he said, Whether they be come out for peace, take them alive; or whether they be come out for war, take them alive. (19) So these young men of the princes of the provinces came out of the city, and the army which followed them. (20) And they slew every one his man: and the Syrians fled; and Israel pursued them: and Ben-hadad the king of Syria escaped on an horse with the horsemen. (21) And the king of Israel went out, and smote the horses and chariots, and slew the Syrians with a great slaughter.

(22) And the prophet came to the king of Israel, and said unto him, Go, strengthen thyself, and mark, and see what thou doest: for at the return of the year the king of Syria will come up against thee.

(23) And the servants of the king of Syria said unto him, Their gods *are* gods of the hills; therefore they were stronger than we; but let us fight against them in the plain, and surely we shall be

---

1 Heb., *are at my feet.*
2 Heb., *word.*
3 Or, *tents.*
4 Or, *Place the engines: And they placed engines.*
5 Heb., *approached.*
6 Or, *servants.*
7 Heb., *bind,* or *tie.*

---

receives the message at a feast, "drinking himself drunk," and, stung by its tone of sarcasm, does not condescend to bestir himself, but orders his servants to an instant attack. The command is given, with a haughty brevity, in a single word ("Set"), which may be "Array troops," or "Place engines," as in the margin. The LXX. translates, "Build a stockade" (for attack on the walls).

(13) **There came a prophet.**—The appearance of this unknown prophet evidently shows (see also chap. xxii. 6, 7) that Ahab's enmity to the prophetic order was over since the great day at Carmel, and that the schools of the prophets were forming themselves again —perhaps not free from connection with the idolatry of Jeroboam, but safe from all attacks from the worshippers of Baal. It is notable that in all these political functions of prophecy Elijah does not appear, reserving himself for the higher moral and religious mission from God. Ahab receives the prophet's message with perfect confidence and reverence; he has returned in profession to the allegiance to Jehovah, which he had, perhaps, never wholly relinquished.

(14) **Who shall order the battle?**—The marginal reading seems right, "Who shall give battle?" "Who shall begin the fray?"

(15) **The young men**—*i.e.*, the attendants or armour-bearers of the territorial chiefs, no doubt picked men and well armed. The whole garrison is stated as seven thousand—enough, perhaps, to man the walls, but wholly unfit to take the field. The sally is made at noon, when (as Josephus relates) the besiegers were resting unarmed in the heat of the day.

(20) **And they slew . . .**—The attack of this handful of men, supported by a sally of the whole garrison, is not unlike the slaughter of the Philistine garrison and host in the days of Saul (1 Sam. xiv.), or the still earlier rout of the army of Midian by the night attack of Gideon (Judg. vii. 16—23). Probably, as in these cases, the Israelites may have risen from various lurking-places to join in the pursuit and slaughter. It does not necessarily follow that the event was miraculous. Such dispersions of vast Oriental armies are not uncommon in history. The lesson is that drawn with noble simplicity by Jonathan: "There is no restraint to the Lord to save by many or by few" (1 Sam. xiv. 6).

(22) **The return of the year.**—The early part of the next year, after the winter was over, "when kings go out to battle" (2 Sam. xi. 1).

(23) **Gods of the hills.**—The idea of tutelary gods, whose strength was greatest on their own soil, is naturally common in polytheistic religions, which, by the very multiplication of gods, imply limitation of the power of each. Now the greater part of the territory where Jehovah was worshipped was a hill-country. Samaria in particular, the scene of recent defeat, lay in the mountain region of Ephraim. The Israelite armies, moreover, being mostly of infantry—having, indeed, few or no cavalry, except in the time of Solomon—naturally encamped and fought, as far as possible, on the hills; as Barak on Mount Tabor (Judges iv. 6—14), Saul on Mount Gilboa (1 Sam. xxxi. 1), and Ahab himself (in verse 27). Perhaps the worship of Jehovah in the "high places" may have also conduced to this belief

stronger than they. (24) And do this thing, Take the kings away, every man out of his place, and put captains in their rooms: (25) and number thee an army, like the army ¹that thou hast lost, horse for horse, and chariot for chariot: and we will fight against them in the plain, *and* surely we shall be stronger than they. And he hearkened unto their voice, and did so. (26) And it came to pass at the return of the year, that Ben-hadad numbered the Syrians, and went up to Aphek, ²to fight against Israel. (27) And the children of Israel were numbered, and ³were all present, and went against them: and the children of Israel pitched before them like two little flocks of kids; but the Syrians filled the country.

(28) And there came a man of God, and spake unto the king of Israel, and said, Thus saith the LORD, Because the Syrians have said, The LORD *is* God of the hills, but he *is* not God of the valleys, therefore will I deliver all this great multitude into thine hand, and ye shall know that I *am* the LORD.

(29) And they pitched one over against the other seven days. And *so* it was, that in the seventh day the battle was joined: and the children of Israel slew of the Syrians an hundred thousand footmen in one day. (30) But the rest fled to Aphek, into the city; and *there* a wall fell upon twenty and seven thousand of the men *that were* left.

And Ben-hadad fled, and came into the city, ⁴⁵into an inner chamber. (31) And his servants said unto him, Behold now, we have heard that the kings of the house of Israel *are* merciful kings: let us, I pray thee, put sackcloth on our loins, and ropes upon our heads, and go out to the king of Israel: peradventure he will save thy life. (32) So they girded sackcloth on their loins, and *put* ropes on their heads, and came to the king of Israel, and said, Thy servant Ben-hadad saith, I pray thee, let me live. And he said, *Is* he yet alive? he *is* my brother. (33) Now the men did diligently observe whether *any thing would come* from him, and did hastily catch *it*: and they said, Thy brother Ben-hadad. Then he said, Go ye, bring him. Then Ben-hadad came forth to him; and he caused him

---

¹ Heb., *that was fallen.*
² Heb., *to the war with Israel.*
B.C. 900.
³ Or, *were victualled.*
⁴ Or, *from chamber to chamber.*
⁵ Heb., *into a chamber within a chamber.*

---

that the "gods of Israel were gods of the hills," whose power vanished in the plains; where, of course, the Syrian armies of chariots and horsemen would naturally fight at advantage. Shrewd policy might, as so often is the case, lurk in the advice of Ben-hadad's counsellors under the cover of superstition; as, indeed, it seems also to show itself in seizing the opportunity to increase the central power, by organising the troops of the tributary kings under officers of his own.

(26) **Aphek.**—The name, signifying simply a "fortress," as applied to several different places. There are two places which suit well enough with the Aphek of this passage and 2 Kings xiii. 17, as being a battlefield in the plain country between Israel and Syria. One is the Aphek of 1 Sam. xxix. 1, evidently in the plain of Esdraelon; the other a place on the road to Damascus, about six miles east of the Sea of Galilee.

(27) **Were all present.** — The marginal reading "were victualled," or, perhaps, more generally, "were supplied," with all things necessary for war, seems correct. The comparatively small number of the Israelite forces, even after the great victory of the year before, appears to show that, previous to the siege of Samaria, Ahab had suffered some great defeats, which had broken the strength of Israel.

(28) **A man of God**—apparently not the same as before. We see from verse 35 that the prophetic order was now numerous. The vindication of the majesty of God before the Syrians, as well as before Israel—like the more celebrated case of the rebuke of the blasphemy of Sennacherib (2 Kings xix. 16—34)—is in accordance with the prayer of Solomon, or the similar utterances in the Psalms (Pss. lxvii. 2, cii. 15, cxxxviii. 4), "That all the people of the earth may know thy name, to fear thee;" and also with such prophetic declarations as those of Ezek. xx. 9, "I wrought for my Name's sake, that it should not be polluted before the heathen." It is a foreshadowing of that view of all nations, as in some degree having knowledge of God and probation before Him, which is afterwards worked out fully in the prophetic writings. The intense and powerful Monotheism of the religion of Israel, in spite of all its backslidings, could hardly have been without influence over the neighbouring nations (see 2 Kings v. 15), especially at a time when the remembrance of Solomon's vast empire, and still wider influence, would yet linger through the tenacious traditions of the East.

(30) **A wall**—properly, *the wall of the city*, whether falling by earthquake, or in the storming of the place, by Israel. The numbers in the text are very large, as in many other instances. It is possible (see Introduction) that there may be corruption, although the same numbers are found in the ancient versions. But the massing in small space of Oriental armies, and the extraordinary slaughter consequent on it, are well illustrated in history; as, for instance, in the Greek wars with Persia, or even our own experience in India.

(31) **Ropes upon our heads**—like "the ropes round the necks" of the burghers of Calais, in the days of Edward III. The envoys offer themselves as naked, helpless criminals, to sue for mercy.

(33) **Now the men.**—There has been much discussion of the meaning here, and some proposals of slight emendations of the reading. But the general sense seems accurately rendered by our version. "The men watched" ("as for augury," says the LXX.), "and hasted, and caught up" (so as to make it sure) "what fell from him." What follows may be a question,

to come up into the chariot. (34) And *Ben-hadad* said unto him, The cities, which my father took from thy father, I will restore; and thou shalt make streets for thee in Damascus, as my father made in Samaria. Then *said Ahab*, I will send thee away with this covenant. So he made a covenant with him, and sent him away.

(35) And a certain man of the sons of the prophets said unto his neighbour in the word of the LORD, Smite me, I pray thee. And the man refused to smite him. (36) Then said he unto him, Because thou hast not obeyed the voice of the LORD, behold, as soon as thou art departed from me, a lion shall slay thee. And as soon as he was departed from him, a lion found him, and slew him. (37) Then he found another man, and said, Smite me, I pray thee. And the man smote him, [1] so that in smiting he wounded *him*. (38) So the prophet departed, and waited for the king by the way, and disguised himself with ashes upon his face. (39) And as the king passed by, he cried unto the king: and he said, Thy servant went out into the midst of the battle; and, behold, a man turned aside, and brought a man unto me, and said, Keep this man: if by any means he be missing, then shall thy life be for his life, or else thou shalt [2] pay a talent of silver. (40) And as thy servant was busy here and there, [3] he was gone. And the king of Israel said unto him, So *shall* thy judgment *be;* thyself hast decided *it*. (41) And he hasted, and took the ashes away from his face; and the king of Israel discerned him that he *was* of the prophets. (42) And he said unto him, Thus saith the LORD, *a* Because thou hast let go out of *thy* hand a man whom I appointed to utter destruction, therefore thy life shall go for his life, and thy people for his people. (43) And the king of Israel went to his house heavy and displeased, and came to Samaria.

---

1 Heb., *smiting and wounding.*

2 Heb., *weigh.*

3 Heb., *he was not.*

a ch. 22. 36.

---

"Is Ben-hadad thy brother?" but probably the simple acceptance of the title is better. The whole description is graphic. The Syrians speak of "thy slave Ben-hadad." Ahab, in compassion or show of magnanimity, says, "my brother." Eagerly the ambassadors catch up the word, which, according to Eastern custom, implied a pledge of amity not to be recalled; and Ahab accepts their inference, and seals it publicly by taking the conquered king into his chariot. (Comp. 2 Kings x. 15, 16.)

(34) **Make streets**—properly, *squares*, or *quarters of a city*. This concession implies a virtual acknowledgment of supremacy; for the right to have certain quarters for residence, for trade, perhaps even for garrison, in the capital of a king, belongs only to one who has sovereignty over him. Hence it goes beyond the significance of the restoration of the cities—conquered, it would seem, from Omri, unless, indeed, taking "father" in the sense of predecessor, the reference is to the Syrian victories in the days of Baasha. (See chap. xv. 20.) The narrative seems to convey an idea that the covenant was made hastily, on insufficient security. The great point, however, was that a war, victoriously conducted under prophetic guidance, should not have been concluded without prophetic sanction.

(35) **A certain man** — according to Josephus, Micaiah, the son of Imlah. This tradition, or conjecture, agrees well with the subsequent narrative in chap. xxii.

**The sons of the prophets.**—This phrase, constantly recurring in the history of Elijah and Elisha, first appears here. But the thing designated is apparently as old as the days of Samuel, who is evidently surrounded by "a company" of disciples. (See 1 Sam. x. 5, 10, xix. 20.) The prophetic office seems never to have been, like the priesthood or kingship, hereditary. "Sonship," therefore, no doubt means simply discipleship; and it is likely enough that the schools of the sons of the prophets were places of higher religious education, including many who did not look for the prophetic vocation; although the well-known words of Amos (Amos vii. 14), "I was no prophet, neither was I a prophet's son," clearly indicate that from their ranks, generally though not invariably, the prophets were called. Probably the institution had fallen into disuse, and had been revived to seal and to secure the prophetic victory over Baal-worship. To Elijah the "sons of the prophets" look up with awe and some terror; to Elisha, with affectionate respect and trust.

(36) **A lion shall slay thee.**—It is obvious to compare the example of chap. xiii. 24.

(38) **Ashes upon his face.**—It should be a "bandage over his head," to cover his face, and to accord with the appearance of a wounded soldier. Unless the wound had some symbolic significance in application to Ahab or Israel, it is difficult to see what purpose it could serve.

(39) **Thy servant.**—The parable is, of course, designed (like those of 2 Sam. xii. 1—4, xiv. 5—11) to make Ahab condemn himself. In Ahab, however, it excites not compunction, but characteristic sullenness of displeasure, like that of chap. xxi. 4.

(42) **A man whom I appointed**—properly, *a man under my curse*. The rash action of Ahab, like the deliberate disobedience of Saul (1 Sam. xv.), may have been due partly to compassion, partly to weakness. In either case it had no right to stand unauthorised between God's judgment and him on whom it was pronounced; for even soft-heartedness, as in the case of Eli, may be treason to the cause of righteousness. The prophet (like Elisha, in 2 Kings xiii. 19) speaks partly as a patriot, jealous—and, as the event proved, with a sagacious jealousy—of the lenity which left the deadly enemy of Israel unsubdued; but he speaks also as the representative of God's stern and righteous judgment, which Ahab, after signal deliverance, had treated as of

*Ahab desires*          I. KINGS, XXI.          *Naboth's Vineyard.*

CHAPTER XXI.—(1) And it came to pass after these things, *that* Naboth the Jezreelite had a vineyard, which *was* in Jezreel, hard by the palace of Ahab king of Samaria. (2) And Ahab spake unto Naboth, saying, Give me thy vineyard, that I may have it for a garden of herbs, because it *is* near unto my house: and I will give thee for it a better vineyard than it; *or*, if it ¹seem good to thee, I will give thee the worth of it in money. (3) And Naboth said to Ahab, The LORD forbid it me, that I should give the inheritance of my fathers unto thee.

(4) And Ahab came into his house heavy and displeased because of the word which Naboth the Jezreelite had spoken to him: for he had said, I will not give

B.C. 899.

¹ Heb., *be good in thine eyes.*

thee the inheritance of my fathers. And he laid him down upon his bed, and turned away his face, and would eat no bread.

(5) But Jezebel his wife came to him, and said unto him, Why is thy spirit so sad, that thou eatest no bread? (6) And he said unto her, Because I spake unto Naboth the Jezreelite, and said unto him, Give me thy vineyard for money; or else, if it please thee, I will give thee *another* vineyard for it: and he answered, I will not give thee my vineyard. (7) And Jezebel his wife said unto him, Dost thou now govern the kingdom of Israel? arise, *and* eat bread, and let thine heart be merry: I will give thee the vineyard of Naboth the Jezreelite. (8) So she

no account. (For the fulfilment of his words, see chap. xxii. 34—36.)

### XXI.

The narrative of this chapter, clearly drawn once more from the prophetic record of Elijah's life and mission, returns to the same vividness of style and lofty spiritual teaching perceptible in chaps. xviii., xix. It describes the turning-point of Ahab's probation, which, like the great crisis of David's history, is an act of unrighteous tyranny, so common in Eastern despotism, that it would hardly be recorded by an ordinary historian. So in the prophetic writings moral evils, especially profligacy and bloodshed and oppression of the weak, are denounced at least not less severely, and even more frequently, than religious unfaithfulness. The whole description is strikingly illustrative of Ahab's character, in its essential weakness and subservience, more fatal in high place of authority than resolute wickedness. It might be painted in the well-known description of Felix by Tacitus, as "swaying the power of a king with the temper of a slave" (*jus regium servili ingenio exercuit*).

(1) **Which was in Jezreel.**—The LXX. omits these words, and makes the vineyard to be " hard by the threshing-floor of Ahab, king of Samaria "—the word being the same as that rendered "void place" in chap. xxii. 10—apparently near the palace of Ahab in Samaria, not in Jezreel. The Vulgate renders "who was" instead of "which was" in Jezreel. The question of the position of the vineyard, apparently the scene of Naboth's murder, is difficult. The "plot of ground" of Naboth referred to in 2 Kings ix. 25, 26 —not, however, called "a vineyard"—is clearly at Jezreel, where, as a native of the place, Naboth would be likely to hold land. But the vineyard may have been an outlying property near Samaria, which Ahab might naturally suppose Naboth, even for that reason, likely to sell. In favour of this supposition—which is, perhaps, on the whole the more probable—is the very emphatic prediction of verse 19, which in chap. xxii. 38 is declared to have been fulfilled at the pool of Samaria. Moreover, the whole action of the chapter, as far as Ahab is concerned, seems to have been at Samaria; and, indeed, if we take verse 18 literally, this is actually declared to be the case. On the other side, however, we have the reading of the text, the more obvious interpretation of the words "his city" in verses 8, 11; and the reference to the prophecy of Elijah, in connection with the casting of the body of Jehoram into the plot of ground at Jezreel (2 Kings ix. 25, 26). It is, perhaps, impossible to clear up the discrepancy entirely with our present knowledge.

(2–4) **And Ahab spake.**—The whole history is singularly true to nature. At first, as the desire of Ahab was natural, so his offer was courteous and liberal. The refusal of Naboth—evidently grounded on the illegality, as well as the natural dislike, of alienation of "the inheritance of his fathers" (see Lev. xxv. 13—28; Num. xxxvi. 7), and therefore not only allowable, but right—has nevertheless about it a certain tone of harshness, perhaps of unnecessary discourtesy, implying condemnation, as well as rejection, of the offer of the king. It is characteristic of the weak and petulant nature of Ahab, that he neither recognises the legality and justice of Naboth's action, nor dares to resent the curt defiance of his refusal. Like a spoilt child, he comes back sullen and angry, throws himself on his bed, and will eat no bread. All that he has is as nothing, while the little plot of ground is refused; as to Haman all was worthless, while Mordecai the Jew sat in the king's gate (Esth. v. 13). This temper of sullen, childish discontent is the natural seedplot of crime, under the instigation of more determined wickedness.

(7) **Dost thou now.**—The scorn of Jezebel is, like the impatience of Lady Macbeth, expressed in a striking boldness of emphasis. First comes the bitter irony of the question, "Dost thou govern the kingdom of Israel, and yet suffer a subject to cross thy will?" expressing her scornful wonder at one who "lets I dare not, wait upon I would." Then in the invitation, "eat bread, and let thine heart be merry," there seems the same half-contemptuous recognition of a self-indulgent weakness of nature, which may be traced in Elijah's words in chap. xviii. 41, "Get thee up, eat and drink, for there is a sound of abundance of rain." Ahab is fit only to desire and to revel; it is for bolder spirits to act for good or for evil.

(8) **Sealed them with his seal**—with the name, or token, of the king, engraved on stone, and impressed (see Job xxxviii. 14) on a lump of clay attached to the

wrote letters in Ahab's name, and sealed *them* with his seal, and sent the letters unto the elders and to the nobles that *were* in his city, dwelling with Naboth. (9) And she wrote in the letters, saying, Proclaim a fast, and set Naboth ¹on high among the people: (10) and set two men, sons of Belial, before him, to bear witness against him, saying, Thou didst blaspheme God and the king. And *then* carry him out, and stone him, that he may die.

(11) And the men of his city, *even* the elders and the nobles who were the inhabitants in his city, did as Jezebel had sent unto them, *and* as it *was* written in the letters which she had sent unto them. (12) They proclaimed a fast, and set Naboth on high among the people. (13) And there came in two men, children of Belial, and sat before him: and the men of Belial witnessed against him, *even* against Naboth, in the presence of the people, saying, Naboth did blaspheme God and the king. Then they carried him forth out of the city, and stoned him with stones, that he died. (14) Then they sent to Jezebel, saying, Naboth is stoned, and is dead.

(15) And it came to pass, when Jezebel heard that Naboth was stoned, and was dead, that Jezebel said to Ahab, Arise, take possession of the vineyard of Naboth the Jezreelite, which he refused to give thee for money: for Naboth is not alive, but dead. (16) And it came to pass, when Ahab heard that Naboth was dead, that Ahab rose up to go down to the vineyard of Naboth the Jezreelite, to take possession of it.

(17) And the word of the LORD came to Elijah the Tishbite, saying, (18) Arise, go

¹ Heb., *in the top of the people.*

---

letter. The sealing (as the modern sense of "signature" implies) was the pledge of authenticity and authority. (See Gen. xxxviii. 18; Neh. ix. 38, x. 1; Esth. iii. 10, 12, viii. 28; Dan. vi. 17, &c.) The use of the seal—ordinarily worn or carried on the person—implies Ahab's knowledge that something is being done in his name, into which he takes care not to inquire.

**In his city.**—This would be most naturally interpreted as Jezreel; but if Naboth dwelt or sojourned at Samaria, it may be Samaria. Jezebel naturally desires that neither Ahab nor she herself, though close at hand, should appear in the matter; but gives the necessary authority in writing, because without it the deed could not be done.

(9) **Proclaim a fast.**—This might be only to cover all that was to be so foully done with a cloak of religious observance, or, perhaps more probably, to imply that some secret sin had been committed, which would draw down vengeance on the whole city, and so to prepare for the false accusation. There is a like ambiguity as to the explanation of the command, " set Naboth on high," as either an exaltation of pretended honour, or the " lifting up his head " (Gen. xl. 20) for accusation. It may be noted that the whole scheme implies a return of the people to at least the outward observance of the Law of the Lord.

(10) **Two men**—in accordance with Num. xxxv. 30; Deut. xvii. 6.

**Sons of Belial.**—See Judges xix. 22, xx. 13; 1 Sam. i. 16, ii. 12, x. 27, xxv. 17, 25, xxx. 22; 2 Sam. xvi. 7, xx. 1, &c.; properly, "children of lawlessness, or worthlessness."

**Blaspheme.**—The word is the same used in Job i. 5, 11, ii. 5, there rendered "curse." It properly signifies " to bless ;" thence, to "part from with blessing;" finally to part from, or " disown." It is, rather, therefore, " to renounce " than " to blaspheme." The punishment, however, was stoning, as for positive blasphemy. (See Lev. xxiv. 16; Deut. xiii. 9, 10.)

(11) **And the men of his city . . . did.**—The pains taken in the invention of this foul plot, and the ready acquiescence of the rulers of the city in carrying it out, are characteristic of the baser forms of organised Eastern despotism—not venturing to take life by simple violence without some cause apparently shown, and yet always able to poison the springs of justice, and do murder under form of law. In Israel, where the king was held to be but a vicegerent of God, subject, in theory, under the old constitution or "manner of the kingdom" (1 Sam. x. 25), to the supreme law, the need of clothing crime with legal form would be especially felt.

(13) **Carried him forth**—as usual, in order to avoid polluting the city with blood—possibly to his own ground, the coveted vineyard itself.

(15) **Take possession.**—Naboth's sons (see 2 Kings ix. 26) were murdered with him, so that there was none to claim the inheritance. Even had this not been so, the property of executed traitors would naturally fall to the king, although no enactment to this effect is found in the Law.

(16) **When Ahab heard.**—It is characteristic of Ahab that he takes care to ask no question about Naboth's death, desirous "to be innocent of the knowledge," and yet tacitly to "applaud the deed." The guilt is Jezebel's; the fruit, his own. In the LXX. there is here a curious and striking insertion: " he rent his clothes and put on sackcloth," representing Ahab as struck with momentary horror, and then, after thus salving his conscience, still resolving to carry out his desire for the coveted vineyard. The picture is equally true to nature, especially to such a nature as his. But the insertion has little authority, and is probably a mistaken interpolation from verse 27.

(17) **Elijah.**—We have heard nothing of him since the call of Elisha, as though he had once more retired to solitude. In the mere political service of the preceding chapter, important in the eyes of the world, he takes no part; but emerges now for the higher moral duty of rebuking crime, and avenging innocent blood, in what Eastern tyranny would deem a very trivial matter. Ahab's address to him seems to imply wonder at his unusual appearance among men.

(18) **Which is in Samaria.**—These words are almost unmeaning, unless they literally signify that Ahab was then in Samaria, not in Jezreel. To interpret them as

down to meet Ahab king of Israel, which *is* in Samaria: behold, he is in the vineyard of Naboth, whither he is gone down to possess it. (19) And thou shalt speak unto him, saying, Thus saith the LORD, Hast thou killed, and also taken possession? And thou shalt speak unto him, saying, Thus saith the LORD, In the place where dogs licked the blood of Naboth shall dogs lick thy blood, even thine.

(20) And Ahab said to Elijah, Hast thou found me, O mine enemy? And he answered, I have found *thee*: because thou hast sold thyself to work evil in the sight of the LORD. (21) Behold, *a* I will bring evil upon thee, and will take away thy posterity, and will cut off from Ahab *b* him that pisseth against the wall, and *c* him that is shut up and left in Israel, (22) and will make thine house like the house of *d* Jeroboam the son of Nebat, and like the house of *e* Baasha the son of Ahijah, for the provocation wherewith thou hast provoked me to anger, and made Israel to sin. (23) And *f* of Jezebel also spake the LORD, saying, The dogs shall eat Jezebel by the ¹wall of Jezreel. (24) Him that dieth of Ahab in the city the dogs shall eat; and him that dieth in the field shall the fowls of the air eat.

(25) But there was none like unto Ahab, which did sell himself to work wickedness in the sight of the LORD, whom Jezebel his wife ²stirred up. (26) And he did very abominably in following idols, according to all *things* as did the Amorites, whom the LORD cast out before the children of Israel.

(27) And it came to pass, when Ahab heard those words, that he rent his clothes, and put sackcloth upon his flesh, and fasted, and lay in sackcloth, and went softly. (28) And the word of the LORD came to Elijah the Tishbite, saying, (29) Seest thou how Ahab humbleth himself before me? because he humbleth himself before me, I will not bring the evil in his days: *but* in his

*a* ch. 14. 10; 2 Kings 9. 8.

*b* 1 Sam. 25. 22.

*c* ch. 14. 10.

*d* ch. 15. 29.

*e* ch. 16. 3.

*f* 2 Kings 9. 36.

1 Or, *ditch*.

2 Or, *incited*.

---

simply part of Ahab's title, or as signifying the country, not the town of Samaria, is to explain them away.

(19) **Hast thou killed, and also taken possession?**—The stern, indignant brevity of the accusation, at once shaming the subterfuge by which Ahab shifts his guilt to Jezebel, and unmasking the real object of the whole crime, leaves the king speechless as to defence, unable to stay the sentence which at once follows. The marked particularity and emphasis of that sentence, "In the place where the dogs licked the blood of Naboth shall dogs lick *thy blood, even thine*," preclude all explanations, which would seek its fulfilment in the fate of Jehoram (2 Kings ix. 25); nor can such explanations be justified by reference to verse 29, for it is not this part of the sentence which is deferred by Ahab's repentance. (See Note on chap. xxii. 38.)

(20) **Hast thou found me, O mine enemy?**— The cry is partly of dismay, partly of excuse. Ahab, having no word of defence to utter, endeavours to attribute Elijah's rebuke and condemnation to simple enmity, much as in chap. xviii. 17 he cries out "Art thou he that troubleth Israel?" The crushing answer is that the prophet came not because he was an enemy, but because Ahab had "sold himself"—had become a slave instead of a king—under the lust of desire and the temptation of Jezebel.

(21–24) **Behold, I will bring evil.**—Distinct from that message of personal judgment is the doom of utter destruction pronounced on the dynasty of Omri—the same in substance, and almost in word, as that already pronounced in chaps. xiv. 10, 11, xvi. 3, 4. It is, indeed, called forth by the last sin of Ahab, but the ground assigned for it (verse 22) extends to the whole course of idolatry and apostasy, "making Israel to sin." It is only this more general sentence which is postponed by the repentance of Ahab (verse 29).

(25) **The dogs shall eat Jezebel.**—In all his address to Ahab, Elijah has, as yet, disdained to name the instigator, on whom the coward king, no doubt, threw his guilt. Ahab stands revealed as the true culprit before God, without a shred of subterfuge to veil his ultimate responsibility. Now, briefly and sternly, the prophet notices the bolder criminal, pronouncing against her a doom of shame and horror, seldom falling upon a woman, but rightly visiting one who had forsworn the pity and modesty of her sex. In the "ditch" (see margin) outside the walls, where the refuse of the city gathers the half-wild dogs—the scavengers of Eastern cities—her dead body is to be thrown as offal, and to be torn and devoured.

This verse and the next are evidently the reflection of the compiler, catching its inspiration from the words of Elijah in verse 20. There is in them a tone not only of condemnation, but of contempt, for a king most unkingly—thus selling himself to a half-unwilling course of crime, against the warnings of conscience, not disbelieved but neglected, for the sake of a paltry desire—thus moreover, grovelling under the open dominion of a woman, which, to an Eastern mind, familiar enough with female intrigues, but not with female imperiousness, would seem especially monstrous.

(26) **As did the Amorites.**—The reference is probably not only to the idolatry and worship of false gods, but to the nameless abominations always connected with such worship.

(27) **And went softly.**—The translation seems correct; the meaning is variously conjectured. The LXX. (in some MSS.) has "bent down" in sorrow; the Vulgate similarly "with head bent down;" the Eastern versions and Josephus, "barefooted," which seems far the most probable meaning.

(29) **How Ahab humbleth himself.**—As there is something entirely characteristic of Ahab's impressible nature in this burst of penitence; so in the acceptance of it there is a remarkable illustration of the Divine mercy. The repentance might seem not

*Ahab gathers*           I. KINGS, XXII.           *the Prophets.*

son's days will I bring the evil upon his house.

CHAPTER XXII.—<sup>(1)</sup> And they continued three years without war between Syria and Israel. <sup>(2)</sup> And it came to pass in the third year, that <sup>a</sup>Jehoshaphat the king of Judah came down to the king of Israel. <sup>(3)</sup> And the king of Israel said unto his servants, Know ye that Ramoth in Gilead *is* our's, and we *be* [1]still, *and* take it not out of the hand of the king of Syria? <sup>(4)</sup> And he said unto Jehoshaphat, Wilt thou go with me to battle to Ramoth-gilead? And Jehoshaphat said to the king of Israel, <sup>b</sup>I *am* as thou *art*, my people as thy people, my horses as thy horses.

<sup>(5)</sup> And Jehoshaphat said unto the king of Israel, Enquire, I pray thee, at the word of the LORD to day. <sup>(6)</sup> Then the king of Israel gathered the prophets together, about four hundred men, and said unto them, Shall I go against Ramoth-gilead to battle, or shall I forbear? And they said, Go up; for the Lord shall deliver *it* into the hand of the king.

<sup>(7)</sup> And Jehoshaphat said, *Is there* not here a prophet of the LORD besides, that we might enquire of him? <sup>(8)</sup> And the king of Israel said unto Jehoshaphat, *There is* yet one man, Micaiah the son of Imlah, by whom we may enquire of the LORD: but I hate him; for he doth not prophesy good concerning me, but evil. And Jehoshaphat said, Let not the king say so.

<sup>(9)</sup> Then the king of Israel called an [2]officer, and said, Hasten *hither* Micaiah the son of Imlah. <sup>(10)</sup> And the king of Israel and Jehoshaphat the king of

*a* 2 Chron. 18. 1, &c.

B.C. 897.

1 Heb., *silent from taking it.*

*b* 2 Kings 3. 7.

2 Or, *eunuch.*

---

only to come too late, but to be the mere offspring of fear—more sensible of the shame of discovery than of the shamefulness of sin. Man's judgment would despise it; God sees in its imperfection some germs of promise, and His partial remission of penalty shows it to be not disregarded in His sight. Ahab himself is still to suffer the predicted doom; but he is to die in honour, and the utter destruction waits, till Jehoram shall fill up the measure of iniquity.

### XXII.

Chap. xxii. is the continuation of chap. xx. (which in the LXX. immediately precedes it) in record of the Syrian war, but in tone far grander and spiritually instructive, a fit catastrophe of the tragedy of Ahab's reign. In it, for the first time since chap. xv. 24, the history of Judah is touched upon; and there is an almost verbal coincidence with 2 Chron. xviii.

<sup>(1)</sup> **Three years without war.**—The period is clearly reckoned from the rash peace made by Ahab with Ben-hadad in chap. xx. 34. Evidently the king of Syria has recovered his independence, if not superiority; he has not restored Ramoth-gilead according to his promise; and his revived power is sufficient to cope with the united forces of Israel and Judah. The sagacity of the prophetic rebuke of chap. xx. 42 has been amply justified.

<sup>(2)</sup> **Jehoshaphat the king of Judah came down.** —The fuller account of the Chronicles (2 Chron. xvii.) notices that the early part of his reign had been marked by a continuance or increase of the prosperity of Asa; but (chap. xviii. 1) adds, in significant connection, he "had riches and honour in abundance, and joined affinity with Ahab," so that this prosperity was, at any rate in part, dependent on a change of policy from enmity to alliance, with apparently some measure of dependence, dangerous alike spiritually and politically, but probably thought to be a necessity. The visit of Jehoshaphat (2 Chron. xviii. 2) was one of festivity, of which Ahab took advantage.

<sup>(3)</sup> **Ramoth in Gilead.**—The city is first mentioned (in Deut. iv. 43; Josh. xx. 8, xxi. 38) as a city of refuge in the territory of Gad; then (in 1 Kings iv. 13) as the centre of one of the provinces of Solomon, including the towns of Jair, and the strong hill country of Argob. In the Syrian wars it appears as a frontier fortress, taken and retaken. It had fallen into the hands of the Syrians, and had not been restored according to promise. The defeat and death of Ahab were subsequently avenged by Jehuram, who took it, and held it against all the attacks of the enemy (2 Kings ix. 1—14).

<sup>(4)</sup> **I am as thou art.**—The answer is apparently one of deference, as well as friendship, to the stronger kingdom. It must be remembered that, as the whole chapter shows, Ahab had now returned to the worship of the Lord.

<sup>(6)</sup> **Prophets . . . four hundred.**—These were clearly not avowed prophets of Baal, or the Asherah ("groves"), as is obvious from the context and from their words in verse 12. But Jehoshaphat's discontent makes it equally clear that they were not in his view true prophets of Jehovah. Probably they were devoted, like the old prophet of Bethel, to the service of the idolatry of Jeroboam.

<sup>(7)</sup> **Is there not here a prophet of the Lord.**— The rendering of the great name "Jehovah" by "the Lord" obscures the sense of the passage. In the previous utterance of the prophets the word (*Adonai*) is merely "Lord" in the etymological sense, which might mean the Supreme God of any religion. Jehoshaphat, struck with their shrinking from the distinctive name Jehovah, asks, "Is there not a prophet of Jehovah?"—one who is not ashamed or afraid to speak in His awful name?

<sup>(8)</sup> **Micaiah** ("who is like Jehovah")—the name being the same as Micah. According to Josephus, he was the prophet of chap. xx. 35–43, who had "prophesied evil" of Ahab for his rash action towards Ben-hadad, and had already been imprisoned by him. The whole description, and especially the words of verse 26, seem to confirm this account.

<sup>(10)</sup> **Each on his throne.**—The description evidently implies that, having reluctantly consented to send for Micaiah, Ahab seeks to overawe him by display not only of royal pomp, but of prophetic inspiration, professing to come, like his own, from the Lord Jehovah.

Judah sat each on his throne, having put on their robes, in a ¹void place in the entrance of the gate of Samaria; and all the prophets prophesied before them. ⁽¹¹⁾ And Zedekiah the son of Chenaanah made him horns of iron: and he said, Thus saith the LORD, With these shalt thou push the Syrians, until thou hast consumed them. ⁽¹²⁾ And all the prophets prophesied so, saying, Go up to Ramoth-gilead, and prosper: for the LORD shall deliver *it* into the king's hand.

⁽¹³⁾ And the messenger that was gone to call Micaiah spake unto him, saying, Behold now, the words of the prophets *declare* good unto the king with one mouth: let thy word, I pray thee, be like the word of one of them, and speak *that which is* good. ⁽¹⁴⁾ And Micaiah said, *As* the LORD liveth, what the LORD saith unto me, that will I speak. ⁽¹⁵⁾ So he came to the king.

And the king said unto him, Micaiah, shall we go against Ramoth-gilead to battle, or shall we forbear? And he answered him, Go, and prosper: for the LORD shall deliver *it* into the hand of the king. ⁽¹⁶⁾ And the king said unto him, How many times shall I adjure thee that thou tell me nothing but *that which is* true in the name of the LORD? ⁽¹⁷⁾ And he said, I saw all Israel scattered upon the hills, as sheep that have not a shepherd: and the LORD said, These have no master: let them return every man to his house in peace.

⁽¹⁸⁾ And the king of Israel said unto Jehoshaphat, Did I not tell thee that he would prophesy no good concerning me, but evil?

⁽¹⁹⁾ And he said, Hear thou therefore the word of the LORD: I saw the LORD sitting on his throne, and all the host of heaven standing by him on his right hand and on his left. ⁽²⁰⁾ And the LORD said, Who shall ²persuade Ahab, that he may go up and fall at Ramoth-gilead? And one said on this manner, and another said on that manner. ⁽²¹⁾ And there came forth a spirit, and stood before the LORD, and said, I will

1 Heb., *floor.*

2 Or, *deceive.*

---

⁽¹¹⁾ **Zedekiah.**—The name itself ("righteousness of Jehovah") must certainly imply professed devotion to the true God, whose Name here is first uttered by him. Symbolic action was not unfrequent in the prophets. (See Note on chap. xi. 30.) The use of the horns, as emblems of victorious strength, is also familiar, as in the utterance of Balaam (Num. xxiii. 22), in the blessing of Moses (Deut. xxxiii. 17), in the song of Hannah (1 Sam. iii. 1), in the visions of Daniel and Zechariah (Dan. viii. 3—10; Zech. i. 18, 19).

⁽¹²⁾ **For the Lord shall deliver it.**—The prophets, led by Zedekiah, now venture to use the Name of Jehovah, from which they had at first shrunk. The description, however, of their united reiteration of the cry, evidently with increasing excitement, reminds us of the repeated "O Baal, hear us" of Mount Carmel, and stands in similar contrast with the calm, stern utterance of the true prophet.

⁽¹³⁾ **Behold now.**—In the whole history, as especially in the words of the officer, there is evidence of the strange confusion of idea, so common in superstition at all times, which in some sense believes in the inspiration of the prophets as coming from God, and yet fancies that they can direct it as they will, and that accordingly they can be bribed, or beguiled, or coerced, to "prophesy smooth things." The extremest form of this infatuation is exemplified in Simon Magus, who believed that the Apostles were the medium for conferring the highest spiritual gifts from God, and yet madly persuaded himself that this power could be bought for money (Acts viii. 18, 19). The natural result is a mingled awe and contempt, such as Balak feels for Balaam. The delusion is, of course, silenced at once by such declarations as the stern reply of Micaiah, which even Balaam could convey (Num. xxii. 18). But, as all false religions and corruptions of true religion show, it is never rooted out, except by real spiritual knowledge of God and of His dealings with the soul.

⁽¹⁵⁾ **Go, and prosper.**—Micaiah is a true disciple of Elijah in the defiant irony of the tone in which he takes up and mocks the utterance of the false prophets, so bitterly as at once to show Ahab his scorn of them and him. But his message is couched in metaphor and symbolic vision, unlike the stern directness of the style of Elijah.

⁽¹⁹⁻²²⁾ The symbolic vision of Micaiah, which naturally recalls the well-known description in Job i. 6—12 of the intercourse of Satan with the Lord Himself, is to be taken as a symbol, and nothing more. (Josephus, characteristically enough, omits it altogether.) The one idea to be conveyed is the delusion of the false prophets by a spirit of evil, as a judgment of God on Ahab's sin, and on their degradation of the prophetic office. The imagery is borrowed from the occasion. It is obviously drawn from the analogy of a royal court, where, as is the case before Micaiah's eyes, the king seeks counsel against his enemies.

⁽²¹⁾ **A spirit.**—It should be *the spirit.* The definite article is explained by some, perhaps rather weakly, as simply anticipatory of the description which follows. Others take the phrase to signify "the spirit of prophecy," a kind of emanation from the Godhead, looked upon as the medium of the prophetic inspiration, which is an expression conceivable, but certainly unprecedented. Perhaps without introducing into this passage the distinct idea of "the Satan," *i.e.,* the enemy, which we find in Job i., ii.; 1 Chron. xxi. 1; Zech. iii. 1, 2, it may be best to interpret it by the conception, common to all religions recognising the terrible existence of evil in the world, of a spiritual power of evil (called

persuade him. <sup>(22)</sup> And the LORD said unto him, Wherewith? And he said, I will go forth, and I will be a lying spirit in the mouth of all his prophets. And he said, Thou shalt persuade *him*, and prevail also: go forth, and do so. <sup>(23)</sup> Now therefore, behold, the LORD hath put a lying spirit in the mouth of all these thy prophets, and the LORD hath spoken evil concerning thee.

<sup>(24)</sup> But Zedekiah the son of Chenaanah went near, and smote Micaiah on the cheek, and said, *a* Which way went the Spirit of the LORD from me to speak unto thee? <sup>(25)</sup> And Micaiah said, Behold, thou shalt see in that day, when thou shalt go ¹into ²an inner chamber to hide thyself.

<sup>(26)</sup> And the king of Israel said, Take Micaiah, and carry him back unto Amon the governor of the city, and to Joash the king's son; <sup>(27)</sup> and say, Thus saith the king, Put this *fellow* in the prison, and feed him with bread of affliction and with water of affliction, until I come in peace. <sup>(28)</sup> And Micaiah said, If thou return at all in peace, the LORD hath not spoken by me. And he said, Hearken, O people, every one of you.

<sup>(29)</sup> So the king of Israel and Jehoshaphat the king of Judah went up to Ramoth-gilead. <sup>(30)</sup> And the king of Israel said unto Jehoshaphat, ³ I will disguise myself, and enter into the battle; but put on thy robes. And the king of Israel disguised himself, and went into the battle. <sup>(31)</sup> But the king of Syria commanded his thirty and two captains that had rule over his chariots, saying, Fight neither with small nor great, save only with the king of Israel. <sup>(32)</sup> And it came to pass, when the captains of the chariots saw Jehoshaphat, that they said, Surely it *is* the king of Israel. And they turned aside to fight against him: and Jehoshaphat cried out. <sup>(33)</sup> And it came to pass, when the captains of the chariots perceived that it *was* not the king of Israel, that they

*a* 2 Chron. 18. 23.

¹ Or, *from chamber to chamber.*

² Heb., *a chamber in a chamber.*

³ Or, *when he was to disguise himself, and enter into the battle.*

---

euphemistically, "the spirit") overruled to work out the judgments of God. The absolute subordination of such spirits of evil in every notice of them in the Old Testament precludes all danger of the monstrous dualism of so many Eastern religions. The reference of the power of divination to such spirits is found in the New Testament also. (See Acts xvi. 16—18.)

<sup>(23)</sup> **The Lord . . . the Lord.**—The emphatic repetition of the Name Jehovah here is an implied answer to the insinuation of mere malice in verses 8, 18.

<sup>(24)</sup> **Smote Micaiah on the cheek.**—The act is not only the expression of contempt (see Isa. l. 6; Micah v. 1; Matt. v. 39), but of professed indignation at words of blasphemy against God, or of contempt for His vicegerents; as is seen clearly, when it is recorded as directed against Our Lord or against St. Paul (John xviii. 22, 23; Acts xxiii. 2). The words which accompany it evidently convey a sarcastic reference to the knowledge of the secret dealings of God, implied in Micaiah's vision, with a view to turn it into ridicule. Micaiah's answer accordingly passes them by, and merely declares the shame and terror, with which Zedekiah shall find out hereafter the truth of the prophecy of evil. Josephus has a curious addition, that Zedekiah challenged Micaiah to wither up his hand, like the hand of Jeroboam at Bethel, and scouted his prophecy as inconsistent with that of Elijah (*Antt.* viii. 15, § 4).

<sup>(26)</sup> **Joash the king's son**, of whom we know nothing hereafter, is apparently entrusted (like the seventy sons of 2 Kings x. 1) to the charge of the governor of the city, perhaps in theory left in command of Samaria with him.

<sup>(27)</sup> **Bread of affliction . . .**—Comp. Isa. xxx. 20. This is a command of severe treatment, as well as scanty fare. Ahab's affectation of disbelief—which his subsequent conduct shows to be but affectation—simply draws down a plainer and sterner prediction, accompanied moreover, if our text be correct, by an appeal to the whole assembly to bear witness of it. Of Micaiah's fate we know nothing; but it is hard to suppose that his bold and defiant testimony could escape the extreme penalty of death, when Ahab's fall gave opportunity of revival to the ruthlessness of Jezebel.

<sup>(28)</sup> **Hearken, O people.**—It is a curious coincidence that these are the opening words of the prophetic Book of Micah. They are not found in some MSS. of the LXX., and are supposed by some to be an early interpolation in this passage from that book.

<sup>(29)</sup> **So . . . Jehoshaphat.**—The continued adhesion of Jehoshaphat, against the voice of prophecy, which he had himself invoked (severely rebuked in 2 Chron. xviii. 31), and, indeed, the subservient part which he plays throughout, evidently indicate a position of virtual dependence of Judah on the stronger power of Israel, of which the alliance by marriage—destined to be all but fatal to the dynasty of David (2 Kings xi. 1, 2)—was at once the sign and the cause.

<sup>(30)</sup> **I will disguise myself.**—The precaution of Ahab is almost ludicrously characteristic of his temper of half-belief and half-unbelief. In itself it is, of course, plainly absurd to believe that God's judgment has in all probability been pronounced, and yet to suppose that it can be averted by so puerile a precaution. But, as experience shows, it is not the less on that account true to human nature, especially such a nature as his, always "halting between two opinions."

<sup>(31)</sup> **His thirty and two captains.**—See chap. xx. 16, 24. The power of Syria had already recovered itself, and is directed with singular virulence against the person of the king who had unwisely spared it. Ahab is represented as the mover of the whole war, and as fighting bravely to the death.

<sup>(32)</sup> **Cried out**—*i.e.*, to rally his people round him. In 2 Chron. xviii. 31 it is added, "And the Lord helped him; and God moved them to depart from him."

*The Death of Ahab.*  I. KINGS, XXII.  *Jehoshaphat's Reign.*

turned back from pursuing him. (34) And a *certain* man drew a bow ¹at a venture, and smote the king of Israel between the ²joints of the harness: wherefore he said unto the driver of his chariot, Turn thine hand, and carry me out of the host; for I am ³wounded. (35) And the battle ⁴increased that day: and the king was stayed up in his chariot against the Syrians, and died at even: and the blood ran out of the wound into the ⁵midst of the chariot. (36) And there went a proclamation throughout the host about the going down of the sun, saying, Every man to his city, and every man to his own country. (37) So the king died, and ⁶was brought to Samaria; and they buried the king in Samaria. (38) And *one* washed the chariot in the pool of Samaria; and the dogs licked up his blood; and they washed his armour; according *a*unto the word of the LORD which he spake.

(39) Now the rest of the acts of Ahab, and all that he did, and the ivory house which he made, and all the cities that he built, *are* they not written in the book of the chronicles of the kings of Israel? (40) So Ahab slept with his fathers; and Ahaziah his son reigned in his stead.

(41) And *b*Jehoshaphat the son of Asa began to reign over Judah in the fourth year of Ahab king of Israel. (42) Jehoshaphat *was* thirty and five years old when he began to reign; and he reigned twenty and five years in Jerusalem. And his mother's name *was* Azubah the daughter of Shilhi. (43) And he walked in all the ways of Asa his father; he turned not aside from it, doing *that which was* right in the eyes of the LORD:

*Marginal notes:* 1 Heb., *in his simplicity.* 2 Heb., *joints and the breastplate.* 3 Heb., *made sick.* 4 Heb., *ascended.* B.C. 914. 5 Heb., *bosom.* 6 Heb., *came.* a ch. 21. 19. b 2 Chron. 20. 31.

---

(34) **A certain man.**—Josephus says, "a young man named Naaman." (Comp. 2 Kings v. 1: "because by him the Lord had given deliverance to Syria.")

**The driver of his chariot.**—In the Egyptian and Assyrian monuments, as subsequently in the Greek of the Homeric days, the war-chariot holds but two, the warrior and the charioteer. This is the first place where the chariot, introduced by Solomon from Egypt (chap. x. 29), is mentioned as actually used in war. (See subsequently, 2 Kings ix. 16, 21, xxiii. 30; and compare the proverbial expression of this period, "The chariot of Israel and the horsemen thereof," 2 Kings ii. 12, xiii. 14.)

(35) **The king was stayed up . . .**—Ahab's repentance, imperfect as it was, has at least availed to secure him a warrior's death, before "the evil came" on his house and on Israel. Evidently he conceals the deadliness of his hurt, though it disables him from action, and bravely sustains the battle, till his strength fails. Then the news spreads, and the army disperses; but the subsequent history seems to show that no fatal defeat was incurred. This union of desperate physical bravery with moral feebleness and cowardice is common enough in history, and (as Shakspeare has delighted to show in his Macbeth) most true to nature.

(38) **They washed his armour.**—There seems little doubt that this is a mistranslation, and that the LXX. rendering (supported also by Josephus) is correct: "And the harlots bathed in it," that is, in the blood-stained pool, the usual public bathing-place of their shamelessness. The dog and the harlot are the animal and human types of uncleanness.

**According unto the word of the Lord.**—The reference to the emphatic prophecy of Elijah is unmistakable, and the context fixes its fulfilment plainly as having taken place in Samaria. The difficulty is, of course, the notice in 2 Kings ix. 25, where the dead body of Jehoram is cast "in the portion of the field of Naboth," evidently at Jezreel; with quotation of the "burden of the Lord laid upon him," "I will requite thee in this plot, saith the Lord." The reconcilement is, with our knowledge, difficult, if not impossible. But the reference in the text is so much clearer, that it must outweigh the other. Naboth, in any case, is likely to have had land in his native place, which would be forfeited to the king; and there would still be an appropriate judgment in making it also the scene of the dishonoured death of the last king of Ahab's house. We may notice, moreover, that the quotation in 2 Kings ix. is not taken from Elijah's words against Ahab, nor does it contain the characteristic notice of the "dogs licking the blood;" though it is noticed as a fulfilment of the subsequent prophecy of chapter xxi. 24 against Ahab's house.

(39) **The ivory house.**—See Amos iii. 15. We note that now, for the first time since the days of Solomon (chap. x. 18—20, 39), the use of ivory—in this case for inlaying the walls of houses—so characteristic of Zidonian art, is mentioned. The "undesigned coincidence," in relation to the renewed intercourse with Zidon, is remarkable.

**All the cities . . .**—Possibly the cities ceded by Ben-hadad, and rebuilt as strongholds. The description shows that Ahab's reign was externally one of power and prosperity, as yet unimpaired even by his death and disaster at Ramoth-gilead. The fruits of spiritual corruption had not yet ripened.

(41) **Jehoshaphat.**—The narrative here, so far as it is full and continuous, centres round the prophetic work of Elijah and Elisha, the scene of which was in Israel; and the compiler contents himself with the insertion of a few brief annalistic notices of the kingdom of Judah, taking up the thread of the narrative of chapter xv. 24, except where (as in 2 Kings iii.) it becomes again connected with the history of Israel. In the Chronicles, on the contrary, there is a full and interesting account of the reign of Jehoshaphat, and especially of his great religious revival (2 Chron. xvii.—xx.), coinciding with this chapter, almost verbally, in the account of the battle at Ramoth-gilead. The brief notices here of the religious work of Jehoshaphat, his "might," and his "wars," agree entirely with this fuller record.

(43) **The high places were not taken away.**—This agrees with 2 Chron. xx. 33, and stands in apparent contradiction with 2 Chron. xvii. 6: "He took

nevertheless the high places were not taken away; *for* the people offered and burnt incense yet in the high places. (44) And Jehoshaphat made peace with the king of Israel.

(45) Now the rest of the acts of Jehoshaphat, and his might that he shewed, and how he warred, *are* they not written in the book of the chronicles of the kings of Judah? (46) And the remnant of the sodomites, which remained in the days of his father Asa, he took out of the land.

(47) *There was* then no king in Edom: a deputy *was* king.

(48) Jehoshaphat ¹made ships of Tharshish to go to Ophir for gold: but they went not; for the ships were broken at Ezion-geber. (49) Then said Ahaziah the son of Ahab unto Jehoshaphat, Let my servants go with thy servants in the ships. But Jehoshaphat would not.

(50) And Jehoshaphat slept with his fathers, and was buried with his fathers in the city of David his father: and Jehoram his son reigned in his stead.

(51) Ahaziah the son of Ahab began to reign over Israel in Samaria the seventeenth year of Jehoshaphat king of Judah, and reigned two years over Israel. (52) And he did evil in the sight of the LORD, and walked in the way of his father, and in the way of his mother, and in the way of Jeroboam the son of Nebat, who made Israel to sin: (53) for he served Baal, and worshipped him, and provoked to anger the LORD God of Israel, according to all that his father had done.

¹ Or, *had ten ships.*

B.C. 889.

B.C. 913.
B.C. 898.

---

away the high places and groves out of Judah." Probably the key to the apparent discrepancy lies in the words " and groves" (Asherah). The high places taken away were those connected with the base Asherah worship; those which were simply unauthorised sanctuaries remained, at any rate in part.

(44) **And Jehoshaphat.**—This verse is chronologically out of place. It refers to the policy of Jehoshaphat, pursued apparently from the beginning, of exchanging the chronic condition of war with Israel in the preceding reigns, for peace and alliance.

(46) **The remnant . . .**—See chaps. xiv. 24, xv. 12.

(47) **There was then no king in Edom.**—This notice is apparently connected with the following verses; for Ezion-geber is a seaport of the Edomite territory. Whatever may have been the influence of Hadad in the last days of Solomon (chap. xi. 14), Edom does not seem to have regained independence till the time of Jehoram, son of Jehoshaphat (2 Chron. xxi. 8—10); although in the confederacy against Jehoshaphat, those " of Mount Seir" are included with the Moabites and Ammonites (2 Chron. xx. 10, 22). The " king of Edom," of 2 Kings iii., who is evidently a subject ally, not regarded in consultation (see verses 6—9), must be " the deputy" of this passage.

(48) **Ships of Tharshish to go to Ophir.**—See Note on chap. x. 22. We note that this revival of maritime enterprise coincides with the renewed alliance through Israel with Tyre. The account in 2 Chron. xx. 35—37 makes the brief narrative of these verses intelligible. The fleet was a combined fleet of Judah and Israel, built at Ezion-geber, which belonged to Judah; the alliance was denounced and judgment threatened by the prophet Eliezer. After the wreck of the fleet, manned, it would seem, by the subjects of Jehoshaphat, Ahaziah of Israel desires to renew the enterprise with the aid of Israelite and probably Tyrian sailors; but Jehoshaphat now refuses.

(51) **Ahaziah.**—In this short reign the influence of Jezebel, evidently in abeyance in the last days of Ahab, revives; and the idolatry of Baal resumes its place side by side with the older idolatry of Jeroboam, and (see 2 Kings i. 2) with the worship of the Canaanitish Baalzebub.

# THE SECOND BOOK OF THE KINGS

# THE SECOND BOOK OF THE KINGS

COMMONLY CALLED

## THE FOURTH BOOK OF THE KINGS

CHAPTER I.—<sup>(1)</sup> Then Moab rebelled against Israel <sup>a</sup> after the death of Ahab. <sup>(2)</sup> And Ahaziah fell down through a lattice in his upper chamber that *was* in Samaria, and was sick : and he sent messengers, and said unto them, Go, enquire of Baal-zebub the god of Ekron whether I shall recover of this disease. <sup>(3)</sup> But the angel of the LORD said to Elijah the Tishbite, Arise, go up to meet the messengers of the king of Samaria, and say unto them, *Is it* not because *there is* not a God in Israel, *that* ye go to enquire of Baal-zebub

B.C. cir. 896.

a ch. 3. 5.

---

The division of the Book of Kings at this point is inartificial and arbitrary. The present narrative obviously continues that of 1 Kings xxii. 51—53.

1. THE REIGN OF AHAZIAH CONTINUED. EPISODE CONCERNING ELIJAH.

<sup>(1)</sup> **Then.**—*And.*

**Moab rebelled against Israel.**—David reduced Moab to vassalage (2 Sam. viii. 2; comp. chap. xxiii. 20). After that event, Scripture is silent as to the fortunes of Moab. It probably took occasion of the troubles which ensued upon the death of Solomon, to throw off the yoke of Israel. The famous Moabite stone supplements the sacred history by recording the war of liberation which Mesha, king of Moab, successfully waged against the successors of Ahab. The inscription opens thus : " I am Mesha, son of Chemosh-gad, king of Moab the Dibonite. My father reigned over Moab thirty years, and I reigned after my father. And I made this *bamah* (" high place," " pillar ") for Chemosh in Korha, a *bamah* of salvation, for he saved me from all the assailants, and let me see my desire upon mine enemies . . . Omri, king of Israel, and he oppressed Moab many days, for Chemosh was angry with his land. And his son (*i.e.*, Ahab) succeeded him, and he, too, said, ' I will oppress Moab.' In my days he said (it), but I saw my desire upon him and his house, and Israel perished utterly for ever. And Omri occupied the land of Medeba, and dwelt therein, and (they oppressed Moab he and) his son forty years. And Chemosh looked (?) on it (*i.e.*, Moab) in my days." From this unique and unhappily much injured record it appears that Omri had reduced Moab again to subjection, and that Ahab, who, like his father, was a strong sovereign, had maintained his hold upon the country. The death of Ahab and the sickness of Ahaziah would be Moab's opportunity. The revolt of Moab is mentioned here parenthetically. The subject is continued in chap. iii. 4—27. (See the Notes there.)

(2—16) A new and (according to Ewald and Thenius) later fragment of the history of Elijah.

<sup>(2)</sup> **Through a lattice.**—Rather, *the lattice, i.e.*, the latticed window of the chamber on the palace roof, looking into the court below. The word rendered " through " (*bĕ‘ad*) implies that Ahaziah was leaning out over the window-sill. (Comp. chap. ix. 30; Ps. xiv. 2.) He perhaps fell into a gallery underneath, as the palace would be several storeys high, and he was not killed by his fall. The word *sĕbākhāh* means " net " in Job xviii. 8, and decorative " network " in metal in 1 Kings vii. 18; 2 Chron. iv. 12. The Rabbis explain it here as a sort of skylight to the chamber beneath the upper chamber, or a spiral stairway; both improbable.

**He sent messengers.**—By Jezebel's advice. (S Ephrem.)

**Baal-zebub.**—Here only in the Old Testament. " Lord of Flies " is generally compared with the Greek Ζεὺς ἀπομυῖος, or μυίαγρος, the " fly-averting Zeus " of the Eleans (Paus., viii. 26, 4), and it is no doubt true that flies are an extraordinary pest in the East. But when we remember that " myiomancy," or divination by watching the movements of flies, is an ancient Babylonian practice, we can hardly doubt that this is the true significance of the title " Baal-zebub." In the Assyrian deluge tablet the gods are said to have gathered over Izdubar's sacrifice " like flies " (*kima zumbie*). The later Jewish spelling (Βεελζεβούλ) probably contains an allusive reference to the Talmudic words *zebel* (" dung "), *zibbūl* (" dunging ").

**Ekron.**—*Akir* (Josh. xiii. 3). Of the five Philistine cities it lay farthest north, and so nearest to Samaria.

**Recover.**—Literally, *live from,* or *after*.

**Disease.**—*Sickness,* viz., that occasioned by his fall. The LXX. adds, " and they went to inquire of him."

<sup>(3)</sup> **But the angel . . . said.**—Rather, *Now the angel . . . had said.* " The angel " is right. (Comp. chap. xix. 35.) Reuss strangely renders : " Mais une révélation de l'Eternel parla ; " and adds the note, " Et non pas un ange " (!).

**Arise, go up.**—Samaria lay on a hill, and the prophet was to meet the messengers at the gates.

**King of Samaria.**—Not *Israel,* a mark of Judæan feeling.

**And say.**—Literally, *speak.* LXX., Vulgate, and Arabic add " saying," but comp. 1 Kings xxi. 5, 6.

**Is it not because.**—Omit " not." So verse 6.

**Ye go.**—*Are going.*

**A God in Israel.**—Comp. Micah iv. 5: " For all peoples will walk every one in the name of his god, and we will walk in the name of Jehovah our God for ever and ever."

the god of Ekron? ⁽⁴⁾ Now therefore thus saith the LORD, ¹Thou shalt not come down from that bed on which thou art gone up, but shalt surely die. And Elijah departed.

⁽⁵⁾ And when the messengers turned back unto him, he said unto them, Why are ye now turned back? ⁽⁶⁾ And they said unto him, There came a man up to meet us, and said unto us, Go, turn again unto the king that sent you, and say unto him, Thus saith the LORD, *Is it* not because *there is* not a God in Israel, *that* thou sendest to enquire of Baal-zebub the god of Ekron? therefore thou shalt not come down from that bed on which thou art gone up, but shalt surely die. ⁽⁷⁾ And he said unto them, ²What manner of man *was he* which came up to meet you, and told you these words? ⁽⁸⁾ And they answered him, He *was* an hairy man, and girt with a girdle of leather about his loins. And he said, It *is* Elijah the Tishbite. ⁽⁹⁾ Then the king sent unto him a captain of fifty with his fifty. And he went up to him: and, behold, he sat on the top of an hill. And he spake unto him, Thou man of God, the king hath said, Come down. ⁽¹⁰⁾ And Elijah answered and said to the captain of fifty, If I *be* a man of God, then let fire come down from heaven, and consume thee and thy fifty. And there came down

1 Heb., *The bed, whither thou art gone up, thou shalt not come down from it.*

2 Heb., *What was the manner of the man?*

---

⁽⁴⁾ **Now therefore.**—For this act of faithlessness, and to prove by the event that there is a God in Israel, whose oracle is unerring. (Comp. 1 Kings xviii. 24, *seq.*)

**Thus saith.**—Or, *hath said*. After these words the prophetic announcement comes in rather abruptly. Perhaps the verse has been abridged by the compiler, and in the original account from which he drew, the words of verse 6 may have followed here, "Go, return to the king . . . Ekron."

**And Elijah departed.**—On the Lord's errand. The LXX. adds, "and said unto them," or "told them," which is perhaps due to a copyist's eye having wandered to the words "unto him," or "unto them," in next verse (*Thenius*).

⁽⁵⁾ **Turned back unto him.**—Unto Ahaziah, as the Syriac and Vulgate actually read. Literally, *And the messengers returned unto him, and he said*, &c. Though Elijah was unknown to the envoys, such a menacing interposition would certainly be regarded as a Divine warning, which it was perilous to disregard.

**Why are ye now turned back?**—*Why have ye returned?* with emphasis on the "Why."

⁽⁶⁾ **Thou sendest.**—*Art sending*. Elijah had said, *ye are going*, in his question to the messengers (verse 3). (See Note on verse 4.) Bähr is wrong in supposing the servants anxious to shift the prophet's blame from themselves to their lord, or that Elijah had addressed them as accomplices in the king's guilt. They had no choice but to obey the royal mandate.

⁽⁷⁾ **He said.**—*Spake*. (See Note on verse 3.)

**What manner of man?**—See margin. The word *mishpat* here denotes the *external* characteristics and visible peculiarities by which a man is *distinguished* (*shāphat*) from his fellows. (Comp. our expressions "sort," "fashion," "style," and the Vulgate, "Cujus figuræ et habitus est vir ille?" LXX., ἡ κρίσις. Syriac, "appearance," "look." Targum, νόμος.)

⁽⁸⁾ **Answered.**—*Said unto*.

**An hairy man.**—Literally, *a lord of hair*. This might refer to length of hair and beard (so LXX., δασύς, "hirsute," "shaggy"); or to a hairy cloak or mantle. The second alternative is right, because a hairy mantle was a mark of the prophetic office from Elijah downwards. (Comp. Zech. xiii. 4, "a rough garment;" and Matt. iii. 4, where it is said of John Baptist—the second Elias—that "he was clad in camel's hair," and had "a leather girdle about his loins.") The girdle, as Thenius remarks, would not be mentioned alone. The common dress of the Bedawis is a sheep or goat's skin with the hair left on.

**Girt with a girdle of leather.**—Such as only the poorest would wear. The girdle was ordinarily of linen or cotton, and often costly. The prophet's dress was a sign of contempt for earthly display, and of sorrow for the national sins and their consequences, which it was his function to proclaim. (Comp. Isa. xx. 2.)

⁽⁹⁾ **Then the king sent.**—Heb., *And he sent*. With hostile intentions, as is proved by his sending soldiers, and by the words of the angel in verse 15. (Comp. 1 Kings xviii. 8, xxii. 26, *seq.*)

**He sat.**—*Was sitting*. The LXX. has "Elias was sitting," which is probably original.

**A captain of fifty.**—The army of Israel was organised by thousands, hundreds, and fifties, each of which had its "captain" (*sar*). (Comp. Num. xxxi 14, 48; 1 Sam. viii. 12.)

**On the top of an hill.**—Rather, *the hill, i.e.,* above Samaria. Others think, Carmel, from 1 Kings xviii. 42; chap. ii. 25.

**He spake.**—LXX., "the captain of fifty spake."

**Thou man of God.**—Heb., *man of the god, i.e.,* the true God. (So in verses 11, 13, *infra*.)

**The king.**—In the Hebrew emphatic, as if to say, the king's power is irresistible, even by a man of God. The true God was thus insulted in the person of His prophet.

**Come down.**—Or, *Pray come down*—in a tone of ironical politeness (*rĕdāh*, precative).

⁽¹⁰⁾ **And Elijah answered and said.**—So Syriac and LXX. Heb., *and spake*.

**If.**—Heb., *And if a man of the god I* (truly be). This "and" closely connects the prophet's reply with the captain's demand. All the versions except the LXX. omit it, with some Hebrew MSS.

**Then.**—Omit.

**Let fire come down from heaven.**—A phrase found only here and in 2 Chron. vii. 1. Ewald considers this a mark of the later origin of this tradition about Elijah. The words "come down" are at any rate appropriate, as repeating the captain's bidding to the prophet.

**Consume.**—*Eat*, or *devour*. (Comp. 1 Kings xviii. 38.) Here, as there, Jehovah is represented as vindi-

fire from heaven, and consumed him and his fifty. <sup>(11)</sup> Again also he sent unto him another captain of fifty with his fifty. And he answered and said unto him, O man of God, thus hath the king said, Come down quickly. <sup>(12)</sup> And Elijah answered and said unto them, If I be a man of God, let fire come down from heaven, and consume thee and thy fifty. And the fire of God came down from heaven, and consumed him and his fifty. <sup>(13)</sup> And he sent again a captain of the third fifty with his fifty. And the third captain of fifty went up, and came and ¹fell on his knees before Elijah, and besought him, and said unto him, O man of God, I pray thee, let my life, and the life of these fifty thy servants, be precious in thy sight. <sup>(14)</sup> Behold, there came fire down from heaven, and burnt up the two captains of the former fifties with their fifties: therefore let my life now be precious in thy sight. <sup>(15)</sup> And the angel of the Lord said unto Elijah, Go down with him: be not afraid of him. And he arose, and went down with him unto the king.

<sup>(16)</sup> And he said unto him, Thus saith the LORD, Forasmuch as thou hast sent messengers to enquire of Baal-zebub the god of Ekron, *is it* not because *there is* no God in Israel to enquire of his word? therefore thou shalt not come down off that bed on which thou art gone up, but shalt surely die.

<sup>(17)</sup> So he died according to the word of the LORD which Elijah had spoken. And Jehoram reigned in his stead in the second year of Jehoram the son of Jehoshaphat king of Judah; because he

¹ Heb., *bowed.*

B.C. 896.

---

cating His own cause by the means most adequate to the necessities of the time, viz., a manifest miracle.

<sup>(11)</sup> **Again also he sent.**—Although he had heard what had befallen his former envoys.

**He answered.**—LXX., "went up" (*way-ya'al* for *way-ya'an*), as in verses 9 and 13.

**And said.**—Heb., *spake*. Yet some MSS., and Vulgate, Syriac, Arabic, as Authorised Version.

**Thus hath the king said.**—Or, *commanded* (*'āmar*).

**Come down quickly.**—"Impudentior fuit hic ... priore; tum quia audito ejus supplicio non resipuit, tum quia auxit impudentiam addendo 'Festina'" (*a Lapide*). (But see Note on verse 12.)

<sup>(12)</sup> **Said (spake) unto them.**—LXX. and Syriac, "unto him," which seems original.

**The fire of God.**—"The" is not in the Hebrew. The LXX., Vulgate, Arabic, and Targum, with some MSS., omit "of God." The phrase occurs in the sense of lightning (Job i. 16).

**Consumed him and his fifty.**—According to Thenius, the story of the destruction of the captains and their companies emphasises (1) the authority properly belonging to the prophet; (2) the help and protection which Jehovah bestows on His prophets. The captains and their men are simply conceived as *instruments of a will opposing itself to Jehovah*, and are accordingly annihilated. These considerations, he thinks, render irrelevant all questions about the moral justice of their fate, and comparative degrees of guilt. (Comp. chaps. ii. 23, *seq.*, vi. 17.)

<sup>(13)</sup> **A captain of the third fifty.**—Literally, *a captain of a third fifty*. But verse 11, "another captain of fifty," and the phrase which follows here, "the third captain of fifty," indicate the right reading, "a third captain of fifty." (So LXX. and Vulg.)

**Fell.**—Margin. (Comp. Isa. xlvi. 1, "Bel boweth down.")

**Besought him.**—*Begged favour, grace,* or *compassion of him* (Gen. xlii. 21; Hosea xii. 5).

**These fifty thy servants.**—Or, *these thy servants, fifty* (*men*), laying stress on the number of lives.

**Be precious in thy sight.**—Comp. Ps. lxxii. 14; 1 Sam. xxvi. 21.

<sup>(14)</sup> **Burnt.**—*Eat*, or *devoured* (verses 10, 12).

**The two captains of the former fifties.**—Rather, *the former two captains of fifties*.

**Therefore let my life now.**—*And now* (*i.e.*, this time) *let my life*. Some MSS., and LXX., Vulg., and Arabic *add* the precative "now," that is, "I pray," as in verse 13 ("I pray thee" = *na'*).

<sup>(15)</sup> **Said.**—So LXX. (εἶπε). Heb., *spake*. Vulgate and Arabic add "saying." (See Note on verse 3.)

**Go down.**—From the mountain top into the city.

**With him.**—*'Othô,* later form for *'ittô,* which some MSS. read here.

**Be not afraid of him**—*i.e.,* the captain. The former two, as being the willing tools of the king, might have shown their zeal by instantly slaying the prophet. (Comp. the case of the knights who murdered St. Thomas of Canterbury.)

<sup>(16)</sup> **And he said.**—Heb., *spake*. The LXX. adds, "and Elijah said."

**Is it not because.**—Omit "not." The question is here parenthetic, the connection of the main sentence being, "Forasmuch as thou hast sent . . . therefore thou shalt not come down," &c.

**Off.**—*From,* as in verses 4 and 6. The words of the oracle are thrice repeated verbally.

"Here, just as in other cases," says Bähr, "Elijah reappears suddenly and disappears again, and no one knows whence he comes or whither he goes." The peculiar form of the story suggests that it was derived in the first instance from oral tradition rather than from a written source.

<sup>(17, 18)</sup> Concluding remarks added by the compiler.

<sup>(17)</sup> **And Jehoram.**—LXX. (Alex.), Syriac, and Vulgate add "his brother," an expression which has fallen out of the Hebrew text, owing to its resemblance to the next (*tahtāw*, "in his stead"). (Comp. chap. iii. 1, "son of Ahab.")

**In the second year of Jehoram.**—Vat. LXX., "in the eighteenth year," which is probably right. (Comp. 1 Kings xxii. 52, "Ahaziah . . . reigned over Israel in . . . the seventeenth year of Jehoshaphat . . . and he reigned two years." Either, therefore, our present Heb. text is corrupt, or the compiler followed a different source in this place.) Thenius proposes the

had no son. ⁽¹⁸⁾ Now the rest of the acts of Ahaziah which he did, *are* they not written in the book of the chronicles of the kings of Israel?

CHAPTER II.—⁽¹⁾ And it came to pass, when the LORD would take up Elijah into heaven by a whirlwind, that Elijah went with Elisha from Gilgal. ⁽²⁾ And Elijah said unto Elisha, Tarry here, I pray thee; for the LORD hath sent me to Beth-el. And Elisha said *unto him, As* the LORD liveth, and *as* thy soul liveth, I will not leave thee. So they went down to Beth-el. ⁽³⁾ And the sons of the prophets that *were* at Beth-el came forth to Elisha, and said unto him, Knowest thou that the LORD will take away thy master from thy head to day? And he said, Yea, I know *it;* hold ye your peace. ⁽⁴⁾ And Elijah said unto him, Elisha, tarry here, I pray thee; for the LORD hath sent me to Jericho. And he said, *As* the LORD liveth, and *as* thy soul liveth, I will not leave thee. So they came to Jericho.

---

reading, "in the twenty-second year of Jehoshaphat," in place of "in the second year of Jehoram the son of Jehoshaphat."

⁽¹⁸⁾ **The acts.**—*Dibrê, i.e.,* history.

**Which he did.**—Some MSS. and the Syriac read "and all that he did," which seems correct.

**The book of the chronicles of the kings.**—See *Introduction*, and 1 Kings xiv. 19.

### II.

THE CLOSE OF THE HISTORY OF ELIJAH. HE IS SUCCEEDED BY ELISHA.

(1—18) Elijah is miraculously taken away from the earth.

⁽¹⁾ **And it came to pass . . . whirlwind.**—The compiler has prefixed this heading to the following narrative by way of connection with the general thread of the history. It *seems* to be indicated that the event happened in the beginning of the reign of Jehoram; but see Note on 2 Chron. xxi. 12.

**When the Lord would take up.**—*When Jehovah caused Elijah to go up*, or *ascend*. This anticipates the conclusion of the story.

**Into heaven.**—Heb., accusative of direction, as in verse 11. The LXX. renders, ὡς εἰς τὸν οὐρανόν, "as into heaven," perhaps to suggest that not the visible heavens, but God, was the real goal of the prophet's ascension.

**By a whirlwind.**—*In the storm.*

**Gilgal.**—Heb., *the Gilgal, i.e.*, the Ring (comp. Isa. xxviii. 28, "wheel"), a descriptive name of more than one place. Here, Gilgal in Ephraim, the present *Jiljilia*, which stands on a hill south-west of *Seilûn* (Shiloh), near the road leading thence to Jericho. (See Deut. xi. 30; Hosea iv. 15; Amos iv. 4.) Hosea and Amos connect Gilgal with Bethel, as a sanctuary. It was probably marked by a *ring* of stones like those at Stonehenge and Avebury. From this spot the mountain land of Gilead, the Great Sea, and the snowy heights of Hermon, were all visible; so that the prophet could take from thence a last look at the whole country which had been the scene of his earthly activity.

⁽²⁾ **Said.**—Not *spake*, as throughout the account in chap. i. 2—16; a mark of different origin.

**Tarry here, I pray thee.**—This was said, not to test Elisha's affection, nor from a motive of humility, that Elisha might not witness his glorious ascension, but because Elijah was uncertain whether it was God's will that Elisha should go with him. (Comp. verse 10.) Elisha's *threefold* refusal to leave him settled the doubt. (Comp. John xxi. 15, *seq.*)

**The Lord hath sent me to Beth-el.**—Why? Not merely to "see once more this holiest place in Israel, the spiritual centre of the kingdom of the ten tribes" (*Ewald*), but to visit the prophetic schools, or guilds, established there, and at Gilgal and Jericho, and to confirm their fidelity to Jehovah. Gilgal and Beth-el, as ancient Canaanite sanctuaries, were centres of illegal worship of the God of Israel. The guilds of the prophets may have been intended to counteract this evil influence at its head-quarters (*Bähr*).

**As the Lord liveth, and as thy soul liveth.**—Chap. iv. 30; 1 Sam. xx. 3. A more solemn and emphatic oath than "As the Lord liveth" (Judges viii. 19), or "As thy soul liveth" (1 Sam. i. 26). Literally, *By the life of Jehovah and by the life of thy soul (i.e., of thyself, thine own life).*

**They went down.**—From Gilgal. The phrase proves that the Gilgal between the Jordan and Jericho cannot be meant in verse 1. (See Josh. iv. 19, v. 10.)

⁽³⁾ **The sons of the prophets.**—See Notes on 1 Kings xx. 35; 1 Sam. x. 10, xix. 20. There was a guild of prophets at Beth-el.

**Came forth to Elisha.**—Who probably walked a little way before his master, to announce his approach.

**And said unto him.**—The prophetic college had been divinely forewarned of Elijah's departure.

**The Lord will take away . . . to day.**—"To day" is emphatic. "Knowest thou that this day Jehovah is about to take away thy lord *from beside thee?*" The word "head" may signify *self*, or *person*, like the word "soul," and other terms. (Comp. Gen. xl. 13; 1 Sam. xxviii. 2; 2 Sam. i. 16.) Others explain "from over thy head," *i.e.*, from his position of superiority over thee as thy master and teacher. (See 1 Kings xix. 21; Acts xxii. 3.) Others again, but very improbably, take the words literally as a reference to Elijah's ascension, "away over thine head."

**Yea, I know.**—Rather, *I, too, know.*

**Hold ye your peace.**—Elisha says this, not to prevent the gathering of a crowd to witness the spectacle of Elijah's departure, nor yet to intimate that his master's modesty will be shocked by much talk of his approaching exaltation, but simply to suggest that the subject is painful both to him and to his beloved master. The Hebrew term, *hehĕshû*, imitates the sound, like our "hush!"

⁽⁴⁾ **And Elijah said.**—The exact repetition of the language of verses 2, 3 in this and the next two verses, appears to indicate that the narrative had originally been handed on by oral tradition, probably in the prophetic guilds at the local sanctuaries.

*Elijah Divides*        II. KINGS, II.        *the Jordan.*

(5) And the sons of the prophets that were at Jericho came to Elisha, and said unto him, Knowest thou that the LORD will take away thy master from thy head to day? And he answered, Yea, I know *it*; hold ye your peace. (6) And Elijah said unto him, Tarry, I pray thee, here; for the LORD hath sent me to Jordan. And he said, As the LORD liveth, and *as* thy soul liveth, I will not leave thee. And they two went on. (7) And fifty men of the sons of the prophets went, and stood [1] to view afar off: and they two stood by Jordan. (8) And Elijah took his mantle, and wrapped *it* together, and smote the waters, and they were divided hither and thither, so that they two went over on dry ground.

(9) And it came to pass, when they were gone over, that Elijah said unto Elisha, Ask what I shall do for thee, before I be taken away from thee. And Elisha said, I pray thee, let a double portion of thy spirit be upon me. (10) And he said, [2]Thou hast asked a hard thing: *nevertheless*, if thou see me *when I am* taken from thee, it shall be so unto thee; but if not, it shall not be *so*.

(11) And it came to pass, as they still went on, and talked, that, behold, *there appeared* a chariot of fire, and horses of fire, and parted them both asunder;

1 Heb., *in sight, or, over against.*

2 Heb., *Thou hast done hard in asking.*

---

(5) **Came.**—*Drew near.*
**Answered.**—*Said.*

(6) **Said unto him.**—Syriac adds, " unto Elisha ; " Arabic, as verse 4, and so three MSS.
**And he said.**—LXX., " and Elisha said "—an improvement.
" Not only Elisha, the intimate companion and future successor of Elijah, but all the disciples of the different 'schools of the prophets,' have the presentiment of the loss which threatens them. The Spirit has warned them all; they communicate their fears, but Elisha forbids them to give free course to their sorrow. A respectful silence, a resignation not exempt from foreboding, suits this condition of things. Elisha clings to his master, as though he could keep him back ; the disciples follow them with their eyes. The monotony of the successive scenes adds to the solemn effect of the total description " (*Reuss*).

(7) **And fifty . . . went.**—*Now fifty . . . had gone.*
**Stood to view.**—*Taken their stand opposite,* i.e., directly opposite the place where the two were standing by the brink of the river, yet at some distance behind. They wished to see whether and how the companions would cross the stream at a point where there was no ford.

(8) **His mantle.**—The hairy *'addèreth,* which characterised him as prophet. Zech. xiii. 4, *'addèreth sĕ'ār,* "mantle of hair ; " Syriac and Arabic, " head-dress " (wrongly).
**Wrapped it together.**—*Rolled it up.* Here only. (Comp. " my substance," or " mass," Ps. cxxxix. 16; "blue mantles," Ezek. xxvii. 24, from the same root.) LXX., εἴλησε; Vulg., "involvit;" Syriac, "rolled it up."
**Smote the waters.**—A symbolical action like that of Moses smiting the rock, or stretching out his rod over the sea. (Comp. also the use of Elisha's staff, chap. iv. 29.) In all these cases the outward and visible sign is made the channel of the invisible and spiritual force of faith.
**They were divided hither and thither.**—Exod. xiv. 16, 21, 22 ; Josh. iv. 22, *seq.*
**So that.**—*And.*

(9) **I pray thee, let . . .**—Literally, *And* (*i.e.*, well, then) *let there fall, I pray thee, a portion of two in thy spirit, unto me.*
**A double portion.**—The expression used in Deut. xxi. 7 of the share of the firstborn son, who by the Mosaic law inherited two parts of his father's property. Elisha asks to be treated as the firstborn among " the sons of the prophets," and so to receive twice as great a share of " the spirit and power " of his master as any of the rest. " Let him be the firstborn among thy spiritual sons ; " " Make me thy true spiritual heir ; " not " Give me twice as great a share of the spirit of prophecy as thou possessest thyself," as many have wrongly interpreted. The phrase, " a mouth of two," seems to be a metaphor derived from the custom of serving honoured guests with double, and even greater, messes (Gen. xliii. 34).
**Ask what I shall do for thee . . . from thee.** —As a dying father, Elijah might wish to bless his spiritual son ere his departure (Gen. xxvii. 4). (Comp. verse 12 *infra,* " My father, my father.")

(10) **Thou hast asked a hard thing.**—Because to grant such a petition was not in Elijah's own power, but in God's only. And therefore in the next words the prophet connects the fulfilment of his follower's wish with a condition depending entirely upon the Divine will : " If thou see me when I am taken from thee, it shall be so unto thee " (*Keil*). " ' If the Lord think thee worthy to witness my departure, thou wilt be worthy to win thy boon.' Elijah thus disclaims power to fulfil the request. At the same time, it is implied that his departure will be something exalted above the perception of ordinary men " (*Thenius*).
**When I am taken.**—Literally, *taken* (participle *pu'al,* shortened form, as in Exod. iii. 2 ; Isa. xviii. 2).

(11) **And it came to pass. . . talked.**—Literally, *And it came to pass, they* (emphatic) *were walking a walking and talking,* i.e., were going on farther and farther, talking as they went. *Whither* they went is not told ; probably some height of the mountains of Gilead, Elijah's native country, was the scene of his departure. (Comp. Deut. xxxiv. 5 ; Num. xx. 28.)
**That, behold, there appeared . . . fire.**—Literally, *and, behold, chariots of fire and horses of fire.* *Rèkeb* is generally collective ; so the Targum here. (Comp. chap. vi. 17 : " Horses and chariots of fire round about Elisha.")
**Parted them both asunder.**—Or, *made parting between them twain,* i.e., the appearance of fiery chariots and horses came between Elijah and Elisha, surrounding the former as with a flaming war-host. (Comp. chap. vi. 17.)
**Elijah went up by a whirlwind into heaven.** —Rather, *Elijah went up in the storm heavenward,* or, perhaps, *into the air. Sĕ'ārāh,* properly *storm-blast*; and

and ᵃElijah went up by a whirlwind into heaven. ⁽¹²⁾ And Elisha saw *it*, and he cried, ᵇMy father, my father, the chariot of Israel, and the horsemen thereof. And he saw him no more: and he took hold of his own clothes, and rent them in two pieces. ⁽¹³⁾ He took up also the mantle of Elijah that fell from him, and went back, and stood by the ¹bank of Jordan; ⁽¹⁴⁾ and he took the mantle of Elijah that fell from him, and smote the waters, and said, Where *is* the LORD God of Elijah? and when he also had smitten the waters, they parted hither and thither: and Elisha went over. ⁽¹⁵⁾ And when the sons of the prophets which *were* ᶜto view at Jericho saw him, they said, The spirit of Elijah doth rest on Elisha. And they came to meet him, and bowed themselves to the ground before him. ⁽¹⁶⁾ And they said unto him, Behold now, there be with thy servants fifty ²strong men; let them go, we pray

ᵃ Ecclus. 48. 9; 1 Macc. 2. 58.

ᵇ ch. 13. 14.

¹ Heb., *lip*.

ᶜ ver. 7.

² Heb., *sons of strength*.

---

so *storm, thunderstorm*. (Comp. Ezek. i. 4, *seq.*, where Jehovah appears in a "whirlwind," which is described as a great fiery cloud; and Job xxxviii. 1, where He answers Job "out of the whirlwind;" and Neh. i. 3: "The Lord hath His path in whirlwind and in storm (*sĕ'ārāh*), and the clouds are the dust of His feet.") The Hebrew mind recognised the presence and working of Jehovah in the terrific phenomena of nature; the thunder-cloud or storm-wind was His chariot, the thunder His voice, the lightning His arrow. (Comp. Pss. xviii. 6—15, civ. 3.) We must therefore be cautious of taking the words before us in too literal a sense. The essential meaning of the passage is this, that God suddenly took Elijah to Himself, amid a grand display of His power in and through the forces of nature. The popular conception, which we see embodied in such pictures as William Blake's *Translation of Elijah*, that the prophet ascended to heaven in a fiery car drawn by horses of fire, is plainly read into, rather than gathered from, the sacred text.

**Went up.**—Bähr *may* be right in asserting that '*ālāh* here means "disappeared, was consumed" (like the German *aufgehen*). He compares Judges xx. 40, "The whole city *went up heavenward*," *i.e.*, was consumed, and the Hebrew name of the burnt offering ('*ōlāh*). But the same phrase ("to go up to heaven") is used in Psalm cvii. 26 of a ship rising heavenward on the stormy waves.

As regards the miraculous removal of Elijah and Enoch (Gen. v. 24), Von Gerlach remarks: "All such questions as whither they were removed, and where they now are, and what changes they underwent in translation, are left unanswered by the Scriptures." It may be added, that the ascension of Elijah into heaven is nowhere alluded to in the rest of the Bible.

⁽¹²⁾ **And Elisha . . . cried.**—Literally, *And Elisha was seeing, and he* (emphatic) *was shouting*. (Comp. verse 10, "If thou see me taken away.")

**My father, my father.**—Expresses what Elijah was to Elisha. (See Note on verse 9.)

**The chariot** (*chariots*—*rĕkeb*) **of Israel, and the horsemen thereof.**—Expressing what Elijah was to the nation. The Targum paraphrases, "My master, my master, who was better to Israel than chariots and horsemen by his prayers." The personal work and influence of a prophet like Elijah was the truest safeguard of Israel. The force of the expression will be seen, if it is remembered that chariots and horsemen constituted, in that age, the chief military arm, and were indispensable for the struggle against the Aramean states. (Comp. chaps. vii. 6, x. 2, xiii. 14; 1 Kings xx. 1; Ps. xx. 7.)

**He saw him no more.**—After his outcry. He *had* seen him taken up.

**Rent them in two pieces.**—From top to bottom, in token of extreme sorrow. (For the phrase, comp. 1 Kings xi. 30.)

⁽¹³⁾ **The mantle of Elijah.**—See verse 8, and comp. 1 Kings xix. 19. The badge of the prophet's office was naturally transferred to his successor.

**The bank.**—Literally, *lip*. So χεῖλος is used in Greek (Herod. ii. 70).

⁽¹⁴⁾ **Where is the Lord God of Elijah?**—Has He left the earth with His prophet? If not, let Him now show His power, and verify the granting of my request (verse 9). The words are a sort of irony of faith. Elisha "seeks" Jehovah as the only source of power. (Comp. Jer. ii. 6, 8, where the priests and prophets are blamed for having recourse to idols, instead of asking, "Where is Jehovah?")

**And when he also had smitten.**—The Hebrew is, *also* (or, *even*) *he—and he smote*. There is clearly something wrong. The LXX. does not render the Hebrew '*aph hû*', "also he," but copies the words in Greek (ἀφφώ). Keil connects them with the foregoing question, "Where is Jehovah, the God of Elijah, even He?" Thenius objects that this use of '*aph* is doubtful, and supports Houbigant's correction, '*ēphô*, an enclitic *then*—"Where, then, is Jehovah, the God of Elijah? and he smote," &c. Perhaps '*ēphōh* ("where") was the original reading: "Where is Jehovah, the God of Elijah? Where?"—an emphatic repetition of the question. Or it may be that the words '*aph hû*' *wayyakkeh* should be transposed: "and he smote—he also (like Elijah)," &c. The Vulgate has the curious rendering, "And with the cloak of Elias which had fallen from him, he smote the waters, and they were not divided; and he said, Where is the God of Elias now also? And he smote the waters, and they were divided," &c. Such also is the reading of the Complutensian LXX.; but the variation is simply an old attempt to account for the twofold "and he smote the waters."

⁽¹⁵⁾ **To view.**—*Opposite, over against*. LXX., ἐξεναντίας; Vulg., "e contra" (Deut. xxxii. 52). It is not clear whether these sons of the prophets are the fifty who "went and stood opposite afar off" (verse 7), or not. On the whole, it seems likely that *all* the guild residing at Jericho is meant. Awaiting Elisha's return, they had assembled at the river side, and witnessed the miracle, which was evidence to them that Elisha was to be their future head.

**The spirit of Elijah doth rest on Elisha.**—*Hath alighted, i.e.*, settled, rested. The proof was that Elisha had just repeated his master's miracle.

⁽¹⁶⁾ **And they said unto him.**—After he had told them of the Assumption of Elijah (*Thenius*).

**Fifty strong men.**—See margin. Perhaps these were attendants on the members of the prophetic guild.

*The Search for Elijah.*           II. KINGS, II.           *Healing the Waters.*

thee, and seek thy master: lest peradventure the Spirit of the LORD hath taken him up, and cast him upon ¹some mountain, or into some valley. And he said, Ye shall not send. ⁽¹⁷⁾ And when they urged him till he was ashamed, he said, Send. They sent therefore fifty men; and they sought three days, but found him not. ⁽¹⁸⁾ And when they came again to him, (for he tarried at Jericho,) he said unto them, Did I not say unto you, Go not?

⁽¹⁹⁾ And the men of the city said unto Elisha, Behold, I pray thee, the situation of this city *is* pleasant, as my lord seeth: but the water *is* naught, and the ground ²barren. ⁽²⁰⁾ And he said, Bring me a new cruse, and put salt therein. And they brought *it* to him. ⁽²¹⁾ And he went forth unto the spring of the waters, and cast the salt in there, and said, Thus saith the LORD, I have healed these waters; there shall not be from thence any more death or barren *land.* ⁽²²⁾ So the waters were healed unto this day, according to the saying of Elisha which he spake.

1 Heb., *one of the mountains.*

2 Heb., *causing to miscarry.*

---

(Comp. Elisha's servant Gehazi, and the fifty sons of the prophets, in verse 7.) Their being "sons of valour" was important, as the search in the mountains would involve danger.

**The Spirit of the Lord hath taken him up.**—Comp. 1 Kings xviii. 12; Acts viii. 39, 40. This suggestion of the sons of the prophets is a good comment on verses 11, 12. It shows that what is there told is certainly *not* that Elijah ascended a fiery chariot and rode visibly into heaven, as the popular notion is.

**Upon some mountain, or into some valley.**—Literally, *on to one of the mountains, or into one of the valleys*, of the land of Gilead. The motive of the disciples was not a desire to pay the last honours to the body of the departed master, as Keil suggests; for they rather expected to find Elijah alive. After the words "cast him," the LXX. has "into the Jordan," which may be authentic. In that case, the disciples may have thought the prophet was hidden somewhere among the reeds and rushes of the river bank, in order to escape some threatened danger.

**Ye shall not send.**—Or, *Ye must not, ye should not*, or *ought not, to send*.

⁽¹⁷⁾ **Urged him.**—Gen. xxxiii. 11.

**Till he was ashamed.**—Literally, *unto being ashamed.* The pronoun is not expressed in the Hebrew. "They pressed upon him, '*ad bōsh*," means "until he was embarrassed, disconcerted, put out of countenance." (Comp. chap. viii. 11; Judges iii. 25.) Thenius prefers "they carried their importunity to a shameless length;" Keil and Bähr, "until he was disappointed in the hope of dissuading them." (Comp. Ps. xxii. 5.)

⁽¹⁸⁾ **For he tarried.**—*Now he* (emphatic) *was abiding in Jericho* (while they were searching).

**Did I not say.**—Or, *command.* Elisha could now fairly remind them of his authority. So the phrase "Go not" is, in the Hebrew, imperative. (Comp. "Ye shall not send," verse 16.) With these words, the history of Elijah significantly closes. "Elias resembled Moses in courage and eloquence, and no other prophet was his equal. But when he withdrew from the world, that Providence which guided the destinies of Israel did not, therefore, forsake His people. A portion of Elijah's spirit passed to his disciples; and they are forbidden to seek their departed master in the desert: they must find among themselves the means of carrying on his work" (*Reuss*).

Thenius considers the entire section (chaps. i. 2—ii. 18) to be a distinct fragment of a lost history of Elijah. Its contents, he says, betray the same *poetical* (?) spirit as 1 Kings xvii.—xix.

(19—25) Elisha, as prophet, heals the waters of Jericho, and curses the scorners of Beth-el.

⁽¹⁹⁾ **The men of the city.**—Not "the sons of the prophets," but the citizens make this trial of the prophet's miraculous powers.

**The situation of this** (Heb., *the*) **city is pleasant** (Heb., *good*).—Jericho, "the city of palms" (Deut. xxxiv. 3), had a fine position, "rising like an oasis from a broad plain of sand."

**The water is naught.**—Heb., *bad.* "Naught" *i.e.*, "naughty."

**And the ground barren.**—Verse 21 ("from thence") shows that the waters, not the soil, were the cause of the evil complained of. "The ground," or rather, *the land* is here put for its *inhabitants*, including the lower animals; and what is said is either "the country bears dead births," or, "the country has *many* miscarriages" (*pi'el* may be either *factitive* or *intensive*). (Comp. Exod. xxiii. 26; Mal. iii. 11.) The use of different waters is said to have good and bad effects upon the functions of conception and parturition (*not* "a popular superstition," as Reuss suggests). "The ground is barren," or unfruitful, is therefore an incorrect translation.

⁽²⁰⁾ **A new cruse.**—*Vessel*; either *dish, bowl,* or *cup* (*çĕlōhîth*); only here. (Comp. *çĕlāhôth*, 2 Chron. xxxv. 16: and the Targum, *çĕlúhîthā.*) A new one, because the holy purpose demanded an instrument uncontaminated by use. (Comp. Num. xix. 2; 2 Sam. vi. 3.)

**Salt.**—As an antiseptic, an appropriate sacramental medium of the Divine influence which was to expel the corruption of the spring.

⁽²¹⁾ **The spring of the waters.**—Now called *Ain es Sultân* ("the Sultan's Fountain"), a fine spring of sweet water, which irrigates the neighbouring plain.

**Thus saith the Lord.**—Not the prophet's own power, nor the natural virtues of the salt, but *the Divine creative will* was effectual to the healing of the spring.

**There shall not be.**—Many MSS., and all the versions, save LXX., read "and there shall not be," or, "arise."

**Death.**—Caused by the unwholesome water, either to the people, or to their unborn offspring.

**Or barren land.**—The same word as in verse 19. Literally, *and making* (or, *multiplying*) *abortion,* which is apparently used as a substantive here (*i.e.*, cause of abortion).

**Unto this day.**—The time when the narrative was first committed to writing.

*Elisha Mocked.*        II. KINGS, III.        *Jehoram Reigns.*

<sup>(23)</sup> And he went up from thence unto Beth-el: and as he was going up by the way, there came forth little children out of the city, and mocked him, and said unto him, Go up, thou bald head; go up, thou bald head. <sup>(24)</sup> And he turned back, and looked on them, and cursed them in the name of the LORD. And there came forth two she bears out of the wood, and tare forty and two children of them. <sup>(25)</sup> And he went from thence to mount Carmel, and from thence he returned to Samaria.

B.C. 896.

1 Heb., *statue.*

CHAPTER III. — <sup>(1)</sup> Now Jehoram the son of Ahab began to reign over Israel in Samaria the eighteenth year of Jehoshaphat king of Judah, and reigned twelve years. <sup>(2)</sup> And he wrought evil in the sight of the LORD; but not like his father, and like his mother: for he put away the ¹image of Baal that his father had made. <sup>(3)</sup> Nevertheless he cleaved unto the sins of Jeroboam the son of Nebat, which made Israel to sin; he departed not therefrom.

<sup>(4)</sup> And Mesha king of Moab was a sheepmaster, and rendered unto the

---

<sup>(23)</sup> **Went up.**—From Jericho, in the plain, Elisha goes now to visit the prophetic community established at Beth-el, the chief seat of the illicit *cultus.*

**By the way.**—*The* way *par excellence;* the highroad leading directly up to the gates of the town.

**Little children.**—*Young boys* (or, *lads*). *Naʻar* is not used rhetorically here, as in 1 Chron. xxix. 1; 2 Chron. xiii. 7. The boys who mocked Elisha might be of various ages, between six or seven years and twenty. "Little children" would not be likely to hit upon a biting sarcasm, nor to sally forth in a body to insult the prophet (verse 24).

**Mocked.**—Hab. i. 10. In Syriac and Chaldee the root implies "to praise, and to praise ironically," *i.e.,* to deride.

**Go up.**—Not "as Elijah was reported to have done;" for the Bethelites knew no more of that than the prophets of Jericho. The word obviously refers to what Elisha was himself doing at the time (verse 23). He was probably going up the steep road slowly, and his prophet's mantle attracted attention.

**Thou bald head.**—Baldness was a reproach (Isa. iii. 17, xv. 2), and suspicious as one of the marks of leprosy (Lev. xiii. 43). Elisha, though still young—he lived fifty years after this (chap. xiii. 14)—may have become bald prematurely.

<sup>(24)</sup> **He turned back.**—The boys were following him with their jeers. Thenius says, "The wanton young people, who had not courage to attack except in the rear, had stolen round him."

**Cursed them.**—"To avenge the honour of Jehovah, violated in his person" (*Keil*). (Comp. Exod. xvi. 8; Acts v. 4.)

**And there came forth.**—Whether at once, and in the presence of Elisha, or not, is uncertain. Thenius supposes that on some occasion or other a terrible calamity had fallen on some person or persons after such a mockery of Elisha, or of some other prophet (!); and that in the desire to magnify the divinely maintained inviolability of the prophetic office, the author of the above narrative has overlooked the immoral character of cursing, especially in the case of wanton *children.* He then contrasts the behaviour of the "historical" David (2 Sam. xvi. 10). But (1) the curse of a prophet was an inspired *prediction* of punitive disaster; (2) Beth-el was a chief seat of idolatry (1 Kings xii. 29, *seq.*; Amos iv. 4, v. 5, vii. 10), and the mobbing of the new prophetic leader may have been premeditated; (3) at all events, the narrative is too brief to enable us to judge of the merits of the case; and (4) what is related belongs to that dispensation in which judgment was made more prominent than mercy, and directly fulfils the menace of Lev. xxvi. 21, *seq.*

**Two she bears.**—Hosea xiii. 8; Prov. xvii. 12; Amos v. 19. (Comp. chap. xvii. 25.) Wild beasts were common in Palestine in those days.

**Forty and two.**—This may be a definite for an indefinite number. It shows that the mob of young persons who beset the prophet was considerable.

<sup>(25)</sup> **To mount Carmel.**—To cultivate the memory of his master in solitude. Elijah had often lived there (comp. 1 Kings xviii.), as its caves were well fitted for solitude and concealment. Elisha may have retired thither to prepare himself for his public ministry by prayer and fasting. (Comp. Matt. iv. 1, *seq.*)

**To Samaria.**—Where he had his permanent abode. (Comp. chap. vi. 32.)

III.

THE REIGN OF JEHORAM OF ISRAEL, AND HIS EXPEDITION AGAINST MOAB, IN WHICH JEHOSHAPHAT OF JUDAH TAKES PART.

<sup>(1)</sup> **Began to reign.**—Literally, *reigned.*

**The eighteenth year.**—Comp. Note on chap. i. 17, and viii. 16.

<sup>(2)</sup> **Wrought evil.**—*Did the evil in the eyes,* &c., *i.e.,* maintained the illicit worship of the bullock at Beth-el (verse 3).

**Like his mother.**—Jezebel lived throughout his reign (chap. ix. 30), which explains why he did not eradicate the Baal-worship (chap. x. 18—28).

**For he put away.**—*And he removed,* scil., from its place in the temple of Baal. (Comp. 1 Kings xvi. 31, 32.) It must have been afterwards restored, probably by the influence of Jezebel. (Comp. chap. x. 26, 27, and Notes.)

**The image.**—*Pillar.* (Comp. 2 Chron. xxxiv. 4.) The LXX., Vulg., and Arabic read "pillars" (a different pointing); and the LXX. adds at the end, "and brake *them* in pieces." This seems original. Ahab would be likely to set up more than one pillar to Baal.

<sup>(3)</sup> **He cleaved unto the sins of Jeroboam.** —1 Kings xii. 28, *seq.,* xvi. 2, 26.

**Therefrom.**—Heb., *from it* (a collective feminine). So in chap. xiii. 2, 6, 11.

<sup>(4)</sup> The revolt of Moab, continued from chap. i. 1. Ahaziah did not reign two full years, and his accident seems to have prevented any attempt on his part to reduce the Moabites.

**Mesha.**—The name means "deliverance, salvation," and occurs on the monument set up by this king, de-

*Jehoram and Jehoshaphat* — II. KINGS, III. — *March against Moab.*

king of Israel an hundred thousand lambs, and an hundred thousand rams, with the wool. <sup>(5)</sup> But it came to pass, when <sup>a</sup>Ahab was dead, that the king of Moab rebelled against the king of Israel. <sup>(6)</sup> And king Jehoram went out of Samaria the same time, and numbered all Israel. <sup>(7)</sup> And he went and sent to Jehoshaphat the king of Judah, saying, The king of Moab hath rebelled against me: wilt thou go with me against Moab to battle? And he said, I will go up: <sup>b</sup>I am as thou art, my people as thy people, and my horses as thy horses. <sup>(8)</sup> And he said, Which way shall we go up?

a ch. 1. 1.

B.C. 895.

b 1 Kings 22. 4.

<sup>1</sup> Heb., *at their feet.*

And he answered, The way through the wilderness of Edom. <sup>(9)</sup> So the king of Israel went, and the king of Judah, and the king of Edom: and they fetched a compass of seven days' journey: and there was no water for the host, and for the cattle <sup>1</sup>that followed them. <sup>(10)</sup> And the king of Israel said, Alas! that the LORD hath called these three kings together, to deliver them into the hand of Moab! <sup>(11)</sup> But Jehoshaphat said, *Is there* not here a prophet of the LORD, that we may enquire of the LORD by him? And one of the king of Israel's servants answered and said, Here *is* Elisha the son of Shaphat, which poured

---

scribing his victories and buildings. (See Note on chap. i. 1.)

**A sheep-master.**—Heb., *nôgēd* (Amos i. 1). In Arabic, *naqad* means a kind of sheep of superior wool; *naqqâd*, the owner or shepherd of such sheep. The land of Moab is mountainous, but well watered, and rich in fertile valleys, and thus specially suited for pasture; and the Arabian wilderness lay open to the Moabite shepherds and their flocks.

**Rendered.**—*Used to render* (*waw* conversive of the perfect); scil., year by year. This tribute is referred to in Isa. xvi. 1.

**With the wool.**—Rather, *in wool* (an accusative of *limitation*). The word rendered "lambs" (*kārīm*) means lambs fatted for food. The expression "in wool," therefore, relates only to the *rams*. Mesha's annual tribute was paid in kind, and consisted of a hundred thousand fatted lambs and the fleeces of a hundred thousand rams. This was a heavy burden for a country no larger than the county of Huntingdon. (Comp. Mesha's own allusions to the "oppression" of Moab by Omri and Ahab, chap. i. 1, Note.) The LXX. adds, ἐν τῇ ἐπαναστάσει ("in the revolt"); implying that the present rebellion was distinct from that of chap. i. 1, and that this tribute was imposed as an indemnity for the former revolt. The addition is probably due to a transcriber.

<sup>(5)</sup> **But.**—*And.*

**When.**—So some MSS. The ordinary text has, "about the time of Ahab's death" (*ke* for *be*).

**Rebelled**—*i.e.*, refused payment of the annual tribute.

<sup>(6)</sup> **The same time.**—Literally, *in that day*; which, in Hebrew, is a much less definite phrase than in English. The time intended is that when the Moabite refusal of tribute was received by Jehoram, who, on his accession, would demand it afresh.

**Numbered.**—*Mustered, made a levy of.*

<sup>(7)</sup> **Wilt thou go.**—So Ahab asks Jehoshaphat in 1 Kings xxii. 4, and he replies as here, "I am as thou art," &c. This indicates that the present section was originally composed by the same hand as 1 Kings xx. 1—34 and xxii. 1—37 (*Thenius*). Jehoshaphat assented, in spite of the prophetic censures of his alliance with Ahab and Ahaziah (2 Chron. xix. 2, xx. 37); perhaps because he was anxious to inflict further punishment on the Moabites for their inroad into Judah (2 Chron. xx.), and to prevent any recurrence of the same (*Keil*).

**Against Moab to battle?**—Or, *into Moab to the war?*

<sup>(8)</sup> **And he said**—*i.e.*, Jehoram said.

**Which way.**—They might cross the Jordan, and attack the northern frontier of Moab, or they might round the southern end of the Dead Sea, and invade Moab from the side of Edom. The former was the shortest route for both kings. But Moab's strongest defences were on the north frontier, and the allies would be liable to attacks from the Syrians in Ramoth-gilead (chap. viii. 28). The longer and more difficult southern road may have been chosen partly on these grounds, and partly because Jehoshaphat wished to march as far as might be within his own territory, and to get a contingent from Edom, which was at this time subject to him (1 Kings xxii. 48), and perhaps to hold it in check. Moreover, the Moabites were less likely to be on their guard on the southern border, which was more difficult of access.

**And he answered.**—*Said*—*i.e.*, Jehoshaphat.

<sup>(9)</sup> **The king of Edom.**—A vassal king appointed by Jehoshaphat (1 Kings xxii. 48).

**They fetched a compass.**—*Went round* (scil., the Dead Sea) *a journey of seven days*. The confederates appear to have lost their way among the mountains of Seir. They would, in any case, be greatly delayed by the cattle which it was necessary to take with them for subsistence. It is evident from the context that the distress began *after* the Edomite contingent had joined.

**For the host, and for the cattle that followed them.**—The stopping is wrong. It should be, *and there was not water for the army and for the cattle which followed them.* "Them," *i.e.*, the kings. (Comp. Judges v. 15.) "The cattle," *i.e.*, the herds and flocks for the maintenance of the army.

The allies appear to have marched through the deep, rocky glen of *El-Ahsy* (or *El-Qurâhy*), between Moab and Edom. They expected to find water there, as is usually the case, even in the dry season; but on this occasion the water failed.

<sup>(10)</sup> **That.**—Omit (*kī*, emphatically introducing the assertion).

**Together.**—Omit.

<sup>(11)</sup> **But** (*and*) **Jehoshaphat . . . by him?**—The same question is asked by Jehoshaphat in 1 Kings xxii. 7.

**By him.**—Heb., *from with him* (*mē'ōthô* for *mē'ittô*, both here and in the parallel place—a mark of the same hand). Jehoshaphat is for "seeking Jehovah" through

water on the hands of Elijah. ⁽¹²⁾ And Jehoshaphat said, The word of the LORD is with him. So the king of Israel and Jehoshaphat and the king of Edom went down to him. ⁽¹³⁾ And Elisha said unto the king of Israel, What have I to do with thee? get thee to the prophets of thy father, and to the prophets of thy mother. And the king of Israel said unto him, Nay: for the LORD hath called these three kings together, to deliver them into the hand of Moab. ⁽¹⁴⁾ And Elisha said, As the LORD of hosts liveth, before whom I stand, surely, were it not that I regard the presence of Jehoshaphat the king of Judah, I would not look toward thee, nor see thee. ⁽¹⁵⁾ But now bring me a minstrel. And it came to pass, when the minstrel played, that the hand of the LORD came upon him. ⁽¹⁶⁾ And he said, Thus saith the LORD, Make this valley full of ditches. ⁽¹⁷⁾ For thus saith the LORD, Ye shall not see wind, neither shall ye see rain; yet that valley shall be filled with water, that ye may drink, both ye, and your cattle, and your beasts. ⁽¹⁸⁾ And this is *but* a light thing in the sight of the LORD: he will deliver the Moabites also into your hand. ⁽¹⁹⁾ And ye shall smite every fenced city, and every choice city, and shall fell

---

a prophet, in contrast with Jehoram, who at once despairs. (Comp. Amos v. 4, 8; and Note on 1 Chron. xiii. 3; 2 Chron. xv. 2.)

**One of the king of Israel's servants.**—One of the king's staff, who, like Obadiah (1 Kings xviii. 3), was perhaps a friend of the prophets of Jehovah.

**Here is Elisha.**—The prophet must have followed the army of his own accord, or rather, as Keil suggests, under a Divine impulse, in order that, when the hour of trial came, he might point Jehoram to Jehovah as the only true God.

**Which poured water on the hands of Elijah.** —Was the personal attendant of that greatest of prophets. The phrase alludes to the well-known Oriental custom of the servant pouring water from a ewer on his master's hands to wash them.

⁽¹²⁾ **The king of Israel and Jehoshaphat.**— All the versions except the Targum add, "the king of Judah." Jehoshaphat said what follows either on the ground of *Elijah's* reputation, or because the news of Elisha's succession had already reached Judah.

The proper names, Shaphat and Jehoshaphat, are identical (*He* judgeth, *i.e.*, Jah judgeth). (Comp. Ahaz and Jehoahaz.)

**Went down to him.**—From the royal tents, which were probably pitched on an eminence, so as to overlook the camp. The three kings go to consult the prophet as persons of ordinary station might do. This shows the estimation in which he was held. Keil says they were humbled by misfortune.

⁽¹³⁾ **Unto the king of Israel.**—As the leader of the confederacy; or as Elisha's sovereign, who might be supposed to have brought the others to the prophet.

**The prophets of thy father**—*i.e.*, the Baal prophets (comp. 1 Kings xviii. 19) and false prophets of Jehovah (1 Kings xxii. 6, 11). Elisha's sarcasm indicates that the former had not been wholly rooted out.

**Nay.**—Heb., *'al*; Greek, μή. "Say not so;" or, "Repulse me not." (Comp. Ruth i. 13.)

**These three kings.**—And not one (myself) only, emphasising the word *three*. Or else Jehoram would rouse compassion by the *magnitude* of the imminent disaster.

⁽¹⁴⁾ **Before whom I stand.**—As a minister. (Comp. 1 Kings xvii. 1, xviii. 15.)

**Surely.**—*Kî* (for); used as in verse 10 ("I cry, alas!" "I thus swear," *for*, &c.). Jehoshaphat is accepted because of his faithful dependence on Jehovah (verse 11). Jehoram still maintained or tolerated the cultus of Bethel and Dan. (See verse 3.)

**Regard the presence.**—Literally, *lift the face.* (Comp. Gen. xix. 21; xxxii. 21.)

⁽¹⁵⁾ **Bring me a minstrel.** — *Měnaggēn*—*i.e.*, a harper, player on a stringed instrument (*něgīnāh*). Elisha called for music as a natural means of calming his perturbed spirit (verses 13, 14). Composure and serenity of soul were essential, if the prophet was to hear the voice of God within. Cicero tells us that the Pythagoreans were wont to tranquillise their minds after the strain of thought with harp music and singing (*Tusc.* iv. 2). (Comp. 1 Sam. x. 5; 1 Chron. xxv. 1, Note.) The incident is a striking mark of the *historical* truth of the narrative.

**And it came to pass.**—Perfect with *weak waw*: a later idiom. (Comp. 1 Sam. xvii. 48.)

**The hand of the Lord came upon him.**— Targum and some MSS., "the Spirit of the Lord;" but comp. 1 Kings xviii. 46.

⁽¹⁶⁾ **Make.** — Right (infinitive, equivalent to an energetic imperative).

**Valley.**—*Nahal*, wady, torrent-bed, gully. According to Thenius, "the brook Zered" of Deut. ii. 13 is meant; the present *Wady el-Ahsy*, (or *el-Hasa*) which forms the natural southern boundary of Moab, and from which several gorges lead up into the Moabite highlands. (See Isa. xv. 7.)

**Full of ditches.** — Literally, *pits, pits.* (Comp. Gen. xiv. 10: "Wells, wells of bitumen.") The pits were to gather the water, which otherwise would soon have run away in the bed of the torrent (Jer. xiv. 3, 4). The style of the oracle is stamped with the liveliness and originality of historic truth.

⁽¹⁷⁾ **Ye shall not see wind.**—Which in the east is the usual precursor of rain.

**Yet that valley.**—*And that wady.* He says "*that* (*hû*) valley," meaning "the one of which I spoke" (verse 16). Contrast "*this* (*zeh*) valley," *i.e.*, "the one in which we are" (verse 16).

**Your cattle.**—*Miqneh*: flocks and herds, as distinguished from, "beasts" (*běhēmāh*), *i.e.*, probably, beasts of burden.

⁽¹⁸⁾ **Is but a light thing.**—*Will be a light thing* (1 Kings xvi. 31).

**He will deliver the Moabites.**—The contrary of Jehoram's expectation (verses 10, 13).

⁽¹⁹⁾ **And ye shall smite . . . shall fell . . .**— These verbs are continuative of those in the last verse, *i.e.*, they do not *command* a course of action, but *foretell* it.

*The Victory*          II. KINGS, III.          *over the Moabites.*

every good tree, and stop all wells of water, and ¹mar every good piece of land with stones. <sup>(20)</sup> And it came to pass in the morning, when the meat offering was offered, that, behold, there came water by the way of Edom, and the country was filled with water. <sup>(21)</sup> And when all the Moabites heard that the kings were come up to fight against them, they ²gathered all that were able to ³put on armour, and upward, and stood in the border. <sup>(22)</sup> And they rose up early in the morning, and the sun shone upon the water, and the Moabites saw the water on the other side *as* red as blood: <sup>(23)</sup> and they said, This *is* blood: the kings are surely ⁴slain, and they have smitten one another: now therefore, Moab, to the spoil. <sup>(24)</sup> And when they came to the camp of Israel, the Israelites rose up and smote the Moabites, so that they fled before them: but ⁵they went forward smiting the Moabites, even in *their* country. <sup>(25)</sup> And they beat down the cities, and on every good piece of land cast every man his stone, and filled it; and they stopped all the

<sup>1</sup> Heb., *grieve.*
<sup>2</sup> Heb., *were cried together.*
<sup>3</sup> Heb., *gird himself with a girdle.*
<sup>4</sup> Heb., *destroyed.*
<sup>5</sup> Or, *they smote in it even smiting.*

---

(Comp. chap. viii. 12, 13.) Taken as *commands*, they appear to conflict with Deut. xx. 19, where the felling of an enemy's *fruit trees* for the purposes of siege-works is forbidden. Keil, however, explains that the law relates to Canaanite territory which the Israelites were to occupy, whereas Moab's was an enemy's country, and therefore not to be spared.

**Fenced city . . . choice city.**—There is a *paronomasia*, or play on words of similar sound, in the Hebrew: *'îr mibçār . . . 'îr mibhôr.*

**Every good tree**—*i.e.,* fruit-bearing trees.

**Stop.**—Gen. xxvi. 15, 18.

**Mar.**—Literally, *make to grieve*: a poetical expression. An *unfruitful* land is said to *mourn* (Isa. xxiv. 4; Jer. xii. 4).

**Every good piece of land.**—*All the good demesne* (literally, *portion, allotment*).

<sup>(20)</sup> **When the meat offering was offered.**—Comp. 1 Kings xviii. 29, 36. A more exact definition of the time. The reckoning by *hours* was unknown before the captivity. According to the Talmud, the morning sacrifice was offered in the Temple the moment it became light. (Ewald assumes that "the meat offering" was offered on this occasion in the camp.) That help came to the distressed army just at the hour of morning worship was a striking coincidence. (This allusion to the law of Exodus xxix. 38, *seq.*, may be an *indirect* hit at the northern kingdom.)

**There came water.**—*Water was coming from the way* (direction) *of Edom.* It would seem that a sudden storm of rain had fallen on the mountains of Seir, at some distance from the camp (Josephus says at a distance of three days' march); and the water found its natural outlet in the dry wady. Reuss thinks this explanation "superfluous," in the face of "the author's intention to describe a *miracle;*" but there are different kinds of miracle, and, in the present instance, the miraculous element is visible in the prophet's prediction of the coming help, and in the *coincidence* of the natural phenomena with the needs of the Israelites. (Comp. chap. vii. 1, 2, *seq.*) [This statement seems to preclude also the naturalistic explanation founded on the meaning of the Arabic name of the locality. *Hisyun, hasyun, hasan,* mean water which gathers on a hard bottom under the sand in certain localities, and which the Arabs get at by scooping holes in the ground. See Lane, *Arab. Eng. Lex.* s.v.]

<sup>(21)</sup> **And when . . . heard . . . they gathered.** —*Now all the Moabites had heard . . . and had gathered themselves*: literally, *had been summoned, called together* (Judges vii. 23).

**All that were able to put on armour.**—*From every one girding on a girdle, and upwards*—*i.e.,* all of adult age, all who could bear arms. It was a levy *en masse* of the male population for the defence of the country.

**Stood in.**—*Had taken their stand on the frontier.*

<sup>(22)</sup> **They rose up early.**—The Moabite camp on the frontier mountains.

**And the sun shone upon the water.**—A parenthesis (*now the sun had risen upon the water*). The red sunrise tinged the water with the same colour.

**On the other side.**— *Min-nèged,* "opposite," "over against them" (chap. ii. 7, 15). The sun rose behind the Moabites.

**Red.**—*'Adōm.* There may be an allusion to the red earth of the locality (Edom), which would further redden the water.

<sup>(23)</sup> **The kings are surely slain.**—*Have surely fought with* (or *destroyed*) *one another.* LXX., ἐμαχέσαντο. The supposition was not improbable. Confederates of different races not seldom had been known to fall out among themselves (comp. Judges vii. 22; 2 Chron. xx. 23, and Note), and in this case the old enmity of Edom towards Israel, and the suppressed jealousies between Israel and Judah, made such a result very likely. The Moabites would know also that the wady had been waterless, so that their mistake was natural. When once their instinct for plunder was aroused they did not stop to think, but with a wild cry of "Moab, to the spoil!" they rushed in disorder upon the Israelite camp.

<sup>(24)</sup> **Smote the Moabites.**—Who were unprepared for resistance.

**But they went forward smiting . . . country.** —The Hebrew text (*Kethib*) has, *and he went* (*wayyābô,* spelt defectively, as in 1 Kings xii. 12) *into it* (*i.e.,* the land of Moab), *and smote* (literally, *smiting* an infinitive for a finite form) *Moab.* This is better than the Hebrew margin (*Qeri*), *and they smote it* (*i.e.* Moab), or the reading of some MSS. and the Targum and Syriac, "and they smote them, and smote Moab," which is tautologous. The original reading is perhaps represented by that of the LXX., καὶ εἰσῆλθον εἰσπορευόμενοι καὶ τύπτοντες τὴν Μωάβ, "and they entered the country, destroying as they went on." (In Hebrew the participles would be infinitives.)

<sup>(25)</sup> **And they beat down the cities.**—Rather, *And the cities they would overthrow,* describing what happened again and again.

**On every . . . filled it.**—Literally, *And every good plot, they would cast each man his stone, and fill*

wells of water, and felled all the good trees: ¹only in Kir-haraseth left they the stones thereof; howbeit the slingers went about *it*, and smote it.

(26) And when the king of Moab saw that the battle was too sore for him, he took with him seven hundred men that drew swords, to break through *even* unto the king of Edom: but they could not. (27) Then he took his eldest son that should have reigned in his stead, and offered him *for* a burnt offering

¹ Heb., *until he left the stones thereof in Kir-haraseth*.

upon the wall. And there was great indignation against Israel: and they departed from him, and returned to *their own* land.

CHAPTER IV.—(1) Now there cried a certain woman of the wives of the sons of the prophets unto Elisha, saying, Thy servant my husband is dead; and thou knowest that thy servant did fear the LORD: and the creditor is come to take unto him my two sons to be bond-

*it; and every fountain of water they would stop, and every good tree they would fell.* All this as Elisha foretold, verse 19.

**Only in Kir-haraseth left they the stones thereof.**— Literally, as margin, *until one left her stones in Kir-harèseth.* This clause connects itself with the opening statement, "And the cities they would overthrow (or, kept overthrowing) until her stones were left in Kir-harèseth," i.e., the work of destruction stopped before the walls of this, the principal stronghold of the country. In the other cities the invaders had not left one stone upon another.

**Kir-haraseth.**—Called "Kir-moab," Isa. xv. 1, and "Kir-hères," Isa. xvi. 11. The Targum on Isa. xv. calls it "Kerak (*castle*) of Moab," and it still bears that name. It stands upon a steep cliff of chalk.

**Howbeit the slingers went about it.**—*And the slingers went round, surrounded it.*

**And smote it**—*i.e.*, shot at the men on the walls with deadly effect.

(26) **The battle was too sore for him.**—The garrison was giving way under the destructive fire of the slingers.

**To break through even unto the king of Edom.**—Because the Edomite contingent seemed to be the most vulnerable point in the allied army, or because he hoped that these unwilling allies of Israel would allow him to escape through their ranks.

(27) **Then.**—*And.*

**His eldest son**—*i.e.*, the despairing king of Moab took his own son and heir.

**Offered him for a burnt offering.** — To Chemosh, without doubt, by way of appeasing that wrath of the god which seemed bent on his destruction. (Comp. the words of Mesha's inscription: "Chemosh was angry with his land." Note, chap. i. 1.) There is a reference to such hideous sacrifices in Micah vi. 7, "Shall I give my firstborn for my transgressions?" In dark times of national calamity the Hebrews were prone, like their neighbours, to seek help in the same dreadful rites. (Comp. the case of Manasseh, 2 Chron. xxxiii. 6; see also Ps. cvi. 37–39.) From the cuneiform records we learn that the sacrifice of children was also a Babylonian practice. (Amos ii. 1 refers to a totally different event from that recorded in the text.)

**Upon the wall.**—Of Kir-haraseth. This was done that the besiegers might see, and dread the consequences, believing, as they would be likely to do, that the Divine wrath was now appeased.

**And there was great indignation against Israel.**—Or, *And great wrath fell upon Israel.* This phrase always denotes a visitation of Divine wrath. (Comp. 2 Chron. xix. 10, xxiv. 18.) The manifestation of wrath in the present case was apparently a successful sortie of the Moabite garrison, whose faith in this terrible expedient of their king inspired them with new courage, while the besiegers were proportionally disheartened. The result was that "they (*i.e.*, the allied forces) departed from him (raised the siege), and returned to the land" (of Israel). Why did Divine wrath fall upon Israel rather than upon Moab? upon the involuntary cause rather than the voluntary agents in this shocking rite? If the wrath of Jehovah be meant, we cannot tell. But, as the present writer understands the words of the text, they rather indicate that the object of the dreadful expiation was attained, and that *the wrath of Chemosh* fell upon the Hebrew alliance. It is certain that belief in the supremacy of Jehovah did not hinder ancient Israel from admitting the real existence and potency of foreign deities. (See Note on 1 Chron. xvi. 25, 26; xvii. 21; and comp. Num. xxi. 29; Judges xi. 24.) This peculiar conception is a token of the antiquity of the record before us. In the second half of Isaiah the foreign gods are called nonentities.

After the events described in this verse we may suppose that Mesha's successes continued, as described on the stone of Dibon. (See Note on chap. i. 1.)

## IV.

IV.—VIII. THE WONDROUS WORKS OF ELISHA THE PROPHET.

(1–7) He multiplies the widow's oil. (Comp. 1 Kings xvii. 12 *seq.*)

(1) **Of the wives of the sons of the prophets.** —This shows that "the sons of the prophets" were not young unmarried men leading a kind of monastic life under the control of their prophetic chief. Those who were heads of families must have had their own separate homes. (See Note on 1 Kings xx. 35.)

**Thou knowest that thy servant did fear the Lord.**—She makes this the ground of her claim on the prophet's assistance. In 1 Kings xviii. 3, 12 it is said of Obadiah, Ahab's steward, that he "feared the Lord," and on account of this slight resemblance, the Targum, Josephus, and Ephrem Syrus identify the dead man of this verse with Obadiah, who is supposed to have spent all his property in maintaining the prophets (1 Kings xviii. 4) (!) Possibly the widow meant to say that her husband's debts were not due to profligate living (*Thenius*).

**The creditor is come to take unto him my two sons.**—According to the law (Lev. xxv. 39). They would have to continue in servitude until the year of jubilee. The ancient Roman law was more severe, for it contained no provision for the future release of the unhappy debtor. (Comp. also Matt. xviii. 26, and Notes.)

*The Widow's*      II. KINGS, IV.      *Oil Multiplied.*

men. <sup>(2)</sup> And Elisha said unto her, What shall I do for thee? tell me, what hast thou in the house? And she said, Thine handmaid hath not any thing in the house, save a pot of oil. <sup>(3)</sup> Then he said, Go, borrow thee vessels abroad of all thy neighbours, *even* empty vessels; <sup>1</sup>borrow not a few. <sup>(4)</sup> And when thou art come in, thou shalt shut the door upon thee and upon thy sons, and shalt pour out into all those vessels, and thou shalt set aside that which is full. <sup>(5)</sup> So she went from him, and shut the door upon her and upon her sons, who brought *the vessels* to her; and she poured out. <sup>(6)</sup> And it came to pass, when the vessels were full, that she said unto her son, Bring me yet a vessel. And he said unto her, *There is* not a vessel more.

<sup>1</sup> Or, *scant not.*

<sup>2</sup> Or, *creditor.*

<sup>3</sup> Heb., *there was a day.*

<sup>4</sup> Heb., *laid hold on him.*

And the oil stayed. <sup>(7)</sup> Then she came and told the man of God. And he said, Go, sell the oil, and pay thy <sup>2</sup>debt, and live thou and thy children of the rest. <sup>(8)</sup> And <sup>3</sup>it fell on a day, that Elisha passed to Shunem, where *was* a great woman; and she <sup>4</sup>constrained him to eat bread. And *so* it was, *that* as oft as he passed by, he turned in thither to eat bread. <sup>(9)</sup> And she said unto her husband, Behold now, I perceive that this *is* an holy man of God, which passeth by us continually. <sup>(10)</sup> Let us make a little chamber, I pray thee, on the wall; and let us set for him there a bed, and a table, and a stool, and a candlestick: and it shall be, when he cometh to us, that he shall turn in thither.

<sup>(11)</sup> And it fell on a day, that he came

---

(2) **What hast thou?**—The form of the pronoun here, and in verses 3, 7, 16, 23 *infra*, is peculiar, and points, as the present writer believes, to the northern origin of the narrative, rather than to later composition.

**A pot of oil.**—Usually explained, *vas unguentarium*, an "oil-flask." Keil says that *'āsûk* rather denotes "anointing," *unctio*, and *'āsûk shèmen*, "an anointing in (or with) oil," *i.e.*, oil enough for an anointing. But it seems better to take the word as a verb: "save (whereby) I may anoint myself with oil" (Micah vi. 15). Vulgate, "parum olei, quo ungar." The Jews, like the Greeks and Romans, anointed themselves after the bath (2 Sam. xii. 20).

(3) **Abroad.**—Literally, *from the outside* (of the house); out of doors.

**Borrow not a few.**—See margin. *Do not scant*, or *stint*, namely, to borrow.

(4) **And when . . . thou shalt shut.**—*And go in and shut the door.* The object was to avoid disturbance from without; perhaps, also, because publicity was undesirable in the case of such a miracle. (Comp. our Lord's injunction of secrecy on those whom He healed, and His exclusion of the people, in Luke viii. 51, 54.)

**Thou shalt set aside.**—By the help of thy sons (verses 5, 6).

(5) **From him.**—*Mē'ittô*, the correct form. (Comp. chap. iii. 11.)

**Who brought . . . poured out.**—There should be a semicolon at "sons." The rest is literally, *They were bringing to her, and she was pouring continually* (*mĕyaççĕqeth*, only here). She did not leave her pouring. The story is evidently abridged in this verse.

(6) **Her son.**—Probably the eldest. The LXX. has plural here and in the verb that follows.

**Stayed.**—Heb., *stood*—*i.e.*, halted, stopped. (Comp. Luke viii. 44, ἡ ῥύσις ἔστη.) Bähr makes the word mean *continued*—*i.e.*, to flow (!).

(7) **Then she came.**—*And she went in.*

**He said.**—LXX., "Elisha said."

**Thy debt.**—Right. Margin incorrect.

**And live thou and thy children.**—Heb., *and thou—thy sons—thou mayest live.* Clearly "and" has fallen out before the second word. Many MSS. and all the versions have it.

**Thou.**—*'Atti*, an archaism, perhaps retained in the dialect of northern Israel (1 Kings xiv. 2).

**Of the rest.**—*On what is left over*—*i.e.*, of the price of the oil.

(8—37) The Shunammitess and her son.

(8) **And it fell on a day.**—Rather, *And it came to pass at that time.* Literally, *during that day*, referring to the period of the miracle just related. Perhaps, too, the contrast of the poor and rich woman is intentional.

**Passed.**—*Crossed over*—scil., the plain of Jezreel, which he would have to do, whether he went from Samaria, or from Carmel to Shunem, which lay on the slope of Little Hermon, about midway between the two.

**A great woman**—*i.e.*, of high rank, or rich (1 Sam. xxv. 2; 2 Sam. xix. 33). Rabbinic tradition identifies her with Abishag the Shunammite of 1 Kings i. 3 (!). In that case she must have been at this time more than 200 years old.

**So it was.**—*It came to pass.*

**Passed by.**—*Crossed over*, as above.

**He turned in.**—*He would turn aside* (frequentative). For the phrase, see Gen. xix. 2.

(9) **An holy man of God.**—The term "holy" is not a merely ornamental or conventional epithet of the "man of God" (*i.e.*, prophet) as such, but denotes the special moral elevation of Elisha.

**Continually.**—*At stated intervals, regularly.*

(10) **A little chamber . . . on the wall.**—Rather, *a little upper chamber* (*'aliyāh*) *with walls*—*i.e.*, a chamber on the roof of the house, walled on each side as a protection against the weather. (Comp. 1 Kings xvii. 19.) Here the prophet would be secure from all interruption or intrusion on his privacy, and so would be likely to honour the house longer with his presence.

**A bed.**—The four things mentioned are the only essentials in Oriental furnishing.

**A stool.**—*A chair of state.* The same word means *throne.*

**Candlestick.**—*Lamp-stand.*

(11) **And it fell on a day.**—See Note on verse 8.

**Chamber.**—*Upper chamber.*

**Lay**—*i.e.*, lay down to rest.

*The Shunammite*          II. KINGS, IV.          *and her Son.*

thither, and he turned into the chamber, and lay there. (12) And he said to Gehazi his servant, Call this Shunammite. And when he had called her, she stood before him. (13) And he said unto him, Say now unto her, Behold, thou hast been careful for us with all this care; what *is* to be done for thee? wouldest thou be spoken for to the king, or to the captain of the host? And she answered, I dwell among mine own people. (14) And he said, What then *is* to be done for her? And Gehazi answered, Verily she hath no child, and her husband is old. (15) And he said, Call her. And when he had called her, she stood in the door. (16) And he said, *a* About this ¹season, according to the time of life, thou shalt embrace a son. And she said, Nay, my lord, *thou* man of God, do not lie unto thine handmaid. (17) And the woman conceived, and bare a son at that season that Elisha had said unto her, according to the time of life.

(18) And when the child was grown, it fell on a day, that he went out to his father to the reapers. (19) And he said unto his father, My head, my head. And he said to a lad, Carry him to his mother. (20) And when he had taken him, and brought him to his mother, he sat on her knees till noon, and *then* died. (21) And she went up, and laid him on the bed of the man of God, and shut *the door* upon him, and went out. (22) And she called unto her husband, and said, Send me, I pray thee, one of the young men, and one of the asses, that I may run to the man of God, and come again. (23) And he said, Wherefore wilt

*a* Gen. 18. 10.

¹ Heb., *set time.*

---

(12) **Gehazi his servant.**—First mentioned here. His name means "valley of vision," and is perhaps derived from his native place, which may have got its name from being a haunt of prophets.

**His servant.**—*His young man* (Gen. xxii. 3).

**She stood before him**—*i.e.*, before Gehazi. The sentence, "And when he had called her, she stood before him," is an anticipation of the result, and might be placed within a parenthesis.

(13) **And he said unto him**—*i.e.*, Elisha, as he lay on the bed (verse 11), had charged Gehazi to say this when he called their hostess. It is hardly likely that Elisha communicated with her through his servant in order to save his own dignity. He may have thought she would express her wishes more freely to Gehazi than to himself.

**Thou hast been careful . . . with all this care.**—Literally, *trembled all this trembling.* Comp. Luke x. 41 (τυρβάζη).

**Wouldest thou be spoken for to the king?**—Literally, *is it to speak for thee to the king?* that is, dost thou stand in need of an advocate at court? Is there any boon thou desirest from the king? This shows what influence Elisha enjoyed at the time; but it does not *prove* that Jehu, whom he anointed, was already on the throne, for Jehoram respected and probably feared the prophet.

**The captain of the host.**—The commander-in-chief, who was the most powerful person next the king.

**I dwell among mine own people.**—Literally, *In the midst of my people I am dwelling*—*scil.*, far from the court and courtly interests. I have nothing to seek from such exalted personages; I am a mere commoner living quietly in the country.

(14) **And he said**—*i.e.*, when Gehazi had reported the woman's reply.

**She hath no child.**—Which was at once a misfortune and a reproach. (Comp. Gen. xxx. 23; 1 Sam. i. 6, 7; Luke i. 25; Deut. vii. 13, 14; Ps. cxxvii. 3, 4.)

(15) **Call her.**—The Shunammite is now summoned into the presence of the prophet himself.

**She stood.**—Or, *took her stand.* Modesty, or reverence for Elisha, prevented her from going farther.

(16) **About this season.**—*At this set time.*

**According to the time of life.**—Rather, *at the reviving time*—*i.e.*, next spring; or, *when the time revives*—*i.e.*, in the following year: a phrase occurring in Gen. xviii. 10, 15. Böttcher renders, "when the year has revolved," assuming the ground meaning of the term "life" to be something *joined in a circle.*

**Thou shalt embrace.**—*Thou art about to embrace.*

**Do not lie**—*i.e.*, raise no delusive hopes. (Comp. Isa. lviii. 11.) We can imagine the emotion with which this would be said. (Comp. the incredulity of Sarah, Gen. xviii. 12, 13.)

(17) **And the woman conceived.**—Comp. with this verse Gen. xxi. 2.

**Said.**—*Promised.*

**According to the time of life.**—See Note on verse 16.

(18) **It fell on a day.**—See Note on verse 8.

(19) **My head, my head.**—The boy had a sunstroke. It was the hot season of harvest, and his head was probably uncovered.

**A lad.**—Rather, *the young man.* The servant waiting on him.

(20) **Taken.**—*Carried.*

**Brought him.**—*Brought him in*—*i.e.*, in-doors.

**Till noon.**—We gather from this that the boy was hurt in the forenoon.

(21) **Laid him on the bed of the man of God.** —She wished to keep the death secret, and the corpse inviolate, during her intended absence.

(22) **One of the young men.**—To lead and drive the ass.

**Asses.**—*She-asses.*

**That I may run.**—Notice the striking *naturalness* of the language, in which she promises to be back soon.

(23) **Wilt thou go.**—*Art thou going.* Archaic forms of the pronoun and participle are here used.

**It is neither new moon, nor sabbath.**—Comp. Amos viii. 5. This remark is interesting, because it implies that the faithful in the northern kingdom were wont to visit prophets on these holy days for the sake of religious instruction and edification. Thenius suggests a doubt whether the later practice of resorting to the

thou go to him to day? *it is* neither new moon, nor sabbath. And she said, *It shall be* ¹well. ⁽²⁴⁾ Then she saddled an ass, and said to her servant, Drive, and go forward; ²slack not *thy* riding for me, except I bid thee. ⁽²⁵⁾ So she went and came unto the man of God to mount Carmel.

And it came to pass, when the man of God saw her afar off, that he said to Gehazi his servant, Behold, *yonder is* that Shunammite: ⁽²⁶⁾ run now, I pray thee, to meet her, and say unto her, *Is it* well with thee? *is it* well with thy husband? *is it* well with the child? And she answered, *It is* well. ⁽²⁷⁾ And when she came to the man of God to the hill, she caught ³him by the feet: but Gehazi came near to thrust her away. And the

¹ Heb., *peace.*
² Heb., *restrain not for me to ride.*
³ Heb., *by his feet.*
⁴ Heb., *bitter.*

man of God said, Let her alone; for her soul *is* ⁴vexed within her: and the LORD hath hid *it* from me, and hath not told me. ⁽²⁸⁾ Then she said, Did I desire a son of my lord? did I not say, Do not deceive me? ⁽²⁹⁾ Then he said to Gehazi, Gird up thy loins, and take my staff in thine hand, and go thy way: if thou meet any man, salute him not; and if any salute thee, answer him not again: and lay my staff upon the face of the child. ⁽³⁰⁾ And the mother of the child said, *As* the LORD liveth, and *as* thy soul liveth, I will not leave thee. And he arose, and followed her.

⁽³¹⁾ And Gehazi passed on before them, and laid the staff upon the face of the child; but *there was* neither voice, nor

---

Scribes on these days has not here been transferred by an anachronism to the days of Elisha. (Comp. Num. xviii. 11 *seq.*; Lev. xxiii. 3, for the legal mode of observing new moons and Sabbath days.)

**It shall be well.**—Omit *it shall be*. The expression may be equivalent to our common "all right;" admitting the truth of what is said, yet persisting in one's purpose. She did not want to be delayed, nor to have her faith shaken by argument.

⁽²⁴⁾ **Then she saddled an ass.**—*And she saddled the ass*—i.e., which the young man brought, and probably saddled at her bidding.

**Slack not thy riding for me.**—Literally, *restrain me not from riding*—i.e., do not stop, or slacken speed. A halt for rest might naturally be taken, as the distance was considerable.

⁽²⁵⁾ **To mount Carmel.**—Elisha, then, must have dwelt there at least occasionally. (Comp. verse 9.) Carmel probably served as a fixed centre of prophetic teaching for the north, as Gilgal, Beth-el, and Jericho for the south. (Comp. also Elisha's sacrifice there, 1 Kings xviii. 31 *seq.*)

**Afar off.**—The same word (*minnèged*) as *to view* (chap ii. 7, 15).

**Shunammite.**—Syriac, *Shulamite.*

⁽²⁶⁾ **Run now, I pray thee, to meet her.**—This perhaps indicates the respect in which Elisha held the Shunammites. But it may denote surprise and apprehension at an *unusual* visit. Hence the inquiries about each member of the family.

**It is well.**—She said this merely to avoid further explanation. She would open her grief to the prophet's own ear, and to none other.

⁽²⁷⁾ **To the hill.**—Probably to the summit.

**She caught him by the feet.**—*She laid hold of* (clasped) *his feet.* Assuming the posture of an humble and urgent suppliant, and no doubt pouring out a flood of passionate entreaties for help.

**But (*and*) Gehazi came near to thrust her away.**—He thought her vehemence a trespass upon the dignity of his master. (Comp. Matt. xix. 13; John iv. 27.)

**The Lord hath hid it from me.**—Supernatural knowledge of every event was not a characteristic of the gift of prophecy. (Comp. 2 Sam. vii. 3 *seq.* for a somewhat similar case of ignorance on the part of a prophet.)

⁽²⁸⁾ **Then.**—*And*; so in verses 29, 35.

**Did I desire (*ask*) a son of my lord?**—Only the conclusion of her appeal is given. She says, Better to have had no son, than to have had one and lost him. The opposite of our poet's

"'Tis better to have loved and lost,
Than never to have loved at all."

But this last is the fruit of reflection; *her* words are the spontaneous outflow of a mother's poignant sorrow. Or, perhaps, we should understand that grief does not allow her to specify the cause directly; she leaves the prophet to infer *that* from her questions.

⁽²⁹⁾ **If thou meet any man, salute him not.**—An injunction of utmost *haste*. (Comp. the similar words of our Saviour, Luke x. 4.) A short greeting might end in a long halt. "Orientals lose much time in tedious salutations" (*Keil*).

**Lay my staff upon the face of the child.**—It seems to be implied that if the mother had had faith this would have sufficed for raising the child. (Comp. chap. ii. 8; Acts xix. 12.) Keil supposes that the prophet foresaw the failure of this expedient, and intended by it to teach the Shunammites and his followers generally that the power of working miracles was not *magically* inherent in himself or in his staff, as they might imagine, but only in Jehovah, who granted the temporary use of that power to faith and prayer. In other words, Elisha was seeking to lift the minds of his disciples to higher and more spiritual conceptions of the prophetic office. But this seems doubtful.

⁽³⁰⁾ **I will not leave thee.**—She wished the prophet himself to go to her child. The writer appropriately substitutes "the mother of the child" for "the Shunammite" or "the woman" in connection with this impassioned utterance, which induced the prophet to yield to her wishes.

⁽³¹⁾ **There was neither voice, nor hearing.**—1 Kings xviii. 29; see margin, and Isa. xxi. 7.

**Wherefore he went again.**—*And he came back to meet him* (Elisha).

**The child is not awaked.**—*The lad woke not.* The Rabbis explain Gehazi's failure by assuming that he had disobeyed his master's injunction by loitering on the way. This is contradicted by the narrative itself. He had acted with all despatch. Others blame him on

¹hearing. Wherefore he went again to meet him, and told him, saying, The child is not awaked. ⁽³²⁾ And when Elisha was come into the house, behold, the child was dead, *and* laid upon his bed. ⁽³³⁾ He went in therefore, and shut the door upon them twain, and prayed unto the LORD. ⁽³⁴⁾ And he went up, and lay upon the child, and put his mouth upon his mouth, and his eyes upon his eyes, and his hands upon his hands: and he stretched himself upon the child; and the flesh of the child waxed warm. ⁽³⁵⁾ Then he returned, and walked in the house ²to and fro; and went up, and stretched himself upon him: and the child sneezed seven times, and the child opened his eyes. ⁽³⁶⁾ And he called Gehazi, and said, Call this Shunammite. So he called her. And when she was come in unto him, he said, Take up thy son. ⁽³⁷⁾ Then she went in, and fell at his feet, and bowed herself to the ground, and took up her son, and went out.

⁽³⁸⁾ And Elisha came again to Gilgal: and *there was* a dearth in the land; and the sons of the prophets *were* sitting before him: and he said unto his servant, Set on the great pot, and seethe pottage for the sons of the prophets. ⁽³⁹⁾ And one went out into the field to gather herbs, and found a wild vine, and gathered thereof wild gourds his lap full, and came and shred *them* into the pot of pottage: for they knew *them* not.

1 Heb., *attention.*
B.C. cir. 891.
2 Heb., *once hither and once thither.*

---

other grounds, which, in the absolute silence of the text, cannot be substantiated. The prophet says no word of censure when he receives the announcement of the failure. Bähr thinks that Elisha himself was at fault in supposing he could transfer the spirit and power of a prophet to his servant; and acted in over-haste without a Divine incentive. (Comp. 2 Sam. vii. 3 seq.)

The true explanation is suggested in the Note on verse 29. (Bähr is wrong in taking *the staff* to be other than a *walking* staff. A different word would be used for *rod* or *sceptre*.)

⁽³³⁾ **He went in therefore.**—Comp. the narrative of Elijah's raising the widow's son (1 Kings xvii. 17—24), which is imitated in the present account.

**Them twain.**—Himself and the body.

⁽³⁴⁾ **He went up.**—Upon the bed (chap. i. 6).

**And lay upon the child.**—Comp. 1 Kings xvii. 21. What is hinted at there is described here (*Thenius*).

**Stretched himself upon the child.**—*Bowed himself.* So LXX., Syriac, and Vulg. (Comp. 1 Kings xviii. 42.) This expression summarises the preceding details.

**The flesh of the child waxed warm.**—The life of the Divine Spirit which was in Elisha was miraculously imparted by contact to the lifeless body. (Comp. Gen. ii. 7.)

⁽³⁵⁾ **He returned.**—From off the bed.

**Walked in the house to and fro.**—Or, *in the chamber.* Elisha's walking to and fro is an index of intense excitement. He was earnestly expecting the fulfilment of his prayer. Cornelius à Lapide thinks the prophet walked "ut ambulando excitaret majorem calorem quem puero communicaret" (!)

**The child sneezed.**—The verb occurs here only. It denotes a *faint* rather than a *loud* sneeze. (Heb., '*atishāh*; Job xli. 10.) It is omitted by the LXX., which has, "and he bowed himself over the boy until seven times." The repeated sneezing was a sign of restored respiration. (Comp. Luke vii. 15.)

Keil supposes that whereas Elijah raised the widow's son at once, his successor only restored the Shunammite's son by degrees; and that this betokens an inferiority on the part of Elisha. But the narrative in 1 Kings xvii. 17 seq. is plainly abridged.

⁽³⁶⁾ **Take up thy son.**—So our Lord "delivered to his mother" the young man whom He raised from death by His word (Luke vii. 15).

⁽³⁷⁾ **Then she went in.**—*And she came.*

**Bowed herself to the ground.**—In deep veneration for the prophet of Jehovah.

(38—44) Elisha among the sons of the prophets at Gilgal during the famine.

⁽³⁸⁾ **And Elisha came again.**—*Now Elisha had returned,* commencing a new narrative. The word "return" refers to the prophet's annual visit. (Comp. verse 25, and chap. ii. 1, Notes.) The story is not put in chronological sequence with the foregoing.

**And there was a dearth.**—*And the famine was.*

**The sons of the prophets were sitting before him.**—As disciples before a master; probably in a common hall, which served for lecture, work, and dining-room. (Comp. chap. vi. 1; Ezek. viii. 1, xiv. 1; Acts xxii. 3.)

**His servant.**—Perhaps not Gehazi, but one of the sons of the prophets. So in verse 43.

**Seethe pottage.**—Gen. xxv. 29.

⁽³⁹⁾ **Herbs.**—A rare word. (See Isa. xxvi. 19.) The Targum renders "greens." The LXX. retains the Hebrew word; the Syriac and Arabic render "mallows." Thenius thinks that 'αριώθ, the reading of the LXX., points to another word derived from a different root, and meaning "to pluck," so that the word would denote *legumina.*

**A wild vine.**—Vulg., "quasi vitem silvestrem," *i.e.,* a running plant, like a vine.

**Wild gourds.**—In 1 Kings vi. 18 a related word is used to describe one of the decorations of the Temple ("knops").

Wild gourds, or cucumbers (*cucumeres agrestes,* or *asinini*), are oval in shape, and taste bitter. Their Hebrew name (*paqqû'ôth*) is expressive of the fact that when ripe they are apt to *burst* upon being touched. If eaten they act as a violent purgative. They were mistaken on the present occasion for edible gourds, a favourite food of the people (Num. xi. 5). The Vulg. renders "colocynth," or coloquintida, a plant of the same family, bearing large orange-like fruits, which

(40) So they poured out for the men to eat. And it came to pass, as they were eating of the pottage, that they cried out, and said, O thou man of God, *there is* death in the pot. And they could not eat *thereof*. (41) But he said, Then bring meal. And he cast *it* into the pot; and he said, Pour out for the people, that they may eat. And there was no ¹harm in the pot.

(42) And there came a man from Baal-shalisha, and brought the man of God bread of the firstfruits, twenty loaves of barley, and full ears of corn ²in the husk thereof. And he said, Give unto the people, that they may eat. (43) And his servitor said, What, should I set this before an hundred men? He said again, Give the people, that they may eat: for thus saith the LORD, ᵃThey shall eat, and shall leave *thereof*. (44) So he set *it* before them, and they did eat, and left *thereof*, according to the word of the LORD.

CHAPTER V.—Now Naaman, captain of the host of the king of Syria, was a great man ³with his master, and ⁴⁵honourable, because by him the LORD had given ⁶deliverance unto Syria: he

B.C. cir. 891.

1 Heb., *evil thing*.
2 Or, *in his scrip, or, garment*.
a John 6. 11.
3 Heb., *before*.
4 Or, *gracious*.
5 Heb., *lifted up, or, accepted in countenance*.
6 Or, *victory*.

---

are very bitter, and cause colic (*cucumis colocynthi*, L.). Keil supposes this to be the "wild vine" intended.

**They knew them not.**—And so did not stop the young man from his shredding.

(40) **There is death in the pot.**—The bitter taste, and perhaps incipient effect of the pottage, made them think of poison.

(41) **Then bring meal.**—Keil says, "the meal was only the material basis for the spiritual activity which went out from Elisha, and made the poisonous food wholesome." Thenius, however, supposes that "the meal softened the bitterness, and obviated the drastic effect." But Reuss appears to be right in saying, "by mistake a poisonous (not merely a bitter) plant had been put into the pot, and the prophet neutralises the poison by means of an antidote whose *natural* properties could never have had that effect." The "meal" here, therefore, corresponds to the "salt" in chap. ii. 21.

**And he said, Pour out.**—The LXX. adds, "to Gehazi, his servant;" probably a gloss.

(42) **Baal-shalisha.**—Probably the same as Beth-shalisha, mentioned by Jerome and Eusebius, fifteen Roman miles north of Lydda-Diospolis, and not far west of Gilgal and Bethel. (Comp. "the land of Shalisha," 1 Sam. ix. 4. Its name, Shalisha—as if *Three-land*—seems to allude to the three wadies, which there meet in the *Wády Qurâwá*.)

**Bread of the firstfruits.**—Comp. Num. xviii. 13; Deut. xviii. 4, according to which all firstfruits of grain were to be given to the priests and Levites. Such presents to prophets appear to have been usual in ordinary times. On the present occasion, which was "a time of dearth" (verse 42 is connected by the construction with the preceding narrative), one pious person brought his opportune gift to Elisha.

**And full ears of corn in the husk thereof.** —Heb., *and karmel in his wallet*. The word *karmel* occurs besides in Lev. ii. 14, xxiii. 14. The Targum and Syriac render "bruised grain;" the Jewish expositors "tender and fresh ears of corn." In some parts of England unripe corn is made into a dish called "frumenty." The word *çiqlôn* only occurs in this place. The Vulg. renders it by *pera* ("wallet"). The LXX. (Alex.) repeats the Hebrew in Greek letters. The Vatican omits the word. It reads: "twenty barley loaves and cakes of pressed fruit" (παλάθας). The Syriac gives "garment."

**And he said**—*i.e.*, Elisha said.

**Give unto the people.**—Comp. Matt. xiv. 16.

(43) **Servitor.**—*Minister*, or attendant.

**What, should I set this before an hundred men?**—Or, *How am I to set?* &c. (Comp. Matt. xiv. 33.)

**He said again.**—*And he said*.

**They shall eat, and shall leave thereof.**—Heb., *eating and leaving!* an exclamatory mode of speech, natural in hurried and vehement utterance.

(44) **And they did eat, and left thereof.**—Comp. our Lord's miracles, already referred to. Bähr denies any miraculous increase of the food. He makes the miracle consist in the fact that the one hundred men were satisfied with the little they received, and even had some to spare. Similarly, Thenius thinks that the provisions were not inconsiderable for a hundred men (?), and that the emphasis of the narrative lies rather on Elisha's absolute confidence in God than on His wonder-working powers; but this is certainly opposed to the sacred writer's intention. Keil rightly calls attention to the fact that Elisha does not *perform*, but only *predicts*, this miracle.

V.

ELISHA HEALS NAAMAN THE SYRIAN'S LEPROSY, AND PUNISHES GEHAZI THEREWITH.

(1) **Now.**—The construction implies a break between this narrative and the preceding. Whether the events related belong to the time of Jehoram or of the dynasty of Jehu is not clear. Evidently it was a time of peace between Israel and Syria.

**Naaman** (*beauty*).—A title of the sun-god. (See Note on Isa. xvii. 10.)

**A great man with his master.**—Literally, *before his lord*. (Comp. Gen. x. 9.)

**Honourable.**—In special favour. Literally, *lifted up of face*. (Comp. chap. iii. 14, Note; Isa. iii. 3.)

**By him the Lord had given deliverance unto Syria.**—Notice the high prophetic view that it is Jehovah, not Hadad or Rimmon, who gives victory to Syria as well as Israel. (Comp. Amos ix. 7.) It is natural to think of the battle in which Ahab received his mortal wound (1 Kings xxii. 30, *seq*.). The Midrash makes Naaman the man who "drew the bow at a venture" on that occasion. The "deliverance" was victory over Israel.

**He was also a mighty man in valour, but he was a leper.**—Literally, *and the man was a brave warrior, stricken with leprosy*. His leprosy need not have been so severe as to incapacitate him for military duties. The victor over Israel is represented as a leper

was also a mighty man in valour, *but he was* a leper. ⁽²⁾ And the Syrians had gone out by companies, and had brought away captive out of the land of Israel a little maid; and she ¹waited on Naaman's wife. ⁽³⁾ And she said unto her mistress, Would God my lord *were* ²with the prophet that *is* in Samaria! for he would ³recover him of his leprosy. ⁽⁴⁾ And *one* went in, and told his lord, saying, Thus and thus said the maid that *is* of the land of Israel.

⁽⁵⁾ And the king of Syria said, Go to, go, and I will send a letter unto the king of Israel. And he departed, and took ⁴with him ten talents of silver, and six thousand *pieces* of gold, and ten changes of raiment. ⁽⁶⁾ And he brought the letter to the king of Israel, saying, Now when this letter is come unto thee, behold, I have *therewith* sent Naaman my servant to thee, that thou mayest recover him of his leprosy. ⁽⁷⁾ And it came to pass, when the king of Israel had read the letter, that he rent his clothes, and said, *Am* I God, to kill and to make alive, that this man doth send unto me to recover a man of his leprosy? wherefore consider, I pray you, and see how he seeketh a quarrel against me.

⁽⁸⁾ And it was *so*, when Elisha the man of God had heard that the king of Israel had rent his clothes, that he sent to the king, saying, Wherefore hast thou rent

---

¹ Heb., *was before*.
² Heb., *before*.
³ Heb., *gather in*.
⁴ Heb., *in his hand*.

---

who has to seek, and finds, his only help in Israel (*Thenius*).

(2) **The Syrians.**—Heb., *Aram*, the word rendered "Syria" in verse 1.

**By companies.**—Or, *in troops*, referring to a marauding incursion made at some time prior to the events here recorded.

**Brought away captive . . . a little maid.**—Comp. the reference in Joel iii. 6 to the Phœnician traffic in Jewish slaves.

(3) **Would God.**—*O that!* '*Ahalê* here; in Ps. cxix. 5, '*Ahalay*. The word seems to follow the analogy of '*ashrê*, "O the bliss of!" (Ps. i. 1). It perhaps means "O the delight of!" the root '*ahal* being assumed equivalent to the Arabic *halâ*, Syriac *hali*, "dulcis fuit."

**For he would recover him.**—*Then he would receive him back*. (Comp. Num. xii. 14, 15.) In Israel lepers were excluded from society. Restoration to society implied restoration to health. Hence the same verb came to be used in the sense of healing as well as of receiving back the leper. Thenius, however, argues that as the phrase "from leprosy" is wanting in Num. xii., the real meaning is, "to take a person away from leprosy," to which he had been, as it were, delivered up.

(4) **And one went in.**—*And he* (i.e., Naaman) *went in* : scil., into the palace. Some MSS.: "and she went in and told."

**Thus and thus.**—To avoid repetition of her actual words.

(5) **Go to, go.**—*Depart thou* (thither), *enter* (the land of Israel).

**A letter.**—Written, probably, in that old Aramean script of which we have examples on Assyrian seals of the eighth century B.C., and which closely resembled the old Phœnician and Hebrew characters, as well as that of the Moabite stone (chap. i. 1, Note).

**With him.**—*In his hand*. (Comp. the expression "to fill the hand for Jehovah"—i.e., with presents; 1 Chron. xxix. 5.)

**Changes of raiment.**—Or, *holiday suits*. Reuss, *habits de fête*. (See the same word, *haliphôth*, in Gen. xlv. 22.) Curiously enough, similar expressions (*nahlaptum*, *hitlupatum*) were used in the like sense by the Assyrians (Schrader).

**Ten talents of silver.**—About £3,750 in our money. The money talent was equivalent to sixty minas, the mina to fifty shekels. The shekel came to about 2s. 6d. of our money.

**Six thousand pieces of gold.**—Heb., *six thousand* (*in*) *gold* : i.e., six thousand gold shekels = two talents of gold, about £13,500. The gold shekel was worth about 45s. of our currency. The total sum appears much too large, and the numbers are probably corrupt, as is so often the case.

(6) **Now.**—Heb., *And now*, continuing an omitted passage. Only the principal sentence of the letter is given. The message pre-supposes a not altogether hostile relation between the two kings; and the words of the next verse, "He seeketh a quarrel against me," point to the time of comparative lull which ensued after the luckless expedition to Ramoth-gilead (1 Kings xxii.), and the short reign of the invalid Ahaziah; *i.e.*, to the reign of Jehoram, *not* to that of Jehoahaz, in which Israel was wholly crushed by Syria (chap. xiii. 3—7). Schenkel thinks the Syrian inroads (verse 2) indicate the reign of Jehu, and that *Hazael* was the king who wrote the letter, as he was personally acquainted with Elisha (chap. v. 5, *seq.*). But, as Thenius remarks, he forgets that the relations between Jehu and Syria were throughout strained to the last degree; so that such a friendly passage between the two kings as is here described is not to be thought of.

(7) **He rent his clothes.**—As if he had heard blasphemy. (Comp. Matt. xxvi. 65.)

**Am I God, to kill and to make alive?**—Deut. xxxii. 39, "I kill, and I make alive;" 1 Sam. ii. 6, "The Lord killeth, and maketh alive." Leprosy was a kind of living death. (Comp. Num. xii. 12, Heb., "Let her not become as the dead, who, when he cometh forth of his mother's womb, hath half his flesh consumed.")

**Wherefore.**—Heb., *For only know* (i.e., notice), *and see*. Plural verbs are used, because the king is addressing his grandees, in whose presence the letter would be delivered and read.

**He seeketh a quarrel.**—This form of the *verb* (*hithpael*) occurs here only. (Comp. the *noun*, Judges xiv. 4.) Jehoram was hardly in a position to renew the war, after the severe defeat of his father (1 Kings xxii. 30, *seq.*).

(8) **There is a prophet.**—With stress on *there is* (*yēsh*) : *scil.*, as his message pre-supposes.

**When Elisha . . . had heard.**—He was in Samaria at the time (verse 3), and would hear of the

*Elisha's Message.*     II. KINGS, V.     *Naaman is Healed.*

thy clothes? let him come now to me, and he shall know that there is a prophet in Israel. ⁽⁹⁾ So Naaman came with his horses and with his chariot, and stood at the door of the house of Elisha. ⁽¹⁰⁾ And Elisha sent a messenger unto him, saying, Go and wash in Jordan seven times, and thy flesh shall come again to thee, and thou shalt be clean. ⁽¹¹⁾ But Naaman was wroth, and went away, and said, Behold, ¹ ² I thought, He will surely come out to me, and stand, and call on the name of the LORD his God, and ³ strike his hand over the place, and recover the leper. ⁽¹²⁾ *Are not* ⁴ Abana and Pharpar, rivers of Damascus, better than all the waters of Israel? may I not wash in them, and be clean? So he turned and went away in a rage. ⁽¹³⁾ And his servants came near, and spake unto him, and said, My father, *if* the prophet had bid thee *do some* great thing, wouldest thou not have done *it*? how much rather then, when he saith to thee, Wash, and be clean? ⁽¹⁴⁾ Then went he down, and dipped himself seven times in Jordan, according to the saying of the man of God: and his flesh came again like unto the flesh of a little child, and *ᵃ* he was clean.

1 Heb., *I said.*
2 Or, *I said with myself, He will surely come out, &c.*
3 Heb., *move up and down.*
4 Or, *Amana.*
a Luke 4. 27.

coming of the great Syrian captain and of the king's alarm. Why did not Jehoram think at once of Elisha? King and prophet were not on good terms with each other. (Comp. chap. iii. 14.) Besides, Elisha had not as yet done any miracle of this sort; and his apprehensions may have made the king unable, for the moment, to think at all.

⁽⁹⁾ **With his horses and with his chariot.**—*Chariots.* (See on chap. ii. 11, 12; and comp. verse 15, *infra.*) The proper term for a single chariot is used in verse 21. The magnificence of his retinue is suggested.

**Stood.**—*Stopped.* The text hardly conveys, as Bähr thinks, the idea that Elisha's house in Samaria was "a poor hovel," which the great man would not deign to enter, but waited for the prophet to come forth to him. The prophet had "a messenger" (verse 10) at his command.

⁽¹⁰⁾ **Elisha sent a messenger.**—Avoiding personal contact with a leper. (Comp. verse 15, where Naaman, when restored, goes in and stands before the prophet.) Perhaps reverence held back those who consulted a great prophet from entering his presence (comp. chap. iv. 12); and therefore, Naaman stopped with his followers outside the house. Keil suggests that Elisha did not come out to Naaman, because he wished to humble his pride, and to show that his worldly magnificence did not impress the prophet. But, as Thenius says, there is no trace of pride about Naaman.

**Go.**—Infinitive, equivalent to the imperative. (Comp. chap. iii. 16; and perhaps chap. iv. 43.)

**Wash in** (the) **Jordan.**—This command would make it clear that Naaman was not cured by any external means applied by the prophet. "The Syrians knew as well as the Israelites that the Jordan could not heal leprosy" (*Bähr*). Naaman was to understand that he was healed *by the God of Israel*, at His prophet's prayer. (Comp. verse 15.)

**Thy flesh shall come again to thee, and thou shalt be clean.**—Literally, *and let thy flesh come back to thee, and be thou clean.* Leprosy is characterised by raw flesh and running sores, which end in entire wasting away of the tissues.

⁽¹¹⁾ **But (and) Naaman was wroth.**—Because, as his words show, he thought he was mocked by the prophet.

**I thought.**—*I said to myself.*

**Strike his hand.**—Rather, *wave his hand towards the place.* (Comp. Isa. x. 15, xi. 15.) He would not *touch* the unclean place.

**Recover the leper.**—Or, *take away the leprous* (*part*). So Thenius; but everywhere else *mĕçōrā'* means "leprous man," "leper" (Lev. xiv. 2).

⁽¹²⁾ **Abana.**—So Hebrew text; Hebrew margin, *Amana*; and so many MSS., Complut., LXX., Targum, Syriac. (Comp. Amana, Cant. iv. 8, as name of a peak of the Lebanon, which is common in the Assyrian inscriptions also.) The river is identified with the present *Burâda*, or *Barady* ("the cold"), which descends from the Anti-Lebanon, and flows through Damascus in seven streams. (The Arabic version has *Bardâ.*)

**Pharpar.**—*Parpar* ("the swift"), the present *Nahr el-Awâj*, which comes down from the great Hermon, and flows by Damascus on the south. Both rivers have clear water, as being mountain streams, whereas the Jordan is turbid and discoloured.

**Rivers of Damascus.**—Add *the.* Damascus is still famous for its wholesome water.

**May I not wash in them, and be clean?**—If mere washing in a river be enough, it were easy to do that at home, and to much better advantage.

⁽¹³⁾ **Came near.**—Comp. Gen. xviii. 23.

**My father.**—A title implying at once respect and affection. (Comp. 1 Sam. xxiv. 11; chap. vi. 21.) Perhaps, however, the word is a corruption of *im* ("if"), which is otherwise not expressed in the Hebrew.

**Great thing.**—Emphatic in the Hebrew.

**Wouldest thou not have done?**—Or, *wouldest thou not do?*

**He saith.**—*He hath said.*

**Be clean?**—*i.e.*, thou shalt be clean: a common Hebrew idiom.

⁽¹⁴⁾ **Then went he down.**—*And he went down:* scil., from Samaria to the Jordan bed. The Syriac and Arabic, and some Hebrew MSS., read "and he departed;" probably an error of transcription.

**Seven times.**—"Because *seven* was significant of the Divine covenant with Israel, and the cure depended on that covenant; or to stamp the cure as a Divine work, for *seven* is the signature of the works of God" (*Keil*). In the Assyrian monuments there is an almost exact parallel to the above method of seeking a cure. It occurs among the so-called exorcisms, and belongs to the age of Sargon of Agadê (Accad), before 2200 B.C. Merodach is represented as asking his father Hea how to cure a sick man. Hea replies that the sick man must go and bathe in the sacred waters at the mouth of the Euphrates. It thus appears that in bidding Naaman bathe seven times in the Jordan, Elisha acted

(15) And he returned to the man of God, he and all his company, and came, and stood before him: and he said, Behold, now I know that *there is* no God in all the earth, but in Israel: now therefore, I pray thee, take a blessing of thy servant. (16) But he said, *As* the LORD liveth, before whom I stand, I will receive none. And he urged him to take *it*; but he refused. (17) And Naaman said, Shall there not then, I pray thee, be given to thy servant two mules' burden of earth? for thy servant will henceforth offer neither burnt offering nor sacrifice unto other gods, but unto the LORD. (18) In this thing the LORD pardon thy servant, *that* when my master goeth into the house of Rimmon to worship there, and he leaneth on my hand, and I bow myself in the house of Rimmon: when I bow down myself in the house of Rimmon, the LORD pardon thy servant in this thing. (19) And he said unto him, Go in peace. So he departed from him [1]a little way.

(20) But Gehazi, the servant of Elisha the man of God, said, Behold, my master hath spared Naaman this Syrian, in not receiving at his hands that which he brought: but, *as* the LORD liveth, I will run after him, and take somewhat of him. (21) So Gehazi followed after Naa-

[1] Heb., *a little piece of ground.*

---

in accordance with ancient Semitic belief as to the healing virtue of running streams.

(15) **Company.**—Heb., *camp, host.* Naaman's following consisted of "horses and chariots" (verse 9).

**Came.**—*Went in*: into Elisha's house. Gratitude overcame awe and dread.

**Behold, now.**—*Behold, I pray thee.* The "now" belongs to "behold," *not* to "I know."

**I know that . . . in Israel.**—Naaman, like most of his contemporaries, Jewish as well as Syrian, believed in locally restricted deities. The powerlessness of the Syrian gods and the potency of Jehovah having been brought home to his mind by his marvellous recovery, he concludes that there is no god anywhere save *in the land of Israel.* In other words, his local conception of deity still clings to him. What a mark of historic truth appears in this representation!

**Now therefore.**—*And now.*

**Take a blessing of.**—*Accept a present from* (Gen. xxxiii. 11).

(16) **But.**—*And* (both times).

**I will receive none.**—Theodoret compares our Lord's "Freely ye have received, freely give" (Matt. x. 8). (Comp. Acts viii. 20.) Such may have been Elisha's feeling. His refusal, strongly contrasting with the conduct of ordinary prophets, Israelite and heathen (comp. 1 Sam. ix. 6—9), would make a deep impression upon Naaman and his retinue.

(17) **Shall there not then.**—Rather, *If not, let there be given, I pray thee.* LXX., καὶ εἰ μή.

**Two mules' burden of earth?**—Literally, *a load of a yoke of mules' (in) earth.* It was natural for Naaman, with his *local* idea of divinity, to make this request. He wished to worship the God of Israel, so far as possible, *on the soil of Israel,* Jehovah's own land. He would therefore build his altar to Jehovah on a foundation of this earth, or construct the altar itself therewith. (Comp. Exod. xx. 24; 1 Kings xviii. 38.)

**Burnt offering nor sacrifice.**—*Burnt offering nor peace offering.*

**Offer.**—Literally, *make.*

(18) **In this thing.**—*Touching this thing* (but *in* at the end of the verse). The LXX. and Syriac read, "*and* touching this thing," an improvement in the connection.

**To worship.**—*To bow down* (the same verb occurs thrice in the verse).

**The house of Rimmon.**—The Assyrian Rammânu (from *ramāmu,* "to thunder"). One of his epithets in the cuneiform is *Râmimu,* "the thunderer;" and another is *Barqu* (= *Bâriqu*), "he who lightens." Rimmon was the god of the atmosphere, called in Accadian, AN. IM ("god of the air or wind"), figured on bas-reliefs and cylinders as armed with the thunderbolt. His name is prominent in the story of the Flood (*e.g.,* it is said *Rammânu irmum,* "Rimmon thundered"); and one of his standing titles is *Râhiçu* ("he who deluges"). The Assyrians identified Rammân with the Aramean and Edomite Hadad. (Comp. the name Hadad-rimmon, Zech. xii. 11; and Tabrimon, 1 Kings xv. 18.) A list of no fewer than forty-one titles of Rimmon has been found among the cuneiform tablets.

**Leaneth on my hand.**—A metaphor denoting the attendance on the king by his favourite grandee or principal adjutant. (Comp. chap. vii. 2, 17.)

**When I bow down myself.**—An Aramaic form is used. The clause is omitted in some Hebrew MSS.

**The Lord pardon thy servant.**—Naaman had solemnly promised to serve no god but Jehovah for the future. He now prays that an unavoidable exception—which will, indeed, be such only in appearance—may be excused by Jehovah. His request is not, of course, to be judged by a Christian standard. By the reply, "Go in peace," the prophet, as spokesman of Jehovah, acceded to Naaman's prayer. "Naaman durst not profess conversion to the foreign *cultus* before the king, his master; so he asks leave to go on assisting at the national rites" (*Reuss*).

**The Lord pardon.**—In the current Hebrew text it is *the Lord pardon, I pray.* The LXX. appears to have had the same reading; but very many MSS. and all the other versions omit the precative particle. It is, however, probably genuine.

(19) **A little way.**—Heb., *a kibrāh of ground* (Gen. xxxv. 16). It seems to mean "a *length* of ground," "a certain distance," without defining exactly how far. Had it been a *parasang,* as the Syriac renders, Gehazi could not have overtaken the company so easily.

(20) **Said**—*i.e.,* thought.

**This Syrian.**—He justifies his purpose on the principle of "spoiling the Egyptians."

**But, as the Lord liveth, I will run.**—Rather, *by the life of Jehovah, but I will run.* (Comp. Note on chap. iv. 30.)

(21) **He lighted down from the chariot to meet him.**—An Oriental mark of respect. Literally, *fell from off the chariot*: an expression denoting haste

man. And when Naaman saw *him* running after him, he lighted down from the chariot to meet him, and said, ¹*Is* all well? ⁽²²⁾ And he said, All *is* well. My master hath sent me, saying, Behold, even now there be come to me from mount Ephraim two young men of the sons of the prophets: give them, I pray thee, a talent of silver, and two changes of garments. ⁽²³⁾ And Naaman said, Be content, take two talents. And he urged him, and bound two talents of silver in two bags, with two changes of garments, and laid *them* upon two of his servants; and they bare *them* before him. ⁽²⁴⁾ And when he came to the ²tower, he took *them* from their hand, and bestowed *them* in the house: and he let the men go, and they departed. ⁽²⁵⁾ But he went in, and stood before his master. And Elisha said unto him, Whence comest thou, Gehazi? And he said, Thy servant went ³no whither. ⁽²⁶⁾ And he said unto him, Went not mine heart *with thee*, when the man turned again from his chariot to meet thee? *Is it* a time to receive money, and to receive garments, and oliveyards, and vineyards, and sheep, and oxen, and menservants, and maidservants? ⁽²⁷⁾ The leprosy therefore of Naaman shall cleave unto thee, and unto thy seed for ever.

1 Heb., *Is there peace?*
2 Or, *secret place*.
3 Heb., *not hither or thither*.

---

(Gen. xxiv. 64). The LXX. has "he turned," which implies an ellipsis of "and descended."

**Is all well?**—Naaman feared something might have befallen the prophet. The LXX. omits this.

⁽²²⁾ **Even now.**—Or, *this moment, just*.

**Mount Ephraim.**—*The hill-country of Ephraim,* or *highlands of Ephraim*, where Gilgal and Bethel were situate.

**Changes of garments.**—The same phrase as in verse 5.

⁽²³⁾ **Be content.**—*Be willing, consent to take.* The Vatican LXX. omits; the Alexandrian renders οὐκοῦν, owing to a transposition of the Hebrew letters (*hălô'* for *hô'êl*).

**Bound.**—Deut. xiv. 25.

**Bags.**—Only here and in Isa. iii. 22, where it means "purses."

**Laid them upon two.**—*Gave them to two of his* (i.e., Naaman's) *young men*. The courtesy of the act is obvious.

**Before him.**—Gehazi.

⁽²⁴⁾ **The tower.**—Heb., the *'ōphel, the mound*, on which the prophet's house may have stood. There would be no window in the exterior wall from which Gehazi and his companions might have been observed approaching. Perhaps, however, a fortified hill, forming part of the system of defences surrounding Samaria, like the Ophel at Jerusalem, is to be understood. (Comp. 2 Chron. xxvii. 3.) Elisha's house lay within the city wall (chap. vi. 30, *seq.*). Keil explains the hill on which Samaria was built. (Comp. Isa. xxxii. 14, and Cheyne's Note; Micah iv. 8: "And thou, O tower of the flock; O mound of the daughter of Zion.") This note of *place* is also a note of historical truth.

**Bestowed them in the house.**—*Stowed them away, laid them up carefully in the* (prophet's) *house.* LXX., παρέθετο.

**Let the men go.**—*Before* he "bestowed" their burdens in the house.

⁽²⁵⁾ **But he.**—*And he himself* (after putting away his ill-gotten gains).

**Went in.**—Into his master's chamber. Gehazi was already in the house.

**Stood before.**—*Came forward to* (2 Chron. vi. 12).

**Thy servant went no whither.**—Literally, *Thy servant went not away hither nor thither*.

⁽²⁶⁾ **Went not mine heart . . . meet thee?**—Rather, *Nor did my heart (i.e.,* consciousness) *go away, when a man turned* (and alighted) *from his chariot to meet thee*. The prophet, in severe irony, adopts Gehazi's own phrase: Maurer, "Non abierat animus meus;" "I was there in spirit, and witnessed everything." The sentence has given the commentators much trouble. (See the elaborate Note in Thenius. We might have expected *wĕlô*, and *w* may have been omitted, owing to the preceding *w*; but it is not absolutely necessary.) The Authorised Version follows the LXX. (Vat.), which supplies the expression "with thee" (μετὰ σοῦ), wanting in the Hebrew text. The Targum paraphrases: "By the spirit of prophecy I was informed when the man turned," &c. The Syriac follows with, "My heart informed me when the man turned," &c.

**Is it a time to receive.**—Comp. Eccles. iii. 2, *seq*. The LXX., pointing the Hebrew differently, reads: καὶ νῦν ἔλαβες τὸ ἀργύριον, καὶ νῦν ἔλαβες τὰ ἱμάτια κ.τ.λ. ("And now thou receivedst the money," &c.). So also the Vulg. and Arabic, but not the Targum and Syriac. Böttcher, retaining the interrogative particle of the Hebrew, adopts this: "Didst thou then take the money?" &c. But the Masoretic pointing appears to be much more suitable. The prophet's question comes to this: "Was that above all others a proper occasion for yielding to your desire of gain, when you were dealing with a *heathen*? Ought you not to have been studiously *disinterested* in your behaviour to such an one, that he might learn not to confound the prophets of Jehovah with the mercenary diviners and soothsayers of the false gods?" The prophet's disciple is bound, like his master, to seek, not worldly power, but spiritual; for the time is one of ardent struggle against the encroachments of paganism.

**And oliveyards . . . maidservants?**—The prophet develops Gehazi's object in asking for the money he wished to purchase lands, and live stock, and slaves—whatever constituted the material wealth of the time. The Targum inserts the explanatory: "And thou thoughtest in thy heart to purchase oliveyards," &c. So Vulg.: "ut emas oliveta."

⁽²⁷⁾ **Shall cleave.**—Or, *cleave! i.e.*, let it cleave. The prophetic sentence is naturally expressed as an imperative.

**A leper as white as snow.**—Comp. Exod. iv. 6. Num. xii. 10. A sudden outbreak of leprosy may follow upon extreme fright or mortification (*Michaelis*).

**Unto thy seed for ever.**—Like other skin diseases, leprosy is hereditary. If it be thought that the sentence is too strong, it should be remembered that

*Elisha causes* **II. KINGS, VI.** *Iron to swim*

And he went out from his presence a leper *as white* as snow.

CHAPTER VI.—⁽¹⁾ And the sons of the prophets said unto Elisha, Behold now, the place where we dwell with thee is too strait for us. ⁽²⁾ Let us go, we pray thee, unto Jordan, and take thence every man a beam, and let us make us a place there, where we may dwell. And he answered, Go ye. ⁽³⁾ And one said, Be content, I pray thee, and go with thy servants. And he answered, I will go. ⁽⁴⁾ So he went with them.

And when they came to Jordan, they cut down wood. ⁽⁵⁾ But as one was felling a beam, the ¹ax head fell into the water: and he cried, and said, Alas, master! for it was borrowed. ⁽⁶⁾ And the man of God said, Where fell it? And he shewed him the place. And he cut down a stick, and cast *it* in thither; and the iron did swim. ⁽⁷⁾ Therefore said he, Take *it* up to thee. And he put out his hand, and took it.

⁽⁸⁾ Then the king of Syria warred against Israel, and took counsel with his servants, saying, In such and such a

B.C. cir. 892.

¹ Heb., *iron*.

---

the prophet is really pronouncing inspired judgment upon the *sin* of Gehazi, and milder language might have produced erroneous impressions. Covetousness and lying are never spared in Scripture, and it is well for mankind that it is so. (Comp. Acts v.)

### VI.

THE HISTORY OF ELISHA'S MIGHTY WORKS CONTINUED.

(1–7) The prophet causes an iron ax-head to float in the Jordan.

(1) **And the sons of the prophets said.**—The form of the verb implies connection with the preceding narrative; but as the section refers to Elisha's activity among the sons of the prophets, it was probably connected originally with chap. iv. 44. The compiler may have transferred it to its present position in order, as Thenius suggests, to indicate the lapse of some time between the events described here and there; and further, to separate the account of the renewed warfare between Syria and Israel (verse 8, *seq.*) from that of Elisha's good deed to Naaman the Syrian.

**The place where we dwell with thee.**—Rather, *the place where we sit before thee*: scil., habitually, for instruction. The phrase occurred in chap. iv. 38. The common hall is meant; whether that at Gilgal or at Jericho is uncertain. Jericho was close to the *Jordan* (verse 2), but that does not *prove* that it is meant here. The prophet's disciples did not live in a single building, like a community of monks. Their settlement is called "dwellings" (*nāyôth*) in the plural (1 Sam. xix. 18); and they could be married (chap. iv. 1).

**Too strait.**—Their numbers had increased. (Comp. chap. iv. 43.)

(2) **Take thence every man a beam.**—The Jordan valley was well wooded. Its present bed is still "overarched by oleanders, acacias, thorns, and similar shrubbery." If all were to take part in felling the trees, the work would soon be done.

**Where we may dwell.**—Literally, *to sit* (or, *dwell*) *there*. The reference seems still to be to *sitting* in the hall of instruction.

(3) **One.**—Heb., *the one*, whoever it was.

**Be content.**—*Consent*, or, *be willing*.

**Go with thy servants.**—To superintend their work, and help them in case of unforeseen difficulty.

(4) **Wood.**—Heb., *the timber*: scil., which they required.

(5) **But.**—Heb., *and it came to pass, the one was felling the beam*. Not necessarily "the one" of verse 3, but *the* one (whoever it was) to whom the mishap occurred, as presently related.

**The ax head fell.**—Heb., *and as for the iron, it fell*. The subject of the verb is made prominent by being put first in the accusative. It is thus implied that something *happened to* the iron. Perhaps, however, it is better to consider that the particle, which usually marks the object of the verb, in cases like the present has its etymological meaning of "something" (*'eth* being regarded as equivalent to *yath*, and so to *yēsh*). (See Winer, *Chaldäische Grammatik*, ed. Fischer.)

**Master!**—*My lord*, Elisha. He instinctively appeals to *Elisha* for help.

**For it was borrowed.**—Heb., *and that one was borrowed*. Vulg., "et hoc ipsum mutuo acceperam."

(6) **Where.**—*Whereinto?* or, *Where fell it in?*

**The iron did swim.**—*He caused the iron to float*. (Comp. Deut. xi. 4 for the verb.) The iron ax-head did not swim, but simply rose to the surface. It had fallen in near the bank. Elisha's throwing in the stick was a symbolical act, intended to help the witnesses to realise that the coming up of the iron was not a natural, but a supernatural, event, brought about through the instrumentality of the prophet. As in the case of the salt thrown into the spring at Jericho, the symbol was appropriate to the occasion. It indicated that iron could be made to float *like wood* by the sovereign power of Jehovah. The properties of material substances depend on His will for their fixity, and may be suspended or modified at His pleasure. The moral of this little story is that God helps in small personal troubles as well as in great ones of larger scope. His providence cares for the individual as well as the race.

(7) **Therefore.**—*And he said*.

(8–23) Elisha baffles several predatory attempts of the Syrians, and strikes with blindness those sent to seize him.

(8) **Then the king of Syria warred.**—Rather, *Now the king of Syria* (Aram) *was warring*, i.e., continually. The time intended cannot be the reign of Jehoahaz, for here the Syrians achieve nothing of importance. (Comp. verse 32.)

**Took counsel with.**—Comp. 2 Chron. xx. 21.

**Such and such.**—The compound Hebrew expression (*pĕlônî 'almônî*) means "a certain one, I will not mention which;" the Greek, ὁ δεῖνα.

**My camp.**—Heb., *tahănôthî*; a difficult expression, found only here. Its form is anomalous, and probably corrupt. The Targum renders "house of my camp;"

*Elisha Warns the King.*  II. KINGS, VI.  *The Syrians encompass Dotham.*

place *shall be* my ¹camp. (9) And the man of God sent unto the king of Israel, saying, Beware that thou pass not such a place; for thither the Syrians are come down. (10) And the king of Israel sent to the place which the man of God told him and warned him of, and saved himself there, not once nor twice. (11) Therefore the heart of the king of Syria was sore troubled for this thing; and he called his servants, and said unto them, Will ye not shew me which of us *is* for the king of Israel? (12) And one of his servants said, ²None, my lord, O king: but Elisha, the prophet that *is* in Israel, telleth the king of Israel the words that thou speakest in thy bedchamber. (13) And he said, Go and spy where he *is*, that I may send and fetch him. And it was told him, saying, Behold, *he is* in Dothan. (14) Therefore sent he thither horses, and chariots, and a ³great host: and they came by night, and compassed the city about. (15) And when the ⁴servant of the man of God was risen early, and gone forth, behold, an host compassed the city both with horses and chariots. And his servant said unto him, Alas, my master! how shall we do? (16) And he answered, Fear not: for ᵃthey that *be* with us *are* more than they that *be* with them. (17) And Elisha prayed, and said, LORD, I pray thee, open his eyes, that he may see. And the LORD opened the eyes of the young man; and he saw: and, be-

1 *encamping.*
2 Heb., *no.*
3 Heb., *heavy.*
4 Or, *minister.*
a 2 Chron. 32. 7.

---

but the Syriac, "Set ye an ambush, and lurk;" the Vulg., "ponamus insidias:" and similarly the Arabic. This has suggested that the true reading is "hide ye," *i.e.*, lie in ambush (*tēhābû, i.e., tēhābě'û*: Thenius). It is, however, a more obvious change to read, "ye shall go down" (*tinhāthú*: Ps. xxxviii. 3). This agrees better with the construction, "*Unto ('el)* such and such a place shall ye go down," *i.e.*, on a plundering incursion.

(9) **Pass.**—*Pass over, across, or through.*

**Such a place.**—*This place.*

**Thither.**—*There.*

**Come down.**—*Coming down.* Another anomalous Hebrew form (*nĕhittim*). Some would recognise here again a corruption of the same verb as in verse 8, and render, "for there the Syrians are *about hiding*" (*nehbim, i.e., nehbě'im*). This is supported by the LXX., "ὅτι ἐκεῖ Συρία κέκρυπται;" the Syriac and Arabic, "are lurking;" the Vulg., "in insidiis sunt;" and the Targum, "are hidden." But the word (Heb.) is really an irregular participial formation from *nahath*, "to descend," and the Authorised Version is therefore correct. The versions have deduced the idea of hiding from that of *going down*, as if *crouching on the ground* were meant.

(10) **Sent.**—A sufficient force to hold the place, so that the Syrians had to return unsuccessful.

**Warned.**—Ezek. iii. 19; 2 Chron. xix. 10.

**Saved himself.**—*Was wary; on his guard* (verse 9).

**Not once nor twice** refers to the statement of the entire verse. On more than one occasion, and in regard to different inroads of the Syrians, Elisha gave the king forewarning.

(11) **Troubled.**—Literally, *storm-tost*. The phrase is not found elsewhere in the Old Testament. (Comp. the use of the same verb in Jonah i. 11, 13; Isa. liv. 11.)

**Which of us is for the king of Israel?**—"Which of us?" is an expression only found here (*mishehellānû*). Pointed differently, the word would give the sense of the LXX., τίς προδίδωσί με βασιλεῖ Ἰσραήλ—"Who betrays me to the king of Israel?"—*malshinēnû*, "our betrayer," an Aramaic term. (Comp. Prov. xxx. 10.) Better still is Böttcher's correction: "Who leads us astray unto the king of Israel?" (*mashlēnû*). This would be the natural supposition of the Syrian king when he found himself unexpectedly confronting an armed Israelitish force, and harmonises well enough with the LXX. and Vulg. The received text, which the Targum, Syriac, and Arabic support, can only mean, "Which of those who belong to us inclines to the king of Israel?" (Comp. Ps. cxxiii. 2.) The Syriac follows the Hebrew exactly; the Targum and Arabic add a verb—"reveals secrets"—before "to the king of Israel."

(12) **One of his servants.**—The old interpreters thought of Naaman, but Elisha's fame may have been otherwise known at Damascus.

**None.**—*Nay.*

**The words.**—The LXX. and Vulg., "all the words."

**Telleth.**—From time to time, as the Hebrew form denotes.

(13) **Fetch.**—*Take.*

**Dothan.**—A contracted dual (equivalent to Dothain· LXX., Dothaim). It lay on a hill, twelve Roman miles north-east of Samaria, in a narrow pass (Judith iv. 5, vii. 3, viii. 3), on the caravan route from Gilead to Egypt (Gen. xxxvii. 17). The old name survives in a *Tell*, covered with ruins, south-west of the modern *Jenin*.

(14) **A great host.**—Of infantry. Not, however, an *army*, but a *company*. (See verse 23.)

**They came by night.**—So as to take the city by surprise.

(15) **The servant of the man of God.**—*One waiting on* (i.e., a minister of) *the man of God*. Not Gehazi, who is never called Elisha's *minister*, and is usually mentioned by name.

**Was risen early.**—For the Hebrew construction, comp. Ps. cxxvii. 2; Isa. v. 11; Hos. vi. 4.

**Gone forth.**—To the outside of the house, which commanded a view of the valley below, where the Syrians lay.

**And his servant said.**—On returning into the house. The narrative is contracted.

(16) **They that be with us . . . with them.**—Comp. Num. xiv. 9; Ps. iii. 6, "I will not be afraid of ten thousands of people that have set themselves against me round about"; and 2 Chron. xxxii. 7, 8, with Notes.

(17) **And the Lord opened the eyes of the young man; and he saw.**—Just as the Lord had opened Elisha's own eyes to see the like vision of unearthly glory when his master was taken away (chap. ii. 10, 12) (Comp. also Num. xxii. 31.)

hold, the mountain *was* full of horses and chariots of fire round about Elisha. (18) And when they came down to him, Elisha prayed unto the LORD, and said, Smite this people, I pray thee, with blindness. And he smote them with blindness according to the word of Elisha. (19) And Elisha said unto them, This *is* not the way, neither *is* this the city: ¹follow me, and I will bring you to the man whom ye seek. But he led them to Samaria. (20) And it came to pass, when they were come into Samaria, that Elisha said, LORD, open the eyes of these *men*, that they may see. And the LORD opened their eyes, and they saw; and, behold, *they were* in the midst of Samaria. (21) And the king of Israel said unto Elisha, when he saw them, My father, shall I smite *them?* shall I smite *them?* (22) And he answered, Thou shalt not smite *them:* wouldest thou smite those whom thou hast taken captive with thy sword and with thy bow? set bread and water before them, that they may eat and drink, and go to their master. (23) And he prepared great provision for them: and when they had

¹ Heb., *come ye after me.*

---

**The mountain.**—On which Dothan stood.

**Horses and chariots of fire.**—Literally, *horses and chariots,* to wit, *fire.* Fire was the well-known symbol of Jehovah's visible presence and protective or destroying might, from the days of the patriarchs onwards (Gen. xv. 17; Exod. iii. 2, xiii. 21, *seq.,* xix. 16, *seq.*; Isa. xxix. 6, xxx. 30, 33, xxxiii. 14). As fiery chariots and horses parted Elijah from Elisha (chap. ii. 12), so now a similar appearance surrounds and protects the latter. "It is a fine thought," says Thenius, "that on this occasion the veil of earthly existence was lifted for a moment for one child of man, so as to allow him a clear glimpse of the sovereignty of Providence." The form of the supernatural appearance was, no doubt, conditioned by the circumstances of the time. Chariots and horses were the strength of the Aramean oppressors of Israel; therefore, Jehovah causes His earthly ministers to see that He also has at His command horses and chariots, and that *of fire.*

(18) **And when they came down to him.**—This would mean that *the Syrians came down* to Elisha. But the prophet was, to begin with, in the city, which lay on the top of the hill; and the heavenly host intervened between him and his enemies, so that the latter must have occupied the lower position. The reading of the Syriac and Josephus is, "and they (*i.e.,* Elisha and his servant) went down *to them*"—*i.e.,* to the Syrian force; and this is apparently right. The sight of the heavenly host guarding his master had inspired the prophet's follower with courage to face any danger in his master's company.

**Elisha prayed.**—*And Elisha prayed*—mentally, as he approached his foes.

**This people.**—Perhaps in the sense of *multitude.*

**Blindness.**—*Sanwêrîm:* the term used in Gen. xix. 11, and nowhere besides. It denotes not so much blindness as a dazing effect, accompanied with mental bewilderment and confusion. "They saw, but knew not what they saw" (*Rashi*). Ewald pronounces the passage in Genesis the model of the present one.

(19) **This is not the way, neither is this the city.**—These words pre-suppose, according to Josephus, that the prophet had asked them whom they were seeking, and that they had replied, "The prophet Elisha." Thenius and Bähr accept this. Keil says, "Elisha's words contain a falsehood, and are to be judged of in the same way as every ruse by which an enemy is deceived." Thenius declares that "there is no untruth in the words of Elisha, strictly taken; for his *home* was not in Dothan (where he had only stayed for a time), but in Samaria; and the phrase 'to the man' might well mean 'to his house.'" Surely it is easier to suppose that the "dazing" had caused the Syrians to go wandering about in the valley at the foot of the hill, vainly seeking to find the right way up to the city gate. (Comp. Gen. *l.c.,* "They wearied themselves to find the door.") If the prophet found them in this plight, his words would be literally true.

**The man whom ye seek.**—An irony.

**Bring you.**—*Lead you.*

**But he led.**—*And he led* (or, *guided*).

**To Samaria.**—Heb., *Shômĕrônāh.* The Assyrian spelling is Shâmerīna; and this, compared with the Greek Σαμάρεια, suggests that the original name was *Shâmirin* ("the warders"). The final *ô* in the present Hebrew form may be due to confounding *y* with *w*.

(20) **Behold, they were in the midst of Samaria.**—Michaelis wonders how such a host could be led *into* the city without putting themselves on their guard. He overlooks the supernatural bewilderment which had fallen upon them. When their eyes were opened, and they realised their whereabouts, dismay and astonishment would paralyse their energies.

(21) **My father.**—Comp. chaps. ii. 12, viii. 9 ("Thy son Ben-hadad"), xiii. 14.

**Shall I smite them? shall I smite them?**—Or, *May I smite? may I smite, my father?* The repetition expresses the king's eagerness to slay his powerless enemies. He asks the prophet's permission. (Comp. chap. iv. 7.)

(22) **Thou shalt not.**—Or, *thou must not.*

**Wouldest thou smite . . . thy bow?**—The Hebrew order is, "An quos ceperis gladio et arcu percussurus es?" (Comp. Gen. xlviii. 22.) Elisha says, "These men are virtually prisoners of war, and therefore are not to be slain in cold blood."

The LXX., Targum, Syriac, and Vulg., ignore the interrogative particle. The Targum and Syriac render, "Lo those whom thou hast taken captive with thy sword, &c., thou dost (or mayst) kill." (Comp. Deut. xx. 13.) The Vulg., "neque enim cepisti eos, ut percutias," and the Arabic, "Didst thou take them captive with thy sword, &c., that thou shouldest slay them?" come to the same thing. These renderings are interesting, as they make Elisha deny the king's right of disposal of these prisoners of Jehovah. The purpose of the miracle would have been frustrated by killing the Syrians. That purpose was to force their king and them to acknowledge the might of the true God.

(23) **He.**—The king of Israel.

**Prepared great provision.**—Or, *a great feast.* The Hebrew verb (*kārāh*) occurs nowhere else in this

eaten and drunk, he sent them away, and they went to their master. So the bands of Syria came no more into the land of Israel. ⁽²⁴⁾ And it came to pass after this, that Ben-hadad king of Syria gathered all his host, and went up, and besieged Samaria. ⁽²⁵⁾ And there was a great famine in Samaria: and, behold, they besieged it, until an ass's head was *sold* for fourscore *pieces* of silver, and the fourth part of a cab of dove's dung for five *pieces* of silver. ⁽²⁶⁾ And as the king of Israel was passing by upon the wall, there cried a woman unto him, saying, Help, my lord, O king. ⁽²⁷⁾ And he said, ¹If the LORD do not help thee, whence shall I help thee? out of the barnfloor, or out of the winepress? ⁽²⁸⁾ And the king said unto her, What aileth thee? And she answered, This woman said unto me, Give thy son, that we may eat him to day, and we will eat my son to morrow. ⁽²⁹⁾ So ᵃwe boiled my son, and did eat him: and I said unto her on the ²next day, Give thy son, that we may

1 Or, *Let not the LORD save thee.*

a Deut. 28. 53.

2 Heb., *other*.

sense. The noun (*kĕrāh*) is cognate with it, and the root meaning seems to be *union*: such as takes place at a common meal. Thenius renders *kĕrāh* by "das Gastrund"—*i.e.*, the *circle* of guests.

**So the bands of Syria came no more.**—The stress lies on the word "bands." The Syrians, dreading Elisha, did not make any further *clandestine* attempts to injure Israel, like those above described, which only involved the despatch of predatory bands. They now resolved to try the fortunes of regular war with the whole strength of their army (verse 24). It is evident, therefore, that we must not think of any gratitude on their part for the clemency of Jehoram.

**Into the land.**—Syriac, "into the border;" Targum, "into the border of the land." (Comp. 1 Sam. vii. 13.)

(24—chap. vii. 20) THE SIEGE OF SAMARIA AND THE FAMINE. THE DELIVERANCE, AS FORETOLD BY ELISHA.

⁽²⁴⁾ **After this.**—*Afterwards.* The term plainly implies *chronological* sequence.

**Ben-hadad.**— Ben-hadad II., who had besieged Samaria in the reign of Ahab (1 Kings xx. 1). He is mentioned on the monuments of Shalmaneser II., now in the British Museum, under the designation of *Rammânu-hidri*, or *idri*. Now, as the Assyrians identified their god *Rammânu* (Rimmon) with the Syrian deity, *Adad, Addu,* or *Dadi*, this title might be equivalent to *Adad-idri*, or *Addu-idri*. Further, in three contract tablets in the reign of Nabonidus, Mr. Pinches has read the names *Bin-Addu-natânu* and *Bin-Addu-amara*—*i.e.*, " Bin-Addu gave," and " Bin-Adău commanded." Bin (or, *Tur*)-Addu, "son of Addu," is clearly the name of a god, like *abal Esarra*, "son of Esarra," in the name Tiglath Pileser; and is, in fact, the Assyrian equivalent of Ben-hadad. The Syrian king's full name, therefore, would seem to have been *Ben-hadad-idri*, "The son of Hadad is my help" (Syriac *'adar*, "to help"). (Comp. the name *Hadad-ezer*.) The Assyrians omitted the first element, the Hebrews the last.

⁽²⁵⁾ **And there was.**—*There arose.* In consequence of the siege.

**Besieged.**—*Were besieging.*

**Fourscore pieces.**—Eighty shekels—*i.e.*, about £10. Ass's flesh would not ordinarily be eaten at all, and the head of any animal would be the cheapest part. Plutarch mentions that during a famine among the Cadusians an ass's head could hardly be got for sixty drachms (about £2 10s.), though ordinarily the entire animal could be bought for about half that sum. And Pliny relates that when Hannibal was besieging Casalinum, a mouse was sold for 200 denarii (£6 5s.).

**The fourth part of a cab of dove's dung.**—The *cab* was the smallest Hebrew dry measure. It held, according to the Rabbis, one-sixth of a *seah* (chap. vii. 1), or a little over a quart (ξέστης.—Josephus, *Antt.* ix. 4, § 4). The term *dove's dung*, in all probability, denotes some kind of common *vegetable* produce, perhaps a sort of pulse or pease, which was ordinarily very cheap. Such a designation is not unparalleled. The Arabs call the herb *kali* " sparrow's dung;" and *Assafœtida* is in German " devil's dung." In some places in England a species of wild hyacinth is called " dead man's hands," from the livid markings on the flower. The shape and colour of the species of pulse mentioned in the text may similarly account for its name. It naturally occurs that so long as there were any " doves" left in the city it would not be necessary to eat their *dung*. When Josephus wrote that dung was eaten in the siege of Jerusalem, he probably had the present passage in his mind.

**Five pieces of silver.**—*Five* (shekels in) *silver;* about 12s. 6d.

⁽²⁶⁾ **The king ... was passing by upon the wall.**—On the broad rampart of the city, which was like that which we see at such old places as Chester. The king went round to encourage the garrison and to superintend the defence. A woman in the street below, or perhaps on a housetop near the rampart, appeals to him for justice against her neighbour.

⁽²⁷⁾ **If the Lord do not help thee.**—This is right. The marginal rendering, "Let not the Lord help thee!" —*i.e.*, "May the Lord destroy thee!" would be possible in another context. Another rendering is, "Nay (*i.e*, do not supplicate me), let the Lord help thee!"

**Out of the barnfloor.**—Comp. Hosea ix 2: "The floor and the winepress shall not feed them, and the new wine shall fail in her." Jehoram, in the irony of despair, reminds the woman of what she well knows—viz., that the corn and wine, the staple foods of the time, are long since exhausted. The words, "If the Lord do not help thee," may be compared with chap. iii. 10, "Alas! that the Lord hath called," &c. The character of Jehoram is consistently drawn. But perhaps the point is : " Jehovah alone is the giver of corn and wine (Hosea ii. 8, 9). Appeal not to me for these."

⁽²⁸⁾ **And the king said.**—When she had explained what she wanted. With the hideous facts here recorded, comp. Deut. xxviii. 56, *seq.* Similar things were done during the sieges of Jerusalem by Nebuchadnezzar (Sam. iv. 10; Ezek. v. 10), and by Vespasian and Titus (Josephus, *Bell. Jud.* vi. 3, 4).

⁽²⁹⁾ **She hath hid her son.**—Perhaps to save him. (Comp. 1 Kings iii. 26.)

*The King's Oath.*        II. KINGS, VII.        *Elisha Prophecies Plenty.*

eat him: and she hath hid her son. <sup>(30)</sup> And it came to pass, when the king heard the words of the woman, that he rent his clothes; and he passed by upon the wall, and the people looked, and, behold, *he had* sackcloth within upon his flesh. <sup>(31)</sup> Then he said, God do so and more also to me, if the head of Elisha the son of Shaphat shall stand on him this day. <sup>(32)</sup> But Elisha sat in his house, and the elders sat with him; and *the king* sent a man from before him: but ere the messenger came to him, he said to the elders, See ye how this son of a murderer hath sent to take away mine head? look, when the messenger cometh, shut the door, and hold him fast at the door: *is* not the sound of his master's feet behind him? <sup>(33)</sup> And while he yet talked with them, behold, the messenger came down unto him: and he said, Behold, this evil *is* of the LORD; what should I wait for the LORD any longer?

CHAPTER VII. — <sup>(1)</sup> Then Elisha said, Hear ye the word of the LORD; Thus saith the LORD, To morrow about this time *shall* a measure of fine flour *be sold* for a shekel, and two measures of barley for a shekel, in the gate of Sa-

---

<sup>(30)</sup> **And he passed.**—*Now he was passing.* The people in the streets below would see him well as he passed along the rampart.

**Looked.**—*Saw.*

**He had sackcloth.**—Rather, *the sackcloth was.* "The sackcloth"—*i.e.*, the well-known garb of penitence and woe (1 Kings xxi. 27). Jehoram had secretly assumed this ascetic garment in order to appease the wrath of Jehovah. That the king should wear sackcloth was a portent in the eyes of his subjects. The prophets wore it *over* the tunic as an official dress.

**Within.**—Under his royal robes, "upon his flesh" —*i.e.*, next the skin. (Comp. Isa. xx. 2, 3.)

<sup>(31)</sup> **Then he said.**—*And he (i.e.,* the king*), said.*

**God do so . . . to me.**—Literally, *So may God do to me, and so may he add*: a common form of oath. (Comp. Ruth. i. 17; 1 Sam. iii. 17; 1 Kings ii. 23.)

**If the head of Elisha . . . this day.**—The king's horror at the woman's dreadful story is succeeded by indignation against Elisha, who had probably counselled an unyielding resistance to the foe, in the steadfast faith that Jehovah would help His own; and who, prophet though he was, and endued with miraculous powers, had yet brought no help in this hour of urgent need. (Comp. with the oath that of Jezebel against Elijah, 1 Kings xix. 2.)

<sup>(32)</sup> **But Elisha sat . . . with him.**—Rather, *Now Elisha was sitting in his house, and the elders were sitting with him.* This shows the important position which the prophet occupied at the time. The elders, who were the nobles and chiefs of Samaria, were gathered round him in his house to learn the will of Jehovah, and to receive comfort and counsel from his lips. (Comp. the way in which Zedekiah and his princes consulted Jeremiah during the last siege of Jerusalem— Jer. xxi. 1, 2; xxxviii. 14, *seq.*)

**And the king sent a man.**—To behead the prophet, according to his oath.

**From before him.**—Comp. chap. v. 16, iii. 14; 1 Kings x. 8. One of the royal attendants—probably a soldier of the guard—is meant.

**But ere.**—"But" is wanting in the Hebrew. (The conjunction *wĕ* has, perhaps, fallen out after the preceding *w.*)

**He said to the elders.**—Elisha foreknew what was about to happen. (Comp. chap. v. 26.) The *he* is emphatic: "*He* (the prophet) said."

**This son of a murderer.**—Referring to Ahab's murder of Naboth (1 Kings xxi. 19) and the prophets of Jehovah; as if to say, "The son takes after his father" (*filius patrissat*). At the same time, we must not forget the idiom by which a man is called a *son* of any quality or disposition which he evinces. (Comp. "son of Belial," "sons of pride," "sons of wickedness;" 2 Sam. vii. 10; Job xli. 34).

**Hold him fast at the door.**—Literally, *press him back with the door.* The door opened *inwards,* and the prophet bade his friends the elders hold the door against the messenger of death.

**Is not the sound . . . behind him?**—Elisha's reason for bidding the elders hold the door. He foresaw that Jehoram would hasten in person after his messenger, to see that his savage order was carried out. (Bähr and Keil think, with Josephus, that Jehoram repented, and hurried off to restrain the sword of his minister.)

<sup>(33)</sup> **Yet talked.**—*Was still speaking.*

**The messenger.**—Ewald's correction, "the king" (*melek* for *mal'āk*), is certainly right. In the rapid progress of the story, the arrival and momentary exclusion of the messenger is understood. The approach of the king may have been seen from the upper part of Elisha's house.

**Came down.**—*Was coming down,* to the prophet's house, from the ramparts. (Comp. chap. v. 24.)

**And he said.**—That is, the *king said.*

**Behold, this evil is of the Lord.**—Rather, *Behold, such (this) is the distress from Jehovah.* Things have come to this pitch by the will of Jehovah.

**What** (rather, *why*) **should I wait for the Lord any longer?**—As I have hitherto done, at your persuasion. Why should I not now surrender to the Syrians, and slay the prophet who has so long deluded me with vain hopes?

VII.

<sup>(1)</sup> **Then Elisha said.**—*And Elisha said.* The division of the chapters is unfortunate, there being no break in the story here. The prophet addresses *the king* and his attendants (verse 18).

**A measure.**—Heb., *a seah*: the most usual corn measure. (Comp. 1 Kings xviii. 32; chap. vi. 25.) The prophet's words are more abrupt in the original: "Thus hath Jehovah said, About this time to-morrow a seah (in) fine flour at a shekel, and two seahs (in) barley at a shekel, in the gate of Samaria!"

**Fine flour.**—Gen. xviii. 6.

**Barley.**—Not only as fodder for the horses (Thenius), but also for human consumption, in the shape of barley cakes, &c. (Judges vii. 13).

*The Leprous Men.*  II. KINGS, VII.  *Flight of the Syrians.*

maria. ⁽²⁾ Then ¹ a lord on whose hand the king leaned answered the man of God, and said, Behold, *if* the LORD would make windows in heaven, might this thing be? And he said, Behold, thou shalt see *it* with thine eyes, but shalt not eat thereof.

⁽³⁾ And there were four leprous men at the entering in of the gate: and they said one to another, Why sit we here until we die? ⁽⁴⁾ If we say, We will enter into the city, then the famine *is* in the city, and we shall die there: and if we sit still here, we die also. Now therefore come, and let us fall unto the host of the Syrians: if they save us alive,

¹ Heb., *a lord which belonged to the king, leaning upon his hand.*

we shall live; and if they kill us, we shall but die. ⁽⁵⁾ And they rose up in the twilight, to go unto the camp of the Syrians: and when they were come to the uttermost part of the camp of Syria, behold, *there was* no man there. ⁽⁶⁾ For the Lord had made the host of the Syrians to hear a noise of chariots, and a noise of horses, *even* the noise of a great host: and they said one to another, Lo, the king of Israel hath hired against us the kings of the Hittites, and the kings of the Egyptians, to come upon us. ⁽⁷⁾ Wherefore they arose and fled in the twilight, and left their tents, and their horses, and their asses, even the

---

**The gate.**—The corn market, therefore, was held in the open space just within the gate.

⁽²⁾ **Then a lord.**—*And the adjutant* (*shâlish*: comp. 2 Sam. xxiii. 8; 1 Kings ix. 22; 1 Chron. xi. 11), or *aide-de-camp* or *esquire* (equerry).

**On whose hand . . . leaned.**—Comp. the similar expression in reference to Naaman (chap. v. 18).

**Leaned.**—*Was leaning.*

**Behold, if the Lord . . . this thing be?**—This may be correct. Even granting the very unlikely supposition that Jehovah is about to make windows (Gen. vii. 11) in the sky, to rain down supplies through them, the promised cheapness of provisions can hardly ensue so soon. Or we may render, "Behold, Jehovah is going to make windows in the sky [*i.e.*, to pour down provisions upon us]. Can this thing come to pass?" In any case, the tone is that of scoffing unbelief. Reuss renders, with French point, "Voyez donc. Iaheweh en fera pleuvoir! Est ce que c'est chose possible?"

**Behold, thou shalt see.**—Literally, *Behold, thou art about* (*i.e.*, destined) *to see*. Elisha partly imitates the speech of the scoffer, which begins in the Hebrew with "Behold, Jehovah is about to make windows." (Comp. chap. v. 26.)

⁽³⁾ **And there were four leprous men.**—Literally, *And four men were lepers.*

**At the entering in of the gate.**—And so outside of the city. (Comp. Lev. xiii. 46; Num. v. 2, 3.) Rashi says they were Gehazi and his sons (!)

**Why sit we?**—Or, *Why are we abiding?* Nobody brought them food any longer, owing to the pressure of the famine.

⁽⁴⁾ **Fall unto**—*i.e., desert, go over to.*

**If they save us alive.**—And give us food, for pity's sake.

**We shall but die.**—As we shall if we stop here, or if we go into the city. (The "but" is not in the Hebrew.)

⁽⁵⁾ **In the twilight**—*i.e.*, at nightfall. (See verses 9 and 12.) They waited till then, that their departure might not be noticed from the walls.

**The uttermost part**—*i.e.*, the *outskirts* or *verge* of the camp nearest to Samaria.

⁽⁶⁾ **For.**—*Now:* introducing a new paragraph.

**Even the noise.**—Rather, *a noise*. The Syriac and the Arabic, as well as some Hebrew MSS., read "*and* a noise." This is preferable. (Comp. chap. vi. 14, where chariots and horses and a host [of infantry] are distinguished from each other.) The word *qôl* (literally, "voice") is commonly used of thunder. (Comp. Ps. xxix., *passim*.) The noise the Syrians heard was doubtless a sound in the air among the neighbouring hills.

**The kings of the Hittites.**—Comp. 1 Kings ix. 20, x. 29. The tract of north Syria between the Euphrates and the Orontes was the cradle of the Hittite race, and it was over this that these kings of the several tribes bore sway. In the thirteenth century (B.C.) their power extended over great part of Asia Minor, as rock inscriptions prove. Carchemish, Kadesh, Hamath, and Helbon (*Aleppo*) were their capitals. Rameses II. made a treaty of peace with *Heta-sira*, the prince of the Hittites. In the time of Tiglath Pileser I. (B.C. 1120), the Hittites were still paramount from the Euphrates to the Lebanon. Shalmaneser II. mentions a Hittite prince, Sapalulme, king of the *Patinâa*, a tribe on the Orontes. The Hittites from whom Solomon exacted forced labour were those who were left in the land of Israel (comp. Gen. xxiii., xxvi. 34; 1 Sam. xxxi. 6), *not* the people of the great cities mentioned above, which remained independent, as we know from the Assyrian inscriptions. (Comp. Amos vi. 2; 2 Chron. viii. 4 for *Hamath*.) Tiglath Pileser II. conquered Hamath (B.C. 740). Twenty years later it revolted under *Yahubihdi* ("Jah is around me;" comp. Ps. iii. 3), but was again reduced, and made an Assyrian prefecture by Sargon, who afterwards stormed Carchemish (B.C. 717). (Comp. chap. xvii. 24, 30.)

**The kings of the Egyptians.**—The plural may be rhetorical. (Comp. 2 Chron. xxviii. 16: "The kings of Assyria," and Note.) Little is known of the state of Egypt at this time (towards the close of the twenty-second dynasty). The Syrians were seized with panic, under the idea that they were about to be attacked on all sides at once. Some such wild rumour as that expressed by the words of the text must have been spread through the camp; but we need not press the *literal* accuracy of the statement, for who was there to report the exact nature of the alarm to the historians of Israel? Moreover, it is evident from the style of the narrative in chapters vi. and vii. that it rests upon *oral tradition*, so that it would be a mistake to press subordinate details. Prof. Robertson Smith considers that the sudden retreat of the Syrians is explained by the fact that the *Assyrians* were already pressing upon them.

⁽⁷⁾ **Wherefore (and) they arose.**—The verse gives a vivid picture of a wild flight, in which everything was forgotten except personal safety.

camp as it *was*, and fled for their life. ⁽⁸⁾ And when these lepers came to the uttermost part of the camp, they went into one tent, and did eat and drink, and carried thence silver, and gold, and raiment, and went and hid *it;* and came again, and entered into another tent, and carried thence *also,* and went and hid *it*. ⁽⁹⁾ Then they said one to another, We do not well: this day *is* a day of good tidings, and we hold our peace: if we tarry till the morning light, ¹some mischief will come upon us: now therefore come, that we may go and tell the king's household. ⁽¹⁰⁾ So they came and called unto the porter of the city : and they told them, saying, We came to the camp of the Syrians, and, behold, *there was* no man there, neither voice of man, but horses tied, and asses tied, and the tents as they *were*. ⁽¹¹⁾ And he called the porters; and they told *it* to the king's house within.

⁽¹²⁾ And the king arose in the night, and said unto his servants, I will now shew you what the Syrians have done to us. They know that we *be* hungry; therefore are they gone out of the camp to hide themselves in the field, saying, When they come out of the city, we shall catch them alive, and get into the city. ⁽¹³⁾ And one of his servants answered and said, Let *some* take, I pray thee, five of the horses that remain, which are left ²in the city, (behold, they *are* as all the multitude of Israel that are left in it: behold, *I say,* they *are* even as all the multitude of the Israel-

B.C. 885.

1 Heb., *we shall find punishment.*

2 Heb., *in it.*

---

**As it was.**—"Camp" is feminine here and in Gen. xxxii. 9 only.

**For their life.**—1 Kings xix. 3.

⁽⁸⁾ **And when . . . tent.**—Literally, *And* (so) *those lepers came to the edge of the camp, and they went into one tent;* taking up the thread of the narrative again at verse 5, where it was broken by the parenthesis about the panic flight of the Syrians.

**Went and hid it.**—A common practice of Orientals, with whom holes in the ground or in the house wall supply the place of banks.

⁽⁹⁾ **Some mischief will come upon us.**—Literally, *guilt will find us:* we shall incur blame. Vulg., "we shall be accused of wrong-doing."

**Now therefore.**—*And now:* the inferential use of "now." (Comp. Ps. ii. 10.)

⁽¹⁰⁾ **The porter.**—The Oriental versions may be right in reading "porters," *i.e.*, warders. The plural is implied by "they told *them*," which immediately follows, and actually occurs in verse 11. But the reading of the LXX. and Vulg., "gate," implies the same consonants differently pointed, as those of the word "porter." This attests the antiquity of the reading. Probably, therefore, the word "porter" is here used collectively.

**No man . . . voice of man.**—The first word (*'ish*) denotes an individual man, the second word (*'ādām*) denotes the *species*, and so includes women and children.

**Horses.**—*The horses.* Similarly, *the asses.* Both words are singular (collectives) in the Hebrew.

**Tied**—*i.e.*, tethered and feeding.

**The tents.**—Omit *the*.

⁽¹¹⁾ **And he called the porters.**—Rather, *And the porters called.* The verb in the Hebrew is singular, and may be used impersonally: "And one called, viz., the warders." But the LXX., Targum, Arabic, and some Hebrew MSS., read the plural. The Syriac has, "And the porters drew near, and told the house of the king."

**And they told it.**—The king's palace may have been near to the ramparts. If not, the sentries at the gate shouted their news to other soldiers near them, who conveyed it to the palace. The word "within" seems to indicate the former. (The Authorised Version, which is Kimchi's rendering, cannot be right, because in that case the Hebrew verb would require the preposition "unto," as in verse 10.)

⁽¹²⁾ **I will now shew you.**—"Suspicax est miseria" (*Grotius*). Such stratagems as Jehoram suspected are, however, common enough in warfare.

**To hide themselves in the field.**—Both expressions in the Hebrew follow the later modes of inflection. Such forms may be due to transcribers rather than to the original writer.

⁽¹³⁾ **Let some take.**—Literally, *And* (*i.e.*, then) *let them take.* (Comp. chaps. ii. 9, iv. 41.)

**Five.**—Used as an indefinite *small* number, like our "half a dozen." (Comp. Lev. xxvi. 8; Isa. xxx. 17.) The *actual* number taken was two pairs (verse 14).

**The horses that remain, which are left in the city.**—Literally, *the remaining horses that remain in it.* The repetition dwells pathetically on the fewness of those that survive. Instead of "in it," the LXX. and Arabic read "here," which may be right, as the two Hebrew terms closely resemble each other.

**Behold, they are as all . . . consumed.**—The king's adviser supposes two contingencies : the horses (and their drivers) may return safe, in which case they share the fortune of "all the multitude of Israel that are left" (*i.e.*, have survived the famine, but are likely to die of it); or they may be taken and slain by the enemy, in which case they will be "even as all the multitude that are consumed" (*i.e.*, by the famine and fighting). The sense is thus the same as in verse 4. The servant is not much more sanguine than the king : he says, "They have to perish in any case; whether here by famine, or there by the sword, makes little difference." "However it may turn out, nothing worse can happen to the men we send out than has already happened to many others, or than will yet happen to the rest." But perhaps Reuss is right in seeing here simply a reference to the wretched condition of the horses. "Qu'attendre de chevaux qui sont exténués de faim ?" A natural doubt whether the starving animals are adequate to the service required of them. "Consumed," then, means *spent, exhausted.*

**The multitude of Israel.**—The article with the first word in the Hebrew is the error of a transcriber, who, as often occurs, wrote the same letter twice.

ites that are consumed:) and let us send and see. ⁽¹⁴⁾ They took therefore two chariot horses; and the king sent after the host of the Syrians, saying, Go and see. ⁽¹⁵⁾ And they went after them unto Jordan: and, lo, all the way *was* full of garments and vessels, which the Syrians had cast away in their haste. And the messengers returned, and told the king.

⁽¹⁶⁾ And the people went out, and spoiled the tents of the Syrians.ᵃ So a measure of fine flour was *sold* for a shekel, and two measures of barley for a shekel, according to the word of LORD. ⁽¹⁷⁾ And the king appointed the lord on whose hand he leaned to have the charge of the gate: and the people trode upon him in the gate, and he died, as the man of God had said, who spake when the king came down to him. ⁽¹⁸⁾ And it came to pass as the man of God had spoken to the king, saying, Two measures of barley for a shekel, and a measure of fine flour for a shekel, shall be to morrow about this time in the gate of Samaria: ⁽¹⁹⁾ and that lord answered the man of God, and said, Now, behold, *if* the LORD should make windows in heaven, might such a thing be? And he said, Behold, thou shalt see it with thine eyes, but shalt not eat thereof. ⁽²⁰⁾ And so it fell out unto him: for the people trode upon him in the gate, and he died.

CHAPTER VIII.—⁽¹⁾ Then spake Elisha unto the woman, ᵃ whose son he had restored to life, saying, Arise, and go thou and thine household, and sojourn wheresoever thou canst sojourn: for the LORD hath called for a famine; and it shall also come upon the land

*a* ch. 4. 35.

---

**The Israelites.**—*Israel.* Syriac: "Let them bring five of the horsemen who are left: if they are taken, they are accounted of as all the people of Israel who have perished; and let us send and see."

⁽¹⁴⁾ **Two chariot horses.**—Literally, *two chariots* (*of*) *horses*, *i.e.*, teams for two chariots, or two pairs of horses. The chariots and their drivers are implied, not mentioned. Two chariots were sent, so that if attacked they might make a better resistance; or perhaps in order that, if one were captured by the enemy, the other might escape with the news.

⁽¹⁵⁾ **In their haste.**—Comp. 1 Sam. xxiii. 6; Ps. xlviii. 6, civ. 7—passages which prove that the Hebrew text is right here, and the Hebrew margin wrong.

**Unto Jordan.**—Not all the way to the river, which would be at least twenty miles, but *in the direction* of it.

⁽¹⁶⁾ **The tents.**—Rather, *the camp.*

**So**—*And it came to pass.*

⁽¹⁷⁾ **And the king appointed.**—Rather, *Now the king had appointed.*

**The lord.**—*The adjutant* (verse 2).

**To have the charge of the gate.**—To maintain order as the famished crowd poured out of the city.

**Trode upon him.**—*Trampled him down,* as he was trying to discharge his duty. This probably happened, as Thenius suggests, when the crowd was *returning* from the Syrian camp, wild with excess of food and drink, after their long abstinence. Thus he "saw the plenty with his eyes, but did not eat thereof" (verse 2). Reuss thinks *the charge of the gate* is equivalent to *the charge of the market*, as the market was held on the space adjoining the gate.

**Had said.**—*Spake.*

**Who spake.**—This is probably a spurious repetition. It is wanting in some Hebrew MSS., and in the Syriac, Vulg., and Arabic versions. If retained in the text, we must render, "And he died, according to that which the man of God spake, *which he spake* when the king," &c. But perhaps the reading of one Hebrew MS. is correct: "And he died, *according to the word* of the man of God, which he spake," &c.

⁽¹⁸⁾ **To the king.**—The LXX. and Syriac have, "to the messenger." (See Note on chap. vi. 23.)

In this and the following verse the author repeats the prediction and its fulfilment with obvious satisfaction. The moral is a warning against unbelief.

⁽¹⁹⁾ **That lord.**—*The adjutant.*

**Now.**—*And.*

**Might such a thing be?**—Literally, *Might it happen according to this word?* But the LXX., Syriac, and Vulg., with many Hebrew MSS., read, as in verse 2, "Might this thing (or word) be?"

⁽²⁰⁾ **For the people trode upon him.**—*And the people trampled him down,* or *under foot.*

VIII.

⁽¹⁻⁶⁾ How the kindness of the Shunammite woman to Elisha was further rewarded through the prophet's influence with the king.

⁽¹⁾ **Then spake Elisha.**—Rather, *Now Elisha had spoken.* The time is not defined by the phrase. It was *after* the raising of the Shunammite's son (verse 1), and *before* the healing of Naaman the Syrian, inasmuch as the king still talks with Gehazi (verse 5).

**Go thou.**—The peculiar form of the pronoun points to the identity of the original author of this account with the writer of chap. iv. Moreover, the famine here foretold appears to be that of chap. iv. 38, *seq.*, so that the present section must in the original document have preceded chap. v. Thenius thinks the compiler transferred the present account to this place, because he wished to proceed chronologically, and supposed that the seven years' famine came to an end with the raising of the siege of Samaria.

**For a famine.**—*To the famine.* The sword, the famine, the noisome beasts, and the pestilence were Jehovah's "four sore judgments," as we find in Ezek. xiv. 21.

**And it shall also come upon.**—*And, moreover, it cometh into.*

**Seven Years.**—Perhaps not to be understood literally, any more than Dante's

"O caro Duca mio che *più di sette Volte* m'hai sicurtà renduta."—*Inferno* 8. 97.

seven years. (2) And the woman arose, and did after the saying of the man of God: and she went with her household, and sojourned in the land of the Philistines seven years. (3) And it came to pass at the seven years' end, that the woman returned out of the land of the Philistines: and she went forth to cry unto the king for her house and for her land. (4) And the king talked with Gehazi the servant of the man of God, saying, Tell me, I pray thee, all the great things that Elisha hath done. (5) And it came to pass, as he was telling the king how he had restored a dead body to life, that, behold, the woman, whose son he had restored to life, cried to the king for her house and for her land. And Gehazi said, My lord, O king, this *is* the woman, and this *is* her son, whom Elisha restored to life. (6) And when the king asked the woman, she told him. So the king appointed unto her a certain [1]officer, saying, Restore all that *was* her's, and all the fruits of the field since the day that she left the land, even until now.

(7) And Elisha came to Damascus; and Ben-hadad the king of Syria was sick; and it was told him, saying, The man of God is come hither. (8) And the king said unto Hazael, Take a present in thine hand, and go, meet the man of God, and enquire of the LORD by him,

[1] Or, *eunuch*.

---

(2) **After the saying.**—*According to the word.*

**In the land of the Philistines.**—The lowlands of the coast were not so subject to droughts as the limestone highlands of Israel. (Comp. Gen. xii. 10, xxvi. 1.) The Philistines, besides, dealt with foreign traders who put in to their shores. (Comp. Joel iii. 4—6.)

(3) **At the seven years' end.**—Omit *the*.

**She went forth.**—From Shunem to Samaria.

**For her house and for her land.**—Literally, *with regard to her house*, &c. She found them in the possession of strangers. The State may have occupied the property as abandoned by its owner; or, as is more likely, some neighbouring landowner may have encroached upon her rights. She therefore appealed to the king.

(4) **And the king talked.**—*And the king was speaking unto*.

**Gehazi.**—He, therefore, was not yet a leper (chap. v. 27). So Keil and some earlier expositors. But lepers, though excluded from the city, were not excluded from *conversation* with others. (Comp. Matt. viii. 2; Luke xvii. 12.) Naaman was apparently admitted into the royal palace (chap. v. 6). The way, however, in which Gehazi is spoken of as "the servant of the man of God" (comp. chap. v. 20) seems to imply the priority of the present narrative to that of chap. v.

**Tell me, I pray thee, all the great things.**—"The history of Elijah and Elisha has a distinctly popular character; it reads like a story told by word of mouth, full of the dramatic touches and vivid presentations of detail which characterise all Semitic history that closely follows oral narration. The king of Israel of whom we read in 2 Kings viii. 4, was, we may be sure, not the only man who talked with Gehazi, saying, 'Tell me, I pray thee, all the great things that Elisha hath done.' By many repetitions the history of the prophets took a fixed shape long before it was committed to writing, and the written record preserves all the essential features of the narratives that passed from mouth to mouth, and were handed down orally from father to child." (Prof. Robertson Smith, *The Prophets of Israel*, p. 116.)

(5) **A dead body.**—*The dead*.

**Cried.**—*Was crying*. Literally, the Hebrew runs, *And it came to pass, he* (emphatic) *was telling . . . and behold the woman was crying*, &c. The woman came in, and began her prayer to the king, while he was talking with Gehazi about her and her son.

**This is her son.**—Who was now grown up, and came as his mother's escort.

(6) **Told.**—*Related to him*, *i.e.*, the story. So in verses 4 and 5.

**Officer.**—Literally, *eunuch* (*sâris*). (Comp. Note on Gen. xxxvii. 36; 1 Chron. xxviii. 1.)

**Fruits.**—Literally, *revenues, produce* in kind, which must have been paid out of the royal stores. This seems to imply that her land had been annexed to the royal domains.

(7—15) Elisha's visit to Damascus, and its consequences.

(7) **And Elisha came to Damascus.**—In the fragmentary condition of the narrative, *why* he came is not clear. Rashi suggests that it was to fetch back Gehazi, who had fled to the Syrians (!), an idea based upon 1 Kings ii. 39, *seq*. Keil and others think the prophet went with the intention of anointing Hazael, in accordance with a supposed charge of Elijah's. (Comp. 1 Kings xix. 15, where Elijah himself is bidden to anoint Hazael). Ewald believes that Elisha retreated to Damascene territory, in consequence of the strained relations existing between him and Jehoram, owing to the latter's toleration of idolatry. Obviously all this rests upon pure conjecture. It is clear from verse 7 that Elisha's visit was not expected in Damascus, and further, that there was peace at the time between Damascus and Samaria. We do not know how much of Elisha's history has been omitted between chap. vii. 20 and chap. viii. 7; but we may fairly assume that a *divine impulse* led the prophet to Damascus. The revelation, of which he speaks in verses 10 and 13, probably came to him at the time, and so was not the occasion of his journey.

**Ben-hadad . . . was sick.**—According to Josephus, on account of the failure of his expedition against Samaria (?).

**The man of God.**—As if Elisha were well known and highly esteemed in Syria.

**Is come hither.**—This certainly implies that Elisha had entered Damascus itself.

(8) **Hazael.**—See Note on verse 15. In 1 Kings xix. 15, 17 the name is written *Hăzā'ēl*; here it is spelt with an etymological allusion, *Hăzāh'ēl*, *i.e.*, "El hath

saying, Shall I recover of this disease? (9) So Hazael went to meet him, and took a present ¹with him, even of every good thing of Damascus, forty camels' burden, and came and stood before him, and said, Thy son Ben-hadad king of Syria hath sent me to thee, saying, Shall I recover of this disease? (10) And Elisha said unto him, Go, say unto him, Thou mayest certainly recover: howbeit the LORD hath shewed me that he shall surely die. (11) And he settled his countenance ²stedfastly, until he was ashamed: and the man of God wept. (12) And Hazael said, Why weepeth my lord? And he answered, Because I know the evil that thou wilt do unto the children of Israel: their strong holds wilt thou set on fire, and their young men wilt thou slay with the sword, and wilt dash their children, and rip up their women with child. (13) And Hazael said, But what, *is* thy servant a dog, that he should do this great thing? And Elisha answered, The LORD hath shewed me that thou *shalt be* king over Syria. (14) So he departed from Elisha, and came to his master; who said to him, What said Elisha to thee? And he answered, He told me *that* thou should-

¹ Heb., *in his hand.*
² Heb., *and set it.*

---

seen" (foreseen). Hazael appears to have been the highest officer in Ben-hadad's court; Josephus says, "the trustiest of his domestics."

**Take a present in thine hand.**—Comp. Num. xxii. 7; 1 Sam. ix. 7; 2 Kings v. 5; 1 Kings xiv. 3.

**Go, meet the man of God.**—Literally, *go to meet him.* This does not imply, as some have supposed, that Elisha was still on the road to Damascus, nor even that he happened to be at the time on his way to the palace, for how could Ben-hadad know that? What is meant is "Go to the place where the prophet is to be found; seek an interview with him."

**Enquire of the Lord by him.**—A different construction is used in chap. 1, 2.

**By him.**—Literally, *from with him.* (Comp. Note on chap. i. 15.)

**Shall I recover of this disease?**—Comp. chap. i. 2.

(9) **A present with him**—*i.e.*, in money. (Comp. chap. v. 5, and see the margin here.)

**Even of every good thing.**—Rather, *and every kind of good thing*; in addition to the present of money. Damascus was a great centre of traffic between Eastern and Western Asia. (Comp. Ezek. xxvii. 18; Amos iii. 12.) *Damask* silk was originally imported from Damascus, and the Damascene sword-blades were famous in mediæval Europe.

**Forty camels' burden.**—To be understood of an actual train of forty camels, carrying the presents of Ben-hadad. The Orientals are fond of making the most of a gift in this way. Chardin remarks, that "fifty persons often carry what a single one could very well carry" (*Voyage*, iii. 21).

**Came.** — Or, *went in, i.e.,* into the house where Elisha was.

**Thy son Ben-hadad.**—Comp. chap. xiii. 14, v. 13, iv. 12, vi. 21. "Father" was a respectful mode of addressing the prophet.

(10) **Unto him.** — The reading of some Hebrew MSS., of the Hebrew margin, and of all the versions, as well as of Josephus.

The ordinary Hebrew text has "not" (*lô*', instead of *lô*), so that the meaning would be, "Thou shalt *not* recover." But (1) the position of the negative *before* the adverbial infinitive is anomalous; and (2) Hazael's report of Elisha's words, in verse 14, is without the negative particle. (See the Note there.) The Authorised Version is, therefore, right.

**Thou mayest certainly recover.** — Rather, *Thou wilt certainly live.* Elisha sees through Hazael's character and designs, and answers him in the tone of irony which he used to Gehazi in chap. v. 26, "Go, tell thy lord—as thou, the supple and unscrupulous courtier wilt be sure to do—he will certainly recover. *I* know, however, that he will assuredly die, and by thy hand." Others interpret, "Thou *mightest* recover" (*i.e.,* thy disease is not mortal); and make the rest of the prophet's reply a confidential communication to Hazael. But this is to represent the prophet as deceiving Ben-hadad, and guilty of complicity with Hazael, which agrees neither with Elisha's character nor with what follows in verses 11, 12. The Syriac and Arabic, with some MSS., read, "*thou* wilt die" for "*he* will die."

(11) **And he settled his countenance stedfastly.**—Literally, *and he* (Elisha) *made his face stand, and set* (it upon Hazael).

**Until he was ashamed.**—Literally, *unto being ashamed.* This may mean either *in shameless fashion,* or *until Hazael was disconcerted.* We prefer the latter. Hazael, conscious that Elisha had read his thoughts aright, shrank from that piercing gaze. (Comp. chap. ii. 17.)

(12) **The evil that thou wilt do unto the children of Israel.**—Fulfilled in chaps. x. 32, 33, xiii. 3, 4. The cruelties enumerated here were the ordinary concomitants of warfare in that age. (Comp. Amos i. 3, 4, 13; Hosea x. 14, xiii. 16; chap. xv. 16.)

**Set on fire.**—Literally, *send into the fire* (Judg. i. 8).

**Young men.**—*Chosen warriors.*

**Dash.**—*Dash in pieces.*

(13) **But what, is thy servant a dog, that he should do this great thing?**—Rather, (*Thou canst not mean it;) for what is the dog thy servant that he should do,* &c. Hazael answers in a tone of pretended amazement and self-depreciation. The exaggerated humility of his language betrays the hypocrite.

**The Lord hath shewed me.**—Comp. 1 Kings xix. 15, where this same fact was revealed to Elijah. Literally, *Jehovah hath made me see thee king.* How Hazael took this announcement we are not told. Bähr says, "Startled by the revelation of his secret plans, Hazael turned away without answering the earnest words of the prophet."

(14) **That thou shouldest surely recover.**—Rather, *Thou wilt certainly live,* repeating Elisha's actual words, but *not* the tone and gesture which accompanied them.

*Murder of the King of Syria.*     II. KINGS, VIII.     *Jehoram Reigns in Judah.*

est surely recover. (15) And it came to pass on the morrow, that he took a thick cloth, and dipped *it* in water, and spread *it* on his face, so that he died: and Hazael reigned in his stead.

(16) And in the fifth year of Joram the son of Ahab king of Israel, Jehoshaphat *being* then king of Judah, <sup>a</sup>Jehoram the son of Jehoshaphat king of Judah ¹began to reign. (17) Thirty and two years old was he when he began to reign; and he reigned eight years in Jerusalem. (18) And he walked in the way of the kings of Israel, as did the house of Ahab: for the daughter of Ahab was his wife: and he did evil in the sight of the LORD. (19) Yet the LORD would not destroy Judah for David his servant's sake, <sup>b</sup>as he promised him to give him alway a ²light, *and* to his

*B.C. 885.*

*a* 2 Chron. 21. 4.

¹ Heb., *reigned.*

*b* 2 Sam. 7. 13.

² Heb., *candle,* or, *lamp.*

---

(15) **He took**—*i.e., Hazael*, the nearest subject. Ewald objects that if Hazael were meant, his name would not occur where it does at the end of the verse. But the objection does not hold, for in relating who succeeded to the throne, it was natural to give the name of the new king. Further, a considerable pause must be understood at "he died." The Judæan editor of Kings then appropriately concludes: "So Hazael reigned in his stead." The mention of the name significantly reminds us that Elisha had designated Hazael as the future king. Besides, after the words "and he died," it would have been more ambiguous than usual to add, "and *he* reigned in his stead."

**A thick cloth.**—Rather, *the quilt*, or *coverlet.* So the LXX., Vulg., Targum, and Arabic. The Syriac renders "curtain;" and, accordingly, Gesenius and others translate, "mosquito net." The Hebrew term (*makbēr*) means, etymologically, something *plaited* or *interwoven.* It is not found elsewhere, but a word of the same root occurs in 1 Sam. xix. 13. It is clear from the context that the *makbēr* must have been something which when soaked in water, and laid on the face, would prevent respiration.

Josephus says Hazael *strangled* his master with a mosquito net. But this and other explanations, such as that of Ewald, do not suit the words of the text. The old commentator, Clericus, may be right when he states Hazael's *motive* to have been *ut hominem facilius suffocaret, ne vi interemptus videretur.* And, perhaps, as Thenius supposes, the crown was offered to Hazael as a successful warrior. (Comp. chap. x. 32, *seq.*) When Duncker (*Hist. of Antiq.*, i. 413) ventures to state that Elisha *incited* Hazael to the murder of Ben-hadad, and afterwards renewed the war against Israel, not without encouragement from the prophet as a persistent enemy of Jehoram and his dynasty, he simply betrays an utter incapacity for understanding the character and function of Hebrew prophecy. The writer of Kings, at all events, did not intend to represent Elisha as a deceiver of foreign sovereigns and a traitor to his own; and this narrative is the only surviving record of the events described.

**Hazael reigned in his stead.**—On the Black Obelisk of Shalmaneser II. (B.C. 860—825), now in the British Museum, we read: "In my 18th regnal year for the 16th time I crossed the Euphrates. Haza'ilu of the land of Damascus came on to the battle: 1,121 of his chariots, 470 of his horsemen, with his stores, I took from him." And again: "In my 21st year for the 21st time I crossed the Euphrates: to the cities of Haza'ilu of the land of Damascus I marched, whose towns I took. Tribute of the land of the Tyrians, Sidonians, Giblites, I received."

(16—24) The reign of Jehoram, king of Judah. (Comp. 2 Chron. xxi.)

(16) **In the fifth year of Joram the son of Ahab.**—See Note on chap. i. 17.

The name Joram is an easy contraction of Jehoram. In this verse and in verse 29 the king of Israel is called Joram, and the king of Judah Jehoram; in verses 21, 23, 24 Joram is the name of the king of Judah. In chap. i. 17 and 2 Chron. xxii. 6, both kings are called Jehoram.

**Jehoshaphat being then king of Judah.**—Literally, *and Jehoshaphat king of Judah*; so that the meaning is, "In the fifth year of Joram . . . and of Jehoshaphat." Were the reading correct, it would be implied that Jehoram was for some reason or other made king or co-regent in the lifetime of his father, just as Esarhaddon united his heir Assurbanipal with himself in the government of Assyria. But the clause should be omitted as a spurious anticipation of the same words in the next line. So some Hebrew MSS., the Complut., LXX., the Syriac, and Arabic, and many MSS. of the Vulg. The clause as it stands is an unparalleled insertion in a common formula of the compiler, and there is no trace elsewhere of a co-regency of Jehoram with his father. Ewald, after Kimchi, would turn the clause into a sentence, by adding the word *mêth*, "had died:" "Now Jehoshaphat the king of Judah had died," an utterly superfluous remark.

(17) **Thirty and two years old . . . in Jerusalem.**—Comp. the similar notices in chap. xii. and the succeeding chapters. How different are these short annalistic summaries, the work of the Judæan compiler, from the rich and flowing narratives about Elijah and Elisha!

(18) **In the way of the kings of Israel.**—This is further explained by the following clause, "As did the house of Ahab," or rather, *to wit, as the house of Ahab acted, i.e.*, Jehoram, as son-in-law of Ahab and Jezebel, lent his countenance to the *cultus* of the Tyrian Baal. Under the influence of his wife Athaliah, as it may be surmised, Jehoram slew his six brothers directly after his accession to the throne (2 Chron. xxi. 4). In this connection the remarks of Michaelis are interesting: "In the reign of Jehoram falls the building of Carthage; Dido, her husband Sichæus, her brother Pygmalion, king of Tyre, and murderer of Sichæus. By marriage Tyre brought its then prevalent spirit, and a vast amount of evil, into the two Israelitish kingdoms." (The Syriac, Arabic, and Vulg. read "in the ways.") The reason why the details added in Chronicles are here omitted is to be found in the studied brevity of the compiler in the case of less important characters.

(19) **To give him alway a light.**—Comp. 1 Kings xv. 4, xi. 36; and for the promise to David, 2 Sam. vii. 12—16.

**And to his children.**—The reading of many Heb. MSS., the LXX., Vulg., and Targum. Thenius calls this a reading devised for the removal of a difficulty, and

children. <sup>(20)</sup> In his days Edom revolted from under the hand of Judah, and made a king over themselves. <sup>(21)</sup> So Joram went over to Zair, and all the chariots with him: and he rose by night, and smote the Edomites which compassed him about, and the captains of the chariots: and the people fled into their tents. <sup>(22)</sup> Yet Edom revolted from under the hand of Judah unto this day. Then Libnah revolted at the same time.

<sup>(23)</sup> And the rest of the acts of Joram, and all that he did, *are* they not written in the book of the chronicles of the kings of Judah? <sup>(24)</sup> And Joram slept with his fathers, and was buried with his fathers in the city of David: and *<sup>a</sup>*Ahaziah his son reigned in his stead.

<sup>(25)</sup> In the twelfth year of Joram the son of Ahab king of Israel did Ahaziah the son of Jehoram king of Judah begin to reign. <sup>(26)</sup> Two and twenty years old *was* Ahaziah when he began to reign; and he reigned one year in Jerusalem. And his mother's name *was* Athaliah, the daughter of Omri king of Israel. <sup>(27)</sup> And he walked in the way of the house of Ahab, and did evil in the sight of the LORD, as *did* the house of Ahab: for he *was* the son in law of the house

B.C. 885.

*a* 2 Chron. 22. 1.

---

asserts that the promise was made to *David* alone. He would omit the conjunction, and render, "To give him alway a lamp in respect of (*i.e.*, through) his sons." (See 2 Chron. xxi. 7, Note.) Keil adopts the same reading, but translates, "To give him, that is, his sons, a lamp," making "to his sons" an explanatory apposition.

<sup>(20)</sup> **In his days Edom revolted.**—The connection of ideas is this: Although Jehovah was not willing to extirpate Judah, yet He suffered it to be seriously weakened by the defections recorded in verses 20—22.

**Made a king over themselves.**—Josephus says they slew the vassal king appointed over them by Jehoshaphat (1 Kings xxii. 48). Edom appears to have been subject to the hegemony of Judah from the time of the disruption under Rehoboam.

<sup>(21)</sup> **So Joram went over to Zair.**—No town called Zair is otherwise known. Hitzig and Ewald would read Zoar, but Zoar lay in Moab, not in Edom. (Jer. xlviii. 34; Isa. xv. 5; Gen. xix. 30, 37.) The Vulg. has *Seira*, and the Arabic *Sá'ira*, which suggest an original reading, "to Seir," the well-known mountain chain which was the headquarters of the Edomite people. Perhaps the form of the text *Çâ'irāh* represents a dialectic pronunciation. (Comp. the forms *Yishāq* and *Yiçhāq* for Isaac.)

**And he rose by night.**—There may be a *lacuna* of a few lines in the text here, or the compiler, in his desire to be brief, may have become obscure. Jehoram appears to have been hemmed in by the Edomites in the mountains, and to have attempted escape under cover of night.

**Smote the Edomites which compassed him about.**—Cut his way through their ranks.

**And the captains of the chariots.**—Part of the object of the verb "smote." Jehoram smote (cut his way through) the Edomites—that is to say, the captains of the Edomite war-chariots which hemmed him and his army in.

**And the people fled into (*unto*) their tents.**—That is to say, the army of Jehoram was glad to escape from the scene of its ill success, and made its way homeward as best it could. (Comp. for the proverbial expression, "to their tents," 1 Sam. xx. 1; 1 Kings viii. 66.) From Joel iii. 19 ("Edom shall be a desolate wilderness for the violence against the children of Judah, because they have shed innocent blood in their land") it has been conjectured that when the Edomites revolted they massacred the Jews who had settled in the country in the time of subjection. (Comp. Gen. xxvii. 40.)

<sup>(22)</sup> **Yet.**—Rather, *and* (*i.e.*, so).

**Unto this day.**—Down to the time of composition of the original account from which this epitome is extracted. This notice is borne out by the Assyrian monuments. Esarhaddon and Assurbanipal mention *Qa'us-gabri* king of *Udumu* (Edom), along with Manasseh of Judah, among their tributaries. Esarhaddon also states that his father Sennacherib had reduced "*Adumû,* a fortified city of Arabia."

**Then Libnah revolted at the same time.**—The point of the statement is that the success of Edom encouraged Libnah to throw off the Judæan supremacy. For the locality see Josh. x. 29 *seq.*, xv. 42, xxi. 13. Keil thinks the revolt of Libnah coincided with (it was probably supported by) the Philistine invasion recorded in 2 Chron. xxi. 16, and continued until Uzziah reduced the Philistines (2 Chron. xxvi. 6 *seq.*). From the time of Hezekiah, Libnah again belonged to Judah (chap. xix. 8, xxiii. 31, xxiv. 18).

<sup>(23)</sup> **The rest of the acts.**—Or, *history.* (See especially 2 Chron. xxi. 11—19, and the Notes there.)

<sup>(24)</sup> **Was buried with his fathers in the city of David.**—But not in the royal tombs (2 Chron. xxi. 20).

<sup>(25—29)</sup> The reign of Ahaziah king of Judah. His expedition with Joram of Israel against Hazael at Ramoth-gilead. (Comp. 2 Chron. xxii. 1—6.)

**Two-and-twenty years old.**—He was Jehoram's youngest son (2 Chron. xxi. 17, xxii. 1), and, as his father died at the age of thirty-nine or forty (verse 17), he must have been begotten in Jehoram's seventeenth or eighteenth year. There is no difficulty in this, nor even in the supposition that Jehoram had begotten sons before Ahaziah, as Thenius seems to imagine. He may have become a father at thirteen or fourteen, and Athaliah was certainly not his only wife.

<sup>(26)</sup> **Ahaziah.**—Called Jehoahaz (2 Chron. xxi. 17) Ewald thinks he assumed the name of Ahaziah on his accession.

**The daughter of Omri**—*i.e.*, granddaughter. Omri is mentioned rather than Ahab as the founder of the dynasty, and the notorious example of its wickedness. (Comp. Micah vi. 16: "The statutes of Omri are kept.")

<sup>(27)</sup> **The son-in-law of the house of Ahab.**—Comp. 2 Chron. xxii. 4, "his mother was his counsellor to do wickedly;" and notice the threefold repetition of the words "the house of Ahab."

*Ahaziah Visits Joram.*        II. KINGS, IX.        *A Messenger sent to Jehu.*

of Ahab. <sup>(28)</sup> And he went with Joram the son of Ahab to the war against Hazael king of Syria in Ramoth-gilead; and the Syrians wounded Joram. <sup>(29)</sup> And king Joram went back to be healed in Jezreel of the wounds ¹which the Syrians had given him at Ramah, when he fought against Hazael king of Syria. And Ahaziah the son of Jehoram king of Judah went down to see Joram the son of Ahab in Jezreel, because he was ²sick.

B.C. 884.

¹ Heb., *wherewith the Syrians had wounded.*

² Heb., *wounded.*

³ Heb., *chamber in a chamber.*

*a* 1 Kings 19. 16.

CHAPTER IX.—<sup>(1)</sup> And Elisha the prophet called one of the children of the prophets, and said unto him, Gird up thy loins, and take this box of oil in thine hand, and go to Ramoth-gilead: <sup>(2)</sup> and when thou comest thither, look out there Jehu the son of Jehoshaphat the son of Nimshi, and go in, and make him arise up from among his brethren, and carry him to an ³inner chamber; <sup>(3)</sup> then *a*take the box of oil, and pour *it*

---

<sup>(28)</sup> **And he went with Joram.**—By the persuasion of his mother and her family (2 Chron. xxii. 4). Ewald would omit the preposition *with*, on the assumption that Ahaziah took no part in the war at Ramoth, but only, as verse 29 relates, visited Jehoram when lying ill of his wounds at Jezreel. But (1) all the MSS. and versions have the preposition; (2) if this verse related only to Joram king of Israel we should expect at the end of the verse, "and the Syrians wounded *him*," rather than "wounded Joram;" and in verse 29, "and *he* went back," rather than "and king Joram went back;" (3) the chronicler (2 Chron. xxii. 5) expressly states that Ahaziah accompanied Joram to Ramoth.

**Against Hazael . . . in Ramoth-gilead.**—Which strong fortress Ahab had vainly tried to wrest from Ben-hadad (1 Kings xxii. 6 *seqq*.).

**Wounded.**—Literally, *smote*.

<sup>(29)</sup> **Joram went back.**—With a few personal attendants. He left the army at Ramoth (chap. ix. 14) under the command of the generals, and perhaps of Ahaziah.

**In Jezreel.**—The seat of the court at this time. (Comp. chap. x. 11, 13.) To reach *Samaria*, moreover, Joram would have had to cross a mountainous country, while he could be carried to Jezreel by an easier route through the valley of the Jordan.

**Which the Syrians had given.**—The verb is imperfect. Ewald suggests that the Hebrew letters may indicate a dialectic pronunciation of the perfect. It is more likely that the imperfect is here used in the sense of *repetition*, implying that Joram was wounded on more than one occasion.

**Ramah.**—*Height*. The same as Ramoth, *heights*.

**And Ahaziah . . . went down.**—Or, *now Ahaziah had gone down*—scil., when the following events happened. The Hebrew construction indicates the beginning of a new paragraph. The division of chapters is again at fault, there being no real break in the narrative between this verse and what follows in chapter ix.

Ahaziah went down either from Ramoth or from Jerusalem; probably from the former, as no mention is made of his having left the seat of war and returned to Jerusalem.

**Because he was sick.**—The same verb as in chap. i. 2. The margin here is wrong.

### IX.

JEHU ANOINTED BY ELISHA'S MESSENGER AS KING OF ISRAEL. HE SLAYS JEHORAM. AHAZIAH AND JEZEBEL. (Comp. 2. Chron. xxii. 7—9.)

<sup>(1)</sup> **And Elisha the prophet called.**—Rather, *meanwhile Elisha had called*—i.e., while Joram was lying ill of his wounds. The Hebrew construction again indicates not so much *succession* as *contemporaneousness*.

**One of the children** (*sons*) **of the prophets.**—Rashi says it was *Jonah*, who is mentioned in chap. xiv. 25.

**Box.**—The same word occurs again only in 1 Sam. x. 1. Render, *phial*.

<sup>(2)</sup> **And when thou comest thither.**—Rather, *And enter into it*—i.e., into the town of Ramoth. This makes it clear that the Israelites had retaken Ramoth from the Syrians (comp. also the mention of "chambers" and "the door" in verse 3, and the order, verse 15, to "let no man escape out of the city") probably before Joram returned to Jezreel (verse 14). Josephus expressly asserts this.

**Jehu.**—Probably left in supreme command of the forces at Jehoram's departure, as being the ablest of the generals (so Josephus).

**The son of Jehoshaphat.**—It is curious that the father of Jehu who executed the sentence of Jehovah upon the house of Ahab should have borne this name ("Jehovah judgeth"). Nothing is known of Jehu's origin. He is twice mentioned by Shalmaneser II., king of Assyria, as one of his tributaries. In a fragment of his Annals relating to the campaign against Hazael, undertaken in his eighteenth year (see Note on chap. viii. 15), the Assyrian monarch states that, after besieging Damascus, and ravaging the Haurân, he marched to the mountains of *Baal-rôsh*, the foreland of the sea (Carmel?), and set up his royal image thereon. "In that day the tribute of the land of the Tyrians (and) Sidonians, (and) of Ya'ua (Jehu), son of Humri, I received." On the Black Obelisk there is a representation of Jehu's tribute-bearers, and, perhaps, of Jehu himself, kneeling before Shalmaneser. The superscription is: "Tribute of Ya'ua, son of Humri (Omri)—(ingots of) silver and gold, a bowl of gold, ewers of gold, goblets of gold, buckets of gold, (ingots of) lead, a rod of the hand of the king, spears—I received it."

**Go in.**—Into Jehu's house.

**From among his brethren**—i.e., his comrades in arms; his fellow-captains.

**Carry him.**—Literally, *cause him to enter*. The object was secrecy.

**An inner chamber.**—Literally, *a chamber in a chamber*. A phrase which occurred in 1 Kings xx. 30, xxii. 25. Thenius thinks this a mark of identity of authorship.

<sup>(3)</sup> **Then.**—*And* (both times).

**Thus saith the Lord . . . over Israel.**—Only the chief part of the message to Jehu is here given, to avoid publicity. (See *infra*, verses 6—9.)

**Over Israel.**—Literally, *unto Israel*, both here and in verse 12. But a great number of MSS., and all the versions in both places, read *over Israel*.

on his head, and say, Thus saith the LORD, I have anointed thee king over Israel. Then open the door, and flee, and tarry not. ⁽⁴⁾ So the young man, *even* the young man the prophet, went to Ramoth-gilead.

⁽⁵⁾ And when he came, behold, the captains of the host *were* sitting; and he said, I have an errand to thee, O captain. And Jehu said, Unto which of all us? And he said, To thee, O captain. ⁽⁶⁾ And he arose, and went into the house; and he poured the oil on his head, and said unto him, Thus saith the LORD God of Israel, I have anointed thee king over the people of the LORD, *even* over Israel. ⁽⁷⁾ And thou shalt smite the house of Ahab thy master, that I may avenge the blood of my servants the prophets, and the blood of all the servants of the LORD, ᵃat the hand of Jezebel. ⁽⁸⁾ For the whole house of Ahab shall perish: and ᵇI will cut off from Ahab him that pisseth against the wall, and him that is shut up and left in Israel: ⁽⁹⁾ and I will make the house of Ahab like the house of ᶜJeroboam the son of Nebat, and like the house of ᵈBaasha the son of Ahijah: ⁽¹⁰⁾ and the dogs shall eat Jezebel in the portion of Jezreel, and *there shall be* none to bury her. And he opened the door, and fled.

⁽¹¹⁾ Then Jehu came forth to the servants of his lord: and *one* said unto him, *Is* all well? wherefore came this mad *fellow* to thee? And he said unto them, Ye know the man, and his communication. ⁽¹²⁾ And they said, It is

*a* 1 Kings 21. 15.
*b* 1 Kings 14. 10, & 21. 21.
*c* 1 Kings 14. 10, & 21. 22.
*d* 1 Kings 16. 3.

---

**Tarry not.**—So as to avoid all questioning, and to give greater force to the act.

⁽⁴⁾ **Even the young man the prophet.**—Rather, *the young man of the prophet—i.e.*, Elisha's minister. The construction, however, is unusual, and some MSS., the LXX. and the Syriac, omit *the young man* in the second place. This gives the suitable reading: "So the young man, the prophet, went," &c.

⁽⁵⁾ **And when he came, behold.**—Rather, *And he went in, and behold.* He went into Jehu's headquarters.

**The captains of the host were sitting.**—In council with Jehu.

⁽⁶⁾ **And he arose**—*i.e.*, Jehu arose.

**Into the house.**—The council of war was sitting in the court.

**I have anointed thee.**—The commission to Elijah (1 Kings xix. 16) was thus fulfilled by his successor.

**Over the people of the Lord.**—Israel being Jehovah's people, Jehovah was Israel's true king, and therefore it was within His sovereign right to appoint whom He would as His earthly representative. Reuss asserts that this account of the anointing of Jehu, like that of the anointing of Hazael (chap. viii. 13), is substituted in the present narration for what another document related of *Elijah*. This is pure conjecture. It is easier to suppose that Elijah had instructed his successor to carry out the commission intrusted to himself, although the narrative nowhere says so. He goes on to remark that there is no need to try to clear Elisha of the charge of being a revolutionary and a regicide, for that the new dynasty would make use of his name by way of legitimising itself, exactly as the houses of Kish and of Jesse made use of that of the prophet Samuel. This is being considerably wiser than our only authorities.

⁽⁷⁾ **The house of Ahab thy master.**—*Not* Ahab thy master, *but* the house of Ahab thy lords. The LXX. adds, *from before me*.

**The blood of my servants the prophets.**—See 1 Kings xviii. 4, 13.

**The blood of all the servants of the Lord.**—We are not told elsewhere, but the thing is in itself probable, that Jezebel persecuted to the death those who clung to the *exclusive* worship of Jehovah.

**At the hand of Jezebel.**—Comp. Gen. ix. 5. Jezebel (Heb., *'Izêbel*) means *immaculata—i.e., virgo.* Is it the original of Isabel, Isabella, Isbel?

⁽⁸⁾ **For.**—*And.*

**Shall perish.**—Syriac, Arabic, Vulg., "I will cause to perish" (different Hebrew points). The LXX. has, "and at the hand of all the house of Ahab," a difference of reading which favours the ordinary Hebrew text.

**Him that is shut up and left** (*and him that is left*).—Reuss imitates the alliteration of the original: "qu'il soit caché ou lâché en Israel."

For the rest of the verse see 1 Kings xxi. 21, and comp. 1 Kings xiv. 10.

⁽⁹⁾ **Baasha.**—See 1 Kings xiv. 10, xvi. S, 4. Shalmaneser II. mentions a king of Ammon named *Ba'sa*.

⁽¹⁰⁾ **And the dogs shall eat Jezebel.**—Literally, *and Jezebel the dogs shall eat.* (Comp. Elijah's threat, 1 Kings xxi. 23.)

⁽¹¹⁾ **The servants of his lord.**—Jehoram's captains.

**And one said.**—Many MSS. and all the versions, except the Targum, have " and they said."

**Is all well?**—They dreaded some sinister news.

**This mad fellow.**—They were struck by his wild demeanour and furious haste. Or, perhaps, "this inspired one," in a tone of ridicule. (Comp. Hosea ix. 7.)

**Ye know the man.**—There is emphasis on the *ye*. Jehu apparently implies that the man was sent to him by his fellow-generals—that they had planned the whole thing. His purpose is to find out their disposition. Or, more probably, his reply may simply mean: "Why ask me, when you yourselves must have divined the right answer to your question?"

**His communication.**—Or, *his meditation* (comp. 1 Kings xviii. 27)—*i.e.*, the thing he had in his mind, his *purpose* in coming. Corn. à Lapide: "Ye know that he is mad, and accordingly what he says is mad, and therefore neither to be credited nor repeated." LXX., "Ye know the man and his babble;" the Targum, "and his story;" the Syriac, "and his folly;" the Vulg., "and what he said;" the Arabic, "and his news."

⁽¹²⁾ **It is false.**—This is rather too strong, and does not convey the exact force of the reply. The captains

false; tell us now. And he said, Thus and thus spake he to me, saying, Thus saith the LORD, I have anointed thee king over Israel. (13) Then they hasted, and took every man his garment, and put *it* under him on the top of the stairs, and blew with trumpets, saying, Jehu ¹is king. (14) So Jehu the son of Jehoshaphat the son of Nimshi conspired against Joram. (Now Joram had kept Ramoth-gilead, he and all Israel, because of Hazael king of Syria. (15) But ᵃking ²Joram was returned to be healed in Jezreel of the wounds which the Syrians ³had given him, when he fought with Hazael king of Syria.) And Jehu said, If it be your minds, *then* ⁴let none go forth *nor* escape out of the city to go to tell *it* in Jezreel. (16) So Jehu rode in a chariot, and went to Jezreel; for Joram lay there. And Ahaziah king of Judah was come down to see Joram. (17) And there stood a watchman on the tower in Jezreel, and he spied the company of Jehu as he came, and said, I see a company. And Joram said, Take an horseman, and send to meet them, and let him say, Is it

¹ Heb., *reigneth.*
ᵃ ch. 8. 29.
² Heb., *Jehoram.*
³ Heb., *smote.*
⁴ Heb., *let no escaper go, &c.*

---

reply to Jehu's "Oh, you know all about it!" with the one word, "trickery!" *i.e.,* "you are pretending!" "mere evasion!" They then assume a tone of persuasion: "Do tell us." Even if they had really guessed the import of the prophet's visit, their manner now convinced Jehu that he might safely trust them.

(13) **Then** (*and*) **they hasted.**—LXX., "and they heard, and hasted." This is probably original, the sense being that the moment they heard it, they hastily took up their outer garments, and laid them as a carpet for Jehu to walk upon. (Comp. Luke xix. 36.) The instantaneous action of the generals shows that there must have existed a strong feeling against Joram in the army and an enthusiasm for Jehu which only required a word from him to precipitate a revolution.

**Put it under him on the top of the stairs.** —So Kimchi, "at the uppermost step." The words are much discussed by commentators. The LXX. has, "and put it underneath him on the *garem* of the steps" (retaining the Hebrew word *gèrem*); the Syriac, "and put it under him on a seat of steps;" the Targum, "at the steps of the hours," *i.e.*, a flight of steps which served as a sundial (comp. chap. xx. 11); the Vulg., "and each one, taking his cloak, put it under his feet *in similitudinem tribunalis*," *i.e.*, in the fashion of a rostrum, or elevated platform; the Arabic, "on the steps of the rise" (or "elevation").

The word *gèrem*, rendered "top," can hardly have that meaning. In Hebrew it rarely occurs (Prov. xvii. 22; xxv. 15), and means *bone*, for which in Aramaic it is the usual term (Dan. vi. 25). In Arabic the word means "body," and it is usually so explained in one passage of the Bible (Gen. xlix. 14), "Issachar is a strong ass;" literally, *an ass of body*. As the Aramaic *garmá* is used in the sense of "self," some would render the present phrase, "on the stairs themselves." But perhaps we may better translate on the analogy of the Arabic word, "They put (their cloaks) under him, on to ('*el*) the body of the stairs." The stairway on the outside of the house, leading to the roof, served as an extemporised throne, or rather platform, for the king. (Comp. chap. xi. 14.) Some Hebrew MSS. have "upon" for "on to." (Comp. 2 Sam. xxi. 10, "on the rock.")

(14, 15) **Now Joram had kept Ramoth-gilead . . . But king Joram was returned.**—Rather, *Now Joram had been on guard in Ramoth-gilead . . . And Jehoram the king returned.* The whole is a parenthesis intended to explain Jehu's words in verse 15: "Let none go forth . . to *tell it in Jezreel.*" Although substantially a repetition of chap. viii. 28, 29, it was hardly "superfluous" (*Thenius*) to remind the reader at this point of Joram's absence—a material element in the success of the conspiracy. Graf's conjecture that *Jehu* should be read instead of *Joram* is an obvious one, but hardly correct.

**Because of Hazael.**—Rather, *against Hazael.*

(15) **If it be your minds.**—Literally, *if it be your soul;* some MSS., "if it be with your soul," as in Gen. xxiii. 8. The Vulg. paraphrases correctly, *si vobis placet.*

**Let none go forth.**—Literally, *let not a fugitive go forth.* This proves that Ramoth was in the hands of the Israelite army. If they were *besieging* the city, as Josephus relates, Jehu's command is unintelligible.

(16) **Lay.**—*Was lying.* His wounds were not yet quite healed.

**Ahaziah king of Judah was come down.**— See chap. viii. 29. After relating what had meanwhile occurred with the army at Ramoth, the narrative returns to that point. Instead of *Joram was lying there*, the LXX. has, "Joram king of Israel was being healed in Jezreel of the shots wherewith the Arameans shot him in Ramoth, in the war with Hazael king of Syria, because he was mighty and a man of might." The first sentence, "Joram king of Israel . . . king of Syria," was probably a marginal note of a different reading of the first half of verse 15. This was inadvertently inserted by some transcriber in connection with *Joram* in the present verse. The sentence, "Because he was mighty and a man of might," was originally a marginal note on the words "Hazael king of Syria" (verse 14), but in like manner came to be erroneously connected with the same words in the various reading of verse 15 (*Thenius*).

(17) **And there stood a watchman.**—Literally, *and the watchman was standing.* The tower was attached to the palace, and the latter was, perhaps, near the eastern wall of the town.

**The company of Jehu.**—The word (*shiph'āh*) literally means *overflow*, and so a *multitude* of waters (Job xxii. 11), of camels (Isa. lx. 6), of horses (Ezek. xxvi. 10). Jehu was accompanied, therefore, by a considerable force.

**Joram said.**—Not to the watchman, but to one of his courtiers. The narrative is very concise.

**Is it peace?**—This hardly represents the force of the original. Joram is not yet apprehensive. His question merely means, "What is the news?" He expects news from the army at Ramoth. Thenius, however, explains "Come ye with friendly or hostile intention?" In that case, would the king have sent *a single horseman* to ascertain the truth?

| | | |
|---|---|---|
| *The Messengers Return not.* | II. KINGS, IX. | *Death of Jehoram.* |

peace? <sup>(18)</sup> So there went one on horseback to meet him, and said, Thus saith the king, *Is it* peace? And Jehu said, What hast thou to do with peace? turn thee behind me. And the watchman told, saying, The messenger came to them, but he cometh not again. <sup>(19)</sup> Then he sent out a second on horseback, which came to them, and said, Thus saith the king, *Is it* peace? And Jehu answered, What hast thou to do with peace? turn thee behind me. <sup>(20)</sup> And the watchman told, saying, He came even unto them, and cometh not again: and the ¹driving *is* like the driving of Jehu the son of Nimshi; for he driveth ²furiously. <sup>(21)</sup> And Joram said, ³Make ready. And his chariot was made ready. And Joram king of Israel and Ahaziah king of Judah went out, each in his chariot, and they went out against Jehu, and ⁴met him in the portion of Naboth the Jezreelite.

<sup>(22)</sup> And it came to pass, when Joram saw Jehu, that he said, *Is it* peace, Jehu? And he answered, What peace, so long as the whoredoms of thy mother Jezebel and her witchcrafts *are so* many? <sup>(23)</sup> And Joram turned his hands, and fled, and said to Ahaziah, *There is* treachery, O Ahaziah. <sup>(24)</sup> And Jehu ⁵drew a bow with his full strength, and smote Jehoram between his arms, and the arrow went out at his heart, and he

¹ Or, *marching.*
² Heb., *in madness.*
³ Heb., *Bind.*
⁴ Heb., *found.*
⁵ Heb., *filled his hand with a bow.*

---

<sup>(18)</sup> **One on horseback.**—Literally, *the rider of the horse.*

**What hast thou to do with peace?**—A rough evasion: "What business is it of yours, on what ground I am come?" Conscious of his strength, Jehu can despise the royal message, and the messenger durst not disobey the fierce general, when ordered summarily to the rear. Of course Jehu wished to prevent an alarm being raised in Jezreel.

**Came to them.**—Literally, *came right up to them.* (The Hebrew text should be corrected from verse 20.)

<sup>(19)</sup> **Then.**—Literally, *And he sent a second rider of a horse.*

**Is it peace?**—So the versions, many editions, and some MSS. The ordinary Hebrew text gives it as a salutation: "Peace!" but wrongly. Joram is still unsuspicious of evil. Some accident might have detained his first messenger.

<sup>(20)</sup> **Driving.**—Correct. The margin is wrong.

**The son of Nimshi.**—Jehu was *son of Jehoshaphat* son of Nimshi. The former phrase may have fallen out of the text here. (Yet comp. chap. viii. 26, "Athaliah daughter of Omri.") The Syriac and Arabic call Jehu "the son of Nimshi" in verse 2 also.

**He driveth furiously**—i.e., the foremost charioteer so drives. The word rendered "furiously" is related to that rendered "mad fellow" in verse 11. (Comp. margin here.) Jehu's chariot *swayed* unsteadily as he drove madly on. LXX., ἐν παραλλαγῇ. The Targum explains in an exactly opposite sense, "quietly;" and so Josephus: "Jehu was driving rather slowly, and in orderly fashion" (perhaps confounding *shiggā'ôn,* "madness," Deut. xxviii. 28, with *shiggāyôn,* "a slow, mournful song," or elegy).

<sup>(21)</sup> **Make ready.**—Literally, *bind*—i.e., the horses to the chariot.

**And his chariot was made ready.**—Literally, *And one bound his chariot.*

**Against Jehu.**—Rather, *to meet Jehu.* Joram was curious to know why his messengers had not returned, as well as why the commander-in-chief had left the seat of war. Had he suspected treachery, he would hardly have left the shelter of the walls of Jezreel, and ventured forth without a guard.

**In the portion of Naboth.**—Naboth's vineyard, which now formed part of the pleasure-grounds of the palace. (See 1 Kings xxi. 16.)

<sup>(22)</sup> **Is it peace, Jehu?**—Joram meant, "Is all well at the seat of war?" Jehu's reply left no doubt of his intentions. He assumes the part of champion of the legitimate worship against Jezebel and her foreign innovations, and the lawless tyrannies by which she sought to enforce them. (Comp. verses 25, 26.)

**What peace . . . are so many?**—Rather, *What is the peace during the whoredoms of thy mother, and her many witchcrafts*—i.e., so long as they continue?

**Whoredoms.**—In the spiritual sense, i.e., idolatries. (See Note on 1 Chron. v. 25.)

**Witchcrafts.**—*Sorceries*; the use of spells and charms, common among Semitic idolaters. (Comp. the prohibitions in the Law (Exod. xxii. 18; Deut. xviii. 10, 11.) A great number of the Assyrian tablets contain magical formulas, incantations, and exorcisms. Babylonia was the home of the pseudo-science of magic; and the oldest collection of such formulas is that of Sargina king of Agadê (Accad), compiled in seventy tablets, about 2200 B.C.

<sup>(23)</sup> **And Joram turned his hands**—i.e., turned the horses round. (Comp. 1 Kings xxii. 34.)

**There is treachery.**—Literally, *Guile,* or *fraud, Ahaziah!* Joram shouted these two words of warning to his companion as he was turning his horses to fly.

<sup>(24)</sup> **And Jehu drew . . . strength.**—See margin, which, however, is not quite accurate. Rather it should be, *And Jehu had filled his hand* (with an arrow) *on the bow*—i.e., had meanwhile put an arrow on his bow ready to shoot. Keil explains, "filled his hand with the bow," i.e., seized the bow. The phrase "to fill a bow" means to *stretch* it, both in Hebrew (Zech. ix. 13) and in Syriac (Ps. xi. 2). In Ps. lxiv. 4. Symmachus renders the Hebrew, "they have aimed their arrow," by the Greek, ἐπλήρωσαν τὸ τόξον, "they have filled the bow."

**Between his arms**—i.e., between the shoulders, as he was flying; Vulg., "inter scapulas."

**The arrow went out at his heart.**—Or, *came out from his heart.* It struck him obliquely between the shoulders, and went right through the heart. (The word for "arrow" is *hêçi,* an ancient form, occurring thrice in 1 Sam. xx. 36–38.) Ewald, on this account, refers both passages to the oldest narrator of the history of the kings.

**Sunk down.**—See margin (Isa. xlvi. 1).

¹sunk down in his chariot. (25) Then said Jehu to Bidkar his captain, Take up, *and* cast him in the portion of the field of Naboth the Jezreelite: for remember how that, when I and thou rode together after Ahab his father, ᵃthe LORD laid this burden upon him; (26) surely I have seen yesterday the ²blood of Naboth, and the blood of his sons, saith the LORD; and I will requite thee in this ³plat, saith the LORD. Now therefore take *and* cast him into the plat *of ground*, according to the word of the LORD.
(27) But when Ahaziah the king of Judah saw *this*, he fled by the way of the garden house. And Jehu followed after him, and said, Smite him also in the chariot. *And they did so* at the going up to Gur, which *is* by Ibleam. And he fled to Megiddo, and died there. (28) And his servants carried him in a chariot to Jerusalem, and buried him in his sepulchre with his fathers in the

1 Heb., *bowed.*
ᵃ 1 Kings 21. 29.
2 Heb., *bloods.*
3 Or, *portion.*

**In his chariot.**—LXX., "on his knees," owing to a partial obliteration of one letter in their Hebrew text.

(25) **Then said Jehu.**—Literally, *And he said.*

**Bidkar.**—The Syriac gives *Bar-dĕkar,* "son of stabbing," *i.e.,* "stabber," "slayer," a very suitable name for Jehu's squire. The Hebrew name is, therefore, a contraction of *Ben-dekar.* (Comp. Bedan, "son of Dan," *i.e,* Danite, 1 Sam. xii. 11; and Bedad, "son of Hadad," in 1 Chron. i. 46.)

**Captain.**—*Adjutant, aide-de-camp,* chief (chap. vii. 2).

**Remember how that, when I and thou rode together.**—This gives the sense of the Hebrew correctly. Literally, *remember thou me and thee riding together.* The word rendered "together" probably means *riding side by side* on horseback in attendance on the king. The Targum, Vulg., and Kimchi interpret, *riding together in the same chariot* ; Josephus, *riding together in Ahab's chariot behind him.*

**The Lord laid this burden upon him.**—Rather, *Jehovah uttered this* (prophetic) *utterance upon* (*i.e.,* about) *him.* (Comp. the oracle uttered by Elijah against Ahab when taking possession of Naboth's vineyard, 1 Kings xxi. 17, *seq.,* 29.)

(26) **Surely.**—Literally, *if not;* a formula of emphatic asseveration, which originally must have run somewhat as follows: "If I have not seen, may I perish." The inappropriateness of such an expression in the mouth of the Deity is obvious; but that only shows how completely the original meaning of the formula was forgotten in everyday usage.

**Yesterday.**—So that Ahab seized the vineyard the day after the murder of Naboth, a detail not exactly specified in 1 Kings xxi. 16.

**The blood.**—The plural (margin) implies *death by violence* (Gen. iv. 10).

**And the blood of his sons.**—The murder of the sons of Naboth is neither stated nor implied in 1 Kings xxi., an omission which has needlessly troubled the minds of commentators. As to the fact, it would be quite in accordance with ancient practice to slay the sons of one accused of blasphemy along with their father (comp. Josh. vii. 24, 25); and the crafty Jezebel would not be likely to spare persons whose wrongs might one day prove dangerous. The difference in the two narratives is accounted for by the circumstance that the present is the *exact* version of an eye-witness, viz., Jehu himself, while the former was probably derived from a less direct source.

**Saith the Lord.**—Literally, *is the thing uttered of Jehovah.* This phrase, which is uncommon except in the writings of the prophets, and the word rendered "burden" in the last verse, which also belongs to prophetic terminology, together establish the historical authenticity of the short oracle of Elijah, recorded in this verse. Its brevity and the solemnity with which it was pronounced would, we may be sure, stamp it ineffaceably upon the memory of those who heard it. (Comp. 1 Sam. ii. 30; and chap. xix. 33, *infra.*)

**I will requite thee in this plat.**—Another important detail not given in the former account.

**Plat.**—*Portion,* as in verse 25 (twice).

(27) **But when . . . saw this.**—*Now Ahaziah . . . had seen it; and he fled, &c.*

**By the way of the garden house**—*i.e.,* in the direction of the garden house, which was probably a sort of arbour or drinking pavilion near the gates of the palace gardens, of which Naboth's vineyard formed a part. Ahaziah wished to escape from the royal park as fast as he could.

**Smite him also in the chariot.**—The Hebrew is much more suited to the excitement of the occasion: *Him too! shoot him in the chariot!* (Here and in verse 13, *supra,* '*el,* "into," seems equivalent to '*al,* "upon.")

**And they did so.**—Some such words as these may have fallen out of the Hebrew text. So the Syriac: "Him also! slay him! and they slew him in his chariot, on the ascent of Gur," &c. But the rendering of the LXX. involves the least change, and is probably right: "Him too! And he smote him in the chariot, in the going up," &c. This is more graphic. Jehu simply ejaculates, "Him too!" and, after a hot pursuit, shoots his second victim, at the ascent or declivity of Gur, where Ahaziah's chariot would be forced to slacken speed.

The ascent of Gur is not mentioned elsewhere. Ibleam lay between Jezreel and Megiddo. (Comp. Judg. i. 27; Josh. xvii. 11.)

**And he fled to Megiddo, and died there.**—See the Note on 2 Chron. xxii. 9, where a different tradition respecting the end of Ahaziah is recorded. The definite assignment of localities in the present account is a mark of greater trustworthiness. The way in which Rashi, whom Keil follows, attempts to combine the two accounts, is revolting to common sense. It would be better to assume a corruption of the text in one or the other narrative.

**Megiddo.**—Identified in the cuneiform inscriptions as *Magidû* or *Magadû.*

(28) **Carried him in a chariot.**—Literally, *made him ride.* After this verb the LXX., Syriac, and Vulg. supply what the Hebrew text almost demands, "and brought him."

**In his sepulchre.**—*In his own sepulchre,* which he had in his lifetime prepared, according to the custom of antiquity.

*Jezebel Killed,*  II. KINGS, IX.  *and Eaten by Dogs.*

city of David. (29) And in the eleventh year of Joram the son of Ahab began Ahaziah to reign over Judah.

(30) And when Jehu was come to Jezreel, Jezebel heard *of it;* and she ¹painted her face, and tired her head, and looked out at a window. (31) And as Jehu entered in at the gate, she said, *Had* Zimri peace, who slew his master? (32) And he lifted up his face to the window, and said, Who *is* on my side? who? And there looked out to him two or three ²eunuchs. (33) And he said,

B.C. cir. 886.

B.C. cir. 884.

¹ Heb., *put her eyes in painting.*

² Or, *chamberlains.*

Throw her down. So they threw her down: and *some* of her blood was sprinkled on the wall, and on the horses: and he trode her under foot. (34) And when he was come in, he did eat and drink, and said, Go, see now this cursed *woman,* and bury her: for she *is* a king's daughter. (35) And they went to bury her: but they found no more of her than the skull, and the feet, and the palms of *her* hands. (36) Wherefore they came again, and told him. And he said, This *is* the word of the

---

(29) **In the eleventh year of Joram.**—Chap. viii. 25 says "in the twelfth year of Joram." Such a difference is not remarkable, inasmuch as the synchronisms between the reigns of the two kingdoms are not based upon exact records. Moreover, different computations might make the same year the eleventh or twelfth of Joram. (The verse is a parenthesis, and perhaps spurious.)

(30) **And when Jehu was come.**—Rather, *And Jehu came*—i.e., after the slaughter of Ahaziah, as the Hebrew construction implies.

**Jezebel heard of it.**—Rather, *Now Jezebel had heard*—scil., the news of the death of the two kings. There should be a stop after Jezreel.

**And she painted her face.**—Rather, *and she set her eyes in paint*—i.e., according to the still common practice of Oriental ladies, she painted her eyebrows and lashes with a pigment composed of antimony and zinc (the Arabic *kohl*). The dark border throws the eye into relief, and makes it appear larger (*Bähr*). Pliny relates that in his day this pigment (*stibium*) was called platyophthalmon (comp. Jer. iv. 30), because it dilates the eye (Plin. *Hist. Nat.* xxxiii. 34).

**Tired.**—An old English word, meaning *adorned* with a *tire* or head-dress. (Comp. Isa. iii. 18.) *Tire* might seem to be the Persian *tiara,* but is much more probably connected with the German *zier* and *zieren.* (See Skeat's *Etym. Dict.,* s.v.) Jezebel put on her royal apparel in order to die as a queen. Comp. the similar behaviour of Cleopatra:—

"Show me, my women, like a queen. Go fetch
My best attires. I am again for Cydnus,
To meet Marc Antony . . . Bring our crown, and all.
 *   *   *   *   *
Give me my robe, put on my crown; I have
Immortal longings in me."
*Antony and Cleop.,* act v., scene 2.

**A window.**—*The window,* looking down upon the square within the city gate. Others think of a window looking down into the courtyard of the palace.

Ewald's notion (after Ephrem Syrus), that Jezebel thought to captivate the conqueror by her charms, is negatived by the consideration that she was the grandmother of Ahaziah, who was twenty-two years old when Jehu slew him, and the fact that Oriental women fade early.

(31) **And as . . . she said.**—*And Jehu had come into the gate, and she said.*

**Had Zimri . . . master?**—Rather, *Art well* (literally, *Is it peace*), *thou Zimri, his master's murderer?* The "Is it peace?" which Jezebel addresses to Jehu, appears to be an ironical greeting. Thenius explains: "Is there to be peace or war between me and thee,

the rebel?" referring to the same phrase in verses 17, 18, 19, 22, *supra.* The phrase is vague enough to admit of many meanings, according to circumstances. Perhaps Jezebel, in her mood of desperate defiance, repeats the question which Jehoram had thrice asked of Jehu, as a hint that *she* herself is now the sovereign to whom Jehu owes an account of his doings. She goes on to call him a second *Zimri*—i.e., a regicide like him who slew Baasha, and likely to enjoy as brief a reign as he. (See 1 Kings xvi. 15—18.)

(32) **Who is on my side? who?**—This hardly implies, as Thenius thinks, that Jezebel had made preparations for resistance. Jehu knew that the imperious and cruel queen was well hated by the palace officials. The "two or three eunuchs," who a moment before had crouched in servile dread before Jezebel, would now be eager to curry favour with the regicide, and, at the same time, wreak their malice upon their former tyrant. (The repetition, "Who is on my side? who?" accords well with Jehu's character. The LXX. has the strange reading, "he saw her, and said, Who art thou? Come down with me." Josephus adopts this; but Thenius shows clearly that it has originated in easy corruptions of the present Hebrew text.)

(33) **Throw her down.**—Comp. Note on 1 Chron. xiii. 9.

**Was sprinkled on.**—*Spirted on to.*

**He trode her under foot.**—All the versions have *they*—i.e., the horses—*trode.* Thenius supposes they were excited by the blood being sprinkled upon them. But "*he*"—i.e., Jehu—"*trode* her under foot," plainly means, *he drove over her fallen body.* Ewald goes beyond the text in stating that Jehu spurned her with his own feet. (For the verb, comp. chap. vii. 20.)

(34) **And when . . . drink.**—Rather, *And he went in* (into the palace), *and ate and drank.* Jehu takes possession of the palace, having slain its former occupants. Savage warrior as he was, he forgot all about the victim of his violence until he had appeased the demands of his appetite. Then he could remember that even Jezebel was of royal rank, and perhaps a touch of remorse may be discerned in the mandate for her burial.

**Go, see now.**—Rather, *Look, I pray, after.*

**This cursed woman.**—Jehu was thinking of the curse pronounced on Jezebel by the prophet Elijah. (See next verse.)

**She is a king's daughter.**—Compare 1 Kings xvi. 31.

(35) **Her hands.**—Heb., *the hands.*

(36) **This is the word of the Lord.**—See 1 Kings xxi. 23, where this oracle of Elijah is given.

LORD, which he spake ¹by his servant Elijah the Tishbite, saying, ᵃIn the portion of Jezreel shall dogs eat the flesh of Jezebel: ⁽³⁷⁾ and the carcase of Jezebel shall be as dung upon the face of the field in the portion of Jezreel; so that they shall not say, This *is* Jezebel.

CHAPTER X.— ⁽¹⁾ And Ahab had seventy sons in Samaria. And Jehu wrote letters, and sent to Samaria, unto the rulers of Jezreel, to the elders, and to ²them that brought up Ahab's *children*, saying, ⁽²⁾ Now as soon as this letter cometh to you, seeing your master's sons *are* with you, and *there are* with you chariots and horses, a fenced city also, and armour; ⁽³⁾ look even out the best and meetest of your master's sons, and set *him* on his father's throne, and fight for your master's house. ⁽⁴⁾But they were exceedingly afraid, and said, Behold, two kings stood not before him: how then shall we stand? ⁽⁵⁾ And he that *was* over the house, and he that *was* over the city, the elders also, and the bringers up *of the children*, sent to Jehu, saying, We *are* thy servants, and will do all that thou shalt bid us; we will not make any king: do thou *that which is* good in thine eyes.

¹ Heb., *by the hand of.*

ᵃ 1 Kings 21. 23.

B.C. 884.

² Heb., *nourishers.*

---

**Portion**—*i.e.*, domain, territory (*hēleq*). In 1 Kings xxi. 23, the word *is* "wall" (*hēl*), an error due to the loss of the final letter; not an original difference, as Keil assumes.

**Dogs.**—*The dogs.*

⁽³⁷⁾ **And the carcase of Jezebel.**—This continuation of the prophecy is not given in 1 Kings xxi. 23. It is probably original; not "a free expansion" by Jehu, as Keil asserts.

**Shall be.**—It is questionable whether the Hebrew text is to be read as a rare ancient form (*wᵉhāyāth*), or simply as an instance of *defective* writing (*wᵉhāyᵉthā*). We prefer the second view.

**As dung.**—Comp. Ps. lxxxiii. 10.

**So that they shall not say.**—Comp. Gen. xi. 7 for the construction. The sense is, So that men will no longer be able to recognise her mangled remains.

X.

JEHU MASSACRES THE FAMILY OF AHAB, THE KINSMEN OF AHAZIAH, AND THE BAAL-WORSHIPPERS.

⁽¹⁾ **Ahab had seventy sons.**—His posterity in general are meant. Ahab had been dead about fourteen years (chap. iii. 1; 1 Kings xxii. 51), and had had two successors on the throne. The name *Ahab* seems to be used here as equivalent to *the house of Ahab.* Many of the number might be strictly sons of Ahab, as he no doubt had a considerable harem.

**Jehu wrote letters, and sent to Samaria.**—Jehu was crafty as well as fierce. He could not venture to the capital without first sounding the inclinations of the nobles of the city.

**Unto the rulers of Jezreel.**—"Jezreel" is an ancient error. The LXX. has "unto the rulers of Samaria." So Josephus. Thenius accordingly suggests that the original reading was, "and sent from Jezreel to the princes of Samaria." The Vulg. gives "ad optimates civitatis," which seems preferable. Before "the elders" we must restore "and unto" with some MSS., the LXX., Syriac, and Vulg. The original text would then run: "and sent to the princes of the city and unto the elders," &c. Reuss, on the other hand, reads "Israel" for "Jezreel."

**Them that brought up Ahab's children.**—Literally, *them who brought up Ahab* (*i.e.*, the house of Ahab). The word occurs in Num. xi. 12; Isa. lxix. 23 ("nursing father"). The nobles entrusted with this charge would be responsible for the good behaviour of their wards. Ahab may have dreaded the evils of an education in the harem, and possible disputes about the succession.

⁽²⁾ **Now as soon as this letter cometh.**—Rather, *And now when this letter cometh.* Only the conclusion of the letter, containing the gist of it, is reported here. (Comp. chap. v. 6.)

**Seeing your master's sons . . . look even out** (verse 3).—Rather, *there are with you both your master's sons, and the chariots and the horses, and a fenced city, and the armoury: so look out the best,* &c.

**A fenced city.**—All the versions but the Arabic have "fenced cities;" and so Josephus. There is a tone of mocking *irony* in Jehu's challenge to the nobles of Samaria, who were probably as luxurious and cowardly now as in the days of Amos, a few years later (Amos iii. 12, vi. 3–6). (Comp. also Isa. xxviii. 1–10.) By his careful enumeration of their resources, he as good as says that his defiance is not the fruit of ignorance.

⁽³⁾ **The best and meetest**—*i.e.*, the one you think best qualified in every sense (not merely in the *moral* sense).

**Your master's sons.**—"Your master" need not mean Jehoram. The story relates to *Ahab* (verse 1).

**His father's throne**—*i.e., Ahab's* throne. (Comp. 2 Chron. xvii. 3, xxi. 12, xxix. 2, where David is called the father of Jehoshaphat, Jehoram, and Hezekiah in turn.)

**Fight for your master's house.**— Jehu thus declares his own warlike intentions, leaving the nobles, whom his prompt and decisive action had taken by surprise, no choice between improvised resistance and instant submission. Knowing Jehu's character as a soldier, they chose the latter.

⁽⁴⁾ **But they were exceedingly afraid.**—Literally, *And they feared mightily, mightily.* (Comp. Gen. vii. 19.)

**Two kings.**—Rather, *the two kings.* The word *kings* is emphatic.

⁽⁵⁾ **He that was over the house.**—The prefect of the palace, or *major-domo.* A similar official is mentioned on the Egyptian monuments. His position and influence would resemble that of the great chamberlain of the Byzantine court.

**He that was over the city.**— The prefect or governor of the city, called in 1 Kings xxii. 26 "the prince (*sar*) of the city." These two are the "rulers" (*sārīm*) of verse 1.

*Slaying of*          II. KINGS, X.          *Ahab's Sons.*

(6) Then he wrote a letter the second time to them, saying, If ye be [1] mine, and *if* ye will hearken unto my voice, take ye the heads of the men your master's sons, and come to me to Jezreel by to morrow this time. Now the king's sons, *being* seventy persons, *were* with the great men of the city, which brought them up. (7) And it came to pass, when the letter came to them, that they took the king's sons, and slew seventy persons, and put their heads in baskets, and sent him *them* to Jezreel. (8) And there came a messenger, and told him, saying, They have brought the heads of the king's sons. And he said, Lay ye them in two heaps at the entering in of the gate until the morning. (9) And it came to pass in the morning, that he went out, and stood, and said to all the people, Ye *be* righteous: behold, I conspired against my master, and slew him: but who slew all these? (10) Know now that there shall fall unto the earth nothing of the word of the LORD, which the LORD spake concerning the house of Ahab: for the LORD hath done *that* which he spake [a][2] by his servant Elijah.

(11) So Jehu slew all that remained of the house of Ahab in Jezreel, and all

---

1 Heb., *for me.*

*a* 1 Kings 21. 29.

2 Heb., *by the hand of.*

---

(6) **The second time.**—Some MSS., the LXX., and the Arabic read "a second letter."

**Take ye the heads.**—Jehu knew his men. The cool cynicism of his savage order is worthy of a Sulla or a Marius.

**The heads of the men your master's sons.**—Literally, *the heads of the sons of your master.* Some MSS., the Syriac, Arabic, and Vulg., as well as the MSS. mentioned by Origen, omit the word *men*. Thenius thinks that this word is used to indicate that only *male* descendants of Ahab were to be put to death (?). The Alexandrian LXX. omits *sons*; and four Hebrew MSS. read instead *house*. The Authorised Version, however, is a permissible interpretation of the Hebrew.

**Come.**—LXX., *bring* (them), which is a natural conjecture.

**To Jezreel.**—A journey of more than twenty miles.

**By to morrow this time.**—Jehu is urgent for despatch, because time is all-important. He wishes to convince the people of Jezreel as soon as possible that none of the royal princes were left to claim the crown, and that the nobles of Samaria have joined his cause.

**Now the king's sons . . . brought them up.**—This is a correct translation. According to the Masoretic punctuation, and supposing that the particle *'eth* (rendered "with") might here be used merely to introduce the subject, we might render: "Now the king's sons were seventy persons; the great men of the city were bringing them up." But such a usage of *'eth* is very doubtful. (Comp. chap. vi. 5.) The sentence, in any case, is only a parenthetic reminder of what was stated in verse 1. The total seventy is, perhaps, not to be taken as exact, seventy being a favourite *round* number. (See Note on 1 Chron. i. 42.)

(7) **And slew.**—Rather, *butchered*, or *slaughtered.* The way in which the writer speaks of this massacre—"they took the king's sons, and butchered seventy persons"—shows that he did not sympathise with Jehu's deeds of blood. His interest rather centres in the fact that the predictions of Elijah were fulfilled by the wickedness of Jehu. (See verse 10.)

**In baskets.**—Rather, *in the baskets.* The word (*dûd*) means a "pot" elsewhere (1 Sam. ii. 14). In Ps. lxxxi. 6, the LXX. renders κόφινος; here it gives κάρταλλοι ("pointed baskets").

(8) **There came a messenger.**—Literally, *and the messenger came in.* Josephus says Jehu was giving a banquet.

**Heaps.**—The noun (*çibbûr*) occurs nowhere else in the Old Testament. In the Talmud it means "congregation," as we say colloquially "a *heap* of persons." The verb (*çâbar*) means "to heap up." (See Exod. viii. 10.)

**At the entering in of the gate.**—The place of public business, where all the citizens would see them. (Comp. chap. vii. 3; 1 Kings xxii. 10.) But perhaps not the city gate, but the gate of the palace is to be understood. Parallels to this deed of Jehu are not wanting in the history of modern Persia. (Comp. 1 Sam. xvii. 54; 2 Macc. xv. 30; and the comparatively recent custom in our own country of fixing up the heads of traitors on London Bridge.)

(9) **And stood.**—Or, *took his place*—*i.e.* (according to Reuss), sat as judge in the palace gateway, according to royal custom, and gave audience to the people.

The citizens would naturally be struck with consternation at the sight of the two ghastly pyramids in front of the palace, and would crowd together in expectancy at the gates. Jehu goes forth to justify himself, and calm their fears.

**Ye be righteous**—*i.e.*, guiltless in respect of the deaths of these men, and therefore have nothing to dread. Thenius explains: "Ye are just, and therefore will judge justly." Others render: "Are ye righteous?" implying that Jehu wished to make the people guilty of the massacre of the princes, while owning his own murder of the king.

**I.**—Emphatic: *I on my part*; or, *I indeed.*

**But who slew all these?**—*Slew* should be *smote.* Jehu professes astonishment, by way of self-exculpation. He hints that as Jehovah had foretold the destruction of the house of Ahab, He must have brought it to pass; and therefore nobody is to blame. (See next verse.)

(10) **Fall unto the earth.**—As a dead thing; man, bird, or beast. (Comp. Matt. x. 29.)

**Nothing of the word of the Lord.**—No part of Elijah's prediction shall fail of accomplishment.

**For the Lord hath done.**—Rather, *and Jehovah, He hath done*; or, *and Jehovah it is who hath done.*

(11) **So.**—Rather, *And.* The verse relates further massacres.

**In Jezreel.**—The seat of the court.

**His great men**—*i.e.*, high officials of his court; persons who owed their exaltation to him.

**Kinsfolks.**—Rather, *his friends* (literally, *his known ones*; "familiares ejus").

**Priests.**—See Notes on 2 Sam. viii. 18; 1 Kings iv. 5; 1 Chron. xviii. 17.

his great men, and his ¹kinsfolks, and his priests, until he left him none remaining. ⁽¹²⁾ And he arose and departed, and came to Samaria. *And* as he *was* at the ²shearing house in the way, ⁽¹³⁾ Jehu ³met with the brethren of Ahaziah king of Judah, and said, Who *are* ye? And they answered, We *are* the brethren of Ahaziah; and we go down ⁴to salute the children of the king and the children of the queen. ⁽¹⁴⁾ And he said, Take them alive. And they took them alive, and slew them at the pit of the shearing house, *even* two and forty men; neither left he any of them.

| | |
|---|---|
| 1 Or, *acquaintance.* | |
| 2 Heb., *house of shepherds binding sheep.* | |
| 3 Heb., *found.* | |
| 4 Heb., *to the peace of, &c.* | |
| 5 Heb., *found.* | |
| 6 Heb., *blessed.* | |

⁽¹⁵⁾ And when he was departed thence, he ⁵lighted on Jehonadab the son of Rechab *coming* to meet him: and he ⁶saluted him, and said to him, Is thine heart right, as my heart *is* with thy heart? And Jehonadab answered, It is. If it be, give *me* thine hand. And he gave *him* his hand; and he took him up to him into the chariot. ⁽¹⁶⁾ And he said, Come with me, and see my zeal for the LORD. So they made him ride in his chariot.

⁽¹⁷⁾ And when he came to Samaria, he slew all that remained unto Ahab in Samaria, till he had destroyed him, ac-

---

**None remaining.**—*No survivor.*

⁽¹²⁾ **And he arose ... and came.**—So the Syriac, rightly. The common Hebrew text has, "And he arose and came and departed."

**And as he was at the shearing house in the way.**—Rather, *He was at Beth-eqed-haroim on the way.* The Targum renders: "He was at the shepherds' meeting-house on the way." The place was probably a solitary building, which served as a *rendezvous* for the shepherds of the neighbourhood. (The root '*aqad* means "to bind," or "knot together;" hence the common explanation of the name is "the shepherds' *binding house*," *i.e.,* the place where they *bound* their sheep for the shearing. But the idea of *binding* is easily connected with that of *meeting, gathering together*: comp. our words *band, knot.*) The LXX. has: "He was at Baith-akad (or *Baithakath*) of the shepherds." Eusebius mentions a place called *Beithakad,* fifteen Roman miles from Legio (*Lejjûn*), identical with the present *Beit-kâd,* six miles east of *Jenin,* in the plain of Esdraelon; but this seems too far off the route from Jezreel to Samaria, which passes *Jenin.*

⁽¹³⁾ **Jehu met with.**—Literally, *And Jehu found.*

**The brethren of Ahaziah king of Judah**—*i.e.,* Ahaziah's *kinsmen.* His brothers, in the strict sense of the word, were slain by a troop of Arabs, in the lifetime of his father Jehoram (2 Chron. xxi. 17, xxii. 1). (See the Notes on 2 Chron. xxii. 8.)

**We go down.**—Rather, *we have come down.*

**To salute**—*i.e.,* to inquire after their health, to visit them.

**The children of the king**—*i.e.,* the sons of Joram.

**The children of the queen.**—Literally, *the sons of the mistress (gebirah)*—*i.e.,* the sons of the queen-mother, Jezebel, and so Joram's brothers. Both these and the former are included in the "sons of Ahab" whom Jehu slew.

The news of the taking of Ramoth, and of Joram's convalescence, may have reached Jerusalem, and induced these princes to make a visit of pleasure to the court of Jezreel, not suspecting the events which had meanwhile happened with the headlong rapidity characteristic of Jehu's action.

⁽¹⁴⁾ **Take them alive.**—Perhaps they made some show of resistance. Jehu slew them because of their connection with the doomed house of Ahab. Keil thinks he dreaded their conspiring with the partisans of the fallen dynasty in Samaria.

**Slew them at the pit of the shearing house.** —Literally, *slaughtered them into the cistern of Beth-*

eked. Either they cut their throats over the cistern, or threw the corpses into it.

**Two and forty.**—Curiously parallel with chap. ii. 24; and perhaps a definite for an indefinite number.

⁽¹⁵⁾ **Jehonadab the son of Rechab.**— Comp. Jer. xxxv. 6—11; and 1 Chron. ii. 55. Ewald supposes that the Rechabites were one of the new societies formed after the departure of Elijah for the active support of the true religion. Their founder in this sense was Jonadab, who, despairing of being able to practise the legitimate worship in the bosom of the community, retired into the desert with his followers, and, like Israel of old, preferred the rough life of tents to all the allurements of city life. Only unusual circumstances could induce them (like their founder, in the present instance) to re-enter the circle of common life. "The son of Rechab" means *the Rechabite.*

**And he saluted him.**—It was important to Jehu to be seen acting in concert with a man revered for sanctity, and powerful as a leader of the orthodox party.

**Is thine heart right, as my heart is with thy heart?**—The Hebrew is: *Is there with thy heart right (sincerity)?* but this does not agree with the rest of the question. Some MSS. omit the particle *'eth* ("with"); but the original reading is probably preserved in the Vatican LXX : "Is thy heart right [*i.e.,* sincere, honest] with my heart, as my heart with thy heart?" This secures a parallelism of expression. (Syriac: "Is there in thy heart sincerity, like that of my heart with thy heart?")

**If it be.**—Literally, *An it be* (the old English idiom, *i.e., and it be*). Jehu makes this reply. The LXX. (Alex.) has: "And Jehu said;" Vulg., *saith he;* Syriac, "It is, and it is ; and he said to him" (perhaps an accidental transposition).

**Give me thine hand.**—As a pledge of good faith and token of amity. Striking hands sealed a compact. (Comp. Isa. ii. 6; and Cheyne's Note.)

⁽¹⁶⁾ **See.**— Rather, *look on at.*

**My zeal for the Lord.**—Jehu addresses Jehonadab as a notoriously staunch adherent of the old faith.

**They made him ride.**—The Syriac, LXX., and Arabic read, "he made him ride;" the Vulg. is ambiguous; the Targum agrees with the Hebrew text, which may mean that Jehu's followers assisted Jehonadab (who was probably an aged sheikh) to mount the chariot.

⁽¹⁷⁾ **And when he came ... he slew.**—Literally, *And he entered Samaria, and smote.*

cording to the saying of the LORD, which he spake to Elijah.

(18) And Jehu gathered all the people together, and said unto them, Ahab served Baal a little; *but* Jehu shall serve him much. (19) Now therefore call unto me all the prophets of Baal, all his servants, and all his priests; let none be wanting: for I have a great sacrifice *to do* to Baal; whosoever shall be wanting, he shall not live. But Jehu did *it* in subtilty, to the intent that he might destroy the worshippers of Baal. (20) And Jehu said, ¹Proclaim a solemn assembly for Baal. And they proclaimed *it*. (21) And Jehu sent through all Israel: and all the worshippers of Baal came, so that there was not a man left that came not. And they came into the house of Baal; and the house of Baal was ²full from one end to another. (22) And he said unto him that *was* over the vestry, Bring forth vestments for all the worshippers of Baal. And he brought them forth vestments. (23) And Jehu went, and Jehonadab the son of Rechab, into the house of Baal, and said unto the worshippers of Baal, Search, and look that there be here with you none of the servants of the LORD, but the worshippers of Baal only. (24) And when they went in to offer sacrifices and burnt offerings, Jehu appointed fourscore men without, and said, *If any of the men*

1 Heb., *Sanctify*.

2 Or, *so full, that they stood mouth to mouth*.

---

**Ahab.**—Again put for the house or family so called. Some MSS. and the Syriac express it so, reading "the house of Ahab." (Comp. 1 Kings xv. 29.)

(18) **Ahab served Baal a little; but Jehu shall serve him much.**—Ahab had, as the people well knew, served Baal more than a little; but the antithesis was not too strong for Jehu's hidden meaning. He was thinking of his intended holocaust of human victims (verse 25).

(19) **Call unto me all the prophets of Baal.**—Comp. the similar convocation of the prophets of the Baal and Asherah by the prophet Elijah, 1 Kings xviii. 19 seq.

**His servants.**—The same word as "worshippers," *infra*.

**To do.**—Omit.

**To Baal.**—*For the Baal*.

**But Jehu did it.**—Or, *Now Jehu had done it*; a parenthesis.

**In subtilty.**—Or, *in guile, treacherously*. The word ('*oqbāh*) occurs only here. It is connected with the proper name *Jacob*. (See Gen. xxv. 26; Hosea xii. 4.) The LXX. renders literally, ἐν πτερνισμῷ, "in heeling"—*i.e.*, striking with the heel, tripping up.

(20) **Proclaim a solemn assembly.**—Rather, *Sanctify a solemn meeting* (Isa. i. 13). Every person who wished to attend would have to "sanctify," or purify, himself in due form.

**They proclaimed**—*i.e.*, gave notice of the festival by criers "through all Israel" (verse 21).

(21) **Sent through all Israel.**—The Vatican LXX. *adds*, "saying: And now all his servants, and all his priests, and all his prophets, let none be wanting; because I make a great sacrifice. Whoever shall be wanting he shall not live." This is another instance (comp. chap. ix. 16) of the insertion in the text of a marginal note belonging to another place. The note preserves the reading of the first half of verse 19 according to another MS. (See Thenius *ad loc*.)

**Was full from one end to another.**—Right as to the sense. The figure is taken from a full vessel; as if we were to say, "The house was brimful." The rim of a vessel was its *mouth*. The rim of the contents reached the rim of the vessel. Schulz explains "head to head" (comp. the margin), Gesenius, "from corner to corner" (comp. chap. xxi. 16); LXX. literally, στόμα εἰς στόμα, "mouth to mouth."

(22) **The vestry.**—The word (*meltāhāh*) occurs here only. The Targum has *chests* (*qumtrayyâ*—*i.e.*, κάμπτραι, "caskets"; comp. Latin, *capsa*). The LXX. does not translate the word.

The Syriac has, "And he said to the treasurer" (*gizbârâ*). The Vulg., "And he said to those who were over the vestments." Thenius thinks the word merely means "cell" or "storechamber," like *lishkāh*, the root of which may be cognate (1 Chron. xxviii. 12). It is said that there is an Ethiopic word, meaning "linen robe," which is connected with this curious term. Thus it would be literally "vestry."

**Brought them forth vestments.**—Literally, *the vestments*—viz., those which were customary on such occasions. Thenius supposes that festival attire from Jehu's palace is meant, rather than from the wardrobe of the Baal temple. But it seems more natural to understand that Jehu simply gives directions that all the priests and prophets should be careful to wear their distinctive dress at the festival, which was to be a specially great one. (Comp. Herod. v. 5; Sil. Ital. iii. 24 *seq*.)

(23) **And Jehu went . . . into the house**—*i.e.*, into the outer court before the temple, where all the worshippers were waiting.

**That there be here with you none of the servants of the Lord.**—This precaution of Jehu's suggests suspicion to a modern reader, but it would suggest the very contrary to the Baal-worshippers—viz., an extraordinary reverence for Baal; a dread lest some *profane* person should be present in his sanctuary.

**Servants of the Lord.**—*Worshippers of Jehovah*.

(24) **When.**—Omit.

**They went in.**—The priests and prophets went into the inner court of the Baal temple, which probably resembled in general construction that of Jehovah at Jerusalem.

**Sacrifices and burnt offerings**—*i.e.*, peace offerings and burnt offerings, which could only be offered in an open court.

**Jehu appointed fourscore men without.**—Rather, *now Jehu had set him on the outside* (of the building) *fourscore men*.

**If any of the men . . . life of him.**—Literally, *The man that escapeth of the men whom I am bringing into your hands—his life for his life!* This is a little incoherent, as is natural in energetic speech, but the

*Death of the*     II. KINGS, X.     *Prophets of Baal.*

whom I have brought into your hands escape, *he that letteth him go,* his life *shall* be for the life of him. (25) And it came to pass, as soon as he had made an end of offering the burnt offering, that Jehu said to the guard and to the captains, Go in, *and* slay them; let none come forth. And they smote them with ¹ the edge of the sword; and the guard and the captains cast *them* out, and went to the city of the house of Baal. (26) And they brought forth the ² images out of the house of Baal, and burned them. (27) And they brake down the image of Baal, and brake down the house of Baal, and made it a draught house unto this day.

(28) Thus Jehu destroyed Baal out of Israel. (29) Howbeit *from* the sins of Jeroboam the son of Nebat, who made Israel to sin, Jehu departed not from after them, *to wit,* the golden calves that *were* in Beth-el, and that *were* in Dan.

(30) And the LORD said unto Jehu, Because thou hast done well in executing *that which is* right in mine eyes, *and* hast done unto the house of Ahab according to all that *was* in mine heart, thy children of the fourth *generation* shall sit on the throne of Israel. (31) But Jehu ³ took no heed to walk in the law of the LORD God of Israel with all his

¹ Heb., *the mouth.*
² Heb., *statues.*
³ Heb., *observed not.*

---

sense is clear. Thenius, however, suggests that the verb "escapeth" should be pointed as a *transitive* form (*pihel* instead of *niphal*). This gives: "The man that letteth escape any of the men," &c., an improvement that may be right, although the old versions agree with the present Hebrew pointing of the word.

(25) **As soon as he had made an end.**—The Syriac has, *when they* (i.e., the Baal priests) *had made an end.* This is probably right. (Comp. the beginning of verse 24). We can hardly suppose with Ewald that Jehu personally offered sacrifices in the character of an ardent Baal-worshipper. For the massacre Jehu chose the moment when all the assembly was absorbed in worship.

**To the guard and to the captains.**—Literally, *to the runners* (or *couriers*) *and to the adjutants* (or *squires*; chap. ix. 25). (Comp. 1 Kings ix. 22.) The royal guardsmen and their officers are meant.

**Cast them out.**—That is, threw the dead bodies out of the temple. This is the explanation of the Targum and the other versions. Thenius asks why this should be specially mentioned, and proposes to understand the verb intransitively, "rushed out," which suits very well with what follows.

**And went to the city of the house of Baal.**—The word *city* has here its original meaning, which is also that of the Greek πόλις—viz., *citadel, stronghold*; properly, a place surrounded by a ring-fence or rampart. Jehu's guards, after the completion of their bloody work in the court of the temple, rushed up the steps into the sanctuary itself, which, like the temple of Solomon, resembled a fortress. ("Ex atrio irruperunt satellites Jehu in ipsam arcem templi."—Sebastian Schmidt.) Gesenius explains the word as meaning the *temenos* or sacred enclosure of the temple, but that does not suit the context. (The origin of the word '*ir*, "city," obscure in Hebrew, is revealed by the cuneiform inscriptions in the Accadian word *erim* or *eri,* meaning "foundation," and *Uru—i.e.,* Ur, a proper name, meaning "the city.")

(26) **The images.**—Rather, *the pillars*; which were of wood, and had a sacred significance. (Comp. Hosea iii. 4.) "In primitive times a pillar was the distinguishing mark of a holy place. Idolatrous pillars were commanded to be destroyed (Exod. xxiii. 24), but most critics think that pillars to Jehovah were quite allowable till the time of Hezekiah or Josiah, to which they assign the Book of Deuteronomy. (Comp. Deut. xvi. 21, 22.) At any rate, the prophet (Isaiah) gives an implicit sanction to the erection of a sacred pillar in Egypt" (*Cheyne's* Note on Isaiah xix. 19). The LXX. has the singular here (τὴν στήλην) and the plural in the next verse. The Syriac has the singular "statue" in both.

(27) **The image of Baal.**—Again the word is *pillar,* which in this case is the conical pillar of stone representing the Baal himself. The wooden pillars of verse 26 probably symbolised companion deities (πάρεδροι συμβώμοι) of the principal idol.

**Made it a draught house.**—By way of utter desecration. (Comp. Ezek. vi. 11; Dan. ii. 5.)

**Unto this day.**—On the bearing of this phrase, see the Introduction to the Books of Kings.

(28) **Thus Jehu destroyed Baal.**—Objectively considered, the slaughter of the servants of Baal was in perfect harmony with the Law; but, subjectively, the motive which influenced Jehu was thoroughly selfish. The priests and prophets of Baal in Israel, as depending entirely on the dynasty of Ahab, the king who had originally introduced the Baal-worship, might prove dangerous to Jehu. By exterminating them he might hope to secure the whole-hearted allegiance of the party that stood by the legitimate worship. His maintenance of the *cultus* established by Jeroboam (verse 29) proves that he acted from policy rather than religious zeal.

(29—36) Jehu's reign and death.

(29) **Howbeit from the sins of Jeroboam.**—Comp. 1 Kings xii. 28, *seq.,* xv. 26, 30, 34. Jehu maintained the worship at Bethel and Dan on the same grounds of state policy as the kings who preceded him.

**Howbeit.**—*Only*; the word constantly used by the redactor to qualify his estimate of the conduct of the kings. (Comp. chap. xii, 3, xiv. 4, xv. 4.) The verse is, therefore, a parenthetic qualification of the approval implied in verse 28.

(30) **And the Lord said.**—Perhaps through Elisha.

**And hast done.**—So the Syriac and Arabic versions. The Hebrew wants the *and.*

**Thy children of the fourth generation.**—The fulfilment of this oracle is noticed in chap. xv. 12. (Comp. the words of the commandment, "visiting the sins of the fathers upon the children unto the third and fourth generation;" Exod. xx. 5.)

(31) **But Jehu took no heed.**—Or, *Now Jehu had not been careful.* This verse, rather than the next, begins a new paragraph.

*Death of Jehu.*  II. KINGS, XI.  *Joash hidden.*

heart: for he departed not from the sins of Jeroboam, which made Israel to sin.

(32) In those days the LORD began ¹to cut Israel short: and Hazael smote them in all the coasts of Israel; (33) from Jordan ²eastward, all the land of Gilead, the Gadites, and the Reubenites, and the Manassites, from Aroer, which is by the river Arnon, ³ even Gilead and Bashan.

(34) Now the rest of the acts of Jehu, and all that he did, and all his might, *are* they not written in the book of the chronicles of the kings of Israel? (35) And Jehu slept with his fathers: and they buried him in Samaria. And Jehoahaz his son reigned in his stead. (36) And ⁴the time that Jehu reigned over Israel in Samaria *was* twenty and eight years.

CHAPTER XI.—(1) And when ᵃAthaliah the mother of Ahaziah saw that her son was dead, she arose and destroyed all the ⁵seed royal. (2) But Jehosheba, the daughter of king Joram, sister of Ahaziah, took Joash the son of Ahaziah, and stole him from among the king's sons which were slain; and they hid him, *even* him and his nurse, in the bed-

---

1 Heb., *to cut off the ends.*
B.C. cir. 860.
2 Heb., *toward the rising of the sun.*
3 Or, *even to Gilead and Bashan.*
B.C. 884.
4 Heb., *the days were.*
a 2 Chron. 22. 10.
5 Heb., *seed of the kingdom.*
B.C. 856.

---

**To walk in the law**—*i.e.*, the Mosaic law, which forbids the use of images, such as the "calves."

**With all his heart.**—This is explained by the next sentence. He had done honour to Jehovah by extirpating the foreign Baal-worship, but he supported the irregular mode of worshipping Jehovah established by Jeroboam as the state religion of the Northern kingdom.

**For.**—Not in the Hebrew.

(32) **In those days.**—As a vassal and ally of Assyria (see Notes on chap. ix. 2), Jehu drew upon himself the active hostility of Hazael. (See Note on chap. viii. 15.) Schröder remarks that it was quite natural for the Israelite sovereign to "throw himself into the arms of distant Assyria, in order to get protection against his immediate neighbour Syria, Israel's hereditary foe." Comp. the similar conduct of Ahaz as against Pekah and Rezin (chap. xvi. 7). From the point of view of the sacred writer, this verse states *the consequence* of Jehu's neglect of "walking in Jehovah's instruction with all his heart" (verse 31).

**The Lord began.**—Through Hazael and the Syrians. (Comp. Isa. vii. 17, 20, x. 5, 6.)

**To cut Israel short.**—Literally, *to cut off in Israel*—*i.e.*, to cut off part after part of Israelite territory. (The verb means *to cut off the extremities*, Prov. xxvi. 6.) This refers to the conquests of Hazael. The Targum explains, "The wrath of the Lord began to be strong against Israel;" and the Vulg. has, "tædere super Israel." Thenius conjectures from this that we should read, "to be wrathful with Israel;" but the construction would not then be usual.

**In all the coasts.**—Rather, *on the whole border*—*scil.*, conterminous with Syria.

(33) **From Jordan eastward.**—This verse defines the border land which Hazael ravaged, and, in fact, occupied. It was the land east of the Jordan, that is to say, all the land of Gilead, which was the territory of Reuben, Gad, and the half tribe of Manasseh.

**From Aroer.**—Aroer, now *'Arâ'îr*, on the Arnon, was the southern limit of Gilead, which extended northward to Mount Hermon, and included Bashan. "Even (both) Gilead and Bashan," is added to make it clear that the whole of the land east of the Jordan, and not merely Gilead in the narrower sense, was conquered by Hazael. These conquests of Hazael were characterised by great barbarity. (Comp. Amos i. 3—5, and Elisha's prediction of the same, chap. viii. 12, *supra*.) Ewald thinks Hazael took advantage of the internal troubles at the outset of the reign to effect his conquests. But a man of Jehu's energy must soon have established domestic tranquillity.

(34) **All his might.**—Comp. chap. xx. 20; 1 Kings xv. 23; some MSS., the Targum, and Vulg. omit "all." The LXX. *adds*: "and the conspiracies which he conspired."

(36) **In Samaria.**—The Hebrew puts this phrase last, perhaps to indicate by emphasis that Jehu made Samaria, *and not Jezreel*, the seat of his court.

XI.

ATHALIAH USURPS THE THRONE OF JUDAH, BUT IS DEPOSED AND SLAIN, AND HER GRANDSON JOASH CROWNED, THROUGH THE INSTRUMENTALITY OF THE HIGH PRIEST JEHOIADA. (Comp. 2 Chron. xxii. 10, xxiii. 21.)

(1) **And when Athaliah . . . saw.**—Rather, *Now Athaliah . . . had seen.* (The *and*, which the common Hebrew text inserts before the verb, is merely a mistaken repetition of the last letter of Ahaziah. Many MSS. omit it.)

As to Athaliah and her evil influence on her husband Jehoram, see chap. viii. 18, 26, 27. By her ambition and her cruelty she now shows herself a worthy daughter of Jezebel.

**Her son.**—Ahaziah (chap. ix. 27). The history of the Judæan monarchy is resumed from that point.

**Destroyed all the seed royal.**—"The seed of the kingdom" (see margin) means all who might set up claims to the succession. Ahaziah's brothers had been slain by the Arabs (2 Chron. xxi. 17); and his "kinsmen" by Jehu (chap. x. 14). Those whom Athaliah slew would be for the most part Ahaziah's own sons, though other relatives are not excluded by the term.

(2) **But Jehosheba . . . sister of Ahaziah.**—By a different mother (see Josephus). Athaliah would not have allowed *her* daughter to marry the high priest of Jehovah. (Comp. verse 3 with 2 Chron. xxii. 11.) This marriage with a sister of the king shows what almost royal dignity belonged to the high priest's office.

**The king's sons which were slain.**—Rather, *which were to be put to death.* At the time when the order for slaying the princes had been given, Jehosheba (or Jehoshabeath; Chronicles) concealed the infant Joash. The fact of his infancy caused him to be overlooked. [The Hebrew text here reads by mistake a word meaning deaths (Jer. xvi. 4). Chronicles supports the Hebrew margin.]

chamber from Athaliah, so that he was not slain. ⁽³⁾ And he was with her hid in the house of the LORD six years. And Athaliah did reign over the land.

⁽⁴⁾ And ᵃthe seventh year Jehoiada sent and fetched the rulers over hundreds, with the captains and the guard, and brought them to him into the house of the LORD, and made a covenant with them, and took an oath of them in the house of the LORD, and shewed them the king's son. ⁽⁵⁾ And he commanded them, saying, This *is* the thing that ye shall do; A third part of you that enter in on the sabbath shall even be keepers of the watch of the king's house; ⁽⁶⁾ and a third part *shall be* at the gate of Sur; and a third part at the gate behind the

*a* 2 Chron. 23. 1.

B.C. 878.

---

**And they hid him.**—This clause is out of its place here. The Hebrew is, *him and his nurse in the chamber of the beds; and they hid him from Athaliah, and he was not put to death.* Clearly the word, "and she put," supplied in Chronicles, has fallen out before this. The Targum and Syriac read, "and she hid him and his nurse," &c.

**In the bedchamber.**—*In the chamber of beds*, *i.e.*, the room in the palace where the mattresses and the coverlets were kept, according to a custom still prevalent in the East. This chamber being unoccupied was the nearest hiding-place at first. The babe was afterwards secretly conveyed within the Temple precincts.

⁽³⁾ **And he was with her**—*i.e.*, with Jehosheba his aunt. The words "in the house of the Lord" should immediately follow. The word "hid" is connected with "six years" in the Hebrew, and relates to the infant prince only. Joash was with his aunt "in the house of the Lord"—*i.e.*, in one of the chambers allotted to the priests, perhaps even in the high priest's residence, which may have been within the sacred precincts. Thenius assumes that the statement of Chronicles, that Jehosheba was wife of the high priest, has no other ground than a "traditional interpretation" of these words; and asserts that Jehosheba was herself obliged to share the asylum of the infant prince in order to escape the vengeance of Athaliah. But it is certain that the chronicler had better authority than mere tradition for his important additions to the history of the kings. (See Note on 2 Chron. xxii. 11.)

**Did reign.**—*Was reigning.*

⁽⁴⁾ **And the seventh year.**—When perhaps discontent at Athaliah's tyranny had reached a climax.

**Jehoiada.**—The high priest (verse 9). The curious fact that his rank is not specified here upon the *first* mention of his name, suggests the inference that in the original authority of this narrative he had been mentioned as high priest, and husband of Jehosheba, at the outset of the story, as in 2 Chron. xxii. 11.

**The rulers over hundreds, with the captains and the guard.**—Rather, *the centurions of the Carians and the Couriers*—*i.e.*, the officers commanding the royal guard. The terms rendered "Carians" and "Couriers" are obscure. Thenius prefers to translate the first "executioners." (Comp. Notes on 1 Kings i. 38; 2 Sam. viii. 18, xv. 18, xvi. 6; 1 Chron. xviii. 17.) Thenius argues against the idea that so patriotic and pious a king as David could have employed foreign and heathen soldiers as his body-guard. But did not David himself serve as a mercenary with Achish, king of Gath, and commit his parents to the care of the king of Moab? And would not the mercenaries who enlisted in the guard of the Israelite sovereigns adopt the religion of their new country? (Comp. the case of Uriah *thè Hittite*.) The apparently *gentilic* ending of the words rendered "Cherethites and Pelethites" in Samuel, and that rendered "captains" in this place, Thenius explains as marking an adjective denoting *position* or *class*. It may be so, but *sub judice lis est*.

**Made a covenant with them.**—The chronicler gives the names of the centurions. His account of the whole transaction, while generally coinciding with that given here, presents certain striking differences, of which the most salient is the prominence assigned to the priests and Levites in the matter. These deviations are explicable on the assumption that the chronicler drew his information from a large historical compilation somewhat later than the Books of Kings, and containing much more than they contain, though mainly based upon the same annalistic sources. The compilers of the two canonical histories were determined in their choice of materials and manner of treatment by their individual aims and points of view, which differed considerably. (See the Introductions to Kings and Chronicles.) At the same time, it must not be forgotten that the account before us is the older and more original, and, therefore, the more valuable regarded as mere history.

⁽⁵, ⁶⁾ Three companies of the guards to be stationed at the three approaches to the palace.

⁽⁵⁾ **A third part of you . . . king's house.**—Rather, *the third of you who come in on the Sabbath shall keep the ward of the king's house.* (Reading *v'shām'rû*, as in verse 7.) The troops of the royal guard regularly succeeded each other on duty just as they do in modern European capitals. That the Sabbath was the day on which they relieved each other is known only from this passage; but the priestly and Levitical guilds did the same, and their organisation in many ways resembled that of an army.

**The watch of the king's house.**—There were two places to be occupied for the success of the present movement—viz., the royal palace and the Temple, "the king's house" and "the house of the Lord." In the former was Athaliah, the usurping queen, whose movements must be closely watched, and whose adherents must be prevented from occupying and defending the palace; in the latter, the young heir to the throne, who must be protected from attack. That "the king's house" here means the palace proper is evident from verses 16 and 19, and, indeed, from the whole narrative. The LXX. adds, "at the entry" (ἐν τῷ πυλῶνι) —*i.e.*, the grand entrance to the palace itself. This is at least a correct gloss, and may be part of the original text.

⁽⁶⁾ **And a third part shall be at the gate of Sur.**—Or, *and the third* (shall be on guard) *at the gate of Sur.* Instead of *Sûr* ("turning aside") Chronicles has *Jesôd* ("foundation"). The gate Sur was apparently a *side exit* from the court of the palace, such as may be seen in the old Egyptian palaces at

guard: so shall ye keep the watch of the house, ¹that it be not broken down. ⁽⁷⁾ And two ²³parts of all you that go forth on the sabbath, even they shall keep the watch of the house of the LORD about the king. ⁽⁸⁾ And ye shall compass the king round about, every man with his weapons in his hand: and he that cometh within the ranges, let him be slain: and be ye with the king as he goeth out and as he cometh in.

⁽⁹⁾ And the captains over the hundreds did according to all *things* that Jehoiada the priest commanded: and they took every man his men that were to come in on the sabbath, with them that should go out on the sabbath, and came to Jehoiada the priest. ⁽¹⁰⁾ And to the captains over hundreds did the priest give king David's spears and shields, that *were* in the temple of the LORD. ⁽¹¹⁾ And the guard stood, every man with his weapons in his hand, round about the king, from the right ⁴corner of the temple to the left corner of the temple, *along* by the altar and the temple. ⁽¹²⁾ And he brought forth the king's son, and put the crown upon him, and *gave him* the testimony; and they made him king, and anointed him; and they

1 Or, *from breaking up.*
2 Or, *companies.*
3 Heb., *hands.*
4 Heb., *shoulder.*

---

*Medinat-Abû* and *Karnak.* "Jesod" is another name for the same side-door, or, as is far more likely, a textual corruption of "Sur."

**And a third part at the gate behind the guard.**—Literally, *and the third at the gate behind the Couriers.* In verse 19 "the gate of the Couriers" is mentioned, apparently as the principal entrance to the palace enclosure. That gate and this one are probably the same. It is here called "the gate *behind* the Couriers" because a guard was usually stationed in front of it. Perhaps the word "behind" has originated in a mere echo of the word "gate" (*'aḥar, sha'ar*), and should be omitted as an error of transcription.

**So shall ye keep the watch of the house.**—Thus shall ye—the three divisions of the guards, entering on duty on the Sabbath—guard the entrances and exits of the royal palace.

**That it be not broken down.**—The Hebrew is only the one word *massāh*, which occurs nowhere else. It appears to mean "repulse," "warding off," and is probably a marginal gloss on "watch" (*mishmèreth*), explaining its nature—viz., that the guards were to keep back any one who tried to enter the palace buildings. Gesenius paraphrases, "ad depellendum populum" (*zum Abwehren*). Thenius suggests the reading "and repel"! *scil.,* "all comers" (*ûnᵉsôah* for *massāh*). He should have written *wᵉnāsôah.*

(7, 8) The whole body of guards relieved on the Sabbath are to guard the Temple and the young prince.

⁽⁷⁾ **And two parts of all you . . . sabbath.**—Rather, *and the two branches among you, all that go out on the Sabbath.* The two "branches" means the two fundamental divisions—viz., Carians (or executioners) and Couriers. The troops relieved on the Sabbath were not to be posted in three companies at three different points, like those who came on duty in their place; but they were to form in two ranks—Carians on one side and Couriers on the other—for the purpose of guarding the Temple, and especially the king's person.

**About.**—Literally, *in the direction of*—i.e., with regard to, over. "The house of the Lord" is obviously contrasted with "the king's house" (verse 5).

⁽⁸⁾ **Ye shall compass the king round about.**—They were to form two lines, between which the king might walk safely from the Temple to the palace.

**The ranges.**—Rather, *the ranks—scil.,* the two lines of the guard formed for the protection of the king. If any one attempted to force his way through the ranks in order to attack the king he was to be slain.

**Be ye with the king . . . cometh in.**—When he leaves the Temple, and when he enters the palace.

(9, 10) The preparations for carrying out the above arrangements.

⁽⁹⁾ **The captains over the hundreds**—i.e., the centurions of the royal guard (verse 4). So in verse 10.

**Commanded.**—*Had commanded.*

⁽¹⁰⁾ **King David's spears and shields.**—The Hebrew has *spear,* but Chronicles has the plural, which appears correct. "Shields" should perhaps be *arms.* (Comp. 2 Sam. viii. 7; 2 Chron. xxiii. 9.) The arms which David had laid up in the Temple as spoils of war were now to be used, appropriately enough, for the restoration of David's heir to the throne. Possibly, as Bähr suggests, the guards who came off duty at the palace had left their weapons there.

⁽¹¹⁾ **The guard.**—Literally, *the Couriers;* not therefore the Levites.

**Corner.**—Rather, *side.*

**Along by.**—*At.*

**And the temple.**—*And at the Temple.* The guard formed in two lines, extending from the south wall to the north wall of the court, one line standing at the altar of burnt offering, which was near the entrance, the other at the sanctuary itself. The words "round about the king" are anticipative.

⁽¹²⁾ **And he brought forth the king's son.**—When the two lines were formed, cutting off the interior of the Temple from the court, Jehoiada led forth the young prince into the protected space between them; perhaps from a side chamber, or perhaps from the sanctuary itself.

**And gave him the testimony.**—The Hebrew has simply *and the testimony.* Kimchi explains this to mean *a royal robe;* other rabbis think of a phylactery on the coronet. (See Deut. vi. 8.) Thenius says, *the Law*—i.e., a book in which were written Mosaic ordinances, and which was held in a symbolic manner over the king's head after he had been crowned. (See Note on 2 Chron. xxiii. 11.)

**Anointed him.**—The chronicler says it was "Jehoiada and his sons" who did it. It is difficult to see what objection can fairly be taken to this explanatory addition, unless we are to suppose that, although the high priest was present, the soldiers of the guard

*Athaliah*      II. KINGS, XI.      *is Slain.*

clapped their hands, and said, ¹God save the king. <sup>(13)</sup> And when Athaliah heard the noise of the guard *and* of the people, she came to the people into the temple of the LORD. <sup>(14)</sup> And when she looked, behold, the king stood by a pillar, as the manner *was*, and the princes and the trumpeters by the king, and all the people of the land rejoiced, and blew with trumpets: and Athaliah rent her clothes, and cried, Treason, Treason. <sup>(15)</sup> But Jehoiada the priest commanded the captains of the hundreds, the officers of the host, and said unto them, Have her forth without the ranges: and him that followeth her kill with the sword. For the priest had said, Let her not be slain in the house of the LORD. <sup>(16)</sup> And they laid hands on her; and she went by the way by the which the horses came into the king's house: and there was she slain.

<sup>(17)</sup> And Jehoiada made a covenant between the LORD and the king and the people, that they should be the LORD'S people; between the king also and the

1 Heb., *Let the king live.*

---

poured the sacred oil on the king's head. Yet Thenius adduces it as an instance of the "petty spirit of the chronist," accusing him of inserting the words "for fear anybody should think of an anointing by unconsecrated hands." Surely such criticism as this is itself both "petty" and "wilful." The words probably stood in the chronicler's principal source.

**God save the king.**—Literally, *Vivat rex.* (1 Kings i. 25.)

<sup>(13)</sup> **Of the guard and of the people.**—This is correct. The *and* has fallen out of the Hebrew text.

**The guard.**—The Aramaic form of the plural, rare in prose, occurs here. (Comp. 1 Kings xi. 33.) In 2 Chron. xxiii. 11 the words are transposed. This gives a different sense—viz., "of the people *running together*," to which is added, "and acclaiming the king." The chronicler may have found this in the work he followed, but the text before us seems preferable, as the word "runners" (Couriers) throughout the account means the royal guard.

**The people.**—See Note on verse 14.

**She came . . . into the temple.**—Evidently, therefore, the palace was hard by the Temple. (See Note on verse 16.)

<sup>(14)</sup> **And when she looked.**—Having entered the court, the whole scene met her astonished gaze.

**The king stood by a pillar.**—Rather, *the king was standing on the stand.* (Comp. chap. xxiii. 3.) The stand (Vulg., "tribunal") was apparently a dais reserved for the king only, which stood before the great altar, at the entrance to the inner court (2 Chron. xxiii. 13, vi. 13). Thenius maintains that the king stood on the top of the flight of steps leading into the sanctuary. Why, then, does not the text express this meaning more exactly? (Comp. chap. ix. 13.)

**As the manner was**—*i.e.*, according to the custom on such occasions.

**The princes.**—The chiefs of the people, *not* the centurions of the royal guard, who have their *full* designation throughout the chapter. (See verses 4, 9, 10, 15, 19.) The present account is nowhere stated that the nobles were present in the Temple; but this sudden mention of them, as if they had been present throughout the proceedings, is in striking harmony with the chronicler's express assertion that, after their conference with Jehoiada, the centurions of the guard assembled the Levites and *the heads of the clans* in the Temple (2 Chron. xxiii. 3). (The LXX. and Vulg. render "singers," because they read *shārīm*, "singers," instead of *sārīm*, "princes.")

**The trumpeters.**—Literally, *the trumpets*; as we speak of "the violins," meaning *the players* on them.

The sacred trumpets or clarions blown on solemn occasions by the priests are intended. (Comp. chap. xii. 14; Num. x. 2; 1 Chron. xv. 24.) This is an indication that the priests and Levites were present as the chronicle so conspicuously represents, and as, indeed, was to be expected on an occasion when the high priest took the lead, and when the scene of action was the Temple. The acting classes of priests and Levitical musicians, warders, and priestly attendants must certainly have participated in the proceedings.

**All the people of the land.**—Secrecy was no longer necessary, as Thenius supposes, when once the centurions of the guard had heartily taken up with the plot.

**Rejoiced . . . blew.**—*Rejoicing . . . blowing.*

**Treason.**—Literally, *Conspiracy.*

<sup>(15)</sup> **The captains of the hundreds, the officers of the host.**—The centurions of the royal guard are called "the officers of the host" (comp. Num. xxxi. 14) to signify that it was they who gave effect to the high priest's orders by communicating them to their troops.

**Have her forth without the ranges.**—Rather, *Cause her to go out between the ranks*—*i.e.*, escort her out of the sacred precincts with a guard on both sides.

**Him that followeth her**—*i.e.*, whoever shows any sympathy with her, or attempts to take her part. There might have been some of her partisans in the large gathering in the Temple court.

**For the priest had said.**—This is a parenthetic statement accounting for the order just given; and "had said" may mean "thought."

<sup>(16)</sup> **They laid hands on her.**—So the LXX. and Vulg. The Hebrew phrase means: *and they made room for her on both sides*—*i.e.*, the crowd fell back, and a lane was formed for her exit (so the Targum and Rashi).

**She went . . . king's house.**—*She entered the palace by way of the entry of the horses.* Athaliah was conducted to the royal stables which adjoined the palace, and there put to death.

<sup>(17)</sup> **A covenant.**—Rather, *the covenant.* The high priest solemnly renewed the original compact between Jehovah and the king and people—a compact which had been violated by the Baal-worship of recent reigns.

**That they should be the Lord's people.**—Comp. Deut. iv. 20; Exod. xix. 5, 6.

**Between the king also and the people.**—For the protection of their mutual rights and prerogatives. (Comp. 1 Sam. x. 25.) The king was bound to govern according to the law of Jehovah—"the testimony" which had been put upon him (verse 12),

*The Worship*           II. KINGS, XII.           *of God Restored.*

people. <sup>(18)</sup> And all the people of the land went into the house of Baal, and brake it down; his altars and his images brake they in pieces thoroughly, and slew Mattan the priest of Baal before the altars. And the priest appointed ¹officers over the house of the LORD. <sup>(19)</sup> And he took the rulers over hundreds, and the captains, and the guard, and all the people of the land; and they brought down the king from the house of the LORD, and came by the way of the gate of the guard to the king's house. And he sat on the throne of the kings. <sup>(20)</sup> And all the people of the land rejoiced, and the city was in quiet: and they slew Athaliah with the sword *beside* the king's house.

<sup>(21)</sup> Seven years old *was* Jehoash when he began to reign.

CHAPTER XII.—<sup>(1)</sup> In ªthe seventh year of Jehu Jehoash began to reign; and forty years reigned he in Jerusalem. And his mother's name *was* Zibiah of Beer-sheba. <sup>(2)</sup> And Jehoash did *that which was* right in the sight of the LORD all his days wherein Jehoiada the priest

1 Heb., *offices.*

B.C. 878.

a 2 Chron. 24. 1.

---

(Comp. Note on 2 Chron. xxiii. 16.) The people were to be loyal to the house of David.

<sup>(18)</sup> **All the people of the land went into the house of Baal.**—Immediately after the covenant had been renewed, of which the extirpation of the foreign Baal-worship was a consequence. In the fervour of their newly-awakened enthusiasm for Jehovah, the assembly may have hurried off at once to the work of demolition. It seems to be implied that the "house of Baal" stood on the Temple mount, in ostentatious rivalry with the sanctuary of Jehovah. (Comp. the introduction of idolatrous altars into the Temple itself by Manasseh, chaps. xxi. 4, 5, 7, xxiii. 12.) This house of Baal had, perhaps, been built by Athaliah. (Comp. 1 Kings xvi. 31, 32.)

**His altars . . . his images.**—Or, *its* (the Temple's) *altars . . . its images.*

**And the priest appointed officers over the house of the Lord.**—The obviously close connection of this statement with what precedes, almost proves that the sanctuary of Baal had stood within the Temple precincts, probably in the outer court. After the destruction of it, Jehoiada appointed certain overseers—probably Levites of rank—to prevent any future desecration of the Temple by the practice of idolatrous rites (comp. Ezek. viii. 5—16), or by wanton attacks of the Baal-worshippers, who might be cowed, but were certainly not exterminated (comp. 2 Chron. xxiv. 7); and to see that the legitimate *cultus* was properly carried out. (The sentence tells us what was done some time afterwards, in consequence of the reformation; thus finishing the subject in hand at the expense of the strict order of time.)

**Mattan.**—Mattan is short for Mattanbaal, "gift of Baal," a Phœnician name occurring in Punic and Assyrian inscriptions (the Muthumballes of Plautus). Comp. also *Mitinna* and *Matténa*, as names of Tyrian kings (Inscr. of Tig. Pil. ii.; Herod. vii. 98).

<sup>(19)</sup> **And he took the rulers . . . the land.**—Jehoiada now arranges a procession to escort the king in triumph from the Temple to the palace.

**The rulers . . . guard.**—Rather, *the captains of the hundreds* (the centurions) *and the Carians and the Couriers;* or, as Thenius prefers, *the lictors and the satellites.*

**They brought down the king from the house of the Lord.**—*Down* from the Temple to the bridge connecting Moriah with Zion.

**And came by the way . . . king's house.**—Rather, *and entered the king's house by way of the gate of the Couriers.* This gate, therefore, belonged not to the Temple, but to the palace, and was probably the chief entrance thereto.

**And he sat on the throne.**—The proceedings ended with the solemn enthronement of the king in the palace of his fathers. (The LXX. reads more suitably: "And they seated him on the throne;" so Chronicles.)

<sup>(20)</sup> **All the people of the land . . . the city.**—Thenius calls this an "evident contrast between the soldiery and the citizens; the former exulting in their work, the latter not lifting a finger while the idolatrous tyrant was being put to death" (connecting the first half of the verse with the second; after Ewald). But his assumption that "all the people of the land," here and in verse 14, means "the soldiery" ("die ganze in Jerusalem anwesende Kriegerische Landesmannschaft—Die Kriegsmannschaft") is certainly wrong. "The people of the land" are plainly opposed to the royal guards—"the Prætorians"—who effected the revolution, as civilians to soldiers.

**The city was in quiet.**—The citizens of Jerusalem accepted the revolution without attempting any counter movement. No doubt there was a strong element of Baal-worshippers and partisans of Athaliah in the capital. "The people of the land" (*i.e.*, probably, the people whom the centurions had called together from the country, at the instance of Jehoiada, according to 2 Chron. xxiii. 2) are contrasted with the burghers of Jerusalem. The phrase, "the city was in quiet" (or "had rest," Judges v. 31), may, however, possibly refer to the deliverance from the tyranny of Athaliah.

**And they slew Athaliah.**—Rather, *and Athaliah they had slain;* an emphatic recurrence to the real climax of the story (verse 16), by way of conclusion.

**Beside.**—Rather, *in, i.e.,* within the palace enclosure.

<sup>(21)</sup> **Seven years old was Jehoash.**—The Hebrew editions connect this verse with chapter xii.

### XII.

THE REIGN OF JEHOASH, OR JOASH. (Comp. 2 Chron. xxiv.)

<sup>(1)</sup> **Forty years.**—A common round number. David and Solomon are each said to have reigned forty years.

**His mother's name.**—The author of these short abstracts generally gives this particular in regard to the kings of Judah.

**Beer-sheba.**—A famous Simeonite sanctuary, and resort of pilgrims (Amos v. 5, viii. 14).

<sup>(2)</sup> **All his days wherein Jehoiada the priest instructed him.**—The Hebrew is ambiguous, but may certainly mean this, which is the rendering of the LXX. and Vulg. (The accent dividing the verse ought

instructed him. ⁽³⁾ But the high places were not taken away: the people still sacrificed and burnt incense in the high places.

⁽⁴⁾ And Jehoash said to the priests, All the money of the ¹²dedicated things that is brought into the house of the LORD, *even* the money of every one that passeth *the account*, ³the money that every man is set at, *and* all the money that ⁴cometh into any man's heart to bring into the house of the LORD, ⁽⁵⁾ let the priests take *it* to them, every man of his acquaintance: and

1 Or, *holy things*.
2 Heb., *holinesses*.
B.C. 856.
3 Heb., *the money of the souls of his estimation*.
4 Heb., *ascendeth upon the heart of a man*.
5 Heb., *in the twentieth year and third year*.

let them repair the breaches of the house, wheresoever any breach shall be found.

⁽⁶⁾ But it was *so, that* ⁵in the three and twentieth year of king Jehoash the priests had not repaired the breaches of the house. ⁽⁷⁾ Then king Jehoash called for Jehoiada the priest, and the *other* priests, and said unto them, Why repair ye not the breaches of the house? now therefore receive no *more* money of your acquaintance, but deliver it for the breaches of the house. ⁽⁸⁾ And the priests consented to receive no *more*

---

to fall on "the Lord" rather than on "his days.") Perhaps the peculiar form of the sentence arose in this way: the writer first set down the usual statement concerning kings who supported the worship of Jehovah, and then, remembering the evils which ensued upon the death of the high priest (2 Chron. xxiv. 17), added as a correction of that statement, "during which Jehoiada the priest instructed him." Thenius says the words *can* only be rendered, *all his life long, because Jehoiada had instructed him*. They certainly *can*, however, be rendered as our version renders them, and further, thus: "And Jehoash did . . . all his days, *whom Jehoiada the priest instructed*." But the ambiguity of the statement gave an opportunity for discrediting the chronicler.

⁽³⁾ **But.**—*Save that*; as at chap. xv. 4. (For the statement of the verse, comp. 1 Kings xv. 14.)

**Sacrificed . . . burnt.**—*Were wont to sacrifice . . . burn*. The worship of the high places continued even under the *régime* of Jehoiada.

(4—16) The restoration of the Temple.

⁽⁴⁾ **The money of the dedicated things.**—Comp. 1 Kings xv. 15.

**Is brought**—*i.e.*, from time to time. All the silver given for the purposes of the sanctuary is meant.

**Even the money of every one that passeth the account.**—Rather, *to wit, current money* (Gen. xxiii. 16). The currency at this period consisted of pieces of silver of a fixed weight. There was no such thing as a Hebrew coinage before the exile. The reason "current money" was wanted was that it might be paid out immediately to the workpeople employed in the repairs.

**The money that every man is set at.**—Literally, *each the money of the souls of his valuation, i.e.*, every kind of redemption money, such as was paid in the case of the first-born (Num. xviii. 16) and of a vow (Lev. xxvii. 2, *seq.*). In the latter case, the priest fixed the amount to be paid.

**And all the money that cometh into any man's heart to bring**—That is, all the free-will offerings in money. In 2 Chron. xxiv. 6 the revenues here specified are called "the tax of Moses . . . for the tabernacle," implying that Moses had originally instituted them. The chronicler's language, indeed, appears to indicate that he understood the money collected to have been chiefly the tax of half a shekel, which the law ordered to be paid by every male on occasion of the census (Exod. xxx. 12—16), for the good of the sanctuary.

⁽⁵⁾ **Every man of his acquaintance.**—See 2 Chron. xxiv. 5. From that passage it is evident that the chronicler understood that the priests were required to collect such moneys, each in his own city and district, year by year. Our text, taken alone, would seem to imply that persons going to the Temple to have the value of vows estimated, or to make free-will offerings, resorted to the priests whom they knew. (The word rendered "acquaintance" only occurs in this account.)

**The breaches of the house.**—The dilapidations of the Temple were serious, not because of its age—it had only stood about 130 years—but owing to the wanton attacks of Athaliah and her sons (comp. 2 Chron. xxiv. 7), who had, moreover, diverted the revenues of the sanctuary to the support of the Baal-worship.

⁽⁶⁾ **In the three and twentieth year.**—Jehoash may have ordered the restoration in his twentieth year, when he came of age. It is noticeable that he and not Jehoiada takes the initiative in the matter. The chronicler states that the king had ordered the priests *and the Levites* "to hasten the matter," but that "the Levites hastened it not."

⁽⁷⁾ **Now therefore receive no more money.**—The account of the whole transaction is not very clear, and commentators disagree upon the question of the degree of blame attaching to the priests for their neglect. It is evident, however, that the king now took the control of the funds and the work out of their hands. Probably the revenues of the sanctuary had been in a very languishing condition during the late reigns; and the priesthood had used whatever offerings they received for their own support. They would now very naturally be unwilling to appropriate any part of the revenues which they had come to regard as their own, to the work of repair. From the account in Chronicles it would not appear that any money was collected for the purpose of restoration before the king took the matter into his own hands. The idea of Thenius, that Joash wished to humble the pride of the priests by diminishing their revenues, is not contained in either narrative. But it is in itself likely that the moral tone of the whole order had degenerated in the late period of apostasy.

**But deliver it for the breaches of the house.**—Rather, *For to the dilapidation of the house ye should give it*; scil., and not apply it to any other purposes. The king's words certainly seem to throw suspicion on the priests.

⁽⁸⁾ **And the priests consented.**—No doubt they made some such explanation as is suggested in the Note

money of the people, neither to repair the breaches of the house. ⁽⁹⁾ But Jehoiada the priest took a chest, and bored a hole in the lid of it, and set it beside the altar, on the right side as one cometh into the house of the LORD: and the priests that kept the ¹door put therein all the money *that was* brought into the house of the LORD. ⁽¹⁰⁾ And it was *so*, when they saw that *there was* much money in the chest, that the king's ²scribe and the high priest came up, and they ³put up in bags, and told the money that was found in the house of the LORD. ⁽¹¹⁾ And they gave the money, being told, into the hands of them that did the work, that had the oversight of the house of the LORD: and they ⁴laid it out to the carpenters and builders, that wrought upon the house of the LORD, ⁽¹²⁾ and to masons, and hewers of stone, and to buy timber and hewed stone to repair the breaches of the house of the LORD, and for all that ⁵was laid out for the house to repair *it*. ⁽¹³⁾ Howbeit there were not made for the house of the LORD bowls of silver, snuffers, basons, trumpets, any vessels of gold, or vessels of silver, of the money *that was* brought into the house of the LORD: ⁽¹⁴⁾ but they gave that to the workmen, and repaired therewith the house of the LORD. ⁽¹⁵⁾ Moreover they reckoned not with the men, into whose hand they delivered the money to be bestowed on workmen: for they dealt faithfully. ⁽¹⁶⁾ The trespass money and sin money was not brought into the house of the LORD: it was the priests'.

1 Heb., *threshold*.
2 Or, *secretary*.
3 Heb., *bound up*
4 Heb., *brought it forth*.
5 Heb., *went forth*.

---

on verse 7, by way of clearing themselves from the suspicion of fraud; after which, they agreed to resign all connection with the business.

(9) **But.**—*And.*

**Jehoiada the priest took a chest.**—By order of the king (2 Chron. xxiv. 8).

**Beside the altar, on the right side as one cometh into the house of the Lord.**—Chronicles says: "in the gate of the house of the Lord outwards." This can hardly refer to the same position. It probably describes where the chest, which became a permanent feature of the sanctuary, stood in the time after the return from the Captivity. The chronicler adds that offerings were asked by proclamation throughout the country, and that the princes and people readily contributed.

**Put.**—Rather, *used to put*. The chest was kept locked, and the Levitical doorkeepers received the money from those who offered it, and dropped it at once into the chest. This obviated all suspicion of a possible misapplication of the contributions.

(10) **And it was so.**—Rather, *And it came to pass.* Whenever the chest was full the royal secretary and the high priest went up into the Temple, and emptied it.

**Put up in bags, and told.**—Literally, *they bound up and counted.* They put the pieces of silver into bags of a certain size, and then counted the bags, weighed, and sealed them up. These would be paid out as money. (Comp. chap. v. 23.) Instead of "they bound up," Ewald prefers the word used in Chronicles, "they emptied," which is very similar in Hebrew writing. The royal secretary came, as the king's representative, to make a record of the amount.

(11) **They gave.**—Rather, *And they used to give, i.e.,* every time they had emptied the chest.

**Being told.**—Rather, *which was weighed.*

**Them that did the work.**—Not the actual workmen, but, as is immediately explained, "those who had the oversight of the house," or were charged with the superintendence of the work.

**That wrought.**—Literally, *who were making.*

(12) **Masons . . . hewers.**—Heb., *the masons . . . the hewers.*

**Hewed stone.**—Or, *quarry stone.*

**That was laid out.**—The Hebrew tense implies that it was done *repeatedly.*

**To repair it.**—Rather, *for repair.* The word (*chozqah*) does not recur in this sense.

(13) **There were not made.**—Rather, *there used not to be made.*

**For the house.**—Literally, *in the house.*

**Bowls . . . basons.**—Comp. 1 Kings vii. 50, where the same three terms occur.

**Trumpets**—*i.e.,* the straight priestly trumpets.

**Of the money that was brought.**—The plain meaning is that the whole amount offered was expended on the *necessary* work of restoring the Temple fabric.

(14) **But they gave that to the workmen.**—Literally, *for to the doers of the work they used to give it, and they used to repair,* &c. In Chronicles it is added that, *after the repairs were finished,* the money that was left was applied to the purpose of making "spoons and vessels of gold and silver" for the house of the Lord. This certainly has the appearance of having been added to the original account, for the purpose of edifying the chronicler's contemporaries. He may, however, have found it in the compilation on which he mainly depended.

(15) **Moreover they reckoned not.**—Rather, *and they were not wont to reckon.*

**To be bestowed on workmen.**—Literally, *to give to the doers of the work.* Here the phrase "doers of the work" obviously means the artisans, not the superintendents, as in verse 11.

**They dealt faithfully.**—This is not a covert thrust at the priests, as Thenius imagines. The statement of the verse is repeated in chap. xxii. 7, in connection with the restoration of the Temple under Josiah, where the priests are not concerned in the matter at all. All that is meant is, that the officials entrusted with the oversight of the work were above suspicion, and did not belie their reputation.

(16) **The.**—The definite article should be omitted.

**Trespass money and sin money.**—See Lev. v. 15—18; Num. v. 8; Lev. vi. 26—29.

**Was not brought.**—*Was not wont to be brought; i.e.,* put into the chest for the restoration fund.

(17) Then Hazael king of Syria went up, and fought against Gath, and took it: and Hazael set his face to go up to Jerusalem. (18) And Jehoash king of Judah took all the hallowed things that Jehoshaphat, and Jehoram, and Ahaziah, his fathers, kings of Judah, had dedicated, and his own hallowed things, and all the gold *that was* found in the treasures of the house of the LORD, and in the king's house, and sent *it* to Hazael king of Syria: and he ¹went away from Jerusalem.

(19) And the rest of the acts of Joash, and all that he did, *are* they not written in the book of the chronicles of the kings of Judah? (20) And his servants arose, and made a conspiracy, and slew Joash in ²the house of Millo, which goeth down to Silla. (21) For Jozachar the son of Shimeath, and Jehozabad the son of Shomer, his servants, smote him, and he died; and they buried him with his fathers in the city of David: and Amaziah his son reigned in his stead.

CHAPTER XIII. — (1) In ³the three and twentieth year of Joash the son of Ahaziah king of Judah Jehoahaz the son of Jehu began to reign over Israel

B.C. cir. 840.

1 Heb., *went up.*

B.C. 839.

2 Or, *Beth-millo.*

B.C. 856.

3 Heb., *the twentieth year and third year.*

---

**It was the priests'.**—Literally, *to the priests they* (these moneys) *used to fall,* or *continued to accrue.* The general sense is that the priests were not deprived of their lawful revenues by the new arrangement. They received their ancient dues from the trespass and sin offerings. The change initiated by Jehoash consisted in this, that henceforth gifts intended for the sanctuary itself were kept apart from the gifts intended for the priesthood.

(17—21) Conclusion of the epitome of the reign, broken off at verse 4.

(17) **Then.**—*At that time,* viz., after the events just related. Hazael's invasion of the south followed upon his successes against Jehoahaz, who became king of the northern kingdom in the very year when Jehoash took in hand the restoration of the Temple. (Comp. verse 6 with chap. xiii. 1, 3.) It appears from 2 Chron. xxiv. 23 that the high priest Jehoiada was dead, and Jehoash had already swerved from his counsels.

**Fought against Gath.**—Which, therefore, at the time either belonged to, or was in league with, Judah. Rehoboam had included this town in his system of national defences (2 Chron. xi. 8); and it was perhaps at this time the only important outpost of the capital on the western side. Ewald assumes that the petty Philistine states had invited the intervention of Hazael between themselves and their suzerain, the king of Judah. Gaza, Ashdod, Ascalon, and Ekron, but *not* Gath, appear as Philistine kingdoms in the annals of Sennacherib and Esarhaddon, a century later. This agrees with what is stated in 2 Chron. xxvi. 6 as to Uzziah having destroyed the walls of Gath. (Comp. Amos vi. 2.)

**Set his face.**—Comp. Luke ix. 51.

**To go up to.**—Or, *against.*

(18) **The hallowed things that . . . Jehoram, and Ahaziah . . . had dedicated.**—Although these kings had sought to naturalise the Baal-worship, they had not ventured to abolish the worship of Jehovah. On the contrary, as appears from this passage, they even tried to conciliate the powerful priesthood and numerous adherents of the national religion, by dedicating gifts to the sanctuary. The fact that there was so much treasure disposable is not to be wondered at, even after the narrative of the way in which funds were raised for repairing the Temple; because the treasure in question, especially that of the Temple, appears to have been regarded as a reserve, only to be touched in case of grave national emergency like the present.

**And he went away from Jerusalem**—*i.e.,* withdrew his forces. Thenius asserts that the present expedition of Hazael is distinct from that recorded in 2 Chron. xxiv. 23, *seq.*, which he admits to be historical. But it is not said here that Hazael went in person against Jerusalem. (Comp. verse 17, "set his face to go up," *i.e., prepared* to march thither.) The serious defeat of the army of Jehoash, related in Chronicles, accounts very satisfactorily for the sacrifice of his treasures here specified; while the withdrawal of the Syrians after their victory, as told in Chronicles, is explained by the bribe which Jehoash is here said to have paid them. The two narratives thus supplement each other.

(20) **His servants.**—His immediate attendants. (Comp. chap. viii. 15.)

**Arose**—*i.e.,* against him.

**In the house of Millo.**—Or, *at Beth-Millo.* The precise locality cannot be determined. Thenius supposes that the sorely wounded (?) king had retired for greater safety into "the castle palace." Ewald says the king was murdered while engaged in the fortress. For "the Millo," see 2 Sam. v. 9; 1 Kings ix. 15. The chronicler relates that Jehoash was murdered in his bed.

**Which goeth down to Silla.**—These words convey no meaning to us, the name *Silla* being otherwise unknown. The text is probably corrupt, for *Silla* is almost exactly like *Millo* in Hebrew writing. (The Vatican LXX. omits "which goeth down.")

(21) **For Jozachar . . . smote him.**—Rather, *And Jozachar . . . it was that smote him.* The names are different in Chronicles. (See the Note on 2 Chron. xxiv. 26.) Thenius notices the curious coincidence of the names as given here with the last words of the murdered Zechariah, "Jehovah see, and avenge!" The prophet was avenged by *Jozachar* ("Jehovah remembers"), the son of *Shimeath* ("hearing"), and *Jehozabad* ("Jehovah bestows"), the son of *Shomer* ("watcher").

**With his fathers**—*i.e.,* in the city of David; but "not in the sepulchres of the kings" (2 Chron. xxiv. 25).

### XIII.

(1—3) THE REIGN OF JEHOAHAZ.

(1) **In the three and twentieth year of Joash.** —Josephus makes it the twenty-first year of Joash, but wrongly. According to chap. xii. 1, Joash succeeded in the seventh year of Jehu, and Jehu reigned twenty-eight years (chap. x. 36).

in Samaria, *and reigned* seventeen years. ⁽²⁾ And he did *that which was* evil in the sight of the LORD, and ¹followed the sins of Jeroboam the son of Nebat, which made Israel to sin; he departed not therefrom. ⁽³⁾ And the anger of the LORD was kindled against Israel, and he delivered them into the hand of Hazael king of Syria, and into the hand of Benhadad the son of Hazael, all *their* days. ⁽⁴⁾ And Jehoahaz besought the LORD, and the LORD hearkened unto him: for he saw the oppression of Israel, because the king of Syria oppressed them. ⁽⁵⁾ (And the LORD gave Israel a saviour, so that they went out from under the hand of the Syrians: and the children of Israel dwelt in their tents, ²as beforetime. ⁽⁶⁾ Nevertheless they departed not from the sins of the house of Jeroboam, who made Israel sin, *but* ³walked therein: and there ⁴remained the grove also in Samaria.) ⁽⁷⁾ Neither did he leave of the people to Jehoahaz but fifty horsemen, and ten chariots, and ten thousand footmen; for the king of Syria had destroyed them, and had made them like the dust by threshing.

⁽⁸⁾ Now the rest of the acts of Jehoahaz, and all that he did, and his might, *are* they not written in the book of the chronicles of the kings of Israel?

1 Heb., *walked after*.
2 Heb., *as yesterday, and third day*.
B.C. 849.
3 Heb., *he walked*.
B.C. cir. 842.
4 Heb., *stood*.

---

**Seventeen years.**—This agrees with chap. xiv. 1.

⁽²⁾ **And he did.**—See Notes on chap. iii. 3.

⁽³⁾ **He delivered them into the hand of Hazael.**—Comp. chap. x. 32, *seq.* The meaning is that Jehovah allowed Israel to be defeated in successive encounters with the Syrian forces, and to suffer loss of territory, but not total subjugation. According to the Assyrian *data*, Shalmaneser warred with Hazael in 842 B.C., and again in 839 B.C. (See Notes on chap. viii. 15, ix. 2.)

**All their days.**—Rather, *all the days*, i.e., continually (*not* all the days of Jehoahaz, nor of Hazael and Ben-hadad). The phrase is an indefinite designation of a long period of disaster.

⁽⁴⁾ **Besought.**—Literally, *stroked the face of;* a metaphor which occurs in Exod. xxxii. 11; 1 Kings xiii. 6.

**And the Lord hearkened unto him.**—Not, however, immediately. (See verse 7.) The Syrian invasions, which began under Jehu, were renewed again and again throughout the reign of Jehoahaz (verse 22), until the tide of conquest began to turn in the time of Joash (verse 15), whose incomplete victories (verses 17, 19, 25) were followed up by the permanent successes of his son Jeroboam II. (chap. xiv. 25—28).

The parenthesis marked in verse 5 really begins, therefore, with the words, "And the Lord hearkened." The historian added it by way of pointing out that although the prayer of Jehoahaz did not meet with immediate response, it was not ultimately ineffectual.

**For he saw the oppression.**—Comp. Exod. iii. 7; Deut. xxvi. 7.

**The king of Syria.**—Intentionally general, so as to include both Hazael and Ben-hadad III., his son (verse 24).

⁽⁵⁾ **A saviour.**—Jeroboam II., the grandson of Jehoahaz, a vigorous and successful sovereign, of whom it is said that Jehovah "saved" Israel by his hand (chap. xiv. 27).

**They went out from under the hand.**—Referring to the oppressive supremacy of Syria. From these words, and from those of verse 22, it would appear that Israel was tributary to Syria during some part of this period.

**Dwelt in their tents**—*i.e.*, in the open country. In time of war they were obliged to take refuge in strongholds and fortified cities.

**As before time.**—See Note on 1 Chron. xi. 2; Gen. xxxi. 2.

⁽⁶⁾ **Nevertheless they departed not.**—The restoration of Divine favour did not issue in the abolition of the irregular worship introduced by Jeroboam I. as the state religion of the northern kingdom. This is written, of course, from the point of view of the Judæan editor of Kings, who lived long after the events of which he is writing in the period of the exile. It does not appear from the history of Elijah and Elisha, incorporated in his work, that either of those great prophets ever protested against the worship established at Bethel and Dan.

**The house of Jeroboam**—Some MSS., the Syriac, Targum, and Arabic omit "house." But the specification of the *dynasty* is here very appropriate.

**But walked therein.**—Rather, *therein they walked;* the reading of the LXX. (Alex.), Vulg., and Targum being probably correct. It is the conduct of the *nation* that is being described.

**And there remained the grove also in Samaria.**—Rather, *and moreover the Asherah stood* (*i.e.*, *was set up*) *in Samaria*. The Asherah was the sacred tree, so often depicted in Assyrian art. It symbolised the productive principle of nature, and was sacred to Ashtoreth. With the return of peace, and the renewal of prosperity, luxury also soon reappeared, and the idolatry that specially countenanced it lifted up its head again. (See the Note on chap. xvii. 16.)

⁽⁷⁾ **Neither did he leave of the people to Jehoahaz.**—Rather, *For he had not left to Jehoahaz* (*any*) *people* (*i.e.*, war folk; 1 Kings xvi. 15). The subject appears to be Jehovah. The narrative returns, after the long parenthesis, to the statement of verse 4, "and Jehoahaz besought Jehovah (for he had not left, &c.)." Or we might render, "one had not left," *i.e.*, "there was not left."

**Fifty horsemen, and ten chariots.**—The mention of so small a number appears to indicate the result of the Israelite losses in some great battle, or in successive engagements. The destruction of these particular kinds of forces was equivalent to complete disarmament, and rendered further resistance hopeless, as the Syrians were especially strong in chariots and horsemen. (See Note on chap. ii. 12.)

**Had made them like the dust by threshing.**—Rather, *and set them like the dust to trample on* or *tread underfoot*. Israel was *down-trodden* by the conqueror. (Comp. 2 Sam. xxii. 43; Isa. x. 6.)

⁽⁸⁾ **And his might.**—Or, *prowess*. The reference is to his wars with the Syrians.

*(9)* And Jehoahaz slept with his fathers; and they buried him in Samaria: and Joash his son reigned in his stead.

*(10)* In the thirty and seventh year of Joash king of Judah began Jehoash the son of Jehoahaz to reign over Israel in Samaria, *and reigned* sixteen years. *(11)* And he did *that which was* evil in the sight of the LORD; he departed not from all the sins of Jeroboam the son of Nebat, who made Israel sin: *but he* walked therein. *(12)* And the rest of the acts of Joash, and all that he did, and his might wherewith he fought against Amaziah king of Judah, *are* they not written in the book of the chronicles of the kings of Israel? *(13)* And Joash slept with his fathers; and Jeroboam sat upon his throne: and Joash was buried in Samaria with the kings of Israel.

*(14)* Now Elisha was fallen sick of his sickness whereof he died. And Joash the king of Israel came down unto him, and wept over his face, and said, O my father, my father, the chariot of Israel, and the horsemen thereof. *(15)* And Elisha said unto him, Take bow and arrows. And he took unto him bow and arrows. *(16)* And he said to the king of Israel, ¹Put thine hand upon the bow. And he put his hand *upon it*: and Elisha put his hands upon the king's hands. *(17)* And he said, Open the window eastward. And he opened *it*. Then Elisha said, Shoot. And he shot. And he said, The arrow of the LORD's deliverance, and the arrow of deliverance from Syria: for thou shalt smite the Syrians in Aphek, till thou have consumed *them*. *(18)* And he said, Take the arrows. And he took *them*. And he said unto the king of Israel, Smite upon the ground.

B.C. 839.
B.C. 841.
¹ Heb., *Make thine hand to ride.*
B.C. 825.
B.C. cir. 839.

---

*(9)* **Slept with his fathers.**—Or, *lay down* (*i.e.*, to sleep) *like his fathers, i.e.*, as his fathers had done before him. The same phrase is used even of Amaziah, who came to a violent end (chap. xiv. 22).

*(10—25)* THE REIGN OF JOASH, OR JEHOASH. ELISHA FORETELLS HIS SUCCESSES AGAINST THE SYRIANS.

*(10)* **In the thirty and seventh year.**—This does not agree with verse 1. The Ald. LXX. reads, "thirty-ninth," which is right.

**Began . . . to reign, and reigned sixteen years.**—The Hebrew is briefer, *reigned sixteen years.*

*(11)* **But he walked therein.**—Heb., *in it he walked.* The pronoun is *collective* in force.

*(12)* **And the rest.**—This is repeated, chap. xiv. 15, 16.

**Wherewith he fought.**—Or, *how he fought.* In chap. xiv. 15 *and* is prefixed, and should be restored here.

**Against Amaziah.**—See the account of chap. xiv. 8, *seq.*

*(13)* **Jeroboam sat upon his throne.**—The variation from the stereotyped phrase, "and Jeroboam his son reigned in his stead," is remarkable. (See chap. xiv. 16.) The Talmud (*Seder Olam*) and Kimchi fancy that it is implied that Joash associated Jeroboam with himself on the throne, for fear of a revolt (!).

**Buried in Samaria with the kings of Israel.** —So that there were "tombs of the kings" there, as at Jerusalem.

*(14—21)* The visit of Joash to the dying Elisha.

This section is obviously derived from another documentary source than the preceding. What a fresh and life-like picture it presents in contrast with the colourless abstract which it follows!

*(14)* **He died.**—Rather, *he was to die.*

**Came down to him**—*i.e.*, to his house. Comp. the Note on chap. v. 24, vi. 33.

**Wept over his face.**—As he lay on the bed.

**O my father, my father.**—Comp. the Note on chap. ii. 12. Joash laments the approaching loss of his best counsellor and helper. The prophet, by his teaching and his prayers, as well as by his sage counsel and wonder-working powers, had been more to Israel than chariots and horsemen.

*(15)* **Take bow and arrows.**—From one of the royal attendants.

*(16)* **Put thine hand upon the bow.**—Rather, as margin. In drawing a bow, the left hand "rides" upon it, or closes round it, while the right grasps arrow and string.

**Elisha put his hands upon the king's hands.** —So as to invest the act of shooting with a *prophetic* character; and, further perhaps, to signify the consecration of the king to the task that the shooting symbolised. It is not implied that Elisha's hands were on the king's hands *when he shot.*

*(17)* **The window.**—Or, *lattice.* Probably a lattice opening outwards.

**Eastward.**—In the direction of Gilead, which was occupied by the Syrians (chap. x. 33).

**Shoot.**—The old illustration of declaring war by shooting an arrow into the enemy's country (*Æn.* ix. 57) is not without bearing on this case, though it obviously does not exhaust the meaning of the act.

*(17)* **And he said**—*i.e.*, Elisha said.

**The arrow of the Lord's . . . Syria.**—Literally, *An arrow of victory for Jehovah, and an arrow of victory over Aram!*

**In Aphek.**—Josh. xiii. 4; 1 Kings xx. 26. The scene of former defeats was to become that of triumph.

**Till thou have consumed them.**—Literally, *unto finishing.* The annihilation of the opposing army at Aphek, not of the entire forces of Syria, is predicted. (See verse 19.)

*(18)* **And he said.**—LXX., "and Elisha said unto him," which, as Thenius remarks, is more appropriate here, in introducing the account of the second symbolic action.

**The arrows**—*i.e.*, the bundle of arrows.

**Smite upon the ground.**—Rather, *smite* (or, *strike*) *earthwards*; as if striking an enemy to the earth.

**He smote thrice.**—Three being a sacred number.

*Death of Elisha*  II. KINGS, XIII.  *and of Hazael.*

And he smote thrice, and stayed. (19) And the man of God was wroth with him, and said, Thou shouldest have smitten five or six times; then hadst thou smitten Syria till thou hadst consumed *it*: whereas now thou shalt smite Syria *but* thrice.

(20) And Elisha died, and they buried him. And the bands of the Moabites invaded the land at the coming in of the year. (21) And it came to pass, as they were burying a man, that, behold, they spied a band *of men*; and they cast the man into the sepulchre of Elisha: and when the man ¹was let down, and touched the bones of Elisha, ªhe revived, and stood up on his feet. (22) But Hazael king of Syria oppressed Israel all the days of Jehoahaz. (23) And the LORD was gracious unto them, and had compassion on them, and had respect unto them, because of his covenant with Abraham, Isaac, and Jacob, and would not destroy them, neither cast he them from his ²presence as yet. (24) So Hazael king of Syria died; and Benhadad his son reigned in his stead. (25) And Jehoash the son of Jehoahaz

¹ Heb., *went down*.
ª Ecclus. 48. 14.
B.C. cir. 838.
² Heb., *face*.
B. C. cir. 839.

---

(19) **The man of God was wroth with him.**—Because his present want of zeal augured a like deficiency in prosecuting the war hereafter. The natural irritability of the sick man may also have had something to do with it. Thenius well remarks on the manifestly *historical* character of the entire scene. It may be added that, to appreciate it fully, we must remember that βελομαντεία, or soothsaying by means of arrows, was a practice of unknown antiquity in the Semitic world. Shooting an arrow, and observing where and how it fell, was one method of trying to fathom the secrets of that Power which overrules events and foreknows the future. The proceedings of David and Jonathan, recorded in 1 Sam. xx. 35, *seq.*, appear to have been an instance of this sort of divination, which in principle is quite analogous to *casting lots*, a practice so familiar to readers of the Bible. The second process—that described in verse 18—seems equally to have depended upon chance, according to modern ideas. The prophet left it to the spontaneous *impulse* of the king to determine the number of strokes; because he believed that the result, whatever it was, would betoken the purpose of Jehovah. "The lot is cast into the lap, but the whole disposing thereof is of the Lord" (Prov. xvi. 33). Elisha's *anger* was the natural anger of the man and the patriot, disappointed at the result of a divination from which he had hoped greater things. In conclusion, it cannot be too often or too forcibly urged upon students of the true religion that the essential differences which isolate it from all imperfect or retrograde systems are to be found not so much in matters of outward organisation, form, and ritual, such as priesthoods and sacrifices, prophets and modes of divination, which were pretty much the same everywhere in Semitic antiquity; but in the inward spirit and substance of its teaching, in the vital truths which it handed on through successive ages, and, above all, in its steady progress from lower to higher conceptions of the Divine character and purposes, and of the right relations of man to God and his fellow-creatures.

(20) **And the bands of the Moabites invaded.**—Rather, *And troops of Moabites used to invade.* They took advantage of the weakened condition of Israel to revenge the devastation of their country described in chap. iii. 25.

**At the coming in of the year.**—So the Targum and the LXX. The Syriac, Vulg., and Arabic understand, "in that (or, 'the same') year." The preposition *bě* has probably fallen out of the Hebrew text: read, *běbō' shānāh*, "when the year came in"—*i.e.*, in the spring. (Comp. 2 Sam. xi. 1.)

(21) **As they were burying.**—*They*—*i.e.*, a party of Israelites. The story is told with vivid *definiteness*.

**A band.**—Rather, *the troop.* The particular troop of Moabites which happened to be making an inroad at the time.

**They cast the man into the sepulchre of Elisha.**—Comp. Mark xvi. 3, 4. In this case, we must suppose that the tomb was more easily opened, as the action was obviously done in haste.

**And when the man was let down, and touched the bones.**—Rather, *and they departed. And the man touched the bones.* The order of words in the original, as well as the sense, supports old Houbigant's conjecture. If the meaning were, "and the man went and touched," the subject in the Hebrew would have followed the first verb, not the second. Moreover, the verb would hardly have been *hālak*.

**He revived.**—Literally, *and he lived.* Thenius thinks that the sacred writer regarded this miracle as a pledge of the fulfilment of Elisha's promise to Joash. Bähr says: "Elisha died and was buried, like all other men, but even in death and in the grave he is avouched to be the prophet and servant of God." Dante's warning may not be out of place here:—

"O voi che avete gl'intelletti sani,
Mirate la dottrina, che s asconde
Sotto il velame degli versi strani."
*Inf.* ix. 61, *sqq.*

(22) **But Hazael . . . oppressed.**—Rather, *Now Hazael . . . had oppressed.* The narrative returns to verse 3.

(23) **And the Lord was gracious.**—The verse is a remark of the compiler's, as is evident from the style, the reference to the Covenant, and the expression "as yet," or rather, *until now*—*i.e.*, the day when he was writing, and when the northern kingdom had finally perished.

**Had respect.**—*Turned.*

(24) **Ben-hadad**—III., not mentioned in the Assyrian inscriptions. His reign synchronises with that of Samas-Rimmon in Assyria, who made no expeditions to the West (B.C. 825—812). The name Ben-hadad does not, of course, signify any connection with the dynasty overthrown by Hazael. It was a Divine title (Comp. Note on chap. vi. 24.)

Benhadad was probably a feebler sovereign than Hazael. The rule, "Fortes creantur fortibus et bonis," is perhaps as often contradicted as corroborated by actual experience.

(25) **The cities, which he had taken**—*i.e.*, which *Hazael* had taken. The cities referred to must have

¹took again out of the hand of Benhadad the son of Hazael the cities, which he had taken out of the hand of Jehoahaz his father by war. Three times did Joash beat him, and recovered the cities of Israel.

CHAPTER XIV.—⁽¹⁾ In the second year of Joash son of Jehoahaz king of Israel, reigned ᵃAmaziah the son of Joash king of Judah. ⁽²⁾ He was twenty and five years old when he began to reign, and reigned twenty and nine years in Jerusalem. And his mother's name *was* Jehoaddan of Jerusalem. ⁽³⁾ And he did *that which was* right in the sight of the LORD, yet not like David his father: he did according to all things as Joash his father did. ⁽⁴⁾ Howbeit the high places were not taken away: as yet the people did sacrifice and burnt incense on the high places. ⁽⁵⁾ And it came to pass, as soon as the kingdom was confirmed in his hand, that he slew his servants ᵇwhich had slain the king his father. ⁽⁶⁾ But the children of the murderers he slew not: according unto that which is written in the book of the law of Moses, wherein the LORD commanded, saying, ᶜThe fathers shall not be put to death for the children, nor the children be put to death for the fathers; but every man shall be put to death for his own sin. ⁽⁷⁾ He slew of Edom in the valley of salt ten thousand, and took ²Selah by war, and called the name of it Joktheel unto this day.

⁽⁸⁾ Then Amaziah sent messengers to Jehoash, the son of Jehoahaz son of Jehu, king of Israel, saying, Come, let us look one another in the face. ⁽⁹⁾ And

---

1 Heb., *returned and took.*
B.C. cir. 836.
a 2 Chron. 25. 1.
B.C. 839.
b ch. 12. 20.
B.C. cir. 827.
c Deut. 24. 16; Ezek. 18. 20.
B.C. cir. 826.
2 Or, *The rock.*

---

been cities on the *west* of Jordan (comp. verses 3 and 7), for the trans-Jordan had been subdued by Hazael in the time of Jehu (chap. x. 32, *seq.*). Jeroboam II., the son of Joash, restored the ancient boundaries of Israel (chap. xiv. 25).

**By war.**—Or, *in the war.*

**Beat him.**—Rather, *smite him* (verse 19).

XIV.

THE REIGN OF AMAZIAH IN JUDAH, AND OF JEROBOAM II. IN ISRAEL.

(1—17) THE REIGN OF AMAZIAH. (Comp. 2 Chron. xxv.)

⁽²⁾ **Jehoaddan.**—The Hebrew text, which is supported by the LXX., has *Jehoaddin* (perhaps, "Jehovah is delight;" comp. Isa. xlvii. 8, and the Divine name *Naaman*).

⁽³⁾ **Yet not like David his father.**—The chronicler paraphrases this reference to the ideal king of Israel: "yet not *with a perfect heart.*"

⁽⁴⁾ **Howbeit.**—The same word was rendered "yet" in the last verse. "Only," or "save that" would be better.

⁽⁵⁾ **As soon as the kingdom was confirmed**—*i.e.*, as soon as he was firmly established on the throne; as soon as he felt his power secure. (Comp. 1 Kings ii. 46.)

**Slew . . .slain.**—Literally, *smote . . . smitten.*

⁽⁶⁾ **The murderers.**—Literally, *the smiters.*

**According unto that which is written . . . law of Moses.**—A quotation of Deut. xxiv. 16. This reference is from the pen of the Judæan editor.

**Shall be put to death.**—So the original passage and the Hebrew margin. Hebrew text, "shall die."

This humane provision of the Jewish law contrasts favourably with the practice of other nations, ancient and modern. Readers of the classics will recollect the hideous story of the treatment of the young daughter of Sejanus (Tac. *Ann.* v. 9).

⁽⁷⁾ **He slew.**—Rather, *he it was that smote.*

**The valley of salt.**—Comp. 2 Sam. viii. 13. *El-Ghôr*, the salt plain of the Dead Sea, which Amaziah would traverse in marching against Edom.

**Ten thousand.**—The number slain in one conflict.

**Selah.**—Heb., the *Sĕlaʿ*, *i.e.*, the crag. The Hebrew name of the famous rock-hewn town of Petra.

**By war.**—Or, *in the battle.* After the decisive engagement, Amaziah's troops forced their way through the narrow defile leading to the Edomite capital, probably meeting no great resistance.

**Joktheel.**—A town of Judah bore this name (Josh. xv. 38). The name probably means *God's ward*, referring to the wonderful strength of the natural position of the town. Others explain, *subjugated of God.*

**Unto this day**—*i.e.*, unto the time when the original document was written, from which the writer derived this notice.

The reduction of the capital implies that of the country. The defeat of Jehoram (chap. viii. 20, *seq.*) was thus avenged. Chronicles gives a more detailed account of the re-conquest of Edom, and its consequences (2 Chron. xxv. 5—16). It is there related that Amaziah hired a large force of mercenaries from the northern kingdom, but sent them home again at the bidding of a prophet. On their way back they attacked and plundered certain of the cities of Judah. The fall of Selah was followed by a massacre of captives. The gods of Edom, which Amaziah carried off, proved a snare to him. (See the Notes on the passage.)

⁽⁸⁾ **Then.**—After the reduction of Edom. The more extended narrative which follows is plainly taken from a different source than that of the brief extract preceding it.

**Come, let us look one another in the face.**—A challenge to battle, the ground of which might be found in the outrages committed by the Israelite mercenaries on their homeward march. It appears likely, however, that Amaziah, intoxicated by his recent success, aimed at nothing less than the recovery of the Ten Tribes for the house of David. So Josephus (*Antt.* ix. 9, § 2), who gives what purport to be the letters which passed between the two kings on this occasion.

⁽⁹⁾ **The thistle.**—Or *bramble* or *briar.* (Comp. Job xxxi. 41; Cant. ii. 2.) The LXX. and Vulg. render "thistle;" the Syriac, "blackthorn" (*Prunus silvestris*).

Jehoash the king of Israel sent to Amaziah king of Judah, saying, The thistle that *was* in Lebanon sent to the cedar that *was* in Lebanon, saying, Give thy daughter to my son to wife: and there passed by a wild beast that *was* in Lebanon, and trode down the thistle. <sup>(10)</sup> Thou hast indeed smitten Edom, and thine heart hath lifted thee up: glory *of this*, and tarry ¹at home: for why shouldest thou meddle to *thy* hurt, that thou shouldest fall, *even* thou, and Judah with thee? <sup>(11)</sup> But Amaziah would not hear. Therefore Jehoash king of Israel went up; and he and Amaziah king of Judah looked one another in the face at Beth-shemesh, which *belongeth* to Judah. <sup>(12)</sup> And Judah ²was put to the worse before Israel; and they fled every man to their tents. <sup>(13)</sup> And Jehoash king of Israel took Amaziah king of Judah, the son of Jehoash the son of Ahaziah, at Beth-shemesh, and came to Jerusalem, and brake down the wall of Jerusalem from the gate of Ephraim unto the corner gate, four hundred cubits. <sup>(14)</sup> And he took all the gold and silver, and all the vessels that were found in the house of the LORD, and in the treasures of the king's house, and hostages, and returned to Samaria. <sup>(15)</sup> Now the rest of the acts of Jehoash which he did, and his might, and how he fought with Amaziah king of Judah, *are* they not written in the book of the chronicles of the kings of Israel?

*Marginal notes:* 1 Heb., *at thy house.* — B.C. cir. 825. — 2 Heb., *was smitten.*

---

**Give thy daughter to my son to wife.**—Perhaps hinting at Amaziah's demand for the surrender of Israel (the "daughter" of Jehoash) to Judah (the "son" of Amaziah).

**And there passed by a wild beast that was in Lebanon.**—Rather, *and the wild beasts that were in Lebanon passed over it.* So LXX. and Vulg. It is obvious to compare with this brief but most pithy parable that of Jotham (Judges ix. 8—15). The contrast between the northern and southern kingdoms in point of military strength and resources, and the disdainful tolerance with which the former regarded the latter, could hardly have found more forcible expression.

<sup>(10)</sup> **Thou hast indeed smitten**—*i.e.*, thou hast *thoroughly* worsted; gained a *brilliant* victory over Edom. (The "indeed" qualifies "smitten.")

**Hath lifted.**—Rather, *lifteth.*

**Glory of this, and tarry at home.**—Literally, *be honoured, and abide in thine own house, i.e.,* be content with the glory thou hast achieved. Rest on thy laurels, and do not risk them by further enterprises which may not turn out so favourably. So the Vulg. Thenius explains: "Show thy might at home," referring to the LXX. (Comp. 2 Sam. vi. 20).

**For why shouldest thou meddle to thine hurt?**—Rather, *and why shouldst thou challenge* or *provoke* (literally, *attack*, Deut. ii. 5) *disaster?*

<sup>(11)</sup> **Looked one another in the face**—*i.e.*, encountered one another; joined battle.

**Beth-shemesh.**—The modern *Ain-shems*, north of which is a great plain now called *Wâdy-es-Surâr*, in which the encounter probably happened. Jehoash proposed to attack Jerusalem from the west, as Hazael also had intended (chap. xii. 17).

<sup>(12)</sup> **To their tents.**—Hebrew text, *to his tent*; so the LXX. and Syriac. Hebrew margin, *to his tents*; so Vulg., and Targum, and Chronicles. The meaning is that the enemy disbanded, as usually after a great defeat. (Comp. chap. viii. 21.)

<sup>(13)</sup> **Amaziah king of Judah, the son of Jehoash the son of Ahaziah.**—Comp. verse 8. Thenius thinks the formal specification of Amaziah's descent indicates that this narrative was derived from "the Book of the Chronicles of the Kings of Israel." At all events, it emphasises the importance of the incident, which is further indicated in the original by the order of the words: "And Amaziah king of Judah . . . did Jehoash king of Israel take . . ."

**Came.**—So the Hebrew margin. The Hebrew text has, *brought him* (*way'bî'ô*; a rare form). So Chronicles and the Vulg., but not the other versions. Jehoash brought Amaziah a prisoner to his own capital.

**Brake down the wall.**—Or, *made a breach in the wall.* No resistance appears to have been offered. Josephus relates that Amaziah was induced by menaces of death to order the gates to be thrown open to the enemy; a needless assumption, considering that the army had been routed and the king was a captive. He adds, that Jehoash rode in his chariot through the breach in the walls, leading Amaziah as a prisoner.

**From the gate.**—So Chronicles and the Syriac, Vulg., and Arabic here. The Hebrew text has, *at the gate*, which is due to the common confusion of the letters *b* and *m* (*be*, "in;" *min*, "from"). The following "unto" shows that "from" is right.

**Of Ephraim.**—This gate lay on the north side of the city, and was also called the "Gate of Benjamin." It answers to the modern Damascus gate.

**The corner gate.**—This gate was at the north-west corner of the wall at the point where it trended southwards.

**Four hundred cubits.**—That is, about 222 yards. The insolence of a victorious enemy is sufficient to account for this conduct of Jehoash. It was also a forcible way of convincing Amaziah that even his strongest city was not proof against the prowess of *Ephraim*. Thenius thinks that Jehoash wanted to make room for the triumphal entry of his troops.

<sup>(14)</sup> **That were found.**—This expression seems to hint that there was not much treasure to carry off. (Comp. chap. xiii. 18.)

**Hostages.**—Literally, *the sons of sureties.* Having humbled the pride of Amaziah, Jehoash left him in possession of his throne, taking hostages for his future good behaviour. Similar acts of clemency are recorded of themselves by the Assyrian kings of the dynasty of Sargon.

<sup>(15, 16)</sup> **Now the rest . . .**—Comp. chap. xiii. 12, 13, where the reign of Jehoash is already summed up, though not altogether in the same phraseology. The compiler probably found verses 15, 16, in their present

(16) And Jehoash slept with his fathers, and was buried in Samaria with the kings of Israel; and Jeroboam his son reigned in his stead.

(17) And Amaziah the son of Joash king of Judah lived after the death of Jehoash son of Jehoahaz king of Israel fifteen years. (18) And the rest of the acts of Amaziah, are they not written in the book of the chronicles of the kings of Judah? (19) Now *they made a conspiracy against him in Jerusalem: and he fled to Lachish; but they sent after him to Lachish, and slew him there. (20) And they brought him on horses: and he was buried at Jerusalem with his fathers in the city of David. (21) And all the people of Judah took <sup>b</sup>Azariah, which was sixteen years old, and made him king instead of his father Amaziah. (22) He built Elath, and restored it to Judah, after that the king slept with his fathers.

(23) In the fifteenth year of Amaziah the son of Joash king of Judah Jeroboam the son of Joash king of Israel began to reign in Samaria, and reigned forty and one years. (24) And he did that which was evil in the sight of the LORD: he departed not from all the sins of Jeroboam the son of Nebat, who made Israel to sin. (25) He restored the coast of Israel from the entering of Hamath unto the sea of the plain, according to the word of the LORD God of Israel, which he spake by the hand of his ser-

*a* 2 Chron. 25. 27.

B.C. 825.

*b* 2 Chron. 26. 1, he is called *Uzziah*.

B.C. 810.

B.C. cir. 825.

---

position in the document from which he derived the entire section, verses 8—17; a document which was not the same as that upon which chap. xiii. depends, as appears from the differences of language in the two passages.

The two verses are almost necessary here as a suitable introduction of the statement of verse 17, that Amaziah survived Jehoash by fifteen years.

(17) **Fifteen years.**—He came to the throne in the second year of Jehoash, who reigned sixteen years (chap. xiii. 10), and reigned twenty-nine years (verse 2). The different *data* are thus self-consistent. Jehoash appears to have died very soon after his victory—perhaps in the following year.

(19) **Now . . . but.**—*And . . . and.*

**They made a conspiracy.**—The fact that no *individual* conspirators are mentioned appears to indicate that Amaziah's death was the result of a general disaffection; and this inference is strengthened by the other details of the record. Thenius supposes that he had incensed the army in particular by some special act. Probably his foolish and ill-fated enterprise against Israel had something to do with it.

**Lachish.**—Now *Um Lákis.* Of old it was a strong fortress. (Comp. 2 Chron. xi. 9; chap. xviii. 14, xix. 8.) Amaziah's flight thither seems to indicate either a popular rising in Jerusalem, or a military revolt.

**They sent after him to Lachish.**—This, too, may point to a military outbreak.

(20) **They brought him on horses.**—Rather, *they carried him upon the horses*—*i.e.,* perhaps in the royal chariot wherein he had fled from Jerusalem. Or, perhaps, the corpse was literally carried on horseback by the regicides.

The orderly method of proceeding, the burial of the king in the royal sepulchres, and the elevation of Azariah, seem to prove that the murder of Amaziah was not an act of private blood-revenge.

(21) **All the people of Judah.**—Thenius explains, all the men of war, as in chap. xiii. 7.

**Took.**—The expression seems to imply that Azariah was *not* the eldest son. As Amaziah was fifty-nine years old at his death he probably had sons older than sixteen. Azariah was therefore chosen as a popular, or perhaps military, favourite.

**Azariah.**—See Note on 2 Chron. xxvi. 1. Thenius thinks the soldiery gave Azariah the name of Uzziah. At all events, the king may have taken a new name on his accession, though which of the two it was we cannot say. (Comp. chap. xxiv. 17.) Sennacherib on investing Esarhaddon with sovereignty named him *Asshurebil-mukin-pal.*

(22) **He built Elath.**—The pronoun is emphatic, *he*, in contrast with his father. "Built," either *rebuilt* or *fortified.* The verse is in close connection with the preceding narrative. Amaziah perhaps had not vigorously prosecuted the conquest of Edom, having been greatly weakened by his defeat in the struggle with Jehoash. He may even have suffered some further losses at the hands of the Edomites; and this, as Thenius supposes, may have led to the conspiracy which brought about his death and the accession of his son. The warlike youth Uzziah took the field at once, and pushed his victorious arms to the southern extremity of Edom, the port of Elath (chap. ix. 26), and thus restored the state of things which had existed under Solomon and Jehoshaphat.

**After that the king slept**—*i.e.,* immediately after the murder of Amaziah. Thenius explains the verse with most success, but this clause is still somewhat surprising.

THE REIGN OF JEROBOAM II. IN SAMARIA (verses 23—29).

(23) **Reigned forty and one years.**—According to the statement of this verse, Jeroboam reigned fourteen years concurrently with Amaziah, who reigned altogether twenty-nine years (verse 2); and thirty-seven years concurrently with Azariah (chap. xv. 8), so that he reigned altogether not forty-one but fifty-one years. (The discrepancy originated in a confusion of the Hebrew letters נא, fifty-one, with מא, forty-one.)

(25) **He restored.**—Rather, *He it was who restored the border,* i.e., he wrested out of the hands of the Syrians the territory they had taken from Israel.

**From the entering of Hamath**—*i.e.,* from the point where the territory of Hamath began. This was the originally determined boundary of Israel on the north (comp. Num. xiii. 21, xxxiv. 8; Josh. xiii. 5), and the prophet Ezekiel specifies it as the future limit (Ezek. xlvii. 16, xlviii. 1). Israel's territory first reached this limit under Solomon, who conquered a portion of the Hamathite domains (2 Chron. viii. 3, 4).

vant ᵃJonah, the son of Amittai, the prophet, which *was* of Gath-hepher. (26) For the LORD saw the affliction of Israel, *that it was* very bitter: for *there was* not any shut up, nor any left, nor any helper for Israel. (27) And the LORD said not that he would blot out the name of Israel from under heaven: but he saved them by the hand of Jeroboam the son of Joash.

(28) Now the rest of the acts of Jeroboam, and all that he did, and his might, how he warred, and how he recovered Damascus, and Hamath, *which belonged* to Judah, for Israel, *are* they not written in the book of the chronicles of the kings of Israel? (29) And Jeroboam slept with his fathers, *even* with the kings of Israel; and Zachariah his son reigned in his stead.

CHAPTER XV.—(1) In the twenty and seventh year of Jeroboam king of Israel began Azariah son of Amaziah king of Judah to reign. (2) Sixteen years old was he when he began to reign, and he reigned two and fifty years in Jerusalem. And his mother's name *was*

B.C. 822.
B.C. 784.
B.C. cir. 810.

ᶜ Matt. 12. 39, 40, called *Jonas*.

---

**The sea of the plain**—*i.e.*, the Dead Sea (Num. iii. 17, iv. 49; Josh. iii. 16). The whole length of the Dead Sea is included (comp. Amos vi. 14, where virtually the same limits are specified), and the country beyond Jordan. (Comp. Note on 1 Chron. v. 17.)

**Jonah, the son of Amittai, the prophet.**—Comp. Jonah i. 1. Ewald remarks that the activity of this prophet must have occupied a very large field, as tradition connects him with Nineveh. Hitzig and Knobel recognise the prophecy referred to here in Isa. xv., xvi. There is no difficulty in the supposition that Isaiah has "adopted and ratified the work of an earlier prophet," as Jeremiah has so often done. (See Cheyne's *Isaiah*, vol. i., p. 93.) But it is easier to prove that these chapters are not Isaiah's, than that they belong to Jonah.

**Gath-hepher.**—Josh. xix. 13. The present *Meshed*, Not far north of Nazareth.

(26) **Affliction.**—Better, *oppression*.

**Bitter.**—So the LXX., Syriac, and Vulg. Better, *stubborn*, and so, *inveterate*, *unyielding*, *enduring*. (Comp. Deut. xxi. 18—20.) Targum, "hard;" Arabic, "strong" or "violent."

**For there was . . . left.**—Comp. Note on 1 Kings xiv. 10.

(27) **Said not.**—By any prophet.

**Blot out the name.**—The figure is taken from blotting out writing. (Comp. Num. v. 23.) The Hebrews used inks that soon faded, and could easily be wiped off the parchment. (Hence the partial obliteration of words and letters which is one of the causes of textual corruption.)

(28) **How he recovered Damascus, and Hamath.**—Jeroboam II. was probably contemporary with Rammân-nirâri, king of Assyria (B.C. 812—783). This king has recorded his exaction of tribute from Tyre and Sidon, "the land of Omri" (*i.e.*, Israel), Edom, and Philistia; and a siege of Damascus, followed by the submission of Mari', its king, and the spoiling of his palace. The prostration of his enemy thus accounts for the permanent success of Jeroboam, who was himself a vassal of Assyria.

**He recovered.**—This verb was rendered "he restored" in verse 25, and that is the meaning here.

**Damascus and Hamath.**—Not the entire states so named, which were powerful independent communities, but portions of their territory, which had belonged to Israel in the days of Solomon. (See Note on 2 Chron. viii. 3, 4.)

**Which belonged to Judah.**—This is really an epithet restrictive of the phrase, "Damascus and Hamath," the sense being, "*Judæan* Damascus and Hamath." (Comp. the Note on chap. xv. 1.)

**For Israel.**—Heb., *in Israel*. The sense is obscure; but the particle "in" appears to refer to the *re-incorporation* of the Damascene and Hamathite districts with Israel. Ewald would cancel "which belonged to Judah," and read "to Israel" (so the Syriac and Arabic. But the LXX., Vulg., and Targum support the existing text.) Others explain: *He restored Damascus and Hamath to Judah* (*i.e.*, to the theocratic people) *through Israel* (*i.e.*, the northern kingdom, to which the recovered districts were actually annexed). No explanation, however, is really satisfactory. It may be that by an oversight the Judæan editor wrote "to Judah," instead of "to Israel," and that some scribe added a marginal note "in Israel," which afterwards crept into the text. It is curious to find certain districts of Hamath leagued with Azariah, king of Judah, against Tiglath Pileser. (See Note on chap. xv. 1.)

(29) **Even with the kings of Israel.**—Probably some words have fallen out, and the original text was, "*and was buried in Samaria* with the kings of Israel." (Comp. verse 16.) The Syriac and Arabic have, "and was buried."

## XV.

(1—7) THE REIGN OF AZARIAH (Uzziah), KING OF JUDAH. (Comp. 2 Chron. xxvi.)

(1) **In the twenty and seventh year of Jeroboam.**—An error of transcription for *the fifteenth year* (טו, 15; כז, 27). The error is clear from chap. xiv. 2, 17, 23. Amaziah reigned twenty-nine years (chap. xiv. 2), fourteen concurrently with Joash, and fifteen with Jeroboam. It was, therefore, in the fifteenth of Jeroboam that Uzziah succeeded his father.

**Azariah.**—An *Azriyâhu* (*Az-ri-ya-a-u*), king of Judah, is mentioned in two fragmentary inscriptions of Tiglath Pileser II. (B.C. 745—727). The most important statement runs: "xix. districts of the city of Hamath (*Hammatti*) with the cities of their circuit, on the coast of the sea of the setting of the sun (*i.e.*, the Mediterranean), which in their transgression had revolted to Azariah, to the border of Assyria I restored, my prefects my governors over them I appointed." The Eponym list records a three years' campaign of Tiglath Pileser against the Syrian state of Arpad in B.C. 742—740. Schrader supposes that Azariah and Hamath were concerned in this campaign. (This conflicts with the ordinary chronology, which fixes 758 B.C. as the year of Azariah's death.)

Jecholiah of Jerusalem. ⁽³⁾ And he did *that which was* right in the sight of the LORD, according to all that his father Amaziah had done; ⁽⁴⁾ save that the high places were not removed: the people sacrificed and burnt incense still on the high places.

⁽⁵⁾ And the LORD smote the king, so that he was a leper unto the day of his death, and dwelt in a several house. And Jotham the king's son *was* over the house, judging the people of the land.

⁽⁶⁾ And the rest of the acts of Azariah, and all that he did, *are* they not written in the book of the chronicles of the kings of Judah? ⁽⁷⁾ So Azariah slept with his fathers; and they buried him with his fathers in the city of David: and Jotham his son reigned in his stead.

⁽⁸⁾ In the thirty and eighth year of Azariah king of Judah did Zachariah the son of Jeroboam reign over Israel in Samaria six months. ⁽⁹⁾ And he did *that which was* evil in the sight of the LORD, as his fathers had done: he departed not from the sins of Jeroboam the son of Nebat, who made Israel to sin. ⁽¹⁰⁾ And Shallum the son of Jabesh conspired against him, and smote him before the people, and slew him, and reigned in his stead.

⁽¹¹⁾ And the rest of the acts of Zachariah, behold, they *are* written in the book of the chronicles of the kings of Israel. ⁽¹²⁾ This was ᵃthe word of the LORD which he spake unto Jehu, saying, Thy sons shall sit on the throne of Israel unto the fourth generation. And so it came to pass.

⁽¹³⁾ Shallum the son of Jabesh began to reign in the nine and thirtieth year of ᵇUzziah king of Judah; and he reigned ¹a full month in Samaria. ⁽¹⁴⁾ For Menahem the son of Gadi went

*a* ch. 10. 30.

B.C. cir. 772.

B.C. cir. 765.

*b* Matt. 1. 9, called Ozias.

1 Heb., *a month of days.*

B.C. cir. 758.

B.C. cir. 772.

B.C. cir. 733.

---

⁽³⁾ **And he did that which was right.**—This statement is repeated word for word in Chronicles. Its exact meaning here, as in other instances, is that Azariah supported the legitimate worship, and lent his countenance to no foreign *cultus.* When the chronicler adds that he "sought God in the days of (the prophet) Zachariah," and that "as long as he sought Jehovah, God made him to prosper," he does not contradict the preceding general estimate of the king's religious policy, but simply gives additional information respecting his life and fortunes.

⁽⁵⁾ **And the Lord smote the king.**—The chronicler relates the reason—viz., because of his usurpation of priestly functions in the sanctuary. This happened towards the end of the reign. Jotham, the regent, was only twenty-five when Azariah died (verse 33).

**Smote.**—Or, *struck.* So we speak of a paralytic *stroke,* and the word *plague* literally means *stroke.*

**In a several house.**—Rather, *in the sickhouse* (or, *hospital*)—*i.e.,* a royal residence outside of Jerusalem (Lev. xiii. 46; chap. vii. 3) set apart for such cases. (Strictly, *in the house of freedom;* because lepers were *emancipated* from all social relations and duties. Gesenius explains the word from an Arabic root said to mean *prostration, weakness;* but Lane gives for that term the special meaning *smallness* (or, *narrowness*) *of the eye; weakness of sight.* See his *Arabic Lexicon,* Bk. I., Pt. II., p. 772.

**Over the house.**—Not apparently as *prefect of the palace* (comp. 1 Kings iv. 6, xviii. 3), but as dwelling in the palace instead of his father.

**Judging the people of the land.**—As his father's representative. (Comp. 1 Sam. viii. 6, 20; 1 Kings iii. 9.) This passage is strong evidence against the assumption of joint sovereignties of princes with their fathers, so often made by way of escaping chronological difficulties in Hebrew history. Jotham is not co-regent but viceroy of Azariah until the latter dies.

⁽⁶⁾ **The rest of the acts of Azariah.**—Such as his wars with the Philistines and Arabs, his improvements in the organisation of the army and the defences of the capital, his fondness for husbandry and cattle-breeding, and his success in all these directions, as well as his intrusion into the Sanctuary to offer incense at the golden altar. (See 2 Chron. xxv. and the Notes there.)

(8—16) THE REIGNS OF ZACHARIAH AND SHALLUM IN SAMARIA.

⁽⁸⁾ **In the thirty and eighth year of Azariah.**—This agrees with the assumption that Jeroboam reigned fifty-one years (chap. xiv. 23).

⁽⁹⁾ **As his fathers**—*i.e.,* the dynasty of Jehu, of which he was the last member. Like all his predecessors, he upheld the illicit worship established by Jeroboam I.

⁽¹⁰⁾ **Son of Jabesh.**—*Not* man of Jabesh Gilead, as Hitzig explains. The father's name is always given in the case of usurpers.

**Before the people.**—Rather, *before people*—*i.e.,* in public. So all the versions except the LXX. The open assassination of the king is noted, in contrast with the secrecy with which former conspiracies had been concerted. It is a symptom of the rapidly-increasing corruption of morals, which allowed people to look on with indifference while the king was being murdered. (The LXX. puts the Hebrew words into Greek letters thus: Κεβλαάμ. The word *qŏbol*—"before"—is Aramaic rather than Hebrew, and only occurs here. Ewald acutely conjectured that *Qŏbol'ām*—"before people"—was really the proper name of another usurper, comparing Zech. xi. 8, "the third king added that month;" but in that case the narrative is hardly coherent or complete. Grätz suggests the correction "in Ibleam."

⁽¹²⁾ **This was the word of the Lord.**—Thenius considers this remark as added by the Judæan editor to the short abstract of Zachariah's reign.

⁽¹³⁾ **A full month.**—Literally, as margin. Thenius says Shallum cannot have reigned a *full* month, as Zech. xi. 8 obviously refers to the three kings Zachriah, Shallum, and Menahem.

⁽¹⁴⁾ **For.**—*And.*

up from Tirzah, and came to Samaria, and smote Shallum the son of Jabesh in Samaria, and slew him, and reigned in his stead.

(15) And the rest of the acts of Shallum, and his conspiracy which he made, behold, they *are* written in the book of the chronicles of the kings of Israel.

(16) Then Menahem smote Tiphsah, and all that *were* therein, and the coasts thereof from Tirzah: because they opened not *to him*, therefore he smote it; and all the women therein that were with child he ripped up.

(17) In the nine and thirtieth year of Azariah king of Judah began Menahem the son of Gadi to reign over Israel, *and reigned* ten years in Samaria. (18) And he did *that which was* evil in the sight of the LORD: he departed not all his days from the sins of Jeroboam the son of Nebat, who made Israel to sin. (19) And *a* Pul the king of Assyria came against the land: and Menahem gave Pul a

B.C. 772.

*a* 1 Chron. 5. 26.

B.C. 771.

---

**Menahem.**—Tiglath Pileser II. records in his annals that in his eighth regnal year (*i.e.*, B.C. 738) he took tribute of "Raçunnu (Rezin) the Damascene, and Menihimmè Samerinâ'a"—*i.e.*, Menahem the Samaritan.

**Gadi.**—Or, *a Gadite*.

**Went up from Tirzah.**—Menahem was Zachariah's general, who at the time was quartered with the troops at Tirzah, near Samaria (1 Kings xiv. 17). On the news of the murder of Zachariah, Menahem marched to the capital. The month of Shallum's reign was probably taken up with preparations for hostilities on both sides. A battle at Samaria decided matters (Josephus). Perhaps, however, Menahem simply entered Samaria with a part of his forces.

(16) **Then.**—After slaying Shallum, and seizing the supreme power.

**Tiphsah.**—The name means *ford*, and elsewhere denotes the well-known Thapsacus on the Euphrates (1 Kings iv. 24). Here, however, an *Israelite* city in the neighbourhood of Tirzah is obviously intended. The course of events was apparently this: after slaying Shallum, Menahem returned to Tirzah, and set out thence at the head of his entire army to bring the rest of the country to acknowledge him as king. Tiphsah resisting his claims, he made an example of it which proved efficient to terrorise other towns into submission. [Thenius would read *Tappuah* for Tiphsah by a slight change in one Hebrew letter. This agrees very well with the local indications of the text (comp. Josh. xvii. 7, 8), though, of course, there *may* have been an otherwise unknown Tiphsah near Tirzah.]

**The coasts thereof.**—Literally, *her borders* (or, *territories*). (Comp. Josh. xvii. 8.)

**From Tirzah**—*i.e.*, starting from Tirzah. This shows that the districts of Tirzah and Tiphsah (or, Tappuah) were conterminous.

**Because they opened not to him.**—Literally, *for one opened not*; an impersonal construction. The meaning is: the gates were closed against him. The *to him* is added by all the versions except the Targum.

**And all the women.**—Comp. chap. viii. 21; Hosea xiii. 16; Amos i. 13.

(17—22) THE REIGN OF MENAHEM. HIS TRIBUTE TO PUL, KING OF ASSYRIA.

(17) **Reigned ten years.**—And some months over. (Comp. verse 23.)

(18) **He did that which was evil.**—Ewald says that at the outset Menahem appeared to be guided by better principles, referring to Zech. xi. 4—8.

**All his days.**—In the Hebrew these words occur at the *end* of the verse. They are not found in any other instance of the common formula which the verse repeats (comp. 1 Kings xv. 26, 34, xvi. 26, xxii. 53; 2 Kings iii. 1, x. 31, &c.), and almost certainly belong to the next verse.

**From the sins.**—Heb., *from upon the sins*, which is peculiar. The reading of the LXX., "from all the sins," appears right.

(19) **And.**—As it stands, the verse begins abruptly. But the reading of the LXX. restores the connection: "*In his days* Pul the king of Assyria," &c. (Comp. verse 29.)

**Pul.**—This name has been read in the cuneiform (*Pu-u-lu, i.e., Pûlu*, an officer of Sargon's). For the identity of Pul, king of Assyria, with Tiglath Pileser II., see Note on 1 Chron. v. 26, and Schrader's *Die Keilinschr. und das Alt. Test.*, pp. 227—240 (2nd edit., 1883). Prof. Schrader gives the following as the result of his elaborate and most interesting discussion: (1) Menahem of Israel and Azariah of Judah were contemporaries, according to the Bible as well as the Inscriptions. (2) According to the Bible, both these rulers were contemporary with an Assyrian king Pul; according to the Inscriptions, with Tiglath Pileser. (3) Berosus calls Pul a Chaldean; Tiglath Pileser calls himself king of Chaldea. (4) Pul-Porus became in 731 B.C. king of Babylon; Tiglath Pileser in 731 B.C. received the homage of the Babylonian king Merodach-Baladan, as he also reduced other Babylonian princes in this year, amongst them Chinzēros of Amukkan. (5) Poros appears in the canon of Ptolemy as king of Babylon; Tiglath Pileser names himself "king of Babylon." (6) Chinzēros became king of Babylon in 731 B.C. according to the canon, and, in fact, along with (or, under) a king of the name of Pōros; the hypothesis that the vanquished king of Amukkan of the same name was entrusted by Tiglath Pileser with the vassal-kingship of Babylon is suggested at once by the coincidence of the chronological data. (7) In the year 727—726 B.C. a change of government took place in Assyria in consequence of the death of Tiglath Pileser, and in Babylonia in consequence of the death of Porus. (8) No king appears in the Assyrian lists by a name like Pul, which is anomalous as a royal designation; we can only identify Pul with some other name in the lists, and, on historical grounds, with Tiglath Pileser only. (9) Pul and Pōros are forms of the same name (comp. *Bâbiru* for *Bâbilu* in Persian inscriptions). (10) From all this, the conclusion is inevitable that Pul and Porus, Pul and Tiglath Pileser, are one and the same person.

**Came against the land.**—Rather, *came upon the land* (Isa. x. 28; Judges xviii. 27). The meaning here is, *occupied* it.

**A thousand talents of silver.**—About £375,000.

**That his hand might be with him.**—Pul (Tiglath Pileser) came at the invitation of Menahem to establish the latter in the sovereignty against other

thousand talents of silver, that his hand might be with him to confirm the kingdom in his hand. (20) And Menaham ¹exacted the money of Israel, *even of* all the mighty men of wealth, of each man fifty shekels of silver, to give to the king of Assyria. So the king of Assyria turned back, and stayed not there in the land.

(21) And the rest of the acts of Menahem, and all that he did, *are* they not written in the book of the chronicles of the kings of Israel? (22) And Menahem slept with his fathers; and Pekahiah his son reigned in his stead.

(23) In the fiftieth year of Azariah king of Judah Pekahiah the son of Menahem began to reign over Israel in Samaria, *and reigned* two years. (24) And he did *that which was* evil in the sight of the LORD: he departed not from the sins of Jeroboam the son of Nebat, who made Israel to sin. (25) But Pekah the son of Remaliah, a captain of his, conspired against him, and smote him in Samaria, in the palace of the king's house, with Argob and Arieh, and with him fifty men of the Gileadites: and he killed him, and reigned in his room.

(26) And the rest of the acts of Pekahiah, and all that he did, behold, they *are* written in the book of the chronicles of the kings of Israel.

(27) In the two and fiftieth year of Azariah king of Judah Pekah the son of Remaliah began to reign over Israel in Samaria, *and reigned* twenty years. (28) And he did *that which was* evil in the sight of the LORD: he departed not from the sins of Jeroboam the son of Nebat, who made Israel to sin.

(29) In the days of Pekah king of

B.C. 759.
B.C. 759.
B.C. 761.
B.C. 740.

¹ Heb., *caused to come forth.*

---

pretenders as a vassal of Assyria. (Comp. Hosea v. 13, vii. 11, viii. 9.) Tiglath Pileser had first reduced Rezin king of Syria-Damascus, which was probably much weakened by the victories of Jeroboam II. (See Note on verse 14.)

(20) **Exacted.**—Literally, *caused to go out;* a word already used in the sense of *to lay out, expend* money (chap. xii. 12). Probably, therefore, *laid (vayyissā)*, *i.e.*, imposed, should be read here (Gen. xxxi. 17).

**Of.**—Heb., *upon.*

**The mighty men of wealth.**—A later use of the Hebrew phrase, which, in older parlance, means "the heroes of the host" (Judges vi. 12; 1 Sam. ix. 1).

**Fifty shekels.**—The talent of silver was worth 3,000 shekels. The payment of 1,000 talents (3,000,000 shekels) therefore implies a total of 60,000 persons able to contribute. Fifty shekels were one *maneh* (Assyrian, *mana*; Greek, μνᾶ, and Latin, *mina*). There was no great Temple treasury to draw from in the northern kingdom, and any palace hoards would have disappeared in the confusions attending the frequent revolutions of the time.

**There.**—Or, *then* (Ps. xiv. 5).

(23—26) THE REIGN OF PEKAHIAH (Heb., *Pěkahyāh*).

(23) **In the fiftieth year.**—The forty-ninth, if verse seventeen were exact.

(25) **But . . . a captain of his.**—*And . . . his adjutant* (or *knight,* chap. vii. 2).

**The palace of the king's house.**—The same expression occurred in 1 Kings xvi. 18. The word *armôn,* rendered "palace," is usually explained as meaning *citadel* or *keep,* from a root meaning *to be high.* (Comp. ἡ ἄκρα in Greek.) Ewald makes it *the harem,* which, as the innermost and most strongly-guarded part of an Oriental palace, is probably meant here. Thither Pekahiah had fled for refuge before the conspirators.

**With Argob and Arieh.**—Pekah slew these two persons, probably officers of the royal guard, who stood by their master, as well as the king himself.

The peculiar names are an indication of the *historical character* of the account. Argob suggests that the person who bore this name was a native of the district of Bashan so designated (1 Kings iv. 13); Arieh ("lion"), like our own Cœur-de-Lion, betokens strength and bravery. (Comp. 1 Chron. xii. 8, "The Gadites, whose faces were as the faces of lions.")

**And with him fifty men of the Gileadites.** —Or, *and with him were fifty,* &c. Pekah was supported by fifty soldiers, probably of the royal guard. Menahem himself was of Gadite origin (verse 17), and so belonged to Gilead. He would therefore be likely to recruit his body-guard from among the Gileadites, who were always famous for their prowess. (Comp. Josh. xvii. 1; Judges xi. 12; 1 Chron. xxvi. 31.) The two names Argob and Arieh agree with this supposition. The LXX. reads, in place of "the Gileadites," ἀπὸ τῶν τετρακοσίων, "of the four hundred," which reminds us of David's six hundred *Gibbôrîm* (2 Sam. xv. 18).

Josephus accounts for the short reign of Pekahiah by the statement that he imitated the cruelty of his father.

(27—31) THE REIGN OF PEKAH, SON OF REMALIAH, IN SAMARIA.

(27) **Reigned twenty years.**—This does not agree with the duration assigned to the reign of Jotham (verse 33), and the year assigned as the beginning of Hoshea's reign (chap. xvii. 1). For, according to verse 32, Pekah had reigned about two years when Jotham succeeded in Judah, and Jotham reigned sixteen years; and, according to chap. xvii. 1, Pekah was succeeded by Hoshea in the twelfth year of Jotham's successor, Ahaz. These data make the duration of Pekah's reign from twenty-eight to thirty years. We must, therefore, either assume, with Thenius, that "the numeral sign for 30 (ל) has been corrupted into 20 (כ)," or, with Ewald, that "and nine" has been accidentally omitted after "twenty."

(29) **Tiglath-pileser.**—This Assyrian sovereign, who reigned from 745 to 727 B.C., is called in his own inscriptions, *Tukulti-* (or *Tuklat*) *'abal-Esarra,* which Schrader renders, "my trust is Adar"—literally, *Trust is the son of the temple of Sarra.* (See Note on 1

Israel came Tiglath-pileser king of Assyria, and took Ijon, and Abel-beth-maachah, and Janoah, and Kedesh, and Hazor, and Gilead, and Galilee, all the land of Naphtali, and carried them captive to Assyria.

(30) And Hoshea the son of Elah made a conspiracy against Pekah the son of Remaliah, and smote him, and slew him, and reigned in his stead, in the twentieth year of Jotham the son of Uzziah.

(31) And the rest of the acts of Pekah, and all that he did, behold, they *are* written in the book of the chronicles of the kings of Israel.

(32) In the second year of Pekah the son of Remaliah king of Israel began *a* Jotham the son of Uzziah king of Judah to reign. (33) Five and twenty years old was he when he began to reign, and he reigned sixteen years in Jerusalem. And his mother's name *was* Jerusha, the daughter of Zadok. (34) And he did *that which was* right in the sight of the LORD: he did according to all that his father Uzziah had done. (35) Howbeit the high places were not removed: the people sacrificed and burned incense still in the high places. He built the higher gate of the house of the LORD.

(36) Now the rest of the acts of Jotham, and all that he did, *are* they not written in the book of the chronicles of the kings of Judah?

(37) In those days the LORD began to send against Judah Rezin the king of Syria, and Pekah the son of Remaliah. (38) And Jotham slept with his fathers,

---

Chron. v. 26.) "The idea we get of this king from the remains of these inscriptions corresponds throughout to what we know of him from the Bible. Everywhere he is presented as a powerful warrior-king, who subjugated the entire tract of anterior Asia, from the frontier mountains of Media in the east to the Mediterranean sea in the west, including a part of Cappadocia" (Schrader, *K.A.T.*, p. 247).

**Took Ijon, and Abel-beth-maachah ... all the land of Naphtali.**—Comp. 1 Kings xv. 20.

**Janoah.**—Not the border-town between Ephraim and Manasseh (Josh. xvi. 6), as the context requires a place in the northernmost part of Israel.

**Kedesh.**—On the western shore of the waters of Merom (Josh. xxi. 37).

**Hazor.**—See 1 Kings ix. 15.

**Gilead.**—See chap. xiv. 25; 1 Chron. v. 26. It was no long time since Jeroboam II. had recovered it for Israel. According to Schrader (*K.A.T.*, pp. 254, *seq.*) the reference of the verse is to Tiglath Pileser's expedition in B.C. 734, called in the Eponym list an expedition to the land of *Pilista* (Philistia). With this Schrader connects a fragment of the annals which begins with a list of towns conquered by Tiglath, and ends thus : . . . "the town of Gaal (ad) . . . (A) bil . . . of the upper part of the land of Beth-Omri (*i.e.*, Samaria) . . . in its whole extent I annexed to the territory of Assyria ; my prefects the sagans I appointed over them." The fragment goes on to mention the flight of Hânûn, king of Gaza, to Egypt, and the carrying off of his goods and his gods by the conqueror. It is added, "The land of Beth-Omri . . . the whole body of his men, their goods, to the land of Assyria I led away, *Pakaha* (*i.e.*, Pekah) their king I *slew* (so Schrader ; ᵖ 'they slew'), and *A-u-si-ha* (*i.e.*, Hoshea) . . . over them I appointed. Ten (talents of gold, 1,000 talents of silver) I received from them."

(30) **Hoshea ... slew him, and reigned in his stead.**—See the inscription of Tiglath Pileser, quoted in the last Note, from which, as Schrader remarks, it is clear that Hoshea only secured his hold on the crown by recognition of the suzerainty of Assyria. The brief record of Kings does not mention this; but chap. xvii. 3 represents Hoshea as paying tribute to Shalmaneser IV., the successor of Tiglath.

**In the twentieth year of Jotham.**—This is a suspicious statement, as not agreeing with verse 33, according to which Jotham reigned sixteen years only.

(32–38) THE REIGN OF JOTHAM IN JERUSALEM. (Comp. 2 Chron. xxvii.)

(32) **In the second year of Pekah.**—Who came to the throne in the last year of Uzziah (Azariah, verse 27).

(34) **According to all that his father Uzziah had done.**—The chronicler qualifies this general statement by adding that Jotham did not, like his father, invade the Holy Place. (Comp. 2 Chron. xxvii. 2, with 2 Chron. xxvi. 16.)

(35) **Howbeit the high places.**—The chronicler generalises this statement: "And the people did yet corruptly."

**He built.**—Rather, *He it was who built.* For "the higher gate," see Note on 2 Chron. xxvii. 3. Thenius considers that the term *higher* denotes rank rather than local position. (See Jer. xx. 2; Ezek. viii. 3, 5, 14, 16; ix. 2; xl. 38—43; and comp. chap. xii. 9.)

(36) **Now the rest of the acts of Jotham.**—Some of these are related in 2 Chron. xxvii. 4—6. We read there how Jotham built towns and castles, and towers of refuge, and how he fought victoriously against Ammon, and exacted from that nation a heavy tribute three years running. Ewald and Thenius admit the historical value of this brief narrative, which is indeed evident on the face of it.

(37) **In those days**—*i.e.*, in the last year of Jotham. The attacks of the allies at first took the form of isolated raids. In the next reign the country was invaded by them in full force. (See chap. xvi. 5, *seq.*, and the Notes there.)

**Rezin.**—Comp. Rezon, Heb., *Rĕzôn* (1 Kings xi. 23), the founder of the dynasty. The present name is spelt in the Hebrew of Kings and Isaiah (vii. 1) *Rĕçin.* The Assyrian spelling in the records of Tiglath Pileser, who conquered and slew Rezin, suggests that the right spelling was *Răçôn* (Assyrian, *Raçunnu*). The first and last kings of the Syrian monarchy thus bore similar names, both, perhaps, meaning "prince."

and was buried with his fathers in the city of David his father: and Ahaz his son reigned in his stead.

CHAPTER XVI.—<sup>(1)</sup> In the seventeenth year of Pekah the son of Remaliah ᵃ Ahaz the son of Jotham king of Judah began to reign. <sup>(2)</sup> Twenty years old *was* Ahaz when he began to reign, and reigned sixteen years in Jerusalem, and did not *that which was* right in the sight of the LORD his God, like David his father. <sup>(3)</sup> But he walked in the way of the kings of Israel, yea, and made his son to pass through the fire, according to the abominations of the heathen, whom the LORD cast out from before the children of Israel. <sup>(4)</sup> And he sacrificed and burnt incense in the high places, and on the hills, and under every green tree.

<sup>(5) ᵇ</sup> Then Rezin king of Syria and Pekah son of Remaliah king of Israel came up to Jerusalem to war: and they besieged Ahaz, but could not overcome him. <sup>(6)</sup> At that time Rezin king of

---

*a* 2 Chron. 28. 1.

B.C. cir. 742.

B.C. 742.

*b* Isa. 7. 1.

---

## XVI.

THE REIGN OF AHAZ. (Comp. 2 Chron. xxviii.)

<sup>(2)</sup> **Twenty years old.**—The number should probably be *twenty-and-five*, according to the LXX., Syriac, and Arabic of 2 Chron. xxviii. 1. Otherwise, Ahaz was begotten when his father was ten (or, eleven) years old—a thing perhaps not impossible in the East, where both sexes reach maturity earlier than among Western races.

<sup>(3)</sup> **But he walked in the way.**—See Notes on 2 Chron. xxviii. 2.

**Made his son to pass through the fire.**—The chronicler rightly explains this as a *sacrifice* by fire. That such an appalling rite is really intended may be seen by reference to chap. xvii. 31; Jer. xix. 5; Ezek. xvi. 20, xxiii. 37; Jer. xxxii. 35. The expression, "To make to *pass through the fire to Moloch*" (Lev. xviii. 21) may have originated, as Movers suggests, in the idea that the burning was a kind of passage to union with the deity, after the dross of the flesh had been purged away; or it may be a mere euphemism. Ahaz appears to have been the first Israelite king who offered such a sacrifice. He, no doubt, regarded it as a last desperate resource against the oppression of his northern enemies. It is absurd to suppose that the king intended it in love to his child, as Thenius suggests. (See Judges xi. 31.) Such dreadful sacrifices were only made in cases of dire extremity. (Comp. chap. iii. 27.)

**The heathen.**—More particularly the *Ammonites*, who made such sacrifices to Molech or Milcom.

<sup>(4)</sup> **In the high places.**—These are evidently distinguished from "the hills," two different prepositions being used in the Hebrew as in the English. A *bāmāh*, or "high-place," was a local sanctuary, and it appears that a sacred pillar or altar might be called a *bāmāh*. Mesha king of Moab speaks of his pillar as "this *bāmath*." (See Note on chap. i. 1.)

**Under every green tree.**—Comp. 1 Kings xiv. 23; Hosea xiv. 8. Thenius says not so much a green as a *thick-foliaged* and *shadow-yielding* tree. "They burn incense . . . under oaks, and poplars, and teil trees, because the shadow thereof is good" (Hosea iv. 13).

THE SYRO-EPHRAIMITIC WAR, AND THE INTERVENTION OF TIGLATH PILESER. (Comp. Isa. vii.—ix. 7, "an epitome of the discourses delivered by the prophet at this great national crisis."—Cheyne.)

<sup>(5)</sup> **Then Rezin king of Syria . . . to war.**—This verse agrees almost word for word with Isa. vii. 1. The *time* is soon after the accession of Ahaz. "Jotham, the last of a series of strong and generally successful princes, had died at a critical moment, when Pekah and Rezin were maturing their plans against his kingdom. The opposing parties in northern Israel suspended their feuds to make common cause against Judah (Isa. ix. 21), and the proud inhabitants of Samaria hoped by this policy to more than restore the prestige forfeited in previous years of calamity (Isa. ix. 9, 10). At the same time the Syrians began to operate in the eastern dependencies of Judah, their aim being to possess themselves of the harbour of Elath on the Red Sea, while the Philistines attacked the Judeans in the rear, and ravaged the fertile lowlands (Isa. ix. 12, verse 6). A heavy and sudden disaster had already fallen on the Judean arms, a defeat in which 'head and tail, palm-branch and rush' had been mown down in indiscriminate slaughter (Isa. ix. 14). Ahaz was no fit leader in so critical a time; his character was petulant and childish, his policy was dictated in the harem (Isa. iii. 12). Nor was the internal order of the state calculated to inspire confidence. Wealth, indeed, had greatly accumulated in the preceding time of prosperity, but its distribution had been such that it weakened rather than added strength to the nation. The rich nobles were steeped in sensual luxury, the court was full of gallantry, feminine extravagance and vanity gave the tone to aristocratic society (Isa. v. 11, iii. 16; comp. iii. 12, iv. 4), which, like the *noblesse* of France on the eve of the Revolution, was absorbed in gaiety and pleasure, while the masses were ground down by oppression, and the cry of their distress filled the land (Isa. iii. 15, v. 7)."—Prof. Robertson Smith.

**They besieged Ahaz.**—The allies wanted to compel Judah to join them in their attempt to throw off the burdensome yoke of Assyria, imposed in 738 B.C. (chap. xv. 19); and thought the best way to secure this was to dethrone the dynasty of David, and set up a creature of their own—"the son of Tabeal" (Isa. vii. 6).

**Could not overcome him.**—Literally, *they were not able to war*, as in Isa. vii. 2. The allies could not storm the city, which had been strongly fortified by Uzziah and Jotham (2 Chron. xxvi. 9, xxvii. 3).

<sup>(6)</sup> **At that time.**—Bähr regards this verse as a parenthesis, so that verse 7 is the strict continuation of verse 5, and "At that time" simply assigns this war as the epoch when Judah lost its only harbour and chief emporium—a grave blow to the national prosperity. It is perhaps impossible to weave the various data of Isaiah, Kings, and Chronicles into a single narrative which shall be free from all objection. But it seems probable that, after the successes recorded in 2 Chron. xxviii. 5, *seq.*, the confederates advanced upon Jerusa-

*Judah Invaded by*        II. KINGS, XVI.        *Israel and Syria.*

Syria recovered Elath to Syria, and drave the Jews from Elath: and the Syrians came to Elath, and dwelt there unto this day. <sup>(7)</sup> So Ahaz sent messengers to Tiglath-pileser king of Assyria, saying, I *am* thy servant and thy son: come up, and save me out of the hand of the king of Syria, and out of the hand of the king of Israel, which rise up against me. <sup>(8)</sup> And Ahaz took the silver and gold that was found in the house of the LORD, and in the treasures of the king's house, and sent *it for* a present to the king of Assyria. <sup>(9)</sup> And the king of Assyria hearkened unto him: for the king of Assyria went up against <sup>1</sup>Damascus, and took it, and carried *the people of* it captive to Kir, and slew Rezin.

<sup>(10)</sup> And king Ahaz went to Damascus to meet Tiglath-pileser king of Assyria, and saw an altar that *was* at Damascus: and king Ahaz sent to Urijah the priest the fashion of the altar, and the pattern

<sup>1</sup> Heb., *Dammesek.*

---

lem, and that Ahaz despatched his envoys to Tiglath Pileser. The allies soon despaired of a siege, and Pekah fell to ravaging the country, while Rezin pushed on to Elath, determined not to return home without having achieved some permanent success. The approach of Tiglath Pileser compelled the two kings to give up their enterprise, and hasten to defend their own frontiers.

**Recovered Elath to Syria . . . the Syrians.**—The words for *Syria* and *Edom*, *Syrians* and *Edomites*, are very much alike in Hebrew writing, and the Hebrew margin, many MSS., the LXX. and Vulg. read *Edomites* for *Syrians* here. If this be correct, we must also restore *Edom* for *Syria*, as many critics propose. The meaning then becomes this: Rezin emancipated the Edomites from the yoke of Judah imposed on them by Uzziah (chap. xiv. 22) in order to win their active co-operation against Judah. Bähr, however, prefers the readings of the ordinary text, and supposes that Rezin simply expelled the Jews from Elath, and established there a commercial colony of Syrians.

<sup>(7)</sup> **So Ahaz sent messengers.**—See Notes on 2 Chron. xxviii. 16, 20.

**Which rise up against me.**—Or, *which are assailing me.* "The vain confidence of the rulers of Judah, described by Isaiah in his first prophetic book, was rudely shaken by the progress of the war with Pekah and Rezin. Unreasoning confidence had given way to equally unreasoning panic. They saw only one way of escape—namely, to throw themselves upon the protection of Assyria." (*Robertson Smith.*)

<sup>(8)</sup> **Ahaz took the silver and gold.**—"He was well aware that the only conditions on which protection would be vouchsafed were acceptance of the Assyrian suzerainty with the payment of a huge tribute, and an embassy was despatched laden with all the treasures of the palace and the Temple. The ambassadors had no difficulty in attaining their object, which perfectly fell in with the schemes of the great king. The invincible army was set in motion, Damascus was taken, and its inhabitants led captive, and Gilead and Galilee suffered the same fate" (*Robertson Smith*). (Comp. chap. xv. 29.) According to Schrader, the expedition "to Philistia" in 734 B.C., was directed against Pekah, who probably saved himself by an instant submission. It was only after Tiglath had settled matters with the northern kingdom, and so isolated Damascus, that he turned his arms against Rezin. Two whole years were spent in reducing him (733—732 B.C.) In an inscription dating from his seventeenth year, Tiglath Pileser mentions that he received tribute from Eniel, king of Hamath, Muthumbaal, king of Arvad, Sanibu of Ammon, Salamanu of Moab, Mitinti of Ascalon, Jahuhazi (Jehoahaz, *i.e.*, Ahaz) of Judah, Qaus-malaka of Edom, Hanun of Gaza, and other princes. This probably relates to the expedition of 734 B.C., in which year, therefore, Ahaz (Jehoahaz) must have put himself under the protection of Assyria (Schrader, *K.A.T.*, p. 257 *seq.*).

<sup>(9)</sup> **Went up against Damascus, and took it.**—We learn from the inscriptions that Damascus stood a two years' siege. (The Eponym-list makes Tiglath Pileser march against Damascus for two successive years, namely 733 and 732 B.C.)

**Carried the people of it captive to Kir.**—(Comp. Amos i. 5, ix. 7.) The name Kir is not found in the fragmentary remains of the annals of Tiglath Pileser. Schrader (p. 261 *seq.*) gives a mutilated inscription, apparently relating to the fall of Damascus.

**And slew Rezin.**—Sir H. Rawlinson found this fact recorded on a tablet of Tiglath Pileser's, since unfortunately lost. In the inscription just referred to Tiglath says: "I entered the gate of his city; his chief officers alive [I took, and] on stakes I caused to lift them up" (*i.e.*, impaled them).

Kir was the aboriginal home of the Arameans, according to Amos ix. 7. It is mentioned along with Elam in Isa. xxii. 6. "It has been generally identified with the district by the river Cyrus (the modern Georgia). But, besides the linguistic objection pointed out by Delitzsch (Qir cannot be equivalent to Kúr), it appears that the Assyrian empire never extended to the Cyrus. We must, therefore, consider Kir to be a part of Mesopotamia." (*Cheyne.*)

<sup>(10)</sup> **Ahaz went to Damascus, to meet Tiglath-pileser.**—The great king appears to have held his court there after the capture of the city, and to have summoned the vassal princes of Palestine thither to do him homage in person before his departure. (See the Note on verse 8.)

**And saw an altar.**—Rather, *and he saw the altar,* namely, that of the principal Temple. Upon the account which follows Prof. Robertson Smith well remarks that the frivolous character of Ahaz "was so little capable of appreciating the dangers involved in his new obligations, that he returned to Jerusalem with his head full of the artistic and religious curiosities he had seen on his journey. In a national crisis of the first magnitude he found no more pressing concern than the erection of a new altar in the Temple on a pattern brought from Damascus. The sundial of Ahaz (2 Kings xx. 11), and an erection on the roof of the Temple, with altars apparently designed for the worship of the host of heaven (2 Kings xxiii. 12), were works equally characteristic of the trifling and superstitious *virtuoso,* who imagined that the introduction of a few foreign novelties gave lustre to a reign which had fooled away the independence of Judah, and sought a

of it, according to all the workmanship thereof. (11) And Urijah the priest built an altar according to all that king Ahaz had sent from Damascus: so Urijah the priest made *it* against king Ahaz came from Damascus. (12) And when the king was come from Damascus, the king saw the altar: and the king approached to the altar, and offered thereon. (13) And he burnt his burnt offering and his meat offering, and poured his drink offering, and sprinkled the blood of ¹his peace offerings, upon the altar. (14) And he brought also the brasen altar, which *was* before the LORD, from the forefront of the house, from between the altar and the house of the LORD, and put it on the north side of the altar. (15) And king Ahaz commanded Urijah the priest, saying, Upon the great altar burn the morning burnt offering, and the evening meat offering, and the king's burnt sacrifice, and his meat offering, with the burnt offering of all the people of the land, and their meat offering, and their drink offerings; and sprinkle upon it all the blood of the burnt offering, and all the blood of the sacrifice: and the brasen altar shall be for me to enquire *by*. (16) Thus did Urijah the priest, according to all that king Ahaz commanded. (17) And king Ahaz cut off the borders of the bases, and removed the laver from off them; and took down the sea from off the brasen oxen that *were* under it, and put it upon a pave-

¹ Heb. *which were his.*

B.C. 739.

---

momentary deliverance by accepting a service the burden of which was fast becoming intolerable" (*Proph. of Israel*, p. 251).

**Urijah the priest**—*i.e.*, the high priest, who appears to be identical with the "credible witness" of Isa. viii. 2. His high official position would secure Urijah's credit as a witness.

**Fashion . . . pattern . . . workmanship.**—These terms indicate that the king's interest in the matter was artistic rather than religious.

(12) **The king approached to the altar, and offered thereon.**—So the Targum renders. But all the other versions: "The king approached to the altar, *and went up* thereon." (Comp. 1 Kings xii. 32, 33.) It thus appears that Ahaz, like Uzziah, personally exercised the priestly function of sacrifice.

(13) **And he burnt his burnt offering . . .**—The verse describes the thank-offering of Ahaz for his late deliverance from deadly peril. From the present narrative it does not appear but that he offered it to Jehovah. The account in 2 Chron. xxviii. 23 must be understood to refer to other sacrifices instituted by Ahaz, who, like most of his contemporaries, thought the traditional worship of Jehovah not incompatible with the *cultus* of foreign deities. (Comp. verses 3, 4.)

(14) **And he brought also the brasen altar . . .**—Literally, *And as for the brasen altar, he brought it near* (to the new one), *away from the front of the house, to wit, from between the* (new) *altar, and the house of Jehovah; and put it at the side of the* (new) *altar northward.* The brasen altar used to stand "before the Lord," *i.e.*, in the middle of the court of the priests, and in front of the Temple proper. The verse seems to imply that Urijah had pushed it forward nearer to the sanctuary, and set the new Syrian altar in its place. Ahaz, not satisfied with this arrangement, which appeared to confer a kind of precedence on the old altar, drew it back again, and fixed it on the north side of his new altar.

(15) **The great altar**—*i.e.*, as we say, "the *high* altar," the new Syrian one. So the high priest is sometimes called "the great priest" (*kôhēn haggādôl*). Ahaz orders that the daily national sacrifices, the royal offerings, and those of private individuals, shall all be offered at the new altar.

**The morning burnt offering, and the evening meat offering.**—Not that there was no meat offering in the morning, and no burnt offering in the evening. (See Exod. xxix. 38—42; Num. xxviii. 3—8.) The morning meat offering is implied in the mention of the burnt offering, because no burnt offering was offered without one (Num. vij. 87, xv. 2—12). On the other hand, the evening meat offering was the only part of the evening sacrifice which the congregation could stay out, for the burnt offering had to burn all the night through (Lev. vi. 9).

**The brasen altar.**—The contrast seems to imply that the new altar was of a different material.

**Shall be for me to enquire by**—*i.e.*, for consulting God. So Rashi. Others (as Keil): "I will think about what to do with it." Perhaps it is simply, "It shall be for me to look at," *i.e.*, an ornamental duplicate of the other altar. (Comp. Ps. xxvii. 4.) Grätz suggests "to draw near" (*i.e.*, to sacrifice), transposing the last two letters of the verb, which does not suit the context; and Thenius would read, "to seek," after the Syriac, which has "to ask" (*i.e.*, to pray), as if the old altar of sacrifice were henceforth to be an altar of prayer. (?)

(17, 18) **And king Ahaz cut off.**—The key to the right understanding of these verses is given in the last words of verse 18. Ahaz spoiled the Temple of its ornamental work, not out of wanton malice, but from dire necessity. He had to provide a present *for the king of Assyria*. Thus these verses are really a continuation of the first statement of verse 10. They inform us how Ahaz managed not to appear empty-handed at Damascus. (So Thenius.) Prof. R. Smith says: "Ahaz, whose treasures had been exhausted by his first tribute, was soon driven by the repeated demands of his masters to strip the Temple even of its ancient bronzework and other fixed ornaments. The incidental mention of this fact in a fragment of the history of the Temple incorporated in the Book of Kings is sufficient evidence of the straits to which the kingdom of Judah was reduced."

**Borders of the bases.**—See 1 Kings vii. 28. Thenius thinks Ahaz replaced them with unadorned plates, and set the laver up in a different fashion; but the text does not *say* so. (Comp., however, chap. xxv. 13, 16; Jer. lii. 17.)

*Death of Ahaz.* II. KINGS, XVII. *Hoshea Imprisoned.*

ment of stones. <sup>(18)</sup> And the covert for the sabbath that they had built in the house, and the king's entry without, turned he from the house of the LORD for the king of Assyria.

<sup>(19)</sup> Now the rest of the acts of Ahaz which he did, *are they* not written in the book of the chronicles of the kings of Judah? <sup>(20)</sup> And Ahaz slept with his fathers, and was buried with his fathers in the city of David: and Hezekiah his son reigned in his stead.

CHAPTER XVII.—<sup>(1)</sup> In the twelfth year of Ahaz king of Judah began Hoshea the son of Elah to reign in Samaria over Israel nine years. <sup>(2)</sup> And he did *that which was* evil in the sight of the LORD, but not as the kings of Israel that were before him. <sup>(3)</sup> Against him came up Shalmaneser king of Assyria; and Hoshea became his servant, and <sup>1</sup> gave him <sup>2</sup> presents. <sup>(4)</sup> And the king of Assyria found conspiracy in Hoshea: for he had sent messengers to So king of Egypt, and brought no present to the king of Assyria, as *he had done* year by year: therefore the king of Assyria shut him up, and bound him in prison.

<sup>1</sup> Heb., *rendered.*
<sup>2</sup> Or, *tribute.*
B.C. 726.
B.C. 725.
B.C. 730.

---

**The brasen oxen.**—These were ultimately carried off by the Babylonians (Jer. lii. 20).

**A pavement of stones**—*i.e.*, a pedestal or foundation of stonework: ἐπὶ βάσιν λιθίνην (LXX.).

<sup>(18)</sup> **The covert for the sabbath.**—A very obscure expression. The best interpretation is "the covered hall (or stand) set apart for the use of the king and his attendants when he visited the Temple on holy days" (reading, with the Hebrew margin, *mûsak*, which is attested by the Vulg., *musach*, and the Syriac "house of the sabbath"). The thing is not mentioned anywhere else.

**In the house**—*i.e.*, in the sacred precincts, probably in the inner forecourt.

**The king's entry without.**—*The outer entry of the king*, *i.e.*, the gate by which the king entered the inner court (Ezek. xlvi. 1, 2).

**Turned he from the house of the Lord.**—Or, *he altered in the house of the Lord*, *i.e.*, stripped them of their ornamental work.

**For.**—Or, *from fear of* . . .—But comp. Gen. vi. 32, "through them." Ahaz durst not appear before Tiglath without a present. It is possible also that he anticipated a visit from the great king.

<sup>(19)</sup> **Which he did.**—Some MSS., and the LXX., Syriac, and Arabic have the usual formula, "and all which he did."

XVII.

THE REIGN OF HOSHEA, THE LAST KING OF SAMARIA. THE FALL OF SAMARIA. CAPTIVITY OF ISRAEL, AND RE-PEOPLING OF THE LAND BY FOREIGNERS.

<sup>(1)</sup> **In the twelfth year of Ahaz.**—If Pekah reigned thirty years (see Note on chap. xv. 27), and Ahaz succeeded in Pekah's seventeenth year (chap. xvi. 1), Ahaz must have reigned thirteen years concurrently with Pekah. Hoshea, therefore, succeeded Pekah in the *fourteenth* year of Ahaz.

**Began Hoshea.**—See the inscription of Tiglath Pileser, quoted at chap. xv. 30, according to which, Hoshea (*A-u-si-ha*) only mounted the throne as a vassal of Assyria. On the news of the death of Tiglath, he probably refused further tribute.

<sup>(2)</sup> **But not as the kings of Israel that were before him.**—The preceding phrase is used of all the northern kings but Shallum, who only reigned a month, and had no time for the display of his religious policy. We can hardly assume that Hoshea abandoned the calf-worship of Bethel, but he may have discountenanced the *cultus* of the Baals and Asheras. The *Seder Olam* states that Hoshea did not replace the calf of Bethel, which, it assumes, had been carried off by the Assyrians in accordance with the prophecy of Hosea (Hosea x. 5). We may remember that the last sovereigns of falling monarchies have not always been the worst of their line—*e.g.*, Charles I. or Louis XVI.

<sup>(3)</sup> **Against him came up Shalmaneser king of Assyria.**—Shalmaneser IV. (*Shalmânu-ushshir*, "Shalman be gracious!"), the successor of Tiglath Pileser II., and predecessor of Sargon, reigned 727–722 B.C. No annals of his reign have come down to us in the cuneiform inscriptions, but a fragment of the Eponymlist notes foreign expeditions for the three successive years 725–723 B.C. This agrees with what Menander states (Josephus, *Ant.* ix. 14, 2), according to whom Shalmaneser made an expedition against Tyre (and no doubt Israel, as the ally of Tyre), which lasted *five years*—*i.e.*, was continued beyond Shalmaneser's reign into that of Sargon. Nothing is known of the death of Shalmaneser.

<sup>(4)</sup> **Conspiracy**—*i.e.*, as is presently explained, a conspiracy with the king of Egypt against his suzerain. Shalmaneser regarded Hoshea, and probably the king of Egypt also, as his "servant." (verse 3). (Comp. chap. xii. 20 and Jer. xi. 9.) Thenius wishes to read "falsehood," after the LXX., ἀδικίαν (comp. Deut. xix. 18; Micah vi. 12), a change involving transposition of two Heb. letters (*shèqer* for *qèsher*); but the change is needless.

**So.**—The Hebrew letters should be pointed differently, so as to be pronounced *Sewè*, or *Sěwē*, as this name corresponds to the Assyrian *Shab'i*, and the Egyptian *Shabaka*, the Greek *Sabaco*, the first king of the XXVth, or Ethiopian dynasty, whom Sargon defeated at Raphia in 720 B.C. Sargon calls him "prince," or "ruler" (*shiltân*), rather than "king" of Egypt; and it appears that at this time Lower Egypt was divided among a number of petty principalities, whose recognition of any central authority was very uncertain—a fact which rendered an Egyptian alliance of little value to Israel. (See Isa. xix., xx.)

**Brought.**—Rather, *offered*. The word elsewhere is always used of *sacrifice*.

**As he had done.**—Omit. The Hebrew phrase (*according to a year, in a year*), which is not found elsewhere, denotes the regular payment of yearly dues. This Hoshea failed to discharge.

**Therefore . . . shut him up.**—Comp. Jer. xxxiii. 1, xxxvi. 5, xxxii. 2, 3. This statement seems to imply that Shalmaneser took Hoshea prisoner *before* the siege

(5) Then the king of Assyria came up throughout all the land, and went up to Samaria, and besieged it three years. (6) *In the ninth year of Hoshea the king of Assyria took Samaria, and carried Israel away into Assyria, and placed them in Halah and in Habor *by* the river of Gozan, and in the cities of the Medes. (7) For *so it was*, that the children of Israel had sinned against the LORD their God, which had brought them up out of the land of Egypt, from under the hand of Pharaoh king of Egypt, and had feared other gods, (8) and walked in the statutes of the heathen, whom the LORD cast out from before the children of Israel, and of the kings of Israel, which they had made. (9) And the children of Israel did secretly *those* things that *were* not right against the LORD their God, and they built them high places in all their cities, from the tower of the watchmen to the fenced city. (10) And they set them up ¹images and groves in every high hill, and under every green tree: (11) and there they burnt incense in all the high places, as *did* the heathen whom the LORD carried away before them; and wrought wicked things to provoke the LORD to anger: (12) for they served idols, whereof the LORD had said unto them, *b*Ye shall not do this thing.

(13) Yet the LORD testified against

B.C. 723.

*a* ch. 18. 10.

1 Heb., *statues.*

*b* Deut. 4. 19.

---

of Samaria: a supposition which finds support in the fact that Sargon, who ended the siege, makes no mention of the capture or death of the Israelite king.

(5) **Then** (*and*) **the king of Assyria came up . . . and besieged it three years.**—Sargon states that he took Samaria (*Samerína*) in his *first* year. Shalmaneser therefore had besieged the city some two years before his death.

The brief narrative before us does not discriminate between the respective shares of the two Assyrian sovereigns in the overthrow of the kingdom of Israel, but it is noticeable that it does *not* say that Shalmaneser "besieged Samaria three years," and "took Samaria." (Comp. chap. xviii. 11.)

(6) **In the ninth year of Hoshea the king of Assyria took Samaria.**—Comp. Hosea x. 5 *seq.*; Micah i. 6; Isa. xxviii. 1—4. In the great inscription published by Botta, Sargon says: "The city of Samaria I assaulted, I took; 27,280 men dwelling in the midst thereof I carried off; 50 chariots among them I set apart (for myself), and the rest of their wealth I let (my soldiers) take; my prefect over them I appointed, and the tribute of the former king upon them I laid."

**Placed them.**—Literally, *made them dwell.* LXX., κατῴκησεν.

**In Halah.**—This place appears to be identical with *Halahhu*, a name occurring in an Assyrian geographical list between *Arrabha* (Arrapachitis) and *Ratsappa* (Rezeph). It probably lay in Mesopotamia, like Rezeph and Gozan. (See Note on 1 Chron. v. 26.)

**In Habor by the river of Gozan.**—Rather, *on Habor the river of Gozan.*

**The cities of the Medes.**—The LXX. seems to have read "mountains of the Medes." (Comp. Notes on 1 Chron. v. 26, where "Hara and the river of Gozan" is probably the result of an inadvertent transposition of "The river of Gozan and Hara.")

(7—23) REFLECTIONS OF THE LAST EDITOR ON THE MORAL CAUSES OF THE CATASTROPHE.

(7) **For so it was.**—Literally, *and it came to pass.*

**Sinned against the Lord . . . Egypt.**—The claim of Jehovah to Israel's exclusive fealty was from the outset based upon the fact that He had emancipated them from the Egyptian bondage—a fact which is significantly asserted as the preamble to Jehovah's laws. (See Exod. xx. 2; and comp. Hosea xi. 1, xii. 9.)

**Had feared other gods.**—Such as the Baals and Asheras of Canaan, which symbolised the productive powers of Nature, and, further, the heavenly bodies. (Comp. Amos v. 25, 26; Ezek. viii. 14, 16.)

(8) **Statutes of the heathen . . . and of the kings of Israel.**—The national guilt was twofold. It comprised: (1) idolatry in the strict sense—*i.e.,* worship of other gods than Jehovah; (2) a heathenish mode of worshipping Jehovah Himself—namely, under the form of a bullock, as Jeroboam I. had ordained. The term "statutes" means religious rules or ordinances. (Comp. Exod. xii. 14, "statutes;" Lev. xx. 23, "manners;" 1 Kings iii. 3, "ordinance.")

**Which they had made**—*i.e.,* the statutes which the kings of Israel had made. (Comp. verse 19 *b.*)

(9) **Did secretly.**—The literal sense is *covered.* In this connection it is natural to remember that Heb. verbs of *covering* and *hiding* are often used in the sense of dealing *perfidiously* or *deceitfully.* (Comp. *mā'al*, 1 Chron. x. 13, with *me'îl*, "mantle;" and *bāgad*, "to deal treacherously," Hosea v. 7, with *beged*, "garment.") The form in the text (the *pihel* of *'hāphā*) is only found here.

**They built them high places.**—First, the institution of unlawful *places* of worship.

**From the tower of the watchmen to the fenced city.**—The towers are such as are mentioned in 2 Chron. xxvi. 10. Here, and in chap. xviii. 8, these solitary buildings, tenanted by a few herdsmen, are contrasted with the embattled cities which protected multitudes. Wherever men were, whether in small or large numbers, these high places were established.

(10) **Images and groves.**—*Pillars and Asheras*—*i.e.,* sacred trunks.

The *second* degree of guilt: the setting up of idolatrous symbols.

(11) **Wrought wicked things.**—Not merely idolatrous rites, but also the hideous immoralities which constituted a recognised part of the nature-worships of Canaan.

(12) **For they served idols.**—Rather, *and they served the dunglings*; a term of contempt used in 1 Kings xv. 19; Deut. xxix. 16, where see Note.

(13) **Yet the Lord testified against Israel.**—Rather, *And Jehovah adjured Israel . . .* The verb means here, *gave solemn warning*, or *charge.* In verse 15 it is repeated, with a cognate noun as object: "His

Israel, and against Judah, ¹ by all the prophets, *and by* all the seers, saying, *ᵃ* Turn ye from your evil ways, and keep my commandments *and* my statutes, according to all the law which I commanded your fathers, and which I sent to you by my servants the prophets. (14) Notwithstanding they would not hear, but hardened their necks, like to the neck of their fathers, that did not believe in the LORD their God. (15) And they rejected his statutes, and his covenant that he made with their fathers, and his testimonies which he testified against them; and they followed vanity, and became vain, and went after the heathen that *were* round about them, *concerning* whom the LORD had charged them, that they should not do like them. (16) And they left all the commandments of the LORD their God, and *ᵈ* made them molten images, *even* two calves, and made a grove, and worshipped all the host of heaven, and served Baal. (17) And they caused their sons and their daughters to pass through the fire, and used divination and enchantments, and sold themselves to do evil in the sight of the LORD, to provoke him to anger.

(18) Therefore the LORD was very angry with Israel, and removed them out of

¹ Heb., *by the hand of all.*
*ᵃ* Jer. 18. 11 & 25. 5, & 35. 15.
*ᵇ* Ex. 32. 8; 1 Kings 12. 28.

---

testimonies which he testified against them;" or, *his charges* (*i.e.*, precepts) *which he had given them.*

**By all the prophets, and by all the seers.**—The Hebrew text is, *by the hand of all his prophets—namely, every seer.* One or two MSS. and the Targum have *prophet*, instead of *his prophets*. The Syriac has "by the hand of all his servants the prophets, and all the seers." The Vulg. and Arabic also have both nouns plural. Seers were such persons as, without belonging to the prophetic order, came forward in times of emergency upon a sudden Divine impulse. Thenius thinks Israel and Judah are mentioned together because the reference is to the time before the partition of the kingdom; more probably, because both apostatised, and prophets were sent to both.

**And which I sent**—*i.e.*, the law which I sent. But—as according to later Jewish ideas, the prophets did not bring the Law, but only interpreted it—it seems better to understand with the Vulg. ("et sicut misi") "*and according to all* that I sent to you (*i.e.*, enjoined upon you) by my servants the prophets."

(14) **Notwithstanding . . . hear.**—Rather, *and they hearkened not.*

**Necks.**—Heb., *neck.* (Comp. Deut. x. 16; Jer. xvii. 23; 2 Chron. xxxvi. 13.)

**Like to the neck.**—LXX. and Syriac, *more than the neck.* One letter different in the Hebrew.

**Did not believe in the Lord their God.**—The reference is not to *intellectual* but to *moral* unbelief, evincing itself as disobedience. Vulg., "qui voluerunt obediren." They did not render the obedience of faith. (Comp. the use of 'ἀπειθεῖν in the Greek Testament.)

(15) **And they followed vanity, and became vain.**—The same expression occurs in Jer. ii. 5. The word "vanity" (*hèbel*) has the article. It denotes strictly *breath*; and then that which is as *transient* as a breath. (Comp. Job vii. 16.) Here the idols and their worship are intended. The cognate verb, "became vain," means "dealt (or, 'talked;' Job xxvii. 12) foolishly." The LXX. has 'ἐματαιώθησαν. (Comp. Rom. i. 21.)

(16) **Molten images.**—1 Kings xii. 28. Literally, *a casting.*

**A grove.**—*An Asherah* (1 Kings xiv 23, xvi. 33). Schlottmann writes: "That Ashera was only another name for the same supreme goddess (*i.e.*, Ashtoreth) is at once shown by the parallelism of 'Baal and Ashtaroth' (Judges ii. 13) with 'Baal and Asherim' (the plural of Ashera) in Judges iii. 7. In quite the same way Baal and Ashera stand side by side in Judges vi. 28, 2 Kings xxiii. 4; and in 1 Kings xviii. 19 the 450 prophets of the Baal and the 400 of the Ashera. Further, in 2 Chron. xv. 16, xxiv. 18, the LXX. render Ashera by Astarte; and in other passages Aquila, Symmachus, and the Peshito do the same thing." He then refers to 1 Kings xiv. 23 and Isa. xvii. 8, xxvii. 9, and continues: "according to these and many other passages, *Ashera* was used as the designation of the commonest material representation of the goddess. It consisted of a block of wood, of considerable size (Judges vi. 26), and resembling a tree, as is shown by the expressions used in connection with it, such as 'setting up,' 'planting,' and 'cutting down' (2 Kings xvii. 10; Deut. xii. 17; Judges vi. 28; 2 Kings xviii. 4, &c.). In Isa. xxvii. 9 the LXX. actually renders 'tree;' and so the Peshito in Deut. vi. 21, Micah v. 13. Hence, we must not think of pillars like the Greek Hermae, but of a *real trunk planted in the ground, rootless, but not branchless*; for which purpose pines and evergreens were preferred. The *tree* signifies, according to an ancient and widespread conception, *nature*, or *the world*, which in this case stands as goddess at the side of the Baal—*the lord* of the world. (Comp. the Norse tree, Yggdrasil, and the Assyrian sacred tree.) Hence, the Ashera was set up by the altar of Baal (Judges vi. 28). (Comp. Deut. xvi. 21.)" Schlottmann adds that Movers is wrong in making Astarte and Ashera two different goddesses, the former being "the stern, cruel virgin," the latter, "the goddess who excites to pleasure;" and he justly observes that, as in the case of Baal, the same deity may be conceived under contrary aspects (Riehm's *Handwörterbuch Bibl. Alterthums*, pp. 111–114). For the Hebrew conception of Astarte see Jer. vii. 18, xliv. 17 *seq.* Kuenen, *Rel. of Isr.* i. 88 *seq.*, agrees with Movers, but hardly proves his case.

**Worshipped all the host of heaven.**—Chap. xxi. 3; comp. xxiii. 4.

(17) **And they caused . . . fire.**—The *cultus* of Moloch (chap. xvi. 3).

**Used divination and enchantments.**—Deut. xviii. 10; Num. xxiii. 23. "Divinationibus inserviebant et auguriis" (Vulg.).

**Sold themselves.**—Idolatry is regarded as a *servitude.* (Comp. 1 Kings xxi. 20, 25.)

(18) **Removed them out of his sight.**—By banishing them from his land (verse 23)—an expression founded upon the old *local* conceptions of deity.

*Sins of Judah.*      II. KINGS, XVII.      *Samaria Re-peopled.*

his sight: there was none left but the tribe of Judah only. (19) Also Judah kept not the commandments of the LORD their God, but walked in the statutes of Israel which they made. (20) And the LORD rejected all the seed of Israel, and afflicted them, and delivered them into the hand of spoilers, until he had cast them out of his sight. (21) For he rent Israel from the house of David; and they made Jeroboam the son of Nebat king: and Jeroboam drave Israel from following the LORD, and made them sin a great sin. (22) For the children of Israel walked in all the sins of Jeroboam which he did; they departed not from them; (23) until the LORD removed Israel out of his sight, as he had said by all his servants the prophets. So was Israel carried away out of their own land to Assyria unto this day.

(24) And the king of Assyria brought *men* from Babylon, and from Cuthah, and from Ava, and from Hamath, and from Sepharvaim, and placed *them* in the cities of Samaria instead of the children of Israel: and they possessed Samaria, and dwelt in the cities thereof.

B.C. cir. 678.

---

**The tribe**—*i.e.,* the kingdom. (Comp. 1 Kings xi. 36.)

(19) **Also Judah kept not . . .**—Judah was no real or permanent exception to the sins and punishment of Israel; she imitated the apostasy of her sister-kingdom, and was visited with a similar penalty.

**The statutes of Israel which they made.**—See Note on verse 8 *supra*, and comp. Micah vi. 16, "the statutes of Omri." According to chap. viii. 27 and xvi. 3, Ahaziah and Ahaz especially favoured the idolatry practised in the northern kingdom. The example of her more powerful neighbour exercised a fatally powerful spell upon Judah.

(20) **And the Lord rejected all the seed of Israel.**—Thenius prefers the reading of the LXX. "and rejected the Lord (as in the last clause of verse 19), and the Lord was angry with all the seed of Israel," &c. It thus becomes plain that the writer goes back to verse 18, after the parenthesis relating to Judah. "Israel" is used in the narrow sense in those verses.

**Into the hand of spoilers**—*e.g.,* the Syrians (chap. x. 32;) and the Assyrians (chap. xv. 19, 29, xvii. 3. The writer probably remembered Judg. ii. 14.

(21) **For he rent . . .**—The verse assigns the *fons et origo mali*; it makes the secession of the Ten Tribes from the house of David the ultimate cause of their ruin. The "for," therefore, refers to what has just been said in verses 18–20.

**He rent Israel.**—The Hebrew as it stands can only mean *Israel rent*. The want of an object after the transitive verb favours the suggestion of Thenius that the *niphal* should be restored: *Israel rent himself away* (comp. the Vulg., "scissus est"). (If *Israel* were the object, *'eth* should be expressed.)

**Drave.**—Hebrew text, *put far away* (Amos ii. 3). Hebrew margin, *misled* (2 Chron. xxi. 11); the Targum and Syriac "caused to stray." The argument obviously is this—separation from Judah led to the calf-worship, and that to idolatry pure and simple.

(22) **The children of Israel walked . . .**—Israel obstinately *persisted* in the sin of Jeroboam, in spite of all warning.

(23) **By all his servants the prophets.**—Comp. Hosea i. 6; ix. 16; Amos iii. 11, 12, v. 27; Isa. xxviii. 1–4.

**So was Israel carried away.**—That the land was not entirely depopulated appears from such passages as 2 Chron. xxx. 1, xxxiv. 9. But henceforth "the distinctive character of the nation was lost; such Hebrews as remained in their old land became mixed with their heathen neighbours. When Josiah destroyed the ancient high places of the northern kingdom he slew their priests, whereas the priests of Judæan sanctuaries were provided for at Jerusalem. It is plain from this that he regarded the worship of the northern sanctuaries as purely heathenish (comp. 2 Kings xxiii. 20 with verse 5), and it was only in much later times that the mixed population of Samaria became possessed of the Pentateuch, and set up a worship on Mount Gerizim, in imitation of the ritual of the second Temple. We have no reason to think that the captive Ephraimites were more able to retain their distinctive character than their brethren who remained in Palestine. The problem of the lost tribes, which has so much attraction for some speculators, is a purely fanciful one. The people whom Hosea and Amos describe were not fitted to maintain themselves apart from the heathen among whom they dwelt. Scattered among strange nations, they accepted the service of strange gods (Deut. xxviii. 64), and, losing their distinctive religion, lost also their distinctive existence." (*Robertson Smith.*)

(24–33) RE-PEOPLING OF THE LAND WITH ALIENS; THEIR WORSHIP DESCRIBED.

(24) **The king of Assyria.**—Sargon (*Sargîna*), who actually records that in his first year (721 B.C.) he settled a body of conquered Babylonians in the land of *Hatti* or Syria. In another passage he speaks of locating certain Arab tribes, including those of Thamûd and Ephah, in the land of Beth-Omri; and in a third passage of his annals he says that he "removed the rest" of these Arab tribes, "and caused them to dwell in the city of Samerina" (Samaria). This notice belongs to Sargon's seventh year (715 B.C.). Kuthah and Sepharvaim were also towns in Babylonia. The former is called *Kutiè* in the cuneiform inscriptions. It had a temple of Nergal and Laz, the ruins of which have been discovered at *Tell-Ibrâhim*, north-east of Babylon. Sepharvaim, in the cuneiform *Sipar* and *Sippar*, means "the two Sipars;" in allusion, probably, to the fact that the town was divided between the two deities, *Samas* (the sun), and *Anunitum*, and bore the names of *Sippar sa Samas* ("Sippara of the Sun"), and *Sippar sa Anunitum* ("Sippara of Anunit"). Rassam discovered ruins of *Eparra*, the great sun-temple, at *Abu Habba*, south-west of Bagdad, on the east bank of the Euphrates.

**Ava** (Heb., *'Avvâ*) may be the same as Ivah (Heb. *Iwwah*) (chap. xviii. 34, xix. 13).

**Hamath.**—Sargon has recorded his reduction, in 720 B.C., of *Itu-bi-'di* (or *Yau-bi-'di*) king of Hamath, and also his settling of colonists in Hamathite territory.

(25) And so it was at the beginning of their dwelling there, that they feared not the LORD: therefore the LORD sent lions among them, which slew some of them. (26) Wherefore they spake to the king of Assyria, saying, The nations which thou hast removed, and placed in the cities of Samaria, know not the manner of the God of the land: therefore he hath sent lions among them, and, behold, they slay them, because they know not the manner of the God of the land. (27) Then the king of Assyria commanded, saying, Carry thither one of the priests whom ye brought from thence; and let them go and dwell there, and let him teach them the manner of the God of the land. (28) Then one of the priests whom they had carried away from Samaria came and dwelt in Beth-el, and taught them how they should fear the LORD.

(29) Howbeit every nation made gods of their own, and put them in the houses of the high places which the Samaritans had made, every nation in their cities wherein they dwelt. (30) And the men of Babylon made Succoth-benoth, and the men of Cuth made Nergal, and the men of Hamath made Ashima, (31) and the Avites made Nibhaz and Tartak, and the Sepharvites burnt their children in fire to Adrammelech and Anammelech, the gods of Sepharvaim. (32) So they feared the LORD, and made unto themselves of the lowest of them priests of the high places, which sacrificed for them in the houses of the high places. (33) *a* They feared the LORD, and served their own gods, after the manner of the

*a* Zeph. 1. 5.

---

It is, therefore, quite likely that he had, as usual, deported the conquered Hamathites, and, in fact, settled some of them in Samaria, as this verse relates.

**Placed them.**—Heb., *made them dwell*, the very phrase used by Sargon himself in describing these arrangements (*usesib*). At a later period Esarhaddon reinforced these colonists (Ezra iv. 2).

(25) **The Lord sent** (the) **lions.**—In the interval between the Assyrian depopulation and the re-peopling of the land, the lions indigenous to the country had multiplied naturally enough. Their ravages were understood by the colonists as a token of the wrath of the local deity on account of their neglect of his worship. The sacred writer endorses this interpretation of the incident, probably remembering Lev. xxvi. 22. (Comp. Exod. xxiii. 29; Ezek. xiv. 15.)

**Which slew.**—The form of the verb implies a state of things which lasted some time. Literally, *and they were killing among them*.

(26) **They spake.**—Rather, *men spake*, i.e., the prefects of the province.

**The manner of the God.**—The word *mishpāt*, "judgment," "decision," here means "appointed worship," or "cultus." In the Koran the word *din*, "judgment," is used in a similar way, as equivalent to "religion," especially the religion of Islam.

(27) **Carry.**—*Cause to go.*

**Let them go and dwell.**—To be corrected after the Syriac and Vulg.: *let him go and dwell*.

**Ye brought.**—*Ye carried away.*

(28) **And taught.**—*And was teaching*, implying a *permanent* work.

**In Bethel.**—Because he was a priest of the calf-worship.

**Fear the Lord.**—Not in the modern *ethical* but in the ancient *ceremonial* sense.

(29) **Howbeit.**—*And.* The colonists did not fear Jehovah in a monotheistic sense; they simply *added* his *cultus* to that of their ancestral deities.

**The houses of the high places.**—The temples or chapels which constituted the sanctuaries of the different cities in the Samaritan territory.

**The Samaritans**—*i.e.*, the people of northern Israel. (Comp. *Samaria* in verse 24.)

**Dwelt.**—*Were dwelling.*

(30) **Succoth-benoth.**—The Hebrew spelling of this name has probably suffered in transmission. The Babylonian goddess *Zirbânit* or *Zarpanitum* ("seed-maker") the consort of Merodach, appears to be meant.

**Nergal.**—The name of the god represented by the colossal *lions* which guarded the doorways of Assyrian palaces. These colossi were called *nirgali*; and a syllabary informs us that Nergal was the god of Kutha.

**Ashima.**—Nothing is known of this idol. Schrader (in *Riehm*) pronounces against identification with the Phœnician *Esmûn*. Lane's lexicon gives an Arabic word, '*usâmatu*, or '*al-usâmatu*, "the lion," which *may* be cognate with Ashima.

(31) **Nibhaz** and **Tartak** are unknown, but the forms have an Assyrio-Babylonian cast. (Comp. Nimrod, Nergal with the former, and Ishtar, Namtar, Merodach, Shadrach, with the latter.) Before Nibhaz the LXX. have another name, *Abaazar*, or *Eblazer* (? '*abal Assûr* "the Son of Assur").

**Adrammelech.**—Comp. chap. xix. 37. Identified by Schrader with the Assyrian *Adar-mâlik*, "Adar is prince" (? *Adrum*).

**Anammelech**—*i.e., Anum-mâlik*, "Anu is prince." Adar and Anu are well-known Assyrian gods.

(32) **They feared.**—*They were fearing.* (See Note on verse 25, 28; supra.)

**Of the lowest of them.**—Rather, *of all orders*, or *promiscuously*. (Comp. 1 Kings xii. 31.) This is another indication that it was *Jeroboam's* mode of worship which was now restored.

**Which sacrificed.**—Heb., *and they used to do.* The verb *do* is used in the sense of *sacra facere*, just like the Greek ποιεῖν, ἔρδειν, ῥέζειν.

**Priests of the high places.**—Rather, *bāmāh-priests* (omit *the*). Bamah-priests are opposed to the priests of Jehovah's Temple.

(33) **They feared . . . gods.**—Literally, *Jehovah were they fearing, and their own gods were they serving.* The verse recapitulates 28—32.

**Whom they carried away from thence.**—Rather, *whence they had been carried away*. Literally, *whence men carried them away*. The meaning

nations ¹ whom they carried away from thence. ⁽³⁴⁾ Unto this day they do after the former manners: they fear not the LORD, neither do they after their statutes, or after their ordinances, or after the law and commandment which the LORD commanded the children of Jacob, ᵃwhom he named Israel; ⁽³⁵⁾ with whom the LORD had made a covenant, and charged them, saying, ᵇYe shall not fear other gods, nor bow yourselves to them, nor serve them, nor sacrifice to them: ⁽³⁶⁾ but the LORD, who brought you up out of the land of Egypt with great power and a stretched out arm, him shall ye fear, and him shall ye worship, and to him shall ye do sacrifice. ⁽³⁷⁾ And the statutes, and the ordinances, and the law, and the commandment, which he wrote for you, ye shall observe to do for evermore; and ye shall not fear other gods. ⁽³⁸⁾ And the covenant that I have made with you ye shall not forget; neither shall ye fear other gods. ⁽³⁹⁾ But the LORD your God ye shall fear; and he shall deliver you out of the hand of all your enemies. ⁽⁴⁰⁾ Howbeit they did not hearken, but they did after their former manner.

⁽⁴¹⁾ So these nations feared the LORD, and served their graven images, both their children, and their children's children: as did their fathers, so do they unto this day.

CHAPTER XVIII.—⁽¹⁾ Now it came to pass in the third year of Hoshea son of Elah king of Israel, that ᶜHezekiah the son of Ahaz king of Judah began to reign. ⁽²⁾ Twenty and five years old was he when he began to reign; and he reigned twenty and nine years in Jerusalem. His mother's name also was Abi, the daughter of Zachariah. ⁽³⁾ And he did *that which was* right in the sight of the LORD, according to all that David his father did. ⁽⁴⁾ He removed the high places, and brake the ²images, and cut down the groves, and brake in pieces the ᵈbrasen serpent that Moses had

---

¹ Or, *who carried them away from thence.*

ᵃ Gen. 32. 28; 1 Kings 18. 31.

B.C. cir. 726.

ᵇ Judges 6. 10.

ᶜ 2 Chron. 28, 27, & 29. 1; He is called *Ezekias*, Matt. 1. 9.

² Heb., *statues.*

ᵈ Num. 21. 9.

---

is: according to the customs of the cities from which Sargon had deported them.

**(34—41) THE RELIGIOUS STATE OF THE MIXED POPULATION OF SAMARIA IN THE TIME OF THE EDITOR.**

⁽³⁴⁾ **They do after the former manners.**—They still keep up the religious customs of the first colonists.

**They fear not the Lord.**—They fear Him not in the sense of a *right* fear; they do not honour Him in the way He has prescribed in the Torah. The LXX. omits both *nots* in this verse.

**After their statutes, or after their ordinances.**—The writer here thinks of the *remnant* of the Ten Tribes who amalgamated with the new settlers (chap. xxiii. 19; 2 Chron. xxxiv. 6, 9, 33; John iv. 12).

**Ordinances.**—Heb., *ordinance,* or *judgment.*

**Or after the law and commandment.**—This pair of terms is exegetical of the preceding pair. Probably, however, the original reading was, "after *the* statutes, and after *the* ordinances," as in verse 37, where the same four terms recur. Then the sense will simply be, that the Samaritans contemporary with the writer do not worship Jehovah according to the Torah.

⁽³⁸⁾ **Neither shall ye fear other gods.**—This formula is repeated thrice (verse 35, 37, 38), as the main point of the covenant between Jehovah and Israel.

⁽³⁹⁾ **And he.**—The pronoun is emphatic: "and He, on His part, will deliver you."

⁽⁴⁰⁾ **They**—*i.e.,* the Ephraimites.

**Did.**—*Continued doing.*

**After their former manner**—*i.e.,* they clung to the old-established cultus of the calves.

⁽⁴¹⁾ **So these nations feared . . . images.**—A variation of verse 33.

**Their children, and their children's children.**—The captivity of Ephraim took place in 721 B.C.

Two generations later bring us to the times of the exile of Judah—the age of the last Redactor of Kings.

**XVIII.—XIX.**

**THE REIGN OF HEZEKIAH IN JUDAH. THE GREAT DELIVERANCE FROM SENNACHERIB.**

⁽¹⁾ **Hezekiah.**—See Note on chap. xvi. 20 and 2 Chron. xxix. 1. The name in this form means, "My strength is Jah" (Ps. xviii. 2), and its special appropriateness is exemplified by Hezekiah's history.

⁽²⁾ **Abi.**—This should probably be Abijah, as in Chronicles and a few MSS.

⁽⁴⁾ **He removed.**—*He it was who removed.* According to this statement, Hezekiah made the Temple of Jerusalem the only place where Jehovah might be publicly worshipped. (Comp. verse 22, and the fuller account in 2 Chron. xxix. 3—36.)

**Brake the images.**—*Shattered the pillars* (1 Kings xiv. 23; Hosea iii. 4; 2 Chron. xiv. 2).

**The groves.**—Heb., *the Asherah.* It should probably be plural, *the Asherim,* as in 2 Chron. xxxi. 1, and all the versions here. (See Note on chap. xvii. 16.)

**Brake in pieces the brasen serpent that Moses had made.**—The attempt of Bähr and others to evade the obvious force of this simple statement is quite futile. It is clear that the compiler of Kings believed that the brasen serpent which Hezekiah destroyed was a relic of the Mosaic times. (See the narrative in Num. xxi. 4—9, and the allusion to the fiery serpents in Deut. viii. 15.) His authority may have been oral tradition or a written document. In ancient Egypt the serpent symbolised the healing power of Deity; a symbolism which is repeated in the Græco-Roman myth of Æsculapius. When Moses set up the Brasen Serpent, he taught the people by means suited to their then capacity that the power of healing lay in the God whose prophet he was—namely, Jehovah; and that

*Prosperity of Hezekiah.* **II. KINGS, XVIII.** *Israel carried Captive.*

made: for unto those days the children of Israel did burn incense to it: and he called it Nehushtan. (5) He trusted in the LORD God of Israel; so that after him was none like him among all the kings of Judah, nor *any* that were before him. (6) For he clave to the LORD, *and* departed not ¹from following him, but kept his commandments, which the LORD commanded Moses. (7) And the LORD was with him; *and* he prospered whithersoever he went forth: and he rebelled against the king of Assyria, and served him not. (8) He smote the Philistines, *even* unto ²Gaza, and the borders thereof, from the tower of the watchmen to the fenced city.

(9) And ᵃit came to pass in the fourth year of king Hezekiah, which *was* the seventh year of Hoshea son of Elah king of Israel, *that* Shalmaneser king of Assyria came up against Samaria, and besieged it. (10) And at the end of three years they took it: *even* in the sixth year of Hezekiah, that *is* ᵇthe ninth year of Hoshea king of Israel, Samaria was taken. (11) And the king of Assyria did carry away Israel unto Assyria, and put them in Halah and in Habor *by* the river of Gozan, and in the cities of the Medes: (12) because they obeyed not the voice of the LORD their God, but transgressed his covenant, *and* all that Moses the servant of the LORD commanded, and would not hear *them*, nor do them.

¹ Heb., *from after him.*

B.C. cir. 721.

² Heb., *Azzah.*

a ch. 17. 3.

B.C. cir. 725.

b ch. 17. 6.

B.C. 723.

---

they must look to Him, rather than to any of the gods of Egypt, for help and healing. (Kuenen does not believe in the great antiquity of this relic. Yet the Egyptian and Babylonian remains which have come down to our time have lasted many centuries more than the interval between Moses and Hezekiah; and some of them were already ancient in the Mosaic age. Our own Doomsday Book is at least as old as the brasen serpent was when it was destroyed. There is really no tangible *historical* ground for this extreme unwillingness to admit the authenticity of anything attributed by tradition to the authorship and handiwork of Moses.)

**And he called it.**—Rather, *and it was called.* Literally, *and one called it.* The impersonal construction, like the German *man nannte.*

**Nehushtan.**—The popular name of the serpent-idol. It is vocalised as a derivative from *nĕʽhōsheth*, "brass," or "copper;" but it may really be formed from *nāʽhāsh*, "serpent," and denote "great serpent" rather than "brass-god." (Comp. the term Leviathan, Job iii. 8.) Further, although the word is certainly not a compound of *nĕʽhōsheth*, "copper," and *tān* (*i.e.*, *tannīn*), "serpent," this may have been the popular etymology of the word. (Comp. the proper name, Nehushta, chap. xxiv. 8.)

(5) **He trusted . . . Israel.**—*In Jehovah, the God of Israel he trusted.* Hezekiah is thus contrasted with idolatrous kings, such as those who trusted in the Nehushtan.

**After him was none like him among all the kings of Judah.**—This does not contradict what is said of Josiah (chap. xxiii. 25). Hezekiah was preeminent for his *trust* in Jehovah, Josiah for his *strict* adherence to the Mosaic Law.

**Nor any that were before him.**—Rather, *nor among those that were before him.*

(6) **For he clave.**—*And he held fast.* Hezekiah's pious *feeling.*

**But kept.**—*And he kept.* Hezekiah's *practice.* The context shows that the "commandments" specially in the writer's mind were those against polytheism.

(7) **And he prospered . . . went forth.**—*Whithersoever he would go forth he would prosper.* (The italicised *and* is needless here, as in verse 6.)

**Prospered.**—Comp. 1 Kings ii. 3; Prov. xvii. 8. *Going forth* denotes any external undertaking or enterprise, especially going forth to war. (Comp. the phrase "going out and coming in.")

**He rebelled against the king of Assyria**—*i.e.*, refused the tribute which Ahaz his father had paid. In this matter also it is implied that Hezekiah succeeded. The mention of Hezekiah's revolt here does not imply that it happened at the *beginning* of his reign, for verses 1—12 are a preliminary sketch of his entire history. The subject here glanced at is continued at large in verse 13 *seq.*

(8) **He smote.**—*He it was who smote.* The reduction of the Philistines was probably subsequent to the retreat of Sennacherib. (Comp. 2 Chron. xxxii. 22; Isa. xi. 14.)

**Unto Gaza.**—The southernmost part of the Philistine territory.

**From the tower of the watchmen . . . city.** —See Note on chap. xvii. 9. The entire land of Philistia was ravaged by the Judean forces.

(9—12) The account of the captivity of northern Israel is repeated here, because the editor faithfully reproduces what he found in the abstract of the *Judæan* history of the kings. (Comp. chap. xvii. 3—6, and the Notes.) We may also see a contrast between the utter overthrow of the stronger kingdom and the deliverance of its smaller and weaker neighbour, because Hezekiah trusted in Jehovah (verse 5).

(10) **They took it**—*i.e.*, the Assyrians took it. This reading is preferable to that of the LXX., Syriac, and Vulg. ("he took it"), as it was Sargon, not Shalmaneser, who took the city. Schrader is too positive in calling this "a certainly false pronunciation" of the Hebrew verb. (Comp. Note on chap. xvii. 5.) Chap. xvii. 6, to which he refers as "decisive" for the singular here also, says that "the king of Assyria" (*not* Shalmaneser) took Samaria.

(12) **Because they obeyed not . . .**—Thenius calls this remark, which properly belongs to the historical abstract from which the compiler drew the narrative of verses 1—12, "the theme" which suggested the reflections of chap. xvii. 7—23. They *may* have been suggested by passages of the Law and Prophets.

(13) Now ᵃin the fourteenth year of king Hezekiah did ¹Sennacherib king of Assyria come up against all the fenced cities of Judah, and took them. (14) And Hezekiah king of Judah sent to the king of Assyria to Lachish, saying, I have offended; return from me: that which thou puttest on me will I bear. And the king of Assyria appointed unto Hezekiah king of Judah three hundred talents of silver and thirty talents of gold. (15) And Hezekiah gave *him* all the silver that was found in the house of the LORD, and in the treasures of the king's house. (16) At that time did Hezekiah cut off *the gold from* the doors of the temple of the LORD, and *from* the pillars which Hezekiah king of Judah had overlaid, and gave ²it to the king of Assyria. (17) And the king of Assyria sent Tartan and Rabsaris and Rab-shakeh from Lachish to king Hezekiah with a ³great host against Jerusalem. And they went up and came to Jerusalem. And when they were come up, they came and stood by the conduit of the upper pool, which *is* in the highway of the fuller's field. (18) And when they had called to the king, there came out to them Eliakim the son of Hilkiah,

B.C. 713.
ᵃ 2 Chron. 32. 1; Isa. 36. 1; Ecclus. 48. 18.

B.C. cir. 710.

1 Heb., *Sanherib.*

2 Heb., *them.*

3 Heb., *heavy.*

---

**And all.**—Omit *and*, with all the versions. "All that Moses . . . commanded" is in apposition with "his covenant."

**And would not . . . do them.**—Literally, *and hearkened not, and did not.*

(13–37) THE INVASION OF SENNACHERIB.

(13) **In the fourteenth year of king Hezekiah.**—The fall of Samaria is dated 722—721 B.C., both by the Bible and by the Assyrian inscriptions. That year was the sixth of Hezekiah, according to verse 10. His fourteenth year, therefore, would be 714—713 B.C. Sennacherib's own monuments, however, fix the date of the expedition against Judah and Egypt at 701 B.C. (See the careful discussion in Schrader's *Keilinschriften*, pp. 313—317.) This divergence is remarkable, and must not be explained away. It must be borne in mind that the Assyrian documents are strictly *contemporary*, whereas the Books of Kings were compiled long after the events they record, and have only reached us after innumerable transcriptions; while the former, so far as they are unbroken, are in exactly the same state now as when they first left the hands of the Assyrian scribes.

**Sennacherib.**—Called in his own annals *Sin-ahi-irib*, or *Sin-ahi-erba*, i.e., "Sin (the moon-god) multiplied brothers." He was son and successor of Sargon, and reigned from 705—681 B.C. He invaded Judah in his *third* campaign.

**All the fenced cities . . . took them.**—See Sennacherib's own words, quoted in the Note on 2 Chron. xxxii. 1.

(14) **Lachish.**—*Um-Lâkis*, in the south-west corner of Judah, close to the Philistine border, and near the high road from Judæa and Philistia to Egypt. The fortress was important to Sennacherib, as it commanded this route. In fact, Sennacherib's chief aim was Egypt, as appears from chap. xix. 24, and Herodotus (ii. 141), and it was necessary for him to secure his rear by first making himself master of the fortresses of Judah, which was in league with Egypt. (See Note on 2 Chron. xxxii. 9.)

**I have offended.**—Literally, *I have sinned.* The term "sin" is constantly used of "revolts" in the Assyrian inscriptions.

**That which thou puttest on me.**—In the way of tribute. A similar phrase occurs on the monuments.

**Three hundred talents of silver, and thirty talents of gold.**—Sennacherib says: "Eight hundred talents of silver, and thirty of gold," estimating the silver by the light Babylonian talent, which was to the heavy Palestinian talent in the ratio of eight to three. The sum mentioned is about a seventh less than that exacted by Pul from Menahem (chap. xv. 19).

(15) **The silver**—*i.e.*, the money.

(16) **Cut off the gold from the doors.**—Literally, *trimmed*, or *stripped the doors* (the word used in chap. xvi. 17 of the similar proceeding of Ahaz). The leaves of the doors of the sanctuary were overlaid with gold (1 Kings vi. 18, 32, 35). Hard necessity drove Hezekiah to strip off this gold, as well as that with which he had himself plated "the pillars," or rather *the framework* of the doors (literally, *the supporters*; others think that the *door-posts* only are meant by this term).

(17) **And the king of Assyria sent . . .**—Apparently in careless violation of his word, as Josephus states.

**Tartan.**—Rather, *the commander-in-chief*; called in Assyrian *tur-ta-nu*, a word of Sumerian origin, imitated in the Hebrew *tartān* here and in Isa. xx. 1.

**Rabsaris and Rab-shakeh.**—Two other official titles. The Rabsaris has not been identified on the Assyrian monuments. The Hebrew word suggests "chief eunuch," or "courtier." (Comp. Jer. xxxix. 3.) Such an official would accompany the *tartan* as scribe. The term *Rab-shakeh*, as a Hebrew expression, signifies "chief cup-bearer;" but it is really only a Hebraised form of the Assyrian title *rab-sak*, "chief officer," applied to superior military commanders or staff officers. In Isa. xxxvi. 2 only the Rabshakeh is mentioned; in 2 Chron. xxxiii. 9 the three foreign titles are naturally displaced by the general expression, "his servants."

**And they went up and came**—*i.e.*, the Assyrian army-corps under the *tartan*, &c.

**And when they were come up, they came.**—Literally, as before, *And they went up and came*. This is omitted in LXX., Syriac, Vulg., and Arabic, but the phrase refers this time specially to the three principals, who came within speaking distance of the walls.

**The conduit . . . field.**—Isa. vii. 3. The upper pool (called Gihon in 1 Kings i. 33) on the "highway of the fuller's field," *i.e.*, the Joppa road, on the west side of the city, is different from the upper pool in the Tyropœon, which is also called "the artificial pool" (Neh. iii. 16), and "the old pool" (Isa. xxii. 11). Below this latter was a pool, dug in Hezekiah's time, called in Isa. xxii. 9 "the lower pool," and in Neh. iii. 15 "the pool of Siloah."

(18) **And when they had called to the king.**—They demanded a parley with Hezekiah himself. The

which was over the household, and Shebna the ¹scribe, and Joah the son of Asaph the recorder. ⁽¹⁹⁾ And Rab-shakeh said unto them, Speak ye now to Hezekiah, Thus saith the great king, the king of Assyria, What confidence is this wherein thou trustest? ⁽²⁰⁾ Thou ²sayest, (but they are but ³vain words,) ⁴I have counsel and strength for the war. Now on whom dost thou trust, that thou rebellest against me? ⁽²¹⁾ Now, behold, thou ⁵trustest upon the staff of this bruised reed, even upon Egypt, on which if a man lean, it will go into his hand, and pierce it: so is Pharaoh king of Egypt unto all that trust on him. ⁽²²⁾ But if ye say unto me, We trust in the LORD our God: is not that he, whose high places and whose altars Hezekiah hath taken away, and hath said to Judah and Jerusalem, Ye shall worship before this altar in Jerusalem? ⁽²³⁾ Now therefore, I pray thee, give ⁶pledges to my lord the king of Assyria, and I will deliver thee two thousand horses, if thou be able on thy part to set riders upon them. ⁽²⁴⁾ How then wilt thou turn away the face of one captain of the least of my master's servants, and put thy trust on Egypt for chariots and for horsemen? ⁽²⁵⁾ Am I now come up without the LORD against this place to destroy it? The LORD said to me, Go up against this land, and destroy it.

1 Or, secretary.
2 Or, talkest.
3 Heb., word of the lips.
4 Or, but counsel and strength are for the war.
5 Heb., trustest thee.
6 Or, hostages.

---

king sent out his chief ministers; as to whom see 1 Kings iv. 1–4. For *Eliakim* and *Shebna* see further, Isa. xxii. 15, 20 *seq*.

⁽¹⁹⁾ **And Rab-shakeh said.**—Tiglath Pileser records that he sent a *rab-sak* as his envoy to Tyre. Thenius supposes the present *rab-sak* may have been a better master of Hebrew than his companions. Schrader says it would have been beneath the *tartan's* dignity to speak, and that such vigorous language as follows would have had a very strange effect in the mouth of a eunuch (the *rabsaris*).

**The great king, the king of Assyria.**—Comp. the usual grandiloquent style of the Assyrian sovereigns: "I, Esarhaddon, the great king, the mighty king, the king of multitudes, the king of the country of Asshur;" and the title, "king of princes," which Hosea applies to the king of Assyria (Hos. viii. 10).

⁽²⁰⁾ **Thou sayest (but they are but vain words).**—Literally, *thou hast said—a mere lip-word it was*—*i.e.*, insincere language, an utterance which thou knewest to be false. (Comp. our expression, "lip-service.")

**I have counsel . . .**—The margin is wrong.

⁽²¹⁾ **The staff of this bruised reed.**—*Cracked* or *flawed* would be better than bruised; because, as is clear from the following words, the idea is that of a reed splitting and piercing the hand that rests upon it. (Comp. Isa. xlii. 3.) As to the Judæan expectations from Egypt, comp. Isa. xx. 1–5, xxx. 1–8, xxxi. 1–4, passages in which such expectations are denounced as implying want of faith in Jehovah.

⁽²²⁾ **But if ye say.**—The address seems to turn abruptly from Hezekiah to his ministers, and to the garrison of Jerusalem in general. But the LXX., Syriac, Arabic, and Isaiah xxxvi. 7 have the singular, "But if thou say," which is probably original. (Hezekiah is presently mentioned in the third person, to avoid ambiguity.)

**In the Lord our God.**—The emphatic words of the clause.

**Whose high places and whose altars Hezekiah hath taken away.**—This is just the construction which a heathen would naturally put on Hezekiah's abolition of the local sanctuaries. (Verse 4; 2 Chron. xxxi. 1.) The Assyrians would appear to have heard of Hezekiah's reformation. As he was a vassal of the great king, no doubt his proceedings were watched with jealous interest.

**Ye shall worship . . . in Jerusalem?**—Literally, *Before this altar shall ye worship, at Jerusalem.* The great altar of burnt offering was to be the *one* altar, and Jerusalem the *one* city, where Jehovah might be worshipped.

⁽²³⁾ **Give pledges to.**—Rather, *make a compact with . . .* So the Syriac; literally, *mingle with . . . have dealings with* (Ps. cvi. 35). Gesenius explains: *join battle with*; literally, *mingle yourselves with*: LXX., μίχθητε δή. Mr. Cheyne prefers, *lay a wager with . . .* The *rab-sak* sneers at Hezekiah's want of cavalry, an arm in which the Assyrians were pre-eminently strong; and further hints that even if horses were supplied him in numbers sufficient to constitute an ordinary troop, he would not be able to muster an equivalent number of trained riders.

⁽²⁴⁾ **How then.**—Literally, *And how.* The connection of thought is: (*But thou canst not*); *and how . . .*

**Turn away the face of . . .**—*i.e.*, repulse, reject the demand of . . (1 Kings ii. 16.)

**One captain of the least of my master's servants.**—Rather, *a pasha who is one of the smallest of my lord's servants.* He means himself. The word we render "pasha" is, in the Hebrew, *pa‘hath*, a word which used to be derived from the Persian, but which is now known to be Semitic, from the corresponding Assyrian words *pahat*, "prefect," "provincial governor," and *pihat*, "prefecture."

**And put thy trust.**—Rather, *but thou hast put thy trust*; assigning a ground for Hezekiah's folly. There should be a stop at "servants." (Comp. Isa. xxxi. 1: "Woe to them that go down to Egypt for help; and stay on horses, and trust in chariots.")

⁽²⁵⁾ **The Lord said to me.**—Michaelis supposed that Sennacherib had consulted some of the captive priests of the Northern kingdom. Others think some report of the menaces of the Hebrew prophets may have reached Assyrian ears. Thenius makes Rab-shakeh's words a mere inference from the success which had hitherto attended the expedition; but the language is too definite for this. In the annals of Nabuna'id, the last king of Babylon, a remarkable parallel occurs. The Persian Cyrus there represents himself as enjoying the special favour of Merodach the chief god of

(26) Then said Eliakim the son of Hilkiah, and Shebna, and Joah, unto Rab-shakeh, Speak, I pray thee, to thy servants in the Syrian language; for we understand *it*: and talk not with us in the Jews' language in the ears of the people that *are* on the wall. (27) But Rab-shakeh said unto them, Hath my master sent me to thy master, and to thee, to speak these words? *hath he* not *sent me* to the men which sit on the wall, that they may eat their own dung, and drink ¹their own piss with you? (28) Then Rab-shakeh stood and cried with a loud voice in the Jews' language, and spake, saying, Hear the word of the great king, the king of Assyria: (29) thus saith the king, Let not Hezekiah deceive you: for he shall not be able to deliver you out of his hand: (30) neither let Hezekiah make you trust in the LORD, saying, The LORD will surely deliver us, and this city shall not be delivered into the hand of the king of Assyria. (31) Hearken not to Hezekiah: for thus saith the king of Assyria, ²³Make *an agreement* with me by a present, and come out to me, and *then* eat ye every man of his own vine, and every one of his fig tree, and drink ye every one the

1 Heb., *the water of their feet?*
3 Or, *Seek my favour.*
4 Heb., *Make with me a blessing.*

---

Babylon; Merodach foretells his march upon the city, and accompanies him thither. Cyrus even declares that he has daily offered prayers to Bel and Nebo, that they might intercede with Merodach on his behalf. From all this it would appear to have been customary with invaders to seek to win the gods of hostile countries to the furtherance of their schemes of conquest. (Comp. the account of the taking of Veii in *Livy*, v. 21, especially the sentence beginning "Veientes ignari se jam ab suis vatibus, jam ab externis oraculis proditos;" and Macrob. *Sat.* iii. 9.) It is not impossible that there was some renegade prophet of Jehovah in the Assyrian camp. At all events, the *form* of the oracle, "Go up against this land, and destroy it," is thoroughly authentic. Comp. the oracle of Chemosh to Mesha: "And Chemosh said unto me, Go thou, seize Nebo against Israel" (*Moabite Stone*, l. 14). Meanwhile, Isaiah x. 5 *seq.* shows how true was the boast of the arrogant invader, in a sense which lay far above his heathenish apprehension.

(26) **Speak, I pray thee . . . in the Syrian language.** — Hezekiah's ministers naturally dread the effect of Rab-shakeh's arguments and assertions upon the garrison of the city. The people, many of whom had always been accustomed to worship at the high places, might very well doubt whether there were not some truth in the allegation that Jehovah was incensed at their removal.

**In the Syrian language.**—*In Aramaic;* which was at that time the language of diplomacy and commerce in the countries of Western Asia, as is proved by the bilingual contract-tablets (in Aramaic and Assyrian) discovered at Nineveh.

**In the Jews' language.**—*In Jewish;* an expression only found in Nehemiah xiii. 24 besides the present narrative. The word "Jew" (*Yehûdî*), from which it is derived, itself occurs only in the later Biblical books; but contemporary Assyrian usage (*mât Ya-u-di* or *Ya-u-du*, "Judah;" *Ya-u-da-a-a*, "the Jews") is in favour of the supposition that the people of the Southern kingdom were even then called *Yehûdîm*, and their language "Jewish" (*Yehûdîth*). The spoken dialect probably differed considerably from other varieties of Hebrew, though not enough to make it unintelligible to other Hebrew-speaking peoples, such as the northern Israelites and the Moabites and Edomites.

(27) **Hath my master . . .**—Rather, *Is it to thy lord and to thee that my lord hath sent me to speak these words?*

**The men which sit on the wall** — *i.e.*, the soldiers on guard.

**That they may eat . . .**—These coarse words are meant to express the *consequence* of their resistance: it will bring them to such dire straits that they will be fain to appease the cravings of hunger and thirst with the vilest garbage. (Comp. chap. vi. 25 *seq.*)

(28) **Stood.**—*Came forward*, *i.e.*, nearer to the wall. (Comp. 1 Kings viii. 22.)

**The word.**—LXX. and Vulg., *words;* so Isaiah.

(29) **Let not Hezekiah deceive you.** — Rab-shakeh was quick-witted enough to take instant advantage of Eliakim's unwary remark, and to come forward in the character of a friend of the people (*Cheyne*). (For the verb, see Gen. iii. 13.)

**His hand.**—To be corrected into " my hand," in accordance with all the versions, save the Targum.

(30) **Neither let Hezekiah make you trust in the Lord.**—Hezekiah cannot save you himself (verse 29); Jehovah will not do so (verse 25). The " Jewish colouring" of the verse is not apparent to the present writer. If Rab-shakeh could speak Hebrew, he would almost certainly know the name of the god of the Jews; and it was perfectly natural for him to assume that Hezekiah and his prophets would encourage the people to trust in the God who had His sanctuary on Zion, and was bound to defend His own dwelling-place. The words are not so exact a reproduction of Isaiah's language (Isa. xxxvii. 35) as to preclude this view.

**Delivered.**—Rather, *given, yielded up.*

(31) **Make an agreement with me by a present.**—Literally, *make with me a blessing*, *i.e.* (according to the Targum and Syriac), " make peace with me." The phrase does not elsewhere occur. Perhaps it is grounded on the fact that the conclusion of peace was generally accompanied by mutual expressions of goodwill. (Gesenius says *peace* is a conception akin to *blessing, weal*.)

**Come out to me.**—From behind your walls; surrender (1 Sam. xi. 3; Jer. xxi. 9).

**And then eat ye.**—Omit *then*. The country-folk who had taken refuge in Jerusalem are invited to return to their farms, and dwell in peace, "until Sennacherib has brought his Egyptian campaign to a close; then, no doubt, they will be removed from their home, but a new home will be given them equal to the old" (*Cheyne*). We might, however, render, according to a well-known Hebrew idiom, *so shall ye eat, every man of his own vine, &c., i.e.,* If ye surrender at once, no

waters of his ¹cistern: ⁽³²⁾ until I come and take you away to a land like your own land, a land of corn and wine, a land of bread and vineyards, a land of oil olive and of honey, that ye may live, and not die: and hearken not unto Hezekiah, when he ²persuadeth you, saying, The LORD will deliver us. ⁽³³⁾ Hath any of the gods of the nations delivered at all his land out of the hand of the king of Assyria? ⁽³⁴⁾ Where *are* the gods of Hamath, and of Arpad? where *are* the gods of Sepharvaim, Hena, and Ivah? have they delivered Samaria out of mine hand? ⁽³⁵⁾ Who *are* they among all the gods of the countries, that have delivered their country out of mine hand, that the LORD should deliver Jerusalem out of mine hand?

⁽³⁶⁾ But the people held their peace, and answered him not a word: for the king's commandment was, saying, Answer him not.

⁽³⁷⁾ Then came Eliakim the son of Hilkiah, which *was* over the household, and Shebna the scribe, and Joah the son of Asaph the recorder, to Hezekiah with *their* clothes rent, and told him the words of Rab-shakeh.

1 Or, *pit*.
2 Or, *deceiveth*.

---

harm shall befall you; but ye shall enjoy your own land, until I remove you to a better. (Comp. 1 Kings v. 5.) Thenius denies the reference to the Egyptian campaign, and makes Sennacherib pose as a father who wishes to make the necessary preparations for the reception of his dear children (!).

⁽³²⁾ **Oil olive.**—The cultivated as distinct from the wild olive, or oleaster (1 Kings vi. 23), which yields less and worse oil.

**That ye may live.**—Or, *and ye shall live*; a general promise of immunity, if they obey. (There should be, in this case, a stop at "honey.")

**When he persuadeth you.**—Or, *if he prick you on* (1 Chron. xxi. 1).

⁽³³⁾ **Hath any . . . his land.**—Literally, *have the gods of the nations at all delivered every one his own land?* If this is to be consistent with verse 25, we must suppose the thought to be that the god of each conquered nation had favoured the Assyrian cause, as Jehovah is here alleged to be doing. But, as verses 34, 35 seem to imply the impotence of the foreign deities when opposed to the might of Assyria, a verbal inconsistency may be admitted. (See Note on 2 Chron. xxxii. 15.)

The *rab-sak* would hardly be very particular about what he said in an extemporised address, the sole aim of which was to work on the fears of the Jews. The connection of thought in his mind may have been somewhat as follows: "Jehovah, instead of opposing, manifestly favours our arms; and even if that be otherwise, as you may believe, no matter! He is not likely to prove mightier than the gods of all the other nations that have fallen before us."

**Out of the hand of the king of Assyria.**—Sennacherib, or his spokesman, thinks of his predecessors as well as of himself, as is evident from chap. xix. 12, 13. (Comp. 2 Chron. xxxii. 13, 14.)

⁽³⁴⁾ **Where are the gods of Hamath, and of Arpad?**—Sargon, Sennacherib's father, had reduced these two cities. The reference to "my fathers" in chap. xix. 12, and the use of the general term, "the king of Assyria" (verse 33), are against Schrader's supposition that the historian has confused the campaigns of Sargon with those of Sennacherib. (Comp. chap. xvii. 24, 30.) Sargon has recorded that *Ya-u-bi-h-di*, king of the Hamathites, induced Arpad, Simyra, Damascus, and Samaria to join his revolt against Assyria. The confederacy was defeated at Qarqar, and Yahubihdi taken and flayed alive (B.C. 720).

**Arpad.**—*Tell-Erfâd*, about ten miles north of Aleppo. The question, "Where are the gods?" &c., may imply that they had been annihilated along with their temples and statues. (Comp. Job xiv. 10.) Sometimes, indeed, the Assyrians carried off the idols of conquered nations, but this need not have been an invariable practice, and Isa. x. 11 seems to imply that they were sometimes destroyed, as was likely to be the case when a city was taken by storm, and committed to the flames.

**Sepharvaim.**—See on chap. xvii. 24. This city revolted with Babylon against Sargon at the beginning of his reign. No account of its fall has been preserved.

**Hena, and Ivah.**—These names do not occur in Isaiah, and are wholly unknown. The words look like two Hebrew verbs ("He hath caused to wander, and overturned"), as at present vocalised; and the Targum translates them as a question: "Have they not made them wander, and carried them away?" Hoffmann thinks the two words are really one (the *niphal* participle of *'av'av*), and should be rendered as an epithet of Sepharvaim, "the utterly perverted;" a nickname given it by the Assyrians, because of its folly in revolting again after its former subjugation. But the mention of Ava and the Avites (chap. xvii. 24, 31) is in favour of the same proper name here, and the LXX., Syriac, Arabic, and Vulg. agree with this. (The Syriac reads *Avva*, as in chap. vii. 24.)

**Have they delivered Samaria . . . ?**—Rather, *How much less have they* (i.e., its gods) *delivered Samaria out of mine hand!* So Ewald, *Gram.*, § 256. The Syriac, Vulg., and Arabic render as the Authorised Version. Perhaps the original reading was not *kî*, but *hăkî*: "Is it the case *that* they have delivered?" &c. (Job vi. 22).

**Out of mine hand?**—Sennacherib speaks as if he were one with his father, a circumstance which lends some support to the suggestion of Schrader, that the successive Assyrian invasions were not kept quite distinct in the Hebrew tradition. If so, the year 714 B.C., assigned as the date of the present expedition (verse 13), may really be that of an earlier expedition under Sargon, who, in fact, invaded the West in 720, 715, and 711 (or 709) B.C.

⁽³⁵⁾ **The countries.**—Which I have myself conquered.

**That the Lord should deliver . . .**—Ewald explains here, as in the last verse, *much less will Jehovah deliver*, &c., taking *kî*, "that," as equivalent to *'aph kî*.

CHAPTER XIX.—<sup>(1)</sup> And <sup>a</sup>it came to pass, when king Hezekiah heard *it*, that he rent his clothes, and covered himself with sackcloth, and went into the house of the LORD. <sup>(2)</sup> And he sent Eliakim, which *was* over the household, and Shebna the scribe, and the elders of the priests, covered with sackcloth, to Isaiah the prophet the son of Amoz. <sup>(3)</sup> And they said unto him, Thus saith Hezekiah, This day *is* a day of trouble, and of rebuke, and <sup>1</sup>blasphemy: for the children are come to the birth, and *there is* not strength to bring forth. <sup>(4)</sup> It may be the LORD thy God will hear all the words of Rab-shakeh, whom the king of Assyria his master hath sent to reproach the living God; and will reprove the words which the LORD thy God hath heard: wherefore lift up *thy* prayer for the remnant that are <sup>2</sup>left. <sup>(5)</sup> So the servants of king Hezekiah came to Isaiah. <sup>(6)</sup> And <sup>b</sup>Isaiah said unto them, Thus shall ye say to your master, Thus saith the LORD, Be not afraid of the words which thou hast heard, with which the servants of the king of Assyria have blasphemed me. <sup>(7)</sup> Behold, I will send a blast upon him, and he shall hear a rumour, and shall return to his own land; and I will cause him to fall by the sword in his own land.

<sup>(8)</sup> So Rab-shakeh returned, and found the king of Assyria warring against Libnah: for he had heard that he was departed from Lachish. <sup>(9)</sup> And when he heard say of Tirhakah king of

*a* Isa. 37. 1.

1 Or, *provocation.*

2 Heb., *found.*

*b* Luke 3. 4, called *Esaias.*

---

## XIX.

<sup>(1)</sup> **Went into the house of the Lord.** — To humble himself before Jehovah and pray for help. (Comp. 2 Chron. xxxii. 20.)

<sup>(2)</sup> **And he sent Eliakim . . .**—See the Note on chap. iii. 12; and comp. chap. xiii. 14, xxii. 14; Jer. xxxvii. 3. Knobel (on Isaiah) remarks that this distinguished embassy speaks for the high estimation in which the prophet stood.

**The elders of the priests**—*i.e.*, the heads of the sacerdotal caste (*proceres*, not *senes*).

<sup>(3)</sup> **Rebuke.**—Rather, *chastisement* (Hosea v. 9). The verb means *to give judgment, punish*, &c. It occurs in the next verse, "will reprove the words," or rather, *punish for the words*.

**Blasphemy.**—Comp. Isa. i. 4, v. 24, where the cognate verb is used; and Neh. ix. 18, 26, where the noun "provocations" is almost identical.

**The children are come . . .**—With this proverb, expressive of the utter collapse of all human resources, comp. the similar language of Hosea (xiii. 13).

<sup>(4)</sup> **It may be.**—The old commentator Clericus well remarks: "Non est dubitantis sed sperantis."

**And will reprove the words.**—See Note on verse 3. The LXX. and Vulg. read, "and to rebuke with the words which the Lord," &c., but the Syriac and Targum agree with the Authorised Version as regards the construction.

**Lift up.**—Heavenwards (2 Chron. xxxii. 2). Or we might compare the phrase "to lift up the voice" (Gen. xxxvii. 38), and render, "to utter" (Num. xxiii. 7).

**Thy prayer.**—*A prayer.*

**The remnant that are left.**—*The existing* (or, *present*) *remnant*. Sennacherib had captured most of the strong cities of Judah, and "the daughter of Zion was left as a hut in a vineyard" (Isa. i. 8). (Comp. Note on 2 Chron. xxxii. 1.)

<sup>(5)</sup> **So the servants . . .**—This verse merely resumes the narrative in a somewhat simple and artless fashion.

<sup>(6)</sup> **The servants.**—Or, *attendants*. The word is rather more special in sense than *servant*, denoting apparently *personal attendant*. Delitzsch renders "squires." (Comp. chaps. iv. 12, v. 20, viii. 4; Exod. xxxiii. 11; Judges vii. 10; 2 Sam. ix. 9; 1 Kings xx. 15.)

**Blasphemed.**—Not the same root as in verse 3. (Ps. xliv. 16; Isa. li. 7; Num. xv. 30.)

<sup>(7)</sup> **Behold, I will send a blast upon him.**—*Behold, I am about to put a spirit within him.* "'A spirit' is probably not to be understood personally (comp. 1 Sam. xviii. 10; 1 Kings xxii. 21 *seq.*), but in the weaker sense of *impulse, inclination.* (Comp. Isa. xix. 14, xxix. 10; Num. v. 14; Hosea iv. 12; Zech. xiii. 2.) The two senses are, however, very closely connected" (*Cheyne*, on Isa. xxxvii. 7). In fact, it may be doubted whether Hebrew thought was conscious of any distinction between them. The prophets believed that all acts and events—even the ruthless barbarities of Assyrian conquerors—were "Jehovah's work." The lowly wisdom of the peasant, as well as the art of good government, was a Divine inspiration (Isa. xxviii. 26, 29, xi. 2).

**And he shall hear . . . return.**—To be closely connected with the preceding words. In consequence of the spirit of despondency or fear with which Jehovah will inspire him, he will hastily retire upon hearing ill news. The "rumour" or report intended is presently specified (verse 9); "for though Sennacherib made one more attempt to bring about the surrender of Jerusalem, his courage must have left him when it failed, and the thought of retreat must have suggested itself, the execution of which was only accelerated by the blow which fell upon his army" (*Keil* and *Thenius*).

<sup>(8)</sup> **So Rab-shakeh returned.**—This takes up the narrative from chap. xviii. 37. It is not said, but is probably to be understood, that Tartan and Rabsaris and the "great host" (chap. xviii. 17) departed with him, having been foiled of their purpose.

**Libnah.**—See Note on chap. viii. 22. The great King had taken Lachish. (See Note on 2 Chron. xxxii. 9.) Its position is not yet determined. Schrader thinks it may be *Tell-es-Sâfieh*, west of Lachish, and north north-west of Eleutheropolis; in which case Sennacherib had already begun his retreat.

<sup>(9)</sup> **Heard say of Tirhakah.**—For the construction, comp. Pss. ii. 7, iii. 2.

**Tirhakah.**—Called in Egyptian inscriptions *Taharka*, in Assyrian *Tarqû*; the Ταρακὸς of Manetho, and

Ethiopia, Behold, he is come out to fight against thee: he sent messengers again unto Hezekiah, saying, ⁽¹⁰⁾ Thus shall ye speak to Hezekiah king of Judah, saying, Let not thy God in whom thou trustest deceive thee, saying, Jerusalem shall not be delivered into the hand of the king of Assyria. ⁽¹¹⁾ Behold, thou hast heard what the kings of Assyria have done to all lands, by destroying them utterly: and shalt thou be delivered? ⁽¹²⁾ Have the gods of the nations delivered them which my fathers have destroyed; *as* Gozan, and Haran, and Rezeph, and the children of Eden which *were* in Thelasar? ⁽¹³⁾ Where *is* the king of Hamath, and the king of Arpad, and the king of the city of Sepharvaim, of Hena, and Ivah?

⁽¹⁴⁾ And Hezekiah received the letter of the hand of the messengers, and read it: and Hezekiah went up into the house of the LORD, and spread it before the LORD. ⁽¹⁵⁾ And Hezekiah prayed before the LORD, and said, O LORD God of Israel, which dwellest *between* the cherubims, thou art the God, *even* thou alone, of all the kingdoms of the earth; thou hast made heaven and earth. ⁽¹⁶⁾ LORD, bow down thine ear, and hear: open, LORD, thine eyes, and see: and hear the words of Sennacherib, which

---

Τεαρκὼς of Strabo. He was the last king of the 25th, or *Ethiopian* (Cushite) dynasty, and son of Shabataka the son of Shabaka (chap. xvii. 4). Sennacherib does not *name* Tirhakah, but calls him "the king of Meluhhu," i.e., Meroë. The two successors of Sennacherib had further wars with Tirhakah. Esarhaddon, according to notices in the annals of Assurbanipal, conquered Tirhakah, "king of Mizraim and Cush," and divided Egypt between a number of vassal kings. A list of twenty names is preserved, beginning with " Necho king of Memphis and Sais." This was Esarhaddon's tenth expedition (circ. 671 B.C.). Tirhakah, however, invaded Egypt once more, for "he despised the might of Asshur, Istar, and the great gods my lords, and trusted to his own power." This led to Assurbanipal's first expedition, which was directed against Egypt. Ewald and Knobel suppose that Isaiah xviii. refers to an embassy from Tirhakah asking the co-operation of Judah against the common foe. If it be alleged that Shabataka was still nominal king of Egypt, we may regard Tirhakah as commanding in his father's name. But Egyptian chronology is too uncertain to be allowed much weight in the question.

(10—13) Sennacherib's second message repeats the arguments of chap. xviii. 29—35.

(10) **Let not thy God . . . deceive thee.**—Through prophets, or dreams, or any other recognised medium of communication.

(11) **All lands, by destroying them utterly.**—*All the countries, by putting them under the ban, i.e.,* solemnly devoting all that lived in them to extermination.

(12) **My fathers.**—Sargon his father founded the dynasty; but he speaks of his predecessors generally as his "fathers."

**Gozan.**—Chap. xvii. 6.

**Haran.**—Also a west Aramean town, mentioned by Tiglath Pileser I. (circ. 1120 B.C.) Shalmaneser II. speaks of its conquest. It had a famous sanctuary of the moon god Sin. (See Gen. xi. 31.)

**Rezeph.**—The Assyrian *Raçappa*, a town of Mesopotamia, often mentioned in the inscriptions.

**The children of Eden.**—Schrader identifies this community with *Bit-Adini* ("the house of Eden"), often mentioned by Assurnâçirpal and Shalmaneser II. The latter records his defeat of *Ahuni*, "son of Eden," a phrase which exactly corresponds to "the children (sons) of Eden" here. It lay on both banks of the middle Euphrates, between the present *Bális* and *Birejik*.

**Thelasar.**—Heb., *Tĕlassar*, the Assyrian *Tul-Assuri* ("Mound of Assur"). More than one place bore the name.

(13) **The king.**—Comp. chap. xviii. 34, from which, as well as from the sequence of thought in verses 12, 13 here, it is clear that "king" is here used as a synonym of *local god.* (Comp. Amos v. 26; Ps. v. 2: "My King, and my God.")

(14) **The letter.**—The Hebrew word is plural, like the Latin *litterae.* The first "it" is plural, the second singular. Verses 10—13 may be regarded as embodying the substance of the letter, which the envoys first delivered orally, and then presented the letter to authenticate it. But perhaps the contents of the letter were not preserved in the Hebrew annals.

**Spread it before the Lord.**—Commentators have taken offence at this act, as if it betokened some heathenish conception of Jehovah. "Très-naïvement, pour que Dieu la lût aussi" (*Reuss*). But one who could think of his God as having "made heaven and earth," and as the *only* God, would not be likely to imagine Him ignorant of the contents of a letter until it had been laid before Him in His sanctuary. Hezekiah's act was a solemn and perfectly natural indication to his ministers and people that he had put the matter into the hands of Jehovah.

(15) **Which dwellest between the cherubims.** —Rather, *which sittest above the cherubim,* or, *the cherub-throned.* (Comp. Exod. xxv. 22; 1 Sam. iv. 4; Ps. xviii. 10; Ezek. i. 26.)

**Thou art the God.**—With emphasis on *Thou. Thou art the true God, thou alone, unto all the kingdoms,* &c.

**Thou hast made.**—*Thou it was that madest.* The thought is, And therefore Thou art—the only God for all the kingdoms (comp. Isa. xl. 18 *seq.*), and "the only ruler of princes."

(16) **Bow down thine ear, and hear.**—Not so much my prayer as the words of Sennacherib.

**Open, Lord, thine eyes, and see.**—Referring, as Thenius says, to Sennacherib's letter; not, however, as if Jehovah's eyes were closed before this prayer. To treat the figurative language of the Old Testament in such a manner does violence to common sense. "Bow thine ear," "Open thine eyes," in Hezekiah's mouth simply meant "Intervene actively between me and my enemy;" although, no doubt, such expressions origi-

*Hezekiah's Prayer.*      II. KINGS, XIX.      *Isaiah's Message.*

hath sent him to reproach the living God. <sup>(17)</sup> Of a truth, LORD, the kings of Assyria have destroyed the nations and their lands, <sup>(18)</sup> and have ¹cast their gods into the fire: for they *were* no gods, but the work of men's hands, wood and stone: therefore they have destroyed them. <sup>(19)</sup> Now therefore, O LORD our God, I beseech thee, save thou us out of his hand, that all the kingdoms of the earth may know that thou *art* the LORD God, *even* thou only.

<sup>(20)</sup> Then Isaiah the son of Amoz sent to Hezekiah, saying, Thus saith the LORD God of Israel, *That* which thou hast prayed to me against Sennacherib king of Assyria I have heard. <sup>(21)</sup> This *is* the word that the LORD hath spoken concerning him;

The virgin the daughter of Zion hath despised thee, *and* laughed thee to scorn; the daughter of Jerusalem hath shaken her head at thee. <sup>(22)</sup> Whom hast thou reproached and blasphemed? and against whom hast thou exalted *thy* voice, and lifted up thine eyes on high? *even* against the Holy *One* of Israel. <sup>(23)</sup> ²By thy messengers thou hast reproached the LORD, and hast said, With the multitude of my chariots I am come up to the height of the mountains, to the sides of Lebanon, and will cut down ³the tall cedar trees thereof, *and* the choice fir trees thereof: and I will enter

<small>1 Heb., *given.*</small>
<small>2 Heb., *By the hand of.*</small>
<small>3 Heb., *the tallness, &c.*</small>

---

nally conveyed the actual thoughts of the Israelites about God.

**Which hath sent him.**—Rather, *which he hath sent.* The "words" are regarded as a single whole, a message.

**The living God.**—In contrast with the lifeless idols of Hamath, Arpad, &c.

<sup>(17)</sup> **Of a truth.**—It is even as Sennacherib boasteth.

**Destroyed.**—Rather, *laid waste.* Perhaps *put under the ban*—the expression of verse 11—should be read.

**Their lands.**—Heb., *their land*, referring to each conquered country.

<sup>(18)</sup> **And have cast (*put*) their gods into the fire.**—Comp. 1 Chron. xiv. 12. The Assyrian's emphatic question, "*Where are the gods?*" implied their annihilation.

**For they were no gods.**—This idea is common in the latter half of the Book of Isaiah. The question has been raised whether the compiler of Kings has not made Hezekiah express a stricter monotheism than had been attained by the religious thought of his days. But if, as Kuenen alleges, no such definite statement of this belief is to be found in Isaiah and Micah (but comp. Isa. ii. 18—21, viii. 10, x. 10 *seq.*) we may still point to the words of a third prophet of that age—namely, Amos the herdman of Tekoah. (Comp. Amos iv. 13, v. 8, ix. 6, 7.) "To Amos . . . the doctrine of creation is full of practical meaning. 'He that formed the mountains and created the wind, that declareth unto man what is His thought, that maketh the morning darkness and treadeth on the high places of the earth, Jehovah, the God of hosts is His name.' This supreme God cannot be thought of as having no interest or purpose beyond Israel. It was He that brought Israel out of Egypt, but it was He too who brought the Philistines from Caphtor and the Arameans from Kir. Every movement of history is Jehovah's work. It is not Asshur but Jehovah who has created the Assyrian empire; He has a purpose of His own in raising up the vast overwhelming strength, and suspending it as a threat of imminent destruction over Israel and the surrounding nations. To Amos, therefore, the question is not what Jehovah as king of Israel will do for His people against the Assyrian, but what the Sovereign of the world designs to effect by the terrible instrument He has created" (*Robertson Smith*). We do not think, however, that the utterance of Hezekiah on this occasion was necessarily recorded in writing at the time. The prayer may well be a free composition put into the king's mouth by the author of this narrative.

<sup>(20)</sup> **Then Isaiah . . .**—The prophet, as Hezekiah's trusted adviser, may have counselled the king to "go up into the house of the Lord," or, at least, would be cognisant of his intention in the matter.

**Against.**—Hebrew text, *in regard to . . . . touching.*

**I have heard.**—The verb has fallen out in Isaiah xxxvii. 21.

<sup>(21)</sup> **This is the word . . .**—The prophecy which follows is well characterised by Cheyne as one "of striking interest, and both in form and matter stamped with the mark of Isaiah."

**Concerning him.**—Or, *against him.*

**The virgin the daughter of Zion.**—A poetic personification of place. Zion here, as Jerusalem in the next line, is regarded as *mother* of the people dwelling there. (Comp. 2 Sam. xx. 19.) The term Virgin naturally denotes the inviolable security of the citadel of Jehovah.

**Hath shaken her head at thee.**—Or, *hath nodded behind thee.* (Comp. Ps. xxii. 8.) The people of Jerusalem nod in scorn at the retiring envoys of Sennacherib.

<sup>(22)</sup> **On high**—*i.e.*, towards heaven (Isa. xl. 26). (Comp. Isa. xiv. 13, 14.)

**The Holy One of Israel.**—A favourite expression of Isaiah's, in whose book it occurs twenty-seven times, and only five times elsewhere in the Old Testament (Pss. lxxi. 22, lxxviii. 41, lxxxix. 19; Jer. l. 29, li. 5).

<sup>(23)</sup> **The multitude.**—The reading of the Hebrew margin, of many MSS., Isaiah, and all the versions. The Hebrew text has "with the chariotry of my chariotry"—obviously a scribe's error.

**I am come up . . . mountains.**—*I* (emphatic) *have ascended lofty mountains.* Such boasts are common in the Assyrian inscriptions.

**To the sides of Lebanon.**—Thenius explains: "the spurs of the Lebanon—*i.e.*, the strongholds of Judæa, which Sennacherib had already captured." "Lebanon, as the northern bulwark of the land of Israel, is used as a representative or symbol for the whole country (Zech. xi. 1)" (*Cheyne*). The language is similar in Isa. xiv. 13.

into the lodgings of his borders, *and into* ¹the forest of his Carmel. (24) I have digged and drunk strange waters, and with the sole of my feet have I dried up all the rivers of ²besieged places.

(25) ³Hast thou not heard long ago *how* I have done it, *and* of ancient times that I have formed it? now have I brought it to pass, that thou shouldest be to lay waste fenced cities *into* ruinous heaps. (26) Therefore their inhabitants were ⁴of small power, they were dismayed and confounded; they were *as* the grass of the field, and *as* the green herb, *as* the grass on the house tops, and *as* corn blasted before it be grown up. (27) But I know thy ⁵abode, and thy going out, and thy coming in, and thy rage against me. (28) Because thy rage against me and thy tumult is come up into mine ears, therefore I will put my hook in thy nose, and my bridle in thy lips, and I will turn thee back by the way by which thou camest.

(29) And this *shall be* a sign unto thee, Ye shall eat this year such things as grow of themselves, and in the second year that which springeth of the same; and in the third year sow ye, and reap, and plant vineyards, and eat the fruits

¹ Or, *the forest* and *his fruitful field.*
² Or, *fenced.*
B.C. 710.
³ Or, *Hast thou not heard how I have made it long ago, and formed it of ancient times? should I now bring it to be laid waste, and fenced cities to be ruinous heaps?*
⁴ Heb., *short of hand.*
⁵ Or, *sitting.*

---

**And will cut down . . .**—Or, *and I will fell the tallest cedars thereof, the choicest firs thereof.* Cedars and firs in Isaiah's language symbolise "kings, princes, and nobles, all that is highest and most stately" (*Birks*), or "the most puissant defenders" (*Thenius*). (See Isa. ii. 13, x. 33, 34.)

**The lodgings of his borders.**—Or, *the furthest lodging thereof*—*i.e.*, Mount Zion or Jerusalem. Isaiah has *height* for *lodging*, either a scribe's error or an editor's correction.

**Carmel**—*i.e.*, pleasure-garden or park (Isa. x. 18). The royal palace and grounds appear to be meant. Thenius compares "the house of the forest of Lebanon" (1 Kings vii. 2).

(24) **I have digged and drunk strange waters.**—Scarcity of water has hitherto been no bar to my advance. In foreign and hostile lands, where the fountains and cisterns have been stopped and covered in (2 Chron. xxxii. 3), I have digged new wells.

**And with the sole . . . places.**—Rather, *and I will dry up with the sole of my feet all the Nile arms of Māçôr*—*i.e.*, Lower Egypt. (Comp. Isa. xix. 5 *seq.*) Neither mountains nor rivers avail to stop my progress. As the style is poetical, perhaps it would be correct to take the perfects, which in verses 23, 24 alternate with imperfects, in a *future* sense: "I—I will ascend lofty mountains . . . I will dig and drink strange waters" the latter in the arid desert that lies between Egypt and Palestine (the *Et-Tîh*). Otherwise, both perfects and imperfects may mark what is *habitual*: "I ascend . . . I dig."

(25) **Hast thou not heard . . . ?**—*Hast thou not heard? In the far past it I made; in the days of yore did I fashion it; now have I brought it to pass.* The "it"—the thing long since foreordained by Jehovah—is defined by the words: "that thou shouldest be to lay waste," &c. (Comp. Isa. xxii. 11, xlvi. 10, 11, x. 5—15.)

(26) **Of small power.**—Literally, *short-handed.* (Comp. Isa. l. 2, lix 1.) Keil compares the well-known title of Artaxerxes I., *Longimanus,* the "long-handed," as if that epithet meant far-reaching in power. Thenius says that a frightened man draws in his arms (?).

**As the grass . . .**—The *as* may better be omitted. *They were field growth and green herbage; grass of the roofs and blasting before stalk.* The sense seems imperfect, unless we supply the idea of *withering away,* as in Pss. xxxvii. 2, xc. 5, 6, cxxix. 6; Isa. xl. 6, 7. Instead of the word *blasting* the parallel text (Isa. xxxvii. 27) has *field*—a difference of one letter. Thenius adopts this, and corrects *stalk* into *east wind,* no great change in the Hebrew. We thus get the appropriate expression: *and a field before the east wind.*

(27) **But I know thy abode . . .**—Literally, *and thy down sitting, and thy going out, and thy coming in I know.* Clearly something has fallen out at the opening of the sentence. Probably the words *before me is thine uprising* have been omitted by some copyist, owing to their resemblance to the words which end the last verse. So Wellhausen. (See Ps. cxxxix. 2.) The thought thus expressed is this: I know all thy plans and thy doings; I see also thy present rebellion against me. What thou hast hitherto done was done because I willed it: now I will check thee.

(28) **Because thy rage . . . is come up.**—Literally, *Because of thy rage . . . and of thy self-confidence* (Isa. xxxii. 9, 11, 18) *which hath come up.* Or else the construction is changed: *Because of thy rage . . . and because that thy self-confidence is come up . . .*

**I will put my hook . . . lips.**—Comp. the Note on 2 Chron. xxxiii. 11, where this threat is shown to be no mere figure of speech. Keil's remark, however, is also to the purpose: "The metaphor is taken from wild animals, which are thus held in check—the ring in the nose of lions (Ezek. xix. 4), and other wild beasts (Ezek. xxix. 4; Isa. xxx. 28), the bridle in the mouth of intractable horses" (Ps. xxxii. 9). This agrees with "I will turn thee back," &c. (With this last comp. chap. xviii. 24).

(29) **And this shall be a sign unto thee.**—The prophet now addresses Hezekiah.

**A sign.**—Rather, *the sign;* namely, of the truth of this prophetic word. "The sign consists in the foretelling of natural and nearer events, which serve to accredit the proper prediction. The purport of it is that this and the next year the country will be still occupied by the enemy, so that men cannot sow and reap as usual, but must live on that which grows without sowing. In the third year, they will again be able to cultivate their fields and vineyards, and reap the fruits of them" (*Keil*). The prophecy was probably uttered in the autumn, so that only one full year from that time would be lost to husbandry.

**Ye shall eat.**—Or, *eat ye.*

**Such things as grow of themselves.**—The Hebrew is a single word, *sāphîah,* "the after-growth" (*Cheyne*; see Lev. xxv. 5. 11).

**That which springeth of the same.**—Again one word in the Hebrew, *sāhîsh,* or as in Isaiah, *shāhîs.*

*Isaiah's Prophecy.*           II. KINGS, XIX.           *The Assyrians are Slain.*

thereof. ⁽³⁰⁾ And ¹the remnant that is escaped of the house of Judah shall yet again take root downward, and bear fruit upward. ⁽³¹⁾ For out of Jerusalem shall go forth a remnant, and ²they that escape out of mount Zion: the zeal of the LORD *of hosts* shall do this.

⁽³²⁾ Therefore thus saith the LORD concerning the king of Assyria, He shall not come into this city, nor shoot an arrow there, nor come before it with shield, nor cast a bank against it. ⁽³³⁾ By the way that he came, by the same shall he return, and shall not come into this city, saith the LORD. ⁽³⁴⁾ For I will defend this city, to save it, for mine own sake, and for my servant David's sake.

⁽³⁵⁾ And ᵃ it came to pass that night, that the angel of the LORD went out, and smote in the camp of the Assyrians an hundred fourscore and five thousand: and when they arose early in the morning, behold, they *were* all dead corpses.

1 Heb., *the escaping of the house of Judah that remaineth.*

2 Heb., *the escaping.*

a Isa. 37. 36; Tob. 1. 21; Ecclus. 48. 21; 1 Mac. 7. 41; 2 Mac. 8. 19.

---

probably synonymous with the preceding term, "after-shoot," *i.e.*, the growth from old roots left in the ground.

⁽³⁰⁾ **The remnant that is escaped of the house of Judah.**—Rather, *the survival (survivors) of the house of Judah that are left.* (Comp. Isa. xi. 11—16.)

**Shall yet again take root.**—Literally, *shall add root, i.e.*, shall take firmer root, like a tree after a storm. The figure naturally follows on the language of verse 29. It is thoroughly in the style of Isaiah. (Comp. Isa. vi. 13, xxvii. 6.)

⁽³¹⁾ **A remnant.**—Isaiah's favourite doctrine of the remnant (Isa. iv. 2, 3, x. 20, 21).

**They that escape.**—*A survival.*

**Out of Jerusalem.**—The ravaged land was to be newly stocked from thence.

**The zeal (jealousy) of the Lord of hosts shall do this.**—Another of the phrases of Isaiah. (See Isa. x. 7.) (The word *hosts*, wanting in the common Hebrew text, is found in many MSS., and all the versions).

⁽³²⁻³⁴⁾ This may be, as Mr. Cheyne supposes, an after *addition* to the original prophecy. Isaiah may have spoken it a little later, in which case it was quite natural for an editor to append it here, as belonging to the same crisis. But it seems better to see here a return to the subject of the king of Assyria, after the parenthetic address to Hezekiah. The repetition of verse 28 in verse 33 favours this view.

⁽³²⁾ **Into this city.**—Or, *unto this city.* Sennacherib shall not come hither to make his intended attack.

**Nor shoot an arrow there** (at it).—In open assault.

**Nor come before it with shield.**—As a storming party advances to the walls under cover of their shields.

**Nor cast a bank against it.**—In regular siege. Comp. 2 Sam. xx. 15; Hab. i. 10). The incidents of warfare here specified may be seen represented on the Assyrian sculptures from Khorsâbad and elsewhere.

⁽³³⁾ **He came.**—So the versions and Isaiah, rightly. The Heb. text here has "he cometh," or "shall come." With the thought comp. verse 28: "I will turn thee back by the way by which thou camest."

**And shall not come into this city.**—*And unto this city he shall not come* (verse 32).

⁽³⁴⁾ **For I will defend.**—*And I will cover* (with *a shield*). (Comp. Isa. xxxi. 5; xxxviii. 6; chap. xx. 6.)

**For my servant David's sake.**—See 1 Kings xi. 12, 13, and the promise in 2 Sam. vii.

⁽³⁵⁻³⁷⁾ THE CATASTROPHE. SENNACHERIB'S RETREAT, AND HIS VIOLENT END.

⁽³⁵⁾ **And it came to pass** (in) **that night.**—This definition of time is wanting in the parallel text; but it is implied by the phrase "in the morning (Isa. xxxvii. 36; verse 35). The night intended can hardly be the one which followed the day when the prophecy was spoken (see verse 29). The expression "in that night," may perhaps be compared with the prophetic "in that day," and understood to mean simply "in that memorable night which was the occasion of this catastrophe." (Thenius sees in this clause an indication that the present section was derived from another source, probably from the one used by the chronicler in 2 Chron. xxxii. 20—23. Reuss thinks this confirmed by the fact that neither the prediction in verse 7, nor that of verses 21—34, speaks of so great and so immediate an overthrow.)

**The angel of the Lord went out.**—The destroying angel, who smote the firstborn of the Egyptians (Exod. xii. 12, 13, 23), and smote Israel after David's census (2 Sam. xxiv. 15—17). These passages undoubtedly favour the view that the Assyrian army was devastated by pestilence, as Josephus asserts. Others have suggested the agency of a simoom, a storm with lightning, an earthquake, &c. In any case a supernatural causation is involved not only in the immense number slain, and that in one night (Ps. xci. 6), but in the coincidence of the event with the predictions of Isaiah, and with the crisis in the history of the true religion:

"Vuolsi così colà, dove si puote
Ciò che si vuole; e più non dimandare."

**In the camp of the Assyrians.**—Where this was is not said. That it was not before Jerusalem appears from verses 32, 33; and the well-known narrative of Herodotus (ii. 141) fixes Egypt, the land of plagues, as the scene of the catastrophe. "Of the details of the catastrophe, which the Bible narrative is content to characterise as the act of God, the Assyrian monuments contain no record, because the issue of the campaign gave them nothing to boast of; but an Egyptian account, preserved by Herodotus, though full of fabulous circumstances, shows that in Egypt, as well as in Judæa, it was recognised as a direct intervention of Divine power. The disaster did not break the power of the great king, who continued to reign for twenty years, and waged many other victorious wars. But none the less it must have been a very grave blow, the effects of which were felt throughout the empire, and permanently modified the imperial policy; for in the following year Chaldæa was again in revolt, and to the end of his

*Hezekiah being Sick* II. KINGS, XX. *seeks the Lord.*

<sup>(36)</sup> So Sennacherib king of Assyria departed, and went and returned, and dwelt at Nineveh. <sup>(37)</sup> And it came to pass, as he was worshipping in the house of Nisroch his god, that Adrammelech and Sharezer his sons smote him with the sword: and they escaped into the land of <sup>1</sup> Armenia. And Esarhaddon his son reigned in his stead.

CHAPTER XX.—<sup>(1)</sup> In <sup>a</sup>those days was Hezekiah sick unto death. And the prophet Isaiah the son of Amoz came to him, and said unto him, Thus saith the LORD, <sup>2</sup>Set thine house in order; for thou shalt die, and not live.

1 Heb., *Ararat.*

a 2 Chron. 32. 24; Isa. 38. 1.

2 Heb., *Give charge concerning thine house.*

3 Heb., *with a great weeping.*

4 Or, *cit*

<sup>(2)</sup> Then he turned his face to the wall, and prayed unto the LORD, saying, <sup>(3)</sup> I beseech thee, O LORD, remember now how I have walked before thee in truth and with a perfect heart, and have done *that which is* good in thy sight. And Hezekiah wept <sup>3</sup>sore. <sup>(4)</sup> And it came to pass, afore Isaiah was gone out into the middle <sup>4</sup> court, that the word of the LORD came to him, saying, <sup>(5)</sup>Turn again, and tell Hezekiah the captain of my people, Thus saith the LORD, the God of David thy father, I have heard thy prayer, I have seen thy tears: behold, I will heal thee: on the third day thou shalt go up unto the house of the LORD.

---

reign Sennacherib never renewed his attack upon Judah" (*Robertson Smith*).

**And when they arose early.**—The few who were spared found, not sick and dying, but corpses, all around them. (Comp. Exod. xii. 33: "They said, we be all dead men.")

<sup>(36)</sup> **Departed, and went.**—*Broke up camp, and marched.* There should be a stop at *returned.*

**And dwelt at Nineveh.**—Or, *and he abode in Nineveh*, implying that he did not again invade the west. Sennacherib records five subsequent expeditions to the east, north, and south of his dominions, but these obviously were nothing to the peoples of Palestine. (See Notes on chap. xx. 12.)

**Nineveh.**—The capital of Assyria, now marked by large mounds on the east bank of the Tigris, opposite Mosul. (The Arabic version has "the king of Mosul," instead of "the king of Assyria.") It is usually called *Ninua* in the inscriptions; sometimes *Niná*, seldom *Ninú* (Greek, Νίνος).

<sup>(37)</sup> **And it came to pass.**—Twenty years afterwards.

**Nisroch.**—This name appears to be corrupt. The LXX. gives Νασαράχ and Μεσεράχ; Josephus, ἐν Ἀράσκῃ, "in Araskè," as if the name were that of the temple rather than the god. The Hebrew version of Tobit (i. 21) gives Dagon as the god. Dagon (*Da-kan, Dagan-nu*) was worshipped at an early date in Babylonia, and later in Assyria; but no stress can be laid on the evidence of a late version of an Apochryphon. Wellhausen thinks the original reading of the LXX. must have been Ἀσσαράχ, which seems to involve the name of Asshur, the supreme god of the Assyrians.

**Adrammelech and Sharezer his sons smote him.**—The Assyrian monuments are silent on the subject of the death of Sennacherib. For Adrammelech, see the Note on chap. xvii. 31. Sharezer, in Assyrian, *Sar-uçur*, "protect the king," is only part of a name. The other half is found in Abydenus (*apud* Eusebius), who records that Sennacherib was slain by his son Adramelos, and succeeded by Nergilos (*i.e.*, Nergal), who was slain by Axerdis (Esarhaddon). From this it appears that the full name was *Nergal-sar-uçur*, "Nergal protect the king!" (the Greek Neriglissar.) (See Jer. xxxix. 3, 13.)

**And they escaped into the land of Armenia.**—Ararat, the Assyrian *Urartu*, was the name of the great plain through which the Araxes flowed. The battle in which Esarhaddon defeated his brothers was fought somewhere in Little Armenia, near the Euphrates, according to Schrader, who gives a fragment of an inscription apparently relating thereto.

**Esarhaddon.**—The Assyrian *Assur-aha-iddina,* "Asshur gave a brother," who reigned 681—668 B.C.

XX.

HEZEKIAH'S SICKNESS AND RECOVERY. THE BABYLONIAN EMBASSY. CONCLUSION.

Parallel accounts may be read in Isa. xxxviii., xxxix.; 2 Chron. xxxii. 24—33.

<sup>(1)</sup> **In those days**—*i.e.*, in the time of the Assyrian invasion. The illness may have been caused, or at least aggravated, by the intense anxiety which this grave peril created. Hezekiah reigned 29 years (chap. xviii. 2), and the invasion began in his 14th year (chap. xviii. 13). In verse 6 he is promised 15 years of life, and deliverance from the king of Assyria. That Hezekiah recovered *before* the catastrophe recorded at the end of the last chapter, is evident from the fact that no allusion to the destruction of his enemies is contained in his hymn of thanksgiving (Isa. xxxviii. 10—20).

**Set thine house in order.**—The margin is right. (Comp. 2 Sam. xvii. 23.)

<sup>(2)</sup> **Then he turned his face.**—*And he turned his face round* (1 Kings xxi. 4). Hezekiah did so to avoid being disturbed in his prayer; and perhaps because grief instinctively seeks a hiding-place.

<sup>(3)</sup> **Remember now how I have walked . . .**—Hezekiah deprecates an untimely death—the punishment of the wicked (Prov. x. 27)—on account of his zeal for Jehovah and against the idols. As Thenius remarks, there is nothing surprising in his apparent self-praise if we remember such passages as Pss. xviii. 20, vii. 8; Neh. xiii. 14. Josephus sets down the poignancy of his sorrow to childlessness, and makes him pray to be spared until he get a son; but this is merely an instance of that "midrashitic" enlargement of the narrative which we find elsewhere in that historian.

<sup>(4)</sup> **Into the middle court.**—This is the reading of some Heb. MSS., and of all the versions. The Hebrew text (*city*; see margin) is wrong. Before Isaiah had left the precincts of the palace, he was bidden to return. (Keil says that here, as in chap. x. 25, the word rendered "city" denotes "castle," *i.e.*, the royal residence.)

<sup>(5)</sup> **The captain of my people.**—Or, *ruler* (*nāgid*); a designation of honour (1 Kings i. 35;

*Hezekiah is Healed,*  II. KINGS, XX.  *and given a Sign.*

(6) And I will add unto thy days fifteen years; and I will deliver thee and this city out of the hand of the king of Assyria; and I will defend this city for mine own sake, and for my servant David's sake. (7) And Isaiah said, Take a lump of figs. And they took and laid *it* on the boil, and he recovered. (8) And Hezekiah said unto Isaiah, What *shall be* the sign that the LORD will heal me, and that I shall go up into the house of the LORD the third day? (9) And Isaiah said, This sign shalt thou have of the LORD, that the LORD will do the thing that he hath spoken: shall the shadow go forward ten degrees, or go back ten degrees? (10) And Hezekiah answered, It is a light thing for the shadow to go down ten degrees: nay, but let the shadow return backward ten degrees. (11) And Isaiah the prophet cried unto the LORD: and *a*he brought the shadow

*a* Isa. 38. 8; Ecclus. 48. 23.

---

1 (Sam. x. 1). This is wanting in Isa. xxxviii., as well as the end of the verse "I will heal thee," &c. That narrative looks like an abbreviated transcript of the present, or of a common original.

**On the third day.**—Comp. Hos. vi. 2. Here, however, there is no ground for understanding the expression other than literally. The precise nature of Hezekiah's malady cannot be ascertained.

(6) **I will add unto thy days fifteen years.**—In the Jewish reckoning fourteen years and a fraction of a year would count as fifteen years. With this very definite prediction comp. Isa. vii. 8, xxiii. 15; Jer. xxv. 11, 12.

**And I will deliver thee . . .**—So that the Assyrians had not yet retired from the West. For the rest of the verse see chap. xix. 34.

(7, 8) In Isaiah these two verses are given at the end of the narrative; a position in which they are obviously out of place. Probably some copyist, after accidentally omitting them where they properly belonged, added them there, "with marks for insertion in their proper places, which marks were afterwards neglected by transcribers" (*Lowth*, cited by *Cheyne*), perhaps because they had become obliterated.

**Take a lump of figs.**—Figs pressed into a cake (1 Sam. xxv. 18). "Many commentators suppose the figs to be mentioned as a remedy current at the time. But surely so simple and unscientific a medicine would have been thought of, without applying to the prophet by those about Hezekiah. The plaster of figs is rather a sign or symbol of the cure, like the water of the Jordan in the narrative of Naaman (2 Kings v. 10)" (*Cheyne*). That in antiquity figs were a usual remedy for boils of various kinds appears from the testimony of Dioscorides and Pliny.

**Laid it on the boil.**—It is not to be supposed that Hezekiah was suffering from the plague and, in fact, the very plague which destroyed the army of Sennacherib. (See Note on verse 1). The word "boil" (*shĕhîn*) denotes leprous and other similar ulcers (Exod. ix. 9; Job. ii. 7), but not plague, which moreover, would not have attacked Hezekiah alone, and would have produced not one swelling, but many.

**And he recovered.**—Heb., *lived*. The result is mentioned here by natural anticipation.

(8) **What shall be the sign . . . ?**—Comp. chap. xix. 29 and note; Isa. vii. 11 *seq.*, where Isaiah requests Ahaz to choose a sign. The sign was obviously a token that the prophet's word would come true.

(9) **Shall the shadow go forward ten degrees, or go back ten degrees?**—Rather, *the shadow hath marched* (or *travelled) ten steps; shall it return ten steps?* This is what the Hebrew text seems to say at a first glance. But Hezekiah's answer apparently implies an alternative; and we *might* render: "the shadow shall have travelled ten steps; or shall it return ten steps?" (Comp. the LXX. πορεύσεται.) The Targum has: "shall the shadow march ten hours or return ten hours?" The Vulgate also makes it a double question. The Syriac is: "the shadow shall march ten steps, or return ten steps."

It is very probable that the Hebrew text is corrupt. We might read the first word as an infinitive instead of a perfect, after the analogy of chap. xix. 29 ("ye shall eat"). Or we might read "shall it march?" as a question (*hă-yēlēk*); or better still, "shall it go up" (*hă-ya'ăleh*), after the hint afforded by the Vulgate: "Vis ut *ascendat* umbra . . . Et ait Ezechias, Facile est umbram *crescere*," &c. It is obvious that a kind of sun-dial is meant, though what kind is not so clear. The word "degrees" (*ma'ălôth*) means "steps" or "stairs" wherever it occurs. (See Exod. xx. 26; Ezek. xl. 6, 22, 26, 31, &c.; 1 Kings x. 20; Neh. iii. 15.) There is probability, therefore, in Knobel's conjecture that "the dial of Ahaz" consisted of a column rising from a circular flight of steps, so as to throw the shadow of its top on the top step at noon, and morning and evening on the bottom step. This, or some similar device, was set up in the palace court, and was probably visible to Hezekiah lying on his sick bed and facing the window. Herodotus (ii. 9) ascribes the invention of the gnomon to the Babylonians. From the inscriptions we know that they divided time into periods of two hours, each called in Sumerian *kasbumi*, and in Assyrian *asli*. Each *kasbu* or *aslu* was subdivided into sixty equal parts.

(10) **It is a light thing for the shadow to go down.**—Because that was the ordinary course of things. As a natural phenomenon, of course, the *sudden* extension of the shadow would have been as wonderful as its retrogression; but what is in any way a familiar occurrence must needs *seem* easier than what has never fallen under observation.

**To go down.**—Rather, *to spread*. The LXX. has κλῖναι, another use of the Hebrew verb. The Targum, Syriac, and Arabic render "to go forward" (march).

(11) **And Isaiah the prophet cried unto the Lord.**—Thus the sign is evidently regarded by the historian as something directly involving the Divine agency, *i.e.*, as a miracle.

**He brought . . . Ahaz.**—Literally, *and he* (*i.e.*, Jehovah) *made the shadow return on the steps, which it had descended in the steps of Ahaz, backward ten steps.* On the question of how it was done, a good many opinions have been expressed, *e.g.*, by means of a mock sun, a cloud of vapour, an earthquake, a contrivance applied by Isaiah (!) to the sun-dial, &c. Ephrem Syrus, and other church fathers, believed that the sun receded in his celestial path; but it is not said that the sun went back, but the shadow. (Isaiah

ten degrees backward, by which it had gone down in the ¹ dial of Ahaz.

(12) "At that time Berodach-baladan, the son of Baladan, king of Babylon, sent letters and a present unto Hezekiah: for he had heard that Hezekiah had been sick. (13) And Hezekiah hearkened unto them, and shewed them all the house of his ²precious things, the silver, and the gold, and the spices, and the precious ointment, and *all* the house of his ³ ⁴armour, and all that was found in his treasures: there nothing in his house, nor in all his dominion, that Hezekiah shewed them not. (14) Then came Isaiah the prophet unto king Hezekiah, and said unto him, What said these men? and from whence came they unto thee? And Hezekiah said, They are come from a far country, *even* from Babylon. (15) And he said, What have they seen in thine house? And

1 Heb., *degrees.*
a Isa. 39. 1.
2 Or, *spicery.*
3 Or, *jewels.*
4 Heb., *vessels.*

---

xxxviii. 8 says "the sun returned," by a perfectly natural *usus loquendi.*) Keil assumes "a wondrous refraction of the sun's rays effected by God at the prayer of Isaiah." Professor Birks and Mr. Cheyne agree with this, assuming, further, that the refraction was local only. (See 2 Chron. xxxii. 31.) Thenius, after arguing at length in favour of an eclipse (that of September 26th, 713 B.C., which, however, will not harmonise with the Assyrian chronology), says : " Notwithstanding all this, I do not insist upon the suggested explanation, but I attach myself, with Knobel and Hitzig, to the *mythical* conception of the narrative." " That the sign was granted, and that it was due to the direct agency of Him who ordereth all things according to His Divine will, is certain. *How* it was effected the narrative does not in any way disclose " (the Editor). Ewald and others wish to see in the retrogression of the shadow a token that "Hezekiah's life-limit was to go back many years;" but the prophet gave the king his choice whether the shadow should go forward or backward.

THE EMBASSY OF MERODACH-BALADAN (verses 12—19).

(12) **At that time Berodach-baladan.**—As to the name, *Berodach* is a transcriber's error for *Merodach* (Jer. l. 2). Some MSS. of Kings, and the LXX., Syriac, and Arabic, as well as Isa. xxxix. 1, and the Talmud, spell the name with *m*, a letter easily confused with *b* in Hebrew. Above all, the cuneiform inscriptions present *Marduk* (or, *Maruduk*)*-abla-iddina* ("Merodach gave a son"). A king of this name occupied the throne of Chaldea at intervals, during the reigns of the four Assyrian sovereigns Tiglath Pileser, Shalmaneser, Sargon, and Sennacherib. He is called in the inscriptions "son of Yâkin," an expression which, like "Jehu son of Omri," is territorial rather than genealogical. *Bît-Yâkin* was the name of the tribal domain of the "sons of Yâkin," just as *Bît-Humria* was that of the territory of which Jehu was king. He is further designated as king of "the land of the sea" (*mât tihâmtim*), *i.e.,* the country at the head of the Persian Gulf, and of "the land of Chaldea" (*mât Kaldi*). He did homage to Tiglath Pileser in 731 B.C. In the first year of Sargon, Merodach-baladan established himself as king of Babylon, and was eventually recognised as such by the Assyrian sovereign. He reigned about twelve years contemporaneously with Sargon, who in 710 and 709 B.C. defeated and captured him, and burnt his stronghold *Dûr-Yâkin.* On the death of Sargon, Merodach-baladan once more gained possession of the throne of Babylon; and perhaps it was at this time (so Schrader) that he sent his famous embassy to seek the alliance of Hezekiah and other western princes. After a brief reign of six months, he was defeated by Sennacherib, and driven back to his old refuge in the morasses of South Chaldea. Belibus was made Assyrian viceroy of Babylon. These events belong to the beginning of Sennacherib's reign. (He says, *ina ris sarrutiya*, "in the beginning of my sovereignty.") There was yet another outbreak before Merodach-baladan was finally disheartened; and later still Esarhaddon mentions that he slew *Nabu-zir-napisti-sutesir*, son of Mardak-abla-iddina, and made his brother *Na'id-Maruduk* king of "the land of the sea" in his stead.

**Son of Baladan.**—The name of Merodach-baladan's father is not mentioned in the cuneiform inscriptions.

**He had heard that Hezekiah had been sick.**—The ostensible business of the embassy was to congratulate Hezekiah on his recovery, and to inquire about the sign that had been vouchsafed him (see 2 Chron. xxxii. 31, and Note); but the Assyrian records make it pretty clear that the real object was to ascertain the extent of Hezekiah's resources, and to secure his alliance against the common enemy.

(13) **Hearkened unto.**—A scribe's error for "was glad of them" (Isaiah, and many MSS. and the versions here).

**The silver, and the gold.**—This, as well as the phrase in verse 17, "that which thy fathers have laid up," appears to contradict chap. xviii. 15, 16. Schrader regards this as an indication that Hezekiah's illness and the embassy of Merodach-baladan belong to the time preceding Sennacherib's invasion. Thenius, however, supposes that Hezekiah simply gave all the *money* in his treasury to Sennacherib's envoys, and stripped off the gold plating of the Temple before them that they might suppose his resources exhausted, when, in fact, he had not touched his real treasures, which were concealed in subterranean chambers. Thenius also refers to the "credible" statement of the chronicler, that presents were made to Hezekiah from all quarters after the retreat of Sennacherib (2 Chron. xxxii. 23). Professor Robertson Smith agrees with Schrader in referring the embassy of Merodach-baladan to the years 704—703 B.C.

**The precious ointment.**—*The fine oil* (*Cheyne*). Perfumed oil used for anointing.

**All that was found in his treasures.**—See 2 Chron. xxxii. 27, 28. Storehouses beyond the precincts of the palace, and beyond Jerusalem. (Comp. the phrase "in all his dominion," which alludes to the resources of Hezekiah in the country, statistics of which he might show to the envoys.)

(14) **What said these men?**—"Isaiah, with that fearless assumption of a superior position which we have noticed in Isaiah vii., at once challenges the king to explain his conduct. Jehovah's will is opposed to all coquetting with foreign powers. (Comp. Isa. xxx. 1.)" [*Cheyne.*]

Hezekiah answered, All *the things that are* in mine house have they seen: there is nothing among my treasures that I have not shewed them. [16] And Isaiah said unto Hezekiah, Hear the word of the LORD. [17] Behold, the days come, that all that *is* in thine house, and that which thy fathers have laid up in store unto this day, *shall be carried into Babylon: nothing shall be left, saith the LORD. [18] And of thy sons that shall issue from thee, which thou shalt beget, shall they take away; and they shall be eunuchs in the palace of the king of Babylon. [19] Then said Hezekiah unto Isaiah, Good *is* the word of the LORD which thou hast spoken. And he said, [1]*Is it not good, if peace* and truth be in my days?

[20] And the rest of the acts of Hezekiah, and all his might, and how he made a pool, and a conduit, and brought water into the city, *are* they not written in the book of the chronicles of the kings of Judah? [21] And Hezekiah slept with his fathers: and Manasseh his son reigned in his stead.

CHAPTER XXI.—[1] Manasseh *was* twelve years old when he began to reign, and reigned fifty and five years in Jerusalem. And his mother's name *was* Hephzi-bah. [2] And he did *that which was* evil in the sight of the LORD, after

*a* ch. 24. 13 & 25. 13; Jer. 27. 19.

1 Or, *Shall there not be peace and truth, &c.*

B.C. cir. 698.

*b* 2 Chron. 33. 1.

---

**From a far country.**—So the Assyrian kings describe Palestine as "a far off land," using the same adjective (*rûqu*).

[17] **Behold, the days come** . . .—Comp. 2 Chron. xxxii. 25, 26, 31. It is there said that Divine wrath fell upon Hezekiah, because his heart was lifted up; and that the Babylonian embassy was an occasion in which God made proof of his inward tendencies. Self-confidence and vanity would be awakened in Hezekiah's heart as he displayed all his resources to the envoys, and heard their politic, and perhaps hyperbolical, expressions of wonder and delight, and himself, it may be, realised for the first time the full extent of his prosperity. But it was not only the king's vanity which displeased a prophet who had always consistently denounced foreign alliances as betokening deviation from absolute trust in Jehovah; and a more terrible irony than that which animates the oracle before us can hardly be conceived. Thy friends, he cries, will prove robbers, thine allies will become thy conquerors. That Isaiah should have foreseen that Assyria, then in the heyday of its power, would one day be dethroned from the sovereignty of the world by that very Babylon which, at the time he spoke, was menaced with ruin by the Assyrian arms, can only be accepted as true by those who accept the reality of supernatural prediction. Thenius remarks: "An Isaiah might well perceive what fate threatened the little kingdom of Judah, in case of a revolution of affairs brought about by the Babylonians." But the tone of the prophecy is not hypothetical, but entirely positive. Besides, Isaiah evidently did not suppose that Merodach-baladan's revolt would succeed. (Comp. Isa. xiv. 29, *seq.*, xxi. 9.)

[18] **Thy sons . . . beget**—*i.e.*, thy descendants. Comp. the fulfilment (Dan. i. 3). Ewald refers to the captivity of Hezekiah's own son Manasseh (2 Chron. xxxiii. 11).

**Eunuchs.**—Rather, *courtiers, palace attendants* (so Josephus). Cheyne, "chamberlains" (so Thenius: *kämmerer*).

[19] **Good is the word of the Lord** . . .—Pious acquiescence in the will of God. (Comp. Eli's: "It is the Lord: let him do what seemeth him good." Comp. also a similar expression in 1 Kings ii. 38.)

**Is it not good, if peace** . . .—This rendering appears to be right. Severe as is the prophetic word of judgment, it contains an element of mercy, in that Hezekiah himself is spared. The words are introduced by *and he said*, to indicate that they were spoken after a pause.

**Peace and truth.**—Rather, *peace and permanence* (or, *security, stability*; Jer. xxxiii. 6). Ewald, Thenius, and Bähr render: "Yea, only may there be peace, &c., in my days." (Comp. the prayer of the church: "Give peace in our time, O Lord.")

[20] **His might.**—See 2 Chron. xxxii.; Isa. xxxiii. 18; Ps. xlviii. 12, 13.

**A pool . . . a conduit . . . water.**—Rather, *the pool . . . the conduit . . . the water*. The pool of Hezekiah is now the *Birket-Hammâm-el-Batrak*. (See Notes on 2 Chron. xxxii. 4, 30, and Isa. vii. 3.)

### XXI.

(1—18) THE REIGN OF MANASSEH IN JUDAH. (Comp. 2 Chron. xxxiii.)

[1] **Manasseh.**—This king was a tributary to Esarhaddon and Assurbanipal successively. (See Schrader, *Keilinschr.*, pp. 354—357, who says: "The conclusion is imperative that during the last period of the reign of Esarhaddon and Assurbanipal, certainly during the first period of the latter, Manasseh was tributary to the great king of Assyria." (See the Notes on 2 Chron. xxxiii. 11.) His name, like that of his successor Amon, suggests Egyptian influence. We know that combinations with Egypt against Assyria were popular during this epoch.

**Twelve years old.**—This early accession to power may help to explain his deviation from the religious policy of his father. It is not necessary to assume (with Thenius) that the queen-mother swayed the government until he reached a riper age. Manasseh may have been older than his years. According to the datum of the text, he was born a year or two after the Assyrian invasion. Whether he was Hezekiah's firstborn son or not cannot be ascertained.

**Hephzi-bah.**—Isa. lxii. 4, as a title of Mount Zion. It means "my delight is in her."

[2] **And he did that which was evil.**—Perhaps under the pernicious influence of his courtiers. (Comp. the case of Rehoboam.)

**After the abominations.**—Comp. Deut. xxix. 17; 1 Kings xi. 5.

the abominations of the heathen, whom the LORD cast out before the children of Israel. ⁽³⁾ For he built up again the high places ᵃ which Hezekiah his father had destroyed; and he reared up altars for Baal, and made a grove, as did Ahab king of Israel; and worshipped all the host of heaven, and served them. ⁽⁴⁾ And ᵇ he built altars in the house of the LORD, of which the LORD said, ᶜ In Jerusalem will I put my name. ⁽⁵⁾ And he built altars for all the host of heaven in the two courts of the house of the LORD. ⁽⁶⁾ And he made his son pass through the fire, and observed times, and used enchantments, and dealt with familiar spirits and wizards: he wrought much wickedness in the sight of the LORD, to provoke *him* to anger. ⁽⁷⁾ And he set a graven image of the grove that he had made in the house, of which the LORD said to David, and to Solomon his son, ᵈ In this house, and in Jerusalem, which I have chosen out of all tribes of Israel, will I put my name for ever: ⁽⁸⁾ neither will I make the feet of Israel move any more out of the land which I gave their fathers; only if they will observe to do according to all that I have commanded them, and according to all the law that my servant Moses commanded them. ⁽⁹⁾ But they hearkened not: and Manasseh seduced them to do more evil than did the nations whom the LORD destroyed before the children of Israel.

⁽¹⁰⁾ And the LORD spake by his servants the prophets, saying, ⁽¹¹⁾ ᵉ because Manasseh king of Judah hath done these abominations, *and* hath done wickedly above all that the Amorites did, which

*a* ch. 18. 4.

*b* Jer. 32. 34.

*c* 2 Sam. 7. 13.

*d* 1 Kings 8. 29 & 9. 3; ch. 23. 27.

*e* Jer. 15. 4.

---

**The heathen ... cast.**—*The nations ... dispossessed*—i.e., the peoples of Canaan (chap. xvii. 8).

⁽³⁾ **For he built up again.**—The LXX. and Vulg. imitate the Hebrew idiom, *and he returned and built*—i.e., *and he rebuilt*.

**The high places ... altars for Baal ... a grove** (*an Ashĕrah*).—"The idols, the sun-pillars, the *ashĕrim*, the sacred trees, and all the other pagan or half-pagan symbols, so plainly inconsistent with the prophetic faith, were of the very substance of Israel's worship in the popular sanctuaries" (*Prof. Robertson Smith*).

**As did Ahab.**—See 1 Kings xvi. 32, 33.

**Worshipped all the host of heaven.**—See Notes on chap. xvii. 16, and comp. chap. xxiii. 12. The Babylonian star-worship and astrology, with concomitant superstitions, had been introduced under Ahaz.

⁽⁴⁾ **He built altars**—i.e., idolatrous altars (verse 5).

**In the house of the Lord**—i.e., in the two courts of it. This verse contains the *general* statement of what is *particularised* in verse 5.

**In Jerusalem will I put my name.**—See 1 Kings xiv. 21.

⁽⁵⁾ **In the two courts.**—Even in the inner and more sacred court, where the sacrifices were offered to Jehovah.

⁽⁶⁾ **And he made his son . . .**—The LXX. has *his sons*; so Chronicles.

**Dealt with familiar spirits . . .**—*made a necromancer*—i.e., formally appointed such a person as a court official (1 Kings xii. 31). (See the Notes on chaps. xvi. 3, xvii. 17, and especially 2 Chron. xxxiii. 6.)

"In the time from Manasseh onwards, Molochworship and worship of the Queen of Heaven appear as prominent new features of Judah's idolatry. It is also probable that the local high places took on their restoration a more markedly heathenish character than before" (*Prof. Robertson Smith*).

⁽⁷⁾ **A graven image of the grove.**—*The graven image of the Ashĕrah* (verse 3).

**In the house of which the Lord said . . .**—See 1 Kings viii. 16, ix. 3. It is meant that the Asherah was erected within the Temple itself, probably in the holy place—an act which was the climax of Manasseh's impiety. (Comp. xxiii. 4; Ezek. xliii. 7; Jer. vii. 30 *seq.*)

⁽⁸⁾ **Neither will I make the feet (***foot***) of Israel move (***wander***) . . .**—Comp. the promise in 2 Sam. vii. 10. The reference is to the migration to Egypt; and the thought is that the permanent possession of the Promised Land depends on the permanent adherence of the nation to Jehovah only.

**Only if.**—*If only.*

**According to all.**—Chronicles rightly has simply (*to do*) *all*; and so LXX., Syriac, Vulg., Arabic here.

**And according to all the law.**—Omit *and*, with Chronicles and the Vatican LXX.

⁽⁹⁾ **Seduced them.**—*Led them astray.* Chronicles renders the same verb *made them to err.*

**To do more evil.**—*To do the evil more . . .* The LXX. adds: "in the eyes of Jehovah." The idolatry of Judah was worse than that of the Canaanites, because *they* worshipped only their national gods, whereas Judah forsook its own God and was ready to adopt almost any foreign *cultus* with which it was brought into contact (Jer. ii. 11).

⁽¹⁰⁾ **By His servants the prophets . . .**—This general expression is used because the historian found no name assigned in his source. It is possible that Isaiah was still living under Manasseh, and protested in the manner here described against his apostasy. More probably, however, the protests in question were those of that great prophet's disciples: the style is not Isaiah's. 2 Chron. xxxiii. 18 refers to the history of the kings of Israel for "the words of the seers who spake to Manasseh;" and the originality of the language in verse 13 might be held to favour the view that we have in verses 11–15, an extract from that work embodying the authentic oracle of a contemporary prophet. (So Ewald.) But it appears much more likely that the passage before us is a sort of *résumé* of the substance of many such prophetic addresses.

⁽¹¹⁾ **And hath done.**—The *and* is not in the Hebrew, though the Syriac and Arabic supply it. It is not wanted, for the sense is, *namely, because he hath done wickedly*, &c.

**The Amorites.**—A general designation of the native races of Canaan, just as in Homer Achaeans.

*were* before him, and hath made Judah also to sin with his idols: (12) therefore thus saith the LORD God of Israel, Behold, I *am* bringing *such* evil upon Jerusalem and Judah, that whosoever heareth of it, both ᵃhis ears shall tingle. (13) And I will stretch over Jerusalem the line of Samaria, and the plummet of the house of Ahab: and I will wipe Jerusalem as *a man* wipeth a dish, ¹wiping *it*, and turning *it* upside down. (14) And I will forsake the remnant of mine inheritance, and deliver them into the hand of their enemies; and they shall become a prey and a spoil to all their enemies; (15) Because they have done *that which was* evil in my sight, and have provoked me to anger, since the day their fathers came forth out of Egypt, even unto this day. (16) Moreover Manasseh shed innocent blood very much, till he had filled Jerusalem ²from one end to another; beside his sin wherewith he made Judah to sin, in doing *that which was* evil in the sight of the LORD. (17) Now the rest of the acts of Manasseh, and all that he did, and his sin that he sinned, *are* they not written in the book of the chronicles of the kings of Judah? (18) And ᵇManasseh slept with his fathers, and was buried in the garden of his own house, in the garden of Uzza: and Amon his son reigned in his stead. (19) Amon *was* twenty and two years old when he began to reign, and he reigned two years in Jerusalem. And his mother's name *was* Meshullemeth, the daughter of Haruz of Jotbah. (20)And he did *that which was* evil in the sight of the LORD, as his father Manasseh did. (21) And he walked in all the way that his father walked in, and served the idols that his father served, and wor-

ᵃ 1 Sam. 3. 11.

¹ Heb., *he wipeth and turneth it upon the face thereof.*

² Heb., *from mouth to mouth.*

ᵇ 2 Chron. 33. 20.

---

Danaans, &c., in turn represent the Greeks. (See Amos ii. 9; Ezek. xvi. 3; and comp. 1 Kings xxi. 26.)

(12) **Whosoever heareth of it.**—Literally, *his hearers.* Many MSS. and the Heb. margin read *her* (*i.e.,* its) *hearer.*

**Both his ears shall tingle.**—The dreadful news shall affect him like a sharp piercing sound. (See the same metaphor in 1 Sam. iii. 11; Jer. xix. 3.)

(13) **And I will stretch over Jerusalem** . . .—Comp. Amos vii. 7—9; Isa. xxxiv. 11; Lam. ii. 8. The sense is, I will deal with Jerusalem by the same rigorous rule of judgment as I have dealt already with Samaria. The figure of the measuring line and plummet suggests the idea that Jerusalem should be levelled and "laid even with the ground."

**As a man wipeth a (the) dish** . . .—The wiping of the dish represents the destruction of the people, the turning it upside down, the overthrow of the city itself. Or perhaps, as Thenius says, the two acts together represent the single notion of *making an end.*

**Wiping it and turning it** . . .—This implies a different pointing of the text (*infinitives* instead of *perfects,* which is probably right).

(14) **Forsake.**—Or, *cast off*; LXX., ἀπώσομαι. Judg. vi. 13.

**The remnant of mine inheritance.** — The Northern Kingdom had already been depopulated.

**A prey and a spoil.**—Isa. xlii. 22.; Jer. xxx. 16.

(15) **Have provoked me.**—*Have been provoking; i.e.,* continually.

**Their fathers came forth.**—The LXX. has probably preserved the original reading: *I brought forth their fathers.*

(16) **Moreover Manasseh shed innocent blood** . . .—The narrative is taken up again from verse 9. The "innocent blood" shed by Manasseh was that of the prophets of Jehovah and their followers. "As the nation fell back into the grooves of its old existence, ancient customs began to reassert their sway. The worship which the prophets condemned, and which Hezekiah had proscribed, was too deeply interwoven with all parts of life to be uprooted by royal decree, and the old prejudice of the country folk against the capital, so clearly apparent in (the pages of the prophet) Micah, must have co-operated with superstition to bring about the strong revulsion against the new reforms which took place under Hezekiah's son, Manasseh. A bloody struggle ensued between the conservative party and the followers of the prophets, and the new king was on the side of the reaction" (*Robertson Smith*). Talmudic tradition relates that Isaiah himself was sawn asunder in the trunk of a cedar tree in which he had taken refuge. (Comp. Heb. xi. 37. This is, perhaps, not impossible, but hardly probable. Ewald considers that Jer. ii. 30, Ps. cxli. 7, and Isa. liii., allude to the persecution of the prophets by Manasseh.

(17) **Now the rest of the acts of Manasseh** . . .—See 2 Chron. xxxiii. 11—19 for the story of his captivity, repentance, and restoration, which is now allowed by the best critics to be genuine history, though at one time it was the fashion to consider it an edifying fiction of the chronicler's.

(18) **In the garden of his own house, in the garden of Uzza.**—His house was apparently not the royal palace built by Solomon, but another which Manasseh had built for himself. Thenius argues that the garden of Uzza lay in the Tyropœon, at the foot of the spur of Ophel. (Comp. 2 Sam. vi. 8; 1 Chron. viii. 7; Ezra ii. 49; Neh. vii. 51).

THE REIGN OF AMON (verses 19—26).

(19) **Amon.**—The Vatican LXX. reads Ἀμώς, Amos (So Josephus Ἀμωσός). The name is perhaps that of the Egyptian sun-god *Amen* (Greek Ἀμμών), as Amon's father was an idolater.

**Meshullemeth.**—Feminine form of Meshullam, "friend" *i.e.,* of God; Isa. xlii. 19. Ewald compares the Latin Pius, Pia, as a proper name.

**Jotbah.**—Thenius imitates the name with *Gutstadt.* St. Jerome says it was in Judah. A similar name occurs in Num. xxxiii. 33; Deut. x. 7.

shipped them: (22) And he forsook the LORD God of his fathers, and walked not in the way of the LORD. (23) And the servants of Amon conspired against him, and slew the king in his own house. (24) And the people of the land slew all them that had conspired against king Amon; and the people of the land made Josiah his son king in his stead.

(25) Now the rest of the acts of Amon which he did, *are* they not written in the book of the chronicles of the kings of Judah? (26) And he was buried in his sepulchre in the garden of Uzza: and *a* Josiah his son reigned in his stead.

CHAPTER XXII. — (1) Josiah *b was* eight years old when he began to reign, and he reigned thirty and one years in Jerusalem. And his mother's name *was* Jedidah, the daughter of Adaiah of Boscath. (2) And he did *that which was* right in the sight of the LORD, and walked in all the way of David his father, and turned not aside to the right hand or to the left.

(3) And it came to pass in the eighteenth year of king Josiah, *that* the king sent Shaphan the son of Azaliah, the son of Meshullam, the scribe, to the house of the LORD, saying, (4) Go up to Hilkiah the high priest, that he may sum the

*a* Matt. 1. 10, called *Josias.*

*b* 2 Chron. 34. 1.

---

(22) **And he forsook the Lord** . . . — *And he forsook Jehovah, the God of his fathers*; abandoned his worship altogether, and gave himself up to foreign superstitions which his father had introduced. It is noteworthy that the long reign of Manasseh-Amon is described by the sacred historian simply on the side of its relation to the religion of Israel. The astonishing corruption of worship which broke out during this period; the perverted hankering after foreign rites, which appears to have been only intensified by the restraints endured under Hezekiah; the bloody persecution of those who maintained the ancient faith; the prophetic menaces of coming retribution—such are the main points of the brief but impressive story. As usual, moral and religious license went hand in hand. The prophet Zephaniah denounces all the ruling classes of "the rebellious and polluted city;" princes and judges, prophets and priests, are involved in the same condemnation (Zeph. i. 4, 5; iii. 1—4; comp. Micah vi. 10 *seq.*, vii. 2—6).

(23) **The servants of Amon** — *i.e.*, according to the common use of the phrase, his courtiers or palace officials. Nothing further is known of the circumstances of the murder. For a conjecture, see 2 Chron. xxxiii. 25.

(24) **The people of the land.** — Thenius thinks these are the militia, as in chap. xi. 14; but in neither case does his opinion appear likely.

(26) **In his sepulchre** . . . —Which he had caused to be prepared near his father's (verse 18)

### XXII.

THE REIGN OF JOSIAH (chaps. xxii., xxiii. 30; comp. 2 Chron. xxxiv., xxxv.)

(1) **Josiah.**—The name seems to mean "Jah healeth." (Comp. Exod. xv. 26; Isa. xxx. 26.)

**Eight years old.**—The queen-mother was probably paramount in the government during the first years of the reign.

**Boscath.**—In the lowland of Judah (Josh. xv. 39).

**He reigned thirty and one years.**—And somewhat over. (Comp. Jer. i. 2; xxv. 1, 3; according to which passages it was twenty-three years from the thirteenth of Josiah to the fourth of Jehoiakim.)

(2) **And walked** . . .—See Note on 2 Chron. xxxiv. 2.

(3) **In the eighteenth year.**—See the Notes on 2 Chron. xxxiv. 3, *seq.* The discourses of Jeremiah, who began his prophetic ministry in the thirteenth year of Josiah, to which Thenius refers as incomprehensible on the assumption that idolatry was extirpated throughout the country in the twelfth year of this king, would be quite reconcilable even with that assumption, which, however, it is not necessary to make, as is shown in the Notes on Chronicles. Josiah did not succeed, any more than Hezekiah, in rooting out the spirit of apostasy. (See Jer. ii. 1, iv. 2). The young king was, no doubt influenced for good by the discourses of Jeremiah and Zephaniah; but it is not easy to account for his heeding the prophetic teachings, considering that, as the grandson of a Manasseh and the son of an Amon he must have been brought up under precisely opposite influences (*Thenius*).

**The king sent Shaphan . . the scribe.**—Chronicles mentions beside Maaseiah, the governor of the city, and Joah the recorder. Thenius pronounces these personages fictitious, because (1) only the scribe is mentioned in chap. xii. 10 (?); (2) Joshua was the then governor of the city (but this is not quite clear: the Joshua of chap. xiii. 8 *may* have been a former governor; or, as Maaseiah and Joshua are very much alike in Hebrew, one name may be a corruption of the other); (3) Maaseiah *seems* to have been manufactured out of the Asahiah of verse 12 (but Asahiah is mentioned as a distinct person in 2 Chron. xxxiv. 20); and (4) Joah the recorder seems to have been borrowed from 2 Kings xviii. 18 (as if anything could be inferred from a recurrence of the same name; and that probably in the same family!). Upon such a basis of mere conjecture, the inference is raised that the chronicler invented these names, in order "to give a colour of genuine history to his narrative." It is obvious to reply that Shaphan only is mentioned here, as the chief man in the business. (Comp. also chap. xviii. 17, xix. 8).

**Go up to Hilkiah the priest.**—The account of the repair of the Temple under Josiah naturally resembles that of the same proceeding under Joash (chap. xii. 10, *seq.*) More than 200 years had since elapsed, so that the fabric might well stand in need of repair, apart from the defacements which it had undergone at the hands of heathenish princes (2 Chron. xxxiv. 11). The text does not say that the repair of the Temple had been "longtemps négligée par l'incurie des prêtres" (*Reuss*).

**Hilkiah.**—See 1 Chron. vi. 13 for this high priest. He is a different person from Hilkiah, the father of Jeremiah, who was *a* priest, but not high priest (Jer. i. 1).

*The Repairing of the Temple.*     II. KINGS, XXII.     *Hilkiah finds a Book of the Law.*

silver which is brought into the house of the LORD, which the keepers of the ¹door have gathered of the people: <sup>(5)</sup> and let them deliver it into the hand of the doers of the work, that have the oversight of the house of the LORD: and let them give it to the doers of the work which *is* in the house of the LORD, to repair the breaches of the house, <sup>(6)</sup> unto carpenters, and builders, and masons, and to buy timber and hewn stone to repair the house. <sup>(7)</sup> Howbeit there was no reckoning made with them of the money that was delivered into their hand, because they dealt faithfully.

<sup>(8)</sup> And Hilkiah the high priest said unto Shaphan the scribe, I have found the book of the law in the house of the LORD. And Hilkiah gave the book to Shaphan, and he read it. <sup>(9)</sup> And Shaphan the scribe came to the king, and brought the king word again, and said, Thy servants have ²gathered the money that was found in the house, and have delivered it into the hand of them that do the work, and have the oversight of the house of the LORD. <sup>(10)</sup> And Shaphan the scribe shewed the king, saying, Hilkiah the priest hath delivered me a book. And Shaphan read it before the king. <sup>(11)</sup> And it came to pass, when the king had heard the words of the book of the law, that he rent his clothes. <sup>(12)</sup> And the king commanded Hilkiah the priest, and Ahikam the son of Shaphan, and Achbor the son of Michaiah, and Shaphan the scribe, and Asahiah a servant of the king's, saying, <sup>(13)</sup> Go ye, enquire of the LORD for me, and for the people, and for all Judah, concerning the words of this book that is found: for great *is* the wrath of the LORD that is kindled against us, because our fathers have not hearkened unto the words of this book, to do according unto all that which is written concerning us.

1 Heb., *threshold.*

2 Heb., *melted.*

---

**That he may sum**—*i.e.*, make up, ascertain the amount of . . . The LXX. reads, *seal up* (σφράγισον), which implies a Hebrew verb, of which that in the present Hebrew text might be a corruption.

**Which the keepers of the door.**— See the Notes on chap. xii. 9, 11, 12, as to the contents of this and the next verse.

<sup>(7)</sup> **Howbeit there was.**—*Only let there be.* The words of verses 6, 7 are part of the royal mandate.

**That was delivered . . . they dealt.**—*That is given . . . they deal.* In chap. xii. 14, 16 the same construction is used in a different sense. (See the Notes there.)

<sup>(8)</sup> **I have found.**—Literally, *the book of the Torah have I found.* The definite form of the expression proves that what the high priest found was something already known; it was not *a* book, but *the* book of the Law. How little the critics are agreed as to the precise character and contents of the book in question is well shown by Thenius: "Neither the entire then existing Scripture (Sebastian Schmidt), nor the Pentateuch (Josephus, Clericus, Von Lengerke, Keil, Bähr,) nor the ordered collection of Mosaic laws contained in Exodus, Leviticus, and Numbers (Bertheau), nor the book of Exodus (Gramberg), nor the book of Deuteronomy (Reuss, Ewald, Hitzig) is to be understood by this expression. All these must have been brought into their present shape at a later time. What is meant is *a collection of the statutes and ordinances of Moses*, which has been worked up (*verarbeitet*) in the Pentateuch, and especially in Deuteronomy. This work is referred to by Jeremiah (Jer. xi. 1–17), and was called "The Book of the Covenant" (chap. xxiii. 2). According to 2 Chron. xvii. 9 it already existed in the time of Jehoshaphat (comp. 2 Kings xi. 12, "the Testimony"); was probably preserved in the Ark (Deut. xxxi. 26), along with which in the reign of Manasseh it was put on one side. When after half a century of disuse it was found again by the high priest in going through the chambers of the Temple with a view to the intended repairs, in the Ark which, though cast aside, was still kept in the Temple, it appeared like something *new*, because it had been wholly forgotten (for a time), so that Shaphan could say: 'Hilkiah has given me *a book*' (verse 10)." (See also the Notes on 2 Chron. xxxiv. 14.)

**And he read it.**—Thenius thinks that this indicates that the book was of no great size, as Shaphan made his report to the king immediately after the execution of his commission (verse 9). But neither does verse 9 say *immediately*, nor does this phrase necessarily mean that Shaphan read the book *through*.

<sup>(9)</sup> **Thy servants.**—Hilkiah and I.

**Have gathered.**—Rather, *have poured out*—*i.e.*, from the alms-chest into the bags.

**In the house.**—In the wider sense of the word, as including the outer court (chap. xii. 9). Chronicles reads "in the house of the Lord," which is probably right. So LXX., Vulg., Arabic here.

<sup>(10)</sup> **Read it before the king.**— Keil suggests such passages as Deut. xxviii. and Lev. xxvi. If it were meant that Shaphan read *the whole* of the book, as Thenius alleges, we should expect "*all* the words of the book" in verse 11.

<sup>(12)</sup> **And the king commanded . . .**—Comp. the similar embassy to Isaiah (chap. xix. 2).

As to *Ahikam* see Jer. xxvi. 24, xl. 5; and for *Achbor*, Jer. xxvi. 22, xxxvi. 12.

**Asahiah a servant of the king's.**—Probably the same officer as "the knight" or *aide-de-camp* who attended on the king (chap. vii. 2, ix. 25.)

<sup>(13)</sup> **Enquire of the Lord.**—Or, *seek ye Jehovah.* Josiah wished to know whether any hope remained for himself and his people, or whether the vengeance must fall speedily.

**For the people.**—Of Jerusalem.

**Written concerning us.**—Thenius conjectures *written therein*, a slight change in the Hebrew. But Josiah identifies the people and their fathers as one nation. (Comp. also Exod. xx. 5.) However,

(14) So Hilkiah the priest, and Ahikam, and Achbor, and Shaphan, and Asahiah, went unto Huldah the prophetess, the wife of Shallum the son of Tikvah, the son of Harhas, keeper of the [1] wardrobe; (now she dwelt in Jerusalem [2] in the college;) and they communed with her. (15) And she said unto them, Thus saith the LORD God of Israel, Tell the man that sent you to me, (16) Thus saith the LORD, Behold, I will bring evil upon this place, and upon the inhabitants thereof, *even* all the words of the book which the king of Judah hath read: (17) because they have forsaken me, and have burned incense unto other gods, that they might provoke me to anger with all the works of their hands; therefore my wrath shall be kindled against this place, and shall not be quenched. (18) But to the king of Judah which sent you to enquire of the LORD, thus shall ye say to him, Thus saith the LORD God of Israel, *As touching* the words which thou hast heard; (19) because thine heart was tender, and thou hast humbled thyself before the LORD, when thou heardest what I spake against this place, and against the inhabitants thereof, that they should become a desolation and a curse, and hast rent thy clothes, and wept before me; I also have heard *thee*, saith the LORD. (20) Behold therefore, I will gather thee unto thy fathers, and thou shalt be gathered into thy grave in peace; and thine eyes shall not see all the evil which I will bring upon this place. And they brought the king word again.

B.C. 624.

[1] Heb., *garments.*

[2] Or, *in the second part.*

a 2 Chron. 34. 30.

[3] Heb., *from small even unto great.*

CHAPTER XXIII.—(1) And *a* the king sent, and they gathered unto him all the elders of Judah and of Jerusalem. (2) And the king went up into the house of the LORD, and all the men of Judah and all the inhabitants of Jerusalem with him, and the priests, and the prophets, and all the people, [3] both small

---

Chronicles has "in this book," and the Arabic here "in it."

(14) **Went unto Huldah the prophetess.**—Why not to Jeremiah or Zephaniah? Apparently because Huldah "dwelt in Jerusalem," and they did not, at least at this time. Anathoth in Benjamin was Jeremiah's town. Huldah, however, must have enjoyed a high reputation, as *prophets* are mentioned in chap. xxiii. 2.

**Keeper of the wardrobe.**—Either the royal wardrobe or that of the priests in the Temple. (Comp. chap. x. 22.) In either case Shallum was a person of consideration, as is further shown by the careful specification of his descent.

**In the college.**—This is the rendering of the Targum, as if *mishneh* ("second") were equivalent to the later Mishna. The word really means *the second part of the city*—i.e., the lower city. (See Neh. xi. 9; Zeph. i. 10.)

(16) **I will bring evil upon . . .**—Literally, *I am about to bring evil unto* . . . Instead of *unto,* the LXX., Vulg., and Chronicles rightly read *upon,* which follows in the next phrase.

**Which the king of Judah hath read.**—The book had been read to him as the chronicler explains. The freedom of expression here warns us against pressing the words of verses 8, 10 ("he read it").

(17) **With all the works** (work) **of their hands.** —With the idols they have made. See 1 Kings xvi. 7, where the same phrase occurs. (Comp. also Isa. xliv. 9–17; Ps. cxv. 4 *seq.*).

**Shall not be quenched.**—Comp. Jer. iv. 4; Amos v. 6; Isa. i. 31.

(19) **Tender.**—See 1 Chron. xxix. 1, xiii. 7; Deut. xx. 8.

**Hast humbled thyself.**—Comp. the behaviour of Ahab (1 Kings xxi. 27 *seq.*).

**Become a desolation and a curse.**—See Jer. xliv. 22. "A curse" is not so much an instance of *causa pro effectu* (Thenius), as a specification of the type such as would be made in blessing and cursing. (Comp. Jer. xxix. 22; Gen. xlviii. 20; Ruth iv. 11, 12.)

(20) **Thy grave.**—So some MSS. and the old versions. But the ordinary Hebrew text, *thy graves,* may be right, as referring to the burial-place formed by Manasseh, which would contain a number of chambers and niches (chap. xxi. 18).

**In peace.**—These words are limited by those which follow: "thine eyes shall not see all the evil," &c. Josiah was slain in battle, as the next chapter relates (verse 29); but he was spared the greater calamity of witnessing the ruin of his people.

### XXIII.

JOSIAH RENEWS THE COVENANT, ROOTS OUT IDOLATRY, AND HOLDS A SOLEMN PASSOVER. HIS END.

(1) **They gathered.**—The right reading is probably that of the Syriac and Vulg., *there gathered.* Chron., LXX., and Arabic have *he gathered.*

**All the elders.**—The representatives of the nation.

(2) **And the prophets.**—That is, the numerous members of the prophetic order, who at this time formed a distinct class, repeatedly mentioned in the writings of Jeremiah (*e.g.,* Jer. ii. 8, v. 31, vi. 13), as well as of older prophets. The Targum has *the scribes,* the γραμματεῖς of the New Testament, a class which hardly existed so early. Chron. and some MSS. reads *the Levites.* (See Note on 2 Chron. xxxiv. 30.)

**All the men of Judah . . . inhabitants of Jerusalem . . . the people.**—A natural hyperbole. Of course the Temple court would not contain the entire population.

**And he read.**—Perhaps the king himself; but not necessarily. (Comp., *e.g.,* chap. xii. 10, 16.) *Qui facit per alium facit per se.* The priests were charged to read the Law to the people (Deut. xxxi. 9, *seq.*) at the end of every seven years.

*The King Renews the Covenant*     II. KINGS, XXIII.     *and Destroys Idolatry.*

and great: and he read in their ears all the words of the book of the covenant which was found in the house of the LORD. <sup>(3)</sup> And the king stood by a pillar, and made a covenant before the LORD, to walk after the LORD, and to keep his commandments and his testimonies and his statutes with all *their* heart and all *their* soul, to perform the words of this covenant that were written in this book. And all the people stood to the covenant.

<sup>(4)</sup> And the king commanded Hilkiah the high priest, and the priests of the second order, and the keepers of the door, to bring forth out of the temple of the LORD all the vessels that were made for Baal, and for the grove, and for all the host of heaven: and he burned them without Jerusalem in the fields of Kidron, and carried the ashes of them unto Beth-el. <sup>(5)</sup> And he [1]put down [2]the idolatrous priests, whom the kings of Judah had ordained to burn incense in the high places in the cities of Judah, and in the places round about Jerusalem; them also that burned incense unto Baal, to the sun, and to the moon, and to the [3]planets, and to all the host of heaven. <sup>(6)</sup> And he brought out the <sup>a</sup>grove from the house of the LORD, without Jerusalem, unto the brook Kidron, and burned it at the brook Kidron, and and stamped *it* small to powder, and cast the powder thereof upon the graves of the children of the people. <sup>(7)</sup> And he brake down the houses of the sodomites, that *were* by the house of the LORD, where the women wove [4]hangings for the grove.

[1] Heb., *caused to cease.*
[2] Heb., *chemarim.*
[3] Or, *twelve signs,* or, *constellations.*
<sup>a</sup> ch. 21.7.
[4] Heb., *houses.*

---

**Small and great**—*i.e.*, high and low. (Comp. Ps. xlix. 2.)

<sup>(3)</sup> **By a pillar.**—*On the stand* or *dais* (chap. xi. 14).

**A covenant.**—*The covenant,* which had so often been broken. Josiah pledged himself "to walk after the Lord," and imposed a similar pledge on the people.

**Stood to the covenant**—*i.e.*, *entered it;* took the same pledge as the king. (Comp. chap. xviii. 28.)

<sup>(4)</sup> **The priests of the second order.**—Thenius is probably right in reading the singular, *the priest of the second rank, i.e.,* the high priest's deputy, after the Targum, unless the heads of the twenty-four classes be intended ("the chief priests" of the New Testament). (See also chap. xxv. 18.)

**The keepers of the door** (threshold).—The three chief warders (chap. xxv. 18.)

**Out of the temple**—*i.e.*, out of the principal chamber or holy place.

**For Baal ... grove.**—*For the Baal ... Ashêrah* (so in verses 6, 7, 15 also).

**Burned them.**—According to the law of Deut. vii. 25; xii. 3. (Comp. 1 Chron. xiv. 12.)

**Without Jerusalem.**—As unclean.

**In the fields of Kidron.**—North-east of the city, where the ravine expands considerably. (Comp. Jer. xxxi. 40; also 1 Kings xv. 13.)

**Carried the ashes of them unto Beth-el.**—This is undoubtedly strange, and Chronicles says nothing about it. If the ashes of the vessels were sent to Beth-el, why not also those of the idols themselves, and the fragments of the altars (verses 6—12)? The text appears to be corrupt.

<sup>(5)</sup> **He put down.**—Syriac and Arabic, *he slew.*

**The idolatrous priests.**—The *kĕmārim,* or *black-robed* priests (Hos. x. 5, of the priests of the calf-worship at Beth-el). Only occurring besides in Zeph. i. 4. Here, as in the passage of Hosea, the word denotes the unlawful priests of Jehovah, as contrasted with those of the Baal, mentioned in the next place. Whether the term really means *black-robed,* as Kimchi explains, is questionable. Priests used to wear *white* throughout the ancient world, except on certain special occasions. Gesenius derives it from a root meaning *black,* but explains, *one clad in black, i.e., a mourner,* an ascetic, and so *a priest.* Perhaps the true derivation is from another root, meaning *to weave: weaver of spells* or *charms;* as magic was an invariable concomitant of false worship. (Comp. chap. xvii. 17, xxi. 6.) It is a regular word for priest in Syriac (*chûmrâ;* Ps. cx. 4; and the Ep. to the Heb., *passim.*)

**To burn incense.**—So Syriac, Vulg., and Arabic. The Hebrew has, *and he burnt incense.* Probably it should be plural, as in the Vatican LXX. and Targum.

**In the places round about.**—1 Kings vi. 29. Omit *in the places.*

**Unto Baal, to the sun.**—*Unto the Baal, to wit, unto the sun.* But it is better to supply *and* with all the versions. *Bel* and *Samas* were distinct deities in the Assyro-Babylonian system. When Reuss remarks that "the knowledge of the old Semitic worships, possessed by the Hebrew historians, appears to have been very superficial, for Baal and the sun are one and the same deity," he lays himself open to the same charge.

**The planets.**—Or, *the signs of the Zodiac.* The Heb. is *mazzâlôth,* probably a variant form of *mazzârôth* (Job xxxviii. 32). The word is used in the Targums, and by rabbinical writers, in the sense of star, *as influencing human destiny,* and so *fate, fortune,* in the singular, and in the plural of the signs of the Zodiac (*e.g.,* Eccl. ix. 3; Esth. iii. 7). It is, perhaps, derived from '*azar,* "to gird," and means "belt," or "girdle;" or from '*azal,* "to journey," and so means "stages" of the sun's course in the heavens. (Comp. Arab. *manzal.*)

<sup>(6)</sup> **And he brought out the grove ...**—The Asherah set up by Manasseh (chap. xxi. 3, 7), and removed by him on his repentance (2 Chron. xxxiii. 15), but restored (probably) by Amon (chap. xxi. 21).

**Unto the brook ... at the brook.**—*Unto the ravine ... in the ravine,* or *wady.*

**The graves of the children** (sons) **of the people**—*i.e.,* the common graves (Jer. xxvi. 23); a mark of utter contempt: 2 Chron. xxxiv. 4 paraphrases, "the graves of them that sacrificed unto them."

<sup>(7)</sup> **The houses ... by the house.**—*The cabins of the Kedêshim ... in the house.* The *Kedêshim* were *males,* perhaps eunuchs, who prostituted themselves like women in honour of the Asherah. (See 1 Kings xiv. 24, xv. 12; Hosea iv. 14.) The passage shows that the

(8) And he brought all the priests out of the cities of Judah, and defiled the high places where the priests had burned incense, from Geba to Beer-sheba, and brake down the high places of the gates that *were* in the entering in of the gate of Joshua the governor of the city, which *were* on a man's left hand at the gate of the city. (9) Nevertheless the priests of the high places came not up to the altar of the LORD in Jerusalem, but they did eat of the unleavened bread among their brethren.

¹⁰ And he defiled Topheth, which *is* in the valley of the children of Hinnom, that no man might make his son or his daughter to pass through the fire to Molech. (11) And he took away the horses that the kings of Judah had given to the sun, at the entering in of the house of the LORD, by the chamber of Nathan-melech the ¹chamberlain,

¹ Or, *eunuch, or, officer.*

---

last infamy of Canaanite nature-worship had been established in the very sanctuary of Jehovah. The revolt of Judah could go no farther.

**Where the women wove hangings for the grove.**—*Wherein the women used to weave tents for the Ashērah.* The word we have rendered *cabins* and *tents* is *bāttim*, "houses." What is meant in the latter case is not clear. Perhaps the female harlots attached to the Temple wove portable tabernacles or sanctuaries of the goddess for sale to the worshippers; or tents (screens) for their own foul rites may be meant.

(8) **And he brought all the priests . . .**—Josiah caused all the priests of the local sanctuaries of Jehovah to migrate to Jerusalem, and polluted the high places to which they had been attached, in order to get rid of the illegitimate worship once for all.

**From Geba.**—The present *Jeba*, near the ancient Ramah (1 Kings xv. 22).

**To Beer-sheba.**—Where was a specially frequented high place (Amos v. 5, viii. 15; and Note on 2 Chron. xxxiv. 6).

**The high places of the gates.**—Altars erected within the gates, that persons entering or leaving the city might make an offering to ensure success in their business.

**That were in the entering in . . .**—Thenius renders, (*the high place*) *which was at the entry of the gate of Joshua the governor of the city, (as well as) that which was on the left in the city gate.* But this assumption of *two* localities is very precarious. The Authorised Version appears to be correct (a similar repetition of the relative referring to the same antecedent occurs in verse 13). Joshua is an unknown personage, and it is not clear whether "the gate of Joshua" was a gate of the city named after him, or the great gate of his residence; nor is it certain that "the gate of the city" was that now called the Jaffa Gate. It is possible that the governor's residence lay near the principal gate of the city, on the left as one entered. Several "high places" stood in the open space in front of it, between it and the city gate. These would naturally be called "the high places of the gates."

(9) **Nevertheless . . . came not up to the altar.**—*Only the priests of the high places used not to offer at the altar.* They were not permitted to do so, being considered to be incapacitated for that office by their former illegal ministrations.

**But they did eat.**—They might not even eat their share of the meat offerings in company with the legitimate priests; but had to take their meals apart, "among their brethren," *i.e.*, in their own company. (Comp. Ezek. xliv. 10—14; Lev. xxi. 21, 22.)

**Eat of the unleavened bread.**—Omit *of the.* The phrase is a technical one, meaning to live upon offerings. (See Lev. ii. 1—11, vi. 16—18, x. 12.) These irregular priests were probably employed in the inferior duties of the Temple.

(10) **Topheth.**—Heb. *the Topheth*; *i.e., the burning place, or hearth,* if the word be rightly derived from the Persian *tŏften,* "to burn." The Hebrew word, however, has been so modified as to suggest a derivation from *tŏph,* "to spit;" so that the epithet would mean "the abomination." (Comp. verse 13.) (Comp. also Job xvii. 6; Isa. xxx. 33; and the Coptic *tāf,* "spittle.")

**The valley of the children of Hinnom.**—Elsewhere called "the valley of the son of Hinnom," and "the valley of Hinnom" (Josh. xv. 8; Jer. vii. 31, 32). Simonis plausibly explained the word *Hinnom* as meaning *shrieking* or *moaning* (from the Arabic *hanna,* arguta voce gemuit, flevit). "The valley of the sons of shrieking" would be a good name for the accursed spot. (Thenius suggests *Wimmer-Kinds-Thal.*)

**That no man . . .**—See Note on chap. xvi. 3.

**To Molech.**—Heb., *to the Molech* (Molech is another form of *melech,* "king"). In 1 Kings xi. 7, the god of the Ammonites is called Molech, but elsewhere, as in verse 13, Milcom, another variation of the same word. The feminine *molecheth,* "queen," occurs as a proper name in 1 Chron. vii. 18.

(11) **He took away.**—The same word as "put down" (verse 5). Here, as there, the Syriac and Arabic render, "he killed," which is possibly a correct gloss.

**The horses . . . the sun.**—These horses drew "the chariots of the sun" in solemn processions held in honour of that deity. (See Herod. i. 189; Xenoph. *Anab.* iv. 5. 34, *seq.*; Quint. Curt. iii. 3. 11.) Horses were also sacrificed to the sun. The sun's apparent course through the heavens, poetically conceived as the progress of a fiery chariot and steeds, explains these usages.

**Had given**—*i.e., had dedicated.*

**At the entering in of the house of the Lord.** —This appears right. Along with the next clause it states where the sacred horses were kept; viz., in the outer court of the Temple, near the entrance. (So the LXX. and Vulgate. This rendering involves a different pointing of the Hebrew text—*mĕbô* for *mibbô*. The latter, which is the ordinary reading, gives the sense, "*so that they should not come* into the house, &c.")

**By the chamber.** — Rather, *towards the cell;* further defining the position of the stalls. As to the cells in the outer court, see the Note on 1 Chron. ix. 26; Ezek. xl. 45 *seq.*

**Nathan-melech the chamberlain,** or, *eunuch,* is otherwise unknown. He may been charged with the care of the sacred horses and chariots. *Melech* was a title of the sun-god in one of his aspects (verse 10.)

*The Defilement of the*  II. KINGS, XXIII.  *High Places and Groves.*

which *was* in the suburbs, and burned the chariots of the sun with fire. (12) And the altars that *were* on the top of the upper chamber of Ahaz, which the kings of Judah had made, and the altars which *a* Manasseh had made in the two courts of the house of the LORD, did the king beat down, and ¹ brake *them* down from thence, and cast the dust of them into the brook Kidron. (13) And the high places that *were* before Jerusalem, which *were* on the right hand of ² the mount of corruption, which *b* Solomon the king of Israel had builded for Ashtoreth the abomination of the Zidonians, and for Chemosh the abomination of the Moabites, and for Milcom the abomination of the children of Ammon did the king defile. (14) And he brake in pieces the ³ images, and cut down the groves, and filled their places with the bones of men. (15) Moreover the altar that *was* at Beth-el, *and* the high place which Jeroboam the son of Nebat, who made Israel to sin, had made, both that altar and the high place he brake down, and burned the high place, *and* stamped *it* small to powder, and burned the grove. (16) And as Josiah turned himself, he spied the sepulchres that *were* there in the mount, and sent, and took the bones out of the sepulchres, and burned *them* upon the altar, and polluted it, according to the *c* word of the LORD which the man of God proclaimed, who pro-

*a* ch. 21. 5.

1 Or, *ran from thence.*

2 That is, the mount of Olives.

*b* 1 Kings 11. 7.

3 Heb., *statues.*

*c* 1 Kings 13. 2.

**Which was in the suburbs.**—Rather, *which was in the cloisters* or *portico. Parwārim* is a Persian word explained in the Note on 1 Chron. xxvi. 18.

**Burned the chariots . . .**—Literally, *and the chariots of the sun he burnt.* The treatment of the chariots is thus contrasted with that of the horses. If the whole had been, as some expositors have thought, a work of art in bronze or other material, placed over the gateway, no such difference would have been made.

(12) **And the altars that were on the top (roof) of the upper chamber of Ahaz.**—The roof of an upper chamber in one of the Temple courts, perhaps built over one of the gateways (comp. Jer. xxxv. 4), appears to be meant. The altars were for star-worship, which was especially practised on housetops. (Comp. Jer. xix. 13, xxxii. 29; Zeph. i. 5.)

**Brake them down from thence.**—The Targum has *removed from thence;* the LXX. *pulled them down from thence* (κατέσπασεν). The Hebrew probably means *ran from thence;* marking the haste with which the work was done. The clause thus adds a vivid touch to the narrative. It is hardly necessary to alter the points with Kimchi and Thenius, so as to read, *he caused to run from thence;* i.e., hurried them away.

**Cast the dust of them.**—Over the wall of the Temple enclosure, into the ravine beneath.

(13) **The high places that were before the city . . .**—See 1 Kings xi. 5—8. "Before" means "to the east of," because, to determine the cardinal points, one faced the sunrise. The right hand was then the south, the left hand the north, and the back the west.

**The mount of corruption.**—The southern summit of the Mount of Olives was so-called, because of the idolatry there practised. It still bears the name of the "Hill of Offence," derived from the Vulg. "*mons offensionis.*" (The word rendered "corruption," *mashhith,* may originally have meant "anointing," from *mashah* "to anoint," and have simply referred to the olive oil there produced. The name would thus be equivalent to the German *Oelberg.* In later times the term was so modified as to express detestation of idol-worship.)

**Did the king defile.**—As it is not said that they were pulled down, these high places may have been merely sacred sites on the mountain, consisting of a levelled surface of rock, with holes scooped in them for receiving libations, &c. Such sites have been found in Palestine; and it is hardly conceivable that *chapels* erected by Solomon for the worship of Ashtoreth, Chemosh, and Milcom, would have been spared by such a king as Hezekiah, who even did away with the high places dedicated to Jehovah (chap. xviii. 3).

(14) **The images . . . the groves.**—*The pillars . . . the ashērahs.* These pillars and sacred trees may have been set up at the high places mentioned in the last verse; but the Hebrew construction does not *prove* this, for comp. verse 10. The reference is probably general.

**Their places.**—*Their place* or *station;* a technical term for the position of an idol (the Heb. *māqôm,* equivalent to Sabæan *maqāmum,* and Arabic *muqām,* which is still the common designation of holy sites in Palestine.

(15) **The altar . . . and the high place.**—The *and* is wanting in the Hebrew, LXX., and Targum. It is supplied in the Syriac, Vulgate, and Arabic, correctly as regards the sense; see below. Grammatically, "the high place" may be in apposition to "the altar," and may include it, as being a more general term.

**Which Jeroboam the son of Nebat . . .**—See 1 Kings xii. 28 *seq.*

**Burned the high place.**—Was it, then, a wooden structure, as Thenius supposes? Perhaps it resembled a dolmen (many hundred such have been found in Palestine); and fire may have been kindled under it, by way of cracking the huge slabs of stone of which it was built. The fragments might then be more easily crushed.

**Burned the grove.**—The present text is, *burned an ashērah.* Perhaps the article has fallen out; especially as this is not the only indication that the text has suffered in this place. Thenius understands the word in the general sense of an *idol-image,* comparing chap. xvii. 29 *seq.* But it is doubtful whether the word *Ashērah* is so used. It is noteworthy that the present passage indirectly agrees with Hosea x. 6, for no mention is made of what used to be the chief object of worship at Beth-el; viz., the golden bullock. It had been carried away to Assyria, as the prophet foretold.

(16—18) These verses are supposed by Stähelin to be a fictitious addition of the compiler's. Thenius does not go so far as this, but assumes that the proper sequel

claimed these words. <sup>(17)</sup> Then he said, What title *is* that that I see? And the men of the city told him, *It is* the sepulchre of the man of God, which came from Judah, and proclaimed these things that thou hast done against the altar of Beth-el. <sup>(18)</sup> And he said, Let him alone; let no man move his bones. So they let his bones ¹ alone, with the bones of the prophet that came out of Samaria.

<sup>(19)</sup> And all the houses also of the high places that *were* in the cities of Samaria, which the kings of Israel had made to provoke *the* LORD to anger, Josiah took away, and did to them according to all the acts that he had done in Beth-el. <sup>(20)</sup> And he ² slew all the priests of the high places that *were* there upon the altars, and burned men's bones upon them, and returned to Jerusalem.

<sup>(21)</sup> And the king commanded all the people, saying, "Keep the passover unto the LORD your God, *as it is* written in the book of this covenant. <sup>(22)</sup> Surely there was not holden such a passover from the days of the judges that judged Israel, nor in all the days of the kings of Israel, nor of the kings of Judah; <sup>(23)</sup> but in the eighteenth year of king Josiah, *wherein* this passover was holden to the LORD in Jerusalem.

¹ Heb., *to escape.*
² Or, *sacrificed.*
*a* 2 Chron. 35. 1; 1 Esd. 1. 1.
*b* Exod. 12. 3; Deut. 16. 2.

---

of 1 Kings xiii. 1—32, has been transferred to this place. He argues that it must be an interpolation here, because (1) the "moreover" of verse 15 (*wĕgam*) corresponds to the "and . . . also" (*wĕgam*) of verse 19, which does not prove much; and because (2) Josiah could not pollute the altar (verse 16) after he had already *shattered it in pieces* (verse 15). This reasoning is not conclusive, because it is obvious that, as is so often the case, the writer has first told in brief what was done to the altar and high place at Bethel, and then related at length an interesting incident that occurred at the time. In short, the statement of verse 15 is anticipatory.

<sup>(16)</sup> **Turned himself.**—So that he caught sight of the tombs on the hill-side opposite—not on the hill where the high place was.

**The man of God proclaimed.**—Some words appear to have fallen out of the Hebrew text here, for the LXX. *adds,* " when Jeroboam stood in the feast at the altar. And he returned and lifted up his eyes upon the grave of the man of God." (A transcriber's eye wandered from one "man of God" to the other.) Josiah *returned,* when on the point of going away.

<sup>(17)</sup> **What title is this?**—*What is yonder monument,* or *memorial stone?* Ezek. xxxix. 15, " sign." Jeremiah uses the same term of a sign-post (Jer. xxxi. 21, "waymarks"). (See 1 Kings xiii. 29 *seq.*)

<sup>(18)</sup> **Let him alone.**—Or, *Let him rest.*

**So they let his bones alone.**—A different verb. *And they suffered his bones to escape,* scil., disturbance.

**With the bones of the prophet . . .**—See 1 Kings xiii. 31, 32.

**That came out of Samaria.**—This simply designates the old prophet who deceived the Judæan man of God, as a citizen of the Northern kingdom, which was called Samaria, after its capital.

<sup>(19)</sup> **The houses also of the high places**—*i.e.,* temples or chapels attached to the high places.

**Josiah took away.**—Comp. 2 Chron. xxxiv. 6, from which it appears that the king's zeal carried him as far as Naphtali. The question has been asked, how it was that Josiah was able to proceed thus beyond the limits of his own territory. It is possible that, as a vassal of Assyria, he enjoyed a certain amount of authority over the old domains of the ten tribes. We have no record of either fact, but his opposition to Necho favours the idea that he recognised the Assyrian sovereign as his suzerain. Moreover, it is in itself likely that the remnant of Israel would be drawn towards Judah and its king as the surviving representatives of the past glories of their race, and would sympathise in his reformation, just as the Samaritans, in the times of the return, were eager to participate in the rebuilding of the Temple. (Comp. 2 Chron. xxxiv. 9.) Another supposition is that, as the fall of the Assyrian empire was imminent, no notice was taken of Josiah's proceedings in the west.

<sup>(20)</sup> **He slew.**—*He slaughtered.* A contrast to his mild treatment of the priests of the Judæan high places (verses 8, 9). *They* were Levites, and these heathenish priests. (Comp. Deut. xvii. 2—5.) Thus was fulfilled the prophecy of 1 Kings xiii. 2. (Thenius considers the event historical, *because* that prophecy " is undoubtedly modelled upon it.")

<sup>(21)</sup> **Keep the passover.**—*Hold a passover* (verse 22). (Comp. 2 Chron. xxxv. 1—19 for a more detailed account of this unique celebration.) Josiah had the precedent of Hezekiah for signalising his religious revolution by a solemn passover (2 Chron. xxx. 1).

**In the book of this covenant.**—Rather, *in this book of the covenant* (verse 2). The book was that which Hilkiah had found in the Temple, and which gave the impulse to the whole reforming movement. (The LXX. and Vulg. read, *in the book of this covenant* —a mere mistake.)

<sup>(22)</sup> **Surely there was not holden . . .**—*For there was not holden* (*a passover*) *like this passover.* This and the next verse constitute a parenthetic remark, in which the historian emphasises the phrase, " As it is written in this book of the covenant." No passover, from the time of the Judges onward had been celebrated in such strict conformity to the prescriptions of the Law. The LXX. omits the particle of comparison: ὅτι οὐκ ἐγενήθη τὸ πάσχα τοῦτο. On the ground of this difference, and the one mentioned in the Note on verse 21, Thenius thinks it not improbable that the text of Kings has been altered to bring into harmony with the account in Chronicles about the restoration of the feast of the passover by *Hezekiah*—a weighty inference from such slight data. The chronicler repeats this very verse at the close of his narrative of Josiah's passover (2 Chron. xxxv. 18).

<sup>(23)</sup> **Wherein.**—Omit this word. As Ewald says, the meaning of these two verses is, that the passover was never so celebrated before, especially as regards (1) the offerings over and above the paschal lamb (Deut. xvi. 2), and (2) the strict *unity* of the place of this

(24) Moreover the *workers with* familiar spirits, and the wizards, and the ¹images, and the idols, and all the abominations that were spied in the land of Judah and in Jerusalem, did Josiah put away, that he might perform the words of ᵃthe law which were written in the book that Hilkiah the priest found in the house of the LORD. (25) And like unto him was there no king before him, that turned to the LORD with all his heart, and with all his soul, and with all his might, according to all the law of Moses; neither after him arose there *any* like him.

(26) Notwithstanding the LORD turned not from the fierceness of his great wrath, wherewith his anger was kindled against Judah, because of all the ²provocations that Manasseh had provoked him withal. (27) And the LORD said, I will remove Judah also out of my sight, as I have removed Israel, and will cast off this city Jerusalem which I have chosen, and the house of which I said, ᵇMy name shall be there.

(28) Now the rest of the acts of Josiah, and all that he did, *are* they not written in the book of the chronicles of the kings of Judah?

(29) ᶜIn his days Pharaoh-nechoh king of Egypt went up against the king of Assyria to the river Euphrates: and king Josiah went against him; and he

---

1 Or, *teraphim.*

ᵃ Lev. 20. 27; Deut. 18. 11.

2 Heb., *angers.*

ᵇ 1 Kings 8. 29, & 9. 3; ch. 21. 7.

ᶜ 2 Chron. 35. 20.

---

festival (Deut. xvi. 5). The assumption that *no passover had ever been held before* (De Wette), is obsolete, even among "advanced critics," and does not merit serious discussion.

(24) **Moreover the workers** . . .—After abolishing public idolatry, Josiah attacked the various forms of private superstition.

**The workers with familiar spirits.**—*The necromancers* ('ôbôth; 1 Sam. xxviii. 3 *seq.*). (See chap. xxi. 6.)

**Images.**—See margin; and Gen. xxxi. 19; Judges xvii. 5; 1 Sam. xix. 13; Zech. x. 2.

**The idols.**—*The dunglings.* Gesenius prefers to render, *idol-blocks*; Ewald, *doll-images.* (See chap. xvii. 12.)

**That were spied** (seen).—A significant expression. Many idols were, doubtless, concealed by their worshippers.

**Put away.**—Or, *put out, did away with* (Deut. xiii. 6, xvii. 7); strictly, *consumed.* (See the law in Lev. xx. 27; Deut. xviii. 9, 10.)

(25) **And, like unto him was there no king before him.**—Comp. chap. xviii. 5, 6, where a similar eulogy is passed upon Hezekiah. It is not, perhaps, necessary to insist upon any formal contradiction which may appear to result from a comparison of the two passages. A writer would not be careful to measure his words by the rule of strict proportion in such cases. Still, as the preceding account indicates, the Mosaic law does not appear to have been so rigorously carried out by any preceding king as by Josiah. (See Note on 2 Chron. xxx. 26.)

**With all his heart** . . .—An echo of Deut. vi. 5. That Josiah's merits did not merely consist in a strict observance of the legitimate worship and ritual, is evident from Jer. xxii. 15, 16, where he is praised for his righteousness as a judge.

(26, 27) The historian naturally adds these remarks to prepare the way for what he has soon to relate—the final ruin of the kingdom; and probably also to suggest an explanation of what must have seemed to him and his contemporaries a very mysterious stroke of providence, the untimely end of the good king Josiah.

(26) **The fierceness of his great wrath . . . kindled.**—*The great heat of his wrath, wherewith his wrath burnt.*

**Because of all the provocations that Manasseh . . .**—Comp. the predictions of Jeremiah (Jer. xv. 4, xxv. 2 *seq.*) and Zephaniah; and see the Note on 2 Chron. xxxiv. 33.

(28—30) Josiah's end. The historical abstract broken off at chap. xxii. 2 is now continued. (Comp. the more detailed account in 2 Chron. xxxv. 20 *seq.*)

(29) **Pharaoh-nechoh.**—Necho II., the successor of Psammetichus, and the sixth king of the 26th or Saite dynasty, called Νεκῶς by Herodotus (ii. 158, 159; iv. 42); he reigned circ. 611—605 B.C., but is not mentioned in the Assyrian records, so far as they are at present known to us.

**The king of Assyria.**—It is sometimes assumed that Necho's expedition was directed against "the then ruler of what *had been* the Assyrian empire" (Thenius and others), and that the king in question was Nabopalassar, the conqueror of Nineveh, who became king of Babylon in 626—625 B.C. If the fall of Nineveh preceded or coincided with this last event, then Nabopalassar must be intended by the historian here. But if, as the chronology of Eusebius and Jerome represents, Cyaraxes the Mede took Nineveh in 609—608 B.C., or, according to the Armenian chronicle, *apud* Eusebius, in 608—607 B.C., then Necho's expedition (circ. 609 B.C.) was really directed against *a king of Assyria* in the strict sense. After the death of Assurbanipal (626 B.C.) it appears that two or three kings reigned at Nineveh, namely, *Assur-idil-ilani-ukinni, Bel-sum-iskun* and *Esar-haddon II.* (the Saracus of Abydenus and Syncellus). Nineveh must have fallen before 606 B.C., as Assyria does not occur in the list of countries mentioned by Jeremiah (Jer. xxv. 19—26) in the fourth year of Jehoiakim, *i.e.*, 606 B.C. The probable date of its fall is 607 B.C. A year or so later Necho made a second expedition, this time against the king of Babylon, but was utterly defeated at Carchemish. (See Schrader, *K. A. T.*, pp. 357—361.) Josephus says that Necho went to wage war with the Medes and Babylonians, who had just put an end to the Assyrian empire, and that his object was to win the dominion of Asia.

**King Josiah went against him.**—Probably as a vassal of Assyria, and as resenting Necho's trespass on territory which he regarded as his own. The Syriac

*Death of Josiah.*      II. KINGS, XXIII.      *Jehoahaz Imprisoned.*

slew him at Megiddo, when he had seen him.ᵃ <sup>(30)</sup> And his servants carried him in a chariot dead from Megiddo, and brought him to Jerusalem, and buried him in his own sepulchre. And "the people of the land took Jehoahaz the son of Josiah, and anointed him, and made him king in his father's stead.

<sup>(31)</sup> Jehoahaz *was* twenty and three years old when he began to reign; and he reigned three months in Jerusalem. And his mother's name *was* Hamutal, the daughter of Jeremiah of Libnah. <sup>(32)</sup> And he did *that which was* evil in the sight of the Lord, according to all that his fathers had done. <sup>(33)</sup> And Pharaoh-nechoh put him in bands at Riblah in the land of Hamath, ¹that he might not reign in Jerusalem; and ²put the land to a tribute of an hundred talents of silver, and a talent of gold. <sup>(34)</sup> And Pharaoh-nechoh made Eliakim the son of Josiah king in the room of Josiah his father, and turned his name to ᵇJehoi-

*a* 2 Chron. 36. 1.

1 Or, *because he reigned.*

2 Heb., *set a mulct upon the land.*

*b* Matt. 1. 11, called *Jakim.*

---

adds: "to fight against him: and Pharaoh said to him, Not against thee have I come; return from me. And he hearkened not to Pharaoh, and Pharaoh smote him." This may once have formed part of the Hebrew text, but is more likely a gloss from Chronicles.

**At Megiddo.**—In the plain of Jezreel (1 Kings iv. 12). (Comp. Zech. xii. 11.) Herodotus calls it Magdolus (ii. 159). The fact that this was the place of battle shows that Necho had not marched through southern Palestine, but had taken the shortest route over sea, and landed at Accho (*Acre*). Otherwise, Josiah would not have had to go so far north to meet him.

**When he had seen him.**—At the outset of the encounter; as we might say, *the moment he got sight of him*. According to the account in Chronicles, which is derived from a different source, Josiah was wounded by the Egyptian archers, and carried in a dying state to Jerusalem (2 Chron. xxxv. 22 *seq.*). Thenius thinks that Jer. xv. 7—9 was spoken on occasion of Josiah's departure with his army from the north, and that the prophet's metaphor, "her sun went down while it was yet day," refers to the eclipse of Thales, which had recently happened, 610 B.C. (Herod. i. 74, 103).

<sup>(30)</sup> **And his servants carried him . . .**—See Notes 2 Chron. xxxv. 24.

**The people of the land.**—Thenius says they were the soldiery who had fled to Jerusalem; but this is doubtful.

**Took Jehoahaz.**—He was not the eldest son (see verse 36), but he may have been thought a more capable prince amid the emergencies of the time, although Jer. xxii. 10 *seq.* shows that this estimate was fallacious.

The Reign of Jehoahaz (31—34).

<sup>(31)</sup> **Jehoahaz.**—Called Shallum (Jer. xxii. 11; 1 Chron. iii. 15), which may have been his name before his accession. (Comp. verse 34, xxiv. 17.) Hitzig suggested that he was so called by Jeremiah in allusion to his brief reign, as if he were a *second* Shallum (chap. xv. 13). It is against this that Shallum was not a Judean prince, but an obscure adventurer who usurped the throne of Samaria a hundred and fifty years previously, so that the allusion would not be very clear.

**Hamutal.**—"Akin to dew." (Comp. Abital, "father of dew," or perhaps, "the father is dew.") *Tal*, however, may be a divine name; the meaning then is, "Tal is a kinsman." (Comp. Hamuel, "El is a kinsman.")

<sup>(32)</sup> **And he did that which was evil . . .**—Comp. Ezekiel's lamentation for the princes of Judah," where Jehoahaz is called a young lion that "devoureth men," alluding to his oppressive rapacity and shameless abuse of power (Ezek. xix. 1—4).

<sup>(33)</sup> **And Pharaoh-nechoh put him in bands . . .**—See Note on 2 Chron. xxxvi. 3. The LXX. here has "removed him," but the other versions "bound him."

**That he might not reign.**—This is the reading of the Hebrew margin, some MSS., and the LXX., Vulg., and Targum. The Syriac and Arabic have, "when he reigned," which is the ordinary Hebrew text. The original text of the whole was perhaps this: "and Pharaoh-nechoh bound him at Riblah . . . and removed him from reigning in Jerusalem;" *i.e.*, he threw him into bonds, and pronounced his deposition. (Comp. the construction in 1 Kings xv. 13.) Riblah (now *Ribleh*) lay in a strong position on the Orontes, commanding the caravan route from Palestine to the Euphrates. Necho had advanced so far, after the battle of Megiddo, and taken up his quarters there, as Nebuchadnezzar did afterwards (chap. xxv. 6, 20, 21). Josephus relates that Necho summoned Jehoahaz to his camp at Riblah. The passage, Ezek. xix. 4, suggests that he got the king of Judah into his power by fraud: "he was taken in their pit." It used to be supposed, on the strength of Herod. ii. 159, that Necho captured *Jerusalem*. What Herodotus says is this: "And engaging the Syrians on foot at Magdolus, Nechoh was victorious. After the battle he took Kadytis, a great city of Syria." Kadytis has been thought to be either *Hadath* ("the new town;" referring to the rebuilding of Jerusalem after the Return), or *el-Kuds* ("the holy;" the modern Arabic title of Jerusalem), or Gaza. In reality it is Kadesh on the Orontes, one of the great Hittite capitals, and not far from Hamath.

**A talent of gold.**—So Chronicles. The LXX. here reads, *an hundred talents of gold* (a transcriber's error). The Syriac and Arabic, *ten talents*, which may be right. (Comp. chap. xviii. 14, where the proportion of silver to gold is ten to one.)

**Tribute.**—The Hebrew word means *fine*. The Vulg. renders rightly, "et imposuit multum terrae."

<sup>(34)</sup> **Turned his name to Jehoiakim.**—A slight change. Eliakim is "El setteth up;" Jehoiakim, "Jah setteth up." Necho meant to signify that the new king was his creature. Eliakim, the elder son, may have paid court to Necho; or the Egyptian may have deposed Jehoahaz, as elected without his consent, and perhaps as likely to prove a stronger king than his brother. Necho may have fancied a resemblance between the name *Yahû* (*i.e., Jah;* so it was then pronounced) and *Aah*, the name of the Egyptian moon-god. (See Note on 1 Chron. iv. 18.)

**And he came to Egypt, and died there.**—LXX. and Vulg. as Chronicles: *and he brought him to Egypt* (by a slight change of the pointing in the Hebrew.) Jeremiah had foretold the fact (Jer. xxii. 10—12).

akim, and took Jehoahaz away: and he came to Egypt, and died there. (35) And Jehoiakim gave the silver and the gold to Pharaoh; but he taxed the land to give the money according to the commandment of Pharaoh: he exacted the silver and the gold of the people of the land, of every one according to his taxation, to give it unto Pharaoh-nechoh.

(36) Jehoiakim *was* twenty and five years old when he began to reign; and he reigned eleven years in Jerusalem. And his mother's name *was* Zebudah, the daughter of Pedaiah of Rumah. (37) And he did *that which was* evil in the sight of the LORD, according to all that his fathers had done.

CHAPTER XXIV.—(1) In his days Nebuchadnezzar king of Babylon came up, and Jehoiakim became his servant three years: then he turned and rebelled against him. (2) And the LORD sent against him bands of the Chaldees, and bands of the Syrians, and bands of the Moabites, and bands of the children of Ammon, and sent them against Judah to destroy it, *a* according to the word of the LORD, which he spake ¹by his servants the prophets. (3) Surely at the commandment of the LORD came *this* upon Judah, to remove *them* out of his sight, for the sins of Manasseh, according to all that he did; (4) and also for the innocent blood that he shed: for he

*a* ch. 20. 17, & 23. 27.

¹ Heb., *by the hand of.*

---

THE REIGN OF JEHOIAKIM (verse 35—chap. xxiv. 7).

(35) **And Jehoiakim gave.**—*And the silver and the gold did Jehoiakim give* . . . He had to pay for his elevation. The raising of the fine of verse 33 is described in this verse.

**But he taxed . . .**—The king kept his pledge to Pharaoh, but not out of his own means. He exacted the money from "the people of the land," *i.e.*, the people of all classes, levying a fixed contribution even upon the poorest of his subjects. As in chap. xi. 14, xiv. 21, xxi. 24, Thenius insists that "the people of the land" are *the national militia*, and he renders: "he exacted the silver and the gold, *along with* (*i.e.*, by the help of) *the people of the land.*" But this is, to say the least, very questionable. (See Note on chap. xi. 14.)

(36) **He reigned eleven years.**—Not eleven full years. (Comp. Jer. xxv. 1 with chap. xxiv. 12; and Jer. lii. with chap. xxv. 8.)

**His mother's name was Zebudah.**—So the Hebrew margin and Targum. Hebrew text, Syriac, Vulg., Arabic, *Zebidah. Zebadiah* may have been the real name. The mother of Jehoahaz was Hamutal (verse 31). Thus Josiah had at least two wives, and probably more. (Comp. chap. xxiv. 15.) He could not have been over fourteen when he begot Jehoiakim.

**Rumah.**—Perhaps Arumah, near Shechem (Judg. ix. 41), as Josephus has *Abumah*. This is interesting as a slight indication that Josiah's power extended over the territory of the former kingdom of Samaria.

(37) **He did that which was evil . . .**—Jeremiah represents him as luxurious, covetous, and violent (Jer. xxii. 13 *seq.*). He murdered Urijah a prophet (Jer. xxvi. 20 *seq.*). Ewald thinks that he introduced Egyptian animal-worship (Ezek. viii. 7 *seq.*), which is rendered highly probable by his relation of dependence on Necho. (Comp. the introduction of Assyrian star-worship under Ahaz.)

XXIV.

(1) **In his days.**—In his fifth or sixth year. In Jehoiakim's fourth year Nebuchadnezzar defeated Necho at Carchemish (Jer. xlvi. 2), and was suddenly called home by the news of the death of Nabopolassar his father, whom he succeeded on the throne of Babylon in the same year (Jer. xxv. 1). From Jer. xxxvi. 9 we learn that towards the end of Jehoiakim's fifth year the king of Babylon was expected to invade the land. When this took place, Nebuchadnezzar humbled Jehoiakim, who had probably made his submission, by putting him in chains, and carrying off some of the Temple treasures (2 Chron. xxxvi. 6, 7). Left in the possession of his throne as a vassal of Babylon, Jehoiakim paid tribute three years, and then tried to throw off the yoke.

(2) **And the Lord sent against him bands of the Chaldees.**—Jehoiakim's revolt was no doubt instigated by Egypt. Whilst Nebuchadnezzar himself was engaged elsewhere in his great empire, predatory bands of Chaldeans, and of the neighbouring peoples the hereditary enemies of Judah, who had submitted to Nebuchadnezzar, and were nothing loth to make reprisals for the power which Josiah had, perhaps, exercised over them, ravaged the Judæan territory (comp. Jer. xii. 8—17, concerning Judah's 'evil neighbours'").

**According to the word of the Lord.**—Isaiah, Micah, Urijah (Jer. xxvi. 20), Huldah, Jeremiah, Habakkuk, and doubtless others whose names and writings have not been transmitted, had foretold the fate that was now closing in upon Judah.

(3) **Surely at the commandment.**—Literally, *Only* (*i.e.*, upon no other ground than) *upon the mouth* (*i.e.*, at the command of; chap. xxiii. 35) *of Jehovah did it happen in Judah.* The LXX. and Syriac read *wrath* instead of *mouth*, which Ewald prefers (so verse 20).

**Out of his sight.**—*From before his face*, *i.e.*, as the Targum explains, from the land where he was present in his Temple.

**For the sins of Manasseh.**—Comp. chaps. xxi. 11 *seq.*, xxiii. 26 *seq.*; Jer. xv. 4.

(4) **The innocent blood.**—Heb., *blood of the innocent*; an expression like *hand of the right*, *i.e.*, the right hand; or, *day of the sixth*, *i.e.*, the sixth day. Thenius thinks the murder of some prominent personage, such as Isaiah, may be intended, and wishes to distinguish between the statement of the first clause of the verse and the second; but chap. xxi. 16, where the two statements are connected more closely, does not favour this view.

**Which the Lord would not pardon.**—Literally, *and Jehovah willed not to pardon.* We must not soften the statement of verses 3, 4, as Bähr does, by asserting the meaning to be that the nation was punished, not for the sins of Manasseh, but for its persis-

filled Jerusalem with innocent blood; which the LORD would not pardon.

(5) Now the rest of the acts of Jehoiakim, and all that he did, *are* they not written in the book of the chronicles of the kings of Judah? (6) So Jehoiakim slept with his fathers: and Jehoiachin his son reigned in his stead. (7) And the king of Egypt came not again any more out of his land: for the king of Babylon had taken from the river of Egypt unto the river Euphrates all that pertained to the king of Egypt.

(8) Jehoiachin *was* eighteen years old when he began to reign, and he reigned in Jerusalem three months. And his mother's name *was* Nehushta, the daughter of Elnathan of Jerusalem. (9) And he did *that which was* evil in the sight of the LORD, according to all that his father had done.

(10) *a* At that time the servants of Nebuchadnezzar king of Babylon came up against Jerusalem, and the city ¹was besieged. (11) And Nebuchadnezzar king of Babylon came against the city, and

*a* Dan. i. 1.

1 Heb., *came into siege.*

---

tence in the same kind of sins. The sins of Manasseh are regarded as a climax in Judah's long course of provocation: the cup was full, and judgment ready to fall. It was only suspended for a time, not revoked, in the reign of the good king Josiah. In short, the idea of the writer is that the innocent blood shed by Manasseh cried to heaven for vengeance, and that the ruin of the kingdom was the answer of the All-righteous Judge. It is no objection to say, that in that case children suffered for their fathers' misdeeds; that was precisely the Old Testament doctrine, until Ezekiel proclaimed another (Ezek. xviii. 19; comp. Exod. xx. 5; Deut. v. 9). Looking at the catastrophe from a different standpoint, *we* may remember that national iniquities must be chastised in the present life, if at all; and that the sufferings of the exile were necessary for the purification of Israel from its inveterate tendency to apostatise from Jehovah.

(5) **Now the rest of the acts of Jehoiakim** ...—Assuming with Hitzig that the passage Hab. ii. 9—14 refers to him, we gather that he severely oppressed his people by his exactions of forced labour upon the defences of Jerusalem. Thenius concludes from the words, "that he may set his nest on high," &c., that Jehoiakim strengthened and enlarged the fortress on Ophel erected by Manasseh. (Comp. also Jer. xxii. 13—17.)

**Are they not written** ...—The last reference to this authority. Bähr concludes that the work did not extend beyond the reign of Jehoiakim.

(6) **So Jehoiakim slept with his fathers.**—The usual notice of the king's burial is omitted, and the omission is significant, considered in the light of Jeremiah's prophecy: "Thus saith the Lord concerning Jehoiakim the son of Josiah king of Judah; they shall not lament for him . . . He shall be buried with the burial of an ass, drawn and cast forth beyond the gates of Jerusalem" (Jer. xxii. 18, 19; comp. chap. xxxvi. 30). Jehoiakim appears to have been slain in an encounter with the bands of freebooters mentioned in verse 2, so that his body was left to decay where it fell, all his followers having perished with him. Ewald supposes that he was lured out of Jerusalem to a pretended conference with the Chaldeans, and then treacherously seized, and, as he proved a refractory prisoner, slain, and his body denied the last honours, his family craving its restoration in vain. (The words of the text do not necessarily imply *a natural and peaceful* death, as Thenius alleges, but simply *death* without further qualification.)

(7) **And the king of Egypt came not again any more** ...—The verse indicates the posture of political affairs at the time when Jehoiachin succeeded his father. Necho had been deprived by Nebuchadnezzar of all his conquests, and so crippled that he durst not venture again beyond his own borders. Thus Judah was left, denuded of all external help, to face the consequences of its revolt from Babylon, which speedily overtook it (verse 10).

**From the river** (torrent) **of Egypt**—*i.e.,* the *Wady-el-Arish.* The details of this campaign of Nebuchadnezzar are not recorded. It is clear, from the statement before us, that before the battle of Carchemish Necho had made himself master of the whole of Syria and the country east of the Jordan.

THE REIGN OF JEHOIACHIN. BEGINNING OF THE BABYLONIAN CAPTIVITY (verses 8—16).

(8) **Jehoiachin.**—"Jah will confirm." Four or five different forms of this name occur in the documents. Ezek. i. 2 gives the contraction *Joiachin.* In Jeremiah we find a popular transposition of the two elements, thus: *Jechonjahu* (once, viz., Jer. xxiv. 1, *Heb.*), and usually the shorter form, Jechoniah (Jer. xxvii. 20; Esther ii. 6); which is further abridged into Coniah (Heb., *Chonjahu*) in Jer. xxii. 24, 28. Ewald thinks this last the original name; but Hengstenberg supposes that the prophet altered the name, so as to make of it a "Jah will confirm" without the "will," in order to foreshadow the fate which awaited this king.

**Nehushta.**—Referring, perhaps, to her complexion (as we say "bronzed").

**Elnathan.**—See Jer. xxvi. 22, xxxvi. 12, 25; one of Jehoiakim's "princes."

(9) **And he did that which was evil** ...—Ezek. xix. 5—9 refers to him, according to Keil and Ewald; but Thenius asks how, in his position, and during his brief reign of ninety (?) days, a considerable number of which must probably be allowed for the siege, he could possibly do what is there described. Hitzig refers the passage to Zedekiah; and so Thenius. Josephus calls Jehoiachin "naturally good and just;" probably misunderstanding the words of Jer. xxii. 24, 28.

(10) **At that time.** — In the spring of the year (2 Chron. xxxvi. 10). Thenius infers from Jer. xiii. 19 ("the cities of the south land are shut up"), that Nebuchadnezzar drew a *cordon* across that part of the country, to cut off any succours from Egypt.

**The servants**—*i.e.,* generals. (Comp. chap. xix. 6.)

**Was besieged.**—See margin; and chap. xxv. 2; Jer. lii. 5.

(11) **Did besiege.** — *Were besieging.* The king arrived after the siege had begun.

*Jerusalem carried*     II. KINGS, XXIV.     *Captive into Babylon.*

his servants did besiege it. <sup>(12)</sup> And Jehoiachin the king of Judah went out to the king of Babylon, he, and his mother, and his servants, and his princes, and his ¹ officers: and the king of Babylon took him in the eighth year of his reign. <sup>(13)</sup> <sup>*a*</sup>And he carried out thence all the treasures of the house of the LORD, and the treasures of the king's house, and cut in pieces all the vessels of gold which Solomon king of Israel had made in the temple of the LORD, as the LORD had said. <sup>(14)</sup> And he carried away all Jerusalem, and all the princes, and all the mighty men of valour, *even* ten thousand captives, and all the craftsmen and smiths: none remained, save the poorest sort of the people of the land. <sup>(15)</sup> And <sup>*b*</sup>he carried away Jehoiachin to Babylon, and the king's mother, and the king's wives, and his ² officers, and the mighty of the land, *those* carried he into captivity from Jerusalem to Babylon. <sup>(16)</sup> And all the men of might, *even* seven thousand, and craftsmen and smiths a thousand, all *that were* strong *and* apt for war, even them the king of Babylon brought captive to Babylon.

<sup>(17)</sup> And <sup>*c*</sup>the king of Babylon made Mattaniah his father's brother king in his stead, and changed his name to

---

B.C. 599.

1 Or, *eunuchs.*

*a* ch. 20. 17; Isa. 39. 6.

*b* 2 Chron. 36. 10; Esther 2. 6.

2 Or, *eunuchs.*

*c* Jer. 37. 1, & 52. 1.

---

**Came against.**—*Came unto.*

<sup>(12)</sup> **And Jehoiachin the king of Judah went out . . .**—Despairing of the defence, he threw himself upon the clemency of Nebuchadnezzar. The queen-mother (Jer. xxii. 2) and all his grandees and courtiers accompanied the king, who probably hoped to be allowed to keep his throne as a vassal of Babylon.

**Took him**—*i.e.*, as a prisoner.

**In the eighth year of his** (*i.e.*, Nebuchadnezzar's) **reign.**—This exactly tallies with the data of Jer. xxv. 1, xlvi. 2.

<sup>(13)</sup> **And he carried out thence . . .**—It is not said, but implied, that Nebuchadnezzar entered the city. He *may* have done so at the time of his invasion under Jehoiakim (verse 1). On that occasion he had carried off some of the sacred vessels (2 Chron xxxvi. 7; Dan. i. 2, v. 2, 3; comp. Ezra i. 7 *seq.*) It is certainly surprising to find that anything was left in the Temple treasury after the repeated spoliations which it had undergone. The fact not only indicates the probable existence of secret (subterranean) store-chambers, but also lends some support to the chronicler's representations of the great wealth stored up in the sanctuary.

**Cut in pieces.**—Chap. xvi. 17; 2 Chron. xxviii. 24. The meaning seems to be that the gold-plating was now stripped off from such "vessels" as the altar of incense, the table of shewbread, and the Ark. (Comp. chap. xviii. 16.)

**As the Lord had said**—*e.g.*, to Hezekiah (chap. xx. 17; comp. Jer. xv. 13, xvii. 3).

<sup>(14)</sup> **All Jerusalem.**— Limited by what follows, and meaning the most important part of the population.

**The princes**—*i.e.*, the nobles, *e.g.*, the grandees of the court, some of the priests (Ezek. i. 1), and the heads of the clans.

**The mighty men of valour.**—This is probably right. Thenius and Bähr prefer to understand the men of property and the artisans, as in chap. xv. 20.

**All the craftsmen and smiths.**—The former were workers in wood, stone, and metal, *i.e.*, carpenters, masons, and smiths. (Comp. Gen. iv. 22.) The "smiths" (properly, "they who shut") answer to what we should call locksmiths. They were makers of bolts and bars for doors and gates (Jer. xxiv. 1, xxix. 2). It is obvious that by deporting "the craftsmen and smiths" the king of Babylon made further outbreaks impossible (comp. 1 Sam. xiii. 19.) Kimchi's explanation of " smiths " is a curiosity of exegesis. He makes of them " learned persons, who *shut other people's* mouths, and propose riddles which nobody else can guess." Hitzig and Thenius derive the word (*masgēr*) from *mas*, " levy," and *gēr*, " alien," so that it would originally mean " statute labourers," " Canaanites compelled to work for the king ; " and afterwards, as here, " manual labourers " in general. But such a compound term in Hebrew would be very surprising.

**The poorest sort.**—Those who had neither property nor handicraft. (Comp. Jer. xxxix. 10.)

<sup>(15)</sup> **And he carried away.**— The form of the verb is different from that in verse 14. We might render: "*Yea*, he carried away;" for verses 15, 16 simply give the *particulars* of what was stated generally in verse 14. In the present verse the "princes" are defined.

**He carried away Jehoiachin to Babylon, and the king's mother.**—Fulfilment of Jer. xxii. 24—27.

**The mighty of the land.** — So the Targum, " the magnates of the land." All who could do so, must have taken refuge in Jerusalem at the approach of the Chaldæan army.

<sup>(16)</sup> **And all the men of might.**—"The mighty men of valour" of verse 14. (The words depend on the verb, "he carried away," in verse 14.) As there were 7,000 of these, and 1,000 " craftsmen and smiths," and the total number of the exiles was 10,000, there were 2,000 belonging to the aristocratic classes. Jer. lii. 28 gives a total of 3,023. Thenius explains his discrepancy as resulting from a transcriber's confusion of a large *y*, *i.e.* 10, with *g*, *i.e.* 3. Josephus has made his total of 10,832 out of the 832 of the second deportation (Jer. lii. 29) added to the 10,000 here assigned.

**All that were strong and apt for war.**— Literally, *the whole, warriors and doers of battle.* This clause refers to both those which precede, and it states that the 8,000 were all men in their prime, and trained in the use of weapons (*Thenius*). But may not the term " strong " (*gibbôrim*, " heroes," " warriors ") refer to the 7,000 as actual fighting men; and the phrase " makers of war " denote the craftsmen as employed in forging weapons and constructing defences? (The Syriac reads, *and all the men that made war.*)

**Even them the king of Babylon brought.** —Literally, *and the King of Babylon brought them.*

<sup>(17)</sup> **Mattaniah his father's brother.**— He was the third son of Josiah (comp. Jer. i. 3, xxxvii. 1), and full brother of Jehoahaz-Shallum (chap. xxiii. 31). Jehoiachin was childless at the time (comp. verses 12

Zedekiah. **(18)** Zedekiah *was* twenty and one years old when he began to reign, and he reigned eleven years in Jerusalem. And his mother's name *was* Hamutal, the daughter of Jeremiah of Libnah. **(19)** And he did *that which was* evil in the sight of the LORD, according to all that Jehoiakim had done. **(20)** For through the anger of the LORD it came to pass in Jerusalem and Judah, until he had cast them out from his presence, that Zedekiah rebelled against the king of Babylon.

*a* Jer. 39. 1, & 52. 4

*b* Jer. 52. 6.

**CHAPTER XXV.**—**(1)** And it came to pass *a* in the ninth year of his reign, in the tenth month, in the tenth *day* of the month, *that* Nebuchadnezzar king of Babylon came, he, and all his host, against Jerusalem, and pitched against it; and they built forts against it round about. **(2)** And the city was besieged unto the eleventh year of king Zedekiah. **(3)** And on the ninth *day* of the *b* fourth month the famine prevailed in the city, and there was no bread for the people

---

and 15 with chap. xxv. 7 and Jer. xxii. 30). In the exile he had offspring (1 Chron. iii. 17, 18). (The LXX. reads, *his son*, υἱὸν, a corruption of θεῖον, *uncle*).

**And changed his name to Zedekiah.**—His former name meant "gift of Jah;" his new one, "Jah is righteousness" (or "my righteousness"). The prophecy of Jeremiah (Jer. xxiii. 1—9), denouncing "the shepherds that destroy and scatter the flock," and promising a future king, whose name shall be "Jehovah is our righteousness" (*Iahweh çidgĕnu*), evidently refers to the delusive expectations connected with Zedekiah's elevation. Nebuchadnezzar's act of clemency in putting another native prince on the throne may have been the execution of a promise made at the surrender of the city.

THE REIGN OF ZEDEKIAH, the last KING OF JUDAH (verse 17—chap. xxv. 7; comp. 2 Chron. xxxvi. 11 *seq.*; Jer. lii).

This section and the parallel in Jeremiah appear to have been derived from the same historical work. The text of Jeremiah is generally, though not always, the best.

**(19) And he did that which was evil . . .**—The evidence of the prophet Jeremiah should be compared with this statement. (See especially Jer. xxiv. 8; xxxvii. 1, 2; xxxviii. 5, and Comp. Note on 2 Chron. xxxvi. 13.) The contemporary state of religion is vividly reflected in the pages of Ezekiel (chaps. viii.—xi.); who, moreover, denounces Zedekiah's breach of faith with the king of Babylon (Ezek. xvii. 11—21).

**According to all that Jehoiakim . . .**—He is not compared with Jehoiachin, who only reigned three months.

**(20) For through . . . in Jerusalem.**—Literally, *for upon the anger of Jehovah it befel Jerusalem.* That which fell upon Jerusalem and Judah like a ruinous disaster was *the evil doing of Zedekiah*, mentioned in verse 19. That such a prince as Zedekiah was raised to the throne was itself a token of Divine displeasure, for his character was such as to hasten the final catastrophe.

**Until he had cast them out.** — See Note on chap. xvii. 23.

**That Zedekiah rebelled.**—Rather, *and Zedekiah rebelled*. There should be a full stop after "presence." Zedekiah expected help from Pharaoh Hophra (Apries), king of Egypt, to whom he sent ambassadors (Ezek. xvii. 15; comp. Jer. xxxvii. 5, xliv. 30.) Moreover the neighbouring peoples of Edom, Ammon, and Moab, as well as Tyre and Zidon, were eager to throw off the Babylonian yoke, and had proposed a general rising to Zedekiah (Jer. xxvii. 3 *seq.*) The high hopes which were inspired by the negotiations may be inferred from the prophecy of Hananiah (Jer. xxviii.). Jeremiah opposed the project of revolt to the utmost of his power; and the event proved that he was right. In the early part of his reign Zedekiah had tried to procure the return of the exiles carried away in the last reign (Jer. xxix. 3); and in his fourth year he visited Babylon himself, perhaps with the same object, and to satisfy Nebuchadnezzar of his fidelity (Jer. li. 59). The date of his open revolt cannot be fixed.

XXV.

**(1) And it came to pass.**—With the account which follows comp. Jer. lii. 4 *seq.*, xxxix. 1—10, xl.—xliii.

**In the ninth year . . . tenth day.**—Comp. the similarly exact dates in verses 3 and 8. Ezek. xxiv. 1, 2, agrees with the present. The days were observed as fasts during the exile (Zech. vii. 3, 5, viii. 19).

**Came . . . against Jerusalem.**—After taking the other strong places of Judah, as Sennacherib had done (Jer. xxxiv. 7; comp. 2 Kings xviii. 13, xix. 8), Zedekiah must have prepared for the siege, as it lasted a year and a half.

**Forts.**—The Hebrew word (*dāyēq*) occurs in Ezek. iv. 2, xvii. 17; xxi. 27; xxvi. 8. Its meaning is some kind of *siege work*, as appears from the context in each case; but what precisely is not clear. The LXX. here has "wall" (τεῖχος); Syriac, "palisade" (*qalqûmê*, i.e., χαράκωμα).

**(2) Unto the eleventh year.**—The siege lasted altogether one year, five months, and twenty-seven days (verse 1 compared with verse 8). The Chaldæans raised the siege for a time, and marched against Pharaoh-Hophra, who was coming to the help of the Jews (Jer. xxxvii. 5 *seq.*; comp. Ezek. xvii. 17, xxx. 20 *seq.*)

**(3) And on the ninth day of the fourth month.**—The text is supplemented from Jer. xxxix. 2, lii. 6. The Syriac, however, has, "And in the eleventh year of King Zedekiah, *in the fifth month*, on the ninth day of the month, the famine prevailed," &c.; which may be original. (Comp. verse 1.)

**The famine prevailed.**—Not that the scarcity was first felt on that day, but that it then had reached a climax, so that defence was no longer possible. The horrors of the siege are referred to in Lam. ii. 11 *seq.*, 19 *seq.*, iv. 3—10; Ezek. v. 10; Baruch ii. 3. As in the famine of Samaria and the last siege of Jerusalem, parents ate their own offspring. (Comp. the prophetic threats of Lev. xxvi. 29; Deut. xxviii. 53 *seq.*; Jer. xv. 2 *seq.*, xxvii. 13; Ezek. iv. 16 *seq.*)

**The people of the land.**—The population of the city, especially the families which had crowded into it from the country. Thenius, as usual, insists that the

*Zedekiah taken and*      II. KINGS, XXV.      *Carried Captive to Babylon.*

of the land. <sup>(4)</sup> And the city was broken up, and all the men of war *fled* by night by the way of the gate between two walls, which *is* by the king's garden : (now the Chaldees *were* against the city round about:) and *the king* went the way toward the plain. <sup>(5)</sup> And the army of the Chaldees pursued after the king, and overtook him in the plains of Jericho: and all his army were scattered from him. <sup>(6)</sup> So they took the king, and brought him up to the king of Babylon to Riblah; and they <sup>1</sup>gave judgment upon him. <sup>(7)</sup> And they slew the sons of Zedekiah before his eyes, and <sup>2</sup>put out the eyes of Zedekiah, and bound him with fetters of brass, and carried him to Babylon.

<sup>(8)</sup> And in the fifth month, on the seventh *day* of the month, which *is* the nineteenth year of king Nebuchadnezzar king of Babylon, came Nebuzaradan, <sup>3</sup>captain of the guard, a servant of the king of Babylon, unto Jerusalem :

<sup>1</sup> Heb., *spake judgment with him.*

<sup>2</sup> Heb., *made blind.*

<sup>3</sup> Or *chief marshal.*

---

militia are meant. But these are the "men of war" (verse 4).

(4) **Broken up.**—Comp. 2 Chron. xxxii. 1. A breach was made in the wall with battering-rams, such as are depicted in the Assyrian sculptures. The Chaldæans forced their entry on the north side of the city, *i.e.*, they took the Lower City (chap. xxii. 14). This is clear from Jer. xxxix. 3, where it is said that, after effecting an entrance, their generals proceeded to assault "the middle gate," *i.e.*, the gate in the north wall of Zion, which separated the upper from the lower city. (See also chap. xiv. 13.)

**All the men of war fled.**—The Hebrew here is defective, for it wants a verb, and mention of the king is implied by what follows. (See Jer. xxxix. 4; lii. 7.) A comparison of these parallels suggests the reading : "And Zedekiah king of Judah and all the men of war fled, and went out of the city by night," &c.

**By the way of the gate between** (*the*) **two walls which is** (*was*) **by the king's garden.**—This gate lay at the south end of the Tyropœon, *i.e.*, the glen between Ophel and Zion ; and is the same as "the Gate of the Fountain" (Neh. iii. 15). The two walls were necessary for the protection of the Pool of Siloam and the water supply ; besides which the point was naturally weak for purposes of defence. Whether "the king's garden" was within or without the double wall is not clear, probably the latter, as Thenius supposes.

**Now the Chaldees . . . round about.**—An indication that even by this route the king and his warriors had to break through the enemy's lines, as the city was completely invested. (Comp. Ezek. xii. 12.)

**And the king went.**—Some MSS. and the Syriac, *and they went.* (So Jer. lii. 7; a correction, after the mention of the king had fallen out of the text.)

**The way toward the plain.**—The Arabah, or valley of the Jordan (Josh. xi. 2 ; 2 Sam. ii. 29).

(5) **In the plains of Jericho.**—In the neighbourhood of Jericho, the Arabah expands to the breadth of eleven or twelve miles. The part west of Jordan was called the "plains" (*Arbôth* plural of *Arabah*) of Jericho ; and that which lay east of the river was known as the plains of Moab (Josh. iv. 13; Num. xxii. 1). The depression between the Dead Sea and the Gulf of Akaba still bears the old name of the Arabah ; between the Dead Sea and the Lake of Tiberias it is called the Ghor.

(6) **To the king of Babylon, to Riblah.**—Chap. xxiii. 33. Nebuchadnezzar was not present at the storm of Jerusalem (Jer. xxxix. 3). He awaited the result in his headquarters.

**And they gave judgment upon him.**—Or, *brought him to trial.* (Comp. Jer. i. 16, iv. 12.) Nebuchadnezzar with the grandees of his court, perhaps including some dependent princes of the country, held a solemn trial of Zedekiah, as a rebel against his liege lord, in which, no doubt, his breach of oath was made prominent (2 Chron. xxxvi. 13 ; Ezek. xvii. 15, 18). The verb is singular in Jeremiah, and the versions. (See next Note.)

(7) **And they slew . . .**—The verbs are all singular in Jer. xxxix. 6, and lii. 10, 11 ; so that the acts in question are attributed directly to Nebuchadnezzar, to whose orders they were due. (So the versions, except that the Targum has "they slew.") The blinding of Zedekiah need not have been done by the conqueror himself, although in the Assyrian sculptures kings are actually represented as blinding and otherwise torturing their captives. It is no argument against the singular, "he carried him to Babylon," to say with Thenius that Zedekiah was sent to Babylon at once, while Nebuchadnezzar remained at Riblah. "Qui facit per alium, facit per se."

**The sons.**—Who fled with him (Comp. Jer. xli. 10). In Jeremiah it is added that all the nobles or princes of Judah were slain also.

**Put out the eyes.**—A Babylonian punishment (Herod. vii. 18). This was the meaning of Ezekiel's prediction; "I will bring him to Babylon . . . *yet shall he not see it*, though he shall die there" (Ezek. xii. 13).

**With fetters of brass.**—Literally, *with the double brass* (2 Chron. xxxiii. 12) ; *i.e.*, with manacles and fetters, as represented on the Assyrian monuments.

**Carried him to Babylon.**—Jer. lii. 11; "and put him in prison till the day of his death." So the Arabic of Kings.

(8) **On the seventh day . . .**—An error for the *tenth* day (Jer. lii. 12), one numeral letter having been mistaken for another. The Syriac and Arabic read *ninth* (perhaps, because, as Thenius suggests, the memorial fasts began on the evening of the ninth day).

According to Josephus the second Temple also was burnt on the tenth of the fifth month (*Bell. Jud.* vi. 4. 8).

**The nineteenth year of Nebuchadnezzar.**—This agrees with Jer. xxxii. 1, according to which the tenth of Zedekiah was the eighteenth of Nebuchadnezzar.

**Nebuzaradan.**—A Hebrew transcript of the Babylonian name *Nabû-zir-iddina,* "Nebo gave seed."

**Captain of the guard.**—Strictly, *chief of executioners.* (See Gen. xxxvii. 36.) This means commander of the Royal Bodyguard, the "Prætorians" of the time ; a corps of picked warriors, answering to the "Cherethites and Pelethites," and the "Carians and Runners" among the Hebrews (chap. xi. 4). Nebuzaradan is not

*Destruction of Jerusalem*     II. KINGS, XXV.     *and Spoiling of the Temple.*

(9) and he burnt the house of the LORD, and the king's house, and all the houses of Jerusalem, and every great *man's* house burnt he with fire. (10) And all the army of the Chaldees, that *were with* the captain of the guard, brake down the walls of Jerusalem round about. (11) Now the rest of the people *that were* left in the city, and the ¹fugitives that fell away to the king of Babylon, with the remnant of the multitude, did Nebuzar-adan the captain of the guard carry away. (12) But the captain of the guard left of the poor of the land *to be* vinedressers and husbandmen.

(13) And ᵃ the pillars of brass that *were* in the house of the LORD, and the bases, and the brasen sea that *was* in the house of the LORD, did the Chaldees break in pieces, and carried the brass of them to Babylon. (14) And the pots, and the shovels, and the snuffers, and the spoons, and all the vessels of brass wherewith they ministered, took they away. (15) And the firepans, and the bowls, *and* such things as *were* of gold, *in* gold, and of silver, *in* silver, the captain of the guard took away. (16) The two pillars, ²one sea, and the bases which Solomon had made for the house of the LORD; the brass of all these vessels was without weight. (17) ᵇ The height of the one pillar *was* eighteen cubits, and the chapiter upon it *was* brass: and the height of the chapiter three cubits; and the wreathen work, and pomegranates upon the chapiter round about, all of brass: and like unto these had the second pillar with wreathen work.

(18) And the captain of the guard took

1 Heb., *fallen away.*

*a* ch. 20. 17; Jer. 27. 22.

2 Heb., *the one sea.*

*b* 1 Kings 7. 15; Jer. 52. 21.

---

mentioned among the other generals in Jer. xxxix. 3. On this ground, and because his *coming* is expressly mentioned here, and because a month elapsed between the taking of the city (verse 4) and its destruction (verses 9, 10), Thenius infers that the city of David and the Temple did not at once fall into the hands of the Chaldeans; but were so well defended under the lead of some soldier like Ishmael (verse 23), that Nebuchadnezzar was compelled to despatch a specially distinguished commander to bring the matter to a conclusion. Verses 18—21 certainly appear to favour this view.

**A servant.**—In Jer. lii., "who stood before the king;" probably the original phrase. (Comp. chap. iii. 14, v. 16).

(9) **He burnt the house . . . king's house.**—Which were in the upper city. (There should be a semicolon after "king's house.")

**And every great man's house.**—Omit *man's*. The phrase limits the preceding one, "all the houses of Jerusalem," that is to say, "every great house" (2 Chron. xxxvi. 19, "all her palaces"). The common houses were spared for the poor who were left (verse 12).

(10) **With the captain.**—The preposition, though wanting in the common Hebrew text, is found in many MSS. and the old versions, as well as Jer. lii.

(11) **The fugitives that fell away**—*i.e.*, the deserters. (See Jer. xxvii. 12, xxxvii. 13 *seq.*, xxxviii. 2, 4, 17, 19.)

**The multitude.**—Probably the rank and file of the fighting-men (Judges iv. 7). The word is *hāmôn*, strictly *a shouting throng*. (The Syriac has "the rest of the army.") Jer. lii. 15, spells the word with *the light breathing* ('*āmôn*—either a dialectic use, or a mistake, not a distinct word).

(12) **Of the poor of the land.**—Chap. xxiv. 14 (Comp. Jer. xxxix. 10.)

**Husbandmen.**—Or, *plowmen*. The word (Hebrew text, *gābîm*) occurs here only. Jer. lii. 16 has a cognate form (*yôgʻbîm*) also unique.

(13) **And the pillars of brass.**—From this point Jer. xxxix. ceases to be parallel with the present narrative. (See the Notes on 1 Kings vii. 15 *seq.*, for the objects enumerated in this and the following verses.) Instead of "brass" we should probably understand *copper* throughout.

(14) **The snuffers.**—Jer. lii. 18 adds: *and the sprinkling-bowls*. The account there is in general more detailed than the present. (See 1 Kings vii. 40, 50.)

**Ministered.**—*Used to minister*. Things belonging to the service of the brazen altar are enumerated in this verse.

(15) **Firepans.**—See 1 Kings vii. 50. Besides "firepans" and "bowls" five other sorts of vessel are given in Jer. lii. 19.

**Such things as were . . . silver.**—A general expression intended to include all other objects of the same material as the two kinds mentioned. The verse treats of the utensils of the holy place. Many such had doubtless been carefully concealed by the priests on the occasion of the first plundering of the Temple (chap. xxiv. 13). (Comp. Jer. xxvii. 19 *seq.*)

(16) **The two pillars,** (*the*) **one sea . . .**—A nominative absolute.

**All these vessels . . .**—Those just mentioned, the two pillars, &c.

**Without weight.**—A natural hyperbole closely resembling one which we often meet with in Assyrian accounts of the plunder carried off from conquered towns: "*spoils without number* I carried off."

(17) **Three cubits.**—An error of transcription for *five*. Five cubits was the height of the capital according to 1 Kings vii. 16; Jer. lii. 22; 2 Chron. iii. 15.

**The wreathen work.**—Lattice-work (1 Kings vii. 17).

**With wreathen work.**—*Upon the lattice-work*. Thenius says this is the residuum of a sentence preserved in Jeremiah—namely, "And the pomegranates were ninety and six towards the outside; all the pomegranates were a hundred upon the lattice-work round about." (Jer. lii. 23). Our text is, at any rate, much abridged.

(18, 19) List of the chief personages taken by Nebuzaradan in the Temple and the city of David. This notice may be regarded as an indirect proof that the upper city was not captured before.

Seraiah the chief priest, and Zephaniah the second priest, and the three keepers of the ¹door: ⁽¹⁹⁾ And out of the city he took an ²officer that was set over the men of war, and five men of them that ³were in the king's presence, which were found in the city, and the ⁴principal scribe of the host, which mustered the people of the land, and threescore men of the people of the land *that were* found in the city: ⁽²⁰⁾ and Nebuzar-adan captain of the guard took these, and brought them to the king of Babylon to Riblah: ⁽²¹⁾ and the king of Babylon smote them, and slew them at Riblah in the land of Hamath. So Judah was carried away out of their land.

⁽²²⁾ ᵃAnd *as for* the people that remained in the land of Judah, whom Nebuchadnezzar king of Babylon had left, even over them he made Gedaliah the son of Ahikam, the son of Shaphan, ruler. ⁽²³⁾ And when all the ᵇcaptains of the armies, they and their men, heard that the king of Babylon had made Gedaliah governor, there came to Gedaliah to Mizpah, even Ishmael the son of Nethaniah, and Johanan the son of Careah, and Seraiah the son of Tanhumeth the Netophathite, and Jaazaniah

---

1 Heb., *threshold.*
2 Or, *eunuch.*
3 Heb., *saw the king's face.*
4 Or, *scribe of the captain of the host.*
a Jer. 40. 5, 9.
b Jer. 40. 7.

---

⁽¹⁸⁾ **Seraiah the chief** (*high*) **priest.**—And grandfather or great-grandfather of Ezra (1 Chron. vi. 14; Ezra. vii. 1).

**Zephaniah the second priest.**—See chap. xxiii. 4, Note; and Jer. xxi. 1, xxix. 25, 29, xxxvii. 3. From the last three passages it is clear that Zephaniah was a priest of high rank, being probably the high priest's deputy.

**The three keepers of the door** (*threshold*).— The chief warders of the principal entrances to the Temple. (See Jer. xxxviii. 13.) All the chief officials of the Temple were apparently taken away together.

⁽¹⁹⁾ **The city.**—Thenius is probably right in explaining *the city of David.*

**An officer that was set over the men of war** —*i.e.*, a royal officer commanding the garrison of the city of David. He was probably not an eunuch (chap. xx. 18, xxiv. 12), though in the Byzantine empire, at all events, eunuchs were sometimes great soldiers—*e.g.*, the heroic Narses.

**And five men of them . . .**—See margin. The phrase is explained by the seclusion affected by Oriental sovereigns. The LXX., Syriac, and Vulg., read *five*; the Targum, *fifty.* Jer. lii. and the Arabic read *seven.* The numeral letter denoting 5 had probably become partially obliterated in the MS. used by the writer of Jer. lii. The persons in question were royal counsellors. They may have dissuaded the king from flight, and so held out to the last (*Thenius*).

**The principal scribe of the host.**—See margin. This scribe was an officer on the staff of the commander-in-chief, who had himself either fallen fighting or accompanied the king in his flight.

**Which mustered the people of the land**—*i.e.*, enrolled the names of such persons as were bound to serve in the army.

**Threescore men of the people of the land . . .**—*i.e.*, apparently the remains of the garrison of the citadel. Keil thinks such as had distinguished themselves above others in the defence, or had been ringleaders in the rebellion.

**That were found . . .**—This expression seems to imply that they were the few survivors of a much larger force.

**In the city.**—Jer. lii. *in the midst of the city,* an expression which seems to point to the city of David, which was the strategical centre of Jerusalem.

⁽²¹⁾ **The king of Babylon smote them . . .**— He was too irritated by the obstinacy of their defence to admire their bravery.

**So Judah was carried away . . .**—This sentence evidently concludes the whole account of the destruction of Jerusalem and the deportation of the people (comp. chap. xvii. 23; Jer. lii. 27); and not merely that of the proceedings of Nebuzaradan. The prophecy of Obadiah refers to the heartless behaviour of the Edomites on occasion of the ruin of Judah. (Comp. Ps. cxxxvii.; Lam. iv. 21, 22.)

(22—26) An extract from Jer. xl.—xliii., relating to the people left in the land.

⁽²²⁾ **Gedaliah the son of Ahikam.**—Ahikam was one of Josiah's princes (chap. xxii. 12). In the reign of Jehoiakim he saved the prophet Jeremiah from the popular fury (Jer. xxvi. 24). Nebuzaradan committed the prophet to the care of Gedaliah, who probably, like his father, sympathised with Jeremiah's views (Jer. xxxix. 13, 14). After hesitating whether to accompany Nebuzaradan to Babylon or not, the prophet finally decided upon repairing to Gedaliah at Mizpah (Jer. xl. 1—6). Gedaliah's magnanimous behaviour in regard to Ishmael (Jer. xl. 16 *seq.*) shows that he was not a traitor and deserter as some have misnamed him. Rather he was a disciple of Jeremiah, and did his utmost to induce the remnant over which he was appointed governor to submit with patience to their divinely-ordered lot, as the prophet urged them to do.

⁽²³⁾ **The captains of the armies.**—Rather, *the army captains;* or, *the captains of the forces.* They and their men had fled with the king, and dispersed themselves over the country (Jer. xl. 7). Now they came out of hiding.

**Their men.**—The Hebrew text has *the men,* but all the versions, and Jer. xl. 7, read rightly, *their men.*

**Mizpah.**—See 1 Kings xv. 22. It was well suited to be the governor's residence, as it lay high, and was a naturally strong position. Moreover, it was the seat of an ancient sanctuary (Judg. xx. 1), which might serve in some sort as a substitute for the destroyed Temple of Jerusalem (Jer. xli. 5).

**Ishmael.**—Grandson of Elishama the royal secretary (verse 25; Jer. xxxvi. 12, 20), and of royal blood (Jer. xli. 1).

**Johanan the son of Careah.**—Jer. xl. 8, "and Johanan and Jonathan the sons of Careah."

**The Netophathite.**—The words, "and the sons of Ophai," have fallen out before this epithet (Jer. xl. 8), and probably the names of these sons of Ophai in both passages. Netophah is mentioned in Ezra ii. 22; Neh.

*Death of Gedaliah.* | **II. KINGS, XXV.** | *Jehoiachin advanced.*

the son of a Maachathite, they and their men. <sup>(24)</sup> And Gedaliah sware to them, and to their men, and said unto them, Fear not to be the servants of the Chaldees: dwell in the land, and serve the king of Babylon; and it shall be well with you.

<sup>(25)</sup> But it came to pass in the seventh month, that Ishmael the son of Nethaniah, the son of Elishama, of the seed [1] royal, came, and ten men with him, and *a* smote Gedaliah, that he died, and the Jews and the Chaldees that were with him at Mizpah. <sup>(26)</sup> And all the people, both small and great, and the captains of the armies, arose, and came to Egypt: for they were afraid of the Chaldees.

<sup>(27)</sup> And it came to pass in the seven and thirtieth year of the captivity of Jehoiachin king of Judah, in the twelfth month, on the seven and twentieth *day* of the month, *that* Evil-merodach king of Babylon in the year that he began to reign did lift up the head of Jehoiachin king of Judah out of prison; <sup>(28)</sup> and he spake [2] kindly to him, and set his throne above the throne of the kings that *were* with him in Babylon; <sup>(29)</sup> and changed his prison garments: and he did eat bread continually before him all the days of his life. <sup>(30)</sup> And his allowance *was* a continual allowance given him of the king, a daily rate for every day, all the days of his life.

B.C. 588.

1 Heb., *of the kingdom.*

*a* Jer. 41. 2.

2 Heb., *good things with him.*

---

vii. 26. It may be *Beit Nettif* south-west of Jerusalem.

**The son of a** (*the*) **Maachathite.**—His father was an alien, and belonged to the Syrian state of Maachah (2 Sam. x. 6, 8).

<sup>(24)</sup> **Fear not to be the servants.**—Rather, *Be not afraid of the servants.* By "the servants of the Chaldees" Gedaliah probably means those who recognised the Chaldeans as their masters—that is to say, himself and those who adhere to him. He promises immunity for the past if only the captains and their men will settle down quietly as subjects of the conqueror.

<sup>(25)</sup> **In the seventh month.**—Only two months after the fall of Jerusalem (verse 8).

**Smote Gedaliah.**—At a friendly meal in the governor's own house (Jer. xli. 1, 2). Perhaps, as Josephus says, when he and his followers were overcome with wine.

**Of the seed royal.**—Perhaps this reveals Ishmael's motive. He thought his claim to the government of the community was greater than Gedaliah's. Baalis king of the Ammonites had incited him to the crime (Jer. xl. 14).

**The Chaldees that were with him.**—They were soldiers left to support his authority (Jer. xli. 3).

**That he died.**—The Jews afterwards observed the day of Gedaliah's death as a day of mourning.

<sup>(26)</sup> **Arose and came to Egypt.**—They took Jeremiah with them (Jer. xliii. 6). This verse only gives the end of the story as it is told in Jeremiah.

<sup>(27–30)</sup> The captivity of Jehoiachin ameliorated by the new king of Babylon. (See Jer. lii. 31–34.)

<sup>(27)</sup> **In the seven and thirtieth year . . .**—Jehoiachin was now fifty-five years old (chap. xxiv. 8, 12).

**On the seven and twentieth day.**—Jer. lii. 31: *five and twentieth,* which is probably right. (See Note on verse 19.)

**Evil-merodach.**—In Babylonian *Amil-marduk,* "man of Merodach." (Comp. the Hebrew Eshbaal, "man of Baal.") There are in the British Museum some contract tablets dated from his regnal years (562,

561, 560, B.C.). He came to the throne 562 B.C., upon the death of Nebuchadnezzar, who had reigned forty-three years. According to the canon of Ptolemy, Evil-merodach reigned two years. He was murdered by his brother-in-law Neriglissar—*i.e.,* Nergal-sharezer.

**Did lift up the head of Jehoiachin . . . out of prison**—*i.e.,* brought him out of prison (Gen. xl. 13, 20). The LXX., Syriac, and Arabic add, "and brought him forth" before the words "out of prison." So Jer. lii. 31.

<sup>(28)</sup> **Set his throne above the throne of the kings . . .**—Gave him precedence of the other captive kings who were kept at the Babylonian court by way of enhancing its glory (comp. Judg. i. 7), and probably marked this precedence by allowing him a higher chair of state in the royal hall. So Cyrus kept Crœsus king of Lydia at his court (Herod. i. 88). We may remember also the chivalrous behaviour of our own Black Prince towards his royal captive John of France.

<sup>(29)</sup> **And changed.**—Rather, *and he* (*i.e.,* Jehoiachin) *changed* his prison garments—that is to say, he discarded them for others more suitable to his new condition. Joseph did the same when taken from prison to the Egyptian court (Gen. xli. 14).

**He did eat bread continually before him . . .**—Jehoiachin became a perpetual guest at the royal table. (Comp. 2 Sam. ix. 10—13.)

<sup>(30)</sup> **His allowance.**—For the maintenance of his little court. Literally, *And* (*as for*) *his allowance a continual allowance was given him from the king, a day's portion in its day.*

**All the days of his** (*Jehoiachin's*) **life.**—He may have died before Evil-merodach was murdered. There would be nothing strange in this, considering his age and his thirty-seven years of imprisonment.

The writer evidently dwells with pleasure on this faint gleam of light amid the darkness of the exile. It was a kind of foreshadowing of the pity which afterwards was to be extended to the captive people, when the divine purpose had been achieved, and the exile had done its work of chastisement and purification. (Comp. Ps. cvi. 46; Ezra ix. 9; Neh. ii. 2.)

# THE FIRST BOOK OF THE CHRONICLES

# INTRODUCTION
## TO
# THE BOOKS OF THE CHRONICLES

§ 1. **Title.**—In the Hebrew MSS. the Books of Chronicles form a continuous work, bearing the general name of *Dibrê hayyâmim* ("Events of the Days," or "History of the Times"), which is no doubt an abridgment of *Sêpher dibrê hayyâmim*—i.e., "The Book of the Events (or History) of the Times." (Comp. 2 Kings xiv. 19; 1 Chron. xxvii. 24; Esther vi. 1, x. 2.) This designation is not given in the text of the work itself, but was prefixed by some unknown editor. Accordingly we find a different title in the LXX., which divides the work into two books, called Παραλειπομένων πρῶτον and δεύτερον ("First and Second [Book] of Things omitted"); or, Παραλειπομένων βασιλέων or, in some MSS., τῶν βασιλείων Ἰουδά, α and β ("First and Second Book of omitted Notices of the Kings or the Kingdoms of Judah"). This title indicates that, in the opinion of the Greek translators, the work was intended as a kind of supplement to the older historical books. In that case, however, great part of Chronicles could only be considered redundant and superfluous, consisting, as it does, in the mere repetition of narratives already incorporated in Samuel and Kings. (See § 5, *infra*.) The name by which we know the work, and which fairly represents the Hebrew designation, is derived from St. Jerome, who says:—"Dibre hayamim, id est, Verba dierum, quod significantius Chronicon totius divinae historiae possumus appellare, qui liber apud nos Paralipomenon primus et secundus inscribitur" (*Prolog. galeat.*). The work, however, is not a mere chronicle or book of annals, although somewhat resembling one in its external form, and deriving its facts from annalistic sources (§ 7, *infra*). In the Vulgate we find the heading, "The First Book of Paralipomena, in Hebrew Dibre Haiamim." In the Peshito-Syriac, "Next the Book of the Rule of Days (*Dûbor yaumâthâ*) of the Kings of Judah, which is called Sephar debar yamîn." In the Arabic, "In the name of God the Merciful, the Compassionate. The First Book of the *Kitâb 'akhbâri 'l 'ayyâmi*—the Book of the Histories of the Days; which is called in the Hebrew, Dibrâ hayyâmin."

That Chronicles was originally a single, undivided work, is evident from the Masoretic note at the end of the Hebrew text, which states that 1 Chron. xxvii. 25 is the middle verse of the whole book. Moreover, Josephus, Origen (ap. Euseb. *Hist. Eccl.* vi. 25), Jerome, and the Talmud reckon but one book of Chronicles. The Peshito-Syriac ends with the remark: "Finished is the book of Debar yamin, in which are 5,603 verses"—implying the unity of the work. The present division into two books, which certainly occurs in the most suitable place, was first made by the LXX. translators, from whom it was adopted by St. Jerome in the Vulgate, and so passed into the other versions and the modern printed editions of the Hebrew Bible.

§ 2. **Relation to the Books of Ezra and Nehemiah.**—An attentive examination of the Hebrew text of the Books of Chronicles, Ezra, and Nehemiah, soon reveals the important fact that the three apparently separate works resemble each other very closely, not only in style and language, which is that of the latest age of Hebrew writing, but also in the general point of view, in the manner in which the original authorities are handled and the sacred Law expressly cited, and, above all, in the marked preference for certain topics, such as genealogical and statistical registers, descriptions of religious rites and festivals, detailed accounts of the sacerdotal classes and their various functions, notices of the music of the Temple, and similar matters connected with the organisation of public worship. These resemblances in manner, method, and matter, raise a strong presumption of unity of authorship, which is accordingly asserted by most modern scholars. As regards Chronicles and Ezra, this result is further indicated by the strange termination of the Chronicles in the middle of an unfinished sentence, which finds its due completion in the opening verses of Ezra. (Comp. 2 Chron. xxxvi. 22, 23 with Ezra i. 1—4.) Had Chronicles been an independent work, it might have ended less abruptly at 2 Chron. xxxvi. 21. But there is no real break in the narrative between 2 Chron. xxxvi. and Ezra i.; and the awkwardness of the existing division simply points to the perplexity of some editor or transcriber, who did not know where to leave off. It is absurd to lay any stress on the two trivial variants between the two passages. They are not marks of an editorial hand, but merely errors of transcription. (See Notes on 2 Chron. xxxvi. 22, 23.)

There are other facts which combine with the above considerations to prove that Chronicles, Ezra, and Nehemiah originally constituted a single great history, composed upon a uniform plan by one author. Thus there is actually extant part of a Greek version of the three books which ignores their division. The Third Book of Esdras is, with certain important omissions and additions, an independent translation of the history from 2 Chron. xxxv. to Neh. viii. 12. In this work the edict of Cyrus occurs but once; and it is evident that the author's Hebrew text did not divide the history into three distinct books.

Further, the ancients did not separate Ezra and Nehemiah in the modern fashion. The Talmudic treatise *Baba bathra* (fol. 15. A), the Masorah, and the Christian fathers Origen and Jerome, regard Ezra-Nehemiah as a single work; and it appears in the

# CHRONICLES.

Vulgate as 1st and 2nd of Esdras, a non-fundamental division like that of Samuel, Kings, and Chronicles, into two books each. Indeed, the Book of Ezra as it stands is an unfinished fragment, which finds its natural continuation in Neh. viii. *seq.*, where the history of Ezra's part in the restoration is further pursued. Lastly, the notes of time in Chronicles and Nehemiah coincide (see § 3 *infra*); and the genealogies of the high priests from Eleazar to Jehozadak in 1 Chron. vi. 4—16, and from Jeshua to Jaddua in Neh. xii. 10, 11, are given in the same form, and are obviously complementary, covering, as they do, when taken together, the whole period from Moses to Alexander the Great.

The LXX. translators found Chronicles already severed from Ezra-Nehemiah. This division is explicable in connection with the formation of the Hebrew Canon. In the Hebrew text the Book of Ezra-Nehemiah precedes Chronicles, apparently because the value of this, the newer and more interesting portion of the whole work, was recognised first. Chronicles may well have been regarded as of less importance, because to a great extent it merely repeats the familiar narratives of Samuel and Kings. In no long time, however, it was perceived that the new relation of the ancient history was animated by the spirit of the age, and its catalogues of family descent, and its detailed treatment of religious matters, won for it first, perhaps, general use as a manual of instruction, and then the last place in the sacred Canon.

§ 3. **Date.**—The orthography and language of the Chronicle, its Levitical tendency, and its position at the end of the Hagiographa, conspire to suggest a comparatively late origin. Other internal evidence of a more definite character enables us to settle the question of date with approximate precision. The partially confused passage, 1 Chron. iii. 19—24, carries the line of David's posterity down to at least the sixth generation from Zerubbabel, who along with the High Priest Jeshua conducted the first return, B.C. 536. According to R. Benjamin in the *Me'or 'enayim* (fol. 153. A, quoted by Zunz), as many as nine generations must be reckoned from Jesaiah to Johanan in this genealogy. In like manner, the LXX. makes eleven generations from Zerubbabel to the last name in the list. This brings the date of the author down to about B.C. 200, if we count thirty years to the generation. This was the opinion of Zunz, whom Nöldeke follows. Kuenen also favours a late epoch, asserting that "the author must have lived about B.C. 250." These views, however, are not accepted by the majority of modern scholars; and they rest upon a highly questionable interpretation of the passage under consideration. (See Notes on 1 Chron. iii. 19, *seq.*)

What is certain is, that both in this genealogy of the house of David, and in that of the high priests, the writer descends several generations below the age of Ezra and Nehemiah, who flourished about B.C. 445. Thus in Neh. xii. 10, 11 the line of the high priests is traced as far as Jaddua, who was the fifth successor of Jeshua the contemporary of Zerubbabel. Josephus informs us that Jaddua came into personal contact with Alexander the Great (*Antiq.* xi. 7, 8). This points to a date about B.C. 330. Again, Neh. xii. 22 appears to speak of Jaddua and "Darius the Persian" (*i.e.*, Codomannus) as belonging to an earlier age than the writer; and Neh. xii. 47 refers to "the days of Zerubbabel and Nehemiah" as to a past already distant.

It is an acute suggestion of Ewald's that the chronicler's designation of Cyrus and Darius as "kings of Persia," indicates that he lived and wrote after the fall of the Persian monarchy. The reckoning by "darics" in 1 Chron. xxix. 7 does not prove authorship *during* the Persian dominion. The Persian coinage would not disappear from use immediately upon the establishment of the Greek supremacy. A few other terms survived in the language as vestiges of the Persian age; and the Temple fortress was still called the *Baris* (comp. the Persian *baru*) in the days of Josephus. On the other hand, Prof. Dillmann is probably right in asserting that "there are no reasons of any sort for fixing the authorship of the Chronicle as late as the third century, or even later." The limits of the two genealogies above considered are evidence against such a conclusion. Upon the whole, it appears likely that the great historical work, of which Chronicles forms the largest section, was compiled between the years B.C. 330 and B.C. 300, and perhaps somewhat nearer the latter than the former date.

§ 4. **Author.**—"Ezra wrote his own book, and the genealogy of the Chronicles down to himself." Such is the assertion of the Talmud (*Baba bathra*, fol. 15. A). But we are no more bound to accept this as fact than the preceding statements which connect Moses with the Book of Job, and—more wonderful still—Adam with the Psalms. The grain of truth embodied in the tradition is simply this, that the compiler of the last great book of history has drawn largely upon the authentic memoirs of Ezra and Nehemiah, incorporating whole sections of their journals in his work. But, as every Hebrew scholar knows, a single hand can be traced throughout the three books now called Chronicles, Ezra, Nehemiah; and the original documents stand out in sharp contrast to their modern setting, wherever the compiler has been contented to transcribe verbally. From the entire tone and spirit of the work, it is reasonably inferred by most critics that it was the production of a Levite attached to the Temple at Jerusalem in the latter half of the fourth century B.C. Ewald further supposes the author to have belonged to one of the guilds of Levitical musicians: a conjecture which is highly probable, considering how much the work has to tell us about the Temple choirs and their music. Keil objects that the porters are mentioned as often as the musicians, and that therefore we might just as well assume the chronicler to have been a porter or Temple-warder. But an acquaintance with musical technicalities such as the writer displays almost certainly proves him to have been a member of one of the musical guilds. Similarly, it is no reply to allege that priests are made quite as prominent in the work as Levitical warders and musicians. The priests are naturally mentioned on all religious occasions as being the principal functionaries. The fact that the inferior ministers are so persistently brought forward in their company—which is not the case in the older history—proves the peculiar interest of the author in these latter.

§ 5. **Contents.**—*Character and Scope of the Work.* The Chronicle opens with an outline of primeval history from Adam to David. The Pentateuchal narratives, however, are not repeated, because the five books were already recognised as canonical, and the writer had nothing to add to them. In like manner, the times of the Judges and the reign of Saul are passed over. The chronicler had no special sources for that period,

# CHRONICLES.

and it did not appear to lend itself easily to the illustration of the particular lesson which he wished to enforce upon his readers. Accordingly the first section of his work takes the driest and most succinct form imaginable, that of a series of genealogies interspersed with brief historical notices (1 Chron. i.—ix.). The writer's extraordinary fondness for genealogical and statistical tables is apparent also in other parts of his history, and is to be explained by reference to the special requirements of the post-exilic age. (Comp. Ezra ii. 59, seq.) Here, after tracing the generations from Adam to Jacob, the writer gives a flying survey of the twelve tribes, lingering longest over Judah, the tribe of David, and Levi, the tribe of the priests; after which (in chaps. viii., ix.) his horizon narrows at once from all Israel to the southern kingdom only (Benjamin, Judah, Jerusalem). Chap. x.—the death of Saul—is transitional to the reign of David, which follows at length (1 Chron. xi.—xxix.).

The second and main portion of the work (1 Chron. xi.—2 Chron. xxxvi.) relates the history of the kings who reigned in Jerusalem from David to Zedekiah, thus covering a period of between four and five centuries (B.C. 1055—588). The third part contains the history of the restored community under Zerubbabel, Ezra, and Nehemiah (B.C. 536—432), and is now known as the Books of Ezra and Nehemiah. (See the *Introduction* to those books.)

When we consider the second part of this great compilation, we are immediately struck by the large space occupied by the reign of David. To the chronicler, as to the prophetic historians before him, that reign, it would seem, was the golden age of his people's history. The greater distance at which he stood from the old heroic times of the monarchy only intensified the spell which they wrought upon his imagination. He does not, however, repeat the familiar tale of David's romantic adventures, of his reign at Hebron, of his sin against Uriah, of the revolt of Absalom, and similar matters. His point of view and the needs of his contemporaries are different from those of the older historians; and it is as the true founder of Jerusalem and the Temple, with its beautiful service of music and song, and as the prime author of the priestly organisation, that the heroic figure of David engages his highest interest. Accordingly, all that refers to the activity of the king in these directions is described with intentional fulness and emphasis. (See 1 Chron. xiii.—xvii., xxii.—xxix.)

The reign of Solomon is treated much more briefly, though at considerably greater length than any subsequent one (2 Chron. i.—ix.). Here again we observe a fuller description of whatever relates to religion and its ministers. In fact, the account of the building and dedication of the Temple occupies by far the largest part of the narrative (chaps. ii.—vii.).

The rest of the history is told from the same standpoint. After the division of the kingdom, the writer follows the fortunes of the Davidic monarchy, which was the more important from a religious, if not from a political, point of view. The northern kingdom he almost entirely ignores, as founded upon apostasy from the orthodox worship, as well as from the legitimate rule of the house of David. Even in this limited field, political, military, and personal facts and incidents are subordinated to the religious interest, and it is obvious that the real subject of the history is everywhere that holy religion which made Israel what it was, and upon which its historical significance wholly depends. Thus the reigns of Asa, Jehoshaphat, Joash, Hezekiah, and Josiah are especially prominent, because they witnessed the initiation of important religious reforms, and the restoration of Jerusalem and its sanctuary to their hereditary rank as the religious centre of the nation. And thus "traditions about the Temple and its worship, the sacerdotal orders and their functions, the merits of the kings and others in the matter of the *cultus*, are presented with great fulness, and the author expatiates with evident pleasure on the sacred festivals of the olden time. Reigns of which little of the sort could be told are briefly treated" (*Dillmann*).

From all this we may gather the aim of the work. The writer has produced not so much a supplement of the older histories, as an independent work, in which the history of the chosen people is related afresh in a new manner, and from a new point of view. That point of view has been characterised as the *priestly-Levitical*, in contradistinction to the *prophetical* spirit of the ancient writers. To understand this, we must remember that in the chronicler's day the political independence of Israel was a thing of the past; and that the religion of the Law was the most precious survival from the great catastrophe which had finally shattered the nation, and the principle of cohesion and the basis of all order, public and private, in the new community. The writer's main object, therefore, is to urge upon his contemporaries a faithful observance of the Mosaic Law; and he seeks to impress his lesson by presenting a picture of times and occasions when, with the Temple as its centre, and the priests and Levites as its organs, the legitimate worship flourished and brought blessing upon the land.

§ 6. **Documental Authorities. Relation to the Books of Samuel and Kings.**—Besides a number of narratives running parallel to those of Samuel and Kings, the Books of Chronicles contain other important accounts which are without parallel in the older histories. Such are many of the genealogical and statistical tables, as well as certain supplementary details and stories inserted in different reigns. The former, which possessed a very special interest for the chronicler's contemporaries, were ultimately derived from those ancient taxation rolls or assessment lists, which were so highly valued by the Jews in the times immediately preceding and subsequent to the captivity (Ezra ii. 59, 62). These catalogues may in some cases have been preserved independently, but it is probable that the chronicler found most of them already incorporated in the historical compilations which constituted his principal authorities. (Comp. 1 Chron. v. 17, vii. 2, ix. 1, xxiii. 3, 27, xxvi. 31, xxvii. 24; Neh. xii. 23, vii. 5.) The censuses, for instance, to which reference is made in 1 Chron. v. 17, vii. 2, were doubtless entered in the state annals.

The second, and to us more important, historical element peculiar to Chronicles is equally based upon trustworthy records of an earlier period. The writer refers from time to time to documents which he presumes to be well known to his readers, for further details upon subjects which he does not himself care to pursue. At first sight the number of these documents appears to be so considerable as to excite surprise, especially when we remember that the compiler of Kings mentions only two or three such primary documents. For almost every reign a different source appears to be cited; which is the more remarkable, inasmuch as the titles indicate that more than one of the histories referred to must have contained the entire history of

# CHRONICLES.

the kings of Jerusalem. The references in question are:

1. The History of Samuel the seer,
2. The history of Nathan the prophet, } in 1 Chron xxix. 29, for David.
3. The history of Gad the seer,
4. The prophecy of Ahijah the Shilonite,
5. The vision of Je-edi or Je-edo the seer, against Jeroboam ben Nebat, } in 2 Chron. ix. 29, for Solomon.
6. The history of Shemaiah the prophet,
7. The history of Iddo the seer, } in 2 Chron. xii. 15, for Rehoboam.
8. The Midrash of the prophet Iddo, in 2 Chron. xiii. 22, for Abijah.
9. The book of the kings of Judah and Israel, in 2 Chron. xvi. 11, xxv. 26, xxviii. 26, for Asa, Amaziah, and Ahaz.
10. The history of Jehu the son of Hanani, inserted in the book of the kings of Israel, in 2 Chron. xx. 34, for Jehoshaphat.
11. The Midrash of the book of the Kings, in 2 Chron. xxiv. 27, for Joash.
12. The history of Uzziah, by Isaiah the prophet, 2 Chron. xxvi. 22.
13. The book of the kings of Israel and Judah, in 2 Chron. xxvii. 7, xxxv. 27, xxxvi. 8, for Jotham, Josiah, and Jehoiakim. Perhaps also in 1 Chron. ix. 1.
14. The vision of Isaiah the prophet, the son of Amoz, in the books of the kings of Judah and Israel, 2 Chron. xxxii. 32, for Hezekiah.
15. The history of the kings of Israel, 2 Chron. xxxiii. 18,
16. The history of Hozai (or, The words of the Seers), 2 Chron. xxxiii. 19, } for Manasseh.

Six reigns, viz., those of Jehoram, Ahaziah, Athaliah, Jehoahaz, Jehoiachin, Zedekiah, are without any such references.

The similarity of some of these sixteen titles favours the supposition of their being merely variations of each other. "The book of the kings of Judah and Israel" (9) may at once be equated with "the book of the kings of Israel and Judah" (13). "The history (*words*) of the kings of Israel" (15) is an expression tantamount to "the book of the kings of Israel" (10). Five at least, then, of the above citations refer to a single work, a "history of the kings of Judah and Israel." This work appears to have been a compilation based upon the same annalistic sources as the canonical books of Kings —viz., "the book of the chronicles of the kings of Israel," and "the book of the chronicles of the kings of Judah." It was probably younger than the canonical Kings, and was perhaps in some degree influenced by the form and contents of that work. That it was not identical therewith, as used to be assumed, is certain, because it contained much which is not found there— *e.g.*, genealogical and other lists, and the account of Manasseh's captivity and restoration (2 Chron. xxxiii. 18); and the chronicler often refers to this work for fuller information in cases where the narrative in the existing Book of Kings is even briefer than his own. (Comp. 2 Chron. xxvii. with 2 Kings xv. 32–38.)

The references to prophetic "words" (*dibrê*), or rather histories, are by some supposed to imply the existence of a number of historical monographs written by the prophets with whose names they are connected. But "the history of Jehu the son of Hanani" (10) is expressly cited, not as an independent work, but as a section of the great Book of the Kings; and "the vision of Isaiah the prophet" (14) is another section of the same work. Moreover, when the chronicler does not refer to the history he generally mentions a prophetic account, but *never* both for the same reign (unless 2 Chron. xxxiii. 18, 19 be an exception). It is likely, therefore, that the other prophetic histories (numbers 1—7) were integral parts of the same great compilation, and are merely cited in briefer form, perhaps as the chronicler found them already cited in that his principal source. We do not know what were the grounds which determined the selection of a work by the unknown collectors of the Canon, but it seems certain that had a number of separate writings of such prophets as Samuel, Nathan, Gad, and Isaiah been extant in the chronicler's age, they would have been included in the Canon.

The "history of Uzziah, which Isaiah the prophet the son of Amoz wrote" (12; see 2 Chron. xxvi. 22), does not appear to be an exception to the above general inference. Whether, as Prof. Dillmann thinks, the chronicler himself supposed Isaiah to have been the author of the history of Uzziah as embodied in the great Book of the Kings (comp. Isa. vi. 1), or whether, as is more likely, he merely copies the reference from that source, makes no difference. On the other hand, it is, of course, quite possible that an independent monograph of Isaiah's did exist and was known to the chronicler, although no trace of it is to be recognised in the canonical Books of Kings or Isaiah. Similar considerations would apply to "the history of Hozai" (16; see 2 Chron. xxxiii. 19), which is apparently contrasted in 2 Chron. xxxiii. 19 with "the history of the kings of Israel," were it not likely that the text of that passage is unsound.

Lastly, the chronicler refers besides to a "Midrash of the prophet Iddo" (8), and a "Midrash of the book of the Kings" (11). The former may have been a section of the latter work. In this, as in the preceding cases, it was natural to cite a particular passage of a large book of history, by mentioning the name of the prophet with whose activity it was chiefly concerned; because the division of the canonical books into sections and chapters was unknown to antiquity (comp. our Lord's reference in Mark xii. 26, "in the bush," *i.e.*, in the section relating to the burning bush; and St. Paul's "in Elias," Rom. xi. 2.)

The term "Midrash" occurs nowhere else in the Old Testament. It means "search," "investigation," "study," and is the neo-Hebraic term for the Rabbinical exegesis of the sacred books. A *Beth-midrash* is a school in which the Law and other scriptures are studied under the lead of a Rabbi, whose disciples are called *talmidîm*, a word first occurring in 1 Chron. xxv. 8. "The Midrash of the book of the Kings" was probably a kind of commentary or expository amplification of the great "history of the Kings of Judah and Israel"; and the chronicler may have derived other narratives from this source, besides the two for which he cites it. But it is pure dogmatism to say, with Reuss, that "his work from one end to the other is drawn from a Midrash; and it is this Midrash that is responsible for all that provokes our doubts, including the history of Uzziah written by Isaiah." The Midrash which the chronicler consulted may really have been an early predecessor of that series of works so well known to students of Rabbinical Hebrew as the Midrashim (*Bereshith rabba, Shemoth rabba,* &c. &c.); but its intrinsic superiority to all these later works is evident from the extracts preserved in the Chronicles.

We have now characterised the two principal sources of the accounts peculiar to the Books of Chronicles. The compiler may, of course, have had at his command other documents besides those to which he refers by name; but probably they were few in number, and certainly of subordinate importance.

It remains to ask what is the precise relation between the forty or more passages of Chronicles which are more or less exact duplicates of parallel passages in Samuel and Kings?

This question can hardly be answered with certainty. The negative criticism which flourished in Germany at the beginning of the present century found an easy offhand reply in the theory that the chronicler transcribed his parallel accounts directly from the canonical Books of Samuel and Kings. All deviations and peculiarities were results of misunderstanding, fictitious embellishment, and wilful perversion of the older history. It would hardly be worth while to revive the memory of this unhistorical and obsolete criticism, were it not still salutary to signalise the former errors of scholars whose theories for a time enjoyed unbounded influence, by way of suggesting caution to such persons as are inclined to accord a too hasty acceptance to similarly destructive hypotheses advocated by men of acknowledged ability at the present day. What is certain is, (1) that the chronicler must have known the great history now divided into the Books of Samuel and Kings; (2) that many of his narratives at different points verbally coincide with these books, and so far *might* have been transcribed from them; but (3) these coincidences may be accounted for by the supposition advanced above, viz., that the same ancient state annals were the principal source from which both the compiler of the older canonical history, and the compiler of that "book of the kings of Judah and Israel" which supplied the chronicler with so much of his narrative, derived the staple of their history; and further, that the "book of the kings of Judah and Israel" may have been in part constructed on the model of the already existing Books of Samuel and Kings. At the same time we may freely admit that the form into which the history was already cast in the older work would naturally exert some, and perhaps a considerable, influence upon the mind and work of the latest historian of Israel.

### § 7. The Historical Value of Chronicles.—

This question has in part been already decided by the results at which we arrived in discussing the prior question of the sources. All that remains to be determined is, whether and how far the chronicler was faithful to his authorities. Whatever charges of distortion, misinterpretation, falsification, fictitious embellishment, &c. &c., of the ancient history have been levelled against him by earlier critics, have been amply disproven by their successors. Such charges depended for the most part upon the assumption that he had no other documents than the canonical books of the Old Testament—an assumption sufficiently rebutted by impartial examination of internal evidence. Comparing the parallel sections with their duplicates in Samuel and Kings, we find in general an assiduous and faithful reproduction of the sources, which warrants us in supposing that the important passages of the narrative which are peculiar to Chronicles were likewise extracted with substantial accuracy from other historical records no longer extant. Often, indeed, in such passages the style is so much purer than that which we identify as the chronicler's own, as to suggest at once that he is simply transcribing from an ancient document; though more usually he has recast what he found in his authority. It is admitted that the chronicler wrote with a distinct purpose, and that his aim was not so much history for its own sake, as edification. He writes neither as a modern scientific historian, nor as a mere annalist, but with a distinctly didactic and hortatory object. Accordingly, in the exercise of his lawful discretion, he omits some well-known passages of the ancient history, and adds others more to his purpose. He habitually inserts remarks of his own, which put the facts narrated into relation to the working of Divine Providence, and so bring into prominence the religious aspect of events, while religious conceptions prevalent in his own age naturally find expression through his pages. (Comp. 1 Chron. xxi. 1 with 2 Sam. xxiv. 1.) Moreover, he does not hesitate, nor would any writer of his time have hesitated, to put appropriate speeches into the mouths of leading personages, some of which betray their ideal character by a close similarity in form and matter; and although in some cases he undoubtedly had genuine tradition at his command, and simply followed his documents, in others he has freely expanded the meagre records of the past, and developed the fundamental thoughts of the speakers according to his own taste. In the description of ancient religious solemnities he has reasonably enough been influenced by his minute professional knowledge of the ritual of his own day, and has thus succeeded in his purpose of lending animation to the dry memoranda of the past. Yet it must not be forgotten that he probably had substantial precedents for this mode of treatment, and, further, that in antiquity religious custom is the least likely sphere of innovation. Besides all this, the chronicler has considered the needs and tastes of his own time by substituting current for obsolete Hebrew words, phrases, and constructions, and by interpretation, paraphrase, and correction of what seemed obscure or faulty in the ancient texts. The mode of spelling (*scriptio plena*), and the Aramaisms which characterise his work, are what were to be expected from a writer of his age. In these latter respects the Chronicle already foreshadows the Targum or "Chaldee" Paraphrase.

Many deviations from the older canonical history, especially in the matter of names and numbers, are due to errors of transcription in one or the other text; and many may be ascribed to the licence of editors and copyists, which in those early times far exceeded what would now be considered allowable. To appreciate this argument, it is only necessary to examine the LXX. translation of the Books of Samuel, which obviously represents a Hebrew original differing in many important particulars from the present Masoretic Recension. Discrepancies due to such causes obviously do not affect the credibility of the chronicler. And with regard to excessive numbers, in particular, we have to bear in mind "the tendency of numbers to grow in successive transcriptions," and the fact already demonstrated (§ 6) that Chronicles was only indirectly derived from the same primary sources as Samuel and Kings. The existing text of the older books is itself not free from exaggerated numbers (see 1 Sam. vi. 19; xiii. 5); and in some instances the figures of Chronicles are lower and intrinsically more probable than those of the older history. (Comp. 2 Chron. ix. 25 with 1 Kings v. 6.) After making every allowance upon these and similar grounds, the impartial critic will still acquiesce in the conclusion of Ewald, that "we should deprive ourselves of one of the richest and oldest sources of the Davidical history, if we failed to do justice to the very remarkable remains of the state annals fortunately preserved to us in the Book of Chronicles;" and that "this work, when rightly understood and applied, not only yields very valuable supplements to the history of the (Davidic) monarchy, the foundation of which undoubtedly rested on the original state annals, but also tells us of many prophets, of whose very names we should have otherwise been wholly ignorant" (*Hist. of Israel*, Martineau's Translation, p. 195).

§ 8. **Literature of the Subject.**—A list of the older commentators may be read in Carpzov and in Lange's *Bibelwerk*. The principal modern works known to the present writer are Bertheau's (English Trans. in Clarke's Foreign Library, 2nd ed. 1860); Keil's, also translated in Clarke's series (ed. 1872); Zöckler's, in Lange (English trans., 1876); and that of Reuss (ed. Paris, 1878). He has also had before him L'Abbé Martin's Commentary (ed. Paris, 1880), a recent work by a Roman Catholic priest, which closely follows Keil and Zöckler. The criticisms of Thenius in his *Die Bücher der Könige* (Leipzig, 1873) have always been considered, and specially noticed whenever it seemed advisable.

The following have been consulted upon introductory questions: — Gramberg (*Die Chronik nach ihrem geschichtlichen Charakter*, &c. Halle, 1823). His reasonings are interesting from a historical point of view, but his conclusions are thoroughly unfair, and no longer require refutation. Graf (*Die gesch. Bücher des alt. Test.* Leipzig, 1866). Also a hostile criticism. De Wette's *Einleitung*, as re-edited by Schrader, who modifies the more extreme *dicta* of the original author. Movers (*Kritische Untersuchungen über die bibl. Chronik.* Bonn, 1834); a reply to Gramberg and De Wette. Keil's *Einleitung* (Frankfurt, 1853). Zöckler's *Handbuch der theolog. Wissenschaften* (Nördlingen, 1882). Ewald's *History of Israel* (Martineau's English Transl., Longmans, 1876). Kuenen's *History of Israel* (English Transl., 1875) follows Graf in exaggerating the subjective and unhistorical tendency of the chronicler. Wellhausen's tract, *De gentibus et familiis Judaeis quae 1 Chron. ii. — iv. enumerantur* (Göttingen, 1870), is very important for the right understanding of the genealogies. The article *Chronik*, by Prof. Dillmann, in Herzog's *Real-Encyclopädie* is a specially fair estimate of the work; and the same may be said of Prof. Robertson Smith's *Chronicles* in the *Encyclopædia Britannica*. The writer has also to acknowledge considerable obligations to the same author's *Old Testament in the Jewish Church*, and *The Prophets of Israel*, and to Schrader's *Keilinschriften und das Alte Testament* (Giessen, 1883). For several important suggestions he is indebted to his friend Prof. Sayce, who kindly looked through the Notes on the greater part of the first book.

§ 9. **Ancient Versions. State of the Hebrew Text.**—The translation of Chronicles in the LXX. is carefully and skilfully done, is strictly literal, and one of the best works of those translators, far surpassing the Books of Samuel and Kings, which proceed from another hand. In many passages it still preserves an unquestionably better reading than that of the Masoretic Recension. In too many instances, however, it has had its readings altered into conformity with later Greek versions of the *textus receptus*, and thus its originality has in part been obliterated by the hands of injudicious editors. (See Movers' *Untersuch.*, p. 93.) In the Greek of 2 Chron. xxxv., xxxvi. there are a few interpolations corresponding to passages in 2 Kings xxiii., xxiv.

The old Latin versions, upon which the Vulgate is based, followed the LXX.

The Peshittâ (Peshito) Syriac version presents many surprising peculiarities of omission, interpolation, transposition, and paraphrase, insomuch that it resembles a Jewish Targum rather than a literal version. This phenomenon suggests that Chronicles was perhaps not received with the original collection of sacred books in the Peshito (*Dillmann*).

The Arabic version is a daughter of the Syriac, and possesses little independent value for the criticism of the text.

The Targum is late (seventh century?) and is not printed in the Rabbinical Bibles. Lagardé has recently edited another, which I have not been able to procure. The four versions have been consulted in Walton's *Polyglot*; and for the LXX. Tischendorf's edition has also been used. The unsatisfactory condition of the Hebrew text, due perhaps to the fact that Chronicles was never so highly valued as other portions of the Canon, may in part be remedied by careful comparison of the data of the versions, as well as of the other books of the Old Testament.

# THE FIRST BOOK OF THE
## CHRONICLES

CHAPTER I.—<sup>(1)</sup> Adam, <sup>a</sup>Sheth, Enosh, <sup>(2)</sup> Kenan, Mahalaleel, Jered, <sup>(3)</sup> Henoch, Methuselah, Lamech, <sup>(4)</sup> Noah, Shem, Ham, and Japheth.

B.C. 4004, &c.

a Gen. 5. 3, 9.
b Gen. 10. 2.

<sup>(5)</sup> <sup>b</sup>The sons of Japheth; Gomer, and Magog, and Madai, and Javan, and Tubal, and Meshech, and Tiras. <sup>(6)</sup> And the sons of Gomer; Ashchenaz, and

---

The abrupt opening of the narrative with a series of proper names presupposes that the reader is already acquainted with their historic import. The chronicler intends to give a synopsis of the archæology of man, as recorded in the book of Genesis, by way of fixing the place of Israel in the great human family. Arabian and monkish annalists of the middle ages have followed his precedent, at least so far as regards the external form of their histories. William of Malmesbury, for instance, does not hesitate to trace the line of the Saxon kings to Adam; and the chroniclers of Spain have derived their monarchs from Tubal, a grandson of Noah. Such inventions, of course, bear only an artificial resemblance to the Biblical records, which are undoubtedly survivals of a remote antiquity, a fact which should suggest caution in theorising upon their interpretation.

Chapter i. falls naturally into three sections. (1) The ten generations of the first age of humanity, with a table of races and countries, given in genealogical form according to ancient conceptions (verses 1—23). (2) The ten generations after the Flood, from Shem to Abraham, the second age of man, with a list of the races claiming descent from Abraham (verses 24—42). (3) A catalogue of the kings of Edom anterior to the Israelite monarchy and of the tribal chieftains of that country (verses 43—54).

Verses 1—4 are an abstract of the fifth chapter of Genesis. (See the Notes there.) The arrangement of the names, in three triads and a quartette, is perhaps mnemonic. In our translation the Hebrew spelling is followed more closely here than in Genesis v. Sheth, Enosh, Kenan, Jered, Henoch are nearer the original than Seth, Enos, Cainan, Jared, Enoch (the spelling of the LXX).

<sup>(1)</sup> **Adam** (*man*) is here treated as a proper name; in Gen. v. 1—5 it is an appellative.

The Chaldeans also had a tradition of ten antediluvian patriarchs or kings, beginning with Alorus and ending with Xisuthrus (Hasis-Adra), the hero of the Flood. They made the duration of this first period of human history 432,000 years. Remembering that Abraham, the Hebrew, was from "Ur (Uru, the city) of the Chaldees," we can hardly suppose the two accounts to be independent of each other. The comparative simplicity and, above all, the decided monotheism of the Hebrew relation, give a high probability to the assumption that it represents a more original form of the tradition.

**Sheth, Enosh.**—Those who have imagined the present list to be a mere duplicate of that given in Gen. iv. 17 *sqq.*, and who explain the whole by the fatally easy process of resolving all these different names into a capricious repetition of one original solar figure, are obliged to admit a difficulty in connection with the names of Sheth and Enosh, which are acknowledged "not to belong to mythology at all" (Prof. Goldziher). Considering that most Hebrew names have a distinct and intentional significance, it is obviously a mere exercise of ingenuity to invest them with a mythological character. Meanwhile, such speculations cannot possibly be verified.

<sup>(4)</sup> **Shem, Ham, and Japheth.**—There is no doubt that Ham means black, or sunburnt, and Japheth (Heb., *Yepheth*) is probably the fair-skinned. Shem has been compared with an Assyrian word meaning brownish (*sa'mu*). Thus the three names appear to allude to differences of racial complexion.

Verses 5—23 are an abridgment of Gen. x. The proper names represent, not persons, but peoples and countries. By adding them all together, the old Jewish interpreters made a total of seventy nations for the world. The list is a classified summary of the ethnical and geographical knowledge of Hebrew antiquity.

THE SONS OF JAPHETH THE FAIR—(verses 5—7).

The Oriental theory of political and even social communities refers each to a common ancestor. The Israelites are known as "sons of Israel," the Ammonites as "sons of Ammon" (Authorised version, "children"). In the same way, an Arab tribe is called the "Bêni Hassan" (sons of Hassan), and Assurbanipal styles his subjects "sons of Asshur." Sometimes a people is called "sons" of the land or city they inhabit; *e.g.*, the Babylonians are styled "sons of Babel." The "sons of Japheth" are probably the fair Caucasian race.

<sup>(5)</sup> **Gomer.**—The Cimmerians of the Greek writers; called Gi-mir-ra-a-a in Assyrian inscriptions. Their country was Cappadocia, called *Gamir* by the ancient Armenians. The Arabic version has "Turkey."

**Magog.**—Ezek. xxxviii. 2, 3, 6 speaks of Gog, king of Magog, and suzerain of Tubal, Meshech, Gomer, and the house of Togarmah. With the name Gog compare Gâgu, king of Sahi, mentioned in connection with Assurbanipal's campaign against the Manna-a. Magog appears to be a general name for the peoples north of Assyria, *i.e.*, in Armenia.

¹ Riphath, and Togarmah. ⁽⁷⁾ And the sons of Javan; Elishah, and Tarshish, Kittim, and ² Dodanim. ⁽⁸⁾ The sons of Ham; Cush, and Mizraim, Put, and Canaan. ⁽⁹⁾ And the sons of Cush; Seba, and Havilah, and Sabta, and Raamah, and Sabtecha. And the sons of Raamah; Sheba, and Dedan. ⁽¹⁰⁾ And Cush *a* begat Nimrod: he began to be mighty upon the earth. ⁽¹¹⁾ And Mizraim begat Ludim, and Anamim, and Lehabim, and Naphtuhim, ⁽¹²⁾ and Pathrusim, and Casluhim, (of whom came the Philistines,) and *b* Caphthorim.

¹ Or, *Diphath*, as it is in some copies.
*a* Gen. 10. 8.
² Or, *Rodanim*, according to some copies.
*b* Deut. 2. 23.

---

**Madai.**—The Medes. 2 Kings xvii. 6; Isa. xiii. 17. Assyr., *Ma-da-a-a*.

**Javan.**—The Assyrian *Yavnan*, i.e., Cyprus, mentioned in the Behistun Inscription, as here, along with Media, Armenia, and Cappadocia. (Comp. Joel iv. 6; Isa. lxvi. 19.)

**Tubal and Meshech**, the Tibareni and Moschi of classical writers; and the Muski and Tabali of Assyrian records.

**Tiras** has been compared with the Tyras or Dniester. Perhaps we may compare Tros and the Trojans.

⁽⁶⁾ **Ashchenaz.**—Jer. li. 27, *near or in Armenia*. Apparently the Asguzâa mentioned by Esarhaddon in the account of his campaign against the Cimmerians and Cilicians. The Arabic has *Slavonia*.

**Riphath.**—The reading of Gen. x. 3, some Heb. MSS., the LXX., and Vulg. The common Hebrew text (Van der Hooght's) wrongly reads Diphath (Syriac, *Diphar*). Togarmah seems to be the Tulgarimmē on the border of Tabali, which Sennacherib reduced in his expedition against Cilicia (Smith, *Sennach.*, p. 86).

⁽⁷⁾ **Elishah.**—Usually identified with Hellas, or the Hellenes. Perhaps, however, Carthage is meant: comp. the name Elissa, as a by-name of Dido, Virg. *Æn.* iv. 335.

**Tarshish.**—Usually identified with the Phœnician colony of Tartessus, in Spain. (Comp. Ps. lxxii. 10.)

**Dodanim.**—So many Heb. MSS., the Syriac, Vulg., and Gen. x. 3. The LXX. has "Rhodians," which implies a reading, Rodanim, which we find in the common Hebrew text. Dodanim might be the Dardanians of the Troad, or the Dodoneans (*Dodona*, the seat of an ancient oracle, the fame of which might have reached Phœnician ears).

Thus far the list appears to deal with Asia Minor and adjacent lands; and Japheth, whose name is curiously like the Greek Iäpetus, seems to include the western races so far as known to the Hebrews.

THE SONS OF HAM, THE DARK-SKINNED OR SWARTHY (verses 8—16).

⁽⁸⁾ **Cush.**—The Greek Meroë, Assyrian Miluhha, or Kûsu, south of Egypt, in our Bibles often called Ethiopia (Isa. xix. 1). The Arabic gives *Habesh*, i.e., Ethiopia.

**Mizraim.**—The common Hebrew name of Egypt: strictly, "the two Miçrs"—i.e., Upper and Lower Egypt. But the name should rather be spelt Mizrim—the Egyptians; the form Mizraim being probably a mere fancy of the Jewish punctuators. The Assyrians wrote Muçuru, Muçru, Muçur. The Inscription of Darius has Miçir. Maçôr was the name of the wall which protected Egypt on the north-east. Hence it gave its name to the whole of Lower Egypt.—Cush and Muçur are coupled together in the inscriptions of Esarhaddon and his son Assurbanipal.

**Put.**—Perhaps the Egyptian *Punt*, on the east coast of Africa. King Darius mentioned Pûta and Kûsu as subject to him (Behist. Inscr.). Comp. Nah. iii. 9; Jer. xlvi. 9; Ez. xxx. 5. The Arabic has *Kibtu*, i.e., Coptland.

**Canaan.**—There are many proofs of an early connection between Egypt and Canaan. The Philistines were colonists from the Delta (verse 12), and Ramses II. (*cir.* 1350 or 1450 B.C.) had wars and made alliance with the Hittites.

⁽⁹⁾ **Seba.**—Capital of Meroë. The other names represent Arabian tribes and their districts.

**Sheba.**—The famous Sabæans, whose language, the Himyaritic, has quite recently been deciphered from inscriptions.

⁽¹⁰⁾ **Cush begat Nimrod.**—Micah (v. 6) speaks of the "land of Nimrod" in connection with the "land of Asshur." The land of Nimrod is plainly Babylonia; and some have supposed the primitive inhabitants of Babylonia—"the black-headed race" (*zalmat qaqqadi*) as they styled themselves—to have been akin to the peoples of Muçur and Cush. At all events, Cush in this table of races appears as father of a series of mixed populations, ramifying from the north-west of the Persian Gulf in a southernly direction to the coast of Arabia. The Asiatic Cush represents that primitive Elamitic Sumerian race which occupied the north-west and north coast of the Persian Gulf; or rather that portion of it which attained to empire in Babylonia.

The name Nimrod appears to be identical with Merodach, the Accadian Amar-utu, or Amar-utuki, Assyrian Maruduk. Merodach was the tutelar deity of Babylon, as Asshur was of Assyria; and many Babylonian sovereigns bore his name. (Comp. Merodach-baladan, Isa. xxxix. 1.)

**He began to be.**—*He was the first to become*. Tradition made Nimrod the first founder of a great Oriental empire. The statement about his four cities (Gen. x. 10), the first of which was Babel (Babylon), is omitted here.

**Mighty.**—Literally, *a hero, warrior* (*gibbôr*); a title of Merodach.

(11, 12) The names in these verses are all in the masculine plural, and obviously designate nations. Mizraim, the two Egypts, is said to have begotten the chief races inhabiting those regions — a common Oriental metaphor. The Ludim are the Ludu, or Rudu, of the hieroglyphs (Prof. Sayce thinks, the Lydian mercenaries of the Egyptian sovereigns); the Anamim are perhaps the men of An (On, Gen. xli. 50), Lehabim, the Lybians. The Naphtuhim seem to get their name from Noph, i.e., Memphis, and the god Ptah. Perhaps, however, the name is to be recognised in the town Napata.

⁽¹²⁾ **Pathrusim.**—The men of the south (Egyptian, *pe-ta-res*, "the southland"), or Upper Egypt.

**Casluhim . . . Caphthorim.**—The men of Kaftûra, or the Delta. (See Amos ix. 7: "Have not I brought up Israel out of the land of Mizraim? and the Philistines from Caphtor?" and comp. Deut. ii. 23.) The

*The sons*            I. CHRONICLES, I.            *of Shem.*

<sup>(13)</sup> And Canaan begat Zidon his firstborn, and Heth, <sup>(14)</sup> the Jebusite also, and the Amorite, and the Girgashite, <sup>(15)</sup> and the Hivite, and the Arkite, and the Sinite, <sup>(16)</sup> and the Arvadite, and the Zemarite, and the Hamathite.

<sup>(17)</sup> The sons of <sup>a</sup>Shem; Elam, and Asshur, and Arphaxad, and Lud, and Aram, and Uz, and Hul, and Gether, and <sup>1</sup>Meshech. <sup>(18)</sup> And Arphaxad begat Shelah, and Shelah begat Eber. <sup>(19)</sup> And unto Eber were born two sons: the name of the one was <sup>2</sup>Peleg; because in his days the earth was divided: and his brother's name was Joktan. <sup>(20)</sup> <sup>b</sup>And Joktan begat Almodad, and Sheleph,

1 Or, *Mash*, Gen. 10. 23.
2 That is, *Division*.
a Gen. 10. 23 & 11. 10.
b Gen. 10. 26.

---

Casluhim may have been a leading division of the Caphthorim.

THE CITY ZIDON AND THE TEN RACES OF CANAAN (verses 13—16).

<sup>(13)</sup> **Canaan begat Zidon his firstborn.**—Or, in modern phrase, *Zidon is the oldest city of Canaan.* It is usually mentioned along with Tyre, the ruling city in later times. Sennacherib speaks of the flight of Luli, "king of Zidon," from Tyre. Esarhaddon mentions Baal of Tyre as a tributary. Of the eleven "sons of Canaan" all but three or four have been identified in the cuneiform inscriptions of Assyria.

**And Heth**—that is, the Hittite race, called Heta by the Egyptians, and Hatti by the Assyrians. (See verse 8, Note.) The Hittites were once the dominant race of Syria and Palestine. Carchemish, on the Euphrates, and Kadesh, as well as Hamath, appear to have been Hittite cities. Their kings had commercial relations with Solomon (1 Kings x. 29). Inscriptions, in a kind of mixed hieroglyph, have been found at Hamath and Carchemish, but they still await decipherment.

<sup>(14)</sup> **The Jebusite.**—The men of Jebus, or Jerusalem (chap. xi. 4).

**Amorite.**—The hill-men of the trans-Jordan.

**Girgashite.**—Perhaps of Gergesa (Matt. iii. 28).

<sup>(15)</sup> **Hivite.**—On the slopes of Lebanon (Josh. xi. 3), "under Hermon," but also in Gibeon and Shechem (Josh. ix. 7; Gen. xxxiv. 2). Delitzsch suggests that the name is connected with Hamath (Assyrian, Hammath = Havvath).

**Arkite, and the Sinite.**—Tribes living to the west of northern Lebanon. A fragment of the annals of Tiglath-pileser mentions along with Simyra the towns of Arqâ and Sianu "on the sea-coast" (B.C., 739). Josephus mentions a town Arka, which is otherwise known as the birthplace of the emperor Alexander Severus (Ruins: *Tell 'Arqa*).

<sup>(16)</sup> **Arvadite.**—Arvad, or Aradus, now *Ruâd*, an island off Phœnicia. Assurnâçirpal (B.C. 885) calls it "Arvada in the mid-sea." Its king submitted to Sennacherib.

**Zemarite.**—The people of Simyra, on the coast of Phœnicia, south-east of Arvad. Simyra (Assyrian, Çimirra) was a fortified town commanding the road from the coast to the upper valley of the Orontes (Ruins: *Sumra*).

**Hamathite.**—The people of Hamath (*Hamah*) on the Orontes, a Hittite state which made alliance with David (*circ.* 1040 B.C.).

On a review of verses 8—16 we see that the "sons of Ham" include Ethiopia, Egypt, and the neighbouring shores of Arabia, and perhaps the founders of Babylon (verses 8—10). The tribes of Egypt and Canaan are enumerated in verses 11—16.

THE SONS OF SHEM, OR THE SEMITES (verses 17—23).

<sup>(17)</sup> **Elam.**—The Elamtum of the Assyrian inscription, the classic Susiana, a mountainous land eastward of Babylonia, to which it was subject in the days of Abraham (Gen. xiv.). The names Assurû, Elamû, Kassû, and Accadû occur together in an old Assyrian list of nations. Elama, from which the Assyrian and Hebrew names are derived, is Accadian. The native designation was Ansan. The Sargonide kings of Assyria had frequent wars with Elam.

**Asshur.**—Assyria proper, *i.e.*, a district on the Tigris, about twenty-five miles long, between the thirty-sixth and thirty-seventh parallels of latitude. Asshur was the name of its older capital and tutelar god. The Semitic Assyrians appear to have been settled at Asshur as early as the nineteenth century B.C. They were emigrants from Babylonia (Gen. x. 11). The original name was A-usar, "water-meadow."

**Arphaxad** apparently means Babylonia, or, at least, includes it. Babylonian monarchs styled themselves "King of the Four Quarters" (of heaven); and Arphaxad may perhaps mean land of the four quarters or sides, and be derived from the Assyrian *arba-kisâddi* "**four sides**" (Friedrich Delitzsch). **More probably it is *Arph-chesed*, "boundary of Chaldea."**

**Lud**, usually identified with the Lydians (Assyrian *Luddi*), perhaps their original home in Armenia. The name has also been compared with *Rutennu*, the Egyptian name of the Syrians (*l* and *r* being confused in Egyptian). But comp. Ezek. xxvii. 10, xxx. 5.

**Aram.**—The high land—that is, eastern and western Syria, extending from the Tigris to the Great Sea. The name is constantly used for the Arameans, or Syrians.

**Uz.**—An Arab tribe, called Hâsu by Esarhaddon, who reduced them. Perhaps, however, Uz (Heb., *Ûç*), is the Assyrian *Uçça*, a district on the Orontes, mentioned by Shalmaneser II. (B.C. 860—825). Job lived in the "land of Uz." The remaining names appear to be also those of Arab tribes, who must have lived northward in the direction of Aram; these are called sons of Aram in Gen. x.

**Hul** is the Assyrian *Hûli'a*, which formed a part of the mountain land of Kasiar or Mash (Inscription of Assurnâçirpal, B.C. 885—860). For Meshech Gen. x. has Mash, which is compared with Mount Masius, near Nisibin. (So the Syriac and some Heb. MSS.)

<sup>(18)</sup> **Eber.**—The land on the other side (Gr., ἡ πέραν) Peræa. Here the land beyond the Euphrates is meant, from which "Abraham, the Hebrew" (*i.e.*, Eberite), migrated.

<sup>(19)</sup> **Two sons.**—This indicates the ancient consciousness that the Hebrew and Arabian peoples were akin.

**The earth was divided.**—Or, *divided itself*. (Comp. Deut. xxxii. 7—9.) The words probably refer to a split in the population of Mesopotamia.

<sup>(20)</sup> **Joktan begat Almodad.**—The Joktanite tribes lived along the coast of Hadhramaut (Hazarmaveth) and Yemen, in southern Arabia. The tribes of Yemen call their ancestor Qahtân (= Joktan). The names in verses 20, 21, are all explicable from Arabic sources.

and Hazarmaveth, and Jerah, (21) Hadoram also, and Uzal, and Diklah, (22) and Ebal, and Abimael, and Sheba, (23) and Ophir, and Havilah, and Jobab. All these *were* the sons of Joktan.

(24) *a* Shem, Arphaxad, Shelah, (25) *b* Eber, Peleg, Reu, (26) Serug, Nahor, Terah, (27) *c* Abram; the same *is* Abraham. (28) The sons of Abraham; *d* Isaac, and *e* Ishmael.

(29) These *are* their generations: The *f* firstborn of Ishmael, Nebaioth; then Kedar, and Adbeel, and Mibsam, (30) Mishma, and Dumah, Massa, ¹Hadad, and Tema, (31) Jetur, Naphish, and Kedemah. These are the sons of Ishmael.

(32) Now the sons of Keturah, Abraham's concubine: she bare Zimran, and Jokshan, and Medan, and Midian, and Ishbak, and Shuah. And the sons of Jokshan; Sheba, and Dedan. (33) And the sons of Midian; Ephah, and Epher, and Henoch, and Abida, and Eldaah. All these *are* the sons of Keturah.

*a* Luke 3. 34.
¹ Or, *Hadar*, Ger. 25. 14.
*b* Gen. 11. 15.
*c* Gen. 17. 5.
*d* Gen. 21. 2, 3.
*e* Gen. 16. 11.
*f* Gen. 25. 13 to 17.

---

(22) **Ebal.**—Gen. x. 28 Obal, where, however, the LXX. read Εὐάλ (Ebal). The different spelling is due to the common confusion in MSS. of the Hebrew letters *w* and *y*. Both Ebal and Abimael are unknown.

(23) **Ophir.**—Abhîra, at the mouth of the Indus.

**Jobab.**—Probably a tribe of Arabia Deserta. (Comp. the Arabic *yabâb*, a desert.)

**All these were the sons of Joktan.**—Gen. x. 30 adds a definition of their territory: "Their dwelling was from Mesha" (*Maisânu*, at the head of the Persian Gulf), "until thou comest to Sephar" (probably *Zafâru* or *Isfor*, in South Arabia) "and the mountains of the east" (i.e., *Nejd*, a range parallel to the Red Sea).

From the whole section we learn that the Elamites, Assyrians, Chaldees, Arameans, Hebrews, and Arabs, were regarded as belonging to the great Semitic family. In regard to Elam, modern philologers have questioned the correctness of this view. It is, however, quite possible that at the time when the original of this table of nations was composed, some Semitic tribes were known to have effected a settlement in Elam, just as kindred tribes occupied Babylonia and Assyria.

The fourteen sons of Japheth and the thirty sons of Ham, and the twenty-six sons of Shem, make a total of seventy eponyms of nations. The number seventy is probably not accidental. Comp. the seventy elders (Num. xi. 16); the seventy members of the Sanhedrin; and even the seventy disciples of Christ (Luke x. 1). The seventy nations of the world are often mentioned in the Talmud. Ezekiel's prophecy concerning Tyre, and the peoples that had commerce with her (Ezek. xxvii.), is a valuable illustration of the table.

TEN GENERATIONS FROM SHEM TO ABRAHAM; AN ABSTRACT OF GEN. XI. 10—26, OMITTING ALL HISTORIC NOTICES (verses 24—27).

Between Arphaxad and Shelah the LXX., at Gen. xi. 12, insert Καϊνάν = Heb. *Kênan* (verse 2, above). The name is not contained in our present Hebrew text of Genesis. Kenan may have been dropped originally, in order to make Abraham the tenth from Shem, as Noah is tenth from Adam. The artificial symmetry of these ancient lists is evidently designed. Comp. the thrice fourteen generations in the genealogy of our Lord (Matt. i.).

Verses 28—42 enumerate a second series of seventy tribes or peoples, derived from Abraham through the three representative names of Ishmael, Keturah, and Isaac; just as the seventy peoples of the former series are derived from Noah through Shem, Ham, and Japheth. And as, in the former list, the sons of Japheth and Ham were treated of before the Semitic stocks, so, in the present instance, the sons of Ishmael and Keturah precede Isaac, and of Isaac's sons Esau precedes Israel (35, seq.); because the writer wishes to lead up to Israel as the climax of his presentation.

(29) **These are their generations.**—Or, *their genealogy* or *register of births*. Before a personal name the term *Tôldôth* denotes the "births," i.e., the *posterity* of the man, and the *history* of him and his descendants. Before the name of a thing *Tôldôth* signifies *origin, beginnings* (Gen. ii. 4). The Hebrew expression *sêfer tôldôth* answers to the βίβλος γενέσεως of Matt. i. 1. The twelve sons or tribes of Ishmael (verses 29—31) are given first, in an extract from Gen. xxv. 13—16.

**Nebaioth.**—The Nabateans of Arabia Petræa, and Kedar, the Cedrei of classical writers, are named together, Isa. lx. 7. (Assyrian *Naba'âta* and *Kidrâ'a* reduced by Assurbanipal.)

**Adbeel.**—Both here and in Genesis the LXX. read Nabdeel. But *Adbe'êl* is the Assyrian *Idiba'il* or *Idibi'il* a tribe south-west of the Dead Sea, towards Egypt; mentioned along with Massa and Tema, as paying tribute to Tiglath-pileser II.

(30) **Dumah.**—Isa. xxi. 11, as a name of Edom. There is still a locality bearing this name, "Duma the Rocky," on the borders of the Syrian desert and Arabia.

**Hadad.**—The right reading here and in Genesis.

**Tema.**—*Taimâ'u*, in the north of the Arabian desert. The LXX. confuses it with Teman. (Assyr. *Têmâ'a*).

(31) **Jetur.**—The Itureans beyond Jordan (Luke iii. 1). The other names are obscure.

(32) **The sons of Keturah.**—An extract from Gen. xxv. 1—4.

**Medan** is very likely a mere repetition of Midian, due to a mistake of some ancient copyist. Gen. xxv. 3 adds, "And the sons of Dedan were Asshurim, and Letushim, and Leummim;" which is, perhaps, an interpolation, as the three names are of a different form from the others in the section; and the chronicler would hardly have omitted them had he found them in his text.

**Midian.**—The most important of these tribes. The Midianites dwelt, or rather wandered, in the peninsula of Sinai.

**Sheba, and Dedan.**—See verse 9, where these names appear as sons of Cush. The names may have been common to different tribes settled in different regions. Sheba (Assyr. *Saba'â'a*), Massa, Tema, and Adbeel, are described by Tiglath-pileser as lying "on the border of the sunset lands."

(33) The five clans or tribes of Midian. These, with the seven names of verse 31, make a total of twelve tribes for Keturah.

**Ephah.**—Called *Hâ'âpâ*, or *Hayâpa* by Tiglath-pileser.

*The tribes of Esau*     I. CHRONICLES, I.     *and of Seir.*

(34) And Abraham begat Isaac. The sons of Isaac; Esau and Israel.

(35) The sons of [a] Esau; Eliphaz, Reuel, and Jeush, and Jaalam, and Korah. (36) The sons of Eliphaz; Teman, and Omar, [1] Zephi, and Gatam, Kenaz, and Timna, and Amalek. (37) The sons of Reuel; Nahath, Zerah, Shammah, and Mizzah.

(38) And the sons of Seir; Lotan, and Shobal, and Zibeon, and Anah, and Dishon, and Ezar, and Dishan. (39) And the sons of Lotan; Hori, and [2] Homam: and Timna *was* Lotan's sister. (40) The sons of Shobal; [3] Alian, and Manahath, and Ebal, [4] Shephi, and Onam. And the sons of Zibeon; Aiah, and Anah. (41) The sons of Anah; [b] Dishon. And the sons of Dishon; [5] Amram, and Eshban, and Ithran, and Cheran. (42) The sons of Ezer; Bilhan, and Zavan, *and* [6] Jakan. The sons of Dishan; Uz, and Aran.

(43) Now these *are* the [c] kings that reigned in the land of Edom before *any* king reigned over the children of Israel; Bela the son of Beor: and the name of

*a* Gen. 36. 9, 10.
[1] Or, *Zepho,* Gen. 36. 12.
[2] Or, *Heman,* Gen. 36. 22.
[3] Or, *Alvan,* Gen. 36. 23.
[4] Or, *Shepho,* Gen. 36. 23.
*b* ch. 2. 31.
[5] Or, *Hemdan,* Gen. 36. 26.
[6] Or, *Achan,* Gen. 36. 27.
*c* Gen. 36. 31.

---

(34) **Abraham begat Isaac.**—From Gen. xxv. 19.

**Esau and Israel.**—Esau is named first, not as the elder, but because the tribes of Esau are to be first enumerated. (Comp. Note above on verses 28—42.)

**Israel.**—The more honourable appellation (Gen. xxxii. 28) almost wholly supplanted Jacob as the name of the chosen people, except in poetry and prophecy. Some moderns have seen in such double names as Jacob-Israel, Esau-Edom, a trace of an ancient fusion or amalgamation of distinct races.

(35—42) The tribes of Esau and Seir, extracted from Gen. xxxvi.

(35—37) **The sons of Esau.**—Comp. Gen. xxxvi. 9—13. In verse 36 the name of Timna occurs under the general heading, "Sons of Eliphaz." According to Gen. xxxvi. 12, Timna was a secondary wife of Eliphaz, and mother of Amalek. Strange as this difference may at first sight appear, it is in fact absolutely unimportant. The writer's intention being simply to enumerate the principal branches of the sons of Eliphaz, the statement of the special relations between the different clans might be omitted here, as fairly and naturally as the relations between Noah, Shem, Ham, and Japheth are left unnoticed in verse 4. Comp. also verse 17, where Uz, Hul, &c., are apparently co-ordinated with Aram, although Gen. x. 23 expressly calls them "sons of Aram." The Vatican MS. of the LXX. has our text; the Alexandrine MS. follows that of Gen. xxxvi. 12. It is at least curious that if Timna-Amalek be excluded from account, the sons of Esau are twelve in number. The fact is obscured in the compressed statement of the chronicler; but it becomes evident by reference to Gen. xxxvi. 11—14, where five sons are reckoned to Eliphaz (verse 11), four to Reuel (verse 13), and three to Esau's wife Aholibamah (verse 14), viz.: Jeush, Jaalam, and Korah. Although verse 12 of that passage reckons Amalek with the sons of Adah, mother of Eliphaz, it distinctly separates Timna-Amalek from the sons of Eliphaz. It would seem that Amalek was known to be but remotely connected with the pure Edomite stocks. For the organisation of a people in twelve tribes, &c., comp. Ewald, *Hist. of Israel,* i. 362, and his *Antiq. of Israel,* § 280. However, Gen. xxxvi. 15—19 enumerates Teman, Omar, Zepho, Kenaz, Gatam, and Amalek, sons of Eliphaz; Nahath, Zerah, Shammah, Mizzah, sons of Reuel; and Jeush, Jaalam, Korah, sons of Aholibamah; as chiliarchs (*allūfim*—LXX., φύλαρχοι) or chieftains of Esau-Edom.

(38—42) **The sons of Seir** (from Gen. xxxvi. 20—30).—There is no apparent link between this series and the preceding. Comparison of Gen. xxxvi. 20 shows that Seir represents the indigenous inhabitants of Edom ("the inhabitants of the land," comp. Josh. vii. 9) before its conquest by the sons of Esau. In time a fusion of the two races would result, the tribes of each being governed by their own chieftains, as is indicated by Gen. xxxvi. 20, 21, where the seven sons of Seir (verse 38) are called "chiliarchs of the Horites, the sons of Seir in the land of Edom." Deut. ii. 22 implies not the actual extermination of the Horites (Troglodytes or Cave-dwellers) by their Semitic invaders, the sons of Esau, but only their entire subjugation. The differences of spelling noticed in the margin are unimportant as regards the names Zephi (verse 36), Homam (verse 39), and Alian and Shephi (verse 40); the note on Ebal-Obal (verse 22) explains them. The written *w* and *y* in Hebrew are so similar as to be perpetually confounded with each other by careless copyists. The same fact accounts for the missing conjunction *and* in verse 42, which is expressed in Hebrew by simply prefixing the letter *w* to a word. The *w* in this case having been misread, and transcribed as *y,* the name Jakan (Yaqan) resulted. The Aqan (not Achan) of Gen. xxxvi. 2 is correct. (So some MSS., the LXX., and Arabic.) Amram, in verse 41, is a mistake of the Authorised version. The Hebrew has Hamran, which differs only by one consonant from the Hemdan of Gen. xxxvi. 26; a difference due to the common confusion of the Hebrew letters *d* and *r,* already exemplified in verses 6 and 7 (Riphath — Diphath, Dodanim — Rodanim). Many MSS. and the Arabic read *Hemdan* here.

(39) **And Timna was Lotan's sister.**—This appears to mean that the tribe settled in the town of Timna was akin to the sons of Lotan, but not a subdivision of that tribe. Towns are feminine in Hebrew, and are sometimes called *mothers* (2 Sam. xx. 19), sometimes *daughters*.

(41) **The sons of Anah; Dishon.**—Gen. xxxvi. 25 adds, "and Aholibamah the daughter of Anah." (Comp. verse 52, "the chiliarch of Aholibamah.") Dishon, like Ammon or Israel, being the collective name of a number of tribes or clans, there is nothing strange in the expression, "The sons of Anah; Dishon."

(43—54) The ancient kings and chiliarchs of Edom, a transcript of Gen. xxxvi. 31—43, with only such differences as are incidental to transcribing.

(43) **Before any king reigned over the children of Israel.**—Comp. Num. xx. 14—21, the message of Moses to the king of Edom, asking for a free passage

his city *was* Dinhabah. (44) And when Bela was dead, Jobab the son of Zerah of Bozrah reigned in his stead. (45) And when Jobab was dead, Husham of the land of the Temanites reigned in his stead. (46) And when Husham was dead, Hadad the son of Bedad, which smote Midian in the field of Moab, reigned in his stead: and the name of his city *was* Avith. (47) And when Hadad was dead, Samlah of Masrekah reigned in his stead. (48) *a* And when Samlah was dead, Shaul of Rehoboth by the river reigned in his stead. (49) And when Shaul was dead, Baal-hanan the son of Achbor reigned in his stead. (50) And when Baal-hanan was dead, ¹Hadad reigned in his stead: and the name of his city *was* ²Pai; and his wife's name *was* Mehetabel, the daughter of Matred, the daughter of Mezahab. (51) Hadad died also. And the *b* dukes of Edom were; duke Timnah, duke Aliah, duke Jetheth, (52) duke Aholibamah, duke Elah, duke Pinon, (53) duke Kenaz, duke Teman, duke Mibzar, (54) duke Magdiel, duke Iram. These *are* the dukes of Edom.

*a* Gen. 36. 37.

¹ Or, *Hadar*, Gen. 36. 39.

B.C. cir. 1496.

² Or, *Pau*, Gen. 36. 39.

*b* Gen. 36. 40.

---

for Israel through his domains. As the older people, and as having been earlier established in its permanent home, Edom was naturally a stage beyond Israel in political development. Unhappily brief as it is, this notice is very appropriately inserted here in an introduction to the history of the kings of the house of David.

**Bela the son of Beor.**—Curiously like "Balaam the son of Beor," Num. xxii. 5. In Hebrew, Bela and Balaam are essentially similar words, the terminal *m* of the latter being possibly a mere formative. (Perhaps, however, Balaam—Heb. *Bil'am* = "Bel is a kinsman") comp. Eliam. The prophet whose strange story is read in Num. xxii.—xxiv. may, like Isaiah, have been of royal extraction.

**Dinhabah.**—*Doom-giving*, that is, the place where the king gave judgment (1 Sam. viii. 5).

(44, 45) **Bozrah.**—"Fortress" (the *Byrsa* of Carthage); was one of the capitals of Edom, perhaps identical with Mibzar (fortress, verse 53). Eusebius mentions Mabsara as a large town in Gebalene. It is now represented by the ruins of *Al-Bussireh* in *Jebal*. See Amos i. 12, "I will send a fire upon Teman, which shall devour the palaces of Bozrah;" and Isa. xxxiv. 6.

(46) **Hadad.**—The name of a Syrian deity, a form of the sun-god. (Comp. the royal titles, Ben-hadad and Hadadezer, chap. xviii. 3, and the Note on 2 Kings v. 18.) Hadad is the same as Dadi, a Syrian title of Rimmon. Perhaps the classical Attis is equivalent to Dadis. The cry of the vintagers (*hēdād*) seems to show that Hadad, like Bacchus, was regarded as the giver of the grapes (Isa. xvi. 9, 10).

**Which smote Midian.**—A glimpse of the restless feuds which prevailed from time immemorial between these tribes and peoples of kindred origin. Like the judges of Israel, the kings of Edom seem to have been raised to their position owing to special emergencies.

**The field of Moab.**—That is, *the open country*.

**Avith.**—Like Dinhabah, and Pai, and Masrekah, unknown beyond this passage. In the Hebrew of Chron. it is spelt, *Ayuth*; in Gen. xxxvi. *Awith*. The letters *w* and *y* have been transposed in our text.

(47) **Masrekah** means *place of Sorek vines*.

(48) **Shaul.**—*Saul*, the name of the first king of Israel.

**Rehoboth by the river.**—Probably the same as Rehoboth Ir in Gen. x. 11, *i.e.*, the suburbs of Nineveh. The river is Euphrates.

(49) **Baal-hanan.**—*Baal bestowed*. (Comp. "Johanan," *Iahweh bestowed*; and "Hananiah," and "Hannibal.") This name and that of Hadad indicate the polytheism of ancient Edom.

(50) **Baal-hanan.**—Some MSS. have "ben Achbor," as in Gen. xxxvi. 39; so in verse 51. "Alvah," of Genesis, is more correct than our "Aliah." The Hebrew margin reads "Alvah" (Alwah).

**Pai.**—Many MSS. have "Pau," the reading of Gen., which is right. *Hadar* (Gen. xxxvi. 39), on the other hand, is probably a mistake for Hadad.

**Mehetabel.**—*El benefiteth*. Perhaps Mehetabel was an Israelite, as no other queen of Edom is mentioned. But her name is Aramean.

(51) **Hadad died also.**—Rather, *And Hadad died, and there were* (or *arose*) *chiliarchs of Edom, the chiliarch of Timnah, the chiliarch of Aliah*, &c. This appears to state that Hadad was the last king of Edom, and that after his death the country was governed by the heads of the various clans or tribes, without any central authority. In Gen. xxxvi. 40, the sentence, "And Hadad died," is wanting, and the transition from the kings to the chiliarchs is thus effected: "And these are the names of the chiliarchs of Esau, after their clans, after their places, by their names: the chiliarch of Timnah," &c. The chiliarchs ('*allûphîm*, from '*eleph*, a thousand) were the heads of the thousands or clans (*mishpehôth*) of Edom (Gen. xxxvi. 40). (See Note on chap. xiv. 1.) The names in these verses are not personal, but tribal and local, as the conclusion of the account in Gen. xxxvi. 43 indicates: "These are the chiliarchs of Edom, after their seats, in the land of their domain." Comp. the names of the sons of Esau and Seir (verses 35—42). This makes it clear that Timnah and Aholibamah were towns. The king of Edom is often mentioned elsewhere in the Old Testament. (See Num. xx. 14; Amos ii. 1—8th cent. B.C.; 2 Kings, iii. 9—9th cent.) According to Ewald (*Hist.* p. 46), the chieftains of Edom follow the list of kings, "as if David had already vanquished the last king of Edom, and put it under" merely tribal government, in subordination to himself. "The Hadad who fled very young to Egypt at David's conquest (1 Kings xi. 14—22) may have been grandson of Hadad, the last king."

(54) **These are the dukes (chiliarchs) of Edom.** —Eleven names only are given, whereas there were twelve (or thirteen) chiliarchs of Edom (Gen. xxxvi. 15—19; see Note on verses 35—37). A name may have fallen out of the ancient text from which the chronicler derived the list.

*The sons*  I. CHRONICLES, II.  *of Judah.*

CHAPTER II.—<sup>(1)</sup> These *are* the sons of ¹Israel; *a*Reuben, Simeon, Levi, and Judah, Issachar, and Zebulun, <sup>(2)</sup> Dan, Joseph, and Benjamin, Naphtali, Gad, and Asher.

<sup>(3)</sup> The sons of *b* Judah; Er, and Onan, and Shelah: *which* three were born unto him of the daughter of *c*Shua the Canaanitess. And Er, the firstborn of Judah, was evil in the sight of the LORD; and he slew him. <sup>(4)</sup> And *d*Tamar his daughter in law bare him Pharez and Zerah. All the sons of Judah *were* five. <sup>(5)</sup> The sons of *e*Pharez; Hezron, and Hamul.

<sup>(6)</sup> And the sons of Zerah; ²Zimri, and Ethan, and Heman, and Calcol, and ³Dara: five of them in all. <sup>(7)</sup> And the sons of Carmi; ⁴Achar, the troubler of Israel, who transgressed in the thing *g*accursed. <sup>(8)</sup> And the sons of Ethan; Azariah.

<sup>(9)</sup> The sons also of Hezron, that were

---

1 Or, *Jacob.*
*a* Gen. 29. 32, & 30. 5, & 35. 18, 22, & 46. 8, &c.
*b* Gen. 38, 3 & 46. 12.
*c* Gen. 38. 2.
*d* Gen. 38. 29, 30; Matt. 1. 3.
*e* Ruth 4. 18.
2 Or, *Zabdi,* Josh. 7. 1.
*f* 1 Kings 4. 31.
3 Or, *Darda.*
4 Or, *Achan.*
*g* Josh. 6. 19 & 7. 1, 25.

---

## II.

Dismissing the sons of Esau-Edom, the narrative proceeds with the sons of Israel, who are named in order, by way of introduction to their genealogies, which occupy chaps. ii.—viii.

The rest of chap. ii. treats of the leading tribe of Judah, and its sub-divisions, under the heads of Zerah and Perez (3—41), and Caleb (42—55); while chaps. iii. and iv. complete the account of this tribe, so far as the fragmentary materials at the writer's disposal permitted.

<sup>(1, 2)</sup> **The sons of Israel.**—The list is apparently taken from Gen. xxxv. 23—26, where the heading is, "Now the sons of Jacob were twelve." The chronicler omits the mothers, and puts Dan before instead of after Joseph and Benjamin, as if to hint that Dan was considered Rachel's elder son. (See Gen. xxx. 6.) In the list at Gen. xlvi. 9—23, Gad and Asher follow Zebulun, and Dan follows Joseph and Benjamin. Of course accident may have caused the transposition of Dan with Joseph and Benjamin in our list, especially as it otherwise agrees with Gen. xxxv. 3, 4.

THE FIVE SONS OF JUDAH, FROM GEN. XXXVIII.

<sup>(3)</sup> **The daughter of Shua the Canaanitess.**—Shua was the father of Judah's wife.

**Er, the firstborn of Judah, was** (became, proved) **evil.**—Word for word from Gen. xxxviii. 7. Suppressing other details relating to the sons of Judah, the chronicler copies this statement intact from Genesis, because it thoroughly harmonises with the moral he wishes to be drawn from the entire history of his people.

<sup>(4)</sup> **Tamar.**—Wife of Er. The story of her incest with Judah, the fruit of which was the twins Pharez (Heb., *Perez*) and Zerah (called Zarah, Gen. xxxviii. 30; and Zara, Matt. i. 3), is told in Gen. xxxviii. 8—30.

<sup>(5)</sup> **The sons of Pharez.**—From Gen. xlvi. 12, which also names the five sons of Judah. Num. xxvi. 21 mentions the clans (*mishpahath*) of the Hezronites and Hamulites, as registered in a census held by Moses.

<sup>(6—8)</sup> **The sons of Zerah.**—From this point our narrative ceases to depend entirely upon the data of Genesis.

<sup>(6)</sup> **Zimri.**—This name is probably a merely accidental variant of Zabdi. Both are genuine Hebrew names occurring elsewhere. But the fact that Zimri here, and Zabdi at Josh. vii. 1, are both called sons of Zerah, seems to prove their identity; especially as *m* is often confused with *b*, and *d* with *r*.

**Ethan, and Heman, and Calcol, and Dara.** —It is stated (1 Kings iv. 31) that Solomon was "wiser than all men; than Ethan the Ezrahite, and Heman, and Chalcol, and Darda, the sons of Mahol." It will be seen that the first three names coincide with those of our text, and that Dara is only one letter different from Darda. Further, many MSS. of Chronicles, as well as the Syriac and Arabic versions and the Targum, actually have Darda. The Vatic. LXX. reads Darad. There is thus a virtual repetition of these four names in the passage of Kings, and it is difficult to suppose that the persons intended are not the same there and here. Ethan is called an Ezrahite in Kings, but Ezrah and Zerah are equivalent forms in Hebrew; and the Vatic. LXX. actually calls Ethan a Zarhite—*i.e.*, a descendant of Zerah (Num. xxvi. 13). The designation of the four as "sons of Mahol" presents no difficulty. *Mahol* is a usual word for the sacred dance (Pss. cxlix. 3, cl. 4), and the four Zarhites are thus described as "sons of dancing"— that is, sacred musicians. It is likely, therefore, that these famous minstrels of Judah were adopted into the Levitical clans in which sacred music was the hereditary profession. (See Pss. lxxxviii. and lxxxix., titles.) Whether Ethan and Heman are the persons mentioned in chaps. vi. 33, 44, and xv. 17, 19 as the recognised heads of two of the great guilds of temple musicians is not clear. The Levitical ancestry ascribed to them in chap. vi. would not be opposed to this assumption, as adoption would involve it.

<sup>(7)</sup> **The sons of Carmi.**—See Note on chap. i. 41.

**Achar, the troubler of Israel.**—See Josh. vii. 1, where the man is called "Achan, son of Carmi, son of Zabdi, son of Zerah, of the tribe of Judah." The family of Carmi, therefore, were Zarhites. Josh. vii. 27 calls him "Achan, the son of Zerah," an expression which shows, if other proof were wanting, that we must be cautious of interpreting such phrases literally in all instances.

**Achar . . . troubler of Israel.**—There is a play on the man's name in the Hebrew, which is, "*Achar 'ocher Yisrael.*" So in Josh. vii. 25 Joshua asks, "Why hast thou troubled us?" (*'achartânu*), and in verse 26 the place of Achar's doom is called "the valley of Achor" (trouble). Probably Achan is an old error for Achar.

<sup>(8)</sup> **The sons of Ethan.**—Nothing is known of this Ethanite Azariah. It seems plain that the writer wished to name only the historically famous members of the Zarhite branch of Judah—in verse 6, the four proverbial sages; in verse 7, Achar who brought woe upon Israel by taking of the devoted spoils of Jericho.

<sup>(9—41)</sup> The Hezronites, who were sons of Pharez (verse 5), and their three lines of descent, Jerahmeel, Ram, and Chelubai.

<sup>(9)</sup> **Jerahmeel.**—*God pitieth.*

**Ram.**—Called *Aram* in our Lord's genealogy (Matt. i.) The two names are synonyms, both meaning

born unto him; Jerahmeel, and ¹Ram, and ²Chelubai. ⁽¹⁰⁾ And Ram ᵃ begat Amminadab; and Amminadab begat Nahshon, prince of the children of Judah; ⁽¹¹⁾ and Nahshon begat Salma, and Salma begat Boaz, ⁽¹²⁾ and Boaz begat Obed, and Obed begat Jesse, ⁽¹³⁾ ᵇ and Jesse begat his firstborn Eliab, and Abinadab the second, and ³Shimma the third, ⁽¹⁴⁾ Nethaneel the fourth, Raddai the fifth, ⁽¹⁵⁾ Ozem the sixth, David the seventh: ⁽¹⁶⁾ whose sisters were Zeruiah, and Abigail. And the sons of Zeruiah; Abishai, and Joab, and Asahel, three. ⁽¹⁷⁾ And Abigail bare Amasa: and the father of Amasa was Jether the Ishmeelite. ⁽¹⁸⁾ And Caleb the son of Hezron begat *children* of Azubah *his* wife, and of Jerioth: her sons *are* these; Jesher, and Shobab, and Ardon. ⁽¹⁹⁾ And when Azubah was dead, Caleb took unto him Ephrath, which bare him Hur. ⁽²⁰⁾ And Hur begat Uri, and Uri begat ᶜBezaleel.

⁽²¹⁾ And afterward Hezron went in to the daughter of Machir the father of Gilead, whom he ⁴married when he *was* threescore years old; and she bare him

¹ Or, *Aram*, Matt. 1.3.
² Or, *Caleb*, ver. 18.
ᵃ Ruth 4. 19.
ᵇ 1 Sam. 16. 6.
³ Or, *Shammah*, 1 Sam. 16. 9.
ᶜ Ex. 31. 2.
⁴ heb., *took*.

---

*high*, and are used interchangeably in Job xxxii. 2 (Ram) and Gen. xxii. 21 (Aram).

**Chelubai.**—Strictly, *the Chelubite* or *Calebite*, a gentilic term formed from Caleb (verse 18). This seems to show that we are concerned here not so much with individual sons of Hezron as with families or clans of Hezronites.

I.—(10—17) The descent of David from Amminadab, of the house of Ram. The royal line naturally takes precedence of the other two. Ruth iv. 18—22 gives this line from Pharez to David. (Compare the genealogies of Christ, Matt. i. and Luke iii.) Nahshon is called chief of Judah in Num. ii. 3 (comp. chaps. i. 7, vii. 12), at the time of the Exodus.

(11) **Salma.**—So in Ruth iv. 20; but in verse 21, Matt. i. 4, and Luke iii. 32, Salmon.

(13—17) The family of Jesse (Heb., *Yishai* in verse 12, but *'Ishai* in verse 13).

Seven sons are here named. 1 Sam. xvii. 12, 13 states that Jesse had eight sons; and from 1 Sam. xvi. 6—10 (Heb.) it appears that he had that number. In both passages, Eliab, Abinadab, and Shimma (Heb., *Shim'â*, here and at chap. xx. 7) occur, the last under the form Shammah. He is called Shimei (2 Sam. xxi. 21); but Shimeah = Shim'ah (2 Sam. xiii. 3, 32); and this appears to have been his real name.

(14, 15) **Nethaneel . . . Raddai . . . Ozem.**—Not named elsewhere in the Scriptures. The son of Jesse, omitted in our present Heb. text, is called Elihu in the Syriac version, which makes him seventh and David the eighth. The name Elihu occurs in chap. xxvii. 18 for Eliab.

(13) **Whose sisters were Zeruiah, and Abigail.** —Literally, *And their sisters*, &c. If the reading in 2 Sam. xvii. 25 be correct, these two women were daughters of Nahash, who must therefore have been a wife of Jesse. Abigail (there called Abigal) was mother of the warrior Amasa, who became Absalom's general (2 Sam. xix. 13), and was afterwards assassinated by Joab (2 Sam. xx. 10).

**Abishai.**—*Abshai*, here and elsewhere in the chronicle.

**Joab**, the famous commander-in-chief of David's forces (see chap. xi. 6—8); and for Joab and Abishai, who, like Asahel, was one of David's heroes (chap. xi. 20, 26), comp. chaps. xviii. 12, 15, xix. 10 *seq.*, xxi. 2 *et seq.*, xxvii. 24. David's champions were thus his immediate kin, just as Abner was to Saul.

(17) **Jether the Ishmeelite.**—Incorrectly called "Ithra an Israelite" in 2 Sam. xvii. 25. The later abhorrence of alien marriages seems to have been unknown in the age of David. The name of Zeruiah's husband is unknown.

II.—The Calebite stock (verses 18—24).

(18) **And Caleb the son of Hezron begat children of Azubah his wife.**—The Heb. text, as it stands, does not say this. The *primâ facie* rendering is, "And Caleb son of Hezron begat Azubah a woman, and Jerioth: and these (are) her sons; Jesher, and Shobab, and Ardon." But verse 19 continues: "And Azubah died, and Caleb took to himself (as wife) Ephrath," which of course suggests that Azubah was not daughter but a former wife of Caleb. Verse 18 has also been translated, "And Caleb son of Hezron caused Azubah a wife and Jerioth to bear children." (Comp. Isa. lxvi. 9.) It seems best to read, "his wife, daughter of Jerioth" ('ishtô-bath-Ierioth), instead of the text (ishshah ve'eth Ierioth); and to render: "And Caleb son of Hezron begat sons with Azubah daughter of Jerioth" (*eth*, the particle before Azubah, is ambiguous, and might be either the mere sign of the accusative, or the prep. "with," *cum*, μετὰ). The Syriac partly supports this version, for it reads: "And Caleb begat of Azubah, his wife, Jerioth," making Jerioth Azubah's daughter. The LXX. has, "And Caleb took Azubah a wife and Jerioth," which only shows that the corruption of the text is ancient.

(19) **Ephrath.**—In verse 50 Ephratah; so also iv. 4. The town of Bethlehem was so called (Micah v. 1).

(20) **Hur begat Uri . . . Bezaleel.**—See Exod. xxxi. 2, which states that: "Bezaleel, son of Uri, son of Hur, of the tribe of Judah," was divinely qualified for building the Tent of Meeting. Bezaleel is no doubt a person, but Hur is probably a Calebite clan, established at "Ephrath, which is Beth-lehem" (Gen. xxxv. 19).

(21—24) This short section, concerning other Hezronites than those of the house of Caleb, is a parenthesis relating to a Hezronite element in Manassite Gilead.

(21) **And afterward Hezron went in to the daughter of Machir.**—This appears to mean, after the birth of the three sons mentioned in verse 9.

**Machir.**—The firstborn of Manasseh (Gen. l. 23), to whom Moses gave the land of Gilead (Num. xxxii. 40; Deut. iii. 15). This explains the term "father of Gilead." The great clan of Machir was the ruling clan in Gilead. Comp. Num. xxvi. 28, which mentions

Segub. ⁽²²⁾ And Segub begat Jair, who had three and twenty cities in the land of Gilead. ⁽²³⁾ ᵃAnd he took Geshur, and Aram, with the towns of Jair, from them, with Kenath, and the towns thereof, *even* threescore cities. All these *belonged to* the sons of Machir the father

of Gilead. ⁽²⁴⁾ And after that Hezron was dead in Caleb-ephratah, then Abiah Hezron's wife bare him Ashur the father of Tekoa.

⁽²⁵⁾ And the sons of Jerahmeel the firstborn of Hezron were, Ram the firstborn, and Bunah, and Oren, and Ozem, *and*

ᵃ Num. 32. 41; Deut. 3.14; Josh. 13. 30.

---

the clan of the Machirites, and adds that "Machir begat Gilead," which perhaps means to say that the Israelite settlers in Gilead were of the clan Machir.

**Whom he married when he was threescore.**—It is possible to see here a metaphorical statement of the fact that a branch of Hezronites amalgamated with the Machirites of Gilead. The "daughter of Machir" would then mean the clan so named. Comp. the expressions, "daughter of Zion" (Isa. xxxvii. 22), "daughter of Judah" (Lam. i. 15), "daughter of Babylon" (Isa. xlvii. 1).

⁽²²⁾ **And Segub begat Jair . . .**—The Havoth-jair (tent-villages of Jair) are several times mentioned in the Pentateuch. In the passage Num. xxxii. 39–42 it is related—(1) That the Manassite clan of the sons of Machir took Gilead from the Amorites; (2) That Moses then formally assigned Gilead "to Machir son of Manasseh," and the clan accordingly settled there; (3) That Jair son of Manasseh had taken their (*i.e.*, the Amorite) tent-villages, and called them Havoth-jair. Comp. Deut. iii. 14, 15: "Jair son of Manasseh had taken all the region of Argob unto the bounds of the Geshurite and the Maachathite; and he called them (that is, Bashan) after his own name, Havoth-jair, unto this day. And to Machir I gave Gilead."

Verses 21—23 show a connection between Jair and the two tribes of Judah and Manasseh thus:—

```
Judah                    Manasseh
  |                          |
Pharez                       |
  |                          |
Hezron married the daughter of Machir, chief of Gilead
                   |
                Segub
                   |
                 Jair
```

Jair is of course the name of a group of kindred families or clans, settled in the twenty-three cities.

⁽²³⁾ **And he took . . . of Gilead.**—Rather, *And Geshur and Aram took the Havoth-jair from them—Kenath and her daughters, sixty cities: all these* (were) *sons of Machir, chief of Gilead*.

**Geshur, and Aram.**—That is, the Aramean state of Geshur, north-west of Bashan, near Hermon and the Jordan, which was an independent kingdom in the age of David (2 Sam. iii. 3). The Geshurites "took the tent-villages of Jair *from them*"—*i.e.*, from the sons of Jair, or the Jairites; at what date is unknown. Comp. Deut. iii. 14, 15, above cited.

**With Kenath.**—The Hebrew particle before "Kenath" may be either the sign of the object of the verb, or the preposition "with." In the latter case, the statement of the verse will be that the twenty-three villages of Jair, together with the (thirty-seven) places called Kenath and her daughters, amounting in all to sixty towns, were taken by the Geshurites. See Num. xxxii. 41, 42, where it is said that Jair occupied the Havoth-jair, and "Nobah went and took Kenath and her daugh-

ters, and called it Nobah after his own name." Kenath is the modern *Kanwat*, on the western slope of *Jebel Hauran*.

It is difficult to reconcile all the different statements about the Havoth-jair. Judges x. 3, 4, for example, speaks of Jair the Gileadite, who judged Israel twenty-two years, and "had thirty sons that rode on thirty ass colts," and, moreover, possessed "thirty cities, which are called Havoth-jair unto this day." Josh. xiii. 30 seems to make the Havoth-jair sixty towns. Comp. 1 Kings iv. 13; also verse 21, where Hezron is sixty when he marries the Gileadite daughter of Machir.

Of course the number of places included in the "camps of Jair" may have varied at different epochs.

**All these belonged to the sons of Machir.**—Or, *all these were sons of Machir*—*i.e.*, the clans and families that came of the union of Hezron with the daughter of Machir. (See Note on verse 21; and Josh. xix. 34.)

⁽²⁴⁾ **And after that Hezron was dead . . .**—Or, "And after the death of Hezron in Caleb-ephratah—and the wife of Hezron was Abiah—and she bare him Ashur . . ." The text is evidently corrupt. The best suggestion is based on the reading of the LXX.: καὶ μετὰ τὸ ἀποθανεῖν Ἐσρὼν ἦλθεν Χαλὲβ εἰς Ἐφραθά; "And after Hezron's death Caleb went to Ephrath." Some very slight changes in the Hebrew, affecting only three letters of the entire sentence, will give the sense, "And after Hezron's death Caleb went in to Ephrath, the wife of his father Hezron (verse 19); and she bare him Ash-hur, father (founder, or chief) of Tekoah." (Comp. Gen. xxxv. 22.)

**Ashur** (Heb., *Ash-hur*) means "man of Hur"—that is, the chief of the clan of the Hurites, settled at Ephrath or Bethlehem (verse 19). Comp. Ashbel "man of Bel." (*Ash* is the elder form of *Ish* "man"; as appears from the Phœnician inscriptions.)

That "Caleb" in this verse means the house of Caleb is evident if we consider that the genealogy makes him great grandson of Judah, whereas the individual Caleb son of Jephunneh took part in the conquest of Canaan, more than four centuries after Judah went down to Egypt.

III.—The Jerahmeelites (verses 25—41). Comp. I Sam. xxvii. 10, "the south (land) of the Jerahmeelites," in the territory of Judah.

⁽²⁵⁾ **Ram the firstborn.**—Not the same as the Ram, brother of Jerahmeel, of verse 9. (See Note at end of section.)

**And Ahijah.**—This is probably a mistake, as the conjunction is wanting in the Hebrew. The LXX. has, "his brother" the Hebrew for which might easily be misread Ahijah. So the Syriac and Arabic read, "and Ozem their sister." But the statement of verse 26, "Jerahmeel had also another wife," &c., makes it likely that the first wife was mentioned here; and, therefore, it is conjectured that Ahijah—usually a man's name—is the former wife,

*The Posterity of Jerahmeel*  I. CHRONICLES, II.  *and of Sheshan.*

Ahijah. (26) Jerahmeel had also another wife, whose name *was* Atarah; she *was* the mother of Onam. (27) And the sons of Ram the firstborn of Jerahmeel were, Maaz, and Jamin, and Eker. (28) And the sons of Onam were, Shammai, and Jada. And the sons of Shammai; Nadab, and Abishur. (29) And the name of the wife of Abishur *was* Abihail, and she bare him Ahban, and Molid. (30) And the sons of Nadab; Seled, and Appaim: but Seled died without children. (31) And the sons of Appaim; Ishi. And the sons of Ishi; Sheshan. And the children of Sheshan; Ahlai. (32) And the sons of Jada the brother of Shammai; Jether, and Jonathan: and Jether died without children. (33) And the sons of Jonathan;

*a* ch. 11. 41.

Peleth, and Zaza. These were the sons of Jerahmeel. (34) Now Sheshan had no sons, but daughters. And Sheshan had a servant, an Egyptian, whose name *was* Jarha. (35) And Sheshan gave his daughter to Jarha his servant to wife; and she bare him Attai. (36) And Attai begat Nathan, and Nathan begat *a* Zabad, (37) and Zabad begat Ephlal, and Ephlal begat Obed, (38) and Obed begat Jehu, and Jehu begat Azariah, (39) and Azariah begat Helez, and Helez begat Eleasah, (40) and Eleasah begat Sisamai, and Sisamai begat Shallum, (41) and Shallum begat Jekamiah, and Jekamiah begat Elishama.

(42) Now the sons of Caleb the brother of Jerahmeel *were*, Mesha his firstborn,

---

and that the right reading is "from Ahijah," which requires merely the restoration of the prefix *m* (*me-Ahiyah*), which has fallen out, as in other instances, after the *m* of Ozem immediately preceding.

(26) **Atarah.**—The word means *corona*, here and in verse 54; probably, the ring-fence or fortifications round a city. So στέφανος was used in Greek (Pindar, *Olymp.* viii. 42, of the wall of Troy). The plural Ataroth occurs as the name of a town in Num. xxxii. 3; Josh. xvi. 5.

**The mother of Onam.**—See verses 28—34 for the ramifications of this clan.

(30) **Seled died without children.**—That is, the clan Seled did not multiply, and subdivide into new groups. (Comp. verse 32.)

(31) **The children of Sheshan; Ahlai.** — See Note on chap. i. 41, "Dishon." Ahlai is the name of a clan, not of an individual. Others would explain such phrases by assuming that "sons of so-and-so" is a conventional expression, used even where only one person has to be registered; or that the chronicler has in such cases abbreviated the contents of his source, by omitting all the names but one. Both assumptions are antiquated.

(33) **These were the sons of Jerahmeel.**—Subscription of the list contained in verses 25—33. It is noteworthy that the total of the names from Judah to Zaza again amounts to about seventy. (Comp. chap. i. ; see also Gen. xlvi. 27.)

(34) **Now Sheshan had no sons, but daughters.**—Comp. verse 31 above, "And the children of Sheshan; Ahlai." Those who insist upon a literal understanding of these lists reconcile the two statements by making Ahlai a daughter; others suppose that the chronicler has preserved for us in the present section fragments of at least two independent accounts.

(35—41) The line of Sheshan-Jarha is pursued for thirteen generations of direct descent, but nothing is known of any of its members from any other source. Elishama, the last name (verse 41), is the twenty-fourth generation specified from Judah. The list thus extends over a period of at least 720 years; and if we reckon from the Exodus (circ. 1330 B.C.), we get B.C. 610 as an approximate date for Elishama. Now an Elishama was living about that time, who is mentioned (Jerem. xxxvi. 12) as one of the princes of Jehoiakim, king of Judah;

Jerem. xli. 1 perhaps mentions the same person again, calling him "of the seed of the kingdom." It is at least a coincidence that several of the names recur in the house of David: Nathan (verse 36) in chap. iii. 5; Obed, as David's grandfather in verse 12; Azariah, as a by-name of King Uzziah, in chap. iii. 12; Shallum, as a son of Josiah, in chap. iii. 15; Jekamiah, as a brother of Salathiel (Shealtiel), in chap. iii. 18; and Elishama, as a son of David, in chap. iii. 8—a coincidence of six out of thirteen names. The passage Deut. xxiii. 7, 8 rules that in the third generation persons of Egyptian blood are to be treated as full Israelites. This whole section proves that an Egyptian element was recognised in Judah. (Compare Exod. xii. 38; Num. xi. 4.) Even the name Jarha has an Egyptian cast (comp. *Iarō*, the Memphitic name of the Nile, with the Vulg. spelling of the word Jeraa); perhaps it is *Iar-aa*, great river, (*i.e.*, the Nile).

(42—55) These verses revert to the Calebite stocks. Interpreted as merely bearing upon the extraction of individuals about whom, for the most part, nothing whatever is known beyond what these brief notices reveal, the section presents great difficulties. The key to it appears to be the assumption that it is an ancient record of the relations between certain great branches of the tribe of Judah, and their various settlements; in other words, these lists are tribal and topographical, rather than genealogical.

I.—Verses 42—45 : Caleb brother of Jerahmeel = Caleb son of Hezron (verse 18) = Chelubai (verse 9).

(42) **Mesha.**—The name of a king of Moab (2 Kings iii. 4), whose monument of victory, the famous Moabite stone, was found in 1868 at Dibon. Here the name is probably that of a principal Calebite clan, settled at Ziph, near Hebron (Josh. xv. 54, 55 ; 1 Sam. xxiii. 14).

**Father of Ziph.** — Comp. verses 21, "father of Gilead," and 24.

**And the sons of Mareshah the father of Hebron.**—The statement of the verse is, "the sons of Mareshah were sons of Caleb," that is, the Mareshathites, or people of Mareshah (Josh. xv. 44), a town in the Shephelah, were a Calebite clan. This branch of

which *was* the father of Ziph; and the sons of Mareshah the father of Hebron. ⁽⁴³⁾ And the sons of Hebron; Korah, and Tappuah, and Rekem, and Shema. ⁽⁴⁴⁾ And Shema begat Raham, the father of Jorkoam: and Rekem begat Shammai. ⁽⁴⁵⁾ And the son of Shammai *was* Maon: and Maon *was* the father of Beth-zur. ⁽⁴⁶⁾ And Ephah, Caleb's concubine, bare Haran, and Moza, and Gazez: and Haran begat Gazez. ⁽⁴⁷⁾ And the sons of Jahdai; Regem, and Jotham, and Gesham, and Pelet, and Ephah, and Shaaph. ⁽⁴⁸⁾ Maachah, Caleb's concubine, bare Sheber, and Tirhanah. ⁽⁴⁹⁾ She bare also Shaaph the father of Madmannah, Sheva the father of Machbenah, and the father of Gibea: and the daughter of Caleb *was* ᵃAchsa.

⁽⁵⁰⁾ These were the sons of Caleb the son of Hur, the firstborn of Ephratah; Shobal the father of Kirjath-jearim,

1 Josh. 15. 17.

---

Caleb is called "father of Hebron," because it had the chief part in colonising that old Canaanite city.

⁽⁴³⁾ **Korah.**—Elsewhere the name of a subdivision of the Kohathite Levites; in chap. i. 35 it was a tribe of Edomites. In this place, therefore, it may be a clan of Hebronites.

**Tappuah.**—A town in the Shephelah (Josh. xv. 34, xvi. 8).

**Rekem.**—A Benjamite city (Josh. xviii. 27); in chap. vii. 16, a Machirite chieftain or clan.

**Shema.**—Occurs several times in the chronicle. In chaps. v. 8 and viii. 13 it appears to be the name of a clan; in chap. xi. 44 and Neh. viii. 4 a person is meant.

⁽⁴⁴⁾ **Jorkoam.**—Occurs nowhere else in the Old Testament. The LXX. (Alex.) has Ἰεκλάν, Jeklan. Probably, therefore, the correct reading is Jokdeam. For the change of Hebrew *d* to Greek *l* see 1 Kings v. 11, where Hebrew *Darda* is represented by Δαρωλά.) Jokdeam was a town in the hill-country of Judah (Josh. xv. 56). The chief or clan Raham is here called its father or founder.

**Rekem.**—The LXX. (Alex.) again has Jeklan (Jokdeam), which is as likely to be right as Rekem.

**Shammai.**—See verse 28.

⁽⁴⁵⁾ **Maon . . . Beth-zur.** — Towns in the hill-country of Judah (Josh. xv. 55, 58). Maon, now *Main*, south of Hebron. Beth-zur (2 Chron. xi. 7), now *Beit-sûr*. In Judges x. 12 Midianites, not Maonites, is the better reading.

II.—Verses 46—49: The sons of Ephah and Maachah, two concubines of Caleb.

⁽⁴⁶⁾ **Ephah, Caleb's concubine . . .**—These sons of concubines appear to represent mixed populations or tribal groups considered to be of less pure descent than the chief houses of Caleb. The same title of inferiority might cover a relation of dependence, something like that of the clients of the great Roman houses. The name Ephah occurred in chap. i. 33 as a tribe of the Midianites. It is likely, therefore, that we have before us a record of the admixture of a Midianite element with the southern Judeans.

**Haran.**—Abraham's brother (Gen. xi. 26); a place in Mesopotamia where Abraham settled (Gen. xi. 31). It is the Assyrian *harranu* (high-road). The Midianites claimed descent from Abraham (chap. i. 33), this name therefore might well be borne by a semi-Midianite clan.

**Moza.**—Occurs in Josh. xviii. 26 as a town in Benjamin.

**Haran begat Gazez.**—Comp. verse 24, Note. Gazez was probably a branch of the clan Haran. The LXX. (Vat.) omits the clause.

⁽⁴⁷⁾ **The sons of Jahdai.** — Heb., *Yohdai*, or *Yehdai*. The connection of these tribal groups with the foregoing is not clear; but from verse 46 it appears that they were Calebites with a foreign admixture. It is curious to find the Midianite name Ephah recurring among them.

⁽⁴⁸⁾ **Maachah, Caleb's concubine, bare . . .**—The Heb. is peculiar, "Caleb's concubine Maachah—he bare Sheber," &c. There is another reading, "she bare." Maachah was a well-known Syrian state (Deut. iii. 14). (Comp. 2 Sam. iii. 3; chaps. xi. 43, xix. 6, 7; and 2 Kings xxv. 23.) These Calebites, it would seem, were of partly Aramean origin. The masculine verb "he bare" is intelligible if Maachah means not a woman, but a race. (Comp. chap. xix. 15, "Aram hath fled" = the Syrians have fled; 16, "Aram saw," &c.)

⁽⁴⁹⁾ **Madmannah.**— A town of southern Judah, mentioned along with Ziklag in Josh. xv. 31. The Shaaf who settled here are different from those mentioned in verse 47.

**Machbenah,** an unknown place in Judah, and Gibeah in the hill-country (Josh. xv. 57) were settlements of the mixed Calebites called Sheva.

**The daughter of Caleb was Achsa.**—In Josh. xv. 13—19 the father of Achsah is called Caleb son of Jephunneh. This Caleb son of Jephunneh is associated with Joshua in the Pentateuch (Num. xii. 6, 8), and took a prominent part in the conquest of Canaan.

As he represents Judah (Num. xii. 6; comp. Judg. i. 10—12), it is reasonable to see in Caleb son of Jephunneh the chief of the tribal division of Hezron-Caleb in the time of Joshua.

Already in these curious lists we have met with special memorials of remarkable members of clans (comp. verses 6, 7, and 20), and we may see in the brief clause "and Achsah, daughter of Caleb" a similar notice that this famous person was a Calebite.

III.—Verses 50—55: A third register of Calebite clans and settlements.

⁽⁵⁰⁾ **The sons of Caleb the son of Hur, the firstborn of Ephratah.**—See verses 19, 20 and Notes. The statement "These were the sons of Caleb" should be connected with verse 49, as a subscription or concluding remark to the list, verses 42—49. (Comp. verse 33.) A fresh start is then made with "the sons (so the LXX.) of Hur, firstborn of Ephratah," reverting to the Caleb of verse 19 *seq.*, just as verse 34 returns to Jerahmeel in the Sheshanite branch.

**Shobal the father of Kirjath-jearim.**—Shobal is named at chap. iv. 1 as a chief clan or sub-tribe of Judah, along with Hur.

**Kirjath-jearim.**—"City of woods," one of the four cities of the Gibeonites (Josh. ix. 17), also called Kirjath-Baal and Baalah (Josh. xv. 9, 60), in the hill-country of Judah.

*The Posterity of*  I. CHRONICLES, III.  *Caleb the Son of Hur.*

⁽⁵¹⁾ Salma the father of Beth-lehem, Hareph the father of Beth-gader. ⁽⁵²⁾ And Shobal the father of Kirjath-jearim had sons; ¹Haroeh, *and* ²half of the Manahethites. ⁽⁵³⁾ And the families of Kirjath-jearim; the Ithrites, and the Puhites, and the Shumathites, and the Mishraites; of them came the Zareathites, and the Eshtaulites. ⁽⁵⁴⁾ The sons of Salma; Beth-lehem, and the Netophathites, ³Ataroth, the house of Joab, and half of the Manahethites, the Zorites. ⁽⁵⁵⁾ And the families of the scribes which dwelt at Jabez; the Tirathites, the Shimeathites, ʌnd Suchathites. These *are* the ᵃKenites that came of Hemath, the father of the house of ᵇRechab.

CHAPTER III.—⁽¹⁾ Now these were the sons of David, which were born unto him in Hebron; the firstborn ᶜAmnon,

¹ Or, *Reaiah*, ch. 4. 2.
² Or, *half of the Menuchites*, or, *Hatsi-hammenuchoth*.
³ Or, *Atarites*, or, *crowns of the house of Joab.*

B.C cir. 1471, &c.

a Judg. 1. 16.
b Jer. 35. 2.
c 2 Sam. 3. 2.

---

⁽⁵¹⁾ **Salma the father of Beth-lehem.**—See verse 11, where *Salma* may be the father-house (clan) of which Boaz was a member. The present Salma, however, is a Calebite, whereas the Salma of verse 11 is a Ramite.

**Beth-gader** (*géder*).—Josh. xii. 13, Geder; Josh. xv. 36, Gederah: or perhaps Gedor (Josh. xv. 58).

⁽⁵²⁾ **Haroeh, and half of the Manahethites.**—Haroeh is probably a relic of Jehoraah (LXX., 'Ἀραδ)=Reaiah (see chap. iv 2) and perhaps *hatsi-hammenuhoth* should be altered to *hatsi-hammanahti* (see verse 54), which would give the sense of the Authorised Version. As the Hebrew stands, the Vulg. is a literal rendering of it: *qui videbat dimidium requietionum* (!). The Manahathites were the people of Manahath (chap. viii. 6), a town near the frontier of Dan and Judah (verse 54).

⁽⁵³⁾ This verse is really a continuation of the last, and a comma would be better than a full stop after the word Manahathites. The "families" (clans or groups of families, *mishpehôth*) dwelling in the canton of Kirjath-jearim, viz., the Ithrites, Puhites (Heb., *Puthites*), &c., were also sons of Shobâl. Two of David's heroes, Ira and Gareb (chap. xi. 40), were Ithrites. The three other clans are nowhere else mentioned.

**Of them came the Zareathites, and the Eshtaulites.**—Rather, *from these went forth the Zorathites,* &c. The men of Zorah and Eshtaôl were subdivisions of the clans of Kirjath-jearim. Zorah (Judges xiii. 2), a Danite town, the home of Samson, now *Sura*. Eshtaôl, also a Danite town, near Zorah (Judges xvi. 31, xviii. 11, 12), the present *Um-Eshteiyeh*. Both were on the western border of Judah, a few miles west of Kirjath-jearim.

⁽⁵⁴⁾ **The sons of Salma; Beth-lehem.**—In verse 51 Salma is called "father of Bethlehem," and according to verse 50, Salma is a son of Hur and a grandson of Ephratah, *i.e.*, Beth-lehem (see verse 19, Note). The recognition of the ethnographical and geographical significance of these expressions at once removes all difficulty. Salma was the principal clan established in Bethlehem-Ephratah; branches of which were settled at Netophah, a neighbouring township (chap. ix. 16; 2 Sam. xxiii. 28, 29), important after the return (Ezra ii. 22; Neh. vii. 26).

**Ataroth, the house of Joab.**—Rather, *Atroth-beth-Joab* (comp. Abel-beth-Maáchah); an unknown town, whose name means "ramparts of the house of Joab," *i.e.*, "Joab's castle," perhaps a strong city where Joab's family was settled. (See verse 26.)

**Half of the Manahethites** were sons of Salma, the other half sons of Shobal (verse 52).

**The Zorites.**—A by-form of Zorathites (verse 53). The word really belongs to the next verse, as the sons of Salma are arranged in pairs.

⁽⁵⁵⁾ **The families** (*mishpehôth*=clans) **of the scribes which dwelt at Jabez.**—Among the clans calling themselves sons of Salma were three groups of Sopherim (Authorised version, "scribes") settled at Jabez (Heb., *Ia'bêç*), a town of northern Judah, near to Zorah. (See chap. iv. 9, Note.) The three clans were known as those of Tir'ah, Shimeah, and Suchah. The Vulg. treats these names as appellatives, and renders *canentes atque resonantes et in tabernaculis commorantes,* that is, "singing and resounding, and dwelling in tents." This translation is assumed to be due to Jerome's Rabbinical teachers, and is justified by reference to the words *terû'āh*, "trumpet-blare;" *shim'āh*, "report;" or the Aramaic *Shema'tâ* "legal tradition" and *sûkāh* (= *sukkah*), "a booth." Hence the conclusion has been drawn that the Sopherim of Jabez were, in fact, ministers of religion, discharging functions precisely like those of the Levites. So Wellhausen, who refers to Jer. xxxv. 19, and the title of Ps. lxx. in the LXX., and to one or two late fragmentary notices of the Rechabites. On the face of it the supposition is unlikely; nor does it derive any real support from the Kenite origin of these Sopherim, for it is a mere fancy that the house of Jethro, the Kenite priest of Midian, became temple-ministers in Israel. Besides, the etymologies of the names are hardly cogent; and if we try to extract history from etymology here, we might as well do so in the case of the clans of Kirjath-jearim (verse 53), and make the Ithrites a guild of ropers (*yether*, "cord, bowstring"), the Puthites hinge-makers (*pôthôth*—1 Kings i. 50— "hinges"), and the Shumathithes garlic-eaters (*shûm*, "garlic," Num. xi. 5). The Vulg. often makes the blunder of translating proper names. (See verses 52, 54).

**These are the Kenites that came of Hemath** (Heb., *Hammath*), **the father of the house of (Beth-) Rechab.**—The three clans of Sopherim were originally Kenites, and traced their descent from Hammath, the traditional founder of the Rechabite stock. When, or under what circumstances these Rechabite Kenites amalgamated with the Calebite clan of Salma is unknown; but comp. Judges i. 11—16.

### III.

Chap. iii. resumes the genealogy of the Hezronite house of Ram, suspended at chap. ii. 17. (1) The nine sons of David (verses 1—9). (2) The Davidic dynasty from Solomon to Zedekiah (10—16). (3) The line of Jechoniah-Jehoiachin,. continued apparently to the ninth generation (17—24).

I.—**The sons of David.**—This section is parallel to 2 Sam. iii. 2—5 (comp. verses 1—4) and 2 Sam. v. 14 —16 (verses 5—9), with which comp. 1 Chron. xiv. 3—7.

*The Sons of David*  I. CHRONICLES, III.  *Born in Hebron and Jerusalem.*

of Ahinoam the *a* Jezreelitess; the second ¹Daniel, of Abigail the Carmelitess: ⁽²⁾ the third, Absalom the son of Maachah the daughter of Talmai king of Geshur: the fourth, Adonijah the son of Haggith: ⁽³⁾ the fifth, Shephatiah of Abital: the sixth, Ithream by *b* Eglah his wife.

⁽⁴⁾ *These* six were born unto him in Hebron; and there he reigned seven years and six months: and in Jerusalem he reigned thirty and three years. ⁽⁵⁾ *c* And these were born unto him in Jerusalem; ² Shimea, and Shobab, and Nathan, and Solomon, four, of ³Bath-shua the daughter of ⁴Ammiel: ⁽⁶⁾ Ibhar also, and ⁵Elishama, and Eliphelet, ⁽⁷⁾ and Nogah, and Nepheg, and Japhia, ⁽⁸⁾ and Elishama, and ⁶Eliada, and Eliphelet, nine. ⁽⁹⁾ *These were* all the sons of David, beside the sons of the concubines, and *d* Tamar their sister.

*a* Jos. 15. 56.
¹ Or, *Chileab*, 2 Sam. 3. 3.
*b* 2 Sam. 3. 5.
*c* 2 Sam. 5. 14.
² Or, *Shammua*, 2 Sam. 5. 14.
³ Or, *Bathsheba*, 2 Sam. 11. 3.
⁴ Or, *Eliam*, 2 Sam. 11. 3.
⁵ Or, *Elishua*, 2 Sam. 5. 15.
⁶ Or, *Beeliada*, ch. 14. 7.
*d* 2 Sam. 13. 1.

---

(1—4) **The six sons born in Hebron.** The sons and mothers agree with those of the parallel passage in Sam., with the one exception of the second son, who is here called Daniel, but in Samuel, Chileab. The LXX. (2 Sam. iii. 3) has Δαλουία, which may represent Heb. *Delaiah* (*Iah hath freed*), though in our verse 24 that name is spelt Δαλααία, or Δαλαία. In the present passage the Vatican LXX. has Δαμνιήλ, the Alex. Δαλουία. Perhaps Daniel is a corruption of Delaiah, as this name recurs in the line of David. Chileab may have had a second name (comp. Uzziah-Azariah, Mattaniah-Zedekiah), especially as Chileab appears to be a nickname, meaning "dog." (Comp. the Latin Canidius, Caninius, as a family name.)

(1) **Amnon.**—For his story see 2 Sam. xiii.
**Of Ahinoam.**—Literally, *to Ahin*. (1 Sam xxv. 43).
**The second Daniel of Abigail the Carmelitess.**—Better, *A second, Daniel, to Abigail*, &c. Sam. adds, "wife of Nabal the Carmelite." (See 1 Sam. xxv. for her story.)

(2) **Absalom.**—David's favourite and rebellious son (2 Sam. xv.—xix.). The common Heb. text has "to Absalom;" but a number of MSS. and all the old versions read Absalom. Rabbi D. Kimchi gives the characteristic explanation that L-ABSHALOM alludes to LO-ABSHALOM, "not Absalom"—that is, not a "father of peace," but a rebel.
**Maachah . . . Geshur.**—See chap. ii. 23.
**Adonijah the son of Haggith.**—Who would have succeeded his father, and was put to death by Solomon (1 Kings i., ii. 19—25).

(3) **Eglah** (*heifer*) **his wife.**—Eglah is not marked out as principal wife of David. The expression "his wife" is added simply to balance the clause, to make up for the absence of details respecting her connexions, such as are given in the case of some of the other wives. Jewish expositors have groundlessly identified Eglah with Michal, daughter of Saul (1 Sam. xviii. 20).

(4) **These six were born unto him in Hebron.**—Literally, *Six were born*. 2 Sam. iii. 5: "These were born."
**And there he reigned seven years.**—This notice of the time David reigned first in Hebron, the Judean capital, and then in Jerusalem over all Israel, is not read in the parallel section of Samuel; but see 2 Sam. ii. 11, v. 5 for the same statements.

(5—8) **The thirteen sons born in Jerusalem.** See 2 Sam. v. 14—16, and chap. xiv. 4—7, where this list is repeated with some variations (verse 5). The four sons of Bath-sheba, called here Bath-shua, a weakened form, if not, a copyist's error. By a similar change the Elishama of verse 6 appears in Samuel as Elishua.

Shimea ("report") was a son of Jesse (chap. ii. 13). Perhaps, therefore, Shammua ("famous") is correct here, as in Samuel.
**Ammiel** and Eliam are transposed forms of the same name, meaning "El is a tribesman" ('*am*= *gens*, *el* = *deus*). (Comp. Ahaziah and Jehoahaz, Nethaniah and Jehonathan, and many similar transpositions.) So in Gr. Theodoros and Dorotheos, Philotheos and Theophilos exist side by side.

(6) **Ibhar.**—"He" (*i.e.*, God) "chooseth."
**Elishama.**—Spelt Elishua in both of the parallel passsages. (See Note on verse 5.) The recurrence of Elishama ("God heareth") in verse 8 is no argument against the name here.
**Eliphelet** ("God is deliverance") also occurs twice, and David may have chosen to give names so expressive of his own peculiar faith and trust to the sons of different wives. (See Ps. xviii. 2, 6.) This Eliphelet (called Elphalet—Heb., *Elpèlet*, chap. xiv. 5; a by-form, as Abram is of Abiram, or Absalom of Abishalom, or Abshai of Abishai) is omitted in Samuel. So also is Nogah (*brightness*, *i.e.*, of the Divine Presence, Ps. xviii. 13—a hymn which is certainly David's). (Comp. *Japhia*, "the Shining One.") *Nepheg* means "shoot, scion."

(8) **Eliada.**—("God knoweth") The Beeliada ("Lord knoweth") of chap. xiv. 7 is probably more ancient, though Samuel also has Eliada. God was of old called Baal as well as El; and the former title was only discarded because it tended to foster a confusion between the degrading cultus of the Canaanite Baals, and the true religion of Israel. So it came to pass in later times that men were unwilling to write or speak the very name of Baal, and in names compounded therewith they substituted either El or Iah as here; or the word *bosheth* (shame) as in Ishbosheth instead of Eshbaal, Jerubbesheth instead of Jerubbaal.

(9) **Sons of the concubines.**—David's concubines (*pilagshim*, παλλακαί) are mentioned several times in Samuel (*e.g.*, 2 Sam. xii. 11), but their sons here only. However repugnant to modern ideas, it was and is part of the state of an Oriental potentate to possess a harem of many wives.
**And Tamar** (was) **their sister.**—Not the only one, but the sister whose unhappy fate had made her famous (2 Sam. xiii.).

A comparison of the above lists of David's sons with the parallels in Sam. makes it improbable that they were drawn from that source; for (1) the Hebrew text of the chronicle appears, in this instance, to be quite as original as that of Samuel; (2) Some of the names differ, without our being able to pronounce in favour of one or the other text; (3) The form of the lists is different, especially that of the second. The chronicler alone gives the number of the four and nine sons, assigning the former

*The Sons of Solomon*     I. CHRONICLES, III.     *and of Jeconiah*

(10) And Solomon's son was ᵃRehoboam, ¹Abia his son, Asa his son, Jehoshaphat his son, (11) Joram his son, ²Ahaziah his son, Joash his son, (12) Amaziah his son, ³Azariah his son, Jotham his son, (13) Ahaz his son, Hezekiah his son, Manasseh his son, (14) Amon his son, Josiah his son. (15) And the sons of Josiah were, the firstborn ⁴Johanan, the second ⁵Jehoiakim, the third ⁶Zedekiah, the fourth Shallum. (16) And the sons of ᵇJehoiakim : ⁷Jeconiah his son, Zedekiah ᶜhis son.

(17) And the sons of Jeconiah ; Assir, ⁸ Salathiel ᵈhis son, (18) Malchiram also, and Pedaiah, and Shenazar, Jecamiah,

*a* 1 Kin. 11. 43 & 15. 6.
1 Or, *Abijam*, 1 Kin. 15. 1.
2 Or, *Azariah*, 2 Chr. 22. 6 & 21. 17.
3 Or, *Uzziah*, 2 Kin. 15. 30.
4 Or, *Jehoahaz*, 2 Kings 23. 30.
5 Or, *Eliakim*, 2 Kings 23. 34.
6 Or, *Mattaniah*, 2 Kings 24. 17.
*b* Matt. 1. 11.
7 Or, *Jehoiachin*, 2 Kings 24. 6 ; or, *Coniah*, Jer. 22. 24.

*c* 2 Kings 24. 17, being his uncle.     8 Heb., *Shealtiel*.     *d* Matt. 1. 2.

---

to "Bathshua the daughter of Ammiel," and arranging the latter in three triads. Verse 9 also is wanting in Samuel.

II.—The kings of the house of David, as otherwise known from the books of Kings (verses 10—16).

(10) **Rehoboam.**—So LXX. Ροβοάμ. Heb., *Rĕhab-'ām* ("the Kinsman," *i.e.*, God hath enlarged).
**Abia.**—LXX., Αβιά ; Heb., *Abiyāh* (*Iah is father*), of which *Abijam* (*Abíyām*) is a *mimmated* form.
**Asa.**—*Healer*.
**Jehoshaphat.**—*Iahweh judgeth*.
(11) **Joram**— Jehoram. *Iahweh is high*.
**Ahaziah.**—*Iah holdeth* (Luke i. 54, ἀντελάβετο, "he hath holpen").
**Joash.**—(?) *Iahweh is a hero.* Cf. *Ashbel* = "man of Bel," and Exod. xv. 3.
(12) **Amaziah.**—*Iah is strong.*
**Azariah.**—*Iah helpeth.*
**Jotham.**—*Iahweh is perfect.*
(13) **Ahaz.**—Abbreviation of Jehoahaz, which = Ahaziah.
**Hezekiah.**—Heb., *Hizkiyāhû*, "my strength is Iahu."
**Manasseh** (?) Perhaps of Egyptian origin.
(14) **Amon.**—Probably the Egyptian sun-god Amen or Amun.
**Josiah.**—*Iah comforteth.*
In this line of fifteen successive monarchs, the usurper Athaliah is omitted between Ahaziah and Joash (verse 11).

(15) **And the sons of Josiah.**—The regular succession by primogeniture ceases with Josiah.
The **firstborn Johanan** (*Iahweh bestowed*) never ascended the throne of his fathers. He may have died early. He is not to be identified with Jehoahaz, who was two years younger than Jehoiakim (2 Kings xxiii. 31, 36), and therefore could not have been the *firstborn* of Josiah.
The **second Jehoiakim, the third Zedekiah, the fourth Shallum.**—The order of succession to the throne after Josiah was this :—First, Shallum (= Jehoahaz, 2 Kings xxiii. 30; comp. Jer. xxii. 11); then Jehoiakim (= Eliakim, 2 Kings xxiii. 34 ; Jer. xxii. 18) ; then Jeconiah, son of Jehoiakim (= Jehoiachin, Jer. xxii. 24) ; and, lastly, Zedekiah (= Mattaniah, 2 Kings xxiv. 17).
The **third Zedekiah.**—Zedekiah was much younger than Shallum. Shallum was twenty-three when he came to the throne, which he occupied eleven years. Zedekiah succeeded him at the age of twenty-one (2 Kings xxiii. 31, xxiv. 18). The order of verse 15 is not wholly determined by seniority any more than by the actual succession. If age were considered, the order would be Jehoiakim, Shallum, Zedekiah ; if the actual succession, it would be, Shallum, Jehoiakim, Zedekiah. The order of the text may have been influenced by the two considerations—(1) That Jehoiakim and Zedekiah each enjoyed a reign of eleven years, while Shallum reigned only three months ; (2) That Shallum and Zedekiah were full brothers, both being sons of Hamutal, whereas Jehoiakim was born of another of Josiah's wives, viz., Zebudah.

(16) **Jeconiah** (*Iah establish !*)= Jehoiachin (*Iahweh establisheth*) = Coniah (Jer. xxii. 24, 28—an abbreviation of Jeconiah), was carried captive to Babylon by Nebuchadnezzar (1 Kings xxiv. 15), and Zedekiah his father's brother, became king in his stead. Hence the supposition that "Zedekiah his son" means "Zedekiah his successor" on the throne. (Comp. margin.) But (1) the phrase "his son" has its natural sense throughout the preceding list ; and (2) there really is nothing against the apparent statement of the text that Jeconiah the king had a son named Zedekiah, after his great-uncle. As, like Johanan (verse 15), he did not come to the throne, this younger Zedekiah is not mentioned elsewhere. (See verse 17, Note.)

III.—The posterity of Jeconiah after the exile (verses 17—24). This section is peculiar to the chronicle.

(17) **Assir.** — This word means prisoner, captive ; literally, *bondman*. It so occurs in Isa. x. 2, xxiv. 22. Accordingly the verse may be rendered, "And the sons of Jeconiah when captive—Shealtiel (was) his son." This translation (1) accords with the Masoretic punctuation, which connects the term *assir* with Jeconiah ; and (2) accounts for the double reference to the offspring of Jeconiah, first in verse 16, "Zedekiah his son," and then again here. Zedekiah is thus separated from the sons born to Jeconiah in captivity. The strongest apparent objection against such a rendering is that the expression "the sons of Jeconiah the captive" would require the definite article to be prefixed to the word *assir*. No doubt it would ; but then "the sons of Jeconiah the captive" is not what the chronicler intended to say. He has said what he meant—viz., "the sons of Jeconiah *when in captivity*," or "*as a captive*." The Talmudic treatise, *Sanhedrin*, gives "Assir his son ;" but another, the *Seder Olam*, does not mention Assir, who is likewise wanting in the genealogy of our Lord (Matt. i. 12 ; see the Notes there).
**Salathiel.**—The form in the LXX., Σαλαθιήλ ; and Matt. i. 12, Heb., *Shealti-el* ("request of God ") ; Hag. i. 12, Shalti-el.

(18) **Malchiram also, and Pedaiah.**—According to our present Hebrew text these six persons, arranged as two trios, are sons of Jeconiah, and brothers of Shealtiel.
**Shenazar**—Heb., *Shen'azzar* ; LXX., Σανεσάρ—is a compound Babylonian name, like Belteshazzar (Dan. i. 7), of which the last part means "protect," and the first is, perhaps, "Sin" (comp. Σαναχάριβος), the moon-

228

*The Posterity of Jeconiah*      I. CHRONICLES, III.      *after the Exile.*

Hoshama, and Nedabiah. [19] And the sons of Pedaiah were, Zerubbabel, and Shimei: and the sons of Zerubbabel; Meshullam, and Hananiah, and Shelomith their sister: [20] and Hashubah, and Ohel, and Berechiah, and Hasadiah, Jushab-hesed, five. [21] And the sons of Hananiah; Pelatiah, and Jesaiah: the sons of Rephaiah, the sons of Arnan, the sons of Obadiah, the sons of Shechaniah. [22] And the sons of Shechaniah; Shemaiah: and the sons of Shemaiah; Hattush, and Igeal, and Bariah, and Neariah, and Shaphat, six. [23] And the sons of Neariah; Elioenai, and [1]Hezekiah, and Azrikam, three. [24] And the sons of Elioenai were, Hodaiah, and Eliashib, and Pelaiah, and Akkub, and Johanan, and Dalaiah, and Anani, seven.

[1] Heb., *Hizkijahu.*

---

god. Such a name as "Sin protect" may well have been given to this Jewish prince at the court of Babylon, just as Daniel and his three companions received idolatrous designations of the same sort from Nebuchadnezzar. This fact seems to support our rendering of the word *Assir* (verse 17).

**Hoshama.**—A contraction of Jehoshama (*Iahweh hath heard*), like Coniah for Jeconiah.

[19] **And the sons of Pedaiah were, Zerubbabel, and Shimei.**—Zerubbabel, the famous prince who, with Joshua the high priest, led the first colony of restored exiles from Babylon to Canaan, under the edict of Cyrus (B.C. cir. 536). Zerubbabel (LXX., Ζοροβάβελ), means *born at Babel.* His father is appropriately named Pedaiah (*Iah hath redeemed*). Zerubbabel is called son of Shealtiel (Hag. i. 1, &c.; Ezra iii. 2, v. 2—part of the chronicle it should be remembered; Matt. i. 12). Hence some expositors, ancient and modern, have assumed that the six persons named in verse 18, including Pedaiah, the father of Zerubbabel, were sons, not brothers of Salathiel (Shealtiel). In this way they bring Zerubbabel into the direct line of descent from Shealtiel. But our Hebrew text, though peculiar, can hardly mean this. It makes Zerubbabel the son of Pedaiah, and nephew of Shealtiel. If Zerubbabel, for reasons unknown, became adopted son and heir of Shealtiel, his uncle, the seemingly discordant statements of the different passages before us are all reconciled; while that of our text is the more exact.

**And the sons of Zerubbabel.**—The Hebrew received text has "*and the son.*" This is not to be altered, although some MSS. have the plural. (Comp. verses 21 and 23.) This use of the singular is characteristic of the present genealogical fragment (see verses 17 and 18), "And the sons of Jeconiah captive—Salathiel his son, and Malchiram," &c.

**Meshullam, and Hananiah, and Shelomith their sister.**—This seems to mean that the three were the offspring of one wife.

[20] These five sons form a second group of Zerubbabel's children, probably by another wife. The *v* of union seems to have fallen out before the last name, Jushab-hesed.

The names of the last kings (Shallum, *recompense;* Zedekiah, *Iah is righteousness*) were parables of the judgment that should come to pass in Judah. (Comp. Isa. x. 22: "A consumption is doomed, overflowing with righteousness.") Those of the kindred and sons of Zerubbabel indicate the religious hopefulness of his people at the dawn of the restoration. His father is Pedaiah (*Iah redeemeth*) (see Isa. li. 11); his son Meshullam (*devoted to God*) recalls Isa. xlii. 19, where the pious remnant of Israel is so designated. The name Ohel, "tent," is probably an abbreviation of Oholiah, or Oholiab, and refers to the sacred dwelling of Jehovah, which was for ages a tent. (See Isa. xxxiii. 20; Ezek. xxxvii. 27.)

**Jushab-hesed** (*mercy will be restored*) is a prophecy of faith in Him who in wrath remembereth mercy (Hab. iii. 2).

[21] **And the sons of Hananiah; Pelatiah, and Jesaiah.**—Heb., *son;* but some MSS. and all the versions read *sons.* Pelatiah means *Iah is deliverance.* Jesaiah is the same name as Isaiah, meaning *Iah is salvation.*

**The sons of Rephaiah.**—The ancient versions represent here an important various reading. The LXX. have rendered the whole verse thus: "And sons of Anania; Phalettia, and Jesias his son, Raphal his son, Orna his son, Abdia his son (Sechenias his son.)" The Syriac reads: "Sons of Hananiah: Pelatiah and Ushaiah. Arphaia his son, Arnun his son, Ubia his son —viz., Ushaia's; and his son, viz., Shechaniah's Shemaiah," &c. The difference between "sons" and "his son" in Hebrew writing is simply that between *y* and *w.* (See Note on chap. i.)

This various reading presents a form of genealogy like that which prevails in verses 10—16, and occurs also in verse 17, at the beginning of the present section. But it is probable that this reading is really an ancient correction of the Hebrew text, which, as it stands, appears to leave undefined the relation between Hananiah and the four families mentioned in this verse. The truth, however, would seem to be that the expression "the sons of Hananiah" includes not only Pelatiah and Jesaiah, but also the four families named after Rephaiah, Arnan, Obadiah, and Shechaniah (comp. chap. ii. 42, and Note). The four founders of these families were perhaps brothers of Pelatiah and Jesaiah, though not necessarily so; for these families may have been subdivisions of those of Pelatiah and Jesaiah.

**Rephaiah.**—*Iah healeth* (Isa. xxx. 26; Exod. xv. 26). See Note on verse 20.

[22] **The sons of Shechaniah; Shemaiah.**—See Note on chap. i. 41.

**Hattush.**—Probably the Hattush "of the sons of David, of the sons of Shechaniah," mentioned by Ezra as one of those who went up with him from Babylon in the second return, 457 B.C. (Ezra viii. 2, 3). If we have rightly understood verse 21, Hattush is of the fourth generation after Zerubbabel (Hananiah, Shechaniah, Shemaiah, Hattush), and so might well have been a youthful companion of Ezra.

**Six.**—As the text gives only five names, one must have been omitted by an oversight.

[23] **Elioenai**—*unto Iah* (*are*) *mine eyes*, Ps. cxxiii. 1, 2—is an expansion of the same idea. (Comp. also Ps. xxv. 15.) An Elioenai went up with Ezra (Ezra viii. 4).

[24] **The sons of Elioenai . . . Hodaiah.**—These sons of Elioenai are the sixth generation from

CHAPTER IV.—<sup>(1)</sup> The sons of Judah; *Pharez, Hezron, and ¹Carmi, and Hur, and Shobal. <sup>(2)</sup> And ²Reaiah the son of Shobal begat Jahath; and Jahath begat Ahumai, and Lahad. These *are* the families of the Zorathites. <sup>(3)</sup> And these *were of* the father of Etam; Jezreel, and Ishma, and Idbash: and the name of their sister *was* Hazelelponi: <sup>(4)</sup> and Penuel the father of Gedor, and Ezer the father of Hushah. These *are* the sons of Hur, the firstborn of Ephratah, the father of Beth-lehem. <sup>(5)</sup> And ᵇAshur the father of Tekoa had two wives, Helah and Naarah. <sup>(6)</sup> And Naarah bare him Ahuzam, and Hepher, and Temeni, and Haahashtari. These *were* the sons of Naarah. <sup>(7)</sup> And the sons of Helah *were*, Zereth, and Jezoar, and Ethnan. <sup>(8)</sup> And Coz begat Anub, and Zobebah, and the families of Aharhel the son of Harum.

*a* Gen. 38. 29 & 46. 12.

1 Or, *Chelubai*, ch. 2. 9; or, *Caleb*, ch. 2. 18.

2 Or, *Haroeh*, ch. 2. 52.

*b* ch. 2. 24.

---

Zerubbabel (536—515 B.C.), that is to say, they were living about 345 B.C., under Artaxerxes Ochus. If the reading of the LXX. in verse 21 be correct, their date is four generations later, or about 225 B.C. The result is to bring down the date of the chronicle a century lower than the best critics approve. (See Introduction.)

## IV.

Chap. iv. comprises (1) a compilation of fragmentary notices relating to the clans of Judah, their settlements and handicrafts, at an epoch which is not determined: this section serves at once as a supplement to the account of Judah already given in chaps. ii. and iii., and as a first instalment of the similar survey of the other tribes which follows (chap. iv. 24—27); (2) similar notices relating to the tribe of Simeon (24—38).

<sup>(1)</sup> **The sons of Judah.**—Pharez only of these five was literally a *son* of Judah, chap. ii. 3, 4. We have, however, seen that all these names, with the possible exception of Carmi, represent great tribal divisions or clans; and as such they are called sons of Judah. For Carmi it is proposed to read the more famous name of Chelubai (chap. ii. 9). This would give a line of direct descendants from Judah to the fifth generation, according to the genealogical presentation of chap. ii. 4, 9, 18, 19. But the result thus obtained is of no special value. It has no bearing on the remainder of the section. Moreover, Carmi is mentioned (chap. ii. 7) among the great Judean houses, and might have been prominent in numbers and influence at the unknown period when the original of the present list was drafted.

(2—4) Branches and settlements of the Hurites.

<sup>(2)</sup> **Reaiah** (*or* Jehoraah) **the son of Shobal . . .**—See chap. ii. 52, which also calls Shobal "father of Kirjath-jearim." Chap. ii. 53 adds that the Zorathites (Authorised Version, *Zareathites*) came of the clans of Kirjath-jearim. The present verse supplements the data of chap. ii., by putting the clans of Zorah in immediate genealogical connection with Shobal. Their names—Ahumai and Lahad—occur nowhere else.

<sup>(3)</sup> **And these were of the father of Etam.**—Heb., *And these* (were) *the father of Etam*. Some MSS., the LXX., and the Vulg. read "and these (were) the sons of Etam;" other MSS., with the Syriac and Arabic versions, have "the sons of the father of Etam." Both variants look like evasions of a difficulty. The unusual expression "and these—Abi-Etam" may be a brief way of stating that the clans whose names are given were the dominant houses of Etam (or Abi-etam; compare Abiezer, Judg. vii. 11,

viii. 2). Etam is known from the history of Samson (Judg. xv. 8, and 2 Chron. xi. 6); Jezreel—not Ahab's capital—from Josh. xv. 56, and as the city of Ahinoam, wife of David, from chap. iii. 1. Both places were in the hill-country of Judah. The other three names are unknown.

**Their sister.**—*Their sister-town* (see chap. i. 39, 52, and Notes).

**Hazelelponi.**—Means "make shadow, O thou that regardest me!"

<sup>(4)</sup> **And Penuel the father of Gedor.**—Penuel occurs as a trans-Jordan town in Judg. viii. 8, and elsewhere. Here a Judean town or clan is meant.

**Gedor.**—See chap. ii. 51, and Note; Josh. xv. 58. Now the ruin called Jedur.

**Ezer the father of Hushah.**—Ezer occurs as a name of clans and localities, as well as of persons. (Comp. Judg. vii. 24, Abi-ezri; chap. viii. 2, Abi-ezer; and 1 Sam. iv. 1, Eben-ezer.) In chap. xii. 9 and Neh. iii. 19 it is a man's name.

**Hushah.**—The place is unknown, but several celebrated persons are called Hushathites—*e.g.*, Sibbechai, one of David's heroes, chap. xi. 29.

**These are the sons of Hur.**—A subscription to the short list of verses 2—4. Both the Shobalite clans of Zorah (verse 2) and those enumerated in verses 3—4 were sons of Hur.

**The firstborn of Ephratah.**—See chap. ii. 19 and 50.

**The father of Beth-lehem.**—At chap. ii. 51, Salma, son of Hur, is called father of Bethlehem.

FAMILIES THAT CAME OF ASH-HUR (verses 5—7).

<sup>(5)</sup> **And Ashur the father of Tekoa.**—See chap. ii. 24, and Notes. If Ashur means the Hurites, the two wives, Helah and Naarah, may designate two settlements of this great clan.

<sup>(6)</sup> **Hepher.**—A district of southern Judah, near Tappuach (Josh. xii. 17; 1 Kings iv. 10).

**Temeni** is a Gentilic name, formed from the word Têmân, "the south." This clan was called "the Southrons," and doubtless lived with the others in the south of Judah.

**Haahashtari** is another *nomen gentilicium*, meaning the Ahashtarites ("muleteers;" comp. Esth. viii. 10).

<sup>(7)</sup> The sons of Helah are unknown from other sources.

**Jezoar** should be Zohar, according to the Hebrew margin. The Heb. text has Izhar.

**Ethnan.**—*Harlot's hire* (Hos. ix. 1). There may have been a foreign element in this clan or township.

<sup>(8)</sup> **Coz begat Anub.**—Coz (*thorn*) is unknown. **Anub.**—LXX., Ἐνώβ. Comp. Anâb, (Josh. xi. 21, xv. 50), a town in the hill-country near Debir (Kirjath-sepher). The word appears to mean "grape-town"

*The Prayer of Jabez.*   I. CHRONICLES, IV.   *The Men of Rechah.*

(9) And Jabez was more honourable than his brethren: and his mother called his name ¹Jabez, saying, Because I bare him with sorrow. (10) And Jabez called on the God of Israel, saying, ²Oh that thou wouldest bless me indeed, and enlarge my coast, and that thine hand might be with me, and that thou wouldest ³keep *me* from evil, that it may not grieve me! And God granted him that which he requested. (11) And Chelub the brother of Shuah begat Mehir, which *was* the father of Eshton. (12) And Eshton begat Bethrapha, and Paseah, and Tehinnah the father of ⁴Irnahash. These *are* the men of Rechah. (13) And the sons of Kenaz; Othniel, and Seraiah: and the sons of

1 That is, *Sorrowful.*
2 Heb., *If thou wilt, &c.*
3 Heb., *do me.*
4 Or, *The city of Nahash.*

---

so that "Coz begat Anub" reminds us of Matt. vii. 16. Comp. Isa. v. 6, vii. 23.

**Zobebah.**—Heb., *ha-zobebah,* "she that goeth (or floweth) softly." Perhaps so called from a neighbouring brook. Comp. Isa. viii. 6.

**The families of Aharhel the son of Harum.**—The word Aharhel signifies "behind the rampart;" Harum, "the elevated." Perhaps Harum (ἡ ἄκρα) was the citadel of the clans of Aharhel. Notice the expression, "Coz begat the clans of Aharhel son of Harum," which is hardly intelligible if taken literally.

(9–10) **And Jabez was more honourable than his brethren.**—Jabez (Heb., *Ia'bêç*) was a town of Judah (chap. ii. 55), inhabited by certain clans of Sopherim, of the lineage of Salma son of Hur (chap. ii. 50, 54, 55). This is important, as giving a clue to the connection here, which is by no means clear upon the surface. It seems to prove that verses 8—10 are to be regarded as part of the list which begins at verse 5: we may thus fairly assume, although the chronicler does not expressly state it, that verse 8 also concerns some clans of the Hurites (or Ash-hurites). Coz is not put into genealogical connection with the other Hurite houses; but it is reasonable to suppose that at the date of the present list the name was well known among the Hurites. "And Coz" may have fallen out of the Heb. text, as the same expression follows immediately (verse 8).

(9) **More honourable than his brethren.**—Comp. what is said of Hamor son of Shechem in Gen. xxxiv. 19.

**His brethren.**—Perhaps the sons of Coz. The form of the Hebrew verb implies connection with verse 8.

**His mother called his name . . .**—Comp. Gen. xxix. 32—35, and especially Gen. xxxv. 18.

**With sorrow.**—Rather, *pain.*

(10) **Jabez called on the God of Israel.**—Comp. Jacob's vow at Bethel, Gen. xxviii. 20—22, and his altar, El-'elohē Israel, "El is the God of Israel," chap. xxxiii. 20. Some have supposed that the peculiar phrase, "God of Israel," indicates that the original Canaanite population of Jabez proselytised.

**Oh that thou wouldest bless me indeed.**—Literally, "*if indeed thou wilt bless me.*"

**My coast.**—My border or domain (*fines*).

**And that thine hand.**—Rather, *and if thine hand will be with me, and thou wilt deal without* (Heb. *away from*) *evil, that I suffer not!*—The prayer is expressed in the form of a condition, with the consequence ("then will I serve thee," comp. Gen. xxviii. 22) suppressed.

The name Jabez is twice explained; in verse 9 it is made to mean "he paineth," in verse 10 Jabez prays to be saved from pain. Comp. the frequent allusions in the book of Gen. to the meaning of the name Isaac (Yiçhâq, "he laugheth"); Gen. xvii. 17, Abraham's laughter; chap. xviii. 12, Sarah's incredulous laughter; chap. xxi. 6, Sarah's joy at the birth; chap. xxvi. 8, Isaac's own mirth. These features of likeness to the language and thought of Genesis, prove the originality and antiquity of the section.

**And God granted.**—Literally, *and God brought* (*caused to come*). Hence Jabez was "honoured above his brethren," verse 9. If the Sopherim of Jabez (chap. ii. 55) were, as their name implies, writers or men of letters, we can understand that Jabez, like Kirjath-sepher, was a place of books, and was honoured accordingly. The art of writing among the peoples of Babylonia ascends to an unknown antiquity. The oldest inscription we possess in the Phœnician character is of the ninth century B.C., and the development of that character from its Egyptian prototype must have occupied some centuries. Perhaps this very tradition concerning their founder originally emanated from the "families of the scribes which dwelt at Jabez."

(11–12) A fragment relating to the "men of Rechah," a name which occurs nowhere else, and for which Rechab appears a plausible correction. So the Vat., LXX. Ρηχάβ. Compare chap. ii. 55, where the Sopherim of Jabez are called Rechabites, and see Notes on the passage. These Rechabites united with the Salmaite branch of Hurites; and Hur was a son of Caleb, chap. ii. 19. Hence it is likely that the Chelub of verse 11 is identical with the Caleb-Chelubai of chap. ii., who represents a main division of the Hezronites. Others suppose that the epithet, "brother of Shuah" (Shuhah), is meant to obviate this identification. The other names in this short section are wholly unknown. But their form shows at once that Beth-rapha and Ir-nahash (serpent city) are towns.

**Paseah** (lame; comp. Latin Claudius as a family name) recurs Neh. iii. 6; and as the name of a clan of Nethinim, Ezra ii. 49, Neh. vii. 51. The subscription, "these are the men of Rechah" (Rechab), probably looks back as far as verse 8.

(13–15) **The sons of Kenaz**—*i.e.,* the Kenizzite element in Judah. Kenaz was the name of an Edomite clan, chap. i. 53, and of an old Canaanite race.

**Othniel.**—Judg. i. 13, one of the heroes of the conquest; Judg. iii. 9, he vanquishes Chushan-rishathaim, king of Aram-naharaim. In both passages he is called "son of Kenaz, Caleb's younger brother." The Kenizzites, who cast in their lot with the Calebites of Judah, were naturally called "younger brothers" of their new kindred.

**Seraiah** is unknown.

**The sons of Othniel, Hathath.**—Hathath means *dread,* Job vi. 21. Comp. the name Hittites, from the same root. The sons of Othniel (lion of God) would be a terror to their foes.

"**And Meonothai**" has perhaps been accidentally omitted at the end of this verse, before the same phrase in verse 14. Or the genealogist may have purposely omitted it, as implied by what follows verse 14. Meonothai is apparently a gentilic name, *i.e.,* Meon-

*The Posterity of*  I. CHRONICLES, IV.  *Othniel and Caleb.*

Othniel; ¹Hathath. ⁽¹⁴⁾ And Meonothai begat Ophrah: and Seraiah begat Joab, the father of the ²valley of ³Charashim; for they were craftsmen. ⁽¹⁵⁾ And the sons of Caleb the son of Jephunneh; Iru, Elah, and Naam: and the sons of Elah, ⁴even Kenaz. ⁽¹⁶⁾ And the sons of Jehaleleel; Ziph, and Ziphah, Tiria, and Asareel. ⁽¹⁷⁾ And the sons of Ezra *were*, Jether, and Mered, and Epher, and Jalon: and she bare Miriam, and Shammai, and Ishbah the father of Eshtemoa. ⁽¹⁸⁾ And his wife ⁵Jehudijah bare Jered the father of Gedor, and Heber the father of Socho, and Jekuthiel the father of Zanoah. And these *are* the sons of Bithiah the daughter of Pharaoh, which Mered took. ⁽¹⁹⁾ And the sons of *his* wife ⁶Hodiah the sister of Naham, the father of Keilah the Garmite, and Esh-

1 Or, *Hathath, and Meonothai, who begat, &c.*
2 Or, *inhabitants of the valley.*
3 That is, *Craftsmen.*
4 Or, *Uknaz.*
5 Or, *The Jewess.*
6 Or, *Jehudijah,* mentioned before.

---

othites. The name Maon occurs Josh. xv. 55 as a Judæan town; and Maon was the residence of the Calebite Nabal, 1 Sam. xxv. 2, 3.

**Ophrah.**—Occurs several times as the name of a town; in Jud. vii. as the city of Gideon, who belonged to Manasseh; in Josh. xviii. 23, as a place in Benjamin. The latter may be meant here, as the boundaries of the tribes varied at different epochs.

**Joab, father of the valley of Charashim.**—Charashim means workers in wood, or metal, or stone, chap. xiv. 1, 2 Chron. xxiv. 12, 1 Chron. xxii. 15. This valley of craftsmen (Val-aux-forges, as Reuss translates it) is mentioned again, Neh. xi. 35. Lod, that is Lydda-Diospolis of Roman times, was situate here; a place occupied by Benjamites after the return. In Neh. vii. 11, Ezr. ii. 6, in a list of those who returned with Zerubbabel, mention is made of some "sons of Joab." For the term *father* in this connection, comp. Gen. iv. 20, 21.

**They**—*i.e.*, the sons of Joab, were craftsmen or smiths.

⁽¹⁵⁾ **The sons of Caleb, son of Jephunneh.**—Caleb son of Jephunneh is called the Kenizzite, Josh. xiv. 6—14. He obtained "a part among the children of Judah" (Josh. xv. 13), "because that he wholly followed the Lord God of Israel" (Josh. xiv. 14). If Caleb the Kenizzite and his clan were received among the Hezronite houses of Judah, this new division of the Hezronites would henceforth be known as "the house of Caleb," 1 Sam. xxv. 3; or simply "Caleb" (= Chelubai, the Calebite). (See Notes on chap. ii. 42, 49.)

**Elah** occurred chap. i. 52, as an Edomite princedom, like Kenaz in verse 53.

**Naam** is perhaps Naamah, Josh. xv. 41, a town in the Shephelah.

**And the sons of Elah, even Kenaz.**—The Heb. is, *and the sons of Elah and Kenaz*, that is, two clans of Calebites called Elah and Kenaz. Comp. verse 13, and chaps. ii. 42, iii. 21. Some MSS., the LXX., Vulg., and Targum omit *and* before Kenaz. But the word *Elah*, with different points, might be read *elleh*, "these." It may be suggested, therefore, that we have in this last sentence the subscription to the list begun at verse 13, *'elleh bnê Qnaz*, "these are the sons of Kenaz." Others suppose a name omitted, and render: "and the sons of Elah . . . and Kenaz." Jehaleleel may have dropped out after the like-sounding Elah.

⁽¹⁶⁾ **The sons of Jehaleleel.**—Heb., *Yehallel-êl*, "he praiseth God."

**Ziph** is known, from Josh. xv. 21, 24, as one of the cities of the children of Judah, "towards the border of Edom, southwards." Perhaps, therefore, the sons of Jehallel-el also were Edomite-Kenizzites. Another Ziph, perhaps our Ziphah, is mentioned as in the hill-country, Josh. xv. 55.

**Asareel** is perhaps a dialectic form of Israel. (See chap. xxv. 2 and 14.) A foreign clan might take the name of its adopted people.

⁽¹⁷⁾ **And the sons of Ezra.**—Heb., *son*, but some MSS. have *sons* (see Note on chap. iii. 19, 21). Ezra means *help* = Ezer, verse 4.

**Jether** occurred chap. ii. 32, as a Jerahmeelite.

**Epher** recurs chap. v. 24, as a Manassite name.

**Jalon** and **Mered** occur nowhere else.

**And she bare.**—Literally, *conceived*. Who bare the three sons, whose names follow, is not clear from the preceding statement, which includes none but male appellations. The LXX. reads, "And Jether bare Maron (Miriam)," &c., and the Syriac and Arabic omit verses 17, 18. This confirms our suspicion that the text is faulty.

⁽¹⁸⁾ **And his wife Jehudijah** [Margin is right, *the Jewess*] **bare Jered.**—It is obvious that a contrast with the sons of some non-Jewish wife is intended, and these latter ought already to have been mentioned. Clearly, therefore, the sentence "And these are the sons of Bithiah, the daughter of Pharaoh, which Mered took"—a sentence which is meaningless in its present position—must be restored to its original place after the first statement of verse 17. We thus get the sense: "And the sons of Ezra were Jepher and Mered, and Epher and Jalon. And these [the following] are the sons of Bithiah, daughter of Pharaoh, whom Mered took [to wife]; she conceived Miriam and Shammai and Ishbah the father of Eshtemoa. And his [Mered's] wife the Jewess bare Jered . . . Zanoah." Thus the house of Mered son of Ezra bifurcates into a purely Judæan and a mixed Egyptian group of families. Eshtemoa (verse 17) lay south of Hebron, in the hill country (Josh. xv. 50).

**Gedor.**—See verse 4, where Penuel is called father of Gedor. The two lists may, and probably do, refer to different epochs.

**Socho.**—Josh. xv. 35; in the Shephelah, south-west of Jerusalem.

**Zanoah.**—Two Judæan towns were so named, one in the Shephelah, the other in the highlands (Josh. xv. 34, 56).

**Jekuthiel** occurs here only; but comp. Joktheel (Josh. xv. 38), a town in the Shephelah.

**Bithiah the daughter of Pharaoh.**—Bithiah is apparently Hebrew, "daughter of Iah," that is, a convert to the religion of Israel. It may be a Hebraized form of Bent-Aah, daughter of the Moon, or some like native name. Daughter of Pharaoh, if the nomenclature be tribal, need only mean an Egyptian clan which amalgamated with that of Mered. On the other hand, comp. 2 Chron. viii. 11 and 1 Kings ix. 24, where the phrase is used in its literal sense.

⁽¹⁹⁾ **And the sons of his wife Hodiah.**—The existing Hebrew text says, *And the sons of Hodiah's*

*The Posterity*  I. CHRONICLES, IV.  *of Shelah.*

temoa the Maachathite. (20) And the sons of Shimon *were*, Amnon, and Rinnah, Ben-hanan, and Tilon. And the sons of Ishi *were*, Zoheth, and Ben-zoheth. (21) The sons of Shelah *a* the son of Judah *were*, Er the father of Lecah, and Laadah the father of Mareshah, and the families of the house of them that wrought fine linen, of the house of Ashbea, (22) and Jokim, and the men of Chozeba, and Joash, and Saraph, who had the dominion in Moab, and Jashubi-lehem. And *these are* ancient things. (23) These *were* the potters, and those that dwelt among plants and hedges: there they dwelt with the king for his work.

(24) The sons of Simeon *were*, ¹Nemuel,

*a* Gen. 38. 1. 5.

¹ Or, *Jemuel*. Gen. 46. 10; Ex. 6. 15.

---

*wife*. Hodiah recurs as a man's name in Neh. viii. 7, ix. 5; but a very slight change—the addition of three letters—in the Hebrew would give the sense: "And sons of his Jewish wife, the sister of Naham, were the father of Keilah the Garmite, and Eshtemoa," &c.

**Naham** is unknown.

**Keilah** is a town in the Shephelah (Josh. xv. 44), well known as the scene of David's prowess and peril (1 Sam. xxiii.).

**Eshtemoa** occurred in verse 17, in connexion with Ishbah, son of Ezra by Bithiah. (See Note there.) The Garmites and Maachathites are unknown clans. The former founded or were settled at Keilah. It appears that *abi* ("father of") has dropped out of the text before Eshtemoa; the sense being that the Maachathites were settled at Eshtemoa; which, of course, they may have been, side by side with the half-Egyptian clan Ishbah. Maachah is mentioned, chap. ii. 48, as a concubine of Caleb. The list is still dealing with the Calebite division of Hezron.

(20) **The Sons of Shimon.**—Nothing is said elsewhere of them, or of the sons of Ishi. Ishi (chap. ii. 31) is a Jerahmeelite name; but as throughout the section (verses 2—19) we have found indications that the ramifications of the house of Caleb are the principal subject, and as verse 20 is appended to the rest, without any opposing remark, it, is highly probable that it also refers to some Calebite clans and towns.

II.—SONS OF SHELAH, THIRD SON OF JUDAH, verses 21—23 (omitted by Syriac version).

The Shelanite clans were not noticed in chap. ii. (See Gen. xxxviii. 5 and chap. ii. 3.)

(21) **Er.**—This Er who founded Lecah is, of course, distinct from Er "the firstborn of Judah." Lecah is unknown. Mareshah, a town in the lowlands of Judah, is connected with Caleb (chap. ii. 42). Such statements are not contradictory. At different periods different tribal divisions might have been settled in the same city. The present statement need only mean that Mareshah was a Shelanite foundation.

**The families of the house of them that wrought fine linen.**—"The clans of the house of Byssus work at Beth-Ashbea." Beth-Ashbea is an unknown place. It was the seat of some Shelanite houses engaged in growing flax and weaving linen. Such industries in ancient times were confined to hereditary guilds, which jealously guarded their methods and trade secrets.

(22) **Jokim.**—Comp. Jakim (chap. viii. 9). Both are probably equivalent to Joiakim (Jehoiakim).

**Chozeba.**—Perhaps Chezib (Gen. xxxviii. 5), called Achzib (Josh. xv. 44), the birthplace of Shelah; now the ruins of *Kesâba*. It was a town of the Shephelah.

**And Joash, and Saraph, who had the dominion in Moab.**—The passage is obscure, because we know nothing further of Joash and Saraph. The LXX. render the whole verse: "And Joakim, and men of Chozeba, and Joas, and Saraph, who settled in Moab;" adding the meaningless words, καὶ ἀπέστρεψεν αὐτοὺς ἀβεδηρὶν ἀθουκίμ. The word rendered "had the dominion" occurs sixteen times, and in twelve cases at least means "to marry." Probably Isa. xxvi. 13, Jer. iii. 14 and xxxi. 32 are not exceptions. The right translation here, therefore, would seem to be "who married Moab," a metaphor expressing settlement in that country (LXX., κατῴκησαν).

**And Jashubi-lehem.**—We have here a vestige of some form of the verb *shûb* ("to return"), as the LXX. (ἀπέστρεψεν) indicates; and "lehem" (Heb., *lahem*) may either signify "to them," or represent the second half of the name Bethlehem. Reading (with one MS.) *wayyâshûbû*, we might translate, *and they returned to themselves*, i.e., to their Judæan home. (Comp. the story of the sojourn of Elimelech and his family in Moab, and the return of Naomi to Judah.) But *Bêth* might easily have fallen out before *lahem*, and if so, the statement is, *and they returned to Bethlehem*—another point of likeness to the story of the Book of Ruth. (2) Others render, "Reduced Moab and requited them" (*wayyashîbû lahem*); referring the notice to a supposed subjugation of Moab by two chieftains of Judah. (3) Others, again, have proposed: "Who married into Moab, and brought them home (wives)." (Comp. the story of Mahlon and Chilion in Ruth.) The Vulg. translates all the proper names, and continues: "*Qui principes fuerunt in Moab, et qui reversi sunt in Lahem.*" (Comp. also Ezr. ii. 6.)

**And these are ancient things.**—*And the events are ancient*, that is, those just recounted.

(23) **These were the potters.**—Viz., the clans enumerated in verse 22.

**And those that dwelt among plants and hedges.**—Rather, *and inhabitants of Netaim and Gederah*. Netaim means "plantations" (Isa. xvii. 10). Solomon had pleasure-gardens near Bethlehem. See also the notice of Uzziah's farms and vineyards (2 Chron. xxvi. 10). Gederah (Josh. xv. 36), a town in the Shephelah.

**There they dwelt with the king.**—Literally, *with the king in his work they dwelt there*. This seems to say that the potteries of Netaim and Gederah were a royal establishment, as those of Sévres used to be. Perhaps the linen-weaving of Beth-Ashbea (verse 21) should be included.

III.—THE TRIBE OF SIMEON: ITS CLANS, AND THEIR SETTLEMENTS AND CONQUESTS (verses 24—43).

(24) **The sons of Simeon.**—The Pentateuch contains three lists of sons of Simeon, viz., Gen. xlvi. 10, Exod. vi. 15, and Num. xxvi. 12. Genesis and Exodus name six sons; Numbers agrees with the Chronicles in

*The Posterity*   I. CHRONICLES, IV.   *and Cities of Simeon.*

and Jamin, Jarib, Zerah, *and* Shaul: (25) Shallum his son, Mibsam his son, Mishma his son. (26) And the sons of Mishma; Hamuel his son, Zacchur his son, Shimei his son. (27) And Shimei had sixteen sons and six daughters; but his brethren had not many children, neither did all their family multiply, ¹like to the children of Judah. (28) And they dwelt at ᵃBeer-sheba, and Moladah, and Hazar-shual, (29) and at ²Bilhah, and at Ezem, and at ³Tolad, (30) and at Bethuel, and at Hormah, and at Ziklag, (31) and at Beth-marcaboth, and ⁴Hazar-susim, and at Beth-birei, and at Shaaraim. These *were* their cities unto the reign of David. (32) And their villages *were*, ⁵Etam, and Ain, Rimmon, and Tochen, and Ashan, five cities: (33) and all their villages that *were* round about the same cities, unto ⁶Baal. These *were* their habitations, and ⁷ their genealogy. (34) And Meshobab, and Jamlech, and Joshah the son of Amaziah, (35) And Joel, and Jehu the son of Josibiah, the son of Seraiah, the son of Asiel, (36) And Elioe-

B.C. 1300, &c.

1 Heb., *unto*.
ᵃ Josh. 19. 2.
2 Or, *Balah*, Josh. 19. 3.
3 Or, *Eltolad*, Josh. 19. 4.
4 Or, *Hazarsusah*, Josh. 19. 5.
5 Or, *Ether*, Josh. 19. 7.
6 Or, *Baalath-beer*, Josh. 19. 8.
7 Or, *as they divided themselves by nations among them.*

---

naming five, the Ohad of Genesis and Exodus being omitted. In place of our Jarib Numbers has Jachin; the other names are the same. Genesis and Exodus read Jemuel and Zohar for Nemuel and Zerah. Exodus vi. 15 calls Shaul "son of a Canaanitess." The mixed race of Shaul was the only Simeonite clan that became populous (verses 25—27). The other clans are not further noticed by this genealogy.

(27) **His brethren had not many children.**—His brethren, *i.e.*, his fellow-tribesmen. The other Simeonite clans (Num. xxvi. 12), are meant.

**Neither did all their family multiply.**—Rather, *nor did they multiply their whole clan.* The word clan (*mishpahath*) is here used in the wider sense of tribe. This remark is borne out by what we otherwise know of the tribe of Simeon. It was never historically important, and appears to have ultimately been absorbed by Judah, within which its domain was included (Josh. xix. 1). (Comp. Gen. xlix. 7: "I will divide them in Jacob, and scatter them in Israel.")

II.—THE SEATS OF THE SIMEONITES UNTIL THE REIGN OF DAVID (verses 28—33).

This list is parallel to Josh. xix. 2—8. There are some variations, partly accidental.

(28) **Beer-sheba, and Moladah, and Hazar-shual.**—Josh. xix. 2 adds Sheba after Beer-sheba—an obviously mistaken repetition, making fourteen towns in all, whereas verse 3 concludes, "thirteen cities and their villages." Beer-sheba is *Bir-esseba*; Moladah, *Tel-Milh*, south of Hebron; Hazar-shual (fox-village) is unknown.

(29) Many of the places assigned to Simeon in this list are reckoned among the towns of the extreme south of Judah in Josh. xv. 26, *et seq.* Bilhah, or Balah, is, perhaps, Baalah (Josh. xv. 29); Ezem (Authorised Version, *Azem*) and Eltolad are also mentioned there. Their sites are unknown.

(30) **Bethuel.**—Called Chesil in Josh. xv. 30; Josh. xix. 4 has Bethûl, a contraction like Hamul for Hamuel (verse 26; comp. chap. ii. 5).

**Hormah.**—The ancient Zephath (Judges i. 17), now *Sepata*.

**Ziklag.**—Now *Kasluj*, east of Sepata (Josh. xv. 30, 31; 1 Sam. xxvii. 6).

(31) **Beth-marcaboth** = "house of chariots."

**Hazar-susim** = "village of horses;" for which Hazarsusah is an equivalent (*susah* being used as a collective word).

**Beth-birei.**—Probably a corrupt writing of Beth-lebaoth, "house of lionesses" (Josh. xix. 6), for which Josh. xv. 32 has the contraction Lebaoth. There were lions in the wilds of Judah (1 Sam. xvii. 34). (Comp. Judges xiv. 5; 1 Kings xiii. 24.)

**Shaaraim** (two gates) is Sharuhen (Josh. xix. 6), and Shilhim (Josh. xv. 32). Sharuhen is known from Egyptian inscriptions (*Sharuhuna*).

**These were their cities unto the reign of David, and their villages.**—Josh. xix. 6 shows that this is the right punctuation: "And Beth-lebaoth and Sharuhen: thirteen towns, and their villages."

**Unto the reign of David.**—Does this mean that in the age of David the thirteen cities passed from the possession of the Simeonites? Ziklag, at all events, was at that time a Philistine borough (1 Sam. xxvii. 6).

(32) **And their villages.**—This belongs to verse 31. The verb should be cancelled.

**Etam, and Ain, Rimmon . . .**—Why are these five cities separated from the former thirteen? The old Jewish expositors Rashi and Kimchi assert, that whereas the thirteen were lost to the Simeonites from the time of David, these five remained in their possession. The separation is made in Josh. xix. as well as here. (Many MSS. read "and Rimmon.")

**Five cities.**—Josh. xix. 7: "Ain, Rimmon, and Ether, and Ashan; four cities and their villages." Etam may be a mistake for Ether. But there were two Etams, one in the hills of Judah, south of Bethlehem (see verse 3, Note; 2 Chron. xi. 6), and one in the south of Judah (Judges xv. 8)—perhaps the place intended here. Ether occurs in Josh. xv. 42 along with Ashan. Both were in the lowlands of Judah. Ain and Rimmon are spoken of as one place (Neh. xi. 29): they must have been close to each other (comp. Buda-Pesth). Tochen only here.

(33) **Unto Baal.**—Called in Josh. xix. 8 Baalathbeer ("lady of the well"). The same passage adds what appears to be the name of this group of villages, viz., Ramath-negeb, or Ramah of the southland. (Comp. 1 Sam. xxx. 27.)

**These** (Heb., *this*) **were their habitations.**—A conclusion of the list of towns of Simeon.

**And their genealogy.**—Heb., *and they had their own registration* (or, *enrolment*); that is, though their settlements lay within the territory of Judah, their clans were registered as belonging to a distinct tribe.

III.—EMIGRATION OF THE SIMEONITES: THEIR CONQUESTS (verses 34—43).

(34—37) The thirteen princes (emirs) of Simeon who headed the expedition of their tribe in the age of Hezekiah (fl. 710 B.C.). None of them are otherwise known.

(36) **Jaakobah.**—Literally, *to Jacob*; a patronymic derived from Jacob, like the English Jacobs.

*The Conquests*        I. CHRONICLES, V.        *of Simeon.*

nai, and Jaakobah, and Jeshohaiah, and Asaiah, and Adiel, and Jesimiel, and Benaiah, <sup>37</sup> and Ziza the son of Shiphi, the son of Allon, the son of Jedaiah, the son of Shimri, the son of Shemaiah; <sup>(38)</sup> these <sup>1</sup>mentioned by *their* names were princes in their families: and the house of their fathers increased greatly. <sup>(39)</sup> And they went to the entrance of Gedor, *even* unto the east side of the valley, to seek pasture for their flocks. <sup>(40)</sup> And they found fat pasture and good, and the land *was* wide, and quiet, and peaceable; for *they* of Ham had dwelt there of old. <sup>(41)</sup> And these written by

<sup>1</sup> Heb., *coming.*

name came in the days of Hezekiah king of Judah, and smote their tents, and the habitations that were found there, and destroyed them utterly unto this day, and dwelt in their rooms: because *there was* pasture there for their flocks. <sup>(42)</sup> And *some* of them, *even* of the sons of Simeon, five hundred men, went to mount Seir, having for their captains Pelatiah, and Neariah, and Rephaiah, and Uzziel, the sons of Ishi. <sup>(43)</sup> And they smote the rest of the Amalekites that were escaped, and dwelt there unto this day.

CHAPTER V.—<sup>(1)</sup> Now the sons of

---

<sup>(38)</sup> **These mentioned by their names.**—Literally, *these who have come (forward) with names,* that is, have been adduced by name.

**Were princes in their families.**—*Ameers* or *chieftains in their clans.*

**And the house of their fathers increased.**—*And their father-houses had spread greatly.* Finding their territory too strait for them under these conditions, and probably also because of the encroachments of their powerful neighbours, the Judæans and Philistines, the Simeonite chieftains went forth at the head of their clans to seek new settlements.

**And (so) they went to the entrance of Gedor, even unto the east side of the valley.**—Gedor can hardly be the town of that name in the hill country of Judah (Josh. xv. 58). The LXX. read Gerar (Γέραρα).

**Even unto the east side of the valley.**—*So far as to the east of the valley,* that is, apparently, the valley of or near the unknown Gedor, or Gerar. The only considerable valley south-east of Judah is the Arabah, below the Dead Sea. That this locality is meant appears likely from the vicinity of Mount Seir and the Amalekites (verse 42).

**To seek pasture for their flocks.**—This statement is of interest as proving that even so late as the reign of Hezekiah, those Israelite clans which bordered on the desert were still nomades, like the Beidawis. (Comp. Gen. xiii. 5—12).

<sup>(40)</sup> **And they found fat pasture and good.**—If Gerar was the right reading in verse 39, we might compare Gen. xxvi. 17 *seq.*

**And the land was wide.**—Gen. xxxiv. 21. Literally, *broad of both hands*—i.e., on both sides. An open plain is meant.

**And quiet and peaceable.**—Like Laish, which the Danites took by surprise (Judg. xviii. 7, 28).

**They of Ham had dwelt there of old.**—That is, *they who were then dwelling there were Hamites or Canaanites* (chap. i. 8).

**Of old.**—Literally, *before (lephānīm);* that is, *before the Simeonite invasion.*

<sup>(41)</sup> **These who were written by name.**—The Ameers enumerated in verses 34—37.

**Smote their tents.**—These Hamites, like the men of Laish, were nomades.

**And the habitations that were found there.**—Heb. text, *the wells*: Heb. marg., *the Maonites,* in Hebrew a very similar word. LXX., τοὺς Μιναίους, the Maonites or Minaeans. The text may be com-

pared with the Syriac, which reads, "And all springs of water that were there they stopped up." But the Margin is probably correct, as the verb which the Syriac supplies is wanting in the Hebrew. The Maonites appear to have been sojourners from Maon, south of the Dead Sea, near Petra, now called *Maân.* (Comp. 2 Chron. xx. 1.)

**Destroyed them utterly.**—*Devoted them to God for destruction;* Josh. vi. 17, "the city shall be accursed unto the Lord." This practice was not peculiar to Israel, but was common to the Semitic races. Mesha, king of Moab, in like manner devoted the inhabitants of Nebo, 7,000 in number, to destruction in the name of 'Ashtar-Chemosh. (See the Stele of Dibân, lines 14—17, in Dr. Ginsburg's *The Moabite Stone.*)

**Unto this day**—That is, *to the time when this record was first written, long before the chronicler borrowed it from his sources.*

<sup>(42)</sup> **Went.**—Or, *had gone* (marched). The time of this expedition to mount Seir is not expressed; but for that very reason it is likely to have been nearly contemporaneous with the events just described. The band of five hundred would seem to have belonged to the clans which had already smitten the Hamites. Neither Ishi (*Yish'i*) nor his sons are otherwise known. If a totally different expedition were intended, the expression, "and of them—of the sons of Simeon—five hundred men," would be a needlessly misleading periphrasis for, "And some of the sons of Simeon." "Of them" can only refer to the clans whose emigration in the days of Hezekiah has been the subject of this section.

<sup>(43)</sup> **The rest of the Amalekites that were escaped.**—Literally, *the remnant of the survivors (pelêtâh,* an abstract collective word) *belonging to Amalek.* These Amalekites are usually supposed to have been some who had taken refuge in Seir from Saul and David's exterminating wars (1 Sam. xiv. 48, xv. 7; 2 Sam. viii. 12. Comp. chap. i. 36, where Amalek appears as a partly Edomite stock.)

V.

The tribes east of Jordan—Reuben, Gad, and half-Manasseh, with short notices of their conquest, and their final captivity.

I.—THE REUBENITES (verses 1—10).

<sup>(1)</sup> **Reuben the firstborn of Israel.**—See Gen. xlix. 3: "Reuben, my firstborn thou! my strength, and firstfruits of my manhood;" also Gen. xxix. 32.

*The Posterity*                I. CHRONICLES, V.                *of Reuben.*

Reuben the firstborn of Israel, (for he *was* the firstborn; but, forasmuch as he defiled his father's bed, his birthright was given unto the sons of Joseph the son of Israel: and the genealogy is not to be reckoned after the birthright. (2) For Judah prevailed above his brethren, and of him *came* the 'chief ¹ ruler; but the birthright *was* Joseph's :) (3) the sons, *I say*, of ᵈReuben the firstborn of Israel *were*, Hanoch, and Pallu, Hezron, and Carmi. (4) The sons of Joel; Shemaiah his son, Gog his son, Shimei his son, (5) Micah his son, Reaia his son, Baal his son, (6) Beerah his son, whom ²Tilgath-pilneser king of Assyria carried away *captive* : he *was* prince of the Reubenites. (7) And his brethren by their families, when the genealogy of their generations was reckoned, *were* the chief, Jeiel, and Zechariah, (8) and Bela the son of Azaz, the son of ³Shema, the

*a* Gen. 35. 22 & 49. 4.
*b* Gen. 49. 9, 10.
*c* Mic. 5. 2; Matt. 2. 6.
1 Or, *prince.*
*d* Gen. 46. 9; Ex. 6. 14; Num. 26. 5.
2 Or, *Tiglath-pileser*, 2 Kin. 15. 29 & 16. 7.
3 Or, *Shemaiah*, ver. 4.

**For he was the firstborn.**—The parenthesis is an assertion of the legitimacy of the Davidic monarchy, as against the fact that both Reuben and Joseph had claims prior to those of Judah.

**He defiled his father's bed.**—Gen. xlix. 4. Jacob's curse: "Bubbling like the waters, excel thou not! For thou wentest up thy father's couches. Then thou defiledst my bed." (See Gen. xxxv. 22).

**His birthright was given to the sons of Joseph.**—The reading of some MSS., and the Syriac and Arabic, "to Joseph," is probably original. This transfer of the rights of primogeniture is not elsewhere mentioned. It is, however, a fair inference from Jacob's curse, and from the special blessing of Joseph (Gen. xlix. 22—26) and of his two sons (Gen. xlviii. 15—20), considered in the light of historical fulfilment. Ephraim was always a leading tribe (Judges ii. 9, iv. 5, v. 14, viii. 1, 2, xii. 1, 15).

**And the genealogy is not to be reckoned after the birthright.**—Rather, *though he was not to be registered as firstborn* (literally, *according to the primogeniture*). The subject is Joseph or the sons of Joseph, who received the forfeited rights of Reuben, but not the first place in lists of the tribes. What those rights were is defined by Deut. xxi. 15—17, which rules that the son of a hated wife—if he be firstborn (the case of Reuben, son of Leah), shall inherit a double portion, "for he is the firstfruits of his strength, the right of the firstborn is his;" words obviously referring to Gen. xlix. 4, 5.

(2) **For Judah prevailed above his brethren.**—Literally, *was mighty among his brethren*. Comp. Jacob's blessing (Gen. xlix. 8—10): "Judah, thou—thy brethren shall praise thee, Thy hand shall be on the neck of thy foes, Thy father's sons shall bow before thee. Sceptre shall not depart from Judah, Nor doom-staff from between his feet," &c. (See also Judges i. 1, 2, where Judah is divinely commissioned to lead the attack upon the Canaanites.) At the census of Moses, Judah greatly outnumbered any other single tribe (Num. i. 27).

**And of him came the chief ruler.**—"And from him (one was to become) prince." Literally, *and for a prince—out of him.* (Comp. Micah v. 1.) LXX., εἰς ἡγούμενον ἐξ αὐτοῦ. David is meant, as in 1 Sam. xiii. 14. We may also remember the word of the apostolic writer: "It is evident that our Lord sprang out of Judah" (Heb. vii. 4). The prophecy concerning the royal dignity of Judah is only thus exhausted of its meaning.

**But the birthright was Joseph's,** who actually received the "double portion" in the two tribal domains of Ephraim and Manasseh.

(3) **Hanoch, and Pallu, Hezron, and Carmi.**—So Gen. xlvi. 9; Exod. vi. 14; Num. xxvi. 5—7. Considering the prominence of Hezron and Carmi among the clans of Judah, it is remarkable to find their names recurring among the main branches of Reuben.

(4—6) **The sons of Joel.**—The connection of this leading house with one of the four sons just mentioned, is implied but not stated. The line of Joel is traced through seven generations to Beerah, who was transported to Assyria by Tiglath Pileser II., 734 B.C., in the reign of Pekah, king of Israel. Supposing there are no gaps in the series, Joel flourished 280 years (7 × 40) before that date; that is, about 1014 B.C., under David and Solomon.

(4) The LXX. read: "Sons of Joel Shemaiah, and Banaia (Benaiah) his son; and sons of Gog, son of Shemaiah, his son Micah," &c.

(5) **Baal.**—Compare the names of Saul's posterity Eshbaal and Meribbaal; and David's son Beeliada (Heb., *Baalyada*).

(7) **Tilgath-pilneser.**—The Assyrian monarch known as Tiglath Pileser II. See 2 Kings xv. 29, for his deportation of the people of the northern and trans-Jordanic districts of Israel, in the reign of Pekah. Some MSS., with LXX. and Syriac, read Tiglath, which is more correct than Tilgath. Vat., LXX., Θαγλαφαλλασὰρ, Syr., *Teglath-Palsar.* The Assyrian name, of which these forms are transcripts, is *Tukulti-pal-Esarra*, "the servant of the son of Esarra." (The "Son of Esarra" is a title of the god Ninip.) Tilgath-Pilneser (Vulg., *Thelgath-Phalnasar*) is the invariable spelling of Chronicles.

**He was prince of the Reubenites.**—Beerah was tribal prince of Reuben, and not merely chief of a Reubenite clan, as some will have it. The Hebrew construction is parallel to that of Num. vii. 24, 30 *seq.*, with which comp. Num. vii. 18.

(7) **And his brethren by their families.**—"And his fellow-tribesmen, each after his clan (Num. ii. 34), in the registration after their pedigrees, were the chief, Jeiel, and Zechariah." Jeiel was the chief of the second Reubenite clan, as Beerah of the first, Zechariah and Bela were heads of the other chief houses. It appears that these four chieftains correspond to the four divisions of Reuben mentioned in verse 3. Num. xxvi. 7 says expressly that "the Hanochite, the Palluite, the Hezronite, and the Carmite" were "the clans of the Reubenite."

(8) **Bela.**—His descent is traced, like that of Beerah, but through fewer names. This does not necessarily imply that Bela and Beerah were not contemporaries. Intermediate names are often omitted in genealogies. (See Josh. vii. 18: "Achan son of Carmi son of Zabdi son of Zerah," and verse 24, "Achan son of Zerah," and the different lengths of the pedigrees of Heman, Asaph, and Ethan in chap. vi. 33—47.) It is not

son of Joel, who dwelt in ªAroer, even unto Nebo and Baal-meon : ⁽⁹⁾ and eastward he inhabited unto the entering in of the wilderness from the river Euphrates : because their cattle were multiplied in the land of Gilead. ⁽¹⁰⁾ And in the days of Saul they made war with the Hagarites, who fell by their hand : and they dwelt in their tents ¹throughout all the east *land* of Gilead.

⁽¹¹⁾ And the children of Gad dwelt over against them, in the land of ᵇBashan unto Salcah : ⁽¹²⁾ Joel the chief, and Shapham the next, and Jaanai, and Shaphat in Bashan. ⁽¹³⁾ And their brethren of the house of their fathers *were*, Michael, and Meshullam, and Sheba, and Jorai, and Jachan, and Zia, and Heber, seven. ⁽¹⁴⁾ These *are* the children of Abihail the son of Huri, the son of Jaroah, the son of Gilead, the son of Michael, the son of Jeshishai, the son of Jahdo, the son of Buz ; ⁽¹⁵⁾ Ahi the son of Abdiel, the son of Guni, chief of the house of their fathers. ⁽¹⁶⁾ And they dwelt in Gilead in Bashan, and in her towns, and in all the suburbs of ᶜSharon, upon ²their borders. ⁽¹⁷⁾ All these

---

*a* Josh. 1⅔ 15, 16.

¹ Heb., *upon all the face of the east.*

*b* Josh. 13. 11.

*c* ch. 27. 29,.

² Heb., *their goings forth.*

---

likely that the Joel of verse 8 is the same as the Joel of verse 4, in spite of the further coincidence of Shema-Shemiah.

**Who dwelt.**—*He was dwelling*, that is, *he and his clan.*

**Aroer.**—Now *Arā'ir*, on the north bank of the Arnon (Josh. xii. 2).

**Nebo**, a place on the famous mount Nebo, in the region east of the Dead Sea (now *Jebel Neba*, Deut. xxxiv. 1), over against Jericho (Num. xxxii. 38).

**Baal-meon.**—Or, *Beth-baal-meon*, now *Ma'in*, about two miles south-east of Heshbon. Aroer gives the southern Nebo, and Baalmeon the northern, limits of the tribe. All three places are mentioned on the Stone of Mesha, kings of Moab (2 Kings. iii. 4—27).

⁽⁹⁾ **And eastward he inhabited unto the entering in of the wilderness.**—As their flocks and herds increased, the Reubenites gradually spread eastward, to the great desert lying between the Euphrates and Syria. This desert was a painful memory to the restored exiles. Ezra took four months to cross it (Ezra vii. 9, viii. 22). The form of the expression, "unto the entrance into the wilderness from the river Euphrates," seems to indicate that this account was written originally in Babylonia.

**Because their cattle were (had) multiplied in the land of Gilead.**—Gilead, in Old Testament usage, means all Israelite territory east of the Jordan.

⁽¹⁰⁾ **And in the days of Saul they made war with the Hagarites.**—The great extension of the tribe in an easterly direction took place in the reign of Saul, the first king of Israel. Bela and his clan victoriously fought with the Hagarites (Heb., *Hagri'im*) or Hagarenes (see Ps. lxxxiii. 7, *Hagrim*), that is, *the sons of Hagar*, for possession of the pasture-grounds east of Gilead. This Arab nation is mentioned in the Assyrian inscriptions. (The LXX. has τοὺς παροίκους, *i.e.*, haggārim, " sojourners," " nomads.")

**They dwelt in their tents.**—This phrase first occurs in Gen. ix. 27. The Belaites occupied the territory of the Hagarites.

**Throughout all the east land of Gilead.**—Rather, *on the whole eastern side* or *border of Gilead.* This includes the new settlements of Bela beyond the border.

(11—17) THE SONS OF GAD, THEIR CLANS, TERRITORY, AND REGISTRATION.

⁽¹¹⁾ **And the children of Gad dwelt over against them.**—That is, *adjoining them on the east of Jordan.*

**In the land of Bashan unto Salcah.**—(Josh. xiii. 11.) Bashan, the ancient dominion of the giant Og (Num. xxi. 33—35; Deut. iii. 1—12). Salcah, now *Sulkhad*, on the south-east slope of *Jebel Hauran* in the extreme east of Gilead.

⁽¹²⁾ **Joel the chief** (or, *first*; literally, *head*), **and Shaphan the next** (or *second.*)—Gen. xlvi. 15 enumerates seven sons of Gad, a number corresponding with the clans of verse 13; but none of the names are the same.

**In Bashan.**—This expression goes to prove that clans, not individuals, are intended.

Joel is also the head Reubenite house (verse 4).

⁽¹³⁾ **And their brethren of the house of their fathers.**—*And their kinsmen* (fellow-tribesmen), *according to their father-houses* (clans). The verse names seven inferior clans of the Gadites, whose seats are assigned in verse 16.

**These**, viz., the clans of verse 13, were sons of Abihail, whose line is retraced through seven generations to Buz, of whom nothing further is known. The name has occurred Gen. xxii. 21 as that of a son of Nahor; and Job xxxii. 2, as that of the clan of Elihu the Buzite.

⁽¹⁵⁾ **Ahi the son of Abdial, the son of Guni** (was) head of their clans. Perhaps Ahi was chieftain or prince of the sons of Abihail at the time when this register was drawn up (verse 17).

⁽¹⁶⁾ **And they dwelt in Gilead.**—The seats of the Gadites of verse 13 were *in the country east of Jordan.*

**In Bashan**, defines the locality more precisely. It was the northern region of Gilead.

**And in her towns.**—Heb., *her daughters.*

**And in all the suburbs of Sharon.**—Rather, *pasture-grounds* or *sheep-walks.*

**Sharon.**—The well-known plain of this name lay *west* of Jordan, between Carmel and Joppa, along the coast of the Great Sea. The old conjecture that Shirion, *i.e.*, mount Hermon (Deut. iii. 9; Ps. xxix. 6) should be read, is probably right.

**Upon their borders.**—That is, *their extremities* (Num. xxxiv. 4, 5). The Gadites fed their flocks in the glens opening out at the foot of the mountains, here called their *exits* or *outlets.*

⁽¹⁷⁾ **All these.**—That is, *the Gadite clans.*

**Were reckoned by genealogies** (or *registered*) **in the days of Jotham king of Judah**, *i.e.*, after 757 B.C., according to Biblical chronology.

**And in the days of Jeroboam** (the second), **king of Israel**, who reigned from 825—784, according to the *data* of Kings. Clearly, therefore, more than

were reckoned by genealogies in the days of ªJotham king of Judah, and in the days of Jeroboam king of Israel.

(18) The sons of Reuben, and the Gadites, and half the tribe of Manasseh, ¹ of valiant men, men able to bear buckler and sword, and to shoot with bow, and skilful in war, *were* four and forty thousand seven hundred and threescore, that went out to the war. (19) And they made war with the Hagarites, with ᵇ Jetur, and Nephish, and Nodab. (20) And they were helped against them, and the Hagarites were delivered into their hand, and all that *were* with them: for they cried to God in the battle, and he was intreated of them; because they put their trust in him. (21) And they ²took away their cattle; of their camels fifty thousand, and of sheep two hundred and fifty thousand, and of asses two thousand, and of ³men an hundred thousand. (22) For there fell down many slain, because the war *was* of God. And they dwelt in their steads until the captivity.

(23) And the children of the half tribe of Manasseh dwelt in the land: they increased from Bashan unto Baal-hermon

*a* 2 Kings 15. 5, 32.

¹ Heb., *sons of valour.*

*b* Gen. 25. 15.

² Heb., *led captive.*

³ Heb., *souls of men,* as Num. 31. 35.

---

one registration is the basis of the above statistics. That of Jeroboam was the earlier in point of time; but the chronicler names the king of Judah first *honoris causâ.* Jeroboam II., a vigorous king, who "restored the border of Israel from the entry of Hamath to the sea of the Arabah" (2 Kings xiv. 25), may have taken this census of the tribes east of Jordan, with a view to fiscal purposes. Jotham or his father, the great Uzziah, appears to have recovered Gad for Judah during the anarchy that succeeded the fall of Jehu's dynasty in the northern kingdom.

(18—22) A war of conquest between the three tribes east of Jordan, and their Arab neighbours. The date is not given.

(18) **Of valiant men.**—" *All that were valiant men, bearing shield and sword, and drawing bow, and trained in warfare, were 44,760, going out to the host.*" Comp. what is said in chap. xii. 8, 21, of the Gadites and Manassites, who joined fortunes with David. The number of the warriors of the three tribes nearly corresponds to the number (40,000) assigned in Josh. iv. 13. It evidently rests upon some official census, of which the chronicler had the record or among his authorities. The data of the Pentateuch (Num. i. and xxvi.) are quite different.

(19) **Hagarites.**—See verse 10.

**Jetur, and Nephish, and Nodab.**—In chap. i. 31, Jetur, Naphish, and Kedemah are the last three of the twelve tribes of Ishmael. As *Nodab* is mentioned nowhere else, the word may be a corruption of Kedemah, or rather Kedem. The first two letters might have been mistaken for *k,* the *d* is common to both words, and *b* and *m* are often confused in Hebrew writing. Jetur is the original of the classical name Ituræa, the modern *El-Jedur.*

(20) **And they were helped against them.**—The same word recurs in chap. xv. 26: "And when God helped the Levites that bare the Ark." In both places strictly natural events are regarded as providential. Here the Divine hand is recognised as controlling the issues of an invasion; there as permitting the Ark to be successfully removed from its temporary resting place.

**For they cried to God in the battle.**—No doubt the Arab warriors also cried to their gods in the fierce struggle for life; and their faith, such as it was, gave them strength for the battle. (Comp. Ps. xviii. 3—6 and verse 41.) The whole sentence to the end of the verse looks like a reason added to the narrative by the chronicler himself.

(21) **And they took away their cattle.**—The numbers are large, but not at all incredible. Flocks and herds naturally constituted the chief wealth of these nomade tribes. Comp. the annual tribute in kind paid by Mesha, king of Moab, to Ahab of Israel (2 Kings iii. 4): "a hundred thousand lambs, and a hundred thousand rams in fleeces."

**Sheep.**—The Heb. word denotes both sheep and goats; *pecora.*

**Of men an hundred thousand.**—*And persons* (*soul of man,* a collective expression) *a hundred thousand.* In Num. xxxi. 32—35 the booty taken from Midian is far greater, but only 32,000 virgins were saved from the general slaughter of the vanquished. The number here may be corrupt, but we do not know enough about the numerical strength of the Arabian peoples to be able to decide. The captives would be valuable as slaves. Sennacherib boasts that he took 200,150 persons "small and great, male and female," from the cities of Judah.

(22) **There fell down many slain.**—Hence the richness of the plunder. The warriors of the Arabian allies were probably exterminated.

**The war was of God.**—Comp. 2 Chron. xxv. 20. This accounts for the completeness of the Arabian overthrow. It is a human instinct to see tokens of Divine activity in great national catastrophes, as well as in the more awful phenomena of nature. In prophetic language, a "day of the Lord" had overtaken the sons of Hagar and their kindred.

**And they dwelt in their steads until the captivity.**—When they were carried away to Assyria by Tiglath-Pileser, verses 6 and 26.

(23, 24) The sons of half-Manasseh "in the land" east of Jordan. The translation should be: "And the children . . dwelt in the land, from Bashan unto Baal-hermon and Senir and mount Hermon. These were many." Their territory extended from "Bashan," the domain of Gad, in the south, to the mountains of Hermon, or Antilibanus, in the north.

(23) **Baal-hermon.**—Perhaps the same as Baal-gad (Josh. xii. 7, xiii. 5), the modern town of *Banias.*

**Senir.**—The Amorite name of the range of Hermon (Deut. iii. 9). The principal summit is now called *Jebel esh-Sheikh,* "hill of the chief," and *Jebel eth-Thelj,* "Snow Hill."

and Senir, and unto mount Hermon. (24) And these *were* the heads of the house of their fathers, even Epher, and Ishi, and Eliel, and Azriel, and Jeremiah, and Hodaviah, and Jahdiel, mighty men of valour, ¹famous men, *and* heads of the house of their fathers. (25) And they transgressed against the God of their fathers, and went a ᵃwhoring after the gods of the people of the land, whom God destroyed before them. (26) And the God of Israel stirred up the spirit of ᵇPul king of Assyria, and the spirit of Tilgath-pilneser king of Assyria, and he carried them away, even the Reubenites, and the Gadites, and the half tribe of Manasseh, and brought them unto ᶜHalah, and Habor, and Hara, and to the river Gozan, unto this day.

¹ Heb., *men of names.*

B.C. cir. 771.

*a* 2 Kings 17. 7.

B.C. cir. 740.

*b* 2 Kings 15. 19.

*c* 2 Kings 17. 6.

---

(24) **And these were the heads . . . (name lost) Epher, and Ishi . . .**—Of these seven "valiant warriors, men of renown, heads for their clans" nothing further is recorded. The meagre memorial of their names has at least this value: it proves that abundant materials for the history of Israel once existed, of which our canonical books have preserved authentic fragments.

(25, 26) The captivity of the three eastern tribes. A fuller account may be read in 2 Kings xvii. 6—18.

(25) **They transgressed against the God of their fathers.**—Rather, *were faithless* or *untrue to* Him (Josh. vii. 1, "committed a trespass").

**Went a whoring after the gods of the people** (peoples).—Jehovah was the true Lord (*Ba'al*) and Husband (*Ish*) of Israel. Apostasy from Him is, in the prophetic language, whoredom. (See Hos. chaps. i. and ii., especially ii. 16, and chap. iii.) According to Kings *l.c.* the fatal sin of Israel evinced itself: (1) in the worship of the high places; (2) in adoration of the heavenly bodies, and the productive powers of nature; (3) in the practice of magic and divination.

**The people of the land, whom God had destroyed before them.**—Comp. Num. xxi. 21—35, and Josh. xii. 6; Ps. cxxxv. 10—12. The reduction of the Canaanites was, to the mind of the chronicler, a Divine work. He is not thinking only of such extraordinary events as were told of the battle of Bethhoron (Josh x. 11—14). All the incidents of the conquest were the Lord's doing, whether He acted through the agency of sun and moon, or storm and tempest, or the good swords of Joshua and his warriors. From the same standpoint, he ascribes the Assyrian invasions to a direct impulse from the God of Israel (verse 26). The Assyrian kings themselves were wont to regard their campaigns as a fulfilment of the bidding of their Divine protectors, Istar, Bel, and other imaginary beings. It was not given to them to attain to the higher vision of the Hebrew prophets and priests, who saw but one guiding and controlling power at the summit of the world. (Comp. Isa. x. 5—15.)

(26) **Stirred up** (or woke) **the spirit.**—So 2 Chron. xxi. 16, and Ezr. i. 1, 5. For the thought, Isa. xliv. 28, xlv. 1—13.

**Pul king of Assyria, and . . . Tilgathpilneser king of Assyria.**—No trace of Pûl as distinct from Tiglath-pileser has been found in the Assyrian monuments, which, it must be remembered, are contemporary. In 2 Kings xv. 19 we read that, "Pul king of Assyria came against the land," in the reign of Menahem, who recognised the Assyrian monarch as his suzerain, and paid a tribute of 1,000 talents of silver. Now Tiglath-pileser II. actually claims to have received tribute of Menahem (*Menahimmu*). Pûl appears to have been the original name of Tiglathpileser, which, upon his accession to the throne of Assyria (745 B.C.), he discarded for that of the great king who had ruled the country four centuries before his time. The name Pûl has been identified by Dr. Schrader with the Porus of Ptolemy's Canon, *Pôr* being the Persian pronunciation of Pûl. The Syriac here omits "Pul king of Assyria." The LXX. (Vat.) has Φαλώχ, and the Arabic *Bâlaq*. Perhaps the chronicler meant to indicate the identity of Pûl and Tiglath: "The spirit of Pul *and* (= that is) the spirit of Tiglath, and *he* carried them away."

**And he carried them away.**—Tiglath-pileser is meant. (See 2 Kings xv. 29: "In the days of Pekah king of Israel, came Tiglath-pileser king of Assyria, and took Ijon, and Abel-beth-maachah . . . and *Gilead,* and Galilee . . . and carried them captive to Assyria.") From the Assyrian records we learn that (*circ.* 734–732 B.C.) Tiglath-pileser received the homage of Ahaz (Yahu-haçi, Jeho-ahaz), king of Judah, slew Rezin (Raçunni) of Damascus, and reduced Pekah (Paqahú), king of Samaria, to vassalage. This supplements the Biblical account. Gilead, in 2 Kings xv. 29, represents the trans-Jordanic tribes. (See verses 10 and 16 above.) The transportation of entire populations was a common practice with the Assyrian kings. Assurbanipal (Sardanapalus) removed the men of Karbit from the mountains east of Assyria, and settled them in Egypt.

**Brought them unto Halah, and Habor. . . .**—The same localities are mentioned (2 Kings xvii. 6) as those to which Shalmaneser IV., or rather his successor Sargon, transported the other tribes of the northern kingdom (*circ.* 721 B.C.). There is nothing unlikely in the statement of either text. Sargon might have thought fit to strengthen the Israelite settlements in Northern Assyria by sending thither the new bodies of compulsory colonists. It is arbitrary to suppose that two different events have been confounded by the sacred annalists.

**Halah.**—See Note on 2 Kings xvii. 6.

**Habor.**—Probably a district of North Assyria, not far from Halah, named after the river *Habûr* which rises near the upper *Zab* and falls into the Tigris.

**Hara.**—Kings, *l.c.*, "cities of Media." Hara here is perhaps an Aramaic name for the Median highlands, but more probably the reading is a relic of "the mountains of Media" (*hârê Mâdai*); comp. the LXX. at 2 Kings xvii. 6. The Syriac here has "*cities* of Media;" the LXX. omits the word.

**The river Gozan.**—Rather, *the river of Gozan.* Shalmaneser mentions the country Guzana in Mesopotamia, the Greek Gauzanitis. An Assyrian list connects it with Naçibina (Nisibis). The "river of Gozan" is the *Habur.*

CHAPTER VI.—(1) The sons of Levi; [a]1Gershon, Kohath, and Merari. (2) And the sons of Kohath; Amram, Izhar, and Hebron, and Uzziel. (3) And the children of Amram; Aaron, and Moses, and Miriam. The sons also of Aaron; [b]Nadab, and Abihu, Eleazar, and Ithamar. (4) Eleazar begat Phinehas, Phinehas begat Abishua, (5) and Abishua begat Bukki, and Bukki begat Uzzi, (6) and Uzzi begat Zerahiah, and Zerahiah begat Meraioth, (7) Meraioth begat Amariah, and Amariah begat Ahitub, (8) and Ahitub begat Zadok, and [c]Zadok begat Ahimaaz, (9) and Ahimaaz begat Azariah, and Azariah begat Johanan, (10) and Johanan begat Azariah, (he *it is* that executed the priest's office [2]in the [d]tem-

B.C. cir. 1300, &c.

a Gen. 46. 11; Ex. 6. 16.
1 Or, *Gershom*, ver. 16.
b Lev. 10. 1.
c 2 Sam. 15. 27.
2 Heb., *in the house.*
d 1 Kings 6; 2 Chron. 3.

---

## VI.

The tribe of Levi, its principal genealogies, and its cities. (1) The genealogy of Aaron, including his descent from Levi, and his successors in the line of Eleazar until the Babylonian exile (verses 1—15). (2) A double series of the sons of Gershon, Kohath, and Merari, the three sons of Levi, to whom also the ancestry of Heman, Asaph, and Ethan is traced (verses 16—48). (3) A repetition of the line of Aaron, from Eleazar to the age of David and Solomon, as prelude to the account of the cities of the Levites (verses 49—81).

(1—15) THE LINE OF AARON THROUGH ELEAZAR TO JEHOZADAK.

(1—3) Aaron's descent from Levi.

(1) **The sons of Levi; Gershon . . .**—So Gen. xlvi. 11; Exod. vi. 16, and uniformly in the Pentateuch. In verse 16 we have the spelling *Gershom*, which perhaps indicates a difference of source.

(2) **The sons of Kohath.**—The names are the same as in Exod. vi. 18. Kŏhath, or Kĕhath, was the chief house of Levi. The name is put second in the series, perhaps for euphonic reasons. (Comp. "Shem, Ham, and Japhet" with Gen. ix. 24 and x. 21.)

(3) **And the children.**—Heb., sons (*bnê 'Amrâm*).
**Aaron, and Moses.**—Exod. vi. 20.
**And Miriam.**—Num. xxvi. 59: "the prophetess, the sister of Aaron" (Exod. xv. 20).
**The sons also of Aaron.**—Heb., *'Ahărôn*; Arab., *Hârûn*. Exod. vi. 23, Num. xxvi. 60 name the four sons of Aaron in the same order as here. "Nadab and Abihu died when they offered strange fire before the Lord" (Num. xxvi. 61). A fuller account is given in Lev. x. 1—7.

(4—15) Twenty-two successors of Aaron, for the interval between his death and the Babylonian exile (*circ.* 588 B.C.). How many centuries that interval comprises is uncertain. The Exodus has been placed at various dates from 1648 B.C. (*Hales*), and 1491 (*Usher*) to *circ.* 1330 (*Lepsius* and other modern scholars), and even so late as 1265. It is premature, therefore, to object, as some have done, that twenty-two generations are too few for the period they are supposed to cover. If the later dates assigned for the Exodus be nearer the truth, an allowance of about thirty years to the generation would justify the list. At least we have no right to say that the list *requires* a reckoning of forty or fifty years to the generation. On the other hand, it may well be the case that some links in the chain are wanting. Comp. Ezra vii. 1—7, where this list recurs in an abridged form, giving only fifteen names instead of twenty-two.

(4) **Eleazar begat Phinehas.**—Num. xx. 22—28 tells how Moses, by Divine command, made Eleazar priest in Aaron's room. Josh. xiv. 1, xvii. 4 represent him as acting with Joshua in Canaan. Josh. xxiv. 33 records his death and place of burial. For Phinehas, son of Eleazar, see Exod. vi. 25; Num. xxv. 7, 11; Jud. xx. 28 (as ministering before the Ark at Beth-el). The list before us appears to ignore the line of Ithamar, Aaron's remaining son. Chap. xxiv. 1—6, however, proves that the chronicler was well aware that there had been other personages of high-priestly rank besides those registered here (see especially verse 5: "for there had been princes of the sanctuary and princes of God, of the sons of Eleazar and of the sons of Ithamar"). The line of Eleazar alone is here recorded as being at once the elder and legitimate, and also the permanent one from the time of Solomon onwards.

(5) **Uzzi** is assumed to have been contemporary with Eli, whose immediate descendants to the fourth generation exercised the office of the high-priest, according to the data of the Books of Samuel and Kings. The line of Eli is as follows: Eli, Phinehas, Ahitub, Ahimelech, Abiathar. (See 1 Sam. i. 28, ii. 4, 11, xiv. 3, xxii. 9, 20; 1 Kings ii. 26, 27.)

(6) **Zerahiah begat Meraioth.**—Scripture is silent as regards the six persons named in verses 6, 7. That the line of Eleazar abstained from the priestly functions during the ascendency of the house of Ithamar-Eli, is probably nothing more than a groundless guess on the part of Josephus (*Antiq.* viii. 1, 3). The indications of the Scriptures point the other way. Zadok and Abiathar enjoyed a co-ordinate authority in the time of David (1 Sam. xx. 25), and proofs are not wanting of the existence of more than one recognised sanctuary, in which the representatives of both houses might severally officiate. (See Note on chap. xvi. 39.)

(8) **Zadok** was appointed sole high-priest by Solomon, who deposed Abiathar (1 Kings ii. 27, 35).
**Ahimaaz.**—2 Sam. xv. 36, xvii. 17 *sqq.*, xviii. 27. In all these passages Ahimaaz appears as a young man and a fleet runner, who did service to David in the time of Absalom's revolt. He nowhere appears as high-priest.
**Azariah.**—See 1 Kings iv. 2, which mentions "Azariah son of Zadok the priest," in a list of Solomon's grandees. The remark in verse 10, "he who served as priest in the house that Solomon built in Jerusalem," enigmatical where it stands, is intelligible if connected with Azariah son of Ahimaaz; contrasting him with his grandfather, Zadok, who had ministered at *Gibeon* (chap. xvi. 39); and with the other high-priests who were his namesakes, as the *first* Azariah. Solomon reigned forty years. Azariah, therefore, may have succeeded to the priesthood before his death.

(10) **Johanan begat Azariah.**—Johanan is unknown. The name Azariah occurs thrice in the present

*The Line of the Priests.*     I. CHRONICLES, VI.     *The Family of Gershom.*

ple that Solomon built in Jerusalem :) <sup>(11)</sup> and Azariah begat Amariah, and Amariah begat Ahitub, <sup>(12)</sup> and Ahitub begat Zadok, and Zadok begat <sup>1</sup> Shallum, <sup>(13)</sup> and Shallum begat Hilkiah, and Hilkiah begat Azariah, <sup>(14)</sup> and Azariah begat *a* Seraiah, and Seraiah begat Jehozadak, <sup>(15)</sup> and Jehozadak went *into captivity,* *b* when the LORD carried away Judah and Jerusalem by the hand of Nebuchadnezzar.

<sup>(16)</sup> The sons of Levi; *c* <sup>2</sup> Gershom, Kohath, and Merari. <sup>(17)</sup> And these *be* the names of the sons of Gershom; Libni, and Shimei. <sup>(18)</sup> And the sons of Kohath *were,* Amram, and Izhar, and Hebron, and Uzziel. <sup>(19)</sup> The sons of Merari; Mahli, and Mushi.

And these *are* the families of the Levites according to their fathers.

<sup>(20)</sup> Of Gershom; Libni his son, Ja-

---

1 Or, *Meshullam,* ch. 9. 11.

*a* Neh. 11. 11.

*b* 2 Kings 25. 18.

*c* Ex. 6. 16.

2 Or, *Gershon,* ver. 1.

---

list—viz., in verses 9, 10, and 13. We have already identified the first with the son, or rather grandson, of Zadok, who is mentioned in 1 Kings iv. 2. A highpriest (Azariah) withstood King Uzziah's assumption of priestly privilege (2 Chron. xxvi. 17), *circ.* 740 B.C. The Jewish exegetes Rashi and Kimchi supposed him to be identical with Azariah son of Johanan, fancifully explaining the remark, "he it is that executed the priest's office in the temple," &c., as a reference to his bold defence of the priestly prerogative against the king himself. If this were right, several names would be omitted in verses 9, 10. But we have seen that the remark in question really belongs to a former Azariah, and has been transposed from its original position in verse 9 by the inadvertence of some copyist. Another Azariah is mentioned (2 Chron. xxxi. 10) as "chief priest of the house of Zadok," early in the reign of Hezekiah. Him, too, we fail to identify with either of the Azariahs of the present list. (See verse 13, Note.)

<sup>(11)</sup> **Azariah begat Amariah.** — Perhaps the Amariah of 2 Chron. xix. 11, who was high-priest under Jehoshaphat.

<sup>(12)</sup> **And Ahitub begat Zadok, and Zadok begat Shallum.**—See verse 8: "And Ahitub begat Zadok." The recurrence of names in the same families is almost too common to require notice, except where confusion of distinct persons has resulted or is likely to result, as in the instance of those among our Lord's immediate followers, who bore the names of Simon, Judas, and James.

Somewhere about this part of the list we miss the name of Jehoiada, the famous king-maker, who put down Athaliah and set up Joash (2 Chron xxiii.). In like manner, Urijah, the too compliant highpriest of the reign of Ahaz, who flourished a generation or so later, is conspicuous here by omission (2 Kings xvi. 10—16).

Urijah *may* have been omitted because of his unworthy connivance in an unlawful worship, not, however, as "an unimportant man," as Keil thinks. (Comp. Isa. viii. 2.) But if the list is a list of actual high-priests, Jehoiada can only have been omitted by accident, unless indeed he is represented in it by an unrecognised *alias.* Double names are common in Scripture, from Jacob-Israel, Esau-Edom, downwards.

<sup>(13)</sup> **Hilkiah begat Azariah.**—Hilkiah is probably the well-known high-priest who "found the Book of the Law," which led to the great reformation of Josiah's reign (2 Kings xxii. 8, *seq.*). Azariah, his son, is not elsewhere mentioned. The Azariah of 2 Chron. xxxi. 10, who figures as high-priest under Hezekiah, at least eighty years earlier, is absent from this list.

<sup>(14)</sup> **Seraiah begat Jehozadak.** — Seraiah was still high-priest at the moment of the fall of Jerusalem (588 B.C.). Nebuchadnezzar caused him to be put to death at Riblah (2 Kings xxv. 18—21; Jer. lii. 24, *seq.*)

From Azariah (verse 10) to Seraiah we find only ten names. In the list of the kings of Judah for about the same interval eighteen names occur (see chap. iii. 10—16). This fact undoubtedly suggests the omission of some generations from the list before us.

The use of the word "begat" throughout the series is not to be pressed to the contrary conclusion. Like the term "son" in Ezra vii. 3 ("Azariah, *son* of Meraioth," though six intermediate names are given in Chron.), it is a somewhat elastic technical formula in these genealogies.

<sup>(15)</sup> **And Jehozadak went into captivity.**—The Heb. is *went away.* Our version rightly supplies *into captivity.* (Comp. Jer. xlix. 3.) Jehozadak was presumably a child at the time; half a century later a son of his, the high-priest Jeshua or Joshua, returned with Zerubbabel at the head of the first colony of restored exiles, 536 B.C. (Hag. i. 1; Ezra iii. 2).

**When the Lord carried away Judah and Jerusalem by the hand of Nebuchadnezzar.** —The chronicler is generally charged with a strong Levitical and priestly bias, in unfavourable contrast to the "prophetical" tendency of the writers of Samuel and Kings. The sentiment of this verse, however, and of many other passages, is thoroughly accordant with the point of view of the greater prophets. Isaiah, *e.g.,* never wearies of proclaiming that the Assyrian conquerors were mere instruments in the hands of Jehovah, unconsciously executing His fore-ordained purposes.

**Nebuchadnezzar.**—So the name is spelt in Kings, Chronicles, and Daniel, but incorrectly. Jer. xxiv. 2, &c., reads Nebuchadrezzar, which is nearer the true name, *Nabium-kudurri-uçur* (Nebo protect the crown).

<sup>(16—19)</sup> The three branches of Levi with their main subdivisions. Parallel passages, Exod. vi. 16—19; Num. iii. 17—20.

<sup>(16)</sup> **Gershom.**—See Note on verse 1. In the Pentateuch, Gershom is son of Moses; Gershon, son of Levi.

<sup>(19)</sup> **And these are the families of the Levites according to their fathers.**—The word "families" (Heb., *mishpehôth*) does not mean single households, but groups of households, or clans. The sentence concludes the short list of the great Levitical houses, just as at Exod vi. 19. (See also Num. iii. 20, where a like formula appears to introduce what follows.)

<sup>(20, 21)</sup> The genealogy of the Gershonites in seven successive generations. It does not occur in the Pentateuch. This and the two following lists of Kohathites and Merarites are symmetrical in plan, but not in the number of names included.

<sup>(20)</sup> **Of Gershom.**—Literally, *to*—*i.e.,* belonging to Gershom.

*The Family*       I. CHRONICLES, VI.       *of Kohath.*

hath his son, *a* Zimmah his son, (21) ¹ Joah his son, ² Iddo his son, Zerah his son, Jeaterai his son. (22) The sons of Kohath; ³ Amminadab his son, Korah his son, Assir his son, (23) Elkanah his son, and Ebiasaph his son, and Assir his son, (24) Tahath his son, Uriel his son, Uzziah his son, and Shaul his son. (25) And the sons of Elkanah; *b* Amasai, and Ahimoth. (26) *As for* Elkanah; the sons of Elkanah; ⁴ Zophai his son, and Nahath his son, (27) Eliab his son, Jeroham his son, Elkanah his son. (28) And the sons of

*a* ver. 42.
¹ Or, *Ethan*, ver. 42.
² Or, *Adaiah*, ver. 41.
³ Or, *Izhar*, ver. 2. 18.
*b* See ver. 35, 36.
⁴ Or, *Zuph*, 1 Sam. i. 1.

---

Libni his son.—See Num. iii. 21, "To Gershon, the clan of the Libnite, and the clan of the Shimeite; these are the clans of the Gershonite."

The names Jahath, Zimmah, and Zerah recur in the line of Asaph, verses 41—43 below (see the Note there). Jeaterai, in whom the present series culminates, is wholly unknown. At the time when the list was first drawn up, the name may have represented a famous chieftain or family. It has the ending of a patronymic or gentilic term, and perhaps should be read with different vowels, *we 'Ithrai*, or *'Ithri*, "and the Ithrite" (comp. 'Ishai for Yishai), a clan of which came two of David's heroes (chap. xi. 40).

(22—23) **The sons of Kohath.** As the text stands we have here a threefold list, each portion of which is isolated from the rest, and begins afresh with the word *bnê* (the sons of).

(22) **Amminadab his son.**—Amminadab is not mentioned as a son of Kohath in the Pentateuch or elsewhere. Korah, here called son of Amminadab, is called son of *Izhar*, son of Kohath, Exod. vi. 21. (See verse 18, *supra*, and verse 38, *infra*.) Some assume that Amminadab is a "by-name" of Izhar (so Margin). It is more likely that the name Izhar has dropped out of the text of verse 22.

(22, 23) **Assir his son, Elkanah his son, and Ebiasaph his son.**—Comp. Exod. vi. 24: "And the sons of Korah, Assir, and Elkanah, and Abiasaph, these are the sons of Korah." The connection, then, is as follows:—

```
        Kohath
          |
        Izhar
          |
        Korah
   _____|_____
  |       |       |
Assir  Elkanah  Ebiasaph.
```

The conjunction *and*, in verse 23, seems to hint that the connection is no longer one of direct descent, but that the three, Assir, Elkanah, and Ebiasaph, are to be regarded as brothers.

(23) **And Assir his son.**—Comp. verse 37 below, in the line of Heman, which in great part coincides with the present series. There we read, "Assir, son of Ebiasaph, son of Korah." The present Assir is therefore son of Ebiasaph, and nephew of the former Assir (verse 22). The form of a direct descent is now resumed and continued with Tahath, son of Assir (verse 24).

(24) In the corresponding verse of the genealogy of Heman below (verse 38) the names are Tahath, Zephaniah, Azariah, and Joel. It is easy to suppose that as the two series diverge after Tahath, Uriel and Zephaniah are two different sons of Tahath. But we notice (1) that Uzziah (verse 24) may = Azariah, verse 36 (comp. King Uzziah=Azariah, 2 Kings xv. 1; 2 Chron. xxvi. 1); (2) that although there is an apparent break between verses 24 and 25, so that a new list begins with the sons of Elkanah (verse 25), yet verses 35 and 36 speak of an "Amasai, son of Elkanah," in exact agreement with verse 25; and (3) that the correspondence between the two lists (verses 22—30 and 33—38) is so close, that it is difficult not to assume their substantial identity. Uriel *may* have been also known as Zephaniah, and Shaul as Joel.

(25) **And the sons of Elkanah; Amasai.**—See last Note. It is natural to identify the Elkanah of verse 36 with this one. The posterity of both are so nearly the same; otherwise we might have taken the present Elkanah for the person mentioned in verse 23.

(26) The Hebrew text reads: "Elkanah his son—Elkanah—Zophai his son," &c. Zophai might mean the Zophite. The LXX. has (verse 25) "And sons of Elkanah, Amessi and Ahimoth;" (verse 26) "Elkanah his son, Souphi his son," &c. So the Syriac. That this is correct appears from comparison of Heman's pedigree (verse 35). The second Elkanah in verse 26 is therefore an intrusion, due perhaps to some scribe who remembered 1 Sam. i. 1, where Zophim occurs just before Elkanah. In verse 35 Elkanah is a son of Mahath, son of Amasai. Perhaps Mahath is identical with the Ahimoth of verse 25; if so, the true reading of verses 25, 26 would be: "And sons of Elkanah: Amasai his son, Ahimoth (Mahath) his son, Elkanah his son, Zophai his son," &c. Zophai is to Zuph (verse 35) as Chelubai (chap. ii. 9) to Chelub (chap. iv. 11). Nahath looks like a transformation of Toah (verse 34), and Eliab (verse 27)—"*El* is father"—may be a by-form of Eliel (*ibid.*) "*El* is el." Jeroham and Elkanah go back to Eliel in verse 34, just as they spring from Eliab here. The two series again coincide.

(28) **And the sons of Samuel.**—Heb., *Shemuel.* The third break in the Kohathite list.

We see from verses 33, 34 that Samuel (Shemuel, *name of God*) is son of Elkanah, son of Jeroham; hence we might suppose that the clause "Samuel his son" has been accidentally omitted at the end of verse 27. But it is quite possible that the writer assumed the connection to be too well known to require specification, or that he has here thrown together three independent genealogical fragments. Comp. with verses 27, 28 the pedigree of Elkanah, 1 Sam. i. 1: "Elkanah son of Jeroham son of Elihu son of Tohu son of Zuph." Here again the names vary, yet not so as to obliterate their identity. Elihu ("*El* is He") = Eliab, Eliel; Tohu, a fuller form of Toah = Nahath.

**The firstborn Vashni, and Abiah.**—Vashni is not a proper name, but a corrupt form of the Hebrew phrase "and the second" (*shēni*, *secundus*). The sons of the prophet Samuel were Joel, the firstborn, and Abiah, 1 Sam. viii. 2 (see also verse 33 below). Joel has fallen out of the text here; it should run, "Joel the firstborn, and the second Abiah."

Reviewing the Kohathite list (22—28) we conclude that it represents three statistical fragments which have been put in juxtaposition by the chronicler or the author whom he has followed, and that in accordance with the real connection between the members, as appears on comparison with the continuous list which

*The Family of Merari.*  **I. CHRONICLES, VI.**  *The Pedigree of Heman.*

Samuel; the firstborn ¹Vashni, and Abiah.

⁽²⁹⁾ The sons of Merari; Mahli, Libni his son, Shimei his son, Uzza his son, ⁽³⁰⁾ Shimea his son, Haggiah his son, Asaiah his son.

⁽³¹⁾ And these *are they* whom David set over the service of song in the house of the LORD, after that the *ᵃark had rest. ⁽³²⁾ And they ministered before the dwelling place of the tabernacle of the congregation with singing, until Solomon had built the house of the LORD in Jerusalem: and *then* they waited on their office according to their order.

⁽³³⁾ And these *are* they that ²waited with their children. Of the sons of the Kohathites: Heman a singer, the son of Joel, the son of Shemuel, ⁽³⁴⁾ the son of Elkanah, the son of Jeroham, the son of Eliel, the son of Toah, ⁽³⁵⁾ the son of Zuph, the son of Elkanah, the son of Mahath, the son of Amasai, ⁽³⁶⁾ the son of Elkanah, the son of Joel, the son of Azariah, the son of Zephaniah, ⁽³⁷⁾ the son of Tahath, the son of Assir, the son

¹ Called also Joel, ver. 33 & 1 Sam. 8. 2.

B.C. cir. 1296, &c.

ᵃ ch. 16. 1.

² Heb., *stood.*

---

immediately follows in verses 33—38. The fact that "Samuel his son" is the missing link between verses 27, 28, makes it likely that "Elkanah his son" is the true connection between verses 24 and 25.

From Levi to the sons of Samuel about twenty generations are reckoned. Usher's chronology dates the descent of Jacob and his sons into Egypt at 1706 B.C. Twenty generations are six hundred years. The sons of Samuel would, according to this, be living about 1106 B.C. and later. Ruth iv. 18—22 reckons only ten generations from Judah to Jesse, the father of David. This again shows that in their genealogical tables the Hebrews did not uniformly supply every link, but were often content with a statement of the principal names.

(29, 30) A short list of Merarite names. (Comp. Num. iii. 20, and verse 14, *supra*, for the two sons of Merari, Mahli and Mushi, after whom the clans of the Merarites were designated. The present list traces the line of Mahli to the seventh generation; all the names are alike unknown. Below, verses 44—47, we have another line going back to Mushi, brother of Mahli. Why has the chronicler preserved the three lists of verses 19—30? The process from Levi to the worthless sons of Samuel, and the utterly unknown names of Jeaterai and Asaiah, reads like an anti-climax. But it is not to be forgotten that these no longer significant fragments are genuine relics of ancient family registers, and as such may have had more than a merely antiquarian value in the days of the chronicler.

Verses 31, 32 are a prelude to the pedigrees of Heman, Asaph, and Ethan, the three great masters of David's choirs (33—48). The nature, time, and place of their special duties are described.

(31) **Set over the service of song.**—Literally, *made stand by the sides (hands) of song,* as if to minister to the sacred music. (Comp. chap. xxv. 2, 3, where the same peculiar phrase recurs, and Ps. cxxiii. 2, "as the eyes of slaves are unto the hand of their Lord." Comp. also the common heading of the Psalms, "to the conductor or precentor;" Authorised Version, "chief musician.")

**In the house of the Lord.**—In David's time, a tent, as next verse declares.

**After that the ark had rest.**—Perhaps locative: *at the resting-place of the Ark* (comp. Gen. viii. 9). From the time of its capture by the Philistines (2 Sam. vi. 17), the Ark had no certain dwelling till it was lodged in the tent which David spread for it on Mount Zion.

(32) **And they ministered.**—"And they continued ministering, before the dwelling of the Tent of Meeting, with the music."

**The dwelling place of the tabernacle.**—A defining genitive, like River of Jordan, or City of Jerusalem. In the court *before* this sacred dwelling wherein the Lord met His people, the services of sacrifice and song were carried on. The tent of the Ark in the city of David (see chap. xvi. 1) is here called by the old name of the Mosaic Tabernacle, *'ōhel mō'ēd*, "tent of tryst, or meeting," *i.e.*, of God with man. The ancient tent appears to have stood at Shiloh, and at Bethel (Judges xx. 26—28) in the days of the Judges, at Nob in the reign of Saul, and later at Gibeon. (See chap. xxi. 29, and 2 Chron. i. 3.)

**Until Solomon had built the house.**—The Ark, and the worship of which it was the centre, were then transferred to the more august abode of Solomon's Temple.

**And then they waited.**—Omit *then* and read "and they stood at their service according to their privilege." The place and precedence of the choirs and their leaders were fixed by David (chap. xvi. 37). *Standing* was the normal posture for singing.

(33) **And these are they that waited** (*stood*) **with their children.**—The main sentence which began at verse 31, and was suspended by the parenthetic verse 32, is now resumed. The persons meant are the three chiefs of the Levitical guilds of musicians, Heman, Asaph, and Ethan; their "children" are the members of those guilds. (Comp. the phrase, "sons of the prophets," *i.e.*, members of prophetic guilds, 2 Kings ix. 1; Amos vii. 14.) Chap. xxv. 1—7 supplies the names of the principal "sons" of the three masters. Their Levitical descent is shown in the genealogies here traced up from themselves to Levi. First we have the pedigree of Heman (verses 33—38) the Kohathite.

**Heman a singer.**—Rather, *the singer* or *minstrel*. Heman, as representing the chief branch of the Levites, is *primus inter pares* as regards the other master singers. His choir occupied the centre, having on its right that of the Gershonite Asaph, on its left that of the Merarite Ethan (verses 39, 44), so that Heman would conduct the whole body of musicians, when the three choirs chanted in concert. The word "minstrel" is more appropriate than "singer" because the original term (*ham'shôrēr*) implies singing which the singer himself accompanies with an instrument of music. (See chap. xxv. 6; LXX., ὁ ψαλτῳδός.)

**Son of Joel, the son of Shemuel.**—It is interesting to learn that Heman, the great minstrel, was a grandson of Samuel the great prophet. (For the connection between music and prophecy, see 2 Kings iii. 15; 1 Sam. x. 5, 6; and below, chap. xxv. 1, Note.)

243

of ᵃEbiasaph, the son of Korah, ⁽³⁸⁾ the son of Izhar, the son of Kohath, the son of Levi, the son of Israel.

⁽³⁹⁾ And his brother Asaph, who stood on his right hand, *even* Asaph the son of Berachiah, the son of Shimea, ⁽⁴⁰⁾ the son of Michael, the son of Baaseiah, the son of Malchiah, ⁽⁴¹⁾ the son of Ethni, the son of Zerah, the son of Adaiah, ⁽⁴²⁾ the son of Ethan, the son of Zimmah, the son of Shimei, ⁽⁴³⁾ the son of Jahath, the son of Gershom, the son of Levi.

*a* Ex. 6. 24.

¹Or, *Kushaiah*, ch. 15. 17.

⁽⁴⁴⁾ And their brethren the sons of Merari *stood* on the left hand: Ethan the son of ¹Kishi, the son of Abdi, the son of Malluch, ⁽⁴⁵⁾ the son of Hashabiah, the son of Amaziah, the son of Hilkiah, ⁽⁴⁶⁾ the son of Amzi, the son of Bani, the son of Shamer, ⁽⁴⁷⁾ the son of Mahli, the son of Mushi, the son of Merari, the son of Levi. ⁽⁴⁸⁾ Their brethren also the Levites *were* appointed unto all manner of service of the tabernacle of the house of God.

---

Considering that some have denied that Samuel was a Levite, the point of contact here noted looks like an undesigned coincidence.

⁽³⁸⁾ **Son of Israel.**—Asaph and Ethan are traced to Levi. It was not needful to repeat "son of Israel" in each case. For further remarks on the names in verses 34—38 see above Notes on 22—28, the lines being identical. The numerous variants, however, seem to imply that the author drew from different documents.

⁽³⁹⁻⁴³⁾ The pedigree of Asaph the Gershonite, traced back through thirteen names to Levi. That of Heman names twenty ancestors for the same period of time. This is one more illustration of the common usage of overleaping names in these genealogies.

⁽³⁹⁾ **His brother Asaph.**—Asaph was Heman's brother (1) as a Levite; (2) as a choir-master.

The striking agreement of the line of Heman with that of the Kohathites, detailed in verses 22—28 above, has led critics to look for a like coincidence between the line of Asaph as given here, and that of the Gershonites in verses 20, 21. There, however, we have only seven names, here there are thirteen. Still we observe that in the former passage the three names, Jahath, Zimmah, and Zerah appear in *the same order of lineal descent* from Gershon as in the present list; while the Adaiah of verse 41 obviously answers to the Iddo of verse 21, and Ethni (verse 41) is in Hebrew writing not unlike Jeaterai; and we are already familiar with the fact that genealogies sometimes recur in abbreviated forms. (Comp. Ezra vii. 1—5, with the line of Aaron in the present chapter.) Upon the whole, therefore, if the suggested identifications be correct, it appears that Asaph's pedigree has really been partially anticipated in verses 20, 21.

⁽⁴⁴⁻⁴⁷⁾ The pedigree of Ethan the Merarite, traced back through twelve names to Levi. Ethan is no doubt the same as Jeduthun, chap. xxv. 1; 2 Chron. xxxv. 15.

⁽⁴⁴⁾ **And their brethren the sons of Merari.**—We should say their *comrades* or *kinsmen* (see Note on verse 39). "Brethren," or "brothers," is the natural style for the members of a guild, whether religious like the monastic bodies, or commercial like the city companies of London, or benevolent like the Freemasons. The plural pronoun refers to the two preceding guilds of Heman and Asaph. The Ethanites stood on the left of the Hemanites in the sanctuary, as the Asaphites stood on their right, and this arrangement was hereditary.

**Kishi** is a contraction of Kushaiah, like Zabdi of Zebadiah.

⁽⁴⁷⁾ **Son of Mahli, the son of Mushi.**—In verse 19 Mahli and Mushi appear as two sons of Merari; so also at Lev. iii. 20. Mahli son of Mushi here must be nephew of the Mahli of those two passages, if the genealogical form is in each case to be understood literally. It is difficult on a first inspection to perceive any connection between the present list and that of the Merarites in verses 29, 30. The series there is:

Mahli, Libni, Shimei, Uzza, Shimea, Haggiah, and Asaiah.

Here we have:

Mushi, Mahli, Shamer, Bani, Amzi, Hilkiah, Amaziah, Hashabiah, Malluch, Abdi, Kishi, and Ethan.

Now it is quite possible that both lines spring from Mushi son of Merari. We have only to suppose that the name of Mushi has either dropped out or been omitted by design in verse 29. In that case, of course, Mahli in each line becomes identical. Next we remark that Libni in Hebrew adds but one letter (l) to Bani; and these two may be variants of the same name. The second line is again more complete than the first, as it supplies Shamer (Shemer) between Mahli and Bani-Libni. Further, Uzzi and Amzi express the same idea—that of strength—and may therefore indicate identity of person. The names Shimei and Shimeah are perhaps inadvertent duplicates of each other; which may also be the case with Amzi and Amaziah in the second series. Haggiah perhaps answers to Hilkiah.

Thus it may be right to regard this pedigree of Ethan as related to the Merarite line of verses 29, 30, in the same way as those of Heman and Asaph are related to the first drafts of the Kohathite and Gershonite lines of descent, although the connection is not so evident in the present instance, owing perhaps to corruption of the text.

Verses 48, 49 constitute the transition from the pedigrees of the three Levitical choir-masters to the line of the sons of Aaron—Eleazar, which is here repeated from Aaron to Ahimaaz. The form of the list is, however, different. Instead of "Eleazar *begat* Phinehas," it runs "Phinehas *his son*," &c. It is more likely that the chronicler found this list already connected with what follows in the source which he used for this section, than that he merely chose to repeat part of what he had already given under a slightly altered form.

⁽⁴⁸⁾ **Their brethren also the Levites.**—That is, *the Levites who were not musicians—the remaining Levites*.

**Appointed.**—Literally, *given*—that is, to Aaron and his sons as their assistants; Num. iii. 9 (Heb.), "And thou shalt give the Levites to Aaron and to his sons,

(49) But Aaron and his sons offered ᵃupon the altar of the burnt offering, and ᵇon the altar of incense, *and were appointed* for all the work of the *place* most holy, and to make an atonement for Israel, according to all that Moses the servant of God had commanded. (50) And these *are* the sons of Aaron; Eleazar his son, Phinehas his son, Abishua his son, (51) Bukki his son, Uzzi his son, Zerahiah his son, (52) Meraioth his son, Amariah his son, Ahitub his son, (53) Zadok his son, Ahimaaz his son. (54) Now these *are* their dwelling places throughout their castles in their coasts, of the sons of Aaron, of the families of the Kohathites: for their's was the lot. (55) And they gave them Hebron in the land of Judah, and the suburbs thereof round about it. (56) But the fields of the city, and the villages thereof, they gave to Caleb the son of Jephunneh. (57) And to the sons of Aaron they gave the cities of Judah, *namely*, Hebron, *the city* of refuge, and Libnah with her suburbs, and Jattir, and Eshtemoa, with their suburbs, (58) and ¹Hilen with her suburbs, Debir with her suburbs, (59) and ²Ashan with her suburbs, and Beth-shemesh with her suburbs: (60) and out of the tribe of Benjamin; Geba with her suburbs, and ³Alemeth with her suburbs, and Anathoth with her suburbs. All their cities

B.C. 1444, &c.

ᵃ Lev. 1. 9.

ᵇ Ex. 30. 7.

¹ Or, *Holon.* Josh. 21. 15.

² Or, *Ain,* Josh. 21. 16.

³ Or, *Almon,* Josh. 21. 18.

---

given are they to him from amongst the sons of Israel." The word is *nethûnim*. (Comp. *nethînim*, an identical form, as the name of a well-known class of Temple-servants.)

**Tabernacle.**—Rather, *dwelling-place* (*mishkan*).

(49) **But Aaron and his sons offered.**—Literally, *And Aaron and his sons were offering.* The participle denotes unintermitted action. "Aaron and his sons" is a technical name for the priests, to whom, according to this passage, three functions pertained: (1) sacrifice on the altars of burnt-offering and incense; (2) the work of the most holy place (Holy of holies); (3) atonement for Israel by special rites of sacrifice and purification.

**According to all that Moses . . . commanded.**—This refers to the entire ministry of the priests. The time in question is the Davidic age.

**The servant of God.** — Comp. Deut. xxxiv. 5; Josh. i. 1, 13. After his death, Moses is thrice called "servant of Jehovah," in whose earthly household he had been faithful as a servant (Heb. iii. 5). He forefigures in grand if imperfect outline that other servant of Jehovah, of whom the second half of Isaiah has so much discourse. "Servant of *God*" (*Elohim*) the chronicler writes, because in his day the NAME was held in ever-increasing awe.

(50—53) If the chronicler, and not his source, be held responsible for this repetition of the Aaronite line, we may regard it as an instance of his inartificial method of making a new start. He is about to pass from the Levitical genealogies to their cities and domains, and he first partially recapitulates the line of Aaron's sons, because their seats are to be described first. (Comp. verses 1, 2 with 16, 18.) He stops at Ahimaaz, who lived in the age of David and Solomon, because, apparently, the preceding section was mainly concerned with the Levites of that epoch.

(54—81) The Levitical cities, beginning with those of the Aaronites, the principal branch of the Kohathite clan. This list deals with the same topic as Josh. xxi. 3—40, with which, upon the whole, it is in substantial agreement. Verses 54—60 are parallel to Josh. xxi. 10—19.

(54) Render, "And these were their seats according to their encampments within their border." This, as the heading to all that follows, should be stopped off therefrom. It does not occur in Josh. xxi., and may indicate an intermediate source used by the chronicler. The variant spellings of proper names, many of which are not mere copyists' blunders, point in the same direction.

**Of the sons of Aaron.**—Rather, "to the sons of Aaron, of the clan of the Kohathites—for to them had fallen the lot—they gave to them Hebron," &c. Josh. xxi. 10 has, " for to them the lot had fallen first."

(55, 56) Closely answering to Josh. xxi. 11, 12.

(55) **Hebron.**—Josh., "the city of Arba, the father of the Anak, that is, Hebron."

**In the land of Judah.**—Josh., "hill-country" (*har for ha'areç*).

**Suburbs.**— The Hebrew *migrashim*, pastures or commons, as opposed to arable land (Authorised version, "fields;" Heb., *sadeh*). Num. xxxv. 3—5 defines the extent of the Levitical domain round the cities where they dwelt.

(56) **To Caleb the son of Jephunneh.**—Josh. adds "as his posesssion."

(57) **They gave the cities of Judah.**—Heb. text, *the cities of refuge, Hebron and Libnah, and her pastures.* Of the cities mentioned only Hebron was an asylum for the manslayer. The other cities of refuge were Kedesh-Naphtali, Shechem, Bezer, Ramoth-Gilead, and Golan. (See Josh. xx. 7, 8.) Here our translators have adopted the Hebrew marginal correction of the text. (Comp. Josh. xxi. 13, which reads, "The manslayer's city of refuge, Hebron.") The same inaccuracy recurs in verse 67, below.

**With her suburbs.**—*With her pastures.* The phrase has been omitted after Jattir (Josh. xxi. 13).

(58) **Hilen.**—Holon, which twice occurs in Josh. xv. 51, xxi. 15, is a more natural form.

**Debir.**—Oracle, the inmost sanctuary; anciently, Kirjath-sepher (Book Town).

(59) **Ashan** (smoke); in Joshua, Ain (fountain). The place may have had both names, from a fountain rising like a column of smoke. "Juttah and her pastures" has fallen out here (Josh. xxi. 16). At the end of the verse Joshua adds, "Nine cities out of these two tribes," viz., Judah and Simeon.

(60) "Gibeon and her pastures" is omitted; probably an oversight, due to the similarity of sound and form

throughout their families *were* thirteen cities.

(61) And unto the sons of Kohath, *which were* left of the family of that tribe, *were cities given* out of the half tribe, *namely, out of* the half *tribe* of Manasseh, ᵃ by lot, ten cities.

(62) And to the sons of Gershom throughout their families out of the tribe of Issachar, and out of the tribe of Asher, and out of the tribe of Naphtali, and out of the tribe of Manasseh in Bashan, thirteen cities.

(63) Unto the sons of Merari *were given* by lot, throughout their families, out of the tribe of Reuben, and out of the tribe of Gad, and out of the tribe of Zebulun,

ᵇ twelve cities. (64) And the children of Israel gave to the Levites *these* cities with their suburbs. (65) And they gave by lot out of the tribe of the children of Judah, and out of the tribe of the children of Simeon, and out of the tribe of the children of Benjamin, these cities, which are called by *their* names.

(66) And *the residue* of the families of the sons of Kohath had cities of their coasts out of the tribe of Ephraim. (67) ᶜ And they gave unto them, *of* the cities of refuge, Shechem in mount Ephraim with her suburbs; *they gave* also Gezer with her suburbs, (68) and Jokmeam with her suburbs, and Bethhoron with her suburbs, (69) and Aijalon

ᵃ Josh. 21. 5.
ᵇ Josh. 21. 7, 34.
ᶜ Josh. 21. 21.

---

between Gibeon and Geba. Alemeth and Almôn are each valid formations, and perhaps represent an older and younger name of the place.

**Thirteen cities.**—The list in its present shape contains eleven. This *proves* that Juttah and Gibeon should be restored to the text.

(61–63) These verses correspond to Josh. xxi. 5–7. They supply short statements of the *number* of cities in the various tribes assigned to the non-Aaronic Kohathites, to the Gershonites, and the Merarites.

(61) **And unto the sons of Kohath, which were left of the family of that tribe.**—A comparison with Josh. xxi. 5 shows that the text is again mutilated. That passage reads (Heb.), " And unto the sons of Kohath which were left, out of the families [clans] of the tribe of Ephraim, and out of the tribe of Dan, and out of the half of the tribe of Manasseh, by the lot, ten cities." The curious redundancy of the present text of verse 61, " Out of the half of the tribe of the half of Manasseh "—a phrase which occurs nowhere else—suggests bad emendation of a corrupt reading. The passage from Joshua undoubtedly gives the meaning here. (Comp. verses 66 and 67, below.)

(62) **Gershom** (Josh., *Gershon*) **throughout their families.**—Heb., *to* [*i.e.*, with regard to, after] *their clans* (so verse 63). In verse 60, "throughout their families" represents Heb. *in their clans.*

**Tribe of Manasseh in Bashan.**—Joshua, "half-tribe."

(63) This verse is word for word the same as Josh. xxi. 7, omitting the one term " by lot."

(64, 65) " So the sons of Israel gave to the Levites the cities and their pastures. And they gave by the lot, out of the tribe of the sons of Judah, and out of the tribe of the sons of Simeon, and out of the tribe of the sons of Benjamin, those cities which are called by names;" named, that is, in the list of verses 55—60, above. This is clearly a summing up of the whole account so far. The eleven tribes have all been mentioned in verses 61—65.

The " cities " of verse 64 are those included in verses 61–63. So the parallel verse (Josh. xxi. 8) refers back to Josh. xxi. 5–7, which is parallel to our verses 61–63. Josh. xxi. 9 (= our verse 65) *introduces* the names of the cities which fell to the Aaronites. But there is no real divergence between that account and this; because verse 65 also refers back to the list of the same cities in verses 55—60. The chronicler adds Benjamin, with reference to verse 60, to make his tribal list complete.

(66–81) The names of the cities numbered in verses 61—64. (Comp. Josh. xxi. 20—26.)

(66) **And the residue of the families.**—The Hebrew text can hardly mean this; and Josh. xxi. 20 shows that it is incorrect. The original text must have been, " And to the families of the sons of Kohath : —— and the cities of their border were of the tribe of Ephraim." The construction breaks off, and a new start is made by the words " and the cities," &c. The verse is abridged as compared with Joshua, *l.c.*

(67) **And they gave unto them, of the cities of refuge . . .**—The correct version of the Hebrew text is, " And they gave unto them the cities of refuge, Shechem and her pastures, in the hill-country of Ephraim; and Gezer and her pastures." Perhaps both here and in verse 57 above " city " (*'iyr*), and not " cities " (*'arey*), is the original reading. We have already noticed many indications of textual corruption in this and the former section. Gezer was not a city of refuge. (See Note on verse 57.) Josh. xxi. 21 has the singular.

(68) **Jokmeam.**—Joshua has Kibzaim, a name omitted by the LXX. Vatic. Jokmeam is probably right. The other might easily be a misreading of it, owing to confusion of similar letters. The site is unknown. The four cities of verses 67, 68 lay in Ephraim. Beth-horon, Gibeon, and Aijalon, the scenes of the great and providentially determined overthrow of the five kings of the Amorites, were appropriately assigned to the sacred tribe of Levi.

(69) **Aijalon with her suburbs . . .**—Josh. xxi. 23, 24, " And out of the tribe of Dan, Eltekeh and her pastures, Gibbethon and her pastures, Aijalon and her pastures, Gath-rimmon and her pastures; four cities." Clearly there is a *lacuna* in our text between verses 68 and 69. It has been supposed that the chronicler omits mention of the tribe of Dan, here and elsewhere, owing to a religious prejudice, because of the illicit form of worship of which the city Dan was the centre. It is more likely that such omissions are not chargeable to the chronicler, but either to the im-

*The Cities of the Children* I. CHRONICLES, VI. *of Gershom and Merari.*

with her suburbs, and Gath-rimmon with her suburbs: <sup>(70)</sup> and out of the half tribe of Manasseh; Aner with her suburbs, and Bileam with her suburbs, for the family of the remnant of the sons of Kohath.

<sup>(71)</sup> Unto the sons of Gershom *were given* out of the family of the half tribe of Manasseh, Golan in Bashan with her suburbs, and Ashtaroth with her suburbs: <sup>(72)</sup> and out of the tribe of Issachar; Kedesh with her suburbs, Daberath with her suburbs, <sup>(73)</sup> and Ramoth with her suburbs, and Anem with her suburbs: <sup>(74)</sup> and out of the tribe of Asher; Mashal with her suburbs, and Abdon with her suburbs, <sup>(75)</sup> and Hukok with her suburbs, and Rehob with her suburbs: <sup>(76)</sup> and out of the tribe of Naphtali; Kedesh in Galilee with her suburbs, and Hammon with her suburbs, and Kirjathaim with her suburbs.

<sup>(77)</sup> Unto the rest of the children of Merari *were given* out of the tribe of Zebulun, Rimmon with her suburbs, Tabor with her suburbs: <sup>(78)</sup> and on the other side Jordan by Jericho, on the east side of Jordan, *were given them* out of the tribe of Reuben, <sup>1</sup>Bezer in the wilderness with her suburbs, and Jahzah with her suburbs, <sup>(79)</sup> Kedemoth also with her suburbs, and Mephaath with her

<sup>1</sup> Or, *Bozor*, Josh. 21. 36.

---

perfection of his sources, or to the carelessness, and perhaps malpractice, of his copyists and editors. (See further Note on chap. vii. 12.)

<sup>(70)</sup> **Aner ... Bileam.**—Josh. xxi. 25 reads, "Taanach [see Josh. xvii. 11] and Gath-rimmon." The latter is a mere repetition from the preceding verse. Bileam is a man's name, being the Hebrew spelling of Balaam. It should be Ibleam (Josh. xvii. 11). So the LXX. Aner (Gen. xiv. 13) is also a man, one of Abraham's allies. Taanach is probably right, the last three letters of the Hebrew word closely resembling those of Aner.

**For the family.**—Better, *unto the family of the sons of Kohath who were left.* This depends on the idea of *giving* (verse 67). The phrase is a sort of subscription to the whole list of verses 67—70. For "family" the plural should be read, as in Josh. xxi. 26.

THE CITIES OF THE GERSHONITES. (Comp. Josh. xxi. 27—33.) Verses 71—76.

<sup>(71)</sup> **Unto the sons of Gershom.**—Supply *they gave*, from verse 67.

**Golan in Bashan** (comp. the classical Gaulanitis, a district east of the sea of Galilee) was a city of refuge, like Hebron and Shechem.

**Ashtaroth.**—*Images of Ashtoreth* (Astarte, queen of heaven); a name like Anathoth (verse 60), which means "images of Anath," or *Anatum*, the consort of *Anum* (the sky). The two cities must have been ancient seats of the worship of Ashtoreth and Anath. The names still survive in *Tell-Ashtereh* and *Anâta*. Joshua (*l.c.*) reads Be'eshterah—perhaps a popular pronunciation of Beth-Ashterah (house of Ashtoreth).

<sup>(72)</sup> **Kedesh** means "sanctuary." Josh. xix. 20 and xxi. 28 has Kishion, which may have borne the other name, as being the seat of a famous sanctuary.

<sup>(73)</sup> **Ramoth.**—In Josh. xxi. Jarmuth, but in Josh. xix. 21 Remeth. Jarmuth occurs in Josh. xii. 11, and is probably right.

**Anem.**—Josh. xxi. 29 and xix. 21 has En-gannim. Josh. xv. 34 mentions a Judæan city called ha-Enam (the two fountains), and that not far from En-gannim (fount of gardens). Anem is very much like Enam.

<sup>(74)</sup> **Mashal** is perhaps a popular pronunciation of Mish'al (Josh. xxi. 30, xix. 26). (Comp. Shêlâh = She'êlâh.)

<sup>(75)</sup> **Hukok.**—Helkath (Josh. xix. 25). Hukkôk was a city of Naphtali (Josh. xix. 34).

<sup>(76)</sup> **Kedesh in Galilee.**—A city of refuge (Josh. xxi. 32); the modern *Kedes*.

**Hammon** = Hammoth-dor, "hot springs of Dor" (Josh. xxi. 32); also called Hammath (Josh. xix. 35).

**Kirjathaim.**—In Josh. xxi. 32 Kartan; a contracted form of the dual of Kereth (=Kirjah), like Dothan for Dothaim. (Dothain, Gen. xxxvii. 17.)

THE CITIES OF THE MERARITES. (Comp. Josh. xxi. 34—38.) Verses 77—81.

<sup>(77)</sup> **Unto the rest of the children of Merari.**—Rather, *Unto the sons of Merari, the remaining Levites*, as at Josh. xxi. 34. The cities of the Kohathites and Gershonites having been rehearsed, it was natural to speak of the Merarites as "those who were left."

**Were given.**—*They gave*, as before (verse 71).

**Rimmon ... Tabor.**—Heb. *Rimmônô*. The reading of Josh. xxi. 34, 35 is quite different. We there find mention of Jokneam, Kartah, Dimnah, and Nahalal, "four cities." The first pair of names may be accidentally omitted from our text. Dimnah, in Joshua, should probably be Rimmonah, answering to the present Rimmono or Rimmon (Josh. xix. 13). Rimmon, the Assyrian *Rammânu*. (See Note on 2 Kings v. 18.) Nahalal is mentioned again (Josh. xix. 15) as a city of Zebulun; while Tabor is only known as the name of the mountain which rises north-east of the plain of Esdraelon, and is famous as the traditional scene of the Transfiguration (Judges viii. 18; Ps. lxxxix. 12). Nahalal means "pasture," or "sheep-walk" = Nahalôl (Isa. vii. 19); and the original reading of our text may have been, *Nahalal-tabôr* (*pasturage of Tabor*) — a compound proper name like Hamm-thôdôr, and many others.

<sup>(78, 79)</sup> **Bezer in the wilderness.**—A city of refuge (Deut. iv. 43). The phrase "on the east of Jordan" fixes the meaning of the indefinite expression "on the other side Jordan."

**Jahzah** is a form of Jahaz, originally meaning, "to Jahaz." (Comp. the modern names Stamboul = ἐς τὰν πόλιν, Stanchio = ἐς τὰν χίω.) Jahaz was assigned to Reuben at the partition of Canaan (Josh. xiii. 18), along with Kedemoth and Mephaath. Mesha, king of Moab, recovered it from Israel (see Note on 2 Kin. i. 1). Mephaath belonged to Moab temp. Jeremiah (Jer. xlviii. 21). It was, according to Jerome, a garrison town in the Roman age. (See also Josh. xiii. 18, xxi. 37; Deut. ii. 26.)

suburbs: (80) and out of the tribe of Gad; Ramoth in Gilead with her suburbs, and Mahanaim with her suburbs, (81) and Heshbon with her suburbs, and Jazer with her suburbs.

CHAPTER VII.—(1) Now the sons of Issachar were, ªTola, and Puah, Jashub, and Shimrom, four. (2) And the sons of Tola; Uzzi, and Rephaiah, and Jeriel, and Jahmai, and Jibsam, and Shemuel, heads of their father's house, to wit, of Tola: they were valiant men of might in their generations; ᵇ whose number was in the days of David two and twenty thousand and six hundred. (3) And the sons of Uzzi; Izrahiah: and the sons of Izrahiah: Michael, and Obadiah, and Joel, Ishiah, five: all of them chief men. (4) And with them, by their generations, after the house of their fathers, were bands of soldiers for war, six and thirty thousand men: for they had many wives and sons. (5) And their brethren among all the families of Issachar were valiant men of might, reckoned in all by their genealogies fourscore and seven thousand.

ª Gen. 46. 13; Num. 26. 23.

ᵇ 2 Sam. 24. 1. 2.

---

(80) **Ramoth in Gilead.**—A city of refuge (Josh. xxi. 36). Jazer, Heshbon, Mahanaim, were given by Moses to the Gadites (Josh. xiii. 25, 26). Ramoth Gilead (see 1 Kings xxii.; 2 Chron. xviii., and 2 Kings viii. 28). Its position is unknown.

**Mahanaim,** now *Maneh,* lay on the north border of Gad.

(81) **Heshbon,** now *Hesbân,* on the south border of Gad. (See also Isa. xv. 4; Jer. xlviii. 2.)

**Jazer** belonged to Moab in the eighth century (Isa. xvi. 8, 9; Jer. xlviii. 32).

In regard to this entire list of the Levitical cities, it has been asserted that it is based upon a theory which is historically false; the theory, namely, that certain towns with their pasture-grounds were assigned by lot to the Levites for their exclusive possession. The objection is irrelevant, for the sacred records neither affirm nor imply that none but Levitical families dwelt in the forty-eight Levitical cities. It is à priori probable that the bulk of their population would be ordinary Israelites of the tribes in which they were situated. (Comp. Lev. xxv. 32—34, and verses 55—57 *supra,* and Num. xxxv. 1—5.)

Variations in local names, such as we have noted in comparing this list with those in Joshua, are not at all surprising, when it is remembered that centuries elapsed between the composition of the two books; and that names of places, like other names, are liable to phonetic change in the course of time. Something also must be allowed for errors of transcription.

### VII.

THE GREAT CLANS OF ISSACHAR, BENJAMIN, NAPTHALI, WEST MANASSEH, EPHRAIM, AND ASHER.

(1—5) The tribe of Issachar, its clans and their military strength.

(1) **Now the sons of Issachar.**—Heb., *and to the sons*—i.e., "and as for the sons of Issachar, Tola, Puah, &c., four were they." The Vatic., LXX., has the dative; the Alex. the nominative, which is perhaps a correction. The four names are given Gen. xlvi. 13, where the second is Puwwah, the third Iôb; and Num. xxvi. 23, where also the second name is Puwwah, but the third Iâshûb (*he returns*). The Heb. text here is Iâshîb (*he makes return*); the Hebrew margin, adopted by the Authorised Version, is the same as the text of Num. xxvi.

(2—6) These verses supply names and facts not found elsewhere. We have here some of the results of the census of David (2 Sam. xxiv., and below, chap. xxi.).

(2) **Heads of their father's house.**—Rather, *chiefs of their father-houses* (septs or clans).

**Of Tola.**—*Belonging to Tola,* that is, to the great clan or sub-tribe so called.

**In their generations.**—*According to their registers* or *birth-rolls.*

**Whose number.**—The number of the warriors of all the six groups of the Tolaite branch of Issachar.

**In the days of David.**—See the census (chap. xxi.).

(3) **Izrahiah . . .**—All these names contain a divine element. Izrahiah means "Iah riseth (like the sun)" (comp. Mal. iv. 2); Michael, "who like God?" (Comp. Isa. xl. 18, 25.) Before Ishiah *and* has fallen out.

**Five: all of them chief men.**—Heb., *five chiefs* (heads) *altogether* (all of them). But perhaps the punctuation should be as in the Authorised Version. verse 7.)

(4) **By their generations.**—Heb., *after* or *according to their birth-rolls* or *registers.* The census of the Uzzite warriors was taken "according to their birth-rolls and their father-houses" (septs or clans).

**Bands of soldiers.**—Heb., *troops of the host of war* or *of the battle-host.*

**For they had many wives and sons.**—They are the clans represented by the hereditary chiefs Izrahiah, Michael, and the rest.

(5) **And their brethren.**—Fellow-tribesmen.

**Families.**—Clans (*mishpehôth*). The verse states the number of warriors for the whole tribe of Issachar in David's census at 87,000. Render: "And their kinsmen, of all the clans of Issachar, valiant warriors. Eighty-seven thousand was their census for the whole (tribe)."

**Reckoned in all by their genealogies.**—Heb., *hithyahsâm,* a difficult word peculiar to the chronicler in the Old Testament, but reappearing in the Rabbinic Hebrew. The present form is a verbal noun with suffix pronoun, and means "their enrolling" or "enrolment," their census; cp. ἀπογράφεσθαι (Luke ii. 1). As the Tolaites were 22,600, and the sons of Izrahiah 36,000, the other son of Issachar must have amounted to 28,400, to make up the total of 87,000 for the tribe. At the first census of Moses (Num. i. 29), the warriors of Issachar were 54,400; at the second (Num. xxvi. 25) they were 64,300. (Comp. Judges v. 15 and x. 1 for the ancient prowess of Issachar.)

*The Sons of*      I. CHRONICLES, VII.      *Benjamin.*

(6) The sons of ᵃBenjamin; Bela, and Becher, and Jediael, three. (7) And the sons of Bela; Ezbon, and Uzzi, and Uzziel, and Jerimoth, and Iri, five; heads of the house of *their* fathers, mighty men of valour; and were reckoned by their genealogies twenty and two thousand and thirty and four. (8) And the sons of Becher; Zemira, and Joash, and Eliezer, and Elioenai, and Omri, and Jerimoth, and Abiah, and Anathoth, and Alameth. All these *are* the sons of Becher. (9) And the number of them, after their genealogy by their generations, heads of the house of their fathers, mighty men of valour, *was* twenty thousand and two hundred. (10) The sons also of Jediael; Bilhan: and the sons of Bilhan; Jeush, and Benjamin, and Ehud, and Chenaanah, and Zethan, and Tharshish, and Ahishahar. (11) All these the sons of Jediael, by the heads of their

ᵃ Gen. 46. 21.

---

(6—11) The tribe of Benjamin.

(6) **Benjamin.**—Before this word *bnê* (sons of . . .) has been lost, because Benjamin in Hebrew begins with the same three letters. The present list of the sons of Benjamin may be compared with three others, that of Gen. xlvi. 21, that of Num. xxvi. 38—41, and that of the next chap., verses 1—5.

(1) Gen. xlvi. 21—
Bela and Becher and Ashbel, Gera and Naaman, Ehi and Rosh, Muppim and Huppim and Ard.

(2) Num. xxvi. 38—
    Bela. Ashbel. Ahiram. Shephupham. Hupham.
    |
Ard. Naaman.

(3) 1 Chron. viii. 1—
    Bela. Ashbel. Ahrah. Noha. Rapha.
    |
Addar. | Abihud. | Naaman. | Gera. | Huram.
Gera.   Abishua.   Ahoah.   Shephupham.

All the lists make Bela the first of Benjamin's sons. In other respects they differ greatly. Verse 6 assigns him two brothers—Becher and Jediael. Of these, Becher occurs in Gen. xlvi., Jediael here only.

(6) **Becher** with different vowels would mean *firstborn*; and the original reading in Gen. xlvi. may have been *Bela bechoro*—"Bela his firstborn," as in 1 Chron. viii. 1.

**Jediael**, *friend of God*, may be a substitute for *Ashbel*, i.e., Eshbaal, *man of Bel* or *Baal*. (Comp. chap. iii. 8, Eliada for Beeliada.) Ashbel is the second son of Benjamin in Num. xxvi. and chap. viii., and the third (perhaps second) in Gen. xlvi.

(7) **And the sons of Bela.**—The names are wholly different in chap. viii. 3, 4. The reason would seem to be that the names before us represent the chieftains and clans of Bela as they existed at a given epoch, viz., the time of David's census. The list of chap. viii. belongs to another period. Here, as elsewhere, it is evident enough that the chronicler has faithfully followed or rather transcribed his sources, without a thought of harmonising their apparent inconsistencies.

**Heads of . . . fathers.**—Rather, *heads of their father-houses*, i.e., chieftains.

**And were reckoned by their genealogies.**—*And their census was* 22,034. This number represents the fighting strength of the Belaites, who are here identified with their heads.

(8) Nine sons of Becher.

**The sons of Becher.**—See Note on verse 6. The nine Benjamite houses here enumerated might have been known as "sons of the firstborn." They are nowhere else recorded. The remarkable name Elioenai is frequent in the Chronicles. (See chaps. iii. 23, iv. 36, vii. 8; Ezra x. 22, 27; uncontracted, Eliohenai, chap. xxvi. 3, Ezra viii. 4.)

**Anathoth and Alameth** (Alemeth) were Levitical *towns* in Benjamin (chap. vi. 60).

**Jerimoth**, or Jeremoth (a son of Bela, verse 7), looks like another local name. (Comp. Jarmuth and Ramoth.) It also occurs often in the Chronicles (eight or nine times). The clans may have borne the names of their seats.

(9) **And the number . . .**—Render, "And their census (*hithyahsâm*) according to their birth-rolls, heads of their clans, valiant warriors, was 20,200." This means that the total number of the warriors of Becher, chiefs with clans, was 20,200. "Their census:" that is, the census of the chiefs who are regarded as one with their clans. Others assume that the names in these registers are merely those of supposed founders of the clans; eponyms like Hellen, Ion, Dorus, &c., or Italus, Latinus, Romulus, and Remus.

(10) Eight sons of Jediael.

**Bilhan.**—Chap. i. 42, a son of Seir. Perhaps an Edomite element in Benjamin. (Comp. chaps. ii. 34, iv. 18, ii. 46, and especially the case of Caleb the Kenizzite.)

**Jeush.**—So Heb., margin. Text, Jeish; a son of Esau (chap. i. 35).

**Benjamin.**—It is curious that a Benjamite clan should have borne the tribal name. (Comp. iv. 16, Asareel and Note.)

**Ehud.**—A namesake of Ehud the judge, who slew Eglon the Moabite oppressor of Israel (Judges iii. 15). Ehud the judge was a son of Gera, and Gera was a division of Bela (chap. viii. 3, 5).

**Chenaanah** (Canaanitess) is perhaps a Canaanite house which had amalgamated with the bnê Jediael.

**Tharshish.**— Elsewhere the name of a famous Phœnician colony in Spain. The name occurs once again as a personal name (Esther i. 14, one of the seven Persian princes). In Exod. xxviii. 20, and six other places, it is the name of a gem.

**Ahishahar.**—*Brother of dawn*. (Comp. Shaharaim—*double dawn*, chap. viii. 8, and Isa. xiv. 12, ben-shahar—*son of dawn*.) Perhaps the common Arab designation bnê *qedem*—"sons of the east"—is similar.

(11) **All these the sons of Jediael.**—Render, "All these were sons of Jediael; (according) to the heads of the clans, valiant warriors; 17,200 going out in host to the battle." Perhaps the particle (*according to*) should be omitted. In any case, the chiefs or the clans are regarded as one with their warriors.

The sum of the warriors of Benjamin is thus 54,434. The Mosaic census (Num. xxvi. 41) gave 45,600. An increase of barely 14,000 in the course of at least

fathers, mighty men of valour, *were seventeen thousand and two hundred soldiers*, fit to go out for war *and* battle. <sup>(12)</sup> Shuppim also, and Huppim, the children of ¹Ir, *and* Hushim, the sons of ²Aher.

<sup>(13)</sup> The sons of Naphtali; Jahziel, and Guni, and Jezer, and Shallum, the sons of Bilhah.

<sup>(14)</sup> The sons of Manasseh; Ashriel, whom she bare : (*but* his concubine the Aramitess bare Machir the father of Gilead: <sup>(15)</sup> and Machir took to wife *the sister* of Huppim and Shuppim, whose

¹ Or, *Iri*, ver 7.
² Or, *Ahiram*, Num. 26. 38.

---

three centuries may seem too small. But the tribe was well-nigh exterminated in the vengeance which Israel took for the crime of Gibeah (Judges xx. 47).

<sup>(12)</sup> **Shuppim also, and Huppim, the children of Ir.**—Literally, *and Shuppim and Huppim sons of Ir; Hushim sons of Aher.* The copulative *and* suggests that "Shuppim and Huppim" are other Benjamite clans thrown in at the end of the account. We have seen (see Note on verses 6—11) that Gen. xlvi. 21 names "Muppim and Huppim" as sons of Benjamin, and that Num. xxvi. has "Shephupham and Hupham" corresponding to the same pair of names. Lastly, chap. viii. 5 mentions "Shephuphan and Huram" among the sons of Bela, son of Benjamin. It is clear that "Muppim" is a mere slip of the pen for "Shuppim," to which the name Shephupham is really equivalent. From Shephupham, according to Num. xxvi., sprang the clan of the "Shuphami" (Shuphamite), as from "Hupham" the clan of the Huphami. Shupham and Hupham are quite natural variants of Shuppim and Huppim. The "Huram" of chap. viii. 5 is a scribe's error for "Hupham." Shuppim and Huppim, called sons of Benjamin in Genesis and Numbers, and sons of Bela in chap. viii., are here called "sons of Ir;" verse 7 above informs us that Ir or Iri (? the Irite) was a son of Bela. There is no more contradiction here than there would be in calling the same person a son of David, son of Judah, and son of Abraham.

**Hushim, the sons of Aher.**—The name Hushim (a *plural* form) recurs at chap. viii. 8, 11, as a Benjamite clan. Aher looks like a variant of the Ahiram of Numbers, and the Ahrah of chap. viii., and perhaps of the Ehi-Rosh of Genesis. From this it would appear that the whole verse is an appendix to the genealogy of Benjamin. The word Aher, however, happens to mean *another*, and if the reading were certain (comp. the variants Ahiram, Ahrah, &c.), would be very singular as a proper name. The clause has been rendered "Hushim, sons of another;" and this odd expression has been taken to be a veiled reference to the tribe of Dan, whose name is omitted in the present section. Gen. xlvi. 23, "And the sons of Dan, Hushim," a statement occurring like the present clause between that of the sons of Benjamin and the sons of Naphtali, is cited in support of this view. This last coincidence is certainly remarkable; but the following considerations are decidedly adverse to the view in question: 1. Num. xxvi. 42 calls the offspring of Dan, Shuham, not Hushim, though there also Dan follows Benjamin. 2. Dan is, indeed, omitted here, but so also is Zebulun, just as Gad and Asher are omitted in chap. xxvii. 16—22; and Naphtali here has only one verse. 3. The chronicler's dislike of the tribe of Dan is probably an unfounded supposition, suggested by some accidental omissions; he has mentioned that tribe by name in chaps. ii. 2, xii. 35, xxvii. 22. If the omission in the present list be neither accidental nor due to imperfect MSS., it may be ascribed to later editors of the book. (Comp. Judges xviii. and Rev. vii. 5—8.)

<sup>(13)</sup> **The sons of Naphtali.**—See Num. xxvi. 48 seq., and Gen. xlvi. 24, which read Jahzeel and Shillem.

**Sons of Bilhah.**—Dan and Naphtali were her sons (Gen. xlvi. 25). That does not, however, prove that a reference to Dan is intended here. Both in Genesis, *l.c.*, and in the present text, grandsons are reckoned as sons.

THE TRIBE OF WEST MANASSEH (verses 14—19).

Verses 14—15 are very obscure.

<sup>(14)</sup> **The sons of Manasseh.**—Translate, *the sons of Manasseh, Asriel, whom his Aramean concubine bare.* (*She bare Machir, father of Gilead.*) Num. xxvii. 1, Josh. xvii. 3, give the line

Manasseh.
|
Machir.
|
Gilead.
|
Hepher.
|
Zelophehad.

Zelophehad has five daughters, but no sons. Num. xxvi. 29—33 gives the same line with additions thus:—

Manasseh.
|
Machir.
|
Gilead.
|
Jeezer. Helek. Asriel. Shechem. Shemida. Hepher.
|
Zelophehad.

This last passage is important, because it expressly declares that the names all represent clans, with the exception of Zelophehad, who "had no sons, but daughters." It also shows that Asriel was great-grandson of Manasseh. The parenthesis of verse 14, therefore, appears to be intended to warn the reader that Asriel was the "son" of the Aramean concubine of Manasseh, mediately through descent from Machir.

<sup>(15)</sup> **And Machir took to wife.**—The Hebrew cannot mean this. Translate, *now Machir took a wife of Huppim and of Shuppim* (the two Benjamite clans of verse 12); *and the name of the first* (read 'ahath) *was Maachah, and the name of the second* (read shēnith) *was . . . ."* (the name is omitted). It is tempting to make Zelophehad the other wife, who had only daughters, whereas Maachah bore a son (verse 16); but Numbers, *l.c.*, and Josh., *l.c.*, make Zelophehad a man. We must, therefore, suppose a *lacuna* of some few words, which gave the name of Machir's second wife, and the descent of Zelophehad from her. The expression "of Huppim and of Shuppim" is literally "to Huppim and to Shuppim," that is, belonging to. So "of Tola," (verse 2).

We have no means of further elucidating the import of this curious tribal record. That it relates to West Manasseh is inferred from its position here, as well

*The Sons of*     I. CHRONICLES, VII.     *Ephraim.*

sister's name *was* Maachah;) and the name of the second *was* Zelophehad: and Zelophehad had daughters. <sup>(16)</sup> And Maachah the wife of Machir bare a son, and she called his name Peresh; and the name of his brother *was* Sheresh; and his sons *were* Ulam and Rakem. <sup>(17)</sup> And the sons of Ulam; *ᵃBedan. These *were* the sons of Gilead, the son of Machir, the son of Manasseh. <sup>(18)</sup> And his sister Hammoleketh bare Ishod, and Abiezer, and Mahalah. <sup>(19)</sup> And the sons of Shemidah were, Ahian, and Shechem, and Likhi, and Aniam.

<sup>(20)</sup> And the sons of Ephraim; Shu-thelah, and Bered his son, and Tahath his son, and Eladah his son, and Tahath his son, <sup>(21)</sup> and Zabad his son, and Shuthelah his son, and Ezer, and Elead, whom the men of Gath *that were* born in *that* land slew, because they came down to take away their cattle. <sup>(22)</sup> And Ephraim their father mourned many days, and his brethren came to comfort him. <sup>(23)</sup> And when he went into his wife, she conceived, and bare a son, and he called his name Beriah, because it went evil with his house. <sup>(24)</sup> (And his daughter *was* Sherah, who built Beth-horon the nether, and the upper, and

*ᵃ* 1 Sam. 12. 11.

---

as from the fact that chap. v. 23, 24 treated of East Manasseh. (See also Josh. xvii. 1—5.) The name of Gilead, however, points to the transjordanic half of the tribe. The whole passage seems to assert an Aramean and a Benjamite element in the population of Western Manasseh.

<sup>(16)</sup> **Peresh . . . Sheresh** occur nowhere else.

**Ulam and Rakem** (Rekem) were probably sons of the elder, Peresh, whose line would naturally be continued, as usual.

<sup>(17)</sup> **Bedan** (*i.e., ben Dan* "the Danite") in 1 Sam. xii. 11 is a judge between Jerubbaal and Jephthah. Here a clan is meant, not a person.

**These were the sons of Gilead, the son of Machir, the son of Manasseh.**—These words appear to refer to a series of names which has dropped out of the text, but which may be inferred from Num. xxvi. 30—32 to have included Abiezer (of which Jeezer is a contraction) and Shemidah. (See the genealogy, verse 14, Note.) Verses 17 *b* and 18 may thus have read, "These were the sons of Gilead, &c. Abiezer . . . Shemidah. (Now his sister Hammoleketh had borne Ish-hôd and Abiezer and Mahalah.) And the sons of Shemidah were," &c. (verse 19).

**Hammoleketh**—or, *the queen,* as the Vulg. renders it, may be conceived of here as a half-sister and consort of Gilead.

**Ishod** = *Man of majesty.*

<sup>(19)</sup> **Shechem.**—See Josh. xvii. 2. The name points to West Manasseh.

**Ahian, Likhi,** and **Aniam,** are not mentioned elsewhere.

THE TRIBE OF EPHRAIM (verses 20—29).

**Shuthelah** (Num. 26, 35) was head of the first of the four Ephraimitic clans (*mishpehôth*). The names of six successive chieftains of his line appear to be given in verses 20 and 21, ending with his namesake Shuthelah. It is likely, however, that these names really represent clans, as in other similar cases. (Comp. Num. xxvi. 29—33.) "Bered" (Gen. xvi. 14) is a local name, a place in the desert of Shûr. But Bered may be a mistake for Becher. So "Tahath" (Num. xxxiii. 26) was a desert station of Israel. But Tahath may well be a corruption of Tahan, son of Ephraim (verse 25, and Num. xxvi. 35).

<sup>(21)</sup> **Ezer** and **Elead.**—Apparently these names are coördinated with the Shuthelah of verse 20, as sons of Ephraim. Elead is a masculine form of Eleadah.

**Whom the men of Gath . . . .**—Literally, *and the men of Gath who were born in the land slew them; for they had come down to take their cattle.*

**Born in the land**—That is, aborigines of Canaan as contrasted with the Ephraimites, who were foreign invaders. Others think the real aborigines of Philistia, the Avim of Deut. ii. 23, are meant. In verses 21, 22 we have a brief memorial of an ancient raid of two Ephraimite clans upon the territory of Gath, for the purpose of lifting cattle, much as the Highland freebooters used to drive off the herds of their Lowland neighbours.

**They came down.**—The reference of the pronoun is not quite clear. Conceivably the Gittites were the aggressors. The expression "came down" is often used of going from Canaan to Egypt, but not *vice versâ.* It can hardly, therefore, apply to an invasion of Gath by Ephraimites from Egypt. And the phrase "born in the land" excludes an expedition of Gittites to Goshen. It seems, then, that the descent was made upon Philistia from the hill country of Ephraim, in the early days of the settlement of the tribe in Canaan.

<sup>(22—23)</sup> This is either what we should call a metaphorical description of the enfeebling of the tribe of Ephraim by the disaster which had befallen two of its chief houses, and of its subsequent recovery owing to the natural increase of its numbers, and the formation of a new and populous clan, that of Beriah; or if this be deemed too bold an interpretation of the archaic record, we have nothing for it but to suppose that the whole account relates to an expedition from Goshen, under two sons of Ephraim, during the lifetime of that patriarch; who, after the death of Ezer and Elead, begat another son, Beriah.

<sup>(23)</sup> **Because it went evil.**— Beriah is derived from a root, *baraʻ,* and apparently means *gift.* Heb., *because in evil it* (*i.e.,* the birth of Beriah) *happened in his house.* There is an allusive play on the words *Beriah* ("gift") and *beraʻah* ("in evil") such as we often meet with in Genesis (see Gen. v. 29, xi. 9). To call such plays on words derivations would be a tasteless anachronism. Their purpose is to point a moral, not to teach etymology.

<sup>(24)</sup> **His daughter**—*i.e.,* Ephraim's.

**Built** may mean rebuilt, or restored, or fortified (Josh. vi. 26; Ps. cii. 16; 2 Chron. xi. 6).

**Beth-horon the nether, and the upper.**—The two Beth-horons (Josh. x. 10) were apparently a

I. CHRONICLES, VII.

Uzzen-sherah.) (25) And Rephah was his son, also Resheph, and Telah his son, and Tahan his son, (26) Laadan his son, Ammihud his son, Elishama his son, (27) ¹Non his son, Jehoshuah his son.

(28) And their possessions and habitations were, Beth-el and the towns thereof, and eastward ᵃNaaran, and westward Gezer, with the ²towns thereof; Shechem also and the towns thereof, unto ³Gaza and the towns thereof: (29) and by the borders of the children of ᵇManasseh, Beth-shean and her towns, Taanach and her towns, ᶜMegiddo and her towns, Dor and her towns. In these dwelt the children of Joseph the son of Israel.

(30) ᵈThe sons of Asher; Imnah, and Isuah, and Ishuai, and Beriah, and Serah their sister. (31) And the sons of Beriah; Heber, and Malchiel, who is the father of Birzavith. (32) And Heber begat Japhlet, and Shomer, and Hotham, and Shua their sister. (33) And the sons of Japhlet; Pasach, and Bimhal, and Ashvath. These are the children of Japhlet. (34) And the sons of Shamer; Ahi, and

¹ Or, *Nun*, Num. 13. 8.
ᵃ Josh. 16. 7.
² Heb., *daughters*.
³ Or. *Adasa*, 1 Mac. 7. 45.
ᵇ Josh. 17. 7.
ᶜ Josh. 17. 11.
ᵈ Gen. 46. 17.

---

Canaanite foundation. They are now *Beit ur et-Tahta* and *Beit-ur el-Fariqa—i.e.*, Lower and Upper Beitur.

**Uzzen-sherah.**—Sherah's ear, or peak, only mentioned here. The relation of Sherah to Beth-horon may be compared with that of Achsah to the Negeb of Judah (Josh. xv. 19. Cf. also Josh. xvii. 4).

(25) **And Rephah his son; and Resheph and Telah his son.**—(Heb. text). This seems to mean that Rephah was son of Beriah. But perhaps a son of Ephraim is intended. Rephah does not occur among the sons of Ephraim (Num. xxvi. 35, 36). The word "his son" (*benô*) may have fallen out after Resheph. Otherwise Resheph is brother and Telah son of Rephah (the elder). Resheph, which means "arrow," "lightning," "fever," was a title of the Phœnician Baal. "Tahan," a son of Ephraim (Num. xxvi. 35: "the clan of the Tahanites").

(26) **Elishama son of Ammihud** was tribal prince or Emir of Ephraim in the time of Moses (Num. vii. 47).

(27) **Non.**—Everywhere else Nun, the father of Joshua the servant and successor of Moses. Verses 25—27 trace his ancestry, as it would seem, through seven or eight generations to Rephah, son of Beriah or Ephraim. At chap. vi. 1—3 only two names are given between Levi, uncle of Ephraim, and Moses, Joshua's elder contemporary. But abundant reason has already been shown for not interpreting these genealogies in a slavishly literal spirit, and without regard to their own contrary indications. It is obvious to common sense that when it is said that Moses was "son of Amram, son of Kohath, son of Levi," the meaning cannot be that only two generations intervened between the tribal patriarch and the age of Moses. Moreover, it is, to say the least, doubtful that the names in verse 25 represent a lineal descent of individuals, and not a group of variously connected clans. "Telah" looks like a fragment of Shuthelah (verse 20); and perhaps the true reading of verse 25 is, "And Rephah his son, and Shuthelah his son, and Tahan his son," *we-Reshef, we-Thelah* being a possible distortion of *we-Shuthelah*.

THE BOUNDS OF EPHRAIM AND WEST MANASSEH (verses 28, 29).

Comp. chap. vi. 54, *sqq.*, where a list of the cities of the Levites is similarly added to their tribal registers.

(28) **And their possessions.**—Heb., *and their domain and their seats were Bethel and her daughters;* "their domain," that is, the domain of both divisions of the tribe of Joseph.

**Bethel**—originally assigned to Benjamin (Josh. xviii. 22), belonged later to the northern kingdom. The present list appears therefore to be younger than the disruption of Solomon's empire.

**Naaran,** or Naarah (Νααρά) (Josh. xvi. 7) was a town north-east of Jericho. Gezer lay on the south-west border of Ephraim (Josh. xvi. 3), Shechem (*Nablûs*, Νεάπολις) on the north. Gaza: so the LXX., Vulg. (Aza which represents the Hebrew '*Azzâh, i.e.*, Gaza), and Targum; but a great number of MSS. and seventeen editions read Ayyah, a place not mentioned elsewhere, but doubtless lying on the north-west border of Ephraim.

(29) **And by the borders of the children of Manasseh.**—Literally, *and by the hands of the sons* of Manasseh, a favourite phrase with the chronicler, occurring nine times in Chronicles and once in Ezra. (See Note on chap. vi. 31.) The four cities lay within the territory of Issachar and Asher, but were assigned to Manasseh (Josh. xvii. 11). They mark the northward marches of the two houses of Joseph, as the cities of verse 28 mark the southward. They long withstood the Israelite occupation (Josh. xvii. 12—16; see also Judg. v. 19. "Then fought the kings of Canaan, in Taanach, by the waters of Megiddo.")

THE TRIBE OF ASHER (verses 30—40).

(30, 31) **The sons of Asher; Imnah .... Malchiel.**—This is a literal transcript of Gen. xlvi. 17. Comp. also Num. xxvi. 44—46, where the clan (*mishpahath*) of each eponym is assigned; but the name of Isaah (Heb., *Yishwâh*) does not appear.

**Beriah.**—Also the name of an Ephraimitic stock (ver. 23). Malchiel is called the "father (chief or founder) of Birzavith" only here. The Heb. margin has Birzayith, perhaps "well of olive" (*be-er zayith*); the text, Berazôth or Barzûth. It is probably the name of a place.

(32—34) The race of Heber (spelt differently from Heber, Abraham's ancestor). Nothing is known of any of these families. The name Japhleti (the Japhletite) occurs as a clan (Josh. xvi. 3), but far away from the bounds of Asher.

(34) **Shamer** (pausal form of Shemer) probably identical with Shomer, the second son of Heber (verse 32).

**Jehubbah.**—Heb. margin has *we-Hubbah,* "and Hubbah," which is correct according to the prevailing form of this list (*and* before each name).

**Aram** is the ordinary name of the Syrians east and west of the Euphrates. It may here designate a clan of half-Aramean extraction.

Rohgah, Jehubbah, and Aram. ⁽³⁵⁾ And the sons of his brother Helem; Zophah, and Imna, and Shelesh, and Amal. ⁽³⁶⁾ The sons of Zophah; Suah, and Harnepher, and Shual, and Beri, and Imrah, ⁽³⁷⁾ Bezer, and Hod, and Shamma, and Shilshah, and Ithran, and Beera. ⁽³⁸⁾ And the sons of Jether; Jephunneh, and Pispah, and Ara. ⁽³⁹⁾ And the sons of Ulla; Arah, and Haniel, and Rezia. ⁽⁴⁰⁾ All these were the children of Asher, heads of *their* father's house, choice *and* mighty men of valour, chief of the princes. And the number throughout the genealogy of them that were apt to the war *and* to battle *was* twenty and six thousand men.

*a* Gen. 46. 21; Num. 26. 38.

¹ Or, *Ard*, Gen. 46. 21.

CHAPTER VIII.—⁽¹⁾ Now Benjamin begat *ᵃBela his firstborn, Ashbel the second, and Aharah the third, ⁽²⁾ Nohah the fourth, and Rapha the fifth. ⁽³⁾ And the sons of Bela were, ¹Addar, and Gera, and Abihud, ⁽⁴⁾ and Abishua, and Naa-

---

**(35—39) And the sons of his brother Helem.**—Apparently the offshoots of Helem, "brother" of Shemer-Shomer. If we construe *brother* in the strict sense, we must assume that Helam is the same as Hotham (verse 32), and that one or the other name is corrupt. But Helem may be the name of another chief house of Asher not directly connected with that of Heber. The brotherhood then would be that of the tribe, not of the clan or family.

(36) The branches of Helem through Zophah the elder house. Eleven names of the sons of Zophah. The second, "Harnepher," has a name which looks like pure Egyptian: *Har nefer*, "the beauteous Horus," or morning sun. Comp. the case of the Egyptian slave Jarha (chap. ii. 34), and the marriage of Mered with "Pharaoh's daughter" (chap. iv. 18). (See also the Notes on verse 10.)

(38) **The sons of Jether.**—Jether and Ithran (verse 37) are virtually the same name, and perhaps to be identified here. This will connect verse 38 with the preceding line of the sons of Zophah.

**Jephunneh.**—The name of the father of Caleb the Kenizzite.

(39) **The sons of Ulla.**—Apparently Ulla is not connected with the foregoing genealogy. But he seems to be the same as *Ara* (verse 38). '*Arā*' is a very curious form, and may be due to a copyist's eye having wandered to *Be-era* at the end of last verse; '*Ullā*' is intelligible, and probably correct. If the identification be allowed, we get a complete concatenation from verses 30 to 39.

**Arah** is in Hebrew quite different from Ara.

(40) The summing up of the list. "All these were sons of Asher, picked chiefs of the father-houses, valiant warriors, chiefs of the princes." This declares that the names in the foregoing series are those of the chiefs of the different Asherite clans. They are called "choice," picked men, *eximii*, and chiefs of the princes or emirs. The clans appear to be identified with their chieftains.

**And the number throughout the genealogy.** —Better, *and their census, in the host, in the battle—their number in men was 26,000.*" Perhaps we should render *in the case of service in war*. The census here given has reference only to the number of males qualified for military service. In the Mosaic census (Num. i. 41) the total of males of the tribe of Asher was 41,500; and a generation later, the fighting men were 53,000 (Num. xxvi. 47). The date of the present census is not assigned. If it be that of David, which appears likely, the tribe may have declined in numbers and importance by his day. (Comp. Judg. v. 17. "Asher continued at the sea-shore, and abode on his creeks;" *i.e.*, did not bestir himself for the war).

### VIII.

The narrative returns to the tribe of Benjamin. The present register is quite different from that preserved in chap. vii. 6—12, which, as we have seen, is an extract from a document drawn up for military purposes. Apparently based on a topographical register, this new list agrees better than the other with the data of the Pentateuch (Gen. xlvi.; Num. xxvi.), allowance being made for the mistakes of generations of copyists. The chronicler may well have thought the short section of chap. vii. too meagre as an account of a tribe which had furnished the first royal house, and had afterwards inseparably linked its fortunes with those of the legitimate dynasty. Here, therefore, he supplements his former notice. Perhaps, also, he returns to Benjamin by way of introduction to the royal genealogy with which the section concludes. In short, he begins, as his manner is, at the beginning; and having to tell of Saul, starts from the tribal patriarch to whom the house of Saul traced back its long descent.

THE SONS OF BENJAMIN AND BELA (verses 1—5). (See Notes on chap. vii. 6, 7.)

**Bela his first-born.**—The Hebrew word for "first-born" in Gen. xlvi. 21 may have been turned into the proper name Becher, by an ancient mistake of the scribes. (See Note on chap. vii. 6.)

**Ashbel.**—Probably the same as Jediael.

**Aharah** the same as Ahiram and Ehirosh.

(2) **Nohah and Rapha.**—These names do not occur in either of the other lists. The present series agrees with Num. xxvi. 38 in assigning *five* sons to Benjamin, of whom Bela is the first, and Ashbel the second. Further, there is enough likeness between the name Aharah here and Ahiram there to warrant our assumption of their original identity. But we cannot hence conclude that the Nohah and Rapha of our list answer to the Shephupham-Shupham and Hupham of the other. It is more likely that Nohah and Rapha represent different clans, which were prominent at the time when the present list was draughted. *Rapha* reminds us of the valley of Rephaim, south-west of Jerusalem, chap. xi. 15.

(3—5) The sons of Bela here are *nine*, like the sons of the suspected *Becher*, chap. vii. 8. But none of the names correspond.

(3) **Addar** the same as Ard, who in Num. xxvi. is eldest son of Bela, but in Gen. xlvi. apparently his youngest brother.

**Gera** appears as brother of Bela in Gen. xlvi. 21. The name is repeated in verse 5, probably by a scribe's

man, and Ahoah, (5) and Gera, and 6 Shephuphan, and Huram. (6) And these *are* the sons of Ehud: these are the heads of the fathers of the inhabitants of Geba, and they removed them to *a* Manahath: (7) and Naaman, and Ahiah, and Gera, he removed them, and begat Uzza, and Ahihud. (8) And Shaharaim begat *children* in the country of Moab, after he had sent them away; Hushim and Baara *were* his wives. (9) And he begat of Hodesh his wife, Jobab, and Zibia, and Mesha, and Malcham, (10) and Jeuz, and Shachia, and Mirma. These *were* his sons, heads of the fathers. (11) And of Hushim he begat Abitub, and Elpaal. (12) The sons of Elpaal; Eber, and Misham, and Shamed, who built Ono, and Lod, with the towns thereof: (13) Beriah also, and Shema, who *were* heads of the fathers of the inhabitants of Aijalon, who drove away the inhabitants of Gath:

1 Or, *Shupham*, Num. 26. 39.

*a* ch. 2. 52.

---

inadvertence; though there may have been two great Benjamite houses so designated.

**Abihud** (4) **and Abishua** are peculiar to the present list.

**Naaman** is a son of Bela in Num. xxvi., a brother in Gen. xlvi.

**Ahoah** is peculiar, unless he be identified with the Ehi of Gen. xlvi.

**Shephupham and Huram,** younger sons of Bela in the present series, are in Gen. and Num. his younger brothers Muppim (Shuppim) and Huppim, or Shephupham and Hupham. These fluctuations of statement are worth observing, because they demonstrate the vagueness of terms denoting various degrees of kindred, when used in describing tribal and clan relationships.

(6) **And these are the sons of Ehud.**—The Authorised Version makes no distinction between this *Ehud* and *Ehud son of Gera*, the famous Benjamite judge (Judg. iii. 15). The difference in the Heb. is so slight, that perhaps we may assume an original identity of the two names. In that case we get a link between the *sons of Ehud* and the house of *Gera*, verse 5. Others identify the present Ehud with the Abihud of verse 3, which is possibly correct. (Comp. Nadab-Abinadab, Dan and Abidan, Num. i. 11.)

**These are the heads of the fathers.**—Heads of father-houses, *i.e.*, of groups of kindred families or clans. The Hebrew text of the rest of this verse, and verses 7—8, is unusually obscure, partly owing to the construction, but chiefly because of the historical allusions which are no longer explicable with any certainty. Most interpreters assume a parenthesis after the words "and these are the sons of Ehud," extending to the words "he removed them," in verse 7.

**Uzza and Ahihud** are then "the sons of Ehud" referred to in verse 6.

**Removed them.**—Rather, *carried them captive*, or *transported them*. The same expression denotes the Babylonian exile or transportation, and was used in chap. v. 26 of the Assyrian removal of the transjordanic tribes.

(7) **And Naaman, and Ahiah, and Gera, he removed them.**—The three clans here mentioned are commonly regarded as the authors of the expatriation of the people of Geba. Of Gera it is specially said "*he* removed them," because Gera was the leading clan of the three. According to this interpretation the two verses (6—7) may be rendered: "And these are the sons of Ehud. (These are heads of clans belonging to the inhabitants of Geba, and men carried them away to Manahath—both Naaman, and Ahijah, and Gera, he it was who carried them away.) He begat Uzza and Ahihud." That is to say, Uzza and Ahihud, two chiefs of clans settled at Geba (chap vi. 45), were forcibly removed by three other Benjamite clans to Manahath (see chap. ii. 52, 54). '*Al manahath* might perhaps be rendered "for the sake of peace," referring to feuds between the clans of Geba.

(8) **And Shaharaim begat children in the country of Moab.**—Shaharaim is apparently out of all connection with the other Benjamite houses. He has been identified with Ahi-Shahar, chap. vii. 10, because his name has a similar meaning, and even with the mysterious Aher (hypothetically Shaher) of chap. vii. 12. It is simpler to suppose that *we'eth-Shaharaim*, "and Shaharaim," has dropped out at the end of verse 7 (see Note on verse 31). Expelled from Geba, Shaharaim found a refuge in Moab. (Comp. Ruth i.; 1 Sam. xxii. 3, 4.)

**After he had sent them away; Hushim and Baara were his wives.**—The Heb. is certainly corrupt. The easiest correction is to read *'eth-Hushim* instead of *'otham Hushim*: "and Shaharaim begat in the country of Moab, after divorcing Hushim and Baara his wives, he begat (verse 9) of Hodesh his wife, Jobab," &c. This is supported by the LXX. The emigration of the clan Shaharaim, from its old home in Geba of Benjamin is called a divorce, in the figurative style of these genealogies; just as the amalgamation of clans is marriage. *Hushim*, in chap. vii. 12, is a Benjamite clan. In Moab, Shaharaim branched off into seven clans, whose names are given in verses 9—10.

(9) **Hodesh his wife.**—The new Moabite wife or settlement of Shaharaim. The names of two of the sons begotten in Moab have a Moabite cast—viz., *Mesha'*, comp. Mesha' king of Moab, 2 Kings iii. 4; and *Malcham*, comp. Malcham (Milcom) as a title of the god of Moab and Ammon, Jer. xlix. 1 (Heb.).

(10) **Heads of the fathers.**—See Note on verse 6.

(11) **And of Hushim he begat . . .**—The offspring of Shaharaim by Hushim before her divorce; in other words, two offshoots of the clan Shaharaim settled in the vicinity of Lod or Lydda (verse 12), which took no part in the emigration to Moab.

(12) **Shamer,** or *Shemer*, occurred in chap. vii. 34 as a clan of Asher.

**Who built Ono and Lod . . . .**—Literally, *he built Ono and Lod and her daughters*. The clause is a parenthesis referring to Shemer.

**Ono,** now *Kefr Auna*, recurs in Ezra ii. 33, Neh. vii. 37, and xi. 35, but is not found elsewhere in the Old Testament. It is always coupled with Lod, and must have been near it.

**Lod,** the Lydda of Acts ix. 32, is now the village of *Ludd*, north of Ramleh, between Jaffa and Jerusalem.

(13) **Beriah also, and Shema.**—After these two names the Masoretic punctuators have put a stop. Thus verses 12—13 give five sons of Elpaal. Or verse 13

## I. CHRONICLES, VIII.

(14) and Ahio, Shashak, and Jeremoth, (15) and Zebadiah, and Arad, and Ader, (16) and Michael, and Ispah, and Joha, the sons of Beriah; (17) and Zebadiah, and Meshullam, and Hezeki, and Heber, (18) Ishmerai also, and Jezliah, and Jobab, the sons of Elpaal; (19) and Jakim, and Zichri, and Zabdi, (20) and Elienai, and Zilthai, and Eliel, (21) and Adaiah, and Beraiah, and Shimrath, the sons of [1]Shimhi; (22) and Ishpan, and Heber, and Eliel, (23) and Abdon, and Zichri, and Hanan, (24) and Hananiah, and Elam, and Antothijah, (25) and Iphedeiah, and Penuel, the sons of Shashak; (26) and Shamsherai, and Shehariah, and Athaliah, (27) and Jaresiah, and Eliah, and Zichri, the sons of Jeroham. (28) These were heads of the fathers, by their generations, chief *men*. These dwelt in Jerusalem.

(29) And at Gibeon dwelt the [2]father of Gibeon; whose [a]wife's name *was* Maachah: (30) and his firstborn son Abdon, and Zur, and Kish, and Baal, and Nadab, (31) and Gedor, and Ahio, and

[1] Or, *Shema*, ver. 13.
[2] Called *Jehiel*, ch. 9, 35.
[a] ch. 9. 35.

---

may be disconnected from verse 12, and Beriah and Shema regarded as beginning a new series of Benjamite clans.

**Who were heads of the fathers . . . .** Rather, "THEY *were heads of the clans of the inhabitants of Aijalon*; THEY *put to flight the inhabitants of Gath.*" The pronoun is emphatic in both cases. The clans of Beriah and Shema, who were settled at Ajalon (*Yalo*), near Gibeon, appear to have expelled a Gittite population from Ajalon, and dwelt in their stead. At all events, there is evident allusion to some famous exploit, in which the two Benjamite houses were more fortunate than the Ephraimites Ezer and Elead (chap. vii. 21). We must not identify this Benjamite Beriah with the Ephraimite Beriah of chap. vii. 23. There was also an Asherite clan of Beriah (chap. vii. 30).

(14—16) Apparently nine sons of Beriah. But (1) in verse 14, the LXX. reads ὁ ἀδελφὸς αὐτοῦ instead of *Ahio*. With different vowels the Hebrew term would mean this. (2) All the other names in this list are connected by the conjunctive particle. It is therefore likely that this was once the case with Shashak. (3) Verses 14—27 give five groups of Benjamite clans—viz., the sons of Beriah, the sons of Elpaal, the sons of Shimhi, the sons of Shashak, and the sons of Jeroham, all dwelling in Jerusalem. Apparently, their eponymous heads are named in verses 13, 14—viz., Beriah (Elpaal ? omitted by accident), Shema (the same as Shimhi; there is no *h* in the Heb.), Shashak, and Jeremoth (probably the same as Jeroham).

If this combination hold, the text of verse 14 may be thus restored: "And Elpaal his brother, and Shashak and Jeroham." Elpaal will then be brother of Beriah (verse 13), and perhaps son of Elpaal (verse 12). Shashak and Jeremoth-Jeroham, and the six following names, are sons of Beriah.

(17—18) Seven sons of Elpaal.

(19—21) Nine sons of Shimhi (Shimei being the same as Shema). This is the same Hebrew name as that which at 2 Sam. xvi. 5 *seq.* the Authorised Version renders by Shimei.

(22—25) Eleven sons of Shashak (verse 14), followed by six sons of Jeroham (Jeremoth, verse 14) in verses 26—27. The recurrence of the same names in the five groups is noticeable. Thus, a Zichri appears among the sons of Shimei (verse 19), among the sons of Shashak (verse 23), and among the sons of Jeroham (verse 27). Of course the name may have been thus frequent among the Benjamite clans dwelling in Jerusalem. But it is possible to see in the fact an indication that, at the time when the present register was framed, some of these houses were no longer able to trace their pedigrees with certainty to one famous name rather than another.

(28) **These were . . . chief men.**—*These were chiefs of clans; according to their birth-rolls, chiefs.* All the names from verse 14 to verse 27 are included in this summation. The repetition of the word "chiefs" (Heb., *heads*) is peculiar. The writer can hardly have meant other than to warn his readers against the idea that the preceding names represent individual members of single families, whereas, in truth, they are "heads of clans." ("Heads" in Hebrew may denote "companies," or "divisions," as at Judg. vii. 16, "And he divided the three hundred men into three heads.")

**These dwelt in Jerusalem.**—This statement contrasts the five branches of Benjamin, whose subdivisions have just been enumerated, with the clans that dwelt in Geba and Manahath (verse 6), in Moab (verses 9, 10), in Lod and Ono (verse 12), and in Ajalon (verse 13), as well as with those who dwelt in Gibeon (verse 29).

THE FAMILIES OF GIBEON, ESPECIALLY THE ROYAL HOUSE OF SAUL (verses 29—40).

Verses 29—38 recur at chap. ix. 35—44.

(29) **At Gibeon dwelt the father of Gibeon.**—His name (Jehiel) has been accidentally omitted. (See chap. ix. 35.) The verb *dwelt* is plural, "they dwelt;" a sufficient indication that the "father of Gibeon" merely represents the original population of that place under a collective name. Maachah would be a place in the neighbourhood.

**Gibeon.**—Now *el-Jib*, about eight miles north-west of Jerusalem.

(30) The sons of Abi-Gibeon—that is, the Benjamite clans of Gibeon. The name of *Ner* has fallen out between Baal and Nadab. (Comp. chap. ix. 36.) That of *Baal* is interesting. Comp. verses 33, 34, where we find Eshbaal and Merib-baal (rather *Meri-baal*, *i.e.*, "man of Baal"); comp. *Merbal* in Herod. vii. 88. It appears from Hos. iii. 16 that the title Baal (lord) was once applied to Jehovah in common speech: "Thou shalt call me *Ishi*, and shalt no more call me *Baali.*" After the name had become associated with a foreign and idolatrous *cultus*, it was discarded in favour of the synonymous Adon (Adonai).

(31) **Ahio.**—The recurrence of this name here lends some support to the Authorised Version in verse 14.

**Zacher.**—Heb., *Zecher* (comp. Shamer-Shemer), the Zechariah of chap. ix. 37, which is in fact the full form of the name. Such abbreviations are common. (See

*The Stock of Saul*  I. CHRONICLES, VIII.  *and Jonathan.*

¹Zacher. ⁽³²⁾ And Mikloth begat Shimeah. And these also dwelt with their brethren in Jerusalem, over against them. ⁽³³⁾ And ᵃNer begat Kish, and Kish begat Saul, and Saul begat Jonathan, and Malchi-shua, and Abinadab, and ³Esh-baal. ⁽³⁴⁾ And the son of Jonathan was ⁴Merib-baal; and Merib-baal begat Micah. ⁽³⁵⁾ And the sons of Micah were, Pithon, and Melech, and ⁵Tarea, and Ahaz. ⁽³⁶⁾ And Ahaz begat Jehoadah; and Jehoadah begat Alemeth, and Azmaveth, and Zimri; and Zimri begat Moza, ⁽³⁷⁾ and Moza begat Binea: Rapha was his son, Eleasah his son, Azel his son: ⁽³⁸⁾ and Azel had six sons, whose names are these, Azrikam, Bocheru, and Ishmael, and Sheariah, and Obadiah, and Hanan. All these were the sons of Azel. ⁽³⁹⁾ And the sons of Eshek his brother were, Ulam his firstborn, Jehush the second, and Eliphelet the third. ⁽⁴⁰⁾ And the sons of Ulam were mighty men of valour, archers, and had many sons, and sons' sons, an hundred and fifty. All these are of the sons of Benjamin.

1 Or, *Zechariah,* ch. 9. 37.
2 Or, *Shimeam,* ch. 9. 38.
a 1 Sam. 14. 51.
3 Or, *Ishbosheth,* 2 Sam. 2. 8.
4 Or, *Mephibosheth,* 2 Sam. 4. 4.
5 Or, *Tahrea,* ch. 9. 41.

---

chap. v. 26, Note.) After Zecher, the phrase *and Mikloth* has dropped out of the text, because verse 32 begins with the same words. (See chap. ix. 33.)

⁽³²⁾ **Shimeah** is essentially the same word as *Shimeam* (chap. ix. 38). The latter is a *mimmated* form (i.e., a more ancient form of the noun, with the original ending *m*).

**And these also dwelt with their brethren in Jerusalem, over against them.**—Literally, *And they also, before their brethren, dwelt in Jerusalem with their brethren.* The verse seems to tell us that of all the stock of Gibeon only the branch of Mikloth-Shimeah settled in Jerusalem. When, we are not informed. Some think the reference is to the repeopling of Jerusalem after the Restoration (Neh. xi. 1). "Before their brethren."—*Before* in Heb. means east, as *behind* means west. The clans in question dwelt in Jerusalem, to the east of their fellow-tribesmen in Gibeon.

**With their brethren**—that is, with the other Benjamite clans settled in Jerusalem (verses 16—28).

⁽³³⁾ The house of Saul. It is not said here that Saul's immediate family was settled at Gibeon. From 1 Sam x. 26, xv. 34, and 2 Sam. xxi. 6, we learn that Gibeah, or "Gibeah of Saul," was the seat of the king. It is gratuitous to suppose that the chronicler has confounded two different places.

**And Ner begat Kish.**—1 Sam. ix. 1 gives the following pedigree of Kish : Kish son of Abiel, son of Zeror, son of Bechorath, son of Aphiah; and 1 Sam. xiv. 51 states that Kish the father of Saul, and Ner the father of Abner, were sons of Abiel. The omission of intermediate names is not uncommon in these lists. We may, therefore, suppose that some members of the genealogical series are here omitted between Ner and Kish. The father of Abner was, of course, only a namesake of the present *Ner*, which is perhaps a clan, not an individual.

**Saul begat Jonathan.**—So 1 Sam. xiv. 49, and xxxi. 2; save that the former passage has Ishui for Abinadab. This seems to be a case of double naming. Others identify Ishui with Ishbosheth.

**Abinadab.**—Comp. Nadab, verse 30. Both are probably Divine titles, meaning "the father (i.e., Jehovah) is noble." Comp. *Kammusu Nadbi*, "Chemosh is my prince," the name of a Moabite king, mentioned by Sennacherib. *Ner* and *Kish* also both occurred in verse 30 as Gibeonite clans. Here they (or at least Kish) may be said to be personal names.

**Esh-baal.**—2 Sam. ii. 8, Ish-bosheth, David's rival king. Esh-baal ("man of Baal") is the true name. Ish-bosheth ("man of shame") is a sort of euphemism, avoiding the very mention of an idol. So the Merib-baal ("Baal strives;" rather, perhaps, Meri-Baal, "man of Baal") of verse 34 appears in 2 Sam. iv. 4, ix. 6, &c., as Mephibosheth, where probably the right reading is Meribbosheth. In like manner, idols are styled "abominations." 1 Kings xi. 5: "Milcom the abomination (i.e., god) of the sons of Ammon," and elsewhere. Beth-el, the sanctuary of the golden calf, or rather bullock, is called Beth-aven. The "house of God" is a "house of wickedness" (Hos. iv. 15, v. 8; Josh. vii. 2.) (See Note on verse 30.)

⁽³⁵⁾ **Tarea.**—*Ta'rea.* Tahrea (chap. xxix. 41) is a harder pronunciation of the same name. The name Shime'ah, or Shime'am (verse 32) appears to be a similar softening of the name Shime'ah (2 Sam. xiii. 3).

⁽³⁶⁾ **Jehoadah.**—Heb., *Jeho'addah.* Chap. ix. 42 gives Jarah (Heb., *Ja'rah*), a mistake arising from the common confusion of the Heb. *d* and *r*. The name there should be read, "Jo'addah," a contraction of the present form.

**Alemeth.**—In chap. vii. 8 a son of Becher; in chap. vi. 60 a Levitical town. The name is apparently personal here.

⁽³⁸⁾ **Bocheru.**—Some MSS. read "his firstborn," with which, with different points, the LXX. and the Syriac agree. This seems right, as the conjunctive particle is wanting between Azrikam and the doubtful word, and Bocheru would be anomalous as a proper name. (See Note on verse 40.)

**Azel.**—A place near Jerusalem was so called (Zech. xiv. 5; Mic. i. 11).

⁽³⁹⁾ **Eshek his brother**—that is, the brother of Azel, and son of Eleasah (verse 37). The elder line is first developed.

⁽⁴⁰⁾ **And the sons of Ulam were mighty men of valour, archers.**—The ancient prowess of the Benjamites is recorded in Judg. xx. Their left-handed slingers were famous. (See also Judg. iii. 15 seq.)

**Archers.**—Literally, *treaders of the bow* (chap. v. 18). The meaning is that they drew their bows by resting the foot against them, the bows being large.

**Had many sons, and sons' sons, an hundred and fifty.**—What was their date? If we may assume that no names have been omitted, we are concerned with the fourteenth generation from Jonathan, the friend of David. The era of David has been fixed at about 1055—1045 B.C.; so that the great-grandsons of Ulam may have flourished about 635—625 B.C. (1055 *minus* 420), in the reign of Josiah. The omission

*Original of the Genealogies.*     I. CHRONICLES, IX.     *Dwellers in Jerusalem.*

CHAPTER IX.—<sup>(1)</sup> So all Israel were reckoned by genealogies; and, behold, they *were* written in the book of the kings of Israel and Judah, *who* were carried away to Babylon for their transgression.

<sup>(2)</sup> Now the first inhabitants that *dwelt* in their possessions in their cities *were*, the Israelites, the priests, Levites, and the Nethinims.

<sup>(3)</sup> And in <sup>a</sup>Jerusalem dwelt of the children of Judah, and of the children of Benjamin, and of the children of Ephraim, and Manasseh; <sup>(4)</sup> Uthai the son of Ammihud, the son of Omri, the son of Imri, the son of Bani, of the children of Pharez the son of Judah. <sup>(5)</sup> And of the Shilonites; Asaiah the firstborn, and his sons. <sup>(6)</sup> And of the sons of Zerah; Jeuel, and their brethren, six hundred and ninety. <sup>(7)</sup> And of the sons of Benjamin; Sallu the son of Meshullam, the son of Hodaviah, the son of Hasenuah, <sup>(8)</sup> and Ibneiah the son

*a* Neh. II. 1.

---

of names, however, is as possible and as likely in the present series as elsewhere; and it is obvious that one or two additional members would carry the list past the exile (B.C. 588). There are reasons for believing that the posterity of Ulam really represent a family of the period of the Return. Their number is favourable to the supposition. Comp. Ezr. ii. 18, 21, 23, 27, 30 for families of about the same dimensions, which returned with Zerubbabel. Further, the reference in verse 8—10 to a sojourn of certain Benjamite houses in Moab may be connected with the mention in Ezra ii. 6, viii. 4; Neh. iii. 11, and elsewhere, of the "sons of the Pasha of Moab" (*Pahath Mo'ab*. This word *pahath* used to be reckoned among the indications of the late origin of the Chronicle. Now, however, it is known to be an ancient Semitic term. Comp. the Assyrian *pihatu*). *Ono and Lod* (verse 12) may be compared with Ezra ii. 33, and the singular names *Elam* (verse 24) and *Azmaveth* (verse 36), with the "sons of Elam" (Ezra ii. 7), and "the sons of Azmaveth," or "Beth-azmaveth" (Ezra ii. 24; Neh. vii. 28). The name *Bocheru* (in verse 38) has been classed with Gashmu (Neh. vi. 6), but the latter is an Arab, and there is seemingly no MS. authority for Bocheru. *Ishmael* (verse 38) reminds us of "Ishmael son of Nethaniah, of the seed royal" (2 Kings xxv. 25), who survived the fall of Jerusalem.

### IX.

<sup>(3)</sup> **And in Jerusalem dwelt** (some) **of the children of Judah, and** (some) **of the children of Benjamin.**—This sentence is word for word the same with Neh. xi. 4*a*. The next clause, "and some of the children of Ephraim, and Manasseh," is not found in Nehemiah, and nothing further is said in the present chapter concerning these two tribes. But so far from proving the clause to be a figment of the chronicler's, this fact only indicates that he has chosen to use the ordinary freedom of a compiler in transcribing from the fuller document which supplied him with materials here and in Neh. xi. His source dealt with the neighbouring townships as well as Jerusalem; the latter is the sole subject of the chronicler's extracts here.

<sup>(4)</sup> **Uthai the son of Ammihud, the son of Omri, the son of Imri, the son of Bani.**—Neh. xi. 4 traces this line thus: "Athaiah son of Uzziah, son of Zechariah, son of Amariah, son of Shephatiah, son of Mahalaleel, of the children of Perez." Uthai is equivalent to Athaiah, and Imri to Amariah, by a common contraction. The other intermediate names in the two series do not coincide; but this does not prove that Uthai and Athaiah are different clans. Many more than five or six members would obviously be required to constitute a complete genealogical stem, reaching from post-exilic times to the age of the tribal patriarchs. We may therefore conclude that the compiler has chosen to select different names in each case from a longer list, which comprised both series.

<sup>(5)</sup> **And of the Shilonites.** — Shilonite means "man of Shiloh," the ancient capital of Ephraim; whereas verses 4—6 have to do with Judah. The three sons of Judah, after whom three great sub-tribal divisions were named, were Pharez, Shelah, and Zarah (Gen. xxxviii.). The clan of Shelah was called the Shelanite (Num. xxvi. 20), and that is doubtless the correct reading here (see chaps. ii. 3, iv. 21), supported as it is by the LXX. (Σηλωνὶ) and the Targum.

**Asaiah** ("Jah hath wrought") is essentially the same as "Maaseiah" ("Work of Jah") in Neh. xi. 5, where six progenitors are enumerated.

**The firstborn.**—That is, the leading clan.

**His sons.**—The members of the clan.

<sup>(6)</sup> **Of the sons of Zerah.**— The Zarhites are omitted in the parallel passage of Nehemiah, where we read, instead of the present statement, that "all the sons of Perez that dwelt at Jerusalem were four hundred threescore and eight valiant men." The common source of both the narratives must have contained information about the Zarhites, as well as their brother clansmen, the Parzites and Shelanites. We see from the verse before us that the Zarhites were more numerous in Jerusalem than the Parzites. The chronicler has again exercised his own discretion in the choice and rejection of details.

**Jeuel, and their brethren.**—The plural pronoun clearly hints that Jeuel is a Zarhite father-house or clan. The passage of Nehemiah just cited shows that six hundred and ninety is the total of the Zarhites only. The number of the Parzites and Shelanites is not here specified.

<sup>(7)</sup> **And of the sons of Benjamin.**—The parallel passage (Neh. xi. 7) starts with "Sallu the son of Meshullam," but continues, "the son of Joed, the son of Pedaiah," and carries the ancestry four generations further back.

**The son of Hodaviah, the son of Hasenuah.** —Perhaps we should read "and Hodaviah," instead of "son of Hodaviah." (See Note on verses 9, 10.) The name Hodaviah, which occurred chap. v. 24, is a peculiar Aramaizing form of Hoduyah ("Thank the Lord"). Perhaps here the true reading is *wihudah*, "and Judah." Comp. Neh. xi. 9, "Judah the son of Senuah" (Heb. *ha-Senuah*).

<sup>(8)</sup> Three other Benjamite houses.

**Ibneiah** is much the same name as "Ibnijah" at the end of the verse. Both mean "Jah buildeth," *i.e.*, maketh offspring. (Comp. Assyrian *Ea-Ibni*, "Ea made," *i.e.*, a son.)

*The Dwellers*     I. CHRONICLES, IX.     *in Jerusalem.*

of Jeroham, and Elah the son of Uzzi, the son of Michri, and Meshullam the son of Shephathiah, the son of Reuel, the son of Ibnijah; <sup>(9)</sup> and their brethren, according to their generations, nine hundred and fifty and six. All these men *were* chief of the fathers in the house of their fathers.

<sup>(10)</sup> And of the priests; Jedaiah, and Jehoiarib, and Jachin, <sup>(11)</sup> and Azariah the son of Hilkiah, the son of Meshullam, the son of Zadok, the son of Meraioth, the son of Ahitub, the ruler of the house of God; <sup>(12)</sup> and Adaiah the son of Jeroham, the son of Pashur, the son of Malchijah, and Maasiai the son of Adiel, the son of Jahzerah, the son of Meshullam, the son of Meshillemith, the son of Immer; <sup>(13)</sup> and their brethren, heads of the house of their fathers, a

---

**Son of Jeroham.**—The sons of Jeroham dwelt in Jerusalem before the exile as well as after it (chap. viii. 27).

**Michri** should perhaps be Zichri. (Comp. chap. viii. 19, 23, and 27.)

Verses 7—9 correspond to Neh. xi. 7—9; but after tracing the ascending line of Sallu son of Meshullam (verse 7) through six degrees, the latter account continues (Neh. xi. 8): "And after him Gabbai, Sallai, nine hundred twenty and eight." This apparently is quite a different statement from that of our verse 8. Gabbai, Sallai, however (note the absence of a conjunction), may be corrupt. Gabbai perhaps conceals Bani or Ibni, a contracted form of Ibneiah; and Sallai might have originated out of Shallum or Meshullam, under the influence of the preceding Sallu (verse 7). Neh. xi. 9 continues, "And Joel son of Zikri was their overseer, and Judah son of Hasenuah was over the second part of the city." "Joel son of Zikri" may be our "Elah son of Uzzi son of Michri" (verse 8); for Joel ("Jah is El") may be compared with Elah, which is perhaps a disguise of Elijah ("El is Jah;" only *yod*, the smallest Hebrew letter, is wanting). "Judah son of Hasenuah," may be the equivalent of "Hodaviah son of Hasenuah." If these combinations be accepted, the list here is brought into strict harmony with its parallel—five Benjamite clans being named in each, viz., Sallu, Hodaviah (Judah), Ibneiah (Bani), Joel (Elah), and Meshullam.

**And their brethren, according to their generations.**—The members of the five Benjamite clans amounted to nine hundred and fifty-six, according to their family registers. Neh. xi. 8 gives a total of nine hundred and twenty-eight. If the numbers are both genuine, our text may refer to a date a little subsequent to the time intended in Nehemiah.

**All these men.**—Translate, *all these men were chiefs of their respective clans*. This appears to be the subscription to verses 4—9. It states that the proper names are representatives of clans, and, so to speak, collective personalities.

(10—13) The priests resident in Jerusalem. (Comp. Neh. xi. 10—14.)

<sup>(10)</sup> **And of the priests; Jedaiah, and Jehoiarib, and Jachin.**—These three names do not designate persons, but three of the priestly courses, or classes, instituted by David according to chap. xxiv, of which Jehoiarib was the first, Jedaiah the second, and Jachin the twenty-first. Neh. xi. 10 has "Jehoiarib son of Jedaiah," a mistake of the scribe. (Comp. verse 7 and Note; cf. also Ezra ii. 36; Neh. xii. 6.)

<sup>(11)</sup> **And Azariah the son of Hilkiah, the son of Meshullam.**—See chap. vi. 12, 13. The names coincide so far as Zadok; but either Meraioth and Ahitub have been transposed (see chap. vi. 7), or perhaps Meraioth has been omitted in chap. vi. 12. Instead of Azariah, the parallel in Neh. xi. 11 has Seraiah, the rest of the verse being *verbatim* the same as here. A list of priests who went up with Zerubbabel and Joshua begins with Seraiah (Neh. xii. 1), and in Neh. x. 2 Seraiah and Azariah are priests who sealed the covenant with Nehemiah the Tirshatha, about seventy years later. Neh. xii. 12 shows that Seraiah was the name of a priestly clan. Perhaps the name Seraiah should be read in the present passage before, or instead of, Azariah. (Comp. chap. vi. 13, 14.) If, however, the name is official, not personal, like the names in the preceding verse, this supposition is hardly necessary. Either Azariah or Seraiah might equally represent the priestly house intended.

<sup>(12)</sup> **And Adaiah the son of Jeroham.**— Neh. xi. 12 runs: "And their brethren, doers of the work of the house, 822; and Adaiah son of Jeroham, son of Pelaliah, son of Amzi, son of Zechariah, son of Pashur, son of Malchijah." Thus the line of Adaiah as given there exactly corresponds with the present passage, save that it inserts three names here wanting between Jeroham and Pashur: another illustration of the freedom of the compiler in dealing with these lists.

**Malchijah** was the fifth of the twenty-four priestly classes.

**Maasiai the son of Adiel . . . son of Immer.**—Immer was the sixteenth course of the priests. The parallel (Neh. xi. 13) reads: "And his brethren, heads of clans, 242; and Amashsai son of Azareel, son of Ahzai, son of Meshillemoth, son of Immer, and their brethren, mighty men of valour, 128; and their overseer was Zabdiel son of Haggedolim." Amashsai and Maasiai are variants of the same name, and perhaps both bad spellings of Amasai (chaps. vi. 35, xii. 18). Adiel may well be a mistake for Azareel. Jahzerah and Ahzai are evidently two forms of one name, Ahzai,—Ahaziah being perhaps more correct. Meshullam in our line is either an additional link, or a copyist's anticipation of part of the following name. The line in Nehemiah is therefore originally identical with the present. Verses 10—12 show that at the date of the present register three entire courses of the priests, and two clans representing two other courses, as well as the ruler or president of the Temple, dwelt in Jerusalem.

<sup>(13)</sup> **And their brethren, heads of the house of their fathers.**—We can hardly suppose so many as 1,760 priestly clans dwelling in the holy city. Either the phrase "heads of their father-houses" belongs to the last verse, and has been accidentally brought into its present position; or in this instance it means simply "heads of single families;" or "their brethren, heads of their (respective) clans," refers to other father-houses not mentioned by name, and the number 1,760 refers to all the guilds and clans of verses 10—13, and should be separated from the preceding phrase by a semicolon.

thousand and seven hundred and threescore; ¹very able men for the work of the service of the house of God.

⁽¹⁴⁾ And of the Levites; Shemaiah the son of Hasshub, the son of Azrikam, the son of Hashabiah, of the sons of Merari; ⁽¹⁵⁾ and Bakbakkar, Heresh, and Galal, and Mattaniah the son of Micah, the son of Zichri, the son of Asaph; ⁽¹⁶⁾ and Obadiah the son of Shemaiah, the son of Galal, the son of Jeduthun, and Berechiah the son of Asa, the son of Elkanah, that dwelt in the villages of the Netophathites. ⁽¹⁷⁾ And the porters were, Shallum, and Akkub, and Talmon, and Ahiman, and their brethren: Shallum was the chief; ⁽¹⁸⁾ who hitherto waited in the king's gate eastward: they were porters in the companies of the children of Levi. ⁽¹⁹⁾ And Shallum the son of Kore, the son of Ebiasaph, the son of Korah, and his brethren, of the house of his father, the Korahites, were over the work of the service, keepers of the ²gates of the tabernacle: and their fathers, being over the host of the LORD,

B.C. 1200, &c.

1 Heb., *mighty men of valour*.

2 Heb., *thresholds*.

---

This last explanation is probably right. The total number given in Neh. xi. 10—14 for the priests is 1,192. (See Note on verse 9.)

**Very able men.**—See Margin, and chap. vii. 9.

**For the work.**—"For" is wanting in the Hebrew. Perhaps "doers of" (Neh. xi. 13) has fallen out.

⁽¹⁴⁻¹⁷⁾ The Levites resident in Jerusalem (Neh. xi. 15—19).

⁽¹⁴⁾ Word for word the same with Neh. *l.c.*, save that here Shemaiah is ultimately deduced from the clan of the Merarites, whereas there one more ancestor (Bunni) follows Hashabiah, and the phrase "of the sons of Merari" is omitted.

⁽¹⁵, ¹⁶⁾ The chronicler here omits the verse Neh. xi. 16, after which follows, "And Mattaniah son of Micha son of Zabdi son of Asaph, the leader of praise, who used to give thanks after the prayer; and Bakbukiah the second among his brethren, and Abda son of Shammua, son of Galal, son of Jeduthun."

**Bakbakkar** and **Bakbukiah** are clearly variants of the same name, the latter being probably right.

**Heresh, and Galal** are omitted in Neh. xi.

**Zichri** here is doubtless "Zabdi" there: a confusion of similar letters, k, b, r, d.

**Obadiah the son of Shemaiah** is the same as "Abda son of Shammua."

**Berechiah the son of Asa, the son of Elkanah.**—Unmentioned in Neh. xi. As the name Elkanah appears in the pedigree of Heman (chap. vi. 34), it is supposed that Berechiah represents the Hemanite guild, which is otherwise conspicuous here by its omission. Perhaps "son of Heman" has dropped out of the text, as there are two names between Mattaniah and Asaph, Obadiah and Jeduthun. It thus appears that verses 15, 16 are concerned with the Levitical choirs; comp. verse 33.

**Villages of the Netophathites.**—Netophah was near Bethlehem (Neh. vii. 26; chap. ii. 54).

⁽¹⁷⁾ **And the porters were, Shallum, and Akkub, and Talmon, and Ahiman.**—Comp. Neh. xi. 18, 19, which sums up thus: "All the Levites in the holy city were two hundred fourscore and four. Moreover the porters, Akkub, Talmon, and their brethren that kept the gates, were an hundred seventy and two." Shallum does not appear.

**Ahiman** may have originated out of the following:

**Their brethren.**—Heb., *aheihem*. Comp. also Neh. xii. 25, 26, where we are told that (Mattaniah and Bakbukiah, Obadiah and) Meshullam (*i.e.*, Shallum), Talmon, and Akkub were porters keeping ward at the storehouses of the Temple gates, in the times of Joiakim son of Jeshua son of Jozadak, and of Nehemiah and Ezra. It is clear that the names of the porters likewise represent families or guilds, which had hereditary charge of the Temple gates. In fact, all the Levitical functions appear to have descended in the same families from father to son, like the various civil offices in the Roman empire; and tradition ascribed the entire arrangement to David, the second founder of the national worship. At this point the correspondence with Neh. xi. ceases.

**Shallum was the chief.**—This really belongs to verse 18, and introduces a description of the duties of the Levites, which extends over verses 18—34. Translate, *Shallum is the chief even unto this day in the king's gate, on the east side.* Shallum ("recompense") is called "Shelemiah" (chap. xxvi. 14), which, again, is a curtailment of Meshelemiah ("Jah recompenseth"), chap. xxvi. 1; verse 21 *infra*. The fact that Shallum—Meshelemiah—is spoken of as warder in David's day as well as in the post-exilic age, proves that a guild or clan, not an individual, is in question. The eastern gate was the post of honour (Ezek. xlvi. 1, 2), and the royal entry. The old name of the King's Gate would naturally be retained in the restored Temple.

⁽¹⁸⁾ **They were porters in the companies of the children of Levi.**—Rather, *They are warders for the camps of the sons of Levi.* (Comp. Num. iii. 23 *et seq.*, where it is prescribed that the Levites encamp on the four sides of the tabernacle.) The primitive terminology is used in order to convey the idea that the Levitical wardership of the Temple went back historically to that of the Mosaic sanctuary.

⁽¹⁹⁾ **And Shallum the son of Kore, the son of Ebiasaph, the son of Korah.**—Comp. chap. xxvi. 1, which makes "Meshelemiah son of Kore, of the sons of Asaph" a guild of warders under David.

**Ebiasaph**—"The Father (*i.e.*, God) gathered," is a fuller form of *Asaph*, "He gathered."

**And his brethren, of the house of his father.** —That is, the Korahites, as is immediately explained: *his kinsmen belonging to his father-house* or *clan*.

**The work of the service** (of Shallum),—That is, of the guild so called, is defined as that of "wardens of the thresholds of the tent," that is, of the Temple, which had taken the place of the old Tent of Meeting.

**And their fathers, being over the host of the Lord, were keepers of the entry.**—"Their fathers" are the ancestors of the Korahite clan of Shallum.

**The host of the Lord.**—Or, rather, *the encampment of Jehovah*, means the tabernacle, or Tent of Tryst, which had only one entrance, over which, according to this passage—the Pentateuch is silent—the house of

*were* keepers of the entry. (20) And Phinehas the son of Eleazar was the ruler over them in time past, *and* the LORD *was* with him. (21) *And* Zechariah the son of Meshelemiah *was* porter of the door of the tabernacle of the congregation.

(22) All these *which were* chosen to be porters in the gates *were* two hundred and twelve. These were reckoned by their genealogy in their villages, whom David and Samuel the seer ¹did ordain in their ²set office. (23) So they and their children *had* the oversight of the gates of the house of the LORD, *namely*, the house of the tabernacle, by wards. (24) In four quarters were the porters, toward the east, west, north, and south. (25) And their brethren, *which were* in their villages, *were* to come after seven days from time to time with them. (26) For these Levites, the four chief porters, were in *their* ³set office, and were over the ⁴chambers and treasuries of the house of God. (27) And they lodged round about the house of God, because the charge *was* upon them, and the opening thereof every morning *pertained* to them. (28) And *certain* of them had the charge of the ministering

¹ Heb., *founded*.
² Or. *trust*.
³ Or, *trust*.
⁴ Or, *Storehouses*.

---

Shallum stood guard. 2 Chron. xxxi. 2 applies the same archaic nomenclature to the Temple in Hezekiah's reign, speaking of "the gates of the camps of Iahweh."

(20) **And Phinehas the son of Eleazar was the ruler over them in time past.**—Or, *of yore*. Phinehas may have held this office of president (*nagid*, verse 11) of the warders before he became high priest, just as Eleazar had held a similar position during the lifetime of Aaron (Num. iii. 32). Nothing is said of it elsewhere.

**And the Lord was with him.**—Rather, *The Lord be with him!* a pious ejaculation, such as the Jews of later times were wont to use in speaking of a departed worthy; and of interest to us as indicating a belief in continued existence after death. (Comp. chap. xxii. 11, 16.)

(21) **And.**—Omit. The verse returns abruptly from the Mosaic to the Davidic age.

**Zechariah the son of Meshelemiah** had charge of the north gate under David (chap. xxvi. 12).

**Was porter of the door of the tabernacle of the congregation.**—*Was a doorkeeper of the tent of meeting.* The verse seems to refer the functions of Zechariah to Mosaic antiquity; but comp. Note on verse 19. The relation of this company to those mentioned in verse 17 is indeterminate.

(22) **All these which were chosen to be porters in the gates** (Heb., *thresholds*) **were two hundred and twelve.**—This seems to assign the number of warders at the epoch of which the chronicler, or, rather, his source, is writing. Neh. xi. 19 makes the total of the porters one hundred and seventy-two. According to Ezra ii. 42, one hundred and thirty-nine returned with Zerubbabel. Under David, the number of warders was ninety-three (chap. xxvi. 8—11).

**These were reckoned by their genealogy in their villages.**—Rather, *these—in their villages was their registration*.

**These.**—That is, their ancestors. Guilds and corporations do not die.

**Whom David and Samuel the seer did ordain in their set office.**—*These David and Samuel had ordained in their office of trust*, or, *in permanence.* No mention is made elsewhere of Samuel's part in arranging the Levitical service. He died before David's accession (1 Sam. xxv. 1). Tradition doubtless associated him with David in the work of religious reform, and from what is known of his relation to the sovereigns of his day, the statement of the text may be held true in spirit, if not in the letter.

(23) **Namely, the house of the tabernacle.**—For the Temple was not built in David's day.

**By wards.**—*For Watches.*

(24) **In four quarters were the porters.**—"To the four winds used the warders to stand" (to be), viz., on the four sides of the tent of meeting, and from the age of Solomon on the four sides of the square enclosure of the Temple.

(25) **And their brethren, which were in their villages.**—The families of the Temple warders, like those of the singers, lived on their farms in the villages round Jerusalem, and came up for their duties in weekly rotation (verse 16; Neh. xii. 29).

**After seven days.**—*Every seventh day*; that is, on the Sabbath, when each class entered on its duties.

(26) **For these Levites, the four chief porters, were in their set office.**—The Heb. says, or seems to say, "For in fixed position (or trust) were they, viz., the four heroes of the warders." (See verse 17. which apparently names four chief "porters.") The temporary chiefs of the warder guilds abode in the Temple; the mass of their members was settled in the neighbouring villages, and occupied with pastoral pursuits.

**And were over the chambers and treasuries of the house of God.**—This statement belongs to the following verse. The preceding account of the porters or warders seems to terminate with the words, "For in fixed position are they, the four stalwart warders; *they* are the Levites;" that is, *the* Levites *par excellence. And they were over the cells and over the treasuries of the house of God* (viz., the warders); *and they used to pass the night* (verse 27) *in the places round the house of God, for upon them was the ward, and they were over the opening* (key) *every morning*—a brief recapitulation of the main duty of the Levitical warders. Some have proposed to alter the text of verse 26*b*, and to read, " And some of the Levites were over the cells," &c., thus constituting a new paragraph, although verse 27 obviously recurs to the warders. Probably the paragraph mark should be transferred to verse 28. From this point to verse 34 we have a review of the other special charges of the Levites.

(28) The care of the sacred vessels of gold and silver. These were counted when brought out of the storerooms, and when replaced, to make sure that none was purloined. (Comp. Ezra viii. 20 *et seq.*)

vessels, that they should ¹bring them in and out by tale. (29) *Some* of them also *were* appointed to oversee the vessels, and all the ²instruments of the sanctuary, and the fine flour, and the wine, and the oil, and the frankincense, and the spices. (30) And *some* of the sons of the priests made *a*the ointment of the spices. (31) And Mattithiah, *one* of the Levites, who *was* the firstborn of Shallum the Korahite, had the ³set office over the things that were made ⁴in the pans. (32) And *other* of their brethren, of the sons of the Kohathites, *were* over the ⁵shewbread, to prepare *it* every sabbath. (33) And these *are* the singers, chief of the fathers of the Levites, *who* remain- ing in the chambers *were* free: for ⁶they were employed in *that* work day and night. (34) These chief fathers of the Levites *were* chief throughout their generations; these dwelt at Jerusalem. (35) And in Gibeon dwelt the father of Gibeon, Jehiel, whose wife's name *was* ⁵Maachah: (36) and his firstborn son Abdon, then Zur, and Kish, and Baal, and Ner, and Nadab, (37) and Gedor, and Ahio, and Zechariah, and Mikloth. (38) And Mikloth begat Shimeam. And they also dwelt with their brethren at Jerusalem, over against their brethren. (39) *c* And Ner begat Kish; and Kish begat Saul: and Saul begat Jonathan, and Malchi-shua, and Abinadab, and

---

1 Heb., *bring them in by tale, and carry them out by tale.*
2 Or, *vessels.*
a Ex. 30. 23.
3 Or, *trust.*
4 Or, *on flat plates, or, slices.*
5 Heb., *bread of ordering.*
6 Heb., *upon them.*
b ch. 8. 29.
c ch. 8. 33.

---

**Tale.**—"Reckoning," "number:"—

"And every shepherd tells his *tale*
Under the hawthorn in the dale."

Literally, *for by number they used to bring them in* (to the sanctuary), *and by number they used to take them out.*

(29) Care of the ordinary vessels; that is, all those which were used in the daily service of the sanctuary ("vessels . . . instruments:" the same Hebrew term, *kêlim*, vasa, σκεύη); as also supervision of the stores of flour, wine, oil, incense, and spicery, which were adjuncts of meat offerings and libations, and the holy unguents (Exod. xxv. 6).

(30) A parenthetic remark. The Levites had charge of the stores of spicery, but only the priests might lawfully prepare the holy ointment and oil wherewith the sacred tent, the ark, the table, &c., were anointed (Exod. xxx. 23—29).

(31) The narrative returns to the functions of the Levites. "And Mattithiah, one of the Levites (he was the firstborn of Shallum the Korahite), was (or is) in fixed charge over the making of the pancakes."

**Mattithiah . . . firstborn of Shallum the Korahite.**—The son of Shallum, or Meshelemiah, is called Zechariah (chap. xxvi. 2). If Zechariah was the chief branch of Shallum in the days of David, Mattithiah may have been so in the time of the chronicler or of his authority here.

**Had the set office.**—In other words, the duty of baking the sacred cakes for the meat offerings was hereditary in this branch of the family of Shallum.

**Things that were made in the pans**—*i.e.*, "pancakes." The Hebrew term (*hăbittim*) occurs here only, but its meaning is fixed by the related word "baking-pan" (Ezek. iv. 3; *mahăbath*).

(32) "Some of the sons of the Kohathites, some of their brethren." The Korahites, to which house Shallum and Mattithiah belonged, were a subdivision of the great clan of Kohath.

**The shewbread.**—See Lev. xxiv. 5—9. Here it is called "Bread of the Pile;" another name was "Bread of the Presence."

**To prepare it every sabbath.**—The Levites had to get it ready for the priests to lay it fresh on the golden table, after removing the old bread, every Sabbath.

(33, 34) A general subscription, or concluding statement, with reference to the preceding account of the Levites (verses 14—32).

(33) Refers to the singers treated of in verses 14—16: *And these (above mentioned) are the minstrels, heads of Levitical families; in the Temple cells (they lived), exempt from all other charge; for day and night they were over them in the work.* The Hebrew is harsh, and perhaps corrupt, but the meaning seems to be clear. It is hardly meant that the service of song in the Temple was uninterrupted (comp. Rev. iv. 8), but only that the choristers were under obligation to perpetually recurring service.

**They were employed in that work.**—Rather, *They were over them in the work.* They—that is, the leaders for the time being—lived, like the chief warders, in the Temple cells, presiding continually over the guilds of singers.

(34) **These chief . . . generations.**—Literally, *These are the heads of the Levitical houses, according to their birth-rolls, heads.* (Comp. chap. viii. 28 for the meaning.)

**These dwelt in Jerusalem.**—A final remark concerning *all* the Levites of verses 14—32. The proper names are regarded as chiefs, under whom their numerous clansmen are *subsumed.*

(35—44) A duplicate of chap. viii. 29—38. The genealogy of Saul seems to be repeated, according to the chronicler's habit (comp. chap. vi. 4 *et seq.* with chap. vi. 50 *et seq.;* chap. vii. 6 *et seq.* with chap. viii. 1 *et seq.*), as a transition or introduction to something else, viz., the account of that king's final ruin in chap. x. The present list is identical with the former, so far as it extends (chap. viii. 39—48 is wanting here), but is, on the whole, in better preservation, supplying, as we have seen, several omissions in the other copy. Only the name of Ahaz has fallen out (verse 41). The correspondence of the two lists appears to be too exact to justify an assumption of different original sources; but the chronicler may have found the repetition already existing in the principal document from which he drew his materials.

(36) **Zur.**—"Rock," a Divine title. (Comp. Pedahzur, "the Rock hath ransomed;" Zurishaddai, "the Rock is the Lofty One;" if we may connect the difficult

*The Stock of Jonathan.*     I. CHRONICLES, X.     *Saul's overthrow.*

Esh-baal. <sup>(40)</sup> And the son of Jonathan was Merib-baal : and Merib-baal begat Micah. <sup>(41)</sup> And the sons of Micah were, Pithon, and Melech, and Tahrea, <sup>a</sup> and Ahaz. <sup>(42)</sup> And Ahaz begat Jarah ; and Jarah begat Alemeth, and Azmaveth, and Zimri ; and Zimri begat Moza ; <sup>(43)</sup> and Moza begat Binea ; and Rephaiah his son, Eleasah his son, Azel his son. <sup>(44)</sup> And Azel had six sons, whose names *are* these, Azrikam, Bocheru, and Ishmael, and Sheariah, and Obadiah, and Hanan : these *were* the sons of Azel.

*a* ch. 8. 35.

*b* 1 Sam. 31. 1, 2

1 Or, *wounded*.

2 Or, *Ishui*, 1 Sam. 14. 49.

3 Heb., *shooters with bows*.

4 Heb., *found him*.

CHAPTER X. — <sup>(1)</sup> Now <sup>b</sup> the Philistines fought against Israel ; and the men of Israel fled from before the Philistines, and fell down <sup>1</sup>slain in mount Gilboa. <sup>(2)</sup> And the Philistines followed hard after Saul, and after his sons ; and the Philistines slew Jonathan, and <sup>2</sup>Abinadab, and Malchi-shua, the sons of Saul. <sup>(3)</sup> And the battle went sore against Saul, and the <sup>3</sup>archers <sup>4</sup>hit him, and he was wounded of the archers. <sup>(4)</sup> Then said Saul to his armourbearer, Draw thy sword, and thrust me through therewith ; lest

---

Shaddai with the Assyrian term *sadu,* "mountain." But it seems better to explain it from the root *shādāh*, "to pour out," which is found in Aramaic and Arabic ; so that *Shaddai* would signify "giver of rain." (Comp. Joel ii. 23.)

Baal has been compounded with Nadab, to form a single name, Baal-nadab, "Baal is prince." (Comp. Baal-gad, "Baal is Gad ; " Baal-hanan, "Baal is bounteous," chap. i. 49.) In that case Ner is out of place.

<sup>(43)</sup> Rephaiah appears in the contracted form Rapha in chap. viii.

<sup>(44)</sup> With the omission of the sons of Eshek and Ulam here, comp. the similar abridgment of the list in chap. vi. 4—15, when repeated in the same chap. at verses 50—53. This suggests that the present omission is not due to inadvertence, but either to the design of the chronicler or to a like omission in his source.

Chaps. x.—xxix.—The history of King David, who made Jerusalem the political and religious centre of Israel, organised the Levitical ministry in its permanent shape, and amassed great stores of wealth and material for the Temple, which his son and successor was to build.

X.

A Brief Narrative of the Overthrow and Death of Saul, by way of Prelude to the Reign of David.

Verses 1—12 are parallel to 1 Sam. xxxi. 1—13. The general coincidence of the two texts is so exact as to preclude the supposition of independence. We know that the chronicler has drawn much in his earlier chapters from the Pentateuch ; and as he must have been acquainted with the Books of Samuel, it is *à priori* likely that he made a similar use of them. At the same time, a number of small variations—on an average, three at least in each verse—some of which can neither be referred to the freaks or mistakes of copyists nor to the supposed caprice of the compiler, may be taken to indicate the use of an additional source, or perhaps of a text of Samuel differing in some respects from that which we possess. (See *Introduction.*)

<sup>(1)</sup> Now the Philistines fought against Israel.—For a similarly abrupt beginning, comp. Isa. ii. 1. The battle was fought in the plain of Jezreel, or Esdraelon, the scene of so many of the struggles of ancient history. (Comp. Hosea ii. 10 : "I will break the bow of Israel in the valley of Jezreel.")

The men of Israel.—Heb., *man*—a collective expression, which gives a more vivid image of the rout. They fled as one man, or in a body. Samuel has the plural.

Fell down slain in mount Gilboa.—The Jebel Faku'a rises out of the plain of Jezreel to a height of one thousand seven hundred feet. The defeated army of Saul fell back upon this mountain, which had been their first position (1 Sam. xxviii. 4), but were pursued thither. "Slain" is right, as in verse 8.

<sup>(2)</sup> The Philistines followed hard after Saul. —Literally, *clave to Saul*, that is, hotly pursued him. (Comp. 1 Kings 22, 31.) The destruction of the king and his sons would make their triumph complete.

The sons of Saul.—Omit *the.* Eshbaal, Saul's fourth son, was not in the battle (2 Sam. ii. 8. Comp. chap. viii. 33). Like Zedekiah, the last king of Judah, Saul may have witnessed the death of his sons (2 Kings xxv. 7). Jonathan, at least, would not be far from him in the last struggle. "In their deaths they were not divided."

<sup>(3)</sup> The battle went sore against Saul.—Literally, *was heavy upon* (Samuel, "unto") *him*, like a burden weighing him to the earth.

And the archers hit him.—Literally, *And they that shoot with the bow came upon him ; and he shuddered* (Sam., "greatly") *before the shooters.* "He shuddered or trembled" (Deut. ii. 25). The verb is properly to writhe, travail (Isa. xxiii. 4). Saul's deadly terror was natural. He believed himself forsaken of God, and stood now, after a lost battle, beset by murderous foes, whom he could not reach. There was no chance of a fair hand to hand encounter. The Heb. word for "archers" is the same in both places in Sam. (*mōrîm*) ; here a rarer form (*yōrîm*, 2 Chron. xxxv. 23) fills the second place. The Philistines were from Egypt, and the bow was a favourite Egyptian arm. The hieroglyph for "soldier" (*menfat*) is a man with bow and quiver.

<sup>(4)</sup> And Saul said.—So Abimelech (Judges ix. 54). Lest these uncircumcised come.—Sam. adds " and thrust me through." An inadvertent repetition there, or omission here, is possible. Or, we might say, Saul preferred death by a friendly stroke to the thrusts of insulting foemen.

And abuse me.—The Hebrew means, strictly, "to make a toy of," "sport with." "How I have made a toy of Egypt" (Exod. x. 2) ; and is used (Jer. xxxviii. 19) of insulting a fallen foe, as here.

Took a sword.—Literally, *the sword*—*i.e.,* his sword.

*Death of Saul.*  I. CHRONICLES, X.  *The Philistine's Triumph.*

these uncircumcised come and ¹abuse me. But his armourbearer would not; for he was sore afraid. So Saul took a sword, and fell upon it. ⁽⁵⁾ And when his armourbearer saw that Saul was dead, he fell likewise on the sword, and died. ⁽⁶⁾ So Saul died, and his three sons, and all his house died together. ⁽⁷⁾ And when all the men of Israel that *were* in the valley saw that they fled, and that Saul and his sons were dead, then they forsook their cities, and fled: and the Philistines came and dwelt in them.

⁽⁸⁾ And it came to pass on the morrow,

1 Or, *mock me.*

when the Philistines came to strip the slain, that they found Saul and his sons fallen in mount Gilboa. ⁽⁹⁾ And when they had stripped him, they took his head, and his armour, and sent into the land of the Philistines round about, to carry tidings unto their idols, and to the people. ⁽¹⁰⁾ And they put his armour in the house of their gods, and fastened his head in the temple of Dagon.

⁽¹¹⁾ And when all Jabesh-gilead heard all that the Philistines had done to Saul, ⁽¹²⁾ they arose, all the valiant men, and took away the body of Saul, and the bodies of his sons, and brought them to

---

⁽⁵⁾ **He fell likewise on the sword.**—Sam., "his sword," *i.e.*, the sword of the armour-bearer.

**And died.**—Samuel adds "with him," which seems to be omitted here for brevity, which may be the reason of other similar omissions. Loyalty to his chief, and perhaps dread of the foe, were the armour-bearer's motives.

⁽⁶⁾ **And all his house died together.**—Instead of this Samuel reads "and his armour-bearer; also all his men on that day together." The LXX. adds "on that day" here, while in Samuel it omits "all his men," thus minimising the differences of text. It is mere pedantry to press the phrases "all his men," "all his house." The strength of these expressions indicates the completeness of the overthrow.

The chronicler was fully aware that some of Saul's house were not engaged in this battle (chap. ix. 35). And in any case, the chief warriors of his household, and immediate followers, died with the king.

⁽⁷⁾ **That were in the valley.**—Rather, *the plain*, in which the main battle was fought—that of Jezreel. Samuel has "that were on the other side of the plain, and on the other side of the Jordan." The curt phrase "who (dwelt) in the plain," may be compared with chap. ix. 2. The people of the surrounding districts are meant; who, when they "saw that they" (viz., Saul's army, "the men of Israel," Samuel) "fled," or had been routed, deserted "their (Samuel, 'the,' perhaps a transposition of letters) cities" which were then occupied by the Philistines.

**Dwelt in them.**—The pronoun here is masculine, in Samuel, feminine, which is correct.

⁽⁸⁾ **His sons.**—Samuel, "his three sons." Otherwise the two verses are word for word the same.

⁽⁹⁾ **And when they had stripped him.**—Better, *and they stripped him, and carried off his head*, &c. Samuel, "and they cut off his head, and stripped his armour off." With the phrase "carried off his head," comp. Gen. xl. 19, "Pharaoh will lift thy head from off thee," where the same Hebrew verb is used (*yissá*).

**And sent** (Saul's head and armour) **to carry tidings unto their idols.**—The verb *bassēr* is used of good and bad tidings, especially of the former, as in 2 Sam. xviii. 19, 20.

**Unto their idols.**—Samuel, "house of their idols." But the LXX. reading there is the same as here, τοῖς εἰδώλοις. The expression of Samuel looks original, though it may have been copied by mistake from verse 10. Note the strictly local conception of deities implied in this act of the Philistines; as if their idols could neither see nor hear beyond their own temples. (Comp. 1 Kings xx. 23, 28; Ps. xciv. 9.)

⁽¹⁰⁾ **In the house of their gods.**—Or god, as LXX. Samuel, "house of Ashtaroth," which the chronicler or his source paraphrases, perhaps from a repugnance to mentioning the idol's name. Ashtoreth had a great temple at Ascalon, as "Heavenly Aphrodite" (Herod., *Hist.* i. 108). The "Queen of Heaven" (Jer. vii. 18) was worshipped by the Semitic races generally. Under the name of *Ishtar*, she was a chief goddess of the Assyrians, and had famous temples at Nineveh and Arbela. The Sabæans worshipped her as *Athtár*; and the name *Ashtár* is coupled with Chemosh on the Moabite Stone.

**Fastened his head in the temple of Dagon.**—Literally, *and his skull* (*gulgōleth*—comp. Golgotha, Matt. xxvii. 33) *they fastened in the house of Dagon.* Instead of this, we read in Samuel, "and his corpse they fastened to the wall of Beth-shan." It is hardly likely that the one reading is a corruption of the other. The chronicler has omitted the statement about Saul's corpse, which is not mentioned in verse 9, and supplied one respecting his head, which has been already spoken of in that verse. He found the fact in his additional source, if the clause in question has not dropt out of the text of Samuel.

The Accadians worshipped Dagon, as we learn from the cuneiform inscriptions: comp. the name Ismi-Dagan (*Dagon hears*).

⁽¹²⁾ **All the valiant men.**—Literally, *every man of valour*. Samuel adds, "and marched all the night."

**Took away.**—*Carried off.* Samuel has "took," (*ceperunt*).

**The body.**—A common Aramaic word, *gûfāh*, only read here in the Old Testament, for which Samuel has the pure Hebrew synonym *g'wiyah*. Samuel adds, "from the wall of Beth-shan."

**And brought them.**—Samuel, "and came to Jabesh, and burnt them there." To burn a corpse was a further degradation of executed criminals (Josh. vii. 25; Lev. xx. 14, xxi. 9), and as the Jews did not ordinarily practise cremation, it is supposed that the phrase "burnt them," in 1 Sam. xxxi. means "made a burning for them" of costly spices, as was done at the funerals of kings (Jer. xxxiv. 5; 2 Chron. xvi. 14, xxi. 19). But perhaps the bodies were burnt in this exceptional case because they had been mutilated by the enemy.

**Buried their bones.**—Samuel, "took and buried." The phrase "their bones," contrasted with their

Jabesh, and buried their bones under the oak in Jabesh, and fasted seven days. <sup>(13)</sup> So Saul died for his transgression which he <sup>1</sup>committed against the LORD, *<sup>a</sup>even against the word of the LORD*, which he kept not, and also for asking *counsel of one that had* a familiar spirit, *<sup>b</sup>to enquire of it;* <sup>(14)</sup> and enquired not of the LORD: therefore he slew him, and turned the kingdom unto David the son of <sup>2</sup>Jesse.

B.C. 1048.

1 Heb., *transgressed*.
*a* 1 Sam. 15. 23.
*b* 1 Sam. 28. 7.
2 Heb., *Isai*.
*c* 2 Sam. 5. 1.
3 Heb., *both yesterday and the third day*.
4 Or, *rule*.

CHAPTER XI.—<sup>(1)</sup> Then *<sup>c</sup>*all Israel gathered themselves to David unto Hebron, saying, Behold, we *are* thy bone and thy flesh. <sup>(2)</sup> And moreover <sup>3</sup>in time past, even when Saul was king, thou *wast* he that leddest out and broughtest in Israel: and the LORD thy God said unto thee, Thou shalt <sup>4</sup>feed my people Israel, and thou shalt be ruler over my people Israel. <sup>(3)</sup> Therefore came all the elders of Israel to the king to Hebron; and David made a

---

"corpses," certainly seems to imply that the latter had been burnt.

**The oak.**—Heb., *terebinth*, or *turpentine tree*. Samuel, "tamarisk." The difference points to another source used by Chronicles.

**And fasted seven days.**—In token of mourning. (Comp. the friends of Job, Job ii. 11—13; and Ezekiel among the exiles at Tel-abib, Ezek. iii. 15.) For the behaviour of the men of Jabesh, comp. 1 Sam. xi.

(13, 14) A concluding reflection from the mind of the chronicler himself. He sums up his extract concerning the ruin of Saul by assigning the moral ground of it, viz., Saul's "unfaithfulness whereby he showed himself unfaithful to Jehovah." The same charge was made against the Transjordan tribes in chap. v. 25, and against the people of Judah in chap. ix. 1.

<sup>(13)</sup> **Even against the word of the Lord.**—Saul's unfaithfulness was twofold: (1) he did not observe the prophetic word of Jehovah (comp. 1 Sam. xiii. 13, xv. 11); and (2) he consulted a necromancer, to the neglect of consulting Jehovah (1 Sam. xxviii.).

**And also for asking counsel.**—*And also by consulting the necromancer in order to get a response.* "Turn ye not to the necromancers" (Lev. xix. 31). (See also Isa. viii. 19.) Saul broke the general law of his people, as well as special commands addressed to himself. No allusion is made to his cruel slaughter of the priests (1 Sam. xxii. 18), nor to his implacable hatred of David.

<sup>(14)</sup> **And enquired not of the Lord.**—Saul had, in fact, enquired of Jehovah before resorting to the witch of En-dor, "but the Lord answered him not, neither by the dreams, nor by the Urim, nor by the prophets" (1 Sam. xxviii. 6). We shall not be reading a meaning of our own into the text if we say that Saul's natural impatience (1 Sam. xiii. 13) on this occasion betrayed him again; he at once despaired of help from his God, instead of seeking it with self-humiliation and penitence. His character is consistently drawn throughout the history. The sin that ruined the first king was essentially that which led to the final ruin of the nation, viz., unfaithfulness to the covenant-God. The same word characterises both. (Comp. verse 13 with chaps. v. 25, ix. 1.)

**Therefore he slew him.**—God acts through the instrumentality of His creatures. In this case He employed the Philistines, and the suicidal hand of Saul himself; just as He employed the Assyrian conquerors of a later age to be the scourge of guilty peoples (Isa. x. 5—15), and raised up Cyrus to be His servant, who should fulfil all His pleasure (Isa. xliv. 28, xlv. 1—13).

**Turned the kingdom unto David.**—By means of the warriors of Israel (chap. xii. 23). This sentence shows that chap. x. is transitional to the history of David as king.

XI.

The chapter contains (1) the election of David in Hebron, and his conquest of Jerusalem (verses 1—9); (2) a list of David's chief warriors, with short notices of their famous deeds (verses 10—47).

(1—9) Parallel to 2 Sam. v. 1—10.

<sup>(1)</sup> **Then all Israel gathered themselves.**—Literally, *and*. "Then" is too definite a mark of time. The chronicler passes over the subsequent history of the house of Saul, and its decline under the feeble Ishbosheth, who reigned at Mahanaim as a puppet-king in the hands of Abner his powerful kinsman and general (2 Sam. ii.—iv.).

**All Israel.**—This proves that the allusion is not to David's election by Judah (2 Sam. ii. 4).

**Hebron**, the burial-place of the patriarchs, was the capital of Judah, the tribe of David.

**Thy bone and thy flesh.**—A proverb first of physical, then of moral unity (Gen. ii. 23; Judges ix. 2). It was not as if David were some valiant foreigner, like certain of his own heroes. Moreover, the affection and sympathy of the tribes were with him, whose life of struggle and success had marked him out as their divinely chosen leader.

<sup>(2)</sup> **In time past.**—*Yesterday*, or *three days since*. A very indefinite phrase, used in Gen. xxxi. 2 of a time fourteen years since, and 2 Kings xiii. 5 of more than forty years ago.

**Leddest out.**—To battle.

**Broughtest in.**—Of the homeward march. David had thus already discharged kingly functions. (Comp. 1 Sam. viii. 20, xviii. 6, 13, 27; 2 Sam. iii. 18.)

**The Lord thy God said unto thee.**—1 Sam. xvi. 13.

**Thou shalt feed my people.**—Literally, *shepherd* or *tend them*. The same term is used of the Lord Himself (Isa. xl. 11; Ps. lxxx. 1). The king then is God's representative, and as such his right is really Divine (Rom. xiii. 1). The cuneiform documents reveal the interesting fact that the term "shepherd," as applied to sovereigns, is as old as the pre-Semitic stage of Babylonian civilisation (the second millennium B.C.).

<sup>(3)</sup> **Therefore came all the elders of Israel.**—The assembly of elders, the Senate of Israel, make a contract with David concerning his prerogative and the rights of his people, thus formally determining "the manner of the kingdom." (Comp. 1 Sam. viii. 9 seq., x. 25.) Representative institutions appear to have been

*David Anointed.*      I. CHRONICLES, XI.      *Joab made Chief.*

covenant with them in Hebron before the LORD; and they anointed David king over Israel, according to the word of the LORD [1] by [a] Samuel.

(4) And David and all Israel [b] went to Jerusalem, which *is* Jebus; where the Jebusites *were*, the inhabitants of the land. (5) And the inhabitants of Jebus said to David, Thou shalt not come hither. Nevertheless David took the castle of Zion, which *is* the city of David.

(6) And David said, Whosoever smiteth the Jebusites first shall be [2] chief and captain. So Joab the son of Zeruiah went first up, and was chief. (7) And David dwelt in the castle; therefore they called [3] it the city of David. (8) And he built the city round about, even from Millo round about: and Joab [4] repaired the rest of the city. (9) So David [5] waxed greater and greater: for the LORD of hosts *was* with him.

[1] Heb., *by the hand of.*
[a] 1 Sam. 16. 13.
[b] 2 Sam. 5. 6.
[2] Heb., *head.*
[3] That is, *Zion*, 2 Sam. 5. 7.
[4] Heb., *revived.*
[5] Heb., *went in going and increasing.*

---

the rule in the best period of Israel's national existence. The elders or hereditary heads of the tribal subdivisions met in council to discuss and settle matters of national concern. (Comp. chap. xii. 23.)

**Before the Lord.**—In the presence of the high priest, and perhaps before the ark; comp. Exod. xxi. 6; 1 Sam. ii. 25, where the priestly judge is called God, as representing the authority of the Divine judge (Exod. xxii. 28).

**According to the word of the Lord by Samuel.**—A reflection added by the chronicler, and based upon the facts related in 1 Sam. xv. 28, xvi. 1—13.

(4—9) THE CAPTURE OF ZION BY JOAB'S VALOUR, AND DAVID'S SETTLEMENT THERE.

The accession of the new king is followed by a warlike enterprise, according to the precedent of Saul (1 Sam. xi.). This agrees with the reason assigned for the election of a king (1 Sam. viii. 20), as well as with what we know of Assyrian custom, and is a mark of historic truth.

(4) **And David . . . land.**—Samuel is briefer: "And the king and his men went to Jerusalem, to the Jebusite, the inhabitant of the land." The chronicler adds the explanatory "that is Jebus," because of the after-mention of the Jebusite. He then further modifies the form of the original statement, continuing "and there (lived) the Jebusite (*collect.*), the inhabitants," &c.

**Jerusalem** means city of Salem; Assyrian, *Ursalimmê*. But in Hebrew the name has been so modified as to suggest "vision of peace." In Greek the name became Hierosolyma, "Sacred Solyma."

**Inhabitants of the land.**—A standing name of the native Canaanites, and equivalent to indigenæ, or Ἀυτόχθονες.

(5) **Thou shalt not come hither.**—A jeer. (Comp. 2 Sam. v. 6.) "And one spake unto David, saying, Thou shalt not come in hither. The blind and the lame will have kept thee out!" The Jebusites trusted in the strength of their fortress. Even the weakest defence would be sufficient to repel David's assault.

(6) **Whosoever smiteth the Jebusites first.**—The account diverges more and more from the parallel passage. 2 Sam. v. 8, reads, "And David said in that day, Whosoever smiteth the Jebusite, let him hurl down the waterfall (Ps. xlii. 7), both the lame and the blind, the hated of David's soul! Therefore they say, Blind and lame must not enter the house" (*i.e.*, the Temple). Such is the simplest rendering of an obscure, but evidently original record. The chronicler appears to have followed another and clearer account, which made Joab play at the storm of Jebus the part of Othniel at that of Kirjath-sepher (Judges i. 12, 13).

**Chief and captain.**—Literally, *shall become a head and a captain.*

**Joab the son of Zeruiah** is not mentioned at all in the parallel passage. Joab already appears as David's general, while Ishbosheth is yet reigning at Mahanaim (2 Sam. ii. 13, iii. 23). Perhaps the phrase here used means head and governor of Jerusalem. (Comp. verse 8.)

**Went up.**—Scaled the rampart, "and became a head."

(7) **Castle.**—*Stronghold, fastness.* (Comp. 2 Sam. v. 7.) In verse 5 the form is *meçûdāh*, here it is the rare masculine form, *meçād*: comp. Ar. *maçād, cacumen montis.*

**They called it.**—Samuel (Hebrew), "one called it;" both in a general sense.

**City.**—Comp. Greek, *polis* = acropolis.

(8) **And he built the city round about.**—Literally, *and he built* (or rebuilt or fortified) *the city all round, from the Millo even unto the* (complete) *round.* The Millo was probably a tower or citadel, like the Arx Antonia of later times. According to the chronicler David started from that point, and brought his line of defences round to it again. Samuel has simply, "And David built around, from the Millo, and inward." This seems to mean that he carried his buildings from the fortress towards the interior of the city. Both statements may, of course, be true.

(9) This verse corresponds word for word with Samuel, only omitting "God" after "Lord." Literally, *and David walked on, a walking and growing great*—a common Hebrew metaphor of gradual and progressive increase or decrease. (Comp. Gen. viii. 5, and the use of the term *andante*, "walking," in music.)

**Lord of hosts was with him.**—The Lord of Hosts is doubtless a contracted form of the fuller expression, Lord God of Hosts, as it appears in Samuel. The Lord (or God) of Hosts is a title derived from God's supremacy over the host of heaven, *i.e.*, the stars, worshipped as deities by the races environing Israel, insomuch that the very word for *God* in the old Babylonian is represented by a star (✱); and in the later Assyrian character *star* was represented by the symbol for *God* thrice repeated. Assur, the supreme deity of the Assyrian Pantheon, is called in the inscriptions "king of the legions of heaven and earth," or "of the great gods." Similar titles were given to the Babylonian Nebo and Merodach. The Hebrew phrase is therefore, in one sense, equivalent to a concise assertion of the statement, "Jehovah your God is God of gods, and Lord of lords" (Deut. x. 17: comp. also Ps. xcv. 3, xcvii. 7). That the hosts in question are the stars appears from Ps. xxxiii. 6; Isa. xl. 26; Judges v. 20.

# I. CHRONICLES, XI.

*David's*                      *Mighty Men.*

(10) <sup>a</sup>These also *are* the chief of the mighty men whom David had, who <sup>1</sup>strengthened themselves with him in his kingdom, *and* with all Israel, to make him king, according to the word of the LORD concerning Israel. (11) And this *is* the number of the mighty men whom David had; Jashobeam, <sup>2</sup>an Hachmonite, the chief of the captains: he lifted up his spear against three hundred slain *by him* at one time. (12) And after him *was* Eleazar the son of Dodo, the Ahohite, who *was* one of the three mighties. (13) He was with David at <sup>3</sup>Pas-dammim, and there the Philistines were gathered together to battle, where was a parcel of ground full of barley; and the people fled from

*a* 2 Sam. 23. 8.
1 Or, *held strongly with him.*
2 Or, *son of Hachmoni.*
B.C. 1047.
3 Or, *Ephesdammim,* 1 Sam. 17. 1.

---

Very anciently the stars were conceived of as the army of heaven, marshalled in orderly array. (Comp. Isa. xl. 26, xxiv. 21, xiv. 12, 13.) The Lord of the hosts of heaven is *a fortiori* Lord of all earthly hosts; hence the fitness of the phrase in passages like the present. Lastly, we may observe that it is a grand idea of revealed religion that He who guides the stars in their courses guides also the destinies of individual men, elevating one and abasing another, according to the eternal principles of goodness and truth (Isa. lvii. 15).

(10—44) A list of the warriors who helped David to win and maintain his kingdom. This catalogue answers to that of 2 Sam. xxiii. 8—39, which, however, breaks off with Uriah the Hittite; whereas our text communicates sixteen additional names. This fact proves that the chronicler had either a fuller source, or a different recension of Samuel. The numerous variant spellings are in general mistakes of transcription.

(10) **These also are the chief of the mighty men.**—Rather, *And these were the heads of the warriors* (*i.e.*, the chief warriors, other warriors of lower rank being enumerated in chap. xii.) *who showed themselves strong in his support* (with him, Dan. x. 21; Ps. xii. 4), *in the matter of his kingdom, in common with all Israel, in order to make him king* (and maintain him as such: comp. their exploits, noticed below). This description of the heroes is not given in Samuel, the connection there being different.

**According to the word of the Lord concerning Israel.**—Comp. Note on verse 3. David was made king (1) for his own sake. It was work for which he was best fitted, and a reward of his faithfulness. (2) For Israel's sake: "So he led them with a faithful and true heart" (Ps. lxxviii. 70—72).

(11) **And this is the number of the mighty men.**—The heading of the catalogue in Samuel is merely, "These are the names of the warriors whom David had." The chronicler resumes, after the parenthetic explanation of the last verse, with "These, the number of the warriors." The word "number" (*mispar*) seems to refer to the fact that the corps was originally known as the Thirty (comp. verse 12). In chap. xii. 23, the plural (*mispᵉrê*) is used.

**Jashobeam, an Hachmonite.**—Literally, *Jashobeam, son of a Hakmonite*; but *ben* may be spurious, as in chap. ix. 7, and Neh. xi. 10. The Hebrew of 2 Sam. xxiii. 8 has *yoshebbashshebeth Tahkᵉmoni*, which has been supposed to be a corruption of *Ishbosheth ha-hakmoni* ("Ishbosheth the Hachmonite"). If this guess be right, the Jashobeam of our text may be a disguise of Eshbaal. This seems to be borne out by the readings of the Vatican LXX. here and at chap. xxvii. 2: Ἰεσεβαδά and Ἰσβοάζ. The Alex. MS., however, reads Ἰσβαδμ and Ἰσβοδμ, that is, Jashobeam.

**The chief of the captains.**—The Hebrew text has "head of the Thirty," and so the LXX. and Syriac. "Captains" ("knights," or "members of the royal staff,") is the reading of Samuel and the Hebrew margin here. The corps of the Thirty may also have been called the Knights; but the two Hebrew words might easily be confused (*shᵉlôshim, shalishim*). It is possible that the original reading was "head of the Three" (*shᵉlôshah*), as verses 11—14 describe an exploit of three champions.

**He lifted up his spear.**—Literally, *he it was who brandished his lance over three hundred slain in a single encounter*. Samuel says eight hundred, but the text there is otherwise very faulty. Yet as verse 20 records that the lesser hero, Abishai, slew three hundred, the greater number may be correct here. (Comp. the like exploit of Shamgar (Judges iii. 31), and the feats ascribed to Rameses II. and to the heroes of the Iliad.) A well-armed champion might cut down whole companies of ordinary fighting-men.

(12) **Eleazar the son of Dodo.**—For Dodo the LXX. has Dodai; so chap. xxvii. 4, and the Hebrew text of Samuel; but Syriac and Vulgate "his uncle," a translation of *dodo*.

**The Ahohite**—*i.e.*, of the clan Ahoah; perhaps the Benjamite house of this name (chap. viii. 4).

**Who was one of the three mighties.**—"He was among the three heroes," *i.e.*, one of the first or leading trio of warriors, whose names were Jashobeam (Eshbaal), Eleazar, and Shammah (2 Sam. xxiii. 11).

(13) **He was with David at Pas-dammim.**—Or Ephes-dammim, between Shochoh and Azekah in the Mountains of Judah, where David encountered Goliath. The name does not now appear in 2 Sam. xxiii. 5, being probably concealed under the word rendered "when they defied."

**And there the Philistines were gathered together to battle.**—After these words several lines have been lost, as may be seen by comparison of 2 Sam. xxiii. 9, 10. The text may be restored thus: "He was with David at Pas-dammim, and there the Philistines had gathered to the battle; and the men of Israel went up (perhaps, up the mountain side, in retreat). And he stood his ground, and smote the Philistines until his hand was benumbed, and clave to the sword. And Iahweh wrought a great victory on that day. And the people began returning (from flight) behind him, only to spoil (the slain). And after him (was) Shammah ben Agè, an Hararite. And the Philistines gathered together unto Lehi (Judges xv. 9). And there there was a parcel, etc.," verse 13. The cause of this serious omission was perhaps the double occurrence of the phrase "the Philistines gathered together." The eye of some copyist wandered from one to the other. What was originally told of Eleazar the second hero, was that his prowess turned the flight at Pas-dammim into a victory.

**Where was a parcel of ground full of barley.**—The scene of the exploit of the third hero,

*David's*          I. CHRONICLES, XI.          *Mighty Men.*

before the Philistines. (14) And they [1] set themselves in the midst of *that* parcel, and delivered it, and slew the *a* Philistines; and the LORD saved *them* by a great [2] deliverance.

(15) Now [3] three of the thirty captains went down to the rock to David, into the cave of Adullam; and the host of the Philistines encamped in the valley of Rephaim. (16) And David *was* then in the hold, and the Philistines' garrison *was* then at Bethlehem. (17) And David longed, and said, Oh that one would give me drink of the water of the well of Beth-lehem, that *is* at the gate! (18) And the three brake through the host of the Philistines, and drew water out of the well of Beth-lehem, that *was* by the gate, and took *it*, and brought *it* to David: but David would not drink *of* it, but poured it out to the LORD, (19) and said, My God forbid it me, that I should do this thing: shall I drink the blood of these men [4] that have put their lives in jeopardy? for with *the jeopardy of* their lives they brought it. Therefore he would not drink it. These things did these three mightiest.

(20) And Abishai the brother of Joab, he was chief of the three: for lifting up his spear against three hundred, he slew *them*, and had a name among the three. (21) *b* Of the three, he was more honourable than the two; for he was

---

1 Or, *stood.*

*a* 2 Sam. 23. 13.

2 Or, *salvation.*

3 Or, *three captains over the thirty.*

4 Heb., *with their lives.*

*b* 2 Sam. 23. 19, &c.

---

Shammah, son of Agê. "Perhaps the Philistines were intent on carrying off the crop (1 Sam. xxiii. 1). Samuel reads lentils. The Hebrew words for barley and lentils are very similar. We cannot tell which text is right.

(14) **And they set themselves . . . and delivered . . . and slew.**—These verbs should be singular, as describing the exploit of Shammah (2 Sam. xxiii. 12). After the omission just noticed had become perpetuated in the text, some editor must have altered the words into the plural, supposing that they referred to David and Eleazar (verse 13).

**Saved them.**—Samuel, "made a great deliverance": transpose one letter, and the Hebrew words are identical. LXX. and Syriac agree with Samuel.

(15—19) Three unnamed heroes who fetched water for David from the well at Bethlehem.

(15) **Now three of the thirty captains.**—Literally, *and a three out of the thirty chiefs went down*; a mode of description which appears to distinguish this trio from the former (verses 11—14). The form of the verb, however, connects this exploit with the same war. (Comp. 2 Sam. xxiii. 13—17.)

**To the rock.**—'*Al haç-çûr* (later use of '*al*, "on"). Samuel has "at (or towards) harvest," '*el qaçir*. In Hebrew writing the phrases are very similar. Our phrase looks like a correction of that in Samuel. At any rate, the Syriac, Targum, Arabic, and probably the LXX., read *qaçir* in the MSS. of Samuel. Here the LXX. has "to the rock;" Syriac omits the phrase.

**Cave of Adullam.**—See 1 Sam. xxii. 1.

**Encamped.**—*Were camping.*

**Valley of Rephaim.**—See Josh. xv. 8, Note. It lay south-west of Jerusalem, in the direction of Bethlehem. It may have got its name from the aboriginal Rephaim, Deut. iii. 11 (Authorised Version, giants), Josh. xvii. 15. It was a rich corn land (Isa. xiii. 5). (Comp. verse 13.)

(16) **The hold.**—The stronghold or rock-fortress of Adullam (2 Sam. v. 17, xxiii. 14).

**The Philistines' garrison.**—An outpost; for their army was camping near Jerusalem.

(17) **That is at (in) the gate!**—No such well is now known. The so-called "David's well" is half a mile north-east of the town.

(18) **Brake through the host.**—Not the main army, but the outpost in front of Bethlehem. There were heroes before Agamemnon, and there was chivalry before the Crusades.

**By the gate.**—Heb., *in*.

**Poured it out.**—As a libation or drink-offering. The technical term is used, as in Gen. xxxv. 14. An act of free sacrifice, done under a sudden impulse of thankfulness, and not according to any formal prescription of the Law.

(19) **Shall I drink the blood of these men?** —Literally, *the blood of these men should I drink in their lives* (souls)?

**Their lives** appears to be spurious here, as it occurs again immediately, and is read only once in Samuel. David regards the water as blood: it had been obtained at the hazard of life, and "the life is the blood" (Gen. ix. 4). The question in Samuel runs: "The blood of the men who went in (= at the risk of) their lives?" The verb seems to have fallen out by accident.

**For with the jeopardy of their lives they brought it.**—Literally, *in their lives*. This remark is not found in Samuel, and looks like an explanation of the words, "shall I drink the blood of these men?"

**These things did these three mightiest.**— Rather, *these things did the three mighty men* (or, *warriors*). The Hebrew text of this narrative presents only a few verbal differences from 2 Sam. xxiii. 13—17.

(20—25) Feats of Abishai and Benaiah. (Comp. 2 Sam. xxiii. 18—23, of which the present passage is little more than a duplicate.)

(20) **Abishai the brother of Joab.**—Heb., Abshai, but in Samuel, Abishai. (Comp. Abram and Abiram.) Samuel adds "son of Zeruiah" after Joab. (Comp. chap. ii. 16 and chap. xviii. 12, xix. 11 ff. for other deeds of Abishai.)

**He was chief of the three.**—Apparently the second triad, one of whose famous exploits has just been related (verses 15—19). The Hebrew text of Samuel seems to read "knights," but some MSS., the Hebrew margin, and all the versions, agree with Chronicles.

**For lifting up . . .**—Literally, *and he had brandished his spear over three hundred slain*. The exploit of Jashobeam (verse 11).

**And had a name among the three.**—That is, among the second triad, of which he was captain.

(21) **Of the three, he was more honourable than the two.**—The Hebrew text here varies from

their captain: howbeit he attained not to the *first* three. ⁽²²⁾ Benaiah the son of Jehoiada, the son of a valiant man of Kabzeel, ¹who had done many acts; he slew two lionlike men of Moab: also he went down and slew a lion in a pit in a snowy day. ⁽²³⁾ And he slew an Egyptian, ²a man of *great* stature, five cubits high; and in the Egyptian's hand *was* a spear like a weaver's beam; and he went down to him with a staff, and plucked the spear out of the Egyptian's hand, and slew him with his own spear. ⁽²⁴⁾ These *things* did Benaiah the son of Jehoiada, and had the name among the three mighties. ⁽²⁵⁾ Behold, he was honourable among the thirty, but attained not to the *first* three: and David set him over his guard.

⁽²⁶⁾ Also the valiant men of the armies *were*, Asahel the brother of Joab, El-

¹ Heb., *great of deeds.*
² Heb., *a man of measure.*

---

Samuel, which has "Above (or out of) the three, was he not honoured?" The reading of Chronicles seems to be an exegetical alteration of this, and should probably be rendered, "Above the three of the second rank he was honoured," *i.e.*, he was the most honoured member of the second triad. So the Vulg., *et inter tres secundos inclitus.* The LXX. has ἀπὸ τῶν τριῶν ὑπὲρ τοὺς δύο ἔνδοξος ("Of the three, renowned above the two"). But the Hebrew expression, which means literally, "in the two," seems plainly to indicate a second group of three. Otherwise, we might translate: "Of the three he was honoured among the two," that is, above the other two members of his triad. Both here and in verse 20 the Syriac reads thirty instead of three: "Above the thirty he was honoured, and he became chief over them and warlike; the thirty he used to make" (verse 21). The Arabic is more correct: "And he was mightier than the two, and chief over them twain, and he came not to the three."

**Howbeit he attained not . . .**—Literally, *but to the three he came not*, *i.e.*, the first triad of warriors (verses 11—14).

**(22—25) Benaiah the son of Jehoiada.**—Captain of the royal guard (chap. xviii. 17) and third "captain of the host" (chap. xxvii. 5, 6).

**Son of a valiant man.**—"Son" is probably a spurious addition here, as elsewhere. The Syriac has "Benaiah son of Joiada, a strong warrior." The LXX., however, reads, "son of a mighty man."

**Kabzeel.**—A town of southern Judah, site unknown (Josh. xv. 21); Neh. xi. 25 (Jekabzeel).

**Who had done many acts.**—The margin is correct. This poetic phrase only occurs in this and the parallel passage.

**He slew two lionlike men of Moab.**—See chap. xviii. 2. So the Syriac: "He slew two giants of Moab." The Hebrew has, "He smote the two Ariel of Moab." Ariel, "lion of God"—a title of heroes with the Arabs and Persians—appears to be used as an appellative (Isa. xxxiii. 7): "Lo, the heroes (*'ariēlim*) cry without!" (Heb.) The LXX. of 2 Sam. xxiii. 20 reads, "The two sons of Ariel of Moab;" whence some think that Ariel denotes here the king of Moab; but the former sense is better.

**Also he went down and slew a lion.**—Literally, *And he (it was who) went down and smote the lion in the middle of the cistern in the day of snow.* The article pointedly refers to some well-known feat of Benaiah's.

**(23) And he slew an Egyptian . . .**—Literally, *and he it was who smote the Egyptian, a man of measure, five in the cubit.* Samuel has only "who (was) a sight;" or "a man to look at" (Heb. margin). The chronicler says why.

**Like a weaver's beam.**—Not in Samuel. Perhaps due to a recollection of the combat of David and Goliath. (Comp. also 2 Sam. xxi. 19.) Yet the LXX. of 2 Sam. xxiii. 21 has "like the beam of a ship's ladder" (ξύλον διαβάθρας); and this may be original.

**Went down.**—To the combat. (Comp. Latin: *descendere in aciem*, &c.) The staff (*shēbet*) of Benaiah differs from David's (*maqqēl*, 1 Sam. xvii. 40, 43); and the similarity of the two accounts, so far as it extends, is a similarity not of fiction, but of fact.

**With a staff.**—Rather, *the staff*, which he happened to carry.

**(24) And had the name.**—Literally, *and to him (was) a name among the three heroes*, viz., the second triad.

**(25) Behold, he was honourable among the thirty.**—Rather, *above the thirty behold he was honoured.*

**But attained not to the first three.**—For he was a member of the second triad of heroes. The third member is omitted here, as in the case of the first triad.

**Over his guard.**—Literally, *over his obedience;* an abstract for concrete, as in Isa. xi. 14 (= vassals). The Cherethites and Pelethites, a small corps probably of foreigners, who constituted David's body-guard, and were under his direct orders, appear to be meant here. (See 2 Sam. viii. 18, xx. 23.) The word has this precise sense only in this place and its parallel.

**(26—47) A catalogue of forty-eight "doughty warriors."** Sixteen names are here added to the list as given in Samuel. The chronicler, therefore, possessed a source more complete than our Book of Samuel. Variations of spelling abound in the names common to the two texts, the transcription of proper names being especially liable to error.

**(26) Also the valiant men of the armies.**—The Heb. phrase has this meaning (chap. xii. 8); but elsewhere it denotes "valiant heroes" (chap. vii. 5, 7, &c.), and so here. 2 Sam. xxiii. 24 has "Asahel brother of Joab was among the thirty." It thus appears that the warriors of this list are none other than the famous band of thirty warriors already spoken of (verses 15, 25). From having been the original number, *thirty* may have become the conventional name of the corps even when its limits had been enlarged. It is noticeable that so far as to verse 41 the heroes are arranged in pairs, and that the gentilic or cantonal name is usually added to that of the hero. They mostly belong to Judah and Benjamin; whereas the sixteen additional names, so far as known, belong to the transjordanic tribes, and the northern tribes are not represented at all.

**Elhanan.**—*Dodo* is very much like *David.* Is this a third *alias* of the slayer of Goliath? See Note on chap. xx. 5.

| David's | I. CHRONICLES, XI. | Mighty Men |

hanan the son of Dodo of Beth-lehem, <sup>(27)</sup> Shammoth the ¹Harorite, Helez the Pelonite, <sup>(28)</sup> Ira the son of Ikkesh the Tekoite, Abiezer the Antothite, <sup>(29)</sup> Sibbecai the Hushathite, Ilai the Ahohite, <sup>(30)</sup> Maharai the Netophathite, Heled the son of Baanah the Netophathite, <sup>(31)</sup> Ithai the son of Ribai of Gibeah, *that pertained* to the children of Benjamin, Benaiah the Pirathonite, <sup>(32)</sup> Hurai of the brooks of Gaash, Abiel the Arbathite, <sup>(33)</sup> Azmaveth the Baharumite, Eliahba the Shaalbonite, <sup>(34)</sup> the sons of Hashem the Gizonite, Jonathan the son of Shage the Hararite, <sup>(35)</sup> Ahiam the son of Sacar the Hararite, Eliphal the son of Ur, <sup>(36)</sup> Hepher the Mecherathite, Ahijah the Pelonite, <sup>(37)</sup> Hezro the Carmelite, Naarai the son of Ezbai, <sup>(38)</sup> Joel the brother of Nathan, Mibhar ²the son of Haggeri,

1 Or, *Harodite*, 2 Sam. 23. 25.

2 Or, *the Haggerite*.

---

<sup>(27)</sup> **Shammoth the Harorite.**—Samuel has "Shammah (of which Shammoth is plural) the Harodite." A place called Harod occurs in Judges vii. 1. (Comp. also chap. xxvii. 8, Note.) 2 Sam. xxiii. 26 adds another Harodite, Elika (? Elikam), omitted here by accident.

**Helez the Pelonite.**—Samuel, "the Paltite," perhaps more correctly. The Syriac and Arabic read "of Palton" and 'Faltûna.' Beth-pelet was a town of Judah (Neh. xi. 26), but chap. xxvii. 10 calls Helez "the Pelonite of the sons of Ephraim." The Heb. *peloni* (Authorised Version, Pelonite), means *so-and-so*, and may be a scribe's substitute for an illegible name.

<sup>(28)</sup> **Ira . . . Tekoite**, of Tekoa, in Judah.

**Abi-ezer**, of Anathoth, in Benjamin. (Comp. chap. xxvii. 9, 19.)

<sup>(29)</sup> **Sibbecai.**—The correct name. (See chap. xxvii. 11.) He slew the giant Saph (2 Sam. xxi. 18). Samuel calls him Mebunnai, by confusion of similar letters. Sibbecai was a Zarhite, *i.e.*, of clan Zerah. Hushah, his township, was in Judah (chap. iv. 4).

**Ilai.**—Samuel has Zalmon, which may be correct, letters having faded.

**Ahohite.**—See verse 12.

<sup>(30)</sup> **Maharai the Netophathite**, of Netophah, a Levitical canton (chap. ix. 16). By family Maharai was a Zarhite (chap. xxvii. 13).

**Heled.**—More correct than (Heleb) Samuel. Called Heldai (chap. xxvii. 15). He was of the clan Othniel.

<sup>(31)</sup> **Ithai.**—Samuel, "Ittai," an older pronunciation. Not to be confused with "Ittai the Gittite" (2 Sam. xv. 19).

**Gibeah . . . of Benjamin** was near Ramah.

**Benaiah the Pirathonite.**—Chap. xxvii. 14. Of course different from Benaiah son of Jehoiada. "Pirathon in the land of Ephraim" (Judges xii. 15) may be the modern *Ferâta*, south-west of Shechem.

<sup>(32)</sup> **Hurai of the brooks of Gaash** seems better than "Hiddai" (Samuel), cf. "Hur" (Exod. xvii. 10). "d" and "r" are often confused in Hebrew writing.

**Brooks.**—Heb., *Nahalê* (gullies or wadys). Nahalê-Gaash was no doubt a place on or near Mount Gaash (Josh. xxiv. 30) in the highland of Ephraim, but the site is not identified.

**Abiel the Arbathite.**—Samuel, "Abi-'albon." Perhaps Abi-baal was the original reading, which was corrupted in the text of Samuel, and altered by the chronicler's authority after the manner of Beeliada —Eliada.

**Arbathite**—of "Beth-arabah" (Josh. xv. 62), in the desert of Judah.

<sup>(33)</sup> **Baharumite**—of Bahurim, the town of Shimei (2 Sam. xvi. 5, iii. 16), in Benjamin. Samuel has the transposed form, "Barhumite."

**Eliahba**—*God hideth*.

**Shaalbonite**—of Shaalbim (Judges i. 35; Josh. xix. 42), a Danite town near Ajalon.

<sup>(34)</sup> **The sons of Hashem the Gizonite.**—Samuel has "the sons of Jashen, Jonathan" (Heb.). Here the Syriac and Arabic have "the sons of Shēm of 'Azûn, Jonathan son of Shaga of Mount Carmel." The word "sons" (*bnê*) is an accidental repetition of the last three letters of the Hebrew word for Shaalbonite. "Jashen the Gizonite" is probably the right reading.

**Jonathan the son of Shage the Hararite.**—This appears more correct than the text of Samuel, "Shammah the Hararite." "Shammah son of Age the Hararite" was the third hero of the first triad (2 Sam. xxiii. 11). Perhaps, therefore, the original reading here was "Jonathan son of Age (or Shammah) the Hararite." The Syriac and Arabic, however, support Shage.

<sup>(35)</sup> **Sacar** (*wages*) is probably right, not "Sharar" (Samuel). LXX. Vat. has "Achar," but Alex. "Sachar." Syriac, "Sacham."

Instead of **Hararite**, Samuel has "Ararite," or "Adrite" (Syr.).

**Eliphal, the son of Ur.**—Instead of this, Samuel reads, "Eliphelet son of Ahasbai son of the Maachathite." Eliphelet (the name of a son of David) seems right.

<sup>(36)</sup> **Hepher the Mecherathite.** — Wanting in the present text of Samuel. Mecherah is unknown as a place, and a comparison with Samuel (verse 34) suggests "Hepher the Maachathite," *i.e.*, of Abel-beth-Maachah, or perhaps the Syrian state of Maachah (2 Sam. x. 8).

**Ahijah the Pelonite.**—Instead of this, Samuel has "Eliam son of Ahithophel the Gilonite." For Ahithophel, see 2 Sam. xv. 31.

**The Pelonite**—*i.e.*, *so-and-so*, may indicate either that Ahithophel's name had become obscure in the chronicler's MS., or that he was unwilling to mention the traitor. Ahijah (*Jah is a brother*) and Eliam (*God is a kinsman*) might be names of one person.

<sup>(37)</sup> **Hezro.**—Syriac, "Hezri," and so perhaps Samuel, margin; but Samuel, text, "Hezro."

**Carmelite.**—Of Carmel (*Kurmul*), a town south of Hebron (Josh. xv. 55).

**Naarai the son of Ezbai.**—Samuel, "Paarai the Arbite." Arab also was a town south of Hebron, in the hill country of Judah (Josh. xv. 52).

<sup>(38)</sup> **Joel the brother of Nathan.**—Samuel, "Jigal (a name found in Num. xiii. 7) son of Nathan of Zobah." This is probably correct. Zobah was a Syrian state.

**Mibhar the son of Haggeri.**—"Mibhar" (*choice*) is unlikely as a proper name, and is probably a corruption of *Miççobah*, "of Zobah," as in Samuel. After this word Samuel adds "Bani the Gadite." The name "Bani" has fallen out of our text. "Haggeri" is an easy corruption of *Haggadi* "the Gadite."

(39) Zelek the Ammonite, Naharai the Berothite, the armourbearer of Joab the son of Zeruiah, (40) Ira the Ithrite, Gareb the Ithrite, (41) Uriah the Hittite, Zabad the son of Ahlai, (42) Adina the son of Shiza the Reubenite, a captain of the Reubenites, and thirty with him, (43) Hanan the son of Maachah, and Joshaphat the Mithnite, (44) Uzzia the Ashterathite, Shama and Jehiel the sons of Hothan the Aroerite, (45) Jediael the [1]son of Shimri, and Joha his brother, the Tizite, (46) Eliel the Mahavite, and Jeribai, and Joshaviah, the sons of Elnaam, and Ithmah the Moabite, (47) Eliel, and Obed, and Jasiel the Mesobaite.

B.C. cir. 1058.

1 Or, *Shimrite.*

a 1 Sam. 27. 1.

2 Heb., *being yet shut up.*

3 Or, *Hasmaah.*

CHAPTER XII.—(1) Now *these are* they that came to David to Ziklag, [2]while he yet kept himself close because of Saul the son of Kish: and they *were* among the mighty men, helpers of the war. (2) *They were* armed with bows, and could use both the right hand and the left in *hurling* stones and *shooting* arrows out of a bow, *even* of Saul's brethren of Benjamin. (3) The chief *was* Ahiezer, then Joash, the sons of [3]Shemaah the Gibeathite; and Jeziel, and Pelet, the sons of Azmaveth; and Berachah, and Jehu the Antothite, (4) and Ismaiah the Gibeonite, a mighty man among the thirty, and over the

---

(39) **Zelek the Ammonite.**—Many of David's warriors were aliens. (Comp. "Uriah the Hittite;" "Ittai the Gittite;" and "Ithmah the Moabite," verse 46.

**Berothite.**—Of Beeroth in Benjamin (Josh. xviii. 25).

(40) **The Ithrite.**—Of Jether, one of the clans of Kirjath-jearim (chap. ii. 53).

(41) **Uriah the Hittite.**—His history, omitted by Chronicles, is told in 2 Sam. xi. The list of heroes in Samuel closes with this name, adding by way of summation, "all, thirty and seven."

The sixteen names which follow may indicate a later revision of the catalogue. They are not given elsewhere.

(42) **A captain of the Reubenites** (or, *chief;* Heb., *head*) **and thirty with him** (besides him).— Literally, *upon him*. So LXX. Syriac reads "and he was commanding thirty men," which gives the apparent meaning of the verse. If, as seems likely, the "thirty" were the officers of David's guard of six hundred warriors (1 Sam. xxiii. 13, xxx. 10; 2 Sam. xv. 18), called "the mighty men," or heroes (2 Sam. x. 7, xx. 7; 1 Kings i. 8), each captain would lead about twenty men. Adina's corps is mentioned perhaps as being larger than usual.

(43) **Joshaphat the Mithnite.**—The LXX. has "the Mathanite," or "the Bethanite." Syriac, "Azi of Anathoth"!

(44) **Ashterathite.**—Of Ashtaroth, a town in Bashan (chap. vi. 71).

**Jehiel.**—Heb., *Jeuel.* Margin, "*Jeiel.*"

**Hothan.**—A misprint of the Authorised Version for *Hotham.* There was an *Aroer* in Reuben, and another in Gad (Josh. xiii. 16, 25).

(45) **Jediael.**—Perhaps the Manassite who joined David at Ziklag (chap. xii. 20).

(46) **Eliel.**—Perhaps the Gadite of chap. xii. 11.

**The Mahavite.**—Probably a corruption of "the Mahanaimite." Mahanaim was in Gad.

(47) **Eliel.**—LXX., "*Daliel.*"

**The Mesobaite.**—The word is corrupt. Perhaps it should be "of Zobah." Syriac has *and Ashkir.*

### XII.

Chap. xii. is a sort of supplement to chap. xi., and is throughout peculiar to the Chronicle. It contains two registers: (1) of the warriors who successively went over to David during his outlaw career (1 Sam. xxii. ff.), verses 1—22; and (2) of the tribal representatives who crowned David at Hebron (forming an appendix to chap. xi. 1—3), verses 23—40.

The first of these registers sub-divides into three smaller lists, viz., verses 1—7, 8—18, 19—22.

(1—7) Men of Benjamin and Judah who joined David at Ziklag. (Comp. 1 Sam. xxvii.)

(1) **To Ziklag.**—A place within the territory of Judah allotted to Simeon (Josh. xix. 5; chap. iv. 30). The Philistines seized it, and Achish of Gath gave it to David, whose headquarters it remained sixteen months, until the death of Saul.

**While he yet kept himself close.**—The Hebrew is concise and obscure, but the Authorised Version fairly renders it. David was still *shut up* in his stronghold, or *restrained* within bounds, *because of, i.e.*, from dread of King Saul. Or perhaps the meaning is "banished from the presence of Saul."

**Helpers of the war.**—*The helpers in war,* allies, or companions in arms of David. They made forays against Geshur, Gezer, and Amalek (1 Sam. xxvii. 8; comp. also verses 17 and 21 below).

(2) **Armed with bows.**—Literally, *drawers of the bow* (2 Chron. xvii. 17).

**And could use.**—They were ambidextrous "with stones, and with arrows on the bow." The left-handed slingers of Benjamin were famous from of old. (Comp. Judges xx. 16, and also chap. iii. 15.)

**Of Saul's brethren**—*i.e.,* his fellow-tribesmen.

**Of Benjamin** is added to make it clear that Saul's immediate kinsmen are not intended. (Comp. verse 29.)

(3) **The chief was Ahiezer.**—Captain of the band. Heb., *head.*

**Shemaah.**—Heb., *Hashsh<sup>e</sup>maah.*

**The Gibeathite.**—Of "Gibeah of Saul," between Ramah and Anathoth (Isa. x. 29); also called "Gibeah of Benjamin" (chap. xi. 31; Judges xx. 4).

**Jeziel.**—So Hebrew margin; Hebrew text, *Jezûel.* (Comp. Peniel and Penuel.)

**Azmaveth.**—Perhaps the warrior of Bahurim (chap. xi. 33).

**Jehu the Antothite**—of Anathoth, now *Anâta* (chap. xi. 28).

(4) **Ismaiah the Gibeonite.**—Gibeon belonged to Benjamin (chap. ix. 35), and verse 2 proves that Ismaiah was a Benjamite, not a Gibeonite in the strict sense of the term.

**A mighty man among the thirty.**—The "thirty" must be the famous corps (chap. xi. 25). Ismaiah's name does not occur in the catalogue, perhaps because he died before it was drawn up.

*The Companies that*     I. CHRONICLES, XII.     *came to Ziklag*

thirty; and Jeremiah, and Jahaziel, and Johanan, and Josabad the Gederathite, (5) Eluzai, and Jerimoth, and Bealiah, and Shemariah, and Shephatiah the Haruphite, (6) Elkanah, and Jesiah, and Azareel, and Joezer, and Jashobeam, the Korhites, (7) and Joelah, and Zebadiah, the sons of Jeroham of Gedor.

(8) And of the Gadites there separated themselves unto David into the hold to the wilderness men of might, *and* men ¹of war *fit* for the battle, that could handle shield and buckler, whose faces *were like* the faces of lions, and *were* ²as swift as the roes upon the mountains;

(9) Ezer the first, Obadiah the second, Eliab the third, (10) Mishmannah the fourth, Jeremiah the fifth, (11) Attai the sixth, Eliel the seventh, (12) Johanan the eighth, Elzabad the ninth, (13) Jeremiah the tenth, Machbanai the eleventh. (14) These *were* of the sons of Gad, captains of the host: ³one of the least *was* over an hundred, and the greatest over a thousand. (15) These *are* they that went over Jordan in the first month, when it had ⁴overflown all his ªbanks; and they put to flight all *them* of the valleys, *both* toward the east, and toward the west.

1 Heb., *of the host.*
2 Heb., *as the roes upon the mountains to make haste.*
3 Or, *one that was least could resist an hundred, and the greatest a thousand.*
4 Heb., *filled over.*
a Josh. 3. 15.

---

**Over the thirty** may mean that at one time he was captain of the band, or it may simply denote comparison—" a hero above the thirty."

**Josabad the Gederathite**; of Gederah in the lowland of Judah (Josh. xv. 36). Josabad is perhaps the same as Zabad ben Ahlai (chap. xi. 41), one of the thirty.

(5) **Jerimoth.**—A Benjamite name (chap. vii. 7, 8).

**Bealiah.**—*Baal is Jah.* (Comp. Note on chap. viii. 33.) Such names indicate that "Baal" was once a title of the God of Israel.

**The Haruphite.**—Neh. vii. 24 mentions the "sons of Hariph" just before the "sons of Gibeon." The Hebrew margin here is "*Hariphite.*"

(6) Five members of the Levitical clan Korah. The name "Elkanah" occurs thrice in the lineage of Heman, the Korhite musician (chap. vi. 33 ff.), and in that of Samuel (vi. 22 ff.).

**Jesiah.**—Heb., *Yishshiyâhû*; "Jahu is my possession." (Comp. Ps. xvi. 5.)

**Azareel** is a priestly name. (See Neh. xi. 13.) There must have been Levites about the Tabernacle at Gibeon. But these Korhites *may* have been members of the Judean clan Korah, mentioned in chap. ii. 43, but otherwise unknown.

**Jashobeam** occurred as chief of the Three Heroes (chap. xi. 11).

(7) **Sons of Jeroham of Gedor.**—Jeroham is the name of a Benjamite clan (chap. viii. 27); and two Benjamite chiefs are called "Zebadiah" (chap. viii. 15, 17). On the other hand, "Gedor" was a town of Judah, south-west of Bethlehem (chap. iv. 4). Some account for the appearance of Judæan names in a list purporting to relate to Benjaminites, by the assumption that the chronicler has welded two lists into one; but towns did not always continue in the hands of the tribes to whom they were originally intended, and some Judæan towns may have contained a partially Benjaminite population.

(8—18) A list of Gadites, and an account of a band of Judæans and Benjaminites who joined David in the stronghold (chap. xi. 14) towards the desert of Judah.

(8) **Separated** themselves from the royalists of Gad, who clung to Saul.

**Into the hold to** (towards) **the wilderness.** —Perhaps the cave of Adullam (1 Sam. xxii. 1, 4), or one of David's other haunts, the wooded Mount of Hachilah (1 Sam. xxiii. 19), or the crag of Maon, or the rocks of En-gedi (1 Sam. xxiii. 25, 29). "Caves and holds" are mentioned together as refuges (Judg. vi. 2). In the earlier period of his outlawry, David found refuge in the natural fastnesses of Judæa.

**Men of might.**—"Mighty men of valour" (chap. v. 24), and "valiant men of might" (chap. vii. 2). Heb., "*the* valiant warriors," whose names follow.

**Men of war fit for the battle.**—Literally, *men of service or training,* i.e., veterans, *for the war.*

**That could handle shield and buckler.**—Heb., *wielding* (or presenting) *shield and spear.* (Comp. Jer. xlvi. 3.)

**Buckler** (*mâgén*) is the reading of some old editions, but against the MSS., which have *rômah* (lance).

**Whose faces were like the faces of lions.** —Literally,

⁴ And face of the lion, their face;
And like gazelles on the mountains they speed."

The poetic style of this betrays its ancient source. The chronicler is clearly borrowing from some contemporary record. (Comp. David's own description of Saul and Jonathan, 2 Sam. i. 23; and the term Ariel, lion of God, *i.e.*, hero or champion, chap. xi. 22; and Isa. xxix. 1.)

**Swift as the roes.**—Comp. what is said of Asahel (2 Sam. ii. 18).

(9) **The first.**—*The chief*, verse 3 (*har'osh*).

(9—13) Eleven heroes of Gad.

(14) **These were.**—Subscription.

**Captains of the host.**—Literally, *heads of the host,* i.e., chief warriors.

**One of the least was over an hundred.**—The margin is correct. David's band at this time was about 600 strong. The rendering of the text is that of the Syr. and Vulg. The LXX. closely intimates the Heb. εἰς τοῖς ἑκατὸν μικρὸς κτλ. For the true meaning, comp. Deut. xxxii. 30; and Lev. xxvi. 8. The Heb. says: "One to a hundred, the little one; and the great one to a thousand." This, too, is poetic, or, at least, rhetorical in character, and quite unlike the chronicler's usual style.

(15) **When it had overflown.**—A proof of their valour. They did not wait till summer had made the Jordan shallow, but crossed it in spring, when perilously swollen with the rains and the melted snows of Lebanon. (Comp. Josh. iii. 15.)

**In the first month.**—March—April; in Heb., Abib or Nisan.

*The Companies that*     I. CHRONICLES, XII.     *came to Ziklag.*

<sup>(16)</sup> And there came of the children of Benjamin and Judah to the hold unto David. <sup>(17)</sup> And David went out ¹to meet them, and answered and said unto them, If ye be come peaceably unto me to help me, mine heart shall ²be knit unto you: but if *ye be come* to betray me to mine enemies, seeing *there is* no ³wrong in mine hands, the God of our fathers look *thereon,* and rebuke *it.* <sup>(18)</sup> Then ⁴the spirit came upon Amasai, *who was* chief of the captains, *and he said,* Thine are we, David, and on thy side, thou son of Jesse: peace, peace *be* unto thee, and peace *be* to thine helpers; for thy God helpeth thee. Then David received them, and made them captains of the band.

<sup>(19)</sup> And there fell *some* of Manasseh to David, when he came with the Philistines against Saul to battle: but they helped them not: for the lords of the Philistines upon advisement sent him away, saying, ªHe will fall to his master

¹ Heb., *before them.*
² Heb., *be one.*
³ Or, *violence.*
⁴ Heb., *the spirit clothed Amasai.*
ª 1 Sam. 29. 4.

---

**Had overflown.**—*Was filling* or *brimming over.*

**And they put to flight all . . . the valleys.**—Literally, *and they made all the valleys flee:* that is, their inhabitants, who were hostile to their enterprise, both *to the sunrise and the sunset,* or on both sides of the river.

(16—18) Some Benjamite and Judæan accessions. The names are not given, why we cannot tell.

<sup>(16)</sup> **To the hold.**—See Note on verse 8.

<sup>(17)</sup> **And David went out to meet them.**—From his fastness or hiding-place in the hill or wood. Literally, *before them, i.e.,* confronted them. (Comp. same phrase, chap. xiv. 8.)

**And answered and said unto them.**—The familiar New Testament phrase, καὶ ἀποκριθεὶς εἶπεν αὐτοῖς. David's speech and the answer of Amasai have all the marks of a genuine survival of antiquity. "If for peace ye have come unto me to help me." *For peace, i.e.,* with friendly intent. (Comp. Ps. cxx. 7.)

**To help me.**—Comp. verse 1, where David's comrades are called "helpers of the war," σύμμαχοι.

**Mine heart shall be knit unto you.**—Literally, *I shall have* (fiet mihi) *towards you a heart for union,* or *at unity:* that is, a heart at one with and true to you. (Comp. "one heart," verse 38, and Ps. cxxxiii. 1, and terms like *unanimis,* ὁμόφρων.)

**If ye be come to betray me.**—Literally, *and if to beguile me for my foes,* that is, to betray me to them, as Authorised Version. The false part of Sextus Tarquinius at Gabii, or of Zopyrus at Babylon. (Comp. Ps. cxx. 2.)

**Seeing there is no wrong in mine hands.**—*Although* (there be) *no violence in my palms.* (Comp. Job xvi. 17; Ps. vii. 4; Isa. liii. 9.)

**The God of our fathers . . . behold and punish.**—The verbs are jussive or optative. (Comp. 2 Chron. xxiv. 22.) The psalms of David breathe a confidence that Jehovah is a righteous judge, who never fails to vindicate innocence, and punish highhanded violence and treacherous cunning. (Comp. Pss. ix. 12, x. 14 xviii. 20.)

<sup>(18)</sup> **Then the spirit came upon Amasai.**—Literally, *and spirit clothed Amasai.* The term for "God" (*Elohim*) has probably fallen out of the Heb. text. (Comp. 2 Chron. xxiv. 20, and Judg. vi. 34.) We, in these days, may word it differently, and say, Under a sudden impulse of enthusiasm, Amasai exclaimed, &c. But if we look deeper, and seek a definite interpretation of our terms, we shall allow that the impulses of spirit are spiritual, and that enthusiasm for truth and right is indeed a sort of divine possession. The Syriac renders: "The spirit of valour clothed Amasai." (Comp. Isa. xi. 2.) The spirit of Jehovah is the source of true courage, as of all other spiritual gifts.

**Amasai.**—Perhaps the same as Amasa (chap. ii. 17), son of Abigail, David's sister, whom Joab murdered out of jealousy (2 Sam. xvii. 25, xx. 4—10).

**Chief of the captains.**—The Heb. text reads, "head of the Thirty," with which the LXX., Syr., and Vulg. agree. The Heb. margin (*Qri*) has "knights," or "chariot-soldiers" (Authorised Version, "captains"), which is less probable. Amasai's name is not given in the catalogue of the Thirty (chap. xi.), and he is here called "chief of the Thirty" by anticipation.

**Thine are we, David.**—The structure of Amasai's inspired utterance is poetical—

> "To thee, David!
> And with thee, son of Ishai!
> Peace, peace to thee,
> And peace to thine helper;
> For thy God hath holpen thee!"

**On thy side.**—Heb., *with thee.* (Comp. chap. xi. 10; and our Saviour's "He that is not with me is against me.")

**Peace, peace be unto thee.**—David had said, "If ye be come for peace"—that is, with friendly intent. Amasai answers, We will be fast friends with thee, and with all who befriend thee, because God is on thy side. (Comp. the usual Oriental greeting, *Salâm 'alaikum*—Peace to you!) David's past history gave ample evidence of Divine support.

**Then David received them.**—A late Heb. word (*qibbēl*). The chronicler resumes his narrative.

**Made them captains of the band.**—Literally, *and bestowed them among the heads of the band*—made them officers of his little army, which was continually growing by such adhesions. (Comp. 1 Sam. xxii. 2, and xxiii. 13.)

(19—22) The seven Manassite chieftains who went over to David on the eve of Saul's last battle.

<sup>(19)</sup> **There fell.**—The regular term for desertion of one cause for another (2 Kings xxv. 11).

**When he came with the Philistines.**—(Comp. 1 Sam. xxix. 2—11.) This verse is a summary of the narrative of 1 Sam. xxix. 2—xxx. 1.

**They helped them not.**—David and his men helped not the Philistines. Perhaps the right reading is *he helped them* ('*azarām*), not *they helped them* ('*azarûm*).

**Upon advisement.**—After deliberation (Prov. xx. 18).

**To the jeopardy of our heads.**—*At the price of our heads* (chap. xi. 19). By betraying us he will make his peace with his old master.

*The Armies that came*     I. CHRONICLES, XII.     *to David at Hebron.*

Saul ¹to *the jeopardy of* our heads. ⁽²⁰⁾ As he went to Ziklag, there fell to him of Manasseh, Adnah, and Jozabad, and Jediael, and Michael, and Jozabad, and Elihu, and Zilthai, captains of the thousands that *were* of Manasseh. ⁽²¹⁾ And they helped David ²against the band *of the rovers:* for they *were* all mighty men of valour, and were captains in the host. ⁽²²⁾ For at *that* time day by day there came to David to help him, until *it was* a great host, like the host of God.

⁽²³⁾ And these *are* the numbers of the ³ ⁴bands *that were* ready armed to the war, *and* came to David to Hebron, to turn the kingdom of Saul to him, according to the word of the LORD. ⁽²⁴⁾ The children of Judah that bare shield and spear *were* six thousand and eight hundred, ready ⁵armed to the war. ⁽²⁵⁾ Of the children of Simeon, mighty men of valour for the war, seven thousand and one hundred. ⁽²⁶⁾ Of the children of Levi four thousand and six hundred. ⁽²⁷⁾ And Jehoiada *was* the leader of the

1 Heb., *on our heads.*
2 Or, *with a band.*
3 Or, *captains, or, men.*
4 Heb., *heads.*
5 Or, *prepared.*

---

⁽²⁰⁾ **As he went to Ziklag.**—On his dismissal by the Philistine princes, David returned with his men to Ziklag (1 Sam. xxx. 1). On the way he was joined by the Manassite chieftains, probably before the battle which decided the fate of Saul and his sons (1 Sam. xxix. 11).

**Jozabad.**—The repetition may be a scribe's error. (Comp. verses 10 and 13, where we find the name Jeremiah given twice over.)

**Captains of the thousands that were of Manasseh.**—(Comp. Numb. xxxi. 14; and chap. xiii. 1, xv. 25, xxvi. 26.) The term "thousand" interchanges with "father-house" (clan); and perhaps each clan originally furnished 1,000 warriors to the tribal host.

⁽²¹⁾ **And they helped David against the band of the rovers.**—So the Vulg. and Syr. The Heb. text has been called "brief and unintelligible," and its explanation has been sought in 1 Sam. xxx. 8 and 15, where "the band" (*hagg'dûd*, as here) of Amalek, which had captured and burnt Ziklag in David's absence, is spoken of. But why may we not render, "And these helped David *over* the band," *i.e.*, in the joint command of his forces. (Comp. verse 18, "made them captains of the band.") It is pretty clear that the names enumerated (verses 1—20) are those of captains and chiefs, not of ordinary warriors. (Comp. verses 14 and 18.) Consequently verses 21, 22 form a subscription or concluding remark to the entire list.

⁽²²⁾ **For at that time day by day . . .**—Literally, *For at the time of each day (i.e., every day) men used to come to David to help him; amounting to a mighty camp, like a camp of God.* The verse explains why David required so many captains as have been enumerated, and why the term "army" was used of his troop in the last verse.

**A great host, like the host of God.**—Literally, *camp.* The phrase has an antique colouring. Comp. Gen. xxxii. 1, 2: "And Jacob went on his way, and the angels of God met him. And when Jacob saw them, he said, This is God's camp (*mahănĕh 'Ĕlôhîm*): and the name of that place was called Mahanaim (*i.e.*, two camps). Mahanaim was a place in Manasseh (Josh. xiii. 30). Ancient Hebrew denotes excellence by reference to the Divine standard, which is the true ideal of all excellence. Comp. Ps. xxxvi. 6: "Thy righteousness is like the hills of God"; and so elsewhere we find the expression, "cedars of God" (Ps. lxxx. 11). The verse appears to include the considerable accessions to David's forces which followed upon the defeat and death of Saul.

II. THE NUMBER OF THE WARRIORS WHO MADE DAVID KING IN HEBRON AFTER SAUL'S DEATH (verses 23—40).

⁽²³⁾ **And these are the numbers of the bands that were ready armed to the war.**—Literally, *And these are the numbers of the heads of the equipped for warfare.* "Heads" may mean (1) polls, or individuals, as in Judg. v. 30, though "skull" (*gulgôleth*) is more usual in this sense; or (2) it may mean "totals," "bands," as in Judg. vii. 16. The latter seems preferable here. The Vulg. and LXX. render "chiefs of the army"; but no chiefs are named in the list, except those of the Aaronites (verses 27, 28); and we cannot suppose, on the strength of a single ambiguous term in the heading, that the character of the entire list has been altered by the chronicler. The Syriac version omits the whole verse.

**And came to David.**—"And" is wanting in the Heb. "They came to David at Hebron," &c., is a parenthesis, unless the relative has fallen out.

**To turn the kingdom.**—Literally, *to bring it round* out of the direct line of natural heredity (chap. x. 14).

**According to the word.**—Literally, *mouth* (chap. xi. 3, 10). What Jehovah had spoken by Samuel was virtually the word of his own mouth.

⁽²⁴⁾ **The sons of Judah.**—The following list proceeds from south to north, and then passes over to the trans-Jordanic tribes.

**That bare shield and spear.**—Comp. verse 8.

**Ready armed to the war.**—*Equipped for warfare.* The tribe of Judah, which had acknowledged the sovereignty of David for the last seven years, had no need to appear in full force on the occasion of his recognition by the other tribes.

⁽²⁵⁾ **Mighty men of valour for the war.**—Rather, *for warfare, or military service.*

⁽²⁶⁾ **Of the children of Levi** Literally, *Of the sons of the Levite;* the article shows that the name is gentilic or tribal here, not personal. These martial Levites remind us of the priestly warriors of the crusades. That Levites might be soldiers, and in fact must have been such for the defence of the sanctuaries, is noted at chap. ix. 13, 19, and 2 Chron. xxiii.

⁽²⁷⁾ **And Jehoiada . . .**—Literally, *And Jehoiada the prince* (*hannagid,* chap. ix. 11, 20) *belonging to Aaron.* Aaron is used as the name of the leading clan of Levi. Jehoiada is perhaps father of the Benaiah of chap. xi. 22. He was not high priest (Abiathar, 1 Sam. xxiii. 9), but head of the warriors

Aaronites, and with him *were* three thousand and seven hundred; (28) and Zadok, a young man mighty of valour, and of his father's house twenty and two captains. (29) And of the children of Benjamin, the ¹kindred of Saul, three thousand: for hitherto ²the greatest part of them had kept the ward of the house of Saul. (30) And of the children of Ephraim twenty thousand and eight hundred, mighty men of valour, ³famous throughout the house of their fathers. (31) And of the half tribe of Manasseh eighteen thousand, which were expressed by name, to come and make David king. (32) And of the children of Issachar, *which were men* that had understanding of the times, to know what Israel ought to do; the heads of them *were* two hundred, and all their brethren *were* at their commandment. (33) Of Zebulun, such as went forth to battle, ⁴expert in war, with all instruments of war, fifty thousand, which could ⁵keep rank: *they were* ⁶not of double heart. (34) And of Naphtali a thousand captains, and with them with shield and spear thirty and seven thousand. (35) And of the Danites expert in war twenty and eight thousand and six hundred. (36) And of Asher, such as went forth to battle, ⁷expert in war, forty thousand. (37) And on the other side of Jordan, of the Reubenites, and the Gadites, and of the half tribe of

1 Heb., *brethren.*
2 Heb., *a multitude of them.*
3 Heb., *men of names.*
4 Or, *rangers of battle,* or, *ranged in battle.*
5 Or, *set the battle in array.*
6 Heb., *without a heart and a heart.*
7 Or, *keeping their rank.*

---

of his clan. It is not clear whether the 3,700 are included in the 4,600 of verse 26 or not. Probably not.

**Was . . . were.**—Omit.

(28) **And Zadok, a young man mighty of valour.**—*And Zadok, a youth, a valiant warrior.* Perhaps the successor of Abiathar (1 Kings ii. 26, 27, iv. 4), *and his father-house* (family), *princes twenty and two.* The sub-clan or family of Eleazar must have been strong at this time to be able to furnish all these captains, and their implied companies of warriors. But the sum total of the Levites is not given.

(29) **Kindred.**—Fellow-tribesmen.

**Hitherto.**—*Up to that time.* (Comp. same phrase, chap. ix. 18.)

**Had kept.**—*Were still keeping guard over the house of Saul.* For the phrase comp. Num. iii. 38. The Benjamites, as a whole, were still jealously guarding the interests of their own royal house. This remark, as well as the preceding expression, "Saul's fellow-tribesmen," is intended to explain the comparative smallness of the contingent from Benjamin. The tribe's reluctance to recognise David survived the murder of Ish-bosheth.

(30) **Famous throughout the house of their fathers.**—Rather, *men of name* (renown, as in Gen. vi. 4), arranged *according to their clans.* The phrase "men of renown" is a natural addition to "valiant heroes," and need occasion no surprise. Doubtless their renown was collective. The comparative smallness of Ephraim's contingent is noticeable. If this tribe was not already declining within the Mosaic period (comp. Num. i. 33, xxvi. 37), it may have been greatly reduced by the last wars of Saul with the Philistines (comp. 2 Sam. ii. 9).

(31) **Which were expressed by name.**—See the same phrase, chap. xvi. 41; Num. i. 17. Literally it is *pricked down,* or entered in a list, *by names.* The men had been levied by the tribal chiefs, and enrolled in lists for this particular service.

(32) **And of the children of Issachar . . .**—Rather, *And of the sons of Issachar* (came) *men sage in discernment for the times* (tempora, critical junctures), *so as to know what Israel ought to do; viz., their chiefs two hundred* (in number), *and all their fellow-clansmen under their orders.* The old Jewish expositors concluded, from the former part of this verse, that the tribe of Issachar had skill in astrology, so that they could read in the heavens what seasons were auspicious for action, as the ancient Babylonians professed to do. But all that the text really asserts is that those men of Issachar who went over to David thereby showed political sagacity. No similar phrase occurs elsewhere in the Old Testament.

**At their commandment.**—*Upon their mouth.* (Comp. Num. iv. 27.) The clansmen marched with their chieftains. The total number of Issachar's contingent is not assigned.

(33) **Expert in war . . .**—*Marshalling* (or ordering) *battle with all kinds of weapons of war, and falling into rank* (la'adōr, forming in line) *without a double heart.* The expression "falling into rank" occurs only here and in verse 38. Nine MSS. read instead "helping" (la'azōr), and the LXX. and Vulg. so translate. The Syriac has "to make war with those who disputed the sovranty of David." The phrase "falling into rank without a heart and a heart," asserts the unwavering fidelity and resolute courage of these warriors of Zebulun (comp. Ps. xii. 3, "a speech of smooth things with heart and heart they speak"; they think one thing and say another; are double-minded). The number of warriors assigned to Zebulun and Naphtali has been thought surprising, because these tribes "never played an important part in the history of Israel" (comp., however, Judges v. 18). The numbers here given are, at all events, not discordant with those of Num. i. 31, 43; xxvi. 27, 50.

(34) **Spear** (*hănith*).—A different word from that in verse 24 (*rômah*). Perhaps the former was thrown, the latter thrust.

(35) **The Danites.**—Literally, *the Danite,* as in verse 26, the *Levite.* Comp. Note on chap. vii. 12. Dan is not omitted in the present list.

(36) **Expert in war.**—Literally, *to order or marshal battle* (ad aciem struendam). The same phrase occurred in verses 33, 35. The margin (verse 33), "rangers of battle," is good.

(37) **On the other side.**—Better, *from the other side;* that is, from Peræa.

**With all manner of instruments of war for the battle.**—*With all kinds of weapons of warlike service.* The large total of 120,000 for the two and a half Eastern tribes is certainly remarkable. But, admitting the possibility of corruption in the ciphers

*The Armies at Hebron.*  I. CHRONICLES, XIII.  *Preparing to bring the Ark.*

Manasseh, with all manner of instruments of war for the battle, an hundred and twenty thousand. <sup>(38)</sup> All these men of war, that could keep rank, came with a perfect heart to Hebron, to make David king over all Israel: and all the rest also of Israel were of one heart to make David king. <sup>(39)</sup> And there they were with David three days, eating and drinking: for their brethren had prepared for them. <sup>(40)</sup> Moreover they that were nigh them, *even* unto Issachar and Zebulun and Naphtali, brought bread on asses, and on camels, and on mules, and on oxen,

B.C. 1048.

1 Or, *victual of meal.*

2 Heb., *let us break forth and send.*

3 Heb., *in the cities of their suburbs.*

*and* <sup>1</sup>meat, meal, cakes of figs, and bunches of raisins, and wine, and oil, and oxen, and sheep abundantly: for *there was* joy in Israel.

CHAPTER XIII.—<sup>(1)</sup> And David consulted with the captains of thousands and hundreds, *and* with every leader. <sup>(2)</sup> And David said unto all the congregation of Israel, If *it seem* good unto you, and *that it be* of the LORD our God, <sup>2</sup>let us send abroad unto our brethren every where, *that are* left in all the land of Israel, and with them *also* to the priests and Levites *which are* <sup>3</sup>in their

---

here and elsewhere, the want of other documents, with which the text might be compared, renders further criticism superfluous.

(<sup>38</sup>) Conclusion of the list of verses 23—37.

**All these men of war.** — Rather, *All the above, being men of war, forming line of battle with whole heart, came to Hebron to make David king.* The phrase "forming line of battle," repeats the verb of verse 33, and supplies its proper object ('*ôděrê ma'ărākhāh, aciem struentes*). The Hebrew indicates a stop at "line of battle;" it is better to put it after "with whole heart" (comp. verse 33). "They formed in line with fearless intrepidity;" literally, *corde integro*.

**And all the rest also of Israel,** who did not appear personally at Hebron.—"The rest (*shěrith*) is a term used here only. The Hebrew says, "the remainder of Israel (was) one heart," *i.e.*, was unanimous. (Comp. 2 Chron. xxx. 12.)

Allowing the average for Issachar, the total of the warriors assembled at Hebron was upwards of 300,000. This will not surprise us if we bear in mind that in those days every able-bodied man was, as a matter of course, trained in the use of arms, and liable to be called out for the king's wars. Thus "man" and "warrior" were almost convertible terms. The present gathering was not a parade of the entire strength of the nation; comp. the 600,000 warriors of the Exodus, and the 1,300,000 of David's census. The main difficulty—that of the relative proportions of the various tribal contingents—has been considered in the preceding Notes. The suggestions there made are, of course, uncertain, the fact being that we really do not know enough of the condition of the tribes at that epoch to justify us in pronouncing upon the relative probability of the numbers here assigned to them. That being so, it is a hasty and uncritical exaggeration to say that "it is absolutely inconceivable that the tribes near the place of meeting, notably that of Judah, should have furnished so small a contingent, while the figures are raised in direct proportion to the distance to be traversed" (*Reuss*).

(<sup>39—40</sup>) The coronation feast. Comp. 1 Kings i. 9, 19, 25; the usurpation of Adonijah.

**Their brethren.** — Fellow-tribesmen of Judah; especially those living at and around Hebron.

**Had prepared** victuals.—2 Chron. xxxv. 14.

(<sup>40</sup>) **They that were nigh them.**—The tribes bordering on Judah (LXX. οἱ ὁμοροῦντες), and even the northern tribes, contributed provisions.

**Brought,** *were bringing.*

**Asses . . . camels . . . mules . . . oxen,** but not horses, were the usual beasts of burden in rocky Canaan.

**Meat, meal.**—Rather, *food of flour.*

**Bunches.**—Rather, *cakes of raisins;* masses of dried figs and raisins were, and are, a staple article of food in the East (comp. 1 Sam. xxv. 18; Amos. viii. 1). The simple diction of the narrative, reminding us of Homer's feasts, is a mark of its ancient origin.

Chaps. xiii.—xvi. form a complete section relating to the transfer of the Ark from Kirjath-jearim to its new sanctuary at Jerusalem. The continuity of the narrative is only suspended by the short parenthetic chap. xiv. Chap. xiii. is closely parallel to 2 Sam. vi. 1—11. The introduction, however (verses 1—5), is much fuller than that of Samuel, which is condensed into one brief sentence.

XIII.

(<sup>1</sup>) **And David consulted.** — This consultation took place some time after the coronation at Hebron (comp. 2 Sam. vi. 1), "And David gathered together again every chosen man in Israel, thirty thousand." This is all that Samuel has corresponding to our verses 1—5. It is by no means necessary to assume that, "according to the context, we are still at Hebron in the assemblage of 350,000 warriors" (*Reuss*). Samuel implies the contrary.

**Captains of thousands.**—*The thousands* (comp. chap. xii. 20).

**And the hundreds.**—Comp. Num. xxxi. 14. The hundreds were the smaller military divisions of the tribe, representing, perhaps, the warlike strength or the houses, as the thousands represented that of the clans or sub-tribes.

**And with every leader.**—Rather, *viz. with every prince (nagid)* or chief. These chiefs constituted the Great Council of the nation.

(<sup>2</sup>) **All the congregation of Israel.**—As represented by the Council of Chiefs, who, according to the passage in Samuel, were 30,000 in number.

**And that it be.**—Rather, *and if it be.* The clause is not dependent. David says: "If before you (the thing be) good, and if (the motion come) from Jehovah." The former phrase recurs in Neh. ii. 5, 7, and is late Hebrew; the latter is illustrated by Gen. xxiv. 50.

**Let us send abroad.**—Literally, *break we forth, send we, i.e.,* let us send with all despatch.

*The bringing up of*     I. CHRONICLES, XIII.     *the Ark from Kirjath-jearim.*

cities *and* suburbs, that they may gather themselves unto us: <sup>(3)</sup> and let us ¹bring again the ark of our God to us: for we enquired not at it in the days of Saul. <sup>(4)</sup> And all the congregation said that they would do so: for the thing was right in the eyes of all the people.

<sup>(5)</sup> So <sup>a</sup>David gathered all Israel together, from Shihor of Egypt even unto the entering of Hemath, to bring the ark of God from Kirjath-jearim. <sup>(6)</sup> And David went up, and all Israel, to <sup>b</sup> Baalah, *that is*, to Kirjath-jearim, which *belonged* to Judah, to bring up thence the ark of God the LORD, that dwelleth *between* the cherubims, whose name is called *on it.* <sup>(7)</sup> And they ²carried the ark of God in a new cart out of the house of Abinadab: and Uzza and Ahio drave the cart. <sup>(8)</sup> And David and all Israel played before God with all *their* might, and with ³singing, and with harps, and with

¹ Heb., *bring-about.*
*a* 1 Sam. 7. 1; 2 Sam. 6. 2.
*b* Josh. 15. 9.
² Heb., *made the ark to ride.*
³ Heb., *songs.*

---

**Everywhere.**—Not in the Hebrew.

**Land.**—Hebrew, *lands* or *territories*, *i.e.*, of the various tribes. Comp. Gen. xxvi. 3, 4, where the same plural implies the partition of Canaan into many smaller national domains.

**In their cities and suburbs.**—*In the cities of their pastures.* The Levites appear to have occupied themselves with pastoral pursuits when not engaged in the services of religion (comp. chap. vi. 57 *seq.*).

**That they may gather themselves unto us.**—The result would be a great addition to an already large gathering. However, it does not follow that every one to whom the summons came would be willing or able to obey it. The invitation was, in fact, a kind of formal proclamation to the entire people of a solemn act of national importance.

<sup>(3)</sup> **Let us bring again.**—*Bring we round:* transfer it from Kirjath-jearim to Jerusalem, as the throne was transferred (same verb) from Saul to David (chap. x. 14, xii. 23).

**The Ark of our God to us.**—The Ark was at Kirjath-jearim, a city of Judah, David's own tribe. But the king wished to establish it as the centre of the national worship in his new capital and royal residence, Jerusalem.

**For we enquired not at it.**—Rather, *we sought it not*, that is, neglected it, cared nothing about it. The Ark had been left in the house of Abinadab at Kirjath-jearim, for twenty years, after the Philistines sent it back (1 Sam. vii. 2). There may be a reference to Saul's despairing neglect of consulting the Lord (chap. x. 13); and, perhaps, we should translate, "we sought *Him* not," referring the suffix to God (comp. chap. xv. 13; Isa. ix. 12). There is no clear evidence that the Ark itself was ever used as an oracle (comp. Exod. xxv. 10—22; 1 Kings viii. 9).

<sup>(4)</sup> **All the assembly said**, So should we do (comp. for the construction chap. v. 5, ix. 25). **The thing**, the proposal.

<sup>(5)</sup> **So David gathered all Israel.**—*Assembled*; a different word in verse 2.

**Shihor of Egypt.**—The boundary between Egypt and Canaan is elsewhere called *Nahal Miçrayim* (Authorised Version, River of Egypt; Isa. xxvii. 12; 2 Chron. vii. 8). It is the modern *Wady el Arish.* Josh. xiii. 3 also calls this winter torrent the Shihor (Blackwater); but, in Isa. xxiii. 3, Shihor means the Nile.

**The entering of Hemath.**—*Hamath.*—This was the usual designation of the north boundary of Palestine, as the "torrent of Egypt" was that of the south (1 Kings viii. 65). Hamath was the seat of an ancient kingdom, independent of, but friendly to David. The prophet Amos (eighth century B.C.) calls it Hamath Rabbah, Great Hamath (Amos. vi. 2). A revived interest attaches to Hamath in our day, owing to the discovery of five curious inscriptions at *Hâmah*, written in a peculiar hieroglyphic character, which has been pronounced to be Hittite, but still awaits decipherment.

<sup>(6)</sup> From this point our narrative coincides with that of 2 Sam. vi. 2—11. The original text was plainly the same, whether the chronicler drew directly from the Book of Samuel, or from another source. Such differences as appear consist of abridgments, paraphrases, and corrections.

**All Israel.**—Samuel, "All the people that were with him."

**To Baalah.**—Josh. xviii. 14, "Kirjath-baal, which is Kirjath-jearim." "Baal's town" was doubtless the original name. "Town of woods" describes the position of the place. Our text appears more correct than that of Samuel, which has, "And David rose and went, and all the people that were with him, from Baalê-Judah." The Targum, LXX., and Syriac, translate that which the Authorised Version gives as a proper name, "The people that were with him of the { cities lords men } of Judah." If this be right, perhaps "Baalah" has fallen out of the text of Samuel owing to its resemblance to the word *baalê*, lords. Kirjath-jearim is the modern '*Erma*, four miles east of *Ain Shems* (Bethshemesh).—*Palestine Exploration Fund Quarterly Statement, October,* 1881.

**The Lord, that dwelleth between the cherubims.**—Rather, *Jehovah, who sitteth upon the cherubim* (comp. Ps. xviii. 11, lxxx. 2; Isa. xxxvii. 16).

**Whose name is called on it.**—The Hebrew is, "who (or which) is called Name." The Israelites in later days avoided all mention of the Divine name of *Jehovah*, and substituted *hashshêm* "the Name" (comp. Lev. xxiv. 16, and the Third Commandment). A comparison with 2 Sam. vi. 2, however, suggests that a word meaning "upon it" (*ālâw*), has fallen out. In that case the literal rendering will be, *upon which* (*i.e.*, the Ark) *the Name* (of Jehovah) *is called*=which is called by the name (of Jehovah). The Ark was often called "the Ark of Jehovah" (chap. xv. iii). The Hebrew and Targum of Samuel favour this. Some MSS. of Chron. read "there" (*shām*) instead of "name" (*shēm*). This gives the meaning, *who is invoked there* (at the Ark). Comp. the LXX. οὗ ἐπεκλήθη ὄνομα αὐτοῦ.

<sup>(7)</sup> Abridged form of the fuller text preserved in 2 Sam. vi. 3 (see Notes there).

**Drave.**—*Were driving.* 2 Sam. vi. 4, is wholly omitted by the Chronicles. "Ahio" may mean *his brother*, or, with different points, *his brothers* (so LXX. and Syriac).

<sup>(8)</sup> **Played.**—*Were dancing* (to music).

**With all their might, and with singing.**—So LXX. and Syriac. Samuel has "with all woods

276

psalteries, and with timbrels, and with cymbals, and with trumpets. ⁽⁹⁾ And when they came unto the threshingfloor of ¹Chidon, Uzza put forth his hand to hold the ark; for the oxen ²stumbled. ⁽¹⁰⁾ And the anger of the LORD was kindled against Uzza, and he smote him, because he put his hand to the ᵃark: and there he died before God. ⁽¹¹⁾ And David was displeased, because the LORD had made a breach upon Uzza: wherefore that place is called ³Perez-uzza to this day. ⁽¹²⁾ And David was afraid of God that day, saying, How shall I bring the ark of God *home* to me? ⁽¹³⁾ So David ⁴brought not the ark *home* to himself to the city of David, but carried it aside into the house of Obed-edom the Gittite.

⁽¹⁴⁾ And the ark of God remained with the family of Obed-edom in his house three months. And the LORD blessed ᵇthe house of Obed-edom, and all that he had.

CHAPTER XIV.—⁽¹⁾ Now ᶜHiram king of Tyre sent messengers to David, and timber of cedars, with masons and

1 Called *Nachon,* 2 Sam. 6. 6.

2 Or, *shook it.*

a Num. 4. 15.

3 That is, The *breach of Uzza.*

4 Heb., *removed.*

b As chap. 26. 5.

c 2 Sam. 5. 11, &c.

---

of cypresses;" a strange expression, probably due to confusion of similar letters, and transposition. The LXX. there has "in strength."

**Cymbals and trumpets.**—Samuel (Hebrew) has *sistrums* (a kind of rattle) *and cymbals.* The former word only occurs there. The Chronicle has a later term for *cymbals* (*meçiltayim* for *çilçᵉlim*).

⁽⁹⁾ **Chidon.**—So one MS. of LXX. Syriac and Arabic, *Rāmīn.* The *Nachon* of Samuel seems right. The Targum, Syriac, and Arabic of Samuel have, "prepared threshing-floor (s)," treating *nākōn* as a participle.

**Put forth his hand to hold the ark.**—An explanatory paraphrase of the more ancient text, "Uzza put forth unto the ark of God, and held thereon" (Samuel).

**Stumbled.**—Or, *plunged.* The margin is wrong. The verb is used transitively, in 2 Kings ix. 33, "Throw her down."

⁽¹⁰⁾ **And he smote him.**—Abridged from "and God smote him there" (Samuel).

**Because he put his hand to the ark.**—"Because he put" is in the Heb., *'al 'asher shalah.* For this Samuel has *'al hashshal,* an obscure phrase, occurring nowhere else in the Old Testament. The similarity of letters in the two phrases can hardly be accidental, but whether the chronicler has given the original text of the passage as he found it preserved in his source, or whether he has himself made a guess at the true reading, cannot be determined. The Syriac of Samuel reads, "because he put forth his hand;" and so the Arabic, adding, "to the ark." The Targum, "because he sinned" (using a word like *hashshal*). The Vat. LXX. omits the phrase.

**Before God.**—Samuel, "by the ark of God." This explains the same phrase in verse 8. (Comp. for the event 1 Sam. vi. 19.)

⁽¹¹⁾ **Made a breach.**—*Broken forth against.* The same verb recurs in chap. xiv. 11. (Comp. Exod. xix. 22.)

**Wherefore that place is called.**—Heb., *and he* (one) *called that place.*

**To this day.**—It is not implied necessarily that the place was known by this name in the days of the Chronicles. The same phrase occurs in the parallel verse of Samuel, and the chronicler has merely given an exact transcript of his source.

⁽¹²⁾ **God . . . ark of God.**—Here and in verses 8 and 14, &c. Samuel has *Jehovah.* The chronicler or his authority has avoided the frequent use of that most holy Name.

**Saying.**—Samuel, "and said."

**How.**—*Hēk,* an Aramaic form, perhaps due to a transcriber rather than to the author.

**Shall I bring.**—Samuel, "shall come." Two different voices of the same verb.

⁽¹³⁾ **Brought not . . . home.**—A different verb from that in verse 12. Literally, *And David caused not the ark to turn aside unto himself.* Slightly abridged. (See Samuel.)

**Obed-edom the Gittite.**—As, according to chap. xxvi. 1—4, Obed-edom was a Korhitic Levite, the term "Gittite" is generally assumed to mean native of Gath-rimmon, a Levitical township (Josh. xxi. 24) belonging to the great clan of Kohath, which was charged with the carriage of the Ark, and of which Obed-edom was a member (Num. iv. 15).

⁽¹⁴⁾ **With the family.**—*By* (near) *the house.* The preposition is wanting in Samuel, according to older usage.

**In his house.**—*In its own house* (shrine). Instead of this, Samuel has "the Gittite," and for the concluding words, "And the Lord blessed Obed-edom, and all his house." (Comp. 2 Sam. vi. 12.) As to the nature of the blessing, see chap. xxvi. 4—8; and comp. Ps. cxxvii.

XIV.

This section is a duplicate of 2 Sam. v. 11—25. In the older work it follows immediately upon the account of the taking of Jebus (2 Sam. v. 6—10), and precedes that of the removal of the Ark. Neither Samuel nor the chronicler has observed the order of chronology. The chronicler may have transposed the two accounts, in order to represent the removal of the Ark to the new capital in immediate connection with the acquisition of the city.

The chapter treats (1) of David's palace building and family; (2) of his two victories over the Philistines in the valley of Rephaim.

⁽¹⁾ **Hiram.**—So the Hebrew text of Chronicles spells the name, and the LXX. and all the other ancient versions both of Samuel and Chronicles have it so. But the Hebrew margin of Chronicles writes "Huram."

**Messengers.**—Ambassadors.

**Timber of cedars.**—Felled from the Lebanon, and sea-borne to Joppa (2 Chron. ii. 16).

**With masons and carpenters.**—Literally, *and craftsmen of walls, and craftsmen of timber.* 2 Sam. v. 11 has "craftsmen of wood, and craftsmen of stone of wall."

carpenters, to build him an house. <sup>(2)</sup> And David perceived that the LORD had confirmed him king over Israel, for his kingdom was lifted up on high, because of his people Israel.

<sup>(3)</sup> And David took ¹more wives at Jerusalem: and David begat more sons and daughters. <sup>(4)</sup> Now these *are* the names of *his* children which he had in Jerusalem; Shammua, and Shobab, Nathan, and Solomon, <sup>(5)</sup> and Ibhar, and Elishua, and Elpalet, <sup>(6)</sup> and Nogah, and Nepheg, and Japhia, <sup>(7)</sup> and Elishama, and ²Beeliada, and Eliphalet.

<sup>(8)</sup> And when the Philistines heard that <sup>a</sup> David was anointed king over all Israel, all the Philistines went up to seek David. And David heard *of it*, and went out against them. <sup>(9)</sup> And the Philistines came and spread themselves in the valley of Rephaim. <sup>(10)</sup> And David enquired of God, saying, Shall I go up against the Philistines? and wilt thou deliver them into mine hand? And the LORD said unto him, Go up; for I will deliver them into thine hand. <sup>(11)</sup> So they came up to Baal-perazim; and David smote them there. Then David said, God hath broken in upon mine enemies by mine hand like the breaking forth of waters: therefore they called the name of that place

1 Heb., *yet.*
2 Or, *Eliada,* 2 Sam. 5. 16.
*a* 2 Sam. 5. 17.

---

**To build him an house.**—Samuel, "and they built a house for David." (2 Sam. v. 11.)

**House.**—Palace. So the Temple was called "the house" (*hab-bayith*) as well as "the palace" (*hēkāl;* comp. the Accadian *e-gal,* "great house"). We may think of the numerous records of palace building which the Assyrian and Babylonian sovereigns have left us. The cedar of Lebanon (*Labnānu*) was a favourite material with them.

<sup>(2)</sup> **And David perceived ..,**—*And David knew that Jehovah had appointed him.* The willing alliance of the powerful sovereign of Phœnician Tyre was so understood by David. The favour of man is sometimes a sign of the approval of God—always, when it results from well-doing (Gen. xxxix. 21; Luke ii. 52).

**For his kingdom was lifted up on high.**—Samuel, "and (he knew) that he had lifted up his kingdom." Perhaps our text should be rendered, viz., that his kingdom was lifted up on high."

**Lifted up.**—Aramaic form (*nissēth*).

**Because of.**—*For the sake of.*

**On high.**—A favourite intensive expression with the chronicler (chaps. xxii. 5, xxiii. 17, &c.).

**Kingdom.**—The Hebrew term (*malkūth*) is more modern than that in Samuel (*mamlākhāh*).

This verse helps us to understand how David was "a man after God's own heart." His innate humility recognises at once the ground of his own exaltation as not personal, but national.

<sup>(3)</sup> **And David took more wives.**—The verse is considerably abbreviated as compared with Samuel, which reads, "concubines and wives from Jerusalem, after he had come from Hebron." The concubines are not omitted because of offence, for they are mentioned in chap. iii. 9.

<sup>(4)</sup> **His children.**—Literally, *the born.* Samuel has a different word from the same root; and omits the relative pronoun and its verb. (For the names, comp. chap. iii. 5—9, Notes, and 2 Sam. v. 14—16.) The list is repeated here because it occurred at this point in the document which the historian was copying, and perhaps also as an instance of David's prosperity, which is the topic of the section.

**Nathan.**—"And Nathan" (Samuel) must be right. The conjunction occurs throughout the list. Joseph, "the husband of Mary, of whom was born Jesus," traced his descent from this son of David (Luke iii. 23—31).

II.—DAVID'S TWO VICTORIES OVER THE PHILISTINES (verses 8—16; 2 Sam. v. 17—25).

Although placed here after the account of the palace building, this invasion must have occurred earlier in the reign of David, and probably soon after the storming of Jerusalem, a proof of capacity, which would rouse the Philistines to combined action against the new sovereign of Israel. (Comp. 1 Sam. xiii.)

<sup>(8)</sup> **David was anointed.**—Samuel, "they had anointed David." The verb in each case is *mashah*, from which is derived *Mashiah*=Messiah.

**Over all Israel.**—The word "all," omitted in Samuel, contrasts David's second election with his first as king of Judah only.

**To seek David.**—With hostile intent. The verb is so used in 1 Sam. xxvi. 2.

**Went out against them.**—Literally, *before them* (chap. xii. 17). Samuel has, "went down to the stronghold." The term "stronghold" (*mĕçūdāh*) designates the "castle of Zion" (chap. xi. 5, 7), and also David's old refuge, the rock and cave of Adullam, in the valley of Elah. The latter is probably intended here. As on former occasions, the Philistine forces were likely to choose the route through the valley of Elah (comp. 1 Sam. xvii. 1, 2), and David "went down" from Zion "to meet them" there.

<sup>(9)</sup> **And the Philistines came.**—*Now the Philistines had come.* The narrative goes back to verse 8a. The invaders had approached by another road than usual, and encamped in the valley of Rephaim (chap. xi. 15).

**Spread themselves.**—The chronicler has given an easier term than that used in Samuel.

<sup>(10)</sup> **And David enquired of God.**—How? Through the high priest Abiathar, who sought Divine direction by means of the Urim and Thummim, or sacred lots, which he carried in a pouch on his breast, which was fastened to the ephod, or priestly mantle. (See Exod. xxviii. 30, xxxix. 21; Lev. viii. 8; Num. xxvii. 21; 1 Sam. xiv. 18, 19, 37, 41, xxiii. 9, xxviii xxx. 7. 8.)

**Against.**—Samuel, "unto." There should be a comma, not a query, at "Philistines;" the whole sentence forms but one question in the Hebrew. Samuel gives two distinct questions, disconnected from each other. The rest of the verse is abridged here. (Comp. Samuel.)

<sup>(11)</sup> **So they came up to Baal-perazim.**—*And they:* that is, David and his troops. Samuel, "And

<sup>1</sup> Baal-perazim. <sup>(12)</sup> And when they had left their gods there, David gave a commandment, and they were burned with fire. <sup>(13)</sup> And the Philistines yet again spread themselves abroad in the valley. <sup>(14)</sup> Therefore David enquired again of God; and God said unto him, Go not up after them; turn away from them, <sup>a</sup> and come upon them over against the mulberry trees. <sup>(15)</sup> And it shall be, when thou shalt hear a sound of going in the tops of the mulberry trees, *that* then thou shalt go out to battle: for God is gone forth before thee to smite the host of the Philistines. <sup>(16)</sup> David therefore did as God commanded him: and they smote the host of the Philistines from Gibeon even to Gazer.

<sup>1</sup> That is, *A place of breaches.*

<sup>a</sup> 2 Sam. 5. 23.

---

David came into Baal-perazim." The locality is unknown. The prophet Isaiah (chap. xxviii. 21) refers to these two victories of David: "For *Jehovah* shall rise up as in Mount Perazim, he shall be wroth as in the valley of Gibeon, that he may do his work, his strange work; and bring to pass his act, his strange act." Such a reference proves the great moment of the events so briefly chronicled here.

**God hath broken in upon mine enemies.**—Samuel has "Jehovah" here and in verse 10*a*, and again in verses 14 and 15. (See Note, chap. xiii. 12.) True to his character, David owns the mighty hand of God in the results of his own valour. (Comp. chap. xvii. 16, *sqq.*) He is conscious of being God's instrument. Contrast the haughty self-confidence of the Assyrian conqueror (Isa. x. 5--15).

**By mine hand.**—Samuel, "before me;" and so the Syriac and Arabic here. The Hebrew phrases are probably synonymous. (Comp. 1 Sam. xxi. 14, "in their hand," *i.e., before them.*) In Arabic, "between the hands" means *before*. Our text seems the more original here.

**Like the breaking forth of waters.**—David's forces probably charged down the slopes of Mount Perazim (Isa. xxviii. 21), like a mountain torrent, sweeping all before it.

**They called.**—An explanation of Samuel, which has "he [*i.e.,* one] called." The remark indicates the antiquity of the narrative. (Comp. the frequent verbal plays of this kind in the stories of the Book of Genesis.)

**Baal-perazim.**—*Lord, or owner, of breaches,* or *breakings forth.* "Baal" may refer to *Jehovah* (comp. chap. ix. 33, Note); and *perazim* may have also meant the *fissures* or gullies on the mountain-side. It is the plural of the word *perez* (chap. xiii. 11).

<sup>(12)</sup> **And when they had left their gods there.**—Samuel, "their images." Our word is explanatory.

**David gave a commandment, and they were burned with fire.**—Samuel, "And David and his men carried them off" (Heb.). The two statements are not incompatible, and may both have existed in the same original text. The chronicler is careful to record David's compliance with the law of Deut. vii. 25.

(13—16) A second Philistine invasion and defeat (2 Sam. v. 22—25).

<sup>(13)</sup> **In the valley**—"of Rephaim" (Samuel). Slightly abridged.

<sup>(14)</sup> **Therefore David enquired.**—The first half of this verse is fuller and clearer than in Samuel. The second half must be adjusted by comparison with the older text, which reads, "Thou must not go up [LXX., "to meet them"]; go round to their rear, and come upon them in front of the *baca* trees." Probably the terms rendered "after them" and "from them" should be slightly modified and transposed in our text. This will give, "Go not up against them; go round to their rear," &c., as in Samuel.

**Mulberry trees.**—The traditional Jewish rendering of *beka'im,* a Hebrew word only occurring here and in the parallel passage of Samuel. Probably the kind of balsam tree called *bākā* by the Arabs is meant. It sheds a gum like tears, whence its name. (Heb., *bākā,* "to weep.") (Comp. Ps. lxxxiv. 6.)

<sup>(15)</sup> **A sound of going.**—Rather, *the sound of marching.* The sign may have been a natural one. David was to listen for the wind rustling in the tops of the *bacas*—a sound like that of walking on dead leaves—and then to make his attack. (But comp. 2 Kings vii. 6.) But we are reminded, in connection with this fragment of David's history, that all ancient people attached a prophetic import to the motion and rustling of leaves. Omens from trees are mentioned in the table of contents of the great Assyrian work on terrestrial omens, compiled by order of Sargon of Agadē or Accad (about 2200 B.C.). Comp. also the speaking oaks of Dodona, the laurel of Delos (Virg. *Æn.* iii. 91), and that of Delphi (*Hymn to Apollo,* 393). The "oak of the diviners" (Judg. ix. 37), and perhaps Deborah's palm-tree, and even the burning bush, must be referred to the same order of ideas. The Arabs believe the thorny bushes of the *gharqud* capable of uttering prophetic words; and with them the *samûra,* or Egyptian thorn, is sacred. These analogies, however, do not militate against the reality or the miraculous character of the Biblical occurrence. The Divine communications with man always assume the form best adapted for striking the mind amidst reigning ideas. Biblical visions, *e.g.,* always have the colour of the seer's environment: those of Joseph are Egyptian; those of Ezekiel in the Exile, Assyrian. (See, further, Lenormant, *La Divination en Chaldée.*)

**Then thou shalt go out to battle.**—A paraphrase of the term used in Samuel.

**For God is gone forth.**—"Then" (Samuel), viz., "when thou hast heard the signal."

<sup>(16)</sup> **David therefore.**—*And David did.* Samuel adds "so."

**And they smote the host** (camp).—Samuel, "and he smote the Philistines." (Comp. verse 11.)

**From Gibeon.**—The present Hebrew text of Samuel has Geba. The LXX. agrees with Chronicles in reading Gibeon, but the Targum, Syriac, and Arabic read Geba. Gibeon lay about six miles north-west of Jerusalem, between the valley of Rephaim and Gezer. Isa. xxviii. 21 supports this reading.

**Even to Gazer** (or Gezer).—Gazer is the so-called *pausal* form. Comp. Pharez (Perez) and Japhet (Yepheth): The text of Samuel has, "until thou come to Gezer;" the Chronicles, "even unto Gezer-ward." (See Josh. xii. 12; 1 Kings ix. 15—17.)

(17) And the fame of David went out into all lands; and the LORD brought the fear of him upon all nations.

CHAPTER XV.—(1) And *David* made him houses in the city of David, and prepared a place for the ark of God, and pitched for it a tent. (2) Then David said, ¹None ought to carry the *a* ark of God but the Levites: for them hath the LORD chosen to carry the ark of God, and to minister unto him for ever. (3) And David gathered all Israel together to Jerusalem, to bring up the ark of the LORD unto his place, which he had prepared for it. (4) And David assembled the children of Aaron, and the Levites: (5) of the sons of Kohath; Uriel the chief, and his ² brethren an hundred and twenty: (6) of the sons of Merari; Asaiah the chief, and his brethren two hundred and twenty: (7) of the sons of Gershom; Joel the chief, and his brethren an hundred and thirty: (8) of the sons of Elizaphan; Shemaiah the chief, and his brethren two hundred: (9) of the sons of Hebron; Eliel the chief, and his brethren fourscore: (10) of the sons of Uzziel; Am-

1 Heb., It is not to carry the ark of God, but for the Levites.

*a* Num. 4. 2, 15.

B.C. 1042.

2 Or, *kinsmen.*

B.C. cir. 1042.

---

(17) This verse is not in Samuel. It looks like a concluding reflection of the chronicler's, similar to 2 Chron. xvii. 10, xx. 29.

**The fame of David went out.**—*David's name.* The same phrase recurs in 2 Chron. xxvi. 15.

**All lands.**—*All the lands.* (Comp. Ps. xix. 4.)

**And the Lord brought the fear of him upon all nations.**—Yet this fear was, as we should say, the natural effect of his victories. In the view of the chronicler, David's success in arms, with all its consequences, was the work of Jehovah. The Hebrew phrase is similar to that in Esther viii. 17.

### XV.

The thread of the narrative dropped at chap. xiii. 14 is now resumed, and the subject of this and the following chapter is the solemn transfer of the Ark from the house of Obed-edom by the lawful ministry of priests and Levites. The elaborate account here presented corresponds to a brief section of eight verses in Samuel (2 Sam. vi. 12—20a), which it incorporates, subject to certain variations, noticed in their place (chaps. xv. 25—xvi. 3, and 43).

Chap. xv. relates—I. David's preparations for the ceremony of the transfer: (1) by erection of a tent for the Ark (verse 1); (2) by assembling representatives of all Israel, and especially the priests and Levites, and consulting with the latter (verses 2—16); (3) by choice of individuals to conduct the proceedings (verses 17—24). II. The incidents of the procession (verses 25—29).

(1) **And David made him houses.**—Or, *and he made* (*i.e.,* finished) *a palace* (plural, intensive) *for himself,* referring back to chap. xiv. 1. Others think of fresh buildings required for his additional wives, which is less likely. David had the example of Egyptian and Babylonian monarchs for his palace-building.

**City of David.**—Castle of Zion (chap. xi. 5, 7).

**And prepared a place for the ark.**—Comp. 2 Sam. vi. 17.

**A place.**—Probably within the palace precincts.

**Pitched** (or spread) **for it a tent** (or tabernacle). —The old one was at Gibeon, and Zadok ministered as high priest therein (chap. xvi. 39). Abiathar, of the house of Ithamar, who had hitherto followed the fortunes of David, probably ministered before the Ark in the new tent.

(2) **Then.**—This word is here a real note of time. It seems to denote the end of the three months' interval mentioned in chap. xiii. 14.

**None ought to carry the ark of God but the Levites.**—See Num. iv. 5—15, where the Kohathite Levites are appointed to carry the Ark and other sacred objects; and the more definite Deut. x. 8: "At that time the Lord separated the tribe of Levi, to bear the ark of the covenant of the Lord, to stand before the Lord to minister unto him, and to bless in his name, unto this day." David's enunciation of the law is a tacit acknowledgment that on the former occasion (chap. xiii. 7—10) it had not been observed. That the Ark was now duly carried by bearers is expressly stated in the older account (2 Sam. vi. 13), though their being Levites is not noticed.

(3) **And David gathered all Israel.**—Comp. 2 Sam. vi. 15: "So David and *all the house of Israel* brought up the ark." Samuel does not mention Jerusalem as the meeting-place. Of course, only a full *representation* of the people is signified. (Comp. chap. xiii. 2, 5.)

**Unto his place.**—The Ark's. The neutral *its* is unknown to the Authorised version.

(4) **And David assembled.**—He confers separately with the priestly order respecting their part in the procession.

**The children of Aaron.**—The sons of Aaron, *i.e.,* the high priests, Zadok and Abiathar (verse 11).

**The Levites**—*i.e.,* the six chieftains—Uriel, Asaiah, Joel, heads of the clans of Kohath, Merari, and Gershom respectively; and Shemaiah, Eliel, and Amminadab, additional Kohathite chiefs: all the six being at the head of their clansmen ("brethren," verses 5—10). There were four Kohathite houses to one of Merari and Gershom, because the sub-tribe of Kohath was the elder house, and had special charge of the Ark and other most holy vessels of the sanctuary (Num. iv. 4).

(5) **Of the sons of Kohath.**—Kohath comes first, as the senior clan, to which the priestly house of Aaron itself belonged.

(5—7) **Uriel** (*El is light*), **Asaiah** (*Iah made*), **Joel** (*Iah is El*) occur as Levitical names in chap. vi. 24, 30, 33, and elsewhere.

(8) **Of the sons of Elizaphan; Shemaiah.**— Elzaphan was son of Uzziel, the fourth son of Kohath (Exod. vi. 18, 22). Of this Kohathite family, Shemaiah was chief in David's time (chap. xxiv. 6).

(9) **Of the sons of Hebron.**—Hebron was third son of Kohath (Exod. vi. 18). (Comp. chap. vi. 2, above.)

(10) **Of the sons of Uzziel.**—Uzziel was fourth son of Kohath (chap. vi. 2). Exodus vi. 22 names three sons of Uzziel—Mishael, Elzaphan, and Zithri. The

minadab the chief, and his brethren an hundred and twelve.

<sup>(11)</sup> And David called for Zadok and Abiathar the priests, and for the Levites, for Uriel, Asaiah, and Joel, Shemaiah, and Eliel, and Amminadab, <sup>(12)</sup> and said unto them, Ye *are* the chief of the fathers of the Levites: sanctify yourselves, *both* ye and your brethren, that ye may bring up the ark of the LORD God of Israel unto *the place that* I have prepared for it. <sup>(13)</sup> For because ye *did it* not at the first, the LORD our God made a breach upon us, for that we sought him not after the due order. <sup>(14)</sup> So the priests and the Levites sanctified themselves to bring up the ark of the LORD God of Israel. <sup>(15)</sup> And the children of the Levites bare the ark of God upon their shoulders with the staves thereon, as <sup>a</sup> Moses commanded according to the word of the LORD.

<sup>(16)</sup> And David spake to the chief of the Levites to appoint their brethren *to be* the singers with instruments of musick, psalteries and harps and cym-

*a* Ex. 25. 14.

---

family of Elzaphan has already been represented (verse 8). The term "sons of Uzziel," therefore, in this verse represents the two other Uzzielite houses, which may have amalgamated in one. As Elzaphan is mentioned first, the elder line of Mishael may have become extinct. At any rate, chaps. xxiii. 20 and xxiv. 24 imply the existence of only two Uzzielite stocks.

<sup>(11)</sup> David's instructions to the eight spiritual chiefs.

**Zadok and Abiathar the priests** were of co-ordinate rank, as representing the two lines of Eleazar and Ithamar. (Comp. Notes on chaps. vi. 4, *sqq.*, and xxiv. 3.) On verse 5 the meanings of three of these names have been suggested. Of the others, **Zadok** imports *just*, perhaps equivalent to Zedekiah, *Jah is just;* **Abiathar,** *the Father* (*i.e.,* God) *excels;* **Shemaiah,** *Jah heareth;* **Eliel,** *God* (and none else) *is God* (*i.e.*, Divine); **Amminadab,** *the Clansman* (*i.e.*, the Lord) *is bounteous.* Thus the very names of those who conducted this great religious event expressed to themselves and others the high spiritual truths that Jehovah the Lord is righteous, the Author and Bestower of all knowledge and excellence and working power; that He alone is God; and that He hears prayers, as being a gracious Father unto all His creatures.

<sup>(12)</sup> **Chief of the fathers.**—*Heads of the father-houses.* They were the heads of the chief divisions in each sub-group of the tribe.

**Sanctify yourselves.**—Special purifications appear to have been prescribed in connection with all sacrifice and worship. (Comp. Gen. xxxv. 2; Exod. xix. 10, 15, xxx. 17—21.) Bathing the person, and washing or changing the garments, and keeping oneself aloof from whatever was regarded as defiling, were the main requisites. And all this was needful to teach Israel that the All-pure requires purity in His worshippers. (Comp. 2 Chron. xxx. 3.)

**The ark of the Lord** (Jehovah) **God of Israel.** —Contrast the simpler expression, "ark of God" (chap. xiii. and chap. xiv. 1, 2). Here David uses a specially solemn title, by way of warning. Further, the term "God of Israel" suggests that the undertaking is national, and that the nation's future welfare depends on its due performance (1 Sam. ii. 30). Israel's vocation was to be "a kingdom of priests, and an holy nation" (Exod. xix. 6), as the chronicler has well understood.

**Unto the place that I have prepared for it.** —*Unto* (that) *I have prepared for it.* The relative is omitted. (Comp. chap. xxix. 3 and 2 Chron. i. 4.)

<sup>(13)</sup> **For because ye did it not at the first.**— The Hebrew seems to mean, *for because on the first occasion it was not you* (that is, the heads of the Levitical houses)—*scil.,* who carried up the ark, but Uzza and Ahio, sons of Abinadab (2 Sam. vi. 3). The phrase so rendered only occurs here (*lĕmabbārîshônāh* = "because at the first").

**Our God made a breach.**—*Broke out upon us;* referring to the sudden death of Uzza (chap. xiii. 10). (Comp. Exod. xix. 22, 24, same phrase.)

**We sought him not** (chap. xiii. 3) **after the due order.**—The Ark was carried on a cart, instead of being borne by the sons of Kohath "on their shoulders, with the staves thereon" (verse 15; Num. iv. 15). Even the Kohathites themselves were forbidden to "touch any holy thing," as Uzza had ventured to do. It has been said that the "sanctity of institutions," as opposed to the "sanctity of a people under the government of a righteous God," is the leading idea of the Chronicles. It would be difficult to show how the sanctity of a people is to be secured, and how the government of a righteous God is to be realised, except in and through Divine institutions. As there is a "due order" by which God rules the physical world, so is there a corresponding order whereby His will is fulfilled in the spiritual sphere. There are positive institutions in Christianity as well as in Mosaism; and if we abolish the Divine authority of the one, why not of the other also?

<sup>(15)</sup> **And the children of the Levites bare the ark of God.**—The priests and Levites, having purified themselves (verse 14), duly and rightly discharged their sacred office of bearing the Ark. This statement anticipates verse 25, *sqq.* Such brief anticipative summaries of a series of events afterwards described in detail are very common in Hebrew narrative.

**Upon their shoulders with the staves thereon.**—Literally, *with their shoulder, with the poles upon themselves.*

**As Moses commanded according to the word of the Lord.**—Num. vii. 9, iv. 15; Exod. xxv. 13—15.

<sup>(16)</sup> **David spake to the chief.**—*Ordered the chiefs* (*sārîm*).

**To appoint their brethren to be the singers.** —*To station* or *assign places to their clansmen, the minstrels.*

**Psalteries and harps.**—*Harps and lutes,* or *guitars* (*nĕbālîm* and *kinnôrôth*).

**Sounding, by lifting up the voice with joy.** —So far as grammar goes, the participle *sounding* (Heb., *causing to hear—i.e.,* making a loud noise) might refer to the musicians, or to all the instruments mentioned, or to the last kind (the cymbals) only. The third reference is the best, because of the special sense

*The Musicians*          I. CHRONICLES, XV.          *Appointed*

bals, sounding, by lifting up the voice with joy. (17) So the Levites appointed *a* Heman the son of Joel; and of his brethren, *b* Asaph the son of Berechiah; and of the sons of Merari their brethren, *c* Ethan the son of Kushaiah; (18) and with them their brethren of the second *degree,* Zechariah, Ben, and Jaaziel, and Shemiramoth, and Jehiel, and Unni, Eliab, and Benaiah, and Maaseiah, and Mattithiah, and Elipheleh, and Mikneiah, and Obed-edom, and Jeiel, the porters. (19) So the singers, Heman, Asaph, and Ethan, *were appointed* to sound with cymbals of brass; (20) and Zechariah, and Aziel, and Shemiramoth, and Jehiel, and Unni, and Eliab, and Maaseiah, and Benaiah, with psalteries on Alamoth; (21) and Mattithiah, and Elipheleh, and Mikneiah, and Obed-edom, and Jeiel, and Azaziah, with harps [1] on the Sheminith to excel. (22) And Chenaniah, chief of the Levites, [2] *was* for [3] song: he instructed about the song, because he *was* skilful. (23) And Berechiah and Elkanah *were* doorkeepers for the ark. (24) And Shebaniah, and Jehoshaphat, and Nethaneel, and Amasai, and Zecha-

*a* ch. 6. 33.
*b* ch. 6. 39.
*c* ch. 6. 44.
[1] Or, *on the eighth to oversee.*
[2] Or, *was for the carriage: he instructed about the carriage.*
[3] Heb., *lifting up.*

---

of the verb. (Comp. verse 19 and Ps. cl. 5: "loud cymbals," *i.e., cymbals of sound or hearing.*) Translate: "harps and lutes and clashing cymbals, in order to swell the sound for gladness:" that is, to express and enhance the rejoicing. (Comp. 2 Chron. v. 13.)

(17) **Heman . . . Asaph . . . Ethan** (or Jeduthun) were the precentors of David's three choirs of Levitical minstrels (chap. vi. 31—44). Heman was of Kohath, and Asaph of Gershon, as Ethan of Merari.

(18) **And with them their brethren of the second degree.**—So chap. xvi. 5: "Asaph the leader, and his second Zechariah." Fourteen minstrels of the second rank—that is, subordinate to the first three—are named here.

**Ben** (son) is not a proper name. That of Zechariah's father may have fallen out after it (comp. the Syriac and Arabic: "Zechariah *son of Ne'ael*"), or it may be due to a scribe's inadvertence. The LXX. omits it.

**Shemiramoth.**—This peculiar name resembles the Assyrian *Sammurramat*, the classical Semiramis. Delitzsch suggests that it is a compound of *sammîm* ("spices"), and *râ'imat* ("loving"): a suitable name for a woman, and actually borne by a lady of the court of *Rammân-nirâri* (B.C. 812), king of Assyria.

**Jaaziel.**—Called Jeiel by mistake in chap. xvi. 5.

**And Jeiel.**—The LXX. adds, "and Azaziah" (Ozias). (Comp. verse 21.) Perhaps this should be read, and "the porters" omitted. (See verse 24.)

(19—21) The minstrels named in verses 17, 18, classified according to their instruments.

(19) The cymbal-players.

**Were appointed to sound with cymbals of brass.**—Rather, *with cymbals of bronze for clashing.* Furnished with these instruments, the three chiefs were to lead and accentuate the music.

Verses 19—25 give the order of the procession thus:—

I. The three master-singers, and two bands of seven each (verses 19—21).
II. Chenaniah, marshal of the bearers.
III. Two warders of the Ark.
IV. Seven priests, with trumpets.

THE ARK.

V. Two warders of the Ark.
VI. The king, with the heads of the nation.

(20) The eight harpers. Perhaps Maaseiah or Benaiah belongs to the next verse. This would give seven (comp. verse 24) in each band.

**Aziel** should be Jaaziel, as in verse 18.

**Jehiel.**—*God liveth.* Jeiel = Jeuel (chap. ix. 6, 35), *Remembered of God.*

**With psalteries on Alamoth.**—"With harps after the mode of maidens:" that is, probably, of soprano compass or pitch. The same expression occurs in the heading of Ps. xlvi.

(21) The six lute-players.

**With harps on the Sheminith.**—"With lutes (or lyres) in the bass." Literally, *after the mode of the eighth*—*i.e.,* an octave below the tenor—*al ottava bassa.*

**To excel.**— *To* lead the orchestra, *to precent.* (Comp. Ps. vi., heading.)

(22) Rather, *And Chenaniah, captain (i.e., conductor) of the Levites in bearing* (that is, the sacred vessels), *was conducting the bearing, because he was skilled*—*scil.,* in the traditional regulations connected with bearing the Ark duly and rightly.

**Chenaniah.**—Verse 27, and chap. xxvi. 29.

**Chief of the Levites.**—Not one of the six princes (verses 5—10), or heads of houses, but *president of the carriage of the Ark.*

**Was for song.**—So the LXX., which reads "leader of the songs;" but the Syriac has "bore the burden daily," and although the word *massâ*—*i.e.,* "lifting up," or "bearing"—might mean "lifting up the voice," (1) the context is against that meaning here; for Heman, Asaph, and Ethan were conductors of the singing and music; (2) Chenaniah is nowhere else associated with music (see Note on chap. xxvi. 29); (3) the word *massâ*, "bearing," has the sense we have given it when used in relation to Levites (Num. iv. 19; 2 Chron. xxxv. 3).

**He instructed.**—The Hebrew has an ambiguous form, which may be an infinitive—*instructing, correcting* (*yăsar*); or an imperfect of a different verb—*was prince over, superintendent of* (*sārar*).

**He was skilful.**—Comp. chap. xxv. 7; 2 Chron. xxxiv. 12.

(23) **Doorkeepers for the ark.**—"Porters" (verse 18). Warders are meant. Obed-edom and Jehiah were also warders of the Ark (verse 24). In the procession two may have walked in front of it and two behind. They would be responsible for the prevention of all unauthorised approach to the Ark of God.

(24) Seven priestly trumpeters.

**The priests, did blow with the trumpets.**—*Were blowing.* (Comp. Num. x. 2.) A pair of silver clarions were blown by the priests "for the calling of the assembly, and the journeying of the camps." (See also chap. xvi. 6.) The seven priests perhaps walked immediately before the Ark, as in Josh. vi. 4.

riah, and Benaiah, and Eliezer, the priests, did blow with the trumpets before the ark of God: and Obed-edom and Jehiah *were* doorkeepers for the ark. <sup>(25)</sup> So <sup>a</sup>David, and the elders of Israel, and the captains over thousands, went to bring up the ark of the covenant of the LORD out of the house of Obed-edom with joy. <sup>(26)</sup> And it came to pass, when God helped the Levites that bare the ark of the covenant of the LORD, that they offered seven bullocks and seven rams. <sup>(27)</sup> And David *was* clothed with a robe of fine linen, and all the Levites that bare the ark, and the singers, and Chenaniah the master of the <sup>1</sup>song with the singers: David also *had* upon him an ephod of linen. <sup>(28)</sup> Thus all Israel brought up the ark of the covenant of the LORD with shouting, and with sound of the cornet, and with trumpets, and with cymbals, making a noise with psalteries and harps. <sup>(29)</sup> And it came to pass, *as* the ark of

*a* 2 Sam. 6. 12, 13, &c.

1 Or, *carriage.*

---

**And Obed-edom and Jehiah were doorkeepers for the ark.**—Comp. verse 23. It is hardly likely that these persons were identical with the minstrels Obed-edom and Jeiel of verses 18 and 21, for (1) verses 19—24 appear to describe the order of the procession, according to which two "doorkeepers" walked before and two behind the ark (verses 23, 24), whereas Obed-edom and Jeiel the minstrels walked, playing their lutes, two places before even the first pair of doorkeepers (verse 21); (2) the name "Jeiel" is different in form and meaning from "Jehiah," *Jah liveth*; (3) the recurrence of names has been too frequent to allow us to be much surprised at a second Obed-edom. (Comp. chap. xvi. 38.)

<sup>(25)</sup> **So David, and the elders of Israel.**—Literally, *And it was David and the elders of Israel and princes of the thousands who were walking to bring up the Ark,* &c. The preparations for the ceremony are now complete, and the procession starts. A slight change in the Hebrew (omission of the article; so Syriac and one MS. of LXX.) will improve the sense: "And it came to pass, David and the elders . . . were walking to bring up the Ark."

**To bring up the ark.**—"Into the city of David" (Samuel).

**The ark of the covenant of the Lord.**—A special title of the Ark, which has not occurred before in this history. It is not read in the parallel passage of Samuel, where we find only "ark of God," and "ark of Jehovah." The phrase may therefore indicate that the chronicler had another source besides that book. (Comp. Josh. iii. 3, 17.) The parallel (2 Sam. vi. 12) makes no mention of "the elders and captains," but merely states in brief and somewhat abrupt fashion that David went and brought up the Ark, because he had heard of its bringing a blessing upon the house of Obed-edom.

**With joy.**—With set rejoicings and festal mirth.

<sup>(26)</sup> **When God helped the Levites that bare the ark.**—Comp. 2 Sam. vi. 13, "And it was so, that when the bearers of the ark of the Lord had gone six paces, he sacrificed oxen and fatlings" (sing. collect.). God had been adverse to those who conducted the Ark on the former occasion (chap. xiii. 9), as was inferred from the sudden death of Uzza. Now, when the Levites had undertaken the work in due order, and no harm had befallen, it was understood that the Divine goodwill was with the enterprise. That they had borne the holy Ark six paces without any sign of wrath was enough to call forth the grateful offerings of hearts relieved from a dread which only ceased to haunt them when the event proved it to be groundless. Our text, more exact than Samuel, gives the number and kind of the victims then sacrificed. Others refer the two accounts to different sacrifices, taking Samuel to mean that at every six paces a bullock and a fat sheep were slain by priests stationed all along the course, while they suppose our text to refer to a final sacrifice, offered when the Ark had reached its destination. This solution of the difficulty appears incredible, especially as regards the supposition of priests not mentioned in the narrative. Another view understands our text in this sense, but makes the offering in Samuel an initial sacrifice of consecration. But it is not likely that the two sacrifices are really different: (1) because the narrative here is generally parallel with Samuel; and (2) the chronicler may have intentionally paraphrased the older text for the sake of explanation. (Comp. Num. xxiii. 1, 29 for the sacrifice.)

<sup>(27)</sup> **And David was clothed with a robe of fine linen.**—Samuel reads, "And David was dancing before *Jehovah* with all might" (Heb.). The Hebrew of our text may be a corruption or intentional alteration of this. The word for "clothed" is the Aramaic (Daniel iii. 21, *měkurbāl*), which might easily be, by inadvertence or design, substituted for the rare word *měkarkēr* (Sam.), "dancing."

**A robe of fine linen.**—Heb., *a me'il of byssus.* The *me'il* was an upper garment worn by persons of rank (2 Sam. xii. 18; 1 Sam. xv. 27; Job xxix. 14).

**And all the Levites . . . and the singers, and Chenaniah.**—*Scil.,* were clothed with *a me'il of byssus.*

**The master of the song.**—Rather, *the chief* (overseer) *of the bearing.* (Comp. verse 22.)

**With the singers.**—Omit, as an accidental repetition. The word "with" is wanting in the Hebrew, which is ungrammatical as it stands. The entire clause, "and all the Levites . . . with the singers," is not read in the parallel account.

**David also had upon him an ephod of linen.**—Literally, *and upon David* (was) *an ephod of linen.* (See 2 Sam. vi. 14.) The ephod, a sort of cope, was distinctive of the priests (1 Sam. xxii. 18).

<sup>(28)</sup> **Thus all Israel brought.**—*And all Israel were bringing.* Samuel has "and David and all the house of Israel," and "ark of the Lord."

**Cornet.**—Rather, *trumpet.*

The rest of this verse is wanting in Samuel, but all the additional instruments have already been mentioned (verses 16—21).

**Trumpets.**—Clarions, or straight trumpets.

The last clause should be rendered, "and with clanging cymbals, with harps and lutes." (Comp. Ps. cl. 3, 4.)

<sup>(29)</sup> **And it came to pass.**—The verse reads in the Hebrew like a modernised form of 2 Sam. vi. 16.

the covenant of the LORD came to the city of David, that Michal the daughter of Saul looking out at a window saw king David dancing and playing: and she despised him in her heart.

CHAPTER XVI.—⁽¹⁾ So ᵃ they brought the ark of God, and set it in the midst of the tent that David had pitched for it: and they offered burnt· sacrifices and peace offerings before God. ⁽²⁾ And when David had made an end of offering the burnt offerings and the peace offerings, he blessed the people in the name of the LORD. ⁽³⁾ And he dealt to every one of Israel, both man and woman, to every one a loaf of bread, and a good piece of flesh, and a flagon of wine.

⁽⁴⁾ And he appointed *certain* of the Levites to minister before the ark of the LORD, and to record, and to thank and praise the LORD God of Israel: ⁽⁵⁾ Asaph the chief, and next to him Zechariah, Jeiel, and Shemiramoth, and Jehiel, and Mattithiah, and Eliab, and Benaiah, and Obed-edom: and Jeiel [1] with psalteries and with harps; but Asaph made a sound with cymbals; ⁽⁶⁾ Benaiah also and Jahaziel the priests with trumpets continually before the ark of the covenant of God.

ᵃ 2 Sam. 6. 17.

[1] Heb., *with instruments of psalteries and harps.*

---

**As the ark of the covenant of the Lord came.**—Rather, *The ark had come so far as to the city, and Michal had looked forth by the lattice, and she saw . . .*

**Dancing and playing.**—In the Hebrew two common words have been substituted for the two obsolete ones occurring in Samuel.

**Playing.**—The Hebrew word denotes dancing combined with singing and playing (Jer. xxx. 19; 1 Sam. xviii. 6, 7).

**She despised him.**—Because he seemed forgetful of his royal and manly honour, in dancing like a woman.

### XVI.

⁽¹⁾ **So they brought the ark of God.**—Verses 1—3 are wrongly separated from the concluding verses of chap. xv. The narrative is still parallel to 2 Sam. (17—19*a*). The differences are unimportant.

**God.**—Samuel, *Jehovah*.

**And set it.**—Samuel adds, "in its place."

**And they offered burnt sacrifices.**—Samuel, "and *David* offered [a different word] burnt sacrifices before *Jehovah*." Our narrative takes care to make it clear that *the priests and Levites* ministered in the sacrifices.

⁽²⁾ **The burnt offerings.**—Heb., *the burnt offering*, as if one great holocaust were meant. This verse is identical with 2 Sam. vi. 18, only omitting *Sabaoth* at the end, a Divine title which was perhaps obsolete in the chronicler's day.

**He blessed the people in the name of the Lord.**—Comp. Num. vi. 22—27; 1 Kings viii. 14, 55; Deut. xxxiii. 1.

⁽³⁾ **To every one . . .**—Literally, *to every man of Israel from man unto woman.* Samuel has, "to all the people, to all the multitude of Israel, from man," &c.

**A loaf** (*kikkar*).—*A round cake* (1 Sam. ii. 36). The parallel in Samuel has a less common word (*hallath*), meaning a sacrificial cake punctured all over. (Comp. Exod. xxix. 23.)

**A good piece of flesh.**—A single Hebrew term, found only here and in Samuel (*'eshpār*). It seems to mean "a portion," *i.e.*, of the victims slain for the "peace offerings." (The "burnt offerings" were wholly consumed on the altar.) Syriac, "a portion." Arabic, "a slice of flesh." Others interpret, "a measure of wine."

**A flagon of wine.**—Rather, *a raisin-cake*—*i.e.*, a mass of dried grapes (Hosea iii. 1); Isa. xvi. 7, "raisin-cakes of Kir-hareseth."

⁽⁴⁻⁴²⁾ THE INSTITUTION OF A MINISTRY FOR THE ARK. THE ODE SUNG ON THE DAY OF INSTITUTION.

This entire section is peculiar to the Chronicle. Verse 43 is almost identical with 2 Sam. vi. 19, 20. Compared, then, with the older text, this relation of the chronicler's looks like a parenthesis interpolated from another source into the history, as narrated in 2 Sam. vi. 12—20.

⁽⁴⁾ **And he appointed certain of the Levites.** —Literally, *put, placed* (Gen. iii. 12).

**To minister.**—Literally, *ministering—i.e., as ministers.* The object of the appointment is defined by the words which follow: "both to remind, and to thank, and to praise Jehovah, the God of Israel." Each verb expresses a distinct kind of duty in the service of song.

**To record** is the technical term for chanting the psalms which accompanied the sacrificial burning of the *Azkārāh*, that is, the part of the meat offering that was presented on the altar (Lev. ii. 2). (Comp. the use of the cognate verb in the titles of Pss. xxxviii., lxx.)

**To thank** was to perform psalms of invocation, and confession of benefits received.

**To praise** was to sing and play hymns of hallelujah such as Ps. cxlvi.—cl.

These Levites were to minister thus before the Ark in the sacred tent of Mount Zion.

⁽⁵, ⁶⁾ The names of the persons appointed — ten Levites and two priests—all of whom but one, Jahaziel, were in the procession described in chap. xv. 19—21.

**Asaph the chief, and next to him** (his second) **Zechariah.**—See chap. xv. 18.

**Jeiel.**—A scribe's error for "Jaaziel" (chap. xv. 18).

**With psalteries and with harps.**—*With instruments of harps and lutes* (appositive or defining genitive).

**But Asaph made a sound with cymbals.**— Literally, *and Asaph with cymbals clanging.*

⁽⁶⁾ **Jahaziel.**—Not mentioned in chap. xv., unless he be the Eliezer of verse 24. The number of these musicians is twelve, suggesting the twelve tribes of Israel.

**With trumpets.**—Clarions, or straight trumpets.

**Continually.**—The Hebrew term is a special one, denoting *at fixed and regularly recurring services.*

(7) Then on that day David delivered first *this psalm* to thank the LORD into the hand of Asaph and his brethren. (8) ª Give thanks unto the LORD, call upon his name, make known his deeds among the people. (9) Sing unto him, sing psalms unto him, talk ye of all his wondrous works. (10) Glory ye in his holy name: let the heart of them rejoice that seek the LORD. (11) Seek the LORD and his strength, seek his face continually. (12) Remember his marvellous works that he hath done, his wonders, and the judgments of his mouth; (13) O ye seed of Israel his servant, ye children of Jacob, his chosen ones. (14) He *is* the LORD our God; his judgments *are* in all the earth. (15) Be ye mindful always of his covenant; the word *which* he commanded to a thousand generations; (16) *even of the* ᵇ *covenant* which he made with Abraham, and of his oath unto Isaac; (17) and hath confirmed the same to Jacob for a law, *and* to Israel *for an*

a Ps. 105. 1.

b Gen. 17. 2, & 26. 3, & 28. 13.

---

(7—36) An ode of thanksgiving appropriate to the occasion.

(7) **Then on that day David delivered first this psalm.**—Rather, *On that day then* (viz., after the Ark had been placed in its tent, and the minstrels appointed) *David originally committed the giving of thanks to Jehovah into the hands of Asaph and his brethren.* Thus understood, the verse merely asserts that this was the occasion when "Asaph and his brethren" were first charged with the duties described in verses 4—6. But the words seem really intended to introduce the long ode which follows, and therefore we should perhaps render, "On that day, then David gave for the first time into the hands of Asaph and his brethren, for giving thanks to Jehovah, 'Give thanks unto the Lord,'" &c., the whole psalm being regarded as the object of the verb. It may be that this composite hymn was sung in the time of the compiler, on the anniversary of the removal of the Ark, which may in after-times have been commemorated by a special service. Hence it was easy to infer that it was the ode sung at the original service under David. The words "then" (*'âz*) and "on that day" certainly seem to introduce the psalm. (Comp. their use, Exod. xv. 1, and Judges v. 1. Comp. also 2 Chron. vii. 6.)

But the ambiguity of verse 7 may be taken along with other considerations to indicate that this ode does not constitute an original part of the Chronicles, but has been inserted by a later hand. For (1) the Psalm is clearly a *cento* consisting of portions of three others extant in the Psalter, and so loosely patched together that the seams are quite visible; (2) the Psalter itself does not refer the three psalms in question to David; if, however, the editors of the Psalter had read in the Chronicles a clear assertion of Davidic authorship, they would hardly have left them anonymous; (3) all critics agree that it is not here expressly said that David composed this ode, and, in fact, its ideas and language betray a later origin than the Davidic age; and (4) it contains no specific allusion to the occasion for which it purports to have been written. If no record was preserved of the psalms actually sung at the festival, it was natural that some editor should attempt to supply the apparent *lacuna* from the Psalter.

(8—22) The first four strophes of Ps. cv. (verses 1—15.)

(8) **Give thanks.**—The same Hebrew verb as in verse 4, "to thank." Ps. cv. is a *tôdāh*, or thanksgiving, hence its use here.

**Call upon his name.**—Invoke His help, appealing to Him by His revealed name of Jehovah. (Comp. Pss. iii. 1—7, v. 1, vii. 6, and many others.)

**Make known.**—Israel's mission.

**Deeds.**—*Feats, exploits,* deeds of wonder; a poetic word.

**People.**—*Peoples.*

(9) **Sing psalms.**—The word implies a musical accompaniment.

**Talk ye.**—A third term for *singing. Chant ye.*

**His wondrous works.**—*His wonders,* or *miracles.* The word means *things separate, distinct,* and so *out of the common* (Exod. iii. 20).

(10) **That seek the Lord.**—Comp. chaps. xiii. 3, xv. 13, where a synonymous term is used. Both occur in verse 11.

(11) **And his strength.**—Comp. Exod. xv. 2, Isa. xxvi. 4: "Jah, Jehovah is a rock of ages" (Heb.).

**His face.**—His presence, especially in the sanctuary. True devotion is the secret of moral strength.

(12) The second strophe of Psalm cv.

**Marvellous works.**—*Wonders,* as in verse 9.

**His wonders.**—*His portents;* τέρατα of the New Testament.

**The judgments of his mouth.**—His judicial utterances, which execute themselves. (Comp. Gen. i. 3; Exod. xii. 12.)

**Of his mouth.**—Psalm cv. 5 has a different form of the pronoun.

(13) **Seed of Israel.**—Psalm cv. 6 reads, "Abraham." "Israel" improves the parallelism, and is probably a correction. Syriac and Arabic have "Abraham."

**His servant.**—LXX., "his servants." (Comp. "servant of Jehovah" as a title of Israel in Isaiah.)

(14) The grand thought of Israel that, though Jehovah is their God, He is not theirs exclusively: He governs the wide world.

(15) **Be ye mindful.**—Psalm cv. 8, third strophe, begins, "He hath remembered," that is, "He will certainly remember" His ancient covenant; and the exile and oppression of His people can only be transitory (Comp. Ps. cxi. 5.) The expression is modified here, to suit different circumstances, and perhaps in view of verse 12.

**The word which he commanded to . . .** Rather, *the promise which he established for . . .*

(16) **Even of the covenant.**—These words should be cancelled. The object is still *the word* of promise.

**Which he made.**—Literally, *he cut.* Same phrase as in Haggai ii. 5.

**With Abraham.**—Gen. xxii. 16.

**Unto Isaac.**—Heb., *Yiçhāq.* Psalm cv. 9 has the weaker form, *Yishāq* (Amos vii. 9).

(17) **And hath confirmed.**—In Psalm cv. the sense is future.

**The same.**—*It*—*i.e.,* the word (verse 15).

**For a law** = as a fixed decree.

everlasting covenant, (18) saying, Unto thee will I give the land of Canaan, ¹ the lot of your inheritance; (19) when ye were but ² few, *even a few, and strangers in it. (20) And *when* they went from nation to nation, and from *one* kingdom to another people; (21) he suffered no man to do them wrong: yea, he *b* reproved kings for their sakes, (22) *saying*, *c* Touch not mine anointed, and do my prophets no harm. (23) *d* Sing unto the LORD, all the earth; shew forth from day to day his salvation. (24) Declare his glory among the heathen; his marvellous works among all nations.

1 Heb., *the cord.*
2 Heb., *men of number.*
a Gen. 34. 30.
b Gen. 12. 17 & 20. 3.
c Ps. 105. 15.
d Ps. 96. 1.
e Lev. 19. 4.

(25) For great *is* the LORD, and greatly to be praised: he also *is* to be feared above all gods. (26) For all the gods *e* of the people *are* idols: but the LORD made the heavens. (27) Glory and honour *are* in his presence; strength and gladness *are* in his place. (28) Give unto the LORD, ye kindreds of the people, give unto the LORD glory and strength. (29) Give unto the LORD the glory *due* unto his name: bring an offering, and come before him: worship the LORD in the beauty of holiness. (30) Fear before him, all the earth: the world also shall be stable, that it be not

---

(18) **The land of Canaan.**—In the Hebrew the rhythm is marred here by omission of a particle (*eth*), found in Psalm cv. 11.

**The lot.**—Literally, *as the measuring line* (comp. Ps. xvi. 5), *i.e.*, as your measured or apportioned domain.

(19) The fourth strophe of Psalm cv. begins here.

**When ye were but few.**—The psalm has "when they [that is, your fathers] were but few;" and so LXX. here.

**Few.**—Literally, *men of number* = easily counted. (Comp. Gen. xxxiv. 30.)

**Strangers in it.**—*Sojourners*, μέτοικοι (Gen. xxiii. 4).

(20) **And when they went from nation to nation.**—*And they went*. This shows that the third plural ("when they were") is original in the last verse. The reference is to the wanderings of the patriarchs.

**And from one kingdom.**—The conjunction is prosaic, and is not read in Psalm cv. 13.

(21) This verse was originally the apodosis to verse 19, as in Psalm cv.: "When they were but few . . . and went from nation to nation . . . he suffered no man," &c.

**He suffered no man.**—Heb., *he permitted to no man*, as in 2 Sam. xvi. 11. Psalm cv. has the mere accusative, and a different word for "man" (*'ādām*).

(22) **Saying.**—Omitted in the Hebrew, as in Psalm ii. 6, and perhaps at the end of verse 7, *supra*.

**Mine anointed** (ones).—Plural of *Messiah*. Abraham and Sarah were to be progenitors of *kings* (Gen. xvii. 16). (Comp. Gen. xxiii. 6.)

**My prophets.**—Literally, *do no harm against my prophets*—a construction unparalleled elsewhere. Psalm cv. has the usual expression, "to my prophets." (See Gen. xii., xx., xxvi. for the passages of patriarchal history to which allusion is here made.)

We have now reached the first "seam" in this composite ode. Psalm cv. naturally continues its historic proof of Jehovah's faithfulness, by reference to the sojourn in Egypt, the Exodus, the wanderings, and the occupation of Canaan. Here, however, this train of thought is abruptly broken off, and a fresh start made in verse 23 with Psalm xcvi. The author, or authors, who compiled this hymn of praise "strung together familiar psalms as a sort of mosaic, to give approximate expression to the festive strains and feelings of the day" (*Delitzsch*).

(23–33) See Psalm xcvi. This psalm, in the Psalter, consists of five strophes or stanzas of six lines each—an artistic arrangement which has been violated here.

The subject is the extension of Jehovah's kingdom over all the world, a thought familiar to the readers of the Book of Isaiah, where most of the ideas and phrases of the psalm may be found.

(23) **Sing unto the Lord, all the earth.**—The second line of the psalm. The spirited opening of the psalm is purposely weakened, by omission of the first and third lines, in order to make it fit in here. Strophe I. is thus compressed into four lines (verses 23, 24).

**All the earth.**—*All the land* (of Israel).

**Shew forth.**—Heb., *tell the* (good) *news of.*

**His salvation.**—*Deliverance* (from exile).

(24) **Heathen.**—*Nations* (verse 31).

(25–27) Strophe II. of the psalm. Jehovah is the Creator; other gods are nonentities.

(25) **He also.**—*And he.* The conjunction is not in Psalm xcvi., and is a prosaic addition of the compiler. (Comp. verse 20.)

(26) **People.**—*Peoples.*

**Idols** (*'ĕlilim*).—A favourite expression in Isaiah.

(27) **Strength and gladness are in his place.** —Ps. xcvi. 6: "Strength and beauty are in his sanctuary." The psalmist's idea of the heavenly temple seems to have been understood of the earthly; and then his phrase was altered as unsuitable.

**Gladness** (*hedwāh*).—A late word, occurring again in Neh. viii. 10 only. "Beauty" (*tiph'ĕreth*) is ancient.

**His place**—*i.e.*, the tent of the Ark on Mount Zion. (Comp. chap. xv. 1, 3.)

(28, 29) Strophe III. of the psalm, mutilated. A call to all nations to come and worship in the Temple of Jehovah.

(28) **Kindreds of the people.**—*Clans* (races) *of the peoples.*

(29) So far each verse of this ode has symmetrically consisted of two clauses. The present verse has three —another mark of awkward compilation.

**Come before him.**—Ps. xcvi., "into his courts," that is, the Temple courts: an expression modified here to suit another application.

**Worship the Lord in the beauty of holiness.** —Rather, *bow ye down to Jehovah, in holy vestments.* This line ought to be the first of the next couplet.

(30) **Fear** (plural).—Literally, *Writhe ye.*

**Before him.**—The preposition is a compound form common in the Chronicles; in the psalm it is simple.

*The Psalm of*          I. CHRONICLES, XVI.          *Thanksgiving.*

moved. <sup>(31)</sup> Let the heavens be glad, and let the earth rejoice: and let *men* say among the nations, The LORD reigneth. <sup>(32)</sup> Let the sea roar, and the fulness thereof: let the fields rejoice, and all that *is* therein. <sup>(33)</sup> Then shall the trees of the wood sing out at the presence of the LORD, because he cometh to judge the earth. <sup>(34)</sup> *a*O give thanks unto the LORD; for *he is* good; for his mercy *endureth* for ever. <sup>(35)</sup> And say ye, Save us, O God of our salvation, and gather us together, and deliver us from the heathen, that we may give thanks to thy holy name, *and* glory in thy praise. <sup>(36)</sup> Blessed *be* the LORD God of Israel for ever and ever.

And all *b* the people said, Amen, and praised the LORD.

<sup>(37)</sup> So he left there before the ark of the covenant of the LORD Asaph and his brethren, to minister before the ark continually, as every day's work required: <sup>(38)</sup> and Obed-edom with their brethren, threescore and eight; Obed-edom also the son of Jeduthun and Hosah *to be* porters: <sup>(39)</sup> and Zadok the priest, and his brethren the priests,

*a* Ps. 107. 1, & 118. 1, & 136. 1.

*b* Deut. 27. 15.

---

**The world also shall be stable.**—A line, which precedes this in the psalm, is omitted here, to the detriment of the sense. That line—"Say ye among the nations, Jehovah is king"—begins the fourth strophe of the original hymn, but is here strangely transferred to verse 31.

<sup>(31)</sup> **Let the heavens be glad, and let the earth rejoice.**—In the Hebrew, the initial letters of these words form an acrostic of the sacred Name of Jehovah; and those of the first half of verse 32 make up *Iahu*, another form of the Name.

**And let men say.**—An adaptation of Ps. xcvi. 10: "*Say ye among the nations.*"

<sup>(32)</sup> **Let the fields rejoice.**—Here begins the fifth strophe of the original psalm.

**Fields.**—Heb., *the field*, or *open country*. Psalm xcvi. has an archaic spelling of the word (*sādai*), which is here modernised (*sādèh*).

**Rejoice.**—*Exult* (not the same word as in verse 31).

<sup>(33)</sup> **At the presence of.**—The compound preposition of verse 30. The climax of the psalm—"He shall judge the world in righteousness, and peoples in his faithfulness"—is here omitted; and this long and heterogeneous composition terminates with verses borrowed from a third source.

<sup>(34)</sup> **O give thanks unto the Lord . . .**—Several of the later psalms begin with this beautiful liturgic formula. (See Pss. cvi., cvii., cxviii., cxxxvi.; and comp. Jer. xxxiii. 11.) The ode thus concludes with the thought from which it started (verse 8).

<sup>(35, 36)</sup> See Ps. cvi. 47, 48.

<sup>(35)</sup> **And say ye.**—Not in Ps. cvi. 47. The compiler or interpolator has added it here in order to connect verse 34 (Ps. cvi. 1) with verse 35 (Ps. cvi. 47). It was doubtless suggested by Ps. xcvi. 10: "Say ye among the nations, The Lord reigneth."

**O God of our salvation.**—The psalm has "Jehovah our God."

**Gather us.**—The phrase used in Jer. xxxii. 37, and many other places, of Israel's restoration from exile.

**And deliver us.**—Not in the psalm, where the words "gather us from among the heathen" certainly refer to the dispersion. This reference is eliminated by the compiler's insertion.

**Glory in thy praise.**—"Glory" (*hishtabbēah*) is a common Aramaic word, found only here (and in Ps. cvi.) in the Old Testament.

<sup>(36)</sup> **Blessed be the Lord God of Israel.**—The *Bĕrāchāh* or benedictory close of the fourth book of the Psalter. This doxology did not form part of the original psalm, which closed with verse 35 (Ps. cvi. 47). After the psalms had been edited in their present arrangement of five books, each concluding with a doxology, these doxologies came in time to be sung in liturgical service as integral parts of the psalms to which they were appended.

**And all the people said, Amen.**—Ps. cvi. 48 has, "And let all the people say, Amen. Hallelujah." The chronicler, or rather the interpolator of his work, has altered a liturgical direction, or rubric, into a historical statement suitable to the occasion to which his long ode is assigned. Instances of a like free handling of fixed formulas may be seen in 2 Chron. v. 13 and Ezra iii. 11.

Those who hold the chronicler himself responsible for this thanksgiving ode, find in it a weighty indication of the fact that the Psalter already existed in its present shape at his epoch. The historian might, of course, have inserted such a composition in his work, as fairly and freely as such writers as Thucydides and Livy have put ideal speeches into the mouths of their leading characters; but, for reasons already stated, we do not think that the ode should be ascribed to his pen.

<sup>(37–42)</sup> Resumption and conclusion of the narrative suspended at verse 7.

<sup>(37)</sup> **So (and) he left there.**—Were the above ode interposed by the chronicler himself, he might better have written, "And David left."

**As every day's work required.**—Literally, *for a day's business in its own day*—*i.e.*, to perform the services appointed for each day. (Comp. Exod. v. 13.)

<sup>(38)</sup> **And Obed-edom with (and) their brethren.**—The pronoun *their* shows that a word or words have fallen out. It is simplest to supply "Hosah," and render: *And* (he left there) *Obed-edom and Hosah and their brethren, sixty-eight persons.* The construction, however, is altered from that of verse 37: "Asaph and his brethren." (Comp. verse 39.)

**Obed-edom also the son of Jeduthun.**—This repetition is tautologous, but hardly obscure. Chap. xxvi. 8 assigns sixty-two members to the house of Obed-edom.

**Jeduthun.**—Not the Merarite minstrel (chap. vi. 44, Ethan). Obed-edom was a Korhite, *i.e.*, a Kohathite (chap. xxvi. 1—4).

<sup>(39)</sup> The narrative now passes from the tent on Zion to the Mosaic tabernacle at Gibeon. The establishment of the Ark in its new abode was the inauguration of a new national sanctuary. But the old one at Gibeon was not therefore abandoned. On the contrary, David

before the tabernacle of the LORD in the high place that *was* at Gibeon, <sup>(40)</sup> to offer burnt offerings unto the LORD upon the altar of the burnt offering continually ¹ morning and evening, and *to do* according to all that is written in the law of the LORD, which he commanded Israel; <sup>(41)</sup> and with them Heman and Jeduthun, and the rest that were chosen, who were expressed by name, to give thanks to the LORD, because his mercy *endureth* for ever; <sup>(42)</sup> and with them Heman and Jeduthun with trumpets and cymbals for those that should make a sound, and with musical instruments of God. And the sons of Jeduthun *were* ² porters. <sup>(43)</sup> And all the people departed every man to his house: and David returned to bless his house.

CHAPTER XVII.—<sup>(1)</sup> Now *it came to pass, as David sat in his house, that David said to Nathan the prophet, Lo, I dwell in an house of cedars, but the ark of the covenant of the LORD *remaineth*

¹ Heb., *in the morning and in the evening.*
² Heb., *for the gate.*
*a* 2 Sam. 7. 1, &c.

---

either instituted or formally recognised the priesthood of Zadok therein.

**And Zadok.**—The name is preceded in the Hebrew by the sign of the accusative case, and therefore depends on the verb *he left* (verse 37).

**The priest.**—*Par excellence*—*i.e.*, the High Priest (1 Sam. i. 9, ii. 11; 2 Kings xi. 9, 15).

**In the high place.**—See 1 Kings iii. 3, 4.

<sup>(40)</sup> **Continually morning and evening.**—The *Tamid*, or regular burnt offering of a lamb at dawn and sunset, with its food offering and drink offering, as prescribed in Exod. xxix. 38, *sqq.*, and Num. xxviii. 3, *sqq.*

**And to do.**—Literally, *and for everything that is written*, viz., all the other prescribed sacrifices and duties of the priests. Nothing is here said of similar duties of the priests before the Ark on Zion. But it ought not to be argued from this omission that in the chronicler's opinion only choral services took place there. If, as we have supposed, Abiathar was attached to David's sacred tent, sacrifice must have been offered there as well as at Gibeon. (Comp. chap. xviii. 16.) The present account says nothing of this, because the writer is mainly interested in the service of song. (See 1 Kings viii. 1—4.)

<sup>(41)</sup> The narrative returns to its principal topic—the Levitical minstrels.

**And with them** (Zadok and his brethren) **Heman and Jeduthun.**—These two masters of song ministered in the tabernacle at Gibeon, as their colleague Asaph did in the tent on Zion.

**Who were expressed** (enrolled) **by name.**—Chap. xii. 31. Their names are not given here, but they may be partially included in the list of chap. xv. 19—24. Asaph's corps has been individually specified at verse 5, perhaps as the more important body.

**To give thanks to the Lord.**—In describing the chief function of the choirs stationed at Gibeon, the chronicler repeats the liturgical formula of verse 34; probably with an allusion to odes like Ps. cxxxvi., in which these words constitute a continual refrain.

<sup>(42)</sup> **And with them Heman and Jeduthun.**—The last verse began with the same words, a fact which renders them suspicious here. The LXX., Syriac, and Arabic omit the proper names.

**With trumpets . . . with musical instruments.**—The prepositions are wanting in the Hebrew text, which might be rendered thus: "And with them [viz., Heman and Jeduthun] were clarions and cymbals for persons playing aloud [comp. chap. xvi. 5], and instruments of sacred music." From chap. xv. 9, compared with chap. xvi. 5, it appears that the three conductors (Asaph, Heman, and Jeduthun) played cymbals only, to accent the time; and from chap. xv. 24 and chap. xvi. 6, we know that the clarions were blown by priests. Omitting as spurious the names of the two leaders, who are not likely to have had the custody of the various instruments of their choirs, the meaning of the verse is simply that the Levitical minstrels were provided with proper instruments to accompany their singing.

**Musical instruments of God.**—Literally, *instruments of song of God*—*i.e.*, of sacred music. Harps and lutes are meant.

**Sons of Jeduthun.**—See verse 38. Obed-edom, son of Jeduthun, was a warder before the Ark. Thus the warders of both sanctuaries belonged to the same clan.

<sup>(43)</sup> This verse is a duplicate of 2 Sam. vi. 19, 20*a*.

**Departed.**—Plural; Samuel has singular.

**Returned.**—Rather, *went round* (chap. x. 14). Samuel has "returned," which in Hebrew is very similar.

The incident which in 2 Sam. vi. 20—23 here follows (Michal's encounter with David) is omitted by the chronicler as a matter of purely domestic interest, and therefore out of place in his history, which is mainly concerned with the sacred institutions. Chap. xv. 29. however, plainly *implies* the story.

### XVII.

1. David, desiring to build a house for God, receives from Nathan a Divine promise of perpetual dominion (verses 1—15). 2. His prayer (verses 16—27). This section is a duplicate of 2 Sam. vii. The differences are mostly verbal rather than essential, and are due, as usual, to a natural tendency to interpret and simplify archaisms and obscurities in the original narrative.

<sup>(1)</sup> **Now it came to pass, as David sat in his house.**—In both texts the story of this chapter naturally follows that of the removal of the Ark, although the events themselves appear to belong to a later period of David's reign, "when the Lord had given him rest round about from all his enemies" (2 Sam. vii. 1; comp. 1 Chron. xvii. 8). Verses 11—14 indicate some time before the birth of Solomon, but the date cannot be more exactly determined.

**David.**—Thrice in verses 1, 2, for which Samuel has "the king." The chronicler loves the name of his ideal sovereign.

**Sat.**—Dwelt.

**Lo.**—Samuel, "See, now."

**An house.**—The house—viz., that which Hiram's craftsmen had built (chap. xiv. 1, *sqq.*).

**Of cedars.**—A vivid allusion to the splendour of the palace, with its doors, walls, and ceilings of cedar wood.

*The Lord Forbids*     I. CHRONICLES, XVII.     *David to Build a Temple.*

under curtains. <sup>(2)</sup> Then Nathan said unto David, Do all that *is* in thine heart; for God *is* with thee.

<sup>(3)</sup> And it came to pass the same night, that the word of God came to Nathan, saying, <sup>(4)</sup> Go and tell David my servant, Thus saith the Lord, Thou shalt not build me an house to dwell in: <sup>(5)</sup> for I have not dwelt in an house since the day that I brought up Israel unto this day; but ¹ have gone from tent to tent, and from *one* tabernacle *to an-other.* <sup>(6)</sup> Wheresoever I have walked with all Israel, spake I a word to any of the judges of Israel, whom I commanded to feed my people, saying, Why have ye not built me an house of cedars? <sup>(7)</sup> Now therefore thus shalt thou say unto my servant David, Thus saith the Lord of hosts, I took thee from the sheepcote, *even* ² from following the sheep, that thou shouldest be ruler over my people Israel: <sup>(8)</sup> and I have been with thee whithersoever thou hast walked, and have cut off all thine enemies from before thee, and have made thee a name like the name of the great men that *are* in the earth. <sup>(9)</sup> Also I will ordain a place for my people Israel, and will plant them, and they shall dwell in their place, and shall be moved no more; neither shall the children of

<sup>1</sup> Heb., *have been.*
<sup>2</sup> Heb., *from after.*

---

" Cedar of Labnana " (Lebanon) was in great request with the Assyrian monarchs of a later age for palace-building.

**Under curtains**—*i.e.*, in a tent (Hab. iii. 7). Samuel has, "dwelleth amid the curtain" (collect.). The verb is omitted here for brevity.

<sup>(2)</sup> **Do.**—Samuel, "Go, do."

**All that is in thine heart.**—According to Hebrew ideas, the heart was the seat of the mind and will, as well as of the emotions. But even the great Greek Aristotle, seven centuries later than David, supposed the brain to be merely a kind of cooling counterpoise to the heat of the liver.

**God.**—Samuel, "Jehovah;" but in last verse, "ark of God."

<sup>(3)</sup> **The same night.**—The words indicate a dream as the method of communication (Job iv. 13; 1 Sam. xxvii. 6).

<sup>(4)</sup> **David my servant.**—Samuel, "unto my servant, unto David."

**Thou shalt not build me an house to dwell in.**—Rather, *It is not thou that shalt build me the house to dwell in.* Samuel, interrogatively, implying a negation, "Wilt *thou* build me a house for me to dwell in?" The chronicler, thinking of the famous Temple of Solomon, writes, "*the* house."

<sup>(5)</sup> **Since the day that I brought up Israel** ("out of Egypt," Samuel) **unto this day.**—The construction, as compared with Samuel, is simplified, and the sentence abbreviated.

**But have gone . . .**—Literally, *and I became from tent to tent, and from dwelling.* This is clearly too brief for sense; some words must have fallen out, or the reading of Samuel may be original here. The phrase " and I became " almost demands a participle, and the one actually read in Samuel may be here disguised under the expression translated "from tent." A slight further change (in the prepositions) will give the sense: "And I continued walking in a tent and in a dwelling." Perhaps, however, the original text was, "and I walked from tent to tent, and from dwelling to dwelling;" alluding to the various sanctuaries anciently recognised, such as Bethel (Judges xx. 18, 26), Mizpeh (Judges xi. 11; 1 Sam. x. 17), and Shiloh. The word " dwelling " (*mishkân*) is a more general term than tent. It includes the sacred tent and its surrounding court.

<sup>(6)</sup> **Wheresoever.**—*As long as . . .* Literally, *In all that . . .*

**With** (in) **all Israel.**—Samuel, "in (among) all the sons of Israel." (Comp. Lev. xxvi. 11, 12; Deut. xxiii. 15.)

**The judges of Israel.**—Samuel has "tribes." The term " judges " would be more intelligible in later times, and has probably been substituted for the more difficult original expression. The following clause seems to refer to individual rulers, but is not really incompatible with a reference to the ascendency or hegemony of different tribes at different epochs of Israelite history. (Comp. Gen. xlix. 10; 1 Chron. xxviii. 4; Ps. lxxviii. 67, 68.) The word " tribe " (*shêbet*) might only denote *clan,* or *house,* as in Judges xx. 12 (Heb.).

**To feed.**—*Shepherd,* or *tend*—*i.e.*, to govern. (Comp. Ps. lxxviii. 71.)

<sup>(7)</sup> **I took thee from the sheepcote . . .**—Comp. Ps. lxxviii. 70—72. The pronoun is emphatic: " I it was who took thee from the pasture."

**From following.**—Heb., *from behind.* Samuel has the older form of this preposition.

**That thou shouldest be.**—*That thou mightest become.*

**Ruler.**—*Nāgîd* (chap. ix. 11, 20). (Comp. chap. xi. 2.)

<sup>(8)</sup> **Whithersoever thou hast walked.**—Same phrase as in verse 6, " wheresoever," *i.e.*, throughout thy whole career.

**And have cut off all thine enemies.**—This appears to refer not merely to the death of Saul and the overthrow of his house, but also to the successful conclusion of some of the wars recorded in the following chapters. (Comp. also chap. xiv. 8—17.)

**And have made thee.**—Rather, *and I will make thee.*

**The great men.**—The sovereigns of Egypt and Babylon, of Tyre, and the Hittite states.

<sup>(9)</sup> **I will ordain a place for my people Israel, and will plant them.**—Comp. Exod. xv. 17; Ps. xliv. 2, 3. Although Israel had effected a settlement in Canaan, the history seems to show that down to the times of David the tribal boundaries were subject to great fluctuation, and the inroads of surrounding peoples made their tenure very uncertain.

**Them . . . they . . . their.**—Heb., *him . . . he . . . his*; Israel, the subject, being singular.

**In their place.**—*In his own stead,* or fixed habitation. (Comp. homestead, farmstead.)

**Shall be moved.**—*Shall be troubled,* or *disturbed.*

**Children of wickedness.**—*Sons of wickedness, i.e.*, wicked men; like " sons of Belial " (worthlessness).

*David is promised*     I. CHRONICLES, XVII.     *Blessings in his Seed.*

wickedness waste them any more, as at the beginning, <sup>(10)</sup> and since the time that I commanded judges *to be* over my people Israel. Moreover I will subdue all thine enemies. Furthermore I tell thee that the LORD will build thee an house. <sup>(11)</sup> And it shall come to pass, when thy days be expired that thou must go *to be* with thy fathers, that I will raise up thy seed after thee, which shall be of thy sons; and I will establish his kingdom. <sup>(12)</sup> He shall build me an house, and I will stablish his throne for ever. <sup>(13)</sup> *a* I will be his father, and he shall be my son: and I will not take my mercy away from him, as I took it from *him* that was before thee: <sup>(14)</sup> but I will settle him in mine house and in my kingdom for ever: and his throne shall be established for evermore.

<sup>(15)</sup> According to all these words, and according to all this vision, so did Nathan speak unto David.

*a* 2 Sam. 7. 14, 15.

---

**Waste them.**—An Aramaic usage of the verb. Samuel, "afflict them," which seems original. (Comp. Gen. xv. 13.)

**As at the beginning.**—Referring to the bondage in Egypt.

<sup>(10)</sup> **And since the time that I commanded judges.**—Heb., *from days that* . . . Samuel, more definitely, "from the day that I appointed judges over my people." This whole clause should not have been separated from verse 9, which it properly concludes. The allusion is to the oppressions undergone in the period of the judges, and the troubles of the former reign.

**Moreover** (and) **I will subdue all thine enemies.**—A continuation of the promises at the beginning of verse 9. "I will subdue the foes of the king, as I subdued the foes of the shepherd and the outlaw." (Comp. verse 8.) Instead of this, Samuel has, "And I will give thee rest from all thy enemies."

**Furthermore I tell thee** . . .—Literally, *And I have told thee, and a house will Jehovah build thee;*" that is, I have foretold it. (Comp. Isa. xl. 21, xlv. 21.) That which follows is a sort of ironical inversion of David's wish to build a house for the Lord. The term "house" is figurative (offspring), as in Ps. cxxvii. 1. (Comp. Gen. xxx. 3.) The reading of Samuel is, "And Jehovah hath [now] told thee [by my mouth] that a house will Jehovah make for thee." This looks original, with its rare construction of the perfect, which the chronicler has altered; its repetition of the most holy Name; and its less exact "make," which Chronicles improves into "build," with an eye to verses 4 and 6, as well as to the play on the word (*bānāh*, build; *bānim*, sons).

<sup>(11)</sup> Omit the mark indicating the beginning of a paragraph (¶).

**And it shall come to pass.**—In accordance with the promise, "The Lord will build thee an house" (verse 10). The phrase is wanting in Samuel, and should probably be supplied, with LXX.

**Be expired.**—*Are fulfilled* (perfect; Samuel has imperfect tense).

**That thou must go to be with thy fathers.**—Literally, *to go with thy fathers*—an unusual expression, for which Samuel has the ordinary, "and thou lie down with thy fathers." (Comp. 1 Kings ii. 2: "Go the way of all the earth.")

**Which shall be** (shall arise or come, Gen. xvii. 16) **of thy sons.**—Samuel has the more original, "which shall go forth from thy bowels." The chronicler has paraphrased this, to suit the taste of a later age.

**His kingdom.**—Heb., *malkûthô*—a later word than the synonym in Samuel (*mamlaktô*).

<sup>(12)</sup> **He.**—The emphatic word.

**Build me.**—Samuel, "for my name." (See 1 Kings viii. 29, ix. 3.)

**His throne.**—Samuel, "throne of his kingdom"—a characteristic abridgment.

<sup>(13)</sup> **I will be his father** . . .—Heb., *I* (on my part) *will become a father unto him, and he* (on his part) *shall become a son to me.* (Comp. Ps. ii. 7.) After these words, Samuel adds : "If he commit iniquity I will chasten him with the rod of men, and with the stripes of the children of men." The omission is probably not a mere abridgment. The reference in this prophecy looks beyond Solomon to Him of whom the greatest princes of the house of David were but imperfect types. The warning here omitted was amply fulfilled in the history of Solomon and his successors; but it could not apply to the true Anointed of Jehovah, and is therefore suppressed as a transitory element in the prophecy.

**And I will not take my mercy away.**—Samuel, "and my mercy shall not depart"—the same verb in a different form. But the LXX., Syriac, and Vulgate there agree with Chronicles.

**As I took it** (away) **from him that was before thee.**—Samuel, "as I took it away from Saul whom I took away from before thee;" repeating the same verb thrice. Our text is probably more correct. So Vulg. and LXX. virtually; but Syriac, "My mercies shall not depart from him, as I made [them] depart from Saul who was before thee."

<sup>(14)</sup> **But I will settle him** (Heb., *make him stand*) **in mine house and in my kingdom.**—Samuel, "and thine house and thy kingdom shall be maintained for ever *before thee;* thy throne," &c.; where, however, the LXX. and Syriac have "before me," which agrees better with our text. The change of persons in our verse brings out more clearly the theocratic nature of the Davidic kingdom. Solomon and his successors were to reign as vicegerents of Jehovah.

<sup>(15)</sup> **According to all these words, and according to all this vision.**—The matter of this prophecy (verses 3—15) undoubtedly rests upon authentic tradition. Neither the compiler of Samuel, however, nor the chronicler professes to give an exact report of the words of Nathan, as if they had been taken down on the spot, as they were uttered, by some shorthand reporter. The modern demand for literal accuracy was unknown to Oriental antiquity. Where the two narratives vary, sometimes Samuel, sometimes the Chronicle, contains the more original form of the tradition. Verse 15 (2 Sam. vii. 17), in fact, seems to imply that the essence rather than the actual words of the oracle is given.

2. David's prayer (verses 16—27). The remarks on verse 15 apply generally to this section also. The prayer

*David's Prayer*      I. CHRONICLES, XVII.      *and Thanksgiving.*

(16) And David the king came and sat before the LORD, and said, Who *am* I, O LORD God, and what *is* mine house, that thou hast brought me hitherto? (17) And yet this was a small thing in thine eyes, O God; for thou hast *also* spoken of thy servant's house for a great while to come, and hast regarded me according to the estate of a man of high degree, O LORD God. (18) What can David *speak* more to thee for the honour of thy servant? for thou knowest thy servant. (19) O LORD, for thy servant's sake, and according to thine own heart, hast thou done all this greatness, in making known all *these* [1] great things. (20) O LORD, *there is* none like thee, neither *is there any* God beside thee, according to all that we have heard with our ears. (21) And what one nation in the earth *is* like thy people Israel, whom God went to redeem *to be* his own people, to make thee a name of greatness and terribleness, by driving out nations from before thy people, whom thou hast redeemed out of Egypt? (22) For thy people Israel didst thou make thine own people for ever; and

[1] Heb. *greatnesses.*

---

undoubtedly breathes the genuine Davidic spirit, even if it be merely an ideal soliloquy. But why may not David himself have recorded the substance of it as a memorial?

**(16) Sat before the Lord.**—In the tent of the Ark.
**And said.**—Comp. Ps. xviii., title.
**Who am I.**—The longer form of the pronoun *I* is used in Samuel (*dnokhî;* here *'ani*).
**O Lord God.**—Heb., *Jehovah Elohim.* Samuel has "Adonai Jehovah," which is more original. David addresses God as "my Lord, Jehovah;" just as in verses 4, 7, God speaks of David as "my servant." (Comp. the frequent style of the Assyrian kings, who speak of their wars as undertaken in the service of the gods their lords.)
**Mine house.**—My family.
**Hitherto.**—To this pitch of greatness. With this and the next verse, compare David's last words (2 Sam. xxiii. 5).

**(17) And yet.**—Samuel has the word here supplied in italics. David says, "My unlooked-for exaltation was not enough: thou hast also revealed to me the far future of my offspring."
**O God.**—Here and at the end of the verse Samuel again has "my Lord, Jehovah."
**Also.**—Samuel has this word in the text.
**And hast regarded me according to the estate of a man of high degree.**—The Hebrew is obscure. Samuel has simply, "and this [is] the law of man, my Lord Jehovah." The word "law" (*tôrāh*) has been supposed to mean *manner* or *custom* in this place, but it is not used in that sense elsewhere. Its strict sense is *teaching.* (Comp. Isa. viii. 16, 20, where the oracles delivered to the prophet are called *tôrāh.*) The rendering therefore is, *and this* (thy gracious revelation) *is a lesson to mankind.* Our text demands one slight alteration, in accordance with this. Read *tôrāh* for *tôr*, and then we may translate: *"and thou regardest me* (LXX., ἐπεῖδες: comp. Luke i. 48) *like man's teaching* (Ps. xxxii. 8) *that bringeth up* (same verb, Ezek. xix. 2), O Lord God;" that is to say, Thy revelation is a part of my moral discipline, like the instruction which men give their children. David was not allowed to build the Temple, which was so far a check; but encouragement was added to the prohibition by the wisdom of his heavenly Teacher. If we might assume the other sense of *tôrāh*, we might render: *and thou regardest me after the manner of men that exalteth,* that is, as human benefactors help on those whom they favour. The old versions give no help.

**(18)** Samuel has the omitted "speak." (Comp. Ps. cxx. 3.) The word translated "for the honour," may be a corruption of that for "to speak."

**Of thy servant?**—The Hebrew term is in the accusative case, and should be omitted as a mistaken repetition of the same word at the end of the verse.

**(19) O Lord.**—Not in Samuel. Probably belongs to end of last verse.
**For thy servant's sake.**—Comp. Ps. cxxxii. 10; 2 Chron. vi. 42. Samuel has the more original "for thy word's sake." (Comp. verse 23, and chap. xvi. 15.)
**Heart**—*i.e.*, purpose, intent.
**In making known all these great things** (greatnesses).—The repetition "greatness . . . greatnesses" is probably a scribe's error. Samuel has the right text: "Thou hast done all this greatness" (work of power, δύναμις), viz., informing Thy servant of what shall be hereafter. Isaiah makes the miracle of prediction a special difference between the true God and idols (Isa. xli. 21—29, xlv. 11, 21).

**(20)** One or two words are omitted. (See 2 Sam. vii. 22: "Wherefore thou art great, O Lord God, for there is none," &c. Comp. Isa. xlvi. 9, xlv. 18, 5, 6, &c.; Deut. xxxiii. 26; and for the end of the verse, Ps. xliv. 1; Exod. x. 2; Deut. iv. 9.)

**(21) And what one nation in the earth.**—Rather, *And who is like Thy people Israel, a single* (isolated) *race on the earth?* (Comp. Num. xxiii. 9.)
**Nation** (*gôy*)—*i.e.*, race; a people considered as united by common blood, speech, country.
**People** ('*ām*)—*i.e.*, a political community, social union, or state, owning one sovereign.
**Whom God went . . .**—Literally, *which God went* (marched) *to redeem to Himself as a people.* Samuel has "which gods went."
**To make thee a name.**—That is, for Thyself, God. Samuel has "for him," in the same sense.
**A name of greatness and terribleness.**—Both nouns are plural, and imply renown for great and terrible deeds.
**By driving.**—*To drive;* parallel with "to redeem" and "to make."
**Nations.**—Samuel adds, "and his gods." The text of this verse in Samuel is corrupt (comp. the LXX.), and perhaps the added phrase is spurious. But, on the other hand, the chronicler may have omitted it because, like Isaiah, he regarded the heathen deities as non-entities. In earlier times, foreign gods were spoken of as real beings, subordinate to Jehovah. (Comp. the LXX. rendering of Deut. xxxii. 8.)

**(22) For thy people Israel . . .**—Literally, *And Thou gavest* (Samuel, *confirmedst it*) *Thy people Israel unto Thyself for a people.* Our reading is probably a result of partial obliteration.

thou, LORD, becamest their God. <sup>(23)</sup> Therefore now, LORD, let the thing that thou hast spoken concerning thy servant and concerning his house be established for ever, and do as thou hast said. <sup>(24)</sup> Let it even be established, that thy name may be magnified for ever, saying, The LORD of hosts *is* the God of Israel, *even* a God to Israel: and *let* the house of David thy servant *be* established before thee. <sup>(25)</sup> For thou, O my God, <sup>1</sup> hast told thy servant that thou wilt build him an house: therefore thy servant hath found *in his heart* to pray before thee. <sup>(26)</sup> And now, LORD, thou art God, and hast promised this goodness unto thy servant: <sup>(27)</sup> now therefore <sup>2</sup> let it please thee to bless the house of thy servant, that it may be before thee for ever: for thou blessest, O LORD, and *it shall be* blessed for ever.

CHAPTER XVIII. — <sup>(1)</sup> Now after this <sup>a</sup>it came to pass, that David smote the Philistines, and subdued them, and took Gath and her towns out of the hand of the Philistines. <sup>(2)</sup> And he smote Moab; and the Moabites became

<sup>1</sup> Heb., *hast revealed the ear of thy servant.*

<sup>2</sup> Or, *it hath pleased thee.*

B.C. cir. 1040.

*a* 2 Sam. 8. 1, &c.

---

**And thou, Lord . . .**—Literally, *and Thou, Jehovah, becamest unto them for a God.* (See Gen. xvii. 7, 8, xxviii. 21; Exod. vi. 3, 7.)

<sup>(23)</sup> **Lord.**—Samuel adds "God."

**Let the thing . . . be established.**—*Let the word* (promise) *be upheld, maintained, assured.* Samuel has a different verb, "establish thou."

<sup>(24)</sup> **Let it even be established.**—"Yea, let it be assured." This repetition is wanting in Samuel.

**The Lord of hosts is the God of Israel . . .**—"Jehovah Sabaoth, God of Israel, is God to Israel." "God of Israel" is not read here in Samuel, but in the next verse.

**And let the house of David . . . be established.**—"Let be" is wanting in the Hebrew, and the sentence might be taken as part of what men are to say hereafter in praise of God: "The house of David thy servant is established before thee." Samuel, however, inserts the verb "let it become," or "shall become."

<sup>(25)</sup> **O my God.**—Samuel: "Jehovah Sabaoth, God of Israel."

**Hast told thy servant that thou wilt build him an house.**—Literally, *hast uncovered the ear of Thy servant, to build him a house.* Samuel has the more usual construction: "saying, A house I will build thee." (Comp. 1 Sam. ix. 15.)

**Hath found in his heart.**—Rather, *hath found his heart*—*i.e.,* hath taken courage. The noun is expressed in Samuel. As to its omission here, comp. chap. xiv. 1. The phrase is unique in Hebrew.

**To pray.**—Samuel adds, "this prayer."

<sup>(26)</sup> **Lord, thou art God.**—*Jehovah, Thou art the* (true) *God.* Samuel: "my Lord Jehovah." The chronicler omits the clause which follows in Samuel: "and thy words become truth" (prove true).

<sup>(27)</sup> **Now therefore let it please thee.**—Rather, *and now Thou hast willed to bless.* Samuel: "and now be willing, and bless."

**For thou blessest, O Lord.**—*For Thou, Jehovah, hast blessed.* Samuel is, as usual, fuller: "For thou, my Lord Jehovah, hast spoken [promised], and in virtue of thy blessing thy servant's house shall be blessed for ever." Num. xxii. 6 illustrates our text.

### XVIII.—XX.

This section represents the warlike aspect of David's character, just as chaps. xv.—xvii. portrayed him from the religious point of view, as zealous for the due observance of the Divine order in worship. The narratives are closely parallel to the corresponding ones in 2 Samuel, and are given in the same order. The variations, such as they are, may be accounted for (1) by mistakes of copyists; (2) by the chronicler's habit of explaining difficult expressions, abridging what appeared needlessly prolix, and adding here and there small details from another source.

### XVIII.

1. A summary account of David's wars of conquest (verses 1—13). 2. His internal administration (verses 14—17). (Comp. 2 Sam. viii., and the Notes on that chapter.)

(1—3) Reduction of the Philistines, Moabites, and Arameans of Zobah.

<sup>(1)</sup> **Now after this it came to pass.**—Literally, *And it befel afterwards.* This expression does not put the contents of this chapter into direct chronological sequence with those of the last. (Comp. Note on chap. xvii. 1.) The formula of the original history, from which both Samuel and Chronicles have derived a chief part of their substance, has been taken over without modification, after the manner of Oriental compilers. We may, therefore, regard the phrase as a mere mark of transition in the narrative.

**Gath and her towns.**—Heb., *her daughters,* that is, outlying dependencies. Samuel has, "And David took the bridle [control, supremacy] of the metropolis [mother-city] out of the hand," &c. The chronicler or his authority has interpreted this curious expression (*mètheg hā'ammāh*). If at the time Gath was the chief city of Philistia, and David made it recognise his suzerainty by payment of tribute, the phrases of both books are intelligible. In Solomon's time Gath was ruled by a king, Achish (1 Kings ii. 39), but he was hardly independent of Solomon. (Comp. 1 Kings iv. 24.) The general sense is the same if *mètheg hā'ammāh* be rendered *the bridle of the arm*—*i.e.,* the sovereign control, or supremacy.

<sup>(2)</sup> Much abridged, as compared with Samuel. After the words "he smote Moab," we read there of a partial massacre of the conquered. The omission is scarcely due to any unfair bias on the part of the chronicler. Indeed, as a Jew, possessed with all the national exclusiveness and hatred of the aliens who always misunderstood and sometimes cruelly oppressed his people, he was not likely to regard the slaughter of captive Moabites from a modern point of view. (Comp. Ezra vi. 21, ix., x.; Neh. ii. 19, iv., vi., xiii.) Besides, he has related the cruel treatment of the Ammonite prisoners (chap. xx. 3). (See the prophecy, Num. xxiv. 17.)

David's servants, *and* brought gifts. ⁽³⁾ And David smote ¹Hadarezer king of Zobah unto Hamath, as he went to stablish his dominion by the river Euphrates. ⁽⁴⁾ And David took from him a thousand chariots, and seven thousand horsemen, and twenty thousand footmen: David also houghed all the chariot *horses*, but reserved of them an hundred chariots. ⁽⁵⁾ And when the Syrians of ²Damascus came to help Hadarezer king of Zobah, David slew of the Syrians two and twenty thousand men. ⁽⁶⁾ Then David put *garrisons* in Syria-damascus; and the Syrians became David's servants, *and* brought gifts. Thus the LORD preserved David whithersoever he went. ⁽⁷⁾ And David took the shields of gold that were on the servants of Hadarezer, and brought them to Jerusalem. ⁽⁸⁾ Likewise from ³Tibhath, and from Chun, cities of Hadarezer, brought David very much brass, wherewith *Solomon made the

¹ Or, *Hadadezer*, 2 Sam. 8. 3.

² Heb., *Darmesek*.

³ Called in the book of Samuel *Betah and Berothai*.

*a* 1 Kings 7. 23; 2 Chr. 4. 15.

---

**And the Moabites became.**—Literally, *and they became*—viz., Moab. The name of the country denotes the people. Samuel has "and Moab [*i.e.*, the country] became" (verb singular feminine).

**David's servants.**—Samuel, "to David for servants."

**And brought gifts.**—Literally, *bringers of an offering*—i.e., tribute. Similar notices are common in the Assyrian inscriptions. (Comp. 1 Kings iv. 21; 2 Kings iii. 4; and the famous Moabite inscription of which the fragments are now in the Louvre, and which records Mesha's revolt against the successor of Ahab.)

⁽³⁾ **Hadarezer.**—Samuel, "Hadadezer" (*Hadad is help*), which is correct. Hadad was a Syrian god, identical with Dadda (Rimmon), worshipped from the Euphrates to Edom and North Arabia. Comp. the royal names Benhadad and Abdadad (*i.e.*, servant of Hadad, like Obadiah, servant of Iahu), which last occurs on Syrian coins, and the Notes on 2 Kings v. 18; 1 Chron. i. 46. Samuel adds, "son of Rehob."

**Zobah unto Hamath.**—Rather, *Zobah towards Hamath*. The word (*Hămáthāh;* not in Samuel) defines the position of Zobah. (Comp. 2 Sam. viii. 8; Ezek. xlvii. 16.) The town of Zobah lay somewhere near Emesa (*Homs*), and not far from the present *Yabrúd*, north-east of Damascus. (The Assyrian monarch Assurbanipal mentions the towns of *Yabrudu* and *Çubiti*—i.e., Zobah—in his Annals.) Its kings are spoken of in 1 Sam. xiv. 47. Hadadezer appears to have brought the whole country under a single sceptre.

**Hamath.**—See chap. xiii. 5, and 2 Chron. viii. 4. The town lay in the valley of the Upper Orontes, west of Zobah, and north of Hermon and Damascus.

**As he** (Hadarezer) **went.**—The occasion intended appears to be that whereof the particulars are given at chap. xix. 16—19.

**To stablish his dominion.**—Heb., *to set up his hand*—*i.e.*, "his power." Samuel has a different word, *to recover* his power, or *repeat* his attack.

**The river Euphrates.**—The Hebrew text of Samuel has "the river." Our text explains.

⁽⁴⁾ **A thousand chariots, and seven thousand horsemen.**—Hebrew text of Samuel, "a thousand and seven hundred horsemen." The territory of Zobah lay somewhere in the great plain of Aram. Hadadezer would, therefore, be strong in chariots and horses, and our reading is probably correct. (Comp. chap. xix. 18.)

**Houghed.**—*Hamstrung*—*i.e.*, cut the sinews of the hind legs, so as to disable them.

**Chariot horses.**—The same Hebrew term has just been rendered *chariots*. It means also chariot soldiers.

David reserved a hundred chariots, with their horses, probably for his own use. Horses were always a luxury in Israel. (Comp. Isa. ii. 7.) Solomon recruited his stud from Egypt. (Comp. the prohibition, Deut. xvii. 16.)

⁽⁵⁾ **And when the Syrians of Damascus came.**—Literally, *And Aram of Damascus came*. The verb is masculine here, feminine in Samuel. (Comp. verse 2.)

**Damascus.**—Heb., *Darmèseq*, a late form, occurring again in 2 Chron. xxviii. 5, 23 (= ancient *Dammèseq*). In Syriac the name is similar: *Darmèsûq*. The Arabic is *Dimashqu*, the cuneiform *Dimashqa* or *Dimmasqa*.

**David slew of the Syrians.**—Literally, *smote in Aram*. The preposition is partitive.

⁽⁶⁾ **Put garrisons.**—The noun here omitted in the Hebrew, probably by an oversight, occurs in Samuel. In chap. xi. 16 and 2 Chron. xvii. 2 it means "outpost," or "garrison;" in 1 Kings iv. 19, "prefects," or "pashas." The Targum of Samuel gives *strategi*, "generals;" Syriac and Arabic, "prefects" and "collectors;" LXX. and Vulg., "garrison." The Arabic here has "collectors and guards;" the Syriac, "commanders."

**Syria-damascus.**—*Aram of Damascus* (verse 5). (Comp. verse 2 for the next clause.)

**David's servants.**—*To David servants*—the order in Samuel.

**Thus.**—*And*.

**Preserved.**—Made victorious.

**Preserved David.**—Samuel has *'eth-David*—*i.e.*, the simple accusative; Chronicles, *le-David*, a late construction.

**Whithersoever he went.**—Same phrase as in chap. xvii. 6, 8.

**Shields.**—*Shiltê*. Probably "armour" or "arms." (Comp. 2 Kings xi. 10; 2 Chron. xxiii. 9, "the spears, and the shields, and the *sh'lātim;*" Ezek. xxvii. 11; Cant. iv. 4; Jer. li. 11, "quivers.") LXX. here, "golden collars" (Samuel, "bracelets"); Syriac and Arabic, "golden plates which hung on the horses;" Vulg., "quivers" (Samuel, "golden arms").

Hadadezer was not dethroned, but became a vassal king.

⁽⁷⁾ **On.**—Samuel, "to" = belonging to.

⁽⁸⁾ **Tibhath, and . . . Chun.**—Two unknown places. The names in Samuel are Betah and Berothai. Tebah occurs as an Aramean name in Gen. xxii. 24, of which "Tibhath" is a feminine form, and "Betah" probably a corruption. Syriac, "Tĕbah" and "Bĕrŭthi" in both places. So Arabic of Samuel, "Tābah" and "Barûti" (here "Himsa" and "Baalbec," probably by way of an explanation). The readings of the LXX., "Metebak" (or Masbach) in Samuel, and "Matebeth" here, support Tebah. Vulgate in Samuel, "Bete," but here "Thebath," obviously equivalent to Tibhath.

*The Presents*      I. CHRONICLES, XVIII.      *Dedicated to the Lord.*

brazen sea, and the pillars, and the vessels of brass. (9) Now when ¹Tou king of Hamath heard how David had smitten all the host of Hadarezer king of Zobah; (10) he sent ²Hadoram his son to king David, ³to enquire of his welfare, and ⁴to congratulate him, because he had fought against Hadarezer, and smitten him; (for Hadarezer ⁵had war with Tou;) and *with him* all manner of vessels of gold and silver and brass. (11) Them also king David dedicated unto the LORD, with the silver and the gold that he brought from all *these* nations; from Edom, and from Moab, and from the children of Ammon, and from the Philistines, and from Amalek. (12) Moreover Abishai the son of Zeruiah slew of the Edomites in the valley of salt eighteen thousand. (13) And he put garrisons in Edom; and all the Edomites became David's servants. Thus the LORD preserved David whithersoever he went. (14) So David reigned over all Israel, and executed judgment and justice among all his people. (15) And Joab the son of Zeruiah *was* over the host; and Jehoshaphat the son of Ahilud, ⁶recorder. (16) And Zadok the son of Ahitub, and ⁷Abimelech the son of Abiathar, *were* the priests; and ⁸Shavsha

<sub>1 Or, *Toi*, 2 Sam. 8. 9.</sub>
<sub>2 Or, *Joram*, 2 Sam. 8. 10.</sub>
<sub>3 Or, *to salute*.</sub>
<sub>4 Heb., *to bless*.</sub>
<sub>5 Heb., *was the man of wars*.</sub>
<sub>6 Or, *remembrancer*.</sub>
<sub>7 Called *Ahimelech*, 2 Sam. 8. 17.</sub>
<sub>8 Called *Seraiah*, 2 Sam. 8. 17, and *Shisha*, 1 Kin. 4. 3.</sub>

---

"Chun" is doubtless corrupt. All the versions support "Berothai" (LXX., "chosen cities;" comp. Heb., *bārōth*) except Arabic and Vulg. here.

**Much brass.**—*Copper* (as Job xxviii. 2), or *bronze* (an alloy of copper and tin, which was well known to the ancients). Samuel, "copper in abundance" (*harbēh*), an older form of expression.

**Wherewith Solomon made** . . .—Not in the Hebrew of Samuel, though LXX. adds it.

(9, 10) The King of Hamath's embassy to David.

(9) **Now when** . . .—*And Tou king of Hamath heard.* Samuel, "Toi." The Hebrew letters answering to *w* and *y* are often confused in MSS. Tō-ū is right; so LXX. and Vulg. in Samuel; Syriac, "Thŭ;" Arabic, "Tû'u." The Syriac here has "Phûl king of the Antiochenes" (!); the Arabic, "Phàwil king of Antioch," an apparent allusion to Pul the Assyrian (chap. v. 26). Professor Sayce believes he has read the name *Tu-ve-es*—that is, Toū—on the stones from Hamath, now in the British Museum.

(10) **He sent.**—Heb., *and he sent.*

**Hadoram.**—Samuel, "and Toi sent Joram" (LXX., "Jeddŭram"). Vulg., "Adoram;" but Syriac and Arabic, "Joram." Hadoram, or Adoram (*Hadar* or *Adar, is high*), seems right; but Joram, *i.e.*, Jehoram (*Jehovah is high*), may be correct, for it appears from an inscription of Sargon that the God of Israel was not unknown to the Hamathites. Sargon calls their king *Iahu-bihdi.*

**To congratulate.**—*Bless*—*i.e.*, pronounce him happy.

**Had war with Tou.**—*A man of wars* (a foeman) *of Tou was Hadadezer.*

**And** . . . **all manner** . . .—Samuel, "and in his hand [were] vessels of silver, and vessels of gold," &c. The clause is here curtailed.

(11) **He brought.**—Samuel, "dedicated." Chronicles avoids the tautology.

**These nations.**—*The nations*—*scil.*, "whom he had reduced" (Samuel).

**From Edom.**—Samuel, "from Aram," but LXX., Syriac, and Arabic, "Edom;" (Targum and Vulg., "Aram"). All the versions read "Edom" here, which appears correct. Edom and Moab were conterminous, and the reference includes *all* the nations whom David conquered and despoiled.

**And from Amalek** may refer to 1 Sam. xxx. 16, *seq.*, but more probably to an unrecorded campaign.

Samuel adds, "and from the spoil of Hadadezer son of Rehob, king of Zobah," which Chronicles omits, as implied already in verses 7, 8.

(12, 13) The reduction of Edom. The paragraph mark should be at verse 12, not verse 13.

(12) **Moreover Abishai** . . .—Heb., *And Abishai son of Zeruiah had smitten Edom in the Valley of Salt, eighteen thousand.*

In Samuel we read something quite different: "And David made a name, when he returned from his smiting Aram." "Aram" should be read Edom, as the LXX., Syriac, and Arabic have it. Perhaps, also, the text of Samuel is further corrupted. (Comp. 1 Kings xi. 15, and Ps. lx., title.) From a comparison of the three passages it appears that Edom took advantage of David's absence to invade Judah, whereupon the king detached a column of his forces, and sent them south under Joab and Abishai to repulse the new enemy.

**Valley of salt.**—2 Kings xiv. 7.

(13) **And he put garrisons** (or "prefects," verse 6) **in Edom.**—Samuel adds, "in all Edom he set garrisons," thus marking the complete subjugation of the country.

**Thus the Lord preserved David.**—See verse 6. David was victorious on all sides, north (verses 3—8), and south, and east, and west (verse 11). The six peoples whom he reduced had been the foes of his ill-fated predecessor (1 Sam. xiv. 47, 48).

(14—17) David's internal administration and high officers of state.

(14) **Executed.**—*Was doing*; a permanent state of things.

**Judgment and justice.**—*Right and justice*. The former is the quality, the latter the conduct which embodies it.

**Among.**—*For*, or *unto*.

(15) **Recorder.**—Literally, *Remembrancer*. LXX. and Vulg. render the word "over, or writer of, memoranda." Syriac and Arabic of Samuel have "leader," "director;" here they render literally. (Comp. 2 Sam. viii. 16; 2 Kings xviii. 18; 2 Chron. xxxiv. 8.)

(16) **Zadok**, of the line of Eleazar (chap. vi. 4—8). (Comp. chaps. xii. 28, xvi. 39; 2 Sam. viii. 17, xv. 24, xix. 11; 1 Kings i. 8, iv. 4.)

**Abimelech the son of Abiathar.**—Read *Ahimelech the son of Abiathar*. Samuel has "Ahimelech the son of Abiathar." Elsewhere Zadok and Abiathar figure as the priests of David's reign (comp. 2 Sam.

was scribe; <sup>(17)</sup> and Benaiah the son of Jehoiada *was* over the Cherethites and the Pelethites; and the sons of David were chief [1] about the king.

CHAPTER XIX.—<sup>(1)</sup> Now [a] it came to pass after this, that Nahash the king of the children of Ammon died, and his son reigned in his stead. <sup>(2)</sup> And David said, I will shew kindness unto Hanun the son of Nahash, because his father shewed kindness to me. And David sent messengers to comfort him concerning his father. So the servants of David came into the land of the children of Ammon to Hanun, to comfort him. <sup>(3)</sup> But the princes of the children of Ammon said to Hanun, [2] Thinkest thou that David doth honour thy father, that he hath sent comforters unto thee? are not his servants come unto thee for to search, and to overthrow, and to spy out the land? <sup>(4)</sup> Wherefore Hanun took David's servants, and shaved them, and cut off their garments in the midst hard by their buttocks, and sent them away. <sup>(5)</sup> Then there went *certain*, and told David how the men were served. And he sent to meet them : for the men were greatly ashamed. And the king said,

[1] Heb., *at the hand of the king.*

[a] 2 Sam. 10. 1, &c.

[2] Heb., *In thine eyes doth David, &c.*

---

xv. 29, 35), and as Abiathar was a son of the Ahimelech who was slain at Nob by Saul's orders (1 Sam. xxii. 20), it has been proposed to read here and in the parallel passage, "Abiathar the son of Ahimelech." The correction, however, is far from certain, inasmuch as an "Ahimelech son of Abiathar," who was priest in David's time, is mentioned thrice in chap. xxiv. 3, 6, 31, and this Ahimelech may have been acting as *locum tenens* for his father at the time when this brief list was drawn up. In the absence of details, it would be arbitrary to alter the text of four different passages of the Chronicles. In Samuel the Syriac and Arabic read "Abiathar son of Ahimelech," but here LXX., Vulg., Syriac, Arabic, all have "Ahimelech son of Abiathar."
Abiathar was of the lineage of Ithamar.
**Shavsha.** — Besides the variants in the margin, 2 Sam. xx. 25 has "Shĕva" (Heb. margin, *Shĕya*). *Seraiah* (with which comp. Israel) appears to be the original name. (Comp. Syriac and Arabic, "Sariyā.")
<sup>(17)</sup> **Cherethites and the Pelethites.**—2 Sam. viii. 18. The royal body-guard, for which office Oriental kings have always employed foreign mercenaries. Josephus calls them the body-guard (*Antiq.* vii. 5, § 4). The names are tribal in form, and as the Cherethites recur (Ezek. xxv. 16; Zeph. ii. 5) in connection with the Philistines (comp. 1 Sam. xxx. 14), and the name Pelethites resembles that of Philistines, it is natural to assume that David's guard was recruited from two Philistine tribes. (Comp. 2 Sam. xv. 18, where the Cherethites and Pelethites are mentioned along with a corps of Gittites.) The Targum of Samuel, and Syriac and Arabic of Chronicles, render "archers and slingers."
**Chief about the king.**—Heb., *the first at the king's hand*, or *side*, a paraphrase of what we read in Samuel: "were chief rulers" (*kôhănim*). *Kôhănim* is the common and only word for "priests," and has just occurred in that sense (verse 16). In 1 Kings iv. 5, as well as here, the term is said to denote not a sacerdotal, but a secular "minister." But this theory seems to be opposed to the facts of history. Under the monarchy the priests were brought into close relations with the king, owing to their judicial duties; and the chief priest of a royal sanctuary became one of the great officials of state (Amos vii. 11, 13). Such a position would be of sufficient importance to be filled by the princes of the blood. The chronicler, writing from the point of view of a later age, has substituted for the original term a phrase that would not offend contemporary feeling. In Samuel the LXX. renders "chief courtiers;" the other versions have "magnates," except the Vulg., which has "priests." Syriac of Chronicles, "magnates."

XIX.

The war with the sons of Ammon and their Aramæan allies. The chapter is a duplicate of 2 Sam. x. The story of David's kindness to Mephibosheth (2 Sam. ix.), creditable as it was to David, is omitted by the chronicler, as belonging rather to the private than the public history of the king.

<sup>(1)</sup> **Now it came to pass after this.**—The same phrase as at chap. xviii. 1; it has no chronological significance (see Note there). The conflict with Ammon, which has been glanced at in chap. xviii. 11, is now to be described at length (chaps. xix. 1—xx. 3), and in connection therewith the overthrow of Hadadezer (chap. xviii. 3—8) is again related, with additional details.

<sup>(2)</sup> **Nahash** Samuel omits, but adds "Hanun." The omissions in each are perhaps accidental. Saul's first campaign was against Nahash (1 Sam. xi.).
**Children of Ammon.** — Sons of Ammon, like "sons of Israel." The title calls attention to their tribal organisation.
**Because.**—*For.* Samuel, "according as."
**Shewed kindness to me.**—The Hebrew phrase, which answers to the Greek of Luke i. 72. (See Revised Version.)
The rest of the verse is made more perspicuous than in 2 Sam. x. 2 by slight changes and additions.

<sup>(3)</sup> **Are not his servants come . . . for to search, and to overthrow, and to spy out the land?**—Literally, *Is it not for to search . . . that his servants are come unto thee?* This is hardly an improvement on Samuel : "Is it not to search the city (Rabbath-Ammon, the capital), and to spy it out, and to overthrow it, that David hath sent his servants unto thee?" The Syriac and Arabic agree with Samuel in reading "city;" LXX. and Vulg., "land."

<sup>(4)</sup> **Shaved them**—*i.e.*, *the half of their beards* (Samuel).
**Hard by their buttocks.**—Literally, *unto the extremities.* The chronicler has substituted a more decorous term for the one which appears in Samuel.
**Cut off their garments.**—To look like captives (Isa. xx. 4).

<sup>(5)</sup> **Ashamed.**—Not the usual term (*bôsh*), but a stronger word, *confounded* (*niklam*; properly, *pricked,*

295

Tarry at Jericho until your beards be grown, and *then* return. ⁽⁶⁾ And when the children of Ammon saw that they had made themselves ¹odious to David, Hanun and the children of Ammon sent a thousand talents of silver to hire them chariots and horsemen out of Mesopotamia, and out of Syria-maachah, and out of Zobah. ⁽⁷⁾ So they hired thirty and two thousand chariots, and the king of Maachah and his people; who came and pitched before Medeba. And the children of Ammon gathered themselves together from their cities, and came to battle. ⁽⁸⁾ And when David heard *of it*, he sent Joab, and all the host of the mighty men. ⁽⁹⁾ And the children of Ammon came out, and put the battle in array before the gate of the city: and the kings that were come *were* by themselves in the field. ⁽¹⁰⁾ Now when Joab saw that ²the battle was set against him before and behind, he chose out of all the ³choice

---

¹ Heb., *to stink.*
² Heb., *the face of the battle was.*
³ Or, *young men.*

---

*wounded*). (Comp. Ps. xxxv. 4. where it forms a climax to the other.)

**Be grown.**—*Sprout*, or *shoot* (Judges xvi. 22, of Samson's hair).

**Jericho** lay on their road to the capital.

⁽⁶⁾ **And when the children of Ammon.**—Up to this point the narrative has substantially coincided with 2 Sam. x., and might have been derived immediately from it; but this and the following verses differ considerably from the older account, and add one or two material facts, which suggest another source.

**Made themselves odious.**—"Had become in bad odour." A unique (Aramaized) form of the same verb as is used in Samuel (*hithbā'ăshû* for *nib'ăshû*).

**A thousand talents of silver.**—The talent was a weight, not a coin, coined money being unknown at that epoch. The sum specified amounts to £400,000, estimating the silver talent at £400. This detail is peculiar to the Chronicles.

**Out of Mesopotamia, and out of Syria-maachah, and out of Zobah.**—*Out of Aram-naharaïm, and out of Aram-maachah*, &c. Samuel has, "And they hired Aram-beth-rehob and Aram-zobah, 20,000 foot, and the king of Maachah, 1,000 men, and the men (or *chieftain*) of Tôb, 12,000 men." Aram-naharaïm, *i.e.*, Aram of the two rivers, was the country between the Tigris and Euphrates (see Judges iii. 8); Aram-beth-rehob may have been one of its political divisions, and is perhaps to be identified with Rehoboth-hannahar (chap. i. 48), on the Euphrates. Another Rehoboth ("Rehoboth-ir," Gen. x. 11) lay on the Tigris, north-east of Nineveh, and was a suburb of that great city. Aram-maachah imply the dominions of "the king of Maachah," who is mentioned in verse 7; and Zobah, the Aram-zobah of Samuel. The chronicler makes no separate mention of the "men of Tôb" (Judges xi. 3), perhaps because they were subject to Hadadezer, and as such, included in his forces. The Syriac and Arabic here have "from Aram-naharaïm, Haran, Nisibis, and Edom."

⁽⁷⁾ **So they hired thirty and two thousand chariots, and the king of Maachah and his people.**—The account which the chronicler has followed here did not state the relative strength of the contingents, yet its estimate of the total number of the allied forces is in substantial accord with that of Samuel. The chronicler puts the total at 32,000 + the Maachathite contingent; Samuel at 32,000 + 1,000 Maachathites. The expression "32,000 chariotry" (*rèkeb*) is not to be pressed. The writer wished to lay proper stress on the chariots and cavalry as the chief arm of the Aramæan states, and at the same time to be as concise as possible. That he was not thinking of 32,000 chariots in the literal sense is clear, (1) because he must have known that an army would not consist of chariots only; (2) in chap. xviii. 4 he had already assigned to the army of Zobah its natural proportions of chariots, cavalry, and infantry. (Comp. verse 18, below.) The present text of Samuel can hardly be right, as it makes the whole army consist of infantry. (Comp. 2 Sam. viii 4.) The great plains of Aram were a natural training-ground for horsemen and charioteers.

**Who came and pitched** (their camp) **before Medeba.**—Another detail peculiar to the Chronicles. Medeba, the meeting-place of the Aramæan forces, lay south-east of Heshbon, on a site now known as *Madibiya*.

**And the children of Ammon gathered themselves...**—The muster of the Ammonites is not mentioned in Samuel.

⁽⁸⁾ **All the host of the mighty men.**—So the Hebrew text. The Hebrew margin and Samuel read "all the host," viz., the mighty men. The "mighty men" (*gibbôrîm*) were a special corps. (Comp. 1 Sam. xxiii. 13, xxvii. 8; 2 Sam. ii. 3, xvi. 6; 1 Kings i. 8.) Either, then, the term has a general sense here, or we must read, "and the mighty men."

⁽⁹⁾ **Before the gate of the city.**—Literally, *in the outlet of the city*. Samuel has "in the outlet of the gate." The city appears to have been Medeba (verse 7).

**And the kings that were come.**—Samuel repeats the names: "And Aram-zobah and Rehob, and the men of Tôb and Maachah."

**Were.**—Rather, *put the battle in array* (to be supplied from the former sentence).

**In the field.**—In the open country, or plain (*mishôr*) of Medeba (Josh. xiii. 9, 16), where there was room for the movements of cavalry and chariots.

⁽¹⁰⁾ **The battle was set against him before and behind.**—Literally, *the front of the battle had become towards him, front and rear*. The order of words is different in Samuel, and a preposition added ("on front and on rear"). The Ammonites lay in front of the city, their Aramæan allies at some distance away, in the plain. For Joab to attack either with his entire army would have been to expose his rear to the assault of the other. He therefore divided his forces.

**The choice of Israel.**—Literally, *the chosen* or *young warriors* (singular collective) *in Israel* (*i.e.*, in the Israelitish army). These Joab himself led against the Aramæans, as the most dangerous enemy, while he sent a detachment, under his brother Abishai, to cope with the Ammonites.

**Put them in array.**—Rather, *set the battle in array*, or *drew up against* ... (verse 17; chap. xii. 33). The same Hebrew phrase recurs in verse 11.

of Israel, and put *them* in array against the Syrians. (11) And the rest of the people he delivered unto the hand of ¹Abishai his brother, and they set *themselves* in array against the children of Ammon. (12) And he said, If the Syrians be too strong for me, then thou shalt help me: but if the children of Ammon be too strong for thee, then I will help thee. (13) Be of good courage, and let us behave ourselves valiantly for our people, and for the cities of our God: and let the LORD do *that which is* good in his sight.

(14) So Joab and the people that *were* with him drew nigh before the Syrians unto the battle; and they fled before him. (15) And when the children of Ammon saw that the Syrians were fled, they likewise fled before Abishai his brother, and entered into the city. Then Joab came to Jerusalem.

(16) And when the Syrians saw that they were put to the worse before Israel, they sent messengers, and drew forth the Syrians that *were* beyond the ²river: and ³Shophach the captain of the host of Hadarezer *went* before them. (17) And it was told David; and he gathered all Israel, and passed over Jordan, and came upon them, and set *the battle* in array against them. So when David had put the battle in array against the Syrians, they fought with him. (18) But the Syrians fled before Israel; and David slew of the Syrians seven thousand *men which fought in* chariots, and forty thousand footmen, and killed Shophach

1 Heb., *Abshai*.

2 That is, *Euphrates*.

3 Or, *Shobach*, 2 Sam. 10. 16.

---

(11) **They set themselves in array.**—Samuel, singular, as in verse 10.

(12) Literally, *If Aram prevail over me, thou shalt become to me for succour.* The word "succour" here is *tĕshû‘āh*, a less frequent synonym of *yĕshû‘āh*, the term in Samuel.

**I will help (succour) thee.**—Samuel, "I will march to succour thee." This verb is often rendered "to save," and the cognate noun, "salvation."

(13) **Be of good courage.**—The same verb was rendered "be strong" in verse 12.

**Let us behave ourselves valiantly.**—The same verb again, in reflexive form. Thus the whole runs literally: *Be strong, and let us shew ourselves strong!*

**And let the Lord do . . .**—Literally, *And Jehovah—the good in his own eyes may he do!* The order in the Hebrew of Samuel is that of the Authorised Version here. The chronicler lays stress on the auspicious word "good." There is also emphasis on "Jehovah," as leaving the issue in His hands who is Lord of hosts and God of battles; and on the verb, expressive of a pious wish that right may not miscarry. Evidently the spirit which inspired the prayer, "Thy will be done," was not unknown to the warriors of the old theocracy.

(14) **Before the Syrians.**—Rather, *against Aram;* so Samuel, with the more classical construction. The preposition used here was rendered *to meet* (chap. xii. 17).

(15) **And when the children of Ammon saw.**—The Hebrew construction is quite different from that of verse 6. Render, *Now the sons of Ammon had seen that Aram was routed.*

**They likewise.**—An explanatory addition to the text, as read in Samuel. So also "his brother."

**Then Joab came . . .**—Abridged. (Comp. Samuel.)

(16—19) The last effort of the Arameans. They are defeated, and become vassals to David.

(16) **They sent messengers.**—Samuel, "Hadarezer sent and drew forth" (literally, *made to come out: i.e.,* to war, chap. xx. 1). The name "Hadarezer" (Hadadezer) is important, as helping us to identify this campaign with that of chap. xviii. 3—8.

**Beyond the river.**—The Euphrates, called Purât, Purâtu, by the Babylonians and Assyrians, Furât by the Arabs, and Ufrâtus by the ancient Persians. The name is derived from the Accadian Pura-nunu (great river). The Assyrian Purât, Hebrew Pĕrâth, is simply the word Pura with a feminine ending; so that this well-known name means "The River" *par excellence.* (Comp. Gen. xv. 18; Isa. viii. 7.)

The use of this phrase, "beyond the river," to denote the position of the Eastern Aramæans, shows that the narrative here borrowed by the chronicler was originally written in Palestine. The Syriac and Arabic add here, "and they came to Hîlâm." (So Samuel; see next verse.)

**Shophach.**—Samuel, "Shobach." The letters *p* and *b* are much alike in Hebrew. The Syriac has Sh'bûk. Shophach may be compared with the Arabic *safaka*, "to shed blood" (*saffâk*, a shedder of blood).

**Went before them.**—Commanded them. It thus appears that the suzerainty of Hadadezer was recognised by some Aramæan States lying east of the Euphrates.

(17) **Came upon them.**—Samuel, "came to Hêlâm." The chronicler seems to have substituted an intelligible phrase for the name of an unknown locality. Professor Sayce has suggested to the writer that this mysterious Helam is no other than Aleppo, the *Halman* of the Assyrian monuments.

**Upon them . . . against them.**—Literally, *unto them ('aléhem).* The Hebrew term, "to Helam" (*Helâmah*), contains the same consonants as this prepositional phrase, with one extra. Perhaps, however, the term Helâmah was understood as a common noun implying *to their army* (hayil, hêl, army).

**So when David had put the battle in array against the Syrians.**—Literally, *And David set the battle,* &c., a needless repetition of the last clause. Probably Samuel is right: "And Aram put the battle in array against David."

(18) **Seven thousand men which fought in chariots, and forty thousand footmen.**—Heb., *seven thousand chariotry* (rĕkeb), &c. Samuel reads, "seven hundred chariotry, and forty thousand horsemen." Such deviations seem to indicate independent sources. We can hardly choose between the two ac-

*Israel led by Joab*  I. CHRONICLES, XX.  *to destroy Rabbah.*

the captain of the host. (19) And when the servants of Hadarezer saw that they were put to the worse before Israel, they made peace with David, and became his servants: neither would the Syrians help the children of Ammon any more.

CHAPTER XX.—(1) And ᵃit came to pass, that ¹after the year was expired, at the time that kings go out *to battle*, Joab led forth the power of the army, and wasted the country of the children of Ammon, and came and besieged Rabbah. But David tarried at Jerusalem. And Joab smote Rabbah, and destroyed it. (2) And David ᵇ took the crown of their king from off his head, and found it ²to weigh a talent of gold, and *there were* precious stones in it; and it was set upon David's head: and he brought also exceeding much spoil out of the city. (3) And he brought out the people that *were* in it, and cut *them* with saws, and with harrows of iron, and with

B.C. cir. 1035.

ᵃ 2 Sam. 11. 1.

1 Heb., *at the return of the year.*

ᵇ 2 Sam. 12. 26.

2 Heb., *the weight of.*

---

counts; but "horsemen" may be more correct than "footmen." (See chap. xviii. 4, 5.)

**And killed Shophach . . .**—Abridged statement. (Comp. 2 Sam. x. 18.)

(19) **And when the servants of Hadarezer.**—Samuel is fuller and clearer: "And all the kings, servants of Hadarezer." The tributaries of Hadadezer now transferred their fealty to David.

**They made peace with David.**—Samuel, "with Israel."

**And became his servants.**—Literally, *and served him.* Samuel, "and served them." To the writer of Samuel God's people is the main topic; to the chronicler the divinely-anointed king. The difference, therefore, though slight, is characteristic.

**Neither would the Syrians' help.**—*And Aram was not willing to come to the help of the sons of Ammon.* Samuel, "And Aram feared to come to the help," &c.

XX.

(1) The siege and storm of Rabbah. Completion of the Ammonite campaign (verses 1–3). (2) A fragment, relating how three heroes of Israel slew three Philistine giants (verses 4–8).

Section (1) is parallel to 2 Sam. xi. 1 and xii. 26, 30, 31. The chronicler omits the long intervening account of David's guilt in relation to Uriah and Bathsheba, not because he had any thought of wiping out the memory of David's crimes (an object quite beyond his power to secure, even if he had desired it, unless he could first have destroyed every existing copy of Samuel), but because that story of shame and reproach did not harmonise with the plan and purpose of his work, which was to pourtray the bright side of the reign of David, as founder of the legitimate dynasty and organiser of the legitimate worship.

(1) **After the year was expired.**—Heb., *at the time of the return of the year*: *i.e.*, in spring. (See 1 Kings xx. 22, 26.)

**At the time that kings go out.**—See chap. xx. 16. Military operations were commonly suspended during winter. The Assyrian kings have chronicled their habit of making yearly expeditions of conquest and plunder. It was exceptional for the king to "remain in the country."

**Joab led forth the power of the army.**—Samuel gives details: "David sent Joab and his servants (? the contingents of tributaries, chap. xix. 19), and all Israel" (*i.e.*, the entire national array).

**Wasted the country.**—An explanation of Samuel: "wasted the sons of Ammon."

**Rabbah**, or Rabbath Ammon, the capital. (See 2 Sam. xi. 1; Amos i. 14; Jer. xlix. 2, 3.)

**But David tarried** (Heb., *was tarrying*) **at Jerusalem.**—While Joab's campaign was in progress. In 2 Sam. xi. 1 this remark prepares the way for the account which there follows of David's temptation and fall.

**And Joab smote Rabbah, and destroyed it.**—A brief statement, summarizing the events related in 2 Sam. xi. 27–29. From that passage we learn that, after an assault which doubtless reduced the defenders to the last stage of weakness, Joab sent a message to David at Jerusalem to come and appropriate the honours of the capture. Our verse 2, which abruptly introduces David himself as present at Rabbah, obviously implies a knowledge of the narrative as it is told in Samuel, and would hardly be intelligible without it. Whether the chronicler here and elsewhere borrows directly from Samuel, or from another document depending ultimately on the same original as Samuel, cannot certainly be decided.

(2) **The crown of their king.**—Or, "of Milcom" or "Moloch," their god. The Heb. *malkâm*, "their Melech" (*i.e.*, king), occurs in this sense (Zeph. i. 5. Comp. Amos. v. 26.) The same title is applied by the prophets to Jehovah (Isa. vi. 5, xliv. 6, "Iahweh, the king [melech] of Israel." Comp. Zeph. iii. 15, and John i. 49, xii. 15; 2 Sam. xii. 12; Pss. v. 2, lxxxix. 18; Isa. viii. 21; and Jer. x. 10). The LXX. here has "Molchom, their king"; Vulg., "Melchom"; Arabic, "Malcha, their god;" all confirming our rendering.

**A talent of gold.**—The Arabic Version says one hundred pounds. Modern scholars consider the "talent of gold" as about one hundred and thirty-one pounds troy. If the weight was anything like this, the crown was obviously more suited for the head of a big idol than of a man.

**And there were precious stones in it.**—Samuel includes their weight in the talent.

**And it was set** (Heb., *became*) **upon David's head.**—Vulg., "he made himself a crown out of it." This may be the meaning; or else the weighty mass of gold and jewels may have been held over the king's head by his attendants on the occasion of its capture.

**Exceeding much spoil.**—Comp. the continual boast of the Assyrian conquerors: "spoils without number I carried off" (*sallata la mani aslula*).

(3) **And he brought.**—Better, "*And the people that were in it he brought out, and sawed with the saw, and with the iron threshing-drags* (Isa. xli. 15), *and with the axes.*"

**Sawed.**—The Hebrew is an old word, only found here. Samuel reads, by change of one letter, "set them in," or "among," the saws, &c.

**With the axes.**—So Samuel. Our Hebrew text repeats the word "saw" in the plural, owing to a

axes. Even so dealt David with all the cities of the children of Ammon. And David and all the people returned to Jerusalem.

(4) And it came to pass after this,[a] that there [1][2]arose war at [3]Gezer with the Philistines; at which time Sibbechai the Hushathite slew Sippai, *that was* of the children of [4]the giant: and they were subdued. (5) And there was war again with the Philistines; and Elhanan the son of [5]Jair slew Lahmi the brother of Goliath the Gittite, whose spear staff *was* like a weaver's beam. (6) And yet again [b] there was war at Gath, where was [6]a man of *great* stature, whose fingers and toes *were* four and twenty, six *on each hand*, and six *on each foot*: and he also was [7]the son of the giant. (7) But when he [8]defied Israel, Jonathan the son of [9]Shimea David's brother slew him.

[a] 2 Sam. 21. 18.
[1] Or, *continued.*
[2] Heb., *stood.*
[3] Or, *Gob.*
[4] Or, *Rapha.*
[5] Called also *Jaare-oregim,* 2 Sam. 21. 19.
[b] 2 Sam. 21. 20.
[6] Heb., *a man of measure.*
[7] Heb., *born to the giant,* or, *Rapha.*
[8] Or, *reproached.*
[9] Called *Shammah,* 1 Sam. 16. 9.

scribe's error. The two words differ by a single letter. Samuel adds, "and made them pass through the brick-kiln," or "Moloch's fire" (2 Kings xxiii. 10).

**Even so dealt David.**—Literally, *And so David used to do.* These cruelties were enacted again at the taking of every Ammonite city. There needs no attempt to palliate such revolting savagery; but according to the ideas of that age it was only a glorious revenge. As David treated Ammon, so would the Ammonites have treated Israel, had the victory been theirs. (Comp. their behaviour to the Gileadites, Amos i. 13; comp. also the atrocities of Assyrian conquerors, Hos. x. 14; and of the Babylonians Ps. cxxxvii. 7—9.)

II. This section corresponds to 2 Sam. xxi. 18—22. The chronicler has omitted the history of Absalom's rebellion, with all the events which preceded and followed it, as recorded in 2 Sam. xiii.—xx.; and, further, the touching story of the sacrifice of seven sons of Saul at the demand of the Gibeonites (2 Sam. xxi. 1—14).

(4) **And it came to pass after this.**—Comp. Notes on chaps. xviii. 1, xix. 1. The chronicler has omitted, whether by accident or design, the account with which, in 2 Sam. xxi. 15—17, this fragmentary section begins, and which tells how David was all but slain by the giant Ishbibenob.

**There arose war.**—Literally, *there stood,* an unique phrase, which perhaps originated in a misreading of that which appears in 2 Sam. xxi. 18, "there became again."

**Gezer.**—Samuel, "Gob," an unknown place. Each word (spelling Gôb fully) has three consonants in Hebrew, of which the first is common to both, and the other two are similar enough to make corruption easy. For "Gezer," see Josh. xvi. 3. The Syriac and Arabic here read "Gaza"; but Gezer (so LXX. and Vulg.) seems right.

**Sibbechai the Hushathite.**—See chaps. xi. 29 and xxvii. 11.

**Sippai.**—Samuel, "Saph."

**Of the children of the giant.**—See margin. Render, *Sippai, of the offspring* (a special term—*yĕlidê*—see Numb. xiii. 22; Josh. xv. 14) *of the Rephaites.* "Rapha" was doubtless the collective tribal designation of the gigantic Rephaim (Gen. xiv. 5).

**And they were subdued.**—Added by chronicler.

(5) **There was war again.**—Samuel adds, "in Gob." The proper name is probably a transcriber's repetition; the Syriac and Arabic here are without it.

**Elhanan the son of Jair slew Lahmi the brother of Goliath the Gittite.**—The Hebrew text and LXX. of Samuel have the very different statement: "And Elhanan son of Jaare-oregim the Bethlehemite slew Goliath the Gittite." There are good critics who maintain that we must recognise here a proof that popular traditions fluctuated between David and the less famous hero Elhanan as slayer of Goliath: an uncertainty, supposed to be faithfully reflected in the two accounts preserved by the compiler of Samuel (1 Sam. xvii.; 2 Sam. xxi. 19). Other not less competent scholars believe that the text of Samuel should be corrected from the Chronicles. As regards the name Jaarè-oregim (*forests of weavers*—an absurdity), this is plausible. Whether we proceed further in the same direction must depend on the general view we take of the chronicler's relation to the Books of Samuel. It is easy, but hardly satisfactory, to allege that he felt the difficulty, which every modern reader must feel, and altered the text accordingly. The real question is whether he has done this arbitrarily, or upon the evidence of another document than his MS. of Samuel. Now, it is fair to say that (1) hitherto we have observed no signs of arbitrary alteration; (2) we have had abundant proof that the chronicler actually possessed other sources besides Samuel. There is no apparent reason why "Lahmi" (*i.e.,* Lahmijah) should not be a *nomen individui.* (Comp. Assyrian *Lahmû,* the name of a god, Tablet I., Creation Series.) It is, however, quite possible that Elhanan is another, and, in fact, the original name of *David.* The appellative David, "the beloved" (comp. Dido), may have gradually supplanted the old Elhanan in the popular memory. Solomon we know was at first named Jedidiah, and it is highly probable that the true designation of the first king of Israel has been lost, the name *Saul* ("the asked") having been given in allusion to the fact that the people had *asked* for a king. We may compare, besides, the double names Jehoahaz-Shallum, Mattaniah-Zedekiah, and perhaps Uzziah-Azariah. The Targum on Samuel partly supports this suggestion (see the Note there). I would add that *Jaare* in Hebrew writing is an easy corruption of *Jesse;* so that the original reading of 2 Sam. xxi. 19 may have been, "And Elhanan the son of Jesse the Bethlehemite, slew Goliath," &c. In that case, the reading of Chronicles must be considered an unsuccessful emendation, due probably to the compiler whose work the chronicler followed.

(6) **Man of great stature.**—See Margin. Samuel has a slightly different form.

**Whose fingers . . .**—The Authorised Version here agrees with the Hebrew text of Samuel. The Hebrew text of Chronicles is abridged: "And his digits six and six—twenty and four."

**Was the son of the giant.**—*Was born to the Rephaite:* i.e., the clan so named.

(8) These were born unto the giant in Gath; and they fell by the hand of David, and by the hand of his servants.

CHAPTER XXI. — <sup>(1)</sup> And ᵃSatan stood up against Israel, and provoked David to number Israel. <sup>(2)</sup> And David said to Joab and to the rulers of the people, Go, number Israel from Beersheba even to Dan; and bring the number of them to me, that I may know it. <sup>(3)</sup> And Joab answered, The LORD make his people an hundred times so many more as they be: but, my lord the king, are they not all my lord's servants? why then doth my lord require this thing? why will he be a cause of trespass to Israel? <sup>(4)</sup> Nevertheless the king's word prevailed against Joab. Wherefore Joab departed, and went throughout all Israel, and came to Jerusalem. <sup>(5)</sup> And Joab gave the sum of the number of the people unto David. And all they of Israel were a thousand

*a* 2 Sam. 24. 1, &c.

---

(8) **These** (*ēl*), a rare word, found eight times in the Pentateuch with the article, here only without; perhaps an error of transcription. Samuel, "these four." The chronicler has omitted one giant. (See verse 4.)

**The giant.**—*The Rephaite*: that is, the clan or tribe of Rephaim. They need not have been brothers.

### XXI.

*The census, and consequent plague. The hallowing of the Temple area.* Omitting the magnificent ode which David sang to his deliverer (2 Sam. xxii.), and the last words of David (2 Sam. xxiii. 1—7), as well as the list of David's heroes (2 Sam. xxiii. 8—39), which has already been repeated in chap. xi., the chronicler resumes the ancient narrative at the point coincident with 2 Sam. xxiv. (See the notes there.) Though the two accounts obviously had a common basis, the deviations of our text from that of Samuel are much more numerous and noteworthy than is usual. They are generally explicable by reference to the special purpose and tendency of the writer.

In Samuel the narrative of the census comes in as a kind of appendix to the history of David; here it serves to introduce the account of the preparations for building the Temple, and the organisation of its ministry.

(1—6) The Census.

<sup>(1)</sup> **And Satan stood up against Israel.**—Perhaps, *And an adversary* (hostile influence) *arose against Israel.* So in 2 Sam. xix. 23 the sons of Zeruiah are called "adversaries" (Heb., a *Satan*) to David. (Comp. 1 Kings xi. 14, 25.) When *the* adversary, the enemy of mankind, is meant, the word takes the article, which it has not here. (Comp. Job i., ii. and Zech. iii. 1, 2.)

**And provoked David.**—*Pricked him on, incited him.* 2 Sam. xxiv. begins: "And again the anger of Jehovah burned against Israel, and He (or *it*) incited David against them, saying, Go, number Israel and Judah." It thus appears that the *adversary* of our text, the influence hostile to Israel, was the wrath of God. The wrath of God is the Scriptural name for that aspect of the Divine nature under which it pursues to destruction whatever is really opposed to its own perfection (Delitzsch); and it is only sin, *i.e.*, breach of the Divine law, which can necessarily direct that aspect towards man. If Divine wrath urged David to number Israel, it can only have been in consequence of evil thoughts of pride and self-sufficiency, which had intruded into a heart hitherto humbly reliant upon its Maker. One evil thought led to another, quite *naturally*; *i.e.*, by the laws which God has imposed upon human nature. God did not interpose, but allowed David's corrupt motive to work out its own penal results. (Comp. Rom. i. 18, 24, 26, 28.) The true reading in Samuel may well be, "And an adversary incited David," &c., the word Satan having fallen out of the text. Yet the expression "Jehovah provoked *or* incited against . . ." occurs (1 Sam. xxix. 16).

**To number Israel**—Samuel adds, "and Judah."

<sup>(2)</sup> **And to the rulers** (captains) **of the people.**—Omitted in Samuel, which reads, "Joab, the captain of the host, who was with him." The "captains of the host" are, however, associated in the work of the census with Joab (2 Sam. xxiv. 4). The fact that Joab and his staff were deputed to take the census seems to prove that it was of a military character.

**Go.**—Plural.

**Number.**—*Enrol, or register* (*sifrû*). A different word (*mānāh*) is used in verse 1, and in the parallel place. Samuel has, "Run over, I pray, all the tribes of Israel from Dan to Beersheba," using the very word (*shût*) which, in the prologue of Job (chaps. i. 7, ii. 2) Satan uses of his own wanderings over the earth.

**From Beersheba even to Dan.**—As if the party were to proceed from south to north. (See verse 4.) The reverse order is usual. (See Judges xx. 1; 1 Sam. iii. 20.)

<sup>(3)</sup> **Answered.**—Hebrew, *said.*

**The Lord . . . as they be.**—Literally, *Jehovah add upon his people like them an hundred times,* an abridged form of what is read in Samuel.

**But, my lord the king, are they not . . . ?**—Instead of this, Samuel records another wish, "And may the eyes of my lord the king be seeing," that is, *living* (Gen. xvi. 13).

**Why then doth my lord require this thing?** —So Samuel, in slightly different terms: "And my lord the king, why desireth he this proposal?"

**Why will he be** (why should he become) **a cause of trespass to Israel?**—Not in Samuel. It is an explanatory addition by the chronicler.

<sup>(4)</sup> **Wherefore Joab departed.**—"Went out" *scil.* from the king's presence (Samuel). The chronicler omits the account of the route of Joab and his party, as described in 2 Sam. xxiv. 4—8. They crossed Jordan, and went to Aroer, Jazer, Gilead, and Dan; then round to Zidon, "the fortress of Tyre, and all the cities of the Hivite and Canaanite, and came out at the *nageb* of Judah, to Beersheba." The business occupied nine months and twenty days; and the fact that the generalissimo of David's forces and his chief officers found leisure for the undertaking indicates a time of settled peace. The census, therefore, belongs to the later years of the reign.

<sup>(5)</sup> **The number.**—*Muster*, or census (*miphqăd*). The first clause is identical with Samuel, but has "David" for "the king," as elsewhere.

thousand and an hundred thousand men that drew sword: and Judah *was* four hundred threescore and ten thousand men that drew sword. (6) But Levi and Benjamin counted he not among them: for the king's word was abominable to Joab.

(7) [1] And God was displeased with this thing; therefore he smote Israel. (8) And David said unto God, "I have sinned greatly, because I have done this thing: but now, I beseech thee, do away the iniquity of thy servant; for I have done very foolishly.

(9) And the LORD spake unto Gad, David's seer, saying, (10) Go and tell David, saying, Thus saith the LORD, I [2] offer thee three *things*: choose thee one of them, that I may do *it* unto thee. (11) So Gad came to David, and said unto him, Thus saith the LORD, [3] Choose thee (12) either three years' famine; or three months to be destroyed before thy foes, while that the sword of thine enemies overtaketh *thee*; or else three days the sword of the LORD, even the pestilence, in the land, and the angel of the LORD destroying throughout all the

*Marginal notes:*
[1] Heb., *And it was evil in the eyes of the Lord concerning this thing.*
*a* 2 Sam. 24. 10.
[2] Heb., *stretch out.*
[3] Heb., *Take to thee.*

---

**And all they of Israel.**—*And all Israel became* (came to). The numbers are different in Samuel, which states them as 800,000 for Israel and 500,000 for Judah. The latter may fairly be regarded as a round number (500,000), our text giving the more exact total (470,000). As to the former, we may assume that the 1,100,000 of our text is an error of transcription, or, more probably, that the traditions respecting this census varied, as may easily have happened, inasmuch as the numbers were not registered in the royal archives (chap. xxvii. 24). Perhaps, however, our estimate includes the standing army of David, reckoned (chap. xxvii. 1–15) at a total of 288,000 men (in round numbers, 300,000); thus 800,000 (Sam.) + 300,000 = 1,100,000 (Chron.).

(6) **But Levi . . .**—This verse is wanting in Samuel, but it probably existed in the original source. There is nothing in the style to suggest a later hand; while the word "counted" (*pāqad*), which has not been used before in this chapter, occurs twice in the parallel passage (2 Sam. xxiv. 2, 4). It is noticeable also that the chronicler writes "the king" (not "David") here, as in Samuel.

As regards the fact stated, we may observe that the sacerdotal tribe of Levi would naturally be exempted from a census taken for military or political purposes. (Comp. Numb. i. 47, 49.) And chap. xxvii. 24 expressly asserts that the census was not completed; a result with which Joab's disapprobation of the scheme may have had much to do. The order in which the tribes were numbered (2 Sam. xxiv. 4–8; see verse 4) makes it likely that Judah and Benjamin were to have been taken last, and that, after numbering Judah, Joab repaired to the capital, where he was ordered by the king to desist from the undertaking. Josephus (*Antiq.* vii. 13, 1) speaks as if Joab had not had time to include Benjamin in the census. He may have feared to give offence to the tribe of Saul.

(7–13) The Divine wrath, declared by Gad the seer.

(7) **And God was displeased.**—This verse also is not read in Samuel, which has instead, "And David's heart smote him after that he had numbered the people." The peculiarities of expression in Samuel suggest textual corruption. The chronicler's verse is a sort of general heading, or anticipative summary, to the following narrative. The margin rightly renders the first clause (see Gen. xxi. for the same unusual construction).

(8) **And David said.**—This verse is verbatim the same with its parallel, save that it makes the characteristic substitution of "God" for "Jehovah," and adds the explanatory phrase "this thing" in the first half, and in the second omits the Divine Name altogether.

**Do away.**—*Cause to pass over*, and so *away*. David's conscience misgave him in the night, before his interview with Gad. (See 2 Sam. xxiv. 10, 11.)

(9) **And the Lord** (Jehovah) **spake unto Gad.**—Samuel, "And David arose in the morning. Now a word of Jehovah had come to Gad the prophet, a seer of David, saying—" This appears to be more original than our text.

**David's seer.**—Better, *a seer of David's*, for the same title is applied to Heman (chap. xxv. 5). For Gad, see 1 Sam. xxii. 5, and 1 Chron. xxix. 29. From the latter passage it has been inferred that it was Gad who wrote the original record of the census.

(10) This verse, again, nearly coincides with the parallel in Samuel. The variations look like corrections and explanatory or paraphrastic substitutions. Thus the word "go" is here imperative, instead of the less usual infinitive; "saying" is added by way of clearness; the easier phrase, "I offer thee" (*spread* or *lay before thee*), is given in place of the curious "I lift up" (*i.e.*, impose) "on thee" (*nôteh* for *nôtēl*: a change such as is common in the Targum); and, lastly, the pronoun *of them*, which is masculine in Samuel, is more correctly feminine here.

(11) **And said unto him.**—Samuel has the pleonastic, "And told him, and said," &c.

The following curse from the Annals of Tiglath Pileser I. (circ. 1120 B.C.) well illustrates the three penalties proposed by God to David: "May Assur and Anum, the great gods my lords, mightily rebuke him and curse him with grievous curse . . . The overthrow of his army may they work! In presence of his foes may they make him dwell altogether! May Rimaron with evil pestilence his land cut off! Want of crops, famine, corpses, to his country may be cast!"

**Thus saith the Lord, Choose thee.**—Not in Samuel, which has instead a direct question: "Shall there come to thee seven years' famine in thy land?" Our "choose" (*take*) is a word of later use in Hebrew. The Syriac gives the same term (*qabbél*).

(12) **Three years' famine.**—This appears correct, as harmonising with the three months and three days of the other visitations. Samuel has the reading "seven," which perhaps originated in some scribe's memory of the famine described in Gen. xli. 30, *sqq.*

**To be destroyed.**—Samuel has, "thy flying," and so LXX. and Vulg. here. This is doubtless right, as the word in our Hebrew text might easily be a corrupt form of that in Samuel.

*The Pestilence is sent*     I. CHRONICLES, XXI.     *and stayed.*

coasts of Israel. Now therefore advise thyself what word I shall bring again to him that sent me. <sup>(13)</sup> And David said unto Gad, I am in a great strait: let me fall now into the hand of the LORD; for very ¹great *are* his mercies: but let me not fall into the hand of man. <sup>(14)</sup> So the LORD sent pestilence upon Israel : and there fell of Israel seventy thousand men.

<sup>(15)</sup> And God sent an *a* angel unto Jerusalem to destroy it: and as he was destroying, the LORD beheld, and he repented him of the evil, and said to the angel that destroyed, It is enough, stay now thine hand. And the angel of the LORD stood by the threshing-floor of ²Ornan the Jebusite. <sup>(16)</sup> And David lifted up his eyes, and saw the angel of the LORD stand between the earth and the heaven, having a drawn sword in his hand stretched out over Jerusalem. Then David and the elders *of Israel, who were* clothed in sackcloth, fell upon their faces. <sup>(17)</sup> And David said unto God, *Is it not I that* commanded the people to

---

¹ Or, *many.*

*a* 2 Sam. 24, 16.

² Or, *Araunah,* 2 Sam. 24. 18.

---

While that the sword of thine enemies overtaketh thee.—Literally, *and the sword of thy foes at overtaking.* The word "overtaking" (*massègeth*) only occurs besides in Lev. xiv. 21. Samuel has simply, "and he pursuing thee." Perhaps the right text is, *and he pursue thee to overtaking.* (Comp. the Syriac here: "Three months thou shalt be subdued before thy enemy, and he shall be pursuing thee, and he shall be mastering thee.")

Or else three days the sword of the Lord . . . coasts of Israel.—Samuel has the brief, "Or that there be three days' pestilence in thy land." Our text appears to be an exegetical expansion of the older statement. Others suppose it to be the original, of which Samuel is an epitome, alleging that otherwise "the angel" is introduced in 2 Sam. xxiv. 16 quite suddenly and abruptly. But we must remember that in the thought of those times pestilence and "the sword," or "angel of the Lord," would be suggestive of each other. (Comp. 2 Kings xix. 35; and for the three judgments, Ezek. v. 17, xiv. 13—19, 21; Lev. xxvi. 25, 26.)

Throughout all the coasts.—*In every border.*

Now therefore advise thyself.—*And now see.* Samuel, "Now know and see."

<sup>(13)</sup> And David said.—Almost identical with Samuel. "Let me fall" looks like an improvement of Samuel, "Let us fall." The word "very" (not in Sam.) is perhaps an accidental repetition from the Hebrew of *I am in a great strait.*

Let me not fall.—Samuel has a precative form of the same verb (*'eppōlāh*; here *'eppōl*).

David confesses inability to choose. So much only is clear to him, that it is better to be dependent on the compassion of God than of man; and thus, by implication he decides against the second alternative, leaving the rest to God. Famine, sword, and pestilence were each regarded as Divine visitations, but the last especially so, because of the apparent suddenness of its outbreak and the mysterious nature of its operation.

(14—17) The Pestilence.

<sup>(14)</sup> So the Lord sent pestilence upon Israel. —So Samuel. The rest of our verse is abridged. From Samuel we learn that the plague raged throughout the land from dawn to the time of the evening sacrifice.

<sup>(15)</sup> And God sent an angel unto Jerusalem to destroy it.—The reading of Samuel is probably right, "And the angel stretched out his hand towards Jerusalem, to destroy it." The verb is the same word in each, and the word "God" in our text is substituted for "Jehovah," which, again, is a misreading of part of the Hebrew of Samuel (*yādô ha*), the first word meaning *his hand,* and the second being the definite article belonging to "angel."

To destroy.—A different voice of the same verb as in Samuel.

And as he was destroying, the Lord beheld. Not in Samuel. The words "soften the harshness of the transition from the command to the countermand" (Bertheau).

As he was destroying.—*About* (at the time of) *the destroying;* when the angel was on the point of beginning the work of death. It does not appear that Jerusalem was touched. (Comp. 2 Sam xxiv. 16.)

That destroyed.—Samuel adds, "Among the people." The addition is needless, because the Hebrew implies "the destroying angel." (Comp. Exod. xii. 23.)

It is enough, stay now.—According to the Hebrew accentuation, *Enough now (jam satis), stay* (drop) *thine hand.*

Stood.—*Was standing.* Samuel, "had come to be."

Ornan.—So the name is spelt throughout this chapter. Samuel has the less Hebrew-looking forms *ha-'ôrnah* (text; comp. the LXX. ὄρνα) or *ha-Arawnah,* margin) here, and in verse 18 *Aranyah* (text), elsewhere *Arawnah.* Such differences are natural in spelling foreign names. The LXX. have "Orna," the Syriac and Arabic "Aran."

<sup>(16)</sup> This verse is not read in Samuel, which, however, mentions the essential fact that David "saw the angel that smote the people" (2 Sam. xxiv. 17). There is nothing in the style to suggest suspicion of a later hand; and it is as likely that the compiler of Samuel has abridged the original account as that the chronicler has embellished it.

Having a drawn sword in his hand.—Comp. Num. xxii. 23, where the same phrase occurs. Literally, *and his sword drawn in his hand.*

Stretched out.—See Isa. v. 25, ix. 12, &c., for this term so used of the menace of Divine wrath.

Then David and the elders.—Literally, *and David fell, and the elders, covered with the sackcloth, on their faces.* The elders have not been mentioned before, but wherever the king went he would naturally be accompanied by a retinue of nobles, and their presence on this occasion agrees with the statement of 2 Sam. xxiv. 20, that Araunah saw the *king and his servants* coming towards him. (See verse 21, below.)

Fell upon their faces.—See Num. xxii. 31; Josh. v. 14; Judges xiii. 20.

Clothed in sackcloth.—The garb of mourners and penitents.

<sup>(17)</sup> And David said unto God.—Sam., "Jehovah." Samuel adds, "when he saw the angel that smote the people" (see our verse 16); "and he said."

*David instructed to make*     I. CHRONICLES, XXI.     *an Altar at the Threshing floor.*

be numbered? even I it is that have sinned and done evil indeed; but *as for* these sheep, what have they done? let thine hand, I pray thee, O LORD my God, be on me, and on my father's house; but not on thy people, that they should be plagued. <sup>(18)</sup> Then the *a*angel of the LORD commanded Gad to say to David, that David should go up, and set up an altar unto the LORD in the threshingfloor of Ornan the Jebusite. <sup>(19)</sup> And David went up at the saying of Gad, which he spake in the name of the LORD. <sup>(20)</sup>¹And Ornan turned back, and saw the angel; and his four sons with him hid themselves. Now Ornan was threshing wheat. <sup>(21)</sup> And as David came to Ornan, Ornan looked and saw David, and went out of the threshingfloor, and bowed himself to David with *his* face to the ground. <sup>(22)</sup> Then David said to Ornan, ²Grant me the place of *this* threshingfloor, that I may build an altar therein unto the LORD: thou shalt grant it me for the full price: that the plague may be stayed from the people. <sup>(23)</sup> And Ornan said unto David, Take *it* to thee, and let my lord the king do *that which is* good in his eyes: lo, I give *thee* the oxen *also* for burnt offerings, and the threshing instruments for wood, and the wheat for

*a* 2 Chr. 3. 1.

1 Or, *When Ornan turned back and saw the angel, then he and his four sons with him hid themselves.*

2 Heb., *give.*

---

**Is it not I that commanded the people to be numbered?**—Literally, *to number the people.* In Samuel these words are wanting. They may have been added by the chronicler for the sake of clearness, though they may also have formed part of the original narrative.

**Even I it is that have sinned and done evil indeed.**—Samuel reads, "Lo, *I*" (different pronoun) "have sinned, and *I* have dealt crookedly." Our text here may be paraphrastic, but hardly a corruption of the older one.

**But as for these sheep, what . . . father's house.**—Verbatim as in Samuel, save that the appeal, "O Lord my God," is wanting there. (Literally, *But these, the sheep.* The king was the shepherd.)

**But not on thy people, that they should be plagued.**—Literally, *and on thy people, not for a plague.* The strangeness of this order makes it likely that these words comprise two marginal notes, or glosses, which have crept into the text. They are not read in Samuel.

<sup>(18—27)</sup> The purchase of **Ornan's** threshingfloor as a place of sacrifice.

<sup>(18)</sup> **Then the angel of the Lord commanded Gad to say to David.**—Rather, *Now the angel had told Gad to tell David.* In Samuel, the mediation of the angel is not mentioned. There we read, "And Gad came that day to David, and said unto him, Go up," &c. No doubt it is only in the later prophetical books of the Canon that angels are introduced as the medium of communication between God and His prophets. (See Dan. viii. 16, ix, 21; Zech. i. 9, 12, &c.; but comp. Judges vi. 11, 14, 16, &c., and Gen. xviii. 1, 2, 13, xxxii. 24, 30.)

<sup>(19)</sup> **At the saying.**—Samuel, "according to." The difference is only that of the "one tittle," or small projection, of a letter, mentioned in Matt. v. 18.

**Which he spake in the name of the Lord.**—Samuel reads, "as the Lord commanded." The variation is merely verbal.

<sup>(20)</sup> **And Ornan turned back** (*returned*), **and saw the angel; and his four sons with him hid themselves** (*were hiding*). There can be little doubt that this is corrupt, and that the text of Samuel is right, "And Araunah looked up, and saw the king and his servants passing by him." The LXX. here has "Ornan turned, and saw the king;" the Vulg., "when Ornan had looked up." The Hebrew words for "returned" and "looked up," "angel" and "king," are similar enough to be easily confused in an ill-written or faded MS.

**Now Ornan was threshing wheat.**—This clause does not harmonise with the preceding statement, but its genuineness is made probable by the fact that Ornan was in his threshingfloor at the time. Moreover, the LXX. adds to 2 Sam. xxiv. 15, "And David chose for himself the death; and it was the days of wheat harvest."

<sup>(21)</sup> **And as David came to Ornan, Ornan looked and saw David.**—This is wanting in Samuel. The corruption of the previous verse made some such statement necessary here. The rest of the verse nearly corresponds with 2 Sam. xxiv. 20.

<sup>(22)</sup> **Then** (*and*) **David said to Ornan, Grant me the place of this threshingfloor, that I may build.**—Literally, *Pray give me the place of the threshingfloor.* Samuel, "And Araunah said Why is my lord the king come to his servant? And David said, To purchase from thee the threshingfloor, to build," &c.

**Grant it me for the full price.**—Literally, *At a full price give it me.* These words are not in Samuel. (Comp. Gen. xxiii. 9—Abraham's purchase of the Cave of Machpelah.) The recollection of that narrative may have caused the modification of the present. The last clause is word for word as in Samuel.

<sup>(23)</sup> **Take it to thee.**—Comp. Gen. xxiii. 11.

**Let my lord the king do.**—Samuel, "offer." In the Hebrew only one letter is different; and the word "do" may have the meaning "offer," as in Greek (Comp. Exod. xxix. 38.)

**I give thee.**—Not in Samuel; an exegetical addition.

**For burnt offerings.**—*For the burnt offerings.* Samuel has the singular.

**The threshing instruments,** or drags. Chap. xx. 3 a different word. See Isa. xli. 15 and 2 Sam. xxiv. 22, the only other places where this word (*môraq*) occurs. Samuel adds, "And the instruments (yokes) of the oxen."

**For wood.**—*For the wood* (Gen. xxii. 7).

**And the wheat for the meat offering.**—Not in Samuel, but probably part of the oldest text of this narrative.

**I give it all.**—*The whole I have given.* Samuel (Heb.), "The whole hath Araunah given, O king to the king." The rest of 2 Sam. xxiv. 23 is here omitted;

*David's Prayer is*     I. CHRONICLES, XXI.     *answered by Fire.*

the meat offering; I give it all. <sup>(24)</sup> And king David said to Ornan, Nay; but I will verily buy it for the full price: for I will not take *that* which *is* thine for the LORD, nor offer burnt offerings without cost. <sup>(25)</sup> So *David gave to Ornan for the place six hundred shekels of gold by weight. <sup>(26)</sup> And David built there an altar unto the LORD, and offered burnt offerings and peace offerings, and called upon the LORD; and he answered him from heaven by fire upon the altar of burnt offering. <sup>(27)</sup> And the LORD commanded the angel; and he put up his sword again into the sheath thereof. <sup>(28)</sup> At that time when David saw that the LORD had answered him in the threshingfloor of Ornan the Jebusite, then he sacrificed there. <sup>(29)</sup> For the tabernacle of the LORD, which Moses made in the wilderness, and the altar of the burnt offering, *were* at that season in the high place at <sup>b</sup>Gibeon. <sup>(30)</sup> But David could not go before it to enquire of God: for he was afraid because of the sword of the angel of the LORD.

*a* 2 Sam. 24. 24.
*b* 1 Kin. 3. 4; ch. 16. 39; 2 Chr. 1. 3.

B.C. 1017.

---

"And Araunah said unto the king, The Lord thy God accept thee."

<sup>(24)</sup> **For the full price.**—Samuel simply, "At a price" (different word). The next clause does not appear in Samuel, but may well be original.

**Nor offer burnt offerings without cost.**—So Samuel: "Nor will I offer to the Lord my God burnt offerings without cost." It was of the essence of sacrifice to surrender *something valued* in order to win from God a greater good (*Ewald*).

<sup>(25)</sup> **So David gave to Ornan for the place six hundred shekels of gold by weight.**—Literally, *shekels of gold—a weight of six hundred*. Samuel has, "And David purchased the threshingfloor and the oxen for silver, fifty shekels." The two estimates are obviously discordant. We have no means of calculating what would have been a fair price, for we know neither the extent of the purchase nor the value of the sums mentioned. But comparing Gen. xxiii. 16, where four hundred shekels of silver are paid for the field and cave of Machpelah, fifty shekels of silver would seem to be too little. On the other hand, six hundred shekels of gold appears to be far too high a price for the threshingfloor. Perhaps for "gold" we should read "silver." It has, indeed, been suggested that "the authors were writing of two different things," and that Samuel assigns only the price of the threshingfloor and oxen; whereas the chronicler, when he speaks of "the place," means the entire Mount of the Temple (Moriah), on which the floor was situate. But a comparison of the two narratives seems to identify the things purchased—"the place" (verse 25) is "the place of the threshingfloor" (verse 22); and in both cases Samuel has "the threshingfloor." Tradition may have varied on the subject; and as "there is no positive mention of the use of gold money among the Hebrews" apart from this passage (*Madden*), ours is probably the later form of the story. However this may be, the chronicler has doubtless preserved for us what he found in his original. It is interesting to compare with this sale some of those the records of which are preserved in the Babylonian Contract Tablets. One of these relates how *Dân-sum-iddin* sold a house and grounds in Borsippa for eleven and a-half minæ of silver, *i.e.*, 690 shekels. This was in the second year of Nabonidus the last king of Babylon.

<sup>(26)</sup> **And David built . . . peace offerings.**—Word for word as in Samuel.

**And called upon the Lord.**—Not in Samuel, where the narrative ends with the words, "And the Lord was entreated for the land, and the plague was stayed from Israel."

**From heaven by fire** (*with the fire from the heavens*).—The Divine inauguration of the new altar and place of sacrifice. (See Lev. ix. 24; 1 Kings xviii. 24, 38—Elijah's sacrifice; 2 Chron. vii. 1.) Also a sign that David's prayer was heard.

<sup>(27)</sup> **He put up . . .** —It seems hardly fair to call this verse a "figurative or poetical expression for the cessation of the plague." In verse 16 David *sees* the angel with drawn sword; and the older text (2 Sam. xxiv. 16, 17) equally makes the angel a "real concrete being," and *not* a "personification," as Reuss will have it.

**Sheath** (*nādān*).—A word only found here. A very similar term is applied to the body as the sheath of the soul in Dan. vii. 15; viz., the Aramaic, *nidneh*, which should, perhaps, be read here.

Chaps. xxi. 28—xxii. 1. These concluding remarks are not read in Samuel, but the writer, no doubt, found some basis for them in his special source. They tell us how it was that Ornan's threshingfloor became recognised as a permanent sanctuary, and the site ordained for the future Temple. They thus form a transition to the account of David's preparations for the building (chap. xxii. 2—19).

<sup>(28)</sup> **At that time when David saw . . .**—The use of Ornan's threshingfloor as a place of sacrifice was continued from the time of the cessation of the pestilence. The words "then he sacrificed there" refer to this fact. The answer by fire from heaven (verse 26) was an unmistakable intimation of the Divine will that it should be so. (Comp. also Josh. v. 15.)

<sup>(29, 30)</sup> A parenthesis, relating why it was that David did not rather resort to the ancient Tabernacle, which then stood at Gibeon. (Comp. chap. xvi. 39, 40.)

<sup>(29)</sup> **For the tabernacle.**—*Now the dwelling-place of Jehovah*: in contrast with Ornan's threshingfloor, the new sanctuary.

<sup>(30)</sup> **But (and) David could not go before it**—*i.e.*, the Tabernacle at Gibeon and the altar of burnt offering (chap. xvi. 4, 37, 39).

**To enquire of God.**—*To seek Him*, that is, to seek His favour by sacrifice and prayer. (But comp. chaps. xiii. 3, xv. 13.)

**For he was afraid because of the sword.**—"David could not go to Gibeon," says Keil, "because of the sword of the angel of Jehovah: *i.e.*, on account of the pestilence which raged at Gibeon." Others have thought that the awful vision of the angel had stricken him with some bodily weakness. A more natural explanation is that the menacing aspect of the apparition

# I. CHRONICLES, XXII.

**CHAPTER XXII.**—<sup>(1)</sup> Then David said, This *is* the house of the LORD God, and this *is* the altar of the burnt offering for Israel. <sup>(2)</sup> And David commanded to gather together the strangers that *were* in the land of Israel; and he set masons to hew wrought stones to build the house of God. <sup>(3)</sup> And David prepared iron in abundance for the nails for the doors of the gates, and for the joinings; and brass in abundance without weight; <sup>(4)</sup> also cedar trees in abundance: for the Zidonians and they of Tyre brought much cedar wood to David. <sup>(5)</sup> And David said, *a*Solomon my son *is* young and tender, and the house *that is* to be builded for the LORD *must be* exceeding magnifical, of fame and of glory throughout all countries:

*a* ch. 29. 1.

---

overawed the king, so that he durst not follow the usual course in the present instance. It made, as we should say, an indelible impression upon his mind as to the sanctity of the place where it appeared. (Comp. Gen. xxviii. 17; Exod. iii. 5; Josh. v. 15; Judges vi. 21, 26.)

### XXII.

<sup>(1)</sup> **Then.**—*And.*

**This is the house.**—Better, *This is a house of Jehovah, the* (true) *God, and this* (is) *an altar of burnt offering for Israel.* The verse resumes the narrative suspended at chap. xxi. 28. The place of the apparition is called "a house of God," as in Gen. xxviii. 17. Obviously, we have here the goal of the entire narrative of the census, and the pestilence, which the chronicler would probably have omitted, as he has omitted that of the famine (2 Sam. xxi.), were it not for the fact that it shows how the site of the Temple was determined.

<sup>(2–5)</sup> David gathers craftsmen, and accumulates materials for building the house of God.

<sup>(2)</sup> **And David commanded to gather together the strangers.**—The word rendered "to gather together" (*kānas*) is different from the terms used in chaps. xv. 3, 4 and xix. 7, and is late in this sense.

**The strangers** (*gērim*).—Sojourners, or resident foreigners, such as Israel had been in Egypt (Gen. xv. 13). The Canaanite population are meant, who lived on sufferance under the Israelite dominion, and were liable to forced service if the government required it. (See 2 Chron. viii. 7, 8, and 1 Kings ix. 20, 21.) Solomon found them by census to be 153,600 souls. The census was a preliminary to apportioning their several tasks. (See 2 Chron. ii. 17, 18.) David, probably on the present occasion, had held a similar census of the Canaanite serfs (2 Chron. ii. 17).

**And he set.**—*Appointed* (chap. xv. 16, 17); literally, *caused to stand.*

**Masons.**—*Hewers*; selected, apparently, from among "the strangers."

**Wrought stones.**—"Saxum quadratum," square stones (1 Kings v. 31; Isa. ix. 9).

**To build the house**—*i.e.*, for building it hereafter. It is not said that the work was begun at once, but only that the organisation of the serf labour originated with David.

<sup>(3)</sup> **For the nails.**—*Mismĕrim* happens to occur only in the later books of the Old Testament, but may well be an ancient word. (Comp. the Assyrian *asmarê* "spears," which derives from the same root.)

**For the doors of the gates.**—The doors were to be what we call folding-doors (1 Kings vi. 34, 35).

**For the joinings.**—Literally, *things that couple, or connect* (feminine participle): *i.e.*, iron clamps and hinges. In 2 Chron. xxxiv. 11 the same term is used of *wooden* clamps or braces.

**And brass.**—Bronze, which was much used in the ornamental work of ancient buildings. Comp. the plates of bronze which once adorned the doors of the temple of Shalmaneser II. (B.C. 854), at Balawât, and are now in the British Museum. Sennacherib, in a later age (B.C. 700), describes the doors of his palace at Nineveh as "overlaid with shining bronze."

**Without weight.**—A natural hyperbole. The actual amounts would, of course, be known to the royal treasurers. (Comp. the common use of the phrases *la niba, la mani* "without number," "without measure," in Assyrian accounts of spoils and captives.)

<sup>(4)</sup> **Also cedar trees in abundance.**—Literally, *and beams or logs of cedars without number.* A rhetorical exaggeration, like that which we have just noted. (See also chap. xiv. 1.)

**The Zidonians and they of Tyre** (*i.e.*, the Phœnicians) **brought much cedar wood**—*i.e.*, in the way of ordinary commerce, to barter them for supplies of grain, wine, oil, and other products of the soil, which their own rocky coast-land did not yield in sufficiency. (Comp. chap. xiv. 1.) At a later time Hiram entered into an express contract with Solomon to supply the cedar and other materials required for building the Temple (1 Kings v. 8—11).

<sup>(5)</sup> **Solomon my son is young and tender**—*i.e.*, an inexperienced young man. David repeats the expression (chap. xxix. 1); and it is applied to Rehoboam (2 Chron. xiii. 7) at the age of forty-one. The word here rendered "young," literally, "youth" (*na'ar*), is even more vague than the Latin *adolescens.* It may mean a new-born babe (Exod. ii. 6), a young child (Isa. vii. 16, viii. 4), a youth (Isa. iii. 5; 1 Sam. xviii. 55), or a man in the prime of life (1 Sam. xxx. 17; Exod. xxxiii. 11). Solomon calls himself "a young child" (*na'ar qātôn*) even after his accession to the throne (1 Kings iii. 7), though he was born soon after the time of the Syro-Ammonite war (2 Sam. xii. 24).

**Tender.**—*Timid* (Deut. xx. 8).

**The house that is to be builded . . . exceeding magnifical.**—Literally, *the house to build . . . (one is) to make great exceedingly.* For the infinitival construction, comp. chaps. v. 1, xiii. 4, ix. 25, xv. 2.

**Exceeding.**—Literally, *unto height, upwards;* an adverbial expression, which frequently occurs in the Chronicles. (See chap. xiv. 2: "On high.")

**Of fame and of glory throughout all countries.**—Literally, *for a name and for a glory* (*tiph'ereth*) *for all the lands.* (Comp. Isa. ii. 3, lx. 3, *et seq.*, lxii. 2, 3.) In similar terms the famous Assyrian Sennacherib (Sin-ahi-irba) speaks of his palace as built "for the lodging (*taprati*) of multitudes of men." And of his temple of Nergal he says: "The house

*David instructs*     I. CHRONICLES, XXII.     *Solomon.*

I will *therefore* now make preparation for it. So David prepared abundantly before his death.

(6) Then he called for Solomon his son,ᵃ and charged him to build an house for the LORD God of Israel. (7) And David said to Solomon, My son, as for me, it was in my mind to build an house unto the name of the LORD my God: (8) but the word of the LORD came to me,

saying, " Thou hast shed blood abundantly, and hast made great wars: thou shalt not build an house unto my name, because thou hast shed much blood upon the earth in my sight. (9) Behold, a son shall be born to thee, who shall be a man of rest; and I will give him rest from all his enemies round about: for his name shall be ¹Solomon, and I will give peace and quietness unto Israel in

ᵃ 2 Sam. 7. 13; ch. 28. 3.

¹ That is, *Peaceable.*

---

of Nergal, within the city of Tarbiçu, I caused to be made, and like day I caused it to shine " (*usnammir*).

**I will therefore now make preparation for it.**—Literally, *Let me now prepare for him*—the expression of an earnest desire, and self-encouragement to an arduous task, rather than of mere resolve.

We need not suppose that the verse relates to any actual utterance of David's. It is not said when nor to whom he spoke. The historian is merely representing the king's motive for these preparations. "To say" in Hebrew often means *to think*, by an elliptic construction. (Comp. Exod. ii. 14 with Gen. xvii. 17.)

**So David prepared.**—It is strange, but instructive, to remember that there have been critics so destitute of the historical faculty as to allege that "the whole episode about David's preparations is a fiction of the chronist's" (*Gramberg*), because *the Books of Samuel and Kings are silent on the subject.*

(6—16) David gives formal charge to Solomon to build the Temple.

(6) **Then he called.**—*And he called Solomon.* When? After completing his preparations, and shortly before his death (verse 5). (Comp. 1 Kings ii. 1—9, especially verses 3 and 4, of which we seem to hear echoes in the present speech.) Upon grounds of internal evidence we may pronounce this dying address of David to be an ideal composition, put into the king's mouth by the unknown author whose work the chronicler follows: or rather, perhaps, by the chronicler himself, whose style is evident throughout. (Comp. the addresses attributed to David in chap. xxviii.

**For the Lord God of Israel.**—There ought to be a comma after "Lord." Literally the phrase would run, *For Jehovah, the God of Israel.* Thus the stress lies on the national aspect of the Deity, for whom Solomon was to undertake this national work.

(7) **My son.**—So some MSS., the Hebrew margin, and LXX., Vulg., Targ. rightly. The Hebrew text reads, "His son," which is probably an oversight, due to "Solomon his son" in verse 6.

**As for me, it was in my mind.**—Literally, *I—it became with* (near or *in*) *my heart, i.e.,* it came into my mind, was my intention. The phrase is common in 2 Chronicles, but rare in the older books. (Comp. 1 Kings viii. 17, x. 2; and also Josh. xiv. 7.) It recurs in chap. xxviii. 2 exactly as here.

**Unto the name of the Lord.**—Comp. 1 Kings viii. 29: "My name shall be there," *i.e.,* My real presence. The statement of this and the following verses refers to what is told in chap. xvii. 1—14.

(8) **But the word of the Lord came to me** (upon me).—Literally, *And a word of Jehovah became upon me.* There is a partial correspondence between this "word of the Lord" and that which Nathan is re-

presented as delivering (chap. xvii. 4—14). There, however, David is promised success in war, without any hint that warfare, as such, would unfit him for the sacred task which he longed to undertake. And in 1 Kings v. 3, Solomon implies that David's wars left him no leisure for the work.

**Thou hast shed blood.**—The emphatic word is "blood." Literally, *Blood in abundance hast thou shed, and great wars hast thou made.*

**Because thou hast shed much blood.**—Better. *for torrents of blood* (plural) *hast thou shed earthward before me.* The author of this narrative may well have remembered Gen. ix. 5, 6, and the denunciations of the prophets against men of blood. (Comp. especially Amos i. 3, 13, ii. 1, with David's treatment of the conquered Ammonites, chap. xx. 3. And see also Hosea's denunciation of vengeance upon the house of Jehu for the bloodshed of Jezreel: Hos. i. 4; vii. 7). Or the verse may express the interpretation which David's own conscience put upon the oracle forbidding him to build the Temple.

(9) **Shall be born.**—*Is about to be born* (participle).

**Who shall be.**—*He* (emphatic) *shall become a man of rest,* opposed to "a man of war," such as was David (2 Sam. xvii. 8; 1 Chron. xxviii. 3). The phrase is further explained by what follows.

**And I will give him rest from all his enemies round about**—*i.e.,* the surrounding peoples, who are his natural foes, seeing that they were brought under the yoke by his father, will acquiesce in his dominion. The same words are used, in a somewhat different sense, about David (2 Sam. vii. 1); and in 1 Kings v. 4 Solomon applies them to himself. (Comp. also Prov. xvi. 7.)

**Solomon.**—The emphatic word. (See 2 Sam. xii. 24.) The Hebrew is *Shĕlōmō;* for which the LXX. gives Sălōmōn; Syriac, Shĕleimûn; Arabic, Suleimân (same as "Solyman the Magnificent"). The original form of the word had the final *n* which we see in the cognate languages. The Assyrian *Shalman* (in Shalmaneser) and the Moabite Salamanu seem to be identical. The Vulg. has Pacificus (peace-maker). (Comp. the Greek Irenæus, the German Friederich, our "Frederick," peaceful.) Sŏlŏmon is the New Testament spelling.

It would seem that the original name of Solomon was Jedidiah (2 Sam. xii. 25), but posterity, looking back with fond regret to the palmy days of his reign, remembered him only as Shelomoh, "The Peaceful." (See on chap. xx. 5.)

**And I will give peace and quietness unto Israel in his days.**—Literally, *and peace and quietness will I put upon Israel,* &c. His name will be a Divine augury of the character of his reign.

**Quietness** (*shèqet*).—Only here; but compare the cognate verb (Judges v. 31: " had rest ").

*David instructs*     I. CHRONICLES, XXII.     *Solomon.*

his days. <sup>(10)</sup> He shall built an house for my name; and he shall be my son, and I *will be* his father; and I will establish the throne of his kingdom over Israel for ever. <sup>(11)</sup> Now, my son, the LORD be with thee; and prosper thou, and build the house of the LORD thy God, as he hath said of thee. <sup>(12)</sup> Only the LORD give thee wisdom and understanding, and give thee charge concerning Israel, that thou mayest keep the law of the LORD thy God. <sup>(13)</sup> Then shalt thou prosper, if thou takest heed to fulfil the statutes and judgments which the LORD charged Moses with concerning Israel: be strong, and of good courage; dread not, nor be dismayed. <sup>(14)</sup> Now, behold, ¹in my trouble I have prepared for the house of the LORD an hundred thousand talents of gold, and a thousand thousand talents of silver; and of brass and iron without *a*weight; for it is in abundance: timber also and stone have I prepared; and thou mayest add thereto. <sup>(15)</sup> Moreover *there are* workmen with thee in abun-

*Marginal notes:* 1 Or, *in my poverty.*    *a* As ver. 3.

---

(10) **He shall build an house.**—Comp. chap. xvii.; parts of verses 11, 12, 13 are here repeated. (See the Notes there.)

(11) **The Lord be with thee.**—See chap. ix. 20. (1 Sam. iii. 19; 2 Kings xviii. 7: "The Lord was with him.") The phrase is the origin of the familiar liturgical formula, "The Lord be with you."

**And prosper thou, and build the house.**—Not a command, but a wish, *i.e.,* mayest thou prosper and build. The verb "prosper" (literally, *carry through, make succeed*) is used transitively in 2 Chron. vii. 11 and Gen. xxiv. 40.

**As he hath said of** (upon) **thee.**—This phrase (*dibbèr 'al*) is specially used of Divine threats and promises. (See Gen. xviii. 19; Isa. xxxvii. 22; and comp. verse 8, above: "And the word of the Lord became upon me.")

(12) **Only the Lord give thee wisdom.**—Better, *at least may the Lord give,* &c.; restricting the wish to one supremely important point. (For Solomon's wisdom, comp. 1 Kings iii. 9—15.)

**And give thee charge concerning Israel.**—Rather, *and appoint thee over Israel* (2 Sam. vii. 11). Solomon had been indicated as David's successor, and David intended it so; yet his wish and prayer for the Divine ratification of this Divine appointment was by no means superfluous, unless Solomon were exempt from human liability to err.

**That thou mayest keep.**—Rather, *and mayest thou keep* (the infinitive construct): a favourite continuative construction with the chronicler.

(13) **Then shalt thou prosper.**—The verse makes it quite clear that obedience was an indispensable condition to the full realisation of the promise. (Comp. verse 10 with the actual after-course of history.) Yet the word of the Lord does not return unto Him void; and if the earthly dynasty of David came to an end through disobedience, in due time was born an heir of David and Solomon, who is at this day the Lord of a spiritual dominion which will endure throughout the ages.

**If thou takest heed to fulfil.**—Literally, *if thou keep to do the statutes and judgments:* language which is obviously a reminiscence of Deuteronomy. (Comp. Deut. vii. 11, xi. 32.)

**Be strong, and of good courage.**—Or, *Be stout and staunch!* a frequent phrase in Joshua (chap. i. 7, &c.).

**Dread not, nor be dismayed.**—So Deut. i. 21, xxxi. 8; Josh. i. 9.

**Dismayed.**—*Broken, i.e.,* in spirit: *metu fractus.* (Comp. "Solomon my son is young and timid," verse 5.)

(14) **In my trouble.**—Rather, *by my toil* or *pains.* (Comp. chap. xxix. 2: "I have prepared *with all my might.*") In Gen. xxxi. 42 the same expression is equated with "the labour of my hands." The LXX. and Vulg. wrongly render "in" or "according to my poverty."

**An hundred thousand talents of gold, and a thousand thousand talents of silver.**—The gold talent is usually valued at £6,000, the silver talent at £400 sterling. If this reckoning be approximately correct, the numbers of the text are incredibly large. It is noticeable that the sums are given as round numbers, and expressed in thousands. Further, the figures are such—a hundred thousand and a million —as might easily and naturally be used in rhetorical fashion to suggest amounts of extraordinary magnitude. As David is said to have amassed 100,000 talents of gold and 1,000,000 talents of silver, so he is said, in the same hyperbolical strain, to have hoarded iron and bronze "without weight," and gold and silver "without number" (verse 16): phrases which nobody would think of taking literally. Doubtless, a modern historian would not handle exact numbers in this free manner; but we are not, therefore, bound to construe these vivid Oriental exaggerations according to the strict letter rather than the spirit and general intention. Of course, the numerals may have been corrupted in transmission; but their symmetry is against this hypothesis. (Comp. Dan. vii. 10; Gen. xxiv. 60; Mic. vi. 7, for a like rhetorical use of "thousands.") To take an Egyptian illustration, in the famous poem of Pentaur, Ramses II., beset by the Hittites, calls thus upon his god Amen: "Have I not built thee houses for millions of years? I have slain to thee 30,000 bulls." When the god helps him, he exclaims: "I find Amen worth more than millions of soldiers, one hundred thousand cavalry, ten thousand brothers, were they all joined in one." There are plenty of numerals here, but who would insist on taking them literally?

**And thou mayest add thereto.**—*i.e.,* to the stores of timber and stone. Solomon did so (2 Chron. ii. 3, 8).

**Hewers.**—See verse 2.

**Workers of stone and timber**—See verse 4 and 2 Chron. ii. 7.

**All manner of cunning men . . . work.**—Literally, *and every skilful one in every work.* The word rendered "cunning" is the technical term for a master-craftsman, like Bezaleel, the architect of the Tabernacle (Exod. xxxi. 3, *hākām*; comp. Turkish *hakim,* a doctor).

dance, hewers, and ¹workers of stone and timber, and all manner of cunning men for every manner of work. ⁽¹⁶⁾ Of the gold, the silver, and the brass, and the iron, *there is* no number. Arise *therefore*, and be doing, and the LORD be with thee.

⁽¹⁷⁾ David also commanded all the princes of Israel to help Solomon his son, *saying*, ⁽¹⁸⁾ *Is* not the LORD your God with you? and hath he *not* given you rest on every side? for he hath given the inhabitants of the land into mine hand; and the land is subdued before the Lord, and before his people. ⁽¹⁹⁾ Now set your heart and your soul to seek the LORD your God; arise there-fore, and build ye the sanctuary of the LORD God, to bring the ark of the covenant of the LORD, and the holy vessels of God, into the house that is to be built to the name of the LORD.

CHAPTER XXIII.—⁽¹⁾ So when David was old and full of days, he ᵃmade Solomon his son king over Israel.

⁽²⁾ And he gathered together all the princes of Israel, with the priests and the Levites. ⁽³⁾ Now the Levites were numbered from the age of ᵇthirty years and upward : and their number by their polls, man by man, was thirty and eight thousand. ⁽⁴⁾ Of which, twenty and four thousand *were* ²to set forward the work

*Marginal notes:* 1 That is, *masons and carpenters.* — a ch. 28. 5. — b Num. 4. 3. — 2 Or, *to oversee.*

---

⁽¹⁶⁾ **Arise therefore, and be doing.**—A phrase which recurs at Ezra x. 4.

⁽¹⁷—¹⁹⁾ David invites the coöperation of the chieftains of Israel.

⁽¹⁷⁾ **Saying.**—The absence of this word from the Hebrew text may be compared with the like omission in chaps. xvi. 7, xxiii. 4, 5, xxviii. 19.

⁽¹⁸⁾ **Is not the Lord your God with you?**—The proof appears in what follows.

**And hath he not?**—Rather, *and he hath given you rest* (verse 9).

**He hath given the inhabitants of the land into mine hand.**—The surrounding people, whose reduction is described in chaps. xviii.—xx. (Comp. for the phrase, Josh. ii. 24.)

**And the land is subdued before the Lord . . .**—The chronicler, or his authority, thinks of passages like Numb. xxxii. 22, 29, and Josh. xviii. 1.

⁽¹⁹⁾ **To seek the Lord.**—Hebrew, "to seek *unto* the Lord," as in 2 Chron. xvii. 4; Ezra iv. 2. The older construction, with a simple accusative, occurred in chaps. xvi. 12, xxi. 30.

**Arise therefore, and build.**—Rather, *And arise ye, and build.* The second clause explains how the first was to be carried out. Building the Lord a fair and noble sanctuary was equivalent to seeking His favour. Professions cost nothing, and they were not to serve the Lord "without cost" (chap. xxi. 24).

**To bring the ark.**—From its temporary abode on Mount Zion (chap. xv. 1).

**The holy vessels of God**—*e.g.,* the altar of burnt offering.

**That is to be built.**—The same participal form as in verse 9: "shall be born."

### XXIII.

After a brief notice of Solomon's coronation in the old age of David, the chronicler passes to the main subject of chaps. xxiii.—xxvi., viz., David's organisation of the Priests and Levites. The chapter before us presents (1) a summary account of the number and several duties of the Levites (verses 2—5); and (2) the father-houses or clans of the Levites, with an appendix of remarks about their duties from this time forward (verses 6—32).

⁽¹⁾ **So when David was old and full of days.**—Literally, *Now David had become old and satisfied with days.* (See Gen. xxxv. 29; Job. xlii. 17; where both terms, which are verbs here, appear as adjectives.) Perhaps our pointing is wrong. The expression "satisfied with days" reminds us of Horace, who describes the philosopher as departing this life like a satisfied guest (*ut conviva satur,* etc.).

**He made Solomon his son king.**—Heb., *and he made, &c.* This short statement is all that the chronicler has chosen to repeat from 1 Kings i., a narrative intimately connected with David's family affairs, with which he is not concerned to deal. (Comp. chap. xx., introductory remarks.)

⁽²⁻⁵⁾ The numbering of the Levites and their appointments.

⁽²⁾ **And he gathered together all the princes of Israel.**—The form of the verb (the imperfect with *waw* conversive) implies that this was done in connection with the transfer of the kingdom to Solomon. The following chapters, therefore, relate to arrangements made by David towards the close of his life. (Comp. chap. xxvi. 30, "the fortieth year of the reign of David.")

**The princes of Israel.**—Comp. chaps. xiii. 1, xv. 25, and xxii. 17. "The princes and the priests and the Levites" together constituted, in the conception of the chronicler, the three estates of the realm: the representatives of all spiritual and temporal authority. David consults with the national assembly in a matter of national concern.

⁽³⁾ **Now . . . and**—*i.e.,* after the council had agreed upon it.

**The Levites were numbered from the age of thirty years and upward.**—A census like that which Moses instituted (Numb. iv. 3, 23, 30, &c.), of all Levites " from thirty years old and upward unto fifty years," for the work of the Tabernacle.

**By their polls, man by man.**—Lit., *As to their skulls, as to men.* The second phrase defines the first, and excludes women and children.

⁽⁴⁾ **Of which, twenty and four thousand were to set forward.**—It is clear from verse 5 that David himself is supposed to utter both verses, thus personally assigning their commission to the Levites. The Hebrew here is peculiar. We may render: "Of these let there be for superintending the

*The Levites.* I. CHRONICLES, XXIII. *The Sons of Gershon.*

of the house of the LORD; and six thousand *were* officers and judges: <sup>(5)</sup> Moreover four thousand *were* porters; and four thousand praised the LORD with the instruments which I made, *said David*, to praise *therewith*.

<sup>(6)</sup> And <sup>a</sup>David divided them into <sup>1</sup>courses among the sons of Levi, *namely*, Gershon, Kohath, and Merari.

<sup>(7)</sup> Of the <sup>b</sup>Gershonites *were*, <sup>2</sup>Laadan, and Shimei. <sup>(8)</sup> The sons of Laadan; the chief *was* Jehiel and Zetham, and Joel, three. <sup>(9)</sup> The sons of Shimei; Shelomith, and Haziel, and Haran, three. These *were* the chief of the fathers of Laadan. <sup>(10)</sup> And the sons of Shimei *were*, Jahath, <sup>3</sup>Zina, and Jeush, and Beriah. These four *were* the sons of Shimei. <sup>(11)</sup> And Jahath was the chief, and Zizah the second: but Jeush and

*a* Ex. 6. 16; ch. 6. 1, &c.; 2 Chr. 8. 14 & 29. 25.

1 Heb., *divisions*.

*b* ch. 26. 21.

2 Or, *Libni*, ch. 6. 17.

3 Or, *Zizah*, ver. 11.

---

work of the house of Jehovah twenty-four thousand, and scribes and judges six thousand."

**To set forward.**—An infinitive, as at chap. xxii. 12. The verb is that of which the participle often occurs in the titles of the Psalms. (Authorised Version, "chief musician.") It means "to lead," or "superintend." The Levites had a share in prisoners of war, according to Numb. xxxi. 30. These they could employ in the more menial work of the sanctuary. The Gibeonites were spared on condition of becoming "hewers of wood and drawers of water," *i.e.*, Levitical bondsmen; and other whole cities may have received the same terms (Josh. ix. 23, 27). We have details of the functions of these *superintending* Levites in verses 28—32, below.

**And six thousand were officers and judges.** —See above. "Officers" (*shōtĕrim*) are first mentioned in Exod. v. 6 (see Note there; and comp. Deut. xvi. 18). The word means *writers* (comp. Assyrian *sadhāru*, to write). The progress of the entire people in power and civilisation elevated the Levites also; and from a warlike troop of defenders of the sanctuary, they became peaceful guardians of the great Temple at Jerusalem and its treasures, musicians and artists in its service, instructors and judges scattered throughout the whole country (Ewald).

<sup>(5)</sup> **Moreover four thousand were porters.**— Literally, *and four thousand* (are to be) *warders*. (Comp. chap. ix. 21—27.) Reuss thinks 4,000 warders too many; but the different clans went on duty in turn.

**And four thousand praised the Lord . . .**— Rather, *and four thousand* (are to be) *praising the Lord with the instruments that I have made for praising*. (On "praising," see chap. xvi. 4.) We have here an interesting reference to the fact that David was not only a minstrel and inspired psalmist, but also an inventor of stringed instruments. So the prophet Amos (chap. vi. 5) speaks of the effeminate nobles of Israel, "who prattle on the mouth of the *nebel*, that invent themselves instruments of music, like David." The reference is repeated in Neh. xii. 36.

**Which I have made.**—This expression proves that verses 4, 5 should be within inverted commas, as representing a spoken decree of David. Ewald thinks that the narrative is interrupted in verse 5 by a fragmentary quotation from an ancient poet who speaks in the name of Jehovah, characterising *the musicians* as "those whom I have formed to sing my praise." (But see 2 Chron. vii. 6.)

(6—23) The twenty-four houses of the Levites.

<sup>(6)</sup> **And David divided them into courses.**— Heb., *he divided him them* (reflexive form of verb, with suffix) *into divisions*. (Comp. chap. xxiv. 3, and Gen. xiv. 15.) Others read the simple voice of the verb here, as at chap. xxiv. 4, 5, 2 Chron. xxiii. 18, Neh. ix. 22; others, again, the intensive voice, as at chap. xvi. 3 (only). It is a question of pointing, the consonants remaining the same in each form. "David divided them," *i.e.*, the 2,400 superintendents (verse 4; comp. verse 24). Many of the names here enumerated recur in chaps. xxiv. 20—31 and xxvi. 20 —28; whereas the names of the courses of musicians (chap. xxv. 1—31), warders (chap. xxvi. 1—19), and scribes and judges (chap. xxvi. 29—32), are totally different.

**Among the sons of Levi.**—Rather, *according to the sons of Levi*, viz., *according to Gershon*, &c.: that is, according to the three great sub-divisions of the tribe (chap. vi. 1, 16). Notice the correct spelling, "Gershon" (not Gershom).

<sup>(7)</sup> **Of the Gershonites.**—Verses 7—11 give the names of nine Gershonite houses, or guilds. David's "courses" of Levites were formed according to the natural divisions already existing: *i.e.*, they coincided with the father-houses. They were doubtless twenty-four in number, like those of their brethren the musicians (chap. xxv. 31), and like the priestly classes (chap. xxiv. 4). So states Josephus (*Ant.* vii. 14, 7).

**Laadan, and Shimei.**—See chap. vi. 2, where the two principal branches of the Gershonites are called "Libni" and Shimei. "Laadan" is hardly the same as Libni, but a branch prominent in the time of David.

<sup>(8)</sup> **The sons of Laadan.**—These are named in two groups: viz., first, the three mentioned in this verse; secondly, the three named in verse 9, and called "sons of Shimei." This Shimei is not the same as the Shimei of verse 7, whose sub-divisions are not given till verse 10.

<sup>(9)</sup> **These were the chief of the fathers of Laadan.**—Rather, *heads of the father-houses to Laadan*. The names seem to be at once those of the clans, or guilds, and of their existing chiefs. But perhaps we should render, *These are the chief father-houses*. To Laadan, then, pertained six houses, viz., Jehiel, Zetham, Joel, Shelomith, Haziel, and Haran.

<sup>(10)</sup> **And the sons of Shimei.**—That is, of Shimei the "brother" of Laadan (verse 7). The bnê Shimei formed four houses, but were reckoned as three, because the two last-named, Jeush and Beriah, were numerically weak, and therefore counted as a single house and class (verse 11).

**Zina.**—Verse 11 reads "Zizah" for this name, which is thus spelt quite differently in two consecutive verses. "Zizah" is probably right. (Comp. chap. iv. 37; 2 Chron. xi. 20.) So the LXX. and Vulg.; Syriac and Arabic read "Zabda."

<sup>(11)</sup> **But Jeush and Beriah had not many sons.**—*Now Jeush and Beriah had not multiplied sons; so they became* (one) *father-house* (*bêth-'āb*),

Beriah ¹had not many sons; therefore they were in one reckoning, according to *their* father's house. ⁽¹²⁾ The sons of Kohath; Amram, Izhar, Hebron, and Uzziel, four. ⁽¹³⁾ The sons of ᵃAmram; Aaron and Moses: and ᵇAaron was separated, that he should sanctify the most holy things, he and his sons for ever, to burn incense before the LORD, to minister unto him, and to bless in his name for ever. ⁽¹⁴⁾ ᶜNow concerning Moses the man of God, his sons were named of the tribe of Levi. ⁽¹⁵⁾ ᵈThe sons of Moses *were*, Gershom, and Eliezer. ⁽¹⁶⁾ Of the sons of Gershom, Shebuel *was* the chief. ⁽¹⁷⁾ And the sons of Eliezer *were*, ᵉRehabiah ²the chief. And Eliezer had none other sons; but the sons of Rehabiah ³were very many. ⁽¹⁸⁾ Of the sons of Izhar; Shelomith the chief. ⁽¹⁹⁾ Of the sons of Hebron; Jeriah the first, Amariah the second, Jahaziel the third, and Jekameam the fourth. ⁽²⁰⁾ Of the sons of Uzziel; Micah the first, and Jesiah the second.

⁽²¹⁾ The sons of Merari; Mahli, and Mushi. The sons of Mahli; Eleazar, and Kish. ⁽²²⁾ And Eleazar died, and had no sons, but daughters: and their ⁴brethren the sons of Kish took them. ⁽²³⁾ The sons of Mushi; Mahli, and Eder, and Jeremoth, three.

---

<small>
1 Heb., *did not multiply sons.*
B.C. cir. 1045.
*a* Ex. 6. 20.
*b* Ex. 28. 1; Heb. 5. 4.
*c* Ex. 2. 22.
*d* Ex. 18. 3, 4.
*e* ch. 26. 25.
2 Or, *the first.*
3 Heb., *were highly multiplied.*
4 Or, *kinsmen.*
</small>

---

one class (or muster—*pĕquddāh*). Altogether, then, there were nine Gershonite clans: viz., six of the sons of Laadan, and three of the sons of Shimei, among the 24,000 Levites of verse 4.

⁽¹²⁾ **The sons of Kohath.**—Verses 12—20 give the names of nine Kohathite houses, "Amram, Izhar," &c. (Comp. chap. vi. 2, 18.)

⁽¹³⁾ **And Aaron was separated.**—Aaron and his sons, as priests, are thus excluded from present consideration. They form the proper subject of chap. xxv. 1—19, and are only mentioned here for the sake of completeness in the reckoning.

**That he should sanctify the most holy things.**—Rather, *to hallow* (or *consecrate*) *him as most holy*; literally, *holy of holies* (*qōdesh qŏdāshīm*), an expression not applied to Aaron in any other passage of Scripture. The meaning is that the priests represented a higher grade of holiness, a more thorough consecration, than the mere Levites, because they were called to the discharge of a higher and holier ministry.

**He and his sons.**—All the priests are included with Aaron.

**To burn incense.**—The Hebrew term means to burn victims as well as incense.

**To minister unto him, and to bless in his name.**—The same words occur (Deut. x. 8) with reference to the purpose for which the tribe of Levi was "separated." The tribe obviously includes the Aaronite clan. (Comp. also Deut. xxi. 5.)

**And to bless in his name.**—This appears right from Numb. vi. 23. Others render, *and to bless His name*.

⁽¹⁴⁾ **Now concerning Moses the man of God.** —Rather, *Now Moses, the man of God.*

**His sons were named** (or should be named) **of the tribe of Levi.**—See Gen. xlviii. 6 for the phrase "to be called after" (*niqrâ 'al*). Aaron's sons were priests; but the sons of Moses, his brother, were reckoned as simple Levites, and therefore their houses are here enumerated (verses 15—17).

**The man of God.**—See Deut. xxxiii. 1; Ps. xc.; Josh. xiv. 6. David is so called (2 Chron. viii. 14; Neh. xii. 24). The meaning of the title is one charged with a Divine mission. Hence the prophets were so called in the times of the kings; and St. Paul applies the title to Timothy (1 Tim. vi. 11).

⁽¹⁵⁾ **The sons of Moses.**—See Exod. ii. 22 for "Gershom," Exod. xviii. 3, 4 for both. Gershom means "expulsion" (comp. Gen. iii. 24), and is a variant form of Gershon. What is said in Exod. ii. 22 is an allusive play on the name, not a derivation of it. "Eliezer," *God is help*, a distinct name from "Eleazar" (verse 22), *God hath helped*, or, *is a helper*.

⁽¹⁶⁾ **The sons of Gershom, Shebuel was the chief** (Heb., *head*).—The statement that "Shebuel was the chief" implies that Gershom had other sons not mentioned here, as being reckoned members of the clan the sons of Gershom. Shebuel is called Shubael in chap. xxiv. 20.

⁽¹⁷⁾ **And the sons of Eliezer were, Rehabiah the chief.**—The word "were" (became) ought not to be in italics in the text, as it is expressed in the Hebrew.

**The chief** (head) means founder and eponym of the clan the sons of Rehabiah.

**And Eliezer had none other sons.**—Literally, *And there became not to Eliezer other sons, and the sons of Rehabiah had multiplied exceedingly* (*unto height*, chap. xxii. 5). The clan Rehabiah was very populous.

Thus (verses 16—17) the descendants of Moses were comprised in two father-houses, or clans, viz., Shebuel and Rehabiah.

⁽¹⁸⁾ **The sons of Izhar.**—Second son of Kohath. The sons of Izhar made one clan, that of Shelōmith (or Shelōmōth, chap. xxiv. 22). The same variation occurred in the Hebrew of verse 9, above.

⁽¹⁹⁾ **The sons of Hebron.**—"Of" is wanting in the Hebrew here, as well as in verses 16, 18, and 20. The sons of Hebron comprised four houses, clans, or classes. Their names recur in chap. xxiv. 23.

⁽²⁰⁾ **The sons of Uzziel** constituted two houses and classes. The nine clans of Kohathite Levites are again rehearsed at chap. xxiv. 20—25.

⁽²¹⁾ **The sons of Merari; Mahli, and Mushi.**— See Exod. vi. 19, and Num. iii. 33, and chap. vi. 19.

⁽²²⁾ **And Eleazar died, and had no sons.**—Thus his house merged in that of the sons of Kish, who married his daughters according to the Law (Num. xxxvi. 6—9). The sons of Mahli, then, were represented in David's day by the house of Kish. (See chap. xxiv. 29.)

⁽²³⁾ **The sons of Mushi; Mahli, and Eder, and Jeremoth, three.**—These, with the sons of Kish, make only four Merarite houses, whereas six are required to make up a total of twenty-four Levitical houses. But chap. xxiv. 26, 27 shows that the chronicler's registers named a third son of Merari, viz., Jaaziah, whose descendants constituted the three houses

# The Office     I. CHRONICLES, XXIII.     of the Levites.

(24) These were the sons of <sup>a</sup>Levi after the house of their fathers; *even* the chief of the fathers, as they were counted by number of names by their polls, that did the work for the service of the house of the LORD, from the age of <sup>b</sup> twenty years and upward. (25) For David said, The LORD God of Israel hath given rest unto his people, <sup>1</sup>that they may dwell in Jerusalem for ever: (26) and also unto the Levites; they shall no *more* carry the tabernacle, nor any vessels of it for the service thereof. (27) For by the last words of David the Levites

*a* Num. 10. 24.

*b* Num. 1. 3.

1 Or, *and he dwelleth in Jerusalem,* &c.

---

of Shoham, Zaccur, and Ibri, in the time of David. Adding these, we get seven clans, one too many for our purpose. Perhaps the Mahli of verse 23 is a mistaken repetition from verse 21, due to some ancient scribe. The word "three" at the end of the verse would be added after the mistake had become fixed. It is wanting in chap. xxiv. 30, which otherwise repeats verse 23. Excluding this second Mahli as spurious, we get six clans of Merarites; and thus, altogether, twenty-four classes of Levitical overseers of the work of the sanctuary (verse 4), consisting of nine Gershonite, nine Kohathite, and six Merarite houses. This number of classes or guilds tallies exactly with the total of 24,000 Levites (ver. 4), for it allows a thousand to the class (or clan). See on ch. xiii. 1.

It is right to remark (1) that the passage chap. xxiv. 26, 27, itself needs emendation (see Notes there); (2) that the old versions—viz., the LXX., Vulg., Syriac, and Arabic—have the reading of our present text in verses 21—23, so that the assumed omission of Jaaziah and his sons must be very ancient, and is probably due to an oversight of an early editor, if not of the chronicler himself; (3) in the two other passages of the Old Testament where the sons of Merari are named, only two—viz., Mahli and Mushi—appear; and (4) that the recurrence of the name Mahli in our verse 23 as a son of Mushi is easily paralleled: *e.g.*, in verses 9, 10 ("Shimei" twice). But it is easier to suppose an omission here than an interpolation of unknown names at chap. xxiv. 26, 27. And the correspondence of the present list up to this point with that of chap. xxiv. favours the assumption of an unintentional omission in verse 21.

(24) **These were the sons of Levi after the house of their fathers.**—Rather, *These were the sons of Levi, according to their father-houses* (clans), *heads of the houses* (fathers, *i.e.*, father-houses), *to those mustered of them, in an enumeration of names according to their polls*. This is the subscription to the foregoing list of names of the Levitical houses, as entered in the muster-rolls of David.

**As they were counted.**—Num. i. 21; Exod. xxx. 14. The word is that used in chap. xxi. 6 (*pāqad*).

**By number of names.**—Num. i. 18, iii. 43.

**That did the work for the service of the house of the Lord.**—This description identifies these Levites with the 24,000 mentioned in verse 4.

**That did the work.**—Literally, *doing*. This participle has the form of the singular here and elsewhere in the Chronicles, though the sense demands a plural. It is probably meant as plural, being a variant spelling. (Comp. 2 Chron. xxiv. 12, xxxiv. 10, 13; Ezra iii. 9; Neh. ii. 16.)

**From the age of twenty years and upward.**—Verse 3 states that the Levites were numbered "from the age of thirty and upward." Some would banish discrepancy by the assumption that "thirty" is an ancient error of transcription; others imagine that the chronicler has simply incorporated two divergent statements, as he found them in his authorities. According to Num. iv. 3, 23, 30, 35, 43, 47, the Levites were bound to serve "from thirty years old and upward" to fifty years of age; whereas Num. viii. 24, 25, fixes the age "from twenty and five years old and upward" to fifty; and this, according to Ewald, is the more exact account. It appears from 2 Chron. xxxi. 17, that the later practice, at all events, was for the Levites to enter on their sacred functions at the age of twenty. Accordingly, the older commentators have supposed that David twice numbered the Levites: first, as the Law required, from the age of thirty (verse 3); and again, towards the close of his reign (verse 27), from the age of twenty, because he perceived that the duties had become less onerous, and might therefore be borne by younger men. (Comp. however, Num. i. 3, from which it appears that the military age, *i.e.*, the age of full virile strength, was reckoned "from twenty years old and upward.")

(25) **For David said.**—This verse seems to assign a reason for the extension of the Levitical census.

**The Lord . . . hath given rest unto his people.**—So that they no longer wander from pasture to pasture in the wilderness, nor are any more oppressed by foreign tyrants as in the days of the judges.

**That they may dwell.**—Rather, *And He* (the Lord) *hath settled in Jerusalem for ever.* (Comp. chap. xvii. 5, "I have gone from tent to tent.") Now Jehovah has chosen Zion to be His eternal dwelling-place (Ps. cxxxii. 13.)

(26) **And also unto the Levites; they shall no more carry . . .**—Rather, *And the Levites also have not* (now) *to carry the dwelling and all its vessels for its service*, as they had to do in the wanderings of Israel in the desert. The sacred dwelling-place (*mishkān*) had long been fixed at Gibeon; and the service of the Levites was so much the lighter, as in the olden time they not only had to carry about from place to place, but also to guard the holy tent and its belongings against the attacks of marauders. The inference is that as the duties had become so much less arduous, they might well be undertaken at an earlier age than the ancient custom permitted.

**They shall no more carry.**—Comp. the same infinitival construction in 2 Chron. v. 11.

(27) **For by the last words of David.**—That is, owing to his last commands. So Vulg. (juxta praecepta David novissima) and Syriac.

**The Levites were numbered.**—Literally, *these* (are), *i.e.*, according to the later idiom, *this* (is) *the enumeration of the sons of Levi, from twenty years old and upward.* The verse seems to mean that David towards the end of his reign instituted a census of Levites from twenty instead of thirty years old. Thus, the Authorised Version gives the sense. Others render, *For in the last words* (*i.e.*, records) *of David is the number of the sons of Levi from twenty,* &c., as if the chronicler were referring to some historical work in which this special census was recorded. (Comp. chap. xxix. 29.) The verse is a parenthetic remark of the chronicler, interrupting the speech of David, which

were ¹numbered from twenty years old and above: ⁽²⁸⁾ because ²their office *was* to wait on the sons of Aaron for the service of the house of the LORD, in the courts, and in the chambers, and in the purifying of all holy things, and the work of the service of the house of God; ⁽²⁹⁾ both for the shewbread, and for ᵃthe fine flour for meat offering, and for the unleavened cakes, and for *that which is baked in* the ³pan, and for that which is fried, and for all manner of measure and size; ⁽³⁰⁾ and to stand every morning to thank and praise the LORD, and likewise at even; ⁽³¹⁾ and to offer all burnt sacrifices unto the LORD in the sabbaths, in the new moons, and on the set feasts, by number, according to the order commanded unto them, continually before the LORD: ⁽³²⁾ and that they should keep the charge of the tabernacle of the congregation, and the charge of the holy *place*, and the charge of the sons of Aaron their brethren, in the service of the house of the LORD.

1 Heb., *number.*
2 Heb., *their station was at the hand of the sons of Aaron.*
a Lev. 6. 21; ch. 9. 29, &c.
3 Or, *flat plate.*
c Lev. 10. 1.
c Num. 3. 4 & 26. 61.

CHAPTER XXIV.—⁽¹⁾ Now *these are* the divisions of the sons of Aaron. ᵇThe sons of Aaron; Nadab, and Abihu, Eleazar, and Ithamar. ⁽²⁾ But ᶜNadab and Abihu died before their father, and had no children: therefore Eleazar and

---

however, is resumed in verse 28, and continued to the end of the chapter.

⁽²⁸⁾ **Because their office was to wait on the sons of Aaron.**—*For their appointment* (or *station*) *is at the side of the sons of Aaron* (*i.e.,* the priests). The Levites had no longer to carry the sacred dwelling and its vessels, but to minister, in subordination to the priesthood, in the permanent sanctuary.

**In the courts.**—*Over* (*i.e.,* in charge of) *the courts, and over the cells,* or chambers built around the courts, in which were kept stores and treasures (chap. ix. 26), and in which priests and Levites lived.

**And in** (over) **the purifying of all holy things.** —2 Chron. xxx. 19. They had to cleanse the sacred vessels and the sanctuary itself.

⁽²⁹⁾ **Both for the shewbread, and for the fine flour.**— Rather, *And over the shewbread, and over,* &c. "For" (*lĕ*) continues the sense of "over" (*'al*). The Levitical assistants of the priests had to see to the preparation of the things here enumerated.

**And for that which is baked in the pan.**— Literally, *and over the pan* (Lev. ii. 5).

**And for that which is fried.**—Rather, *and over that which is soaked in oil* (a kind of cake, Lev. vii. 12).

**And for all manner of measure and size.**— The flour and wine and oil, which were the complements of every sacrifice, were measured by the Levites in standard vessels, of which they had the keeping. Exod. xxix. 40 shows that the proportions were fixed for each kind of offering. "Measure" (*mĕsûrāh*), a rare word, implies measure of capacity; "size" (*middāh*), measure of length (*Rashi*).

⁽³⁰⁾ **To thank and praise the Lord.**—This refers to the special function of the 4,000 musicians (verse 5). (Comp. chap. xvi. 4.) Those who slew and flayed the victims could hardly have taken part in the service of song.

⁽³¹⁾ **And to offer all burnt sacrifices.**—Rather, *And over all offering of burnt offerings.* The Levites had to select and prepare the victims, the priests offered them, when ready, upon the altar. The Levites had to do this "by number," *i.e.,* according to the several numbers prescribed by the Law for each occasion. (See Num. xxviii.)

**According to the order commanded unto them.**—*According to the rule concerning them: i.e.,* concerning the sacrifices.

**Continually.**—Heb., *tāmîd,* the technical term in connection with the burnt offerings, which regularly recurred at stated times, *e.g.,* a lamb was offered morning and evening. (Comp. Num. xxviii. 6.)

⁽³²⁾ **And that they should keep.**—This verse sums up the functions of the Levites under three general heads: "And let them keep the charge of the tent of meeting." The words are evidently based upon Num. xviii. 3—5.

**And the charge of the sons of Aaron.**—That is, all that the priests committed to them, and required of them (verse 28) as their appointed assistants. The word rendered "charge" literally means *keeping, guard, watch.*

**In the service.**—*For the service.*

ADDITIONAL NOTE on verses 28 and 32. The law respecting the sacred tent was naturally applied to the future Temple. It is hardly fair to say, with Reuss, that "in the perspective of the author the Tabernacle of David and the Temple of Solomon were confounded with each other." In chap. xvi. 37—39, the chronicler has clearly distinguished two sacred tents: that of the Ark on Mount Zion, and the ancient sanctuary at Gibeon. Throughout that lengthy narrative of the transfer of the Ark, the Temple is not mentioned at all. And if in verse 28 David speaks of "courts" and "chambers," that only shows that the king meant his assignation of the duties of the Levites to be permanent. Nor will it make much difference if we allow that the writer, in speaking of David's tent, has used language more applicable to the Temple of Solomon. The functions of the Levites in both would be essentially the same. The great historian Ewald believed the whole section, ch. xxiii. 24—xxiv. 31 to be an authentic extract from "the Book of Origins," which he refers to the early years of Solomon's reign.

### XXIV.

Chap. xxiv. contains (1) an account of the organisation of the priests in twenty-four classes (verses 1—19); (2) a recapitulation of the Levitical classes, as described in the last chapter (verses 20—31).

⁽¹⁾ **Now these are the divisions.**—Literally, *And for the sons of Aaron, their divisions* (*were as follows*). The sentence forms a superscription to the section (verses 1—19).

**The sons of Aaron** are named above (chap. vi. 3). (Comp. Exod. vi. 23.) As usual, the writer starts *ab ovo.*

⁽²⁾ **But Nadab and Abihu died before their father.**—Lev. x. 1, 2 tells why: viz., because they

Ithamar executed the priest's office. (3) And David distributed them, both Zadok of the sons of Eleazar, and Ahimelech of the sons of Ithamar, according to their offices in their service. (4) And there were more chief men found of the sons of Eleazar than of the sons of Ithamar; and *thus* were they divided. Among the sons of Eleazar *there were* sixteen chief men of the house of *their* fathers, and eight among the sons of Ithamar according to the house of their fathers. (5) Thus were they divided by lot, one sort with another; for the governors of the sanctuary, and governors *of the house* of God, were of the sons of Eleazar, and of the sons of Ithamar. (6) And Shemaiah the son of Nethaneel the scribe, *one* of the Levites, wrote them before the king, and the princes, and Zadok the priest, and Ahimelech the son of Abiathar, and *before* the chief of the fathers of the priests and Levites: one [1] principal household being taken for Eleazar, and *one* taken for Ithamar.

(7) Now the first lot came forth to Jehoiarib, the second to Jedaiah, (8) the

[1] Heb., *house of the father*.

---

offered "strange fire" before the Lord. (See also Num. iii. 4, from which our text appears to be derived.)

**And had no children.**—Literally, *And sons had not become* (been born) *to them.*

**Therefore Eleazar and Ithamar.**—*And Eleazar and Ithamar acted as priests;* Numbers adds, "before the face of Aaron their father." It is implied that the office of the priesthood remained with the two lines, or houses, of Eleazar and Ithamar.

(3) **And David distributed them.**—The same phrase as at chap. xxiii. 3. (See Note there.)

**Both Zadok of the sons of Eleazar, and Ahimelech of the sons of Ithamar.**—This expression forms part of the *subject* of the Hebrew sentence. The construction is like that in verse 2, "And Nadab died, and Abihu." Thus, "And David divided them, and Zadok and Ahimelech," i.e., "And David, with Zadok and Ahimelech, divided them." The meaning is that Zadok and Ahimelech, the heads of the houses of Eleazar and Ithamar, assisted David in the classification of the priests.

**According to their offices.**—Rather, *According to their official class* (chap. xxiii. 11).

(4) **And there were more chief men found.**—Literally, *And the sons of Eleazar were found more numerous as regards the heads of the men than the sons of Ithamar.* The basis of division was not the individual members of the different families, but the heads of them. There were more head men, or heads of households, deriving from Eleazar than from Ithamar.

**Chief men.**—Heb., *heads of the men, i.e.,* heads of single families or households; just as "heads of the fathers" denotes heads of groups of fathers or clans. (Comp. Josh. vii. 14, 16—18.) Of course, as the heads of households were more numerous, the total number of priests claiming descent from Eleazar must likewise have been more numerous than their kinsmen the Ithamarites.

**And thus were they divided . . . fathers.**—Rather, *And they divided them: to the sons of Eleazar, heads of father-houses, sixteen, and to the sons of Ithamar, to their father-houses, eight* (heads). They (i.e., David and the two high priests) divided them (verse 3.)

(5) **Thus were they divided by lot, one sort with another.**—Literally, *And they divided them by lots, these with those: i.e.,* the sons of Eleazar with those of Ithamar, the clans of each standing together, apart from those of the other, and the lots being drawn for each alternately. The object was to decide the question of precedence in the order of ministration (comp. Luke i. 5, 8, 9), the liturgical functions being, of course, the same for all.

**For the governors of the sanctuary . . .**—Better, *for there had arisen holy princes* ("lords spiritual") *and princes of God* (both) *from among the sons of Eleazar, and from among the sons of Ithamar.* The decision was referred to the equal arbitrament of the lot, because there had been, and were, distinguished heads of priestly houses belonging to both lines of descent. "Princes of the sanctuary" (Isa. xliii. 28)—the phrase is equivalent to "princes of the priests" (2 Chron. xxxvi. 14). "Princes of God"—an expression (*sârê 'ĕlôhîm*) not found elsewhere; it is either synonymous with the last, or perhaps denotes the high priests. (Comp. Notes on chap. vi. 4, 5, 6.) The term "Prince of God" (*nĕsî 'ĕlôhîm*) is applied to Abraham (Gen. xxiii. 6), apparently in the sense of *mighty prince,* which may be the meaning here.

(6) **And Shemaiah . . . wrote them.**—Made a list of the names in the order determined by lot, as given below (verses 7—18).

**The chief of the fathers.**—Better, *the heads of the houses* or *clans.*

**One principal household being taken . . .**—The Hebrew text is corrupt, but we may with great probability restore the original reading by the change of a single letter, and translate, *one clan was drawn for Eleazar, and one drawn for Ithamar: i.e.,* alternately. So one Hebrew MS. The LXX. has, "one by one for Eleazar, and one by one for Ithamar." (So some Hebrew MSS. The Syriac and Vulg. read, "one house for Eleazar, and another house for Ithamar.") The chances would be that the Ithamarites would all be drawn before the Eleazarites. (Comp. chap. xxv. 22—31, where ten "sons of the Hemanite" are left over, and drawn last.)

(7—10) The order of the twenty-four classes of priests, as decided by the drawings. We have no means of discovering to which of the lines individual clans belonged, whether to that of Eleazar or to that of Ithamar.

(7) **Jehoiarib . . . Jedaiah.**—See chap. ix. 10. The Maccabean princes were of the house of Jehoiarib (1 Maccab. ii. 1).

**Came forth.**—From the urn (Josh. xvi. 1, xix. 1).

(8) **Harim**—i.e., *hārûm,* flat-nosed. (Comp. Latin *Naso.*) This name recurs in Ezra ii. 39; Neh. iii. 11.

**Seorim** (*barley*)—i.e., bearded (Latin, *Barbatus*), is not found elsewhere.

*The Division of the*     I. CHRONICLES, XXIV.     *Sons of Aaron.*

third to Harim, the fourth to Seorim, <sup>(9)</sup> the fifth to Malchijah, the sixth to Mijamin, <sup>(10)</sup> the seventh to Hakkoz, the eighth to <sup>a</sup> Abijah, <sup>(11)</sup> the ninth to Jeshuah, the tenth to Shecaniah, <sup>(12)</sup> the eleventh to Eliashib, the twelfth to Jakim, <sup>(13)</sup> the thirteenth to Huppah, the fourteenth to Jeshebeab, <sup>(14)</sup> the fifteenth to Bilgah, the sixteenth to Immer, <sup>(15)</sup> the seventeenth to Hezir, the eighteenth to Aphses, <sup>(16)</sup> the nineteenth to Pethahiah, the twentieth to Jehezekel, <sup>(17)</sup> the one and twentieth to Jachin, the two and twentieth to Gamul, <sup>(18)</sup> the three and twentieth to Delaiah, the four and twentieth to Maaziah.

*a* Luke 1. 5.

*b* ch. 23. 19 & 20. 31.

<sup>(19)</sup> These *were* the orderings of them in their service to come into the house of the LORD, according to their manner, under Aaron their father, as the LORD God of Israel had commanded him.

<sup>(20)</sup> And the rest of the sons of Levi *were these*: Of the sons of Amram; Shubael: of the sons of Shubael; Jehdeiah. <sup>(21)</sup> Concerning Rehabiah: of the sons of Rehabiah, the first *was* Isshiah. <sup>(22)</sup> Of the Izharites; Shelomoth: of the sons of Shelomoth; Jahath. <sup>(23)</sup> And the sons *of* <sup>b</sup> Hebron; Jeriah *the first*, Amariah the second, Jahaziel the third, Jekameam the fourth. <sup>(24)</sup> *Of* the sons of Uzziel; Michah: of the sons of Michah;

---

<sup>(9)</sup> **Malchijah.**—Neh. iii. 11.
**Mijamin.**—Looks like *on the right hand*. Perhaps the first syllable is a disguise of *Mê* (water—a metaphorical term for *son*), and then the name would be equivalent to Benjamin (Neh. xii. 5).

<sup>(10)</sup> **Hakkoz.**—*The thorn.* (Comp. *koz*, thorn, chap. iv. 8.)
**Abijah.**—Called "Abia" (Luke i. 5). To this class or course of the priests belonged Zacharias, the father of John the Baptist.

<sup>(11)</sup> **Jeshuah.**—Heb., *Yêshûa'*; in Greek, 'Ιησοῦς, Jesus (Ezra ii. 2). The name only occurs in Chronicles, Ezra, and Nehemiah. The Syriac and Arabic read "Elisha" here.
**Shecaniah.**—Chap. iii. 21. This was a common name in the post-exilic age (*Iah is a neighbour*).

<sup>(12)</sup> **Eliashib** (*God will restore*).—Chap. iii. 27.
**Jakim** (*He, i.e., God, or Jah, will establish*).—Equivalent to Eliakim and Jecamiah (chap. viii. 19).

<sup>(13)</sup> **Huppah.**—(*Covering, canopy*; Isa. iv. 5). Here only as a proper name; but comp. "Huppim" (chap. vii. 12).
**Jeshebeab.**—Only here. It means, *May the Father* (*i.e.*, God) *cause to lead captive!* But the LXX. reads Ἰεσβαάλ, or Ἰοσβαδλ: *i.e., Eshbaal*, "man of Baal." So Vulg., "Isbaab."

<sup>(14)</sup> **Immer.**—Chap. ix. 10; Jer. xx. 1 (perhaps *a lamb*).
**Bilgah.**—Neh. x. 9 ("Bilgai"), xii. 5 (*smiling*; comp. Isaac, *the laugher*).

<sup>(15)</sup> **Hezir.**—*Hog.* (See Neh. x. 21.) The Syriac and Arabic read "Ahaziah;" but Vulg. and LXX. prove "Hezir."
**Aphses.**—Heb., *ha-piççêç* (*the scatterer*): here only. LXX., Ἀφεσή; Vulg., "Aphses;" Syriac and Arabic, "Phasin."

<sup>(16)</sup> **Pethahiah.**—Ezra x. 23, (*Iah openeth, i.e.*, setteth free). (Comp. Jephthah: *He, i.e., Iah, openeth*.)
**Jehezekel.**—Heb., *Yĕhezqél*: Ezekiel.

<sup>(17)</sup> **Jachin.**—Gen. xlvi. 10; 1 Kings vii. 21 (*He, i.e., Jah, setteth up, maketh firm*). The same name as Jehoiachin.
**Gamul.**—Here only as proper name (*weaned*, Isa. xi. 8).

<sup>(18)</sup> **Delaiah.**—Chap. iii. 24, a common post-exilic name (*Jah draws out, i.e., frees*): but comp. Jer. xxxvi. 12, and Note on 1 Chron. iii. 1.
**Maaziah.**—Here only. Perhaps "Maadiah" (Neh. xii. 5) should be read. So Syriac, "Ma'adyâ;" Arabic, "Mi'diyyâ." But LXX. (Vat.), "Maasai" (? Maaseiah); Vulg., "Maaziau."

<sup>(19)</sup> **These were the orderings of them in their service.**—Better, *These were their classes for their service.*
**According to their manner, under Aaron.**—Better, *according to their rule* (or *order*; Vulg., *ritum*), *ordained through Aaron*, &c. (See Num. ii. 1, iv. 1, 17.) All the sacerdotal functions were fixed, and each of the twenty-four classes undertook the weekly discharge of them in rotation with the rest, beginning on the Sabbath (2 Kings xi. 9; 2 Chron. xxiii. 8). Josephus (*Ant.* vii. 14, 7) declares that the arrangements of David lasted down to his own day.

2. Recapitulation of the Levitical classes (verses 20—31). (Comp. chap. xxiii. 12—23.)

<sup>(20)</sup> **And the rest of the sons of Levi were** these.—Rather, *And for the sons of Levi that were left over*; *i.e.*, after the priests had been separately dealt with. The list begins with the Kohathite heads, omitting the Gershonites (chap. xxiii. 7—11), perhaps owing to a *lacuna* in the chronicler's MS. authority.
**Of the sons of Amram; Shubael.**—*For the sons.* Shubael is a variant of "Shebuel" (chap. xxiii. 16). The same variation recurs in chap. xxv. 4, 20. Shebuel was grandson to Moses (chap. xxiii. 16). Here the name represents a Levitical house or class, of which, in David's time, Jehdeiah (*Jah gladdens*) was the head. The name "Jehdeiah" occurs again in chap. xxvi. 30, and nowhere else in the Old Testament. (Comp. "Jahdiel," *God gladdens*, chap v. 24.)

<sup>(21)</sup> **Concerning Rehabiah: of the sons.**—*For Rehabiah: for the sons of Rehabiah, the chief* (head) *was Isshiah.* Chap. xxiii. 17 only says that the sons of Rehabiah were very numerous.

<sup>(22)</sup> **Of the Izharites.**—*For the Izharites.* The Gentilic form of this designation indicates that Shubael, Rehabiah, and others of these proper names, are likewise names of houses or clans.
**Shelomoth** is mentioned in chap. xxiii. 18, but not the chief, "Jahath."

<sup>(23)</sup> **And the sons of Hebron; Jeriah the first.**—The Hebrew text is here mutilated. Our translators have emended it from chap. xxiii. 19. The names of the houses or classes are given, without those of the heads.

<sup>(24)</sup> **The sons of Uzziel . . . of the sons of Michah.**—With verses 24, 25, comp. chap. xxiii. 20. "Jesiah" there is the same Hebrew name as is here

Shamir. **(25)** The brother of Michah *was* Isshiah : of the sons of Isshiah ; Zechariah. **(26)** The sons of Merari *were* Mahli and Mushi: the sons of Jaaziah ; Beno. **(27)** The sons of Merari by Jaaziah; Beno, and Shoham, and Zaccur, and Ibri. **(28)** Of Mahli *came* Eleazar, who had no sons. **(29)** Concerning Kish : the son of Kish *was* Jerahmeel. **(30)** The sons also of Mushi ; Mahli, and Eder, and Jerimoth. These *were* the sons of the Levites after the house of their fathers.

B.C. 1015

**(31)** These likewise cast lots over against their brethren the sons of Aaron in the presence of David the king, and Zadok, and Ahimelech, and the chief of the fathers of the priests and Levites, even the principal fathers over against their younger brethren.

CHAPTER XXV. — **(1)** Moreover David and the captains of the host separated to the service of the sons of Asaph, and of Heman, and of Jeduthun,

---

spelt "Isshiah;" it should be *Yishshiyah* in both places.

**Shamir** and **Zechariah** are the heads of the bnê Micah and bnê Isshiah. Only five heads of the nine Kohathite houses are mentioned, viz., Jehdeiah, Isshiah, Jahath, Shamir, and Zechariah.

(26) **The sons of Merari.**—Verses 26—30 : the Merarite heads. (Comp. chap. xxiii. 21—23.)

**The sons of Jaaziah ; Beno.**— *Beno* is the Hebrew for "his son," and can hardly be a proper name. The clause should be connected immediately with what follows in verse 27, and the whole translated thus: "The sons of Jaaziah his son—that is, sons of Merari belonging to Jaaziah his son—were Shoham, and Zaccur, and Ibri."

**Jaaziah** appears as a third son of Merari, not mentioned elsewhere. (See Note on chap xxiii. 23.) If the Hebrew text is substantially sound, it is implied that there existed in the days of David a group of Merarite houses calling themselves "sons of Jaaziah."

The construction here suggested involves the rejection of the conjunction before "Shoham" in verse 27, and the removal of the paragraphic sign at the beginning of the verse.

(27) **Shoham** (*onyx*) and **Ibri** (*Hebrew*) do not occur as individual names elsewhere, but there is no reason to doubt their genuineness.

Some commentators pronounce verses 26, 27, spurious, against the evidence of the ancient versions.

(28) **Of Mahli came Eleazar.** — Literally, *To Mahli, Eleazar ; and there became not to him sons.* (Comp. chap. xxiii. 22.) The clan Eleazar did not branch out into new clans, but, being few in number, amalgamated with that of Kish-Jerahmeel.

(29) **Concerning Kish.** — Literally, *To Kish, the sons of Kish, Jerahmeel.* The plural, "sons of Kish," as in chap. xxiii. 22.

(30) **The sons also of Mushi.**—So chap. xxiii. 23. (See Notes there.) Only the names of the houses or classes are mentioned, without those of the chiefs. (Comp. verse 23, *supra*.)

**These were the sons of the Levites after the house of their fathers.**—Rather, *according to their father houses* (clans). This subscription proves that the original of verses 20—30 contained a complete catalogue of the Levitical houses or clans, exclusive of the Aaronites. How far the apparent defects of the present Hebrew text reproduce those of its archetype, and how far they are due to errors of transcription, cannot now be decided.

(31) **These likewise cast lots over against their brethren the sons of Aaron.**—Rather, *Just like, in the same way as their brethren*, the priests. The same compound preposition (*le'ummath*) recurs in chap. xxvi. 12, 16. In 2 Sam. xvi. 13 it has the sense of *over against*, or *parallel with*. The lots were cast, as in the case of the priests, to determine the order according to which the classes were to serve in rotation.

**Their brethren the sons of Aaron.**—This expression seems to indicate that the preceding list does not include *all* the Levites, but only those who *assisted the priests* in the Temple services : that is, the 24,000 of chap. xxiii. 4. The chronicler naturally returned to them after his account of the priestly classes. Hence, perhaps, the omission of the Gershonite houses is intentional. The narrative proceeds to treat of the Levites who were not in immediate attendance on the priesthood in chaps. xxv., xxvi.

**The chief of the fathers.**—Rather, *the chiefs of the clans.*

**Even the principal fathers over against their younger brethren.**—Rather, *clans—the chief just like his younger brother*. The word "fathers" (*abôth*) is a brief form of "father-houses" (*bêth-abôth*). The meaning appears to be that all the Levitical houses received their position by lot, senior and junior branches alike. The order, as thus determined, is not communicated ; nor is it expressly stated that the Levitical classes were twenty-four in number, but it appears highly probable, both from the data of the text, and from the analogy of the classes of the priests and the musicians (chap. xxv.).

XXV.

THE TWENTY-FOUR CLASSES OF SINGERS, OR MINSTRELS.

(1) **Moreover (and) David and the captains of the host.**—The latter (" the princes " of chap. xxiv. 6), were also concerned in the arrangement of the priestly classes (chap. xxiii. 2).

**Separated to the service of the sons of Asaph.**—Rather, *separated for service the sons of Asaph, and Heman, and Jeduthun*. These formed three guilds of sacred minstrels, famous to all after times. (Comp. the headings of many psalms in which these names occur, and also chap. vi. 33, *sqq.*, whence it appears that Asaph belonged to the sub-tribe of Gershon, Heman to that of Kohath, and Ethan-Jeduthun to that of Merari, so that all the branches of Levi were represented among the musicians.

**Separated.**—So Num. xvi. 9, and Gen. i. 7. (Comp Acts xiii. 2.)

**Who should prophesy with harps.**—In Hebrew, the verb *to prophesy* is a reflexive form, implying utterance under a spiritual influence. The ancients regarded musical utterance as an effect and proof of direct inspi-

who should prophesy with harps, with psalteries, and with cymbals: and the number of the workmen according to their service was: (2) of the sons of Asaph; Zaccur, and Joseph, and Nethaniah, and [1] Asarelah, the sons of Asaph under the hands of Asaph, which prophesied [2] according to the order of the king. (3) Of Jeduthun: the sons of Jeduthun; Gedaliah, and [3] Zeri, and Jeshaiah, Hashabiah, and Mattithiah, [4] six, under the hands of their father Jeduthun, who prophesied with a harp, to give thanks and to praise the LORD. (4) Of Heman: the sons of Heman; Bukkiah, Mattaniah, [5] Uzziel, [6] Shebuel, and Jerimoth, Hananiah, Hanani, Eliathah, Giddalti, and Romamti-ezer, Joshbekashah, Mallothi, Hothir, and Mahazioth: (5) all these were the sons of Heman the king's seer in the [7] words of God, to lift up the horn. And God gave to Heman

[1] Otherwise called Jesharelah, ver. 14.
[2] Heb., by the hands of the king.
[3] Or, Izri, ver. 11.
[4] With Shimei mentioned, ver. 17.
[5] Or, Azareel, ver. 18.
[6] Or, Shubael, ver. 20.
[7] Or, matters.

---

ration, and we still speak of the higher results of genius as inspired, however we may choose to explain the term away as a mere figure of speech. The power of moving sounds, whether of voice or instrument, is not to be gained by mere study or training; it is commonly spoken of as a "gift," and its products are called "inspirations." Whence come they, if not from the Divine source of life, and of all that makes life glad and beautiful? (James i. 17; 1 Sam. x. 5, xvi. 16, xviii. 10).

**Harps, with psalteries.**—Lutes and harps.

**And the number of the workmen according to their service was.**—Literally, *And the number of them—that is, of the men of work—for their service proved (as follows).*

**Men of work.**—A remarkable appellation. The term "work" is popularly restricted to what is called productive labour, but it is not difficult to see that persons engaged, like these minstrels, in singing and playing to the praise of God are actually helping to produce one of the best of real results, viz., the conservation of the religious spirit: that is, of the right attitude of man towards the Power upon whom his entire welfare absolutely depends.

(2) **Of the sons of Asaph; Zaccur.**—Literally, *To the sons of Asaph belonged Zaccur.* In verses 2—7 the term "sons" appears to mean trained members of the musical guilds, of which the three chiefs, Asaph, Heman, and Jeduthun, were masters.

**Asarelah.**—This singular name is spelt "Jesharelah" in verse 14. Ewald identifies it with "Israel," the unaccented ending *ah* having the force *belonging to*—literally, *towards, unto*—so that Jesharelah is in effect the modern Jewish surname *Israels*. (Comp. "Jaakobah," chap. iv. 36, *to Jacob, i.e., Jacobs*.)

**Under the hands of Asaph.**—Rather, *at the hand of Asaph.* It is implied that the four leaders here named were subordinate to Asaph, and under his direction. (Comp. verses 3, 6; 2 Chron. xxiii. 18, xxix. 27; Ezra iii. 10.)

**Which prophesied according to the order of the king.**—Literally (Asaph), *who prophesied* (or *should prophesy*, the participle, as in verse 1) *at the hands of the king*: that is, either according to the royal arrangements (2 Chron. xxiii. 18), under David's own appointment, or under the royal direction.

**Prophesied.**—That is, made music. (See verse 1.)

(3) **Of Jeduthun: the sons of Jeduthun.**—Rather, *To Jeduthun (i.e., belonging to the guild so called): the sons of Jeduthun were Gedaliah,* &c.

**Zeri.**—The "Izri" of verse 11 is probably right. (Comp. Num. xxvi. 49.) The error here is as old as the ancient versions.

**Six.**—Only five names are now read in the text; that of "Shimei" (verse 17) has fallen out, the only name in verses 9—31 which does not occur in verses 2—4. The Alex. LXX. inserts the name between Jeshaiah and Hashabiah.

**Jeshaiah.**—Elsewhere spelled Isaiah.

**Under the hands** (see last verse) **of their father Jeduthun, who prophesied with a harp.**—Literally, *according to the Hebrew punctuation, at the hands of their father Jeduthun, with the lute (i.e., provided with lutes, chap. xv. 16), who prophesied* (or *was to prophesy*) *for giving thanks and praise to Jehovah.* (Comp. chap. xvi. 4).

**At the hands of their father.**—Under the direction of their conductor.

(4) **Of Heman.**—Rather, *To Heman: the sons of Heman were,* &c. Fourteen names of Hemanite leaders are given. Curiously enough, the last six, excluding the peculiar "Joshbekashah," form, as they stand, a complete poetical couplet, which may be rendered:

"God has come; I have exalted and extolled the help;
I have spoken abundance of visions."

Such words are very suitable in the mouth of a seer, as Heman is called in the next verse, but the arrangement of the names in this order is perhaps only a mnemonic device.

**Uzziel.**—Power of God (Exod. vi. 18); called "Azareel" in verse 18 (*God hath helped*, chap. xii. 6). The words differ in Hebrew by one letter only. The Syriac has "Uzziel" (Azael) in both places. But the difference appears in the LXX. and Vulg.

**Shebuel.**—In verse 20, "Shubael," which the LXX. reads in both places. The Syriac and Vulg. keep the distinction. (Comp. chap. xxiv. 20.)

**Giddalti, and Romamti-ezer.**—That is, perhaps, Giddalti-ezer and Romamti-ezer. But in verse 29 "Giddalti" occurs again without any such addition, and the name as it stands may be compared with "Mallothi." The two verbs, *giddalti* and *romamti*, occur together in Isa. i. 2: "I have nourished and brought up."

(5) **All these were the sons of Heman.**—Literally, *Were sons to Heman.*

**The king's seer in the words of God.**—Or, *in the things of God, in Divine* (that is, liturgical) *matters.* Heman was a prophet as well as a minstrel. (For the connection between music and prophecy, comp. 1 Sam. x. 5, 6; 2 Kings iii. 15; Exod. xv. 20.) Comp. also Note on verse 1, above.

**Seer.**—Heb., *hōzèh.* Literally, *gazer.* The word rendered "seer" in chap. xxvi. 28 and 1 Sam. ix. 9 is different (*rō'èh*). Gad was called "David's seer" (chap. xxi. 9); so also Jeduthun is "the king's seer" (2 Chron. xxxv. 15).

**To lift up the horn.**—That is, according to Bertheau, "to blow the horns loudly." With this he connects the preceding phrase, which he renders "by

fourteen sons and three daughters. (6) All these *were* under the hands of their father for song *in* the house of the LORD, with cymbals, psalteries, and harps, for the service of the house of God, ¹ according to the king's order to Asaph, Jeduthun, and Heman. (7) So the number of them, with their brethren that were instructed in the songs of the LORD, *even* all that were cunning, was two hundred fourscore and eight.

(8) And they cast lots, ward against ward, as well the small as the great, the teacher as the scholar. (9) Now the first lot came forth for Asaph to Joseph: the second to Gedaliah, who with his brethren and sons *were* twelve: (10) the third to Zaccur, *he,* his sons, and his brethren, *were* twelve: (11) the fourth to Izri, *he,* his sons, and his brethren, *were* twelve: (12) the fifth to Nethaniah, *he,* his sons, and his brethren, *were* twelve: (13) the sixth to Bukkiah, *he,* his sons, and his brethren, *were* twelve: (14) the seventh to Jesharelah, *he,* his sons, and his brethren, *were* twelve: (15) the eighth to Jeshaiah, *he,* his sons, and his brethren, *were* twelve: (16) the ninth to Mattaniah, *he,* his sons, and his brethren, *were* twelve: (17) the tenth to Shimei, *he,* his sons, and his brethren, *were* twelve: (18) the eleventh to Azareel, *he,* his sons,

¹ Heb., *by the hands of the king.*

---

God's commands." (Comp. 2 Chron. xxix. 15.) But the horn does not appear elsewhere among the instruments of the Temple musicians, and the phrase "to lift up the horn" of a person is a well-known Hebrew metaphor. (Comp. 1 Sam. ii. 10: "May he give strength to his king, and lift up the horn of his anointed.") Thus it seems that the meaning is that God gave all these "sons"—*i.e.,* proficient disciples—to Heman in order to strengthen him for his work by providing him with a strong body of able assistants.

**And three daughters.**—The mention of "three daughters" is interesting, as an indication that women sustained a part in the service of song. (Comp. Exod. xv. 20; Judges xi. 34; 1 Sam. xviii. 6.) The Syriac omits the whole verse.

(6) **All these were under the hands of their father . . . and harps.**—Rather, *All these were under the direction of their conductor in the music in the house of Jehovah, with cymbals, harps, and lutes.* (See Notes on verses 2, 3.)

**According to the king's order to Asaph, Jeduthun, and Heman.**—Rather, *under the directions of the king* (and), *Asaph, Heman, and Jeduthun.* The meaning is that the arrangement of the duties of the minstrels was accomplished by David with the assistance of the three chief musicians, just as, in the classification of the priests, the king had been helped by the chief priests Zadok and Ahimelech (chap. xxiv. 3).

**All these.** — That is, the twenty-four leading minstrels, enumerated in verses 2—4. Each performed under the supervision of his own "father," *i.e.,* director.

(7) **So the number of them, with their brethren . . . was two hundred fourscore and eight.**—This total of two hundred and eighty-eight skilled musicians (24 × 12) shows that each of the twenty-four leading minstrels, called in verses 2—4 the "sons" of Asaph, Jeduthun, and Heman, was associated with a company of eleven "brethren," who were experts in the chanting of the sanctuary. The twenty-four leaders accompanied the singing of their choirs with instrumental music.

(8) **And they cast lots, ward against ward.**—Rather, *And they cast lots of charge,* that is, for determining the order in which each of the twenty-four guilds, or classes, should take charge of the services. (Comp. the LXX., κλήρους ἐφημεριῶν, "lots of courses;" and see Luke i. 6.) Some Hebrew MSS. and the Targum repeat the word "ward" (*mishmèreth,* "charge"), whence the reading of the Authorised Version. The ancient versions omit the word altogether.

**As well the small as the great.**—Heb., *exactly as the small* (or, *the younger*), *so the great* (or, *the elder*). (Comp. the Vulg., "ex aequo tam major quam minor.") But perhaps *leummath* is here used absolutely: "They cast lots in like manner" (chap. xxiv. 31). The senior houses, or guilds, had no advantage over the juniors, the order of rotation being decided by lot. (Comp. chap. xxiv. 31.)

**The teacher as the scholar.**—Literally, *cunning* (verse 7) *with learner.* According to chap. xxiii. 5, the whole number of Levites appointed for the service of song was 4,000. These were all included in the twenty-four classes, 288 of them being "cunning" men, that is, masters in their art, and the remaining 3,712 forming the rank and file of the choirs under the training of the proficients. The Aramaic word *talmîd* (scholar) occurs nowhere else in the Old Testament. It is the term used of the *disciples* of the Rabbis in the Talmud, and is the exact equivalent of the New Testament word, μαθητής.

(9) **Now the first lot came forth for Asaph to Joseph.**—See verse 2, according to which, Joseph was the second "son" of Asaph. Although not stated in the text, it must have been true of Joseph, as of all the following heads, that "he, and his sons and his brethren were twelve." The specified total of 288 (verse 7) requires it.

**The second to Gedaliah, who with his brethren and sons were twelve.** — Rather, *Gedaliah was the second, he and his brethren and his sons—twelve.* The "brethren" and "sons" of the chiefs, in this and the following verses, are the eleven masters, or proficients, in each class.

**Brethren.**—Fellow-clansmen, or associates.

**Sons.**—Disciples, or subordinates.

Perhaps, however, we should think of elder and younger families, grouped together in one class.

(10) **The third to Zaccur.**—Literally, *The third, Zaccur and his sons and his brethren—twelve.* The same mode of expression is used down to verse 18, except in verse 11, which reads, "The fourth for the Izrite, his sons and his brethren — twelve." The Izrite (not "Izri") is a Gentilic name, and seems to denote a family rather than a person.

(17) **Shimei.**—Omitted by accident from verse 3.

(18) **Azareel.**—Called Uzziel in verse 4. (Comp. Azariah as a variant of Uzziah, chap. iii. 12, and 2 Chron. xxvi. 1.)

and his brethren, *were* twelve: <sup>(19)</sup> the twelfth to Hashabiah, *he*, his sons, and his brethren, *were* twelve: <sup>(20)</sup> the thirteenth to Shubael, *he*, his sons, and his brethren, *were* twelve: <sup>(21)</sup> the fourteenth to Mattithiah, *he*, his sons, and his brethren, *were* twelve: <sup>(22)</sup> the fifteenth to Jeremoth, *he*, his sons, and his brethren, *were* twelve: <sup>(23)</sup> the sixteenth to Hananiah, *he*, his sons, and his brethren, *were* twelve: <sup>(24)</sup> the seventeenth to Joshbekashah, *he*, his sons, and his brethren, *were* twelve: <sup>(25)</sup> the eighteenth to Hanani, *he*, his sons, and his brethren, *were* twelve: <sup>(26)</sup> the nineteenth to Mallothi, *he*, his sons, and his brethren, *were* twelve: <sup>(27)</sup> the twentieth to Eliathah, *he*, his sons, and his brethren, *were* twelve: <sup>(28)</sup> the one and twentieth to Hothir, *he*, his sons, and his brethren, *were* twelve: <sup>(29)</sup> the two and twentieth to Giddalti, *he*, his sons, and his brethren, *were* twelve: <sup>(30)</sup> the three and twentieth to Mahazioth, *he*, his sons, and his brethren, *were* twelve: <sup>(31)</sup> the four and twentieth to Romamti-ezer, *he*, his sons, and his brethren, *were* twelve.

CHAPTER XXVI.—<sup>(1)</sup> Concerning the divisions of the porters: Of the Korhites *was* <sup>1</sup> Meshelemiah the son of Kore, of the sons of <sup>2</sup> Asaph. <sup>(2)</sup> And the sons of Meshelemiah *were*, Zechariah the firstborn, Jediael the second, Zebadiah the third, Jathniel the fourth, <sup>(3)</sup> Elam the fifth, Jehohanan the sixth, Elioenai the seventh. <sup>(4)</sup> Moreover the sons of Obed-edom *were*, Shemaiah the firstborn, Jehozabad the second, Joah the third, and Sacar the fourth, and Nethaneel the fifth, <sup>(5)</sup> Ammiel the sixth, Issachar the seventh, Peulthai the eighth: for God blessed <sup>3</sup> him. <sup>(6)</sup> Also unto Shemaiah his son were sons born, that ruled throughout the house

---

<sup>1</sup> Or, *Shelemiah*; ver. 14.

<sup>2</sup> Or, *Ebiasaph*; ch. 6. 37 & 9. 49.

<sup>3</sup> That is, Obed-edom, as ch. 13. 14.

---

<sup>(19)</sup> **To Hashabiah.**—So the Hebrew.

<sup>(20)</sup> **The thirteenth to Shubael.**—The Hebrew is, *to thirteenth, Shubael, his sons and his brethren, twelve;* and so in the next verse. The meaning seems to be: *as to,* or *as regards, the thirteenth.* Shubael (Shebuel) has occurred before (chaps. xxiii. 16, xxiv. 20).

<sup>(22)</sup> **The fifteenth to Jeremoth.**—Heb., *to fifteenth, to Jeremoth:* i.e., as regards the fifteenth lot, it was for Jeremoth. The construction is the same to the end of the chapter.

Spelling, and probably pronunciation, fluctuated between Jeremoth and Jerimoth (verse 4). (Comp. chaps. xxiii. 23 and xxiv. 30.) The LXX. and Vulg. spell "Jerimoth" in both places here; Syriac, "Jarmûth"; Arabic, "Jārāmāth" and "Jarmûth."

<sup>(31)</sup> An analysis of the whole list shows that the first, third, fifth, and seventh places fell to the four Asaphite guilds, or clans; the second, fourth, eighth, tenth, twelfth, and fourteenth to the six guilds of the sons of Jeduthun, or Ethanites; the sixth, ninth, eleventh, thirteenth, and the remaining ten places, to the fourteen guilds of Heman.

It appears evident that all the lots were thrown into a single urn, and that the Asaphite and Ethanite names were all drawn, as the chances made it likely, before the Hemanites were exhausted. As it happened, only Hemanite names were left after the fourteenth drawing.

## XXVI.

This chapter deals with (1) the classes of the porters, or warders (verses 1—19); (2) the keepers of the treasures of the sanctuary (verses 20—28); (3) the officials charged with external business, and chiefly scribes and judges (verses 29—32).

<sup>(1)</sup> **Concerning the divisions of the porters.** —Literally, (*as*) *to courses to porters.* (Comp. chap. xxiii. 6.) As many as 4,000 Levites were set apart for this function by the king's orders. (Comp. chap. xxiii. 25.)

**Of the Korhites was Meshelemiah.**—*To the Korhites* (sons of Korah) belonged *Meshelemiah son of Kōrĕ.* Meshelemiah is called Shelemiah (verse 14), and Shallum (chap. ix. 19).

**Of the sons of Asaph.**—Not the chief musician Asaph, who was a Gershonite (chap. vi. 39—43); whereas the Korhites were a Kohathite stock (Exod. vi. 21). The name here is evidently an abbreviation of Ebiasaph (chap. ix. 19), as Ahaz of Jehoahaz.

<sup>(2)</sup> **And the sons of Meshelemiah were.**— Rather, *And Meshelemiah had sons, viz., Zechariah the firstborn.* (See chap. ix. 21, and verse 14 below.) The seven "sons" of Meshelemiah-Shallum represent seven guilds of porters.

<sup>(3)</sup> **Jehohanan** (*Jah bestowed*), the full form of Johanan, John.

**Elioenai.**—Heb., *Elyĕhō-ēnai* (*mine eyes are towards Jehovah.* Comp. Ps. cxxiii.), the full form of Elyō-ēnai (chap. iii. 24).

<sup>(4)</sup> **Moreover the sons of Obed-edom.**—*And Obed-edom had sons.* Obed-edom (chap. xv. 24) is called a son of Jeduthun in chap. xvi. 38. This Jeduthun was not the Merarite chief musician, but a Korhite. (Comp. verses 1, 10, 19.)

<sup>(5)</sup> **For God blessed him.**—Comp. chap. xiii. 14, where it is said, "God blessed the house of Obed-edom." His sons' names are all testimonies to his thankful recognition of the Divine favour. The firstborn is Shemaiah, *Jah hath heard* (viz.) *the prayer for offspring;* Jehozabad, *Jah hath bestowed,* is the second; Joah, *Jah is a kinsman,* the third; Sacar, *reward* (Gen. xv. 1), is the fourth; Nethaneel, or Nathanael (Dositheus, Dorotheus, Deusdedit) *God hath given,* the fifth; Ammiel, *a kinsman is God,* the sixth; the seventh, Issachar, *there is a reward;* the eighth, Peulthai (Heb., Pĕullĕthai), *work* or *recompense of Jah.*

<sup>(6)</sup> **That ruled throughout the house of their father.**—Rather, *The lords of their clan.* The word translated "that ruled," is not a verb, but an abstract noun (*mimshāl*), like our expression "the authorities,"

of their father: for they *were* mighty men of valour. <sup>(7)</sup> The sons of Shemaiah; Othni, and Rephael, and Obed, Elzabad, whose brethren *were* strong men, Elihu, and Semachiah. <sup>(8)</sup> All these of the sons of Obed-edom: they and their sons and their brethren, able men for strength for the service, *were* threescore and two of Obed-edom. <sup>(9)</sup> And Meshelemiah had sons and brethren, strong men, eighteen. <sup>(10)</sup> Also Hosah, of the children of Merari, had sons; Simri the chief, (for *though* he was not the firstborn, yet his father made him the chief;) <sup>(11)</sup> Hilkiah the second, Tebaliah the third, Zechariah the fourth: all the sons and brethren of Hosah *were* thirteen. <sup>(12)</sup> Among these *were* the divisions of the porters, *even* among the chief men, having wards one against another, to minister in the house of the LORD. <sup>(13)</sup> And they cast lots, <sup>1</sup> as well the small as the great, according to the house of their fathers, for every gate. <sup>(14)</sup> And the lot eastward fell to <sup>2</sup> Shelemiah. Then for Zechariah his son, a wise counsellor, they cast lots; and his lot came out northward. <sup>(15)</sup> To Obed-

<sup>1</sup> Or, *as well for the small as for the great.*

<sup>2</sup> Called *Meshelemiah,* ver. 1.

---

or "the government." It only occurs besides in Dan. xi. 3, 5.

**Mighty men of valour.**—See Note on chap. ix. 13.

<sup>(7)</sup> **And Obed, Elzabad.**—This is probably corrupt, as the conjunction, which is used with the preceding names, is wanting between Obed and Elzabad. Probably Obed-Elzabad is a corruption of some single name, perhaps Obed-el: (comp. the Syriac and Arabic, *Ubdáël* and *Ufidilu*), or Abdiel (chap. v. 15; Syriac, *Abdáël*; Arabic, *Afádilu*; see Note on verse 12. (Those two versions, however, give six names, while the LXX. gives eight.)

**Whose brethren were strong men.**—The Hebrew has "his brethren." The conjunction appears to be missing again. Read: *And his brethren, sons of strength, Elihu and Semachiah.*

<sup>(8)</sup> **Able men.**—*Were men of power;* in the original, a singular collective.

**For strength.**—Literally, *In the strength,* i.e., ability.

**Were threescore and two . . .**—A distinct sentence: *There were sixty and two* (belonging) *to Obed-edom.* Perhaps the word *kol,* "every," has fallen out before *ish hayil* (comp. chap. x. 12, where the same phrase occurred). In that case render, *All these were of the sons of Obed-edom; they and their sons and their brethren, every man of power in the strength for service.* The "sons and brethren" of the porters may be compared with those of the musicians (chap. xxv. 9, 29).

<sup>(9)</sup> **And Meshelemiah.**—This goes back to verse 2, and forms a kind of supplement to the statement there. The Korhite (*Kohathite*) porters make a total of 80 families; viz., 62 of Obed-edom, and 18 of Meshelemiah.

<sup>(10)</sup> **Also Hosah, of the children of Merari.**—Four chiefs of the sons of Hosah are named, and thirteen assigned as the total number of families belonging to this clan (verses 10, 11). Adding them to the 18 of Meshelemiah and the 62 of Obed-edom, we get a total of 93 principal porters, presiding over the 4,000 Levites appointed to that work (chap. xxiii. 5).

**Simri (Shimri) the chief (for though he was not his firstborn . . .).**—This may mean either that the oldest family had died out, or that none of these families could prove its seniority to the rest.

<sup>(12)</sup> **Among these were the divisions of the porters.**—Rather, *To these, the courses* (chap. xxiii. 6) *of porters, that is, to the heads of the men* (chap. xxiv. 4), were *watches* or charges (chap. xxv. 8) *in common with their brethren* (chap. xxiv. 31), *to minister in the house of Jehovah* (chap. xvi. 37). The statement of this verse makes it evident that the names in verses 2—11 represent the courses of the porters or warders. As the twenty-four sons of Asaph, Heman, and Jeduthun represented the twenty-four courses of musicians in chap. xxv., a similar classification might naturally be expected here. Accordingly, we actually find seven sons of Meshelemiah (verses 2, 3), eight sons of Obed-edom (verses 4, 5), and four sons of Hosah (verses 10, 11), which together make nineteen heads and classes. It remains to add the "sons" of Shemaiah son of Obed-edom. As the text stands, these appear to be six in number, which would give a total of twenty-five (7 + 8 + 4 + 6). But the connection of the Hebrew in verse 7 is so unusual as to suggest at once that something is wrong; and if we assume Obed-Elzabad to represent one original composite name, like Obed-edom, we get five "sons of Shemaiah," and so a total of twenty-four classes or courses of warders. (From this verse to the end of chapter xxvii. the Syriac and Arabic versions fail us.)

<sup>(13)</sup> **And they cast lots.**—Compare chap. xxv. 8.

**As well the small as the great . . .**—Rather, *Small and great* (senior and junior) *alike, according to their houses, for each gate.* The posts of the porters were assigned by lot, without distinction of rank between the various families. The Sanctuary was built square with the four points of the compass, and had four gates, one on each side. The orientation of temples was the rule with the ancient Semites; and the importance attached to the cardinal points is illustrated by the ancient designation of the Babylonian and Assyrian sovereigns as "King of the four quarters," *i.e.*, of heaven (*sar arba'i kiprat*).

<sup>(14)</sup> **And the lot eastward fell to Shelemiah.**—The courses of the sons of Shelemiah (Meshelemiah verses 1, 9, and Shallum ix. 19) received by lot the post of honour on the east side of the Sanctuary.

**Then for Zechariah his son.**—Heb., *And Zechariah his son, counselling with sagacity, they cast lots.* The preposition *for* may have fallen out before Zechariah; or perhaps Zechariah is the real subject of the verb "cast lots," which is plural, because Zechariah is the name of a clan or guild. (Comp. chap. xxiv. 31; xxv, 8). Zechariah, the firstborn of Meshelemiah (verse 2), obtained the charge of the north side. "They cast lots" may mean drew a lot from the urn.

**A wise counsellor.**—This little touch is obviously a mark of truth. The chronicler could have had no motive for so characterising a warder of the Temple, unless he had found it in some older source, of which he has only given extracts.

<sup>(15)</sup> **To Obed-edom** (the lot fell) **southward; and to his sons** (fell by lot) **the house of Asup-**

edom southward; and to his sons the house of ¹Asuppim. ⁽¹⁶⁾ To Shuppim and Hosah *the lot came forth* westward, with the gate Shallecheth, by the causeway of the going ²up, ward against ward. ⁽¹⁷⁾ Eastward *were* six Levites, northward four a day, southward four a day, and toward Asuppim two *and* two. ⁽¹⁸⁾ At Parbar westward, four at the causeway, *and* two at Parbar. ⁽¹⁹⁾ These

¹ Heb., *gatherings.*
² See 1 Kin. 10. 5; 2 Chr. 9. 4.
³ Heb., *holy things.*
⁴ Or, *Libni,* ch. 6. 17.
⁵ Or, *Jehiel,* ch. 23. 8.

are the divisions of the porters among the sons of Kore, and among the sons of Merari. ⁽²⁰⁾ And of the Levites, Ahijah *was* over the treasures of the house of God, and over the treasures of the ³dedicated things. ⁽²¹⁾ *As concerning* the sons of ⁴Laadan; the sons of the Gershonite Laadan, chief fathers, *even* of Laadan the Gershonite, *were* ⁵Jehieli. ⁽²²⁾ The

---

pim.—"Asuppim" occurs only in verses 15 and 17 of this chapter, and in Neh. xii. 25. It seems to mean *collections,* stores of provisions and material for the use of the Temple and its ministers; so that Bêth-hâ-asuppîm is the *storehouse* or *magazine.* Nothing more is known about it. (The Vulgate takes *'asuppim* to mean "Council of Elders;" confusing the word with *'asuppôth,* Eccles. xii. 11.)

⁽¹⁶⁾ **To Shuppim and Hosah.**—No such name as Shuppim (chap. vii. 12) occurs among those of the Levitical warders as given above in verses 1—11. It is almost certainly a mistaken repetition of the last two syllables of Asuppim, which immediately precedes it. (The mistake is as old as the Vulgate; the LXX. has εἰς δεύτερον, perhaps reading *lishnàyim* instead of *le Shuppim.*) Read: *And to Hosah* (the lot fell) *to the west, with the gate Shallèketh on the highway that goeth up.*

**The gate Shalleketh,** mentioned here only. The name means *casting down* (in Isa. vi. 13, it denotes *felling* a tree); and hence this gate has been identified with the "Rubbish" or "Refuse Gate." (Comp. Neh. iii. 13.) It seems an objection to this, that the gate faced *the highway that goeth up* from the lower city to the Temple. Perhaps the name alludes to the drop, or steep descent, from the Sanctuary to the city.

**Ward against ward.**—Heb., *mishmâr lĕ'ummath mishmâr.* Compare the use of the same preposition in verse 12 and chap. xxv. 8, xxiv. 31. Here the meaning seems to be that Hosah had to guard two posts, viz., the western gate of the Temple, and the gate Shalleketh which lay opposite, in the western wall of the Temple area. (The LXX. has φυλακὴ κατέναντι φυλακῆς; the Vulgate *custodia contra custodiam;* implying that Hosah's warders were stationed opposite to each other.) But perhaps these concluding words refer to all four stations, and should be rendered, *ward like ward,* or *ward and ward alike,* or *post over against post.*

⁽¹⁷⁾ **Eastward were six Levites.**—Literally, *To the east the Levites were six; to the northward for the day four; to the southward for the day four; and to the Stores two two* (*i.e., two apiece,* or *two by two*). We must supply *for the day* in the first clause, with the LXX.

**Toward Asuppim two and two.**—The magazine appears to have had two doors, with two warders stationed at each.

⁽¹⁸⁾ **At** (the) **Parbar westward.**—See 2 Kings xxiii. 11, where a plural *Parwârîm* occurs. The meaning of the word is unknown. According to Gesenius (*Thesaur.* p. 1123), "Parwâr" is the right spelling; and the term answers to a Persian word denoting "summer-house," *i.e.,* a building open to light and air. He makes "the Parbar" a cloister running round the court of the Temple, from which the cells were entered. (See Note on chap. xxiii. 28.) Both spellings occur in Persian. Richardson's Persian Dictionary gives as many as fifteen variant forms of the word, besides *Parwâr* and *Parbâr.* His definition of the meaning is, "an open gallery or balcony on the top of a house, an upper room open on all sides to the air; a summer department or habitation; the roof of a house; a private door or entrance to a house."

**At the causeway.**—That is, the highway of verse 16. These four warders, therefore, stood by the gate Shalleketh. Adding together the numbers given in verses 17, 18, we find that there were twenty-four warders on duty every day. The recurrence of the number is curious; but its relation to the twenty-four classes of the porters can hardly be determined. It is likely, however, that the twenty-four warders represent chiefs with their companies rather than individuals (comp. verse 12). Twenty-four would be an insignificant fraction of 4,000 (chap. xxiii. 6).

⁽¹⁹⁾ **These are the divisions of the porters.**—*These are the courses of the porters, belonging to the sons of the Korhite, and to the sons of Merari.* This concluding remark proves that only the Kohathite and Merarite divisions of Levi had part in the duty of Temple-warders. The Gershonites were not represented among the porters (see verses 1 and 10).

II.—THE KEEPERS OF THE TEMPLE TREASURES (verses 20—28).

⁽²⁰⁾ **And of the Levites, Ahijah was over the treasures of the house of God.**—Literally, *And the Levites—Ahijah over the treasures,* . . . a strange beginning, for hitherto none but Levites have been in question. We should have expected at least "the *other* Levites." Further, the name Ahijah is suspicious, because (1) not found among the proper names in chap. xxiii. 7 *sqq.*; (2) it stands alone, without any reference to a family, such as is made in every other case (see verses 21—25); (3) the addition of the single letter *m* at the end of the word, would give the sense "their brethren," which is in fact the reading of the LXX. Read therefore, *And the Levites their brethren were over the treasures;* that is, the Levites other than those whose duties have already been described.

**Treasures of the house of God.**—The ordinary revenues and stores of the Sanctuary, including various kinds of legally prescribed contributions, and special gifts (see Exod. xxx. 11—14; Lev. xxvii.; Num. xviii. 16; 1 Chron. xxix. 7, 8).

**Treasures of the dedicated things.**—See margin and verses 26, 27.

⁽²¹, ²²⁾ These two verses contain one statement, viz:— *The sons of Laadan, i.e., The sons of the Gershonite belonging to Laadan, the heads of the houses of Laadan the Gershonite, Jehieli, that is, the sons of Kehieli, Zetham, and Joel his brother, were over the treasures of the house of Jehovah.* In other words, Zetham and Joel

*The Levites in Charge*     I. CHRONICLES, XXVI.     *of the Treasures.*

sons of Jehieli; Zetham, and Joel his brother, *which were* over the treasures of the house of the LORD. <sup>(23)</sup> Of the Amramites, *and* the Izharites, the Hebronites, *and* the Uzzielites: <sup>(24)</sup> and Shebuel the son of Gershom, the son of Moses, *was* ruler of the treasures. <sup>(25)</sup> And his brethren by Eliezer; Rehabiah his son, and Jeshaiah his son, and Joram his son, and Zichri his son, and Shelomith his son. <sup>(26)</sup> Which Shelomith and his brethren *were* over all the treasures of the dedicated things, which David the king, and the chief fathers, the captains over thousands and hundreds, and the captains of the host, had dedicated. <sup>(27)</sup> <sup>1</sup> Out of the spoils won in battles did they dedicate to maintain the house of the LORD. <sup>(28)</sup> And all that Samuel the seer, and Saul the son of Kish, and Abner the son of Ner, and Joab the son of Zeruiah, had dedicated; *and* whosoever had dedicated *any thing*, it was. under the hand of Shelomith, and of his brethren.

<sup>(29)</sup> Of the Izharites, Chenaniah and his sons *were* for the outward business over Israel, for officers and judges. <sup>(30)</sup> *And* of the Hebronites, Hashabiah and his brethren, men of valour, a thousand and seven hundred, *were* <sup>2</sup> officers among them of Israel on this side Jordan westward in all the business of the LORD, and in the service of the

<sup>1</sup> Heb., *out of the battles and spoils.*

<sup>2</sup> Heb., *over the charge.*

---

the chiefs of the clan Jehiel, which was the leading house of the Laadanite branch of Gershon, had charge of the Temple stores. (Comp. xxiii. 7, 8.) Jehieli looks like the gentilic form of Jehiel, *the Jehielite.*

<sup>(23)</sup> **Of the Amramites, and the Izharites.**—Or, *As for the Amramites,* &c. This enumeration of the four great clans of Kohath is a sort of heading to the rest of the chapter, which relates to Amramites (verses 24—28), Izharites (verse 29), and Hebronites (verses 30—32). (Comp. chap. xxiii. 12—20.)

<sup>(24)</sup> **And Shebuel.**—Rather, *Now Shebuel.* The office of comptroller-in-chief of the treasures was hereditary in the house of this Amramite. Hence he is called "ruler," or rather *prince* (nāgîd, chap. v. 2, xii. 27, xiii. 1); both departments mentioned in verse 20 being subject to his control.

<sup>(25)</sup> **And his brethren by Eliezer.**—*And his* (Shebuel's) *brethren* (kinsmen) *belonging to* (the house of) *Eliezer* (Moses' second son) *were Rehabiah his* (Eliezer's) *son, and Jeshaiah his* (Rehabiah's) *son*, &c. (Comp. chap. xxiii. 17.) The object of the verse is to show the extraction of Shelomith or Shelomoth, whose function is defined in verse 26. Shelomith the Amramite is not to be confused with the Gershomite Shelomith (chap. xxiii. 9), nor with the Izharite (chap. xxiii. 18, and xxiv. 22).

<sup>(26)</sup> **Which Shelomith and his brethen.**—*He,* viz., *Shelomoth and his kinsmen.*

**Chief of fathers.**—*Heads of the clans.*

**The captains over thousands.**—Heb., *to the captains*; a scribe's error.

**Captains of the host.**—Two are mentioned in verse 28, viz., Abner and Joab (see 2 Sam. viii. 16; 1 Chron. xviii. 15, and xxvii. 34).

<sup>(27)</sup> **Out of the spoils won in battles.**—The verse is an explanatory parenthesis. Literally, *Out of the wars, and out of the spoils*; a hendiadys, *i.e., out of the spoils of war.*

**To maintain the house.**—In 2 Kings xii. 8 the verb means *to repair* or *restore.* (Comp. Neh. iii. 4, 7.) Here *to make strong* appears to be the idea. (Comp. chap. xxix. 12.)

<sup>(28)</sup> **And all that Samuel the seer.**—The enumeration of those who had dedicated spoil is resumed from verse 26. The seer (rō'êh), the ancient term for prophet (nābi'). 1 Sam. ix. 9.

**And whosoever had dedicated any thing.**—These words point to a general prevalence of the practice of dedicating to God the spoils of war. (Comp. 2 Sam. viii. 11; 2 Kings xii. 18). The Law, in fact, ordained the dedication of all metals to the endowment of the Sanctuary (Num. xxxi. 22, 23, 50; Josh. vi. 19). These accumulations of spoil in the times preceding David help us to understand how it was that so much wealth was available for building and decorating the Temple (chap. xxii. 14—16).

**Under the hand of Shelomith.**—Comp. the same phrase in chap. xxv. 2, 3.

III. THE LEVITES CHARGED WITH BUSINESS EXTERNAL TO THE SANCTUARY (verses 29—32).

<sup>(29)</sup> **Of the Izharites, Chenaniah and his sons.**—*As to the Izharites, Chenaniah,* &c. Izhar was the second, as Hebron (verse 30) was the third of the Kohathite stocks (chap. xxiii. 12).

**The outward business** is defined as that of "officers" (shoterim, scribes) and judges. Six thousand Levites were set apart for these duties (chap. xxiii. 4). As Nehemiah xi. 16 mentions "the outward business of the house of God," the outward business here spoken of may have been in part connected with the Temple, and included such work as the collection of tithes and taxes.

<sup>(30)</sup> **And of the Hebronites, Hashabiah.**—Rather, *As to the Hebronites, Hashabiah, and his kinsmen, sons of valour* (chap. xxvi. 7), *a thousand and seven hundred, were charged with* (Heb., *over*) *the supervision of Israel on yonder side of the Jordan, westward, for all the work of Iahweh and for the service of the king.*

**Officers.**—*Pĕquddah* (oversight, superintendence). Vulg., *praeërant Israeli*: LXX., ἐπὶ τῆς ἐπισκέψεως τοῦ Ἰσραήλ. (See chaps. xxiii. 11, xxiv. 19 for another meaning of the word.)

**Hashabiah.**—A Kohathite of this name is not mentioned elsewhere.

**On this side Jordan.**—Rather, *on the other side* ('ēber): the western side of the river is so called in Josh. v. 1; xxii. 7. The use of this expression here seems to imply that the source upon which the chronicle is here dependent, was written in some locality east of the Jordan, perhaps at Babylon.

*Officers and Judges.*     I. CHRONICLES, XXVII.     *The Twelve Captains.*

king. <sup>(31)</sup> Among the Hebronites *was* Jerijah the chief, *even* among the Hebronites, according to the generations of his fathers. In the fortieth year of the reign of David they were sought for, and there were found among them mighty men of valour at Jazer of Gilead. <sup>(32)</sup> And his brethren, men of valour, *were* two thousand and seven hundred chief fathers, whom king David made rulers over the Reubenites, the Gadites, and the half tribe of Manasseh, for every matter pertaining to God, and <sup>1</sup> affairs of the king.

<sup>1</sup> Heb., *thing*.

CHAPTER XXVII.—<sup>(1)</sup> Now the children of Israel after their number, to wit, the chief fathers and captains of thousands and hundreds, and their officers that served the king in any matter of the courses, which came in and went out month by month throughout all the months of the year, of every course *were* twenty and four thousand.

<sup>(2)</sup> Over the first course for the first month *was* Jashobeam the son of Zabdiel: and in his course *were* twenty and four thousand. <sup>(3)</sup> Of the children of Perez *was* the chief of all the captains

---

<sup>(31, 32)</sup> **Among the Hebronites was Jerijah the chief.**—Rather, *To the Hebronites there was the head Jeriah (as to the Hebronites, according to their registers, according to families, in the fortieth year of the reign of David, they were sought out; and there were found among them valiant warriors in Jazer-Gilead); and his brethren, sons of might, two thousand seven hundred heads of families: and David the king made them overseers over the Reubenites, &c.* The long parenthesis obscures the meaning or these two verses. The general statement is that other Hebronites were charged with the supervision of the land east of Jordan : the parenthesis accounts for the fact.

<sup>(31)</sup> **Jerijah.**—Chap. xxiii. 19, "Jeriah." The Hebrew is the same (*Yĕriyâh*).

**In the fortieth year of the reign of David.** —This datum is important as fixing the time of these last regulations of David. (Comp. chap. xxiii. 1.) It evidently points to an ancient source.

**Jazer of Gilead.**—A Merarite city (Josh. xxi. 39); whereas the Hebronites were Kohathites. Perhaps we should read, "In the cities of Gilead."

<sup>(32)</sup> **Two thousand and seven hundred chief fathers.**—Rather, *heads of the families, i.e.*, of single households. Sometimes the Hebrew phrase means *heads of father-houses* or *clans;* but it obviously cannot be so here, as the whole number of Levites appointed to be "officers and judges" was only 6,000 (chap. xxiii. 4). The 2,700 fathers mentioned here, with the 1,700 of verse 30, make a total of 4,400. The remaining 1,600 (6,000 minus 4,400) may probably be assigned to Chenaniah (verse 29). It is strange that the house of Hebron should be twice mentioned (verses 30, 31) and the house of Uzziel not at all (see verse 23). Further, of the three great branches of Levi, none but Kohathite houses are named in connexion with "the outward business." The account appears to be incomplete.

## XXVII.

The account of the religious organisation (chaps. xxiii.—xxvi.) is naturally followed here by a sort of outline of the military and civil administration, given in the form of a catalogue of officers and ministers of the king.

I. THE TWELVE ARMY CORPS AND THEIR COMMANDERS (verses 1—15).

<sup>(1)</sup> **Now the children of Israel.**—This first verse is the heading or superscription of the list which follows.

**After their number.**—The stress lies on this phrase. It refers to the twelve courses of twenty-four thousand warriors each.

**Chief fathers.**—*Heads of the clans.*

**Captains of thousands and hundreds.**—See chap. xiii. 1.

**Their officers.**—Scribes, who kept the muster-rolls, and did the work of recruiting sergeants.

**The courses.** — Here, military divisions, *corps d'armée.* The same Hebrew term (*mahlĕgôth*) was used of the Levitical classes in the preceding chapters.

**Which came in and went out.**—Scii. The class or corps which came in and went out. Render: *That which came in and went out every month, for all the months of the year, i.e., the single corps, was twenty and four thousand.* As regards construction, the whole verse, from "the chief fathers" to "of every course," is a long apposition to "the children of Israel."

**Came in and went out month by month.**—Every month, the division whose turn it was stood under arms, as a sort of national guard, ready for immediate service.

<sup>(2)</sup> **Over the first course.**—Jashobeam son of Zabdiel was commander of the army corps appointed to be ready for service during the first month of the year. (See chap. xi. 11.) The names of the twelve generals of division have already occurred in the list of David's heroes contained in that chapter.

**In his course.**—Heb., *upon his course.*

<sup>(3)</sup> **Of the children of Perez.**—The reference is to Jashobeam. He belonged to the branch of Judah called Perez, or Pharez, to which David himself belonged.

**The chief of all the captains of the host for the first month.**—This notice about Jashobeam is obscure. The "captains of the host" (Heb., *hosts*) seem to be the twelve generals of division. (Comp. verse 5.) Jashobeam, as the first of David's heroes, may have enjoyed a kind of precedence among the commanders of the army corps; although he was not commander-in-chief of the entire national forces, which was the function of Joab. Or perhaps it is meant merely to emphasise the fact that Jashobeam was "the first" in the rotation of the generals; so that the phrase "for the first month" explains what precedes it. Or "the captains of the hosts" may possibly mean the officers of the subdivisions of the first army corps, of whom Jashobeam was, of course, the chief. The context appears to favour this last explanation.

of the host for the first month. (4) And over the course of the second month was ¹Dodai an Ahohite, and of his course was Mikloth also the ruler: in his course likewise were twenty and four thousand. (5) The third captain of the host for the third month was Benaiah the son of Jehoiada, a ²chief priest: and in his course were twenty and four thousand. (6) This is that Benaiah, who was "mighty among the thirty, and above the thirty: and in his course was Ammizabad his son. (7) The fourth captain for the fourth month was Asahel the brother of Joab, and Zebadiah his son after him: and in his course were twenty and four thousand. (8) The fifth captain for the fifth month was Shamhuth the Izrahite: and in his course were twenty and four thousand. (9) The sixth captain for the sixth month was Ira the son of Ikkesh the Tekoite: and in his course were twenty and four thousand. (10) The seventh captain for the seventh month was Helez the Pelonite, of the children of Ephraim: and in his course were twenty and four thousand. (11) The eighth captain for the eighth month was Sibbecai the Hushathite, of the Zarhites: and in his course were twenty and four thousand. (12) The ninth captain for the ninth month was Abiezer the Anetothite, of the Benjamites: and in his course were twenty and four thousand. (13) The tenth captain for the tenth month was Maharai the Netophathite, of the Zarhites: and in his course were twenty and four thousand. (14) The eleventh captain for the eleventh month was Benaiah the Pirathonite, of the children of Ephraim: and in his course were twenty and four thousand. (15) The twelfth captain for the twelfth month was ³Heldai the Netophathite, of Othniel: and in his course were twenty and four thousand.

(16) Furthermore over the tribes of Israel: the ruler of the Reubenites was Eliezer the son of Zichri: of the Simeon-

---

1 Or, *Dodo*, 2 Sam. 23. 9.

2 Or, *principal officer*.

a 2 Sam. 23. 20, 22, 23; ch. 11. 24.

3 Or, *Heled*, ch. 11. 30.

---

(4) **Dodai an Ahohite.**—*The Ahohite.* Chap. xi. 11 proves that the right reading is *Eliezer son of Dodai the Ahohite.*

**And of his course was Mikloth also the ruler.**—Literally, *and his course, and Mikloth the prince (nāgîd);* which appears meaningless. Perhaps the "and" before Mikloth is spurious. (Comp. end of verse 6.) The sense may then be that this division included Mikloth "the prince," an unknown personage; or that Mikloth was the chief man in the division. (See chaps. viii. 32, ix. 37, where Mikloth is a Benjamite name.) The LXX. and Vulg. agree with Authorised Version; the Syriac and Arabic are wanting in this chapter.

(5) **The third captain of the host.**—Heb., *captain of the third host.* So Vulg.

**Benaiah.**—See chap. xi. 22.

**The son of Jehoiada, a chief priest.**—Rather, *son of Jehoiada the priest, as head,* viz., of the third army corps. The term "chief," or "head," belongs to Benaiah, not to his father. But perhaps it is an erroneous gloss on Jehoiada. (Comp. 2 Chron. xxiii. 8.) Both LXX. and Vulg. make *Benaiah* the priest.

(6) **This is that Benaiah, who was mighty among the thirty.**—Literally, *he, Benaiah, was a hero of the thirty.* (Comp. chap. xi. 25; 2 Sam. xxiii. 23.)

**And in his course.**—Heb., *and his course. Ammizabad his son.* Comp. the second clause of verse 4. Here, as there, the LXX. and Vulg. give the sense "over his course," as if Ammizabad were coadjutor with his father. The text may be defective in both places.

(7) **The fourth captain for the fourth month.** —Heb., *the fourth, for the fourth month;* an abridged mode of expression, which is preserved from this point to the end of the list.

**Asahel the brother of Joab.**—Chap. xi. 26. Asahel was slain by Abner at the beginning of David's reign (2 Sam. ii. 18—23). The added clause, "And Zebadiah his son after him," evidently refers to this fact. Perhaps the difficult statements about Mikloth and Ammizabad in verses 4 and 6 were originally similar to this one about Zebadiah. The fourth division "may have been called by the name of the fallen hero in honour of his memory" (Bertheau).

(8) **The fifth captain for the fifth month.**— Rather, *the fifth, for the fifth month, was the captain Shamhuth.* Shamhuth is called "Shammoth the Harorite" in chap. xi. 27, and "Shammah the Harodite" in 2 Sam. xxiii. 25.

**The Izrahite.**—Heb., *ha-yizráh,* which is probably a mistake for *ha-zarhî,* "the Zarhite" (comp. verses 11 and 13), i.e., a member of the Judean clan called Zerah. Harod was his town.

(9—14) Comp. chap. xi. 27—31 for the names here given.

(15) **Heldai** (living).—The same as "Heled" (life) in chap. xi. 30.

**Of Othniel.**—Of the clan so called. (Comp. Josh. xv. 17.) His town was Netophah, near Bethlehem.

Of the whole list of twelve generals, it is noticeable that eight—viz., the first, third, fourth, fifth, sixth, eighth, tenth, and twelfth—belonged to the royal tribe of Judah. Of the remaining four, the second perhaps, and the ninth certainly, was a Benjamite; the seventh and eleventh were Ephraimites.

II. THE PRINCES OR EMIRS OF THE TWELVE TRIBES (verses 16—24).

(16) **Furthermore over the tribes of Israel.** Literally, *and over the tribes of Israel . . . the Reubenites had as prince (nāgîd) Eliezer,* etc.

**Eliezer the son of Zichri.**—Originally the emir of the tribe was its leader in war, as well as its chief authority in times of peace. David, as appears by the list (verses 1—15) made the important change of nomi-

*The Princes.*   I. CHRONICLES, XXVII.   *The Numbering Hindered.*

ites, Shephatiah the son of Maachah: (17) of the Levites, Hashabiah the son of Kemuel: of the Aaronites, Zadok: (18) of Judah, Elihu, *one* of the brethren of David: of Issachar, Omri the son of Michael: (19) of Zebulun, Ishmaiah the son of Obadiah: of Naphtali, Jerimoth the son of Azriel: (20) of the children of Ephraim, Hoshea the son of Azaziah: of the half tribe of Manasseh, Joel the son of Pedaiah: (21) of the half *tribe* of Manasseh in Gilead, Iddo the son of Zechariah: of Benjamin, Jaasiel the son of Abner: (22) of Dan, Azareel the son of Jeroham. These *were* the princes of the tribes of Israel.

(23) But David took not the number of them from twenty years old and under: because the LORD had said he would increase Israel like to the stars of the heavens. (24) Joab the son of Zeruiah began to number, but he finished not, because *a* there fell wrath for it against Israel; neither ¹ was the number put in the account of the chronicles of king David.

(25) And over the king's treasures *was* Azmaveth the son of Adiel: and over

*a* 2 Sam. 24. 5, &c.; ch. 21. 7.

¹ Heb., *ascended.*

---

nating the chief commanders himself. The emirs would still manage the internal affairs of their tribes.

(17) **Of the Levites, Hashabiah.**—Levi has two princes, one for the tribe and one for the great Aaronite branch. The literal rendering would be: *To Levi, Hashabiah . . . to Aaron, Zadok.* Zadok was the high priest (chap. xxiv. 3).

(18) **Of Judah, Elihu, one of the brethren of David.**—The LXX. reads "Eliab." Eliab was David's eldest brother (chap. ii. 13). He, therefore, was tribal prince by right of the firstborn, assuming that the house of Jesse was the leading family of Judah. (See Ruth iv. 17—20.)

**Omri the son of Michael.**—Omri was, perhaps, an ancestor of the successful adventurer who founded the dynasty of Ahab (1 Kings xvi. 16; Micah vi. 16).

(20) **Of the half tribe of Manasseh.**—That on the west of Jordan, between Ephraim and Issachar.

(21) **Of the half tribe of Manasseh in Gilead.** —Rather, *towards Gilead, Gilead-ward: i.e.,* on the east of the Jordan, in Gilead and Bashan.

**Iddo the son of Zechariah.**—The prophet Zechariah was a son of Berechiah, son of Iddo, and may have descended from this Iddo.

**Jaasiel the son of Abner,** was, doubtless, a son of Saul's famous marshal.

(22) **Of Dan.**—Dan and Zebulun, omitted in the tribal registers of chaps. iv.—vii., are both mentioned in the present list. On the other hand, Gad and Asher are unnoticed here; why, we cannot say. The total— "twelve"—is made by counting Manasseh as two and Joseph as three tribes. The order of the first six names is that of Gen. xxxv. 23. Why Dan is mentioned last is not clear: some have thought it indicates the chronicler's reprobation of the idolatry of the tribe (2 Kings xii. 29, 30; comp. Judges xviii. 30; Amos viii. 14); but he has probably kept the order of his source.

**These were the princes.**—The same word as "captains" in the former list (*sārim*).

(23) **But David took** (Num. iii. 40, *nāsā'mispar*) **not the number of them.**—This and the next verse contain concluding remarks on the two lists communicated in verses 1—22. The heading of the chapter professes that the "sons of Israel, *according to their number,*" is the subject in hand. This appended note limits that statement to those who were above "twenty years old," that is, to those who were of the military age. The reference is undoubtedly to the census, of which chap. xxi. gave the account; and it is evident that one of the main objects of that census was the military and political organisation here so scantily and obscurely described.

**Because the Lord had said he would increase Israel like to the stars of the heavens.**—The reason why David restricted the census to those who were capable of bearing arms (see Gen. xv. 5, xxii. 17). The idea implied seems to be that to attempt to number Israel would be to evince a distrust of Jehovah's faithfulness; and, perhaps, that such an attempt could not possibly succeed.

(24) **Joab the son of Zeruiah began.**—Or, *had oegun.* This clearly refers to chap. xxi. 6. Joab omitted to number Levi and Benjamin.

**Because there fell wrath for it.**—The same phrase recurs in 2 Chron. xix. 10, xxiv. 18. (Comp. for the fact, chap. xxi. 7, *seq.*) The sense of the Hebrew may be brought out better thus: "*Joab son of Zeruiah had begun to number, without finishing; and there fell,*" &c.

**Neither was the number put in the account of the chronicles of king David.**—Literally, *and the number came not up* ('*ālāh*), was not entered. (Comp. 1 Kings ix. 21; 2 Chron. xx. 34.) The number which Joab ascertained was not recorded, as might have been expected, in the official annals of the reign, here designated as "the account of the chronicles of king David" (*mispar dibrê ha-yāmim*). It is implied that the chronicler had these annals before him in some form or other, probably as a section of the "History of the Kings of Judah and Israel," and that he found the lists of this chapter in that source. Those of chaps. xxiii.—xxvi may have been derived from the same authority. In 2 Kings xii. 20, xiii. 8, 12, and all similar instances, the phrase for "book of the Chronicles" is not *mispar*, but *sēpher dibrê ha-yāmim.* Some suppose that the text here should be altered accordingly; others would render *mispar dibrê ha-yāmim,* "the statistical section of the annals." But *mispar* in Judges vii. 15 means *the telling* or *relation of* a dream, and the transition from such a sense to that of written relation is easy. The phrase rendered "Chronicles" is the same as the Hebrew title of these books.

III.—THE TWELVE OVERSEERS OF THE ROYAL ESTATES AND PROPERTY (verses 25—31).

The number of these officers is noticeable, twelve being a normal number in Israelite institutions.

(25) **And over the king's treasures.**—That is, those of the palace on Zion.

**And over the storehouses.**—The Hebrew has the same word "treasures." The treasures "in the fields" (*sādēh*), or the country, in the cities, the villages,

the storehouses in the fields, in the cities, and in the villages, and in the castles, *was* Jehonathan the son of Uzziah: <sup>(26)</sup> and over them that did the work of the field for tillage of the ground *was* Ezri the son of Chelub: <sup>(27)</sup> and over the vineyards *was* Shimei the Ramathite: <sup>1</sup> over the increase of the vineyards for the wine cellars *was* Zabdi the Shiphmite: <sup>(28)</sup> and over the olive trees and the sycomore trees that *were* in the low plains *was* Baal-hanan the Gederite: and over the cellars of oil *was* Joash: <sup>(29)</sup> and over the herds that fed in Sharon *was* Shitrai the Sharonite: and over the herds *that were* in the valleys *was* Shaphat the son of Adlai: <sup>(30)</sup> over the camels also *was* Obil the Ishmaelite: and over the asses *was* Jehdeiah the Meronothite: <sup>(31)</sup> and over the flocks *was* Jaziz the Hagerite. All these *were* the rulers of the substance which *was* king David's.

<sup>(32)</sup> Also Jonathan David's uncle was a counsellor, a wise man, and a ²scribe: and Jehiel the ³son of Hachmoni was

---

1 Heb., *over that which was of the vineyards*.

2 Or, *secretary*.

3 Or, *Hachmonite*.

---

and the "castles" (*migdālīm*), or towers (2 Chron. xxvi. 10; Micah iv. 8), include all that belonged to David outside the walls of Jerusalem.

**Jehonathan** was comptroller-general of the revenues from these sources.

<sup>(26)</sup> **And over them that did the work of the field.**—Ezri was steward of the arable domains.

<sup>(27)</sup> **Shimei** of Ramah-Benjamin (Josh. xviii. 25) was overseer of the vineyards.

**Zabdi.**—Zebadiah (the New Testament Zebedee), of the south Judean town Shiphmoth (1 Sam. xxx. 28), was "over that which is in the vineyards for the treasures (stores) of wine," *i.e.*, the wine-cellars. So Vulg., *cellis vinariis*. The territory of Judah was famous as a wine-growing land (Gen. xlix. 11). The memorable "grapes of Eshcol" were gathered there (Num. xiii. 23).

<sup>(28)</sup> **Olive trees.**—The same word (*zéthim*) is rendered "olive yards" in Josh. xxiv. 13; 1 Sam. viii. 14, and elsewhere in the Authorised version.

**The sycomore trees that were in the low plains.**—The sycomores that were in the Shephelah or lowland of Judah, between the hills and the sea (Josh. xv. 33). The *Ficus sycomorus*, or fig-mulberry, a beautiful evergreen tree, indigenous to Egypt, was once abundant in Palestine, as appears from 1 Kings x. 27; 2 Chron. i. 15. Its small sweet figs were much eaten by the poor. (Comp. Amos vii. 14.)

**Baal-hanan** ("The Lord bestowed").—An older form of Jehohanan. (Comp. the Phœnician Hannibal.)

**The Gederite.**—Of Geder, or Gedor, a town in the hill-country of Judah (Josh. xii. 13, xv. 58).

**Over the cellars of oil.**—Heb., *treasures*, or stores of oil. The oil was that of the olives. (Comp. Judges ix. 9.)

<sup>(29)</sup> **And over the herds that fed in Sharon.** —Heb., *the oxen that grazed in the Sharon*. The Sharon (*i.e.*, "the Level") was a fertile strip of pasture-land running along the coast of the Mediterranean, between Cæsarea and Joppa. (See Cant. ii. 1; Isa. xxxiii. 9.)

**Shitrai.**—Hebrew margin, *Shirtai*.

**Over the herds that were in the valleys.**—Apparently the valleys of the highlands of Judah. Another reading is "in valleys."

<sup>(30)</sup> **Over the camels also was Obil the Ishmaelite.**—Obil's name means either "owner of camels" or "a good manager of camels," answering exactly to the Arabic '*ibil*. (Comp. Gen. xxxvii. 25; Judges vii. 12.) An "Ishmaelite," *i.e.*, an Arab, would be the fittest person for looking after camels.

**The asses.**—The she-asses. (Comp. Gen. xlix. 14; Judges v. 10; Zech. ix. 9.)

**Jehdeiah the Meronothite.**—Of Merōnōth, a town perhaps near Mizpah (Neh. iii. 7). The LXX. has Merathon, or Marathon.

<sup>(31)</sup> **And over the flocks.**—Of sheep and goats.

**Jaziz the Hagerite.**—See chap. v. 10—19, for the conquest of East Gilead, the home of the Hagrim, or "Hagerites," by the tribe of Reuben, in the days of Saul. David's herds of camels and flocks of small cattle may have grazed in the pastures east of the Jordan, under the charge of his Bedawi overseers.

**All these were the rulers of the substance which was king David's.**—The word rendered "rulers" is *sārīm*, "captains" or "princes." (See verse 22.) The same term is translated "stewards" in chap. xxviii. 1.

**Substance** (*rĕkūsh*) is an old word, denoting especially the moveable wealth of a nomad chief. (Comp. Gen. xii. 5, xiv. 21). The wealth of David consisted partly of flocks and herds, but partly also of the produce of husbandry, and, no doubt, of commerce. (See chaps. xiv. 1, xxii. 4.) The period of the kings saw Israel a settled nation, that had exchanged the purely nomad life for an ordered social existence.

IV.—DAVID'S PRIVY COUNCIL (verses 32—34).

<sup>(32)</sup> **Also Jonathan David's uncle was a counsellor.**—A son of David's brother Shimeah was named Jonathan (chap. xx. 7; 2 Sam. xxi. 21). Nothing further is known of the present Jonathan than what is here related.

**A wise man, and a scribe.**— Rather, *a sage and a scholar was he*. The word rendered "scribe" (*sōphēr*) usually answers to the γραμματεύς of the New Testament, and so the LXX. gives it here. We may remember that in the rude epochs of society mere writing has been esteemed an art, so that a king of England who could write was dubbed Beauclerc, "fine scholar." Charles the Great never got so far as signing his own name, though he made great efforts to do so. But writing goes back to a very ancient period among Semitic races, and *sōphēr* probably means here, as in Ezra vii. 6, "a man of letters," or "skilled in the sacred law." (See chap. ii. 55; Isa. xxxiii. 18; Ps. xlv. 2.) David's official *sōphēr*, or scribe, was Shavsha (chap. xviii. 16).

**Jehiel the son of Hachmoni.**—Rather, *son of a Hachmonite*. (Comp. chap. xi. 11.)

**With the king's sons**—That is, their tutor. The similar lists in 2 Sam. viii. 15—18, 1 Chron. xviii. 15—17, and 2 Sam. xx. 23—26, lack representatives of the two offices mentioned in this verse. Obviously this account is independent of those.

*David Summons and*     I. CHRONICLES, XXVIII.     *Addresses an Assembly.*

with the king's sons: (33) ¹ and Ahithophel *was* the king's counsellor: and Hushai the Archite *was* the king's companion: (34) and after Ahitophel *was* Jehoiada the son of Benaiah, and Abiathar: and the general of the king's army *was* Joab.

CHAPTER XXVIII.—(1) And David assembled all the princes of Israel, the princes of the tribes, and the captains of the companies that ministered to the king by course, and the captains over the thousands, and captains over the hundreds, and the stewards over all the substance and ¹ possession of the king, and of his sons, with the ² officers, and

¹ Or, *cattle.*

² Or, *eunuchs.*

a 2 Sam. 7. 5, 13; 1 Kings 5. 5; ch. 22. 8.

³ Heb., *bloods.*

b Gen. 49. 8; 1 Sam. 16. 13; Ps. 78. 68.

with the mighty men, and with all the valiant men, unto Jerusalem.

(2) Then David the king stood up upon his feet, and said, Hear me, my brethren, and my people: *As for me, I had* in mine heart to build an house of rest for the ark of the covenant of the LORD, and for the footstool of our God, and had made ready for the building: (3) but God said unto me, ᵃThou shalt not build an house for my name, because thou *hast been* a man of war, and hast shed ³ blood. (4) Howbeit the LORD God of Israel chose me before all the house of my father to be king over Israel for ever: for he hath chosen ᵇ Judah *to be* the ruler; and of the house of Judah,

---

(33) **And Ahithophel was the king's counsellor.**—Rather, *a counsellor of the king's*—Ahithophel, the faithless adviser, who committed suicide when his treachery proved unsuccessful (2 Sam. xv. 31 *seq.*, xvii. 23).

**Hushai the Archite.**—The faithful counsellor, who baffled the wisdom of Ahithophel (2 Sam. xvii.).

(34) **And after Ahitophel**—After his death, Jehoiada the son of Benaiah, and Abiathar, the Ithamarite high priest, were David's advisers. Benaiah's father was named Jehoiada (see verse 5, and chaps. xi. 22, xviii. 17), so that David's counsellor Jehoiada bore the name of his grandfather—a common enough occurrence. Others assume that the right reading is "Benaiah the son of Jehoiada," who may have been an adviser of David, as well as captain of his guard.

### XXVIII.

DAVID'S LAST INSTRUCTIONS AND DEATH (chaps. xxviii., xxix.).

David charges Solomon before the National Assembly to build the Temple (verses 1—10), and delivers to him the plans and materials of the building and its furniture (verses 11—21).

(1) **And David assembled all the princes of Israel.**—As he had called the National Assembly before removing the Ark (chaps. xiii. 1, xv. 3). Who the princes (*sārim*) were is defined in the following clauses.

**The princes of the tribes.**—See the list of them in chap. xxvii. 16—22.

**Captains of the companies.**—Rather, *princes of the courses, who served the king* : viz., those enumerated in chap. xxvii. 1—15.

**Stewards.**—See chap. xxvii. 25—31. Both "captains" and "stewards" are *sārim* in the Hebrew.

**Possession** (*miqnèh*).—A word generally used, like the Greek κτῆμα (κτῆνος), of possessions in cattle—live stock.

**And of his sons.**—Perhaps considered as his heirs, or rather, from the old tribal view of property, as sharing the royal domains with him.

**With the officers.**—Heb., *sarīsim*, eunuchs. The word appears to be used in a generalised sense, and to denote simply courtiers or palace officials. (Comp. Gen. xxxvii 36; 1 Sam. viii. 15; 1 Kings xxii. 9; Jer. xxxviii. 7, xli. 16.)

**The mighty men.**—"The heroes" (*ha-gibbôrim*) or "warriors" of chaps. xi. 31—47 and xii. But the LXX. and Vulg. interpret men of rank and wealth, magnates (τοὺς δυνάστας, Luke i. 52).

**And with all the valiant men.**—Literally, *and every mighty man* ("*gibbôr*") *of valour*, a phrase meant to include all other persons of importance. It is noticeable that in this meeting of the estates of the realm all the dignitaries of chap. xxvii. are present (contrast chaps. xv. 25, xxiii. 2, xiii. 1), except the priests and Levites. (But comp. verse 21.)

(2) **Then David the king stood up upon his feet.**—To address the assembly, the king naturally rose from his throne.

**Hear me.**—Calling attention, as in Gen. xxiii. 11—15.

**My brethren, and my people.** — Comp. 1 Sam. xxx. 23; 2 Sam. xix. 12. The words do not so much imply condescension as an acknowledgment of what every one of David's hearers felt to be true—viz., that all Israel were kin, and David the head of the family.

**As for me, I had in mine heart to build.** —See chap. xxii. 7, 8 and the Notes there. Verses 2—7 of this chapter are in substance, and partly in expression, identical with chap. xxii. 7—10 (David's private charge to Solomon).

**An house of rest**—*i.e.*, a permanent abode instead of a sacred tent, which gave the idea of wandering from place to place, like the nomads of the desert. (Comp. Ps. cxxxii. 8.)

**The footstool of our God.** — The so-called mercy-seat, the golden *kappôreth* suspended over the Ark, on which were the cherubim—the throne of Deity (Ps. xcix. 1).

**And had made ready.** — Rather, *and I made ready*, by amassing stores of material (chap. xxii. 2—4, 14—16).

(3) **But God said unto me.**—The emphasis lies on the word *God*, which is in direct contrast with the "I—in my heart it was," of verse 2. (Comp. chap. xxii. 8, of which this verse is a summary.)

(4) **Howbeit the Lord God of Israel chose me.**—Comp. chap. xi. 2 and Notes. The Divine election of David preludes that of Solomon (verse 5).

**For he hath chosen Judah to be the ruler.**—Better, *For Judah it was that he chose for prince*

*David encourages*      I. CHRONICLES, XXVIII.      *Solomon to build the Temple.*

the house of my father; and among the sons of my father he liked me to make *me* king over all Israel: <sup>(5)</sup> <sup>a</sup>and of all my sons, (for the LORD hath given me many sons,) he hath chosen Solomon my son to sit upon the throne of the kingdom of the LORD over Israel. <sup>(6)</sup> And he said unto me, <sup>b</sup> Solomon thy son, he shall build my house and my courts: for I have chosen him *to be* my son, and I will be his father. <sup>(7)</sup> Moreover I will establish his kingdom for ever, if he be <sup>1</sup>constant to do my commandments and my judgments, as at this day. <sup>(8)</sup> Now therefore in the sight of all Israel the congregation of the LORD, and in the audience of our God, keep and seek for all the commandments of the LORD your God: that ye may possess this good land, and leave *it* for an inheritance for your children after you for ever. <sup>(9)</sup> And thou, Solomon my son, know thou the God of thy father, and serve him with a perfect heart and with a willing mind: for <sup>c</sup>the LORD searcheth all hearts, and understandeth all the imaginations of the thoughts: if thou seek him, he will be found of thee; but if thou forsake him, he will cast thee off for ever. <sup>(10)</sup> Take heed now; for the LORD hath chosen thee to build an house for the sanctuary: be strong, and do *it*.

---

*a* ch. 23. 1.

*b* 2 Sam. 7. 13; 2 Chr. i. 9.

<sup>1</sup> Heb., *strong.*

*c* 1 Sam. 16. 7; Ps. 7. 9 & 139. 2; Jer. 11. 20 & 17. 10, & 20. 12.

---

(*nāgîd*), and *in the house of Judah, my father's house.* (Comp. chap. v. 2 and Notes.)

**And among the sons of my father he liked me.**—The expression is scarcely adequate. The verb in the Hebrew is *rāçāh*, which answers to the Hellenistic εὐδοκεῖν, "to be satisfied, well pleased with." Translate, therefore, "It was I in whom He took pleasure." (Comp. Prov. iii. 12.) David uses of himself the very phrase which the Divine voice spoke from heaven at the baptism of the Son of David, the true King of Israel and of mankind (Matt. iii. 17).

(5) **Many sons.**—See chap. iii. 1—9, where nineteen are mentioned by name, "besides the sons of the concubines, and Tamar their sister."

**He hath chosen.**—Heb., *then he chose,* the construction being changed after the parenthesis.

**Solomon my son.**—The son who has the best right to the name. (Comp. chap. xxii. 10.)

**The throne of the kingdom of the Lord.**—This expression is unique in the Old Testament. (Comp. chaps. xxix. 23, xvii. 14.) It brings out into strong relief the idea that the Israelite monarchy was only a vicegerency; not David nor Solomon, but Jehovah being the true and only King. (Comp. Gideon's reply to the offer of the crown, Judges viii. 23; 1 Sam. viii. 7, xii. 12.)

(6) **He shall build.**—Better, *he it is that shall build.* The pronoun is emphatic: *he,* and not *thou.*

**I have chosen him. . . . his father.**—Literally, *I have chosen him for myself as a son, and I—I will become to him a father.*

(7) **Moreover I will establish his kingdom for ever.**—So chap. xxii. 10 (at end).

**If he be constant to do my commandments and my judgments.**—The same condition is attached to the same promise in 1 Kings ix. 4, 5. (Comp. also 1 Kings iii. 14, where the promise is length of days.)

**As at this day.**—As we are doing in our present work. The same words occur in the same sense at the end of Solomon's Prayer (1 Kings viii. 61).

(8) **Now therefore in the sight of all Israel.**—Literally, *And now to the eyes of all Israel . . . and in the ears of our God;* scil. I adjure you. David ends his address to the people by a solemn appeal, like that of Moses (Deut. iv. 26, xxx. 19: "I call heaven and earth to witness," &c.). David's appeal is to the whole nation as represented before him, and to the God whose ear is ever open.

**Seek**—*i.e.,* do not neglect; resort to them always as the rule of right living (same word as chaps. xiii. 3, xv. 13).

**That ye may possess this** (Heb. *the*) **good land.**—Another reminiscence of Deuteronomy (chap. iv. 1, 21).

**And leave it for an inheritance.**—Lev. xxv. 46.

(9) **And thou, Solomon my son.**—The king now turns to his heir, urging a whole-hearted service to his father's God (verses 9, 10).

**Know thou.**—Regard thou, have care for (Ps. i. 6).

**The God of thy father** might mean the God of *Israel* (comp. chap. xxix. 10). But verse 20, where David speaks of "my God," suggests the simpler meaning, God of David, here. (Comp. Ps. xviii. 2, 6, 22; also Gen. xxxi. 29, 42.)

**With a perfect heart.**—The word *shālēm* means *whole, sound, unimpaired;* the Latin *integer.* Hence, what is urged is an undivided allegiance, such as is enjoined by the Decalogue. (Comp. chap. xxix. 9, 19; 1 Kings viii. 61.)

**A willing mind.**—For service is not real unless it be voluntary, and so glad as well as free.

**For the Lord searcheth all hearts.**—Search, *i.e., seek* (verse 8 and below). For the thought, comp. Ps. cxxxix. 1—4, 23; 1 Sam. xvi. 7; Ps. xciv. 9; Acts i. 24; Heb. iv. 13. The Searcher of hearts will at once see through an insincere and half-hearted obedience.

**And understandeth all the imaginations of the thoughts.**—And *every fashioning* (*yēçer,* εἶδος, Bild) or *cast of thoughts he discerneth* (Gen. vi. 5, viii. 21).

**If thou seek him.**—Deut. iv. 29. Seeking Jehovah in earnest always results in finding (Isa. lv. 6). Yet the Divine grace is not *restricted* even by this condition (Isa. lxv. 1).

**If thou forsake him.**—Deliberately and of set purpose, as choosing to live by other laws than His.

**He will cast thee off.**—A strong word (*hizniah*), meaning strictly, *to reject as noisome or foul-smelling.* (Comp. Hosea viii. 3, 5.) The verbal form *hiphil* is peculiar to Chronicles. (See 2 Chron. xi. 14, xxix. 19.)

(10) **Take heed now; for the Lord.**—Or, *See now that Jehovah hath chosen thee;* consider this high commission, weigh it well and realise it thoroughly, then be strong, and act. (See chap. xxii. 13, 16.)

David now, in presence of the Assembly, hands over to his son the plans of the Sanctuary and its vessels,

*David gives Solomon*    I. CHRONICLES. XXVIII.    *Patterns and Gold.*

<sup>(11)</sup> Then David gave to Solomon his son the pattern of the porch, and of the houses thereof, and of the treasuries thereof, and of the upper chambers thereof, and of the inner parlours thereof, and of the place of the mercy seat, <sup>(12)</sup> and the pattern¹ of all that he had by the spirit, of the courts of the house of the LORD, and of all the chambers round about, of the treasuries of the house of God, and of the treasuries of the dedicated things: <sup>(13)</sup> also for the courses of the priests and the Levites, and for all the work of the service of the house of the LORD, and for all the vessels of service in the house of the LORD. <sup>(14)</sup> *He* gave of gold by weight for *things* of gold, for all instruments of all manner of service; *silver also* for all instruments of silver by weight, for all instruments of every kind of service: <sup>(15)</sup> even the weight for the candlesticks of gold, and for their lamps of gold, by weight for every candlestick, and for the lamps thereof: and for the candlesticks of silver by weight, *both* for the candlestick, and *also* for the lamps thereof, according to the use of every

¹ Heb., *of all that was with him.*

---

remarking, as he does so, that the whole is of Divine origin (verse 19).

(11) **Then (and) David gave.**—The description proceeds from the outer to the inner.

**The pattern.**—Heb., *tabnîth*, the word used in Exod. xxv. 9 of the model, plan, or design of the Tabernacle.

**The porch.**—See 1 Kings vi. 3. The Syriac has *prûstidê*: i.e., παραστάδες, colonnade, portico.

**The houses thereof.**—*Its*—*i.e.*, the Temple's— *chambers.* Throughout this verse the word *thereof* refers to the *house* mentioned in verse 10. The two principal rooms of the Temple, the "holy place" and the "Holy of holies," or, as we might say, the nave and the chancel, are called its "houses" (*bāttîm*).

**The treasuries** (*ganzakkîm*), occurring here only. It appears to be a loan word from the Persian (*ghanj*, treasure, treasury; comp. the Latin and Greek *gaza*, treasure. In old Persian *ka* was a noun-ending; comp. *bandaka*, servant). With the singular, *ganzak*, comp. Persian *Ghanjak* (the classical Gazaca), the capital of Atropatene, which was a *treasure-*city. (Comp. also the word *ginzê;* Esther iii. 9, iv. 7; Ezra vii. 20, and *ginzayyā*, Ezra v. 17, vi. 1, meaning *treasures.*) Gesenius (Thesaur., p. 296) assumes that the root G N Z has passed from Semitic into Persian, and not *vice versâ*. This may be true, as the root exists in the principal Semitic tongues, and yet it may be that *ganzak* in Hebrew is a modern loan word. The "treasuries" or store-rooms of the Temple were probably in the side-building of three storeys (1 Kings vi. 5).

**The upper chambers** (*'aliyôth*).—Only here and in 2 Chron. iii. 9. They were probably over the Holy of holies, the ceiling of which was twenty cubits from the floor, whereas the roof of the whole building was thirty cubits from the ground. A space of ten cubits high by twenty wide and twenty long was thus available for the upper chambers.

**The inner parlours.**—The fore-court, or vestibule, and the holy place, or nave, in contrast with "the place of the mercy-seat," or *chamber of the Kappôreth*: *i.e.*, the Holy of holies, the inmost shrine of the whole building.

(12) **And the pattern of all that he had by the spirit.**—Rather, *the pattern of all that was* (or *had come to be*) *in the spirit with him*: *i.e.*, had come into his mind; the whole design as it lay in his mind. (Comp. the phrase in verse 2: "with my heart it was to build." See verse 19, which attributes the design of the Temple to Divine inspiration.)

**Of the courts.**—*For the courts.*

**The chambers.**—*The cells* (*lĕshākhôth*). (Comp. chap. xxiii. 28.)

**The treasuries.**—*For the treasures* (chap. xxvi. 20, and Notes).

(13) **Also (and) for the courses of the priests and the Levites.**—This connects immediately with the phrase "all the chambers round about," in verse 12. The chambers or cells round the Temple court were intended not only for the stowage of the treasures, but also for the use of the priests and Levites who would sojourn in them by course. The LXX. and the Vulg. render (David gave him) *a description of the courses of the priests and Levites*, a sense which the Hebrew admits, and which the Authorised version has adopted; but the former connexion of the words is preferable.

**For all the work of the service.**—Such as cooking the flesh which fell to the priests from the sacrifices, and baking the shewbread. "The vessels of service," that is, the utensils used by the Levites in the work just specified, would naturally be kept in the cells.

The Syriac version paraphrases verses 11—13 as follows:—"And David gave to Solomon his son, the likeness of the porch, and the measure of the house and of the colonnade (*kĕsôstĕrôn* = ξυστός), and of the upper chambers; and of the inner cloisters ('*estĕwê* = στοαι), and of the outer cloisters, and of the upper and of the lower (storeys); and of the treasury (*bêth gazzā*), and of the house of service of the Lord's house, *and of the kitchens, and of the house of the water-carriers* (or cupbearers), *and of the house of lampmen.*" The last words are interesting, as explaining the nature of "the work of the service" (verse 13).

(14) **He gave of gold by weight for things of gold.**—The Hebrew is very concise. Apparently it continues the construction of verse 12, so that the sense is: "He gave him a pattern or description for the golden vessels (literally, *for the gold*), by the weight for the golden vessels (Heb., *for the gold*), for all vessels of each kind of service (*i.e.*, use); and he gave him a pattern for all the silver vessels, by weight, for all vessels of each kind of service." In other words, David gave Solomon an account or schedule of all the different vessels of gold and silver that would be required for the sanctuary, specifying the exact weight of each. (Comp. Ezra viii. 25, seq. 34.)

(15) **Even the weight for the candlesticks of gold.**—Rather, *and a* (specified) *weight for the golden lampstands, and their golden lamps, in the weight of each lampstand and its lamps; and* (a weight) *for the lampstands of silver by weight, for a lamp-*

*David gives Solomon*     I. CHRONICLES, XXVIII.     *Gold and Silver.*

candlestick. (16) And by weight he gave gold for the tables of shewbread, for every table; and *likewise* silver for the tables of silver: (17) also pure gold for the fleshhooks, and the bowls, and the cups: and for the golden basons *he gave gold* by weight for every bason; and *likewise silver* by weight for every bason of silver: (18) and for the altar of incense refined gold by weight; and gold for the pattern of the chariot of the *a* cherubims, that spread out *their wings*, and covered the ark of the covenant of the LORD. (19) All *this*, said David, the LORD made me understand in writing by *his* hand upon me, *even* all the works of this pattern.

(20) And David said to Solomon his son, Be strong and of good courage, and do *it*: fear not, nor be dismayed: for the LORD God, *even* my God, *will be* with thee; he will not fail thee, nor forsake thee, until thou hast finished all the work for the service of the house of the LORD. (21) And, behold, the courses of the priests and the Levites, *even they*

*a* 1 Sam. 4. 4; 1 Kin. 6. 23, &c.

---

stand and its lamps, according to the service of each lampstand. The meaning still is that David gave Solomon a description of the designated articles, fixing the proper weight for each. (Comp. Exod. xxv. 31 *sqq.*, the great golden candelabrum of the Mosaic sanctuary.) No mention of the silver lampstands occurs anywhere else in the Old Testament. According to the Rabbis, they stood in the chambers of the priests.

(16) **And by weight he gave gold.**—*And the gold he gave* (assigned in the schedule or written plan) *a certain weight.*

**For the tables of shewbread.**—Only one table of shewbread is spoken of in the Law. (See Exod. xxv. 23—30, and comp. 1 Kings vii. 48.) The chronicler was well aware of this, as appears from 2 Chron. xxix. 18; and as he states elsewhere that Solomon made ten golden tables, and put them five on the right and five on the left in the holy place (2 Chron. iv. 8), those tables may be intended here. It may even be the case that the term "shewbread" (*hamma'arèketh*) is a gloss which has displaced the word "gold" (*hazzāhāb*), and that the original text was "for the tables of gold." (Comp. "for the tables of silver," at the end of the verse.) The table of shewbread would then be included among the golden tables. (But comp. chap. vi. 57; 2 Chron. xxviii. 16.)

**For the tables of silver.**—The silver tables are not again spoken of in the Old Testament. The rabbis assert that they stood in the court of the Temple, and that the prepared flesh of the sacrificial victims was laid upon them.

(17) **Also pure gold for the fleshhooks, and the bowls, and the cups.**—Rather, *and the forks, and the bowls, and the flagons were* (in the schedule or inventory) *pure gold.* (See Exod. xxvii. 3; 1 Sam. ii. 13, 14.) The bowls were used in lustral sprinkling, the golden flagons in libations (Exod. xxv. 29, xxxvii. 16; Num. iv. 7 only).

**The golden basons.**—Tankards, or lidded pitchers (*kĕphôrim*): a word only found here and in Ezra i. 10, viii. 27 (among the sacred vessels restored by Cyrus).

**By weight.**—*By the* (required) *weight.* The altar of incense stood within the Holiest (the *Dĕbîr*, or Adytum; Exod. xl. 5).

**And gold for the pattern of the chariot of the cherubims, that spread out their wings.**—Rather, *and for the model of the chariot, that is, the cherubim* (he assigned) *gold*; to wit, *for beings outspreading* (their wings) *and overshadowing the Ark of the Covenant of Jehovah.* The two cherubs lying on the (*kappôreth*) above the Ark are here called "the chariot," with obvious reference to such passages as Ps. xviii. 11, where it is said of God, "He charioted on a cherub." (Comp. also Ps. xcix. 1.) The rest of the verse describes the purpose of the symbolical cherubic figures, in terms borrowed from Exod. xxv. 20. (Comp. also Ezekiel's vision, called by the Jews "The Chariot," Ezek. i.)

(19) **All this said David.**—The words with which David delivered the plans of the building and the schedule of its vessels to Solomon. The omission of any introductory formula, such as "And David said," is dramatic. (Comp. chaps. xvi. 8, xxiii. 4, 5.) Literally rendered, after the Hebrew punctuation, the verse runs:—"The whole in a writing from the hand of Jehovah, to me he made clear; all the works of the model." With the expression "a writing from the hand of Jehovah" (comp. Exod. xxxi. 18, xxv. 40), David affirms his "pattern" of the sanctuary and its vessels to have been conceived, and described in writing, under that Divine guidance which he sought and followed in all the great enterprises of his life. Whether "the writing" was a communication "by the hand of" one of David's seers, or merely the description of the Mosaic sanctuary (Exod. xxv. seq.), is not clear. The verb "he taught" (*hiskîl*) requires an object, such as is supplied in the Authorised version: "made me understand." It takes a dative (Prov. xxi. 11), and probably the word rendered "upon me" is really a later equivalent of the same construction. Else we might compare Neh. ii. 8, Ezek. i. 3, and render: "The whole, in a writing from the hand of Jehovah upon me, he taught," implying that David himself sketched out the whole design under Divine inspiration. Perhaps the text is corrupt.

(20) **And David said to Solomon his son.**—The conclusion of the speech begun in verses 9, 10, and interrupted by the transfer of the plans and designs (verses 11—19).

**Be strong and of good courage.**—So chap. xxii. 13. "And do" is added here, because the time for action is imminent.

**Fear not . . . forsake thee.**—From Deut. xxxi. 6, 8. (See also Josh. i. 5, 6).

**My God.**—Recalling, in a single word, all his own wonderful experience of the Divine Helper.

**Fail.**—*Drop, let go,* and so *dismiss, desert.*

**Until.**—The word implies nothing about the time beyond the expressed limit. (Comp. ἕως, Matt. i. 25.)

(21) **And, behold, the courses of the priests and the Levites.**—The form of expression suggests that David pointed to them as he spoke. The representatives of religion would hardly be absent from an assembly of "all the princes of Israel" (verse 1)

*David addresses*     I. CHRONICLES, XXIX.     *the Congregation.*

shall be with thee for all the service of the house of God: and *there shall be* with thee for all manner of workmanship every willing skilful man, for any manner of service: also the princes and all the people *will be* wholly at thy commandment.

CHAPTER XXIX.—⁽¹⁾ Furthermore David the king said unto all the congregation, Solomon my son, whom alone God hath chosen, *is yet* ᵃ young and tender, and the work *is* great: for the palace *is* not for man, but for the LORD God. ⁽²⁾ Now I have prepared with all my might for the house of my God the gold for *things to be made* of gold, and the silver for *things* of silver, and the brass for *things* of brass, the iron for *things* of iron, and wood for *things* of wood; onyx stones, and *stones* to be set, glistering stones, and of divers colours, and all manner of precious stones, and marble stones in abundance. ⁽³⁾ Moreover, because I have set my affection to the house of my God, I have of mine own proper good, of gold and silver, *which* I have given to the house of my God, over and above all that I have prepared for the holy house, ⁽⁴⁾ *even* three thousand talents of gold, of the gold of ᵇ Ophir, and seven thousand talents of refined silver, to overlay the walls of the houses *withal:* ⁽⁵⁾ the gold for *things* of gold, and the silver for *things* of silver, and for all manner of work *to be made* by

*a* ch. 22. 5.

*b* 1 Kings 9. 28.

---

(Comp. chap. xxiv. 5, "princes of God.") They might also be included among "the valiant men." (Comp. chap. ix. 13.)

**And there shall be with thee for all manner of workmanship.**—Rather, *And with thee in every kind of work will be every volunteer with skill, for every kind of service:* that is to say, skilled craftsmen have volunteered for the work (chap. xxii. 15), and will support thy endeavours. The word rendered "volunteer" (*nādîb*) strictly means one who offers free-will offerings. (Comp. Exod. xxxv. 5, 22; and the verb Judges v. 1, *hithnaddēb*.) The phrase "volunteer with wisdom," or artistic skill, is not found elsewhere.

**Also the princes and all the people.**—Spoken, perhaps, with another gesture. The whole assembly would subserve the wishes of Solomon.

**Wholly at thy commandment.**—Literally, *For all thy words:* i.e., orders (Vulg., *praecepta*), or matters, business (chap. xxvi. 32).

XXIX.

CONTINUATION OF PROCEEDINGS IN THE ASSEMBLY.

⁽¹⁾ **Furthermore.**—*And.* David reviews his own preparations, and asks the offerings of the assembly, which are cheerfully accorded (verses 1–9).

**Alone.**—Of all his brothers.

**Young and tender.**—Chap. xxii. 5.

**The palace** (*birāh*).—A word peculiar to the Chronicles, Nehemiah, Esther, and Daniel. It usually means the palace at Susa (comp. the Persian word *bâru,* "citadel"), and this is the only passage of Scripture in which it denotes the Temple. From its august associations, the word was well calculated to convey to the minds of the chronicler's contemporaries some idea of the magnificence of the Temple of Solomon as he imagined it.

⁽²⁾ **Now I have prepared.**—*And with all might have I prepared* (chap. xxii. 14; comp. also Deut. vi. 5, xxviii. 9).

**The gold for things to be made of gold.**—Literally, *the gold for the gold, and the silver for the silver,* &c. (Comp. chap. xxviii. 14.)

**Onyx** (*shōham*).—So Vulg. The LXX. keeps the Hebrew word Σοάμ. (See Gen. ii 12; Exod. xxv. 7, xxviii. 9, 20; Job xxviii. 16.) The uncertainty of meaning is illustrated by the fact that the LXX. in various passages translates *shōham* by onyx, beryl, sardius, emerald, and sapphire.

**Stones to be set** (*'abnê millū'îm*).—Stones of settings; strictly, *fillings;* LXX., πληρώσεως (Exod. xxv. 7, xxxv. 9).

**Glistering stones, and of divers colours.**—Literally, *stones of pûk and riqmāh. Pûk* is the pigment used by Eastern ladies for darkening the eyebrows and lashes (*kohl:* 2 Kings ix. 30). It here seems to denote the colour of the stones in question. Perhaps some kind of decorative marble is intended (comp. Isa. liv. 11). *Riqmāh* stones are veined or variegated marbles, or, perhaps, tesselated work (comp. Ezek. xvii. 3; Judges v. 30). The LXX. renders the phrase "costly and variegated stones."

**All manner of precious stones.**—2 Chron. iii. 6.

**Marble stones.**—Stones of *shâyish,* a word only read here. It means *white marble.* The LXX. and Vulg. have *Parian* marble, but the Targum simply *marmora,* "marbles." (Comp. Esther i. 6; Cant. v. 15, where *shêsh* is equivalent to the present form.)

⁽³⁾ **I have set my affection to the house.**—Chap. xxviii. 4 (he liked, *rāçāh:* Ps. xxvi. 8).

**I have of mine own proper good, of gold and silver.**—I have a personal property in gold and silver. For the word *sĕgullāh,* peculium, see Exod. xix. 5.

**I have given**—i.e., I give (chap. xxi. 23).

**Over and above** (*lĕma'lāh*).—Chap. xxii. 5.

**All that I have prepared.**—The Hebrew again omits the relative. (Comp. chap. xv. 12.)

⁽⁴⁾ **Three thousand talents of gold.**—Comp. chap. xxii. 14. The sum would be about £18,000,000 sterling.

**Gold of Ophir.**—Indian gold, from *Abhîra,* at the mouth of the Indus.

**Seven thousand talents of refined silver.**—About £2,800,000 sterling.

**To overlay.**—Strictly, *to besmear* (Isa. xliv. 18).

**The houses.**—The chambers (chap. xxviii. 11; see 2 Chron. iii. 4–9). The Syriac and Arabic have "a thousand thousand talents of gold," and "twice a thousand thousand talents of silver."

⁽⁵⁾ **The gold for things of gold.**—Literally, *as for the gold, for the gold, and as for the silver, for*

*The Princes and People*     I. CHRONICLES, XXIX.     *Offer Willingly.*

the hands of artificers. And who *then* is willing ¹to consecrate his service this day unto the Lord? ⁽⁶⁾ Then the chief of the fathers and princes of the tribes of Israel, and the captains of thousands and of hundreds, with the rulers of the king's work, offered willingly, ⁽⁷⁾ and gave for the service of the house of God of gold five thousand talents and ten thousand drams, and of silver ten thousand talents, and of brass eighteen thousand talents, and one hundred thousand talents of iron. ⁽⁸⁾ And they with whom *precious* stones were found gave *them* to the treasure of the house of the Lord, by the hand of Jehiel the Gershonite. ⁽⁹⁾ Then the people rejoiced, for that they offered willingly, because with perfect heart they offered willingly to the Lord: and David the king also rejoiced with great joy. ⁽¹⁰⁾ Wherefore David blessed the Lord before all the congregation: and David said, Blessed *be* thou, Lord God of Israel our father, for ever and ever. ⁽¹¹⁾ ᵃThine, O Lord, *is* the greatness, and the power, and the glory, and the victory, and the majesty: for all *that is* in the heaven and in the earth *is thine*;

¹ Heb., *to fill his hand.*

ᵃ Matt. 6. 13; 1 Tim. 1. 17; Rev. 5. 13.

---

*the silver*—Scil., "I give it" (verse 3)—*and for every work by hand of craftsmen.*

**And who then is willing to consecrate his service?**—Literally, *And who volunteers* (Judges v. 1) *to fill his hand to-day for Jehovah?* To fill his hand: that is, with a liberal offering (Exod. xxxii. 29).

⁽⁶⁾ **Then the chief of the fathers**—*And the princes of the clans,* &c., volunteered, showed themselves liberal (*nādîb*: chap. xxviii. 21; comp. Prov. xix. 6).

**Chief ... princes ... captains ... rulers.** —All these words represent a single Hebrew term (*sārîm*). *Princes of the clans or houses = heads of the houses* elsewhere.

**With the rulers of the king's work.**—The stewards or bailiffs of the royal domains (chap. xxvii. 25—31). The construction here is like that in chap. xxviii. 21. The particle rendered "with" (*le*) appears to mean much the same as *'ăd*, "even unto," assigning an inclusive limit.

⁽⁷⁾ **And gave ... of gold.**—*And they gave ... gold, five thousand talents;* between thirty and forty millions sterling (!).

**Ten thousand drams.**—Rather, *Darics.* The Daric (Greek, Δαρεικός) was a Persian gold coin, value about £1 2s., first struck by the great Darius, son of Hystaspes (B.C. 521—485). It remained current in Western Asia long after the fall of the Persian Empire. The Hebrew word (*'ădarkônîm*) occurs again only once, viz., at Ezra viii. 27, where it clearly means *Darics,* and is so rendered by the Syriac (*dărîkûnê*). The *darkôn* (or *darbôn*) is mentioned in the Talmud as a *Persian* coin. The chronicler, or his authority, has evidently substituted a familiar modern term for some ancient expression of value. No real coins are mentioned in Scripture before the age of the exile.

**Silver ten thousand talents.**—About £4,000,000 in modern value (see 1 Kings x. 21, 27); or, according to Schrader, who argues from Assyrian data, £3,750,000. The value of the bronze and the iron must have been much greater then than now. (See Note on chap. xxii. 14.)

⁽⁸⁾ **And they with whom precious stones were found gave them.**—Literally, *And with whom there was found stones, they gave unto the treasure.* (Comp., for this use of the article as a relative, verse 17, chap. xxvi. 28; Ezra viii. 25.)

**The treasure of the house of the Lord.**— Chap. xxvi. 22. (Comp. Exod. xxxv. 27 for a similar contribution of the princes.)

**By the hand of Jehiel.**—Under the charge of Jehiel (*'al yad,* chap. xxv. 2). Jehiel, or Jehieli, was the Gershonite clan in charge of the "treasures of the house of God" (chap. xxvi. 21, 22).

⁽⁹⁾ **Then** (and) **the people rejoiced, for that they offered willingly.**—Comp. Judg. v. 1.

**With perfect heart.**—Chap. xxviii. 9.

⁽¹⁰⁾ **Wherefore.**—*And.* David's Prayer (verses 10 —19). David thanks God because his people are at one with him on the subject nearest his heart. Touching this fine utterance of a true inspiration, which the chronicler—or rather, perhaps, his authority—puts into the mouth of the aged king, we may remark that the spirit which found expression in the stirring odes of psalmists and the trumpet-tones of prophets in olden times, in the latter days, when psalmody was weak and prophecy dead, flowed forth in the new outlet of impassioned prayer.

**Before all.**—*To the eyes of all* (Gen. xxiii. 11), and frequently.

**Lord God of Israel our father.**—The connection is "Israel our father," not "Jehovah our father." (Comp. verses 18 and 20; Exod. iii. 6. Yet comp. also Isa. lxiii. 16, lxiv. 8; Deut. xxxii. 6; Mal. i. 6, ii. 10; Jer. xxxi. 9.) The fatherhood of God, though thus occasionally affirmed in prophetic writings, hardly became a ruling idea within the limits of Old Testament times. (Comp. Matt. xxiii. 9, vi. 9.)

**For ever and ever.**—*From eternity even unto eternity.* (Comp. the doxologies of the first and third books of the Psalter—Pss. xli. 13, cvi. 48—and Ps. ciii. 17.)

⁽¹¹⁾ **Thine, O Lord, is the greatness.**—The point of verses 11, 12 seems to be that David arrogates nothing to himself; but, with the humility of genuine greatness, ascribes everything to God. As if he said, "The greatness of my kingdom, the prowess of my warriors, the splendour and majesty of my throne, are thine, for thine are all things."

**Greatness.**—*Gĕdullāh,* a late word. (Comp. Pss. lxxi. 21, cxlv. 3).

**Power.**—Strictly, *manly strength;* then valour, prowess (Ps. xxi. 13). (Comp. Exod. xv. 3.)

**The glory.**—Ornament, beauty, splendour (Isa. iii. 18, xiii. 19, xlvi. 13; Ps. xcvi. 6).

**Majesty.**—See Pss. xxi. 6, xcvi. 6.

**Victory.**—Glory, splendour (1 Sam. xv. 29). "Victory" is the meaning of the word in Syriac, and so the LXX. and Vulg. render here. But the Syriac version has "beauty," or "glory." With the whole ascription, comp. Rev. iv. 11, v. 12, vii. 12.

thine *is* the kingdom, O LORD, and thou art exalted as head above all. (12) Both riches and honour *come* of thee, and thou reignest over all ; and in thine hand *is* power and might ; and in thine hand *it is* to make great, and to give strength unto all. (13) Now therefore, our God, we thank thee, and praise thy glorious name. (14) But who *am* I, and what *is* my people, that we should ¹be able to offer so willingly after this sort ? for all things *come* of thee, and ² of thine own have we given thee. (15) For we *are* strangers before thee, and sojourners, as *were* all our fathers : ᵃ our days on the earth *are* as a shadow, and *there is* none ³ abiding. (16) O LORD our God, all this store that we have prepared to build thee an house for thine holy name *cometh* of thine hand, and *is* all thine own. (17) I know also, my God, that thou ᵇtriest the heart, and hast pleasure in uprightness. As for me, in the uprightness of mine heart I have willingly offered all these things : and now have I seen with joy thy people, which are ⁴present here, to offer willingly unto thee. (18) O LORD God of Abraham, Isaac, and of Israel, our fathers, keep this for ever in the imagination of the thoughts of the heart of thy people, and ⁵prepare their heart unto thee : (19) and give unto Solomon my son a perfect heart, to keep thy commandments, thy testimonies, and thy statutes, and to do all *these things,* and to build the palace, for the which I have made provision.

1 Heb., *retain, or, obtain strength.*
2 Heb., *of thine hand.*
ᵃ Ps. 39. 12 & 90. 9 ; Heb. 11. 13 ; 1 Pet. 2. 11.
3 Heb., *expectation.*
ᵇ 1 Sam. 16. 7 ; ch. 28. 9.
4 Or, *found.*
5 Or, *stablish.*

---

**All that is in the heavens . . . is thine.**—The pronoun (*lāk*) seems to have fallen out before the following : " Thine (*lĕkā*) is the kingdom." (Comp. for the idea Pss. lxxxix. 11, xxiv. 1.)

**The kingdom.**—The universal sovereignty (Pss. xcvi. 10, xcvii. 1, xxii. 28).

**Thou art exalted as head above all.**—Lit., *And the self-exalted over all as head* (art thou). (Comp. Numb. xvi. 3.) Here also the pronoun (*'attāh*) may have been lost at the end. Ewald, however, explains the apparent participle as an Aramaized infinitive : " And the being exalted over all as head *is* thine." (Comp. Isa. xxiv. 21 for the supremacy of God over all powers of heaven and earth.)

**As head.**—Comp. Deut. xxviii. 13 ; Ps. xviii. 43 ; Col. ii. 10.

(12) **Both riches and honour come of thee.**—Literally, *And the riches and the honour are from before thee.* (Comp. Prov. iii. 16 ; 1 Kings iii. 13.)

**Power and might.**—Power, rendered " might " in verse 2.

**Might.**—Rendered " power " in verse 11. And in thine hand it is to make great (1 Sam. ii. 7, 8 ; Luke i. 52).

(13) **Now therefore, our God, we thank thee.**—*And now, our God, we are thanking thee, and praising* (participles in the Hebrew). *Môdim,* " thanking," occurs nowhere else, though the verb is common in other forms.

**Thy glorious name.**—*The name of thy glory :* here only. (Comp. Isa. lxiii. 14, and Ps. lxxii. 19.)

(14) **But who am I?**—*And, indeed, who am I?* (answering to the Greek καὶ γάρ).

**That we should be able.**—*That we should hold in :* i.e., keep strength (*'ācar kōaḥ*), a phrase confined to six passages in the Chronicles and three in Daniel (chaps. xi. 6, x. 8, 16).

**All things come of thee.**—*For from thee is the whole* (scil.) of our wealth and power. (Comp. verse 16.)

**And of thine own.**—*And out of thine own hand.*

(15) **For we are strangers before thee, and sojourners.**—Ps. xxxix. 12.

**Our days on the earth are as a** (the) **shadow.** —Job viii. 9 ; Ps. cxliv. 4.

**And there is none abiding.**—Rather, *and there is no hope ;* no outlook, no assured future, no hope of permanence. What is the ground for this plaintive turn in the thought ? Merely, it would seem, to emphasise what has just been said. We, as creatures of a day, can have no abiding and absolute possession. Our good things are lent to us for a season only. As our fathers passed away, so shall we.

(16) **All this store.**—Strictly, *multitude ;* and so multitude of goods, riches (Ps. xxxvii. 16).

**Cometh of thine hand, and is all thine own.** —*From thine own hand it is, and thine is the whole.* The whole verse is a clearer expression of the second half of verse 14. (Comp. Ps. civ. 28.)

(17) **Thou triest the heart.**—Pss. xi. 4, vii. 9, xxvi. 2.

**Hast pleasure in.**—Chap. xxviii. 4, verse 3. (Comp. also chap. xxviii. 9.)

**Uprightness.**—Or, *sincerity* (*mêshārîm,* Cant. i. 4).

**In the uprightness** (*yōsher*), integrity (Deut. ix. 5), a synonym of *mêshārîm*. Both literally mean *straightness :* e.g., of a road (Prov. ii. 13, xxiii. 31). The connexion of ideas is this : Thou that lookest upon the heart knowest that my offering has been made without grudging and without hypocrisy ; my motive was not my own interest, but Thy glory. Hence my joyful thanksgiving, because of the free generosity of Thy people.

**Which are present here.**—Literally, *Who have found themselves here* (reflexive verb). (So 2 Chron. v. 11, and other places.)

(18) **Israel.**—Verse 10. (See Gen. xxxii. 28, and Exod. iii. 6.)

**Keep this for ever in the imagination.**—Rather, *preserve this for ever :* to wit, " the cast (chap. xxviii. 9) of the thoughts of the heart of thy people." Give permanence to the frame of mind which has evinced itself in the freewill offerings of to-day.

**Prepare their heart.**—Or, *direct* (1 Sam. vii. 3). (Comp. Ezek. iv. 3, 7, " direct the face towards . . . ." Prov. xvi. 9, " direct his going." Comp. also 2 Chron. xii. 14, xx. 33.)

(19) **To keep thy commandments . . . thy statutes.**—Deut. vi. 17.

**The palace.**—Verse 1.

## I. CHRONICLES, XXIX.

*Solomon is*            *made King.*

(20) And David said to all the congregation, Now bless the LORD your God. And all the congregation blessed the LORD God of their fathers, and bowed down their heads, and worshipped the LORD, and the king. (21) And they sacrificed sacrifices unto the LORD, and offered burnt offerings unto the LORD, on the morrow after that day, *even* a thousand bullocks, and a thousand rams, *and* a thousand lambs, with their drink offerings, and sacrifices in abundance for all Israel: (22) and did eat and drink before the LORD on that day with great gladness. And they made Solomon the son of David king the second time, and *a* anointed *him* unto the LORD *to be* the chief governor, and Zadok *to be* priest. (23) Then Solomon sat on the throne of the LORD as king instead of David his father, and prospered; and all Israel obeyed him. (24) And all the princes, and the mighty men, and all the sons likewise of king David, ¹submitted themselves unto Solomon the king. (25) And the LORD magnified Solomon exceedingly in the sight of all Israel, and *b* bestowed upon him *such* royal majesty as had not been on any king before him in Israel.

*a* 1 Kings 1. 33.

1 Heb., *gave the hand under Solomon.*

*b* 1 Kin. 3. 13; 2 Chr. 1. 12; Eccles. 2. 9.

---

**And to do all these things.**—*And to do the whole;* (scil.) of thy commandments, testimonies, and statutes (comp. chaps. xxii. 13, xxviii. 7), or, *to carry out all my designs.*

**For the which I have made provision.**—*Which I have prepared* (scil.) to build (chap. xxviii. 2).

(20—25) The sacrificial feast and anointing of Solomon.

(20) **Now bless.**—*Bless ye, I pray.* The "now" is not a note of time, but of entreaty.

**Blessed the Lord God of their fathers.**—Probably using a liturgical formula, like the doxologies which close the books of the Psalter (Pss. xli. 13, lxxii. 18, 19, lxxxix. 52, &c.).

**And bowed down their heads.**—Or, *and bowed.* Vulg., *inclinaverunt se;* LXX. here, κάμψαντες τὰ γόνατα, bending the knees; but usually κύψαντες, stooping, bowing.

**Worshipped.**—Prostrated themselves. LXX., προσεκύνησαν. The two expressions "bowed and worshipped" are always united, as here (save in 2 Chron. xx. 18. Comp. Gen. xxiv. 26; Exod. xii. 27). The Syriac renders, "fell down and worshipped."

**And the king.**—As God's earthly representative, David receives the same tokens of reverence and homage. (Comp. 1 Kings i. 31.)

(21) **On the morrow after that day** (*lĕmohŏrath hayyôm hahû*); here only. (Comp. Jonah iv. 7.) That is, on the day after the assembly.

**A thousand bullocks . . .**—Heb., *Bullocks a thousand, rams a thousand,* &c., according to the later mode of speech; *and their libations* (Ps. xvi. 4; Exod. xxix. 40; Lev. xxiii. 13).

**And sacrifices in abundance for all Israel.**—The word "sacrifices" (*zĕbāhim*) occurred in a general sense at the beginning of the verse. Here, in connexion with burnt-offerings, it has the special meaning of "thank-offerings" (*shĕlāmim;* Authorised Version, "peace-offerings," Deut. xii. 6). See for both kinds of sacrifice, Lev. i. 1 *sqq.;* Exod. xx. 24, xxiv. 5.

**For all Israel.**—So that every one present might partake of the sacrificial meal. (Comp. Notes on chap. xvi. 2, 3; Deut. xii. 7; 1 Sam. i. 3—8, 13.)

(22) **And did eat and drink.**—And they ate and drank. (Comp. the account of the feasting at David's coronation, chap. xii. 39, 40.)

**And they made Solomon the son of David king the second time.**—The first time is briefly noticed in chap. xxiii. 1. (Comp. the full account, 1 Kings i. 32—40.)

**And anointed him unto the Lord to be the chief governor.**—*And anointed* (him; perhaps the suffix has fallen out) *for Jehovah as prince (nāgîd,* chap. xxvii. 16; 1 Kings i. 35).

**Anointed.**—Judg. ix. 15; 2 Sam. ii. 4. The expression "for Jehovah" seems to mean, according to His will. (Comp. chap. xxviii. 5.) Or perhaps we should render, *anointed him as prince, and Zadok as priest, to Jehovah.* The king was Jehovah's vicegerent, as Zadok was His priest. The theocratic nature of the Israelite monarchy is again insisted upon. (Comp. chaps. xvii. 14, xxviii. 5.)

**And Zadok to be priest.**—A remarkable notice, peculiar to the Chronicles. Among other things, it vividly illustrates the almost sovereign dignity of the high priest's office; it also explains the deposition of Abiathar (comp. 1 Kings i. 32, ii. 26) as having been already contemplated by David.

(23) **Then.**—And.

**Solomon sat on the throne of the Lord.**—Comp. chap. xxviii. 5.

**As king instead of David his father.**—It is not meant that David abdicated. Verses 23—25 are anticipative of the history of Solomon's reign. At the same time, their introduction here is natural, not only as relating the immediate sequel of Solomon's coronation, but also as showing how David's last wishes in regard to his son were realised.

(24) **And all the princes** (*sārîm*).—The grandees of chaps. xxvii., xxviii. 1, xxix. 6; not members of the royal house, who are designated as "the king's sons."

**Submitted themselves.**—See marginal rendering. The Vulg. has the exegetical expansion, "dederunt manum et subjecti fuerunt Salomoni regi." The Hebrew phrase "put (*nāthan*) hand under . . ." is not met with elsewhere. (Comp. Gen. xxiv. 2, 9.) It appears to be different from "give hand to . . ." in token of good faith or submission. (Comp. 2 Chron. xxx. 8; Lam. v. 6; Ezek. xvii. 18.) An ancient mode of doing homage may be intended. The whole sentence may contain an allusive reference to the attempt of Adonijah (1 Kings i. 5—53).

(25) **And bestowed upon him such royal majesty as had not been on any king before him in Israel.**—Literally, *and put upon him a glory of kingship that had not become on any king over Israel before him.* The phrase "put glory upon . . ." (*nāthan hôd 'al . . .*) occurs in Ps. viii. 2. Only two or, counting Ish-bosheth, three kings had preceded

(26) Thus David the son of Jesse reigned over all Israel. (27) And the time that he reigned over Israel *was* forty years; seven years reigned he in Hebron, and thirty and three *years* reigned he in Jerusalem. (28) And he died in a good old age, full of days, riches, and honour: and Solomon his son reigned in his stead.

(29) Now the acts of David the king, first and last, behold, they *are* written in the [1 2] book of Samuel the seer, and in the book of Nathan the prophet, and in the book of Gad the seer, (30) with all his reign and his might, and the times that went over him, and over Israel, and over all the kingdoms of the countries.

1 Or, *history*.

2 Heb., *words*.

---

Solomon. (Comp. 1 Kings iii. 12; 2 Chron. i. 12.)

(26) **Thus David . . . reigned.**—Rather, *Now David . . . had reigned*.

Verses 26—30.—Concluding remarks upon David's history.

**Over all Israel.**—This alludes to the antecedent reign over Judah only. (See 2 Sam. v. 1—5; chaps. xi. 1, xii. 38.)

(27) **And the time** (Heb., *the days*).

**That he reigned.**—This verse is a duplicate of 1 Kings ii. 11, omitting the words "David" at the beginning and "years" at the end.

**Seven years.**—More exactly, seven and a-half. (See 2 Sam. v. 5.)

(28) **In a good old age.**—Gen. xv. 15.

**Full of days.**—From LXX. and Vulg. (πλήρης ἡμερῶν—*plenus dierum*). Literally, *satisfied with days*. Syriac, "And he was satisfied with the days of his life." (Comp. chap. xxiii. 1; Gen. xxxv. 29.)

**Riches and honour.**—Verse 12. Syriac, "And he was great in the riches of the world, and in the honour thereof."

**And Solomon his son reigned in his stead.**—The regular formula, from 1 Kings xi. 43 to the end of the history of the kings.

(29) **Now the acts of David the king, first and last.**—Literally, *And the words* (dibrê) *of David the king, the former and the latter, behold they are written in* "*the words of Samuel the seer* "(rô-eh), *and in* "*the words of Nathan the prophet,*" *and in* "*the words of Gad the seer*" (hôzeh). For "written in" the Hebrews said "written on." (See Exod. xxxiv. 1; Isa. viii. 1.)

**The acts of David.**—Or, *the matters, history of David*. The Heb. *dābār* is (1) a word, (2) something spoken about, a matter, transaction, or event. (Comp. chap. xvi. 37; 2 Kings xvii. 11; Gen. xv. 1; 2 Sam. xi. 18, 19.) Gesenius renders here: *Et res gestae regis David . . . ecce eae scriptae in libro cui titulus, Res Samuëlis* (Thesaur., p. 722). As to the sources apparently cited by the chronicler in this passage, see the remarks in the Introduction.

(30) **And his might.**—Or, *valour, prowess*. (See verse 11.) His warlike achievements are intended. (Comp. 1 Kings xv. 23; Judg. viii. 21.)

**And the times that went over him.**—Heb., *passed over him*. The seasons of good and evil fortune, the vicissitudes of his own and his people's history. (Comp. chap. xii. 32; Ps. xxxi. 16; Job. xxiv. 1 [= seasons of judgment]; Dan. ix. 25.)

**And over all the kingdoms of the countries.** —Viz., those with which David had relations of friendship or war, such as the Philistines, Aramæans, Hamathites, and other surrounding peoples. (Comp. chap xiv. 17.)

**Kingdoms of the countries.**—2 Chron. xii. 8, xvii. 10, xx. 29; not elsewhere.

The Syriac adds: "Because that David did that which was good before the Lord, and departed not from anything that he commanded him all the days of his life."

# THE SECOND BOOK OF THE CHRONICLES

# THE SECOND BOOK OF THE CHRONICLES

CHAPTER I.—<sup>(1)</sup> And <sup>a</sup>Solomon the son of David was strengthened in his kingdom, and the LORD his God *was* with him, and magnified him exceedingly. <sup>(2)</sup> Then Solomon spake unto all Israel, to the captains of thousands and of hundreds, and to the judges, and to every governor in all Israel, the chief of the fathers. <sup>(3)</sup> So Solomon, and all the congregation with him, went to the high place that *was* at *<sup>b</sup>*Gibeon; for there was the tabernacle of the congregation of God, which Moses the servant of the LORD had made in the wilderness. <sup>(4)</sup> <sup>c</sup>But the ark of God had David brought up from Kirjath-jearim to *the place* which David had prepared for it: for he had pitched a tent for it at Jerusalem. <sup>(5)</sup> Moreover <sup>d</sup>the brasen altar, that Bezaleel the son of Uri, the son of Hur, had made, <sup>1</sup>he put before the tabernacle of the LORD: and Solomon

*Marginal notes:*
B.C. 1015.
a 1 Kings 2. 46.
B.C. 1045.
b 1 Kings 3. 4; 1 Chron. 16. 39, & 21. 29.
c 2 Sam. 6. 2, 17.
B.C. 1015.
d Exod. 38. 1.
1 Or, *was there.*

---

THE REIGN OF SOLOMON (chaps. i.—ix.).

1. Chap. i. describes a national sacrifice at Gibeon, and in connection therewith a dream in which God reveals His will to Solomon (1 Kings iii. 5). A few details are added respecting Solomon's power, wealth, and commerce.

2. Chaps. ii.—vii. are concerned with the principal topic of the writer's presentation, viz., the building and consecration of the Temple.

3. Chaps. viii., ix. supply further particulars of Solomon's public works, his regulation of worship, his foreign relations, his revenues, wisdom, and glory; followed by a reference to authorities, and notice of his death.

### I.

(*a*) The sacrifice at Gibeon, and Solomon's dream (verses 1—13). (*b*) The king's chariots and horsemen, wealth and commerce (verses 14—17).

<sup>(1)</sup> **And Solomon the son of David was strengthened in his kingdom.**—Or, *showed himself strong over his kingdom*; firmly grasped the reins of power, and showed himself a strong ruler. (Comp. chap. xvii. 1; also xii. 13; xiii. 21; xxi. 4.) The chronicler omits all that is related in 1 Kings i., ii., as not falling within the scope of his narrative. Comp. with this opening sentence 1 Kings ii. 46, "And the kingdom was established in the hand of Solomon."

**And the Lord his God was with him.**—Comp. 1 Chron. xi. 9; ix. 20.

**Magnified him exceedingly.**—1 Chron. xxix. 25; xxii. 5.

(2—6) Solomon and the national assembly repair to the Mosaic tabernacle at Gibeon, and sacrifice upon the great altar of burnt offering. (Comp. 1 Kings iii. 4, which the present section supplements and explains.)

<sup>(2)</sup> **Then Solomon spake unto all Israel.**—Or, *commanded all Israel* (1 Chron. xxi. 17; 2 Sam. xvi. 11; 2 Kings i. 11; Vulg., *præcepit*).

**To the captains of thousands . . . chief of the fathers.**—This is an apposition, explaining what is meant by "all Israel" in the first clause, viz., the national representatives. The account in Kings allows only one verse for the sacrifice, and so omits to mention that the princes took part in it (1 Kings iii. 4). The fact, however, is likely in itself. (Comp. the similar assemblies under David, 1 Chron. xiii. 1; xxiii. 2; xxviii. 1.)

**Every governor.**—Heb. *nāsî', prince, emir* of a tribe, or *chief* of a clan. (Comp. Gen. xxiii. 6; Num. vii. 10; 1 Kings viii. 1.)

**The chief of the fathers.**—*The heads of the clans.* This defines the preceding phrase.

<sup>(3)</sup> **The tabernacle of the congregation of God.**—Rather, *God's tent of meeting;* viz., with man (Exod. xxv. 22; xxvii. 21; Num. xvii. 4). Solomon repaired to Gibeon because "that was the great high place" (1 Kings iii. 4). We learn from our text why Gibeon stood pre-eminent above the other high places. (Comp. 1 Chron. vi. 31 *sqq.*; xvi. 39 *sqq.*)

<sup>(4)</sup> **But.**—Or, *But indeed, but no doubt* (*'ăbāl*) (chap. xix. 3; xxxiii. 17). For the transfer of the ark see 1 Chron. xiii. xv.; 2 Sam. vi.

**To the place which David had prepared.**—*Into that David had prepared for it* (the article as relative: comp. 1 Chron. xxvi. 1).

**Pitched.**—Or, *spread* (1 Chron. xv. 1).

<sup>(5)</sup> **Moreover the brasen altar . . . he put before the tabernacle of the Lord.**—Rather, *And the brasen altar . . . was there before the dwelling of Jehovah.* In Hebrew, *shām* is "there"; and *sām*, "he put." Some MSS., supported by the LXX. and Vulg., read the former; most of the MSS. and the Syr., Arab., and Targ., the latter. The former reading is preferable, as it is not likely that David found the brasen altar separated from the Mosaic sanctuary, and restored it to its place. The sentence further explains why Solomon resorted to Gibeon. The presence of the old brasen altar constituted it the legitimate place of sacrifice. With perfect consistency, the chronicler accounted for David's *not* going to Gibeon (1 Chron. xxi. 28—30).

**That Bezaleel the son of Uri . . . had made.**—See Exod. xxxi. 2, 9; xxxviii. 1—8; xxvii. 1—8.

**And Solomon and the congregation sought unto it.**—Rather, *And Solomon and the assembly*

and the congregation sought unto it. ⁽⁶⁾ And Solomon went up thither to the brasen altar before the Lord, which was at the tabernacle of the congregation, and offered a thousand burnt offerings upon it.

⁽⁷⁾ In that night did God appear unto Solomon, and said unto him, Ask what I shall give thee. ⁽⁸⁾ And Solomon said unto God, Thou hast shewed great mercy unto David my father, and hast made me ᵃto reign in his stead. ⁽⁹⁾ Now, O Lord God, let thy promise unto David my father be established: ᵇ for thou hast made me king over a people ¹like the dust of the earth in multitude. ⁽¹⁰⁾ ᶜGive me now wisdom and knowledge, that I may ᵈgo out and come in before this people: for who can judge this thy people, *that is so* great? ⁽¹¹⁾ And God said to Solomon, Because this was in thine heart, and thou hast not asked riches, wealth, or honour, nor the life of thine enemies, neither yet hast asked long life; but hast asked wisdom and knowledge for thyself, that thou mayest judge my people, over whom I have made thee king: ⁽¹²⁾ wisdom and knowledge *is* granted unto thee; and I will give thee riches, and wealth, and honour,

*a* 1 Chron. 28. 5.
*b* 1 Kings 3. 9.
1 Heb., *much as the dust of the earth.*
*c* 1 Kings 3. 11, 12.
*d* Num. 27. 17.

---

**sought Him**—*i.e.,* the Lord. (Comp. 1 Chron. xiii. 3; xv. 13; xxi. 30.) The old versions translate as A. V.

⁽⁶⁾ **And Solomon went up thither to the brasen altar.**—So Vulg. incorrectly. Rather, *And Solomon offered there on the brasen altar*; so LXX. and Syriac.

**Before the Lord.**—The altar stood before the entry of the Lord's dwellingplace (Exod. xl. 6). (Comp. Judges xx. 23, 26.)

**Which was at the tabernacle of the congregation.**—*Which altar belonged to the tent of tryst.* In 1 Kings vi. 22 the golden altar is said in like manner to belong to the Holy of holies, before which it stood. (The Vulg. seems to have read "the brasen altar, before the Lord's tent of meeting"; comp. verse 3.)

**And offered.**—*He offered* (*I say*). The verb is repeated before its object for clearness' sake.

⁽⁷⁻¹³⁾ God's revelation to Solomon by night. (Comp. 1 Kings iii. 5—15.)

⁽⁷⁾ **In that night did God appear unto Solomon.**—Kings, "In Gibeon did Jehovah appear unto Solomon in a dream of the night." Our text fixes the night as that which followed the sacrifices; the parallel passage explicitly states that it was in a dream that God appeared.

**Ask what I shall give thee.**—Rather, *Ask thou! what shall I give thee?* So Kings.

⁽⁸⁾ **Thou hast shewed great mercy unto David.**—Literally, *Thou, thou hast done great kindness with David.* (The regular phrase; comp. Luke i. 72.) From this point the relation here is briefer on the whole than that of Kings. The greater part of the long verse (1 Kings iii. 6) is omitted, and the variations between the two texts become numerous, though the general sense is the same in each.

**And hast made me to reign in his stead.**—Comp. 1 Kings iii. 7; and the similar language of Esarhaddon, king of Assyria (B.C. 681—668): "Ever since Asshur, Samas, Bel, Nebo . . . . made me, Esarhaddon, sit securely on the throne of my father" (*Cuneiform Inscriptions of Western Asia,* iii. 15, col. 2).

⁽⁹⁾ **Now, O Lord God, let thy promise unto David my father be established.**—A reminiscence of 1 Chron. xvii. 23.

**Over a people like the dust of the earth in multitude.**—*Over a people numerous as the dust of the earth.* This last clause freely corresponds with 1 Kings iii. 8. (Comp. the common title of Assyrian monarchs, "king of multitudes," *sar kissāti.*)

⁽¹⁰⁾ **Give me now wisdom and knowledge.**—*Now wisdom and knowledge give thou me;* a petition co-ordinate with that of verse 9: "Now, O Lord God," &c. The clause answers to 1 Kings iii. 9. The word rendered "knowledge" (*maddaʻ*) is late, and occurs besides only in Dan. i. 4, 17; Eccles. x. 20.

**That I may go out and come in before this people.**—See 1 Kings iii. 7; Num. xxvii. 17; Deut. xxxi. 2.

**For who can judge.**—The simple impf.; Kings has, "who is able to judge?"

**This thy people, that is so great** (*gādôl*).—Kings: "This thy numerous (*kābēd*) people." For the king as judge comp. 1 Sam. viii. 20.

⁽¹¹⁾ **Because this was in thine heart.**—For this phrase see 1 Chron. xxii. 7.

**Wealth, or honour.**—Added by chronicler. Wealth (*někāsîm*) is a late word, common in the Targums, and in Syriac (*neksîn*). The phrase "riches, wealth, and honour" occurs in Eccl. vi. 2.

**Long life.**—*Many days.*

**But** (*and*) **hast asked wisdom and knowledge for thyself, that thou mayest judge . . . king.**—An expansion of what we find in Kings: "And hast asked discernment for thyself, to hear judgment." The verb *hast asked* is expressed in better idiom than in Kings.

⁽¹²⁾ **Wisdom and knowledge.**—*The wisdom and the knowledge,* viz., which thou hast asked for.

**Is granted unto thee.**—The Hebrew expression is found only here and in Esther iii. 11. The parallel passage gives three verses for this one (1 Kings iii. 12—14).

**And I will give thee.**—Kings, "I have given." The perfect tense (I will certainly give) is more idiomatic than the chronicler's simple imperfect.

**Such as none of the kings have had that have been before thee . . . the like.**—Rather, *Such as hath not been to the kings before thee, and after thee shall not be.* (Comp. 1 Chron. xxix. 25 and Note.) The Assyrian kings were fond of similar comparisons between themselves and their predecessors. Kings: "That there hath not been (*i.e., shall not be*) a man like thee among the kings, all thy days," a different promise. The conditional promise, "And if thou wilt walk in my ways . . . I will lengthen thy days" (1 Kings iii. 14), is here omitted, although verse 11 has mentioned long life; perhaps because Solomon fell short of it. But comp. chap. vii. 17 *seq.* Of course the omission may be a mere abridgment.

such as ªnone of the kings have had that *have been* before thee, neither shall there any after thee have the like.

(13) Then Solomon came *from his journey* to the high place that *was* at Gibeon to Jerusalem, from before the tabernacle of the congregation, and reigned over Israel. (14) ᵇ And Solomon gathered chariots and horsemen: and he had a thousand and four hundred chariots, and twelve thousand horsemen, which he placed in the chariot cities, and with the king at Jerusalem. (15) ᶜ And the king ¹made silver and gold at Jerusalem as *plenteous* as stones, and cedar trees made he as the sycomore trees that *are* in the vale for abundance. (16) ᵈ And ²Solomon had horses brought out of Egypt, and linen yarn: the king's merchants received the linen yarn at a price. (17) And they fetched up, and brought forth out of Egypt a chariot for six hundred *shekels* of silver, and an horse for an hundred and fifty: and so brought they out *horses* for all the kings of the Hittites, and for the kings of Syria, ³ by their means.

CHAPTER II.—⁽¹⁾ And Solomon determined to build an house for the name

---

*a* 1 Chron. 29. 25; ch. 9. 22; Eccles. 2. 9.

*b* 1 Kings 4. 26, & 10. 26, &c.

*c* 1 Kings 10. 27; ch. 9. 27, 28.

1 Heb., *gave.*

*d* 1 Kings 10. 28; ch. 9. 28.

2 Heb., *the going forth of the horses which* was Solomon's.

3 Heb., *by their hand.*

---

(13) **Then Solomon came from his journey to the high place that was at Gibeon to Jerusalem.**—Heb., *And Solomon came to the high place that was in Gibeon to Jerusalem.* Clearly we should read, "*from* the high place," with the LXX. and Vulgate. The difficulty is as old as the Syriac version, which reads, "And Solomon came to the great high place [reading *bûmsâ*—*i.e.,* βῶμος—with Dr. Payne Smith] that is in Gibeon the city, which is on the east of Jerusalem, from before the tabernacle."

**From before the tabernacle of the congregation.**—See verses 3, 6. Perhaps "to (or *at*) the high place that was at Gibeon," was originally a marginal gloss upon this expression. (Comp. verse 3.) The reading, "And Solomon came to Jerusalem from before the tent of tryst," would be quite intelligible without this addition.

**And reigned over Israel.**—Syr., *over all Israel.* (Comp. 1 Kings iv. 1.) But the remark, "and he reigned over Israel," is by no means "superfluous" (Bertheau), inasmuch as it naturally introduces the following sketch of the reign, which carries us on from God's promise to its fulfilment.

The chronicler does not notice the sacrifices which, on his return, Solomon offered before the ark at Jerusalem (1 Kings iii. 15), nor the story of the king's wise judgment which there follows (1 Kings iii. 16—28). It is unreasonable to seek any other ground of such omissions than the free and legitimate exercise of the compiler's discretion in the choice of his own materials. That he did not depreciate the sanctuary on Mount Zion as a place of sacrifice, is evident from 1 Chron. xxi. 18—xxii. 1.

(14—17) Solomon's "riches, and wealth, and honour" illustrated (comp. 1 Kings x. 26—29). In the parallel passage of Kings, this short section closes the account of Solomon's wealth and glory. 2 Chron. ix. 25—28 is very similar; a fact which will not surprise those who bear in mind that the chronicler is careless of repetition.

(14) **And Solomon gathered chariots and horsemen.**—Word for word as in 1 Kings x. 26; see the Notes there.

**Which he placed.**—*And he placed,* or *bestowed them* (*wayyanhîhem*) (chap. ix. 25). Kings *l.c.* reads, "*and he brought them* into the chariot cities" (*wayyanhem*). The difference turns on the pointing only, and the versions there support our text; LXX., "he put;" Vulg., *disposuit;* Targum, *'ashrinnûn,* "he lodged them;" Syriac, "he left them." The *chariots* (*rekeb;* see 1 Chron. xviii. 4; xix. 6) *and horsemen* were, of course, military. The "chariot cities" probably lay in the south towards Egypt. The Simeonite Beth-marcaboth (*house of chariots*), and Hazar-susim (*court of horses*) may have been included amongst them. (See 1 Chron. iv. 31.)

(15) **Silver and gold . . . stones . . . cedar trees.**—Each of these words has the definite article in the Hebrew.

**And gold.**—Not in 1 Kings x. 27, with which the rest of the verse coincides; nor in chap. ix. 27. The Syriac omits it here also, but the other versions have it, and the phrase is a natural heightening of the hyperbole.

**The sycomore trees that are in the vale.**—(Comp. 1 Chron. xxvii. 28.) The Syriac reads instead: "As the sand which is on the seashore."

(16) **And Solomon had horses brought out . . .**—Rather, *And the outcome* (export) *of horses for Solomon was from Egypt, and the company of the king's merchants—a company* (of horses) *they would fetch at a price.* The same is read in Kings, only that the word *company* (*miqwē*) is there spelt in the ancient fashion (*miqwēh*), and two words are transposed ("they would fetch a company"). *Miqwēh* means *gathering, collection* (Gen. i. 10 [of the waters]). The repetition of this term constitutes a kind of artless play on words, such as is common in the Old Testament. (Comp. Gen. xv. 2; Judges xv. 16.) Both here and in Kings the Vulg. renders the word as a proper name, "from Coa." So also the LXX. in Kings "from Thekkoue" (Tekoa); and the Syriac of Chronicles, "from the city of the Aphelāvē." These variations only prove that the text was felt to be obscure. The "linen yarn" of the Authorised version is a guess based upon the likeness of the word *miqweh* to *qaw,* "rope," and *tiqwāh,* "line" (Josh. ii. 18), and upon the fact that much linen was made in Egypt.

(17) **And they fetched up, and brought forth out of Egypt.**—Literally, *And they caused to come up and to come out.* Kings has: "And there came up and came out a chariot from Egypt." The rest of the verse is identical there and here.

II.

THE BUILDING AND CONSECRATION OF THE TEMPLE (chaps. ii.—vii.).

Preliminary measures: (1) The levy of Canaanite labourers (verses 1, 2, and 17, 18). (2) The treaty with Huram of Tyre (verses 3—16).

(1) **Determined.**—Literally, *said,* which may mean either *commanded,* as in chap. i. 2; 1 Chron. xxi. 17,

*Solomon's Embassage to*     **II. CHRONICLES, II.**     *Huram for Workmen.*

of the LORD, and an house for his kingdom. ⁽²⁾ And Solomon told out threescore and ten thousand men to bear burdens, and fourscore thousand to hew in the mountain, and three thousand and six hundred to oversee them.

⁽³⁾ And Solomon sent to ¹Huram the king of Tyre, saying, As thou didst deal with David my father, and didst send him cedars to build him an house to dwell therein, *even so deal with me.* ⁽⁴⁾ Behold, I build an house to the name of the LORD my God, to dedicate it to him, *and* to burn before him ²sweet incense, and for the continual shewbread, and for the burnt offerings morning and evening, on the sabbaths, and on the new moons, and on the solemn feasts of the LORD our God. This *is an ordinance* for ever to Israel. ⁽⁵⁾ And the house which I build *is* great: for great *is* our God above all gods. ⁽⁶⁾ ᵃBut who ³is able to build him an house, seeing the heaven and heaven of heavens cannot contain him? who *am* I then, that I should build him an house, save only to burn sacrifice before him? ⁽⁷⁾ Send me now therefore a man cunning to work in gold, and in silver, and in brass, and in iron, and in purple, and crimson, and

¹ Or, *Hiram*, 1 Kings 5. 1.

² Heb., *incense of spices.*

ᵃ 1 Kings 8. 27; ch. 6. 18.

³ Heb., *hath retained,* or, *obtained strength.*

---

or *thought, purposed, resolved,* as in 1 Kings v. 5. The context seems to favour the latter sense.

**And an house for his kingdom.**—Or, *for his royalty*; that is, as the Vulg. renders, *a palace for himself.* Solomon's royal palace is mentioned again in verse 12; vii. 11; viii. 1; but the building of it is not related in the Chronicle. (See 1 Kings vii. 1—12.)

⁽²⁾ **And Solomon told out.**—That is, *counted out.* (Comp. Ps. xxii. 17; Exod. v. 8.) For the rest of this verse see Note on verse 18, where its contents are repeated. (Comp. 1 Kings v. 15.)

**To bear . . . to hew . . . to oversee.**—*Bearers of . . . hewers . . . overseers over,* as in verse 18.

⁽²⁾ The treaty with Huram of Tyre (verses 3—16).

⁽³⁾ **And Solomon sent to Huram.**—Comp. 1 Kings v. 2—11, from which we learn that Huram or Hiram had first sent to congratulate Solomon upon his accession. The account here agrees generally with the parallel passage of the older work. The variations which present themselves only prove that the chronicler has made independent use of his sources.

**Huram.**—In Kings the name is spelt *Hiram* (1 Kings v. 1, 2, 7) and *Hirom* (1 Kings v. 10, 18, Hebr.). (Comp. 1 Chron. xiv. 1.) Whether the Tyrian name *Sirōmos* (Herod. vii. 98) is another form of Hiram, as Bertheau supposes, is more than doubtful. It is interesting to find that the king of Tyre bore this name in the time of Tiglath-pileser II., to whom he paid tribute (B.C. 738), along with Menahem of Samaria. (Assyr. *Hi-ru-um-mu,* to which the *Hirôm* of 1 Kings v. 10, 18 comes very near.)

**As thou didst deal . . . dwell therein.**—See 1 Chron. xiv. 1. The sense requires the clause, added by our translators, in italics, "Even so deal with me," after the Vulg. "sic fac mecum." 1 Kings v. 3 makes Solomon refer to the wars which hindered David from building the Temple.

⁽⁴⁾ **I build.**—*Am about to build* (*bôneh*).

**To the name of the Lord.**—1 Kings iii. 2; 1 Chron. xxii. 35; xxii. 7.

**To dedicate.**—Or, *consecrate.* (Comp. Lev. xxvii. 14; 1 Kings ix. 3, 7.) The italicised *and* should be omitted, as the following words define the purpose of the dedication, viz., *for burning before him,* &c. Comp. Vulgate: "Ut consecrem eam ad adolendum incensum coram illo." (See Exod. xxv. 6; xxx. 7, 8.)

**And for the continual shewbread, and for the burnt offerings.**—In the Hebrew this is loosely connected with the verb rendered *to burn,* as part of its object: *for offering before him incense of spices* and a continual pile (of shewbread) *and burnt offerings.* (See Lev. xxiv. 5, 8; Num. xxviii. 4.)

**On the sabbaths, and on the new moons, and on the solemn feasts.**—1 Chron. xxiii. 31. "Solemn feasts:" *set seasons.* These special sacrifices are prescribed in Num. xxviii. 9—xxix.

**This is an ordinance for ever to Israel.**—Literally, *for ever this is* (is obligatory) *upon Israel,* viz., this ordinance of offerings. (Comp. the similar phrase, 1 Chron. xxiii. 31; and the formula, "a statute for ever," so common in the Law, Exod. xii. 14; xxix. 9.)

⁽⁵⁾ **And the house which I build is great.**—1 Chron. xxix. 1.

**Great is our God above all gods.**—Exod. xviii. 11; Deut. x. 17; Ps. lxxvii. 13; xcv. 3. According to modern notions of magnitude, the Temple of Solomon was a small building. (See on 1 Kings vi. 2, 3.) Shelley's

" There once proud Salem's haughty fane
   Reared high to heaven its thousand golden domes,

is pure fancy.

⁽⁶⁾ **But who is able.**—Literally, *who could keep strength?* (See 1 Chron. xxix. 14.)

**The heaven . . . cannot contain him.**—This high thought occurs in Solomon's prayer (1 Kings viii. 27; 2 Chron. vi. 18).

**Who am I then . . . before him?**—That is, I am not so ignorant of the infinite nature of Deity, as to think of localising it within an earthly dwelling. I build not for His residence, but for His worship and service. (Comp. Isa. xl. 22.)

**To burn sacrifice.**—Literally, *to burn incense.* Here, as in verse 4, used in a general sense.

⁽⁷⁾ **Send me now . . .**—*And now send me a wise man, to work in the gold and in the silver* (1 Chron. xxii. 15; verse 13).

**And in (the) purple, and crimson, and blue.**—No allusion is made to this kind of art in chap. iv. 11—16, nor in 1 Kings vii. 13 *seq.,* which describe only metallurgic works of this master, whose versatile genius might easily be paralleled by famous names of the Renaissance.

**Purple** (*'argĕwān*). — Aramaic form. (Heb. *'argāmān,* Exod. xxv. 4.)

**Crimson** (*karmîl*).—A word of Persian origin, occurring only here and in verse 13, and chap. iii. 14. (Comp. our word *carmine.*)

**Blue** (*tĕkēleth*).—*Dark blue,* or *violet.* (Exod. xxv. 4, and elsewhere.)

blue, and that can skill ¹to grave with the cunning men that *are* with me in Judah and in Jerusalem, whom David my father did provide. ⁽⁸⁾ Send me also cedar trees, fir trees, and ²algum trees, out of Lebanon: for I know that thy servants can skill to cut timber in Lebanon; and, behold, my servants *shall be* with thy servants, ⁽⁹⁾ even to prepare me timber in abundance: for the house which I am about to build *shall be* ³wonderful great. ⁽¹⁰⁾ And, behold, I will give to thy servants, the hewers that cut timber, twenty thousand measures of beaten wheat, and twenty thousand measures of barley, and twenty thousand baths of wine, and twenty thousand baths of oil.

⁽¹¹⁾ Then Huram the king of Tyre answered in writing, which he sent to Solomon, Because the LORD hath loved his people, he hath made thee king over them. ⁽¹²⁾ Huram said moreover, Blessed *be* the LORD God of Israel, that made heaven and earth, who hath given to David the king a wise son, ⁴endued with prudence and understanding, that might build an house for the LORD, and an

---

1 Heb., *to grave gravings.*
2 Or, *almuggim,* 1 Kings 10. 11.
3 Heb., *great and wonderful.*
4 Heb., *knowing prudence and understanding.*

---

**Can skill.**—*Knoweth how.*

**To grave.**—Literally, *to carve carvings;* whether in wood or stone. (1 Kings vi. 29; Zech. iii. 9; Exod. xxviii. 9, on gems.)

**With the cunning men.**—The Hebrew connects this clause with the infinitive *to work* at the beginning of the verse. There should be a stop after the words *to grave.*

**Whom David my father did provide** (*prepared,* 1 Chron xxix. 2).—1 Chron. xxii. 15; xxviii. 21.

⁽⁸⁾ **Fir trees.**—The word *bĕrōshim* is now often rendered cypresses. But Professor Robertson Smith has well pointed out that the Phœnician Ebusus (the modern Iviza) is the "isle of *bĕrōshim,*" and is called in Greek Πιτυοῦσαι, *i.e.,* "Pine islets." Moreover a species of pine is very common on the Lebanon.

**Algum trees.**—*Sandal wood;* Heb. '*algummim,* which appears a more correct spelling of the native Indian word (*valgúka*) than the '*almuggim* of 1 Kings x. 11. (See Note on chap. x. 10.)

**Out of Lebanon.**—The chronicler knew that sandal wood came from Ophir, or Abhira, at the mouth of the Indus (chap. x. 10; comp. 1 Kings x. 11). The desire to be concise has betrayed him into an inaccuracy of statement. Or must we suppose that Solomon himself believed that the sandal wood, which he only knew as a Phœnician export, really grew, like the cedars and firs, on the Lebanon? Such a mistake would be perfectly natural; but the divergence of this account from the parallel in 1 Kings leaves it doubtful whether we have in either anything more than an ideal sketch of Solomon's message.

**For I know that thy servants . . .**—Comp. the words of Solomon as reported in 1 Kings v. 6.

⁽⁹⁾ **Even to prepare me timber in abundance.** —Rather, *And they shall prepare,* or, *let them prepare.* (A use of the infinitive, to which the chronicler is partial: see 1 Chron. v. 1; ix. 25; xiii. 4; xv. 2; xxii. 5.) So Syriac, "Let them be bringing to me."

**Shall be wonderful great.**—See margin; and LXX., μέγας καὶ ἔνδοξος, "great and glorious;" Syriac, "an astonishment" (*temhā*).

⁽¹⁰⁾ **And, behold, I will give . . . barley.**—Rather, *And, behold, for the hewers,* that is, *for the woodcutters, I will give wheat as food for thy servants,* viz., *twenty thousand kors, and barley twenty thousand kors,* &c. "For the hewers" may mean "as for the hewers," or perhaps "on account of the hewers" (Gen. iv. 23). The latter sense would bring the verse into substantial harmony with 1 Kings v. 11, where we read: "And Solomon gave Hiram twenty thousand kors of wheat as food for his household, and twenty kors" (LXX., 20,000 baths) "of pure oil: so used Solomon to give to Hiram year by year," *i.e.,* during his building operations.

**Beaten wheat.**—The Hebrew (*hittim makkôth*) is literally *wheat—strokes.* But it is obvious that *makkôth* is a misreading for *makkôleth, food,* the word used in 1 Kings v. 11; and so the LXX. renders. The expression "thy servants" here seems to correspond with the phrase "his household" there; and the drift of the whole passage is that, in return for the services of the Tyrian artificers, Solomon engages to supply Hiram's royal household with provisions of corn and wine and oil.

Others assume, without much likelihood, that the two passages relate to two distinct agreements, by one of which Solomon undertook to supply Hiram's court, and by the other his Tyrian workmen, with provisions.

**Hewers** (*hôtĕbim*).—An old word, not recurring in the chronicle, and therefore explained by the writer.

**Measures** (*kōrim*).—The *kor* was a dry measure = one quarter. (Syriac, *reb'e,* "quarters.") The *bath,* a liquid measure, of six or seven gallons' capacity. Both words occur in the Greek of Luke xvi. 6, 7.

(11–15) Huram's reply. (Comp. 1 Kings v. 7—9.)

⁽¹¹⁾ **Answered in writing.**—*Said in a letter.* This seems to imply that Solomon's message had been orally delivered.

**Because the Lord hath loved his people.**—So chap. ix. 8; 1 Kings x. 9. In the parallel passage Huram blesses Jehovah, on hearing Solomon's message, apparently before writing his reply.

⁽¹²⁾ **Huram said moreover.**—*And Huram said,* that is, in his letter to Solomon.

**Blessed be the Lord God of Israel, that made heaven and earth.**—In 1 Kings v. 7 we read simply, "Blessed be the Lord this day, which hath given unto David a wise son over this great people." The chronicler has perhaps modified the words of his source in a monotheistic sense; although it is quite possible that Jehovah was known to the polytheist Phœnician by the title of "Maker of heaven and earth." (Comp. Gen. xiv. 19.) An inscription of the Persian emperor Xerxes speaks of the Supreme in terms which resemble what Solomon says in verse 5, as well as Huram's language here: "The great god Ahuramazda, great one of the gods, who made this earth, who made these heavens" (inscription on rocks at Elvend).

**An house for his kingdom.**—A royal palace (chap. vii. 11; viii. 1).

house for his kingdom. (13) And now I have sent a cunning man, endued with understanding, of Huram my father's, (14) the son of a woman of the daughters of Dan, and his father *was* a man of Tyre, skilful to work in gold, and in silver, in brass, in iron, in stone, and in timber, in purple, in blue, and in fine linen, and in crimson; also to grave any manner of graving, and to find but every device which shall be put to him, with thy cunning men, and with the cunning men of my lord David thy father. (15) Now therefore the wheat, and the barley, the oil, and the wine, which my lord hath spoken of, let him send unto his servants: (16) and we will cut wood out of Lebanon, [1] as much as thou shalt need: and we will bring it to thee in flotes by sea to [2] Joppa; and thou shalt carry it up to Jerusalem. (17) [a] And Solomon numbered all [3] the strangers that *were* in the land of Israel, after the numbering wherewith David his father had numbered them; and they were found an hundred and fifty thousand and three thousand and six hundred. (18) And he set [b] threescore and ten thousand of them *to be* bearers of burdens, and fourscore thousand *to be*

[1] Heb., *according to all thy need.*

[2] Heb., *Japho.*

[a] As ver. 2.

[3] Heb., *the men the strangers.*

[b] As it is ver. 2.

---

(13) **Endued with understanding.**—See the same phrase in 1 Chron. xii. 32.

**Of Huram my father's.**—Rather, *Huram my father*—*i.e.*, master, preceptor, as in chap. iv. 16, where Huram is called the "father" of Solomon. (Comp. Gen. xlv. 8; Judg. xvii. 10; xviii. 19. So LXX. and Vulgate; Syriac omits.)

(14) **The son of a woman of the daughters of Dan.**—In 1 Kings vii. 14 Hiram is called "son of a widow of the tribe of Naphtali." Bertheau explains, "She was by birth a Danite, married into the tribe of Naphtali, became a widow, and as a widow of the tribe of Naphtali became the wife of a man of Tyre, by whom she had a son Huram. Thus two of the tribes of Israel could boast that on the mother's side Huram belonged to them." But in the Hebrew words "daughters of Dan" it is possible to see a corruption of the word NAPHTALI.

**Skilful.**—This epithet belongs to Huram, not to his Tyrian father.

**To work in gold.**—1 Kings vii. 14 calls Huram simply "a worker in brass," or bronze.

**Purple.**—The strictly Hebrew form (verse 7).

**Fine linen** (*bûç*, byssus).—1 Chron. xv. 27. Neither this material of Huram's art, nor *stone* nor *timber* was mentioned in verse 7. Huram is naturally represented as enhancing the accomplishments of his artist.

**To find out every device which shall be put to him.**—Rather, *to devise any manner of device that may be given him* (to devise); that is, to invent all kinds of artistic objects according to commission. The words are a reminiscence of Exod. xxxi. 4, xxxv. 32, probably interpolated by the chronicler.

**With thy cunning men**—*i.e.*, to work along with them. (Comp. verse. 7.)

**My lord David.**—A touch of Oriental politeness. Huram was independent of David, as of Solomon.

(15) **The wheat, and the barley.**—See verse 10. Huram accepts Solomon's proposed exchange of benefits.

**His servants.**—Huram means himself and his court. The term is the correlative of "lord."

(16) **And we will cut wood.**—The *we* is emphatic, *and we, on our part,* the pronoun being expressed in the Hebrew.

**Wood** (="timber," verses 8, 9, 10, 14).—Properly *trees.*

**As much as thou shalt need.**—See margin. "Need" (*çōrek*) occurs here only in the Old Testament. The word is common in the Targums, and in Rabbinic writings; 1 Kings v. 8 has the classical phrase, "all thy desire."

**In flotes.**—Heb., *raphsōdōth*. Another isolated expression. Rendered "rafts" by the LXX. and Vulgate, but omitted by Syriac and Arabic. 1 Kings v. 9 has *dōbĕrōth*, "rafts," which settles the meaning.

**To Joppa.**—1 Kings v. 9 has the less definite "unto the place that thou shalt appoint me." Joppa (modern Jaffa) was the harbour nearest Jerusalem.

**And thou shalt carry it up to Jerusalem.**—This interprets the curt phrase of 1 Kings v. 9, "*and thou shalt take* (them) *away*."

A comparison of this and the parallel account of Huram's letter makes it clear (1) that the chronicler has not written without knowledge of the older text; (2) that neither text has preserved the exact form of the original documents. From Josephus (*Ant.* viii. 2, 8) it would appear that some record of the negotiations between Huram and Solomon was still extant at Tyre in his day, if only we might trust his authority.

(17, 18) Solomon's levy of Canaanite labourers. (A return to the subject of verse 2.)

(17) **All the strangers.**—The indigenous Canaanite population. (Comp. the use of the term in Gen. xxiii. 4; Exod. xxii. 21; Lev. xvii. 8.)

**After the numbering.**—The word *sĕphár*, "reckoning," "census," occurs here only in the Old Testament.

**Wherewith David his father.**—The former census of the native Canaanites, which had taken place by order of David, is briefly recorded in 1 Chron. xxii. 2. (Comp. 2 Sam. xx. 24, "and Adoram was over the levy," from which it appears that the subject population was liable to forced labour under David; comp. also 1 Kings iv. 6; v. 14; xii. 4—18.)

**And they were found.**—The total of the numbers here given is 153,600, which is the sum of the figures assigned in the next verse, viz., 70,000 + 80,000 + 5,600.

(18) **And he set . . .**—Literally, *and he made seventy thousand of them bearers of burdens, and eighty thousand hewers in the mountains.* This exactly agrees with 1 Kings v. 15.

**And three thousand and six hundred overseers.**—The same number was given in verse 2. In 1 Kings v. 16 we read of 3,300 officers. In the Hebrew, *three* (*shālōsh*) and *six* (*shēsh*) might easily be confused; our reading appears right. The chronicler omits all notice of the levy of 30,000 Israelites, which

*The Place of the Temple.*     II. CHRONICLES, III.     *The Measure and Ornaments.*

hewers in the mountain, and three thousand and six hundred overseers to set the people a work.

CHAPTER III.—<sup>(1)</sup> Then <sup>a</sup> Solomon began to build the house of the LORD at Jerusalem in mount Moriah, <sup>1</sup> where *the LORD appeared unto David his father,* in the place that David had prepared in the threshingfloor of <sup>2</sup> Ornan the Jebusite. <sup>(2)</sup> And he began to build in the second day of the second month, in the fourth year of his reign.

<sup>a</sup> 1 Kings 6. 1, &c.

1 Or, *which was seen of David his father.*

B.C. 1012.

2 Or, *Araunah,* 2 Sam. 24. 18; 1 Chron. 21. 18.

<sup>b</sup> 1 Kings 6. 2.

3 Heb., *founded.*

<sup>c</sup> 1 Kings 6. 3.

<sup>(3)</sup> Now these *are the things wherein* <sup>b</sup> Solomon was <sup>3</sup> instructed for the building of the house of God. The length by cubits after the first measure *was* threescore cubits, and the breadth twenty cubits. <sup>(4)</sup> And the <sup>c</sup> porch that *was* in the front *of the house*, the length *of it was* according to the breadth of the house, twenty cubits, and the height *was* an hundred and twenty: and he overlaid it within with pure gold. <sup>(5)</sup> And the greater house he cieled with fir tree, which he overlaid with fine

---

the parallel passage records (1 Kings v. 13, 14); whether by an oversight, or from disapproval, we cannot say. Adding that number to the 70,000 and 80,000 other labourers, we get a grand total of 180,000, which gives a company of 50 for each of the 3,600 overseers.

**Overseers.**—Heb. *měnaççěhim.* Only here and in verse 2 *supra,* and chap. xxxiv. 13. It is the plural of a participle which occurs only in the titles of the Psalms (including Hab. iii. 19), while the verb is read only in Chronicles and Ezra iii. 8, 9. (See Note on 1 Chron. xv. 21.)

**To set the people a work**—*i.e., on work* or *a-working.* (Comp. "I go a-fishing," John xxi. 3.) Literally, *to make the people work.*

III.

THE BUILDING OF THE TEMPLE AND MAKING OF THE SACRED VESSELS (chaps. iii.—v. 1; comp. 1 Kings vi., vii.).

(*a*) Site and date (verses 1, 2). (*b*) Its dimensions: the porch and the Holy Place, or nave (verses 3—7). (*c*) The Holy of holies, or chancel, with the cherubim and the vail (verses 8—14). (*d*) The two bronze pillars in the porch (verses 15—17).

(*a*) SITE AND DATE (verses 1, 2).

<sup>(1)</sup> **At Jerusalem in mount Moriah.**—Nowhere else in the Old Testament is the Temple site so specified. (Comp. "the land of Moriah," the place appointed for the sacrifice of Isaac, Gen. xxii. 2.)

**Where the Lord appeared unto David his father.**—So LXX.; rather, *who appeared unto David his father.* Such is the meaning according to the common use of words. There is clearly an allusion to the etymology of MORIAH, which is assumed to signify "appearance of Jah." (Comp. Gen. xxii. 14.) Translate, "in the mount of the Appearance of Jah, who appeared unto David his father." The Vulgate reads: "in Monte Moria qui *demonstratus fuerat* David patri ejus;" but *nir'ah* never means *to be shown* or *pointed out.* The Syriac, misunderstanding the LXX. (Ἀμωρία), renders "in the hill of the Amorites."

**In the place that David had prepared.**—This is no doubt correct, as the versions indicate. The Hebrew has suffered an accidental transposition.

**In the threshingfloor of Ornan.**—1 Chron. xxi. 28; xxii. 1.

<sup>(2)</sup> **In the second day of the second month.**—Heb., *in the second month in the second.* The versions omit the repetition, which is probably a scribe's error. "On the second day" would be expressed in Hebrew differently. Read simply, "And he began to build in the second month," *i.e.,* in Zif (or April—May). See 1 Kings vi. 1.

(*b*) DIMENSIONS OF THE TEMPLE; THE PORCH AND THE HOLY PLACE, OR NAVE (verses 3—7).

<sup>(3)</sup> **Now these are the things wherein Solomon was instructed.**—Rather, *And this is the foundation* (or ground-plan) *of Solomon.* The plural pronoun *'ēllè,* "these," is used as a neut. sing. "this" (comp. 1 Chron. xxiv. 19), and the *hophal* infinitive *hiṣṣad,* "to be founded," is used substantively, as in Ezra iii. 11. So Vulgate, "Et haec sunt fundamenta quæ jecit Solomon."

**After the first measure.**—Rather, *in the ancient measure,* an explanation not found in the parallel passage, 1 Kings vi. 2. The ancient or Mosaic cubit was one hand-breadth longer than the cubit of later times (Ezek. xl. 5; xliii. 13). The chronicler has omitted the height, which was thirty cubits (1 Kings vi. 2).

<sup>(4)</sup> **And the porch . . . twenty cubits.**—Heb., *and the porch that was before the length* (*i.e.,* that lay in front of the oblong main building), *before the breadth of the house, was twenty cubits* (*i.e.,* the porch was as long as the house was broad). This curious statement answers to what we read in 1 Kings vi. 3: "And the porch before the hall of the house, twenty cubits was its length, before the breadth of the house." But the Hebrew is too singular to pass without challenge, and comparison of the versions suggests that we ought to read here: "*And the porch which was before it* (Syriac), or *before the house* (LXX.), *its length before the breadth of the house was twenty cubits.*" This would involve but slight alteration of the Hebrew text. (Comp. verse 8.)

**And the height was an hundred and twenty.** This would make the porch four times the height of the main building, which was thirty cubits. The Alexandrine MS. of the LXX., and the Arabic version, read "twenty cubits;" the Syriac omits the whole clause, which has no parallel in Kings, and is further suspicious as wanting the word "cubits," usually expressed after the number (see verse 3). The Hebrew may be a corruption of the clause, "and its breadth ten cubits." (Comp. 1 Kings vi. 3.)

**And he overlaid it within with pure gold.**—See 1 Kings vi. 21.

<sup>(5)</sup> **The greater house.**—Or, *the great chamber, i.e.,* the Holy Place, or nave. (Comp. 1 Chron. xxviii. 11.)

**He cieled with fir tree.**—*He covered with planks of fir;* or, *panelled with fir.* To ciel, or rather *seel*

*The Gold.*        II. CHRONICLES, III.        *The Cherubims.*

gold, and set thereon palm trees and chains. <sup>(6)</sup> And he <sup>1</sup> garnished the house with precious stones for beauty: and the gold *was* gold of Parvaim. <sup>(7)</sup> He overlaid also the house, the beams, the posts, and the walls thereof, and the doors thereof, with gold; and graved cherubims on the walls. <sup>(8)</sup> And he made the most holy house, the length whereof *was* according to the breadth of the house, twenty cubits, and the breadth thereof twenty cubits: and he overlaid it with fine gold, *amounting* to six hundred talents. <sup>(9)</sup> And the weight of the nails *was* fifty shekels of gold. And he overlaid the upper chambers with gold. <sup>(10)</sup> And in the most holy house he made two cherubims <sup>2</sup>of image work, and overlaid them with gold. <sup>(11)</sup> And the wings of the cherubims *were* twenty

<sup>1</sup> Heb., *covered*.

<sup>2</sup> Or, (as some think) *of moveable work*.

---

(from *syle* or *cyll*, a canopy: Skeat, *Etymol. Dict.* s.v.) a room, meant in old English to wainscot or panel it. (Comp. 1 Kings vi. 15, 16.)

**Which he overlaid with fine gold.**—*And covered it* (the chamber) *with good gold.* The cypress wainscoting was plated with gold.

**And set thereon palm trees and chains.**—*Brought up on it* (*i.e.*, carved upon it) *palms and chainwork* (1 Kings vii. 17). (For the palms, see 1 Kings vi. 29; Ezek. xli. 18.) The chain-work must have consisted of garland-like carvings on the fir panels. 1 Kings vi. 18 omits mention of it; LXX., "carved on it palms and chains"; Syriac, "figured on it the likeness of palms and lilies"; Vulgate, "graved on it palms and as it were chainlets intertwining."

<sup>(6)</sup> **Garnished.**—*Overlaid* (verse 4) *the chamber.*

**Precious stones.**—See 1 Chron. xxix. 2; and 1 Kings x. 11, which relates that Hiram's fleet brought "precious stones" from Ophir for Solomon. But no mention of this kind of decoration is made in 1 Kings vi. The Vulgate explains the phrase as meaning a floor of costly marble.

**Gold of Parvaim.**—Perhaps *Farwâ*, an auriferous region in S. Arabia. Others connect the word with the Sanskrit *pûrva*, "eastern," and seek Parvaim, like Ophir, in India. The name does not recur in the Old Testament.

<sup>(7)</sup> **He overlaid also the house.**—*And he covered* (verse 5) *the chamber*—that is, the great chamber or Holy Place. (See 1 Kings vi. 21, 22, 23.)

**The beams.**—Of the roof.

**The posts.**—*The thresholds* (Isa. vi. 4).

**And graved cherubims on the walls.**—See 1 Kings vi. 29, which gives a fuller account of the mural decorations.

**Cherubims.**—*Cherubim*, or *cherubs* (Ps. xviii. 10). Cherubim is the Hebrew plural, for which we have the Chaldee (Aramaic) form "cherubin" in the *Te Deum*. Shakspeare has:—

"The roof of the chamber
With golden cherubins is fretted."
*Cymbeline*, ii. 4.

Why Reuss calls this sketch of the porch and nave "confused" is hardly evident.

(c) THE HOLY OF HOLIES, OR CHANCEL, WITH THE CHERUBIM AND THE VAIL (verses 8–14).

<sup>(8)</sup> **The most holy house.**—*The chamber of the Holy of holies*, or chancel, called also the *oracle* (*Debîr*), 1 Kings vi. 5. (So verse 10.)

**The length whereof was according to the breadth of the house, twenty cubits.**—*Its length before the breadth of the house was twenty cubits.* (See Note on verse 4.)

**And the breadth thereof twenty cubits.**—1 Kings vi. 20 adds that the height also was twenty cubits, so that the chamber formed a perfect cube.

**Six hundred talents.**—The weight of gold thus expended on the plating of the walls of the inner shrine is not given in Kings. Solomon's whole yearly revenue was 666 talents (1 Kings x. 14).

<sup>(9)</sup> **And the weight of the nails was fifty shekels of gold.**—Literally, *And a weight for nails for shekels—fifty in gold.* The LXX. and Vulg. take this to mean that the weight of each nail was fifty shekels; and this is probably right, for fifty shekels as a total would be a trifling sum to record along with six hundred talents. The nails were used to fasten the golden plates to the wooden wainscoting of the edifice.

Whatever may be thought of the apparently incredible quantities of gold and silver stated to have been amassed by David for the Temple (1 Chron. xxii. 14; xxix. 4, 7), it is clear that no inconsiderable amount of the former metal would be required for the plating of the chambers as described in this chapter. And it is well known, from their own monuments, that the Babylonian sovereigns of a later age were in the habit of thus adorning the houses of their gods. Nebuchadnezzar, for instance, who restored the great temple of Borsippa, says: "E-zida, the strong house, in the midst thereof I caused to make, with silver, gold, alabaster, bronze . . . cedar I caused to adorn (or, completed) its *sibir*. The cedar of the roof (?) of the shrines of Nebo with gold I caused to clothe." In another inscription we read: "The shrine of Nebo, which is amid E-Sagili, its threshold, its bolt, and its *babnaku*, with gold I caused to clothe." And again: "The cedar roof of the oracle I caused to clothe with bright silver." The Assyrian Esarhaddon, a century earlier, boasts that he built ten castles in Assyria and Accad, and "made them shine like day with silver and gold."

**And he overlaid.**—*And the upper chambers he covered with gold.* The chambers over the Holy of holies are mentioned in 1 Chron. xxviii. 11. The two statements of this verse are peculiar to the chronicle. The Syriac and Arabic omit the verse.

<sup>(10)</sup> **Two cherubims.**—1 Kings vi. 23—28. They were made of oleaster, plated with gold.

**Of image work.**—Literally, *a work of statuary.* The Hebrew word meaning "statuary" occurs here only, and looks suspicious. The Vulg. renders *opere statuario*; the LXX. "a work of logs"; the Syriac "a durable work." With the last three renderings comp. 1 Kings vi. 23, "wood (or blocks) of oleaster," a specially hard wood. The rendering of the LXX. suggests that the original reading may have been *ma'aseh 'eçîm*, "woodwork."

**And overlaid.**—Heb., *and they overlaid.*

<sup>(11)</sup> **And the wings of the cherubims were twenty cubits long.**—*Their length was, altogether, twenty cubits;* so that, being outspread, they reached from wall to wall of the Holy of holies, which was

cubits long: one wing *of the one cherub* was five cubits, reaching to the wall of the house: and the other wing *was likewise* five cubits, reaching to the wing of the other cherub. (12) And *one wing* of the other cherub *was* five cubits, reaching to the wall of the house: and the other wing *was* five cubits *also*, joining to the wing of the other cherub. (13) The wings of these cherubims spread themselves forth twenty cubits: and they stood on their feet, and their faces were [1] inward.

(14) And he made the [a] vail *of* blue, and purple, and crimson, and fine linen, and [2] wrought cherubims thereon.

(15) Also he made before the house [b] two pillars of thirty and five cubits [3] high, and the chapiter that *was* on the top of each of them *was* five cubits. (16) And he made chains, *as* in the oracle, and put *them* on the heads of the pillars; and made an hundred pomegranates, and put *them* on the chains. (17) And he [c] reared up the pillars before the temple, one on the right hand, and the other on the left; and called the name of that on the right hand [4] Jachin, and the name of that on the left [5] Boaz.

CHAPTER IV.— (1) Moreover he made an altar of brass, twenty cubits

---

1 Or, *toward the house.*
a Matt. 27. 51.
2 Heb., *caused to ascend.*
b 1 Kings 7. 15; Jer. 52. 21.
3 Heb., *long.*
c 1 Kings 7. 21.
4 That is, *He shall establish.*
5 That is, *In it is strength.*

---

twenty cubits wide. Of this breadth each cherub covered half, or ten cubits, with his wings, which were five cubits apiece in length. Obviously the inner wing of each cherub met the inner wing of the other in the middle of the wall.

**One wing . . . other cherub.**—*The wing of the one, extending to five cubits, was touching the wall of the chamber, and the other wing—five cubits—was touching the wing of the other cherub.*

(12) Literally, *And the wing of the one cherub—five cubits—was touching the wall of the chamber, and the other wing—five cubits—was cleaving to the wing of the other cherub.*

(13) **The wings of these cherubims.**—Or, *These wings of the cherubim.*

**Spread themselves forth.**—*Were outspreading* (participle), 1 Chron. xxviii. 18.

**And they stood.**—*Were standing.* They were ten cubits high (1 Kings vi. 26).

**Inward.**— See margin. Translate, *toward the chamber.* The cherubs did not face each other like the cherubim on the mercy seat (Exod. xxv. 20).

(14) **The vail.**—The *Pārōkheth*, or curtain, which divided the holy place from the holy of holies, is not mentioned in the existing text of 1 Kings vi. 21, which passage, however, speaks of the chains of gold by which the vail was probably suspended.

**Blue, and purple, and crimson, and fine linen.**—See Notes on chap. ii. 7, 14.

**Wrought.**—See Note on "set," verse 5. Here raised figures in tapestry or broidered work are meant. (See Exod. xxvi. 31, which gives an identical description of the vail of the tabernacle.)

(d) THE TWO BRONZE PILLARS IN THE PORCH (verses 15—17). Comp. 1 Kings vii. 15—22.

(15) **Before the house.**—Before the holy place, in the porch.

**Two pillars of thirty and five cubits high.**—*Two pillars thirty and five cubits in length.* 1 Kings vii. 15 says "eighteen cubits," so also 2 Kings xxv. 17; Jer. lii. 21; and no doubt correctly. Of the versions, the LXX. and Vulg. have "thirty-five;" the Syriac and Arabic, "eighteen."

**The chapiter**—*i.e.*, *the capital.* French, *chapitre.* Literally, *the ornament.* 1 Kings vii. 16 has "the crown;" so 2 Chron. iv. 12.

(16) **And he made chains, as in the oracle.**—Heb., *And he made chainwork in the oracle,* or chancel, which is clearly corrupt. But if we read *kad-debîr* for *bad-debîr,* an infinitesimal change in Hebrew writing, we get the sense which our version suggests: *And he made chainwork as in the chancel.* It is true that the sacred writer has not told us that the walls of the Holy of Holies were so ornamented, but in verse 5 he states it of the great hall or holy place, and 1 Kings vi. 29 declares that the whole house was adorned with mural carvings. It was quite natural to write, "and he made chainwork as in the oracle," assuming that such decorations really existed in the inner chamber. There seems therefore to be no need to alter *debîr* into *rābîd,* ("collar") as most commentators have done, although the change is very slight in Hebrew writing. The LXX. had the present Hebrew text, but, apparently, not understanding it transliterated the Hebrew words: "He made *serserôth* in the *dabir.*" So Vulg., "as it were chainlets in the oracle." The Syriac and Arabic have "and he made chains of fifty cubits."

**An hundred pomegranates.**—So Jer. lii. 23. (See 1 Kings vii. 20, 42, from which it appears that there were altogether four hundred pomegranates, viz., an upper and lower row of one hundred each upon the chainwork of each pillar. So chap. iv. 13.)

(17) **Before the temple.**—Vulg., *in vestibulo templi.* So 1 Kings vii. 21 has, "at the porch of the temple." 1 Kings vii. 22 adds, "and upon the top of the pillars was lily-work."

**Jachin . . . Boaz.**—See 1 Kings vii. 21. "The description of the two brazen pillars," says Reuss, "much more detailed in 1 Kings vii. 15 ff., has become almost unintelligible, under the pen of the abbreviator." This is a strong exaggeration. He also pronounces the word *bad-debîr* in verse 16 "absolutely unintelligible," and to be accounted "foreign to the text." How little we agree with this hasty decision will be evident from our Note on that verse.

IV.

(a) The principal vessels of the Temple (verses 1—10).
(b) Huram's works in brass (verses 11—18).
(c) Catalogue of golden objects, and conclusion verse 19—chap. v. 1).

a) THE PRINCIPAL VESSELS OF THE TEMPLE (verses 1—10).

THE BRAZEN ALTAR (verse 1).

(1) **An altar of brass.**—The brazen altar, or altar of burnt offering, made by Solomon, is not noticed in the

the length thereof, and twenty cubits the breadth thereof, and ten cubits the height thereof. <sup>(2)</sup> <sup>a</sup>Also he made a molten sea of ten cubits <sup>1</sup>from brim to brim, round in compass, and five cubits the height thereof; and a line of thirty cubits did compass it round about. <sup>(3)</sup> <sup>b</sup>And under it *was* the similitude of oxen, which did compass it round about: ten in a cubit, compassing the sea round about. Two rows of oxen *were* cast, when it was cast. <sup>(4)</sup> It stood upon twelve oxen, three looking toward the north, and three looking toward the west, and three looking toward the south, and three looking toward the east: and the sea *was set* above upon them, and all their hinder parts *were* inward. <sup>(5)</sup> And the thickness of it *was* an handbreadth, and the brim of it like the work of the brim of a cup, <sup>2</sup>with flowers of lilies; *and* it received and held three thousand baths.

<sup>(6)</sup> He made also ten lavers, and put five on the right hand, and five on the

*a* 1 Kings 7. 23, &c.

<sup>1</sup> Heb., *from his brim to his brim.*

*b* 1 Kings 7. 24.

<sup>2</sup> Or, *like a lily flower.*

---

parallel chapters of Kings (1 Kings vi., vii.) which describe the construction of the temple and its vessels of service, but it is incidentally mentioned in another passage of the older work (1 Kings ix. 25), and its existence seems to be implied in 1 Kings viii. 22, 64. This altar stood in the inner court of the temple. It rose from a terraced platform. (Comp. Ezek. xliii. 13—17.) The Hebrew of this verse is such as to suggest that it must have existed in the original document. The style is the same. (Comp. the construction of the numerals with the noun, and note the word *qômāh*, "height," now used for the first time by the chronicler.) It would appear, therefore, that the verse has been accidentally omitted from the text of Kings.

THE BRAZEN SEA (verses 2—5). (Comp. 1 Kings vii. 23—26.)

(2) **Also he made a molten sea.**—*And he made the sea* (i.e., the great basin) *molten*—i.e., of cast metal.

**Of ten cubits . . . thereof.**—*Ten in the cubit from its lip to its lip, circular all round; and five in the cubit was its height.* Word for word as in 1 Kings vii. 23, save that Kings has one different preposition (*'ad*, "unto," instead of *'el*, "to"). "Lip." Comp. "lip of the sea," Gen. xxii. 17; "lip of the Jordan," 2 Kings ii. 13; a metaphor which is also used in Greek.

**And a line of thirty cubits . . .**—*Line, i.e.,* measuring-line, as in Ezek. xlvii. 3. The Hebrew is *qāw*. In Kings we read a rare form, *qāwèh*. The rest of the clause is the same in both texts.

**Did compass.**—*Would compass,* or *go round it.*

(3) **And under it was the similitude of oxen.** —Literally, *And a likeness of oxen* (figured oxen) *under it around surrounding it, ten in the cubit encompassing the sea around: two rows were the oxen, smelted in the smelting of it.* In the parallel passage (1 Kings vii. 24) we read: *And wild gourds underneath its lip around surrounding it,*" &c., as here; *two of rows were the gourds, smelted in the smelting thereof.* The Hebrew words for "oxen" and "gourds" might easily be confused by a transcriber, and accordingly it is assumed by most commentators that the text of the chronicler has suffered corruption, and should be restored from that of Kings. But there seems no reason—unless we suppose that each writer has given an exhaustive description, which is clearly not the case—why the ornamental rows which ran round the great basin should not have included both features, small figures of oxen, as well as wild gourds. Reuss objects on the ground of the diminutive size of the oxen ("ten in a cubit"); but such work was by no means beyond the resources of ancient art. (Comp. the reliefs on the bronze doors of Shalmaneser II. (859—825 B.C.); 1 Kings vii. 29 actually gives an analogous instance.) The word *pĕqā'im*, "wild gourds," only occurs in one other place of Kings, viz., 1 Kings vi. 18. (Comp. *paqqu'ôth*, 2 Kings iv. 39.) A copyist of Kings might have inadvertently repeated the word from the former passage in 1 Kings vii. 24. In any case it is sheer dogmatism to assert that "the copyists (in the Chronicle) have absurdly changed the gourds into oxen" (Reuss). The Syriac and Arabic omit this verse; but the LXX. and Vulg. have it.

(4) **It stood.**—The whole verse coincides verbally with 1 Kings vii. 25, with one slight exception: the common form of the numeral "twelve," *shnêm 'āsār,* is substituted for the rare *shnê 'āsār.*

(5) **And the thickness . . . a cup.**—Identical with 1 Kings vii. 26.

**With flowers of lilies.**—See margin. "Lily" here is *shôshannāh;* in Kings, *shôshān.* LXX., "graven with lily buds." Syriac and Arabic, "and it was very beautiful." Vulg., "like the lip of a cup, or of an open lily."

**And it received and held three thousand baths.**—Literally, *holding* (whole) *baths: three thousand would it contain.* The bath was the largest of Hebrew liquid measures. Perhaps the true reading is, "holding three thousand baths," the last verb being a gloss borrowed from Kings. So Vulg. Syriac and Arabic omit the clause. The LXX. had the present reading. 1 Kings vii. 26 reads, *two thousand baths would it contain.* Most critics assume this to be correct. Some scribe may have read *'alăphim,* "thousands," instead of *'alpayim,* "two thousand," and then have added "three" (*shĕlōsheth*) under the influence of the last verse. But it is more likely that the numeral "three" having been inadvertently omitted from the text of Kings, the indefinite word "thousands" was made definite by turning it into the dual "two thousand." Either mistake would be possible, because in the unpointed text *'alăphim* and *'alpayim* are written alike. The Syriac has the curious addition, "And he made ten poles, and put five on the right and five on the left, and bare with them the altar of burnt offerings." Similarly the Arabic version.

THE TEN LAVERS: THEIR USE, AND THAT OF THE SEA (verse 6). (Comp. 1 Kings vii. 27—39.)

(6) The chronicler now returns to his abbreviating style, and omits altogether the description of the ten bases, or stands, upon which the lavers were placed, and which are described in full and curious detail in

*Candlesticks and Tables.*    II. CHRONICLES, IV.    *The Instruments of Brass.*

left, to wash in them: [1] such things as they offered for the burnt offering they washed in them; but the sea *was* for the priests to wash in. (7) And he made ten candlesticks of gold according to their form, and set *them* in the temple, five on the right hand, and five on the left. (8) He made also ten tables, and placed *them* in the temple, five on the right side, and five on the left. And he made an hundred [2] basons of gold.

[1] Heb., *the work of burnt offering.*
[2] Or, *bowls.*
[3] Or, *bowls.*
[4] Heb., *finished to make.*

(9) Furthermore he made the court of the priests, and the great court, and doors for the court, and overlaid the doors of them with brass. (10) And he set the sea on the right side of the east end, over against the south.

(11) And Huram made the pots, and the shovels, and the [3] basons. And Huram [4] finished the work that he was to make for king Solomon for the house of God.; (12) *to wit,* the two pillars, and

---

1 Kings vii. 27—39. The unusual difficulty of the passage may have determined the omission, but it seems more likely that the sacred writer thought the bases of less importance than the objects described in verses 7—9, the account of which he has interpolated between the first and second half of 1 Kings vii. 39.

**He made also ten lavers.**—*And he made ten pans.* The word *kiyôr* is used in 1 Sam. ii. 14 as a *pan* for cooking, and in Zech. xii. 6 as a *pan* holding fire. Its meaning here and in the parallel place is a pan for washing. (Comp. Exod. xxx. 18, 28.) The LXX. renders λουτῆρας, "baths;" the Syriac, *laqnê*, "flagons" (*lagenae,* λάγηνοι).

**To wash in them.**—This statement, and, indeed, the rest of the verse is peculiar to the chronicler. On the other hand, 1 Kings vii. 38 specifies the size and capacity of the lavers here omitted.

**Such things as they offered for the burnt offering they washed in them.**—This gives the meaning. Literally, *the work* (comp. Exod. xxix. 36, "to do" being equivalent to "to offer") *of the burnt offering they used to rinse* (strictly, *thrust, plunge*) *in them.*

**But the sea was for the priests to wash in.** —The Hebrew words have been transposed apparently. The same infinitive (*lĕrohçāh*) occurs in Exod. xxx. 18; xl. 30, in a similar context. Instead of all this, the Syriac and Arabic versions read: "put them five on the right hand and five on the left, that the priests might wash in them *their hands and their feet,*" which appears to be derived from Exod. xxx. 19; xl. 31.

THE TEN GOLDEN CANDLESTICKS, THE TEN TABLES, THE HUNDRED GOLDEN BOWLS, AND THE COURTS (verses 7—9).

This section is peculiar to Chronicles.

(7) **And he made ten candlesticks of gold according to their form.**—*And he made the golden lampstands ten, according to their rule,* or *prescribed manner.* (Comp. 1 Kings vii. 49; and Exod. xxv. 31—40, where their type is described.) So the Vulg., "secundum speciem quâ jussa erant fieri." Syriac and Arabic, "according to their laws." Others explain "as their use required," which is less likely.

**In the temple.**—And before the chancel (1 Kings vii. 49; verse 20, *infra*).

(8) **He made also ten tables.**—Perhaps the golden candelabra stood upon them. (Comp. 1 Chron. xxviii. 16; and verse 19, *infra*.)

**Side.**—Not in the Hebrew.

**An hundred basons.**—*Bowls* for pouring libations (Amos vi. 6; same word, *mizrāqim*). The Syriac and Arabic make the number of these vessels a hundred and twenty.

The ten tables are not mentioned in the parallel narrative, which speaks of one table only, viz., the table of shewbread (1 Kings vii. 48).

"Basons," or *bowls,* are spoken of in 1 Kings vii. 45, 50 (*mizrāqôth*), but their number is not given.

(9) **The court of the priests.**—See 1 Kings vi. 36; vii. 12, "the inner court;" Jer. xxxvi. 10, "the higher court."

**And the great court.**—*'Azārāh,* "court," a late word, common in the Targums for the classical *hāçēr,* which has just occurred. The *'azārāh* was the outer court of the temple. It is not mentioned at all in the parallel narrative. The LXX. calls it "the great court;" the Vulg., "the great basilica." The Syriac renders the whole verse: "And he made one great court for the priests and Levites, and covered the doors and bolts with bronze." (Comp. Note on verse 3 for this plating of the doors with bronze.) The bronze-plated doors of Shalmaneser's palace at *Balawat* were twenty-two feet high, and each leaf was six feet wide.

(10) **And he set the sea . . .**—Literally, *And he set the sea on the right shoulder, eastward, in front of the southward;* i.e., on the south-east side of the house (1 Kings vii. 39, b.). The LXX. and some MSS. add "of the house," which appears to have fallen out of the text.

(b) HURAM'S WORKS IN BRASS (verses 11—18). Comp. 1 Kings vii. 40—47.

Throughout this section the narrative almost textually coincides with the parallel account.

(11) **And Huram made the pots.**—1 Kings vii. 40 has "lavers" (pans). Our reading, "pots," appears correct, supported as it is by many MSS. and the LXX. and Vulg. of Kings. A single stroke makes the difference between the two words in Hebrew writing. These "pots" were scuttles for carrying away the ashes of the altar.

**Basons.**—"Bowls" (*mizrāqôth*). Probably the same as the *mizrāqim* of verse 8. So *kiyôrôth* (Kings) and *kiyôrim* (Chron.).

**Huram.**—Hebrew text, *Hiram,* as in Kings. The LXX. renders: "And Hiram made the fleshhooks (κρεάγρας) and the firepans (πυρεῖα), and the hearth of the altar and all its vessels."

**The work.**—Kings, "all the work," and so some MSS., LXX., and Vulg. of Chron. The Syriac and Arabic omit verses 11—17 and 19—22.

**He was to make.**—Rather, *he made.*

**For the house.**—*In the house.* Chronicles supplies the preposition *in,* which is not required according to ancient usage.

(12) **And the pommels, and the chapiters**—i.e., *the globes and the capitals.* Kings, Authorised Version.

the pommels, and the chapiters *which were* on the top of the two pillars, and the two wreaths to cover the two pommels of the chapiters which *were* on the top of the pillars; (13) and four hundred pomegranates on the two wreaths; two rows of pomegranates on each wreath, to cover the two pommels of the chapiters which *were* ¹upon the pillars. (14) He made also bases, and ²lavers made he upon the bases; (15) one sea, and twelve oxen under it. (16) The pots also, and the shovels, and the fleshhooks, and all their instruments, did Huram his father make to king Solomon for the house of the LORD of ³ bright brass. (17) In the plain of Jordan did the king cast them, in the ⁴ clay ground between Succoth and Zeredathah. (18) Thus Solomon made all these vessels in great abundance: for the weight of the brass could not be found out. (19) And Solomon made all the vessels that *were for* the house of God, the golden altar also, and the tables whereon the shewbread *was set;* (20) moreover the candlesticks with their lamps, that they should burn after the manner before the oracle, of pure gold; (21) and the

B.C. 1012.

1 Heb., *upon the face.*

2 Or, *caldrons.*

3 Heb., *made bright,* or, *scoured.*

4 Heb., *thicknesses of the ground.*

---

has *bowls*, but in Hebrew the word is the same (*gullôth*, globes). "The globes *of* the capitals" (Kings) is plainly incorrect.

**Which were on the top of the two pillars.**—Heb. (*and the globes and the capitals*), *on the top of the pillars, two;* i.e., two globes and capitals. The word "two" (*shtayim*) is feminine, agreeing with "globes and capitals," which are also feminine; whereas "pillars" is a masculine term.

**Wreaths.**—Heb., *sĕbākhôth*, lattices. (Comp. 2 Kings i. 2.) The Authorised version of 1 Kings vii. 41 gives "network," but the Hebrew word is the same as here.

(13) **Two rows.**—See 1 Kings vii. 42.

(14) **He made also bases.**—*And the bases he made; and the lavers he made upon the bases.* This repetition of the verb is suspicious; and the parallel text shows the right reading to be *and the bases ten* (in number), *and the lavers ten upon the bases.* "Ten" in Hebrew writing closely resembles "he made." The LXX. renders, "And the bases he made ten, and the lavers he made upon the bases;" which shows that the corruption of the text is ancient.

(15) **One sea.**—Heb., *the sea one.* Kings, *and the one sea.*

**And twelve oxen under it.**—*And the oxen, twelve, under it.* Kings, *And the oxen, twelve, under the sea.* The chronicler has abridged the expression.

(16) **The pots also, and the shovels, and the fleshhooks.**—"Fleshhooks", (*mizlāgôth*) should apparently be "bowls" (*mizrāqôth*). (Comp. verse 1, and 1 Kings vii. 45.) But in Exod. xxvii. 3, pots and shovels and bowls and fleshhooks are mentioned in succession as utensils of the altar. Perhaps, therefore, *both* words should be read here and in Kings. LXX., καὶ τοὺς ποδιστῆρας καὶ τοὺς ἀναλημπτῆρας καὶ τοὺς λέβητας καὶ τὰς κρεάγρας. The Vulg. merely repeats verse 11 (*et lebetes et creagras et phialas*). A stop should follow the last; "And all their instruments," &c., being a new sentence.

**And all their instruments.**—1 Kings vii. 45, *and all these instruments,* which appears correct, though the LXX. supports our present reading (πάντα τὰ σκεύη αὐτῶν). "Their instruments" could hardly mean the moulds in which they were cast, as Zöckler suggests. The moulds would not be made in "polished brass."

**Huram his father.**—See Note on chap. ii. 13.

**Bright.**—*Polished.* Jer. xlvi. 4 (*māruq*). Kings has the synonym *mĕmōrāt*. (Comp. Isa. xviii. 2.)

(17) **In the clay ground.**—Heb., *in the thickness of the ground*—i.e., in the stiff or clayey soil. Vulg.. "in argillosa terra." For '*ăbî*, "thickness," see Job xv. 26. Kings has *ma'ăbeh*, which occurs nowhere else.

**Zeredathah.**—Kings, *Zārĕthān* (Josh. iii. 16). *Zĕrēdāthāh* means *towards Zĕrēdāh* (1 Kings xi. 26). The two names denote the same place.

(18) **Thus Solomon made all these vessels in great abundance.**—1 Kings vii. 47, *And Solomon left all the vessels* (unweighed) *from very great abundance.* Our text may be due to a copyist, whose eye wandered to the beginning of the next verse; but it is possible that the chronicler missed the significance of the verb used in Kings, and therefore substituted an easier term. The further changes—"unto great abundance," "for the weight," &c.—suggest this account of the matter.

**Could not be found out.**—*Was not ascertained.*

(*c*) CATALOGUE OF OBJECTS IN GOLD—CONCLUSION (verse 19—chap. v. 1). 1 Kings vii. 48—50.

The narrative still coincides in the main with that of Kings, allowing for one or two remarkable alterations.

(19) **For the house.**—*In the houses* (without preposition, comp. verse 11).

**The golden altar also.**—Literally, *both the golden altar and the tables, and upon them the Presence bread.* So LXX. and Vulg. The parallel passage, 1 Kings vii. 48, says, *and the table on which* (*was*) *the Presence bread* (*in*) *gold.* (See Note on verse 8, *supr.,* and 1 Chron. xxviii. 16.) On the one hand, the chronicler in these three passages consistently speaks of tables, although the book of Kings mentions one table only; and, on the other hand, elsewhere he actually speaks himself of "*the* Pure Table," and "*the* Table of the Pile," as if there were only one such table (2 Chron. xiii. 11; xxix. 18).

The difficulty cannot be solved with certainty; but it seems likely that, finding mention of a number of tables in one of his sources, the chronicler has grouped them all together with the Table of Shewbread, thus gaining brevity at the cost of accuracy. In Ezek. xl. 39 eight tables of hewn stone are mentioned, whereon they slew the sacrificial victims.

(20) **With** (*and*) **their lamps, that they should burn after the manner** (*according to the legal rule*—verse 7). This is added by the chronicler, who omits "five on the right and five on the left" (Kings). The rest is as in Kings.

(21) **And the flowers . . . gold.**—See 1 Kings vii. 49.

flowers, and the lamps, and the tongs, made he of gold, and that ¹perfect gold; ⁽²²⁾ and the snuffers, and the ²basons, and the spoons, and the censers, of pure gold: and the entry of the house, the inner doors thereof for the most holy place, and the doors of the house of the temple, were of gold.

CHAPTER V.—⁽¹⁾ Thus all the work that Solomon made for the house of the LORD was finished: ᵃ and Solomon brought in all the things that David his father had dedicated; and the silver, and the gold, and all the instruments, put he among the treasures of the house of God.

¹ Heb., *perfections of gold.*
² Or, *bowls.*
ᵃ 1 Kings 7. 51.
ᵇ 1 Kings 8. 1, &c.

⁽²⁾ ᵇ Then Solomon assembled the elders of Israel, and all the heads of the tribes, the chief of the fathers of the children of Israel, unto Jerusalem, to bring up the ark of the covenant of the LORD out of the city of David, which *is* Zion. ⁽³⁾ Wherefore all the men of Israel assembled themselves unto the king in the feast which *was* in the seventh month. And all the elders of Israel came; and the Levites took up the ark. ⁽⁵⁾ And they brought up the ark, and the tabernacle of the congregation, and all the holy vessels that *were* in the tabernacle, these did the priests *and* the Levites bring up. ⁽⁶⁾ Also king Solomon,

---

**And that perfect gold.**—*It* was *perfection of gold.* The word *miklôth,* "perfections" (intensive plural) occurs nowhere else. It is derived from *kālāh,* "to be finished," not *kālal* (Bishop Wordsworth). The LXX. omits the clause; not so the Vulg., which renders "all were made of purest gold." This little touch, added to heighten the effect, is quite in the manner of the chronicler, and is certainly not to be suspected, as Zöckler asserts. Perhaps we should read *miklôl,* "perfection" (Ezek. xxiii. 12), instead of the isolated *miklôth.*

**And the snuffers.**—Before this expression, *and the basons* (1 Kings vii. 50) has probably fallen out.

**Snuffers.**—*Shears* or *scissors,* for trimming the lamps.

**The spoons, and the censers.**—Or, *trays and snuff-dishes.*—See 1 Kings vii. 50; Exod. xxv. 38.

**And the entry of the house.**—Including both the doors of the nave or holy place, and those of the chancel or holiest. The words are explained by those which follow: "viz., its inner doors to the holy of holies and the doors of the house—viz., to the nave (*hêkāl,* great hall)." In 1 Kings vii. 50 we read, "And the *hinges* to the doors of the inner house —viz., the holy of holies, (and) to the doors of the house—viz., to the nave, were of gold." The word rendered *hinges* (*pôthôth*) resembles that rendered *entry* (*pethah*); and some have supposed that the latter is a corruption of the former, and would alter our text accordingly. Two reasons seem to be decisive against such a change. (1) *Pôthôth,* "hinges," occurs nowhere else in the Bible; and may not be genuine. It is likely enough that the doors of the Temple were plated with gold (1 Kings vi. 32, 35), but hardly that their hinges were made of gold.

(2) Even if *pôthôth* be correct in Kings, the chronicler might have understood the word to mean *openings,* rather than *hinges,* and so have substituted the common word *pethah,* which has that sense. The resemblance of the one word to the other would be a further consideration in its favour, according to ancient notions of interpretation.

V.

⁽¹⁾ **Thus.**—*And.* This verse is identical with 1 Kings vii. 51. (The chronicler has made three slight corrections of the older text.)

**Brought in all the things . . . dedicated.**— *Brought in the holy* (or *hallowed*) *things of David his father.* (Comp. 1 Chron. xviii. 11; xxvi. 26—28.)

**The implements.**—Or, *vessels.* The word *all* is omitted by some MSS., and by the LXX., Syriac, and Arabic. "The holy things of David" are identical with "the silver and the gold and the vessels."

THE DEDICATION OF THE TEMPLE (chaps. v. 2— vii. 22).

1. Chap. v. 2—14.

NATIONAL CEREMONY OF THE TRANSFER OF THE ARK INTO THE TEMPLE. (Comp. 1 Kings viii. 1—11.)

The chapter is an almost literal duplicate of the parallel text. The desire to explain and abridge accounts for such variations as are not due to the transcribers.

⁽²⁾ **The chief of the fathers.**—Rather, *the chiefs of the clans (father-houses).* Vulg., "capita familiarum;" LXX., τοὺς ἡγουμένους πατριῶν.

**Elders . . . heads.**—Or, *sheikhs . . . ameers.*

**Zion.**—Syr. and Arab., *Hebron.*

**In the feast which was in the seventh month.**—Heb., *in the feast; that (is) the seventh month.* The words "in the month of Ethanim" (Kings) have been accidentally omitted before the expression rendered " in the feast." The Authorised version suggests another mode of emending the text. (Comp. Neh. viii. 14.) Syr., "in the month of the fruits ('*ebbô*) of the feast of Tabernacles; that is the seventh month." The LXX. had the present faulty Hebrew.

⁽⁴⁾ **The Levites.**—Kings has *the priests;* and so Syr. and Arab. here; but LXX. and Vulg., *Levites.* The latter term, as the tribal name, may of course be used to include the priests or Aaronites, as well as their inferior brethren. Verse 7 shows that the priests are intended here.

⁽⁵⁾ **These did the priests and the Levites bring up.**—Heb., *the priests the Levites* (which some explain "the Levitical priests," as in Josh. iii. 3) *brought them up.* But some Hebrew MSS., LXX., and Syriac, read "the priests *and* the Levites;" Arab., "the Levites *and* the priests;" and Vulg., "the priests *with* the Levites." Above all, 1 Kings viii. 4 has, "And the priests and the Levites brought them up." It appears, therefore, that the conjunction is rightly supplied by the Authorised Version.

⁽⁶⁾ **Assembled.**—(*Nō'ad,* to meet at an appointed time and place, Exod. xxv. 22). Not the same word as in verses 2 and 3 (*qāhal*), of which the root meaning is probably *to call together.*

and all the congregation of Israel that were assembled unto him before the ark, sacrificed sheep and oxen, which could not be told nor numbered for multitude. <sup>(7)</sup> And the priests brought in the ark of the covenant of the LORD unto his place, to the oracle of the house, into the most holy *place, even* under the wings of the cherubims: <sup>(8)</sup> for the cherubims spread forth *their* wings over the place of the ark, and the cherubims covered the ark and the staves thereof above. <sup>(9)</sup> And they drew out the staves *of the ark*, that the ends of the staves were seen from the ark before the oracle; but they were not seen without. And <sup>1</sup>there it is unto this day. <sup>(10)</sup> *There was* nothing in the ark save the two tables which Moses *put therein at Horeb, <sup>2</sup>when the LORD made a covenant with the children of Israel, when they came out of Egypt.

<sup>(11)</sup> And it came to pass, when the the priests were come out of the holy *place :* (for all the priests *that were* <sup>3</sup>present were sanctified, *and* did not *then* wait by course: <sup>(12)</sup> <sup>b</sup> also the Levites *which were* the singers, all of them of Asaph, of Heman, of Jeduthun, with their sons and their brethren, *being* arrayed in white linen, having cymbals and psalteries and harps, stood at the east end of the altar, and with them an hundred and twenty priests sounding with trumpets :) <sup>(13)</sup> It came even to pass, as the trumpeters and singers *were* as one, to make one sound to be heard in praising and thanking the LORD; and when they lifted up *their* voice with the trumpets and cymbals and instru-

<sup>1</sup> Or, *they are there, as* 1 Kings 8. 8.

*a* Deut. 10. 2, 5.

<sup>2</sup> Or, *where.*

<sup>3</sup> Heb., *found.*

*b* 1 Chron. 25. 1.

---

**Before the ark.**—By the omission of a single Hebrew word ['*ittô*] before this phrase, the whole form of the sentence is altered from that of Kings. There we read "(were) *with him* before the Ark sacrificing," &c.

**Sacrificed.**—*Were sacrificing.*

**And the priests . . .**—The verse is wholly identical with 1 Kings viii. 6 (see Notes there).

(8) **For the cherubims spread forth their wings.**—Rather, *And the cherubim were spreading forth wings.* Kings has *for* (*kí*); making the sentence an explanation of the last clause of verse 7.

**Covered.**—Kings has the technical term for the cherubim "covering" the ark (Exod. xxv. 20; 1 Chron. xxviii. 18). In Hebrew writing, the difference is marked by the transposition of a single letter. Perhaps, therefore, our present reading is a clerical error.

(9) **And they drew out . . . were seen.** —Rather, *And the staves were so long that the tips of the staves were seen.* &c.

**From the ark.**—1 Kings viii. 8, "from the Holy Place." So the LXX. and four Hebrew MSS. The priests in the great hall could see the tips of the staves projecting within the Holy of Holies; but persons outside ("without") of the great hall could not see them.

**And there it is unto this day.**—*And it* (the ark) *remained there unto this day.* So Vulg., "fuit itaque arca ibi." LXX., Syr., Targ., Arab., *They*—*i.e.,* the poles *were there;* and so some Heb. MSS., and 1 Kings viii. 8. This is no doubt right. A letter has fallen out of the Hebrew text. That the chronicler has preserved this remark without modification to suit altered circumstances, and indeed that the compiler of Kings did the same long before him, is a striking instance of the way in which Oriental historiographers are content to borrow with literal exactitude from the works of predecessors, even in cases where such borrowing appears to the modern mind infelicitous.

(10) **Put therein.**—Heb., *which Moses put—in Horeb.* Kings is fuller and clearer: *which Moses placed there in Horeb.* The chronicler has substituted "put" for "placed;" perhaps remembering Exod. xl. 20 : "And he put the testimony into the ark." The word *shām,* "there" or "therein," has fallen out of the text.

**When the Lord made a covenant.**—*Which* (the two Tables *i.e.,* the Covenant) *the Lord covenanted with the sons of Israel.* (Comp. chap. vi. 11 : "the Ark wherein is the covenant of the Lord," 1 Kings viii. 21.)

(11) **For all the priests.**—From this point to "for his mercy endureth for ever," verse 13, the narrative is peculiar to the chronicler. He has characteristically inserted between the two halves of the short verse (1 Kings viii. 10) a long parenthesis, dwelling upon the Levitical ministrations.

**That were present.**—*That could be found.* So Vulg. (Comp. 2 Kings xix. 4.)

**Were sanctified.**—*Had sanctified* (or purified) *themselves,* for the purpose of taking part in the ceremony (1 Chron. xv. 12).

**And did not wait by course.**—*They had not to observe courses* (1 Chron. xxiv.). Not merely the class of priests then on duty, but all the classes indiscriminately took part in the solemnity.

(12) **All of them of Asaph . . . brethren.**— Heb., *to all of them, to Asaph, to Heman,* &c., &c., *and to their sons, and to their brethren.* This use of the particle *le* (*to, for*) is characteristic of the chronicler, whose style in these verses stands in marked contrast with the former part of the chapter. As to the Levitical guilds of musicians, comp. 1 Chron. xxv. 1—7, xv. 16, *seq.*

**Arrayed in white linen.**—1 Chron. xv. 27.

**Having cymbals and psalteries and harps.** —*With cymbals and nebels and kinnors* (harps and lutes, or guitars). (See 1 Chron. xv. 28.)

**Stood at the east end of the altar.** — *Were standing east of the altar.*

**And with them . . . trumpets.**—*And with them priests, to a hundred and twenty, were trumpeting with trumpets.* (See 1 Chron. xv. 24.)

**An hundred and twenty.**—Thus five to each of the twenty-four classes of the priests.

The mark of parenthesis should be cancelled.

(13) **It came even to pass . . . thanking the Lord.**—*And the trumpeters and the minstrels were to sound aloud, as one man, with one sound, in order to praise and thank the Lord.* This ends the parenthesis-

ments of musick, and praised the LORD, saying, *ᵃFor he is good; for his mercy endureth for ever:* that *then* the house was filled with a cloud, *even* the house of the LORD; ⁽¹⁴⁾ so that the priests could not stand to minister by reason of the cloud: for the glory of the LORD had filled the house of God.

CHAPTER VI.—⁽¹⁾ Then ᵇ said Solomon, The LORD hath said that he would dwell in the ᶜ thick darkness. ⁽²⁾ But I have built an house of habitation for thee, and a place for thy dwelling for ever. ⁽³⁾ And the king turned his face, and blessed the whole congregation of Israel: and all the congregation of Israel stood.

⁽⁴⁾ And he said, Blessed *be* the LORD God of Israel, who hath with his hands fulfilled *that* which he spake with his mouth to my father David, saying, ⁽⁵⁾ Since the day that I brought forth my people out of the land of Egypt I chose no city among all the tribes of Israel to build an house in, that my name might be there; neither chose I any man to be a ruler over my people Israel: ⁽⁶⁾ but I have chosen Jerusalem, that my name might be there; and have chosen David to be over my people Israel. ⁽⁷⁾ Now ᵈ it was in the heart of David my father to build an house for the name of the LORD God of Israel. ⁽⁸⁾ But the LORD said to David my father, Forasmuch as it was in thine heart to build an house for my name, thou didst well in that it was in thine heart: ⁽⁹⁾ notwithstanding thou shalt not build the house; but thy son which shall

*ᵃ Ps. 136.*

*ᵇ 1 Kings 8. 12, &c.*

*ᶜ Lev. 16. 2.*

*ᵈ 2 Sam. 7. 2; 1 Chron. 28. 2.*

---

**Their voice with the trumpets.**—Rather, *A sound with trumpets*, &c.

**And praised the Lord, saying, For he is good.**—For this common liturgical formula see 1 Chron. xvi. 34, 41.

**That then the house was filled with a cloud, even the house of the Lord.**—Omit *that* (1 Kings viii. 10). "Then the cloud filled the house of the Lord." The LXX. reads, "with the cloud *of the glory of the Lord*;" the Vulg. simply, "so that the house of God was filled with a cloud." (The Syriac and Arabic omit verses 12, 13.) The unpointed Heb. text might be rendered, "the house was filled with the cloud of the house of the Lord;" but the Authorised Version is preferable; the phrase, "the house of *the Lord*," being added as a sort of climax. (Comp. chap. iv. 21, *ad fin.*) So Reuss, "Le temple se remplit d'une nuée, le temple *de l'Eternel.*" The emphatic word is *Jehovah*, of whose presence the bright cloud was the standing token.

⁽¹⁴⁾ **House of God.**—Kings, "house of the Lord." See 1 Kings viii. 11, and chap. vii. 2, *infra*.

**Stand to minister.**—*Take their places*, or *approach to minister* (chap. vi. 12). The Syriac adds here, "Ended is the first half of the Chronicles." Before chap. vi. it writes, "The second half of the Book of Chronicles."

## VI.

2. KING SOLOMON BLESSES HIS PEOPLE AND HIS GOD (chap. vi. 1—11.) (Comp. 1 Kings viii. 12—21.)

This section also is in verbal agreement with the parallel account, with a few slight exceptions.

⁽¹⁾ **The thick darkness.**—'*Arăphel*, which is explained as *caligo nubium*, "gloom of clouds." (See Exod. xx. 21; Deut. iv. 11; Ps. xviii. 9. Comp. the Greek, ὀρφνη.) The Targum on 1 Kings viii. 12 reads *Jerusalem*, but this is probably a gloss.

⁽²⁾ **But I have built.**—*And I, on my part, have built.* Kings, "I *have* built" (*bānōh bānîthî*); scil., as "Thou didst indicate." This seems original. So the Syr. here, *mebnō b'nith*, but not LXX. and Vulg.

**Habitation.**—*Zĕbûl*, a poetic word, occurring only five times. (Comp. Hab. iii. 11.)

**And a place.**—*And*, added here, weakens the force of the poetic parallelism.

**A place for thy dwelling.**—(Exod. xv. 17), another poetic expression.

**For ever.**—(Through) *ages*. So only in this account and Ps. lxi. 5.

⁽³⁾ **And the king.**—The verse is word for word as in Kings.

**Turned.**—*Turned round* (1 Chron. x. 14).

**Stood.**—Was *standing*.

⁽⁴⁾ **Who hath with his hands fulfilled . . . David.**—Literally, *who spake* ("promised," *verse* 10), *by his mouth with David my father, and by his hands fulfilled*. (See 1 Chron. xi. 2, xvii. 4—14.) The only variant in this verse is *hands* for *hand*. The unpointed text of Kings might be read in either way. (Comp. verse 15, *infr.*)

⁽⁵⁾ **My people out of the land of Egypt.**—Kings, "My people *Israel* out of *Egypt*." (Comp chap. v. 10.) The Syr. and Arab. have *Israel* here also.

**Neither chose I any man to be a ruler** (*nāgid*) **over my people Israel.**—Neither this sentence nor the following is found in the parallel passage, where the second half of verse 6 forms the last clause of the preceding verse (1 Kings viii. 16). The Syriac and Arabic here follow Kings as often. There is nothing in the language against the supposition that the words originally formed part of the older text.

**Neither chose I any man.**—Saul was originally the people's, not God's, choice. Holy Scripture nowhere teaches that the *vox populi* is identical with the *vox Dei*. (See 1 Sam. viii. 5, and Bishop Wordsworth's Note.)

⁽⁶⁾ **But** (*and*) **I have chosen Jerusalem.**—Some MSS. omit this verse.

⁽⁹⁾ **Notwithstanding thou shalt not build.**—*Only thou, thou shalt not build;* with stress on the pronoun.

**But thy son.**—Heb., *for thy son;* so LXX.; Kings, "but;" and so some MSS. and the Syriac, Vulg., and Arabic here. Otherwise the whole verse is as in Kings.

come forth out of thy loins, he shall build the house for my name. (10) The LORD therefore hath performed his word that he hath spoken : for I am risen up in the room of David my father, and am set on the throne of Israel, as the LORD promised, and have built the house for the name of the LORD God of Israel. (11) And in it have I put the ark, wherein is the covenant of the LORD, that he made with the children of Israel.

(12) And he stood before the altar of the LORD in the presence of all the congregation of Israel, and spread forth his hands : (13) for Solomon had made a brasen scaffold, of five cubits ¹ long, and five cubits broad, and three cubits high, and had set it in the midst of the court: and upon it he stood, and kneeled down upon his knees before all the congregation of Israel, and spread forth his hands toward heaven, (14) and said,

O LORD God of Israel, *a* there is no God like thee in the heaven, nor in the earth ; which keepest covenant, and *shewest* mercy unto thy servants, that walk before thee with all their hearts : (15) thou which hast kept with thy servant David my father that which thou hast promised him ; and spakest with thy mouth, and hast fulfilled *it* with thine hand, as *it is* this day. (16) Now therefore, O LORD God of Israel, keep with thy servant David my father that which thou hast promised him, saying, *b* ² There shall not fail thee a man in my sight to sit upon the throne of Israel ; *c* yet so that thy children take heed to their way to walk in my law, as thou hast walked before me. (17) Now then, O LORD God of Israel, let thy word be verified, which thou hast spoken unto thy servant David.

(18) But will God in very deed dwell with men on the earth ? *d* behold, heaven and the heaven of heavens cannot con-

B.C. 1004.

¹ Heb., *the length thereof*, &c.

*a* Exod. 15. 11.

*b* 2 Sam. 7. 12 ; 1 Kings 2. 4, & 6. 12.

² Heb., *There shall not a man be cut off*.

*c* Ps. 132. 12.

*d* ch. 2. 6 ; Isa. 66. 1 ; Acts 7. 49.

---

(10) **The Lord . . . his word.**—*And Jehovah hath established*, or *ratified, his word.* Literally, *caused to rise up.*

**Spoken**—i.e., promised.

**Set.**—*Seated.* (No variant from Kings.)

(11) **And in it have I put the ark.**—*And I have set there the ark,* abridged from 1 Kings viii. 21, "and I have set there a place for the ark." So Syriac and Arabic, "and I have prepared a place for the ark."

**Wherein is the covenant.**—The two tables of the Law. (See chap. v. 10.)

3. THE KING UTTERS THE PRAYER OF CONSECRATION (verses 12—42). (Comp. 1 Kings viii. 22—53.)

The whole is given as in Kings, save that one verse (13) is added, and the peroration (40—42) is quite different.

(12) **Stood.**—*Took his place.* It is not implied that he remained *standing.* (Comp. 1 Sam. xvii. 51 ; verse 3, *supr.*)

**Spread forth his hands.**—*Towards heaven* (Kings). Syriac and Arabic have both.

(13) **For Solomon had made a brasen scaffold.**—This verse is not in Kings. But it may once have followed 1 Kings viii. 22. At least, marks of the chronicler's individual style are not apparent in it.

**Scaffold.**—Literally, *pan* (*kiyôr*; see chap. iv. 6). The "scaffold" looked like a "laver" turned upside down, and was doubtless hollow underneath. (Comp. Neh. ix. 4 for an analogous structure.)

**Kneeled down upon his knees, and spread forth his hands.**—An attitude of prayer which may be seen figured upon the monuments of ancient Egypt.

**Toward heaven** (*ha-shāmāy'māh*).—The chronicler has used the exact form for the less precise *ha-shāmáyim* of 1 Kings viii. 22.

(14) **In the heaven nor in the earth.**—Abridged from "in the heaven *above*, and *upon* the earth *beneath*" (Kings). Syriac, "Thou art the Lord that sittest in heaven above, and Thy will (pl.) is done on earth beneath ;" apparently a curious reminiscence of the Lord's Prayer. The Assyrians also spoke of their gods as "without an equal" (*sânina la isû*, "a rival he has not").

**Which keepest covenant and shewest mercy.**—Literally, *keeping the covenant and the mercy*; i.e., the covenanted mercy. (Comp. Isa. lv. 3.)

**With thy servant.**—Heb., *for*; so in verse 16. (The verse is word for word as in Kings.)

**And spakest with thy mouth** . . . . Chap. vi. 4.

(16) **Now therefore.**—*And now.* So in verse 17.

**Keep that which thou hast promised**—i.e., Thy further promise. See the fulfilment of the former promise, as described in verse 10, *supr.*

**There shall not fail thee.**— See margin. Authorised Version follows LXX., οὐκ ἐκλείψει σοι ; and Vulg., "non deficiet ex te."

**To sit.**—Heb., *sitting* ; LXX., καθήμενος.

**Yet so that.**—*Only if*; assigning a single condition ; *provided that* . . . . LXX., πλὴν ἐὰν φυλάξωσι; Vulg., "ita tamen si custodierint."

**Take heed to.**—Heb., *keep* (verses 14, 15, 16).

**In my law.**—The only variant from 1 Kings viii. 25. The chronicler has avoided a seeming tautology, as elsewhere. Syriac, "before me in the Law."

(17) **Be verified.**—1 Chron. xvii. 23. LXX. and Syriac add, "I pray" (Heb., *nā*), as in Kings.

**Thy word.**—Or *promise* (verses 10, 15, *supr.*)

**Unto thy servant David.**—Heb., *to thy servant, to David.* Kings, "to thy servant David my father." So Syriac here.

(18) **But will God in very deed.**—Or, *what? will God*, &c.—The LXX. imitates the Hebrew ὅτι εἰ ἀληθῶς κατοικήσει ; Vulg., "ergone credibile est ut habitet Deus ?"

**With men.**—Not in Kings. Syriac, "with his people, Israel ;" Arabic, "with his people." (Comp. Rev. xxi. 3.)

tain thee; how much less this house which I have built! ⁽¹⁹⁾ Have respect therefore to the prayer of thy servant, and to his supplication, O LORD my God, to hearken unto the cry and the prayer which thy servant prayeth before thee: ⁽²⁰⁾ that thine eyes may be open upon this house day and night, upon the place whereof thou hast said that thou wouldest put thy name there; to hearken unto the prayer which thy servant prayeth ¹ toward this place. ⁽²¹⁾ Hearken therefore unto the supplications of thy servant, and of thy people Israel, which they shall ² make toward this place: hear thou from thy dwelling place, even from heaven; and when thou hearest, forgive.

⁽²²⁾ If a man sin against his neighbour, ³ and an oath be laid upon him to make him swear, and the oath come before thine altar in this house; ⁽²³⁾ then hear thou from heaven, and do, and judge thy servants, by requiting the wicked, by recompensing his way upon his own head; and by justifying the righteous, by giving him according to his righteousness.

⁽²⁴⁾ And if thy people Israel ⁴ be put to the worse before the enemy, because they have sinned against thee; and shall return and confess thy name, and pray and make supplication before thee ⁵ in this house; ⁽²⁵⁾ then hear thou from the heavens, and forgive the sin of thy people Israel, and bring them again unto the land which thou gavest to them and to their fathers.

⁽²⁶⁾ When the ᵃ heaven is shut up, and there is no rain, because they have sinned against thee; *yet* if they pray toward this place, and confess thy name, and turn from their sin, when thou dost afflict them; ⁽²⁷⁾ then hear thou from heaven, and forgive the sin of thy servants, and of thy people Israel, when thou hast taught them the good way, wherein they should walk; and send rain upon thy land, which thou hast given unto thy people for an inheritance.

⁽²⁸⁾ If there ᵇ be dearth in the land, if there be pestilence, if there be blasting, or mildew, locusts, or caterpillers; if their enemies besiege them ⁶ in the cities of their land; whatsoever sore or what-

---

1 Or, *in this place.*

2 Heb., *pray.*

3 Heb., *and he require an oath of him.*

4 Or, *be smitten.*

5 Or, *toward.*

a 1 Kings 17. 1.

b ch. 20. 9.

6 Heb., *in the land of their gates.*

---

⁽¹⁹⁾ **Have respect therefore.**—*But turn thou unto.* The Authorised Version follows the LXX. and Vulg., ἐπιβλέψῃ; "ut respicias."

**Before thee.**—Kings adds, "to-day." So LXX., Syriac, Arabic here.

⁽²⁰⁾ **Upon.**—*Unto* or *toward.* "Day and night" (as in Ps. i. 2); Kings, "night and day" (as in Isa. xxvii. 3); for which the chronicler has substituted a more usual phrase. The Syriac and Arabic follow Kings.

**Prayeth.**—*Shall pray,* scil., at any time.

**Toward this place.**—The margin is wrong, though supported by the Syriac, Arabic, and Vulg. The Temple of Jerusalem was, and is, the *Kebla* of the Jew. (Comp. Dan. vi. 10, and verse 34 *infr.*, which is a kind of paraphrase of this expression.)

⁽²¹⁾ **Supplications.**—*Taḥănûnîm,* a word chiefly poetic and late, which nowhere appears in Kings, and only here in Chronicles. Kings has the older synonym *tĕḥinnāh.*

**Hear thou from thy dwelling place, even from heaven.**—*Yea thou—thou shalt hear from the place of thy dwelling, from the heavens.* For "from," in both places, Kings has "unto," an unusual pregnant construction, which is probably original.

⁽²²⁾ **If a man sin.**—Kings, "whatever a man sin."

**And an oath be laid upon him.**—*And he* (i.e., his neighbour or, indefinitely, *people*) *lay an oath upon him.* (See Exod. xxii. 11.)

**And the oath come before thine altar.**—*And he* (the offender) *enter upon an oath before thine altar.* (Comp. Ezek. xvii. 13.) But all the versions have, "*and he come, and swear before thine altar,*" a difference which involves merely the prefixing of one letter (*w*) to the Hebrew word rendered "oath."

⁽²³⁾ **From heaven.**—In Kings we have not the preposition. Perhaps the meaning there is "to heaven," as in verse 30. The chronicler has substituted a more ordinary expression, which, indeed, is found in all the versions of Kings. Similarly in verses 25, 30, 33, 35, 39.

**By requiting the wicked.**—*So as to requite a wicked man.* Kings, "so as to find guilty" (also the Syriac here). The latter is probably original. "To find guilty a guilty man" corresponds to "justifying a just one," in the next clause.

**By justifying.**—*So as to justify;* or *pronounce righteous.*

⁽²⁴⁾ **And if thy people Israel be put to the worse.**—See margin. Kings has a different construction, "when thy people Israel are smitten." (Comp. verse 26.)

**Because they have sinned.**—*When* or *if they sin* (so also in verse 26). LXX., ἐὰν ἁμαρτῶσι. Vulg., "peccabunt enim tibi," as a parenthesis. Syriac and Arabic, "when." Kings, *if ('asher) they sin,* a rarer usage.

⁽²⁷⁾ **Then hear thou from heaven.**—Rather, (*to*) *heaven* or (*in*) *heaven,* as in Kings. (Comp. Note on verse 23.) The versions read "from heaven."

**When thou . . . way.**—*For thou pointest them to the good way.* A construction only found here. Comp. Ps. xxvii. 11, where we see the simple accusation as in Kings, which is probably right here also, *'el* (*to*) being an error for *'eth* (so the versions). Making this change, the verse coincides with 1 Kings viii. 36.

⁽²⁸⁾ **If their enemies besiege them.**—*If his enemies* (Kings, "enemy") *besiege him.* (So in verse 34.)

**In the cities of their land.**—See margin, which correctly renders the Hebrew text. But the expression "in the land of his gates" is strange.

soever sickness *there be*: <sup>(29)</sup> *then* what prayer *or* what supplication soever shall be made of any man, or of all thy people Israel, when every one shall know his own sore and his own grief, and shall spread forth his hands ¹ in this house: <sup>(30)</sup> then hear thou from heaven thy dwelling place, and forgive, and render unto every man according unto all his ways, whose heart thou knowest; (for thou only *a* knowest the hearts of the children of men:) <sup>(31)</sup> that they may fear thee, to walk in thy ways, ² so long as they live ³ in the land which thou gavest unto our fathers.

<sup>(32)</sup> Moreover concerning the stranger, *b* which is not of thy people Israel, but is come from a far country for thy great name's sake, and thy mighty hand, and thy stretched out arm; if they come and pray in this house; <sup>(33)</sup> then hear thou from the heavens, *even* from thy dwelling place, and do according to all that the stranger calleth to thee for; that all people of the earth may know thy name and fear thee, as *doth* thy people Israel, and may know that ⁴ this house which I have built is called by thy name.

<sup>(34)</sup> If thy people go out to war against their enemies by the way that thou shalt send them, and they pray unto thee toward this city which thou hast chosen, and the house which I have built for thy name; <sup>(35)</sup> then hear thou from the heavens their prayer and their supplication, and maintain their ⁵ cause.

<sup>(36)</sup> If they sin against thee, (for *there is* *c* no man which sinneth not,) and thou be angry with them, and deliver them over before *their* enemies, and ⁶ they carry them away captives unto a land far off or near; <sup>(37)</sup> yet *if* they ⁷ bethink themselves in the land whither they are carried captive, and turn and pray unto thee in the land of their captivity, saying, We have sinned, we have done amiss, and have dealt wickedly; <sup>(38)</sup> if they return to thee with all their heart and with all their soul in the land of their captivity, whither they have carried them captives, and pray toward their land, which thou gavest unto their fathers, and *toward* the city which thou hast chosen, and toward the house which I have built for thy name: <sup>(39)</sup> then hear thou from the heavens, *even* from

1 Or, *toward this house.*
*a* 1 Chron. 28. 9.
2 Heb., *all the days which.*
3 Heb., *upon the face of the land.*
*b* John 12. 20; Acts 8. 27.
4 Heb., *thy name is called upon this house.*
5 Or, *right.*
*c* Prov. 20. 9; Eccles. 7. 21; James 3. 2; 1 John 1. 8.
6 Heb., *they that take them captives carry them away.*
7 Heb., *bring back to their heart.*

---

LXX. has, "if the enemy afflict him before their cities;" Vulg., "et hostes, vastatis regionibus, *portas obsederint civitatis*;" Syriac and Arabic, "when enemies press them hard in their land and in their cities." Perhaps "in the land (at) his gates" is right (*Bertheau*).

<sup>(29)</sup> **When.**—Or *if*, as in LXX. Hebrew, '*asher*. (See Note on verse 24.)

**His own sore** (*plague*) **and his own grief.**—Kings, "the plague of his own heart." So Syriac and Arabic. The phrase of the chronicler looks like a gloss on this.

**In this house.**—The margin is right.

<sup>(30)</sup> **Every man.**—*The man.* Distributive use of the article.

**Whose heart thou knowest.**—*Because thou knowest his heart.* So Syriac and Arabic. The Vulg., "which thou knowest him to have in his heart" (as if *eth* meant *with*, here).

**The children of men.**—*All* has dropped out. So some MSS., Syriac, Arabic, and Kings.

<sup>(31)</sup> **To walk in thy ways.**—An explanatory remark added by the chronicler.

<sup>(32)</sup> **Moreover concerning the stranger.**—In this verse, 1 Kings viii. 41, 42, are run together, probably by an error of transcription.

**But is come.**—*And shall come.*

**For thy great name's sake.**—Kings, "for thy name sake (for they will hear of thy great name and thy mighty hand and thy stretched-out arm), and shall come and pray towards this house." So nearly the Syriac and Arabic here.

<sup>(33)</sup> **Then.**—(*And*) Kings omits; but compare verses 30, 27, 23, which have the particle. So also some MSS., as well as the LXX., and Syriac, of Kings.

**People.**—*The peoples.*

**And fear thee.**—Better without *and*; as in Kings, "that they may fear thee." So Syriac.

<sup>(34)</sup> **Toward this city.**—Literally, *the way of this city.* So in verse 38, "the way of their land."

<sup>(35)</sup> **Maintain their cause.**—*Do* (*i.e.*, accomplish) *their right.* Vulg., "avenge" (them).

<sup>(36)</sup> **Their enemies.**—*An enemy.*

**And they carry them away.**—See margin. LXX., αἰχμαλωτεύουσιν αὐτοὺς οἱ αἰχμαλωτεύοντες αὐτούς.

<sup>(37)</sup> **Yet if they bethink themselves.**—Compare margin. *If they take it to heart, i.e.*, repent (Deut. iv. 39).

**We have sinned, we have done amiss, and have dealt wickedly.**—Comp. the same three verbs in Ps. cvi. 6; Dan. ix. 5 (Kings puts the conjunction before the second verb). There is a climax, "we have slipped (or missed the mark), we have done crookedly, we have been godless."

<sup>(38)</sup> **In the land of their captivity, whither they have carried them captives.**—Kings, "in the land of their enemies who carried them captives." The Syriac has, "in the cities of their captors who carried them captive." Perhaps *their captivity* is a corruption of *their captors*; or the relative ('*asher*), rendered *whither*, may refer to *land*, meaning the hostile nation, "in the land of their captivity *which* carried them captive."

<sup>(39)</sup> **Their supplications.**—Kings, sing.; and so some MSS., LXX., Syriac, and Arabic. The plural is found nowhere else, and is probably incorrect here.

thy dwelling place, their prayer and their supplications, and maintain their ¹ cause, and forgive thy people which have sinned against thee. ⁽⁴⁰⁾ Now, my God, let, I beseech thee, thine eyes be open, and *let* thine ears *be* attent ² unto the prayer *that is made* in this place. ⁽⁴¹⁾ Now ᵃtherefore arise, O LORD God, into thy resting place, thou, and the ark of thy strength: let thy priests, O LORD God, be clothed with salvation, and let thy saints rejoice in goodness. ⁽⁴²⁾ O LORD God, turn not away the face of thine anointed: remember the mercies of David thy servant.

CHAPTER VII.—⁽¹⁾ Now ᵇ when Solomon had made an end of praying, the ᶜ fire came down from heaven, and consumed the burnt offering and the sacrifices; and the glory of the LORD

¹ Or, *right.*
² Heb., *to the prayer of this place.*
ᵃ Ps. 132. 9.
ᵇ 1 Kings 8. 54, &c.
ᶜ Lev. 9. 24.

---

**And forgive thy people.**—This is the first clause of 1 Kings viii. 50; and from this point to the end of Solomon's Prayer, the two texts are wholly dissimilar.

(40—42) THE PERORATION.

⁽⁴⁰⁾ **Let, I beseech thee, thine eyes be open.**—Comp. verse 20, *supr.*, and chap. vii. 15; also 1 Kings viii. 52.

**And let thine ears be attent.**—*Attentive, listening* (*qasʻsʻŭbôth*). The same phrase recurs (chap. vii. 15), which is, in fact, a repetition of the whole verse in the shape of a Divine promise. *Qasʻsʻŭbôth* occurs, besides, only in the late Ps. cxxx. 2.

**The prayer that is made in this place.**—See margin. "The prayer of this place" is a strange phrase, only occurring here and in chap. vii. 15.

⁽⁴¹⁾ **Now therefore arise, O Lord God, into thy resting place.**—The two verses (41, 42) are slightly altered from Ps. cxxxii. 8—10. It would seem that the chronicler selected them as forming a more natural and appropriate conclusion to the Prayer of Dedication than that which he found in the older account. The aptness of the quotation may be admitted, without assuming that "for want of this summons to take possession of the sanctuary, the point of the whole prayer is wanting in Kings" (*Zöckler*). The peroration of 1 Kings viii. 50—53 is quite natural, though different; the closing thoughts being a return to those with which the prayer began, so that the prayer forms a well-rounded whole, and the suggestion of a lacuna is out of place. There is no difficulty in this view; the difficulty lies rather in maintaining the originality of all these verses here. (Comp. the free adaptation of several late Psalms in the Hymn of Praise in 1 Chron. xvi. 8, *sqq.*) The versification of the original psalm is neglected here, as there.

⁽⁴¹⁾ **Now therefore.**—*And now*, added by chronicler.

**O Lord God.**—*Iahweh 'ĕlôhîm.* This rare divine title occurs thrice in these two verses, but nowhere else in the prayer. The chronicler uses it as least eight times, but it does not appear at all in the books of Kings. In the Psalm we read simply *Iahweh*.

**Into thy resting place.**—*Nûah.* A late word, found besides only in Esther ix. 16—18 (*nôah*). In the Psalm it is *mĕnûhāh*, a common word.

The idea that *the sanctuary* is God's resting-place is not in keeping with the spirit of the prayer. (Comp. verse 18; and the frequent expression, "Hear Thou *from heaven thy dwelling place.*")

**Let thy priests, O Lord God.**—Ps. cxxxii. 9. The Divine name is *added* here.

**Salvation.**—Or, *prosperity.* The psalm has, "with righteousness;" but the other idea occurs a little after in verse 16.

**Rejoice in goodness.**—*Be glad at the good.* A paraphrase of "shout for joy" in the psalm.

⁽⁴²⁾ **O Lord God.**—Not in the psalm. The triple invocation is used as in the priest's blessing (Num. vi. 24—26).

**Turn not away the face of thine anointed**—*i.e.*, deny not his request (1 Kings ii. 16). Ps. cxxxii. 10:—

"For the sake of David Thy servant,
Turn not away the face of Thine Anointed."

The members of the couplet are transposed, and the language of the first is modified by the chronicler, so as to bring in the phrase, "the mercies of David," that is, Jehovah's mercies promised to David (Isa. lv. 3; Ps. lxxxix. 49).

**Remember** (*zokrāh*).—Only here and five times in Nehemiah.

VII.

4. GOD CONFIRMS THE DEDICATION OF THE TEMPLE (1) BY FIRE FROM HEAVEN; (2) BY SPECIAL REVELATION TO SOLOMON (chap. vii.).

The fire from heaven (verses 1—3). This section is wanting in 1 Kings viii. 54, *sqq.*, where we read instead of it an address of Solomon to the people. All that the king said seems here to be included in the phrase, "when Solomon had made an end of praying."

⁽¹⁾ **When Solomon had made an end of praying.**—(1 Kings viii. 54, "And it came to pass, *when S. had made an end of praying* unto Jehovah all this prayer and supplication.") From this point the divergence between the two accounts begins. There is no objective ground for supposing that the chronicler *invented* the facts here recorded. He must have found them in one of his sources, although we have no means of determining whether or not they were related in the original narrative followed by the author of Kings. It is gratuitous to fancy that the chronicler was more partial to miracle than the older writer. (Comp. 1 Kings viii. 10; xviii. 38.) His greater interest in all that concerned the worship of the Temple is enough to account for the present and similar additions to the older narrative.

**The fire came down from heaven.**— Comp. Lev. ix. 22—24, from which passage it appears likely that the fire descended *after* Solomon had blessed the people. (Comp. also 1 Chron. xxi. 26; 2 Kings i. 10, 12, 14.)

**And the sacrifices.**—The offerings presented when the ark entered the Temple (chap. v. 6).

**And the glory of the Lord filled the house.**—This statement is not a mere duplicate of chap. v. 13, 14. See next verse. The "glory of the

filled the house. (2) And the priests could not enter into the house of the LORD, because the glory of the LORD had filled the LORD's house. (3) And when all the children of Israel saw how the fire came down, and the glory of the LORD upon the house, they bowed themselves with their faces to the ground upon the pavement, and worshipped, and praised the LORD, *saying*, For *he is good*; for his mercy *endureth* for ever. (4) Then the king and all the people offered sacrifices before the LORD. (5) And king Solomon offered a sacrifice of twenty and two thousand oxen, and an hundred and twenty thousand sheep: so the king and all the people dedicated the house of God. (6) ᵃ And the priests waited on their offices: the Levites also with instruments of musick of the LORD, which David the king had made to praise the LORD, because his mercy *endureth* for ever, when David praised ¹ by their ministry; and the priests sounded trumpets before them, and all Israel stood. (7) Moreover Solomon hallowed the middle of the court that *was* before the house of the LORD: for there he offered burnt offerings, and the fat of the peace offerings, because the brasen altar which Solomon had made was not able to receive the burnt offerings, and the meat offerings, and the fat. (8) Also at the same time Solomon kept the feast seven days, and all Israel with him, a very great congregation, from the entering in of Hamath unto ᵇ the river of Egypt. (9) And in the eighth day they made ² a solemn assembly: for they kept the dedication of the

*a* 1 Chron. xvi. 1c.

¹ Heb., *by their hand.*

*b* Josh. 13. 3.

² Heb., *a restraint.*

---

Lord" is apparently a manifestation quite distinct from the "fire."

**(2) And the priests could not enter into the house of the Lord.**—Hardly a different assertion from that of chap. v. 14 ("the priests could not *stand to minister*"); the cause in both instances being the same, and expressed in the same words (1 Kings viii. 11). But it is quite plain that the writer intends to record in chaps. v. and vii. two distinct appearances of the Divine glory, one before and one after the Prayer of Consecration, both of which were attended by the same effects upon the ministering priests.

**(3) Upon the pavement.**—*Riçpāh*; rendered by the LXX. τὸ λιθόστρωτον, which is the word used in John xix. 13; Vulg., "pavimentum stratum lapide." (Comp. Ezek. xl. 17, 18; Esther i. 6, a tesselated pavement.)

**And praised.**—*Gave thanks to Jehovah.* The infinitive is here used for the finite form of the verb, as elsewhere.

**For he is good; for his mercy endureth for ever.**—See 1 Chron. xvi. 34—41, xxiii. 30; 2 Chron. v. 13, xx. 21. The Syriac and Arabic paraphrase, "and they said one to another: Give thanks to the Lord," &c. There is hardly anything in the section, except this last phrase, which can be said to be characteristic of the style of the chronicler.

**(4—10) THE SACRIFICES AND THE FESTIVAL.** (Comp. 1 Kings viii. 62—66.) The two narratives are again mainly coincident.

**(4) Then.**—*And.*

**Offered sacrifices.**—*Were sacrificing a sacrifice.* LXX., θύοντες θύματα. Vulg., "immolabant."

**(5) And King Solomon offered a sacrifice of twenty and two thousand oxen.**—Literally, *the sacrifice of the oxen twenty and two thousand.* Kings, "the sacrifice of *the peace offerings which he sacrificed to Jehovah*, oxen twenty and two thousand." The italicised words seem to have fallen out of our text. The numbers are the same in both accounts.

**The people.**—Kings has the old name, *sons of Israel*, and *house of Jehovah* for *house of God.*

**(6) And the priests.**—This verse is added by the chronicler, after his usual fashion of laying stress on the ritual, especially its choral and musical side. (Comp. chap. v. 11—13.)

**Waited on their offices.**—Literally, *And the priests upon their wards* (*watches*) *were standing*, i.e., stood at their posts. Vulg., "sacerdotes autem stabant in officiis suis."

**Instruments of musick of the Lord**—*i.e.*, of *sacred music*, as we should say. (Comp. 1 Chron. xvi. 42.)

**Which David . . . had made.**—1 Chron. xxiii. 5.

**To praise.**—*Give thanks to.* (Comp. verse 3 *supr.*)

**When David praised by their ministry.**—See margin; and 1 Chron. xvi. 4—7. The LXX., ἐν ὕμνοις Δαυιδ διὰ τῆς χειρὸς αὐτῶν takes *b'hallēl* substantively, as if it meant "in David's psalmody," perhaps with special reference to the great *hallel* of the synagogue. The Authorised Version gives the true meaning, namely, that the Levites were David's ministers of praise.

**Sounded trumpets.**—*Were trumpeting.*

**Stood.**—*Were standing.*

**(7) Moreover.**—*And.* This verse is slightly modified from 1 Kings viii. 64 (see the Notes there).

**Which Solomon had made.**—Chap. iv. 1. Kings, *which was before the Lord.*

**Was not able to receive.**—An explanation of the phrase of Kings, "was too little to receive."

**The burnt offerings . . . meat offerings.**—Both are singular in the Heb.

**(8) Also at the same time.**—Literally, *And Solomon made the feast at that time seven days.* "The feast" was the Feast of Tabernacles. (See Lev. xxiii. 34—36.)

**Seven days.**—The legal time. (See Lev. *l.c.*) The days were counted from the 15th of the seventh month. (Comp. 1 Kings viii. 65.)

**The river.**—*Torrent* or *wady.* LXX., χειμάρρους. Kings adds, "before the Lord our God." So Syriac.

**(9) And in the eighth day**—That is, on the twenty-second of the seventh month (Ethanim, or Tisri; chap. v. 3).

**They made a solemn assembly.**—Comp. Lev. xxiii. 36. Not mentioned in Kings (1 Kings viii. 66

altar seven days, and the feast seven days. [a 1 Kings 9. 1, &c.] <sup>(10)</sup> And on the three and twentieth day of the seventh month he sent the people away into their tents, glad and merry in heart for the goodness that the LORD had shewed unto David, and to [b Deut. 12. 5.] [1 Heb., *upon whom my name is called.*] Solomon, and to Israel his people.

<sup>(11)</sup> Thus <sup>a</sup> Solomon finished the house of the LORD, and the king's house: and all that came into Solomon's heart to make in the house of the LORD, and in his own house, he prosperously effected. [c ch. 6. 40.] [2 Heb., *to the prayer of this place.*]

<sup>(12)</sup> And the LORD appeared to Solomon by night, and said unto him, I have heard thy prayer, <sup>b</sup> and have chosen this place to myself for an house of sacrifice. [d ch. 6. 6.] <sup>(13)</sup> If I shut up heaven that there be no rain, or if I command the locusts to devour the land, or if I send pestilence among my people; <sup>(14)</sup> if my people, [e ch. 6. 16.] [3 Heb., *There shall not be cut off to thee.*] <sup>1</sup> which are called by my name, shall humble themselves, and pray, and seek my face, and turn from their wicked ways; then will I hear from heaven, and will forgive their sin, and will heal their land. <sup>(15)</sup> Now <sup>c</sup> mine eyes shall be open, and mine ears attent <sup>2</sup> unto the prayer *that is made* in this place. <sup>(16)</sup> For now have <sup>d</sup> I chosen and sanctified this house, that my name may be there for ever: and mine eyes and mine heart shall be there perpetually. <sup>(17)</sup> And as for thee, if thou wilt walk before me, as David thy father walked, and do according to all that I have commanded thee, and shalt observe my statutes and my judgments; <sup>(18)</sup> then will I stablish the throne of thy kingdom, according as I have covenanted with David thy father, saying, <sup>e 3</sup> There shall not fail

---

says: "and on the eighth day he dismissed the people," *i.e.*, after this final gathering).

**For they kept the dedication of the altar seven days.**—The seven days preceding the first day of the Feast of Tabernacles, or the 8th to the 14th Ethanim, had been kept as an extraordinary festival on account of the inauguration of the Temple. After this festival, the Feast of Tabernacles was celebrated in due course for seven days more.

This explains the obscure words of 1 Kings viii. 65, "(Solomon and all Israel) kept the feast . . . seven days and seven days, fourteen days," a brief expression which combines the two distinct celebrations. So Syriac, "seven days of the feast, and seven days of the inauguration of the house; these and these, their amount was fourteen days. And on the day of the full moon in the month of Tisri the king sent the people away."

<sup>(10)</sup> **And on the three and twentieth day of the seventh month.**—Beginning with the evening of the twenty-second.

**For the goodness.**—Some MSS., Syriac, and Arabic, "for *all* the goodness," as in 1 Kings viii. 66.

**David, and to Solomon.**—Kings, "David his servant." The mention of Solomon was added by the chronicler. (Comp. chap. vi. 4, 8, 15—17, 42, where all Solomon's success is connected with the promise to David.)

THE LORD'S RESPONSE TO THE PRAYER OF SOLOMON (verses 11—22. Comp. 1 Kings ix. 1—9).

The substance and, for the most part, the language of both passages are the same, but the chronicler paraphrases occasionally, and has added a considerable section not extant in Kings (verses 13—16).

<sup>(11)</sup> **All that came into Solomon's heart to make.**—A paraphrase of *all the desire* (Isa. xxi. 4; 2 Chron. viii. 6) *of Solomon that he willed to do.* The rest of the verse is wanting in Kings.

<sup>(12)</sup> **By night.**—This is *implied* in Kings, which has, "as He had appeared unto him in Gibeon."

**I have heard thy prayer.**—From this point begins the chronicler's addition to the prayer as extant in the older text. Judging by the style, the added section must have formed an integral part of the original text, from which both the editor of Kings and the chronicler drew their narratives.

**An house of sacrifice** (*bêth zābah*).—A phrase occurring nowhere else in the Old Testament.

<sup>(13)</sup> **If I shut up heaven that there be no rain.**—Deut. xi. 17; chap. vi. 26.

**If.**—*Hēn*, as in Jer. iii. 1; Isa. liv. 15.

**The locusts.**—*Hāgāb*, a winged and edible species (Lev. xi. 22). In chap. vi. 28, two other kinds, the *'arbeh* and *hāsîl*, were mentioned.

**If I send pestilence.**—Chap. vi. 28; 1 Chron. xxi.

<sup>(14)</sup> **My people, which are called by my name.**—See margin; chap. vi. 33; Amos ix. 12; Jer. xiv. 9. The sense is: which are dedicated to me.

**Humble themselves.**—Lev. xxvi. 41, in a similar context.

**Seek my face.**—Ps. xxiv. 6, xxvii. 8.

**Turn from their wicked ways.**—Hosea vi. 1; Isa. vi. 10; Jer. xxv. 5.

**Heal their land.**—Ps. lx. 4.

<sup>(15)</sup> **Now mine eyes shall be open.**—Comp. chap. vi. 40, and Notes.

<sup>(16)</sup> **Have I chosen.**—Chap. vi. 6, and verse 12, *supr.*

**Sanctified this house.**—1 Kings ix. 3. The two accounts are again parallel.

**Perpetually.**—*All the days.*

<sup>(17)</sup> **Walked.**—Kings adds, "in perfectness of heart, and in uprightness." So Syriac and Arabic.

**And do.**—So LXX., Vulg., and Arabic. The Heb. is *wĕ-la'asôth*, "and to do," a construction which the chronicler sometimes uses in continuation of a future (imperfect tense). But Kings has "to do," an infinitive defining the former verb; and so the Syriac here.

<sup>(18)</sup> **As I have covenanted with.**—Heb. *kāratti lĕ*, "I cut (a covenant) for." The word *bĕrîth*, "covenant," is omitted, as in chap. v. 10. So LXX., ὡς διεθέμην Δαυιδ τῷ πατρὶ σοῦ. Syriac, "As I sware to David." Kings: "As I spake concerning David" (*kāratti* may be an ancient misreading of *dibbarti*, "I spake;" the two being much alike in Heb. writing).

**Ruler in Israel** (*môshêl*).—Kings, "From upon the throne of Israel." The chronicler has substituted

thee a man *to be* ruler in Israel. <sup>(19)</sup> <sup>a</sup>But if ye turn away, and forsake my statutes and my commandments, which I have set before you, and shall go and serve other gods, and worship them; <sup>(20)</sup> then will I pluck them up by the roots out of my land which I have given them; and this house, which I have sanctified for my name, will I cast out of my sight, and will make it *to be* a proverb and a byword among all nations. <sup>(21)</sup> And this house, which is high, shall be an astonishment to every one that passeth by it; so that he shall say, <sup>b</sup>Why hath the LORD done thus unto this land, and unto this house? <sup>(22)</sup> And it shall be answered, Because they forsook the LORD God of their fathers, which brought them forth out of the land of Egypt, and laid hold on other gods, and worshipped them, and served them: therefore hath he brought all this evil upon them.

CHAPTER VIII.—<sup>(1)</sup> And <sup>c</sup>it came to pass at the end of twenty years, wherein Solomon had built the house of the LORD, and his own house, <sup>(2</sup> that the cities which Huram had restored to Solomon, Solomon built them, and caused the children of Israel to dwell there.

*a* Lev. 26. 14; Deut. 28. 15.

*b* Deut. 29. 21; Jer. 22. 8, 9.

B.C. 992.

*c* 1 Kings 9. 10, &c.

---

a reminiscence of Micah v. 1, probably correcting a defective text, the word *throne* having fallen out. Syriac, "who standeth on the throne of Israel."

<sup>(19)</sup> **But.**—*And.* Kings omits, but emphasises the verb, "If ye *will* turn," or, "if turn ye will."

The order of words in the Heb. implies that *ū-bnêkem*, "and your children," has fallen out of the text: "And if ye turn, ye and your children." So Kings, and Syriac and Arabic here. Kings adds, "From after me."

**And forsake.**—Kings, "and keep not." So Syriac and Arabic.

<sup>(20)</sup> **Then will I pluck them up by the roots** —*i.e., your children* (see last verse). (Comp. Deut. xxix. 27.) Vulg. rightly, "evellam vos de terra mea." The opposite idea is that of *planting* a nation in a land (Jer. xxiv. 6). Kings, "Then will I cut off Israel from upon the face of the land." The chronicler has softened the severity of the expression, *cut off Israel.*

**Will I cast out of my sight.**—Vulg. more literally, "projiciam a facie mea." The exact phrase occurs nowhere else; but comp. Ps. li. 13, which is very similar; also Ps. cii. 11. Instead of *'ashlîk*, "I will cast," Kings has *'ashallah*, "I will send," *i.e.*, throw (Amos ii. 5).

**And will make it.**—A softening down of, *and Israel shall become* (Kings). Comp. Deut. xxviii. 37. So Syriac.

<sup>(21)</sup> **And this house, which is high.**—A correction of Kings: "and this house *shall be high*," which appears meaningless in the context. But the Syriac (and Arabic) here and in Kings has, "And this house shall be laid waste" (*nehwê hreb*); and the Targum of Kings combines both readings thus: "And this house *which is high* shall be laid waste" (*y'hê harîb*). It appears, therefore, that the original reading of the Heb. text was, "And this house shall become *ruinous heaps*" (*'iyîn*, "heaps," not *'elyôn*, "high"). (Comp. Micah iii. 12. The mistake is as old as the LXX., ὁ οἶκος οὗτος ὁ ὑψηλός.)

**Shall be an astonishment to every one that passeth by it.**—*Every one that passeth by it shall be astonished*: πᾶς ὁ διαπορευόμενος αὐτὸν ἐκστήσεται, LXX. Syriac, "Every one that passeth by it shall stop and shake his head, and sway with his hand, and say" . . . Kings adds, "and shall hiss" (certainly original).

<sup>(22)</sup> **And it shall be answered.**—*And men shall say.*

**Hath he brought.** — Kings, "hath Jehovah brought." (So the Syriac and Arabic here.)

### VIII.

SOLOMON'S GOVERNMENT AND EXTERNAL GLORY.—HIS DEATH (chaps. viii.–ix.).

Chap. viii. Solomon's public works.—Forced labour.—Religion.—Maritime commerce. (Comp. 1 Kings ix. 10–28.)

(*a*) PUBLIC WORKS, BUILDING AND FORTIFICATION OF TOWNS (verses 1–6).

<sup>(1)</sup> **And it came to pass.**—The verb is identical with 1 Kings ix. 10, slightly abbreviated.

**Wherein.** — *When.* The "twenty years" are reckoned from the fourth year of the reign (1 Kings vi. 6), and include seven years during which the Temple was building, and thirteen during which the palace was built (1 Kings vi. 38; vii. 1).

<sup>(2)</sup> **Which Huram had restored.** — Literally, *which Huram gave.*

**Solomon built them.**—*Rebuilt* or *restored* and *fortified* (Josh. vi. 26; 1 Kings xv. 17). The parallel passage (1 Kings ix. 11–13) records a contrary transaction; that is to say, it represents Solomon as giving to Huram twenty cities in Galilee, as a return for his past services. It is added that these cities did not please Huram, in consequence of which they got the name of "The Land of Kābûl" (*i.e.*, "Like-nought"). The Authorised Version here assumes that the explanation of Josephus (*Antt.* viii. 5, § 3) is correct. That writer states that Huram restored the despised cities to Solomon, who thereupon repaired them, and peopled them with Israelites. Others assume an exchange of friendly gifts between the two sovereigns; so that Solomon gave Huram twenty Israelite cities (Kings), and Huram gave Solomon twenty Phenician cities (Chronicles): this seems highly improbable. The former explanation appears to be substantially correct. The chronicler, or the authority which he follows here, has omitted to notice a fact which seems to derogate from the greatness of Solomon, viz., the previous surrender of the territory in question to the Tyrian king; and has chosen to speak of Huram's non-acceptance or return of Solomon's present, as a *gift.* He then goes on to tell of the future fate of the twenty cities. Solomon repaired or fortified them, and colonised them with Israelites; for this border-land was chiefly in-

*Solomon's Cities*        II. CHRONICLES, VIII.        *and his Vassals.*

<sup>(3)</sup> And Solomon went to Hamath-zobah, and prevailed against it. <sup>(4)</sup> And he built Tadmor in the wilderness, and all the store cities, which he built in Hamath. <sup>(5)</sup> Also he built Beth-horon the upper, and Beth-horon the nether, fenced cities, with walls, gates, and bars; <sup>(6)</sup> and Baalath, and all the store cities that Solomon had, and all the chariot cities, and the cities of the horsemen, and ¹ all that Solomon desired to build in Jerusalem, and in Lebanon, and throughout all the land of his dominion.

<sup>(7)</sup> *As for* all the people *that were* left of the Hittites, and the Amorites, and the Perizzites, and the Hivites, and the Jebusites, which *were* not of Israel, <sup>(8)</sup> *but* of their children, who were left after them in the land, whom the children of Israel consumed not, them did Solomon make to pay tribute until this day. <sup>(9)</sup> But of the children of Israel did Solomon make no servants for his work; but they *were* men of war, and chief of his captains, and captains of his chariots and horsemen. <sup>(10)</sup> And these *were* the chief of king Solomon's

¹ Heb., *all the desire of Solomon which he desired to build.*

---

habited by Gentiles (Isa. ix. 1, "Galilee of the Gentiles"). A border-land is naturally more exposed to the ravages of an invader; and the cities which Solomon ceded to Huram may have been in a half-ruinous condition. This would account for Huram's disappointment in them. The statement of our text, then, is neither an "effacement," nor a "travesty" (*Reuss*), nor even a "remodelling" of that of the older text "in favour of Solomon" (*Zöckler*). It replaces the older text by another statement which is equally true, and not incompatible with it.

<sup>(3)</sup> **And Solomon went.**—*Marched* (2 Sam. xii. 29).

**Hamath-zobah.**—That is, Hamath bordering on Zobah. (Comp. 1 Chron. xviii. 3.) Solomon's conquest of the kingdom of Hamath, which had been on terms of amity with David, is not mentioned in 1 Kings ix.; nor indeed anywhere else in the Old Testament. Thenius (on 2 Kings xiv. 25) supposes that the text describes not a conquest of Hamath itself, but only the annexation of part of its territory; viz., a part of the highly fruitful plain of Cœle-Syria, called by the Arabs *Ard-el-Beqâa*. This appears to be correct.

**Against it.**—Or, *over it* (a late construction, chap. xxvii. 5; Dan. xi. 5).

<sup>(4)</sup> **And he built Tadmor in the wilderness.**—That is, Palmyra, in the wilderness, on the traders' route between the coast and Thapsacus on the Euphrates. See 1 Kings ix. 18, where *Tamar* or *Tammor* of the Heb. text is explained by the margin to mean Tadmor; and the epithet, "in the wilderness," seems certainly to identify the two names. That Solomon was the founder of Palmyra is the tradition of the country to this day.

**And all the store cities, which he built in Hamath.**—1 Kings ix. 19 mentions these cities, but not their locality. They were no doubt "places of arms," and served as outposts against the hostile neighbouring kingdom of Zobah-Damascus. (See 1 Kings xi. 23—25.) So far as they lay on the caravan route, they would serve also as victualling stations. (Comp. 2 Chron. xxxii. 28.)

<sup>(5)</sup> **Also.**—*And.* 1 Kings ix. 17, "And Solomon built Gezer, and Beth-horon the nether."

**Built**—i.e., *fortified*, as the rest of the verse explains. (See 1 Chron. vii. 24.) He built them *as* (or *into*) *fenced cities*, viz., *walls*, *doors*, and *bar* (Micah vii. 12; Deut. iii. 5). This description is wanting in Kings.

<sup>(6)</sup> **And Baalath.**—1 Kings ix. 18. Like the two Beth-horons, it lay west of Jerusalem, and was a bulwark against the Philistines. (Comp. Josh. xix. 44, a Danite town.) The rest of this verse is identical with 1 Kings ix. 19, which see. (Chronicler has twice added *all.*)

In the above section no mention is made of the fortification of Jerusalem, and the building of Hazor, Megiddo, and Gezer, which last city had been taken by Pharaoh, and given by him to his daughter, Solomon's wife. (See 1 Kings ix. 15, 16.) On the other hand, as we have seen, the chronicler supplies several important details which are wanting in the parallel account.

(*b*) THE FORCED LABOUR OF THE CANAANITES (verses 7—10).

With this section comp. 1 Kings ix. 20—23, and the Notes there. In Kings it stands in more obvious connection with what precedes; for there the account of Solomon's buildings is headed by the words, "And this is the reason of the levy which king Solomon raised, for to build the house of the Lord," &c. (1 Kings ix. 15).

<sup>(7)</sup> **As for all the people that were left.**—The verse agrees with 1 Kings ix. 20.

<sup>(8)</sup> **But.**—Omit. The *of* also is wanting in 1 Kings ix. 21. So Syriac, but not LXX. and Vulgate.

**Consumed not.**—1 Sam. xv. 18. Kings, "were not able to exterminate." The chronicler's reading is probably due to the fading of letters in his MS. authority.

**Them did Solomon make to pay tribute.**—*On them did Solomon levy a tribute.* Kings has the fuller expression, *mas 'ôbēd*, "tribute of labourers." "Solomon en fit de levées pour la corvée" (*Reuss*).

<sup>(9)</sup> **But of the children of Israel.**—See 1 Kings ix. 22. The Heb. text has the relative (*'asher*) after "children of Israel." But some few MSS., and ancient versions, omit it. It is, perhaps, an accidental repetition from the beginning of verse 8.

According to Diod. Sic. i. 56, Sesostris (Rameses II.), the great Egyptian monarch, was wont to inscribe over the temples he built, "No native hath laboured hereon."

After "men of war," Kings adds, " and his servants," which is omitted here as unsuitable, after the preceding statement. It means, however, courtiers and officers.

**Chief of his captains.**—Heb., *captains of his knights;* which appears to be incorrect. Read, " his captains and his knights," or " aides-de-camp," as in Kings. LXX., καὶ ἄρχοντες καὶ οἱ δυνατοί.

<sup>(10)</sup> **The chief of king Solomon's officers.**—"Captains of the overseers," or "prefects," *i.e.*, chief

officers, *even* two hundred and fifty, that bare rule over the people. <sup>(11)</sup> And Solomon *ᵃ* brought up the daughter of Pharaoh out of the city of David unto the house that he had built for her: for he said, My wife shall not dwell in the house of David king of Israel, because *the places are* ¹ holy, whereunto the ark of the LORD hath come. <sup>(12)</sup> Then Solomon offered burnt offerings unto the LORD on the altar of the LORD, which he had built before the porch, <sup>(13)</sup> even after a certain rate every *ᵇ* day, offering according to the commandment of Moses, on the sabbaths, and on the new moons, and on the solemn feasts, *ᶜ* three times in the year, *even* in the feast of unleavened bread, and in the feast of weeks, and in the feast of tabernacles. <sup>(14)</sup> And he appointed, according to the order of David his father, the *ᵈ* courses of the priests to their service, and the Levites to their charges, to praise and minister before the priests, as the duty of every day required: the *ᵉ* porters also by their courses at every gate: for ²so had David the man of God commanded. <sup>(15)</sup> And they departed not from the commandment of the king unto the priests and Levites concerning any matter, or concerning the treasures. <sup>(16)</sup> Now all the

*ᵃ* 1 Kings 3. 1, & 7. 8.

¹ Heb., *holiness.*

*ᵇ* Exod. 29. 38.

*ᶜ* Exod. 23. 14; Deut. 16. 16.

*ᵈ* 1 Chron. 24. 1.

*ᵉ* 1 Chron. 9. 17.

² Heb., *so was the commandment of David the man of God.*

---

overseers, or inspectors of works (Comp. 1 Chron. xviii. 13, and 2 Chron. xvii. 2, for the word *n'çibîm*, prefects.) The Heb. margin suggests *niççābim*, the word used in Kings.

**King Solomon's.**—Literally, *Who were to king Solomon.* Kings, *who were over the work for Solomon.* Clearly the latter has been corrupted into the form presented by our text through a confusion of *mĕlākāh*, "work," with *mèlek*, "king."

**Two hundred and fifty.**—See chap. ii. 17, and 1 Kings ix. 23. In the latter place 550 is the number. The number here is an error of transcription, ה *i.e.*, 550, having been mistaken for נ *i.e.*, 250 (Kennicott).

**Bare rule.**—They were taskmasters. (Comp. Syriac, " who made the people work who were working at the works.")

**The people**—*i.e.*, the Canaanite remnant (verse 7). Kings adds, *who were labouring at the work.* (See Syriac.)

<sup>(11)</sup> **And Solomon brought up the daughter of Pharaoh.**—See 1 Kings ix. 24, which is much briefer than the present notice. The chronicler has not mentioned this princess before (comp. 1 Kings iii. 1, ix. 16), and mentions her here only in connection with Solomon's buildings. (See Note on chap. xii. 2.) Solomon's Egyptian consort was probably a princess of the XXII. Bubastite Dynasty, founded by Shishak, which was of Semitic origin.

**For he said.**—The motive here assigned is wanting in the other text, and is characteristic of the chronicler both in thought and language; though it is too much to say with Thenius that the princess *could* not have lived anywhere else than in the old palace of David, until the new one was built. 1 Kings iii. 1 says only that Solomon brought her "into the city of David."

**King of Israel.**—In contrast with the Egyptian origin of the princess.

**Because the places are holy.**—*For a holy thing is that unto which*, &c. (The plural pronoun *hēmmāh*, "they," is equivalent to a neuter-sing. in the usage of the chronicler.)

(c) REGULATION OF THE TEMPLE WORSHIP (verses 12—16).

This whole section corresponds to the single verse, 1 Kings ix. 25, which the chronicler has paraphrased in verses 12, 13, and extended by the addition of further details in verses 14, 15.

<sup>(12)</sup> **Then.**—After the consecration of the Temple. **Offered.**—Not once, but habitually; according to the prescriptions of the Mosaic Law (verse 13).

**On the altar . . . which he had built.**—And apparently no longer at Gibeon (chap. i. 3).

**Before the porch.**—Not in Kings.

<sup>(13)</sup> **Even after a certain rate every day.**—Literally, *and with a day's matter on a day* (Lev. xxiii. 37) *they had to offer* (infinitive *construct*, as at 1 Chron. xiii. 4, xv. 2), or, perhaps, *he would offer.*

**The solemn feasts.**—Literally, *set seasons,* viz., the three great festivals whose designations follow. (The form *mô'adôth* for *mô'adim* occurs here only.)

<sup>(14)</sup> **And he appointed.**—*Caused to stand.* (1 Chron. vi. 16, xv. 16.)

**According to the order of David his father.** —*Order, i.e.,* ordinance or institution.

**The courses of the priests.**—See 1 Chron. xxiv.

**Charges.**—*Watches, wards, stations.*

**To praise.**—See 1 Chron. xxv. 3.

**And minister before the priests.**—1 Chron. xxiii. 28.

**As the duty of every day required.**—*For a day's matter* (*i.e.*, prescribed work) *on its day.* (Comp. verse 13.)

**The porters also.**—See 1 Chron. xxvi. 1—19. The construction is, *and he appointed*, or stationed, *the warders.*

**For so had David . . .**—See margin. A similar phrase occurs in Neh. xii. 24.

<sup>(15)</sup> **And they departed not from the commandment of the king.**—*From* has fallen out of the Heb. text, and must be restored. So three MSS. and the versions.

**The king**=David.

**Unto.**—*Concerning*; literally, *upon.*

**Concerning any matter, or concerning the treasures.**—*With reference to any matter and* (especially) *with reference to the treasures.* (See 1 Chron. xxvi. 20—28.) Verses 14, 15 assure us that the arrangements of David, as described in 1 Chron. xxiv. —xxvi., were faithfully observed by his successor.

<sup>(16)</sup> **Now.**—*And*, here equivalent to *so.*

**Prepared**=*completed.* (Chaps. xxix. 35, xxxv. 10, 16; a late use of the word *nākôn.*)

**Unto the day of the foundation . . . until it was finished.**—Solomon's activity is apparently divided into two periods, viz., the preparations which he made before and up to the foundation of the Temple

work of Solomon was prepared unto the day of the foundation of the house of the LORD, and until it was finished. So the house of the LORD was perfected.

(17) Then went Solomon to Eziongeber, and to ¹Eloth, at the sea side in the land of Edom. (18) And Huram sent him by the hands of his servant ships, and servants that had knowledge of the sea; and they went with the servants of Solomon to Ophir, and took thence four hundred and fifty talents of gold, and brought *them* to king Solomon.

CHAPTER IX.—(1) And ᵃ when the queen of Sheba heard of the fame of Solomon, she came to prove Solomon with hard questions at Jerusalem, with a very great company, and camels that bare spices, and gold in abundance, and precious stones: and when she was come to Solomon, she communed with him of all that was in her heart. (2) And Solomon told her all her questions: and there was nothing hid from Solomon which he told her not. (3) And when the queen of Sheba had seen the wisdom of Solomon, and the house that he had built, (4) and the meat of his table, and the sitting of his servants, and the attendance of his ministers, and their apparel; his ²cupbearers also, and their apparel; and his ascent by which he went up into the house of the LORD;

1 Or, *Elath*, Deut. 2. 8.

a 1 Kings 10. 1, &c.; Matt. 12. 42; Luke 11. 31.

2 Or, *butlers*.

---

(chap. ii.), and secondly, the prosecution of the work to its completion (chap. iii.—v. 1). (The Heb. is, unto *that day* of the foundation," *i.e.*, that memorable day, see chap. iii. 1—3.) All the versions, however, understand *from* the day of the foundation unto the completion of the Temple, and perhaps '*ad ha-yôm* is, in the chronicler's Hebrew equivalent to *lĕmin ha-yôm*, expressing the *terminus a quo*.

**So the house of the Lord was perfected.**—Omit *so*, and comp. 1 Kings ix. 25, "and he finished [same root as *perfected*] the house." The verse thus closes the entire account of the building and inauguration of the Temple.

(d) THE VOYAGE TO OPHIR (verses 17, 18). Comp. 1 Kings ix. 26—28.

(17) **Then** ('*āz*).—After the completion of the Temple.

**Went Solomon to Ezion-geber, and to Eloth.** —Syr., "Ezion-geber, a city which is over against Eloth." 1 Kings ix. 26 reads, "And a fleet did king Solomon make at Ezion-geber, which is near Eloth."

**The sea.**—Kings, *the Red Sea*. So Vulg. The words of our text do not necessarily imply a *personal* visit on the part of Solomon. He sent his shipwrights to the Idumean port.

(18) **And Huram sent him by the hands of his servants ships.**—When Solomon began to evince an interest in maritime affairs, his Tyrian ally presented him with a number of vessels and their crews of trained seamen. To what port the vessels were sent is not expressly stated. Probably they put in at Joppa (chap. ii. 16). Others assume the meaning to be that the ships were sent from Tyre to Ezion-geber, and then ask whether they were dragged across the desert which divides the Mediterranean from the gulf of Akaba, or whether they circumnavigated Africa. The dilemma is only apparent. The Greek historians of later times often speak of the transport of ships overland; and the galleys of Solomon's age were probably small. Even the circumnavigation of Africa was achieved by a Phœnician expedition sent out by Necho about four centuries later (Herod. iv. 42). But neither alternative seems necessary. If Huram provided Solomon with skilled mariners, they would naturally sail from Tyre to Joppa in their own ships. The Tyrian vessels may have been left at Joppa, while a portion of their crews proceeded, by Solomon's order, to Eziongeber. In short, "ships and servants" means "ships with servants," or "ships conveying servants."

**And they went.**—Huram's mariners. Comp. 1 Kings ix. 27: "And Huram sent in the fleet (which Solomon had built) his servants, men of ships that had knowledge of the sea." So the Syr. and Arab. here.

**To Ophir.**—See 1 Kings ix. 28. LXX., *Sophira*.

**Fifty.**—Kings, *twenty*. The difference may be due to a scribe's error, the letter *kaf* being confused with *nun*.

IX.

(ii) SOLOMON'S WISDOM, WEALTH, AND GLORY. HIS DEATH.

(a) THE VISIT OF THE QUEEN OF SHEBA (verses 1—12). Comp. 1 Kings x. 1—13.

The Hebrew text coincides with Kings, allowing for a few characteristic alterations, the chief of which will be noticed.

(1) **And when the queen of Sheba heard.**—*Now the queen of Sheba had heard.* Kings, *was hearing.*

**The fame of Solomon.**—Kings adds a difficult phrase ("as to the name of Jehovah") which the chronicler omits.

**Hard questions.** — *Riddles, enigmas.* LXX., αἰνίγμασιν (Judg. xiv. 12).

**At Jerusalem.**—An abridgment but not an improvement of Kings. The Syr. agrees with the latter.

**Gold in abundance.**—The chronicler has substituted a favourite expression for the "*very much gold*" of Kings.

(4) **And his ascent by which he went up into the house of the Lord.**—Kings, "And his *burnt offering which he offered* in the house of the Lord." The LXX., Syr., and Vulg. here agree with Kings; and the Arab. reads, "the altar on which he offered." In all other passages, the word used in our text ('*aliyāh*) means not *ascent,* but *upper chamber;* it is likely, therefore, that in the present instance it is merely an error of transcription for the term occurring in Kings ('*ôlāh,* "burnt-offering").

361

there was no more spirit in her. ⁽⁵⁾ And she said to the king, *It was* a true ¹report which I heard in mine own land of thine ²acts, and of thy wisdom: ⁽⁶⁾ howbeit I believed not their words, until I came, and mine eyes had seen *it*: and, behold, the one half of the greatness of thy wisdom was not told me: *for* thou exceedest the fame that I heard. ⁽⁷⁾ Happy *are* thy men, and happy *are* these thy servants, which stand continually before thee, and hear thy wisdom. ⁽⁸⁾ Blessed be the LORD thy God, which delighted in thee to set thee on his throne, *to be* king for the LORD thy God: because thy God loved Israel, to establish them for ever, therefore made he thee king over them, to do judgment and justice. ⁽⁹⁾ And she gave the king an hundred and twenty talents of gold, and of spices great abundance, and precious stones: neither was there any such spice as the queen of Sheba gave king Solomon.

⁽¹⁰⁾ And the servants also of Huram, and the servants of Solomon, which brought gold from Ophir, brought algum trees and precious stones. ⁽¹¹⁾ And the king made *of* the algum trees ³ ⁴terraces to the house of the LORD, and to the king's palace, and harps and psalteries for singers: and there were none such seen before in the land of Judah.

⁽¹²⁾ And king Solomon gave to the queen of Sheba all her desire, whatsoever she asked, beside *that* which she had brought unto the king. So she turned, and went away to her own land, she and her servants.

¹ Heb., *word*.
² Or, *sayings*.
³ Or, *stairs*.
⁴ Heb., *highways*.

---

⁽⁵⁾ **Of thine acts.**—Literally, *words*. LXX., περὶ τῶν λόγων σου. We might render *matters, affairs*.

⁽⁶⁾ **The one half of the greatness of thy wisdom.**—Kings has simply, "the half was not told me." The chronicler has made an explanatory addition. (See 1 Chron. xii. 29, and 2 Chron. xxx. 18, for the word *marbîth*, "increase," "multitude," which occurs thrice in the Chronicles and twice elsewhere.)

**Thou exceedest the fame.**—Literally, *Thou hast added to the report*. Kings, more fully, "Thou hast added wisdom and weal to the report."

⁽⁷⁾ **And happy . . . and hear.**—The conjunctions weaken the rhetorical effect of the verse, and are not read in Kings.

⁽⁸⁾ **On his throne**—*i.e.*, Jehovah's throne. (Comp. 1 Chron. xxviii. 5.) Kings has, "on the throne of Israel."

**To be king for the Lord thy God.**—A further insistance on the idea that Solomon was but the vicegerent of Jehovah. The clause is added by the chronicler, but need not be called "an evidently wilful alteration" (*Thenius*).

**To establish.**—This phrase is wanting in the Hebrew of Kings, but is probably original, as the LXX. there has it.

⁽⁹⁾ **Spices.**—*B'sāmîm*, from which come our words *balsam* and *balm*.

**Great abundance.**—See Note on verse 1. Here *lārōb* is substituted for the ancient *harbēh*.

**Neither was there any such spice.**—Or, *there had not been such spicery*, *i.e.*, in Jerusalem. A defect in the chronicler's MS. authority probably occasioned this deviation from the phrase which we find in the older text, "There came no more such abundance of spicery" (1 Kings x. 10).

⁽¹⁰⁾ **And the servants also of Huram, and the servants of Solomon.**—Kings, "And the fleet also of Huram which carried gold from Ophir." The phrase is altered here to correspond with chap. viii. 18.

**Brought algum trees.**—See chap. ii. 8. LXX., ξύλα πεύκινα; Vulg., "ligna thyina;" Syriac, "acacia (?) wood" ('*eshkor'ō*); Kings, "brought from Ophir *almug trees* in great abundance." In the Mishna '*almûg* is "coral;" and the Rabbis ascribe a *red* colour to the algum wood. The *Pterocarpus Santalinus* has blood-red wood with black streaks, is fragrant, and is used in works of art, as well as for burning. The tree called *Valgu* or *Valgum* is the *Santalum album*, which produces *white* and *yellow* sandalwood. Thenius doubts whether the algum wood of Solomon was not the teak (*Cytharexylon Tectona*), which abounds in East India, and is a hard, yellow-streaked, strongly-scented wood, used in India for temple building.

⁽¹¹⁾ **Terraces.**—*M'sillôth*, which usually means *highways*, that is, raised paths. The word is an interpretation of *mis'ād*, which only occurs in 1 Kings xi. 12. LXX., ἀναβάσεις; Vulg., "gradus;" Arabic, "pillars."

**Singers.**—*The* singers.

**And there were none such seen before in the land of Judah.**—A shortened paraphrase of, "There came no such almug trees, nor were seen unto this day" (Kings). "The land of Judah" is a phrase which indicates how utterly the northern kingdom was excluded from the redactor's thought.

⁽¹²⁾ **Beside that which she had brought unto the king.**—It can hardly be meant that Solomon returned her own presents. If the reading be sound, we may understand *return presents*, *i.e.*, gifts equal in value to those which she had bestowed. Or better, we may regard the clause as a parenthetic note of the chronicler's, to the effect that the giving of presents was *not all on one side*. Solomon showed himself as royally generous as his visitor. Putting the clause first would make this meaning clearer: "And quite apart from what she brought the king, Solomon gave the queen of Sheba all her desire." Bertheau, however, proposes a slight change in the Hebrew text, so as to get the sense, "beside what the king had brought for her." 1 Kings x. 13 is much clearer: "besides what he had given her, according to the hand of king Solomon." LXX. translates, "besides all that she brought to king Solomon;" the Vulg., "and far more than she had brought him," which *may* be a trace of the original reading; the Syriac, "besides what he had given her." Syriac and Arabic add, "and he revealed to her all that was in her heart."

**She turned.**—*Hāphak*, for *pānāh* of Kings, which is more usual in this sense.

(13) Now the weight of gold that came to Solomon in one year was six hundred and threescore and six talents of gold; (14) beside *that which* chapmen and merchants brought. And all the kings of Arabia and ¹governors of the country brought gold and silver to Solomon. (15) And king Solomon made two hundred targets *of* beaten gold; six hundred *shekels* of beaten gold went to one target. (16) And three hundred shields *made he of* beaten gold: three hundred *shekels* of gold went to one shield. And the king put them in the house of the forest of Lebanon. (17) Moreover the king made a great throne of ivory, and overlaid it with pure gold. (18) And *there were* six steps to the throne, with a footstool of gold, *which were* fastened to the throne, and ²stays on each side of the sitting place, and two lions standing by the stays: (19) and twelve lions stood there on the one side and on the other upon the six steps. There was not the like made in any kingdom. (20) And all the drinking vessels of king Solomon *were of* gold, and all the vessels of the house of the forest of Lebanon *were of* ³pure gold: ⁴none *were of* silver; it was *not* any thing accounted of in the days of Solomon. (21) For the king's ships went to Tarshish with the servants of Huram: every three years once came the ships of Tarshish bringing gold, and silver, ⁵ivory, and apes, and peacocks. (22) And king Solomon passed all the

1 Or, *captains.*
2 Heb., *hands.*
3 Heb., *shut up.*
4 Or, there was no silver in them.
5 Or, *elephants' teeth.*

---

(b) SOLOMON'S INCOME, SPLENDOUR, AND DOMINION—(verses 13—28). Comp. 1 Kings x. 14—29, and 1 Kings iv. 26, 27.

(13) **Now the weight of gold.**—See 1 Kings x. 14, with which this verse coincides.

(14) **Besides that which chapmen and merchants brought.**—The Hebrew is difficult, and probably corrupt. Literally it seems to run, *besides the men of the itinerants* (a strange phrase), *and that which the merchants were bringing*; or, perhaps, *apart from the men of the itinerants and the merchants bringing.* The last word may be a clerical error, as it occurs again directly. The conjecture of Thenius on 1 Kings x. 15 seems to be borne out by the ancient Versions. He would read instead of *'anshê ha-tārîm,* "men of the travellers;" *'onshê ha-r'dûyim,* "fines or tributes *of the subjects.*" The Syriac of Chronicles has "tributes of the cities." Perhaps, therefore, the true original reading was *'onshê he'arîm.* The Vulg. renders "envoys of divers peoples;" but the LXX., "men *of the subjected* (states)."

For the second half of the phrase Kings has, "and the merchandise of the pedlars."

**The kings of Arabia.**—Kings, "the kings of the mixed tribes;" that is, the *Bêdâwîs,* bordering on and *mingling* with Israel. (Comp. Exod. xii. 38.) The difference depends on the vowel pointing only. (Comp. Jer. xxv. 24, where both words occur; and Ezek. xxx. 5.)

**Governors.**—*Pachôth, i.e.,* pashas. Thenius is wrong in supposing this word to be a token of the "later composition of the section." (See Note on 2 Kings xviii. 24.)

**Brought.**—*Were bringing* = used to bring. (Comp. verses 23, 24.)

(15) **And king Solomon made.**—Word for word as 1 Kings x. 16.

**Beaten gold.**—Rather, according to Gesenius, *mixed* or *alloyed* gold. But the word (*shahût, i.e., shatûah*) seems to mean gold *beaten out, gold-leaf.* So LXX., ἐλατόν.

**Went to.**—*He put on, i.e.,* he plated the "targets," which were large oblong shields, with gold. (Comp. Amos viii. 10, "And I will *put upon* all loins sackcloth.") So in verse 16.

(16) **Shields.**—*Maginnîm.* The *māgēn* was a round or oval shield, about half the size of the "target" (*çinnah*), with which it is often contrasted; *e.g.,* Ps. xxxv. 2; LXX., ἀσπίδας.

**Three hundred shekels of gold.**—Kings, *three manehs of gold.* The maneh or mina (Assyrian, *mana*), was 1-60th part of a talent, and was equivalent to fifty or sixty shekels. Either the reading of our text is an error of transcription (*sh'losh mē'ôth* for *sh'losheth manim*), or the word *shekels* is wrongly supplied in our version, and we ought rather to read *drachms* (100 drachms = 1 mina). The Syriac reads, "And three minas of gold wrought on the handle of one shield;" so also the Arabic.

(17) **Pure.**—*Tahôr,* a common word, for the once occurring *mûphaz* of Kings.

(18) **With a footstool of gold, which were fastened to the throne.**—Instead of this Kings has, *And the throne had a rounded top behind.* Although the footstool is a prominent object in Oriental representations of thrones, it is quite possible that our text is due to a corruption of that which appears in Kings, and with which the Syriac here agrees. The LXX. renders, "and six steps to the throne, fastened with gold," omitting the footstool. The Heb. is at all events suspiciously awkward.

For the remainder of this and the following verse see 1 Kings x. 19, 20. The chronicler has made two slight verbal corrections in verse 19.

(20) **None were of silver; it was not anything accounted of.**—The *not* appears to be rightly supplied by our version; comp. 1 Kings x. 21, with which the verse otherwise entirely agrees.

(21) **For the king's ships went to Tarshish.**—1 Kings x. 22, "For the king had a Tarshish fleet on the sea, with the fleet of Hiram." It is generally assumed that the words of the chronicler are an erroneous paraphrase of the expression, "Tarshish fleet," *i.e.,* a fleet of ships fitted for long voyages. (Comp. Isa. ii. 16.) The identity of the present fleet with that mentioned above in verse 10 is not evident. Solomon may have had a fleet in the Mediterranean ("the sea" of 1 Kings x. 22) trading westward, as well as in the Red Sea, trading south and east. Some have identified Tarshish with Cape Tarsis in the Persian Gulf. (See Note on chap. xx. 36.)

(22) **And king Solomon.**—See 1 Kings x. 23

**Passed all.**—*Was great above all.*

*Solomon's Presents.* **II. CHRONICLES, X.** *His Death.*

kings of the earth in riches and wisdom. ⁽²³⁾ And all the kings of the earth sought the presence of Solomon, to hear his wisdom, that God had put in his heart. ⁽²⁴⁾ And they brought every man his present, vessels of silver, and vessels of gold, and raiment, harness, and spices, horses, and mules, a rate year by year. ⁽²⁵⁾ And Solomon *a* had four thousand stalls for horses and chariots, and twelve thousand horsemen; whom he bestowed in the chariot cities, and with the king at Jerusalem. ⁽²⁶⁾ And he reigned over all the kings *b* from the ¹river even unto the land of the Philistines, and to the border of Egypt. ⁽²⁷⁾ And the king ²made silver in Jerusalem as stones, and cedar trees made he as the sycomore trees that *are* in the low plains in abundance. ⁽²⁸⁾ *c* And they brought unto Solomon horses out of Egypt, and out of all lands. ⁽²⁹⁾ Now the rest of the *d*acts of Solomon, first and last, *are* they not written in the ³book of Nathan the prophet, and in the prophecy of Ahijah the Shilonite, and in the visions of *e* Iddo the seer against Jeroboam the son of Nebat? ⁽³⁰⁾ And Solomon reigned in Jerusalem over all Israel forty years. ⁽³¹⁾ And Solomon slept with his fathers, and he was buried in the city of David his father: and Rehoboam his son reigned in his stead.

CHAPTER X.—⁽¹⁾ And *f* Rehoboam went to Shechem: for to Shechem were all Israel come to make him king. ⁽²⁾ And it came to pass, when Jeroboam the son of Nebat, who was in Egypt,

*a* 1 Kings 4. 26.
*b* Gen. 15. 18.
¹ That is, *Euphrates.*
² Heb., *gave.*
*c* 1 Kings 10. 28; ch. 1. 16.
*d* 1 Kings 11. 41.
³ Heb., *words.*
*e* ch. 12. 15.
B.C. cir. 975.
*f* 1 Kings 12. 1, &c.

---

⁽²³⁾ **All the kings of the earth.**—Explanatory of "all the earth were seeking" (Kings). *The earth,* an expression defined in verse 26.

⁽²⁴⁾ **And they brought.**—*Used to bring.* (Comp. verse 14.)

**Harness** — *i.e.,* weapons and armour. Compare Macbeth's

"At least we'll die with *harness* on our back."

**A rate year by year.**—Literally, *a year's matter in a year.* Solomon's vassal kings are intended.

⁽²⁵⁾ **And Solomon had four thousand stalls for horses and chariots, and twelve thousand horsemen.**—See 1 Kings iv. 26 (where the number of stalls is erroneously stated at 40,000).

The remainder of the verse coincides with 1 Kings x. 26.

Having already given an account of Solomon's chariots and horses, and his importation of the latter from Egypt, in chap. i. 14—17, an account which is identical with 1 Kings x. 26—29, the chronicler naturally avoids mere repetition of that passage in verses 25—28.

⁽²⁶⁾ **And he reigned over all the kings.**—This verse corresponds to 1 Kings iv. 21.

⁽²⁷⁾ **And the king made silver.**—Identical with 1 Kings x. 27. On this and the following verse, comp. the prohibitions of Deut. xvii. 16, 17.

⁽²⁸⁾ **And they brought.**—*Used to bring.* The verse summarises 1 Kings x. 28, 29 (=2 Chr. i. 16, 17), and adds that Solomon imported horses "out of all the lands," as well as from Egypt.

(*c*) REFERENCE TO DOCUMENTS.—CLOSE OF THE REIGN (verses 29—31). (Comp. 1 Kings xi. 41—43.)

⁽²⁹⁾ **Now the rest of the acts of Solomon.**—Or, *story, history;* literally, *words.* (Comp. 1 Chron. xxix. 29.)

**First and last.**—Or, *the former and the latter.* Instead of this, Kings has, "and all that he did, and his wisdom."

**In the book.**—Or, *history.* For the sources named here, see the Introduction. Kings has simply, "are they not written in the book of the history of Solomon?" His name conveyed the idea of *peace* to the Hebrew ear. But there is no doubt that it was originally identical with Shalman (Assyrian *Salmânu*), the name of a god. Tiglath-pileser II. mentions a *Salamânu* king of Moab. This name exactly corresponds to Solomon.

**Ahijah the Shilonite.**—See 1 Kings xi. 29—39 and xiv. 2—18.

**Iddo.**—Hebrew, *Ie'dî* or *Ie'dô.* This seer is not mentioned in Kings. (See chaps. xii. 15 and xiii. 22 for further references to his works.)

⁽³⁰⁾ **And Solomon reigned.**—So 1 Kings x. 42, "And the days that Solomon reigned," etc., as here.

**Over all Israel**—*i.e.,* the undivided nation.

⁽³¹⁾ **Slept.**—Literally, *lay down.*

**He was buried.**—*They buried him.* Kings has, "he was buried." The two texts are otherwise identical.

X.

(iii) HISTORY OF THE KINGS WHO REIGNED IN JERUSALEM, FROM REHOBOAM TO THE EXILE (chaps. x.—xxxvi.).

(1) The Revolt of the Ten Tribes. The Reign of Rehoboam (chaps. x.—xii.).

(*a*) The Revolt of the Ten Tribes against the Dynasty of David (chaps. x.—xi. 4). Comp. the parallel narrative in 1 Kings xii. 1—24.

Considered by itself, this section might be pronounced a transcript of 1 Kings xii. 1—24. Such differences as appear in the Hebrew text are mostly unimportant, consisting of merely verbal modifications and omissions not affecting the general sense. (See Intro. § 6; and the commentary on the passage in Kings.)

⁽¹⁾ **To Shechem.**—*Sh'kémah,* with accusative ending; Kings, *Sh'kem.* "Were come," pf. plural; Kings, singular.

⁽²⁾ **Who was in Egypt.**—Really a parenthesis, "And it came to pass, when Jeroboam the son of Nebat heard (now he was in Egypt, whither he had fled from the face of Solomon the king), that Jeroboam returned from Egypt." The chronicler has omitted to say he was *still* in Egypt ('*ôdennû,* Kings), because he has

whither he had fled from the presence of Solomon the king, heard *it*, that Jeroboam returned out of Egypt. (3) And they sent and called him. So Jeroboam and all Israel came and spake to Rehoboam, saying, (4) Thy father made our yoke grievous: now therefore ease thou somewhat the grievous servitude of thy father, and his heavy yoke that he put upon us, and we will serve thee. (5) And he said unto them, Come again unto me after three days. And the people departed.

(6) And king Rehoboam took counsel with the old men that had stood before Solomon his father while he yet lived, saying, What counsel give ye *me* to return answer to this people? (7) And they spake unto him, saying, If thou be kind to this people, and please them, and speak good words to them, they will be thy servants for ever. (8) But he forsook the counsel which the old men gave him, and took counsel with the young men that were brought up with him, that stood before him. (9) And he said unto them, What advice give ye that we may return answer to this people, which have spoken to me, saying, Ease somewhat the yoke that thy father did put upon us? (10) And the young men that were brought up with him spake unto him, saying, Thus shalt thou answer the people that spake unto thee, saying, Thy father made our yoke heavy, but make thou *it* somewhat lighter for us; thus shalt thou say unto them, My little *finger* shall be thicker than my father's loins. (11) For whereas my father ¹put a heavy yoke upon you, I will put more to your yoke: my father chastised you with whips, but I *will chastise you* with scorpions.

(12) So Jeroboam and all the people came to Rehoboam on the third day, as the king bade, saying, Come again to me on the third day. (13) And the king answered them roughly; and king Rehoboam forsook the counsel of the old men, (14) and answered them after the advice of the young men, saying, My father made your yoke heavy, but I

1 Heb., *laded*.

---

not alluded before to his flight thither. (See 1 Kings xi. 26—40.)

**That Jeroboam returned out of Egypt.**—Kings continues the parenthesis, "and Jeroboam dwelt in Egypt." The words *dwelt* and *returned* are spelt with the same letters in Hebrew, the difference being one of pointing only.

(3) **And they sent and called him.**—To the assembly. (Comp. 1 Kings xii. 20.)

**All Israel.**—Chron. omits *assembly of*. "Came," singular; Kings, plural.

(4) **Made . . . grievous . . . ease thou.**—*Made hard . . . lighten*.

**Now therefore.**—*And now*. Kings and the Syriac here, "and thou now"—*w'attah 'attah*: an assonance which the chronicler has avoided, at the expense of the proper emphasis, which lies on *thou*. (Some Hebrew MSS. and the Vulgate and Arabic read, *and thou.*) (Comp. verse 10, *and thou . . . lighten it.*)

(5) **Come again unto me after three days.**—Heb., *Yet three days and return unto me*. The verb *go ye* (Kings) seems to have fallen out before the first words. The LXX., Syriac, and Arabic have it.

**Departed.**—Singular; Kings, plural. Contrast verse 1.

(6) **Before Solomon.**—"*Liphnê Sh'lomoh*," the common formula for "*'eth-p'nê Sh'lomoh*" (Kings).

**To return answer to . . .**—Literally, *to return to this people a word;* Kings, "to return this people a word" (double accusative)—a construction preserved in verse 9 below.

(7) **If thou be kind to this people.**—A free paraphrase of, "If *to-day* thou become *a servant* to this people and *serve* them" (Kings)—words which may have seemed inappropriate to the redactor, in connection with *the king*, but which form a pointed antithesis to the last clause of the verse, "they will be *thy servants* for ever."

**And please them.**—*Be propitious to them, receive them graciously* (*raçah*). (Gen. xxxiii. 10.) Kings, "answer them."

(8) **That stood before him.**—The chronicler has omitted a redundant expression (*'asher*).

(9) **And he said unto them.**—The verse agrees with Kings to the letter.

(10) **Spake unto him.**—Heb., *with him*; probably a mistaken repetition. Kings, "unto him," and so LXX.; but Syriac, "with him."

**Answer.**—*Say to*.

**The people.**—*This people* (Kings).

**But make thou it somewhat lighter for us.**—Literally, *And thou lighten from upon us*. LXX., well: καὶ σὺ ἄφες ἀφ' ἡμῶν.

**Thus shalt thou say.**—Kings, "speak."

**My little finger.**—The word "finger" should not be italicised. The word *qôten* means "little finger."

(11) **For whereas . . .**—Literally, *And now, my father . . . and I, I will add to your yoke*.

**Whips . . . scorpions.**—*The whips . . . the scorpions*.

**I will chastise you.**—These words are found in the text of Kings, both here and in verse 14.

(12) **So Jeroboam.**—*Literatim* as Kings.

(13) **Them.**—Kings, "the people."

**Roughly.**—*Hardly*.

**King Rehoboam.**—Not in Kings, which adds, "that they counselled him."

(14) **And answered them.**—*And spake unto them*.

**Advice.**—*Counsel*.

**My father made your yoke heavy.**—The Targum and a large number of Hebrew MSS. read, "I will make heavy." This appears to be an error arising out

will add thereto: my father chastised you with whips, but I *will chastise you* with scorpions. <sup>(15)</sup> So the king hearkened not unto the people: for the cause was of God, that the LORD might perform his word, which he spake by the hand of Ahijah the Shilonite to Jeroboam the son of Nebat.

<sup>(16)</sup> And when all Israel *saw* that the king would not hearken unto them, the people answered the king, saying,

What portion have we in David? and we have none inheritance in the son of Jesse: every man to your tents, O Israel: *and* now, David, see to thine own house.

So all Israel went to their tents. <sup>(17)</sup> But *as for* the children of Israel that dwelt in the cities of Judah, Rehoboam reigned over them.

<sup>(18)</sup> Then king Rehoboam sent Hadoram that *was* over the tribute; and the children of Israel stoned him with stones, that he died. But king Rehoboam [1] made speed to get him up to *his* chariot, to flee to Jerusalem. <sup>(19)</sup> And Israel rebelled against the house of David unto this day.

CHAPTER XI.—<sup>(1)</sup> And *when* Rehoboam was come to Jerusalem, he gathered of the house of Judah and Benjamin an hundred and fourscore thousand chosen *men*, which were warriors, to fight against Israel, that he might bring the kingdom again to Rehoboam. <sup>(2)</sup> But the word of the LORD came to Shemaiah the man of God, saying, <sup>(3)</sup> Speak unto Rehoboam the son of Solomon, king of Judah, and to all Israel in Judah and Benjamin, saying, <sup>(4)</sup> Thus saith the LORD, Ye shall not go up, nor fight against your brethren: return every man to his house: for this thing is done of me. And they obeyed the words of the LORD, and returned from going against Jeroboam.

*a* 1 Kings 11. 29.

[1] Heb., *strengthened himself.*

*b* 1 Kings 12. 21, &c.

---

of a fusion of the two words *'abî hikhbîd* into *'akhbîd*. All the versions have the reading of the text.

**Thereto.**—"To your yoke" (Kings).

<sup>(15)</sup> **The cause was of God.**—*It was brought about by God.* Literally, *it was a turn* or *turning-point (of events) from with God*. The word *n'sibbah* is equivalent to *sibbah* of Kings. Both are isolated in the Old Testament. The latter is the common word for "cause" in Rabbinic, as *sibbath sibbôth—causa causarum*.

**That the Lord might perform his word.**—The chronicler does not deviate from the text of Kings here, although he has not mentioned Ahijah's prophecy to Jeroboam before. (Comp. chap. ix. 29.)

<sup>(16)</sup> **And when all Israel saw.**—*Now all Israel had seen.* Kings: "And all Israel saw." The chronicler makes a new start. (The word "saw" is wanting in very many Hebrew MSS., and in LXX., Vulg., and Targ., and some Hebrew editions.)

**Answered.**—*Returned the king*—scil., *a word*, which Kings supplies.

**Every man to your tents, O Israel.**—Literally, *A man ('îsh) to thy tents,* &c. The word "man" is probably spurious, being due to a repetition of the letters of the preceding proper name Jesse (Heb., *Yishai* or *Ishai*). Kings, LXX., Vulg. are without it, but Syriac has it.

**See to thine own house**—*i.e.*, govern Judah, thine own tribe. Vulg., "pasce domum tuam."

<sup>(18)</sup> **Hadoram.**—Kings, "Adoram." LXX. (Vat.), Adoniram. (Comp. 1 Kings iv. 6.)

**The tribute.**—*The levy (ha-mas).*

**The children of Israel.**—Kings, "all Israel."

**Made speed.**—*Had made speed.*

**His chariot.**—*The (royal) chariot.*

<sup>(19)</sup> **Unto this day.**—Neither the compiler of Kings nor the chronicler saw fit to alter a phrase which no longer applied to the political circumstances of their own day. (Comp. 1 Chron. iv. 41, 43, v. 26.)

XI.

<sup>(1)</sup> **And when Rehoboam.**—*And Rehoboam came . . . and he gathered.* The chronicler omits 1 Kings xii. 20, which relates the call of Jeroboam to the throne of Israel. The present verse is a slightly abridged form of 1 Kings xii. 21.

**The kingdom.**—*Mamlākāh.* Kings, *m'lūkāh.*

<sup>(2)</sup> **The Lord.**—Kings has "God" twice. The chronicler does not always avoid the name *Jehovah*.

**Shemaiah.**—So Kings. The chronicler writes the longer form, *Shemayāhu*; and so *Ahiyāhu* in chap. x. 15.

<sup>(3)</sup> **King of Judah.**—By this significant expression accomplished facts receive at the outset the seal of Divine assent.

**All Israel in Judah and Benjamin.**—Kings, "all the house of Judah and Benjamin, and the remnant of the people;" where the second phrase seems to define the first, for the house of Judah and Benjamin *was* the remnant of Israel that continued loyal to David. In that case, the chronicler's phrase is a mere abbreviation, denoting whatever of Israel was comprised in the two faithful tribes. (Comp. chap. x. 17.) But there may be a hint that Judah and Benjamin were the true Israel, and that the apostate North had forfeited its right to that honourable name. Others suppose a reference to members of Northern tribes dwelling in the territory of Judah and Benjamin. Syriac, "to Rehoboam . . . and to the house of Benjamin, and to all Israel, and to the remnant of the people." LXX., "to all Judah and Benjamin" simply.

<sup>(4)</sup> **Thus saith the Lord.**—The words of the prophecy are reported as in 1 Kings xii. 24, omitting "the sons of Israel" after "your brethren."

**This thing is done of me.**—Literally, *from me became (arose) this matter*; viz., of the revolt of the ten tribes. (Comp. chap. x. 15: "For the cause was of God.")

## II. CHRONICLES, XI.

(5) And Rehoboam dwelt in Jerusalem, and built cities for defence in Judah. (6) He built even Beth-lehem, and Etam, and Tekoa, (7) and Beth-zur, and Shoco, and Adullam, (8) and Gath, and Mareshah, and Ziph, (9) and Adoraim, and Lachish, and Azekah, (10) and Zorah, and Aijalon, and Hebron, which are in Judah and in Benjamin fenced cities. (11) And he fortified the strong holds, and put captains in them, and store of victual, and of oil and wine. (12) And in every several city he put shields and spears, and made them exceeding strong, having Judah and Benjamin on his side. (13) And the priests and the Levites that were in all Israel [1] resorted to him out of all their coasts. (14) For the Levites left their suburbs and their possession, and came to Judah and Jerusalem: for [a] Jeroboam and his sons had cast them off from executing the priest's

[1] Heb., presented themselves to him.

[a] ch. 13. 9.

---

Words.—"Word," Kings and the versions here, no doubt rightly, as this is the usual phrase. But comp. 1 Sam. xv. 1.

From going against Jeroboam.—Kings, "To go away, *according to the word of the Lord*"—a tautology which the chronicler has avoided. The rest of the chapter is wanting in the Syriac and Arabic Versions, which have instead 1 Kings xii. 25—30; xiii. 34; xiv. 1—9, where they break off abruptly, without finishing Ahijah's prophecy.

(b) REHOBOAM STRENGTHENS THE DEFENCES OF HIS KINGDOM (verses 5—12).

This section is peculiar to the chronicler.

(5) **Dwelt in Jerusalem.**—As the capital.

**Cities for defence.**—('*Arîm l'māçōr* = '*arê māçōr*; chap. viii. 5), "embattled cities;" LXX., πόλεις τειχήρεις.

**In Judah.**—Not the territory of the tribe, but the kingdom is intended, for some of the fortresses were in Benjamin (verse 10).

(6) **He built even.**—*And he built*—i.e., fortified.

**Beth-lehem.**—*Beit-lahm*, on a rocky eminence, two hours south of Jerusalem (Gen. xxxv. 19; Micah v. 2; Matt. ii. 6). The birthplace of David and of Christ.

**Etam.**—*Ain Attân*; different from the place mentioned in 1 Chron. iv. 32 and Judges xv. 8, which lay in Simeonite territory.

**Tekoa.**—*Teku'a*; ruins on a hill two hours south of Bethlehem. (See Josh. xv. 59, Note.)

(7) **Beth-zur.**—*Beit-sûr*; a ruin midway between *Urtâs* and Hebron (Josh. xv. 58).

**Shoco.**—Heb., *Sōcō*; *es Suweikeh*, in *Wady Sumt*, three and a-half hours south-west of Jerusalem (Josh. xv. 35; 1 Sam. xvii. 1).

**Adullam.**—Josh. xv. 35. Perhaps *Aid-el-Mieh*.

(8) **Gath.**—Uncertain. Perhaps in the *Wady-el-Gat* north of Ascalon. (See 1 Kings ii. 39 and 1 Chron. xviii. 1, from a comparison of which it appears that, under Solomon, Gath was ruled by a vassal king.)

**Mareshah.**—*Marash*; a ruin two miles south of *Beit-jibrin*, Eleutheropolis (Josh. xv. 44; 2 Chron. xiv. 9).

**Ziph.**—*Tel Zif*; ruins about one hour and a quarter south east of Hebron (Josh. xv. 55; 1 Sam. xxiii. 14, *seqq.*) Another Judean Ziph is mentioned (Josh. xv. 24).

(9) **Adoraim.**—*Dûra*; a village about seven and a-half miles south west of Hebron. Called Ἄδωρα 1 Macc. xiii. 20, and often mentioned by Josephus in connection with Marissa (Mareshah). The name is not found elsewhere in the Old Testament.

**Lachish.**—*Um Lakis*; a ruined city on a round hill, seven hours west of *Beit-jibrin*, on the road from Hebron to Gaza (Josh. x. 3, xv. 39).

**Azekah.**—Uncertain; near Socoh (1 Sam. xvii. 1; Josh. x. 10, xv. 35).

(10) **Zorah.**—*Sur'ah*; a ruin on the ridge north of the *Wady-es-Surar*. The birthplace of Samson.

**Aijalon.**—*Yalo*, north of Sur'ah, four leagues west of Gibeon. Zorah and Aijalon, or Ajalon, may have become Benjamite cities at the epoch of the migration of Dan (Judges xviii.). (See Josh. xix. 41, 42; also Josh. xv. 33, x. 12.) Of the fifteen fortified cities here enumerated these two lay farthest north.

**Hebron.**—*El Khalil* (Gen. xxiii. 2).

**Which are in Judah and in Benjamin.**—This refers to the entire list.

**Fenced cities.**—'*Arê m*<sup>e</sup>*tsûrôth* ("cities of ramparts," or "strongholds"); a phrase peculiar to the chronicler. (Comp. chap. xii. 4.) "The fifteen cities [excluding Zorah and Ajalon] were on the south and west of Jerusalem. Hence Rehoboam appears to have been more afraid of an attack from the south and west—that is, from the Egyptians—than of a war with the northern kingdom." (*Bertheau*.)

(11) **And he fortified.**—Literally, *strengthened*, i.e., put them in an efficient condition for defence, by providing commandants and stores of arms and food.

**The strong holds.**—*M*<sup>e</sup>*tsûrôth*; the word in last verse.

**Captains.**—*N*<sup>e</sup>*gîdim*; leaders, princes (1 Chron. ix. 11). Here it means *commandants*.

(12) **Shields.**—The "targets" of chap. ix. 15.

**Made them exceeding strong.**—*Strengthened them* (the same word as "fortified" in verse 11) *very abundantly* (*l'harbēh m*<sup>e</sup>*ôd*). A form of words only used by the chronicler. (See chap. xvi. 8; and comp. Neh. vi. 18.)

**Having Judah and Benjamin on his side.**—Literally, *and he had* (or, *there fell to him*) *Judah and Benjamin*. A definition of Rehoboam's territory. (Comp. chap. x. 17.)

(c) THE PRIESTS AND LEVITES, AND ALL WHO ARE FAITHFUL TO THE LEGITIMATE WORSHIP, DESERT THE NORTHERN KINGDOM (verses 13—17).

This section also is peculiar to the chronicler, though indirectly confirmed by the notices in 1 Kings xii. 31; xiii. 33.

(13) **Resorted to him.**—*Presented themselves before him* (Job i. 6; ii. 1).

**Coasts.**—*Border, domain*. The term "Levites" is here used in the general sense as including the priests.

(14) **Their suburbs.**—*Pasture-grounds* (Num. xxxv. 1—8).

**And their possession**—i.e., the cities assigned to them among the ten tribes.

*Idolatry of Jeroboam.* II. CHRONICLES, XI. *Rehoboam's Wives.*

office unto the LORD: <sup>(15)</sup> and he ordained him priests for the high places, and for the devils, and for the calves which he had made. <sup>(16)</sup> And after them out of all the tribes of Israel such as set their hearts to seek the LORD God of Israel came to Jerusalem, to sacrifice unto the LORD God of their fathers. <sup>(17)</sup> So they strengthened the kingdom of Judah, and made Rehoboam the son of Solomon strong, three years: for three years they walked in the way of David and Solomon.

<sup>a</sup> 1 Kings 15. 2.

<sup>(18)</sup> And Rehoboam took him Mahalath the daughter of Jerimoth the son of David to wife, *and* Abihail the daughter of Eliab the son of Jesse; <sup>(19)</sup> which bare him children; Jeush, and Shamariah, and Zaham. <sup>(20)</sup> And after her he took <sup>a</sup> Maachah the daughter of Absalom; which bare him Abijah, and Attai, and Ziza, and Shelomith. <sup>(21)</sup> And Rehoboam loved Maachah the daughter of Absalom above all his wives and his concubines: (for he took eighteen wives, and threescore concubines; and begat twenty and

---

Jeroboam and his sons had cast them off from executing the priest's office unto the Lord.—See 1 Kings xii. 26—31. There we are told that, as a matter of policy, Jeroboam established two centres of worship within his own dominions, so that his subjects might cease to visit the Temple of Jerusalem. In appointing priests chosen promiscuously from all classes of the people to minister in the new sanctuaries, Jeroboam struck a direct blow at the Levitical order, and "thrust them out from acting as priests to Jehovah," as our verse declares.

**And his sons.**—Usually explained to mean his successors on the throne. (Comp. 1 Chron. iii. 16.) "For in this matter all the kings of Israel walked in the footsteps of Jeroboam" (*Keil*). Of Jeroboam's own sons Nadab was the only one who reigned (1 Kings xv. 25 *sqq.*); and the narrative of Kings (1 Kings xiv., xv.) mentions but one other son of this king. It does not, however, exclude the possibility of there having been more than these two, and if there were, they may have co-operated with their father in his religious policy.

<sup>(15)</sup> **And he ordained.** — *And had appointed* (1 Chron. xv. 16, 17; xxii. 2).

**For the high places.**—*Bâmôth.* (See Note on 1 Kings xii. 31 *seqq.*) Such local sanctuaries existed not only at Dan and Bethel, but also in other cities of the northern kingdom. (Comp. 2 Kings xvii. 9.)

**And for the devils.**—*Sĕʻirim,* "satyrs" (Isa. xiii. 21). Literally, *goats.* (See Note on Lev. xvii. 7.) The phrase indicates a prevalence of debasing idolatry in the time of Jeroboam.

**And for the calves.**—See Note on 1 Kings xii. 28. The "calves" represented the God of Israel. It appears therefore that Jeroboam encouraged a system of syncretism, or mixture of worships.

<sup>(16)</sup> **And after them**—*i.e.,* following their lead.

**Such as set their hearts.**—The same phrase (*nâthan lebab*) as in 1 Chron. xxii. 19, and nowhere else.

**Came to Jerusalem, to sacrifice.**—And to settle there, as appears from next verse. A similar migration of the faithful worshippers of Jehovah is recorded in the reigns of Asa and Hezekiah. (See chaps. xv. 9; xxx. 11.)

<sup>(17)</sup> **So they strengthened . . . three years**—*i.e.,* during the first three years of the reign. "There is no ground for suspecting the antiquity of this record. On the contrary, it is antecedently probable that the pressure from the north occasioned a proportionally greater earnestness in the religious life of the southern kingdom, and that the former was weakened and the latter strengthened by the migration" (*Bertheau*).

This will explain also Jeroboam's abstention from molesting his rival's territory. (See Note on verse 10.)

**For three years.**—Literally, *for they walked . . . for three years.* The reason of the strengthening.

**They** (*i.e.,* the people of Judah) **walked in the way of David and Solomon**—*i.e.,* served Jehovah according to the system of worship enacted by those monarchs. The countenance which Solomon in his old age gave to foreign religions is here again ignored by the chronicler.

What happened after the three years of faithfulness is told in chap. xii. Here follow

PARTICULARS CONCERNING REHOBOAM'S FAMILY (verses 18—23).

This record also is wanting in the Book of Kings. It appears to have been derived from the sources designated in chap. xii. 15.

<sup>(18)</sup> **The daughter.**—So rightly, LXX., Vulg., and many Hebrew MSS. for the ordinary reading *son.*

**Of Jerimoth the son of David**—Jerimoth does not occur in the list of David's sons (1 Chron. iii. 1—8), unless we suppose the name to be a corruption of "Ithream." Probably he was one of "the sons of the concubines" (1 Chron. iii. 9).

**And Abihail.**—The *and* is not in the present Hebrew text, but is supplied by the LXX. "And of Abihail" is probably the meaning, so that both of Mahalath's parents are named. The LXX. and Vulg. make Abihail a second wife of Rehoboam; but verses 19, 20, as well as the construction of the sentence, make it evident that only one wife is mentioned here. A daughter of David's eldest brother could hardly become the wife of David's grandson.

**Eliab the son of Jesse.**—1 Sam. xvii. 13; 1 Chron. ii. 13.

<sup>(19)</sup> **Which bare.**—*And she* (*i.e.,* Mahalath) *bare.* **Shamariah.**—*Shemariah.* These sons of Rehoboam occur here only.

<sup>(20)</sup> **Maachah the daughter of Absalom**—*i.e.,* granddaughter, as appears from 2 Sam. xiv. 27, where *Tamar* is named as the "one daughter" of Absalom. Josephus says Maachah was daughter of Tamar (*Ant.* viii. 10, 1). (Comp. 2 Sam. xviii. 18; 2 Chron. xiii. 2; 1 Kings xv. 10.)

**Which bare him Abijah.**—Rehoboam's successor, called "Abijam" in Kings. The other three are unknown.

<sup>(21)</sup> **Loved Maachah.**—She probably inherited her mother's and grandfather's beauty.

**For he took**—*Nâsâʼ*, as in chap. xiii. 21; a later usage instead of *lâqah.*

*Abijah Exalted.*       II. CHRONICLES, XII.       *Invasion by Shishak.*

eight sons, and threescore daughters.) <sup>(22)</sup> And Rehoboam made Abijah the son of Maachah the chief, *to be* ruler among his brethren: for *he thought* to make him king. <sup>(23)</sup> And he dealt wisely, and dispersed of all his children throughout all the countries of Judah and Benjamin, unto every fenced city: and he gave them victual in abundance. And he desired ¹many wives.

CHAPTER XII.—<sup>(1)</sup> And it came to pass, when Rehoboam had established the kingdom, and had strengthened himself, he forsook the law of the LORD, and all Israel with him. <sup>(2)</sup> And it came to pass, *that* in the fifth year of king Rehoboam Shishak king of Egypt came up against Jerusalem, *a* because they had transgressed against the LORD, <sup>(3)</sup> with twelve hundred chariots, and threescore thousand horsemen: and the people *were* without number that came with him out of Egypt; the Lubims, the Sukkiims,

B.C. 974.

1 Heb., *a multitude of wives.*

*a* 1 Kings 14. 25.

---

**And threescore concubines.**—Josephus (*l.c.*) says, "thirty," and the difference in Hebrew is only of one letter. The recurrence of the same number immediately ("threescore daughters") is also suspicious.

<sup>(22)</sup> **And Rehoboam made Abijah the son of Maachah . . . brethren.**—Rather, *And Rehoboam appointed Abijah the son of Maachah for head*—to wit, *for prince* (*nagíd*)—*among his brethren.* The expression "head" is explained by the following clause.

**For he thought to make him king.**—This gives the sense of the brief Hebrew phrase, "for—for making him king." In making Abijah heir to the throne, it does not appear that Rehoboam infringed the law of Deut. xxi. 15—17, as the *Speaker's Commentary* suggests. The right of the firstborn was only a double share of a man's property. (Comp. 1 Kings i. 35 for a precedent.)

<sup>(23)</sup> **And he dealt wisely.**—Rehoboam showed his sagacity by providing each of his sons with an independent position and royal establishment in accordance with the notions of the time. In this way he secured their contentment and obviated quarrels for precedence, and intrigues against his destined successor. (Comp. Gen. xxv. 6; and 2 Chron. xxi. 2, 3.) As resident prefects of the fortresses of the kingdom the princes were usefully employed. Ewald compares Ps. xlv. 16.

**The countries.**—*Districts*, or *territories.*

**He gave them victual in abundance.**—No doubt by assigning to each a district which was bound to supply his wants, as was the manner of the later kings of Persia.

**And he desired many wives.**—*And asked* (for them) *a multitude of wives.* This is mentioned, along with the abundant maintenance, as proof of the princely state which he conferred on his sons, a numerous harem being one of the marks of royalty.

XII.

THE EGYPTIAN CONQUEST.

(*a*) SHISHAK'S INVASION OF JUDAH, AND THE PREACHING OF SHEMAIAH (verses 1—12).

The parallel in Kings is much briefer. (See 1 Kings xiv. 25—28.)

<sup>(1)</sup> **When Rehoboam had established the kingdom.**—Rather, *when Rehoboam's kingdom had been established.* The construction is impersonal: *when one had established Rehoboam's kingdom.* The narrative is resumed from chap. xi. 17.

**And had strengthened himself.**—*And when he had become strong* (*hezqāh*, an infinitive, used again at chap. xxvi. 16; Dan. xi. 2, and nowhere else).

**He forsook the law of the Lord**—*i.e.*, lapsed into idolatry. (See 1 Kings xiv. 22—24, where the offence is more precisely described.)

**All Israel.**—The southern kingdom being regarded as the true Israel. (Comp. verse 6.)

<sup>(2)</sup> **And it came to pass.**—See 1 Kings xiv. 25, with which this verse literally coincides, except that the last clause, "because they had transgressed," is added by the chronicler.

**In the fifth year of king Rehoboam.**—The order of events is thus given: For three years Rehoboam and his people continued faithful to the Lord (chap. xi. 17); in the fourth year they fell away; and in the fifth their apostasy was punished.

**Shishak.**—The *Sesonchis* of Manetho, and the *sh-sh-nk* of the hieroglyphs, was the first king of the 22nd dynasty. "His name," says Ebers, "and those of his successors, Osorkon (Zerah) and Takelot, are Semitic, a fact which explains the Biblical notice that Solomon took a princess of this dynasty for his consort, and stood in close commercial relations with Egypt, as well as, on the other hand, that Hadad the Edomite received the sister of Tahpenes the queen to wife (1 Kings xi. 19). In the year 949 B.C. Shishak, at the instigation of Jeroboam, took the field against Rehoboam, besieged Jerusalem, captured it, and carried off a rich booty to Thebes. On a southern wall of the Temple of Karnak, all Palestinian towns which the Egyptians took in this expedition are enumerated" (*Riehm's Handwört. Bibl. Alterth.*, p. 333).

**Because they had transgressed.**—*For they had been faithless to Jehovah.* This is the chronicler's own parenthetic explanation of the event, and expresses in one word his whole philosophy of Israelite history. Of course it is not meant that Shishak had any consciousness of the providential ground of his invasion of Judah.

<sup>(3)</sup> **With twelve hundred chariots.**—The short account in Kings says nothing of the numbers or constituents of the invading host. The totals here assigned are probably round numbers founded on a rough estimate. The cavalry are exactly fifty times as many as the chariots. Thenius finds the numbers "not incredible."

**The Lubims, the Sukkiims, and the Ethiopians.**—Rather, *Lybians, Sukkiyans, and Cushites* (without the definite article). These were "the people"—*i.e.*, the footmen. The Lybians and Cushites are mentioned together as auxiliaries of Egypt in Nah. iii. 9. (Comp. chap. xvi. 8.) The Sukkiyans are unknown, but the LXX. and Vulg. render *Troglodytes*, or cave-dwellers, meaning, it would seem, the Ethiopian Troglodytes of the mountains on the western shore of the Arabian Gulf. (Comp. *sukkò*, "his lair," Ps. x. 9.)

*The Princes humble themselves.*    II. CHRONICLES, XII.    *Plunder of the Temple.*

and the Ethiopians. <sup>(4)</sup> And he took the fenced cities which *pertained* to Judah, and came to Jerusalem.

<sup>(5)</sup> Then came Shemaiah the prophet to Rehoboam, and *to* the princes of Judah, that were gathered together to Jerusalem because of Shishak, and said unto them, Thus saith the LORD, Ye have forsaken me, and therefore have I also left you in the hand of Shishak. <sup>(6)</sup> Whereupon the princes of Israel and the king humbled themselves; and they said, The LORD *is* righteous. <sup>(7)</sup> And when the LORD saw that they humbled themselves, the word of the LORD came to Shemaiah, saying, They have humbled themselves; *therefore* I will not destroy them, but I will grant them <sup>1</sup>some deliverance; and my wrath shall not be poured out upon Jerusalem by the hand of Shishak. <sup>(8)</sup> Nevertheless they shall be his servants; that they may know my service, and the service of the kingdoms of the countries.

<sup>(9)</sup> So Shishak king of Egypt came up against Jerusalem, and took away the treasures of the house of the LORD, and the treasures of the king's house; he took all: he carried away also the shields of gold which Solomon *a*had made. <sup>(10)</sup> Instead of which king Rehoboam made shields of brass, and committed *them* to the hands of the chief of the guard, that kept the entrance of the king's house. <sup>(11)</sup> And when the king entered into the house of the LORD, the guard came and fetched them, and brought them again into the guard chamber. <sup>(12)</sup> And when he humbled himself, the wrath of the LORD turned

*1 Or, a little while.*

*a* ch. 9. 15.

---

<sup>(4)</sup> **He took the fenced cities.**—Those very cities which Rehoboam had fortified as bulwarks against Egypt (chap. xi. 5—12). Fourteen names of cities have disappeared from the Karnak inscription, but Socho, Adoraim, and Ajalon, are still read there.

**Came to** (so far as to) **Jerusalem.**—Comp. Isa. xxxvi. 1, 2. The verse is not in Kings. Thenius (on 1 Kings xiv. 26) says that the chronicler has here made use of "really historical notices." It is self-evident.

<sup>(5)</sup> **Then.**—*And.*

**Shemaiah the prophet.**—The section relating to his mission and its results (verses 5—8) is peculiar to the chronicle.

**The princes of Judah, that were gathered together to Jerusalem.**—Repulsed by the Egyptian arms, they had fallen back upon Jerusalem, to defend the capital. While the invading host lay before the city, Shemaiah addressed the king and princes.

**Ye have forsaken.**—There is emphasis on the pronoun. Literally, *Ye have forsaken me, and I also have forsaken you, in* (into) *the hand of Shishak.* The phrase "to leave into the hand" of a foe occurs Neh. ix. 28. (Comp. also chap. xv. 2 and xxiv. 20; and Deut. xxxi. 16, 17.) Here the words amount to a menace of utter destruction. (Comp. Jonah iii. 4.)

<sup>(6)</sup> **Whereupon.**—*And.*

**The princes of Israel.**—See Note on verse 1. "princes of *Judah*" (verse 5) is the meaning.

**Humbled themselves.**—Literally, *bowed* (chap. vii. 14). (Comp. Jon. iii. 5, 6.)

**The Lord is righteous.**—Comp. Exod. ix. 27 (the exclamation of Pharaoh); and Ezra ix. 15.

<sup>(7)</sup> **But I will grant them some deliverance.** —Rather, *and I will give them a few for a remnant.* (Comp. verse 12, "that he would not destroy him altogether.") For the phrase "to give a remnant," see Ezra ix. 13. The word rendered "few" is *kim'at*. (Comp. 1 Chron. xvi. 19: Isa. i. 9.) The pointing *kim'ăt* is peculiar to this passage.

**My wrath shall not be poured out.**—Or, *pour itself out, wreak itself.* The phrase denotes a judgment of extermination. (Comp. its use in chap. xxxiv. 25.)

**By the hand of Shishak.**—The destruction of Jerusalem was reserved for the hand of Nebuchadnezzar.

<sup>(8)</sup> **Nevertheless they shall be.**—*For they shall become servants* (*i.e.,* tributaries) *to him*; scil., for a while.

**That they may know** (or, *discern*) **my service, and the service of the kingdoms.**—That they may learn by experience the difference between the easy yoke of their God, and the heavy burden of foreign tyranny, which was entailed upon them by deserting Him.

**Kingdoms of the countries.**—See 1 Chron. xxix. 30.

<sup>(9)</sup> **So Shishak king of Egypt came up against Jerusalem.**—The narrative is resumed after the parenthesis relating to Shemaiah by repeating the statement of verse 2.

**And took away the treasures of the house of the Lord.**—See 1 Kings xiv. 26, with which the rest of this verse is identical.

<sup>(10)</sup> **Instead of which king Rehoboam made.** —See Note on 1 Kings xiv. 27, with which this verse coincides.

**Chief of the guard.**—Literally, *captains of the runners,* or *couriers.*

<sup>(11)</sup> **And when.**—*And as often as.*

**The guard came and fetched . . . .**—*The runners came and bare them; and they* (after the royal procession) *restored them to the guard room of the runners.* (See on 1 Kings xiv. 28, which reads, "the runners used to bear them.")

Solomon's golden shields had been kept in "the house of the forest of Lebanon" (chap. ix. 16).

<sup>(12)</sup> **And when he humbled himself, the wrath of the Lord turned from him.**—In fulfilment of the promise of verse 7. This remark, the tone of which is in perfect accord with the chronicler's conception of the real import of Shishak's invasion, is wanting in Kings.

**That he would not destroy him.**— Literally, *and not to destroy.* The infinitive is used as in chap. xi. 22.

**Altogether.**—*Unto consumption,* a phrase only found here and in Ezek. xiii. 13.

from him, that he would not destroy *him* altogether: ¹and also in Judah things went well.

(13) So king Rehoboam strengthened himself in Jerusalem, and reigned: for ªRehoboam *was* one and forty years old when he began to reign, and he reigned seventeen years in Jerusalem, the city which the LORD had chosen out of all the tribes of Israel, to put his name there. And his mother's name *was* Naamah an Ammonitess. (14) And he did evil, because he ²prepared not his heart to seek the LORD.

(15) Now the acts of Rehoboam, first and last, *are* they not written in the ³book of Shemaiah the prophet, and of Iddo the seer concerning genealogies? And *there were* wars between Rehoboam and Jeroboam continually. (16) And Rehoboam slept with his fathers, and was buried in the city of David: and Abijah his son reigned in his stead.

CHAPTER XIII.—(1) Now ᵇin the eighteenth year of king Jeroboam began Abijah to reign over Judah. (2) He reigned three years in Jerusalem. His mother's name also *was* Michaiah the daughter of Uriel of Gibeah.

And there was war between Abijah and Jeroboam. (3) And Abijah ⁴set the battle in array with an army of valiant men of war, *even* four hundred thousand chosen

---

¹ Or, *and yet in Judah there were good things.*
ª 1 Kings 14. 21.
² Or, *fixed.*
³ Heb., *words.*
ᵇ 1 Kings 15. 1, &c.
⁴ Heb., *bound together.*

---

Omit *him*. A general destruction of the country is meant.

**And also in Judah things went well.**—*Moreover in Judah there were good things.* Vulg., "siquidem et in Judah inventa sunt opera bona." The fact that faithfulness to Jehovah was still to be found in Judah is alleged as an additional reason why the Lord spared the land. The same phrase, "good things," recurs in a similar sense chap. xix. 3.

(*b*) SUMMING UP OF THE REIGN (verses 13—16). (Comp. 1 Kings xiv. 21, 22, 29, 31.)

The Syriac and Arabic contain this section.

(13) **So king Rehoboam strengthened himself.**—After the withdrawal of Shishak. In other words, he regained strength after the crushing blow inflicted by the Egyptian invasion. (Comp. the same word in chaps. xiii. 21 and i. 1.)

**And reigned**—*i.e.*, *reigned on* for twelve years longer; *for* he reigned altogether seventeen years.

**Rehoboam was one and forty . . . Naamah an Ammonitess.**—Word for word as in 1 Kings xiv. 21. (See the Notes there).

(14) **And he did evil.**—Syriac adds "before the Lord." The nature of his evil-doing is explained immediately: "for he directed not his heart to seek Jehovah." This estimate of Rehoboam's conduct seems to refer to the early years of his reign, which ended in the catastrophe of Shishak's invasion. 1 Kings xiv. 22, says, "And *Judah* did evil in the eyes of Jehovah"; and then goes on to tell of the acts of apostacy which brought that judgment upon the nation.

The phrase "direct or prepare the heart to seek the Lord." recurs chaps. xix. 3, xxx. 19; Ezra vii. 10.

**The book.**—*History.*

**Concerning genealogies.** — *For registration* (*l'hithyaḥēsh*). On the authorities here named, see the Introduction. The important particulars about the reign which are not given in Kings, *e.g.*, the fortification of the southern cities, the migration of the priests, and Rehoboam's private relations, were probably drawn by the chronicler from these sources.

**First and last.**—*The former and the latter.* (See on, chap. xvii. 3.)

**And there were wars.**—*And the wars of Rehoboam and Jeroboam* [continued] *all the days*, *i.e.*, throughout the reign. So 1 Kings xiv. 30, "Now there had been war between Rehoboam and Jeroboam all the days." Reuss is wrong in regarding this as "a contradiction" of chap. xi. 4. What Shemaiah forbade was a particular attempt to recover the obedience of the northern kingdom by force of arms. The permanent attitude of the rival kings could hardly be other than hostile, especially as Jeroboam appears to have instigated the Egyptian invasion of Judah; and this hostility must often have broken out into active injuries.

(16) **And Rehoboam slept with his fathers.**—Abridged from 1 Kings. xiv. 31, which see.

**Abijah.**—Chap. xi. 22. *Abijam*, the spelling of Kings, is probably due to an accident of transcription.

### XIII.

2. THE REIGN OF ABIJAH. (Comp. 1 Kings xv. 1—8.)

(1) **Now.**—Not in the Hebrew. The verse is nearly identical with the parallel in Kings.

(2) **His mother's name also was Michaiah the daughter of Uriel of Gibeah.**—Kings reads for the names "Maachah the daughter of Abishalom"; and as the chronicler has himself already designated Abijah as son of Maachah, daughter of Absalom (chap. xi. 20—22), there can be no doubt that this is correct, and that "Michaiah," which is elsewhere a man's name, is a corruption of Maachah. This is confirmed by the LXX., Syriac, and Arabic, which read Maachah. As we have already stated (chap. xi. 20), Maachah was *granddaughter* to Absalom, being a daughter of Tamar the only daughter of Absalom. Uriel of Gibeah, then, must have been the husband of Tamar. (See on chap. xv. 16. Uriel of Gibeah is otherwise unknown.)

**And there was war between Abijah and Jeroboam.**—*Now war had arisen.* See 1 Kings xv. 6. "Now war had prevailed [same verb] between Abijam [common Hebrew text incorrectly has *Rehoboam*] and Jeroboam *all the days of his life.*" The chronicler modifies the sense by omitting the concluding phrase, and then proceeds to give a striking account of a campaign in which Abijah totally defeated his rival (verse 3—20); of all which we find not a word in Kings.

(3) **Set the battle in array.**—*Began the battle.* Vulg., "cumque iniisset Abia certamen" (1 Kings xx. 14).

men: Jeroboam also set the battle in array against him with eight hundred thousand chosen men, *being* mighty men of valour.

<sup>(4)</sup> And Abijah stood up upon mount Zemaraim, which *is* in mount Ephraim, and said, Hear me, thou Jeroboam, and all Israel; <sup>(5)</sup> ought ye not to know that the LORD God of Israel gave the kingdom over Israel to David for ever, *even* to him and to his sons by a covenant of salt? <sup>(6)</sup> Yet Jeroboam the son of Nebat, the servant of Solomon the son of David, is risen up, and hath *a* rebelled against his lord. <sup>(7)</sup> And there are gathered unto him vain men, the children of Belial, and have strengthened themselves against Rehoboam the son of Solomon, when Rehoboam was young and tenderhearted, and could not withstand them. <sup>(8)</sup> And now ye think to withstand the kingdom of the LORD in the hand of the sons of David; and ye *be* a great multitude, and *there are* with you golden calves, which Jeroboam *b*made you for gods. <sup>(9)</sup> *c*Have ye not cast out the priests of the LORD, the sons of Aaron, and the Levites, and have made you priests after the manner of the nations of *other* lands? so that whosoever cometh ·¹to consecrate himself with a young bullock and seven rams, the same

*a* 1 Kings 11. 26.

*b* 1 Kings 12. 28.

*c* ch. 11. 14.

¹ Heb., *to fill his hand.*

---

**Four hundred thousand chosen men.**—In David's census, Judah mustered 470,000 fighting men, and Israel 1,100,000, without reckoning Levi and Benjamin (1 Chron. xxi. 5). The numbers of the verse present a yet closer agreement with the results of that census as reported in 2 Sam. xxiv. 9; where, as here, the total strength of the Israelite warriors is given as 800,000, and that of Judah as 500,000. This correspondence makes it improbable that the figures have been falsified in transmission. (See Note on verse 17.)

**Jeroboam also set the battle in array.**—*While Jeroboam had drawn up against him.* Vulg., *instruxit e contra aciem.*

<sup>(4)</sup> **And Abijah stood up upon mount Zemaraim.**—While the two hosts were facing each other, king Abijah addressed his foes from mount Zemaraim, as Jotham addressed the Shechemites from the top of Gerizim in the days of the judges (Judges ix. 7).

**Upon.**—Literally, *from upon to mount Zemaraim*; a mark of the chronicler's hand.

Mount Zemaraim is otherwise unknown A city so called is mentioned (Josh. xviii. 22) as near Bethel, and probably lay a little to the south of it, on the northern frontier of Judah, perhaps upon this mountain.

**Mount Ephraim.**—*The hill country of Ephraim.*

<sup>(5)</sup> **Ought ye not to know.**—Literally, *is it not to you to know?* A construction characteristic of the chronicler. Abijah contrasts the moral position of his adversaries with his own, asserting (1) that their separate political existence is itself an act of rebellion against Jehovah; (2) that they have abolished the only legitimate form of worship, and established in its place an illegal *cultus* and priesthood; whereas (3) he and his people have maintained the orthodox ritual and ministry, and are therefore assured of the divine support.

**By a covenant of salt.**—*As* or *after the manner of a covenant of salt,* i.e., a firm and unalterable compact (see Num. xviii. 19). According to ancient custom, salt was indispensable at formal meals for the ratification of friendship and alliance; and only a "salt treaty" was held to be secure. Salt therefore accompanied sacrifices, as being, in fact, so many renewals of the covenant between man and God. (Lev. ii. 13; Ezek. xliii. 24; Lev. xxiv. 7 in the LXX.)

The antique phrase, "covenant of salt," is otherwise important, as bearing on the authenticity of this speech.

<sup>(6)</sup> **The servant of Solomon.**—See 1 Kings xi. 26.

**Is risen up, and hath rebelled.**—*Arose and rebelled.* (See 1 Kings xi. 26—40).

<sup>(7)</sup> **And there are gathered.**—Omit *are*.

**Vain men** (*rēqîm*, Judges ix. 4, xi. 3).—Said of the followers of Abimelech and the freebooter Jephthah. Neither this nor the following phrase, " the children of Belial" (literally, *sons of worthlessness,* i.e., men of low character and estimation) occurs again in the Chronicles. (See Judges xix. 22, xx. 13; 1 Kings xxi. 10, 13, for the latter.)

**Have strengthened.**—Omit *have*.

**Young and tender-hearted.**—Rather, *a youth and soft of heart, faint-hearted.* A similar phrase occurred 1 Chron. xxix. 1. The expression is somewhat inexact, as Rehoboam was forty-one when he ascended the throne (chap. xii. 13). But Abijah is naturally anxious to put the case as strongly as possible against Jeroboam, and to avoid all blame of his own father. In chap. x. Rehoboam appears as haughty and imperious, rather than timid and soft-hearted.

**Could not withstand them.**—*Did not show himself strong* or *firm* (chap. xii. 13).

**Against them.**—*Before them.* (Comp. 1 Chron. xii. 17; a usage of the chronicler's.)

<sup>(8)</sup> **And now ye think.**—Literally, *say,* i.e., in your hearts (chap. ii. 1).

**To withstand the kingdom.**—Literally, *to show yourselves strong before the kingdom,* as in last verse.

**In** (*through*) **the hand of the sons of David.**—The meaning is, the kingdom which Jehovah holds by the instrumentality of the house of David, as His earthly representatives. (Comp. Vulg., "regno Domini quod possidet per filios David." (See 1 Chron. xxix. 23).

**And there are with you golden calves.**—And therefore you believe yourselves assured of Divine aid, in addition to the strength of numbers. But your trust is delusive, for Jeroboam *made* the objects of your fond idolatry (see Isa. xliv. 9—17); and you have superseded the only lawful worship of Jehovah (verse 9).

<sup>(9)</sup> **The priests of the Lord . . . . and the Levites.**—The Hebrew seems to include the Levites among the priests of the Lord.

**Cast out.**—*Banished* (Jer. viii. 3).

**After the manner of the nations of other lands.**—Literally, *like the peoples of the lands;* that is, priests of all classes of the nation, and not members of the divinely chosen tribe of Levi. (See 1 Kings

Abijah's Speech.        II. CHRONICLES, XIII.        Victory of Judah.

may be a priest of *them that are* no gods. <sup>(10)</sup> But as for us, the LORD *is* our God, and we have not forsaken him; and the priests, which minister unto the LORD, *are* the sons of Aaron, and the Levites *wait* upon *their* business: <sup>(11)</sup> *a* and they burn unto the LORD every morning and every evening burnt sacrifices and sweet incense: the *b* shewbread also *set they in order* upon the pure table; and the candlestick of gold with the lamps thereof, to burn every evening: for we keep the charge of the LORD our God; but ye have forsaken him. <sup>(12)</sup> And, behold, God himself *is* with us for *our* captain, and his priests with sounding trumpets to cry alarm against you. O children of Israel, fight ye not against the LORD God of your fathers; for ye shall not prosper.

<sup>(13)</sup> But Jeroboam caused an ambushment to come about behind them: so they were before Judah, and the ambushment *was* behind them. <sup>(14)</sup> And when Judah looked back, behold, the battle *was* before and behind: and they cried unto the LORD, and the priests sounded with the trumpets. <sup>(15)</sup> Then the men of Judah gave a shout: and as the men of Judah shouted, it came to pass, that God smote Jeroboam and all Israel before Abijah and Judah. <sup>(16)</sup> And the children of Israel fled before Judah: and God delivered them into their hand. <sup>(17)</sup> And

*a* ch. 2. 4.

*b* Lev. 24. 6.

---

xii. 31, xiii. 33). The surrounding heathen had no exclusive sacerdotal castes.

**So that whosoever cometh . . .**—Literally, *every one that cometh, that they may fill his hand, with a steer, son of a herd, and seven rams, becometh a priest unto non-gods.* "To fill a man's hand" was the legal phrase for giving him authority and instituting him as a priest. (See Exod. xxviii. 41, xxix. 9; Judg. xvii. 5.) Every one that came with the prescribed sacrifices (see Exod. xxix.) was admissible to the new priesthood. The phrase "a young bullock and seven rams" is not a full account of the sacrifices required by the law of Moses for the consecration of a priest. Perhaps Abijah did not care to be exact; but it is quite possible that Jeroboam had modified the Mosaic rule.

The compound substantive "no-gods" (*lō' 'elōhîm*) is like *lō' 'ēl* and *lō' 'elōah* (Deut. xxxii. 17, 21). The calves are spoken of as mere idols, although there is little doubt that Jeroboam set them up as representations of the God of Israel.

<sup>(10)</sup> **We have not forsaken him.**—Comp. 1 Kings xv. 3, "he walked in all the sins of his father," "his heart was not perfect with the Lord his God." But that passage is by no means incompatible with the present as some have asserted. What Abijah here states is surely true—viz., that Judah had maintained the Levitical priesthood, and its associated worship. And the following words prove this to be his meaning: "and the priests which minister unto the Lord *are the sons of Aaron*; and *the Levites* wait upon their business," (literally, *are in the work*). The work of the service of Jehovah could be duly performed by none but Levites.

<sup>(11)</sup> **Every morning and every evening.**—For the daily sacrifice, see Exod. xxix. 38—42; for the "sweet incense," or *incense of spices*, Exod. xxx. 7.

**The shewbread also . . .**—Literally, *and a pile of bread on the pure table.* The construction is uncertain. The words seem to depend loosely on the verb *they offer* ("they burn") at the beginning of the sentence. But perhaps they should be taken thus: *and a pile of bread is on the pure table, and the golden lampstand and its lamps they have to light every evening.* (See Exod. xxv. 30, 37; Lev. xxiv. 5—7.) The Syriac reads, "and the golden lampstands and their lamps; and the lamp-boy lighteth them every evening." It is noticeable that only one table and one candlestick are mentioned here. (Comp. chap. iv. 7, 8, 19.)

The observance of these details of ritual is called "keeping the charge of Jehovah" (see Lev. viii. 35), and neglect of them is "forsaking" Him. (See on verse 10).

<sup>(12)</sup> **God himself.**—*The* (true) *God.* So in verse 15. Literally, *and behold there are with us at the head the God and his priests, and the trumpets of alarm to sound alarm against you.* (See Num. x. 9, xxxi. 6.) The trumpets were "the divinely appointed pledges that God would remember them in war." The Syriac gives this verse thus: "But ye have forsaken him, and gone after dead gods, and worshipped and bowed down to them, and forsaken the Lord God of your fathers; and also ye shall not prosper in the world." Then there is a lacuna extending to verse 15.

<sup>(13)</sup> **But Jeroboam caused . . .**—*Now Jeroboam had brought the ambush round, in order to attack* (literally, *approach*) *them in the rear* (literally, *from behind them; so they* (Jeroboam and his main body) *were in front of Judah, and the ambush was in their rear.*

**The ambush.**—The troops which Jeroboam had detached for that service.

<sup>(14)</sup> **And when Judah looked back, behold the battle was before and behind.**—Comp. the account of the ambuscade by which Ai was taken (Josh. viii.); and Gibeah (Judg. xx.).

**Judah looked back.**—*Not prepared* (Bertheau) (See Josh. viii. 20).

**Sounded.**—*Were sounding.* Literally, *trumpeting.*

<sup>(15)</sup> **Then the men of Judah gave a shout.**—The same verb (*hāria'*) occurred in verse 12, in the sense of *sounding an alarm* with the "trumpets of alarm" (*t'rū'ah.*) Here our version gives the right sense. Immediately after the priests had blown a blast upon the trumpets, the warriors raised a shout or war-cry. (Comp. Judg. vii. 18—20).

**God smote Jeroboam and all Israel before Abijah and Judah.**—The wild panic which seized the host of Israel, when they heard the shout of their foes, is thus forcibly described. The same phrase is used in Judg. xx. 35, and again by the chronicler (chap. xiv. 12). (Comp. the Vulg., "perterruit Deus Jeroboam et omnem Israel." Syriac, "the Lord routed," &c.)

<sup>(17)</sup> **Slew them with a great slaughter.**—Literally, *Smote in them a great smiting.* Num. xi. 33.

*Abijah pursues Jeroboam.* **II. CHRONICLES, XIV.** *Death of Jeroboam.*

Abijah and his people slew them with a great slaughter: so there fell down slain of Israel five hundred thousand chosen men. (18) Thus the children of Israel were brought under at that time, and the children of Judah prevailed, because they relied upon the LORD God of their fathers. (19) And Abijah pursued after Jeroboam, and took cities from him, Beth-el with the towns thereof, and Jeshanah with the towns thereof, and Ephrain with the towns thereof. (20) Neither did Jeroboam recover strength again in the days of Abijah: and the LORD struck him, and he died. (21) But Abijah waxed mighty, and married fourteen wives, and begat twenty and two sons, and sixteen daughters. (22) And the rest of the acts of Abijah, and his ways, and his sayings, *are* written in the ¹ story of the prophet ᵃ Iddo.

CHAPTER XIV.—(1) So Abijah slept with his fathers, and they buried him in the city of David: and ᵇ Asa his son reigned in his stead. In his days the

B.C. 957.

¹ Or, *commentary.*

ᵃ ch. 12. 15.

ᵇ 1 Kings 15. 8, &c.

---

**Five hundred thousand chosen men.**—Or more than half of Jeroboam's entire army.

It is hardly true to say that "there is nothing in the original to indicate that this slaughter was all on one day." (*Speaker's Commentary*.) On the contrary, it is perfectly evident from the whole narrative that this verse describes the issue of a single great and decisive encounter of the rival hosts.

The result is certainly incredible, if the numbers be pressed; but it seems more reasonable to see in them "only a numerical expression of the belief of contemporaries of the war, that both kings had made a levy of all the fighting men in their respective realms, and that Jeroboam was defeated with such slaughter that he lost more than half his warriors" (*Keil*). The Syriac reads "five thousand."

The number of slain on the other side is not stated. But it is absurd to talk as Reuss does, of Abijah's 400,000 as being "still intact," and then to ask why they did not proceed to reduce the northern kingdom.

(18) **Were brought under.**—*Were humbled, bowed down* (the same word as in chap. xii. 6). (Judg. iii. 30.)

**Prevailed.**—*Was strong.* (Ps. xviii. 13; Gen. xxv. 23.)

**They relied upon the Lord.**—Isa. x. 20. (Authorised Version, "stay upon.")

(19) **Took cities from him.**—The three cities and their districts were only temporarily annexed to Judah. According to 1 Kings xv. 17—21, Baasha, King of Israel, attempted in the next reign to fortify Ramah, which was only about five miles north of Jerusalem. He had probably recovered these towns before doing so (*Bertheau*).

**Bethel.**—*Beitin.* (Gen. xii. 8; Josh. vii. 2.)

**Jeshanah.**—Not mentioned elsewhere in the Old Testament. Probably identical with 'Ισάνας of Josephus (*Ant.* xiv. 15, § 12); site unknown. Syriac, *Shālā*; Arabic, *Sālā*.

**Ephrain.**—So the Heb. margin; Heb. text, *Ephron*; and so LXX., Vulg., Syriac, Arabic. Mount Ephron (Josh. xv. 9) was situated too far to the south to be intended here. Perhaps Ophrah, near Bethel (Judges vi. 11), or the town called Ephraim (John vi. 54)—especially if Ephrain be the right reading—which also was near Bethel, according to Josephus (*Bell. Jud.* iv. 9, § 9), is to be understood. Ophrah and Ephraim *may* be identical.

The Arabic adds: "And Zāghār with the towns thereof."

(20) **Neither did Jeroboam recover strength.**—*And Jeroboam retained strength no longer.* LXX.,

καὶ οὐκ ἔσχεν ἰσχὺν Ἱεροβοὰμ ἔτι. See 1 Chron. xxix. 14 (the same phrase).

**And the Lord struck him, and he died.**—All that is known of Jeroboam's death is that it took place two years after that of Abijah (1 Kings xv. 8, 9). The expressions of the text cannot mean, as Zöckler suggests, "visited him with misfortune till his death." His death is regarded as a judicial visitation (compare the use of the same Hebrew phrase, 1 Sam. xxv. 38). The verse, then, states that during the rest of Abijah's reign Jeroboam remained powerless to injure his neighbour; and that the circumstances of his death were such that men recognised in them "the finger of God." It is not likely that the reference is to the event of verse 15 (Bertheau), nor to the death of his son (1 Kings xiv. 1—8), as Keil supposes.

(21) **But Abijah waxed mighty.**—*And Abijah strengthened himself,* after his life-and-death struggle with Jeroboam. (See on chap. xii. 13.)

**And married fourteen wives, and begat twenty-two sons and sixteen daughters.**—Abijah reigned only three years altogether. He must, therefore, have had most of these wives and children before his accession. (Chap. xi. 21—23 may be said to imply this; see Note on verse 23.) A stop should be placed after the first clause, thus: "And Abijah strengthened himself. And he took him fourteen wives, and begat twenty-two sons," etc. The two facts are merely placed side by side, though a tacit contrast may be suggested between the number of Abijah's offspring, and the speedy extirpation of the house of Jeroboam.

(22) **And his ways and his sayings.**—Or *works.* The same word has just been rendered *acts.* There is an alliteration in the Hebrew, *u-dᵉrākhav u-dᵉbhārav.*

**Story.**—*Midrash.* See margin. For the source here referred to, see Introduction, § 6.

XIV.

(1) **So Abijah slept . . . in his stead.**—Verbatim as 1 Kings xv. 8 (*Abijam*).

**In his days the land was quiet ten years.**—Mentioned here as a result of Abijah's great victory. "The land was quiet," or "had rest" (Judg. iii. 11; v. 31). The phrase is explained in verse 6, "He had no war in those years."

During this period of repose Asa strengthened the defences of his country (verse 5, comp. chap. xv. 19).

The name Asa may perhaps mean "healer;" (comp. the Syriac '*ōsē* "physician," and chap. xvi. 12); or "spices" (Syriac '*ōsō*; comp. chap. xvi. 14).

land was quiet ten years. (2) And Asa did *that which was* good and right in the eyes of the LORD his God: (3) for he took away the altars of the strange *gods*, and the high places, and brake down the ¹images, and cut down the groves: (4) and commanded Judah to seek the LORD God of their fathers, and to do the law and the commandment. (5) Also he took away out of all the cities of Judah the high places and the ²images: and the kingdom was quiet before him.

(6) And he built fenced cities in Judah: for the land had rest, and he had no war in those years; because the LORD had given him rest. (7) Therefore he said unto Judah, Let us build these cities, and make about *them* walls, and towers, gates, and bars, *while* the land *is* yet before us; because we have sought the LORD our God, we have sought *him*, and he hath given us rest on every side. So they built and prospered. (8) And Asa had an army *of men* that bare targets and spears, out of Judah three hundred thousand; and out of Benjamin, that bare shields and drew bows, two hundred and fourscore thousand: all these *were* mighty men of valour.

(9) *ᵃ*And there came out against them

---

¹ Heb., *statues.*
² Heb., *sun images.*
ᵃ ch. 16. 8.

---

REIGN OF ASA (chaps. xiv.—xvi.)

(a) EFFORTS TO ROOT OUT ILLEGITIMATE WORSHIPS, AND TO STRENGTHEN THE SYSTEM OF NATIONAL DEFENCES (chap. xiv. 2—7; comp. 1 Kings xv. 9—15).

(2) **That which was good and right.**—Literally, *The good and the right*, an expression defined in verses 3, 4. It is used of Hezekiah, chap. xxxi. 20. See 1 Kings xv. 11, "And Asa did the right in the eyes of the Lord, like David his father."

**For (and) . . . the altars of the strange gods.** —Literally, *altars of the alien*. Vulg., "altaria peregrini cultus." Comp. the expression, *gods of the alien* (Gen. xxxv, 2, 4). (Comp. 1 Kings xv. 12*b*, *and he took away all the idols that his fathers had made*; a summary statement, which is here expanded into details.) But both here and in chap. xii. 1, 2, the chronicler has omitted to mention the qᵉdēshim (Authorised Version, "Sodomites") (1 Kings xv. 12a)

**And the high places.**—*i.e.*, those dedicated to foreign religions. It is clear from chap. xv. 17, as well as 1 Kings xv. 14, that high places dedicated to the worship of Jehovah were not done away with by Asa.

**Brake down the images.**—*Brake in pieces* (or *shattered*) *the pillars*. They were dedicated to Baal, and symbolised the solar rays, being, no doubt, a species of obelisk. (See Gen. xxviii. 18; Exod. xxxiv. 13; Judg. iii. 7.)

The "high places, images, and groves" of this verse are all mentioned in 1 Kings xiv. 23.

(4) **And commanded Judah to seek.**—'*amar* with infinitive. (Comp. 1 Chron. xxi. 17.) The chronicler's own style is visible in this verse.

**To seek the Lord God of their fathers.**—The same phrase recurs in chap. xv. 12.

**The law and the commandment.**—Exod. xxiv. 12, "That I may give thee the tables of stone, and *the law and the commandment that I have written*" (Deut. vi. 25).

**And the images.**—*Hammanim*. (Comp. the word *hammah*, "sun.") Pillars or statues to the sun-god, standing before or upon the altars of Baal, are intended (see Lev. xxvi. 30; Isa. xvii. 8; 2 Chron. xxxiv. 4.) Comp. the Phenician deity *Baal-hamman*.

**The kingdom was quiet before him.**—Enjoyed peace under his oversight. Compare the use of the word "before," in Num. viii. 22; Ps. lxxii. 5 ("before the moon").

(6) **And he built fenced cities.**—See chap. xi. 5, xii. 4; and for the expression "had given him rest," 2 Sam. vii. 1.

(7) **Therefore.**—*And.*

**These cities.**—The "fenced cities" of last verse. Their names are unknown. Geba and Mizpah were fortified by Asa; but that was after the war with Baasha, which began in the twenty-sixth year of Asa (1 Kings xv. 33); see chap. xvi. 6. A general system of defence, like that of Rehoboam, who fortified as many as fifteen cities, seems to be indicated.

**Walls.**—*A wall.*

**Gates** (*doors*) **and bars.**—1 Sam. xxiii. 7, and chap. viii. 5, *supra*, where "bars" is, as usual, singular, *bariach*. Here it is plural.

**While the land is yet before us.**—Is open to us, free from hostile occupation. The phrase is apparently borrowed from Gen. xiii. 9. (*Is yet*, '*odennū*, masculine pronoun, instead of feminine; probably a clerical error). Omit *while*, and put a stop at *bars*. "The land is still before us, for we have sought the Lord," appears to be the connection of thought.

**So they built and prospered**—*i.e.*, built prosperously, without let or hindrance.

(8) **Targets and spears.**—*Shield* (or *buckler*) *and lance*. The large shield is meant (see chap. ix. 15). The same phrase is used to describe the warriors of Judah. (1 Chron. xii. 24.)

**That bare shields**—*i.e.*, the short or round shield (chap. ix. 16).

**Drew bows.**—(1 Chron. viii. 40, xii. 2.) The Judæans were the *hoplites*, or heavy-armed; the Benjaminites the light-armed, or *peltasts*, as a Greek writer would have said.

**Three hundred thousand . . . two hundred and fourscore thousand.**—A total of 580,000 warriors. (Comp. Abijah's 400,000, chap xiii. 3.) The entire male population capable of bearing arms must be included in these high figures. Of course, such a thing as a standing army of this strength is not to be thought of.

The proportion of Benjamin relatively to Judah appears much too high. It must, however, be remembered that Benjamin was always famous as a tribe of warriors. (See Gen. xlix. 27; 1 Chron. vii. 6—11.)

(b) INVASION OF THE CUSHITE ZERAH, AND HIS SIGNAL OVERTHROW (verses 9—15)—This Section has no Parallel in Kings.

(9) **Against them.**—Against the army described in last verse. Literally, *unto them* (Gen. iv. 8; Judg. xii. 3).

*Asa smites*          II. CHRONICLES, XIV.          *the Ethiopians.*

Zerah the Ethiopian with an host of a thousand thousand, and three hundred chariots; and came unto Mareshah. <sup>(10)</sup> Then Asa went out against him, and they set the battle in array in the valley of Zephathah at Mareshah. <sup>(11)</sup> And Asa cried unto the LORD his God, and said, LORD, *it is* <sup>a</sup>nothing with thee to help, whether with many, or with them that have no power: help us, O LORD our God; for we rest on thee, and in thy name we go against this multitude. O LORD, thou *art* our God; let not <sup>1</sup>man prevail against thee. <sup>(12)</sup> So the LORD smote the Ethiopians before Asa, and before Judah; and the Ethiopians fled. <sup>(13)</sup> And Asa and the people that *were* with him pursued them unto Gerar: and the Ethiopians were overthrown, that they could not recover themselves; for they were <sup>2</sup>destroyed before the LORD, and before his host; and they carried away very much spoil. <sup>(14)</sup> And they smote all the cities round about Gerar; for the fear of the LORD came upon them: and they spoiled all the cities; for there was exceeding much spoil in them. <sup>(15)</sup> They smote also the tents of cattle, and carried away sheep and camels in abundance, and returned to Jerusalem.

*a* 1 Sam. 14. 6.

1 Or, *mortal man.*

2 Heb., *broken.*

---

**Zerah the Ethiopian.**—Heb., *ha-Kûshi.* (See Note on 1 Chron. i. 8 [Cush].) Zerah is identified with Osorchon II., hieroglyphic Uasarken, who succeeded Shishak as king of Egypt. The name of this king is curiously like that of Sargon, the great Assyrian conqueror of the eighth century. (See Note on chap. xii. 2.) The object of the expedition appears to have been to bring Judah again under the yoke of Egypt. Shishak had made Rehoboam tributary (chap. xii. 8), after reducing his fortresses and plundering Jerusalem. But now Asa had restored the defences of his country, and apparently reorganised the fighting material; steps indicating a desire for national independence.

**A thousand thousand.**—This very large and symmetrical number would probably be best represented in English by an indefinite expression, like "myriads." It is otherwise out of all proportion to the three hundred chariots, which last seems a correct datum. Syriac and Arabic say "20,000 chariots."

**Mareshah.**—One of the fortresses of Rehoboam (chap. xi. 8). It lay in the lowland of Judah, about twenty-six miles south-west of Jerusalem.

<sup>(10)</sup> **Then.**—*And.*

**Against him.**—*Before him* (1 Chron. xii. 17, xiv. 8).

**In the valley of Zephathah at Mareshah.**—This valley is not identified. The LXX. reads: ἐν τῇ φάραγγι κατὰ βορρᾶν Μαρησά, "in the ravine north of Mareshah." This would involve a change of one letter in the present Hebrew. [*Çaphônah* "northward," for *Ç'phathah.*] Syriac and Arabic, "in the wady of Mareshah."

<sup>(11)</sup> **Lord, it is nothing to thee . . . have no power.**—Rather, *Lord, there is none beside,* or *like* [literally, *along with*] *thee to help between strong and powerless,* i.e., in an unequal conflict to interpose with help for the weaker side. *Between strong and* [literally, *to*] *powerless.* The same construction occurs Gen. i. 6, "between waters to waters." Others assume *between . . . to,* to mean *whether . . . or,* which would be in accordance with Rabbinic rather than ancient usage. A very plausible view is that of Kamphausen, who proposes to read *la'çôr* for *la'zôr* ("to retain strength" for "to help"), an expression which actually occurs at the end of the verse, and to render the whole: "Lord, it is not for any to retain (strength) with (*i.e.,* to withstand) Thee, whether strong or powerless." (Comp. chap. xiii. 20; 1 Chron. xxix. 14). The Syriac paraphrases thus: "Thou art our Lord, the helper of thy people. When thou shalt deliver a great army into the hands of a few, then all the inhabitants of the world will know that we rightly trust in thee." This is much more like a Targum than a translation. The difficulty of the text is evaded, not explained.

**We rest.**—*Rely* (chap. xiii. 18).

**We go.**—*We are come.*

**This multitude.**—*Hâmôn*; a term used of Jeroboam's army (chap. xiii. 8), and usually denoting an *armed* multitude.

**Let not man prevail.**—Literally, *Let not mortal man retain* (strength) *with thee.*

**With.**—*Against,* as in the phrase "to fight with."

<sup>(12)</sup> **So the Lord smote . . . before Judah.**—(Comp. chap. xiii. 15, 16.) Thenius remarks that the words of 1 Kings xv. 15, about the spoils dedicated by Asa, help to establish the chronicler's accounts of this victory and that of Abijah.

<sup>(13)</sup> **Pursued them unto Gerar.**—(Gen. xx. 1.) *Kirbet-el-Gerar,* in the Wady Gerar, about eight miles S.S.E. of Gaza, on the route to Egypt (LXX. Gedor).

**And the Ethiopians were overthrown, that they could not recover themselves.**—Literally, *And there fell of Kushites until they had no revival,* or *survival* (Ezr. ix. 8, 9). The latter seems preferable, as a vivid hyperbole, like 2 Kings xix. 35, "When men arose in the morning, behold, they were all dead corpses." So Vulg., "usque ad internecionem."

**Destroyed.**—See margin.

**Before his host.**—Or *camp.* Asa's army is the Lord's army.

<sup>(14)</sup> **And they smote all the cities round about Gerar.**—Philistine cities hostile to Judah. Perhaps they had helped Zerah.

**For the fear of the Lord came upon them.**—Or, *A divine panic had fallen upon them* (1 Sam. xi. 7; chap. xvii. 10; comp. also 1 Sam. iv. 7, 8).

**Spoil.**—*Plunder, booty.* Heb. *bizzah,* a late word, occurring Ezek. xxix. 19. The word in the last verse was *shâlâl,* a classical expression.

<sup>(15)</sup> **They smote also the tents of cattle.**—*And cattle tents* (or *encampments*), *also they smote, i.e.,* hordes of nomad Bedawin whom they encountered in the desert about Gerar. (Comp. 1 Chron. iv. 41, "smote their tents.")

**Sheep and camels in abundance.**—*Sheep in abundance, and camels.* The LXX. adds, καὶ τοὺς Ἀλιμαζονεῖς, apparently as the name of a tribe. Syriac and Arabic render, "And the tents of the Arabs."

CHAPTER XV.—⁽¹⁾ And the Spirit of God came upon Azariah the son of Oded: ⁽²⁾ and he went out ¹to meet Asa, and said unto him, Hear ye me, Asa, and all Judah and Benjamin; The LORD is with you, while ye be with him; and if ye seek him, he will be found of you; but if ye forsake him, he will forsake you. ⁽³⁾ Now for a long season Israel *hath been* without the true God, and without a teaching priest, and without law. ⁽⁴⁾ But when they in their trouble did turn unto the LORD God of Israel, and sought him, he was found of them. ⁽⁵⁾ And in those times *there was* no peace to him that went out, nor to him that came in, but great vexations *were* upon all the inhabitants of the countries. ⁽⁶⁾ And nation was ²destroyed of nation, and city of city: for God did vex them with all adversity. ⁽⁷⁾ Be ye strong therefore, and let not your hands be weak: for your work shall be rewarded.

1 Heb., *before Asa.*

2 Heb., *beaten in pieces.*

---

## XV.

### ASA'S REFORMATION OF RELIGION.
### (a) ADDRESS OF THE PROPHET AZARIAH BEN ODED (verses 1—7).

This section also is peculiar to the Chronicle.

⁽¹⁾ **And the Spirit of God.**—Literally, *And Azariah son of Oded, there fell upon him spirit of God* (i.e., a holy inspiration). The prophet is unknown, except from this chapter. The name Oded comprises the same radical letters as Iddo (chap. ix. 29; xii. 15); but whether the same prophet or another be meant, is beyond decision.

⁽²⁾ **And he went out to meet.**—Literally, *before.* (1 Chron. xii. 17; chap. xiv. 9.) Azariah met the king on his return from battle.

**Hear ye me, Asa, and all Judah.**—(Comp. Abijah's speech, chap. xiii. 4: "Hear ye me, Jeroboam, and all Israel!")

**The Lord is with you, while ye be with him.**—Or, *Jehovah was with you* (in the battle), *because ye were with him* (i.e., clung to him for help; see chap. xiv. 11).

**And if ye seek him . . . forsake you.**—This generalises the preceding statement. It is a favourite formula with the chronicler. (See 1 Chron. xxviii. 9; and for the last clause, chaps. xii. 5, xxiv. 20; comp. also Jer. xxix. 13, 14.)

**He will be found.**—Or, *is found.*

**He will forsake.**—Or, *he forsaketh.*

⁽³⁾ **Now for a long season Israel hath been.**—Literally, *And many days to Israel, without true God, and without teaching priest, and without teaching.* This is clearly an illustration of the general truth asserted in last verse. "Many a time hath Israel been without true God," etc. Periods of religious decline, such as those recorded in the Book of Judges, as well as those of later times, especially since the division of the kingdom, are adduced as historical proof of the statement that the Lord was with Israel while they were with him. (Comp. Judg. ii. 11—19, iii. 7—10; also Hos. iii. 4, 5.)

**Without.**—*Lĕlō'*, only here in this sense.

**The true God.**—Jer. x. 9: "Jehovah is true God" (*'elohîm 'emeth*).

**Teaching priest.**—*Kôhĕn môreh.* (See Lev. x. 11; Deut. xvii. 9, xxxiii. 10, xxiv. 8; Ezek. xliv. 23; Jer. xviii. 18; Mal. ii. 6, 7.) The priests instructed the people in the *Torah*, or divine Law (literally, *teaching*).

⁽⁴⁾ **But when they in their trouble did turn.**—Literally, *and he returned in his straits* (Deut. iv. 30) *unto Jehovah, the God of Israel; they sought him, and,* etc. (See Judg. iii. 9, 15, iv. 3, 15, vi. 6, *sqq.*; Pss. cvi. 44, cvii. 6.)

⁽⁵⁾ **And in those times.**—The "many days" of verse 3; the times of national unfaithfulness.

**There was no peace . . . came in.**—(See Judg. v. 6, 11; vi. 11.)

**But great vexations.**—*For great confusions* (*mᵉhûmôth*). (See Deut. xxviii. 20, where *mᵉhûmah,* "confusion" or "discomfiture," is foretold as a punishment of apostasy. Here the meaning seems to be *tumults,* as in Amos iii. 9. "The countries" are the territories or provinces of Israel, as in chap. xxxiv. 33.

⁽⁶⁾ **And nation was destroyed of nation.**—*And they were crushed, nation by nation and city by city.* The verb *khathath* occurs Isa. ii. 4 ("to beat"); but in its intensive passive form only here. Some MSS. have the (intensive) active form, which is found elsewhere. So LXX. and Vulg.: "And nation shall fight against nation." Nation is *gôy,* i.e., a community of kindred, such as a tribe or clan, rather than a merely political aggregate. The allusion is to the old feuds and contentions between rival tribes, e.g., between Ephraim and Gilead (Manasseh) (Judg. xii.), or between Benjamin and the other tribes (Judg. xx.). The verse vividly pourtrays an internecine strife, like that described in Isa. xix. 2: "And I will set the Egyptians against the Egyptians, and they shall fight every one against his brother, and every one against his neighbour; *city against city, kingdom against kingdom;*" or like that depicted by the same prophet (Isa. ix. 18—21): "No man shall spare his brother . . . they shall eat every man the flesh of his own arm [*i.e.,* of his natural ally]: Manasseh, Ephraim; and Ephraim, Manasseh; and they together shall be against Judah."

**Did vex them with all adversity.**—*Had confounded* (or, *discomfited*) *them with every kind of distress.* (Comp. Zech. xiv. 13: "A great confusion from the Lord.")

⁽⁷⁾ **Be ye strong therefore.**—Rather, *But ye, be ye strong.*

**Be weak.**—*Droop,* or *hang down* (Zeph. iii. 16; 2 Sam. iv. 1).

**Your work shall be rewarded.** — Literally, *there is indeed a reward for your work;* words occurring in Jer. xxxi. 16. We have here the moral of the prophet's address. The ruinous results of not "seeking," and "forsaking," Jehovah (verse 2) have been briefly but powerfully sketched from the past history of the nation. The conclusion is, Do not ye fall away like your forefathers; but let your allegiance to Jehovah be decided and sincere.

**Your work.**—Of rooting out idolatry.

(8) And when Asa heard these words, and the prophecy of Oded the prophet, he took courage, and put away the ¹abominable idols out of all the land of Judah and Benjamin, and out of the cities which he had taken from mount Ephraim, and renewed the altar of the LORD, that *was* before the porch of the LORD. (9) And he gathered all Judah and Benjamin, and the strangers with them out of Ephraim and Manasseh, and out of Simeon: for they fell to him out of Israel in abundance, when they saw that the LORD his God *was* with him. (10) So they gathered themselves together at Jerusalem in the third month, in the fifteenth year of the reign of Asa. (11) And they offered unto the LORD ²the same time, of the spoil *which* they had brought, seven hundred oxen and seven thousand sheep. (12) And they entered into a covenant to seek the LORD God of their fathers with all their heart and with all their soul; (13) that whosoever would not seek the LORD God of Israel *a* should be put to death, whether small or great, whether man or woman. (14) And they sware unto the LORD with a loud voice, and with shouting, and with trumpets, and with cornets. (15) And all Judah rejoiced at the oath: for they had sworn with all their heart, and

1 Heb., *abominations.*

2 Heb., *in that day.*

a Deut. 13. 9.

---

(*b*) THE REFORM OF WORSHIP, AND PUBLIC RENEWAL OF THE COVENANT (verses 8—15).

(8) **And the prophecy of Oded the prophet.**—Heb., *And the prophecy Oded the prophet;* without any connection. This is suspicious, and suggests the idea that "Oded the prophet" is a marginal gloss, which has crept into the text; especially as, according to verse 1, not Oded, but Azariah son of Oded, was the author of the prophecy. Possibly there is a lacuna, and the original text ran: " And the prophecy *which Azariah son of* Oded, the prophet, *spake.*" There is no variation in Heb. MSS., and the readings of the versions only show that the difficulty is ancient. (LXX., Vatic., "the prophecy of Adad the prophet;" but in verse 1: "Azarias son of Oded;" Alex., " Azarias son of Adad the prophet;" Syr., " Azariah son of Azur;" Vulg., " Azariah son of Oded the prophet.") *these words and the prophecy, i.e., these words, even* (or, *that is*) *the prophecy.* Epexegetical use of the conjunction.

**He took courage.** — *Hith^chazzaq, strengthened himself* (chap. xii. 13). The same verb as *be strong* (*^chizqû*), verse 7.

**And put away.**—*Removed* (1 Kings xv. 12).

**The abominable idols.**—*Abominations* (*shiq-qûtsim*): one of the many terms of contempt applied to idols (Deut. xxix. 17; 1 Kings xi. 5, 7; Jer. iv. 1).

**The cities which he had taken from mount Ephraim.**—*The hill-country of Ephraim.* In chap. xvii. 2 we read again: "the cities of Ephraim, which Asa had taken." It is generally assumed that in both passages there is a somewhat inaccurate reference to the conquests of Abijah recorded in chap. xiii. 19; for hitherto *Asa* had had no wars with the northern kingdom (chaps. xiv. 1, 6; xv. 19). But Asa may have annexed some of the towns on his northern border without resistance, after his victory over Zerah. (Comp. the voluntary immigration into Judah described in verse 9.) Thenius, who fixes the date of Baasha's attempt *before* the Cushite invasion, says that Asa seems to have assumed the offensive after Baasha's retreat from Ramah.

**And renewed the altar.**—The context seems to imply that this "renewal" consisted in reconsecration, the altar having been defiled by an illegal *cultus.* So the LXX. and Vulg., ἐνεκαίνισε, dedicavit. The word, however, may only mean *repaired, restored.* The altar had now stood sixty years. (Comp. chap. xxiv. 4.)

(9) **The strangers**—*i.e.*, the non-Judæans; members of the northern kingdom. A similar accession to the southern kingdom had taken place under Rehoboam (chap. xi. 16); and another yet is related in the reign of Hezekiah (chap. xxx. 11, 18).

**And out of Simeon.**—This tribe is again mentioned along with Ephraim and Manasseh in chap. xxxiv. 6, although its territory lay "within the inheritance of the children of Judah" (Josh. xix. 1). Perhaps a portion of the tribe had migrated northward (comp. Judg. xviii.), and some of these now settled again in Judah. Gen. xlix. 7 speaks of Simeon as "divided in Jacob, and scattered in Israel."

Another solution is, that although politically one with Judah, the tribe of Simeon was religiously isolated by its illegal worship established at Beersheba, similar to that at Bethel and Dan (Amos iv. 4, v. 5, viii. 14). But this hardly agrees with the next clause: "They fell to him *out of Israel.*"

**They fell to him.**—(1 Chron. xii. 19; 2 Kings vii. 4.)

**When they saw that the Lord.**—They had heard of his great deliverance from Zerah.

**In the fifteenth year of the reign of Asa.**—This seems to indicate that the Cushite invasion took place not long before, perhaps in the spring of the same year (see Note on 1 Chron. xx. 1).

(11) **The same time.**—*On that day;* viz., the day appointed for the festival, in the third month, *i.e.*, Sivan, corresponding to part of May and June.

**Of the spoil which they had brought.**—The spoil of Zerah, the cities round Gerar, and the nomadic tribes (chap. xiv. 13–15).

(12) **And they entered into a (the) covenant.**—Jer. xxxiv. 10. The phrase means that they bound themselves by an oath (verse 14). Comp. Neh. x. 30.

**To seek the Lord . . . with all their heart . . .** —See the same phrase in Deut. iv. 29.

(13) **That.**—*And.*

**Whosoever would not seek the Lord God . . .**—Part of the solemn oath of the king and people; a sanction prescribed by the law of Deut. xiii. 6, *sqq.*, xvii. 2–6.

(14) **With shouting, and with trumpets, and with cornets.**—See on 1 Chron. xv. 28; chap. xxiii. 13. The acclamations of the people, accompanied by the loud blasts upon trumpet and clarion, naturally enhanced the solemnity of the oath.

(15) **All Judah.**—The entire southern kingdom.

*Maachah deposed.* **II. CHRONICLES, XVI.** *Baasha invades Judah.*

sought him with their whole desire; and he was found of them: and the LORD gave them rest round about. <sup>(16)</sup> And also concerning <sup>a</sup>Maachah the mother of Asa the king, he removed her from *being* queen, because she had made an <sup>1</sup>idol in a grove: and Asa cut down her idol, and stamped *it*, and burnt *it* at the brook Kidron. <sup>(17)</sup> But the high places were not taken away out of Israel: nevertheless the heart of Asa was perfect all his days. <sup>(18)</sup> And he brought into the house of God the things that his father had dedicated, and that he himself had dedicated, silver, and gold, and vessels. <sup>(19)</sup> And there was no *more* war unto the five and thirtieth year of the reign of Asa.

CHAPTER XVI.—<sup>(1)</sup> In the six and thirtieth year of the reign of Asa <sup>b</sup>Baasha king of Israel came up against Judah.

B.C. 941.

a 1 Kings 15. 13.

1 Heb., *horror*.

b 1 Kings 15. 17.

---

**With their whole desire.**—Or, *assent*; with perfect willingness. Vulg., "in tota voluntate."

**And he was found of them.**—Or, *was at hand to them*; in accordance with the promise of Azariah the prophet (verse 2).

**The Lord gave them rest.**—Another period of tranquillity, like that mentioned in chap. xiv. 6, 7; and perhaps of equal duration. (See on chap. xvi. 1.)

<sup>(16)</sup> **And also concerning Maachah.**—Verses 16—18 are a duplicate of 1 Kings xv. 13—15, with a few unimportant variations. See the commentary there.

**The mother of Asa the king**—*i.e.*, his grandmother. (See chap. xiii. 2; and 1 Kings xv. 13). Others have supposed that Maachah the mother of Abijah, and Maachah the "mother" of Asa, were different persons, the former being the daughter of Absalom, the latter the daughter of Uriel of Gibeah. There are really no grounds for this. Maachah, the mother of Abijah, enjoyed the rank of queen-mother not only during his short reign of three years, but also during that of her grandson Asa, until deposed by him on account of her idolatry.

**Queen.**—*Gebîrah*, *lady, mistress*; but always used of a queen. Compare the position of Athaliah (chap. xxii. 2).

**An idol.**—*Miphlètseth*; *a thing of fear*; *a horror*; a term only found here and in 1 Kings xv. 13. (Not as Merx suggests, nor *a phallus*, as others think. Comp. the cognate words in Job. ix. 6, xxi. 6; Jer. xlix. 16.)

**In a grove.**—Rather, *for Ashērah* (2 Kings xvii. 16).

**Stamped it.**—*Crushed it.* A detail added by the chronicler. So Moses treated the golden calf (Exod. xxxii. 20); and Josiah the high place at Bethel (2 Kings xxiii. 15).

<sup>(17)</sup> **But the high places were not taken away.** —See on chap. xiv. 3, 5. An explanation of the discrepancy has been suggested there; but a better one perhaps may be thus stated. The former passage relates what the good king had resolved and attempted to effect; the present records his want of success, owing to the obstinate attachment of his people to their old sanctuaries.

A similar explanation applies to the apparent contradiction of chap. xvii. 6 by chap. xx. 33.

**Out of Israel.**—Not in Kings. The southern kingdom is meant.

**The heart of Asa was perfect.**—Kings adds, *with Jehovah*. The meaning is, that though he failed to get rid of the high places, Asa himself was always faithful to the lawful worship of the Temple. (Comp. 1 Chron. xxviii. 9.)

<sup>(18)</sup> **And he brought into the house of God.**— The verse is identical with 1 Kings xv. 15, substituting *God* for *Jehovah*. "The things that his father had dedicated" were, doubtless, taken from the spoils after Abijah's great victory over Jeroboam (chap. xiii. 16—19); and "the things that he himself had dedicated" were a portion of the Cushite booty (chap. xiv. 13—15).

The brief reference contained in that single verse of Kings is thus an evident confirmation of the chronicler's narrative concerning the victories of Abijah and Asa, which he alone records.

<sup>(19)</sup> **And there was no more war unto the five and thirtieth year of the reign of Asa.**— Literally, *and war arose not until*, etc. This statement appears to refer back to verse 15: "And the Lord gave them rest round about;" and so to assign the limit of that period of peace, which ensued after the defeat of Zerah.

In 1 Kings xv. 16 we find a different statement: "And war continued between Asa and Baasha king of Israel all their days," a statement which is repeated in verse 32 of the same chapter.

The chronicler has evidently modified the older text, in order to assign a precise date to the outbreak of active hostilities between the two monarchs. (Both 1 Kings xv. 16 and the present verse 19 begin with the same two Hebrew words, meaning "and war was," but the chronicler inserts a *not*).

The verse of Kings need not imply more than that no amicable relations were ever established between the two sovereigns. They had inherited a state of war, although neither was in a condition to make an open attack upon the other for some years.

**The five and thirtieth year of the reign of Asa.**—This limit does not agree with the data of Kings (see on chap. xvi. 1). Thenius suggests that the letter *l*, denoting 30, got into the text originally, through some transcriber, who inadvertently wrote the *l* with which the next Hebrew word begins twice over. Later on, some other copyist naturally corrected chap. xvi. 1, to agree with this. Assuming thus that the right readings here were originally *the fifth* and *sixth* years of the reign of Asa, Thenius concludes that in chap. xvi. 1 the letter *v* (*i.e.*, 6) has been shortened into *y* (10); and that Baasha's attempt preceded the invasion of Zerah. The false dates probably existed already in the source which the chronicler followed.

XVI.

THE WAR WITH BAASHA—(verses 1—6). Comp. 1 Kings xv. 17—22.

<sup>(1)</sup> **In the six and thirtieth year of the reign of Asa Baasha king of Israel came up.**—According to 1 Kings xv. 33, xvi. 8, Baasha began to reign in the third year of Asa, reigned twenty-four

and built Ramah, to the intent that he might let none go out or come in to Asa king of Judah. ⁽²⁾ Then Asa brought out silver and gold out of the treasures of the house of the LORD and of the king's house, and sent to Ben-hadad king of Syria, that dwelt at ¹Damascus, saying, ⁽³⁾ *There is* a league between me and thee, as *there was* between my father and thy father: behold, I have sent thee silver and gold; go, break thy league with Baasha king of Israel, that he may depart from me. ⁽⁴⁾ And Ben-hadad hearkened unto king Asa, and sent the captains of ²his armies against the cities of Israel; and they smote Ijon, and Dan, and Abel-maim, and all the store cities of Naphtali. ⁽⁵⁾ And it came to pass, when Baasha heard *it*, that he left off building of Ramah, and let his work cease. ⁽⁶⁾ Then Asa the king took all Judah; and they carried away the stones of Ramah, and the timber thereof, wherewith Baasha was building; and he built therewith Geba and Mizpah.

⁽⁷⁾ And at that time Hanani the seer came to Asa king of Judah, and said unto him, Because thou hast relied on the king of Syria, and not relied on the LORD thy God, therefore is the host of the king of Syria escaped out of thine

1 Heb., *Darmesek.*

2 Heb., *which were his.*

---

years, and died in the twenty-sixth year of Asa. These statements are obviously irreconcileable with that of our verse. We must suppose either that the chronicler has accepted a different calculation from that of the Kings—a calculation which he may have found in one of his documents; or that the text here is unsound, and thirty-six has been substituted by an error of transcription for sixteen, or twenty-six; and that in chap. xv. 19 by a similar mistake thirty-five has taken the place of fifteen or twenty-five. Upon the whole, the latter alternative appears preferable; and if we assume twenty-five and twenty-six to be the correct numerals, we get the following chronology for the reign:—First, ten years of peace (chap. xiv. 1), during which Asa strengthened his defences (chap. xiv. 6—8); then the invasion of Zerah, at what precise date is not clear, but at some time between the eleventh and the fifteenth year (chaps. xiv. 9, xv. 10); then the reformation of religion and renewal of the covenant in Asa's fifteenth year (chap. xv. 10); and lastly, another ten years of peace, until the outbreak of the war with Baasha, in the twenty-fifth or twenty-sixth year.

The idea of the ancient commentators, that the phrase "five and thirtieth year of the reign of Asa" might mean "five and thirtieth year of the kingdom of Judah," is absurd. The phrase "*bishnath . . . lᵉmalkûth*" always denotes the year of a king's reign, not of the duration of his kingdom. (See verse 12 *infra*.)

**And built Ramah.**—*Er-Râm*, about five miles north of Jerusalem. Baasha had probably retaken the cities annexed by Abijah. (See on chap. xv. 8.)

**Built** = fortified it. (See 1 Kings xv. 17 for the rest of the verse.)

⁽²⁾ **Then Asa brought out silver and gold.**—This verse is abridged as compared with 1 Kings xv. 18, but the substance of it is the same. The differences are characteristic. In the first clause Kings reads: "And Asa took *all the silver and the gold that were left* in the treasures of the house of the Lord." The chronicler has purposely weakened this statement. He has also omitted the pedigree of Benhahad ("*ben Tabrimmôn ben Hezyôn*"), and written the Aramaizing form *Darmèseq* for *Dammèseq*. (Syriac, *Darmĕsûq*.)

⁽³⁾ **There is a league.**—*Bĕrith*, "covenant." The verse is the same as 1 Kings xv. 19, omitting the word "a present" before "silver and gold," and making two or three other minute verbal changes.

**As.**—*And*.

**Depart.**—*Go up.* See the Notes on Kings.

⁽⁴⁾ **Abel-maim.** — Kings, "Abel-beth-maachah" (comp. 2 Sam. xx. 14, 15, and 2 Kings xv. 29). This city is nowhere else called Abel-maim, which is, perhaps, an early mistake. The Syriac reads *Abel-beth-maachah*.

**And all the store-cities** (*miskĕnôth*, chap. viii. 4).—Literally, *And all the stores* (magazines) *of the cities of Naphtali*. Kings: "And all *Cinneroth, with all the land* of Naphtali." Cinnèroth is mentioned (Josh. xix. 35) as a town of Naphtali, and the Sea of Galilee was called the Sea of Cinneroth (Josh. xii. 3). Probably the fertile district west of the lake was also called Cinneroth, and this was the country which Benhadad's army laid waste. The present reading of Chronicles may be either a mere textual corruption, or a paraphrase of that of Kings. Some critics assume its originality, which is less likely. We prefer to regard it as a paraphrase or explanation.

⁽⁵⁾ **And it came to pass.**—See 1 Kings xv. 21.

**And let his work cease.** — *Vay-yashbĕth 'eth-mĕlakhtô.* Kings: "*vay-yêsheb bĕthirzah*," "and dwelt in Tirzah." The partial similarity of the Heb. is obvious. Kings appears to be correct, and the tautologous reading of the chronicler is to be ascribed to a fault in the writer's MS.

⁽⁶⁾ **Then.**—*And*.

**Asa the king took all Judah.**—1 Kings xv. 22: "And the king Asa called together all Judah; none was exempted." The chronicler has modified an obscure sentence. The rest of the verse coincides with Kings, save that the latter reads "Geba of Benjamin."

**Mizpah.**—Jer. xli. 9, 10, mentions a great cistern which Asa made in Mizpah "for fear of Baasha king of Israel."

HANANI THE SEER REBUKES ASA, AND IS IMPRISONED (verses 7—10).

⁽⁷⁾ **Hanani the seer.**—*Ha-rô'eh*. (See on 1 Sam. ix. 9.) The use of this term seems to point to an ancient source of this narrative which is peculiar to the chronicler. Nothing beyond what is here told is known of Hanani. He was perhaps the father of the prophet Jehu the son of Hanani, who prophesied against Baasha (1 Kings xvi. 1 *sqq.*) and rebuked Jehoshaphat (2 Chron. xix. 2).

**Because thou hast relied on the king of Syria.**—Hanani's words are in perfect accord with the

hand. (8) Were not *a*the Ethiopians and the Lubims ¹a huge host, with very many chariots and horsemen? yet, because thou didst rely on the LORD, he delivered them into thine hand. (9) For the eyes of the LORD run to and fro throughout the whole earth, ²to shew himself strong in the behalf of *them* whose heart *is* perfect toward him. Herein thou hast done foolishly: therefore from henceforth thou shalt have wars. (10) Then Asa was wroth with the seer, and put him in a prison house; for *he was* in a rage with him because of this *thing*. And Asa ³oppressed *some* of the people the same time. (11) And, behold, the acts of Asa, first and last, lo, they *are* written in the book of the kings of Judah and Israel. (12) And Asa in the thirty and ninth year of his reign was diseased in his feet, until his disease *was* exceeding *great*: yet in his disease he sought not to the LORD, but to the physicians.

*a* ch. 14. 9.

1 Heb., *in abundance.*

2 Or, *strongly to hold with them,* &c.

3 Heb., *crushed.*

---

teachings of the greater prophets, a fact which favours their authenticity. (Comp. Isa. xxx. 2, 7, 15 *sqq.*, xxxi. 1, 3; Jer. xvii. 5; Hosea v. 13, vii. 11, viii. 9, xii. 1.)

**Therefore is the host of the king of Syria escaped out of thine hand.**—Asa had doubtless been afraid that Benhadad would co-operate with Baasha his ally in hostilities against Judah, and therefore bribed the Syrian king at the expense of the Temple treasury (verse 3). This politic act secured its object, but from the prophetic point of view such success was no better than loss and failure; for it had deprived Asa of an assured triumph over the combined forces of Israel and Syria. Not only the defeat of Baasha's schemes, but victory over his formidable ally, would have been conceded to faith (comp. 2 Kings xiii. 14—19). The Syriac renders, "Therefore shall the army of Adûm (Aram) fly from thee." Then follows the curious addition: "And they shall go, and become strong, they and the Hindoos [*Hendewoye*], and the kings that are with them, and they shall become armies and chariots and horsemen, a great multitude; and when thou shalt ask of the Lord God, He will deliver them into thy hands." It continues: "Because the eyes of the Lord see in all the earth. And show yourselves strong, and let your heart be devoted to his fear, and understand ye all his wonders, because the Lord your God maketh war for you. And Asa was wroth against the Seer, and put him in the prison, because he told what he saw not, and stirred the heart of the people." So also the Arabic.

(8) **Were not the Ethiopians and the Lubims** (*Kûshim and Lûbim*) **a huge host?**—An instance confirming what was said in verse 7. Cushites and Lybians were banded together in Zerah's great army, just as Syrians and Israelites might have united in assailing Judah, yet the victory had fallen to Asa (chap. xiv. 9—15).

Cushites and Libyans were among the constituents of Shishak's army (chap. xii. 3). Clearly, therefore, Zerah was master of Egypt.

(The Heb. of this and next verse is unmistakably the chronicler's own. Literally it runs: "Did not the Cushites and the Libyans come to an army, to abundance, (*as*) to chariots and to horsemen, to abounding greatly?")

Neither the Libyan contingent nor the horsemen are mentioned in chap. xiv. Apparently the writer is making extracts from fuller sources.

(9) **For the eyes of the Lord.**—Literally, *For Jehovah, his eyes run,* &c. Run to and fro (comp. Job i. 7, ii. 2). In Zech. iv. 10 we find this very phrase: "The eyes of Jehovah, they run to and fro in all the earth." (Comp. also Jer. v. 1.) The Lord is ceaselessly watchful for occasions of helping the faithful. "He that keepeth Israel neither slumbereth nor sleepeth."

**In the behalf of.**—*With, i.e.,* on the side of. The phrase "to shew oneself strong with," *i.e., strongly to support,* occurred in 1 Chron. xi. 10. (For the Heb. construction, which omits the relative, see 1 Chron. xv. 12.) Out of the twenty-seven occurrences of the form *hithʿhazzaq*, "to show oneself strong," fifteen are found in the Chronicle.

**Whose heart is perfect.**—See Notes on 1 Chron. xii. 38, xxvii. 9, xxix. 19; 1 Kings xv. 14; 2 Chron. xv. 17.

**Herein thou hast done foolishly.**—Literally, *Thou hast shown thyself foolish* (2 Sam. xxiv. 10; 1 Chron. xxi. 8) *in regard to this,* scil., conduct in seeking the help of Syria against Israel.

**Therefore from henceforth thou shalt have wars.**—Instead of peace (chap. xiv. 6, xv. 15). Literally, *For* (the proof of thy folly) *from henceforth,* &c. The sense appears to be that the peace secured by Asa's worldly policy would not be permanent; a prediction verified over and over again in the after-history of the kingdom of Judah (see chap. xxviii. 20, 21). The record is silent as to any future wars in which Asa himself was involved, simply because the writer, having already fulfilled his didactic purpose so far as concerns this reign, presently draws its history to a close.

(10) **Then.**—*And.* In a prison house: *in the stocks.* Literally, *House of the stocks* (Jer. xx. 2, xxix. 26). The word *mahpèkheth* literally means "turning," "distortion," and so an instrument of *torture,* by which the body was bent double, hands and feet being passed through holes in a wooden frame. (See Acts xvi. 24.) The Syriac and LXX. have simply "prison;" Vulgate, "nervus," *i.e.,* stocks. (Comp. the similar behaviour of Ahab to the prophet Michaiah, 1 Kings xxii. 26, 27.)

**Because of this thing**="Herein" of verse 9.

**And Asa oppressed.**—*Riççaç* (Job. xx. 19; comp. 1 Sam. xii. 3).

**The same time.**—*At that time.*

**Some of the people.**—Those who sympathised with Hanani. Asa suppressed their murmurs with violence.

CONCLUSION OF THE REIGN (verses 11—14).
Comp. 1 Kings xv. 23, 24.

(11) **The acts of Asa.**—Or, *history.*

**The book of the kings of Judah and Israel.**—See Introduction, and 1 Kings xv. 23. The mention in that verse of his "might" or "prowess," and of "the cities that he built," confirms the account in chap. xiv. concerning his defensive measures and the invasion of Zerah.

(12) **Diseased in his feet.**—1 Kings xv. 23, "only *in the time of his old age* he was diseased in his feet."

(13) And Asa slept with his fathers, and died in the one and fortieth year of his reign. (14) And they buried him in his own sepulchres, which he had ¹made for himself in the city of David, and laid him in the bed which was filled with sweet odours and divers kinds *of spices* prepared by the apothecaries' art: and they made a very great burning for him.

CHAPTER XVII.—(1) And ᵃJehoshaphat his son reigned in his stead, and strengthened himself against Israel.

¹ Heb., *digged.*

ᵃ 1 Kings 15. 24.

² Heb., *gave.*

(2) And he placed forces in all the fenced cities of Judah, and set garrisons in the land of Judah, and in the cities of Ephraim, which Asa his father had taken. (3) And the LORD was with Jehoshaphat, because he walked in the first ways of his father David, and sought not unto Baalim; (4) but sought to the LORD God of his father, and walked in his commandments, and not after the doings of Israel. (5) Therefore the LORD stablished the kingdom in his hand; and all Judah ²brought to Jehoshaphat

---

The nature of the disease is not specified here or in Kings.

**Until his disease was exceeding great.**—*Unto excess was his disease*: *'ad lĕmà'lah,* a clause added by the chronicler (see on 1 Chron. xxii. 5).

**Yet.**—*And also in his disease,* as well as in his war with Baasha.

**He sought not to the Lord.**—Omit *to.*

**But to the physicians.**—The preposition is expressed here (comp. 1 Chron. x. 13, 14; 2 Kings i. 2). Asa, like Ahaziah, neglected to consult Jehovah through his priests, and preferred to trust in the "Healers" of his day, whose art of healing probably consisted in the use of magical appliances, such as amulets, charms, and exorcisms, as we may infer from the analogous practices of Babylon and Assyria. It is not to be supposed that Israel was more enlightened in such matters than the nations to which it owed so large a share of its civilisation, or, indeed, than Christian England of the seventeenth century.

(13) **And died in the one and fortieth year of his reign.**—Not in 1 Kings xv. 24, which continues, with the usual formula, "and was buried with his fathers in the city of David his father, and Jehoshaphat his son reigned in his stead." (See 1 Kings xv. 10, "And forty and one years reigned he in Jerusalem.")

(14) **And they buried him.**—The particulars of this verse are also added by the chronicler.

**In his own sepulchres.**—Not therefore in the ordinary tombs of the Kings. The plural *sepulchres* indicates a family tomb containing many cells.

**Which he had made.**—*Digged,* or hewn out of the rock. (Comp. Job. iii. 14; Isa. xxii. 16.) Like the Pharaohs, Asa, who was a great and powerful sovereign, prepared his own last resting-place.

**Which was filled.**—Literally, *which one had filled.*

**Sweet odours.**—*Bĕsamim,* " spices " (chap. ix. 1, 9).

**Kinds.** Heb., *zĕnim,* an Aramaic word common in the Targums, but in Old Testament Hebrew only found here and in Ps. cxliv. 13.

**Prepared by the apothecaries' art.**—Literally, *Compounded in a compound of work* (art). The participle *mĕruqqah* only occurs here. The word rendered *compound* means an *ointment* or compost of various spices (1 Chron. ix. 30). The full phrase "compound *of the work of the compounder*" occurs Exod. xxx. 25, 35.

**And they made.**—Literally, *And they burned.*

**Very.**—*'Ad lim·ôd.* Only here, a later equivalent of *'ad mĕ'ôd* (Gen. xxvii. 33). The burning of aromatic woods and spices was usual at the obsequies of kings (see chap. xxi. 19; Jer. xxxiv. 5, and Note on 1 Chron.

x. 12). Asa's distinction as a wealthy and powerful monarch, and the high esteem with which his subjects regarded him, are indicated by the extraordinary amount of spices burnt in his honour. There is no ground for supposing that the chronicler blames " the exaggerated splendour and lavish excess with which this custom was observed at the burial of Asa, as if it were the burial of an Egyptian Pharaoh " (*Zöckler*). His account of the splendour of Solomon proves that he delighted to dwell on the glory of the ancient kings of his people.

XVII.

JEHOSHAPHAT (chaps. xvii.—xx.). PROPHETIC MINISTRY OF MICAH THE SON OF IMLAH AND JEHU THE SON OF HANANI.

Jehoshaphat labours to strengthen his realm internally and externally.

This entire chapter is peculiar to the Chronicle.

(1) **And Jehoshaphat . . . in his stead.**—The last words of 1 Kings xv. 24. The name means *Iah judgeth.*

**And strengthened himself against Israel.**—As described in verse 2. *Israel* is here the northern kingdom. These defensive measures were taken in the early part of the reign, and before Jehoshaphat connected himself by marriage with the northern dynasty (chap. xviii. 1).

(2) **And he placed forces.**—Comp. chap. xi. 12.

**The fenced cities.**—*'Arê ha-bĕtsûrôth.* (Comp. chap. xi. 5 *sqq.,* xiv. 6, 7.)

**And set garrisons.**—*Placed military posts* or *prefects* (*nᵉtsibim*). (1 Chron. xi. 16; chap. xi. 11.) Syriac, "appointed rulers."

**The cities of Ephraim . . . had taken.**—See on chap. xv. 8.

(3) **He walked in the first ways.**—The *former* or *earlier ways* of David, as contrasted with his later conduct—a tacit allusion to the adultery with Bathsheba and other sins of David committed in the later years (2 Sam. xi.—xxiv.). A few MSS. and the LXX. omit *David.*

**And sought not unto Baalim.**—*And sought not the Baals* (*dārash lĕ,* a late construction). The Baals were different local aspects of the sun-god. Here the term no doubt includes the illegal worship of Jehovah under the form of a bullock, as instituted by Jeroboam, and practised in the northern kingdom ("the doing of Israel" verse 4). Syriac, "and prayed not to images."

(5) **Therefore.**—*And* (so " also," " so that," in verses 7, 10).

*Princes and Priests*      II. CHRONICLES, XVII.      *sent to Teach in Judah.*

presents; and he had riches and honour in abundance. <sup>(6)</sup> And his heart ¹was lifted up in the ways of the LORD: moreover he took away the high places and groves out of Judah.

<sup>(7)</sup> Also in the third year of his reign he sent to his princes, even to Ben-hail, and to Obadiah, and to Zechariah, and to Nethaneel, and to Michaiah, to teach in the cities of Judah. <sup>(8)</sup> And with them *he sent* Levites, *even* Shemaiah, and Nethaniah, and Zebadiah, and Asahel, and Shemiramoth, and Jehonathan, and Adonijah, and Tobijah, and Tob-adoni-

¹ That is, *was encouraged*.

² Heb., *was*.

jah, Levites; and with them Elishama and Jehoram, priests. <sup>(9)</sup> And they taught in Judah, and *had* the book of the law of the LORD with them, and went about throughout all the cities of Judah, and taught the people.

<sup>(10)</sup> And the fear of the LORD ²fell upon all the kingdoms of the lands that *were* round about Judah, so that they made no war against Jehoshaphat. <sup>(11)</sup> Also *some* of the Philistines brought Jehoshaphat presents, and tribute silver; and the Arabians brought him flocks, seven thousand and seven hundred rams, and

---

The Lord stablished the kingdom in his hand.—Comp. 2 Kings xiv. 5.

**Presents.**—*Minchah*. This word often means tributary offerings, as in verse 11, but here it obviously denotes the voluntary gifts of loyal subjects, usual at the beginning of a reign (1 Sam. x. 28).

**And he had** (or got) **riches and honour in abundance.**—Like David and Solomon (1 Chron. xxix. 28; chap. i. 12).

<sup>(6)</sup> **And his heart was lifted up.**—*Gabhah lēbh*, which usually, like the phrase of Authorised version, has a bad meaning, as in chap. xxvi. 16. The margin is right here: "his courage rose high," or "he grew bold" *in the ways of Jehovah*, *i.e.*, in the path of religious reform. Vulg., "cum sumpsisset cor ejus audaciam propter vias Domini."

**Moreover.**—*And again, further*. Referring to verse 3. Not only did he not seek the Baals, but more than this, he removed the high places, &c. [This is the common explanation. But the sense may rather be: "And he again removed," referring back to Asa's reforms, chap. xiv. 5.]

**Groves.**—*'Ashērim*, "Asherahs." (Chap. xiv. 3).

THE COMMISSIONERS OF PUBLIC INSTRUCTION IN THE LAW.

<sup>(7)</sup> **He sent to his princes, even to Ben-hail ... to Michaiah.**—Rather, *He sent his princes, Ben-hail and Obadiah ... and Michaiah*. (The *le* "to," in the chronicler's idiom, marking the object of the verb.) If, however, Authorised Version were correct, the construction would not be unique, as the *Speaker's Commentary* asserts. (Comp. 2 Kings v. 7, "this man sendeth to me to recover a man," &c.)

**Princes.**—None of the personages mentioned in this and the following verse are otherwise known. The "five princes" were laymen of rank, and were accompanied by nine (eight) Levites and two priests.

**Ben-hail.**—*Son of valour*. A compound proper name, only occurring here, but analogous to Ben-hur, Ben-deker, and Ben-hesed in 1 Kings iv. 8, 9, 10. The LXX. renders "the sons of the mighty." Syriac, "the chiefs of the forces;" apparently reading *bnê ḥail*.)

**Nethaneel.**—Syriac, Mattanael; Arabic, Mattaniah, Michaiah. Syriac and Arabic, Malachiah.

<sup>(8)</sup> **And with them he sent Levites.**—Rather, *And with them were the Levites*. The construction being changed. So LXX. and the Syriac. (Comp. 1 Chron. xvi. 41, 42, xv. 18, for the same mode of enumeration, which is characteristic of the style of the chronicler.)

**Zebadiah.**—Some MSS. and Syriac and Arabic read *Zechariah*.

**Shemiramoth.**—So LXX. and Vulg. (see 1 Chron. xvi. 5, xv. 18). The Heb. text is probably incorrect. Syriac and Arabic read instead *Natûra*.

**Tob-adonijah.**—This curious name occurs only here, and is perhaps a mere mistake arising out of the preceding Adonijah and Tobijah. The Syriac and Arabic omit it.

**Priests.**—*The priests*.

The commission was a mixed one of civil and ecclesiastical persons (comp. 1 Chron. xiii. 1, 2, xxiii. 2, xxiv. 6.)

**And had the book of the law of the Lord.**—*And with them was the book of the law (teaching) of Jehovah*. For the construction, compare 1 Chron. xvi. 42. The writer evidently means the Pentateuch; and if this notice was derived by him from a contemporary source, *e.g.*, the "words of Jehu the son of Hanani," to which he refers as an authority for the reign (chap. xx. 34), it would constitute an important testimony to the existence, if not of the five books, at least of an ancient collection of laws at this early date (circ. 850 B.C.).

**And taught the people.**—*Taught among the people*.

JEHOSHAPHAT BECOMES A POWERFUL SOVEREIGN.

<sup>(10)</sup> **The fear of the Lord.**—*A dread of Jehovah* (*paḥad*), chaps. xiv. 13, xx. 29. (Comp. Exod. xv. 16; 1 Sam. xi. 7; Isa. ii. 10.) This phrase is not peculiar to the chronicler, as Keil and Bertheau assert. "The kingdoms of the lands" is so (chap. xii. 8; 1 Chron. xxix. 30).

**They made no war.**—The reward of Jehoshaphat's piety (1 Chron. xii. 9; Prov. xvi. 7): "When a man's ways please the Lord, he maketh even his enemies to be at peace with him." (Comp. also Gen. xxxv. 5.)

<sup>(11)</sup> **Brought**—*i.e.*, continually. Such is the force of the participle.

**Presents.**—*An offering*, i.e., tribute (*minchah*, verse 5).

**And tribute silver.**—Rather, *and silver, a load*, or *burden*, *i.e.*, a great quantity (*massā'*), chap. xx. 25. As if, "silver *as much as they could carry*"—a natural hyperbole. Not all the five states of the Philistines were subject to Jehoshaphat. (Comp. 2 Sam. viii. 1.)

**The Arabians.**—*'Arbi'im*, here only equivalent to *'Arbiyim* (chap. xxvi. 7), and *'Arbim* (chap. xxi. 16). They are in each case grouped with the Philistines. The nomad Bedâwin conquered by Asa (chap. xiv. 15)

seven thousand and seven hundred he goats. (12) And Jehoshaphat waxed great exceedingly; and he built in Judah ¹castles, and cities of store. (13) And he had much business in the cities of Judah: and the men of war, mighty men of valour, were in Jerusalem.

(14) And these are the numbers of them according to the house of their fathers: Of Judah, the captains of thousands; Adnah the chief, and with him mighty men of valour three hundred thousand. (15) And ²next to him was Jehohanan the captain, and with him two hundred and fourscore thousand. (16) And next him was Amasiah the son of Zichri, who willingly offered himself unto the LORD; and with him two hundred thousand mighty men of valour. (17) And of Benjamin; Eliada a mighty man of valour, and with him armed men with bow and shield two hundred thousand. (18) And next him was Jehozabad, and with him an hundred and fourscore thousand ready prepared for the war. (19) These waited on the king, beside those whom the king put in the fenced cities throughout all Judah.

¹ Or, *palaces*.

² Heb., *at his hand*.

---

appear to be meant here; or else some tribes which recognised the overlordship of Jehoshaphat after his reduction of Edom (chap. xx. 22, *sqq.*).

**Brought him flocks.**—Comp. Mesha of Moab's tribute to Ahab (2 Kings iii. 4).

(12) **And Jehoshaphat waxed great.**—Literally, *And Jehoshaphat was going on and waxing great*, i.e., became greater and greater. (Comp. 1 Chron. xi. 9.)

**Exceedingly.**—'*Ad lĕmà'lah.* This phrase occurs again in chaps. xvi. 12, xxvi. 8, and nowhere else in the Old Testament. (See on 1 Chron. xiv. 2.)

**And he built.**—Like his predecessors—Solomon, Rehoboam, Asa—he displayed his wealth and power in great public works. The records of the Assyrian and Babylonian sovereigns are largely taken up with similar accounts of temple and palace building.

**Castles.**—*Bìranìyôth*, a derivative from *bìrah* (1 Chron. xxix. 1, 19; comp. Syriac here, *birôthô*). It only recurs at chap. xxvii. 4. It is an Aramaic term. (Comp. *bìranyáthâ*, which in the Targums means "palaces.")

**Cities of stores.**—Comp. chaps. viii. 4, xvi. 4; Exod. i. 11.

(13) **Business.**—Rather, *much goods*, or *stores*; literally, *work* (*mĕlākāh*) and then *produce*. The Hebrew word is so used in Exod. xxii. 7, 10 ("His neighbour's goods"). Stores of provisions and war material seem to be intended. (Comp. chap. xi. 11.)

**And the men of war ... were in Jerusalem.** —Rather, *and* (he had) *men of war ... in Jerusalem.*

**In Jerusalem.**—Not the entire army corps whose numbers are given in verses 14—18, but simply their chiefs.

(14) **And these ... their fathers.**—*And this is their muster* (or census), *according to their father-houses* (*clans*), 1 Chron. xxiv. 3. The warriors were marshalled in the army according to clans, so that men of the same stock fought side by side with their kindred. Perhaps in the original document this heading was followed by a much more detailed scheme of names and divisions than that which the text presents.

**Of Judah.**—*To Judah* (belonged) *captains of thousands*, viz., the three enumerated in verses 14—16: Adnah, Jehohanan, and Amasiah. They were the principal officers, or generals, of the entire forces of Judah.

**Adnah the chief**—*To wit, the captain Adnah.* That Adnah was commander-in-chief is implied by his being named first, and his corps being the largest.

(15) **Next to him.**—*At his hand*, i.e., beside him, and subordinate to him. (Comp. 1 Chron. xxv. 2.)

(16) **Amasiah.**—*Iah carrieth* (Isa. xl. 11); different from Amaziah (*Iah is strong*).

**Who willingly offered himself unto the Lord.**—(Judges v. 2, 9.) An allusion to some noble act of self-devotion, which was doubtless more fully recorded in the source from which the chronicler has drawn this brief account. Such allusions, though no longer intelligible, are important as conducing to the proof of the historical value of the narratives in which they occur. LXX., ὁ προθυμούμενος τῷ κυρίῳ: Vulg., *consecratus Domino*.

(17) **Armed men with bow and shield.**—Literally, *drawing bow and shield*: i.e., as the Targum explains, "drawing bow and grasping shields." (Comp. 1 Chron. xii. 2.) LXX., "Archers and peltasts;" Vulg., "Grasping bow and shield." (Comp. also 1 Chron. viii. 40, for the arms of the Benjaminites.)

(18) **Ready prepared for the war.**—*Equipped for service*. (See on 1 Chron. xii. 23, 24; Num. xxxi. 5, xxxii. 29.) The *hoplites* or heavy-armed infantry are probably meant.

(19) **These waited on the king.**—Rather, *these are they that ministered unto the king*, viz., the five generals above named.

**Beside those whom the king put in the fenced cities**—i.e., the commandants of the fortresses of the kingdom (chap. xi. 11, 23). These latter, as well as the generals of the forces, are called the king's "ministers" (*mĕshārĕthīm*)—a word which is not used of service in the field, but implies their presence at court ("in Jerusalem," verse 13, as the royal staff).

According to the above list, the army of Jehoshaphat was organised in five grand divisions, corresponding perhaps to five territorial divisions of the southern kingdom. The totals are the largest assigned to the two tribes anywhere in the Old Testament; viz., Judah 780,000, and Benjamin 380,000; in all, 1,160,000. At David's census Judah had 500,000 warriors (2 Sam. xxiv. 9), and Israel 800,000. Again, in chap. xiv. 8, Asa's army consists of 300,000 men of Judah and 280,000 Benjaminites: clearly such an increase as our text indicates is unaccountable. At the same time, it is equally clear that the present numbers are not fortuitous results of clerical errors, for they follow each other in the order of relative strength: Judah, 300,000, 280,000, 200,000; Benjamin, 200,000, 180,000; and they are evidently not independent of the estimates of chap. xiv. 8 above quoted.

In the absence of adequate data for modifying these certainly startling figures, it is well to bear in mind that we need not understand by them an army which

*Jehoshaphat joins Ahab*  II. CHRONICLES, XVIII.  *to Invade Ramoth-Gilead.*

CHAPTER XVIII.—<sup>(1)</sup> Now Jehoshaphat had riches and honour in abundance, and joined affinity with Ahab. <sup>(2)</sup> *<sup>a</sup>*And <sup>1</sup> after *certain* years he went down to Ahab to Samaria. And Ahab killed sheep and oxen for him in abundance, and for the people that *he had* with him, and persuaded him to go up *with him* to Ramoth-gilead. <sup>(3)</sup> And Ahab king of Israel said unto Jehoshaphat king of Judah, Wilt thou go with me to Ramoth-gilead? And he answered him, I *am* as thou *art*, and my people as thy people; and *we will be* with thee in the war. <sup>(4)</sup> And Jehoshaphat said unto the king of Israel, Enquire, I pray thee, at the word of the LORD to day. <sup>(5)</sup> Therefore the king of Israel gathered together of prophets four hundred men, and said unto them, Shall we go to Ramoth-gilead to battle, or shall I forbear? And they said, Go up; for God will deliver *it* into the king's hand. <sup>(6)</sup> But Jehoshaphat said, *Is there* not here a prophet of the LORD <sup>2</sup>besides, that we might enquire of him? <sup>(7)</sup> And the king of Israel said unto Jehoshaphat, *There is* yet one man, by whom we may enquire of the LORD: but I hate him; for he never prophesied good unto me, but always evil: the same *is* Micaiah the son of Imla. And Jehoshaphat said, Let not the king say so. <sup>(8)</sup> And the

*a* 1 Kings 22. 2.

B.C. 897.

<sup>1</sup> Heb., *at the end of years.*

<sup>2</sup> Heb., *yet, or, more.*

---

ever actually mustered in the field or on parade, but simply an estimate of the total male population liable to be called out for the national defence; although, even upon that understanding, the total appears to be at least three times too great, considering the small extent of the country.

XVIII.

JEHOSHAPHAT MAKES AFFINITY WITH AHAB, AND TAKES PART IN THE SYRIAN WAR AT RAMOTH-GILEAD.

Comp. 1 Kings xxii. 2—35. Only the introduction of the narrative (verses 1, 2) differs from that of Kings—a change necessitated by the fact that the chronicler is writing the history, not of Ahab, but of Jehoshaphat.

<sup>(1)</sup> **Now Jehoshaphat had.**—*And Jehoshaphat got.*

**Riches and honour in abundance.**—Repeated from chap. xvii. 5.

**And joined affinity with Ahab.**—He married his son Jehoram to Athaliah, daughter of Ahab and Jezebel (chap. xxi. 6; 1 Kings xviii. 8). The high degree of prosperity to which the king of Judah had attained is indicated by the fact that so powerful a monarch as Ahab entered into such an intimate connection with him. (The *vav* of the second clause is not adversative, as Zöckler asserts, but rather consecutive.)

<sup>(2)</sup> **And after certain years.**—See margin. 1 Kings xxii. 2 has: "And it came to pass *in the third year*, that Jehoshaphat went down," &c.—a date which is relative to the three years' truce between Syria and Israel mentioned in the preceding verse. From verse 51 of the same chapter we learn that this visit took place in the sixteenth or seventeenth year of the reign of Jehoshaphat. The marriage of Jehoram and Athaliah preceded the visit by eight or nine years. (Syriac and Arabic, "and after two years.")

**And Ahab killed sheep and oxen for him in abundance.**—This royal hospitality is here represented as part of a deliberate plan for obtaining the co-operation of Jehoshaphat in the projected campaign.

**Persuaded him.**—*Incited, pricked him on* (Judges i. 12); especially to evil; 1 Chron. xxi. 1, Deut. xiii. 7. In 1 Kings xxii. 3, Ahab broaches the subject of the expedition to his court.

**To go up . . . to.**—*To make an expedition against* a town or country (Isa. vii. 1, 6; 1 Kings xv. 17). Comp. Isa. viii. 7, 8.

<sup>(3)</sup> **And Ahab king of Israel.**—This verse is essentially the same as 1 Kings xxii. 4. From this point the two narratives practically coincide. (See the Notes on 1 Kings xxii.)

**To Ramoth-gilead**—*i.e.*, Ramoth of, or in, Gilead. Ramoth ("heights"), or Ramath or Ramah ("height"), was a common name in such a hilly country as Palestine. Kings adds, *to the war.*

**And my people . . . in the war**—The symmetry of this part of the verse has been disregarded by the chronicler, in order to make Jehoshaphat express an apparently more definite assent to Ahab's request. (Comp. Kings: "My people as thy people, my horses *as thy horses*" (*kamôni kamôka, kĕ'ammi kĕ'ammeka, kĕsûsai kĕsûseika*). The Syriac reads: "And *my horses* as thy horses; and I will go with thee to the war." Similarly the Arabic: "My horsemen as thy horsemen."

<sup>(4)</sup> **And Jehoshaphat.**—So exactly 1 Kings xxii. 5.

**Enquire . . . at the word.**—*Seek the word.*

<sup>(5)</sup> **Therefore.**—*And.*

**Of prophets.**—Rather, *the prophets.*

**Four hundred.**—Kings, "*About* four hundred." Also *'Adônai* ("the Lord"), instead of *ha'elôhim* ("the [true] God"); and "I go against" for "we go to," where the former is obviously more appropriate.

<sup>(6)</sup> **But**—*And.* So 1 Kings xxii. 7, literally.

<sup>(7)</sup> **He never prophesied good unto me, but always evil.**—Literally, *He is not prophesying to me for good, but all his days for evil.* Kings: "He prophesieth not to me good but evil." The chronicler has aggravated the idea of opposition, by adding "all his days;" *i.e.*, throughout his prophetic career. (Comp. Homer, *Iliad*, i. 106.)

**Micaiah.**—Heb., *Mîkāyĕhû*, which presupposes an older *Mîkāyăhû* ("Who like Iahu?"). *Iahu* is in all probability the oldest form of the Divine Name, *Iah* being an abridgment of it. Syriac and Arabic, "Micah"—the form in verse 14 (Heb.).

**Imla.**—*He is full*, or, *he filleth*; etymologically right.

**Let not the king say so.**—Jehoshaphat hears in the words a presentiment of evil, and deprecates the omen.

<sup>(8)</sup> **Called for one of his officers.**—Literally, *Called to a eunuch.* (See on 1 Chron. xxviii. 1.)

385

*The Words of the Prophets.*    II. CHRONICLES, XVIII.    *Micaiah's Prophecy.*

king of Israel called for one *of his* ¹officers, and said, ²Fetch quickly Micaiah the son of Imla.

⁽⁹⁾ And the king of Israel and Jehoshaphat king of Judah sat either of them on his throne, clothed in *their* robes, and they sat in a ³void place at the entering in of the gate of Samaria; and all the prophets prophesied before them. ⁽¹⁰⁾ And Zedekiah the son of Chenaanah had made him horns of iron, and said, Thus saith the LORD, With these thou shalt push Syria, until ⁴they be consumed. ⁽¹¹⁾ And all the prophets prophesied so, saying, Go up to Ramoth-gilead, and prosper: for the LORD shall deliver *it* into the hand of the king.

⁽¹²⁾ And the messenger that went to call Micaiah spake to him, saying, Behold, the words of the prophets *declare* good to the king ⁵with one assent; let thy word therefore, I pray thee, be like one of their's, and speak thou good.

⁽¹³⁾ And Micaiah said, *As* the LORD liveth, even what my God saith, that will I speak. ⁽¹⁴⁾ And when he was come to the king, the king said unto him, Micaiah, shall we go to Ramoth-gilead to battle, or shall I forbear? And he said, Go ye up, and prosper, and they shall be delivered into your hand. ⁽¹⁵⁾ And the king said to him, How many times shall I adjure thee that thou say nothing but the truth to me in the name of the LORD?

⁽¹⁶⁾ Then he said, I did see all Israel scattered upon the mountains, as sheep that have no shepherd: and the LORD said, These have no master; let them return *therefore* every man to his house in peace. ⁽¹⁷⁾ And the king of Israel said to Jehoshaphat, Did I not tell thee *that* he would not prophesy good unto me, ⁶but evil? ⁽¹⁸⁾ Again he said, Therefore hear the word of the LORD; I saw the LORD sitting upon his throne, and

¹ Or, *eunuchs.*
² Heb., *Hasten.*
³ Or, *floor.*
⁴ Heb., *thou consume them.*
⁵ Heb., *with one mouth.*
⁶ Or, *but for evil?*

---

**Micaiah**—Hebrew text, *Mikâhû*, a contracted form. The Hebrew margin substitutes the usual spelling.

⁽⁹⁾ **And the king of Israel . . . sat either of them on his throne.**—Rather, *Now the king of Israel . . . were sitting each on his throne.*

**Clothed in their robes.**—The pronoun, which is indispensable if this be the meaning, is wanting in the Hebrew. The Syriac has probably preserved the original reading: "Clothed in raiment spotted white and black." (*Vid. infr.*)

**And they sat.**—*Were sitting.* Explanatory addition by chronicler.

**A void place.**—*A threshingfloor.* LXX., *ἐν τῷ εὐρυχώρῳ*, "in the open ground;" Vulg., "in a threshingfloor." The word is probably corrupt, and may have originated out of *bĕruddim*, "spotted," *i.e.*, perhaps *embroidered*; an epithet of *robes.*

**Prophesied.**—*Were prophesying.* "Vaticinabantur," Vulg.

⁽¹⁰⁾ **Push.**—*Butt* (Dan. viii. 4). Figuratively, as here, Deut. xxxiii. 17.

**Until they be consumed.**—*Unto destroying them.*

⁽¹¹⁾ **Prophesied.**—*Nibbĕ'im*, " were prophesying." Vulg., "prophetabant." In verse 9 the synonym *mithnabbe'im* was used, which also signifies "mad, raving " Jer. xxix. 26). The root meaning of this word is probably visible in the Assyrian *nabû*, "to call, proclaim," so that the *nâbî*, or prophet, was the προφήτης or spokesman of God, the herald of heaven to earth. (Comp. the name of the god Nebo, *Nabî'um*, who answers in the Babylonian Pantheon to the Greek Hermes.)

**And prosper**—*i.e.*, *and thou shalt prosper.* So LXX., καὶ εὐοδωθήσῃ. Vulg., "prosperaberis." (Comp. "This do, and live;" and Gen. xx. 7, "he shall pray for thee, *and live thou !* ")

**For.**—*And.*

⁽¹²⁾ **The words of the prophets ... one assent.** —See margin, and comp. Josh. ix. 2, "they assembled . . . to fight against Israel, one mouth "—*i.e.*, with one consent.)

Probably instead of *dibhrê*, " words," we should read *dibbĕrû*, " they said," a far slighter change in Hebrew writing than in English: " Behold the prophets have with one mouth spoken good unto (or, of) the king." So LXX.

**Like one of their's.**—Literally, *like one of them.* Kings, *like the word of one of them.*

⁽¹³⁾ **Even.**—*Nay, but whatsoever my God shall say.*

**My God.**—Kings, *Jehovah.*

⁽¹⁴⁾ **Shall I forbear.**—Kings, *shall we forbear.* (See Note on verse 5.)

**And he said, Go ye up ... and they shall be delivered.**—Kings repeats the words of verse 11, " Go thou up, and prosper thou, and the Lord," &c. The chronicler has substituted a reply, which states quite definitely that *they* (*i.e.*, the Syrians) shall be delivered into the hands of the allied sovereigns. In verse 11 the object of the verb " deliver " was not expressed. This rather reminds us of the Delphic oracle: " If Crœsus pass the Halys, a mighty empire will be overthrown," though the words of Zedekiah in the preceding verse are plain enough.

⁽¹⁵⁾ **And the king said.**—1 Kings xxii. 16 literatim.

**I adjure thee.**—Compare the words of the high priest to Christ (Matt. xxvi. 63).

⁽¹⁶⁾ **Upon the mountains.**—Kings, "*unto the* mountains."

**As sheep.**—*Like the flock*, both of sheep and goats.

⁽¹⁷⁾ **But evil.**—So Kings. Heb., here as margin. (Comp. verse 7.)

⁽¹⁸⁾ **Again.**—*And.*

**Therefore.**—LXX., *not so,* as if the Hebrew were *lô'kēn* instead of *lākēn.* Vulg., excellently, "at ille: idcirco ait audite verbum domini."

**Hear ye.**—Kings, *hear thou.*

**Standing on his right hand.**—Literally, *were standing.* Kings, *And all the host of heaven was standing by him, on his right hand and on his left.* The chronicler has abridged.

*Micaiah Prophesies*     II. CHRONICLES, XVIII.     *and is cast into Prison.*

all the host of heaven standing on his right hand and *on* his left. <sup>(19)</sup> And the LORD said, Who shall entice Ahab king of Israel, that he may go up and fall at Ramoth-gilead? And one spake saying after this manner, and another saying after that manner. <sup>(20)</sup> Then there came out a *ª*spirit, and stood before the LORD, and said, I will entice him. And the LORD said unto him, Wherewith? <sup>(21)</sup> And he said, I will go out, and be a lying spirit in the mouth of all his prophets. And *the* LORD said, Thou shalt entice *him*, and thou shalt also prevail: go out, and do *even* so. <sup>(22)</sup> Now therefore, behold, the LORD hath put a lying spirit in the mouth of these thy prophets, and the LORD hath spoken evil against thee.

<sup>(23)</sup> Then Zedekiah the son of Chenaanah came near, and smote Micaiah upon the cheek, and said, Which way went the Spirit of the LORD from me to speak unto thee? <sup>(24)</sup> And Micaiah said, Behold, thou shalt see on that day when thou shalt go ¹into ²an inner chamber to hide thyself. <sup>(25)</sup> Then the king of Israel said, Take ye Micaiah, and carry him back to Amon the governor of the city, and to Joash the king's son; <sup>(26)</sup> And say, Thus saith the king, Put this *fellow* in the prison, and feed him with bread of affliction and with water of affliction, until I return in peace. <sup>(27)</sup> And Micaiah said, If thou certainly return in peace, *then* hath not the LORD spoken by me. And he said, Hearken, all ye people.

<sup>(28)</sup> So the king of Israel and Jehoshaphat the king of Judah went up to Ramoth-gilead. <sup>(29)</sup> And the king of Israel said unto Jehoshaphat, I will disguise myself, and will go to the battle; but put thou on thy robes. So the king of Israel disguised himself; and they went to the battle. <sup>(30)</sup> Now the king of Syria had commanded the captains of the chariots that *were* with him, saying, Fight ye not with small or

*ª* Job. 1. 6.

¹ Or, *from chamber to chamber.*

² Heb., *a chamber in a chamber.*

---

<sup>(19)</sup> **And one spake, saying.**—Literally, *and one said* (i.e., it was spoken), *this one saying thus, and that one saying thus.* The text is certainly right.

**After this manner.**—*Kākhāh.* Kings, *běkhōh.* Kings has, *and this one said in this wise, and that one was saying in that wise.*

<sup>(20)</sup> **Then there came out a spirit.**—Rather, *And the spirit came forth.* LXX., καὶ ἐξῆλθε τὸ πνεῦμα.

<sup>(21)</sup> **And be.**—*Become* (*wěhāyithi lě*). Kings omits the particle.

**A lying spirit.**—*A spirit of falsehood.* (Comp. Isa. xi. 2, xix. 14; Ezek. xiv. 9: "And the prophet, if he be deceived, and speak a word, it is I, Jehovah, who have deceived that prophet." The verb "deceive" is that which is rendered "entice" here and in verse 19, *pittah.* LXX., ἀπατήσεις. (See also 2 Thess. ii. 11.)

<sup>(22)</sup> **Now therefore.**—*And now.*

**Of these.**—Kings, *of all these.* So some Hebrew MSS., Vulg., Syriac, Arabic, and one MS. of LXX.

<sup>(23)</sup> **Then.**—*And.*

**And smote.**—*Way-yak,* a correction of *way-yakkèh* (Kings), such as the chronicler often makes.

**Which way.**—Literally, *where is the way the spirit of Jehovah passed.* Kings, *where passed the spirit,* &c.

**Unto thee.**—*With thee.*

<sup>(24)</sup> **Thou shalt see.**—*Thou art to see,* or, *destined to see, on that day when thou shalt enter a chamber in a chamber to hide thyself* (*lěhēchābē'*), correctly. Kings, *lěhēchābēh*). Zedekiah's further history is not recorded—an indication, as Ewald justly observes, that the original narrative contained much more than the present extract from it.

<sup>(25)</sup> **Take ye . . . carry him.**—Kings, *Take thou . . . carry thou,* addressed to some single officer.

**Governor.**—*Sar,* "prefect." LXX., ἄρχοντα. Syriac, *shallit.*

**Carry back**—i.e., *convey back.* Literally, *make him return.*

<sup>(26)</sup> **Bread of affliction, and with water of affliction.**—In the Hebrew the second word (*làhats*) is not a genitive but an accusative, "bread with stint," "water with stint." Literally, *squeezing.* Vulg., "panis modicum et aquae pauxillum." Syriac, "bread (enough) to keep life, and water (enough) to keep life." (Comp. Isa. xxx. 20.)

**Until I return.**—A correction of *until I come* (Kings).

<sup>(27)</sup> **And Micaiah said.**—Literally as 1 Kings xxii. 28.

**If thou certainly return.**—"If thou dost return."

**And he said**—i.e., Micaiah said, turning to the crowd of bystanders, and making them witnesses to his prediction.

**Hearken, all ye people.**—Rather, *Hearken ye, O peoples all!* Literally, *all of them.* The book of the prophet Micah opens with these very words (Micah i. 2). Hitzig thinks they were taken from that passage, and Nöldeke, that they "must be and denote an abbreviation of the entire book." (!) Thenius, on the other hand, justly argues that the whole section before us bears indubitable marks of historical truth, and is probably an extract from the history of Jehoshaphat written by Jehu the son of Hanani (2 Chron. xx. 34).

<sup>(29)</sup> **I will disguise myself, and will go.**—Literally, *disguising myself and entering!* A hurried exclamatory mode of speaking.

**They went.**—Kings, *he* (Ahab) *went into the battle.* So some Hebrew MSS., LXX., Syriac, Vulg., Arabic, and Targum.

<sup>(30)</sup> **That were with him.**—Kings adds, "thirty and two," referring to what is related in 1 Kings xx. 16, 24, a matter which the chronicler has not noticed. The Syriac and Arabic supply the number here.

**With small or great.**—So Kings. Our text is literally, *with the small or the great.*

great, save only with the king of Israel. ⁽³¹⁾ And it came to pass, when the captains of the chariots saw Jehoshaphat, that they said, It *is* the king of Israel. Therefore they compassed about him to fight: but Jehoshaphat cried out, and the LORD helped him; and God moved them *to depart* from him. ⁽³²⁾ For it came to pass, that, when the captains of the chariots perceived that it was not the king of Israel, they turned back again ¹from pursuing him. ⁽³³⁾ And a *certain* man drew a bow ²at a venture, and smote the king of Israel ³between the joints of the harness: therefore he said to his chariot man, Turn thine hand, that thou mayest carry me out of the host; for I am ⁴wounded. ⁽³⁴⁾ And the battle increased that day: howbeit the king of Israel stayed *himself* up in *his* chariot against the Syrians until the even: and about the time of the sun going down he died.

CHAPTER XIX.—⁽¹⁾ And Jehoshaphat the king of Judah returned to his house in peace to Jerusalem. ⁽²⁾ And Jehu the son of Hanani the seer went out to meet him, and said to king Jehoshaphat, Shouldest thou help the ungodly, and love them that hate the LORD? therefore *is* wrath upon thee

1 Heb., *from after him.*
2 Heb., *in his simplicity.*
3 Heb., *between the joints and between the breastplate.*
B.C. 896.
4 Heb., *made sick.*

---

**They compassed about him.**—Or, *came round against him.* Kings, wrongly, "*turned aside* against him." In Hebrew the difference turns on half a letter.

**But Jehoshaphat cried out.**—Probably to bring his followers to the rescue. (1 Kings xxii. 32 ends with these words.)

**And the Lord helped him; and God moved** (literally, *incited,* "persuaded," verse 1) **them ... from him.**—*Drove them away from him.* This addition is evidently from the pen of the chronicler himself. It appears that he understood the verb "cried out" in the sense of a cry to God for help, a sense which it often bears, *e.g.*, Ps. xxii. 6.

How God "drove them off" is explained in the next verse. The captains discovered their mistake and retired.

This perfectly natural event is regarded by the chronicler as providential, and rightly so. Hebrew faith "knows nothing of an order of the world which can be separated even in thought from the constant personal activity of Jehovah."

⁽³³⁾ **Drew a bow.**—*With the bow.*

**At a venture.**—See margin, and comp. 2 Sam. xv. 11, where a similar phrase occurs, which Gesenius interprets "without thought of evil design." The LXX. εὐστόχως, "with good aim," is a bad guess. Syriac, "innocently straight before him." But the explanation of Rashi seems best: "without knowing why he chose that particular man to shoot at."

**And smote.**—See on verse 23.

**Between the joints of the harness.**—Or, *breastplate.* So Syriac, "between the division of his mail"; the LXX. has "in the midst of the lungs and breast"; Vulgate, "between the neck and shoulders"; both mere guesses.

**That thou mayst carry** (literally, *bring*) **me out.**—Kings, *and bring me out.*

⁽³⁴⁾ **Increased.**—Literally, *went up, grew.* (Comp. Gen. xl. 10; Amos vii., the growth of grass.)

**Howbeit the king of Israel stayed himself up in his chariot.**—Literally, *and the king of Israel was* (or, *continued*) *holding himself up in the chariot, facing Aram, until the evening.* 1 Kings xxii. 35 reads: *was held up in the chariot, &c., and he died in the evening.* The reading of Chronicles is preferable, the sense being that Ahab bravely bore up against the pain of his wound, in order not to discourage his own side by retiring from the field. The rest of the narrative which tells of the return of the army and the washing of Ahab's chariot at the pool of Samaria (1 Kings xxii. 36—38) is omitted here, because Jehoshaphat was not concerned in it, and perhaps because the chronicler had a true perception of the real climax of this vivid story of the olden time.

XIX.

JEHU THE SON OF HANANI DENOUNCES THE ALLIANCE WITH AHAB.

The whole chapter is original, so far as regards the Book of Kings.

⁽¹⁾ **Jehoshaphat ... returned to his house in peace.**—A contrast with the fate of Ahab is suggested. (Comp. chap. xviii. 27, 34; and *ibid.* 16.)

**In peace.**—In *wholeness, soundness, i.e., unhurt.*

⁽²⁾ **And Jehu the son of Hanani the seer.**—The seer whose father had suffered for his reproof of Asa (chap. xvi. 7—10), and who had himself already witnessed against Baasha, king of Israel (1 Kings xvi. 1—7).

**To meet him.**—*Unto his presence* (1 Chron. xii. 17; chap. xv. 2).

**King.**—*The king.* The prophets never shrank from facing the highest representatives of earthly power (comp. 1 Kings xxi. 20).

**Shouldest thou help.**—Literally, *to help the ungodly.* The infinitive (as in 1 Chron. v. 1, ix. 25), *i.e., oughtest thou to help.*

**The ungodly.**—The emphatic word. (See Pss. cxxxix. 21, 22; cxix. 158: "I beheld the transgressors *with loathing.*")

**Them that hate the Lord.**—*And haters of Jehovah lovest thou?* (The particle *le* prefixed to the word for "haters" is characteristic of the chronicler's style.)

**Therefore is wrath upon thee.**—See the same phrase, 1 Chron. xxvii. 24. In the case of David, the Divine wrath was embodied in pestilence; what form did it take with Jehoshaphat? The following chapters seem to supply the answer. His land suffered invasion and his fleet shipwreck; his posterity was evil, and came to an evil end (chaps. xx., xxi., xxii.). There may be reference also to the failure of the campaign in which Jehoshaphat had engaged, and his inglorious return to his own land.

from before the LORD. <sup>(3)</sup> Nevertheless there are *ᵃgood things found in thee, in that thou hast taken away the groves out of the land, and hast prepared thine<sup>1</sup> heart to seek God.

<sup>(4)</sup> And Jehoshaphat dwelt at Jerusalem: and <sup>1</sup>he went out again through the people from Beer-sheba to mount Ephraim, and brought them back unto the LORD God of their fathers. <sup>(5)</sup> And he set judges in the land throughout all the fenced cities of Judah, city by city.

<sup>(6)</sup> And said to the judges, Take heed what ye do: for ye judge not for man, but for the LORD, who *is* with you ²in the judgment. <sup>(7)</sup> Wherefore now let the fear of the LORD be upon you; take heed and do *it:* for *there is* no iniquity with the LORD our God, nor *ᵇ*respect of persons, nor taking of gifts.

<sup>(8)</sup> Moreover in Jerusalem did Jehoshaphat set of the Levites, and *of* the priests, and of the chief of the fathers of Israel, for the judgment of the LORD, and for

---

*ᵃ* ch. 17. 4, 6

1 Heb., *he returned and went out.*

2 Heb., *in the matter of judgment.*

*ᵇ* Deut. 10. 17; Job 34. 19; Acts 10. 34; Rom. 2. 11; Gal. 2. 6; 1 Pet. 1. 17.

---

<sup>(3)</sup> **Nevertheless.**—Yet the Divine wrath will not pursue thee to destruction, for *there are good things found in thee.* (So chap. xii. 12; comp. also 1 Kings xiv. 13.)

**Thou hast taken away the groves.**—*Thou hast consumed* (or *exterminated*) *the Ashērahs.* (Deut. xiii. 6; 2 Kings xxiii. 24.) So Asa had done (chap. xvii. 4). (*Ashērôth*, as equivalent to *Ashērîm*, recurs in chap. xxxiii. 3 and in Judg. iii. 7 only.)

**And hast prepared.**—Or, *directed.* The contrary was said of Rehoboam (chap. xii. 14.)

FURTHER PROCEEDINGS IN THE REFORM OF JUSTICE AND RELIGION.

<sup>(4)</sup> **And he went out again.**—This refers to the former Visitation or Royal Commission for the instruction of the people in the sacred Law (chap. xvii. 7—9).

**From Beer-sheba,** the southern, to *the hill country of Ephraim,* the northern limit of his dominions.

**He went out.**—Not necessarily in person, but by his accredited representatives.

**Brought them back.**—*Made them return* (chap. xxiv. 19).

**Unto the Lord God of their fathers.**—From the worship of the Baals and the illicit *cultus* of Jehovah. The local worship of the God of Israel "necessarily came into contact with the Canaanite service of Baal, and, apart from the fact that the luxurious festivals of the latter had a natural attraction for the sensuous Semitic nature of the Hebrews, there was a more innocent motive which tended to assimilate the two worships. The offerings and festivals of Jehovah were acts of homage in which the people consecrated to Him the good things of His bestowing. These were no longer the scanty products of pastoral life, but the rich gifts of a land of corn and wine . . . Thus, the religious feasts necessarily assumed a new and more luxurious character, and, rejoicing before Jehovah in the enjoyment of the good things of Canaan, the Israelites naturally imitated the agricultural feasts which the Canaanites celebrated before Baal. It is not, therefore, surprising that we find many indications of a gradual fusion between the two worships; that many of the great Hebrew sanctuaries are demonstrably identical with Canaanite holy places; that the autumn feast, usually known as the Feast of Tabernacles, has a close parallel in the Canaanite Vintage Feast, that Canaanite immorality tainted the worship of Jehovah; and that at length Jehovah Himself, who was addressed by His worshippers by the same general appellation of 'Baal' or 'Lord' which was the ordinary title of the Canaanite nature-god, was hardly distinguished by the masses who worshipped at the local shrines from the local Baalim of their Canaanite neighbours" (Prof. Robertson Smith, *Prophets of Israel,* p. 38).

<sup>(5)</sup> **And he set.**—*Appointed,* or *stationed.*

**The fenced cities.**—As being the chief centres of each district.

**City by city.**—*For every city,* according to the Law, Deut. xvi. 18, "in all thy gates." (Comp. 1 Chron. xxiii. 4; xxvi. 29.) The judges would be Levites, and probably also priests and family chiefs, as in the case of Jerusalem (verse 8).

<sup>(6)</sup> **Ye judge not for man, but for the Lord.**—*'Tis not for man that ye will judge, but for Jehovah,* as His vicegerents, and ministers of His will. (Comp. Rom. xiii. 1—4.)

**Who is with you in the judgment.**—This rightly gives the sense of the brief words: "and with you in word of doom," *i.e.,* Jehovah will be present with you at the time of your giving sentence. (See on chap. xx. 17, and comp. Ps. lxxxii. 1—4: "God standeth in God's Assembly; in the midst of gods (*i.e.,* judges) He judgeth.") The LXX. and Vulgate misunderstand the passage; but the Syriac renders: "Be strong, and judge true judgment, *and the Lord will be with you* for ever." (Comp. also Deut. i. 17: "The decision belongeth to God"; and Exod. xxi. 6.) The name "Jehoshaphat" denotes *Jehovah judgeth.*

<sup>(7)</sup> **Wherefore.**—*And.*

**The fear of the Lord.**—*A dread,* or *awe, of Jehovah.* (See chap. xvii. 10.)

**Take heed and do** (a *hendiadys, i.e.,* act heedfully, deal warily).

**Iniquity**—*i.e.,* want of equity, unfairness, injustice ('*avlah*). To the marginal references add the prohibition, Deut. xvi. 19. They who judge *for Jehovah* (verse 6) are bound to judge *like* Jehovah.

<sup>(8)</sup> **Did . . . set.**—*Appointed some of the Levites.*

**Chief of the fathers.**—*Heads of the clans* or *families.* (Comp. Exod. xviii. 21—26; Deut. i. 15—17, where the judicial functions of the family chiefs are said to have been ordained by Moses.) The 6,000 Levites set apart by David to be writers (*shôtĕrîm*) and judges (1 Chron. xxiii. 4) appear to have been intended to act as their assessors, as being professional experts in the Law. In this measure, it is probable that David merely systematised traditional usage. Jehoshaphat re-organised the administration of justice throughout the country, and established a superior tribunal, or High Court of Appeal, in the capital, such as Deut. xvii. 8—12 prescribes.

**For the judgment of the Lord.**—Comp. verse 11: "For every matter of Jehovah," *i.e.,* for all ecclesiastical as opposed to civil causes. The latter are here called "controversies" (*rîbh, strife, litigation*), and in verse 11, "every matter of the king."

controversies, when they returned to Jerusalem. <sup>(9)</sup> And he charged them, saying, Thus shall ye do in the fear of the LORD, faithfully, and with a perfect heart. <sup>(10)</sup> And what cause soever shall come to you of your brethren that dwell in their cities, between blood and blood, between law and commandment, statutes and judgments, ye shall even warn them that they trespass not against the LORD, and so wrath come upon you, and upon your brethren: this do, and ye shall not trespass. <sup>(11)</sup> And, behold, Amariah the chief priest is over you in all matters of the LORD; and Zebadiah the son of Ishmael, the ruler of the house of Judah, for all the king's matters: also the Levites shall be officers before you. <sup>1</sup> Deal courageously, and the LORD shall be with the good.

<sup>1</sup> Heb., Take courage and do.

CHAPTER XX.—<sup>(1)</sup> It came to pass after this also, that the children of Moab, and the children of Ammon, and with them other beside the Ammonites, came against Jehoshaphat to battle.

**When.**—*And.* There should be a full-stop at "controversies." "And they returned to Jerusalem" refers to the return of the Royal Commission of verse 4. So Syriac and Arabic, which make the clause begin verse 9: "And he returned to Jerusalem, charged them, and said to them."

<sup>(9)</sup> **Thus.**—Viz., as verse 10 explains.

**Them.**—The members of the Superior Court; just as the ordinary judges had been charged (verses 6, 7).

**Perfect heart.**—*i.e.*, integrity. (See chaps. xv. 17, xvi. 9.)

<sup>(10)</sup> **And.**—*To wit.*

**Cause.**—*Ribh*, "controversy" (verse 8).

**Shall come to you.**—*i.e.*, be referred to you as the Supreme Court of Appeal.

**Of.**—*From your brethren*—*i.e.*, not your judicial brethren, but your fellow-countrymen.

**That dwell in their cities.**—In the various country towns, as opposed to the capital.

**Between blood and blood.**—See Deut. xvii. 8. Questions growing out of cases of homicide—*e.g.*, whether a given crime were murder or manslaughter.

**Between law and commandment, statutes and judgments.**—That is, questions about the interpretation and application of the different legal rules and principles. The phrase "commandment, statutes, and judgments," is a sort of summary of the various kinds of law.

**Ye shall even warn them that they trespass not.**—*Then ye shall instruct them, in order that*, &c.

**Warn.**—*Teach* (Exod. xviii. 20) them the true sense and bearing of the law in the particular case.

**Trespass.**—*Incur guilt*; by giving false judgment.

**And so wrath** (verse 2) **... brethren.**—The miscarriage of justice would involve not only the immediate agents, but the whole people, in guilt and its penal consequences.

**This do ... trespass.**—*Thus shall ye do* (verse 9), *that ye may not incur guilt*.

<sup>(11)</sup> **And behold.**—For the form of the sentence, comp. 1 Chron. xxviii. 21.

**Amariah the chief priest.**—Rather, *High Priest* (*ha-rôsh*), the Head (chap. xxiv. 6). Vulg., "sacerdos et pontifex vester." In 1 Chron. vi. 11 Amariah is the fifth from Zadok, the famous High Priest of David and Solomon's time. As Jehoshaphat was the fifth king from David, the name Amariah probably denotes the same person in both places.

**Over you in all matters of the Lord.**—The High Priest was naturally declared the President of the Court in all spiritual cases (see on verse 8).

**Zebadiah the son of Ishmael** (or, *Zachariah the son of Shemaiah*, Syr. and Arab.) "the ruler of the house of Judah," the *nagid*, emir, or tribal prince, was appointed President of the Court in civil causes ("for all the king's matters").

**Also the Levites shall be officers.**—Literally, *And Writers shall the Levites be*; inferior officials of the Court, such as scribes and notaries.

**Before you.**—In your presence, and under your direction (chap. xiv. 5).

**Deal courageously.**—Literally, *be strong and act*. A favourite locution of the chronicler's. (Comp. 1 Chron. xxviii. 10, 20.)

**The Lord shall be.**—Or, *Jehovah be!* a wish or prayer. This too is a characteristic expression of the writer. (Comp. 1 Chron. ix. 20, xv. 2, xx. 17.)

### XX.

INVASION OF THE MOABITES, AMMONITES, AND MAONITES. THEIR MARVELLOUS OVERTHROW— (verses 1—30).

The chronicler only has preserved an historic account of this great deliverance. But certain of the Psalms have been with much probability supposed to commemorate it. The contents of Psalms xlvi.—xlviii. harmonise well with this assumption; and they are referred by their titles to "the sons of Korah," a fact which corresponds with the statement of verse 19 that certain of the Korahite Levites sang praises to Jehovah on occasion of the prophecy of Jahaziel. Further, Jahaziel himself was an *Asaphite* Levite, and it is noteworthy that Ps. lxxxiii., which is a prayer against a hostile confederacy of Edom, Ammon, Moab, and other races, is headed "A Psalm of Asaph." It may have been composed by the prophet whose name is only recorded in this chapter.

<sup>(1)</sup> **It came to pass after this also.**—Rather, *And it came to pass afterwards*, i.e., after the battle of Ramoth-Gilead, and Jehoshaphat's reformation of law and religion.

**And the children of Ammon, and with them other beside the Ammonites.**—This is an attempt to get a reasonable sense out of a corrupted text. What the Heb. says is: *And the sons of Ammon, and with them some of the Ammonites*. So the Vulg., "et filii Ammon et cum eis de Ammonitis." Transpose a single Hebrew letter, and there results the intelligible reading: *And the sons of Ammon, and with them the Maonites* (Heb., *Meʻûnim*. See on 1 Chron. iv. 41, 42.) The Maonites are mentioned again (chap. xxvi. 7)

(2) Then there came some that told Jehoshaphat, saying, There cometh a great multitude against thee from beyond the sea on this side Syria; and, behold, they be in Hazazon-tamar, which is En-gedi. [1 Heb., *his face*.] (3) And Jehoshaphat feared, and set himself to seek the LORD, and proclaimed a fast throughout all Judah. (4) And Judah gathered themselves together, to ask *help* of the LORD: [2 Heb., *thou*.] even out of all the cities of Judah they came to seek the LORD.

(5) And Jehoshaphat stood in the congregation of Judah and Jerusalem, in the house of the LORD, before the new court. (6) And said, O LORD God of our fathers, *art* not thou God in heaven? and rulest *not* thou over all the kingdoms of the heathen? and in thine hand *is there not* power and might, so that none is able to withstand thee? (7) *Art* not thou our God, *who* didst drive out the inhabitants of this land before thy people Israel, and gavest it to the seed of Abraham thy friend for ever? (8) And they dwelt therein, and have built thee

---

in company with Arabs. They appear to have been a tribe, whose chief seat was Maon, on the eastern slopes of the chain of Mount Seir, after which they are called "sons," or "inhabitants of Mount Seir" in verses 10, 22, 23. Accordingly Josephus (*Ant.* ix. 1, § 2) calls them a multitude of Arabs. [The LXX. reads: "And with them some of the *Minaioi*," a name which possibly represents the *me'inim* of the Heb. text of 1 Chron. iv. 41. Syriac, "and with them men of war;" Arabic, "brave men." Perhaps the expression rendered *and with them—we'immahem*—is a relic of an original reading, *and the Maonites*; and the *some of the Ammonites* (*mēhā'ammōnim*) which follows, is merely a gloss on an obscure name by some transcriber].

(2) **Then there came some that told.**—*And they* (*i.e.*, messengers; Vulg., "nuntii") *came and told*.

**Cometh.**—*Is come.*

**The Sea.**—The Dead Sea, east of which lay the territories of Ammon and Moab; while to the south of it, not far from Petra, was Maon.

**On this side Syria.**—Heb., *from Aram*; and so LXX. and Vulg. But *Edom* is probably the true reading—a name often confused with Aram. As the invaders marched round the southern end of the Dead Sea, they were naturally described as coming from Edom. The Syr. and Arab. have: *from the other side of the Red Sea.*

**Hazazon-tamar.**—See Gen. xiv. 7.

**Engedi** (*Ain-jidy*), midway on the western coast of the Dead Sea (see 1 Sam. xxiii. 29), about thirty-six miles from Jerusalem. The Syr. and Arab. have *Jericho* for Hazazon-tamar (? *meadow of palms*). Jericho was also called "city of palms."

(3) **And Jehoshaphat.**—*And he was afraid* (scil., at the news). *And Jehoshaphat set his face*, &c. Literally, *put* his face—a phrase used in Dan. ix. 3 (comp. 2 Kings xii. 18), and implying *resolved, determined*.

**To seek the Lord.**—The Hebrew construction is that of chap. xv. 13 (*le* is here a sign of the accusative).

**Proclaimed a fast.**—An act of national self-humiliation, implying an admission of guilt, and intended to evoke the Divine pity and succour. (Comp. Judg. xx. 26; Joel ii. 12—17; 1 Sam. vii. 6; Ezra viii. 21.)

(4) **To ask.**—Literally, *to seek* (*baqqēsh*, a synonym of *dārash*, verse 2) *from Jehovah*; scil., help, which Authorised Version rightly supplies.

**Even out of all the cities of Judah.**—Emphasising the fact that the gathering in the Temple represented the whole nation. Syriac and Arabic, "and even from the distant cities."

(5) **And Jehoshaphat stood.**—Comp. chap. vi. 12, 13.

**Judah and Jerusalem.**—So verse 27. Jerusalem is thus mentioned side by side with the country, as being by far the most important part of it. (See also the headings of Isa. i., ii.)

**Before the new court.**—This name, "the New Court," only occurs here. It probably designates the "Great" (chap. iv. 9) or outer court of the Temple, in which the people assembled. Jehoshaphat stood facing the people, in front of the entrance to the Court of the Priests. Perhaps the court was called *New*, as having been recently repaired or enlarged. Syr. and Arab., "before the new gate."

(6) **Art not thou God in heaven.**—So Ps. cxv. 2, 3. Jehovah, the Worship of Israel, is no limited local or tribal deity, but *God over all*. (Comp. also the first clause of the Lord's Prayer.)

**And rulest not thou over all the kingdoms?** —Comp. 1 Chron. xxix. 12 (David's prayer), "and Thou reignest (rulest) over all; and in Thine hand is power and might." This and next sentence should be rendered affirmatively, as in that place. (Comp. also Ps. xlvii. 8: "God reigneth over the heathen.")

**So that none is able to withstand thee.**— Vulg., "nec quisquam tibi potest resistere;" LXX., καὶ οὐκ ἔστι πρὸς σὲ ἀντιστῆναι. Literally, *and there is none against thee to stand up*. For this construction, comp. Ps. xciv. 16: "Who will stand up for me *with* (*i.e.*, against) workers of wickedness. (Comp. also Ps. ii. 2; and the last words of Asa's Prayer, chap. xiv. 11.) Syr. and Arab., "and I am standing and praying before thee."

(7) **Art not thou our God?**—*Didst not Thou, our God, drive out*, &c. (Comp. Josh. xxiii. 5, 9; Deut. iv. 38, xi. 23; and for the form of appeal, Isa. li. 9, 10. Comp. also Ps. xlvii. 3, 4.)

**And gavest it to the seed of Abraham.**— According to the Promise, Gen. xiii. 15, 16, xv. 18.

**For ever.**—Gen. xvii. 8, "for an everlasting possession."

**Thy friend.**—Or, *lover*. So Isa. xli. 8, "seed of Abraham, my friend." This title of Abraham is mentioned again by St. James (chap. ii. 23). Hebron, the patriarch's burial-place, is at this day known to the Muslim world as *el-Khalil*, "the Friend."

(8) **And have built thee a sanctuary therein.** — *And built thee therein a sanctuary for thy name.* "A sanctuary for thy name" is a single expression. (Comp. chap. vi, 5, 6, 7, 8, "that my name might be there.") The *name* of Jehovah designates all that He is to Israel; His revealed character.

a sanctuary therein for thy name, saying, <sup>(9)</sup> ᵃ If, *when* evil cometh upon us, *as* the sword, judgment, or pestilence, or famine, we stand before this house, and in thy presence, (for thy name *is* in this house,) and cry unto thee in our affliction, then thou wilt hear and help. <sup>(10)</sup> And now, behold, the children of Ammon and Moab and mount Seir whom thou ᵇ wouldest not let Israel invade, when they came out of the land of Egypt, but they turned from them, and destroyed them not; <sup>(11)</sup> behold, *I say, how* they reward us, to come to cast us out of thy possession, which thou hast given us to inherit. <sup>(12)</sup> O our God, wilt thou not judge them? for we have no might against this great company that cometh against us; neither know we what to do: but our eyes *are* upon thee. <sup>(13)</sup> And all Judah stood before the LORD, with their little ones, their wives, and their children.

<sup>(14)</sup> Then upon Jahaziel the son of Zechariah, the son of Benaiah, the son of Jeiel, the son of Mattaniah, a Levite of the sons of Asaph, came the Spirit of the LORD in the midst of the congregation; <sup>(15)</sup> and he said, Hearken ye, all Judah, and ye inhabitants of Jerusalem, and thou king Jehoshaphat, Thus saith the LORD unto you, Be not afraid nor dismayed by reason of this great multitude; for the battle *is* not your's, but God's. <sup>(16)</sup> To morrow go ye down against them: behold, they come up by the ¹cliff of Ziz; and ye shall find them at the end of the ²brook, before the wilderness

*ᵃ 1 Kings 8. 37; ch. 6. 28.*
*ᵇ Deut. 2. 9.*
*1 Heb., ascent.*
*2 Or, valley.*

---

<sup>(9)</sup> **If when evil cometh upon us.**—A summary of part of Solomon's Prayer of Dedication (chap. vi. 24—30). The reference to this prayer implies a confidence that it had been accepted in heaven, as the sign that followed it indicated (chap. vii. 1—3). Syriac, "*When the sanctuary is amongst us*, there will not come upon us evil, nor sword, nor judgment, &c., and we will come and stand before this house, and before Thee, because Thy name is invoked in this house; and we will come and pray before Thee in this house and thou wilt hearken to the voice of our prayer, and deliver us." The Hebrew seems to say, "If there come upon us evil —sword (judgment), and pestilence and famine—we will stand (*i.e.*, come forward) before this house, and before Thee, for Thy name is in this house, and we will cry unto Thee out of our distress, and Thou shalt (or *that Thou mayest*) hear and save." The word rendered "judgment" (*shĕphōt*) is not used as a noun anywhere else; and, lacking a conjunction, it spoils the symmetry of the sentence. It is probably an ancient gloss. All the versions have it; and the Vulg. renders, "sword of judgment." (Comp. the Syriac in verse 12, *infra*.)

<sup>(10)</sup> **And (the children of) mount Seir.**—The Maonites are here so called apparently, and thus identified as an Edomite people. (See on verse 1.)

**Whom thou wouldest not let Israel invade.** —See the respective prohibitions (Deut. ii. 4, 9, 19.) Comp. also (Num. xx. 14—21) the king of Edom's refusal of a passage through his territory (Judg. xi. 15, *seq*.) These tribes were recognised as the kindred of Israel, as being sons of Esau and sons of Lot. (The Syriac has "mount Gebel," *i.e., Gebāl,* the name of a tribe living in the northern part of mount Seir, Ps. lxxxiii. 8.)

<sup>(11)</sup> **Behold, I say, how they reward us.**— Literally, *and behold they are requiting us by coming,* &c. (Comp. Ps. lxxxiii. 4—9.)

**Cast.**—*Drive out* (Gen. iii. 24).

**Thy possession.**—The Promised Land is so called nowhere else in the Old Testament.

**Thou hast given us to inherit.**—*Made us possess.* (Comp. Judg. xi. 24.)

<sup>(12)</sup> **Wilt thou not judge them?**—*Exercise judgment in them, i.e., upon them* (here only.) LXX., οὐ κρινεῖς ἐν αὐτοῖς.

**This great company.**—*Multitude* (chap. xiv. 11) Syriac, "for there is not in us might to stand before them: bring the sword of Thy judgment against them."

**Neither know we.**—*And for our part we know not what to do.*

**But our eyes are upon thee.**—*For our eyes are towards thee* ('*al*='*el*). We neither know nor deliberate upon a suitable plan of resistance, for our whole thought is centred upon Thee and Thine omnipotence. For the metaphor, comp. Ps. xxv. 15, "Mine eyes are ever toward ('*el*) Jehovah," and Ps. cxxiii. 2, cxli. 8.

<sup>(13)</sup> **Stood.**—*Were standing.*

**Before the Lord**—*i.e.,* praying with their king. (Comp. the apparent reference to this assembly in Ps. xlviii. 9, "We thought upon Thy lovingkindness, O God, in the midst of Thy Temple.")

<sup>(14)</sup> **Then upon.**—Literally, *and Jahaziel . . . there fell upon him the spirit,* &c., as in chap. xv. 1, "The spirit of courage from the Lord." This Levitical musician is not mentioned elsewhere. His pedigree is traced back for five generations to Mattaniah, which should probably be Nethaniah, a "son of Asaph," who was contemporary with David (1 Chron. xxv. 2, 12).

<sup>(15)</sup> **Hearken ye.**—So Isa. xlix. 1, li. 4, &c.

**Be not afraid nor dismayed.**—Isa. li. 7; Deut. i. 21; Chron. xxii. 3; verse 17, *infr.*

**Great multitude**—*i.e.,* "great company" (verse 12).

**The battle is not your's, but God's.**— Comp. David's words to Goliath. "The battle is Jehovah's" (1 Sam. xvii. 47); and the Divine title Jehovah Sabaoth, *i.e.,* Jehovah, the leader of the hosts of Israel. "It was on the battle-field that Jehovah's presence was most clearly realised."—Prof. Robertson Smith. (Comp. also Ps. xlvi. 2, 7, 9.)

<sup>(16)</sup> **Against them.**—Or, *unto them.*

**They come up by the cliff of Ziz.** — *They are about ascending by the ascent of Hazziz.* Vulg., "ascensuri enim sunt per clivum," &c.

**The brook.**—*The wâdy, ravine, or water-course.*

**The wilderness of Jeruel.**—The name is unknown, but comparing verses 2, 16, 20, it appears that the great stretch of waste, now called *el Husâsah,* from a wady on the north side of it, is intended. The "ascent of Hazziz" would be a pass or mountain path,

of Jeruel. <sup>(17)</sup> Ye shall not *need* to fight in this *battle*: set yourselves, stand ye *still*, and see the salvation of the LORD with you, O Judah and Jerusalem: fear not, nor be dismayed; to morrow go out against them: for the LORD *will be* with you. <sup>(18)</sup> And Jehoshaphat bowed his head with *his* face to the ground: and all Judah and the inhabitants of Jerusalem fell before the LORD, worshipping the LORD. <sup>(19)</sup> And the Levites, of the children of the Kohathites, and of the children of the Korhites, stood up to praise the LORD God of Israel with a loud voice on high.

<sup>(20)</sup> And they rose early in the morning, and went forth into the wilderness of Tekoa: and as they went forth, Jehoshaphat stood and said, Hear me, O Judah, and ye inhabitants of Jerusalem; *a* Believe in the LORD your God, so shall ye be established; believe his prophets, so shall ye prosper. <sup>(21)</sup> And when he had consulted with the people, he appointed singers unto the LORD, and[1] that should praise the beauty of holiness, as they went out before the army, and to say, Praise the LORD; for his mercy *endureth* for ever. <sup>(22)</sup> [2]And when they began [3]to sing and to praise, the LORD

*a* Isa. 7. 9.

1 Heb., *praisers.*

2 Heb., *And in the time that they, &c.*

3 Heb., *in singing and praise.*

---

leading up from Engedi to this desert table-land. (With the name Hazziz, comp. Hakkoz. Perhaps Husâsah preserves a trace of it. The LXX. has Ἀσσεῖς. Syriac and Arabic, "the ascent of dawn," omitting "Jeruel.")

<sup>(17)</sup> **Ye shall not need to fight.**—*It is not for you to fight.* (Comp. 1 Chron. v. 1, xv. 2.)

**In this.**—*Herein, in this instance.* (Comp. for the phrase, chap. xix. 2.)

**Set yourselves** (*i.e.*, "withstand," verse 6).—*Station yourselves, take your stand.* Here the next verb, *stand ye still,* seems added as an explanation, and is, perhaps, a marginal gloss. "Fear not: take your stand, and see the salvation of the Lord," was the command of Moses to Israel at the Red Sea, just before the Great Deliverance (Exod. xiv. 13). (Comp. also the words of Ps. xlvi. 8, "Come, behold the works of the Lord, what desolations he hath made in the earth.")

**The Lord with you.**—Some explain the connection thus: "The Lord (who is) with you." *Iahveh 'immâkhèm* may, perhaps, be compared with *'imnânû ēl,* "with us God" (Isa. vii. 14, viii. 8); it will then be a Divine title, suited to the present emergency. But, more probably, the stop should be at *the Lord;* and *with you, O Judah and Jerusalem!* is an elliptic expression, meaning "He is, or will be with you," &c., as in chap. xix. 6. (Comp. the refrain of Ps. xlvi., "The Lord of hosts is with us! The God of Jacob is our refuge.")

<sup>(18)</sup> **Bowed his head.**—The king "bowed, face earthward," and the people prostrated themselves upon their faces, both "to do worship to Jehovah." (Comp. Lev. ix. 24; Josh. v. 14; 1 Chron. xxi. 16; Exod. xxxiv. 8.)

<sup>(19)</sup> **And the Levites.**—The Levites are the first to rise up, in order to break forth into a hymn of thanksgiving.

**Of the children of the Kohathites, and of the children of the Korhites.**—*Sons of the Kohathites* specifies the clan, and *sons of the Korhites* the house of the musicians who rose up on this occasion. The Korhites were the leading division of Kohath (1 Chron. vi. 22). *And* is explanatory; *even, namely some of the sons of Korah.* The "sons of Korah" were a guild of Levitical minstrels of the first rank. (Comp. the headings of many psalms, *e.g.,* xliv.—xlix., connecting them with their authorship.)

**To praise the Lord God of Israel.**—1 Chron. xvi. 14 (*hallel*).

<sup>(20)</sup> **Went forth into the wilderness of Tekoa.**—Part of the wilderness of Jeruel (verse 16). Tekoa (*Thekua*) is about ten miles south of Jerusalem, and commands a view over the table-land of *el Husâsch.*

**Jehoshaphat stood.**—Or, *came forward.* The king probably stood in the gate at Jerusalem.

**Believe in the Lord your God, so shall ye be established.**—An affirmative way of putting the words of Isaiah to Ahaz: "If ye will not believe, surely ye shall not be established" (Isa. vii. 9).

**Believe his prophets.**—*Believe in,* as before, *i.e.,* put confidence in their advice and leading.

**So shall ye prosper.**—*And prosper ye.* (Comp. chap. xviii. 11.)

<sup>(21)</sup> **And when he had consulted with.**—Or, *advised, given counsel to, warned.* (Comp. 2 Kings vi. 8.) Vulg., "deditque consilium populo, et statuit cantores domini."

**And that should praise the beauty of holiness.**—Rather, *and men praising, in holy apparel,* i.e., Levitical vestments (1 Chron. xvi. 29; Ps. xxix. 2).

**And to say.**—*And saying.*

**Praise the Lord.**—*Give thanks unto Jehovah.* The refrain of the singers. (See on 1 Chron. xvi. 34, 41; 2 Chron. v. 13, vii. 3.) The band of Levitical minstrels were to march before the army (*halûç,* the armed host; Josh. vi. 7).

<sup>(22)</sup> **And when they began.**—Literally, *And at the time when they began with shouting and praise.* (Comp. Deut. xvi. 9, *to begin with.*) They had now reached the neighbourhood of the enemy; and their joyful pæan was the signal for a Divine interposition. (Comp. Josh. vi. 16, 20, and Ps. xlvi. 6.)

**The Lord set ambushments.**—*Jehovah placed liers in wait* (Judges ix. 25). (*nâthan* here is equivalent in meaning to *sâm* there).

**Come against.**—*Come into, i.e.,* invade (verse 10).

**They were smitten.**—Right, according to the ordinary usage. (See 1 Chron. xix. 16, 19, "put to the worse.") This statement anticipates what follows. The ancient translators felt a difficulty here, as is evident from their versions. Thus the LXX. has, "The Lord made the sons of Ammon to war upon Moab and Mount Seir, who came out against Judah; and they were routed." The Vulg., "The Lord turned their ambushment against themselves, viz., that of the sons of Ammon and Moab and Mount Seir, who had gone forth to fight against Judah, and they were smitten."

The Syriac (and Arabic) travesty verse 21 and the first clause of verse 22 thus: "And he stood in the middle of the people, and said, Come, let us give thanks unto the Lord, and let us laud the splendour of his holiness, when he goeth out before our hosts, and maketh war for us with our foes; and be saying, Give

set ambushments against the children of Ammon, Moab, and mount Seir, which were come against Judah; and ¹they were smitten. ⁽²³⁾ For the children of Ammon and Moab stood up against the inhabitants of mount Seir, utterly to slay and destroy *them*: and when they had made an end of the inhabitants of Seir, every one helped ²to destroy another. ⁽²⁴⁾ And when Judah came toward the watch tower in the wilderness, they looked unto the multitude, and, behold, they *were* dead bodies fallen to the earth, and ³none escaped. ⁽²⁵⁾ And when Jehoshaphat and his people came to take away the spoil of them, they found among them in abundance both riches with the dead bodies, and precious jewels, which they stripped off for themselves, more than they could carry away: and they were three days in

¹ Or, *they smote one another.*
² Heb. *for the destruction.*
³ Heb., *there was not an escaping.*

thanks unto the Lord, for he is good, and his goodness endureth for ever. The hills began praising, and the mountains began rejoicing." They then continue as in verse 24, omitting "The Lord set ambushments . . . they were smitten."

The self-destruction of the allied hordes was undoubtedly providential, but it need not have been miraculous. How was it brought about? The answer depends on the meaning of the term "liers in wait." Were *angels* meant, as some have thought (Ewald's *böser Geister*), a more appropriate and less ambiguous term would have been employed to express their agency. Nor is it likely that a *Judean* ambuscade is thus obscurely mentioned without any further reference or explanation: indeed it is evident from verses 15, 17, 24, that the part of the Judeans was that of mere spectators of an accomplished fact. Nor, finally, must we suppose that "the waylaying was done by a section of the confederates themselves, probably certain of the Maonites."

The truth appears to be that some portion of the unwieldy and straggling host was suddenly attacked by a lurking band of Bedawi freebooters. In the providence of God the partial confusion which thus originated speedily became a universal panic. The Ammonites and Moabites instantly suspected their less civilised allies, the Maonites, of treachery, and fell upon them in a frenzy of revenge; after which, maddened by slaughter and mutual suspicion, and the memory of ancient feuds, they turned their reeking swords against each other, and the strife only ended with the self-annihilation of the allies. The occurrence is thus to some extent parallel with the self-destruction of the Midianite hordes, when thrown into confusion by the stratagem of Gideon (Judges vii. 22).

The marvellous result, marvellously predicted, was brought to pass by a perfectly natural sequence of events, just as was Elisha's prophecy of plenty to famine-stricken Samaria, though at the time when it was uttered fulfilment seemed impossible, unless the Lord were to "make windows in heaven," and pour down supplies from thence by a visible miracle. In neither case was the course of events foreseen by the prophet, but only their issue. (See 2 Kings vii.)

⁽²³⁾ **Stood up against.**—'*Amad 'al*, a late usage. (So 1 Chron. xxi. 1.)

**Utterly to slay.**—*To exterminate* (*haᶜharim*), *devote to destruction.*

**Made an end of.**—*Finished with.* (See on verse 22, "begin with," and compare Gen. xliv. 12.)

**Every one helped . . . another.**—Literally, *they helped, each against* (or, *in the case of*) *his fellow, for destruction* (*mashᶜḥîth*, chap. xxii. 4; Ezek. v. 16).

⁽²⁴⁾ **And when Judah came.**—*Now Judah had come*; by the time the slaughter was complete.

**Toward the watch tower.**—*The look-out of the desert.* A height overlooking the wilderness of Jeruel (verse 16). The word *mizpeh* means *watch-tower* in Isa. xxi. 8.

**They looked.**—*And they looked.*

**Behold, they were dead bodies.**—Comp. 2 Kings xix. 35.

**None escaped.**—No survivors were anywhere visible. Vulg., "Porro Juda cum venisset ad speculam quae respicit solitudinem vidit procul . . . nec superesse quemquam qui necem potuisset evadere."

⁽²⁵⁾ **When.**—Omit.

**They found.**—*And found.*

**Among them in abundance both riches.**—Instead of *bāhèm*, "among them," the LXX. reads *bĕhēmāh*, "cattle," which seems preferable. "And found cattle in abundance and substance" (*rĕkûsh*, movable goods of all sorts, including flocks and herds; Gen. xii. 5).

**With the dead bodies.**—*And corpses*, which they stripped of their ornaments and clothing. But *bĕgādim*, "clothes," not *pĕgārim*, "corpses," should be read with some MSS., and apparently the Vulg., "inter cadavera . . . vestes quoque." The Syriac has, "and they found among them a very great spoil and property, and bridles, and horses, and vessels of desire;" the Arabic, "and he found an immense booty, and herds and splendid garments." The LXX. has σκῦλα, "spoils."

**Precious jewels.**—Literally, *vessels of desirable things, i.e.,* costly articles; a phrase only met with here: LXX., well, σκεύη ἐπιθυμητά.

**Which they stripped off for themselves.**—Or, *and they spoiled them, i.e.,* the enemy. (Comp. Exod. iii. 22; LXX., ἐσκύλευσαν ἐν αὐτοῖς.)

**More than they could carry away.**—Literally, *until there was no loading or carrying.*

**Gathering**—*i.e.*, taking away (*bōzĕzim*, "plundering"). Comp. Judges viii. 24—26 (the spoils of Midian). The amount of the spoil is explained by the circumstance that the invaders had intended to effect a permanent settlement in Judah, and so brought all their goods with them (verse 11). (Comp. Ps. lxxxiii. 12.) The invasion was thus similar in character to the migrations of the barbarian hordes, which broke repeatedly over the declining Roman empire, though of course it was on a much smaller scale. Its repulse, however, has proved not less momentous in the history of mankind, than that of the Persians at Marathon, or of the Saracens at Roncesvalles. The greatness of the overthrow may be inferred from the fact that the prophet Joel makes it a type of the coming judgment of Israel's enemies in the "Valley of Jehoshaphat"—a prophetic designation which alludes at once to the catastrophe recorded here, and to the truth that "Jehovah is judge" of all the earth (Joel iii. 2, 12, 14).

gathering of the spoil, it was so much. ⁽²⁶⁾ And on the fourth day they assembled themselves in the valley of ¹ Berachah; for there they blessed the LORD: therefore the name of the same place was called, The valley of Berachah, unto this day.

⁽²⁷⁾ Then they returned, every man of Judah and Jerusalem, and Jehoshaphat in the ² forefront of them, to go again to Jerusalem with joy; for the LORD had made them to rejoice over their enemies. ⁽²⁸⁾ And they came to Jerusalem with psalteries and harps and trumpets unto the house of the LORD. ⁽²⁹⁾ And the fear of God was on all the kingdoms of *those* countries, when they had heard that the LORD fought against the enemies of Israel. ⁽³⁰⁾ So the realm of Jehoshaphat was quiet: for his God gave him rest round about.

⁽³¹⁾ ᵃ And Jehoshaphat reigned over Judah: *he was* thirty and five years old when he began to reign, and he reigned twenty and five years in Jerusalem. And his mother's name *was* Azubah the daughter of Shilhi. ⁽³²⁾ And he walked in the way of Asa his father, and departed not from it, doing *that which was* right in the sight of the LORD. ⁽³³⁾ Howbeit the high places were not taken away: for as yet the people had not prepared their hearts unto the God of their fathers.

⁽³⁴⁾ Now the rest of the acts of Jehoshaphat, first and last, behold, they are written in the ³ book of Jehu the son of Hanani, ᵇ who ⁴ is mentioned in the book of the kings of Israel.

⁽³⁵⁾ And after this did Jehoshaphat king of Judah join himself with Ahaziah

1 That is, *Blessing*.
2 Heb., *head*.
a 1 Kings 22, 41, &c.
3 Heb., *words*.
b 1 Kings 16. 1.
4 Heb., *was made to ascend*.

---

(26) **Valley of Berachah**—*i.e., blessing*. The place is still called *Wady Beraikut*, a wide, open valley west of Tekoa, near the road from Hebron to Jerusalem. St. Jerome speaks of a *Caphar Barucha*, "village of blessing," in the same neighbourhood.

**For there . . . unto this day.**—A notice after the manner of the ancient historians (Gen. xi. 9, xxviii. 19; Exod. xvii. 7; 2 Sam. v. 20).

(27) **Then.**—*And*.

**Every man.**—*All the men* (collective).

**In the forefront of them.**—*At their head*. LXX., ἡγούμενος αὐτῶν.

**To go again . . . with joy.**—They returned, as they came, in festal procession.

**The Lord had made them to rejoice.**—See the same phrase, Ezra vi. 22; Neh. xii. 43. (Comp. Ps. xxx. 2.) LXX., well, ἐν εὐφροσύνῃ μεγάλῃ ὅτι εὔφραινεν αὐτοὺς κύριος ἀπὸ τῶν ἐχθρῶν αὐτῶν.

(28) **With psalteries.**—So Vulg. Rather, *with harps, guitars, and clarions*. (Comp. Ps. xlvii. 5, 6, which may be supposed to commemorate this procession to the Temple.)

(29) **And the fear of God was.**—*And a divine dread fell upon all the kingdoms of the countries* (scil.) around Judah. (See chap. xvii. 10, and Ps. xlviii. 7, "Fear took hold upon them there, and pain as of a woman in travail.")

**The Lord fought.**—Josh. x. 14, 42; Ps. xlvi. 6. That Jehovah had fought for His people was evident from the catastrophe which had befallen their enemies. The warfare of the Divine Being was seen not *apart from*, but *in* a course of events, which, however natural, was almost as marvellous as a visible intervention of angelic hosts.

(30) **So the realm of Jehoshaphat.**—The same is said of Asa's kingdom (chaps. xiv. 5, 6, xv. 15). (Comp. the similar notices in Judges of the rest which followed upon the overthrow of a national enemy, *e.g.*, Judg. iii. 30.)

CONCLUDING NOTICES. END OF THE REIGN (verse 31—chap. xxi. 1).

Comp. 1 Kings xxii. 41—50. A brief section, which constitutes the whole account of the reign of Jehoshaphat in the older narrative.

(31) **And Jehoshaphat reigned over Judah.**—Kings adds: "In the fourth year of Ahab king of Israel." With this omission, our verse coincides with 1 Kings xxii. 41, 42.

(32) **And he walked in the way.**—Kings: "*All* the way."

**From it.**—Here the pronoun is fem., in Kings masc., as in chap. xvii. 3 *supra*.

**Doing.**—*So as to do*.

(33) **For . . . hearts.**—*And the people had not yet directed their heart*. This language is the chronicler's own (see chaps. xii. 14, xix. 3), and is substituted for the statement, "The people were still wont to sacrifice and burn incense on the high places." (Kings). They had not yet accepted the principle of *the one Temple*.

(33) **Howbeit the high places were not taken away.**—This is no contradiction of chap. xvii. 6, "And further (or again), he took away the high places." There the holy places of heathenism, here those of the illegal worship of Jehovah, appear to be meant.

(34) **Now the rest of the acts.**—1 Kings xxii. 45: "Now the rest of the acts of Jehoshaphat, and his might that he shewed, and how he warred, are they not written in the book of the chronicles of the kings of Judah?" The expression *how he warred* hints at his victory over the three allies. "As to the historical foundation of this victory there can be no doubt, after what has been noted by Hitzig on Joel, *Einleit.* u. 4, 2; and by Ewald, *Gesch. Isr.* iii. 510, *ff.*" (*Thenius*).

**In the book** (*story*).—Literally, *words*.

**Who is mentioned.**—*Which is inscribed* (*hŏ·alāh*, see 1 Kings ix. 21; chap. viii. 8), or *entered, in the book*, &c. So the Syriac, "which is written in the book of the kings of Israel." "The words of Jehu the son of Hanani" is the title of a prophetic monograph here referred to as incorporated in the "Book of the Kings of Israel."

(35) **And after this.**—The chronicler has omitted the notice that "Jehoshaphat made peace with the king of Israel" (1 Kings xxii. 44), and now he omits two other short verses of the parallel account, viz., verses 46, 47: "And the remnant of the sodomites,

king of Israel, who did very wickedly: (36) and he joined himself with him to make ships to go to Tarshish: and they made the ships in Ezion-gaber. (37) Then Eliezer the son of Dodavah of Mareshah prophesied against Jehoshaphat, saying, Because thou hast joined thyself with Ahaziah, the LORD hath broken thy works. And the ships were broken, that they were not able to go to Tarshish.

CHAPTER XXI.—(1) Now *a* Jehosha-phat slept with his fathers, and was buried with his fathers in the city of David. And Jehoram his son reigned in his stead. (2) And he had brethren the sons of Jehoshaphat, Azariah, and Jehiel, and Zechariah, and Azariah, and Michael, and Shephatiah: all these were the sons of Jehoshaphat king of Israel. (3) And their father gave them great gifts of silver, and of gold, and of precious things, with fenced cities in Judah: but the kingdom gave he to Jehoram; because he was the firstborn.

B.C. 889.

*a* 1 Kings 22. 50.

B.C. 892.

---

which had remained in the days of his father Asa, he consumed out of the land. There was then no king in Edom: a deputy was king." The former omission is perfectly natural, as the *Qĕdēshīm* were not mentioned in Asa's reign (comp. 1 Kings xv. 12); and the latter is probably due to the fact that it was the religious aspect, and not the political antecedents, of Jehoshaphat's conduct that most interested the chronicler. Hence also the didactic tone of the following verses as compared with 1 Kings xxi. 48, 49. The expression, "after this," can only mean after the overthrow of the three nations (verses 1—30). As Ahaziah began to reign in the seventeenth year of Jehoshaphat, and reigned two years (1 Kings xxii. 51), the league between them was formed in the seventeenth or eighteenth year of the king of Judah.

**Join himself** (*'eth͡chabbar*).—An Aramaism (here only). This verse is peculiar to the chronicle.

**Who did very wickedly.**—*He* (viz., Ahaziah, the pronoun is emphatic) did very wickedly. The implied thought is: And, therefore, Jehoshaphat's alliance was wrong. (Comp. chap. xix. 2.)

(36) **And he joined himself with him.**—Literally, *and he joined him with himself*, an expression only occurring here.

**To make ships to go to Tarshish.**—In 1 Kings xxii. 48, 49, we read: "Jehoshaphat made *ships* (*i.e.*, a fleet) *of Tarshish, to go to Ophir for gold*; and it went not; for the ships were broken (*i.e.*, wrecked) in Ezion-geber. Then said Ahaziah the son of Ahab unto Jehoshaphat, Let my servants go with thy servants in the ships; and Jehoshaphat consented not." There is no mention of a previous alliance and partnership in the ship-building with Ahaziah. Moreover, the expression of our text, "ships to go to Tarshish," appears to be an erroneous paraphrase of "ships of Tarshish," or "*Tarshish-men*," as we might say; a phrase which really means, vessels built for long sea-voyages. According to Kings, the ships were built "to go to Ophir for gold;" in other words, to renew Solomon's traffic with India from the port on the Red Sea.

**And they made the ships in Ezion-gaber.**—The Edomite port at the head of the Gulf of Akaba. If Tarshish means the Phœnician Tartessus in Spain, the fleet could only go thither by doubling the Cape, or crossing the Isthmus of Suez. Therefore some have supposed another Tarshish somewhere in the Persian Gulf or on the north-west coast of India. (See on chap. ix. 21.)

(37) **Then.**—*And*.

**Eliezer the son of Dodavah.**—A prophet who is otherwise unknown.

**Dodavah.**—Heb. *Dôdāvāhû*. (Comp. *Hôdavyāhû*, 1 Chron. iii. 24; LXX., Δωδία, as if the Heb. were *Dôdiyâh*; Vulg., "Dodsu."

**Mareshah.**—See chap. xi. 8.

**Because thou hast joined thyself.**—Comp. Jehu the son of Hanani's similar rebuke of Jehoshaphat for his alliance with Ahab (chap. xix. 2).

**The Lord hath broken.**—*Shattered* (*paraç*). (Comp. chap. xxiv. 7.) The perfect is prophetic, *i.e.*, *will certainly shatter*.

**And the ships were broken.**—*Wrecked* by a gale. (Comp. Ps. xlviii. 7: "With the east wind Thou breakest ships of Tarshish.")

**That they were not able.**—*And kept not strength to go* (chap. xiii. 20, xiv. 10).

After this misadventure, Ahaziah proposed another joint expedition; but the king of Judah declined. (See on verse 36.)

## XXI.

(1) **Now.**—*And*.

**Slept.**—*Lay down*. The verse is literally the same as 1 Kings xxii. 50.

REIGN OF JEHORAM (chap. xxi. 2—18).

THE NEW KING MURDERS HIS SIX BROTHERS (verses 2—4).

(2) **Azariah ... and Azariah.**—Heb. *'Azaryāh ... and Azaryāhû*, different forms of the same name. All the versions give one form only. An old error of transcription may be involved (comp. 1 Chron. iii. 6, 8); but it is also possible that Jehoshaphat named two of his sons Azariah, "Iah helpeth," in pious recognition of two several mercies. *Shephatiah*, "Iah judgeth," repeats his own name in inverted shape.

The other names are—"God liveth," "Iah remembereth," "Who is like God?"—all significant of the king's faith.

**Jehoshaphat king of Israel.**—The southern kingdom is called "Israel" in chaps. xii. 1, 6; xxi. 4; xxviii. 19, 27, and elsewhere, as enjoying the legitimate monarchy, and maintaining the orthodox ritual and priesthood. Here, however, some Hebrew MSS., the LXX., Syriac, Vulg., and Arabic, read "Judah."

(3) **And their father gave them great gifts.**—Jehoshaphat before his death had provided for his sons, as Rehoboam before him had done for his, by appointing them resident governors of the national fortresses, and sending them away with valuable presents (chap. xi. 23).

**Of silver, and of gold.**—The preposition (*le*) belongs to the chronicler's style.

(4) Now <sup>a</sup> when Jehoram was risen up to the kingdom of his father, he strengthened himself, and slew all his brethren with the sword, and *divers* also of the princes of Israel.

(5) Jehoram *was* thirty and two years old when he began to reign, and he reigned eight years in Jerusalem. (6) And he walked in the way of the kings of Israel, like as did the house of Ahab: for he had the daughter of <sup>b</sup>Ahab to wife: and he wrought *that which was* evil in the eyes of the LORD. (7) Howbeit the LORD would not destroy the house of David, because of the covenant that he had made with David, and as he promised to give a ¹light to him and to his <sup>c</sup>sons for ever.

(8) In his days the Edomites revolted from under the ²dominion of Judah, and made themselves a king. (9) Then Jehoram <sup>d</sup>went forth with his princes, and all his chariots with him: and he rose up by night, and smote the Edomites which compassed him in, and the captains of the chariots. (10) So the Edomites revolted from under the hand of Judah unto this day. The same time *also* did

*B.C. 880.*
*a 2 Kings 8. 16, 17.*
*b ch. 22. 2.*
*B.C. 892.*
*1 Heb., lamp, or, candle.*
*c 2 Sam. 7. 12, 13; 1 Kings 11. 36; 2 Kings 8. 19; Ps. 132. 11, &c.*
*2 Heb., hand.*
*B.C. 889.*
*d 2 Kings 8. 21.*

---

**Precious things** (*migdōnóth*; Gen. xxiv. 53).—Such as jewels, robes, and spices.

**Because he was the firstborn.**—This was the rule. (Comp. Deut. xxi. 15—17.) For exceptions, see 1 Chron. xxviii. 5; 2 Chron. xi. 22, xxxvi. 1.

(4) **Now when Jehoram was risen up to the kingdom of his father.**—Literally, *And Jehoram arose over the kingdom*, &c., a peculiar expression, only found here. It seems to mean, *established himself on the throne*. (See Exod. i. 8 for a similar phrase, and comp. the use of the same verb, 1 Sam. xxiv. 20.)

**He strengthened himself.**—Secured his hold of power (chap. i. 1, xii., &c.).

**And slew all his brethren.**—In order to prevent intrigues against himself. Such ruthless crimes have been customary at Oriental accessions, and are one of the natural results of polygamy. (Comp. the conduct of Abimelech (Judges ix. 5) and of Athaliah (chap. xxii. 10). It was thus that Jehoram "strengthened himself."

**And divers also of the princes of Israel.**—Some of the great chiefs of the clans, whose power or sympathy with his murdered brothers Jehoram may have dreaded. Or, like other Oriental despots, Jehoram may have acted from no other motive than a rapacious desire to confiscate their wealth. Some suppose that both his brethren and these "princes" had given signs of dissatisfaction at Jehoram and Athaliah's heathen policy. (Comp. verse 13, "thy brethren . . . which were better than thyself.")

JEHORAM'S IDOLATRY. THE REVOLT OF EDOM AND LIBNAH (verses 5—11).

This section is parallel with 2 Kings viii. 17—22.

(5) **Jehoram was thirty and two years old.**—2 Kings viii. 17, "*he was;*" because the name had just occurred in the former verse.

(6) **And he walked in the way.**—A repetition of 2 Kings viii. 18, *literatim*.

(7) **The Lord would not destroy the house of David . . .**—An exegetical (not *arbitrary*, as Thenius asserts) expansion of "The Lord would not destroy Judah, for the sake of David his servant" (Kings).

**The covenant that he had made with David.**—Literally, *for David*. So Isa. lv. 3, "I will make an everlasting covenant *for* you, even the sure mercies of David." This construction is generally used of the stronger imposing conditions on the weaker. (Comp. Josh. ix. 6; 1 Sam. xi. 1, 2.) In the Pentateuch, God makes a covenant *with* (*im* or *eth*) His people (Gen. xv. 16; Exod. xxiv. 8).

**To give a light to him and to his sons.**—Literally, *a lamp*. Some critics find another " deviation " here, and render 1 Kings viii. 19, " to give a lamp to him *in respect of his sons*." But many Hebrew MSS., and the LXX., Vulg., and Targum of that passage, read, "*and* to his sons," as here. Syriac, " On account of the oaths which he sware to David, to give to him a burning lamp, and to his sons all the days."

**For ever.**—*All the days*.

(8) **In his days the Edomites revolted.**—2 Kings viii. 20. See also 1 Kings xxxii. 47, from which it appears that under Jehoshaphat " a deputy," or viceroy, ruled in Edom. (Comp. chap. xx. 35, Note.)

(9) **Then Jehoram went forth.**—*And Jehoram passed over*.

**With his princes.**—*Captains* ('*im sārāv*); Kings, " to Zair," which appears to be a corruption of " to Seir." The chronicler has substituted an intelligible for an obscure expression.

**And he rose up by night, and smote the Edomites which compassed him in.**—Literally, *and it came to pass, he rose*. Brief as the notice is, it is evident that the verse relates not a victory of Jehoram's, but his desperate escape by cutting his way through the enemy's troops, which had surrounded him and his forces. (See on 2 Kings viii. 21, where it is added, " and the people fled to their tents.") (Syriac, " And Jehoram passed over with his captains; and all his chariots with him. And it came to pass that when he rose in the night, he destroyed the Edomites, and the captains of the chariots came with him.")

(10) **Unto this day.**—See on chap. v. 9. The date thus assigned is some time prior to the captivity. No account is taken of Amaziah's reduction of Edom (chap. xxv. 11—15), which was probably not permanent.

**The same time also.**—Literally, *then revolted Libnah at that time*. 2 Kings viii. 22 ends here. The chronicler adds, " from under his (*i.e.*, Jehoram's) hand," and assigns a moral ground for the successful rebellion: " For he had forsaken Jehovah, the God of his fathers." (Thenius can hardly be right in asserting that the chronicler meant to say that Libnah, *as a city of the priests*, refused obedience to the idolatrous king; nor Hitzig, in explaining the revolt as merely a *religious* secession.) He forsook Jehovah, by "walking in the way of the kings of Israel, as did the house of Ahab," *i.e.*, by adopting and popularising the worship of the Tyrian Baal, to please his wife and her people. In those days

*Elijah's Prophecy*      II. CHRONICLES, XXI.      *against Jehoram.*

Libnah revolt from under his hand; because he had forsaken the LORD God of his fathers. <sup>(11)</sup> Moreover he made high places in the mountains of Judah, and caused the inhabitants of Jerusalem to commit fornication, and compelled Judah thereto.[1] <sup>(12)</sup> And there came a writing to him from Elijah the prophet, saying, Thus saith the LORD God of David thy father, Because thou hast not walked in the ways of Jehoshaphat thy father, nor in the ways of Asa king of Judah, <sup>(13)</sup> but hast walked in the way of the kings of Israel, and hast made Judah and the inhabitants of Jerusalem to go a whoring, like to the whoredoms of the house of Ahab, and also hast slain thy brethren of thy father's house, *which were* better than thyself: <sup>(14)</sup> behold, with [1]a great plague will the LORD smite thy people, and thy children, and thy wives, and all thy goods: <sup>(15)</sup> and thou *shalt have* great sickness by disease of thy bowels, until thy bowels fall out by reason of the sickness day by day.

<sup>(16)</sup> Moreover the LORD stirred up against Jehoram the spirit of the Philistines, and of the Arabians, that *were*

[1] Heb., *a great stroke.*

B.C. cir. 887.

---

friendship with an alien race seems to have involved recognition of their gods. (Comp. Amos i. 9 for the alliance between Tyre and Judah.)

**Libnah.**—Syriac, "the Edomites that lived in Libnah."

<sup>(11)</sup> **Moreover he made.**—There is a stress on the pronoun, "*he* made," in contrast with Asa and Jehoshaphat, his worthier predecessors (chap. xiv. 23, xvii. 6). Or *he himself*, and not the people. LXX., καὶ γὰρ αὐτὸς ἐποίησεν. From this point to the end of the reign the narrative is peculiar to the chronicler.

**High places.**—For the worship of the foreign gods, as well as of the God of Israel.

**Mountains.**—Many Heb. MSS., LXX., and Vulg., "cities" (a similar word); Syriac, "Moreover *he* made high places in the mountain of Judah, and caused the Nazarites of Jerusalem to drink wine, and scattered those who were of the house of Judah."

**And caused the inhabitants of Jerusalem to commit fornication**—*i.e.*, the spiritual fornication of unfaithfulness to Jehovah, the only lawful spouse of Israel. (Comp. Hosea ii. 5, 8, 13, 16, 17, 19; 1 Chron. v. 25.)

**And compelled.**—Or, *seduced* (Deut. xiii. 6, 11). LXX., ἀπεπλάνησε.

ELIJAH'S LETTER TO JEHORAM (verses 12—15).

<sup>(12)</sup> **And there came a writing to him from Elijah the prophet.**—Rather, *to him a writing*. This is the chronicler's only mention of the great prophet of the northern kingdom. Elijah, though a very old man, may have been still alive. His extreme age would account for his sending a written prophecy, rather than going in person to warn Jehoram. If, however, it be supposed that the author of Kings has told the story of Elijah's translation in its right place chronologically, and that the campaign described in the following chapter, in which Jehoshaphat took part, was really subsequent to that event, we may say that this "writing from Elijah the prophet," containing the substance of some last utterances of his directed against Jehoram and Athaliah, was now put into written shape, and forwarded to Jehoram by one of the prophet's pupils, perhaps by his great successor Elisha. (See 2 Kings ii. 15, iii. 11.) This explanation may seem to be favoured by the indefiniteness of the phrase, "a writing from Elijah" (*not* a letter); but 2 Kings iii. 11 is hardly conclusive against the assumption that Elijah was still alive. Elisha's ministry may have begun, probably did begin, some time before his master's ascension, and the description of him in 2 Kings iii. 11, "Elisha the son of Shaphat, who poured water on the hands of Elijah," need not [mean more than "Elisha the son of Shaphat, the servant of Elijah." (Syriac, "And there was brought to him one of the discourses of Elijah the prophet, which said to him." Vulg., wrongly, *a letter*, "allatae sunt autem ei litteræ ab Elia propheta." LXX., καὶ ἦλθεν αὐτῷ ἐν γραφῇ παρὰ 'Ηλιοὺ τοῦ προφήτου λέγων.)

<sup>(13)</sup> **And hast made . . . to go a whoring**—*i.e.*, "caused to commit fornication" (verse 11). Like to the whoredoms, infinitive of the same verb; *as the house of Ahab causeth them to commit fornication*. This verb, *zānāh*, occurred in 1 Chron. v. 25, but the writer does not use it again.

**Hast slain thy brethren.**—Verse 4, *supr.*

<sup>(14)</sup> **Behold, with a great plague will the Lord smite thy people.**—Literally, *Behold, Jehovah is about to smite a great smiting in thy people and in thy sons.* The immediate object of the verb is not expressed. (Comp. verse 18.) It was Jehoram himself who was smitten *in* his people, and *in* his sons, and *in* his wives, and *in* all his goods, as verse 17 shows. The "smiting"—*i.e.*, heaven-sent stroke, or Divine visitation—consisted in an invasion of Philistines and Arabs, who sacked Jerusalem and the royal palace.

<sup>(15)</sup> **And thou shalt have great sickness.**—Literally, *And thou thyself shalt be in great diseases through diseasing of thy bowels*. (Comp. for the two synonyms, Deut. xxviii. 59, Prov. xviii. 14.)

**Fall out.**—*Come out.*

**Day by day.**—Literally, *days upon days*, *i.e.*, probably, "a year upon a year," or "in two years." (Comp. verse 19, and 1 Sam. i. 3; Isa. xxix. 1.)

<sup>(16)</sup> **Moreover.**—*And*, here equivalent to *so*.

**The Lord stirred up against Jehoram.**—Isa. xiii. 17. The phrase, "stirred up the spirit,"—*i.e.*, *the will*—of a man to an undertaking, is found in Jer. li. 11; Hag. i. 14. (Comp. 1 Chron. v. 26; Ezra i. 1.)

**The Philistines, and of the Arabians.**—These are mentioned together elsewhere as enemies of Judah. (See chaps. xxvi. 7, xvii. 11; Jer. xxv. 20.) The invasion of the Philistines and Arabians accords with Joel iii. 4—6, and is certainly historical (Thenius on 2 Kings viii. 23, 24).

**That were near the Ethiopians.**—Literally, *At the hand of* (*i.e.*, beside) *the Cushites*. Some tribes of southern Arabia. There were Cushite settlements on both sides of the Red Sea. LXX., well: τοὺς ὁμόρους τῶν Αἰθιόπων; Vulg., "qui confines sunt Aethiopum."

# Jehoram's Disease — II. CHRONICLES, XXII. — and Death.

near the Ethiopians: (17) and they came up into Judah, and brake into it, and ¹carried away all the substance that was found in the king's house, and his sons also, and his wives; so that there was never a son left him, save ²Jehoahaz, the youngest of his sons.

(18) And after all this the LORD smote him in his bowels with an incurable disease. (19) And it came to pass, that in process of time, after the end of two years, his bowels fell out by reason of his sickness: so he died of sore diseases. And his people made no burning for him, like the burning of his fathers. (20) Thirty and two years old was he when he began to reign, and he reigned in Jerusalem eight years, and departed ³without being desired. Howbeit they buried him in the city of David, but not in the sepulchres of the kings.

CHAPTER XXII.—(1) And the inhabitants of Jerusalem made ᵃAhaziah his youngest son king in his stead: for the band of men that came with the Arabians to the camp had slain all the ᵇeldest. So Ahaziah the son of Jeho-

*Marginal notes:* ¹ Heb., *carried captive.* ² Or, *Ahaziah, ch. 22. 1; or, Azariah, ch. 22. 6.* B.C. 885. B.C. 885. ³ Heb., *without desire.* ᵃ 2 Kings 8. 24, &c. ᵇ ch. 21. 17.

---

(17) **And brake into it.**—Literally, *clave it asunder* (Exod. xiv. 16). Here as in 1 Chron. xi. 18; 2 Sam. xxiii. 16.

**And carried away all the substance . . . his wives.**—This statement implies that the enemy entered Jerusalem, although the chronicler has not expressly said it. In the same way (chap. xii. 9) he omitted to state that Shishak captured the city before plundering the Temple and palace. The desire to be concise accounts for both omissions. (See on chap. xxii. 1.)

**All the substance that was found in the king's house.**—Literally, *that belonged to the king's house.* (Comp. chap. xxxiv. 32 for *in*; comp. also Deut. xxi. 17.) It is not said that the Temple was plundered; but nothing can be inferred from the writer's silence on this point.

**So that there was never a son left him.**—They were not only taken, but slain (chap. xxii. 1).

**Save Jehoahaz.**—Called Ahaziah in chap. xxii. 1, which is the same name with the elements of it reversed. It means "Iah holdeth." The "Azariah" of chap. xxii. 6 seems to be a mistake. LXX., Syriac, Arabic, and Targum, "Ahaziah."

(18) **With an incurable disease.**—This is correct. Literally, *to a disease, to want of healing.* (Comp. chap. xxxvi. 16.) The Syriac and Arabic make verses 16—18 part of the prophecy.

(19) **In process of time.**—Comp. verse 15. Literally, *at days from days*, i.e., "a year after a year," or "after two years."

**After the end of two years.**—This clause more exactly defines the preceding. Literally, *and about the time of the going forth of the end of two years*, i.e., when two full years after the delivery of the prediction had expired. The time of the event exactly coincided with the time predicted. Vulg., well: "*duorum annorum expletus est circulus;*" Syriac, "When the prophet's word was fulfilled touching two years."

**By reason of his sickness.**—Literally, *along with*, i.e., *in, during*, his disease, which appears to have been a violent dysentery.

**So he died of sore diseases.**—*And he died in sore pains* (*tachalu'im*, Deut. xxix. 21).

**And his people made no burning for him.**—The usual honours of a sovereign were withheld in his case. (See on chap. xvi. 14; and comp. Jer. xxii. 19.) So Syriac: "And his people did him no honour, as they did to his fathers."

(20) **Thirty and two years.**—The word "years" has fallen out of the Hebrew text; but some MSS. contain it. The repetition of his age, &c., is curious. (See verse 6.) It seems to indicate that the writer was here transcribing from another source.

**And departed without being desired.**—*And he departed without regret, died unregretted.* *Hemdāh* answers to the Latin *desiderium*. The LXX. and Vulg. render: "And he walked not in approbation," or "rightly." Comp. Jeremiah's prophecy concerning the end of king Jehoiakim: "They shall not lament for him, saying, Ah, my brother!" &c. (Jer. xxii. 18, 19). So Syriac and Arabic.

**Howbeit.**—*And.*

**They buried him.**—LXX., Syriac, and Arabic: "He was buried."

**But not in the sepulchres of the kings.**—Chaps. xxiv. 25, xxvi. 23. Another circumstance of dishonour. It is not mentioned in 2 Kings viii. 17. Thenius asserts that in these additions to the history of Jehoram there is traceable, not only a traditional or legendary element, but also pure *embellishment* on the part of the chronicler. The grounds he alleges, however, by no means necessitate his conclusion, being themselves misinterpretations of the statements of Kings.

## XXII.

THE SHORT REIGN OF AHAZIAH (verses 1—9).
(Comp. 2 Kings viii. 25—29.)

(1) **And the inhabitants of Jerusalem.**—Chap. xxi. 11, 13.

**Made Ahaziah . . . king.**—This variation from the usual formula—"And Ahaziah his son reigned in his stead"—has been supposed to indicate that the succession was disputed, either Athaliah, the queen-mother, or Jehoiada, the high priest, opposing it. It is more likely that the difference of expression simply points to the use of a different source by the writer.

**The band of men that came with the Arabians to the camp.**—The Hebrew is obscure for want of further details. "The troop that came among the Arabs to the camp" appears to have been some party of half-savage warriors, who, after the Jewish camp had been stormed by the invaders and the royal princes taken prisoners, fell upon and slew their captives. (Comp. chap. xxi. 17; and Judges viii. 18, *seq.*; 1 Sam. xv. 32.)

**All the eldest.** — Heb., *the former* (*rishónim*). Syriac: "For all the elder the troop had destroyed them; for the Arabs came and destroyed the camp of Israel."

ram king of Judah reigned. (2) Forty and two years old *was* Ahaziah when he began to reign, and he reigned one year in Jerusalem. His mother's name also *was* ᵃAthaliah the daughter of Omri. (3) He also walked in the ways of the house of Ahab: for his mother was his counsellor to do wickedly. (4) Wherefore he did evil in the sight of the LORD like the house of Ahab: for they were his counsellors after the death of his father to his destruction. (5) He walked also after their counsel, and went with Jehoram the son of Ahab king of Israel to war against Hazael king of Syria at Ramoth-gilead: and the Syrians smote Joram. (6) And he returned to be healed in Jezreel because of the wounds ¹which were given him at Ramah, when he fought with Hazael king of Syria. And ²Azariah the son of Jehoram king of Judah went down to see Jehoram the son of Ahab at Jezreel, because he was sick. (7) And the ³destruction of Ahaziah was of God by coming to Joram: for when he was come, he went out with Jehoram against Jehu the son of Nimshi, ᵇwhom the LORD had anointed to cut off the house of Ahab. (8) And it came to pass, that, when Jehu was executing judgment upon the house of Ahab, and found the princes of Judah, and the sons

*a* ch. 21. 6.

1 Heb., *wherewith they wounded him.*

2 Otherwise called *Ahaziah*, ver. 1; and *Jehoahaz*, ch. 21. 17.

B.C. 884.

3 Heb., *treading down.*

*b* 2 Kings 9. 7.

---

(2) **Forty and two years old.**—An error of transcription. 2 Kings viii. 26, *twenty and two*; and so the Syriac and Arabic: the LXX. has "twenty." Ahaziah could not have been forty when he succeeded, because his father was only forty when he died (chap. xxi. 20).

**Athaliah the daughter of Omri**—*i.e.,* granddaughter, she being daughter of Ahab and Jezebel. Kings adds, "king of Israel," which the chronicler purposely omits. (Comp. Micah vi. 16: "The statutes of Omri," " the works of the house of Ahab.")

(3) **He also.**—The pronoun is emphatic: *he* too, like his father. Kings: "And he walked."

**Walked in the ways of the house of Ahab.**—Chap. xxi. 6, 13; Micah vi. 16.

**For his mother was his counsellor to do wickedly.**—Not in Kings; an explanatory remark added by the chronicler. (Comp. chaps. xx. 35, xxi. 6.) Her influence would be used in support of the Baal worship, which was the symbol of alliance with the northern kingdom.

(4) **Wherefore.**—*And he did the evil.* So 2 Kings viii. 27.

**For they were his counsellors.**—Or, *became.*

**To his destruction.**—Literally, *to destruction to him,* the same peculiar expression being used which occurred in chap. xx. 23. This last half of the verse is evidently the chronicler's own free expansion or interpretation of the words of Kings, "for he was son-in-law of the house of Ahab."

(5) **He walked also after (*in*) their counsel.**—An allusion to Ps. i. 1. He became a close partner in the politics of his ally, and joined in his expedition against the Syrians. The words are not in Kings.

**And went with Jehoram.**—2 Kings viii. 28, " Joram."

**King of Israel.**—Added by chronicler.

**Against.**—Kings, " with."

**Hazael king of Syria.**—See Note on 2 Kings viii. 8, *seq.*; xiii. 3.

**The Syrians.** — Heb., *hărammim,* instead of '*Arammim* (Kings). So Vulg. and Targum. The Syriac, as usual, confuses Aram with Edom. The LXX. renders "the archers," as if the word were the participle of *rāmāh,* "to shoot." Perhaps the chronicler intended *ha-rômim,* "the archers." (Comp. 1 Sam. xxxi. 3; Jer. iv. 29.)

(6) **And he**—*i.e.,* Joram, 1 Kings viii. 29, and LXX.

**Because of the wounds.**—Omit " because." So Kings, and LXX. (ἀπὸ τῶν πληγῶν), Syriac, Arabic, and Targum, as well as some Hebrew MSS. The Hebrew text has " because the wounds," which makes no sense. The word rendered " wounds" (*makkim*) only occurs besides in 2 Kings viii. 29, ix. 15. (*Ki,* " because," has originated out of *min,* "from.")

**Azariah.**—A mistake for " Ahaziah." So Kings, LXX., Vulg., Syriac, Arabic, and some Hebrew MSS.

**Went down.**—Whether from Ramah or Jerusalem is not clear. (See 2 Kings ix. 14.)

**Jehoram.**—Kings, *Joram*; and so the versions.

(7) **And the destruction of Ahaziah was of God.**—Literally, *And from God came the downtreading of Ahaziah, so that he went to Joram.* The coincidence of the visit with Jehu's rebellion revealed the working of Divine providence. It thus came to pass that the three chief representatives of the house of Ahab—Joram, Jezebel, and Ahaziah—were involved in one catastrophe of ruin; Athaliah, however, escaped for the time. " Downtreading" (*tebûsah*) occurs here only. (Comp. *mebûsah,* Isa. xxii. 5.)

**For.**—*And.*

**With Jehoram.**—So 2 Kings ix. 21.

**Against Jehu.**—Rather, *unto Jehu.* Kings, *l.c.,* " to meet Jehu."

**The son of Nimshi**—*i.e.,* grandson. Jehu was son of Jehoshaphat, son of Nimshi (2 Kings ix. 2).

**Whom the Lord had anointed.** — Comp. 1 Kings xix. 16; 2 Kings ix. 1—10.

(8) **When Jehu was executing judgment upon the house of Ahab.**—The Hebrew phrase strictly means *to plead with,* or *argue a cause with.* (Comp. 1 Sam. xii. 7.) When God is said to plead with men, the notion of judicial punishment is often involved, as in Joel iii. 2; Isa. lxvi. 16; and such is the meaning here. Jehu was an instrument of Divine vengeance, even when fulfilling the projects of his own ambition, as were the savage Assyrian conquerors (Isa. x. 5—7).

**And found.**—Rather, *he found.*

**The sons of the brethren of Ahaziah.**—Comp. 2 Kings x. 12—14, where the details are given. The persons whom Jehu slew are there called Ahaziah's " brethren"—*i.e.,* kinsmen (a common use; so LXX. here), and are said to have been forty-two in number. The Hebrew term is wide enough to include cousins and grandsons as well as nephews of the king. The " princes of Judah" who accompanied them would naturally be members of the court in charge of them, and are perhaps to be included in the total of forty-two persons. Thenius, indeed, in his note on 2 Kings x. 13,

*Ahaziah is Slain.*     II. CHRONICLES, XXIII.     *Athaliah Reigns.*

of the brethren of Ahaziah, that ministered to Ahaziah, he slew them. <sup>(9)</sup> *<sup>a</sup>And he sought Ahaziah: and they caught him, (for he was hid in Samaria,) and brought him to Jehu: and when they had slain him, they buried him: Because, said they, he is the son of Jehoshaphat, who sought the* LORD *with all his heart. So the house of Ahaziah had no power to keep still the kingdom.*

<sup>(10)</sup> *<sup>b</sup>But when Athaliah the mother of Ahaziah saw that her son was dead, she arose and destroyed all the seed royal of the house of Judah.* <sup>(11)</sup> *But Jehoshabeath, the daughter of the king, took Joash the son of Ahaziah, and stole him from among the king's sons that were slain, and put him and his nurse in a bedchamber. So Jehoshabeath, the daughter of king Jehoram, the wife of Jehoiada the priest, (for she was the sister of Ahaziah,) hid him from Athaliah, so that she slew him not.* <sup>(12)</sup> *And he was with them hid in the house of God six years: and Athaliah reigned over the land.*

*a* 2 Kings 9. 27.

*b* 2 Kings 11. 1.

B.C. 884.
B.C. 878.

*c* 2 Kings 11. 4, &c.

CHAPTER XXIII.—<sup>(1)</sup> *And <sup>c</sup>in the seventh year Jehoiada strengthened himself, and took the captains of hundreds, Azariah the son of Jeroham, and Ishmael the son of Jehohanan, and Azariah the son of Obed, and Maaseiah the son of Adaiah, and Elishaphat the son of*

---

alleges that we must understand the *real* brothers of Ahaziah, whom the chronicler gets rid of (!) on an earlier occasion (*i.e.*, 2 Chron. xxi. 17, xxii. 1), *because he required a Divine judgment in the lifetime of Jehoram.* Such arbitrary criticism hardly deserves refutation; we may, however, remark that Thenius relies on the untenable assumption that Jehoram could not have begotten any children before Ahaziah, whom he begot in his eighteenth or nineteenth year.

**That ministered to Ahaziah.**—*In attendance on Ahaziah*—*i.e.*, attached to the retinue of Ahaziah as pages, &c.

**He slew them.**—*And slew them.*

<sup>(9)</sup> **And he sought Ahaziah.**—In 2 Kings ix. 27, 28 we find a different tradition concerning the death of Ahaziah. That passage, literally rendered, runs as follows: "And Ahaziah king of Judah had seen it (*i.e.*, the death of Jehoram, verse 24), and he fled by the way of the garden palace, and Jehu pursued after him, and said, Him, too, smite (shoot) ye him in the chariot!—on the ascent of Gûr, beside Ibleam; and he fled to Megiddo, and died there." (Perhaps *and they smote him* has fallen out before the words *on the ascent of Gûr.*) "And his servants brought him in the chariot to Jerusalem, and buried him in his own grave, with his fathers, in the city of David." Such divergences are valuable, because they help to establish the independence of the two accounts.

**For he was hid.**—*Now he was hiding.*

**And when they had slain him.**—*And they put him to death, and buried him; for they said,* &c.

**He is the son of Jehoshaphat, who sought the Lord.**—A didactic remark in the usual manner of the chronicler.

**So the house of Ahaziah had no power to keep still the kingdom.**—Literally, *And the house of Ahaziah had none to retain strength for kingship* (= capable of assuming the sovereignty). Another sentence marked throughout by the chronicler's own style. (Comp. chap. xiii. 20, "retained strength.") It forms the transition to the account of Athaliah's usurpation of the throne.

ATHALIAH SEIZES THE GOVERNMENT (verses 10—12). (Comp. 2 Kings xi. 1—3.)

<sup>(10)</sup> **But when Athaliah.**—See 2 Kings xi. 1, with which this verse nearly coincides.

**Destroyed.**—So Kings and some Hebrew MSS., and all the versions. Hebrew text, *she spake*, a mistake of some scribe.

**All the seed royal.**—Even after the massacres described in verses 1, 8, there would doubtless be left a number of persons more or less nearly connected with the royal family, besides the immediate offspring of Ahaziah, who are, in the first instance, intended by this phrase.

<sup>(11)</sup> **Jehoshabeath.**—Kings, "Jehosheba." (Comp. "Elisheba," Exod. vi. 23; and Ἐλισαβέτ (LXX.), Luke i. 7.)

**The daughter of the king.**—Kings adds "Joram," and "sister of Ahaziah."

**That were slain.**—*That were to be put to death.*

**In a bedchamber.**—Literally, *in the chamber of beds*, *i.e.*, where the bedding was kept. (See Note on 2 Kings xi. 2.)

**The wife of Jehoiada the priest.**—So Josephus. Thenius questions the fact, on the supposed grounds—(1) that the high priest did not live in the Temple; but the passage he alleges (Neh. iii. 20, 21) does not prove this for Jehoiada; and (2) that the chronicler contradicts himself in asserting that the priest's wife also lived within the sacred precinct; but again his reference (2 Chron. viii. 11) is irrelevant. Ewald calls the statement in question "genuinely historical;" and there is not the smallest reason to doubt it.

<sup>(12)</sup> **With them.**—With Jehoiada and his wife. Kings, "with her;" LXX., "with him;" Syriac and Arabic, "with her." (See Note on 2 Kings xi. 3.)

XXIII.

THE FALL OF ATHALIAH, AND SUCCESSION OF JOASH. (Comp. 2 Kings xi. 4—20.)

<sup>(1)</sup> **Jehoiada strengthened himself.**—*Showed himself strong* or *courageous*, *behaved boldly* (1 Sam. iv. 9). The chronicler has substituted a favourite expression (*hithchazzaq*) for the term used in Kings, "Jehoiada *sent.*"

**The captains of hundreds.**—Their names, added here, are not given in 2 Kings xi. 4. On the other hand, Kings reads, "the captains of the hundreds *of the Carians* (or body-guard) *and the Runners* (or couriers *i.e.*, royal messengers)"—terms which were probably obscure to the chronicler.

*Jehoiada makes* II. CHRONICLES, XXIII. *a Covenant with the Levites.*

Zichri, into covenant with him. <sup>(2)</sup> And they went about in Judah, and gathered the Levites out of all the cities of Judah, and the chief of the fathers of Israel, and they came to Jerusalem. <sup>(3)</sup> And all the congregation made a covenant with the king in the house of God. And he said unto them, Behold, the king's son shall reign, as the LORD hath *said of the sons of David. <sup>(4)</sup> This *is* the thing that ye shall do; A third part of you entering on the sabbath, of the priests and of the Levites, *shall be* porters of the <sup>1</sup>doors; <sup>(5)</sup> and a third part *shall be* at the king's house; and a third part at the gate of the foundation: and all the people *shall be* in the courts of the house of the LORD. <sup>(6)</sup> But let none come into the house of the LORD, save the priests, and they that minister of the Levites; they shall go in, for they *are* holy: but all the people shall keep

*a* 2 Sam. 7. 12; 1 Kings 2. 4 & 9. 5; ch. 6. 16 & 7. 18.

1 Heb., *thresholds.*

---

**Azariah . . . and Azariah.**—Heb., '*Azaryāh . . . and 'Azaryāhû.* (Comp. chap. xxi. 2.) These names are introduced in the chronicler's well-known manner (by the prefix *le,* marking the object of the verb). His style is very visible in the additions to the narrative as compared with Kings.

<sup>(2)</sup> **And they went about in Judah.**—Chap. xvii. 9; 1 Sam. vii. 16.

**The chief of the fathers.**—*The heads of the clans,* or *chiefs of houses.*

This and the next verse are added by the chronicler. In Kings the narrative passes at once to the charge of verse 4: "This is the thing that ye shall do," which is there addressed to the "captains of the hundreds," or centurions of the royal guard. In fact, the parallel text is nearly if not altogether silent as to the part played by *the Levites* in the Restoration; and the chronicler appears to have supplemented that account with materials derived from other authorities, and perhaps from Levitical traditions. That he should have done so, is only consistent with his general practice and the special purpose of his history. At the same time, allowing for certain characteristic additions, interpretations, and substitutions of phrase for phrase, which will be specified in these Notes, the narrative of the chronicler absolutely coincides with that of Kings, treating of the same events, and rigidly observing the same limits, as well as maintaining a general identity of language. We conclude, therefore, that in this case, as elsewhere, the chronicler has used as the groundwork of his relation a historical text which contained sections substantially identical with the present narratives of Kings, but accompanied by numerous details not found in those books.

<sup>(3)</sup> **And all the congregation.**—Of the assembled Levites and family chiefs, as well as the royal guard.

**Made a covenant with the king.**—Comp. 2 Kings xi. 4: "And he made a covenant *for* them," *i.e.,* imposed a compact on them, made them swear fidelity to the young prince. (Comp. also 2 Sam. iii. 21, v. 3.)

**The king's son shall reign.**—Or, *Behold the king's son! Let him be king.*

**As the Lord hath said.**—*Spake concerning the sons of David,* in the oracle delivered by the prophet Nathan (2 Sam. vii. 4—17).

<sup>(4)</sup> **This is the thing that ye shall do.**—2 Kings xi. 5: "And he charged them saying, This is the thing," &c. There he charges the captains of the guard as being the leaders of the conspiracy.

**A third.**—*The third.* So verse 5. "The third of you who come in on the Sabbath" is read also in 2 Kings xi. 5. The chronicler has added the explanatory words: "belonging to the priests and to the Levites." This can hardly be harmonised with 2 Kings xii. 4—12. The chronicler may have misunderstood the words, which in the older account designate the royal guard; and it might have appeared to him impossible that any but members of the sacred orders would be called together *in the Temple* by the high priest. (Comp. verses 5, 6 with 2 Kings xi. 4: "brought them *into the house of the Lord."*) But he may also have had before him an account in which the part taken by the sacerdotal caste in the revolution was made much more of than in the account of Kings. Moreover the priests and Levites would be likely to play a considerable part in a movement tending to the overthrow of a *cultus* antagonistic to their own, especially when that movement originated with their own spiritual head, and was transacted in the sanctuary to which they were attached. The chronicler, therefore, cannot with fairness be accused of "arbitrary alterations," unless it be presupposed that his *sole* authority in writing this account was the Second Book of Kings. The priests and Levites used to do duty in the Temple from Sabbath to Sabbath, so that one course relieved another at the end of each week. (See 1 Chron. xxiv.; Luke i. 5.) That the companies of the royal guards succeeded each other on duty in the same fashion is clear from the parallel narrative.

**Shall be porters of the doors.**—*Warders of the thresholds,* that is, of the Temple (1 Chron. ix. 19, 22). 1 Kings xi. 5 says: "The third of you that come in on the Sabbath, they shall keep the *guard of the king's house;*" the latter part of which answers to the first sentence of the next verse: "And the third part (shall be) at the king's house." The king's "house" in Kings means the royal palace; the chronicler appears to mean by it his temporary dwelling within the Temple precincts.

<sup>(5)</sup> **And a third part at the gate of the foundation.**—2 Kings xi. 6 reads: "the gate Sûr," which appears there as a gate of the palace. (LXX., "the middle gate;" Syr. and Arab., "the Butchers' gate.")

**And all the people shall be in the courts of the house of the Lord.**—This appears to be written from the point of view of a strict legalist, according to which none might enter the holy house itself save the priests. It looks like a protest against 2 Kings xi. 4, where it is said that Jehoiada brought the centurions of the royal guard into the house of the Lord.

<sup>(6)</sup> **But let none come into the house of the Lord.**—This verse is not read in Kings. Apparently it is merely an emphatic repetition of the direction of the last verse that all the people were to remain in the courts, and not to break the law by presuming to enter the holy chambers. In 2 Kings xi. 7 we read instead: "And the two parts among you, all that go out on the Sabbath, they *shall keep the watch of the house of*

the watch of the LORD. ⁽⁷⁾ And the Levites shall compass the king round about, every man with his weapons in his hand; and whosoever *else* cometh into the house, he shall be put to death: but be ye with the king when he cometh in, and when he goeth out.

⁽⁸⁾ So the Levites and all Judah did according to all things that Jehoiada the priest had commanded, and took every man his men that were to come in on the sabbath, with them that were to go *out* on the sabbath: for Jehoiada the priest dismissed not the courses. ⁽⁹⁾ Moreover Jehoiada the priest delivered to the captains of hundreds spears, and bucklers, and shields, that *had been* king David's, which *were* in the house of God.

1 Heb., *shoulder*.

2 Heb., *house*.

*a* Deut. 17. 18.

3 Heb., *Let the king live*.

⁽¹⁰⁾ And he set all the people, every man having his weapon in his hand, from the right ¹side of the ²temple to the left side of the temple, along by the altar and the temple, by the king round about. ⁽¹¹⁾ Then they brought out the king's son, and put upon him the crown, and *ᵃgave him* the testimony, and made him king. And Jehoiada and his sons anointed him, and said, ³God save the king.

⁽¹²⁾ Now when Athaliah heard the noise of the people running and praising the king, she came to the people into the house of the LORD: ⁽¹³⁾ and she looked, and, behold, the king stood at his pillar at the entering in, and the princes and the trumpets by the king:

---

*the Lord*, with regard to the king." The last words of the present verse, "And all the people *shall keep the watch of the Lord*," repeat a portion of this, but in a different sense: "Let all the people carefully observe the legal rule against entering the sanctuary."

⁽⁷⁾ **And the Levites shall compass.** — Kings, "And ye (*i.e.*, the centurions of the royal guard) shall compass." (See Note on verse 4.) The chronicler characteristically dwells on the share of the Levites in the matter; but he does not expressly *exclude* the royal guard; and it is utterly unfair to allege that he has metamorphosed the guardsmen of Kings into Levites, "in order to divert to the priesthood the honour which properly belonged to the Prætorians" (*Thenius*). The truth may perhaps be that the high priest Jehoiada brought about a combination of the royal guard with the Levitical warders of the Temple; and that the united body acted under the command of the five centurions of the guard.

**Cometh into the house.**—2 Kings xi. 8 has, "into the ranks;" a rare word (*sᵉdērôth*), occurring only four times, viz., in this narrative thrice, and once in 1 Kings vi. 8 (in a different sense).

**But be ye.**—So Kings. But some MSS. and the LXX., Vulg., Targ., and Arab. read here: "and let them (*i.e.*, the Levites) be." (See Note on 2 Kings xi. 8.)

⁽⁸⁾ **The Levites and all Judah.**—2 Kings xi. 9 reads, "the captains of the hundreds." The rest of the verse is the same in both narratives so far as the words "go out on the Sabbath."

**For Jehoiada the priest dismissed not the courses.**—The companies of priests and Levites, whose weekly duties had been fulfilled, and who under ordinary circumstances would have been formally "dismissed" by the high priest, were detained at the present emergency as auxiliaries to their brethren who were "coming in."

Instead of this clause Kings has: "And they came to Jehoiada the priest," *i.e.*, the captains of the hundreds came to him; a remark which quite naturally preludes the statement of the next verse both there and here.

⁽⁹⁾ **Moreover.**—*And.* This verse is essentially identical with 2 Kings xi. 10: "And the priest delivered to the captains of hundreds the spear and the shields that had been king David's, which were in

the house of Jehovah." The chronicler has added *Jehoiada* and *the bucklers*, and turned *the spear* into *spears*, rightly according to most critics.

**Spears, and bucklers, and shields.**—Each word has the article in the Hebrew.

**That had been king David's.**—Comp. 1 Chron. xviii. 7, 11; also 1 Sam. xxii. 10, xvii. 7.

⁽¹⁰⁾ **And he set all the people.**—2 Kings ix. 11: "And the Couriers stood." By "the people," the chronicler obviously means, not the mass of the congregation, but the armed body who were to "compass the king round about, every man with his weapons in his hand" (verse 7).

**His weapon.**—Or, *his missiles, arms*. LXX., ὅπλα. (Comp. chap. xxxii. 5.) Kings has a commoner word. The remainder of the verse is identical with its parallel.

**Along by.**—*Towards the altar.*

⁽¹¹⁾ **Then.**—*And.* So in verses 14 and 17.

**They brought out . . . and put.**—2 Kings xi. 12: "*he* (Jehoiada) brought out . . . and put."

**Put upon him the crown, and gave him the testimony.**—Literally, *put upon him the crown* (*nēzer*; Exod. xxix. 6; 2 Sam. i. 10) *and the law* (*ha-ʿēdûth*; Exod. xxv. 21, 22, xxxi. 18). Was a scroll of the ten words wrapped round the diadem, or laid on the king's shoulder? (Comp. Vulg., "imposuerunt ei diadema testimonium dederuntque in manu ejus tenendam legem;" as if a copy of the law was solemnly presented to the newly-crowned king.)

**Jehoiada and his sons.**—The chronicler *adds* this to make it clear that it was *the priests* who anointed the king. (Comp. 1 Kings i. 39.)

THE EXECUTION OF ATHALIAH (verses 12–21). (See 2 Kings xi. 13—20.)

⁽¹²⁾ **Now when Athaliah . . . she came.**—*And Athaliah heard . . . and she came.*

**The noise of the people running and praising the king.** — Or, *the noise of the people, the Couriers, and those who were acclaiming the king.* (1 Kings xi. 13, "the noise of the runners, the people;" where *the people* may be an inadvertent repetition, as the same expression follows directly. The rest of the verse is the same as here.)

⁽¹³⁾ **Stood.**—*Was standing.*

*Athaliah is Slain.*     **II. CHRONICLES, XXIII.**     *The Fear of the Lord Restored.*

and all the people of the land rejoiced, and sounded with trumpets, also the singers with instruments of musick, and such as taught to sing praise. Then Athaliah rent her clothes, and said, ¹Treason, treason. ⁽¹⁴⁾ Then Jehoiada the priest brought out the captains of hundreds that were set over the host, and said unto them, Have her forth of the ranges: and whoso followeth her, let him be slain with the sword. For the priest said, Slay her not in the house of the LORD. ⁽¹⁵⁾ So they laid hands on her; and when she was come to the entering of the horse gate by the king's house, they slew her there.

⁽¹⁶⁾ And Jehoiada made a covenant between him, and between all the people, and between the king, that they should be the LORD's people. ⁽¹⁷⁾ Then all the people went to the house of Baal, and brake it down, and brake his altars and his images in pieces, and ᵃslew Mattan the priest of Baal before the altars. ⁽¹⁸⁾ Also Jehoiada appointed the offices of the house of the LORD by the hand of the priests the Levites, whom David had ᵇdistributed in the house of the LORD, to offer the burnt offerings of the LORD, as *it is* written in the ᶜlaw of Moses, with rejoicing and with singing, *as it was ordained* ²by David. ⁽¹⁹⁾ And he set the ᵈporters at the gates of the house of the LORD, that none *which was* unclean in any thing should enter in. ⁽²⁰⁾ And he took the captains of hundreds, and

1 Heb., *Conspiracy.*
a Deut. 13. 9.
b 1 Chron. 24. 1.
c Num. 28. 2.
2 Heb., *by the hands of David.*
d 1 Chron. 26. 1, &c.

---

**At his pillar.**—*On his stand.* So 2 Kings xxiii. 3. Kings here has, "on *the* stand;" LXX., ἐπὶ τῆς στάσεως αὐτοῦ; Vulg., "stantem super gradum."

**At the entering in.**—*In the entry.* LXX., ἐπὶ τῆς εἰσόδου. Kings reads, "according to the custom." So the Syriac and Arabic here.

**And the princes.**—See Note on 2 Kings xi. 14. Some Hebrew MSS. here also read "singers;" one MS. has "Couriers."

**Rejoiced.**—*Were rejoicing and sounding.*

**Also the singers with instruments of musick, and such as taught to sing praise.**—*And the minstrels* (or *musicians*) *with the instruments of music, and men leading the chanting* (literally, *teaching to praise*). This is one of the writer's characteristic additions to the older text.

**Said.**—Kings, "cried," which is more original.

⁽¹⁴⁾ **Then.**—*And.* This verse is the same as 2 Kings xi. 15, with a few formal variations.

**Brought out.**—Kings, "commanded." The Heb. words are so nearly alike that one may easily be a corruption of the other. The Syriac and Arabic agree with Kings. The LXX. gives both readings.

**Have her forth of the ranges.**—*Make her go out between the ranks of guards.*

**Let him be slain.**—An explanation of the form used in Kings (the infinitive).

**Slay her not.**—*Ye must not slay her.* Kings, "Let her not be slain." So the Syriac here.

⁽¹⁵⁾ **So they laid hands on her.**—Rather, *And they made way for her on both sides.* LXX., καὶ ἔδωκαν αὐτῇ ἄνεσιν. Syriac, "And they made room for her."

**To the entering of the horse gate.**—Kings reads: "And she went by the way of the entry of the horses into the king's house." Syriac, "And she entered into the way of the entry of the horses, and was killed there."

RENEWAL OF THE THEOCRATIC COVENANT AND ABOLITION OF BAAL-WORSHIP (verses 16—21).

⁽¹⁶⁾ **A covenant between . . . the king.**—A slight but characteristic variation from 2 Kings xi. 17 : "*the* covenant *between Jehovah* and the king and the people, that they should become a people for Jehovah."

**Between him.**—Or rather, *himself.* The high priest is thus regarded as representing Jehovah in the transaction; and the apparent irreverence of making the Deity a direct co-partner with men in a compact is avoided.

**Be the Lord's people.**—Literally, *become a people for Jehovah.* Kings adds : "and between the king and the people," a not unimportant clause, for it relates to certain limitations of the royal prerogative, which were usually agreed upon at the beginning of a reign (2 Sam. iii. 21, v. 3 ; 1 Sam. x. 25).

⁽¹⁷⁾ **Brake it down.**—*Pulled it down.*

**And brake.**—*And its altars,* &c., *they broke in pieces.* Kings adds, "thoroughly." (See 2 Kings xi. 18.)

⁽¹⁸⁾ **Also Jehoiada appointed.**—This and the next verse are a thoroughly characteristic expansion of the brief notice: "And the priest set officers over the house of the Lord" (Kings). Render, "And Jehoiada put the offices of the house of the Lord into the hand of the priests the Levites." Syriac, "And Jehoiada made prefects (*shallitônê*) in the house of the Lord, and the priests and Levites." The LXX. renders: "And Jehoiada the priest took in hand the works of the house of the Lord, by the hand of priests and Levites."

**Whom David had distributed.**—Divided into courses or classes (1 Chron. xxiii. 6, xxiv., xxv.).

**In the house.**—*For the house.*

**As it is written.**—A reference to the Pentateuch. (Comp. Ezra iii. 2.)

**With rejoicing and with singing, as it was ordained by David.**—See the margin, and comp. the Notes on 1 Chron. xxv. 2, 6, xxiii. 5.

The meaning of all this is that the high priest now restored the regular services of the Temple, as arranged by David, which had been neglected or at least irregularly conducted during the six years of Athaliah's usurpation.

⁽¹⁹⁾ **And he set.**—*Stationed,* or *appointed.*

**At the gates.**—Or, *over the gates.* (See 1 Chron. xxiii. 5, xxvi. 1—19.)

**That none which was unclean . . . should enter.**—Comp. verses 6, and Lev. v. 7; Num. v. 19 ; Deut. xxiv. 1—3, 10, 11.

⁽²⁰⁾ **And he took.**—See 2 Kings xi. 19.

the nobles, and the governors of the people, and all the people of the land, and brought down the king from the house of the LORD: and they came through the high gate into the king's house, and set the king upon the throne of the kingdom. <sup>(21)</sup> And all the people of the land rejoiced: and the city was quiet, after that they had slain Athaliah with the sword.

CHAPTER XXIV.—<sup>(1)</sup> Joash <sup>a</sup>*was* seven years old when he began to reign, and he reigned forty years in Jerusalem. His mother's name also *was* Zibiah of Beer-sheba. <sup>(2)</sup> And Joash did *that which was* right in the sight of the LORD all the days of Jehoiada the priest. <sup>(3)</sup> And Jehoiada took for him two wives; and he begat sons and daughters.

<sup>(4)</sup> And it came to pass after this, *that* Joash was minded ¹to repair the house of the LORD. <sup>(5)</sup> And he gathered together the priests and the Levites, and said to them, Go out unto the cities of Judah, and gather of all Israel money to repair the house of your God from year to year, and see that ye hasten the matter. Howbeit the Levites hastened it not.

<sup>(6)</sup> And the king called for Jehoiada the chief, and said unto him, Why hast thou not required of the Levites to bring in out of Judah and out of Jerusalem the collection, *according to the commandment* of <sup>b</sup>Moses the servant of the LORD,

*a* 2 Kings 12. 1, &c.

B.C. 856.

1 Heb., *to renew.*

B.C. cir. 878.

*b* Exod. 30. 12, 13, 14.

---

**The nobles, and the governors of the people.**—Kings has: "And the Carians and the *Couriers*." (See Note on verse 1.)

**The nobles.**—Comp. Ps. xvi. 3.

**Governors of the people.**—Comp. Isa. xxviii. 14. These "nobles and governors" are perhaps "the heads of the clans" of verse 2, and "the princes" of verse 13; though the phrase certainly looks like an attempt at explaining the obscure titles of the royal guard.

**And they came through the high gate.**—Kings, "And they came by the way of the Couriers' Gate." (See Note on verse 5, *supra.*) The Couriers' Gate may have been called the High Gate, as being the grand entrance to the palace. A gate of the Temple has the same designation in chap. xxvii. 3.

XXIV.

REIGN OF JOASH. (Comp. 2 Kings xii.)
PROPHETIC MINISTRY OF ZECHARIAH BEN JEHOIADA.

The Ascendancy of the High Priest Jehoiada. Repair of the Temple (verses 1—14).

<sup>(1)</sup> **Joash was seven years old.**—This verse coincides with 2 Kings xii. 1, 2, merely omitting the note that his accession took place "in the seventh year of Jehu." There he is called *Jehoash*, of which Joash is a contraction. (Comp. Jehoram-Joram.) The meaning may be "Iahu is fire" (comp. Isa. xxxiii. 14); but more probably it is "Iahu is a man." (Comp. Ashbel.)

<sup>(2)</sup> **And Joash did.**—So 2 Kings xiii. 3.

**All the days of Jehoiada the priest.**—Kings: "all his days, while (or *because*) Jehoiada the priest instructed him." The expression "all his days" is of course relative to the clause which follows it; and the chronicler has accurately given the meaning.

<sup>(3)</sup> **And Jehoiada took for him two wives.**—A statement not found in the parallel narrative, and doubtless taken by the compiler from another source. Instead of this, we read in 2 Kings xii. 4: "Only the high places were not taken away; the people were still wont to sacrifice and burn incense on the high places."

<sup>(4)</sup> **Was minded.**—Literally, *it became with the heart of Joash* (chap. vi. 8, ix. 1; 1 Kings viii. 18).

**To repair.**—See margin to chap. xv. 8. "To restore" is perhaps the best modern equivalent of the Hebrew term. The account of the restoration of the Temple is given here in different language from what we find in the parallel passage, which is not very clear.

The chronicler appears to have paraphrased the account he found in his authority. The *Levites* are not mentioned in Kings.

<sup>(5)</sup> **Go out unto the cities of Judah, and gather of all Israel money.**—This is the chronicler's interpretation of "Let the priests take it to themselves, each from his own acquaintance" (Kings). The priests and Levites of the different districts were to collect the moneys due to the sanctuary, each in his own neighbourhood.

**And see that ye hasten the matter.**—Literally, *and, for your part, hasten ye in regard to the matter* (comp. chap. xviii. 8); *and the Levites hastened not.* This agrees with the statement in 2 Kings xii. 6, 9: "And it was so, *that in the three and twentieth year of king Jehoash* the priests had not repaired the breaches of the house." The remissness of the priestly order is evidently inferable from these words.

<sup>(6)</sup> **And the king called for Jehoiada.**—So 2 Kings xii. 7.

**The chief.**—Literally, *the head, i.e.,* of the sacerdotal caste. Usually *kôhēn*, "priest," is added, as in chaps. xix. 11, xxvi. 20. Kings has simply "the priest," adding "and for the priests."

**Why hast thou not required of the Levites.**—Or, *Why hast thou not attended to the Levites* (comp. chap. xxxi. 9), *that they might bring . . . ?* (*i.e.,* seen about the Levites bringing). LXX., Διὰ τί οὐκ ἐπεσκέψω περὶ τῶν Λευιτῶν τοῦ εἰσενέγκαι, κ.τ.λ.

**The collection.**—Rather, *the tax* (Ezek. xx. 40). "The tax of Moses" is not the poll-tax of half-a-shekel, for the sanctuary, imposed Exod. xxx. 12—16, and collected Exod. xxxviii. 25, 26; but rather a general designation of the moneys mentioned in 2 Kings xii. 25. (See Note on verse 4, *supra.*)

**For the tabernacle of witness.**—Or, *the tent of the testimony* (Num. ix. 15; comp. Note on chap. xxiii. 11); *i.e.,* the "Tent of the Law."

In Kings, the question of Joash is, "Why are ye not repairing the breaches of the house?" He then continues: "And now, receive not money from your acquaintances, for the breaches of the house ye should give it" (scil., instead of appropriating it

and of the congregation of Israel, for the tabernacle of witness? ⁽⁷⁾ For the sons of Athaliah, that wicked woman, had broken up the house of God; and also all the dedicated things of the house of the LORD did they bestow upon Baalim. ⁽⁸⁾ And at the king's commandment they made a chest, and set it without at the gate of the house of the LORD. ⁽⁹⁾ And they made ¹a proclamation through Judah and Jerusalem, to bring in to the LORD the collection *that* Moses the servant of God *laid* upon Israel in the wilderness. ⁽¹⁰⁾ And all the princes and all the people rejoiced, and brought in, and cast into the chest, until they had made an end. ⁽¹¹⁾ Now it came to pass, that at what time the chest was brought unto the king's office by the hand of the Levites, and when they saw that *there was* much money, the king's scribe and the high priest's officer came and emptied the chest, and took it, and carried it to his place again. Thus they did day by day, and gathered money in abundance. ⁽¹²⁾ And the king and Jehoiada gave it to such as did the work of the service of the house of the LORD, and hired masons and carpenters to repair the house of the LORD, and also such as wrought iron and brass to mend the house of the LORD. ⁽¹³⁾ So the work-

¹ Heb., *a voice.*

---

yourselves). In consequence, "the priests obeyed so as not to take money from the people, and not to repair the breaches of the house" (2 Kings xii. 8).

⁽⁷⁾ **For the sons of Athaliah.**—There is nothing corresponding to the statements of this verse in the parallel account. Literally, *For Athaliah, the evildoer* (or, *who did wickedly*, chap. xx. 35), *her sons had broken down* (Isa. v. 5; Ps. lxxx. 14) *the house of God.* Ahaziah and his elder brothers, and perhaps other relatives, may be intended. The young princes thus gratified the queen's hatred of the exclusive *cultus* of Jehovah. (Comp. chap. xxii. 3, 4.) Perhaps some portions of the Temple buildings were demolished, in order to make room for the temple of Baal. (Comp. Notes on 2 Kings xi. 18.)

**The dedicated things**—*i.e.*, the moneys given for the use of the sanctuary.

**Did they bestow upon Baalim.**—Or, *they made into the Baals, i.e.*, used them in making idolatrous images and symbols. (Comp. the same expression, Hosea ii. 8: "Her silver and gold, *which they made into Baal*;" comp. also Hosea viii. 4.)

⁽⁸⁾ **And at the king's commandment they made.**—Literally, *And the king said* (commanded), *and they made.* (Comp. 2 Kings xii. 9: "And Jehoiada the priest took a chest, and bored a hole in its lid;" details characteristic of a more original account.)

**And set it without**—*i.e.*, outside of the Temple proper. The chest stood in the court, just inside the gate.

⁽⁹⁾ **And they made a proclamation.**—Literally, *uttered a voice* (or *cry*) *in Judah.* The phrase (*nathan qól*) occurs here only in this sense. (Comp. Prov. i. 20.)

**To bring in to the Lord.**—Comp. verse 6. The meaning is, To bring into the Temple, for the Lord.

**The collection.**—*Tax*, or *impost.*

This verse, and the next one also, are peculiar to the chronicle. The writer is fond of dwelling on the willingness of the people in the good old time to contribute to the cause of religion; doubtless, by way of suggestion to his own contemporaries. (Comp. 1 Chron. xxix. 6, 9, 14.)

In Kings we read: "And the priests, the warders of the threshold, used to put into it all the money that was brought into the house of the Lord."

**Until they had made an end.**—This is correct. The same phrase recurs, chap. xxxi. 1. The ancient versions wrongly give "until it was filled." *Killāh* does not mean "to make full," as is asserted in Lange's Commentary, but *to finish* any action.

⁽¹¹⁾ **Now.**—*And.*

**At what time the chest was brought.**—Literally, *at the time when one used to bring the chest to the royal inspection* (or, *to the king's officers, pĕquddāh*), *by the hand of the Levites; i.e.,* whenever the chest was brought, &c.

The chronicler, as usual, is careful to record the participation of the Levites in the business.

**The king's scribe and the high priest's officer came and emptied the chest.**—Rather, *the king's scribe* (or *accountant*) *and the high priest's officer would come in and empty the chest ; and they* (*i.e.,* the Levites) *would take it up and restore it to its place.*

Kings has: "The king's scribe *and the high priest* came up, and bound up and counted the money that was found in the house of the Lord." The substitution of "the high priest's officer" for "the high priest" seems to be made in the interest of the high priest's dignity. In the time of the chronicler the high priesthood was invested with all the greater majesty in that the monarchy was a thing of the distant past.

**Day by day.**—That is, time after time, as often as the chest seemed full (*lĕyôm bĕyôm*). The Hebrew phrase only occurs here. (Comp. 1 Chron. xii. 22.)

⁽¹²⁾ **To such as did the work of the service of the house of the Lord.**—Heb., *to the doer* ('*ôséh*) perhaps in a collective sense. Here, as in 1 Chron. xxiii. 24, some MSS., and LXX., Syriac, and Vulgate, read the plural ('*ôsê*). So also the Arabic and Targum here. Those who had charge of the building, probably certain Levitical "inspectors of works," are meant. Vulg.: "Qui praeërant operibus domus." Comp. 2 Kings xii. 11: "into the hand of *the doers of the work,* who were charged with the house of the Lord."

**And hired.**—Rather, *and they* (*i.e.,* the superintendents of works) *were* (from time to time) *hiring masons* (hewers) *and carpenters.* (See 1 Chron. xxii. 15.)

**To mend**—*i.e.,* to repair (verse 4).

The chronicler has abridged here considerably. (Comp. 2 Kings. xii. 12.)

(13, 14) The writer concludes in his own fashion, freely modifying the older account to suit the needs of his contemporaries. (The Syriac and Arabic versions omit both verses.)

*The Temple Repaired.*  II. CHRONICLES, XXIV.  *Jehoiada's Death.*

men wrought, and ¹the work was perfected by them, and they set the house of God in his state, and strengthened it. (14) And when they had finished *it*, they brought the rest of the money before the king and Jehoiada, whereof were made vessels for the house of the LORD, *even* vessels to minister, and ²to offer *withal*, and spoons, and vessels of gold and silver. And they offered burnt offerings in the house of the LORD continually all the days of Jehoiada.

(15) But Jehoiada waxed old, and was full of days when he died; an hundred and thirty years old *was he* when he died. (16) And they buried him in the city of David among the kings, because he had done good in Israel, both toward God, and toward his house.

(17) Now after the death of Jehoiada came the princes of Judah, and made obeisance to the king. Then the king hearkened unto them. (18) And they left the house of the LORD God of their fathers, and served groves and idols: and wrath came upon Judah and Jeru-

*B.C. cir. 850.*

1 Heb., *the healing went up upon the work.*

*B.C. cir. 840.*

2 Or, *pestils.*

---

(13) **So the workmen wrought.**—Literally, *And the makers of the work made.*

**And the work was perfected by them.**—Literally, *and a bandage was applied to the work by their hand.* This curious metaphor, expressive of restoration, is used again in a similar way in Neh. iv. 1, "a bandage was applied to the walls of Jerusalem." Jeremiah had used it before (Jer. viii. 22, xxx. 17; comp. also Isa. lviii. 8) of the national restoration.

**And they set the house of God in his state.**—Rather, *and they made the house of God to stand according to the measure thereof*, i.e., in its original proportions. (Comp. Exod. xxx. 32: *mâthkôneth*, "measure," "proportion.") This verse is not read in Kings.

**Before the king and Jehoiada.**—The expression appears to be characteristic of the present account. (Comp. Note on verse 11.)

(14) **Whereof were made vessels for the house of the Lord.**—Literally, *and he* (i.e., Jehoiada) *made it into vessels for the house of Jehovah, vessels of ministering and of offering,* &c. For "vessels of ministering," comp. Num. iv. 12.

**Spoons.**—*Cups* or *bowls* (*kappôth*, Exod. xxv. 29). The chronicler apparently reverses the statement of 2 Kings xii. 13, 14, "Howbeit there were not made for the house of the Lord, bowls of silver, snuffers, basons, trumpets, any vessels of gold or vessels of silver of the money that was brought into the house of the Lord. But they gave (*used to give*) that to the workmen, and repaired (*used to repair*) therewith the house of the Lord." The solution of the difficulty may be found in the fact that the writer of Kings is relating what was done with the money so long as the repairs of the Temple were in progress, while the chronicler is accounting for the surplus after the restoration was complete. Still the appearance of contradiction is sufficiently curious, and suggests the influence of the *didactic* aims of the later historian.

**And they offered.**—*And they were offering*, i.e., offered habitually, as a matter of regular observance (the same construction as in verse 12, "they were hiring"). The legal ritual was duly carried out in the Temple so long as the influence of Jehoiada was paramount—a remark peculiar to the chronicler. On the other hand, the present writer omits what is stated in closing the account of the Temple repairs (2 Kings xii. 15, 16). There we are told that no reckoning was made with the overseers of the workmen in respect of the moneys entrusted to them, "for they dealt faithfully." It is added that the priests still received the trespass and sin money.

DEATH AND BURIAL OF JEHOIADA. NATIONAL APOSTACY AND MURDER OF ZECHARIAH BEN JEHOIADA THE PROPHET (verses 15—22).

This section is wholly wanting in the Kings. It serves as a moral explanation of the after-history of Joash, recorded there and here (2 Kings xii. 17—21).

(15) **But Jehoiada . . . when he died.**—Literally, *And Jehoiada became old, and was satisfied with days, and he died.* The verb "to be satisfied" is only so used here and in 1 Chron. xxiii. 1. (Comp. Ps. xci. 16.) The ancient expression was adjectival, "full of days" (Gen. xxv. 8, xxxv. 29; Job xlii. 17; 1 Chron. xxix. 28, only).

**An hundred and thirty years old.**—According to some modern physiologists, one hundred and five is the proper limit of human life; that is to say, five times the period usually required for the attainment of full growth. Under favourable conditions it is even supposed that life might extend to half a century longer (M. Flourens, of the French Academy of Sciences). When persons of advanced age (eighty to one hundred) die, it is usually from preventible causes. As a French medical writer has remarked, "Men do not commonly die; they kill themselves." The age of Jehoiada, then, would seem to be not impossible, although an error of transcription in our text is also not impossible.

(16) **Among the kings.**—Literally, *with.* "Because he had done good;" and also, perhaps, as having been regent for so many years, and connected by marriage with the royal house (chap. xxii. 11).

(17) **Came the princes . . . and made obeisance to the king.**—As asking a boon. What their petition was is evident from the context (verse 18). They sought the royal sanction of the idolatrous forms of worship, after which they hankered.

**Then the king hearkened unto them.**—Comp. the influence of the young nobles with Rehoboam, chap. x. 8.

(18) **And they left the house of the Lord.**—*They*, viz., the apostate princes and their following, ceased to attend the legal worship of the Temple.

**And served groves and idols.**—Rather, *the Ashêrim* and *the idols*. (See Note on chap. xiv. 3.)

**And wrath came.**—Chap. xix. 2, 10; 1 Chron. xxvii. 24. In this case the Divine wrath (Num. i. 53) manifested itself in a Syrian invasion (verse 23, *seq.*).

**Upon Judah and Jerusalem.**—The sin of the nobles, allowed and perhaps imitated by the king, involved the nation in its penal consequences (Comp. 1 Chron. xxi.)

*Zechariah is Stoned.*  II. CHRONICLES, XXIV  *The Syrians Invade Judah.*

salem for this their trespass. ⁽¹⁹⁾ Yet he sent prophets to them, to bring them again unto the LORD; and they testified against them: but they would not give ear.

⁽²⁰⁾ And the Spirit of God [1] came upon Zechariah the son of Jehoiada the priest, which stood above the people, and said unto them, Thus saith God, Why transgress ye the commandments of the LORD, that ye cannot prosper? because ye have forsaken the LORD, he hath also forsaken you. ⁽²¹⁾ And they conspired against him, and stoned him with stones at the commandment of the king in the court of the house of the LORD. ⁽²²⁾ Thus Joash the king remembered not the kindness which Jehoiada his father had done to him, but slew his son. And when he died, he said, The LORD look upon *it*, and require it.

⁽²³⁾ And it came to pass [2] at the end of the year, *that* the host of Syria came up against him: and they came to Judah and Jerusalem, and destroyed all the princes of the people from among the people, and sent all the spoil of them unto the king of [3] Damascus. ⁽²⁴⁾ For the army of the Syrians came with a small company of men, and the LORD delivered a very great host into their hand, because they had forsaken the LORD God of their fathers. So they executed judgment against Joash.

[1] Heb., *clothed.*

B.C. 840.

[2] Heb., *in the revolution of the year.*

B.C. 839.

B.C. 840.

[3] Heb., *Darmesek.*

---

⁽¹⁹⁾ **Yet.**—*And.*
**To them.**—*Among them.*
**And they testified against them.**—*Solemnly besought them, exhorted them in the name of God* (Exod. xx. 21; 2 Kings xvii. 13).
**But they would.**—*And they did.*
⁽²⁰⁾ **And the Spirit of God came upon.**—Literally, *clothed, invested.* (See Note on 1 Chron. xii. 18.)
**Zechariah the son of Jehoiada the priest.**—"The priest," *i.e.*, the high priest, is an epithet of Jehoiada, not of Zechariah.
**Which stood above the people.**—Probably on the steps of the inner court of the Temple, facing the people who were assembled in the outer court.
**Why transgress.**—*Wherefore are ye transgressing?*
**That ye cannot prosper.**—Literally, *and will not prosper.*
**Because ye have forsaken . . .**—Rather, *for ye have forsaken the Lord, and He hath forsaken you.* (Comp. the similar language ascribed to the prophets Shemaiah and Azariah ben Oded, chap. xii. 5, xv. 2).
⁽²¹⁾ **And they conspired against him.**—The conspiracy of verse 25 was the Divine recompense for this one.
**And stoned him.**—The legal penalty of idolatry (Lev. xx. 2; Deut. xvii. 2—5).
**At the commandment of the king.**—Probably Zechariah's words had been represented to Joash as treasonable. The Syrian invasion may have been already threatening, when his prophecy was uttered; and in that case it would be easy to allege against the prophet that his "wish was father to his thought." (Comp. the similar case of Jeremiah, Jer. xxxii. 1—5; and 1 Kings xxi. 8—13.)
**In the court of the house of the Lord.**—There is little doubt that the allusion of Christ (Matt. xxiii. 35; Luke xi. 51) to the death of "Zacharias son of Barachias, whom ye slew between the Temple and the altar," refers to this murder. The altar stood in the court, before the Temple. Barachias (Berechiah) may have been Zechariah's father, and Jehoiada his grandfather. Moreover the Lord appears to be thinking of the honourable burial of Jehoiada, in contrast with the murder of his son, in Matt. xxiii. 29—32, verses which immediately precede the mention of Zacharias.

⁽²²⁾ **The Lord look upon it, and require it.**—*Jehovah behold, and avenge!* literally, *seek,* scil., vengeance for the crime (Gen. ix. 5; Ps. x. 4). This dying imprecation is in harmony with the spirit of the older dispensation, which exacted blood for blood. Contrast the prayer of St. Stephen, the first of Christian martyrs (Acts vii. 50). The prayer of Zechariah was also a prophecy destined to speedy fulfilment. (See verse 23, *seq.*)

THE LORD'S VENGEANCE, viz., THE SYRIAN INVASION AND SLAUGHTER OF THE PRINCES, AND THE MURDER OF JOASH (verses 23—27). (Comp. 2 Kings xii. 17—21.)

⁽²³⁾ **At the end of the year.**—*At the running out of the year,* viz., the year of the murder of Zechariah. (See for the phrase, Exod. xxxiv. 22.)
**The host of Syria came up against him.**—Comp. 2 Kings xii. 17. Our passage seems to show that a small part (verse 24) of the besieging army was detached, and sent against Jerusalem. (Comp. 2 Kings xviii. 14, 17.) The princes of Judah (verse 17) at the head of a large force met the invaders in the field; but the Syrians routed them, and "destroyed all the princes of the people from among the people." We may suppose that they made it their special aim to cut off the leaders of the Jewish host. (Comp. chap. xviii. 30.) Thus the apostate princes were overtaken by the prophetic doom. (LXX., "the princes of the people among the people;" Syriac and Vulg. and Arabic omit "from among the people." But comp. Isa. vii. 8.)
**And sent all the spoil of them.**—To Hazael, who was probably still at Gath with the main body of his troops.
⁽²⁴⁾ **For the army of the Syrians.**—This verse is explanatory of verse 23. Literally, *For with fewness of men had the host of Syria come, and Jehovah had given into their hand a host in exceeding abundance.* "Fewness of men" (*miç'ar 'anāshim*) is a phrase not found elsewhere. (Comp. Gen. xix. 20.) The parallel account informs us that Hazael had intended to march against Jerusalem in person, as it would seem, after the battle in which the Syrian division had defeated the Jewish princes. Joash, however, bribed his forbearance by a present of the treasures of the Temple and palace (2 Kings xii. 18).
**So they executed judgment against Joash.**—A phrase always used of Divine requital. (Comp. Exod.

*Joash is slain.* **II. CHRONICLES, XXV.** *Amaziah succeeds him.*

(25) And when they were departed from him, (for they left him in great diseases,) his own servants conspired against him for the blood of the sons of Jehoiada the priest, and slew him on his bed, and he died: and they buried him in the city of David, but they buried him not in the sepulchres of the kings. (26) And these are they that conspired against him; ¹Zabad the son of Shimeath an Ammonitess, and Jehozabad the son of ²Shimrith a Moabitess. (27) Now *concerning* his sons, and the greatness of the burdens *laid* upon him, and the ³repairing of the house of God, behold, they *are* written in the ⁴story of the book of the kings. And Amaziah his son reigned in his stead.

**CHAPTER XXV.**—(1) Amaziah *ᵃwas* twenty and five years old *when* he began to reign, and he reigned twenty and nine years in Jerusalem. And his mother's name *was* Jehoaddan of Jerusalem.

*Marginal notes:*
1 Or, *Jozachar*, 2 Kings 12. 21.
B.C. 839.
2 Or, *Shomer*.
3 Heb., *founding*.
4 Or, *commentary*.
a 2 Kings 14. 1, &c.

---

xii. 12; Ezek. v. 10.) (The construction here is unique: "they did judgments *with* Joash," whereas the ordinary form would be, "they did judgments *in* Joash.")

As compared with Kings, the present narrative regards the Syrian invasion from a prophetic and religious point of view, and, therefore, while it omits certain details which are there clearly specified, it is careful to mention such facts as most vividly point its moral, *e.g.*, the destruction of the idolatrous princes, and the rout of "a great host" by the attack of "a small company."

(25) **And when they were departed from him.**—Omit *were*. The Syrians retired, instead of besieging Jerusalem, as they had purposed to do.

**For they left him in great diseases.**—Some refer this to the wounds which Joash had received from the Syrians in battle. But it is not said that Joash himself was wounded, but only that the destruction of his princes and the defeat of his army were judgments upon him. The word rendered "diseases" (*maḥălûyîm*) only occurs here; but it is obviously a near synonym of the term used of the last sickness of Jehoram (*taḥălû'îm*, chap. xxi. 19), and the probable meaning is "pains," or "suffering." Calamity may have brought about the sickness of Joash, or perhaps the invasion had come upon him when already prostrate with disease, and unable to resist in person.

**His own servants conspired against him.**—2 Kings xii. 20, "And his servants arose and made a conspiracy." Comp. the similar circumstances in the murder of Ishbosheth (2 Sam. iv. 5).

**For the blood of the sons of Jehoiada the priest.**—The LXX. and Vulgate correct this, and read "son," meaning Zechariah the prophet (verse 22), and the plural *may* be due to a transcriber's mistake. More probably it is used *rhetorically*, as in chap. xxviii. 16, and elsewhere.

The writer does not mean to say that revenge for the death of Jehoiada's posterity was the motive which actuated the conspirators, but that their deed was a judgment upon the king for that crime. In Kings the place of the assassination is specified, "Bethmillo that goeth down to Silla." But nothing is there said of the sickness of Joash, and his being murdered in his bed.

**But they buried him not in the sepulchres of the kings.**—See Note on chap. xxi. 20, where the same remark is made about the burial of Jehoram.

(26) **Zabad the son of Shimeath an Ammonitess, and Jehozabad the son of Shimrith a Moabitess.**—2 Kings xii. 21: "Jozachar the son of Shimeath and Jehozabad the son of Shomer." Probably "Jozachar" is right, "Zabad" being an easy corruption of "Zachar," a normal contraction of Jozachar. Yet many MSS. of Kings read "Jozabad." "Shomer" in Kings should probably be Shemer (1 Chron. vii. 32, 34), of which Shimri (1 Chron. iv. 37) and Shimrith might be by-forms. Reuss is incorrect in asserting that the names of the *mothers* are substituted by the chronicler for the names of the *fathers*. Thenius even knows the reason why the chronicler has added the epithets "Ammonitess," "Moabitess." The writer wished to show that the idolatry into which he makes Joash lapse (?), was avenged by two sons of idolatrous wives (!). This is fancy determined by prejudice. The additions "Ammonitess," "Moabitess," indicate the use of another source than the canonical book of Kings; and the same may be said of the strikingly original account of the death of Zechariah (verses 17—22). What that source was the next verse declares, viz., "The Midrash of the book of the Kings."

(27) **Now concerning his sons, and the greatness of the burdens laid upon him, and the repairing of the house of God.**—Rather, *And his sons, and the multitude of oracles upon him, and the founding of the house of God.* The word "burden" (*massa'*) is common in the sense of a threatening prophecy (2 Kings ix. 25; Isa. xiii. 1; Hab. i. 1). In verse 19 it is expressly said that prophets were sent to warn the princes of Judah. If this be the meaning here, the word *massa'* is used collectively. Another possible rendering is, "and the greatness of the tribute laid upon him" by Hazael. (Comp. chap. xvii. 11 for this sense of *massa'*.) The Heb. margin suggests, "and as to his sons, may the burden concerning him multiply;" *i.e.*, may the dying words of Zechariah be fulfilled in them even more disastrously! This is wholly improbable.

**In the story of the book of the kings.**—See margin, and Introduction.

## XXV.

THE REIGN OF AMAZIAH. (Comp. 2 Kings xiv. 1—20.)

DURATION AND CHARACTER OF THE REIGN. EXECUTION OF THE MURDERERS OF JOASH (verses 1—4).

(1, 2) **Amaziah . . . the Lord.**—So 2 Kings xiv. 2. **But not with a perfect heart.**—This is a brief equivalent of the words of the older text: "only not like David his father: according to all that Joash his father had done, he did." The reference to Joash is omitted, perhaps because that king appears to less advantage in the Chronicles than in Kings. In fact, the chronicler's estimate of both princes is less favour-

*Amaziah slays the Traitors.*     II. CHRONICLES, XXV.     *He hires an Army of Israelites.*

(2) And he did *that which was* right in the sight of the LORD, but not with a perfect heart. (3) Now it came to pass, when the kingdom was ¹established to him, that he slew his servants that had killed the king his father. (4) But he slew not their children, but *did as it is* written in the law in the book of Moses, where the LORD commanded, saying, *a*The fathers shall not die for the children, neither shall the children die for the fathers, but every man shall die for his own sin.

(5) Moreover Amaziah gathered Judah together, and made them captains over thousands, and captains over hundreds, according to the houses of *their* fathers, throughout all Judah and Benjamin: and he numbered them from twenty years old and above, and found them three hundred thousand choice *men, able* to go forth to war, that could handle spear and shield. (6) He hired also an hundred thousand mighty men of valour out of Israel for an hundred talents of silver. (7) But there came a man of God to him, saying, O king, let not the army of Israel go with thee; for the LORD *is* not with Israel, *to wit, with* all the children of Ephraim. (8) But if thou wilt go, do *it,* be strong for the battle: God shall make thee fall before the enemy: for God hath power to help, and to cast down. (9) And Amaziah said to the man of God, But what shall we do for the hundred talents which I have given to the ²army of Israel? And the man of God answered, The LORD is able to give thee much more than this. (10) Then Amaziah separated them, *to wit,* the

<small>1 Heb., *confirmed upon him.*

*a* Deut. 24. 16; 2 Kings 14. 6; Jer. 31. 30; Ezek. 18. 20.

2 Heb., *band.*</small>

---

able than that of the older historian. Such differences are perfectly natural, and it is needless to attempt to "reconcile" or eliminate them.

(3) **The kingdom was established to him.**—Or, *The sovereignty* (power) *was confirmed to him.* Vulg., "cumque roboratum videret sibi imperium."

(4) **But he slew not their children.**—The verse coincides almost exactly with 2 Kings xiv. 6. Literally, *And their sons he put not to death; but according to what is written in the Torah, in the book of Moses, which Jehovah commanded,* &c. The reference is evidently to Deut. xxiv. 16, which is more exactly repeated in Kings than here.

**But every man shall die for his own sin.**—Literally, *But, each for (in) his own sin, shall they be put to death.* Kings has the singular.

AMAZIAH'S MILITARY STRENGTH, AND CONQUEST OF EDOM (verses 5—13).

This section is for the most part peculiar to Chronicles. In Kings the conquest of Edom is recorded in a single verse (2 Kings xiv. 7).

(5) **And made them captains over thousands.**—Rather, *And made them stand* (marshalled them) *according to father houses, to wit, according to the captains of thousands and according to the captains of hundreds of all Judah and Benjamin.*

**Numbered.**—*Mustered.*

**Twenty years old.**—The military age: Num. i. 2, 3; 1 Chron. xxvii. 23.

**Three hundred thousand.**—A total immensely below that of the forces of Jehoshaphat (chap. xvii. 14—18), and not much more than half that of Asa's (chap. xiv. 8). All these high numbers are no doubt suspicious; but a certain relative propriety is observable in the present instance, inasmuch as the country had suffered great losses by the disastrous wars of Jehoram, Ahaziah, Joash.

**Able to go forth to war.**—Literally, *going out in the host.* (See Num. *l. c.*)

**That could handle spear and shield.**—*Grasping lance and target, i.e.,* heavy-armed warriors. (Comp. 1 Chron. xii. 8.)

(6) **He hired also . . . out of Israel**—*i.e.,* from the northern kingdom. The number has probably suffered in transmission. Thenius pronounces the fact historical, although not recorded in Kings.

**An hundred talents of silver.**—Worth about £40,000 of our money, reckoning £400 to the talent. What such a sum would represent in the days of Amaziah cannot be determined with certainty.

(7) **The Lord is not with Israel.**—Comp. chaps. xix. 2, xx. 37; also chap. xvi. 7.

**To wit, with all the children of Ephraim.**—Added as an explanation of the term *Israel.* Ephraim was the name of the northern kingdom (Hos. v. 11, 14, vi. 4, and *passim*).

(8) **But if thou wilt go.**—Rather, *But go thyself;* in contrast with the prohibition, "Let not the army of Israel go."

**Do it, be strong for the battle.**—Compare 1 Chron. xxii. 16: "Arise! act!"

**God shall make thee fall.**—Before these words, the expression *welō*', "and not," must have dropped out of the text. "Venture on the expedition by thyself, with a good courage," says the prophet, "and God will not let thee stumble before the foe."

**For God hath power.**—*For there is strength in God, to help and to make to stumble.* (Comp. chap. xx. 6; 1 Chron. xxix. 12; Ps. ix. 3.) The ancient versions were evidently embarrassed by the passage. The LXX. render: "Because if thou think to prevail through them, *then will the Lord rout thee before thy foes;* because it is from the Lord both to be strong and to rout." Vulg.: "But if thou thinkest that wars depend on the strength of an army, *God will make thee to be overcome by the enemy."* Syriac: "Because thou art going to make war, *the Lord will cast thee down before thy foes;* because thou hast not praised the Lord, who is the helper and uplifter." It is noticeable that no version inserts the required negative; the omission, therefore, is ancient.

(9) **What shall we do?**—Literally, *What to do? i.e.,* What is to be done? what must we do?

**The army.**—*The troop* (*gĕdūd*) of mercenaries.

(10) **To wit, the army.**—*The troop* (*le* prefixed, as sign of the accusative).

410

*Victory over the Edomites.* II. CHRONICLES, XXV. *Amaziah's Idolatry.*

army that was come to him out of Ephraim, to go ¹home again: wherefore their anger was greatly kindled against Judah, and they returned home ²in great anger. ⁽¹¹⁾ And Amaziah strengthened himself, and led forth his people, and went to the valley of salt, and smote of the children of Seir ten thousand. ⁽¹²⁾ And *other* ten thousand *left* alive did the children of Judah carry away captive, and brought them unto the top of the rock, and cast them down from the top of the rock, that they all were broken in pieces. ⁽¹³⁾ But ³the soldiers of the army which Amaziah sent back, that they should not go with him to battle, fell upon the cities of Judah, from Samaria even unto Beth-horon, and smote three thousand of them, and took much spoil.

⁽¹⁴⁾ Now it came to pass, after that Amaziah was come from the slaughter of the Edomites, that he brought the gods of the children of Seir, and set them up *to be* his gods, and bowed down himself before them, and burned incense unto them. ⁽¹⁵⁾ Wherefore the anger of the LORD was kindled against Amaziah, and he sent unto him a prophet, which said unto him, Why hast thou sought after the gods of the people, which could

1 Heb., *to their place.*
2 Heb., *in heat of anger.*
3 Heb., *the sons of the band.*

---

**To go home again.**—*To go to their own place.*

**Home in great anger.**—*To their own place in a heat of anger* (Isa. vii. 4). Obviously the dismissed force would be incensed at treatment which seemed to indicate distrust of their honour, and robbed them of the possible fruits of victory. On their way home they revenged themselves by plundering and slaughtering in the cities of Judah (verse 13).

⁽¹¹⁾ **And Amaziah strengthened himself.**—*Shewed himself strong* or *courageous, took courage;* as the prophet had bidden him do (verse 8). (Comp. chap. xv. 8.)

**And went to the valley of salt.**—Comp. 2 Kings xiv. 7: "He it was who smote Edom in the valley of salt ten thousand; and he took Sela in the war, and called its name Joktheel, unto this day." The valley of salt lay to the south-east of the Dead Sea (2 Sam. viii. 13; 1 Chron. xviii. 12).

⁽¹²⁾ **And other ten thousand left alive.**—Rather, *And ten thousand the sons of Judah took alive.* The LXX. renders well: καὶ δέκα χιλιάδας ἐζώγρησαν οἱ υἱοὶ Ἰούδα.

**And brought them unto the top of the rock.**—Or, *of Sela.* Sela, "the crag," was the Edomite capital, known to after ages as Petra, "the rock." The "Head of Sela" may be the name of a cliff overhanging the town. This savage massacre of prisoners is not mentioned in Kings; but it is quite credible, in view of the well-known atrocities of ancient warfare. (Comp. 1 Chron. xx. 3; Ps. cxxxvii. 9; 2 Kings viii. 12; Amos i. 11, 13; 1 Kings xi. 15, 16; Joab "cut off every male in Edom.") It is, however, remarkable that the chronicler does not mention the capture of Sela itself. Thenius, therefore, supposes that the statement of this verse is really the result of an attempt to restore an illegible text of 2 Kings xiv. 7.

⁽¹³⁾ **But the soldiers of the army.**—Literally, *Now the sons of the troop whom Amaziah had caused to return from marching with him to the war, they fell upon,* &c.

**Fell upon.**—The verb used in 1 Chron. xiv. 9, 13: "Spread themselves." Here it means attacked with a view to plunder (Job i. 17).

**From Samaria even unto Beth-horon.**—"Samaria" is probably corrupt. Otherwise we must suppose that the mercenaries first returned home, and then, by order of king Joash, started afresh from Samaria, and invaded the northern districts of the kingdom of Judah. For "Beth-horon," see Note on 1 Chron. vii. 24.

**And smote . . . of them.**—*Of their inhabitants.*

AMAZIAH ADOPTS THE EDOMITE FORM OF WORSHIP, AND SPURNS A PROPHETIC WARNING (verses 14—16).

⁽¹⁴⁾ **From the slaughter.**—*From smiting.*

**Brought the gods.**—The Assyrian inscriptions often refer to this custom of carrying off the idols of conquered countries. Esarhaddon states that he restored the gods of Hazael, king of Arabia, at that prince's entreaty, after engraving on them "the might of Asshur" and his own name. Assurbanipal recovered an image of Nana, which an Elamite sovereign had carried off one thousand six hundred and thirty-five years previously.

**The children of Seir.**—*Bnê Seir,* the tribal designation of the Edomites (1 Chron. i. 38).

**Set them up to be his gods.**—Not necessarily abandoning the worship of Jehovah. (Comp. the conduct of Ahaz, chap. xxviii. 23; 2 Kings xvi. 10, *et seq.;* also 2 Kings xvii. 27—33.) Thenius says this contradicts 2 Kings iv. 3; and it may be allowed that the chronicler portrays Amaziah in a darker light than the older account. This only proves independence of judgment and the possession of additional information. Thenius and Bertheau further suppose that the chronicler, from his theocratic standpoint, merely *inferred* the idolatry of Amaziah from his ill success against Israel. It is more likely that it was mentioned in one of the histories which the compiler had before him.

**Bowed down himself.**—Literally, *And before them would he bow himself, and to them would he offer incense;* relating his habitual practice.

⁽¹⁵⁾ **Could not deliver.**—*Delivered not.* (Comp. the boast of Sennacherib concerning the gods who had failed before him: 2 Kings xviii. 33—35.) The king's object may have been to win their favour, and so retain his hold on what was regarded as their peculiar territory. One of these gods might be *Hadad* (comp. 1 Chron. i. 46, 50; 2 Kings v. 18, vi. 24); another might have been *Kôsh.* (Comp. the Edomite royal names *Qa-us-ma-la-ka, i.e.,* Kosmalak, "Kosh is king," and *Qa-us-gab-ri, i.e.,* Kosgabri, "Kosh is my warrior;" names which are like the Hebrew *Elimelech* and *Gabriel* respectively.) The Hebrew proper name, *Kish,* may be the same as *Kôsh.* Lastly, the name of a king of Edom mentioned by Sennacherib, *Mâlik-rammu, i.e.,* "Moloch is exalted," indicates that Moloch also was worshipped in Edom.

not deliver their own people out of thine hand? ⁽¹⁶⁾ And it came to pass, as he talked with him, that *the king* said unto him, Art thou made of the king's counsel? forbear; why shouldest thou be smitten? Then the prophet forbare, and said, I know that God hath ¹determined to destroy thee, because thou hast done this, and hast not hearkened unto my counsel.

⁽¹⁷⁾ Then ᵃAmaziah king of Judah took advice, and sent to Joash, the son of Jehoahaz, the son of Jehu, king of Israel, saying, Come, let us see one another in the face. ⁽¹⁸⁾ And Joash king of Israel sent to Amaziah king of Judah, saying, The ²thistle that *was* in Lebanon sent to the cedar that *was* in Lebanon, saying, Give thy daughter to my son to wife: and there passed by ³a wild beast that *was* in Lebanon, and trode down the thistle. ⁽¹⁹⁾ Thou sayest, Lo, thou hast smitten the Edomites; and thine heart lifteth thee up to boast: abide now at home; why shouldest thou meddle to *thine* hurt, that thou shouldest fall, *even* thou, and Judah with thee? ⁽²⁰⁾ But Amaziah would not hear; for it *came* of God, that he might deliver them into the hand *of their enemies*, because they sought after the gods of Edom. ⁽²¹⁾ So Joash the king of Israel went up; and they saw one another in the face, *both* he and Amaziah king of Judah, at Beth-shemesh, which *belongeth* to Judah. ⁽²²⁾ And Judah was ⁴put to the worse before Israel, and they fled every man to his tent. ⁽²³⁾ And Joash the king of Israel took Amaziah king of Judah, the son of Joash, the son of Jehoahaz, at Beth-shemesh, and brought him to Jerusalem, and brake down the wall of Jerusalem from the gate of Ephraim to ⁵the corner gate, four hundred cubits. ⁽²⁴⁾ And *he took* all the gold and the silver, and all the vessels that were found in the house of God with Obed-edom, and the treasures of the king's house, the hostages also, and returned to Samaria.

¹ Heb., *counselled.*
ᵃ 2 Kings 14. 8, 9.
² Or, *furze bush, or, thorn.*
³ Heb., *a beast of the field.*
⁴ Heb., *smitten.*
⁵ Heb., *the gate of it that looketh.*

---

⁽¹⁶⁾ **As he talked with him.**—*When he spake unto him.*

**Art thou made of the king's counsel?**—Literally, *A counsellor to the king have we appointed thee?*

**Why shouldest thou be smitten?**—*Wherefore should they smite thee?*

**Hath determined.**—*Hath counselled.* The prophet appropriates the king's own word, and implies his participation in Divine, if not in royal, counsels.

**Because.**—The conduct of Amaziah was proof that God had "counselled to destroy him."

**Thou hast done this.**—*Spurned my warning.* Others say: because thou hast adopted the Edomite gods.

**Unto my counsel.**—Again repeating the king's expression.

AMAZIAH CHALLENGES JOASH OF ISRAEL TO BATTLE, AND SUFFERS DISASTROUS DEFEAT (verses 17—24). (Comp. 2 Kings xiv. 8—14.)

⁽¹⁷⁾ **Then Amaziah . . . took advice.**—*And Amaziah took counsel* (chap. x. 6). Different from the counsel which the prophet would have tendered him (verse 16).

**And sent to Joash.**—See 2 Kings xiv. 8: "Sent *messengers*." The rest of the verse is the same in both passages.

**Let us see.**—*Let us look one another in the face;* as combatants do.

⁽¹⁸⁾ **And Joash king of Israel.**—This verse is the same as 2 Kings xiv. 9. (See Notes there.)

⁽¹⁹⁾ **Thou sayest.**—Slightly altered from 2 Kings xiv. 10. *Thou sayest,* or *thou thinkest,* is added here. The word in Hebrew meaning *Lo* (*hinnêh*) is perhaps a corruption of the word meaning *smiting* (*hakkêh*): "Thou hast indeed smitten."

**To boast.**—*To get glory* (*hakbîd*). Only so used here. Kings, "thine heart lifteth thee up. *Be honoured* (*i.e.,* enjoy thine honours), and abide at home" (*hikkâbêd*). The difference is one of points only, and may be due to a copyist.

⁽²⁰⁾ **But Amaziah would not hear.**—*And Amaziah hearkened not.*

**For it came of God . . . gods of Edom.**—This remark is added by the chronicler, accounting for the infatuation of Joash by reference to the divine predetermination of events. (Comp. verse 16; and chap. xxiv. 24, x. 15; the Syr. and Arab. omit.)

**That he might deliver them into the hand.**—Heb., *into hand;* LXX., "into hands;" Vulg., "into the hands of the enemy." Perhaps the original reading was, *into his hand, i.e.,* the hand of Joash.

**Because they sought.**—*For they had sought.*

⁽²²⁾ **And Judah was put to the worse.**—So 2 Kings xiv. 12. The Syriac and Arabic omit this verse.

⁽²³⁾ **Jehoahaz.**—Several Hebrew MSS. read *Ahaziah,* as in 2 Kings xiv. 13, with which the rest of the verse agrees: see the Notes there. (See Note on chap. xxi. 17.)

**The corner gate.**—So 2 Kings xiv. 13, rightly. Our Hebrew text has, "gate of the turning one," or "gate that turneth;" which would require some word indicating the direction of the turning. (Comp. Ezek. viii. 3, "gate that turneth northward.") Some MSS., and all the versions, agree with Kings. It is merely a matter of different points. (Comp. also chap. xxvi. 9.)

⁽²⁴⁾ **And he took.**—So 2 Kings xiv. 14. The verb has fallen out here. The omission is ancient, as it appears in the LXX. The Vulg. gives the verb *returned* at the end of the verse a transitive form, and renders "he carried back to Samaria" all the things enumerated. The Syriac reads, "and he took the silver," &c.

**With Obed-edom.**—Added by the chronicler, in harmony with what he has stated about the custody of the sacred treasures (1 Chron. xxvi. 15, *seq.*); but

*Amaziah is slain.*      II. CHRONICLES, XXVI.      *Uzziah's Reign.*

<sup>(25)</sup> And Amaziah the son of Joash king of Judah lived after the death of Joash son of Jehoahaz king of Israel fifteen years. <sup>(26)</sup> Now the rest of the acts of Amaziah, first and last, behold, *are* they not written in the book of the kings of Judah and Israel? <sup>(27)</sup> Now after the time that Amaziah did turn away <sup>1</sup>from following the LORD they <sup>2</sup>made a conspiracy against him in Jerusalem; and he fled to Lachish: but they sent to Lachish after him, and slew him there. <sup>(28)</sup> And they brought him upon horses, and buried him with his fathers in the city of <sup>3</sup>Judah.

1 Heb., *from after.*

2 Heb., *conspired a conspiracy.*

3 That is, *the city of David,* as it is 2 Kings 14. 20.

a 2 Kings 14. 21 & 15. 1.

4 Or, *Azariah.*

B.C. 810.

CHAPTER XXVI.—<sup>(1)</sup> Then all the people of Judah took <sup>a 4</sup>Uzziah, who *was* sixteen years old, and made him king in the room of his father Amaziah. <sup>(2)</sup> He built Eloth, and restored it to Judah, after that the king slept with his fathers.

<sup>(3)</sup> Sixteen years old *was* Uzziah when he began to reign, and he reigned fifty and two years in Jerusalem. His mother's name also *was* Jecoliah of Jerusalem. <sup>(4)</sup> And he did *that which was* right in the sight of the LORD, according to all that his father Amaziah did. <sup>(5)</sup> And he sought God in the

---

probably derived from an ancient document. Obed-edom was the name of a Levitical clan.

END OF THE REIGN (verses 25—28.) (Comp. 2 Kings xiv. 17—20.)

<sup>(25)</sup> **And Amaziah.**—Identical with 2 Kings xiv. 17. (See Notes there.)

<sup>(26)</sup> **First and last.**—*The former and the latter.* The chronicler adds his usual formula.

**Behold, are they not written.**—The Hebrew is faulty here. "Behold, they are written" is the customary phrase in the Chronicles (chaps. xx. 34, xxiv. 27); "are they not written" being that of Kings. In the Hebrew text here the two phrases are blended. Some MSS., and the Syriac, Vulg., and Arabic read, "Behold, they are written." But it is possible that *hinnām* ("behold they") is here a corruption of *hēm* ("they"); and that the reading of Kings should be followed, with other Hebrew MSS. and the Targum.

<sup>(27)</sup> **Now after the time that Amaziah did turn away from following the Lord.**—This clause is added by the chronicler, not so much with the aim of assigning a date, as of asserting the real connection between Amaziah's defection from Jehovah, and the calamities that overtook him. Virtually he calls attention to the fulfilment of the prophecy of verse 16.

<sup>(28)</sup> **Upon horses.**—See 2 Kings xiv. 20.

**In the city of Judah.**—A transcriber's mistake for *city of David,* as it is in Kings and all the old versions, as well as some Heb. MSS.

XXVI.

REIGN OF UZZIAH-AZARIAH.

ACCESSION, AGE, AND CONDUCT OF UZZIAH. INFLUENCE OF THE PROPHET ZECHARIAH (verses 1—5). (Comp. 2 Kings xiv. 21, 22; xv. 2, 3.)

<sup>(1)</sup> **Then.**—*And.*

**Uzziah.**—So the chronicler always names him, except in one place (1 Chron. iii. 12), where the name *Azariah* appears, as in 2 Kings xiv. 21; xv. 1, 6, &c. In 2 Kings xv. 13, 30, 32, 34, *Uzziah* occurs (though there also the LXX. reads *Azariah,* thus making the usage of Kings uniform); as also in the headings of the prophecies of Hosea, Amos, and Isaiah. It is not, therefore, to be regarded either as a popular abbreviation or a transcriber's blunder, as Schrader and others suggest. In the Assyrian inscriptions of Tiglath-pileser II. this king is uniformly called *Azriyahu, i.e.,* Azariah. Clearly, therefore, he was known by both names; but to foreigners chiefly by the latter. (Comp. Azareel—Uzziel, 1 Chron. xxv. 4, 18.)

<sup>(2)</sup> **He built.**—*He it was who built.*

**Eloth.**—Kings, *Elath.* The Idumean port on the Red Sea.

The first four verses are identical with the parallel in Kings. (See the Notes there.)

<sup>(5)</sup> **And he sought God.**—*And he continued to seek God* (the Hebrew is an expression peculiar to the chronicler).

**In the days of Zechariah.**—An otherwise unknown prophet.

**Who had understanding in the visions of God.**—Literally, *the skilled in seeing God*—a surprising epithet, occurring nowhere else. Some Hebrew MSS., and the LXX., Syriac, and Arabic versions, and the Targum, read, "in the fear of God." This is doubtless correct; and the text should be rendered: "who had understanding (or *gave instruction*) in the fear of God." So the famous Rabbis, Rashi and Kimchi, long since suggested. Zechariah was thus the guide and counsellor of king Uzziah, and that not only in religious matters, but in what we should call the political sphere; for in those days the distinction between things sacred and secular, civil and ecclesiastical, between Church and State, religion and common life, was wholly unknown.

**And as long as he sought.**—Literally, *in the days of his seeking.*

**The Lord, God . . .**—Such a mode of speech reveals the chronicler's own hand.

Instead of this verse, 2 Kings xv. 4 makes the deduction usual in its estimate of the character of a reign: "Only the high places were not taken away; the people still used to sacrifice and burn incense on the high places."

The power and prosperity of Uzziah are accounted for by the chronicler on the ground that he sought God during the life of Zechariah; although afterwards he offended by rashly intruding upon the priest's office, and was punished with leprosy (verses 16—21).

UZZIAH'S CAMPAIGNS, PUBLIC WORKS, AND MILITARY STRENGTH (verses 6—15).

This section is peculiar to the Chronicles. Although the book of Kings passes over the facts recorded here, they are essential to forming a right conception of the strength and importance of the southern kingdom during the age of Uzziah and Jotham; and they are fully corroborated, not only by comparison with the

days of Zechariah, who had understanding [1] in the visions of God: and as long as he sought the LORD, God made him to prosper. (6) And he went forth and warred against the Philistines, and brake down the wall of Gath, and the wall of Jabneh, and the wall of Ashdod, and built cities [2] about Ashdod, and among the Philistines. (7) And God helped him against the Philistines, and against the Arabians that dwelt in Gurbaal, and the Mehunims. (8) And the Ammonites gave gifts to Uzziah: and his name [3] spread abroad *even* to the entering in of Egypt; for he strengthened *himself* exceedingly.

(9) Moreover Uzziah built towers in Jerusalem at the corner gate, and at the valley gate, and at the turning *of the wall*, and [4] fortified them. (10) Also he built towers in the desert, and [5] digged many wells: for he had much cattle, both in the low country, and in the plains: husbandmen *also*, and vine

[1] Heb., *in the seeing of God.*
[2] Or, *in the country of Ashdod.*
[3] Heb., *went.*
[4] Or, *repaired.*
[5] Or, *cut out many cisterns.*

---

data of Isaiah (Isa. ii.—iv.) upon the same subject, but also by the independent testimony of the cuneiform inscriptions of the period. (See Note on 2 Kings xiv. 28.) Thus we find that the warlike Assyrian Tiglath-pileser II. chastised Hamath for its alliance with Judah during this reign, but abstained from molesting Uzziah himself—"a telling proof," as Schrader says, "for the accuracy of the Biblical account of Uzziah's well-founded power." The name of Uzziah is conspicuously absent from the list of western princes who, in B.C. 738, sent tribute to Tiglath: Hystaspes (*Kushtashpi*), king of Commagene (*Kummuḫa'a*), Rezin, king of the country of the Damascenes, Menahem of the city of the Samaritans, Hiram of the city of the Tyrians, Sibitti-bi'li of the city of the Giblites or Byblos, Urikki of Kui, Pisiris of Carchemish, Eniel of Hamath, Panammu of Sam'al, and nine other sovereigns, including those of Tabal and Arabia. The list thus comprises Hittites and Arameans, princes of Hither Asia, Phœnicia, and Arabia. The omission of Uzziah argues that the king of Judah felt himself strong enough to sustain the shock of collision with Assyria in case of need. He must have reckoned on the support of the surrounding states (also not mentioned in the above list), viz., Ashdod, Ascalon, Gaza, Edom, Ammon, Moab, &c. (Schrader, *Keilinschr.*, p. 252, *seq.*).

(6) **And he went forth and warred against the Philistines.**—At the outset of his reign this able prince had given promise of his future by seizing and fortifying the port of Elath, and thus probably completing the subjugation of Edom, which his father had more than begun. Afterwards he assumed the offensive against the Philistines, Arabs, and Maonites, who had invaded the country under his predecessors (chaps. xxi. 16; xx. 1).

**Brake down the wall of Gath.**—After taking the city. (As to Gath, see 1 Chron. xviii. 1; 2 Chron. xi. 8.)

**Jabneh.**—The *Jamnia* of Maccabees and Josephus; now the village of *Jebnah*, about twelve miles south of Joppa (the same as Jabneel, Josh. xv. 11).

**Ashdod.**—*Esdûd.* (Comp. Josh. xiii. 3.) Like Gath, one of the five sovereign states of the Philistines. It commanded the great road to Egypt; hence its possession was of first-rate importance to the contending military powers of Egypt and Assyria. Sargon captured it B.C. 719. (Comp. Isa. xx. 1.)

**About Ashdod.**—*In Ashdod*, i.e., in the canton so called.

**And among the Philistines.**—That is, elsewhere in their territory. Uzziah appears to have reduced the Philistines to a state of complete vassalage. They were not, however, annexed to Judah, but ruled by their own kings.

(7) **The Philistines, and ... the Arabians.**—They are named together in chap. xvii. 11 also. Their seat, Gur-Baal, only mentioned here, is unknown. The Targum makes it *Gerar*; the LXX. apparently *Petra* (in Edom). The reading *Gedor*-Baal has been proposed.

**The Mehunims** (Heb., *Meʻûnim*) are the Maonites, or people of Maon (*Ma'ân*), near Mount Seir. (See Note on chap. xx. 1.)

(The Syriac and Arabic omit from "wall of Ashdod" verse 6, to "gifts to Uzziah," verse 8.)

(8) **The Ammonites.**—Old enemies of Judah (chap. xx. 1).

**Gave gifts.**—*Paid tribute.* Literally, *gave a present*, or *offering* (*minḥāh*).

**His name spread abroad even to the entering in of Egypt.**—See margin. His name and influence, like Solomon's, extended to the Egyptian border.

**He strengthened himself exceedingly.**—*He showed strength, prevailed, made head* (Dan. xi. 7, 32).

**Exceedingly.**—See the Notes on 1 Chron. xiv. 2, xxix. 25. Syriac, "because he made much war."

(9) **Built towers.**—To defend the approaches.

**At the corner gate.**—*Over*, that is, *commanding* the gate (chap. xxv. 23). Probably the north-west corner of the city wall.

**The valley gate.**—Syriac, "the west gate." In the western wall, the modern Jaffa gate. These two towers protected the most exposed points of the capital.

**At the turning of the wall.**—*Over the angle* (*ha-miqçôa'*), i.e., on the eastern side of Zion, at a bend in the wall. This tower defended both Zion and Moriah against attacks from the south-east. (Neh. iii. 19, 20, 24, 25.)

**And fortified them.**—Literally, *made them* (the gates) *strong.* Or rather, perhaps, *he made the towers strong*, i.e., put them in a posture of defence. (Comp. chap. xi. 11.) The margin is wrong. Syriac, "girded (or bound) them at their corners with clamps (*glidê, i.e., κλεῖδες*) of iron."

(10) **In the desert.**—Or, *grazing country*, i.e., the "wilderness of Judah," on the west of the Dead Sea. The towers were for the protection of the royal herds against the predatory Bedawin. (Comp. Mic. iv. 8: "And thou, O tower of the flock.")

**Digged many wells.**—*Hewed out many cisterns;* to supply his herds with water.

**For he had much cattle.**—Scil. *there*, in the wilderness of Judah. But perhaps we should render thus: "For he had much cattle; and in the lowland and in the plain he had husbandmen; and vinedressers in the mountains and in the glebe land." So Syriac.

*Uzziah's Army*    II. CHRONICLES, XXVI.    *and Engines of War.*

dressers in the mountains, and in ¹Carmel: for he loved ²husbandry. ⁽¹¹⁾ Moreover Uzziah had an host of fighting men, that went out to war by bands, according to the number of their account by the hand of Jeiel the scribe and Maaseiah the ruler, under the hand of Hananiah, one of the king's captains. ⁽¹²⁾ The whole number of the chief of the fathers of the mighty men of valour were two thousand and six hundred. ⁽¹³⁾ And under their hand was ³an army, three hundred thousand and seven thousand and five hundred, that made war with mighty power, to help the king against the enemy. ⁽¹⁴⁾ And Uzziah prepared for them throughout all the host shields, and spears, and helmets, and habergeons, and bows, and ⁴slings to cast stones. ⁽¹⁵⁾ And he made in Jerusalem engines, invented by cunning men, to be on the towers and upon the bulwarks, to shoot arrows and great stones withal. And his name ⁵spread far abroad; for he was marvellously helped, till he was strong.

⁽¹⁶⁾ But when he was strong, his heart was lifted up to his destruction: for he

1 Or, *fruitful fields.*
2 Heb., *ground.*
3 Heb., *the power of an army.*
4 Heb., *stones of slings.*
5 Heb., *went forth.*

---

**Both in the low country.**—*And in the lowland* of Judah; the *Shephēlah*, between the hills and the Mediterranean.

**And in the plains.**—*Plain (mishôr).* "The Plain," *par excellence*, appears to mean the high level east of the Dead Sea and Jordan (Deut. iv. 43; Josh. xx. 8). This was the territory of Reuben, which Uzziah probably recovered from Moab and Ammon (verse 8). (Comp. Isa. xvi. 1, from which it appears that the kings of Judah at this epoch claimed sovereignty over the country on the eastern side of the Jordan.)

**And in Carmel.**—Or, *the fruitful field, the glebe land* (Isa. xxix. 17; xxxii. 15).

With the whole verse comp. the account of David's agricultural and pastoral wealth (1 Chron. xxvii. 25—31).

**He loved husbandry.**—*A lover of land was he*, i.e., of the soil. (Comp. the expression, "man of the land," i.e., husbandman, Gen. ix. 20.)

⁽¹¹⁾ **Moreover . . . fighting men.**—Literally, *And Uzziah had a host making war* (or, *doing battle*).

**That went out to war.**—Literally, *goers forth in the host.*

**By bands.**—Or, *in troops (lig'dûd)*—i.e., in regular array; in organised bodies. Probably each house formed a distinct troop. (See verse 13.)

**According to the number of their account.** —*In the number of their muster (pĕquddāh*, "census").

**By the hand of Jeiel the scribe and Maaseiah the ruler.**—These two royal officials had been entrusted with the draught of the muster rolls. They were "under the hand"—i.e., the direction and superintendence—of Hananiah, who was "one of the king's captains," or staff officers.

**Under the hand.**—Or, *at the side ('al yad)* (1 Chron. xxv. 2).

⁽¹²⁾ **Chief of the fathers.**—*Heads of the families*, or *father-houses.*

**Of the mighty men of valour.**—*To wit, the mighty men of valour*, in apposition with *heads of the families*. The army was marshalled, as of old, according to clans, or houses, the heads of which are here distinguished as "valiant heroes."

⁽¹³⁾ **Under their hand.**—Or, *at their side*, meaning, *under their command.*

**An army.**—See margin. *An armed force*, or, *warlike host (ʽhêl çābā')*; an expression only found besides in 1 Chron. xx. 1.

**Three hundred thousand . . . five hundred.** —This fairly agrees with the statement respecting the total of Amaziah's army (300,000) in chap. xxv. 5.

**That made war with mighty power.**—Literally, *a doer of battle with strength of might* (sturdy strength, *kōaʽh ʽhayil*, a unique phrase). Each chief was thus at the head of about a hundred and twenty men, who formed his troop (*gedûd*, verse 11). (Comp. the expression, "captains of hundreds.") The actual number in each century may have varied, as in the Roman army.

⁽¹⁴⁾ **Throughout.**—*To wit, for all the army*, an apposition.

**Shields, and spears** (*rĕmāʽhim*, "lances"), **and helmets, and habergeons** (*shiryônôth*, "coats of mail," "cuirasses").—For the heavy armed.

"Habergeon" is an old English word, meaning armour for neck and breast.

**Bows, and slings . . . stones.**—For the light armed. (See margin.)

**Slings to cast stones.**—Literally, *stones of slings* (the *le* is the mark of the *accusative*). They are mentioned to show that the equipment was complete.

⁽¹⁵⁾ **Engines, invented by cunning men.**— The first mention of artillery. Literally, *devices, a devising of a deviser.* The word "engine" (i.e., *ingenium*, which is late Latin for *ballista*) fairly represents *ʽhishshābôn.* LXX, μηχανάς. Vulg., *machinas.*

**Bulwarks.**—*Pinnôth.* Zeph. i. 16, "towers."

**To shoot arrows and great stones.**—So that they were like the well-known catapults and ballisters of Roman warfare. An instrument like the ballista is represented on the Assyrian sculptures, and probably both kinds of artillery passed from Assyria to Palestine.

**And his name spread.**—*Went forth* (verse 8).

**He was marvellously helped.**—The Hebrew phrase only occurs here.

**Till.**—*So that he became strong.*

UZZIAH'S PRESUMPTION PUNISHED BY LEPROSY. HIS DEATH (verses 16—23).

This section also is mainly peculiar to the chronicler. 2 Kings xv. 5—7 correspond to verses 21—23 only.

⁽¹⁶⁾ **But when he was strong.**—See verse 15, "till he was strong," and the same phrase, chap. xii. 1.

**His heart was lifted up.**—With pride.

**To his destruction.**—Rather, *even to dealing corruptly ('ad lehashʽhith).*

**For he transgressed.**—*And he was unfaithful to Jehovah* (1 Chron. v, 25).

**Went into the temple . . . to burn incense.** —On the golden altar, in the Holy Place; contrary to the law of Num. xviii. 1—7. Elevated by success,

transgressed against the LORD his God, and went into the temple of the LORD to burn incense upon the altar of incense. (17) And Azariah the priest went in after him, and with him fourscore priests of the LORD, *that were* valiant men: (18) and they withstood Uzziah the king, and said unto him, It *appertaineth* not unto thee, Uzziah, to burn incense unto the LORD, but to the *priests the sons of Aaron, that are consecrated to burn incense: go out of the sanctuary; for thou hast trespassed; neither *shall it be* for thine honour from the LORD God. (19) Then Uzziah was wroth, and *had* a censer in his hand to burn incense: and while he was wroth with the priests, the leprosy even rose up in his forehead before the priests in the house of the LORD, from beside the incense altar. (20) And Azariah the chief priest, and all the priests, looked upon him, and, behold, he *was* leprous in his forehead, and they thrust him out from thence; yea, himself *hasted also to go out, because the LORD had smitten him. (21) *And Uzziah the king was a leper unto the day of his death, and dwelt in a *1several house, *being* a leper; for he was cut off from the house of the LORD: and Jotham his son *was* over the king's house, judging the people of the land.

(22) Now the rest of the acts of Uzziah, first and last, did Isaiah the prophet, the son of Amoz, write. (23) So Uzziah slept with his fathers, and they buried him with his fathers in the field of the burial which *belonged* to the kings; for they said, He *is* a leper: and Jotham his son reigned in his stead.

CHAPTER XXVII.—(1) Jotham *was

*a* Num. 18. 7.
*b* Exod. 30. 7.
*c* As Esth. 6. 12.
*d* 2 Kings 15. 5.
*e* Lev. 13. 46.
1 Heb., *free*.
*f* 2 Kings 15. 32.

---

Uzziah appears to have desired to become supreme pontiff as well as king, and to exercise the same dual functions as the Egyptian Pharaohs were wont to do. Some have thought that he merely revived the precedent of David and Solomon; but it can hardly be proved that those monarchs, though represented as organising the priesthood and ritual, and conducting great religious festivals, ever actually performed the distinctive functions of priests. (Comp. the conduct of Saul, 1 Sam. xiii 9, and its consequences.)

(17) **Azariah the priest**—*i.e.*, the high priest, whose duty it would be to resist such an encroachment on sacerdotal functions. His name does not occur in the list (1 Chron. v. 27—41).

**Valiant men.**—*Sons of valour* (1 Chron. v. 18), so called because they had the moral courage to oppose the king.

(18) **They withstood.**—*'Amad 'al*, a late usage. (Comp. 1 Chron. xxi. 1.)

**It appertaineth not unto thee, Uzziah, to burn incense.**—Comp. the construction (1 Chron. xv. 2).

**Trespassed.**—*Done faithlessly* (*ma'al*), verse 16.

**Neither shall it be . . . Lord God.**—Literally, *and not to thee* (is it) *for honour from Jehovah*; *i.e.*, thine act will not issue in honour, as thou thinkest, but in shame. Or, perhaps, And burning incense belongs not to thee as a prerogative from Jehovah ('*ên*, not *lô*,' would be more natural).

(19) **Then.**—*And*.

**Was wroth.**—*Za'aph*, i.e., foamed with anger.

**And had.**—*And in his hand was a censer* (Ezek. viii. 11).

**Even.**—Omit.

**Rose up.**—*Zarah*. The word is not used in this sense elsewhere.

**From beside**—*i.e.*, near, hard by.

Uzziah's punishment was the same as that which fell upon Miriam (Num. xii. 10) and Gehazi (2 Kings v. 27). Thenius, while asserting the historical character of Uzziah's invasion of the sanctuary, declares that the chronicler has followed *traditional exegesis* in making the king's leprosy a judgment upon his offence. At all events, we may be sure that the chronicler has given the story as he found it in the history of Uzziah, to which he alludes in verse 22.

In Josephus the story is further embellished by the statements that the great earthquake mentioned in Amos i. 1 happened at the moment when Uzziah threatened the opposing priests; and that a ray of sunlight falling upon the king's face through the Temple roof, which was cloven by the shock, produced the leprosy. (Comp. Amos iv. 11; Zech. xiv. 4, 5.)

(20) **Looked upon him.**—*Turned towards him*.

**They thrust him out.**—*Hibhîl*—scared, hurried *him out*. (Comp. Esther vi. 14, "they made haste.") LXX., κατέσπευσαν αὐτὸν ἐκεῖθεν.

**Hasted.**—Literally, *thrust himself*. The Hebrew is a late word occurring thrice in Esther, and not elsewhere.

**The Lord had smitten him.**—2 Kings xiv. 5.

(21) **Was a leper . . . several house.**—2 Kings xiv. 5. Rather, *in the hospital*, or *lazar house*.

**For he was cut off** (Ps. lxxxviii. 5; Isa. liii. 8) **from the house of the Lord.**—This ground of Uzziah's dwelling in a sick house is added by the chronicler. Having been formally excluded as a leper from the sacred precincts, he was obliged to isolate himself from society. (Comp. Lev. xiii. 46.)

(22) **Did Isaiah the prophet, the son of Amoz, write.**—(See Introduction.) Kings, "Are they not written *in the book of the chronicles of the kings of Judah ?*"

(23) **So Uzziah slept.**—2 Kings xv. 7.

**In the field of the burial.**—*In the burial field* or *graveyard* belonging to the kings, and near their sepulchres; but not in the royal tombs themselves, because a leper would have polluted them.

Kings simply says, as usual, "in the city of David."

### XXVII.

REIGN OF JOTHAM. (Comp. 2 Kings xv. 32—38.)
LENGTH AND CHARACTER OF THE REIGN.
PUBLIC WORKS (verses 1—4).

(1) **Jotham was twenty and five years old.**—Word for word as 2 Kings xv. 33, only adding *Jotham*.

twenty and five years old when he began to reign, and he reigned sixteen years in Jerusalem. His mother's name also *was* Jerushah, the daughter of Zadok. (2) And he did *that which was* right in the sight of the LORD, according to all that his father Uzziah did: howbeit he entered not into the temple of the LORD. And the people did yet corruptly. (3) He built the high gate of the house of the LORD, and on the wall of ¹Ophel he built much. (4) Moreover he built cities in the mountains of Judah, and in the forests he built castles and towers. (5) He fought also with the king of the Ammonites, and prevailed against them. And the children of Ammon gave him the same year an hundred talents of silver, and ten thousand measures of wheat, and ten thousand of barley. ²So much did the children of Ammon pay unto him, both the second year, and the third. (6) So Jotham became mighty, because he ³prepared his ways before the LORD his God.

(7) Now the rest of the acts of Jotham, and all his wars, and his ways, lo, they *are* written in the book of the kings of Israel and Judah. (8) He was five and twenty years old when he began to reign, and reigned sixteen years in Jerusalem. (9) And Jotham slept with his fathers, and they buried him in the city of David: and Ahaz his son reigned in his stead.

1 Or, *The tower*.
2 Heb., *this*.
3 Or, *established*.

---

**Jerushah, the daughter of Zadok.**— Perhaps the high priest Zadok of 1 Chron. vi. 12. (Comp. chap. xxii. 11.)

(2) **Howbeit he entered not.**—The chronicler *adds* this reservation upon the preceding general statement. The author of Kings, having said nothing of Uzziah's sacrilege, had no need to make such an exception.

**And the people did yet corruptly.** — *Still used to deal corruptly*; a paraphrase of what we read in 2 Kings xiv. 35, " the people still used to sacrifice and burn incense on the high places." We know further, from the extant utterances of the prophets of those days, that a deep-seated moral corruption was sapping the strength of the nation. (Comp. Mic. iii. 10—12; Hos. iv. 1, 2.)

(3) **He built.**—*He it was that built* (pronoun emphatic). He "built," *i.e.*, restored and beautified. The same statement occurs in 2 Kings xv. 35.

**The high gate.**—Rather, *the upper gate*; *i.e.*, the northern gate of the inner or upper court (Ezek. ix. 2). The north being the holy quarter (Isa. xiv. 13; Ps. xlviii. 2), the north gate would be the principal entrance.

**And on the wall of Ophel he built much.**— The southern slope of the Temple hill was called the Ophel, *i.e.*, "the mound." Its wall would be the line of fortifications connecting Zion with Moriah, on which Uzziah had already laboured (chap. xxvi. 9), with the same object of securing the city against attacks from the south and east. Neither this detail nor the next three verses are found in the parallel account. The style and contents of the passage indicate a good ancient source.

**Much.**—*Larôb*, "to much;" one of the chronicler's favourite words.

(4) **Moreover.**—Literally, *and cities built he in the hill region of Judah*. (Comp. chap. xxvi. 10.)

**Castles.**—*Birâniyôth*; a term explained at chap. xvii. 12. The contemporary prophets denounced the popular confidence in "fenced cities" as a kind of treason against Jehovah, who was Himself the shield and fortress of His people (Psalm xviii. 1; Isa. xii. 2). "Israel hath forgotten his Maker, and buildeth palaces; and Judah hath multiplied fenced cities: but I will send a fire upon his cities, and it shall devour the palaces thereof" (Hos. viii. 14. Comp. Isa. ii. 15, xvii. 3, 4).

(5) **He fought also with the king of the Ammonites.**—"*He* also," like his father, "fought with the king of the sons of Ammon." They no doubt had refused the tribute imposed on them by Uzziah; but Jotham quelled their resistance, and they paid him a fixed contribution for three successive years.

**The same year.**—*In that year*; the year of the revolt.

**Ten thousand measures.**—*Kôrim*. The *kor* was perhaps equivalent to our *quarter*. (Comp. 1 Kings iv. 22; 2 Chron. ii. 10.)

The land of Ammon is fertile of grain even at the present day.

**So much . . . and the third.**—Rather, *This* (tribute) *did the bnê Ammon restore to him* (*i.e.*, after withholding it during the year of rebellion); *and in the second year, and the third*. After three annual payments, the tribute was again suspended, perhaps because the Ammonites took advantage of the outbreak of the Syro-Ephraite war, which took place towards the end of the reign (2 Kings xv. 37). There is no note of time in the text.

(6) **So Jotham became mighty.**—The chronicler's customary phrase. "Strengthened himself," "gained strength" (chap. xiii. 21).

**Because he prepared.**—*For he directed his ways* (Prov. xxi. 29; comp. also chaps. xii. 14, xx. 33). Jotham directed his ways "before," *i.e.*, in the chronicler's usage, "to meet," "towards" Jehovah his God. (Comp. 1 Chron. xii. 17; 1 Sam. vii. 3.) "Direct your heart towards Jehovah." Perhaps, however, "before" simply means "as in the sight of" Jehovah. (Comp. Gen. xvii. 1, "walk before me.")

The verse is a moral reflection of the writer on the preceding facts.

(7) **And all his wars, and his ways.**—See 2 Kings xv. 36, "And all that he did." The chronicler seems to have varied the phrase, in order to hint at the Syro-Ephraite war, mentioned in 2 Kings xv. 37.

(8) **He was five and twenty years old.**—A word for word repetition of 2 Kings xv. 33, omitting the last clause about the queen-mother. Perhaps in one of the chronicler's sources this notice occurred at the beginning, and in another at the end of the reign. This would account for its repetition here, after having been already stated in verse 1.

*Ahaz reigns, and is*     II. CHRONICLES, XXVIII.     *afflicted by the Syrians.*

CHAPTER XXVIII.—<sup>(1)</sup> Ahaz *ᵃwas twenty years old* when he began to reign, and he reigned sixteen years in Jerusalem: but he did not *that which was* right in the sight of the Lord, like David his father: <sup>(2)</sup> for he walked in the ways of the kings of Israel, and made also molten images for Baalim. <sup>(3)</sup> Moreover he ¹burnt incense in the valley of the son of Hinnom, and burnt ᵇhis children in the fire, after the abominations of the heathen whom the Lord had cast out before the children of Israel. <sup>(4)</sup> He sacrificed also and burnt incense in the high places, and on the hills, and under every green tree. <sup>(5)</sup> Wherefore the Lord his God delivered him into the hand of the king of Syria; and they smote him, and carried away a great multitude of them captives, and brought *them* to ²Damascus. And he was also delivered into the hand of the king of Israel, who smote him with a great slaughter. <sup>(6)</sup> For Pekah the son of Remaliah slew in Judah an hundred and twenty thousand in one day, *which were* all ³valiant men; because they had forsaken the Lord God of their fathers.

*ᵃ* 2 Kings 16. 2.
¹ Or, *offered sacrifice.*
*ᵇ* Lev. 18. 21.
B.C. 741.
² Heb., *Darmesek.*
³ Heb., *sons of valour.*

---

XXVIII.

The Reign of Ahaz. (Comp. 2 Kings xvi.) Preliminary Notices of the Length and Character of the Reign (verses 1—4).

<sup>(1)</sup> **Ahaz was twenty years old.**—The verse is identical with 2 Kings xvi. 2; LXX., Syriac, and Arabic, "twenty and five." (See chap. xxix. 1.)

**The Lord.**—Add *his God.* So some MSS. and Syriac; also Kings. The Assyrian monuments call Ahaz *Yahuhazi,* i.e., Jehoahaz, of which Ahaz may be a familiar abridgment. (Comp. Nathan, Jonathan.)

<sup>(2)</sup> **And made also molten images for Baalim.**—*For the Baals,* i.e., the different aspects or avatars of the Canaanite god. This clause is *added* by the chronicler, in explanation of the former one; "the way of the kings of Israel" was the state recognition of Baal worship, side by side with that of Jehovah (chaps. xxi. 6, xxii. 3, 4; comp. chap. xxiii. 17). But possibly both this and the first clause of verse 3 have fallen out of the text of Kings. (So Thenius on that passage.)

<sup>(3)</sup> **Moreover he.**—"And *he* (emphatic) burnt incense" to Moloch, the god of Ammon, for whom Solomon had built a high place (1 Kings xi. 5—8), which was still in existence.

**In the valley of the son of Hinnom.**—Also called simply the valley of Hinnom (Jos., xv. 8), on the west and south of Jerusalem (Jos., xviii. 16), the scene of the cruel rites in honour of

"Moloch, horrid king, besmeared with blood."
—MILTON.

(Jerem. vii. 31, 32, xix. 2—6, where "the Baal" is named as the object of this worship, Moloch being a Baal.) In later times, the term "valley of Hinnom," spelt as one word, and with modified vowels, *Gĕhinnăm,* became the appellation of hell, "the house of woe and pain." It is so used in the Targums, and later in the Talmud, and appears in the New Testament under the Græcised form Γέεννα, whence the Latin Gehenna.

**Burnt his children in the fire.**—Kings, "And even his own son *he made to pass through the fire.*" The chronicler has paraphrased by transposing two Hebrew letters (*baʻar* for *ʻabar*). "His children" is simply a generalised expression, as we might say, "he burnt his own *offspring* or posterity." (Comp. Ps. cvi. 37.) Thenius accuses the chronicler of exaggerating the fact. But this peculiar use of the plural is one of the marks of his style. (Comp. 1 Chron. vi. 57, 67; and verse 16, *infra.*)

The War with Rezin of Syria and Pekah of Israel; or, the Syro-Ephraite Campaign (verses 5—9). (Comp. 2 Kings xvi. 5; Isa. vii. 1.)

<sup>(5)</sup> **Wherefore** (and) **the Lord his God delivered him.**—These opening words help us to understand the ground of the variations of the present account from that of 2 Kings xvi. The chronicler purposes, not so much to describe a campaign, as to select those events of it which most conspicuously illustrate God's chastisements of the apostate Ahaz. Accordingly, throughout the description, the historical is subordinated to the didactic motive. (Comp. the account of the Syrian invasion, chap. xxiv. 23, 24.) Not history for its own sake, but history teaching by example, is what the writer desires to present. At the same time, the events here recorded are above critical suspicion. Thenius characterises the whole section (verses 5—15) as "thoroughly historical."

**Into the hand of the king of Syria.**—Rezin of Damascus. (Comp. 2 Kings xvi. 5.) Instead of relating the joint attempt against Jerusalem, and the seizure of Elath by Rezin, the chronicler prefers to record two severe defeats suffered by Ahaz in the open field, before his retreat behind the walls of Jerusalem. (See Note on chaps. xvii. 17, xxii. 1.) After these successes the confederates converged upon the capital, and the panic inspired by the news of their coming is finely depicted in Isa. vii. 2. Their attempt proved ineffectual, as the prophet had foretold.

**Smote him.**—Literally, smote *in him,* i.e., in his army; *defeated him.* (A similar remark applies in the next sentence.)

**Carried away . . . captives.**—Literally, *and led captive from him a great captivity* (Deut. xxi. 11).

**And he was also delivered.**—A second terrible reverse, which took place, perhaps, while Rezin was absent in Idumæa. "At that time Rezin king of Syria recovered Elath to Syria, and drove the Jews out of Elath: and the Arameans (*or* Edomites) came to Elath, and dwelt there unto this day" (2 Kings xvi. 6).

<sup>(6)</sup> **For.**—*And,* i.e., so.

**Pekah . . . slew in Judah an hundred . . . in one day.**—Details of what is generally stated in the last sentence of verse 5. The totals of slain and of captives (verse 8) are both round numbers. The figures 120,000, if accurate, would show that about a third of the Jewish host (chap. xxvi. 13) had fallen in the battle and pursuit. The ruthlessness of the foe is borne out by the words of the prophet Oded in verse 9: "Ye have

*Judah carried Captive.*     II. CHRONICLES, XXVIII.     *The Word of Oded.*

(7) And Zichri, a mighty man of Ephraim, slew Maaseiah the king's son, and Azrikam the governor of the house, and Elkanah *that was* [1]next to the king. (8) And the children of Israel carried away captive of their brethren two hundred thousand, women, sons, and daughters, and took also away much spoil from them, and brought the spoil to Samaria.

(9) But a prophet of the LORD was there, whose name *was* Oded: and he went out before the host that came to Samaria, and said unto them, Behold, because the LORD God of your fathers was wroth with Judah, he hath delivered them into your hand, and ye have slain them in a rage *that* reacheth up unto heaven. (10) And now ye purpose to keep under the children of Judah and Jerusalem for bondmen and bondwomen unto you: *but are there* not with you, even with you, sins against the LORD your God? (11) Now hear me therefore, and deliver the captives again, which ye have taken captive of your brethren: for the fierce wrath of the LORD *is* upon you. (12) Then certain of the heads of the children of Ephraim, Azariah the son of Johanan, Berechiah the son of

[1] Heb., *the second to the king.*

---

slain them in a rage that reacheth up to heaven." Isa. vii. 6 proves that the allies designed to break wholly the independence of Judah, by abolishing the Davidic monarchy, and setting up a Syrian vassal king.

**In one day.**—In one great engagement. Among the Hebrews and Arabs the word "day" often bears the special force of "day of battle;" *e.g.*, "the day of Midian" (Isa. ix. 4).

**Because they had forsaken.**—Chap. xxvii. 2 Moreover, the idolatrous example of Ahaz would be eagerly followed by large numbers of the people, whose average religious condition was far below the standard which the prophets of Jehovah demanded. The prophetical writings demonstrate this.

(7) **Maaseiah the king's son**—*i.e.*, a prince of the royal house, related to Ahaz, but not his own son; or he would have been too young to be engaged in the battle. (Comp. ch. xviii. 25: "Joash the king's son.")

**Azrikam the governor of the house**—*i.e.*, of the royal house, or palace. Azrikam was *nagid*, "prince" or superintendent of the palace, a high court official. (Comp. 1 Kings iv. 6, xviii. 3.)

**Elkanah . . . next to the king.**—See margin. Elkanah was grand vizier. (Comp. 1 Sam. xxiii. 17; Esther x. 3.) The writer mentions the deaths of these three personages, because of their intimate connection with Ahaz, whose punishment he is describing. The blow which struck them struck the king. (Comp. chap. xxiv. 23.)

(8) **Of their brethren.**—Heightening the barbarity of the deed. So verse 11.

**Two hundred thousand, women, sons, and daughters.**—See Note on verse 6. Sennacherib boasts that in the war against Hezekiah he took forty-six strong cities of Judah, and carried off 200,150 captives. The number of the text is thus corroborated from a foreign and wholly unrelated source. The thrilling narrative of Kings (2 Kings xviii.—xix) says nothing of the carrying away of all these captives by the Assyrian invader, the interest of the writer being centred on Jerusalem. With this omission that of the facts related in the present section may be compared.

THE PROPHET ODED PROTESTS AGAINST RETENTION OF THE JEWISH CAPTIVES, AND THEY ARE SENT HOME (verses 9—15).

(9) **But a prophet of the Lord.**—This whole section is peculiar to the chronicler. The author has told the story in his own way; and perhaps the words of the prophet and the chiefs are mainly his. But there is no ground for doubting the general truth of the narrative.

**Was there.**—In Samaria. It is remarkable that neither here nor in the parallel narrative is any mention made of the great prophet Hosea ben Beeri, who must have been active at this epoch in the northern kingdom. Of *Oded* nothing further is known. He was a "prophet of Jehovah," not of the Baals.

**He went out before.**—*To meet* the hosts, like *Azariah ben Oded* (chap. xv. 2).

**That came.**—*Was coming in.*

**Because the Lord . . . was wroth.**—Literally, *in the wrath of Jehovah . . . against Judah he gave them into your hand.* Your victory was due to the punitive wrath of Jehovah, not to your own valour or intrinsic superiority. You ought to have considered this, and shown compassion to the victims of divine displeasure; but you have, on the contrary, given full rein to the savage dictates of furious hatred.

**Slain them.**—*Slain among them.*

**In a rage.**—Chap. xxvi. 19 (*za'af*).

**That reacheth up unto heaven.**—Gen. xxviii. 12; Isa. viii. 8. Literally, *which even to the heavens did reach;* i.e., a guilty excess of rage, calling to heaven for vengeance, like the blood of Abel (Gen. iv. 10), or the wickedness of Sodom (Gen. xviii. 21). (Comp. also Ezra ix. 6.)

(10) **Ye purpose.**—Literally, *Ye are saying* or *proposing* (chap. i. 18).

**To keep under.**—*Subdue,* or reduce to bondmen. Gen. i. 28 (*kabash*).

**Unto you.**—*Yourselves.*

**But are there not with you.**—An abrupt question: *Are there no trespasses at all with you yourselves?* i.e., "Are you yourselves wholly guiltless, that your indignation was so hot against your brethren? (Gen. xx. 11). Or, "Are there no trespasses with *you* only?" . . . Are you the only guiltless people, so that you are justified in these severities?" (Job i. 15). The reference in either case may be to the calves of Bethel and Dan.

(11) **Now hear me therefore.**—*And now hearken to me* (chaps. xiii. 4, xv. 2). The "and now" is illative, not temporal.

**Deliver . . . again.**—*Cause to return, send back.*

**Fierce wrath.**—*Heat of anger, i.e.*, hot anger. Lev. xxv. 39, expressly forbids the permanent enslaving of Israelites by Israelites.

(12) **Children of Ephraim.**—The ten tribes, as a political whole, are often designated as "Ephraim" by the prophets of that age, *e.g.*, Hosea and Isaiah.

Meshillemoth, and Jehizkiah the son of Shallum, and Amasa the son of Hadlai, stood up against them that came from the war, <sup>(13)</sup> and said unto them, Ye shall not bring in the captives hither: for whereas we have offended against the LORD *already*, ye intend to add *more* to our sins and to our trespass: for our trespass is great, and *there is* fierce wrath against Israel. <sup>(14)</sup> So the armed men left the captives and the spoil before the princes and all the congregation. <sup>(15)</sup> And the men which were expressed by name rose up, and took the captives, and with the spoil clothed all that were naked among them, and arrayed them, and shod them, and gave them to eat and to drink, and anointed them, and carried all the feeble of them upon asses, and brought them to Jericho, <sup>a</sup> the city of palm trees, to their brethren: then they returned to Samaria.

<sup>(16)</sup> At that time did king Ahaz send unto the kings of Assyria to help him. <sup>(17)</sup> For again the Edomites had come and smitten Judah, and carried away <sup>1</sup> captives. <sup>(18)</sup> The Philistines also had invaded the cities of the low country, and of the south of Judah, and had taken Beth-shemesh, and Ajalon, and Gederoth, and Shocho with the villages thereof, and Timnah with the villages thereof,

*a* Deut. 34. 3.

1 Heb., *a captivity.*

---

**Stood up against.**—The Hebrew phrase usually means *opposed*; here *confronted* or *came before those who were coming from the host.*

<sup>(13)</sup> **Ye shall not bring in.**—Into the city.

**Whereas we ... already.**—This is at least a possible rendering. Literally, *at* or *in the trespass of* (against) *Jehovah* (lying) *upon us, ye are proposing to add to our sins,* &c. Others translate, "so that a trespass against Jehovah come upon us." (Comp. Lev. iv. 3.) But the elders admit an already existing trespass, when they add, "for our trespass is great, and there is fierce wrath against Israel." What they deprecate is an aggravation of that trespass.

**Our trespass is great.**—Literally, *a great trespass is ours.* (Syriac omits this clause and next verse. Instead of verse 15 it has: "And they caused the whole captivity to return to Jerusalem." It then continues with verses 23—25, transposing verses 16—21.)

<sup>(14)</sup> **Armed men.**—See chap. xvii. 18.

**The princes,** "the heads" of verse 12.

**The congregation.**—The assembly of the citizens at the gate of Samaria.

<sup>(15)</sup> **The men which ... by name.**—1 Chron. xii. 31, xvi. 41. Certain chiefs formally designated for the office, perhaps including those of verse 12.

**All that were naked.**—Literally, *and all their nakednesses they clad out of the spoil* (*ma'arummim*, "nakednesses," here only).

<sup>(15)</sup> **And arrayed ... shod them.**—*And they clad them, and sandalled them.* (For the miserable destitution of captives, see Isa. iii. 24, xx. 2, 4, "naked and barefoot.")

**Anointed them** (*sûk*, usually intransitive, *e.g.*, 2 Sam. xiv. 2). (Comp. Luke vii. 38.) A different word (*mashah*) was used to express the ceremonial anointing of kings and priests.

**Carried all the feeble of them upon asses.**—Literally, *led them on he-asses, to wit, every stumbling one.* There would be many such, as the captives were mostly women and children.

**To.**—*Beside.*

The writer dwells with manifest pleasure upon the kindness shown by their repentant foes of the northern kingdom to these Jewish captives. He may have intended to suggest a lesson to the Samaritans of his own age, whose bitter hostility had proved so damaging to the cause of the restored exiles (Neh. iv. 2, 7, 8, vi. 1, 2 *sqq.*), and who, according to Rabbinical tradition, endeavoured to prejudice Alexander the Great against the commonwealth of Jerusalem (Talmud, *Yoma*, 69, A).

Some have supposed that our Lord had this passage in His mind when He uttered the parable of the Good Samaritan. The coincidences between the two stories are at any rate curious. (See Luke x. 30, 33, 34.)

The interposition of the Ephraite prophet Oded between the Ephraites and their Judæan captives is precisely parallel to that of the Judæan prophet Shemaiah between his people and the Ten Tribes, as related in 1 Kings xii. 22—24; and granting the truth of the one account, there can be no ground for suspecting the other.

UNDER THE PRESSURE OF NEW ENEMIES, AHAZ ASKS HELP FROM ASSYRIA, BUT RECEIVES HURT (verses 17—21). (Comp. 2 Kings xvi. 7—18.)

<sup>(16)</sup> **At that time.**—Apparently after the events above narrated; how soon after we can hardly decide.

**The kings of Assyria.**—A generalised expression, as in verse 3 (comp. verses 20, 21), where the actual king is named. All the old versions have "king."

<sup>(17)</sup> **For again.**—*And moreover.*

**Smitten Judah.**—*Smitten in Judah*, i.e., inflicted a defeat upon her. After their reduction by Uzziah, the Edomites had probably remained subject to Judah, until Rezin of Syria expelled the Jews from Elath (2 Kings xvi. 6), and restored it to them. After that event, the disasters of Ahaz seem to have encouraged them to make a raid upon his territory.

<sup>(18)</sup> **Invaded**—*i.e.*, "fell upon" (chap. xxv. 13).

**The low country.**—*The shephēlah*, or lowland of Judah, between the hill-country and the Mediterranean.

**The south.**—*The Negeb*, or southland of Judah, nearly co-extensive with the territory assigned to Simeon (2 Sam. xxiv. 7).

**Beth-shemesh.**—See 1 Chron. vi. 59.

**Ajalon.**—1 Chron. vi. 69.

**Gederoth.**—In the lowland (Josh. xv. 41).

**Shocho.**—Rather, *Socho* (chap. xi. 7).

**Timnah.**—Now *Tibna* (Josh. xv. 10).

**Gimzo.**—Now *Jimsu*, between Lydda and Bethhoron (Robinson, iii. 271).

**And the villages thereof.**—*And her daughters.* (See Note on 1 Chron. vii. 28, "and the towns thereof.")

**And they dwelt there.**—Permanently occupied the country. (Comp. 1 Chron. v. 22. See also Isa. xiv. 29, 30.)

Gimzo also and the villages thereof: and they dwelt there. (19) For the LORD brought Judah low because of Ahaz king of Israel; for he made Judah naked, and transgressed sore against the LORD. (20) And Tilgath-pilneser king of Assyria came unto him, and distressed him, but strengthened him not. (21) For Ahaz took away a portion *out* of the house of the LORD, and *out* of the house of the king, and of the princes, and gave *it* unto the king of Assyria: but he helped him not.

(22) And in the time of his distress did he trespass yet more against the LORD: this *is that* king Ahaz. (23) For he sacrificed unto the gods of ¹Damascus, which smote him: and he said, Because the gods of the kings of Syria help them, *therefore* will I sacrifice to them, that they may help me. But they were the ruin of him, and of all

¹ Heb., *Darmesek.*

---

(19) **Ahaz king of Israel.**—Most commentators see an irony in this expression. But, as has been stated before, the southern kingdom *was* Israel in the chronicler's idea; although that of the Ten Tribes was, politically speaking, as much more important, as the cedar of Lebanon was in comparison with the blackthorn growing beside it (chap. xxv. 18. See Note on chaps. xii. 6, xxi. 2). (Some Hebrew MSS., and all ancient versions, read "Judah." Other Hebrew MSS. remark that in seven places "king of Judah" should be read instead of "king of Israel.")

**He made Judah naked.**—Rather, *he behaved loosely, dealt licentiously in Judah* (*hiphri'a*). The verb is so used here only. (Comp. Exod. v. 4, where it is transitive: "Why *loose* ye the people from their works?") (LXX. omits, Authorised version follows the Vulg.)

**Transgressed sore.**—*Done unfaithfulness* (1 Chron. x. 13).

(20) **Tilgath-pilneser** (Heb., *Pilne'eser*). In 2 Kings more correctly called *Tiglath-pileser* (*Pil'eser*). (See Note on 1 Chron. v. 26.) According to the Assyrian Eponym Canon, Tiglath-pileser II. came to the throne B.C. 745, and marched westward against Damascus and Israel, B.C. 734. The importance of these dates for the chronology of the period is obvious.

**Came unto him.**—Comp. the more detailed narrative in 2 Kings xvi. 7–10; and see Note on verse 16. Tiglath was induced by the message and present of Ahaz to undertake a campaign in the west; he captured Damascus, slew Rezin, and transported the population of the city to Kir (Kings, *l.c.*). After this, "king Ahaz went to Damascus to meet Tiglath-pileser king of Assyria" (2 Kings xvi. 10). The chronicler, in the words before us, is estimating the results of this expedition as they affected the interests of Judah. At the prayer of Ahaz the Assyrian had indeed "come to him"; but not with any purpose of strengthening the southern kingdom. Glad of a pretext for interference in the affairs of the west, the ambitious usurper was simply bent on the extension of his own empire; and when the more powerful states of Syria and Israel lay at his feet, he naturally proceeded to require a most unequivocal acknowledgment of vassalage from Ahaz. He thus "distressed" or oppressed him by reducing his kingdom to a mere dependency of Assyria, besides impoverishing him of all his treasure, which Ahaz had sent as the price of this ruinous help.

**Distressed him, but strengthened him not.** —This is correct. A possible rendering is: "and besieged him, and conquered him not"; but the context is against it. (The word *ḥazaq*, "strengthened," everywhere else means *to be strong,* or, *to prevail.* LXX. omits the last words, rendering the whole καὶ ἔθλιψεν αὐτόν. Syriac and Arabic, "besieged him."

The Vulg. has: "et afflixit eum, et nullo resistente vastavit." That Judah now became tributary to Assyria is evident from 2 Kings xviii. 7, 14, 20.

(21) **Took away a portion . . . gave it.**—Rather, *For Ahaz had despoiled the house of the Lord, and the house of the king and the princes, and had given it.* (Comp. 2 Kings xvi. 8.)

**The princes**—*i.e.,* the great courtiers living in the palace, whose valuables as well as those of Ahaz were ransacked to make up the costly bribe. (Syriac and Arabic, "the vessels which were in the house of the Lord, and in the house of the former kings, and in the rich houses.")

**But he helped him not.**—*And it was not for help* (*i.e.,* it resulted not in help) *to him.* His submission to Tiglath brought him no real advantage, but rather hastened the downfall of his kingdom.

"The Assyrians had no regard to the welfare of their vassals. The principle of the monarchy was plunder; and Ahaz, whose treasures had been exhausted by his first tribute, was soon driven, by the repeated demands of his masters, to strip the Temple even of its ancient bronze-work and other fixed ornaments (2 Kings xvi. 17, *seq.*). The time was not far off when the rapacity of the Assyrian could no longer be satisfied, and his plundering hordes would be let loose upon the land" (*Robertson Smith*).

AHAZ ADOPTS THE SYRIAN IDOLATRY, AND CLOSES THE TEMPLE (verses 22–25; comp. 2 Kings xvi. 10–18).

(22) **In the time of his distress.**—*At the time when he* (Tiglath) *oppressed him, i.e.,* at the time when Ahaz went to Damascus to do homage to the Assyrian monarch (2 Kings xvi. 10), probably in reluctant obedience to a peremptory mandate.

**Did he trespass . . . . Ahaz.**—*He dealt yet more unfaithfully towards Jehovah, he, king Ahaz.* The subject is emphatically repeated: "he, king Ahaz," who had already been sorely chastised, sinned yet more. Or "he, king Ahaz," the notorious apostate.

(23) **For** (*and*) **he sacrificed unto the gods of Damascus.**—The statement of this verse is peculiar to the Chronicle; and the same may be said of the next also. Both here and in the preceding account of the relations of Ahaz to Tiglath-pileser, the writer appears to have drawn upon another source than the book of Kings.

**Damascus** may, perhaps, be put for *the Damascenes,* though in that case *Aram* would have been more natural. (Not "at Damascus," as Thenius renders.)

**Which smote him.**—Did the chronicler himself believe that the gods of Aram had any power or real

Israel. (24) And Ahaz gathered together the vessels of the house of God, and cut in pieces the vessels of the house of God, and shut up the doors of the house of the LORD, and he made him altars in every corner of Jerusalem. (25) And in every several city of Judah he made high places ¹to burn incense unto other gods, and provoked to anger the LORD God of his fathers.

(26) Now the rest of his acts and of all his ways, first and last, behold, they *are* written in the book of the kings of Judah and Israel. (27) And Ahaz slept with his fathers, and they buried him in the city, *even* in Jerusalem: but they brought him not into the sepulchres of the kings of Israel: and Hezekiah his son reigned in his stead.

CHAPTER XXIX.—(1) Hezekiah ᵃbegan to reign *when he was* five and twenty years old, and he reigned nine and twenty years in Jerusalem. And his mother's name *was* Abijah, the daughter of Zechariah. (2) And he did *that which was* right in the sight of the LORD, according to all that David his father had done. (3) He in the first year of his reign, in the first month, opened the doors of the house of the LORD, and repaired them. (4) And he brought in

¹ Or, *to offer*.

ᵃ 2 Kings 18. 1.

---

existence? That such was the common belief of the Israelites in the days of Ahaz appears certain. (See Exod. xv. 11; Judg. xi. 24; 1 Sam. xxvi. 19.) In the latter half of Isaiah we find the nothingness of the false gods strongly asserted; but there was also another current opinion, which St. Paul repeats, and which Milton has adopted in *Paradise Lost*, viz., that "the things which the heathen sacrifice, they sacrifice to *demons*" (1 Cor. viii. 4, x. 20; Deut. xxxii. 17).

**Because the gods.**—Omit *because* (the Hebrew particle simply introduces what the speaker said). "The gods of the kings of Aram, *they* help them; *to them* will I sacrifice, that they may help me." Such is the word ascribed to Ahaz, implying a doubt of Jehovah's power or willingness to help. (*Ma‘zĕrîm*, "help," an Aramaised form.)

**But they were the ruin of him, and of all Israel.**—Literally, *and they* (*i.e.*, those very gods) *were to him to make him stumble, and all Israel.* The mode of expression, as well as the thought expressed, is highly characteristic.

Israel = Judah, as usual.

(24) **Gathered together the vessels.**—According to some MSS. the Syriac, Arabic, Vulg., and Targum, *all* the vessels.

**And cut in pieces the vessels.**—Literally, *trimmed* (*qiççaç*), *i.e.*, cut off their metal ornaments. The same word is used in 2 Kings xvi. 17, where it is said, "And king Ahaz cut off the plates of the bases, and removed the laver from upon them, and the sea he took down from off the brazen oxen that were under it, and put it on a pavement of stones."

**And shut up the doors of the house of the Lord.**—Not in Kings. (Comp. chap. xxix. 3—7.) The doors of the sanctuary itself, not those of the great court, must be understood. (Comp. 2 Kings xvi. 15, 16, from which it appears that the new Syrian altar was erected in the inner court near the brazen altar.) By closing the doors Ahaz suspended all rites that could only be duly performed within the Holy Place and the Holy of Holies. (Thenius thinks the verse involves a misunderstanding of 2 Kings xvi. 18.)

**In every corner of (*in*) Jerusalem.**—Wanting in Kings.

(25) **And in every several city of Judah he made high places.**—Comp. verses 2—4.

**And provoked to anger.**—Deut. xxxii. 16. Instead of this verse 2 Kings xvi. 18 obscurely mentions further changes which Ahaz made in the Temple, "for fear of the king of Assyria." It seems probable that the sacrilege described in verse 24 and in 2 Kings xvi. 17, 18, was perpetrated in collecting everything of any value to send to the rapacious Assyrian.

CLOSING NOTICES (verses 26, 27. Comp. 2 Kings xvi. 19, 20).

(26) **Now the rest of his acts, and of all his ways.**—The chronicler has varied the usual formula. (See chaps. xxv. 26, xxvi. 7, &c., and comp. 2 Kings xvi. 19.)

**But (*for*) they brought him not into the sepulchres of the kings of Israel.**—Wanting in Kings. (See Note on chaps. xxi. 20, xxvi. 23.) Thenius supposes that this statement is founded either upon *mistake*, or upon *zeal for the Law*. But why not upon *a written authority*?

XXIX.

HEZEKIAH (chaps. xxix.—xxxii.; 2 Kings xviii.—xx.); Chap. xxix. LENGTH AND SPIRIT OF THE REIGN. THE SOLEMN PURGATION AND HALLOWING OF THE TEMPLE.

(1) **Hezekiah.**—Heb., *Yĕhizqiyāhu*, as if "Strong is Iahu." 2 Kings writes *Hizkiyāh*, "My strength is Iah;" Isa. xxvii., *sqq.*, *Hizkiyāhu*. The annals of Sennacherib present the form *Hazakiyahu*.

**Abijah.**—2 Kings has the shortened form *Abi*. (This verse closely corresponds with 2 Kings xviii. 2.)

(2) **And he did.**—The verse is identical with 2 Kings xviii. 3.

THE KING CHARGES THE LEVITES, AND THEY CLEANSE THE HOUSE OF GOD (verses 3—19).

(3) **In the first month**—*i.e.*, in the month Nisan, the first month of the sacred year; not in the first month of his reign. (Comp. verse 17 and chap. xxx. 23.)

**Opened the doors.**—Which his father had closed (chap. xxviii. 24).

**And repaired them.**—By overlaying them with metal—bronze or gold-leaf (2 Kings xviii. 16).

(4) **Brought in.**—*Caused to come.*

**The east street.**—*The eastern square* or *open space of the East.* (Comp. Ezra x. 9; Neh. viii. 1, 3, 16.) The place of meeting was probably an open area in front of the eastern gate of the sacred enclosure.

*The King's Exhortation*     II. CHRONICLES, XXIX.     *to the Levites.*

the priests and the Levites, and gathered them together into the east street, <sup>(5)</sup> and said unto them, Hear me, ye Levites, sanctify now yourselves, and sanctify the house of the LORD God of your fathers, and carry forth the filthiness out of the holy *place*. <sup>(6)</sup> For our fathers have trespassed, and done *that which was* evil in the eyes of the LORD our God, and have forsaken him, and have turned away their faces from the habitation of the LORD, and ¹turned *their* backs. <sup>(7)</sup> Also they have shut up the doors of the porch, and put out the lamps, and have not burned incense nor offered burnt offerings in the holy *place* unto the God of Israel. <sup>(8)</sup> Wherefore the wrath of the LORD was upon Judah and Jerusalem, and he hath delivered them to ²trouble, to astonishment, and to hissing, as ye see with your eyes. <sup>(9)</sup> For, lo, our fathers have fallen by the sword, and our sons and our daughters and our wives *are* in captivity for this. <sup>(10)</sup> Now *it is* in mine heart to make a covenant with the LORD God of Israel, that his fierce wrath may turn away from us. <sup>(11)</sup> My sons, ³be not now negligent: for the LORD hath ᵃchosen you to stand before him, to serve him, and that ye should minister unto him, and ⁴burn incense.

<sup>(12)</sup> Then the Levites arose, Mahath the son of Amasai, and Joel the son of Azariah, of the sons of the Kohathites: and of the sons of Merari, Kish the son of Abdi, and Azariah the son of Jehalelel: and of the Gershonites; Joah the son of Zimmah, and Eden the son of Joah: <sup>(13)</sup> and of the sons of Elizaphan; Shimri, and Jeiel: and of the sons of Asaph; Zechariah, and Mattaniah:

*Marginal notes:* 1 Heb., *given the neck.*   2 Heb., *commotion.*   3 Or, *be not now deceived.*   *a* Num. 8. 14, & 18. 2. 6.   B.C. 726.   4 Or, *offer sacrifice.*

---

(5) **Hear me.**—Chaps. xv. 2, xx. 15.
**Sanctify now yourselves.**—See Note on 1 Chron. xv. 12, 14.
**Sanctify the house.**—By removing all symbols of idolatry.
**Carry forth the filthiness.**—*Niddah* denotes personal impurity (Lev. xii. 2; Ezek. xviii. 6); and so anything loathsome (Ezek. vii. 19); here probably idols, and things connected with their worship.

(6) **Trespassed.**—*Dealt unfaithfully.*
**Turned away their faces from the habitation of the Lord.**—Comp. Jer. ii. 27: "They have turned their backs unto me, and not their faces." (Comp. also Ezek. viii. 16.)
**Turned their backs.**—Literally, *gave neck* (*nathan 'ōreph*); a phrase here used as equivalent to *turned neck* (*pānāh 'ōreph*), Jer. ii. 27, *et al.* The ordinary meaning is "to put to flight," as in Ps. xviii. 41. It is clear from the next verse that the description is meant to apply to Ahaz and his generation.

(7) **The porch.**—Of the holy place, or nave of the Temple; the only entrance to the two holy chambers.
**Put out the lamps.**—Of the great golden stand, in the holy place.
**Have not burned incense.**—On the golden altar. Literally, *And incense they have not burned, and burnt offering they have not offered in the sanctuary.* The *sanctuary* is not the holy place, or larger chamber of the Temple, but it includes the whole sacred precincts, courts as well as buildings. The burnt offerings presented on the new Syrian altar of Ahaz (2 Kings xvi. 15) are here counted as nought, because they were irregular. (Comp. also 2 Kings xvi. 14.)

(8) **The wrath . . . was** (*i.e., fell*) **upon Judah.**—The phrase of chap. xxiv. 18. (Comp. chap. xix. 2, 10.)
**Delivered them to trouble . . .**—Rather, *made them a horror, an astonishment, and a hissing.* The language is Deuteronomic. (Comp. Deut. xxviii. 25, 37: "Thou shalt become a horror . . . an astonishment." Jer. xxv. 9, 18: "I will make them an astonishment and a hissing," *et al.*)
**As ye see with your** (own) **eyes.**—*For ye behold the disastrous results of the invasions of Aram and Israel, of Edom and the Philistines, and of the appeal to Assyria* (chap. xxviii.).

(9) **For.**—*And.* (See chap. xxviii. 5, 6, 8, 17 for what is here stated.)

(10) **Now it is in mine heart.**—See for this phrase and construction 1 Chron. xxii. 7, xxviii. 2; 2 Chron. vi. 7.
**To make a covenant with.**—The preposition is *for.* (See Note on chap. xxi. 7.)
**Turn away.**—Literally, *return* (Isa. v. 25). "That his fierce wrath may turn away from Israel" (Num. xxv. 4).

(11) **My sons.**—A condescending term from the king; just as *my father* was a term of respect (2 Kings ii. 12, v. 13, xiii. 14).
**Be not now negligent.**—The *Niphal* form of the verb *shalah* ("to be at ease") occurs nowhere else. The margin is incorrect.
**The Lord hath chosen you.**—*You hath the Lord chosen.* The pronoun is emphatic. (Comp. the similar words: 1 Chron. xxiii. 13; Deut. x. 8.)
**To stand before him,** (in order) **to serve him,** is the construction.
**And that ye should minister.**—Literally, *And to become to him ministers and thurifers.*
The thoughts and the style of the royal address make it evident enough that it is a free composition, in the well-known manner of ancient historians.

(12–14) The names of the Levites who received the royal charge.

(12) **Mahath the son of Amasai.**—The verse enumerates two members of each of the three great Levitical sub-tribes—Kohath, Merari, and Gershon. Mahath and Eden recur (chap. xxxi. 13, 15). Kish ben Abdi and Joah ben Zimmah occurred (1 Chron. vi. 21, 44). They appear to be family rather than personal names.

(13) **The sons of Elizaphan.**—Or, *Elzaphan*, ben Uzziel ben Kohath (Exod. vi. 18), who was prince of the bnê Kohath in the time of Moses (Num. iii. 30). Two of this leading house and two of the Gershonite Asaphites were also present.

*Sanctification of the*      II. CHRONICLES, XXIX.      *Temple, the Sacrifices.*

<sup>(14)</sup> and of the sons of Heman; Jehiel, and Shimei: and of the sons of Jeduthun; Shemaiah, and Uzziel. <sup>(15)</sup> And they gathered their brethren, and sanctified themselves, and came, according to the commandment of the king, [1] by the words of the LORD, to cleanse the house of the LORD. <sup>(16)</sup> And the priests went into the inner part of the house of the LORD, to cleanse *it*, and brought out all the uncleanness that they found in the temple of the LORD into the court of the house of the LORD. And the Levites took *it*, to carry *it* out abroad into the brook Kidron. <sup>(17)</sup> Now they began on the first *day* of the first month to sanctify, and on the eighth day of the month came they to the porch of the LORD: so they sanctified the house of the LORD in eight days; and in the sixteenth day of the first month they made an end. <sup>(18)</sup> Then they went in to Hezekiah the king, and said, We have cleansed all the house of the LORD, and the altar of burnt offering, with all the vessels thereof, and the shewbread table, with all the vessels thereof. <sup>(19)</sup> Moreover all the vessels, which king Ahaz in his reign did cast away in his transgression, have we prepared and sanctified, and, behold, they *are* before the altar of the LORD.

<sup>(20)</sup> Then Hezekiah the king rose early, and gathered the rulers of the city, and went up to the house of the LORD. <sup>(21)</sup> And they brought seven bullocks, and seven rams, and seven lambs, and seven he goats, for a *a*sin offering for the kingdom, and for the sanctuary, and for Judah. And he commanded the priests the sons of Aaron to offer *them* on the altar of the LORD. <sup>(22)</sup> So they

[1] Or, *in the business of the Lord.*

*a* Lev. 4. 14.

---

<sup>(14)</sup> **And of the sons of Heman.**—Two Levites of each of the remaining musical guilds—the Kohathite Hemanites and the Merarite bnê Jeduthun (Ethan)—are finally named, making up, with the preceding pairs, a total of seven pairs, or fourteen principal men of the Levitical order. (Comp. 1 Chron. vi. 18—32.)

**Jehiel.**—Repeated (chap. xxxi. 13).

<sup>(15)</sup> **They gathered their brethren.**—As chiefs, or heads of houses, they had the requisite authority. The families mostly concerned would naturally be those residing in Jerusalem.

**According to the commandment of the king, by the words of the Lord**—*i.e.*, through the words of Jehovah; a mandate based on the words of Jehovah, as recorded in the written Law. Comp. 1 Chron. xxv. 5, and chap. xxx. 12. Also verse 25, below: "For by the hand of Jehovah was the commandment" (Note).

<sup>(16)</sup> **The priests went into the inner part.**—Ezek. xli. 3. The interior of the Temple proper is meant, which the Levites might not enter, but only the priests, according to the legal rule.

**Brought out all the uncleanness.**—*Tum'ah* (Lev. v. 3; Jud. xiii. 7). See the Note on the synonymous expression *niddah* (verse 5).

**Took.**—*Received* it; from the hands of the priests (*qibbêl*, a late word).

**Abroad.**—*Outside* (of the Temple precincts).

**Into the brook Kidron.**—Rather, the *Wady* of Kidron (2 Kings xxiii. 12; chaps. xv. 16, xxx. 14).

<sup>(17)</sup> The time the work took. Beginning on the 1st of Nisan with the purification of the courts, they had cleansed them by the 8th of the month, and "came to the porch of the Lord," *i.e.*, to the entry of the holy place. The following eight days were spent in cleansing the two holy chambers, and by the 16th of Nisan the work of purification was done.

<sup>(18)</sup> **They went in.**—Heb., *into the interior* (*pěnimah*, "inner part" verse 16) of the palace.

**Hezekiah.**—*Hizkiyahu.* So also in verse 27; but in verse 30, *Yehizkiyahu.* (See Note on verse 1.)

**The altar of burnt offering.**—Which Ahaz appears to have superseded (2 Kings xvi. 14, 15), besides removing it from its legal position.

**And the shewbread table.**—Literally, *the table of the pile* (of sacred cakes). Only one table is here mentioned. (Comp. 1 Chron. xxviii. 16; chap. iv. 8, 19.) The metal work of all the sacred apparatus would be greatly tarnished, if only from neglect, apart from wanton ill usage.

<sup>(19)</sup> **Cast away.**—The same word as "cast off" in chap. xi. 14. The vessels so treated were the brazen altar, the brazen sea, and the lavers on the stands (2 Kings xvi. 14, 17).

**In his transgression.**—*Unfaithfulness*, or *apostasy.*

**Have we prepared.**—*Ordered aright*, put to rights. (*Hēkannû, i.e., hăkinônû*, 1 Chron. xxix. 16 here only.)

**The altar of the Lord.**—The brazen altar in the court.

THE CONSECRATION SACRIFICES (verses 20—30).

<sup>(20)</sup> **Rose early.**—Comp. Ps. v. 3: "Early in the morning will I direct my prayer unto Thee."

**Gathered the rulers of the city.**—Hezekiah assembled the chief men of Jerusalem, because there was no time to send out a general summons to the country, as he wished to proceed at once with the sacrifices of expiation.

**Went up to the house.**—So 2 Kings xix. 14; chap. ix. 4, and often.

<sup>(21)</sup> **Seven bullocks . . . rams . . . lambs.**—For a burnt offering (*'ôlah*). See the legal prescriptions respecting the sin offering (Lev. iv.). On the present extraordinary occasion, an extraordinary sacrifice was offered. Balak and Balaam offered seven bullocks and seven rams as a burnt offering (Num. xxiii. 1, 2, *seq.*).

**And seven he goats, for a sin offering.**—Comp. Ezra vi. 17, viii. 35; and Lev. iv. 23, 28; also verse 23. *The reigning house and the sanctuary and the people* had all contracted defilement during the late period of idolatry.

**The priests the sons of Aaron to offer.**—In careful accordance with the rule of the Torah.

<sup>(22)</sup> **Received the blood.**—Caught it in bowls of sprinkling (Num. viii. 14).

*The Solemn Sacrifices.*     II. CHRONICLES, XXIX.     *The Work of the Levites.*

killed the bullocks, and the priests received the blood, and *ª sprinkled it* on the altar: likewise, when they had killed the rams, they sprinkled the blood upon the altar: they killed also the lambs, and they sprinkled the blood upon the altar. (23) And they brought ¹ forth the he goats *for* the sin offering before the king and the congregation; and they laid their *ᵇ* hands upon them: (24) and the priests killed them, and they made reconciliation with their blood upon the altar, to make an atonement for all Israel: for the king commanded *that* the burnt offering and the sin offering should be made for all Israel. (25) *ᶜ* And he set the Levites in the house of the LORD with cymbals, with psalteries, and with harps, according to the commandment of David, and of Gad the king's seer, and Nathan the prophet: for *so was* the commandment ² of the LORD ³ by his prophets. (26) And the Levites stood with the instruments of David, and the priests with the trumpets. (27) And Hezekiah commanded to offer the burnt offering upon the altar. And ⁴ when the burnt offering began, the song of the LORD began *also* with the trumpets, and with the ⁵ instruments *ordained* by David king of Israel. (28) And all the congregation worshipped, and the ⁶ singers

*ª* Lev. 8. 14, 15; Heb. 9. 21.
¹ Heb., *near.*
*ᵇ* Lev. 4. 15.
*ᶜ* 1 Chron. 16. 4, & 25. 6.
² Heb., *by the hand of the* LORD.
³ Heb., *by the hand of.*
⁴ Heb., *in the time.*
⁵ Heb., *hands of instruments.*
⁶ Heb., *song.*

---

**And sprinkled it on the altar.**—*Threw it against* (literally, *towards*) *the altar* (Lev. viii. 19, 24).

**Likewise, when.**—*And they slaughtered the rams . . . and they slaughtered the lambs.* The three clauses of the verse are symmetrical. The repetition is a mark of the writer's anxiety to show how carefully the legitimate ritual was observed in each instance.

**Killed.**—*Slaughtered* (*shaḥaṭ*; σφάζω, Gen. xxxvii. 31). Specially used of slaying sacrificial victims (Lev. i. 5).

(23) **Brought forth.**—Rather, *brought near*—viz., to the altar.

**He goats.**—*Se'îrîm* ("hairy ones"). A different term—*çĕphîrê 'izzîm*, "spring-bucks of goats"—was used in verse 21. This latter is properly an Aramean word, and only found in late Heb., *se'îrîm* being the classical term.

**Laid their hands upon them.**—Comp. Lev. 1. 4, iii. 2, iv. 4, from which it appears that the person offering laid his hand upon the head of the victim, whether he were making a burnt offering or a thank-offering or a sin-offering.

The natural fitness of the ceremony in the case of expiatory sacrifices is obvious. "The king and the congregation" performed it, in the present instance, on behalf of the entire nation.

(24) **Made reconciliation with their blood upon the altar.**—Literally, *made sin offering of their blood.* (Comp. Lev. ix. 15.) The meaning may be seen by reference to Lev. iv. 30, *seq.* The priest dipped his finger in the blood of the victim and touched the horns of the altar with it, and then poured the blood at the base of the altar.

**For the king commanded . . . Israel.**—*For for all Israel the king had commanded the burnt offering and the sin offering*; or, *for "For all Israel," said the king, "is the burnt offering and the sin offering."* The expression *all Israel* includes the northern kingdom. (Comp. Hezekiah's invitation to its people to attend the Passover, chap. xxx. 1.)

(25) **He set.**—*Stationed, appointed.* Hezekiah restored the ancient choral worship as established by David (1 Chron. xxiii. 5, xxv.).

**Psalteries.**—*Nĕbâlîm*, a kind of harp; Greek, νάβλα ναβλίον.

**Harps.**—*Kinnôrôth.* Greek, κινύρα, a sort of lyre, or cittern, or guitar.

**Gad . . . Nathan.**—1 Chron. xxix. 29. This is the only place where the institution of the Levitical minstrelsy is ascribed to the injunctions of prophets; but the thing is probable in itself, considering that no important step, whether in civil or ecclesiastical matters, would be likely to be taken by an Israelite king without consulting the Divine will by means of the royal prophets, as we know, from the cuneiform documents, was the uniform practice with the Assyrian and Babylonian sovereigns. Moreover, prophecy was intimately connected with music. (See on 1 Chron. xxv. 1.)

**For so was . . .**—*For by the hand of Jehovah was the commandment; to wit, by the hand of his prophets.* David's command was obeyed because it was Divine, having emanated from the prophets who represented Jehovah. (Comp. verse 15, *supra.*)

(26) **The instruments of David.**—See on 1 Chron. xxiii. 5. The writer's interest in the musical portion of the Temple ritual receives one more illustration in these verses.

(27) **Commanded to offer the burnt offering . . . altar.**—These words are repeated from verse 21, because all that comes between is descriptive of the preparations made for the due performance of the sacrifice. When the victims had been slain, flayed, and cut up, and the altar had been sprinkled with their blood, and when the Levitical musicians had taken their places, instruments in hand, everything was ready, and the sacrifice was ordered to begin. "And at the time when the burnt offering began, the song of Jehovah" (*i.e.*, the chant of the Levites with its musical accompaniment) "began, and the clarions; and that under the lead of the instruments of David king of Israel," *i.e.*, the harps and lyres were dominant throughout, and the clarions subordinate to their music. Or we may render: "And that at the side of (*i.e.*, along with) the instruments of David king of Israel." The phrase is *'al-yĕdê*, "upon the hands." (Comp. 1 Chron. xxv. 2, 3, 6.) The LXX. omits the needless "and that" (*wĕ*); the Syriac renders: "And when the burnt offerings began to be offered, Hezekiah began to chant the praises of the Lord, as from the mouth of David king of Israel." The Vulgate also is very free.

(28) **Worshipped.**—*Were worshipping.* LXX., προσεκύνει.

**The singers.**—Heb., *the song.* So we might say "*the music* was playing;" or even "the song was singing," *i.e.*, being sung.

**The trumpeters sounded.**—*And the clarions were blowing* (literally, *clarioning*). The participle is

sang, and the trumpeters sounded: *and all this continued* until the burnt offering was finished. (29) And when they had made an end of offering, the king and all that were ¹present with him bowed themselves, and worshipped. (30) Moreover Hezekiah the king and the princes commanded the Levites to sing praise unto the LORD with the words of David, and of Asaph the seer. And they sang praises with gladness, and they bowed their heads and worshipped. (31) Then Hezekiah answered and said, Now ye have ²consecrated yourselves unto the LORD, come near and bring sacrifices and thank offerings into the house of the LORD. And the congregation brought in sacrifices and thank offerings; and as many as were of a free heart burnt offerings. (32) And the number of the burnt offerings, which the congregation brought, was threescore and ten bullocks, an hundred rams, *and* two hundred lambs: all these *were* for a burnt offering to the LORD. (33) And the consecrated things *were* six hundred oxen and three thousand sheep. (34) But the priests were too few, so that they could not flay all the burnt offerings: wherefore their brethren the Levites ³did help them, till the work was ended, and until the *other* priests had sanctified themselves: for the Levites *were* more upright in heart to sanctify themselves than the priests. (35) And also the burnt offerings *were* in abundance, with the fat of the peace offerings, and the drink offerings for *every* burnt offering. So the service of the house of the LORD was set in order. (36) And

1 Heb., *found.*

2 Or, *filled your hand.*

3 Heb., *strengthened them.*

---

masculine, although the noun is properly feminine, because here the word "clarions" really stands for the clarion-players. So in modern orchestras they speak of "the violins," or "the 'cellos," meaning the players on those instruments.

**And all this.**—Literally, *the whole, until the burnt offering was finished.*

This passage is highly interesting for the light it throws upon the mode in which the worship of the second Temple was conducted in the fourth century B.C., the probable age of the chronicler; and no doubt also in the times here treated of, for the Temple ritual would naturally be a matter of immemorial tradition. (Comp. chap. vii. 5, 6.)

(29) **Of offering.**—Scil., *the burnt offering,* as the verb implies.

**Bowed themselves.**—Rather, *bowed the knee* (*kara'*). (Isa. xlv. 23; 1 Kings xix. 18.)

(30) **With the words of David, and of Asaph.**—Heb., *in the words.* This appears to mean that the singing (verse 28) consisted in chanting Davidic and Asaphite psalms, and it is usually so explained. But the expression "in the words of David and of Asaph" may be compared with "in the words of Jehovah," verse 15, and "in the command of David and Gad the king's seer," verse 25; and so may be understood to assert merely that the singing was in accordance with the arrangements of David and Asaph. (1 Chron. xxv. 1, 2, 9.)

**Asaph the seer.**—So Heman is called (1 Chron. xxv. 5); and Jeduthun (2 Chron. xxv. 15).

**With gladness.**—Literally, *unto exultation*—i.e., rapturously.

**And they bowed their heads.**—When the song was ended (verse 29).

THE CONSECRATION COMPLETED BY ADDITIONAL SACRIFICES (verses 31—36).

(31) **Answered and said.**—See 1 Chron. xii. 17. The phrase is used as we should use it in Exod. iv. 1; 2 Kings vii. 13.

**Ye have consecrated . . .**—Literally, *ye have filled your hand for Jehovah,* a phrase used of the consecration of priests (Lev. vii. 37). Here it is addressed to the whole assembly, as the following words prove (unless the text be unsound). The congregation, as well as the sacerdotal order, had consecrated themselves anew to Jehovah, by their presence and participation in the previous solemnities. Others suppose that these words are spoken to the priests only, and that then the king turns to the congregation with the words "Come near," &c. (There should be a semicolon after "the Lord.")

**Sacrifices and thank offerings** (*zebahîm wethôdôth*).—The first word means "thank-offerings" (= *zebahîm shelamîm*); the second, a peculiar species of thank-offering, apparently accompanied by a special kind of psalms called *tôdôth* ("thanksgivings"). "Sacrifices *and* thank-offerings" therefore means "sacrifices, that is, thank-offerings." (See Lev. vii. 12, 16, for the three kinds of thank-offerings.)

**As many as were of a free heart.**—Literally, *Every free-hearted one* (1 Chron. xxix. 6, 9).

**Burnt offerings** were a token of greater self-denial and disinterestedness than thank-offerings, because they were wholly consumed on the altar, whereas the worshippers feasted upon the latter.

(33) **The consecrated things.**—That is, the victims for the thank-offerings. (Chap. xxxv. 13.)

(34) **Flay all the burnt offerings.**—In private offerings this was done by the worshipper himself (Lev. i. 6). In national sacrifices it appears to have been the duty of the priests.

**Did help them.**—See margin; and Ezra vi. 22.

**Until the other priests had sanctified.**—*Began to sanctify themselves,* as a body.

**For the Levites . . . in heart.**—The priests, as a class, were probably more deeply involved in the corruption of the last reign.

(35) **And also the burnt offerings were in abundance.**—Another reason why the Levites helped the priests: the latter were so much occupied with the actual service of the altar.

**The fat of the peace** (*thank*) **offerings**—which had to be burned upon the burnt offerings (Lev. iii. 5, vi. 5).

**And the drink offerings.**—Num. xv. 1—16.

(36) **And Hezekiah rejoiced.**—So of David and his people (1 Chron. xxix. 9, 22). (Comp. also chap. vii. 10.)

Hezekiah rejoiced, and all the people, that God had prepared the people: for the thing was *done* suddenly.

CHAPTER XXX.—[1] And Hezekiah sent to all Israel and Judah, and wrote letters also to Ephraim and Manasseh, that they should come to the house of the LORD at Jerusalem, to keep the passover unto the LORD God of Israel. [2] For the king had taken counsel, and his princes, and all the congregation in Jerusalem, to keep the passover in the second *a* month. [3] For they could not keep it at that time, because the priests had not sanctified themselves sufficiently, neither had the people gathered themselves together to Jerusalem. [4] And the thing [1] pleased the king and all the congregation. [5] So they established a decree to make proclamation throughout all Israel, from Beer-sheba even to Dan, that they should come to keep the passover unto the LORD God of Israel at Jerusalem: for they had not done *it* of a long *time in such sort* as it was written.

[6] So the posts went with the letters

*a* Num. 9, 10, 11.

[1] Heb., *was right in the eyes of the king.*

---

**That God had prepared.**—In the Hebrew the article is used instead of the *relative*: a construction characteristic of the chronicler (1 Chron. xxvi. 28). Render: "And Hezekiah rejoiced . . . over that which God had set in order for the people," viz., the long-suspended ordinances of the Temple worship (1 Chron. xii. 39; xv. 1). Perhaps, however, *lā'ām*, "for the people," is the mere accusative after the verb, and the sense is "rejoiced because God had prepared the people" (2 Sam. iii. 30).

**For the thing . . . suddenly.**—Literally, *for on a sudden happened the matter.* "On a sudden," *be-pith'ōm*, here only; elsewhere simply *pith'ōm*. Comp. the synonymous *rega'* and *be-rega'* (Ps. vi. 10; Job xxi. 13). The hand of God was seen in the speed with which the revolution was effected, and the sudden turn of the princes and people from indifference to glad alacrity. (Comp. chap. xxx. 12.)

### XXX.

HEZEKIAH'S PASSOVER—THE ROYAL SUMMONS TO ALL ISRAEL FROM DAN TO BEER-SHEBA (verses 1—12).

[1] **Sent to.**—*'al*, i.e., *'el.* (Jer. xxvi. 15; Neh. vi. 3.)

**Letters.**—*'Iggĕrôth.* Apparently a word of Persian origin. (Comp. *engâre*, "something written;" *'engârîden*, "to paint" or "write;" from which comes the Greek ἄγγαρος, a royal messenger; Esth. ix. 26; comp. Matt. v. 41.) Only used in late Hebrew.

**To Ephraim and Manasseh.**—That is, the northern kingdom. (Comp. verse 10.)

**To keep** (make) **the passover unto the Lord.** —Exod. xii. 48 (same phrase); LXX., ποιῆσαι τὸ φασέκ (Pascha). The first year of Hezekiah was the third of Hoshea, the last king of Samaria, who is described as a better king than his predecessors. Doubtless, therefore, Hoshea did not actively oppose Hezekiah's wish for a really national Passover. (See 2 Kings xviii. 1, xvii. 2.)

[2] **For the king had taken counsel.**—*And the king determined* (chap. xxv. 17). The resolution was taken by the king in council with his grandees and the popular representatives; apparently before the 14th of Nisan, which was the proper time for keeping the feast.

**In the second month.**—And not in the *first* month of the sacred year, as the law prescribes (Num. ix. 1—5). The grounds of the postponement are assigned in the next verse, viz., the legal impurity of many of the priests, and the non-arrival of the people at the proper time. The law permits postponement to the second month in such cases (Num. ix. 6—11). The first month was Nisan; Assyr., *Nisânu*: the second, Iyyar; Assyr., *Âru*.

[3] **At that time.**—The time when the Temple had just been reopened (chap. xxix. 3), in the first month of Hezekiah's first year. The Purification of the Temple was not completed until the 16th of Nisan (chap. xxix. 17); but perhaps the Passover would have been held, had not the hindrances here mentioned prevented it. (See chap. xxix. 34).

**Sufficiently.**—*Lĕmadday.* Literally, *unto what was enough* (*lĕ-mah-dày*), an expression only met with here. (Comp. a similar formation, 1 Chron. xv. 13.) The meaning is that a sufficient number of priests had not observed the legal ceremonies of self-purification in time to hold Passover in Nisan.

[4] **The thing pleased.**—*The matter* (or *proposal*) *was right in the eyes of the king*—i.e., the proposal to keep the Passover in the second month, and to invite the northern tribes.

[5] **So they established a decree.**—*And they decreed a proposal* (*he'ĕmîd dābār*). (Comp. verse 8; Ps. cv. 10, "and hath decreed it unto Jacob for a law.")

**To make proclamation.**—Literally, *to make a voice pass.* (Comp. chaps. xxiv. 9, xxxvi. 22.)

**From Beer-sheba even to Dan.**—Reversing the ancient form of the phrase, to suit the present case. (Comp. Judg. xx. 1; chap. xix. 4.)

**For they had not . . . written.**—Rather, *For not in multitude* (*larōb*) *had they kept it, according to the Scripture.* The people had not been in the habit of "coming in their numbers" to the feast. (Comp. the like use of *larōb* in verses 13, 24.) See the Law respecting the Passover, Exod. xii. 1—20; Deut. xvi. 1—8; from which it appears that the obligation to observe it was *universal,* and according to the latter passage, which is probably referred to in the phrase "according to what is written." Jerusalem was the only legitimate *place* for the festival. It is implied that ever since the division of the kingdom, and perhaps earlier, the Passover had been inadequately celebrated. (Comp. 2 Kings xxiii. 22.) LXX. well, ὅτι πλῆθος οὐκ ἐποίησε κατὰ τὴν γραφήν; Vulg., "multi enim non fecerant, sicut lege praescriptum est; Syriac and Arabic, "because their wealth had grown greatly" (!)

[6] **The posts.**—The *runners*—i.e., couriers (ἄγγαροι). The Syriac uses the Latin word *Tabellarii,* "letter-carriers," which the Arabic mistakes for "folk of

¹ from the king and his princes throughout all Israel and Judah, and according to the commandment of the king, saying, Ye children of Israel, turn again unto the LORD God of Abraham, Isaac, and Israel, and he will return to the remnant of you, that are escaped out of the hand of the kings of Assyria. ⁽⁷⁾ And be not ye like your fathers, and like your brethren, which trespassed against the LORD God of their fathers, *who* therefore gave them up to desolation, as ye see. ⁽⁸⁾ Now ²be ye not stiffnecked, as your fathers *were, but* ³yield yourselves unto the LORD, and enter into his sanctuary, which he hath sanctified for ever: and serve the LORD your God, that the fierceness of his wrath may turn away from you. ⁽⁹⁾ For if ye turn again unto the LORD, your brethren and your children *shall find* compassion before them that lead them captive, so that they shall come again into this land: for the LORD your God *is* ᵃgracious and merciful, and will not turn away *his* face from you, if ye return unto him.

⁽¹⁰⁾ So the posts passed from city to city through the country of Ephraim and Manasseh even unto Zebulun: but they laughed them to scorn, and mocked them. ⁽¹¹⁾ Nevertheless divers of Asher and Manasseh and of Zebulun humbled themselves, and came to Jerusalem. ⁽¹²⁾ Also in Judah the hand of God was to give them one heart to do the com-

¹ Heb., *from the hand.*
² Heb., *harden not your necks.*
³ Heb., *give the hand.*
ᵃ Exod. 34. 6.

---

Tiberias"! The soldiers of the body-guard seem to have acted as royal messengers.

**From the king.**—*From the hand of the king.*

**And according to the commandment.**—The construction appears to be: they went *with the letters . . . . and according to the king's order.* The LXX. and Vulg. omit *and*, but the Syriac has it.

**And he will return.**—*That he may return unto the survivors that are left unto you from the hand of the kings of Assyria.*

**Remnant.**—*Pĕlêṭāh.*—That the word really means *survivors* appears from comparison of the Assyrian *balâṭu*, "to be alive;" *bulluṭu*, "life."

**The kings of Assyria.**—See chap. xxviii. 16, 20. The words are a rhetorical reference to Tiglath-pileser's invasion of the northern kingdom, and the depopulation of Galilee and Gilead. The chronicler's language may have been influenced also by recollection of the last fatal inroad of Shalmaneser II., in the fourth year of Hezekiah (2 Kings xviii 9). (See 2 Kings xv. 29.)

⁽⁷⁾ **And be not ye like your fathers.**—From the days of Jeroboam downwards.

**And like your brethren.**—Of Naphtali and the Trans-Jordan, whom Tiglath-pileser carried captive.

**Trespassed.**—*Were unfaithful to Jehovah.*

**Who therefore gave them up to desolation.**—*And He made them an astonishment* (chap. xxix. 8).

⁽⁸⁾ **Be ye not stiffnecked.**—*Harden ye not your neck like your fathers.* 2 Kings xvii. 14, "and they hardened their neck like their fathers' neck." (Jer. vii. 26; Ps. xcv. 8, 9.)

**But yield yourselves.**—Omit *but*, and place a stop after *fathers*. "Yield ye a hand to Jehovah," *i.e.*, submit to Him. So 1 Chron. xxix. 24. The phrase also means "to make an agreement with" (Ezra x. 19; 2 Kings x. 15). (Comp. Isa. ii. 6.)

**Enter into his sanctuary . . . serve the Lord.**—Comp. Ps. c. 1, 4.

**Which he hath sanctified for ever.**—Chap. vii. 16, 20.

**That the fierceness** (*heat*) **. . . from you.**—Chap. xxix. 10. Such resemblances prove the *ideal* character of these addresses.

⁽⁹⁾ **If ye turn again.**—*When ye return unto Jehovah, your brethren and your sons (shall become) objects of pity (raḥămîm,* "compassion;" here that which inspires it) *before their captors.* (Comp. Ps. cvi. 46, "And he made them *objects of pity before all their captors;*" Neh. i. 11.)

**Gracious and merciful.**—Ps. lxxxvi. 15; Exod. xxxiv. 6; in both places "merciful and gracious." Neh. ix. 17, 31, "gracious and merciful," as here. (Comp. the formula of the Koran: "In the name of God the merciful, the compassionate.")

**Turn away his face.**—Literally, *turn aside face* (a different word from "turn away" in verse 8).

⁽¹⁰⁾ **So the posts passed.**—*And the couriers were passing.*

**Even unto Zebulun.**—This tribe, which lay on the southern border of Naphtali, had suffered from Tiglath-pileser's invasion (Isa. ix. 1). The messengers did not actually travel northward so far as Dan (verse 5). This mention of *Zebulun* as the limit of their journey lends an air of historical truth to the account.

**Laughed them to scorn.**—Literally, *and they were laughing at them* (*hishîq* : here only), *and making mock of them* (Ps. xxii. 7). The verbs imply what the Israelites did continually. Vulg., "cursores pergebant . . . . illis irridentibus et subsannantibus eos."

⁽¹¹⁾ **Nevertheless divers of Asher.**—*But some men of Asher.*—Besides these from Asher, Manasseh, Zebulun, verse 18 mentions others from Ephraim and Issachar. The two and a half tribes of the Trans-Jordan, as well as Naphtali and probably the neighbouring tribe of Dan, had been devastated by Tiglath-pileser; and the couriers went no farther than Zebulun. Part of Asher was contiguous to Zebulun; and the other three tribes mentioned by the chronicler lay south of it, so that the account is self-consistent.

**Humbled themselves**—*i.e.*, repented. (Comp. chap. xii. 6, 7.)

⁽¹²⁾ **Also in Judah . . . was.**—Rather, *Moreover upon Judah was the hand of God*: a phrase here used of a Divine influence for good. (Comp. Ezra viii. 22.) Elsewhere the phrase has the sense of judicial visitation; *e.g.*, Exod. ix. 3.

**The commandment . . . by the word of the Lord.**—Comp. the like phrase, chap. xxix. 15. The

*Idolatrous Altars Destroyed.*     II. CHRONICLES, XXX.     *Hezekiah Prays for the People.*

mandment of the king and of the princes, by the word of the LORD.

(13) And there assembled at Jerusalem much people to keep the feast of unleavened bread in the second month, a very great congregation. (14) And they arose and took away the ᵃaltars that *were* in Jerusalem, and all the altars for incense took they away, and cast *them* into the brook Kidron. (15) Then they killed the passover on the fourteenth *day* of the second month: and the priests and the Levites were ashamed, and sanctified themselves, and brought in the burnt offerings into the house of the LORD. (16) And they stood in ¹their place after their manner, according to the law of Moses the man of God: the priests sprinkled the blood, *which they received* of the hand of the Levites. (17) For *there were* many in the congregation that were not sanctified: therefore the Levites had the charge of the killing of the passovers for every one *that was* not clean, to sanctify *them* unto the LORD. (18) For a multitude of the people, *even* many of Ephraim, and Manasseh, Issachar, and Zebulun, had not cleansed themselves, yet did they eat the passover otherwise than it was written. But Hezekiah prayed for them, saying, The good LORD pardon every one (19) that prepareth his heart to seek God, the LORD God of his fathers, though *he*

ᵃ ch. 28. 24.

¹ Heb., *their standing*.

---

royal command was inspired by the word of the Lord through a prophet.

THE PASSOVER AT JERUSALEM (verses 13—22).

(13) **Much people.**—A very great congregation—*a congregation in great multitude* (*lārôb mĕ'ōd*). (See on verse 5.)

(14) **Took away the altars.**—The altars of burnt offering erected by Ahaz "in every corner" of the city (chap. xxviii. 24).

**Altars for incense.**—*Ha-mĕqaṭṭĕrôth*—literally, *the incense-burners.* The term occurs here only.

**Cast them into the brook Kidron.**—See on chap. xxix. 16. Thus the city was purified as well as the Temple.

(15) **And the priests and the Levites were ashamed, and sanctified themselves.**—Ashamed of their former reluctance to purify themselves from the defilement contracted by their connection with illegal cults and sanctuaries during the late reign (chap. xxix. 34; and verse 3, *supra*). In the former passage the Levites are favourably contrasted with the priests; here they are spoken of in the same terms, a verbal inaccuracy apparently due to the writer's desire to be brief.

(16) **In their place.**—'*Omdām*. This word is used in this sense only in Daniel, Chronicles, Nehemiah. (Comp. chaps. xxxiv. 31, xxxv. 10.)

**After their manner**—*i.e.*, "according to their order" (1 Chron. vi. 31).

**According to the law . . . of God.**—Another reference to the Pentateuchal legislation. (See chaps. xxiii. 18, xxiv. 6, xiv. 4, xvii. 9.)

**Sprinkled . . . Levites.**—Rather, *sprinkling the blood from the hand of the Levites.* On this occasion the Levites, and not the laymen who presented the victims, slew the lambs and handed the blood to the priests to be dashed against the altar. The reason of this breach of the ordinary rule is given in next verse.

(17) **There were many in the congregation that were not sanctified.**—Comp. chap. xxxv. 6, 10, 11, where the Levites are again represented as doing the same work, but not as an exception. The precedent of Hezekiah's Passover would seem to have become the rule. (Comp. also Ezra vi. 20.)

**To sanctify them**—*i.e.*, the lambs, which would have been ceremonially unclean if slain by unclean hands. (Comp. chap. ii. 4, "to dedicate it unto Him;" the same verb.)

(18) **A multitude.**—*Marbîth* (chap. ix. 6; 1 Chron. xii. 29). Only in the Chronicles in this sense. Elsewhere the term means "increase" of children (1 Sam. ii. 33), or of money, *i.e.*, interest (τόκος, Lev. xxv. 37).

**Ephraim . . . Zebulun.**—The names indicate a documental source.

**Had not cleansed themselves.**—As was natural in the case of persons who had long been estranged from the legal religion of Jehovah (*hiṭṭĕhārû*, pausal form of *hiṭṭăhărû*, Ezra vi. 20, occurs here only).

**Yet did they eat . . . written.**—*But ate the Passover in non-accordance with the Scripture*—*i.e.*, in illegal fashion, being themselves unclean. (Comp. Num. ix. 6, *seq.*, according to which unclean persons were bound to abstain from eating the Passover until the fourteenth of the second month.)

**But Hezekiah prayed.**—*For Hezekiah had prayed for them,* and therefore their irregularity was condoned.

**The good Lord.**—*Jehovah the good;* so only here. (Comp. Ps. xxv. 8.)

**Good**—*i.e.*, kind, generous; *benignus, benevolus.*

**Pardon every one.**—Properly, *make atonement on behalf of every one* (*kipper bĕ'ad*): Lev. xvi. 6, 11. In the sense of *forgive* the construction is different: Ps. lxv. 4; Ezek. xvi. 63.

(19) **That prepareth.**—*Hath directed.* The division of verses here is obviously incorrect. (The mistake was doubtless caused by the omission of the relative in the Hebrew between *kol*, "every one," and *lĕbābô hēkîn*, "his heart he hath directed." The construction is parallel to that in 1 Chron. xv. 12, "unto *the place that* I have prepared for it;" so LXX.) The prayer is, "Jehovah the Good atone for every one who hath directed his heart to seek the *true* God, *even* Jehovah, the God of his fathers, albeit not (literally, *and not*) according to the holy purifying"—*i.e.*, although he hath not rigorously observed the law of purification.

**Purification of the sanctuary.**—Or, *holy purification*: a phrase only found here (comp. 1 Chron. xxiii. 28).

The prayer evinces a preference of spiritual sincerity to mere literal observance of legal prescriptions, which is all the more remarkable as occurring in a writer whose

be not *cleansed* according to the purification of the sanctuary. [20] And the LORD hearkened to Hezekiah, and healed the people.

[21] And the children of Israel that were [1]present at Jerusalem kept the feast of unleavened bread seven days with great gladness: and the Levites and the priests praised the LORD day by day, *singing* with [2]loud instruments unto the LORD. [22] And Hezekiah spake [3]comfortably unto all the Levites that taught the good knowledge of the LORD: and they did eat throughout the feast seven days, offering peace offerings, and making confession to the LORD God of their fathers. [23] And the whole assembly took counsel to keep other seven days: and they kept *other* seven days with gladness. [24] For Hezekiah king of Judah [4]did give to the congregation a thousand bullocks and seven thousand sheep; and the princes gave to the congregation a thousand bullocks and ten thousand sheep: and a great number of priests sanctified themselves. [25] And all the congregation of Judah, with the priests and the Levites, and all the congregation that came out of Israel, and the strangers that came out of the land of Israel, and that dwelt in Judah, rejoiced. [26] So there was great joy in Jerusalem: for since the time of Solomon the son of David king of Israel there *was* not the like in Jerusalem.

[1] Heb., *found.*
[2] Heb., *instruments of strength.*
[3] Heb., *to the heart of all, &c.*
[4] Heb., *lifted up,* or, *offered.*

---

principal aim is to foster a due reverence for the external ordinances and traditional customs of religion.

(20) **And the Lord hearkened to Hezekiah.**—Comp. Gen. xx. 17, "And Abraham prayed unto God; *and God healed Abimelech and his wife,*" &c. In the present instance the prayer of Hezekiah is thought of as averting a visitation of Divine wrath in the shape of disease and death. (Comp. Lev. xv. 31, "Thus shall ye separate the children of Israel from their uncleanness; that they die not in their uncleanness, when they defile my dwelling-place, that is among them.")

For the word *heal* in connection with uncleanness comp. Isa. vi. 5, 10. See also chap. vii. 14, *supra;* Hos. v. 13, xiv. 4.

(21) **Kept the feast . . . . with great gladness.**—See 1 Chron. xiii. 8, xv. 16, *seq.,* 28, and similar passages.

**And the Levites.**—With stringed instruments.

**And the priests.**—With clarions.

**Praised.**—*Were praising;* throughout the seven days' festival.

**Singing.**—Omit.

**With loud instruments unto the Lord.**—*With instruments of strength to Jehovah.* This curious phrase apparently means instruments with which *they ascribed* strength to Jehovah; that is to say, with which they accompanied their psalms of praise. (Comp. the many psalms which glorify the strength of the God of Israel—*e.g.,* Ps. xxix. 1, "Ascribe unto Jehovah, ye sons of God, ascribe unto Jehovah glory and strength.")

There is, however, something to be said for the Authorised Version. (Comp. chap. v. 12, 13; 1 Chron. xv. 28, xvi. 42, from which it appears that the chronicler preferred music that was loud and strong.)

(22) **Spake comfortably.**—See margin, and comp. Isa. xl. 2.

**That taught the good knowledge of the Lord.**—Rather, *were showing good skill for* (in honour of) *Jehovah,* in their chanting and playing. The king encouraged the musicians with kindly words of praise.

**They did eat throughout the feast.**—Literally, *they ate the feast,* like "they ate the passover." The meaning is that the assembly ate the sacrificial meals, which were supplied from the flesh of the "peace offerings." The phrase is peculiar to this passage. The LXX. has καὶ συνετέλεσαν, "and they finished:" a difference which implies no great change in the Hebrew writing, but is against the context.

**Making confession.**—LXX. rightly, ἐξομολογούμενοι. The meaning is "yielding hearty thanks," "acknowledging" the Divine goodness. Everywhere else the Hebrew word means "to confess guilt" (Neh. ix. 3; Lev. v. 5; Num. v. 7).

(23) **Took counsel.**—*Determined,* the result of taking counsel (verse 2).

**To keep.**—Literally, *to do* or *make.*

**Other seven days.**—As a prolongation of the festivities. (Comp. chap. vii. 9.)

**With gladness.**—*Simhâh,* an adverbial accusative. But some Hebrew MSS. express the *with,* as in chap. vii. 10. The chronicler is fond of dwelling upon the joy of the ancient festivals, as though he would suggest greater whole-heartedness and magnificence to the people and princes of his own day.

(24) **Did give . . . gave.**—*Had presented* (Exod. xxxv. 24)—*scil.,* for sacrifice as a *terûmâh,* or "heave offering." The gifts of king and princes for the Mazzôth festival were so abundant that they sufficed not only for the feast itself, but also for an additional week of rejoicing.

**And a great number of priests.**—Literally, *and priests had sanctified themselves in multitude,* or *to abundance.* The priests no longer hung back as they had done previously (verses 3 and 15; chap. xxix. 34). There was now no lack of persons duly purified for the sacrifice of so many victims.

(25) **And all the congregation.**—Three classes of persons took part in the festival—(1) the Judæans, including the priests and Levites; (2) their Israelite guests; (3) the "strangers"—*gêrim*—*i.e.,* the proselytes, both those who came from the northern kingdom and those who dwelt in Judah. The word *gêrim* is not the same as *gârim* (chap. xv. 9), with which Lange's comment confuses it. (Comp. Lev. xvii. 12.)

(26) **For since the time of Solomon . . . there was not the like.**—The chronicler himself thus compares this great festival with the twofold Feast of the Dedication of the Temple (chap. vii. 1—10). That festival, like this one, had been prolonged seven days, because the Feast of Tabernacles immediately followed upon it; and "there had been no other since the time

(27) Then the priests the Levites arose and blessed the people: and their voice was heard, and their prayer came *up* to ¹his holy dwelling place, *even* unto heaven.

CHAPTER XXXI.—(1) Now when all this was finished, all Israel that were ²present went out to the cities of Judah, and ᵃbrake the ³images in pieces, and cut down the groves, and threw down the high places and the altars out of all Judah and Benjamin, in Ephraim also and Manasseh, ⁴until they had utterly destroyed them all. Then all the children of Israel returned, every man to his possession, into their own cities.

(2) And Hezekiah appointed the courses of the priests and the Levites after their courses, every man according to his service, the priests and Levites for burnt offerings and for peace offerings, to minister, and to give thanks, and to praise in the gates of the tents of the LORD. (3) *He appointed also* the king's portion of his substance for the burnt offerings, *to wit,* for the morning and evening burnt offerings, and the burnt offerings for the sabbaths, and for the new moons, and for the set feasts, as *it is* written in the ᵇlaw of the LORD.

(4) Moreover he commanded the people that dwelt in Jerusalem to give the portion of the priests and the Levites, that they might be encouraged in the law of the LORD. (5) And as soon as the commandment ⁵came abroad, the children of Israel brought in abundance the firstfruits of corn, wine, and oil, and ⁶honey, and of all the increase of the field; and

---

1 Heb., *the habitation of his holiness.*
2 Heb., *found.*
a 2 Kings 18. 4.
3 Heb., *statues.*
4 Heb., *until to make an end.*
b Num. 28.
5 Heb., *brake forth.*
6 Or, *dates.*

---

of Solomon that could compare with this in respect of duration, or abundance of sacrifices, or number of participants, or the joy that distinguished it" (*Bertheau*).

(27) **Then the priests the Levites.**—*And the Levitical priests*; not any irregular ministrants. Some Hebrew MSS., the LXX., Syriac, and the Vulg. read, "And the priests and the Levites": but comp. chap. xxiii. 18.

**And their voice was heard.**—The priestly blessing was a prayer that Jehovah would bless. (See Num. vi. 22—27.) That the prayer was heard on the present occasion, the writer infers from the progress of reform among the people, and the wonderful deliverance from Assyria, as related in the ensuing chapters.

**Their prayer came up.**—*Entered into His holy dwelling* (comp. Isa. xviii. 6, lxviii. 5) *into the heavens.* Notice the characteristic omission of the sacred Name.

### XXXI.

PROGRESS OF THE RELIGIOUS REFORMATION.

(1) Destruction of the images and high places in both kingdoms. (Comp. 2 Kings xviii. 4.)

**Now when all this was finished.**—*And when they had finished all this*—that is, the business of the Passover.

**All Israel that were present went out.**—Their iconoclastic zeal had been thoroughly roused by the festival in which they had just taken part.

**The images.**—*Maççebôth*, "pillars." (See Hos. iii. 4, and 2 Chron. xiv. 2.)

**The groves.**—*The Ashērim*. The sacred trunks, emblematic of physical fertility. (Comp. Hos. iv. 13.)

**In Ephraim also and Manasseh.**—That is, in the territory of the northern kingdom, which was at this time in the last stage of political weakness, and rapidly drifting towards final ruin. The band of Jewish and Israelite zealots would not, therefore, be likely to encounter any serious opposition.

**Until they had utterly destroyed.**—*'Ad lĕkallēh* (chap. xxiv. 10). Literally, *so far as to finishing.*

(2) **The courses ... their courses.**—Hezekiah restored the system of service in rotation, ascribed to David. (Comp. chap. viii. 14, "according to the order of David.")

**Every man according to his service.**—See the same phrase in Num. vii. 5, 7. Literally, *after the mouth* (*i.e.*, rule, prescription) *of his service.*

**The priests and Levites.**—Literally, *to the priests and Levites.* The words depend upon those which immediately precede. LXX., καὶ τὰς ἐφημερίας ἐκδόντου κατὰ τὴν ἑαυτοῦ λειτουργίαν τοῖς ἱερεῦσι καὶ τοῖς Λευίταις.

**To minister ... praise.**—The chronicler's usual definition of the Levitical functions.

**In the gates ... Lord.**—Literally, *in the gates of the camps of Jehovah.* Comp. 1 Chron. ix. 18, 19, where the phrase is explained.

(3) **He appointed also ... set feasts.**—Rather, *And the king's portion* (*i.e.*, the part he contributed) *from his property was for the burnt offerings*—viz., *for the burnt offerings of the morning and the evening, and the burnt offerings on the Sabbath, and the new moons, the set feasts.* The king gave the victims for the sacrifices prescribed in Num. xxviii., xxix., out of his own revenues. See the account of his wealth (chap. xxxii. 27—29). The "set feasts" were the three great festivals, &c., enumerated in Num. *l.c.*

(4) **Moreover.**—Literally, *And he said to the people,* to wit, *to the dwellers in Jerusalem.* (Comp. chap. xxiv. 8; 1 Chron. xxi. 17.)

**The portion of the priests and the Levites.**—The firstfruits and tithes, ordained in Exod. xxiii. 19; Lev. xxvii. 30—33; Num. xviii. 12, 20—24; Deut. xxvi.

**That they might be encouraged in the law.**—Rather, *that they might stick fast unto the law.* For this use of ᶜḥāzaq, comp. 2 Sam. xviii. 9, "his head stuck fast in the terebinth." The meaning is, that they might be enabled to devote themselves wholly and solely to their religious duties, without being distracted by any secular anxieties. (See Neh. xiii. 10, "And I perceived that the portions of the Levites had not been given, for the Levites and the singers that did the work were fled every one to his field.")

(5) **And ... came abroad.**—Literally, *And when the word broke forth*—*i.e.*, spread abroad.

**The children of Israel.**—Here the people of Jerusalem, who in the chronicler's day had a pre-

the tithe of all *things* brought they in abundantly. ⁽⁶⁾ And *concerning* the children of Israel and Judah, that dwelt in the cities of Judah, they also brought in the tithe of oxen and sheep, and the ᵃtithe of holy things which were consecrated unto the LORD their God, and laid *them* ¹by heaps. ⁽⁷⁾ In the third month they began to lay the foundation of the heaps, and finished *them* in the seventh month. ⁽⁸⁾ And when Hezekiah and the princes came and saw the heaps, they blessed the LORD, and his people Israel. ⁽⁹⁾ Then Hezekiah questioned with the priests and the Levites concerning the heaps. ⁽¹⁰⁾ And Azariah the chief priest of the house of Zadok answered him, and said, Since *the people* began to bring the offerings into the house of the LORD, we have had enough to eat, and have left plenty: for the LORD hath blessed his people; and that which is left *is* this great store. ⁽¹¹⁾ Then Hezekiah commanded to prepare ²chambers in the house of the LORD; and they prepared *them*, ⁽¹²⁾ and brought in the offerings and the tithes and the dedicated *things* faithfully: over which Cononiah the Levite *was* ruler, and Shimei his brother *was* the next. ⁽¹³⁾ And Jehiel, and Azaziah, and Nahath, and Asahel, and Jerimoth, and Jozabad, and Eliel, and Ismachiah, and Mahath, and Benaiah, *were* overseers ³under the

ᵃ Lev. 27. 30; Deut. 14. 28.

¹ Heb., *heaps heaps*.

² Or, *storehouses*.

³ Heb., *at the hand*.

---

eminent right to the name. (See on next verse.) The firstfruits were for the priests (Num. xviii. 12, *seq*., where the oil, wine, and wheat are specified).

**And the tithe . . . abundantly.**—For the Levites (Num. xviii. 21—24).

⁽⁶⁾ **Concerning.**—Omit.

**The children of Israel and Judah, that dwelt in the cities of Judah.**—Contrasted with "the children of Israel" who dwelt in Jerusalem (verse 5). "The children of Israel that dwelt in the cities of Judah" are evidently those who had left the northern kingdom to settle in the south. (Comp. chaps. x. 17, xi. 16, xxx. 25.)

**The tithe of holy things.**—This expression is assumed to be equivalent to "the heave offerings of the holy things" (Num. xviii. 19), which denotes such portions of the sacrificial gifts as were not consumed upon the altar. Taken literally, "tithe of things consecrated" would be a very surprising, as it is a wholly isolated, expression.

The present text of the LXX. appears to contain, not a trace of a different reading, but simply an old error of transcription, suggested probably by the words immediately preceding; for its rendering is, "and tithes of goats" (αἰγῶν for ἁγίων). The Syriac paraphrases freely, but the Vulgate follows the Hebrew (*decimas sanctorum*). (See also Note on verses 10, 12.) There is probably a *lacuna* in the text.

**And laid them by heaps.**—Literally, *and made heaps heaps*—i.e., many heaps. (Comp. Vulg., "fecerunt acervos plurimos.")

⁽⁷⁾ **In the third month.**—And so at the end of wheat-harvest, the third month (Sivan) answering to our May—June. Pentecost, the Feast of Harvest, or Firstfruits, fell in this month.

**To lay the foundation.**—*To found*, or *lay*. Heb., *lissôd*, a curious form only met with here. (Comp. *lisôd*, Isa. li. 16.)

**In the seventh month.**—Tisri (September to October), in which was held the great Feast of Tabernacles, after all the fruits had been gathered in, and the vintage was over.

⁽⁹⁾ **Then Hezekiah questioned with the priests and the Levites.**—*And Hezekiah asked the priests*, &c. The construction is *dārash 'al*. (Comp. 2 Sam. xi. 3; 1 Sam. xxviii. 7.) The king wished to know how it was the heaps of offerings were so large.

⁽¹⁰⁾ **Azariah.**—Possibly the Azariah of chap. xxvi. 17. If not, he is otherwise unknown.

**Since the people began to bring the offerings.**—*Since they began to bring the Tĕrūmāh*: a word which the Authorised Version usually renders "heave offering." (See Note on verse 6.)

**To bring.**—In the Hebrew a contracted form, recurring in Jer. xxxix. 7.

**We have had enough to eat, and have left plenty.**—Literally, *Eating and being satisfied, and leaving over, even unto abundance* (exclamatory infinitives). (Comp. Hosea iv. 2 for this construction.)

**The Lord hath blessed his people.**—So that they were able to give liberally.

**That which is left.**—After the maintenance of the priests has been subtracted.

**This great store.**—In the Hebrew these words are in the accusative case. Probably, therefore, the right reading is, "and there is left this great store" (omitting the article, and reading *wĕ-nôthār*, with Kamphausen).

**Chambers.** — *Cells*; *lĕshākôth*. (See Notes on 1 Chron. ix. 26, xxiii. 28.) The preparation intended is probably nothing but the clearance and cleansing of some of these cells for the reception of the stores.

⁽¹²⁾ **The offerings.**—*The Tĕrûmah* (heave offering; see Note on verse 6) *and the tithe, and the holy things* (verse 5). *Tĕrûmah* seems to mean the firstfruits here (verse 5).

**Faithfully.**—*With faithfulness*, or *honesty* (chap. xix. 9).

**Over which.**—*And over them*—i.e., the stores.

**Shimei.**—Chap. xxix. 14.

**The next.** — *Second* in charge (*mishnèh*). The name Cononiah is, in the Hebrew text, *Kŏnanyāhû*; in the margin, *Kānanyāhû*. The former is correct (*Iahu hath established*).

⁽¹³⁾ **And Jehiel . . . were overseers.**—Nothing is known of these ten Levitical officers; though some of the names occur elsewhere—*e.g.*, Jehiel and Mahath in chap. xxix. 12, 14.

**Under the hand of Cononiah.**—Or, *at the side of* . . . (*miyyad* . . .). The phrase means "under Cononiah's orders."

**At the commandment of Hezekiah.**—An unusual meaning of *miphqād*, which in 1 Chron. xxi. 5 denotes *census*. LXX., καθὼς προσέταξεν Ἐζεκίας.

hand of Cononiah and Shimei his brother, at the commandment of Hezekiah the king, and Azariah the ruler of the house of God. <sup>(14)</sup> And Kore the son of Imnah the Levite, the porter toward the east, *was* over the freewill offerings of God, to distribute the oblations of the LORD, and the most holy things. <sup>(15)</sup> And ¹next him *were* Eden, and Miniamin, and Jeshua, and Shemaiah, Amariah, and Shecaniah, in the cities of the priests, in *their* ²set office, to give to their brethren by courses, as well to the great as to the small: <sup>(16)</sup> beside their genealogy of males, from three years old and upward, *even* unto every one that entereth into the house of the LORD, his daily portion for their service in their charges according to their courses; <sup>(17)</sup> both to the genealogy of the priests by the house of their fathers, and the Levites from twenty years old and upward, in their charges by their courses; <sup>(18)</sup> and to the genealogy of all their little ones, their wives, and their sons, and their daughters, through all the congregation: for in their ³set office they sanctified themselves in holiness: <sup>(19)</sup> also of the sons of Aaron the priests, *which were* in the fields of the suburbs of their cities, in every several city, the men that were expressed by name, to give portions to

1 Heb., *at his hand.*
2 Or, *trust.*
3 Or, *trust.*

---

**Ruler** (*nagîd*) **of the house of God.**—Comp. 1 Chron. ix. 11. Azariah was named in verse 10, *supra*.

<sup>(14)</sup> **The porter toward the east.**—Compare 1 Chron. ix. 18. Korê had charge of "the freewill offerings of God," or voluntary gifts (Deut. xii. 17); and it was his duty "to distribute the oblations of the Lord and the most holy things" to the priests.

**To distribute the oblations.**—*To give the Terûmah of Jehovah*—i.e., the portion of the offerings which, though consecrated to Jehovah, was transferred by Him to the priests (Lev. vii. 14, 32, x. 14, 15).

**And the most holy things**—i.e., that part of the sin and trespass offerings (Lev. vi. 10, 22, vii. 6) and of the meat offerings (Lev. ii. 3, 10) which were to be eaten by the priests in the sanctuary.

<sup>(15)</sup> **Next him.**—*By his hand* (*'al yādô*). (Comp. 1 Chron. xxv. 2, 3.) The meaning is, "subordinate to him."

The six Levites here named as under the direction of Korê had the duty of distributing a proper share of the firstfruits, tithes, and dedicated things to their brethren residing in the sacerdotal cities, where they themselves were stationed.

**In their set office.**—It seems better to connect the phrase so rendered with the following verb: "honestly to give" (comp. verse 12). So Vulg.: "ut fideliter distribuerent fratribus suis partes," &c. Others render *be'emûnah*, "in trust."

**Their brethren by courses.**—Rather, *their brethren in the courses*—i.e., those members of the Levitical classes who, not being on duty at the Temple, were dwelling in their towns; and those who were past service, and young children.

**Great . . . small.**—*Older . . . younger.*

<sup>(16)</sup> **Beside their genealogy.**—The verse is a parenthesis stating an exception, and should rather be rendered, "apart from their register of males from three years old and upward (to wit, the register) of all that came into the house of Jehovah for the daily portion (literally, *for a day's matter in its day*; chap. viii. 13; Neh. xi. 23) for their service in their offices according to their divisions." The meaning is that the Levites who were on duty in the Temple, and whose names were registered as such, along with their male children of three years old and upwards, were not provided for by Cononiah and his associates, as they received their daily portion in the sanctuary itself. Children, it appears, were allowed to accompany their fathers to the Temple, and to eat with them of the sacrifices.

<sup>(17)</sup> **Both to the genealogy.**—The verse is a parenthesis relating to the registration of the priests and Levites, suggested by the occurrence of the word "register" in verse 16. Translate, "And as to the register of the priests, it was according to their clans (Heb., *father-houses*); and the Levites from twenty years old and upwards were in their offices in their divisions." For the latter statement, see 1 Chron. xxiii. 24.

<sup>(18)</sup> **And to the genealogy.**—After the parenthetic statements of verses 16, 17 the thread of the narrative, broken off at verse 15, is taken up again at that point. The six Levites there named were in the priests' cities "to give (their portions) to their brethren," and further (verse 18) "for the registering in the case of all their little ones, their wives and their sons and their daughters, of the whole corporation" (of priests). The board of Levites had to keep a register of all who had claims on the provisions which they had to distribute. The general sense is the same if, as seems better, we trace the connection thus: "to give to their brethren, *and to those who were registered among all their little ones*," &c., explaining *lĕhithyaḥēsh bĕkol-tappām* as a relative sentence with the relative suppressed. (Comp. chap. xxx. 18, 19, and verse 19, *ad fin*.)

**Through all the congregation.**—Or, *to a whole assembly*—scil., of wives and children of the priests and Levites.

**In their set office.**—Or *trust*, or *faithfulness* (*'emûnah*). (See Note on 1 Chron. ix. 22.)

**They sanctified themselves.**—*They used to show themselves holy* (i.e., behave conscientiously) *in regard to the holy* (i.e., the hallowed gifts, which they had to distribute). Perhaps, however, the Authorised Version is here substantially correct, the sense being that the Levites fulfilled their trust with perfect good faith.

<sup>(19)</sup> **Also of the sons of Aaron the priests.**—Officers were likewise appointed to distribute portions to the priests and Levites who dwelt on their farms outside of the sacerdotal cities. Render, "and for the sons of Aaron the priests, in the farms of the pasturage of their cities, in each several city, there were men who were specified by names, to give portions to every male among the priests, and to every one that was registered among the Levites."

**Fields of the suburbs.**—See Lev. xxv. 34; Num. xxxv. 5.

**Expressed by name.**—See 1 Chron. xii. 31; chap. xxviii. 15.

*Sincerity of Hezekiah.*     II. CHRONICLES, XXXII.     *Assyria Invades Judah.*

all the males among the priests, and to all that were reckoned by genealogies among the Levites. (20) And thus did Hezekiah throughout all Judah, and wrought *that which was* good and right and truth before the LORD his God. (21) And in every work that he began in the service of the house of God, and in the law, and in the commandments, to seek his God, he did *it* with all his heart, and prospered.

CHAPTER XXXII.—(1) After *a*these things, and the establishment thereof, Sennacherib king of Assyria came, and entered into Judah, and encamped against the fenced cities, and thought [1]to win them for himself. (2) And when Hezekiah saw that Sennacherib was come, and that [2]he was purposed to fight against Jerusalem, (3) he took counsel with his princes and his mighty men to stop the waters of the fountains which *were* without the city: and they did help him. (4) So there was gathered much people together, who stopped all the fountains, and the brook that [3]ran through the midst of the land, saying, Why should the kings of Assyria come, and find much water? (5) Also he strengthened himself, and built up all

*a* 2 Kings 18. 13, &c.; Isa. 36. 1, &c.
[1] Heb., *to break them up.*
[2] Heb., *his face was to war.*
B.C. 713.
[3] Heb., *overflowed.*

---

To all that were reckoned by genealogies.—*Registered.* The relative is omitted before the verb *hithyaḥēsh,* which is here the perfect as in verse 18, not the infinitive as in verse 16.

(20, 21) Conclusion of the account of Hezekiah's reformation.

(20) Truth (*ha'ĕmeth*).—*Faithfulness,* or *sincerity.*

(21) Commandments.—Heb., *commandment.*

To seek his God.—*In order to seek,* or *by way of seeking.*

He did it with all his heart.—Comp. the frequent phrase, "with a perfect heart" (1 Chron. xxviii. 9, and elsewhere); also "and thou shalt love the Lord thy God with all thine heart," &c. (Deut. vi. 5).

XXXII.

THE INVASION OF SENNACHERIB—HEZEKIAH'S RECOVERY FROM DEADLY SICKNESS—HIS PRIDE AND WEALTH—HIS RECEPTION OF THE EMBASSY FROM BABYLON—END OF THE REIGN.

The narrative is once more parallel to that of Kings (2 Kings xviii. 13—xx. 21), which is repeated in the Book of Isaiah (chaps. xxxvi.—xxxix.).

(1—23) Invasion and Divine overthrow of Sennacherib. (Comp. 2 Kings xviii. 13—xix. 37.) The Assyrian monarch's own record of the campaign may be read on his great hexagonal prism of terra-cotta, preserved in the British Museum, containing an inscription in 487 lines of cuneiform writing, which is lithographed in the *Cuneiform Inscriptions of Western Asia,* III. 38, 39, and printed in G. Smith's *History of Sennacherib.*

(1) After these things, and the establishment thereof.—Rather, *After these matters, and this faithfulness* (chap. xxxi. 20). For the date, see Note on 2 Kings xviii. 13.

Sennacherib.—So the Vulg. The LXX. gives Σενναχηρίμ or είμ; Herodotus, Σαναχάριβος; Josephus, Σενναχήριβος. The Hebrew is *Sanchĕrib.* The real name as given by the Assyrian monuments is *Sin-ahi-iriba,* or *erba* ("Sin," *i.e.*, the moon-god, "multiplied brothers").

And thought to win them for himself.—Literally, *and said to himself that he would break them open* (chap. xxi. 17), or *and commanded to break them open for himself.* Kings states that he fulfilled his purpose; he "came up against all the fenced cities of Judah, *and took them.*" Sennacherib himself boasts as follows: "And Hazakiyahu of the country of the Jews who had not submitted to my yoke, forty-six strong cities of his, fortresses, and the small cities of their neighbourhood, which were without number . . . I approached, I took." The chronicler's object is to relate the mighty deliverance of Hezekiah. Hence he omits such details as would weaken the impression he desires to produce. For the same reason nothing is said here of Hezekiah's submission and payment of tribute (2 Kings xviii. 14—16); and perhaps for the further reason (as suggested by Keil) that "these negotiations had no influence on the aftercourse and issue of the war," but *not* because (as Thenius alleges) the chronicler was unwilling to mention Hezekiah's (forced) sacrilege. They are omitted also in Isaiah, where the account is in other respects abridged as compared with Kings.

PREPARATIONS FOR THE DEFENCE (verses 2—8).

This section is peculiar to the Chronicles. Its contents are "perfectly credible" (*Thenius*), and are borne out by Isa. xxii. 8—11, and 2 Kings xx. 20, and by the inscription of Sennacherib.

(2) And that he was purposed to fight.—Literally, *and his face was for the war.* (Comp. chap. xx. 3; Luke ix. 53.)

To stop.—*To close in* with masonry, so as to conceal. (But comp. 2 Kings iii. 19, 25.) LXX., ἐμφράξαι τὰ ὕδατα.

They did help him.—By "gathering much people together" (verse 4).

(4) The fountains.—*Ma'yānôth.* Verse 3 has "springs" (*'ăyānôth*).

The brook.—*Naḥal.* "The *wâdy.*" The Gihon is meant, a watercourse in the Valley of Hinnom, supplied with water by the springs which Hezekiah closed in and diverted. See Note on verse 30, and 2 Kings xx. 20; comp. Sirach xlviii. 17, "Hezekiah fortified his city, and brought into their midst the Gog" (LXX., Vat.), or, "into its midst water" (LXX., Alex.).

That ran.—*That was flowing over* (Isa. xxx. 28, viii. 8). The overflow of the springs formed the stream.

The kings of Assyria.—A vague rhetorical plural, as in chap. xxviii. 16.

(5) Also he strengthened himself.—*And he took courage.* (Chaps. xv. 8, xviii. 1.)

*Hezekiah Encourages*     II. CHRONICLES, XXXII.     *the People.*

the wall that was broken, and raised *it* up to the towers, and another wall without, and repaired Millo *in* the city of David, and made ¹darts and shields in abundance. ⁽⁶⁾ And he set captains of war over the people, and gathered them together to him in the street of the gate of the city, and ²spake comfortably to them, saying, ⁽⁷⁾ Be strong and courageous, be not afraid nor dismayed for the king of Assyria, nor for all the multitude that *is* with him: for *there be* more with us than with him: ⁽⁸⁾ with him *is* an *ᵃ*arm of flesh; but with us *is* the LORD our God to help us, and to fight our battles. And the people ³rested themselves upon the words of Hezekiah king of Judah. ⁽⁹⁾ *ᵇ*After this did Sennacherib king of Assyria send his servants to Jerusalem, (but he *himself laid siege* against Lachish, and all his ⁴power with him,) unto Hezekiah king of Judah, and unto all Judah that *were* at Jerusalem, saying, ⁽¹⁰⁾ Thus saith Sennacherib king of Assyria, Whereon do ye trust, that ye abide ⁵in the siege in Jerusalem? ⁽¹¹⁾ Doth not Hezekiah persuade you to give over yourselves to die by famine and by thirst, saying, The LORD our God shall deliver us out of the hand of the king of Assyria? ⁽¹²⁾ Hath not the same

---

¹ Or, *swords*, or, *weapons*.

B.C. 710.

² Heb., *he spake to their heart*.

*ᵃ* Jer. 17. 5.

³ Heb., *leaned*.

*ᵇ* 2 Kings 18. 17.

⁴ Heb., *dominion*.

⁵ Or, *in the strong hold*.

---

**Built up all the wall that was broken.**—Isa. xxii. 9, 10, where "many breaches" are spoken of, and it is said that "houses were pulled down to fortify the wall."

**Raised it up to the towers.**—Heb., *and went up on the towers*, or, *and caused to go up on the towers*. A different division of the Hebrew letters will give the sense "and raised upon it towers," which is probably correct. Thenius prefers to keep the ordinary reading, which he understands to mean, *and heightened the towers*; alleging that chap. xxvi. 9 shows that the wall was already furnished with towers. The LXX. has simply καὶ πύργους, "and towers;" the Vulgate, "et exstruxit turres desuper." The Syriac renders, "Let them show themselves strong, and make another wall opposite the wall, and let them stop up the ditch which David made."

**Another wall without.**—Literally, *and on the outside of the wall* (he built) *another*—viz., the wall enclosing the lower city or Acra, which he "built," that is, repaired and strengthened. (See Isa. xxii. 11, "the two walls.")

**Repaired.**—Chap. xi. 11.

**Millo.**—*The rampart.* See Note on 1 Chron. xi. 8.

**In the city of David.**—*To wit, the city of David.*

**Darts.**—*Shelah.* See Note on chap. xxiii. 10, and comp. xxvi. 14. The Hebrew is "missiles in abundance, and shields."

⁽⁶⁾ **Captains of war.**—Literally, *captains of battles*: a phrase found here only.

**In the street.**—*Into the open space.* In like manner, "the open space that was before the water gate" is mentioned in Neh. viii. 1, 16.

**The gate.**—Which gate we are not told; but the LXX. reads, τὴν πλατεῖαν τῆς πύλης τῆς φάραγγος, "the broad place of the gate of the ravine."

**Spake comfortably to them.**—*Encouraged them.* Chap. xxx. 22. (See margin.)

⁽⁷⁾ **Be not afraid . . . the multitude.**—Comp. chap. xx. 15, "Be not afraid nor dismayed for this great multitude." "Be strong and courageous, be not afraid" occurs in Deut. xxxi. 6 (Heb.).

**For there be more with us than with him.** —A reminiscence of 2 Kings vi. 16, "Be not thou afraid; for more are they that are with us than they that are with them." It is not necessary to suppose that the chronicler professes to give the exact words of Hezekiah's exhortation, but only the substance and spirit of it.

⁽⁸⁾ **With him is an arm of flesh.**—A reminiscence of Jer. xvii. 5, "the man that maketh flesh his arm." (Comp. Isa. xxxi. 3: "Their horses are flesh and not spirit.") His power is human, ours superhuman.

**To fight our battles.**—1 Sam. viii. 20, "a king . . . to fight our battles."

**Rested themselves upon.**—*Leaned on*—e.g., a staff, Isa. xxxvi. 6; and so *trusted in*, Isa. xlviii. 2.

(9—21) A brief summary of what is related in 2 Kings xviii. 17—xix.

⁽⁹⁾ **After this did Sennacherib . . . send.**— See 2 Kings xviii. 17.

**But he himself . . . Lachish.** — The verb *nilkham*, "fought," has perhaps fallen out. The great inscription of Sennacherib says nothing about the siege of Lachish; but a bas-relief, now in the British Museum, represents him seated on his throne receiving a file of captives who issue from the gate of a city. Over the king's head is written "Sennacherib, the king of multitudes, the king of the land of Asshur, on a raised throne sate, and caused the spoils of the city of Lachish (*Lakisu*) to pass before him."

**His power.**—Literally, *his dominion* or *realm.* Comp. Jer. xxxiv. 1, "all the kingdoms of the lands of the dominion of his hand." The word *hêl*, "army," may have fallen out.

⁽¹⁰⁾ **Whereon . . . the siege.**—Rather, *Whereon are ye trusting, and why are ye sitting in distress in Jerusalem?* The phrase *sitting* or *abiding in distress* occurs in Jer. x. 17. (Comp. also Deut. xxviii. 53.)

Verses 10—15 reproduce in brief the leading ideas of 2 Kings xviii. 19—25 and 28—35.

⁽¹¹⁾ **Doth not Hezekiah persuade you.**—*Is not Hezekiah inciting you* (2 Kings xviii. 32; 1 Chron. xxi. 1). The verb recurs in verse 15.

**To give over yourselves . . . by thirst.**—*In order to deliver you to dying . . . by thirst.* A softening down of the coarse expression recorded in 2 Kings xviii. 27. Esarhaddon in the record of his Egyptian campaign uses similar language: "siege-works against him I constructed, and food and water, the life of their souls, I cut off."

⁽¹²⁾ **The same Hezekiah.**—*Hezekiah himself.*

**Ye shall worship . . . upon it.**—Literally, *before one altar shall ye worship, and thereon shall ye burn incense.* Comp. 2 Kings xviii. 22: "Is it not He whose high places and altars Hezekiah hath taken away, and commanded Judah and Jerusalem, Before

Hezekiah taken away his high places and his altars, and commanded Judah and Jerusalem, saying, Ye shall worship before one altar, and burn incense upon it? (13) Know ye not what I and my fathers have done unto all the people of *other* lands? were the gods of the nations of those lands any ways able to deliver their lands out of mine hand? (14) Who *was there* among all the gods of those nations that my fathers utterly destroyed, that could deliver his people out of mine hand, that your God should be able to deliver you out of mine hand? (15) Now therefore let not Hezekiah deceive you, nor persuade you on this manner, neither yet believe him: for no god of any nation or kingdom was able to deliver his people out of mine hand, and out of the hand of my fathers: how much less shall your God deliver you out of mine hand? (16) And his servants spake yet *more* against the LORD God, and against his servant Hezekiah.

(17) He wrote also letters to rail on the LORD God of Israel, and to speak against him, saying, As the gods of the nations of *other* lands have not delivered their people out of mine hand, so shall not the God of Hezekiah deliver his people out of mine hand. (18) Then they cried with a loud voice in the Jews' speech unto the people of Jerusalem that *were* on the wall, to affright them, and to trouble them; that they might take the city. (19) And they spake against the God of Jerusalem, as against the gods of the people of the earth, *which were* the work of the hands of man.

(20) And for this *cause* Hezekiah the

---

this altar shall ye worship in Jerusalem?" The chronicler is even more emphatic than Kings in asserting the sole validity of the Brazen Altar in the Temple Court.

(13) **What I and my fathers have done.**—The Assyrian kings are fond of such references to their predecessors.

**The people of other lands.**—Rather, *the peoples of the countries.*

**Those lands.**—*The countries.*

**Their lands.**—*Their country.* The chronicler omits the names of the vanquished states given in 2 Kings xviii. 34, some of which had probably become obscure by lapse of time.

Assurbanipal relates that in his eighth campaign he carried off the gods of Elam with the other spoils: "His gods, his goddesses, his furniture, his goods, people small and great, I carried off to Assyria;" and he adds the names of nineteen of these deities.

(14) **Who was there among all the gods.**—Comp. 2 Kings xviii. 35.

**Utterly destroyed.**—*Put under the ban, devoted to destruction.*

(15) **Neither yet believe him.**—*And believe him not.*

**How much less . . . deliver you.**—Rather, *much less will your gods deliver you*; or, *much more will your gods not deliver you.* (Comp. Isa. xxxvii. 10, 11.) According to ancient conceptions the gods of strong nations were strong gods. Now the Assyrians had vanquished stronger nations than Judah, and therefore, as they ignorantly supposed, stronger deities than the God of Judah. (Some Hebrew MSS. and all the versions have the verb in the singular, which gives the sense, "much less will your god deliver you.")

(16) **Spake yet more.**—See the parallel passages in Kings and Isaiah. The verse shows that the chronicler does not profess to give a full report.

**Against the Lord God.**—Literally, *against Jehovah the* (true) *God.* "Whom hast thou reproached and blasphemed? . . . the Holy One of Israel" (Isa. xxxvii. 23).

(17) **He wrote also letters to rail on.**—*And letters wrote he to reproach* (Isa. xxxvii. 23). Sennacherib wrote to Hezekiah demanding submission, *after* the failure of the mission of the Tartan and his companions (2 Kings xix. 8—14). If, therefore, the chronicler had been careful about the strictly chronological sequence of events, this verse would have followed rather than preceded 18, 19. As it is, the remark is thrown in here as a parenthesis, in the middle of the account of the behaviour of the Assyrian envoys. Something must be allowed for the necessities of abbreviation, which the author has studied in the entire narrative.

**As the gods . . . have not delivered.**—Literally, *Like the gods of the nations of the countries, which have not delivered.* (Comp. 2 Kings xix. 10, 12: "Let not thy God in whom thou trustest deceive thee," &c.) "Have the gods of the nations delivered them," &c.

(18) **They cried . . . on the wall.**—LXX. and Vulg., "he cried" (*i.e.*, the Rab-sak). (See 2 Kings xviii. 26—28.)

**To affright them, and to trouble** (*terrify, scare*) **them; that they might take the city.**—This is the chronicler's own statement of the purpose of the words of the Rab-sak reported in 2 Kings xviii. 28—35.

**To affright.**—The *pi'el* of *yārē*, "to fear," occurs besides, thrice in Neh. vi. 9, 14, 19; and once in 2 Sam. xiv. 15.

(19) **They spake against.**—Or, *spake of.* Literally, *unto.* (Comp. Ps. ii. 7, iii. 2.)

**People.**—*Peoples.*

**The work.**—The versions have "works." Instead of repeating the offers which the Assyrian envoys made to the people of Jerusalem, to induce them to submit, the chronicler dwells on that blasphemy against the God of Israel which was the cause of the Assyrian overthrow.

**The work of the hands of man.**—A reminiscence of 2 Kings xix. 18: "And they put their gods into the fire; for they were no gods, but the work of human hands, wood and stone" (part of Hezekiah's prayer).

(20) **For this cause.**—*Upon this* ('*al zōth*). The reference is to the Assyrian blasphemies against Jehovah, which Hezekiah urged in his prayer for de-

*The Assyrians Slain.*     II. CHRONICLES, XXXII.     *Hezekiah's Sickness.*

king, and the prophet Isaiah the son of Amoz, prayed and cried to heaven. (21) *a* And the LORD sent an angel, which cut off all the mighty men of valour, and the leaders and captains in the camp of the king of Assyria. So he returned with shame of face to his own land. And when he was come into the house of his god, they that came forth of his own bowels ¹ slew him there with the sword. (22) Thus the LORD saved Hezekiah and the inhabitants of Jerusalem from the hand of Sennacherib the king of Assyria, and from the hand of all *other*, and guided them on every side.

B.C. 710.
*a* 2 Kings 19. 35, &c.
B.C. cir. 710.
¹ Heb., *made him fall.*
B.C. 713.
² Heb., *precious things.*
*b* 2 Kings 20. 1; Isa. 38. 1.
³ Or, *wrought a miracle for him.*
⁴ Heb., *the lifting up.*

(23) And many brought gifts unto the LORD to Jerusalem, and ²presents to Hezekiah king of Judah: so that he was magnified in the sight of all nations from thenceforth. (24) *b* In those days Hezekiah was sick to the death, and prayed unto the LORD: and he spake unto him, and he ³ gave him a sign. (25) But Hezekiah rendered not again according to the benefit *done* unto him; for his heart was lifted up: therefore there was wrath upon him, and upon Judah and Jerusalem. (26) Notwithstanding Hezekiah humbled himself for ⁴ the pride of his heart, *both* he and

---

liverance (2 Kings xix. 16), and to which Isaiah referred in his prophetic answer (Isa. xxxvii. 23). The prayer of Hezekiah is given in 2 Kings xix. 15—19; Isa. xxxvii. 15—20. The parallel passages do not say that Isaiah also prayed; but 2 Kings xix. 2—4, and Isa. xxxvii. 2—4, report that the king sent a deputation of nobles to the prophet, requesting his prayers "for the remnant that were left."

**Cried to heaven.**—Comp. chap. xxx. 27; 1 Sam. v. 12.

(21) **And the Lord sent an angel.**—See 2 Kings xix. 35, *seq.*; Isa. xxxvii. 36, *seq.* Hitzig thinks that Pss. xlvi.—xlviii. were composed by Isaiah to commemorate this great natural miracle, an hypothesis which is borne out by the similarity observable between the language and ideas of these psalms and those of Isaiah's prophecies.

**Which cut off . . . valour.**—Literally, *and he hid* (*i.e.*, caused to disappear, destroyed; the Greek ἀφανίζειν; Exod. xxiii. 23) *every valiant warrior, and leader and captain.* (Comp. Ps. lxxvi. 5, a psalm which in the LXX. bears the title ᾠδὴ πρὸς τὸν Ἀσσύριον.) Kings gives the number of those who perished as 185,000.

**With shame of face.**—Ps. xliv. 15, "The shame of my face hath covered me." (Ezra ix. 7.)

**And when he was come . . . with the sword.**—*And he went into the house of his god, and certain of his own offspring there felled him with the sword.* 2 Kings xix. 37 gives the names of the parricides—viz., Adrammelech and Sharezer; and the name of the god—viz., Nisroch—which is probably corrupt. It is added that the assassins "escaped into the land of Ararat." The chronicler as usual suppresses unfamiliar foreign names.

**They that came forth.**—*Some of the issue* (*yāçî*, a verbal noun only found here). (For the whole phrase, comp. Gen. xv. 4; 2 Sam. vii. 12.)

(22) **Thus.**—*And.* The whole verse is the chronicler's own comment on the preceding narrative. (Comp. 2 Kings xviii. 7.)

**The hand of all.**—Some MSS. appropriately add *his enemies*, an expression which may have fallen out of the text.

**And guided them on every side** (*round about*).—A somewhat unusual phrase. The conjecture, "and gave them rest round about (*wayyānah lāhem* for *wayyĕnahălēm*), appears correct. (See chaps. xiv. 6, xv. 15, xx. 30; 1 Chron. xxii. 18.) So the LXX. and Vulg.

(23) **Brought.**—*Were bringing* = used to bring.
**Gifts.**—*An offering* (*minᶜhah*), or tribute.
**Presents to Hezekiah.**—Among those who brought such were the envoys of Merodach Baladan, king of Babylon (2 Kings xx. 12). Probably also the neighbouring peoples—*e.g.*, the Philistines—relieved from the pressure of the Assyrian invaders, would thus evince their gratitude to the God of Israel. (Comp. chap. xviii. 11.)

**So that he was magnified . . . nations.**—Literally, *and he was lifted up, to the eyes of all the nations.*

HEZEKIAH'S SICKNESS—HIS PRIDE AND WEALTH —THE BABYLONIAN EMBASSY—CONCLUSION (verses 24—33).

(24) **In those days Hezekiah was sick.**—This single verse epitomises 2 Kings xx. 1—11; Isa. xxxviii.

**To the death.**—*Unto dying.*

**He spake unto him.**—By the mouth of Isaiah.

**And he gave him a sign.**—The recession of the shadow on the dial of Ahaz. Literally, *and a sign He gave him;* the emphatic word first.

(25) **But Hezekiah.**—For Hezekiah's pride, see the account of his reception of the Babylonian embassy (2 Kings xx. 12—19; Isa. xxxix.).

**According to the benefit done unto him.**—In his illness he promised to walk humbly all his days (Isa. xxxviii. 15); but when he had recovered, "his heart was lifted up."

**Therefore there was wrath upon him.**—*And wrath fell upon him.* The token of this was seen in Isaiah's prophetic rebuke, foretelling that the royal treasures would be carried away to Babylon, and that some of Hezekiah's sons would be eunuchs in the palace there (2 Kings xx. 16—18; Isa. xxxix. 5—7).

**And upon Judah and Jerusalem.**—Which shared in the king's guilty pride and confidence in the arm of flesh. (Comp. 1 Chron. xxvii. 24; chap. xix. 10.)

(26) **Notwithstanding.**—*And.*

**The wrath of the Lord . . . . days of Hezekiah.**—(Comp. Isa. xxxix. 8.) On hearing Isaiah's prophecy of coming evil, Hezekiah humbly acquiesced in the will of Jehovah. "Then said Hezekiah unto Isaiah, Good is the word of the Lord which thou hast spoken. And he said, There shall be peace and permanence in my own days" (2 Kings xx. 19).

*Hezekiah's Wealth*     **II. CHRONICLES, XXXII.**     *and Works.*

the inhabitants of Jerusalem, so that the wrath of the LORD came not upon them in the days of Hezekiah.

<sup>(27)</sup> And Hezekiah had exceeding much riches and honour: and he made himself treasuries for silver, and for gold, and for precious stones, and for spices, and for shields, and for all manner of <sup>1</sup> pleasant jewels; <sup>(28)</sup> storehouses also for the increase of corn, and wine, and oil; and stalls for all manner of beasts, and cotes for flocks. <sup>(29)</sup> Moreover he provided him cities, and possessions of flocks and herds in abundance: for God had given him substance very much. <sup>(30)</sup> This same Hezekiah also stopped the upper watercourse of Gihon, and brought it straight down to the west side of the city of David. And Hezekiah prospered in all his works. <sup>(31)</sup> Howbeit in *the business of* the <sup>2</sup> ambassadors of the princes of Babylon, who *a* sent unto him to enquire of the wonder that was *done* in the land, God left him, to try him, that he might know all *that was* in his heart.

<sup>(32)</sup> Now the rest of the acts of Hezekiah, and his <sup>3</sup> goodness, behold, they *are* written in the vision of Isaiah the prophet, the son of Amoz, *and* in the book of the kings of Judah and Israel. <sup>(33)</sup> And

*Marginal notes:* 1 Heb., *instruments of desire.*   B.C. 712.   2 Heb., *interpreters.*   *a* 2 Kings 20. 12; Isa. 39. 1.   3 Heb., *kindnesses.*

---

<sup>(27)</sup> **Had.**—Or, *got.*

**Riches and honour** (or, *wealth*; *kābôd*).—Comp. 1 Chron. xxix. 28 (David); 2 Chron. i. 12 (Solomon), xvii. 5, xviii. 1 (Jehoshaphat).

**He made himself treasuries.**—Comp. 2 Kings xx. 13; Isa. xxxix. 2, where silver and gold and spices are mentioned among the treasures of Hezekiah.

**Shields.**—Comp. Solomon's golden, and Rehoboam's brazen, shields. No doubt the term is here used to suggest arms in general. Kings and Isaiah mention "his armoury."

**All manner of pleasant jewels.**—Literally, *all vessels of desire.* (Comp. Nah. ii. 10, "wealth of every vessel of desire.") Costly implements and utensils of all sorts are included.

<sup>(28)</sup> **Storehouses also.**—*And magazines* (chap. viii. 4; Exod. i. 11).

**Stalls.**—*'Urāwôth* (Syriac, *'urāwôthō*). (Comp. *ûryôth*, chap. ix. 25; and *'ăwērôth*, "cotes," a word only found here.)

**All manner of beasts.**—*Every kind of cattle.*

**Cotes for flocks.**—Heb., *and flocks for folds.* The words appear to have been transposed by some copyist. (Comp. LXX., καὶ μάνδρας εἰς τὰ ποίμνια, "and folds for the flocks." So Vulg., "et caulas pecorum." Syriac omits.)

<sup>(29)</sup> **Moreover he provided him cities.**—*And he made him watch-towers.* The word rendered "cities" (*'ārîm*) appears in this connection to mean watch-towers or forts for the protection of the flocks and herds. Isa. i. 8 ("a besieged city"); 2 Kings xvii. 9; chap. xxvi. 10.

**Had given.**—*Gave.*

**Substance.**—Wealth in kind, especially cattle (chap. xxxi. 3).

<sup>(30)</sup> **This same Hezekiah also stopped.**—*And he, Hezekiah, had closed in the upper outlet of the waters of Gihon.* (See verse 3.)

**And brought . . . city of David.**—*And conducted them underground to the west of the city of David.* (Comp. 2 Kings xx. 20, where also this great work of Hezekiah is referred to in concluding his history: "He made the pool, and the aqueduct, and brought the waters into the city.") The chronicler gives further details.

**Brought it straight.**—*Directed* or *conducted them* (*wayyashshĕrēm*; the form in the Hebrew margin is a peculiar contraction of the ordinary *piel* form which appears in the text).

**And Hezekiah prospered.**—Chap. xxxi. 21; 1 Chron. xxix. 23.

<sup>(31)</sup> **Howbeit.**—Literally, *And thus;* that is, and when things were thus prosperous with him. In the midst of Hezekiah's prosperity, God left him for a moment to himself, by way of putting him to the proof.

**The princes of Babylon.**—The same vague plural which we have already noticed in chaps. xxviii. 16, xxx. 6, and verse 4, *supra.* The king who "sent letters and a present" to Hezekiah, with congratulations on his recovery from sickness, and overtures of alliance against the common enemy, Assyria, was Merodach-baladan (*Maruduk-abla-iddina*, "Merodach gave a son"). (See the account in 2 Kings xx. 12, *seq.;* Isa. xxxix.)

**Who sent unto him to enquire of the wonder** (Hebrew, *the sign,* as in verse 24).—This is not mentioned in the parallel passage of Kings and Isaiah. But such an inquiry is quite in harmony with what we know of the Babylonians from their own monuments. Babylon was the home of the arts of divination and augury, from observation of all kinds of signs and portents in every department of nature. Moreover, the sign given to Hezekiah would have a special interest for the astrologers and astronomers of the Babylonian temple-towers.

**God left him, to try him, that he might know all that was in his heart.**—"To try," the same word as "to tempt" (Isa. vii. 12; Ps. xcv. 9; and often).

**That he might know**—*i.e.,* in order to bring out and make manifest the latent possibilities of Hezekiah's character. The Searcher of hearts knew the issue beforehand; but we can only conceive of His dealings with man by means of human analogies, such as that of the chemist, who subjects an imperfectly known substance to various combinations of circumstances, by way of ascertaining its nature and affinities. The remark is peculiar to the chronicler.

<sup>(32)</sup> **Now the rest of the acts.**—See 2 Kings xx. 20, 21.

**And his goodness.**—*His good deeds.* So chap. xxxv. 26 (Josiah); Neh. xiii. 14.

**And in the book of the kings.**—Omit *and.* The "vision of Isaiah" is referred to as a section of the "book of the kings of Judah and Israel." (See Introduction.) Kings *l.c.* says, "are they not written in the book of the chronicles of the Kings of Judah?"

<sup>(33)</sup> **And they buried him . . . honour at his death.**—Statements peculiar to the chronicler. They go to prove an authority besides the canonical books of Kings.

Hezekiah slept with his fathers, and they buried him in the ¹chiefest of the sepulchres of the sons of David: and all Judah and the inhabitants of Jerusalem did him honour at his death. And Manasseh his son reigned in his stead.

CHAPTER XXXIII.—⁽¹⁾ Manasseh ²was twelve years old when he began to reign, and he reigned fifty and five years in Jerusalem: ⁽²⁾ but did *that which was evil* in the sight of the LORD, like unto the ᵇabominations of the heathen, whom the LORD had cast out before the children of Israel. ⁽³⁾ For ²he built again the high places which Hezekiah his father had ᶜbroken down, and he reared up altars for Baalim, and made groves, and worshipped all the host of heaven, and served them. ⁽⁴⁾ Also he built altars in the house of the LORD, whereof the LORD had said, ᵈIn Jerusalem shall my name be for ever. ⁽⁵⁾ And he built altars for all the host of heaven in the two courts of the house of the LORD. ⁽⁶⁾ And he caused his children to pass through the fire in the valley of the son of Hinnom: also he observed times, and used enchantments, and used witchcraft, and dealt with a familiar spirit, and with wizards: he wrought much evil in the sight of the LORD, to provoke him to anger. ⁽⁷⁾ And he set a carved image, the idol which he had made, in the house of God, of which God had said to David and to Solomon his son, In ᵉthis house, and in Jerusalem, which I have chosen before all the

*Marginal notes:*
1 Or, *highest*.
a 2 Kings 21. 1, &c.
b Deut. 18. 9.
B.C. 698.
2 Heb., *he returned and built*.
c 2 Kings 18. 4.
d Deut. 12. 11; 1 Kings 8. 29, & 9. 3; ch. 6. 6, & l. 16.
e Ps. 132. 14.

---

**The chiefest.**—Rather, *the ascent*—i.e., *the way up* to the royal tombs. (Comp. chap. xx. 16.) "The sons of David" are the kings of the house of David. Hezekiah may have chosen a favourite spot for his burial-place; but, as his successors Manasseh, Amon, and Josiah likewise, were not laid in the tombs of the kings, it would appear that the old royal sepulchres were full.

**Did him honour at his death.**—The phrase, "did him honour" (*asû kābôd lô*) occurs here only. (Comp. "give honour to," 1 Sam. vi. 5; Ps. xxix. 1.) Probably a great burning of spices was made in honour of Hezekiah as of Asa. (See chaps. xvi. 14, xxi. 19.)

XXXIII.

THE REIGNS OF MANASSEH AND AMON.

(1—20) The history of Manasseh. Duration and character of the reign. Restoration of idolatry (verses 1—10). This section is closely parallel with 2 Kings xxi. 1—10. Verses 1, 2, 5 are word for word the same in both.

⁽³⁾ **For.**—*And*. (See margin.)
**Broken down.**—Chaps. xxiii. 17, xxxi. 1 ("threw down"). Kings has "destroyed" (*'ibbad*).
**Baalim.**—*The Baals*—i.e., the different images of Baal. Kings has the singular, both here and in the next word, "groves," or rather *Asheras* (*'Ashĕrôth*; Kings, *'Ashĕrah*). The latter plural is rhetorical: Manasseh made *such things* as *Asheras*. (Comp. also the use of the plural in chap. xxxii. 31, and the passages there referred to.) Kings adds: "as Ahab king of Israel made."

⁽⁴⁾ **Also he built . . . . In Jerusalem.**—Literally as Kings. Manasseh built altars in the Temple, as Ahaz had done (2 Kings xvi. 10, seq.).
**Shall my name be for ever.**—A heightening of the phrase in Kings, "I will set my name."
⁽⁵⁾ **He.**—Emphatic. Not in Kings.
**Caused his children . . . fire.**—The plural, as in chap. xxviii. 3, is rhetorical. Kings, "his son."
**In the valley of the son of Hinnom.**—Explanatory addition by the chronicler.

**Also he observed times, and used enchantments.**—*And he practised augury and divination*. Forbidden, Lev. xix. 26. The first words seem strictly to mean "observed clouds;" the second, "observed serpents."
**And used witchcraft.**—*And muttered spells or charms*. This word does not occur in the parallel place, but all the offences here ascribed to Manasseh are forbidden in Deut. xviii. 10, 11.
**And dealt with a familiar spirit, and with wizards.**—*And appointed a necromancer and a wizard*. Kings has *wizards*. The source of all these modes of soothsaying was Babylon. Like the first king of Israel, Manasseh appears to have despaired of help or counsel from Jehovah. (Comp. Jer. xliv. 17, 18.) The heavy yoke of Assyria again weighed the nation down, and the great deliverance under Hezekiah was almost forgotten. "To all the Palestinian nations the Assyrian crisis had made careless confidence in the help of their national deities a thing impossible. As life was embittered by foreign bondage, the darker aspects of heathenism became dominant. The wrath of the gods seemed more real than their favour; atoning ordinances were multiplied, human sacrifices became more frequent, the terror which hung over all the nations that groaned under the Assyrian yoke found habitual expression in the ordinances of worship; and it was this aspect of heathenism that came to the front in Manasseh's imitations of foreign religion" (Robertson Smith, *The Prophets of Israel*, p. 366).
**He wrought much evil.**—Literally, *he multiplied doing the evil*. He was worse than his evil predecessors.
⁽⁷⁾ **And he set . . . had made.**—*And he set the carven image of the idol which he had made*. "Idol" (*sĕmel*) explains "Asherah," the term used in Kings. Both "carven image" and "idol" (Authorised Version, *figure*) occur in Deut. iv. 16.
**The house of God.**—Chronicles has added, *of God*, by way of explanation. The Temple proper is meant, as distinct from the courts.
**Before all.**—*Out of all*.
**For ever.**—*Le'ĕlôm*, a form only found here (equivalent to *le'ôlām*).

tribes of Israel, will I put my name for ever: (8) *neither will I any more remove the foot of Israel from out of the land which I have appointed for your fathers; so that they will take heed to do all that I have commanded them, according to the whole law and the statutes and the ordinances by the hand of Moses.

(9) So Manasseh made Judah and the inhabitants of Jerusalem to err, *and* to do worse than the heathen, whom the LORD had destroyed before the children of Israel. (10) And the LORD spake to Manasseh, and to his people: but they would not hearken. (11) Wherefore the LORD brought upon them the captains of the host ¹ of the king of Assyria, which took Manasseh among the thorns, and bound him with ² fetters, and carried him to Babylon. (12) And when he was in affliction, he besought the LORD his God, and humbled himself greatly before the God of his fathers, (13) and prayed unto him: and he was intreated

*a* 2 Sam. 7. 10.

B.C. 677

¹ Heb., *which were the king's.*

² Or, *chains.*

---

(8) **Remove.**—Kings has a less common expression, "cause to wander."

**From out of** (*upon*) **the land** (*ground*) **which I have appointed.**—Kings, with which the versions agree, has the certainly original "from the ground which I gave."

**So that.**—*If only.*

**And the statutes and the ordinances.**—An explanatory addition. Kings has, "And according to all the Torah that Moses my servant commanded them."

**By the hand.**—By the ministry or instrumentality. The phrase is a characteristic interpretation of what we read in 2 Kings xxi. 8; for it carefully notes that the authority of the Lawgiver was not primary but derived.

(9) **So Manasseh . . . heathen.**—Literally, *And Manasseh led Judah and the inhabitants of Jerusalem astray, to do evil more than the nations.* Thenius thinks that the words *and Manasseh . . . . astray*, followed in the primary document immediately upon *and he set the graven image in the house*; the intermediate words being an addition by the editor of Kings.

(10) **And the Lord spake to Manasseh.**—"By the hand of his servants the prophets." See 2 Kings xxi. 10—15, where the substance of the prophetic message is given; and it is added (verse 16) that Manasseh also shed very much innocent blood, "till he had filled Jerusalem from one end to the other." The reaction against the reforms of Hezekiah ended in a bloody struggle, in which the party of reform was fiercely suppressed.

MANASSEH'S CAPTIVITY AND REPENTANCE—HIS RESTORATION AND REFORMS (verses 11—17).

This section is peculiar to the Chronicle, and none has excited more scepticism among modern critics. The progress of cuneiform research, however, has proved the perfect possibility of the facts most disputed, viz., the captivity and subsequent restoration of Manasseh.

(11) **Wherefore.**—*And.*

**The captains of the host of the king of Assyria.**—The generals of Esarhaddon, or rather, perhaps, of Assurbanipal. The former, who reigned from 681—668 B.C., has recorded the fact that Manasseh was his vassal. He says: "And I assembled the kings of the land of Hatti, and the marge of the sea, Baal king of Tyre, Me-na-si-e (or Mi-in-si-e) king of Ya-u-di (*i.e.*, Judah), Qa-us-gabri, king of Edom," &c. "Altogether, twenty-two kings of the land of Hatti [Syria], the coast of the sea, and the middle of the sea, all of them, I caused to hasten," &c. Assurbanipal has left a list which is identical with that of Esarhaddon, except that it gives different names for the kings of Arvad and Ammon. It thus appears that Manasseh paid tribute to him as well as to his father. Schrader (*K.A.T.*, p. 367, *seq.*) thinks that Manasseh was at least suspected of being implicated along with the other princes of Phœnicia-Palestine in the revolt of Assurbanipal's brother *Samar-sum-ukin* (circ. 648—647 B.C.) in which Elam, Gutium, and Meroë also participated; and that he was carried to Babylon, to clear himself of suspicion, and to give assurances of his fidelity to the great king.

**Which took Manasseh among the thorns.**—*And they took Manasseh prisoner with the hooks* (*ba-ḥôḥîm*). The *hooks* might be such as the Assyrian kings were wont to pass through the nostrils and lips of their more distinguished prisoners. Comp. Isa. xxxvii. 29, "I will put my hook in thy nose, and my bridle in thy lips;" and comp. Amos iv. 2, "He will take you away with hooks, and your posterity with fish-hooks." Comp. also Job xli. 2, "Canst thou bore his jaw with a hook?" [The LXX., Vulg., Targ. render the word "chains." Syriac confuses the word with *ḥayyîm*, "life," and renders "took Manasseh in his life."] Perhaps, however, the meaning is, *and they took Manasseh prisoner at Hohim.* There is no reason why Hohim should not be a local name, as well as Coz (1 Chron. iv. 8).

**And bound him with fetters.**—*With the double chain of bronze*, as the Philistines bound Samson (Judg. xvi. 21). So Sennacherib relates: "Suzubu king of Babylon, in the battle alive their hands took him; in fetters of bronze they put him, and to my presence brought him. In the great gate in the midst of the city of Nineveh I bound him fast." This happened in 695 B.C., only a few years before the similar captivity of Manasseh.

**And carried him.**—*Caused him to go,* or *led him away.*

**To Babylon.**—Where Assurbanipal was holding his court at the time, as he appears to have done after achieving the overthrow of his brother the rebellious viceroy, and assuming the title of king of Babylon himself.

(12) **When he was in affliction.**—See this phrase in chap. xxviii. 22.

**He besought.**—Literally, *stroked the face,* a curious realistic phrase occurring in Exod. xxxii. 11.

**The God of his fathers.**—Whom he had forsaken for the gods of aliens. Some MSS., and the Syriac, Targum, and Arabic insert "Jehovah" before this phrase.

(13) **He was intreated of him.**—1 Chron. v. 20.

**And brought him again to Jerusalem.**—The Assyrian monarch after a time saw fit to restore

of him, and heard his supplication, and brought him again to Jerusalem into his kingdom. Then Manasseh knew that the LORD he *was* God.

(14) Now after this he built a wall without the city of David, on the west side of Gihon, in the valley, even to the entering in at the fish gate, and compassed about ¹Ophel, and raised it up a very great height, and put captains of war in all the fenced cities of Judah. (15) And he took away the strange gods, and the idol out of the house of the LORD, and all the altars that he had built in the mount of the house of the LORD, and in Jerusalem, and cast *them* out of the city. (16) And he repaired the altar of the LORD, and sacrificed thereon peace offerings and thank offerings, and commanded Judah to serve the LORD God of Israel. (17) Nevertheless the people did sacrifice still in the high places, *yet* unto the LORD their God only.

(18) Now the rest of the acts of Manasseh, and his prayer unto his God, and the words of the seers that spake to him in the name of the LORD God of Israel, behold, they *are written* in the book of the kings of Israel. (19) His prayer also, and how God was intreated of him, and all his sins, and his trespass, and the places wherein he built high places, and set up groves and graven images, before he was humbled: behold, they *are written* among the sayings of ²the seers. (20) So Manasseh slept with his fathers, and they buried him in his own house: and Amon his son reigned in his stead.

1 Or, *The Tower.*

2 Or, *Hosai.*

---

Manasseh to his throne as a vassal king. The case is exactly parallel to that of the Egyptian king *Nikû* (Necho I.), who was bound hand and foot, and sent to Nineveh; after which Assurbanipal extended his clemency to his captive, and restored him to his former state in his own country. (See Schrader, p. 371.)

**Then.**—And.

**That the Lord he was God.**—*That Jehovah was the true God.* (Comp. 1 Kings xviii. 39, where the same Hebrew words occur twice over.)

(14) **Now after this . . . valley.** — Rather, *And afterwards he built an outer wall to the city of David westward unto Gihon in the ravine.* Manasseh completed the wall begun by Hezekiah (chap. xxxii. 5). This highly circumstantial account of the public works undertaken by Manasseh after his restoration, is utterly unlike fiction, and almost compels the assumption of a real historical source, no longer extant, from which the whole section has been derived.

**Even to the entering in of the fish gate.**— The fish-gate lay near the north-east corner of the lower city (Neh. iii. 3). The direction of the outer wall is described first westward, and then eastward.

**And compassed about Ophel.**—*And surrounded the Ophel* (mound); scil., with the wall, which he carried on from the north-east to the south-east. Uzziah and Jotham had already worked upon these fortifications (chaps. xxvi. 9, xxvii. 3). Manasseh now finished them, "raising them up to a very great height."

**Raised it**—*i.e.,* the outer wall.

**And put captains of war.**—(Comp. chaps. xvii. 2, xxxii. 6.) Literally, *captains of an army* (*sārê ḥayil*).

**Of Judah.**—Heb., *in Judah.* Some MSS. and the Vulgate read as the Authorised Version.

(15) **Took away the strange gods.**—Comp. verses 3—7. For the phrase "strange gods" (*ĕlôhê nēkār*), see Gen. xxxv. 2.

**The idol.**—That is, the Asherah (verses 3, 7; 2 Kings xxi. 7, xvii. 16).

**In the mount of the house.**—The temple hill. Thenius says: the courts with the altars in them (2 Kings xxi. 4, 5).

**Cast them out.**—Comp. chap. xxix. 16, xxx. 14. Manasseh's reform was hardly complete, for some of his altars remained for Josiah to pull down (2 Kings xxiii. 12).

(16) **Repaired.**—Heb., *built, i.e.,* rebuilt. Ewald concludes from this that Manasseh had removed the altar of burnt offering; and from Jer. iii. 16 that he destroyed the ark of the covenant. (Some Hebrew MSS., and many editions read *prepared* instead of *built;* but the Syriac and Arabic have the latter word, which is doubtless right.)

CONCLUSION OF THE REIGN (verses 18—20).

(18) **His prayer unto his God.**—This prayer may or may not have been the basis of the Apocryphal *Prayer of Manasses,* preserved in the LXX.

**The words of the seers that spake to him.** —See Note on verse 10, *supr.* These "words of the seers" were incorporated in the great history of the kings, which is mentioned at the end of the verse, and which was one of the chronicler's principal authorities.

**Written.**—This word, though wanting in our present Hebrew text, is read in some MSS., and in the Syriac, Targum, and Arabic.

**The book.**—*The history,* literally, *words.* 2 Kings xxi. 17 refers, as usual, to the "Book of the Chronicles of the Kings of Judah."

(19) **His prayer also . . . of him.**—*And his prayer, and the hearing him.* Literally, *and the being propitious to him* (the same verb as in verse 13 and Gen. xxv. 21).

**All his sins, and his trespass.**—*All his sin and his unfaithfulness.* 2 Kings xxi. 17 has, "And his sin that he sinned." The chronicler, as usual, heightens the expression.

**Groves.**—*The Ashērim.* (See Note on verse 3.)

**Among the sayings of the seers.**—*In the history of Hozai.* This work was, therefore, the source from which the chronicler derived his additional information about the reign of Manasseh. (See *Introduction.*) The LXX. has "the seers;" but the Vulg., "in sermonibus Hozai," and the Syriac, "in the story of Hanan the prophet." It is pretty clear that *Hozai* is simply a mutilated form of *ha-hôzîm,* "the seers," a term which occurred in verse 17.

(20) **In his own house.**—2 Kings xxi. 18, "and he was buried in the garden of his house, in the garden

*Amon's reign.* **II. CHRONICLES, XXXIV.** *Josiah succeeds him.*

(21) *a*Amon *was* two and twenty years old when he began to reign, and reigned two years in Jerusalem. (22) But he did *that which was* evil in the sight of the LORD, as did Manasseh his father: for Amon sacrificed unto all the carved images which Manasseh his father had made, and served them; (23) and humbled not himself before the LORD, as Manasseh his father had humbled himself; but Amon ¹trespassed more and more. (24) And his servants conspired against him, and slew him in his own house. (25) But the people of the land slew all them that had conspired against king Amon; and the people of the land made Josiah his son king in his stead.

**CHAPTER XXXIV.**—(1) Josiah *b was* eight years old when he began to reign, and he reigned in Jerusalem one and thirty years. (2) And he did *that which was* right in the sight of the LORD, and walked in the ways of David his father, and declined *neither* to the right hand, nor to the left. (3) For in the eighth year of his reign, while he was yet young, he began to seek after the God of David his father: and in the twelfth year he began *c*to purge Judah and

*a* 2 Kings 21. 19, &c.

B.C. 677.

1 Heb., *multiplied trespass.*

*b* 2 Kings 22. 1, &c.

*c* 1 Kings 13. 2.

---

of Uzza." The words, *in the garden of*, seem to have fallen out of our text. So LXX., ἐν παραδείσῳ οἴκου αὐτοῦ; Syriac, "in his house, in the garden of treasure."

THE REIGN OF AMON (verses 21—25. Comp. 2 Kings xxi. 19—26).

(21) **Amon was two and twenty years old.**—So 2 Kings xxi. 19, which adds his mother's name and parentage.

(22) **For Amon sacrificed.**—Literally, *and to all the carven images which Manasseh his father had made did Amon sacrifice*. (Comp. 2 Kings xxi. 21, "and he walked in all the way wherein his father had walked, and served the idols which his father had served, and worshipped them." *Idols* in the above passage is *gillûlîm*, "dunglings," a term nowhere used by the chronicler.) The statement of our text seems to imply that the "carven images" made by Manasseh had not been destroyed, but only cast aside. (See Note on verse 15.) It argues a defect of judgment to say with Reuss that the reforms of Manasseh are rendered doubtful by it. The whole history is a succession of reforms followed by relapses; and the words of the sacred writer need not be supposed to mean that the images which Amon worshipped were the very ones which his penitent father had discarded, but only images of the same imaginary gods.

(23) **And humbled not himself ... more and more.**—This verse is added by the chronicler.

**But Amon trespassed more and more.**—Literally, *for he, Amon, multiplied trespass*.

(25) **Slew.**—*Smote*. The verse is identical with 2 Kings xxi. 24, save that it has "smote" plural instead of singular, which latter is more correct. It may be that the facts thus briefly recorded represent a fierce conflict between the party of religious reform and that of religious reaction, in which the latter was for the time worsted and reduced to a state of suspended activity.

The chronicler has omitted the remarks usual at the end of a reign. See 2 Kings xxi. 25, 26 for a reference to sources, and Amon's burial place ("the garden of Uzza").

### XXXIV.

THE REIGN OF JOSIAH (chaps. xxxiv.—xxxv.).

The history of Josiah, as related here, is in substantial agreement with the narrative of 2 Kings xxii., xxiii. The main difference lies in the fact that the chronicler assigns the various reforms of this king to his eighth, twelfth, and eighteenth years; whereas the compiler of Kings groups them all together, in connection with the repair of the Temple and finding of the Book of the Law, in the eighteenth year of the reign. Our account, moreover, briefly describes the suppression of idolatry, and dwells at great length on the celebration of the Passover; in Kings the contrary is the case.

(1, 2) Length and character of the reign.

(1) **Josiah was eight years old.**—So 2 Kings xxii. 1, which adds, "and his mother's name was Jedidah, the daughter of Adaiah of Boscath."

(2) **And declined ... the left.**—So Kings. Josiah is the only king upon whom this encomium is pronounced. It is equivalent to saying that his observance of the law was perfect. Comp. Deut. v. 32, xvii. 20 (the law of the king), xxviii. 14.

(3—7) Idolatry extirpated. This brief account is parallel to 2 Kings xxiii. 4—20.

(3) **For.**—*Now*.

**In the eighth year.**—The specifications of time in this verse are peculiar to the chronicler.

**While he was yet young.**—Being about sixteen.

**He began to seek.**—Chap. xvii. 3, 4; 1 Chron. xiii. 3.

**And in the twelfth year.**—When, perhaps, he began to govern alone.

**He began to purge.**—It is not said that the whole work was completed in the twelfth year; indeed, verse 33 implies the contrary. But the writer having begun the story of the destruction of idolatrous objects, naturally continues it to its close, though that properly belongs to Josiah's eighteenth year (2 Kings xxii. 3, compared with xxiii. 4 *seq.*). It is *not*, therefore, clear (as Thenius asserts) that the chronicler has put the extirpation of idolatry first, simply to show that the *pious* king needed no special prompting to such a course; or that, as Nöldeke supposes, the writer meant to clear this highly-extolled king from the reproach of having quietly put up with the abomination for full eighteen years.

**The high places.**—2 Kings xxiii. 5, 8, 9, 13.

**The groves.**—*The Asherim* (2 Kings xxiii. 4, 6, 7, 14). There was an Asherah in the Temple, as well as in the high places which Solomon built for Ashtoreth, Chemosh, and Milcom. The carved and molten images are not mentioned in the parallel passage, which, however, gives a much clearer and more original description of the different kinds of idolatry abolished by Josiah.

| *Josiah's good works.* | II. CHRONICLES, XXXIV. | *The Repair of the Temple.* |

Jerusalem from the high places, and the groves, and the carved images, and the molten images. (4) <sup>a</sup>And they brake down the altars of Baalim in his presence; and the <sup>1</sup>images, that were on high above them, he cut down; and the groves, and the carved images, and the molten images, he brake in pieces, and made dust *of them*, and strowed *it* upon the <sup>2</sup>graves of them that had sacrificed unto them. (5) And he burnt the bones of the priests upon their altars, and cleansed Judah and Jerusalem. (6) And so did he in the cities of Manasseh, and Ephraim, and Simeon, even unto Naphtali, with their <sup>3</sup>mattocks round about. (7) And when he had broken down the altars and the groves, and had beaten the graven images <sup>4</sup>into powder, and cut down all the idols throughout all the land of Israel, he returned to Jerusalem. (8) Now in the eighteenth year of his reign, when he had purged the land, and the house, he sent to Shaphan the son of Azaliah, and Maaseiah the governor of the city, and Joah the son of Joahaz the recorder, to repair the house of the LORD his God. (9) And when they came to Hilkiah the high priest, they delivered the money that was brought into the house of God, which the Levites that kept the doors had gathered of the hand of Manasseh and Ephraim, and of all the remnant of Israel, and of all

*a* Lev. 26. 30.

<sup>1</sup> Or, *sun images.*

<sup>2</sup> Heb., *face of the graves.*

<sup>3</sup> Or, *mauls.*

<sup>4</sup> Heb., *to make powder.*

---

(The Syriac has, "he began to root out the altars, and idols, and leopards, and chapels, and collars, and bells, and all the trees which they made for the idols.")

(4) **Of Baalim.**—*Of the Baals.* 2 Kings xxiii. 4, 5, "the Baal."

**In his presence.**—Comp. 2 Kings xxiii. 16, from which it appears that Josiah personally superintended the work of demolition.

**The images.**—*Sun statues* (chap. xiv. 4).

**That were on high above them, he cut down.** —Or, *that were above, from off them he hewed.*

**The molten images.**—Rather, *the* maççebôth, or sacred *pillars.* (See 2 Kings xxiii. 14.)

**Made dust of them.**—2 Kings xxiii. 6 (of an Asherah).

**And shoved . . . unto them.**—Literally, *and sprinkled upon the face of the graves that used to sacrifice unto them,* as if the graves were guilty. 2 Kings xxiii. 6 relates this of the temple Asherah only.

(5) **And he burnt . . . upon their altar.**—See 2 Kings xxiii. 13, 14, 16, 20 for details. Literally, *and bones of priests he burnt.* They were bones taken from the graves of the idolatrous priests, who were thus punished, while their altars were irreparably defiled. (For the horror with which such a violation of the dead was then regarded, see Amos ii. 1.)

**And cleansed** (*i.e.,* "purged," verse 3) **Judah and Jerusalem.**—This phrase does not occur at all in the parallel account.

(6) **And so did he in the cities . . . unto Naphtali.**—See 2 Kings xxiii. 15, 19, according to which Josiah destroyed the sanctuary of Bethel, and the high places "in the cities of Samaria," *i.e.,* the northern kingdom.

Simeon is again mentioned somewhat strangely, as in chap. xv. 9, no doubt because Beersheba, a famous sanctuary within its territory, was a place of pilgrimage for the northern tribes.

**Manasseh and Ephraim,** *i.e.,* the northern kingdom, as in chap. xxxi. 1; Isa. ix. 21.

**With their mattocks.**—Rather, *in their ruins*; reading behorbôthêhem, instead of beharòthêhem, which means "with their swords." (Comp. Ezek. xxvi. 9.) The phrase qualifies the word "cities." The cities of Israel had been ruined by the Assyrians, Sargon, and Shalmaneser, the latter of whom took Samaria, after a three years' siege, and carried the people captive to Assyria, in 721 B.C., replacing them by foreign colonists. This explains how it was that Josiah was able to desecrate the northern sanctuaries, and slay their priests (2 Kings xxiii. 20). The ordinary Hebrew text divides the word thus: behar bôthêhem, so as to suggest the reading behar bâttêhem, "in the hill of their houses." The LXX. has "in their places round about"; the Vulg. omits the phrase; and the Syriac reads "in their streets around." The whole verse should be connected with verse 7, thus: "And in the cities of Manasseh and Ephraim and Simeon, even unto Naphtali, to wit, in their ruins round about, he pulled down the altars and the Asherim; and the carven images he dashed into pieces unto pulverising." *Hedaq* is an unusual form of the infinitive, not a perfect, as Bertheau supposes.

(7) **The idols.**—*Sun-statues* (verse 4). The word does not occur in the parallel account; but verse 5 mentions sun-worship.

(8—13) The cleansing and repair of the Temple. (Comp. 2 Kings xxii. 3—7; and the similar account of the restoration by Joash in chap. xxiv. 11—13).

**When he had purged.**—Omit *had.* (*Lĕtahêr* is apparently co-ordinate with *lĕmolkó,* "in the eighteenth year to his reigning, to purging the land"; as if the work of purification had been co-extensive with the reign. The LXX., however, has, "in order to purge the land," which may be right.)

**He sent Shaphan.**—Who was secretary of state (2 Kings xxii. 3, "the scribe").

**Maaseiah . . . Joah.**—Kings mentions Shaphan only.

**The governor of the city.**—*Sar ha'ir; praefectus urbis.* (Comp. 1 Chron. xi. 6.)

(9) **And when they came . . . they delivered.** —*And they came . . . and they gave.* In 2 Kings xxii. 3—7, the contents of verses 9—12a are given in the form of the king's instructions to Shaphan. Here we are told that those instructions were carried out. "They delivered (*wayyittĕnú*) is substituted for the difficult *wĕyattêm* of Kings (*i.e.,* "and let him pay out").

**From the hand of Manasseh . . . Benjamin.** —Kings, "from the people." Reuss oddly imagines that these words denote "a kind of organised collection throughout all Palestine," and then proceeds to draw an inference unfavourable to the chronicler.

*The Repair of the Temple.*  II. CHRONICLES, XXXIV.  *Hilkiah finds a Book.*

Judah and Benjamin; and they returned to Jerusalem. (10) And they put it in the hand of the workmen that had the oversight of the house of the LORD, and they gave it to the workmen that wrought in the house of the LORD, to repair and amend the house: (11) even to the artificers and builders gave they *it*, to buy hewn stone, and timber for couplings, and ¹ to floor the houses which the kings of Judah had destroyed. (12) And the men did the work faithfully: and the overseers of them *were* Jahath and Obadiah, the Levites, of the sons of Merari; and Zechariah and Meshullam, of the sons of the Kohathites, to set *it* forward; and *other of* the Levites, all that could skill of instruments of musick. (13) Also *they were* over the bearers of burdens, and *were* overseers of all that wrought the work in any manner of service: and of the Levites *there were* scribes, and officers, and porters.

(14) And when they brought out the money that was brought into the house of the LORD, Hilkiah the priest *a* found a book of the law of the LORD *given* ² by Moses. (15) And Hilkiah answered and said to Shaphan the scribe, I have found the book of the law in the house of the LORD. And Hilkiah delivered the book to Shaphan. (16) And Shaphan carried the book to the king, and brought the king word back again, saying, All that

¹ Or, *to rafter.*

*a* 2 Kings 22. 8, &c.

² Heb., *by the hand of.*

---

**And they returned to Jerusalem.**—This is the meaning of the *Qri* or Hebrew margin. The Hebrew text has, "and the inhabitants of Jerusalem," which is correct.

(10) **Put it in.**—*Gave it into.*

**The workmen.**—*The doers of the work,* i.e., the overseers or contractors. See Note on chap. xxiv. 12.

**And they gave it to the workmen ... the house.**—So LXX. and Syriac. The Hebrew text says, *and the doers of the work who were working in the house of Jehovah gave it for restoring and repairing the house.* To whom the masters gave it is stated in next verse.

**To repair.**—*Libdōq,* here only. The term is so used in Syriac. The original form of the verse is 2 Kings xxii. 5, where "the doers of the work" are first the masters, and then the men.

(11) **Even to ... builders.**—*And they gave it to the craftsmen and to the builders.*

**For couplings.**—*For the couplings* or *girders;* an explanation added by the chronicler.

**And to floor ... destroyed.**—Kings, "to repair the house." The reference to the defacement of the Temple buildings by idolatrous kings may be compared with the similar notice concerning Athaliah's sons, chap. xxiv. 7, and Ahaz, chap. xxviii. 24. Perhaps, however, the expression "destroyed" does not mean more than "allowed to go to ruin."

**To floor.**—*To rafter,* or *joist.* (See margin.)

**The houses.**—*The chambers.*

(12) **And the men did the work faithfully.**—Literally, *And the men were working* (or *dealing*) *in good faith in the work.* In 2 Kings xxii. 7 Josiah bids the High Priest not to require any account of the money delivered to the master-workmen, "because they work in good faith."

**And the overseers of them were.**—*And over them were set.* The names of the overseers, and the details added in next verse, are peculiar to and characteristic of the chronicler.

**To set it forward.**—*To lead, conduct, preside;* usually a musical term. (Comp. 1 Chron. xxiii. 4.)

**And other ... musick.**—Literally, *and the Levites,* to wit, *every one skilled in the instruments of song.* (Comp. 1 Chron. xv. 16; xxv. 7.)

(13) **Also.**—*And.*

**They.**—The Levitical musicians.

**Were over the bearers of burdens.**—They probably cheered their labours with song and music; as was the practice in ancient Egypt.

**And were overseers.**—*Leaders, conductors;* see Note on verse 12. Notice the honourable position here assigned to the musical guilds of Levites.

**And of the Levites ... porters.**—In connection, that is, with the work of restoration. But comp. 1 Chron. xxiii. 4, 5. The writer may only intend to say that there were Levitical guilds of "scribes, officers, and porters," as well as of musicians.

**Scribes.**—1 Chron. ii. 55.

(14—19) Hilkiah finds the Book of the Law, and delivers it to Shaphan, who reads it before the king. (Comp. 2 Kings xxii. 8—11.)

(14) **And when they brought out.**—This verse is not in Kings. It supplements the older account, by assigning the occasion of the discovery.

Josephus makes Hilkiah find the book in the treasure-chamber of the Temple which he had entered to get gold and silver for making some sacred vessels. According to Rabbinical tradition it was found hidden under a heap of stones, where it had been placed to save it from being burnt by king Ahaz.

**A book.**—*The book.*

**Given by Moses.**—The Hebrew phrase, "by the hand of Moses," belongs not to "the book," but to "the Law (or teaching) of Jehovah"; and the meaning of the whole expression is, "the Law of Jehovah communicated through the medium or instrumentality of Moses." (Comp. chap. xxxiii. 8.)

**To Shaphan.**—Kings adds, "and he read it." Those words need not mean that Shaphan read the book *through,* as Thenius suggests. (See Note on 2 Kings xxii. 3.)

(16) **Carried.**—*Brought in.*

**Again.**—*Further, besides.*

**Committed to thy servants.**—*Given into the hand of thy servants;* viz. the overseers of the repairs.

**They do it.**—*They are doing.*

"And Shaphan brought the book in unto the king," is only a different pointing of, "and Shaphan the scribe came in unto the king," 2 Kings xxii. 9. The rest of the verse is an addition of the chronicler's. Perhaps the Notes on 2 Kings xii. 11 and chap. xxiv. 11 apply here.

was committed ¹to thy servants, they do it. (17) And they have ²gathered together the money that was found in the house of the LORD, and have delivered it into the hand of the overseers, and to the hand of the workmen. (18) Then Shaphan the scribe told the king saying, Hilkiah the priest hath given me a book. And Shaphan read ³it before the king. (19) And it came to pass, when the king had heard the words of the law, that he rent his clothes. (20) And the king commanded Hilkiah, and Ahikam the son of Shaphan, and ⁴Abdon, the son of Micah, and Shaphan the scribe, and Asaiah a servant of the king's, saying, (21) Go, enquire of the LORD for me, and for them that are left in Israel and in Judah, concerning the words of the book that is found: for great is the wrath of the LORD that is poured out upon us, because our fathers have not kept the word of the LORD, to do after all that is written in this book.

(22) And Hilkiah, and they that the king had appointed, went to Huldah the prophetess, the wife of Shallum the son of Tikvath, the son of ⁵Hasrah, keeper of the ⁶wardrobe; (now she dwelt in Jerusalem ⁷in the college:) and they spake to her to that effect. (23) And she answered them, Thus saith the LORD God of Israel, Tell ye the man that sent you to me, (24) Thus saith the LORD, Behold, I will bring evil upon this place, and upon the inhabitants thereof, even all the curses that are written in the book which they have read before the king of Judah: (25) because they have forsaken me, and have burned incense unto other gods, that they might provoke me to anger with all the works of their hands; therefore my wrath shall be poured out upon this place, and shall not be quenched. (26) And as for the king of Judah, who sent you to enquire of the LORD, so shall ye say unto him, Thus saith the LORD God of Israel concerning the words which thou hast heard; (27) Because thine heart was tender, and thou didst humble thyself before God, when thou heardest his words against this

1 Heb., to the hand of.
2 Heb., poured out, or, melted.
3 Heb., in it.
4 Or, Achbor, 2 Kings 22. 12.
5 Or, Harhas, 2 Kings 22. 14.
6 Heb., garments.
7 Or, in the school, or, in the second part.

---

(17) **Gathered together.**—*Poured out* from the chest or chests. See 2 Kings xxii. 9, where "the doers of the work" are identified with "the overseers."

**And to . . . the workmen.**—*And to . . . the doers of the work.*

Perhaps the *and* is explanatory (*even*, or *that is*).

(18) **Then.**—*And.* The verse is identical with 2 Kings xxii. 10, save that it substitutes "read in it" for "read it," which may mean the same thing. It seems too much to assume that the chronicler altered the phrase, in order to insinuate that the book was of considerable size.

(20—28) The royal message to the prophetess Huldah, and her reply. Comp. 2 Kings xxii. 12—20.

**Abdon the son of Micah.**—Kings, "Achbor the son of Micaiah," which appears right. The Syriac has Abachûr. (See Jeremiah xxvi. 22; xxxvi. 12.)

(21) **Go, enquire of the Lord.**—The verse is virtually identical with 2 Kings xxii. 13.

**For them that are left . . . . Judah.**—An alteration of, "and for the people and for all Judah" (Kings). The chronicler thinks of the remnant in the northern kingdom.

**Poured out.**— Kings, "kindled against." (So LXX.) This was probably the original reading, as the wrath which Josiah dreaded had not yet been *poured out* upon *Judah*. But the chronicler remembered the ruin of the ten tribes.

**Kept.**— Kings, "hearkened to" *shāmĕ'û*, as here, instead of *shāmĕrû*; and so LXX. and Syriac.

(22) **And they that the king had appointed.**—The Hebrew text is defective. We may restore it from the LXX., "and they whom the king had commanded"; or better, perhaps, from the Syriac and Vulg., "and all they whom the king sent." Three MSS. read, "and the king's princes," a plausible correction. 2 Kings xxii. 14 adds the names (verse 20 *supra*).

**Son of Tikvath.**—Heb., *Tŏkahath.* Kings, "Tikvah." The LXX., Θεκωε, the Syriac, *Tekwâ*, and the Vulg., Thecuath, show that Tikvah or Tikvath is right. (The final h and th of Chronicles arise from blending these two equivalent spellings.)

**Son of Hasrah.**—Kings, *son of Harhas.* So the LXX., Ἀράς; but the Syriac (*Hasdâ*) and Vulg. support Hasrah.

**In the college.**—*In the second quarter;* i.e., the lower city.

**To that effect.**—Chap. xxxii. 15 ("on this manner"). Added by the chronicler. The differences in the text of the oracle which follows are mostly due to alteration of the original, which is more exactly given in Kings.

(24) **I will bring.**—*I am about to bring* (participle).

**All the curses . . . the book.**—An explanatory paraphrase of "all the words of the book" (Kings). (See Deut. xxvii. 15 *seq.*, xxviii. 16 *seq.*, xxix. 20, 21, 27, xxx. 19; and comp. Josh. viii. 34.)

(25) **Works.**—"Work" (Kings), and some MSS. and the Syriac version here.

**Poured out.**—"Shall be kindled" (Kings), which agrees better with "shall not be quenched." (See verse 21 for the same alteration. The LXX. here has ἐξεκαύθη) "was kindled."

**Burned incense.**—*Hiphil*, which is much commoner in the chronicle than *piel*, the form in Kings (the forms *piel* and *hiphil* of this word *qatar* are about equally used in Kings.)

(26) **To enquire of the Lord.**—Strictly, *through the Lord.* Kings has the accusative.

**Against this place.**—Kings adds, "that it should become an astonishment and a curse."

place, and against the inhabitants thereof, and humbledst thyself before me, and didst rend thy clothes, and weep before me; I have even heard *thee* also, saith the LORD. (28) Behold, I will gather thee to thy fathers, and thou shalt be gathered to thy grave in peace, neither shall thine eyes see all the evil that I will bring upon this place, and upon the inhabitants of the same. So they brought the king word again.

(29) ᵃThen the king sent and gathered together all the elders of Judah and Jerusalem. (30) And the king went up into the house of the LORD, and all the men of Judah, and the inhabitants of Jerusalem, and the priests, and the Levites, and all the people, ¹great and small: and he read in their ears all the words of the book of the covenant that was found in the house of the LORD. (31) And the king stood in his place, and made a covenant before the LORD, to walk after the LORD, and to keep his commandments, and his testimonies, and his statutes, with all his heart, and with all his soul, to perform the words of the covenant which are written in this book. (32) And he caused all that were ²present in Jerusalem and Benjamin to stand *to it.* And the inhabitants of Jerusalem did according to the covenant of God, the God of their fathers. (33) And Josiah took away all the abominations out of all the countries that *pertained* to the children of Israel, and made all that were present in Israel to serve, *even* to serve the LORD their God. *And* all his days they departed not ³from following the LORD, the God of their fathers.

CHAPTER XXXV.—(1) Moreover ᵇJosiah kept a passover unto the LORD in Jerusalem: and they killed the passover

ᵃ 2 Kings 23. 1.

B.C. 624.

¹ Heb., *from great even to small.*

² Heb., *found.*

³ Heb., *from after.*

ᵇ 2 Kings 23. 21, 22.

---

**And humbledst thyself before me.**—Not in Kings. A characteristic repetition.

**And weep.**—Shorter form of the verb; a correction of Kings (*wattēbk* for *wattebkeh*).

**I.**—Emphatic. (Kings has the longer form *'anokî* for our *'ani.*)

**Saith the Lord.**—*Is the utterance of Jehovah* (*ne'ûm Iahweh*).

**Grave.**—Heb., *graves.* (Comp. chap. xvi. 14.)

**And upon the inhabitants of the same.**—Added by the chronicler.

(29—33) The king reads the Book to the assembly, and renews the covenant. (Comp. 2 Kings xxiii. 1.)

(30) **The Levites.**—The chronicler substituted this for "the prophets" (Kings). It was a natural change to make, seeing that the prophetic order had long been extinct in his day. It may even be the result of an unconscious error, as the phrase "priests and Levites" is so frequent in his pages.

(31) **In his place.**—*'Al 'omdô*, "on his stand;" chap. xxiii. 13 (Authorised Version, "at his pillar"). Kings has *'al hā'ammûd*, which appears to be synonymous; "on the dais."

**A covenant.**—*The covenant.*

(32) **And he caused . . . stand to it.**—Kings, "and all the people stood into (*i.e.,* came into) the covenant." So Syriac: "And everyone that was found in Jerusalem and in Benjamin rose, and the inhabitants of Jerusalem entered into the covenant of the Lord God of their fathers." (The chronicler's reading may be accounted for by the fact that the verbs "he stood" and "he caused to stand" differ only in the vowels, which anciently were not written at all. "All that were present in Jerusalem and Benjamin" is an unusual phrase; and it is likely that "and Benjamin" is really a corruption of "into the covenant" which is required by the context here as much as in Kings.)

**And the inhabitants . . . fathers**—*i.e.,* after they had thus solemnly taken it upon them to do so. The statement is not read in Kings.

(33) **And Josiah took away all the abominations.**—Of idolatry.

**Out of all the countries . . . Israel.**—Out of the territories of the Ten Tribes. The statement glances back to verse 6, and summarises the account of the abolition of heathenish worships, which follows here in 2 Kings xxiii. 4—20.

**And made . . . to serve, even to serve.**—*And made to serve . . . so as to serve;* a unique phrase. The style of the verse is the chronicler's.

**All his days they departed not.**—The king's will secured an outward conformity to the legitimate *cultus,* and open idolatry was for the time being a peril too serious to be thought of. But the unreality of these reformations by royal mandate is proved by the relapse which immediately followed upon the death of Josiah. The moral corruption which at this epoch was preying upon the vitals of the nation, and hurrying it swiftly to destruction, is revealed in the pathetic pages of the prophet Jeremiah. (See Jer. xi., xiii. 27, xvi. 20, xvii. 1, 2, &c.)

### XXXV.

JOSIAH'S PASSOVER (verses 1—19.) (Comp. 2 Kings xxiii., 21—23.)

This event receives brief but emphatic notice in the short section of Kings which records it. The passage is freely copied in 3 Esdras i. 1—22. It is of peculiar importance, as giving a more complete representation of the Passover than the Pentateuchal data supply.

(1) **Moreover.**—*And.* The form of the Hebrew verb implies that this Passover was held subsequently to the renewal of the covenant; and 2 Kings xxiii. 23 fixes the date precisely as "the eighteenth year of king Josiah."

**Kept.**—*Made* (chap. xxx. 1).

**On the fourteenth day of the first month.**—In strict accordance with the law. Hezekiah's Passover was irregular in point of time (chap. xxx. 2, 13).

*Josiah keeps a*      II. CHRONICLES, XXXV.      *Solemn Passover.*

on the <sup>a</sup>fourteenth *day* of the first month. <sup>(2)</sup> And he set the priests in their charges, and encouraged them to the service of the house of the LORD. <sup>(3)</sup> And said unto the Levites that taught all Israel, which were holy unto the LORD, Put the holy ark in the house which Solomon the son of David king of Israel did build; *it shall* not *be* a burden upon *your* shoulders: serve now the LORD your God, and his people Israel, <sup>(4)</sup> and prepare *yourselves* by the <sup>b</sup>houses of your fathers, after your courses, according to the writing of David king of Israel, and according to the <sup>c</sup>writing of Solomon his son. <sup>(5)</sup> And stand in the holy *place* according to the divisions of <sup>1</sup>the families of the fathers of your brethren <sup>2</sup>the people, and *after* the division of the families of the Levites. <sup>(6)</sup> So kill the passover, and sanctify yourselves, and prepare your brethren, that *they* may do according to the word of the LORD by the hand of Moses.

<sup>(7)</sup> And Josiah <sup>3</sup>gave to the people, of the flock, lambs and kids, all for the passover offerings, for all that were present, to the number of thirty thousand, and three thousand bullocks: these *were* of the king's substance. <sup>(8)</sup> And his princes <sup>4</sup>gave willingly unto the people to the priests, and to the Levites: Hilkiah and Zechariah and Jehiel, rulers of the house of God, gave unto the priests for the passover offerings two thousand and six hundred *small cattle*, and three hundred oxen.

*a* Exod. 12. 6.
*b* 1 Chron. 9. 10, & 1 Chron. 23 & 24, & 25 & 26.
*c* ch. 8. 14.
<sup>1</sup> Heb., *the house of the fathers.*
<sup>2</sup> Heb., *the sons of the people.*
<sup>3</sup> Heb., *offered.*
<sup>4</sup> Heb., *offered.*

---

<sup>(2)</sup> **Set the priests in their charges.**—Literally, *over their wards* (chap. viii. 14). The king appointed them to discharge their proper duties in connection with the rite.

**Encouraged them.**—By exhortation and instruction. (See an instance in chap. xxix. 5 *seq.*)

<sup>(3–6)</sup> The king's charge to the Levites.

<sup>(3)</sup> **The Levites that taught all Israel.**—In the law (Neh. viii. 7; comp. also chap. xvii. 8, 9).

**Which were holy unto the Lord.**—Separated to His service (Exod. xxviii. 36, "Holiness to the Lord," the inscription on Aaron's mitre),

**Put the holy ark in the house.**—This command implies that the ark had been removed from its place in the inner sanctuary. The removal probably took place under Manasseh or his son, with the object of saving the sacred symbol from profanation. Or perhaps the repair of the Temple under Josiah had necessitated such a step. A third explanation takes the words in the sense of "Let the ark be, where it stands, in its proper place. Do not give a thought to your ancient function of bearing it about; but set your minds upon present duties." This, however, is too artificial.

**It shall not be a burden.**—Literally, *bearing on the shoulder is not for you.* (Comp. the like statement in 1 Chron. xxiii. 26; see also Numb. iv. 15, vii. 9; 1 Chron. xv. 2.)

**Serve now the Lord . . . and his people.**—In the manner indicated in verses 4—6.

<sup>(4)</sup> **And prepare yourselves.**—The pronoun should not be italicised, for the verb is *niphal* or reflexive, and not *hiphil* or causative, as the Hebrew vowel points wrongly suggest.

**By the houses of your fathers.**—*According to your father-houses.*

**After your courses.**—*In your divisions.* (See 1 Chron. xxiii—xxvi.)

**According to the writing of David . . . Solomon his son.**—Comp. 1 Chron. xxviii. 19, where David refers to such a writing. The words seem to imply the existence of written memorials of the regulations of public worship, which David and Solomon instituted.

("Writing of David" is *kěthâb,* a word only found in Chronicles, Ezra, Nehemiah, and Daniel and Esther. "Writing of Solomon" is *miktab;* see Exod. xxxii. 16).

<sup>(5)</sup> **Stand in the holy place.**—In the Temple court.

**According to the divisions . . . the Levites.** —Rather, *according to the sections of the father-houses of your brethren the sons of the people* (as opposed to "the sons of Levi"); *and, in fact, a portion of a father-house of the Levites;* scil., beside every entire father-house of laymen. The Levites were to slay and skin the lambs, and hand the blood to the priests, and to give their share of the roasted flesh to the people (verses 11, 12).

<sup>(6)</sup> **And sanctify yourselves.**—Probably by washing the hands before handing the blood of sprinkling to the priests. (See chap. xxx. 16 *seq.*)

**Prepare your brethren.**—*Prepare* (the passover) *for your brethren* or the laity.

**That they may do.**—*So as to do.* The Levites themselves are to obey the prescriptions of the Mosaic Law.

<sup>(7–9)</sup> The king and the grandees present the victims. (Comp. chap. xxx. 24.)

<sup>(7)</sup> **Josiah gave.**—As in chap. xxx. 24, *presented as a heave-offering.*

**To the people.**—*To the sons of the people;* i.e., the laity.

**Of the flock.**—Literally, *small cattle, to wit, lambs and sons of goats.*

**All for the passover offerings**—i.e., the thirty thousand small cattle.

**Three thousand bullocks.**—For the peace-offerings and the sacrificial feasting (verse 13).

**The king's substance.**—Chaps. xxxi. 3, xxxii. 29.

<sup>(8)</sup> **And his princes . . . Levites.**—*And his princes for a free-will offering* (Lev. vii. 16) *to the people, to the priests, and to the Levites had presented* heave-offerings. How many victims they gave is not specified. Some words may have fallen out of the text. (Comp. chap. xxx. 24.) Hilkiah is introduced quite abruptly in the text as it stands.

**Rulers of the house of God.**—Chap. xxxi. 13; 1 Chron. ix. 11. Hilkiah was high priest (chap. xxxiv.

*Josiah keeps a* — II. CHRONICLES, XXXV. — *Solemn Passover.*

(9) Conaniah also, and Shemaiah and Nethaniel, his brethren, and Hashabiah and Jeiel and Jozabad, chief of the Levites, ¹gave unto the Levites for passover offerings five thousand *small cattle*, and five hundred oxen. (10) So the service was prepared, and the priests stood in their place, and the Levites in their courses, according to the king's commandment. (11) And they killed the passover, and the priests sprinkled *the blood* from their hands, and the Levites <sup>a</sup>flayed *them*. (12) And they removed the burnt offerings, that they might give according to the divisions of the families of the people, to offer unto the LORD, as *it is* written in the book of Moses. And so *did they* with the oxen. (13) And they <sup>b</sup>roasted the passover with fire according to the ordinance: but the *other* holy *offerings* sod they in pots, and in caldrons, and in pans, and ²divided *them* speedily among all the people. (14) And afterward they made ready for themselves, and for the priests: because the priests the sons of Aaron *were busied* in offering of burnt offerings and the fat until night; therefore the Levites prepared for themselves, and for the priests the sons of Aaron. (15) And the singers the sons of Asaph *were* in their ³place, according to the <sup>c</sup>commandment of David, and Asaph, and Heman, and Jeduthun the king's seer; and the porters <sup>d</sup>waited at every gate; they might not depart from their service; for their brethren the Levites prepared for them. (16) So all the ser-

1 Heb., *offered*.
a See ch. 29. 34.
b Exod. 12. 8, 9.
2 Heb., *made them run*.
3 Heb., *station*.
c 1 Chron. 25. 1, &c.
d 1 Chron. 9. 17, & 26. 14.

---

9); Zechariah perhaps his deputy, "the second priest" (2 Kings xxv. 18); Jehiel may have been the head of the line of Ithamar, which still existed even after the return (Ezra viii. 2).

Oxen, *i.e.*, "bullocks" (verse 7).

(9) **Conaniah also . . . Jozabad.**—The three names Conaniah, Shemaiah, and Jozabad, occurred as belonging to principal Levites under Hezekiah (chap. xxxi. 12—15). They may be names of leading houses rather than persons.

(10) **So the service was prepared.**—The preparations were completed. (See verses 4 and 16).

**In their place.**—*On their stand* (chap. xxx. 16).

(11) **The passover.**—The paschal victims.

**From their hands.**—Heb., *hand*. The hand of the Levites, who caught the blood when they slaughtered the victims, and gave it to the priests.

**Flayed.**—*Were flaying.*—The exception of chap. xxx. 17 has become the rule here.

(12) **They removed.**—Cut off those parts of the victims which had to be consumed on the altar of burnt offering. (Comp. Lev. iii. 9, iv. 31.) These parts are naturally called "the burnt offering," although no special burnt offering was appointed for the evening of the Passover.

**That they might give . . . people.**—*To give them to the sections of the father-houses of the sons of the people.* After separating the proper pieces, the Levites gave them to the sections which they were serving, to be presented in turn to the priests for burning on the altar.

**To offer.**—*Haqrîb*; as in Lev. iii. 9, 14.

**As it is written.**—Referring to the rule that "all the fat is the Lord's" (Lev. iii. 16).

**And so did they.**—*And so for the oxen.* The proper portions of these also were separated for consumption on the brazen altar; the rest of the carcases furnished food for the sacrificial festivities.

(13) **According to the ordinance.**—Exod. xii. 8, 9.

**Roasted with fire.**—*Cooked in the fire.*

**But the other holy offerings sod they . . . pans.**—*And the consecrated things they cooked in the pots, and in the caldrons, and in the pans.*—"The consecrated things" are the oxen (chap. xxix. 33). Their flesh was boiled or fried, and handed with all due haste by the Levites to the laity.

The author tells us here not only what was done on the evening of the fourteenth Nisan, the Passover proper, but also during the seven following days of the Feast of Mazzoth, or Unleavened Bread. On the Passover evening only the paschal lambs and kids would be eaten; the oxen were slain as peace offerings during the subsequent festivities (Deut. xvi. 1—8), and furnished forth the sacrificial meals.

**And divided them speedily . . . the people.**—*And brought them quickly to all the sons of the people,* so that the meat did not get cold. (Comp. Gen. xli. 14.) This little touch of realism calls up a picture. We see the whole busy scene, the different groups of the people scattered here and there about the sacred court, and the Levites bringing them their portions of the savoury meat.

(14) **Afterward.**—After serving the laity with their passover.

**They made ready.**—The Passover (Luke xxii. 8, 9, 13).

**Because the priests . . . until night.**—The reason why the Levites prepared the Passover and the after meals for them.

**In offering of burnt offerings and the fat.**—*In offering the burnt offering and the pieces of fat.* The second phrase seems to define the first (*and, i.e., namely*). The parts of the sheep, goats, and oxen, which in case of peace offerings had to be burnt wholly on the altar were called *hălābîm*, "pieces of fat."

(15) **And the singers the sons of Asaph were in their place.**—"At their post" or station (1 Chron. xxiii. 28). The "sons" of Heman and Jeduthun are omitted for brevity.

**According to the commandment . . . king's seer.**—Comp. 1 Chron. xxv. 1—6.

**They might not depart.**—Rather, *they had no need to depart from their service* (*i.e.*, to leave their posts), in order to prepare their own passover and the subsequent meals, "for their brethren the Levites had prepared for them," and brought it to them at their several stations.

(16) **The same day.**—*On that day, i.e.,* "at that time" (verse 17.)

*The Solemn Passover.*  II. CHRONICLES, XXXV.  *Charchemish Invaded.*

vice of the LORD was prepared the same day, to keep the passover, and to offer burnt offerings upon the altar of the LORD, according to the commandment of king Josiah. <sup>(17)</sup> And the children of Israel that were ¹present kept the passover at that time, and the feast of unleavened bread seven days.

<sup>(18)</sup> And there was no passover like to that kept in Israel from the days of Samuel the prophet; neither did all the kings of Israel keep such a passover as Josiah kept, and the priests, and the Levites, and all Judah and Israel that were present, and the inhabitants of Jerusalem. <sup>(19)</sup> In the eighteenth year of the reign of Josiah was this passover kept.

<sup>(20)</sup> ªAfter all this, when Josiah had prepared the ²temple, Necho king of Egypt came up to fight against Charchemish by Euphrates: and Josiah went out against him. <sup>(21)</sup> But he sent ambassadors to him, saying, What have I to do with thee, thou king of Judah? *I come* not against thee this day, but against ³the house wherewith I have war: for God commanded me to make haste: forbear thee from *meddling with* God, who *is* with me, that he destroy

1 Heb., *found.*
a 2 Kings 23. 29.
2 Heb., *house.*
3 Heb., *the house of my war.*

---

**To offer burnt offerings.**—To burn the fat of the Passover victims, and of the peace offerings. The verse summarises the foregoing account. (Comp. verse 10.)

CHARACTER OF THE PASSOVER THUS HELD, AND ITS DATE (verses 17—19).

<sup>(17)</sup> **At that time.**—The Passover was kept on the evening of the 14th Nisan, and the Mazzoth from the 15th to the 21st of the same month.

<sup>(18)</sup> **And there was no Passover like to that.**—2 Kings xxiii. 22.

**From the days of Samuel the prophet.**—Kings, "from the days of the judges that judged Israel," of whom Samuel was the last and greatest (1 Sam. vii. 15).

**Neither did all the kings of Israel.**—Kings, "and (from) all the days of the kings of Israel and the kings of Judah." (Comp. chap. xxx 26).

**And the priests . . . Jerusalem.**—Not in Kings. A characteristic addition.

**Israel that were present.**—Rather, *Israel that was present,* i.e., the remnant who had come from the ruined kingdom of the ten tribes. (Comp. chap. xxxiv. 33).

<sup>(19)</sup> **In the eighteenth year.**—2 Kings xxiii. 23.

**Kept.**—*Made* (*na'asāh*). For the date, comp. chap. xxxiv. 8. The religious reformation appropriately *culminated* in a splendid celebration of the Passover.

JOSIAH SLAIN IN BATTLE AGAINST NECHO KING OF EGYPT (verses 20—27. Comp. 2 Kings xxiii. 29, 30, and 3 Ezra i. 23—30).

<sup>(20)</sup> **After all this.**—Comp. the similar, "after these matters, and this faithfulness" (chap. xxxii. 1). The phrase calls attention to the difference between the event and what might naturally have been expected. In spite of Josiah's fidelity to Jehovah, *this* was his end.

**Necho king of Egypt came up.**—Kings, "In his days came up Pharaoh Necho, king of Egypt." So LXX. here. Syriac, "Pharaoh the Lame, king of Egypt." *Pharaoh* is simply "the king;" Coptic *Pouro,* or *Perro* (*pi* "the," *ouro* or *r̄ro,* "king"). The Hebrew spelling *Pa'rōh* appears to be due to an assimilation of the Egyptian word to the Hebrew *pěrā'ôth,* "leaders" (Judges v. 1). An inscription of Assurbanipal gives a list of twenty subject kings appointed by Esarhaddon his father to bear rule in Egypt, the first name in the list being that of "*Niku̇ sar ali*

*Mimpi u ali Sáa,*" i.e., "Necho, king of the city of Memphis, and the city of Sais." Assurbanipal twice reinstated this Necho (Necho I., circ. 664 B.C.) after vanquishing Tirhakah.

The Necho of our text is Necho II., who reigned circ. 610 B.C. (See the Note on 2 Kings xxiii. 29.)

**Against Charchemish.**—*At Charchemish.* Syriac and Arabic, "to assault Mabûg," i.e., Hierapolis. Necho's enemy was "the king of Assyria" (2 Kings xxiii. 29; so LXX. here), i.e., Esarhaddon II. (Saracus), the last of the rulers of Nineveh; not Nabopalassar, king of Babylon, for the Assyrian empire had not yet fallen before the united assault of the Medes and the Babylonians. Charchemish has been identified with the modern *Jirbâs,* on the western bank of the middle Euphrates. Its situation, as Schrader observes, suits an intended expedition against Nineveh and Assyria, rather than against Babylon. It was one of the great Hittite capitals, and inscriptions in hieroglyphics, similar to those of Hamath, have recently been disinterred on the site, and brought thence to the British Museum. The name means, "Fortress of Mish." Comp. "Mesha" (Gen. x. 30), the Assyrian *Masu,* i.e., the part of the Syrian desert which ran along the right bank of the Euphrates. The place was also called *Tel-Mish,* "mound of Mish;" Greek, Τελμησσός. (Thenius thinks the phrase, "against Charchemish," was originally a marginal gloss, noting the place of the final and decisive encounter between Necho and the Babylonians).

**Josiah went out against him.**—To this statement Kings only adds that Necho "slew him at Megiddo, when he saw him," i.e., at the outset of the encounter. The chronicler, therefore, has derived the details of the following verses from another source (verses 21—25).

<sup>(21)</sup> **But . . . ambassadors.**—*And . . . messengers.*

**What have I to do with thee?**—Literally, *what to me and to thee?* τί ἐμοὶ καὶ σοί; (LXX.; and Mark v. 7; Luke viii. 28).

**I come not against thee.**—So the old versions. The Hebrew is, "not against thee—thee—to-day." The versions appear to have read *'attāh,* "thee," with different points as *'ōtheh,* "coming." (Comp. Syriac, *ôthê 'nô,* "come I.")

**But against the house . . . war.**—A strange expression. (Comp. 1 Chron xviii. 10.) Probably the reading indicated by 3 Esdr. i. 25 is right (ἐπὶ γὰρ τοῦ Εὐφράτου ὁ πόλεμος μού ἐστί), "but against the Euphrates is my war" (*Perath* for *béth*). Josephus supports this

449

*Josiah is Slain.* **II. CHRONICLES, XXXVI.** *Jehoahaz Succeeds him.*

thee not. (22) Nevertheless Josiah would not turn his face from him, but disguised himself, that he might fight with him, and hearkened not unto the words of Necho from the mouth of God, and came to fight in the valley of Megiddo. (23) And the archers shot at king Josiah; and the king said to his servants, Have me away; for I am sore ¹wounded. (24) His servants therefore took him out of that chariot, and put him in the second chariot that he had; and they brought him to Jerusalem, and he died, and was buried ²in *one of* the sepulchres of his fathers. And ᵃall Judah and Jerusalem mourned for Josiah. (25) And Jeremiah lamented for Josiah: and all the singing men and the singing women spake of Josiah in their lamentations to this day, and made them an ordinance in Israel: and, behold, they *are* written in the lamentations.

(26) Now the rest of the acts of Josiah, and his ³goodness, according to *that which was* written in the law of the LORD, (27) and his deeds, first and last, behold, they *are* written in the book of the kings of Israel and Judah.

CHAPTER XXXVI.—(1) Then ᵇthe people of the land took Jehoahaz the son of Josiah, and made him king in his father's stead in Jerusalem. (2) Jehoahaz *was* twenty and three years old

1 Heb., *made sick.*
2 Or, *among the sepulchres.*
a Zech. 12. 11.
3 Heb., *kindnesses.*
B.C. 610.
b 2 Kings 23. 30, &c.

---

LXX. and Syriac omit; Vulg., "sed contra aliam pugno domum."

**For God . . . haste.**—*And God . . .* The Egyptian kings, like those of Israel, consulted their prophets before undertaking any expedition. So did the Assyrians, as abundantly appears from their inscriptions. So, too, we read on the Moabite stone, "Chemosh said unto me, Go; take Nebo . . . Go up against Horonaim, and take it." These facts sufficiently explain the text, without assuming that Necho had received an oracle *from Jehovah,* or was referring to the God of Israel. (Comp. Herod. ii. 158.)

(22) **But disguised himself.**—Like Ahab (chap. xviii. 29). The LXX. reads, "he strengthened himself," or "persisted" (ἐκραταιώθη). (Comp. 3 Esdr. i. 28.) This implies the reading *hithᶜhazzaq* instead of *hithᶜhappēsh.* It is wholly unlikely that "disguised himself" is used in the figurative sense of "departed from his true character," as Keil and Zöckler think.

**The words of Necho from the mouth of God.**—The warning of Necho was really divine, as the event proved. For "words of Necho," 3 Esdr. i. 26 has, "words of the prophet Jeremiah;" but there is no trace of such a warning in the extant prophecies bearing his name.

**In the valley of Megiddo.**—The valley of the Kishon, where Deborah and Barak had fought in the olden time against Jabin and Sisera. Herodotus (ii. 159) calls the place Magdolus. (See on 2 Kings xxiii. 29.)

(23) **And the archers shot.**—Comp. the death of Ahab (chap. xviii. 33, and of Saul, 1 Chron. x. 3).

**Have me away.**—LXX., ἐξαγάγετέ με. "Take me out" (of the war-chariot).

**For I am sore wounded.**—So Ahab. (chap. xviii. 33.)

(24) **That chariot.**—*The* (war) *chariot.*

**Put him.**—*Made him ride.*

**Brought him to Jerusalem, and he died.**—2 Kings xxiii. 30 says: "And his servants made him ride dead (or *dying*) from Megiddo." Even if it be not permissible to render *mēth* "dying," we cannot agree with the suggestion of Thenius that the account of Chronicles is simply an arbitrary alteration of the older narrative for the sake of literary effect. The divergence proves that the chronicler had special sources of information at his command.

**The second chariot** was no doubt a more comfortable one, reserved in case of such an emergency.

**In one of the sepulchres.**—Omit *one of.* Kings, "in his own sepulchre," which would be a chamber among those of his immediate ancestors, Manasseh and Amon. (See 2 Kings xxi. 18.)

**Mourned.**—*Were mourning.*

(25) **And Jeremiah lamented** —*i.e.,* wrote a dirge. The special mourning of the land over Josiah is not mentioned in Kings.

**The singing men . . . women.**—The LXX. has "the ruling men . . . women," reading *sārím . . . sārôth,* instead of *shārîm . . . shārôth.*

**Spake of Josiah in their lamentations.**—In the dirges which they used to sing on certain anniversaries of disaster.

**And made them an ordinance.**—*And they made them* (i.e. the laments for Josiah) *a standing custom to Israel.*

**They are written in the lamentations.**—The dirges alluding to Josiah's untimely end, and among them Jeremiah's, were preserved in a Book of Dirges (*qinôth*), which may have been extant in the chronicler's day. (Comp. the allusions in Jer. xxii. 10, 18; Zech. xii. 11.)

This collection, however, was quite different from the canonical book of Lamentations, the subject of which is the ruin of Judah and Jerusalem by the Chaldeans.

(26) **His goodness.** — *His pious deeds* (chap. xxxii. 32).

**According to that . . . the Lord.**—Said of no king besides.

**The book . . . and Judah.**—2 Kings xxiii. 28, "the Book of the chronicles of the kings of Judah."

## XXXVI.

THE REIGN OF JEHOAHAZ (verses 1—4). (Comp. 2 Kings xxiii. 30—35; 3 Esdr. i. 32—36.)

(1) **Then.**—*And.*

**The people of the land took Jehoahaz.**—Comp. chap. xxvi. 1; xxxiii. 25. Jehoahaz or Shallum was not the firstborn (1 Chron. iii 15). See Notes on 2 Kings xxiii. 30, with which this verse agrees.

(2) **Jehoahaz was twenty and-three.** — So Kings, adding the mother's name as usual. (So the LXX. here.)

when he began to reign, and he reigned three months in Jerusalem. (3) And the king of Egypt ¹put him down at Jerusalem, and ²condemned the land in an hundred talents of silver and a talent of gold. (4) And the king of Egypt made Eliakim his brother king over Judah and Jerusalem, and turned his name to Jehoiakim. And Necho took Jehoahaz his brother, and carried him to Egypt.

(5) Jehoiakim *was* twenty and five years old when he began to reign, and he reigned eleven years in Jerusalem: and

¹ Heb., *removed him.*
² Heb., *mulcted.*
³ Or, *chains.*
*a* 2 Kings 24. 13; Dan. i. 1, 2.

he did *that which was* evil in the sight of the LORD his God. (6) Against him came Nebuchadnezzar king of Babylon, and bound him in ³fetters, to carry him to Babylon. (7) *a* Nebuchadnezzar also carried off the vessels of the house of the LORD to Babylon, and put them in his temple at Babylon.

(8) Now the rest of the acts of Jehoiakim, and his abominations which he did, and that which was found in him, behold they *are* written in the book of the kings of Israel and Judah:

---

(3) **And the king of Egypt put him down at Jerusalem.**—Rather, *removed him.* 3 Esdr. i. 33 adds "from reigning," which is almost demanded by the context. The LXX. follows the reading of 2 Kings xxiii. 33: "And Pharaoh-necho bound him in Riblah, in the land of Hamath, from reigning (*i.e.*, so that he reigned not) in Jerusalem"; but the Syriac and Vulg. support the existing Hebrew text. The LXX. begins the verse thus: "And he did the evil before the Lord, according to all that his fathers had done;" and adds, after the clause about the fine, "and the king took him away to Egypt."

**Condemned the land in.**—*Fined the land.*—So Kings: "laid a fine upon the land."

Riblah was in Syria, on the river Orontes. Necho may have ordered or enticed Jehoahaz to meet him there.

(4) **And the king of Egypt made Eliakim.**—The verse agrees with 2 Kings xxiii. 34.

**Carried him to Egypt.**—*Made him come.* Kings, "and he came to Egypt, and died there." Comp. Jeremiah xxii. 10—12. The LXX. adds: "and the silver and the gold he gave to the Pharaoh. Then the land began to be assessed, in order to give the money into the mouth of Pharaoh. And each according to ability used to demand the silver and the gold from the people of the land to give to Pharaoh-necho."

THE REIGN OF JEHOIAKIM (verses 5—8). (Comp. 2 Kings xxiii. 36—xxiv. 7; 3 Esdr. i. 37—41; Jer. xxv. xxvi.)

(5) **Jehoiakim . . . in Jerusalem.**—2 Kings xxiii. 36, adding the mother's name. here. So LXX.

**And he did . . . the Lord.**—2 Kings xxiii. 37, which adds "according to all that his fathers had done." So LXX.

**Nebuchadnezzar king of Babylon.**—*Nabium-kudurri-uçur* ("Nebo guard the crown!") son of Nabopalassar, who had founded this dynasty by successful revolt against Assyria. His extant inscriptions chiefly relate to palace and temple building. Schrader gives a short inscription from a brick now in the Zürich Museum. "Nabû-Kudurri-uçur, king of Babylon, restorer of Esagili and Ezida [two famous temples], son of Nabû-abala-uçur, King of Babylon am I." No really historical inscription is known except a fragment relating to his Egyptian campaign in his 37th year (568 B.C.), and an illegible one on the rocks of *Nahr-el-Kelb* near Beirut. The LXX. here interpolates the account of Jehoiakim's three years of vassalage, and his revolt against Nebuchadnezzar, and the other events and reflections contained in 2 Kings xxiv. 1—4. The LXX. makes Jehoiakim, instead of Manasseh, "fill Jerusalem with innocent blood," contrary to the Hebrew text.

**And bound him in fetters.** — *Two bronze* (*chains*), as in chap. xxxiii. 11.

**To carry him to Babylon.**—*To make him go.* It is not said that this intention was carried out. (Comp. chap. xxxiii, 11, "and carried him to Babylon.") Nebuchadnezzar, who, according to Jer. xlvi. 2, had defeated Necho in a great battle at Carchemish, in the 4th year of Jehoiakim, appears to have left the king of Judah to reign as a vassal-king, after inflicting upon him a severe humiliation. (The LXX., 3 Esdr., Vulg., and Arabic, but not the Syriac, read: "and carried him to Babylon.") Thenius says this must be the right reading, and then denies its claim to credibility. He further *asserts* that, "in order to allow ample scope for the fulfilment of the prophecy of Jeremiah" (see Note on verse 8), the chronicler has represented Jehoiakim as carried alive to Babylon in the last year of his reign. This statement rests not upon *objective* historical grounds, but upon *subjective* prejudices against the chronicler.

Dan. i. 1, by a transcriber's error, puts this first capture of Jerusalem by Nebuchadnezzar in the *third* year of Jehoiakim; whereas Nebuchadnezzar only became king in the fourth of Jehoiakim. (2 Kings xxv. 8; Jer. xxv. 1.)

(7) **Nebuchadnezzar also carried.**—*And of the vessels of the house . . . did Nebuchadnezzar bring.* Not mentioned in Kings, but confirmed by Dan. i. 2.

**In his temple.**—The temple of "Merodach, my Lord" (*Bilu, i.e., Bel*), whom his inscriptions so frequently mention. The great temple of Belus (Bel Merodach), which Nebuchadnezzar built, was one of the wonders of the world to Herodotus (Herod. i. 181 *seq.*)

(8) **Now the rest of the acts.**—(Comp. 2 Kings xxiv. 5.)

**And his abominations which he did.** — His crimes against God and man, *i.e.*, probably acts of idolatry and tyranny. (Comp. Jer. xxv. 6, vii. 5—11, xxii. 13—19; covetousness, shedding innocent blood, &c., charged against him.)

**That which was found in him.**—Chap. xix. 3, His general character and conduct.

As in the case of Amon (chap. xxxiii. 25), the last particulars about Jehoiakim are omitted in this flying notice of his reign, which was only memorable because of the invasion of Nebuchadnezzar. The LXX., however, gives instead of this verse 2 Kings xxiv. 5—6, in-

and ¹Jehoiachin his son reigned in his stead. ⁽⁹⁾ ᵃ Jehoiachin *was* eight years old when he began to reign, and he reigned three months and ten days in Jerusalem: and he did *that which was* evil in the sight of the LORD. ⁽¹⁰⁾ And ²when the year was expired, king Nebuchadnezzar sent, and brought him to Babylon, with the ³goodly vessels of the house of the LORD, and made ⁴ Zedekiah his brother king over Judah and Jerusalem.

⁽¹¹⁾ ᵇ Zedekiah *was* one and twenty years old when he began to reign, and reigned eleven years in Jerusalem. ⁽¹²⁾ And he did *that which was* evil in the sight of the LORD his God, *and* humbled not himself before Jeremiah the prophet *speaking* from the mouth of the LORD. ⁽¹³⁾ And he also rebelled against king Nebuchadnezzar, who had made him swear by God: but he stiffened his neck, and hardened his heart from turning unto the LORD God of Israel.

⁽¹⁴⁾ Moreover all the chief of the priests, and the people, transgressed very much after all the abominations of the heathen; and polluted the house of the LORD which he had hallowed in Jerusalem. ⁽¹⁵⁾ ᶜAnd the LORD God of their fathers sent to them ⁵ by his messengers, rising up ⁶betimes, and sending; because he had compassion on his people,

| 1 Or, *Jeconiah,* 1 Chron. 3. 16; or, *Coniah,* Jer. 22. 24. |
| a 2 Kings 24. 8. |
| 2 Heb., *at the return of the year.* |
| 3 Heb., *vessels of desire.* |
| 4 Or, *Mattaniah,* 2 Kings 24. 17; Jer. 37. 1. |
| b Jer. 52. 1, &c.; 2 Kings 24. 18. |
| c Jer. 25. 3, & 35. 15. |
| 5 Heb., *by the hand of his messengers.* |
| 6 That is, *continually and carefully.* |

---

terpolating in the latter "and was buried with his fathers in the garden of Uzza" (ἐν γανοζαῆ or γανοζάν; see 2 Kings xxi. 26). Thenius says "these words *certainly* (!) stood in the original text," but were omitted by the chronicler and the editor of Kings, because *they conflict with the prophecy of* Jeremiah (chaps. xxii. 18, 19, xxxvi. 30)—which is apparently the reason why he is so sure of their genuineness.

JEHOIACHIN (verses 9—10). (Comp. 2 Kings xxiv. 8—17; 3 Esdr. i. 41—44; Jer. xxii. 24—30; Ezek. xix. 5—9.)

⁽⁹⁾ **Jehoiachin was eight years old.**—2 Kings xxiv. 8 has correctly "eighteen;" and so some MSS., LXX. (Alex.), Syriac, Arabic. What the prophet Ezekiel says of him could not apply to a boy of eight. (The difference turns on the omission of the smallest Hebrew letter, namely, *yod*, which as a numeral represents *ten*.)

**Three months and ten days.**—Kings, "three months;" Syriac and Arabic here have "one hundred days," *i.e.*, three months and ten days. Thenius thinks the ten days were added, in order that the catastrophe of Jehoiachin's reign might fall on a *tenth* day of the month, like the investment of Jerusalem and the fall of the city under Zedekiah (chap. xxv. 1, 8).

**He did that which was evil.**—2 Kings xxiv. 9. (See also the above-cited passages of Jeremiah and Ezekiel.) According to the latter prophet, Jehoiachin "devoured men, and forced widows, and wasted cities."

⁽¹⁰⁾ **And when the year was expired.**—See margin. "At the return of the year" means in spring, when kings usually went forth to war. (2 Sam. xi. 1; 1 Kings xx. 22.) Kings gives a full account of the siege and surrender of Jerusalem, and the deportation to Babylon of the king and all his princes and men of war, by "the servants of Nebuchadnezzar."

**With the goodly vessels.**—Chap. xxxii. 27. "Some of the vessels" had already been carried off (verse 7). (See 2 Kings xxiv. 13 and Jer. xxvii. 18—22.)

**Zedekiah his brother.**—Zedekiah was *uncle* of Jehoiachin, being a son of Josiah, and brother of Jehoiakim. Perhaps "brother" is equivalent to "kinsman" here, as elsewhere. (Comp. 1 Chron. iii. 15, where Zedekiah appears as a son of Josiah; and 2 Kings xxiv. 17.) The versions read "his father's brother"—a correction. Thenius thinks the word for "uncle" had become illegible in the MS. here used by the chronicler.

ZEDEKIAH AND THE FINAL CATASTROPHE (verses 11—21). (Comp. 2 Kings xxiv. 18—xxv. 21; Jer. xxxix., lii.; 3 Esdr. i. 44—55.)

⁽¹¹⁾ **Zedekiah was one and twenty.**—So 2 Kings xxiv. 18, adding his mother's name (Hamutal, who was also mother of Jehoahaz).

**Before Jeremiah . . . mouth of the Lord.**—Not in Kings. (Comp. Jer. xxi. xxii. 1—10, xxvii. xxviii., xxxii.—xxxiv., xxxvii., xxxviii.)

Two special sins of Zedekiah are mentioned in this and the next verse—viz., his disregard of Jeremiah's counsel, and his perjury to Nebuchadnezzar.

⁽¹³⁾ **And he also rebelled.**—2 Kings xxiv. 20.

**Who had made him swear by God.**—When Nebuchadnezzar appointed Zedekiah vassal-king of Judah, he would naturally make him swear fealty to himself by the God of his fathers. The fact is not specially recorded in Kings; but the prophet Ezekiel makes it the point of a prophecy against the king and his grandees (Ezek. xvii. 11—21; comp. especially verse 17, "mine oath that he hath despised.")

But (*and*) **stiffened his neck and hardened his heart.**—(Comp. the like expression in Deut. ii. 30; 2 Kings xvii. 14; Jer. xix. 15.) Zedekiah was not personally unfavourable to the prophet Jeremiah, and consulted him more than once; but he was too weak and timorous to stand by the prophetic counsel, in defiance of his princes who were intriguing with Egypt.

SINS OF THE RULING CLASSES WHICH BROUGHT DOWN THE JUDGMENT OF GOD (verses 14—16). (Comp. with this passage 2 Kings xvii. 7—23.)

⁽¹⁴⁾ **The chiefs.**—*The princes.*

**Transgressed very much.**—*Committed manifold unfaithfulness.*

**After all the abominations . . .**—See Ezek. viii. 5—18; where "the princes of the priests and the people" are specially singled out in verses 11 and 16. The twenty-five men of the latter verse are the High Priest and the heads of the twenty-four courses of priests. (Comp. also Jer. xxxii. 32, *seq*).

**His Messengers.**—The prophets (2 Kings xvii. 13).

⁽¹⁵⁾ **Rising up betimes and sending.**—*i.e.*, constantly and earnestly. Jer. xxv. 3, 4: "The Lord hath

*Judah Spoiled*     II. CHRONICLES, XXXVI.     *by the Chaldeans.*

and on his dwelling place: (16) but they mocked the messengers of God, and despised his words, and misused his prophets, until the wrath of the LORD arose against his people, till *there was* no ¹remedy. (17) *ª* Therefore he brought upon them the king of the Chaldees, who slew their young men with the sword in the house of their sanctuary, and had no compassion upon young man or maiden, old man, or him that stooped for age: he gave *them* all into his hand. (18) And all the vessels of the house of God, great and small, and the treasures of the house of the LORD, and the treasures of the king, and of his princes; all *these* he brought to Babylon. (19) And they burnt the house of God, and brake down the wall of Jerusalem, and burnt all the palaces thereof with fire, and destroyed all the goodly vessels thereof. (20) And ² them that had escaped from the sword carried he away to Babylon; where they were servants to him and his sons until the reign of the kingdom of Persia: (21) to fulfil the word of the LORD by the mouth of *ᵇ* Jeremiah, until the land *ᶜ* had enjoyed her sabbaths: *for* as long as she lay desolate she kept sabbath, to fulfil threescore and ten years.

(22) *ᵈ* Now in the first year of Cyrus king

1 Heb., *healing.*
*a* 2 Kings 25. 1, &c.
2 Heb., *the remainder from the sword.*
*b* Jer. 25. 9, 12, & 29. 10.
*c* Lev. 26. 34, 35, 43.
*d* Ezra 1. 1.

---

sent all his servants, the prophets, rising early and sending them." (comp. also Jer. xxvi. 5; xxix. 19; xxxv. 14, 15).

**He had compassion on.**—*He spared, was forbearing with.*

**Dwelling place.**—*Mā̒ôn* (chap. xxx. 27; Ps. xxvi. 8; comp. Jer. xxv. 6).

(16) **But they mocked.**—*And they were mocking, mal'ibim;* only here (an Aramaism).

**Misused.**—*Mitta'te'im,* only here. *Derided,* strictly, *stammered.* Another form of this verb occurs in Gen. xxvii. 12. (Comp. for the fact Isa. xxviii. 9—14; Ezek. xxxiii., 30; Jer. xvii. 15, xx. 7, 8.)

**Till there was no remedy.**—*Healing;* i.e., deliverance, σωτηρία (comp. chap. xxi. 18). God is said to *heal,* when he averts calamity (chap. xxx. 20).

**The wrath . . . arose.**—*Went up ('ālăh),* like smoke (Ps. xviii. 8; 2 Sam. xi. 20).

(17) **Therefore he brought up.**—*And He caused to come up;* alluding to "the wrath . . went up."

**In the house of their sanctuary.**—Which they had polluted (verse 14). The scene of their sin witnessed their destruction.

**Him that stooped for age.**—Rather, *greyheaded, hoary (yāshēsh).* (Comp. Ezek. ix., where the horrors of the capture of Jerusalem are ascribed expressly to the Divine working; see also Jer. xv. 1—9; Deut. xxxii. 25.)

**He gave them all into his hand.**—Comp. Jer. xxxvii. 6, xxxii. 3, 4.

**Them all.**—Literally, *the whole, everything,* τὰ πάντα. "Them all" would be *kullām,* whereas the text is *hakkōl.* (So verse 18, "all these.") Jerusalem was taken 588 B.C.

(18) **All the vessels . . .** (the) **great and** (the) **small.**—See 2 Kings xxv. 13—17, for an inventory of the articles; also Jer. xxvii. 19 *seq.*

(19) **They burnt the house of God.**—2 Kings xxv. 9.

**Brake down the wall . . .**—Jer. xxxix. 8; 2 Kings xxv. 9, 10.

**And destroyed all the goodly vessels.**—Literally, *And all her delightsome vessels were for destroying (lĕhashᶜhith).* (Comp. Isa. lxiv. 11): "all our pleasant things are laid waste." 2 Kings xxv. 13 speaks of the breaking-up of the great vessels of the Temple, for the sake of carrying off their material more easily.

**Servants to him and his sons . . . kingdom of Persia.**—A fulfilment of Jeremiah's prophecy concerning Nebuchadnezzar: "And all nations shall serve him, and his son, and his son's son, until the time of his own land come" (Jer. xxvii. 7). Comp. also Isaiah's word to Hezekiah (2 Kings xx. 18.)

(21) **To fulfil.**—*lĕmallôth* (an Aramaised form).

**The word . . . Jeremiah.**—The seventy years of Babylonian exile are predicted in Jer. xxv. 11—12. (Comp. also Jer. xxix. 10: "Thus saith the Lord, After seventy years be accomplished for Babylon, I will visit you.")

**Until the land had enjoyed her sabbaths.**—"Enjoyed" is *rāçĕthāh,* which Gesenius renders *persolvit,* "made good," "discharged," as a debt. The meaning is that during the long years of the exile, the land would enjoy that rest of which it had been defrauded by the neglect of the law concerning the sabbatical years (Lev. xxv. 1—7). The following words, "as long as she lay desolate she kept sabbath" (literally, *all the days of the desolation she rested*) are taken from Lev. xxvi. 34, 35.

**To fulfil threescore and ten years.**—i.e., in order to fulfil the seventy years of exile foretold by Jeremiah.

We have no right whatever to press the words of the sacred writer, in the sense of assuming that he means to say that when Jerusalem was taken by the Chaldeans exactly seventy sabbatical years had been neglected—that is, that the law in this respect had not been observed for 490 years (70×7), or ever since the institution of monarchy in Israel (490 + 588 = 1,078).

The seventy years are reckoned from the 4th of Jehoiakim, when the prophecy was uttered (Jer. xxv. 1, 12), to the first year of Cyrus, and the return under Zerubbabel, 536 B.C.

THE EDICT OF CYRUS, AUTHORISING THE RETURN (verses 22, 23). (Comp. Ezra i. 1—3; 3 Esdr. ii. 1—5; Isa. xliv. 28, xlv.—xlvii.)

(22) **Now in the first year of Cyrus.**—This verse is the same as Ezra i. 1, save that it has "by the mouth" instead of "from the mouth." The latter is probably correct. (Comp. verse 12 *supra.*) So some MSS. here also.

**That the word . . . Jeremiah.**—Concerning the seventy years.

**Stirred up the spirit.**—1 Chron. v. 26; 2 Chron. xxi. 16.

**That he made a proclamation.**—*And he made a voice pass* (chap. xxx. 5).

of Persia, that the word of the LORD *spoken* by the mouth of *ª Jeremiah might be accomplished,* the LORD stirred up the spirit of Cyrus king of Persia, that he made a proclamation throughout all his kingdom, and *put it* also in writing, saying, <sup>(23)</sup> Thus saith Cyrus king of Persia, All the kingdoms of the earth hath the LORD God of heaven given me; and he hath charged me to build him an house in Jerusalem, which *is* in Judah. Who *is there* among you of all his people? The LORD his God *be* with him, and let him go up.

*a* Jer. 25. 12, 13, & 29. 10.

**Throughout all his kingdom . . . and put it also in writing.**—*Into all . . . and also into a writing.*

**Writing.**—*Miktāb* (chap. xxxv. 4.)

**The Lord.**—*Iahweh.* Instead of this Ezra i. 3 has, *Iehi,* " Be ; " so also 3 Esdr. ii. 5. " The Lord—with him! " (*Iahweh 'immô*) is a frequent formula in the chronicle, and is probably correct here. (Some Hebrew MSS. and the Vulg. unite the readings.)

**And let him go up.**—Whither ? The sentence is abruptly broken off here, but continued in Ezra i. 3. As to the relation between the Chronicles and Ezra, see Introduction.

**Thus saith Cyrus, king of Persia.**—Comp. the words of Darius Hystaspes on the famous Behistun Inscription, which begins " I am Darius, the great king, the king of kings, the king of Persia ; " while every paragraph opens with " Saith Darius the king."

**All the kingdoms . . . given me.**—Comp. the words of Darius: " Saith Darius the king :—By the grace of Ormazd I am king ; Ormazd has granted me the empire."

**The Lord God of heaven.**—*Jehovah, the God of heaven.* " The god of heaven " was a title of Ormazd or Ahuramazda, the Supreme Being according to Persian belief, which was Zoroastrianism. It is not at all wonderful that Cyrus should have identified the God of Israel with his own deity, especially if he had heard of the prophecies Isa. xliv. 28, &c. Such a politic syncretism was the settled practice of the Roman empire in a later age.

# EZRA

# GENERAL INTRODUCTION
## TO
# EZRA AND NEHEMIAH

ALTHOUGH these two books have distinct authors, they describe consecutive periods of the same general stage of Jewish history, and in many respects are closely linked. Hence much of the matter introductory to their exposition must necessarily be common to the two, and equally applicable to both.

I. The names of Ezra and Nehemiah are combined in revelation after a manner of which Moses and Aaron furnish the only parallel. The analogy, though not perfect, will bear to be followed out to a certain extent. Strictly speaking, Zerubbabel and Joshua were the Moses and Aaron of the new Israel redeemed from captivity in Babylon. But these two names fade in the presence of their greater successors, who finished the work they only began. This has been the view of Jewish tradition; and Christian sentiment agrees with Jewish tradition. Here, however, the analogy begins to fail. Judaism has always regarded the priest Ezra alone as the restorer of the law and the polity, making Nehemiah with his book merely an adjunct; just as the Pentateuch was "the book of the law of Moses," Aaron being altogether or almost kept out of view. When we go to the Scriptures themselves, Ezra and Nehemiah, the spiritual and the civil rulers of the new constitution, have an equal dignity, and both are very subordinate characters in comparison with those first organs of Divine revelation. They introduce nothing really original; they bring no new tables from the Mount; they have no Urim and Thummim; and are rather administrators of a revived law than legislators themselves. A few minor institutions owe their origin to Nehemiah. But neither he nor Ezra was directly the founder of the synagogue and other great additions to the Mosaic economy. The greatness of these two names is, in fact, very much the result of wonderful traditions which have been most prodigal in their honour, and especially in the glorification of Ezra.

II. Ezra and Nehemiah are both, though in different ways, connected by Jewish tradition with the final settlement of the Old Testament canon. Among the early Fathers an opinion was current that, when the originals of Scripture were burned with the Temple, Ezra, by inspiration of the Holy Spirit, restored the Law and the Prophets, adding or authenticating the books which were afterwards written. Another tradition is preserved in the Mishna, and has found more favour, that Ezra, or Ezra and Nehemiah, instituted the GREAT SYNAGOGUE, numbering 120 associates, and in conjunction with them settled the limits of the canon. In many parts of the Talmud such a college is referred to; but neither the canonical nor the apocryphal scriptures yield this tradition any real support. The "company of scribes" of 1 Macc. vii. 12 has been supposed to refer to this body. But 2 Macc. ii. 13 gives the tradition a different form. It alludes to and quotes certain "writings and commentaries" of Nehemiah, and describes him as having "established a library" or collection of holy documents, including historical and prophetical books and writings of David, thus not obscurely pointing to the threefold conventional order of our present canonical volume. If we understand the "letters of kings concerning offerings" to mean the decrees of the Persian monarchs that make up a large part of our two books, the tradition may be understood to embrace the whole canon. It will be seen that there are traces in Nehemiah of interpolation as late as the days of Alexander the Great; and the question of the final ratification of the Hebrew canon is one still involved in obscurity.

III. The relation of these two to the other historical books of the canon has been matter of some controversy. Without any support from subsequent Jewish literature, a certain class of critics have invented a later editor, who, living in the time of the Greek Dominion, constructed the Chronicles, Ezra, and Nehemiah as one series of historical works. Agreeing in this, the hypotheses then differ; and their differences are of such a character as to confirm our confidence in the traditional view that the three books are distinct, that their true common editor was Ezra, and that only a very few additions were left for aftertimes. While the end of Chronicles is the beginning of Ezra, a long and unrecorded period comes between; Ezra and Nehemiah give the history of a totally different century of the national life; and they close the inspired historical records of the ancient nation. Malachi alone comes after them; while Haggai and Zechariah immediately precede, or rather they delivered their predictions in the days which the former part of Ezra describes. The last historical books of the Old Testament are works of which the authors were to a great extent editors also; and there is every reason to think that the chief of these editors was Ezra, who put the finishing touches on all that preceded his own annals. It can hardly be maintained that his editorship included the book of Nehemiah, seeing that this contains a long list of names almost entirely coinciding with a similar list in his predecessor.

IV. The authenticity of these two records cannot be reasonably called in question: the only attacks proceed from that style of criticism which makes the entire history of the Old Testament a series of inventions based on but a slight substratum of actual events. There is nothing here but a series of plain statements concerning a great historical fact which cannot be called in question. We observe the same use of public documents and genealogical lists with which the rest of the Bible makes us familiar. The sources are never referred to as such; for both writers, from their position, were above the necessity of giving their authorities. But we may be sure that the history of the first return under Zerubbabel had been preserved, and only required Ezra's abridgment. The Persian documents quoted were in public archives. There is not an incident recorded, nor a character introduced, which is out of keeping with internal probability or external independent vouchers. The simplicity of the narrative and its utter absence of disguise, when recording the humble estate and deep unworthiness of the rescued people, plead irresistibly for the truth of the whole. The very dislocations of the narratives, with the repetition of lists, are in favour of the trustworthiness of the narrators. The want of strict agreement between them in names and numbers here and there simply indicates that the text, especially that of Ezra, is not in a perfect state. It must be admitted that the discrepancies between the two books themselves, as also between both and the Chronicles, are very numerous: no two lists perfectly agree either in order of names or amount of numbers. But a careful and dispassionate examination of the differences will lead to the conclusion that the text of one or the other or of both has suffered through transcription. Besides what has been said on this subject in former Introductions, something in the nature of historical vindication will be found in the course of the exposition itself.

V. As these two books give the history of the return from the Captivity, they cannot be understood without some knowledge of the character of that Captivity. In the last words of inspiration before our history commences the prophecies of Jeremiah are put into an historical form; the people were to be servants in Babylon until the reign of the kingdom of Persia; and the emptied land was to enjoy her Sabbaths, in sad vindication of ages of Sabbath neglect, " to fulfil threescore and ten years." But there was mercy in the great visitation. Though the bondmen were sometimes made to howl (Isa. lii. 5), they were also to have peace in the peace of the place of their captivity for which they prayed (Jer. xxix. 5—7). They rose to wealth in the enjoyment of civil rights; they occupied places of high trust in the courts of their oppressors; they maintained their religious customs as far as they might do so in a strange land; above all, they kept alive their hope of restoration, and in token of this carefully preserved the records of their genealogies. These important facts have their illustration at all points in the books which contain the history of the Return.

VI. It follows that the events of which Ezra and Nehemiah are the historians must be studied in the light of the purposes of God in regard to His ancient people, and can be understood only in that light. In other words, they form a chapter in the history of redemption. It must needs be that the " holy seed "—holy because of it Christ was to come according to the flesh—should be kept undefiled among the nations, that the " holy land " should be ready to become the land of Immanuel, that the " holy city " should both welcome and reject Him as its king, and that the " holy place " should receive the true High Priest, and be closed by His voice. Generally speaking, it was necessary, for the fulfilment of prophecy, for the maintenance of true religion in the world, and for the preparation of the earthly sphere of the Incarnate Son, that the ancient polity should be renewed and kept up until the " fulness of time." Their relation to the future Saviour of the world—its present Saviour not yet revealed—gave to the Jewish remnant, and to everything connected with their history, an immeasurable importance. We may not be able to see the precise bearing on this of many details in these books and that of Esther; nor is it necessary to believe that many of them—in a certain sense the greater part of the minute narrative, with its genealogical and other lists—had any such precise bearing. Granted the general necessity for the new life of the people, as a witness of the past and the future, the particulars of its new history become on that account important. To sum up, if we consider the re-establishment of the people and the revival of the worship of Zion as a record of past prophecy fulfilled, as a means of keeping up the knowledge of God and the hope of His Kingdom in the present, and as part of the great preparation for the supreme future of finished redemption—these three in one—then scarcely any detail in these narratives will be thought to be without its meaning. Nothing is more needful as a preparation for the study of our history than the deep conviction of this principle.

VII. It is a narrower view of the same subject that sees in these histories the foundation of that Judaism of the interval with which the Gospel narrative and the Christian Church are so intimately bound up. To understand this we must remember that with Ezra and Nehemiah and Esther are to be connected the final post-exile prophets, Haggai, Zechariah, and Malachi. The entire cycle, taken as a whole, reveals the tendencies of the Judaism which grew up after prophetic inspiration had ceased, and the finished development of which our Saviour found so utterly wanting. But in the process we must distinguish between the good and the evil. The good elements were many: the ancient Scriptures were restored to their place in the popular heart; Ezra was the first of an order of scribes entirely devoted to its exposition; and the synagogue worship, unknown in the Old Testament, was based on a revival of Sabbath devotion throughout the land. And the dispersion soon began to claim its rights beyond the land itself. Though Ezra and Nehemiah rebuilt the Temple and threw walls around Jerusalem—giving no hint themselves that the kingdom of God was on its way to the Gentiles—the prophets of their new economy were less restricted. And when the intermediate "fulness of time" came, Greek Scriptures and a Jewish service in Egypt and other lands paved the way for the Gospel. The evil elements were also very many. An internal, hard, ceremonial religion became, after four centuries, what the Lord found in Pharisaism; the scepticism which Malachi rebuked developed into Sadduceeism; and the descendants of the " perfect scribe " laid more than the foundation of Talmudical Rabbinism.

VIII. Out of this arises another canon, namely, that this portion of the history of the one CIVITAS DEI which runs through all ages has, like every other, its lessons to teach the Christian Church. In regard to this expositors have run into the usual opposite extremes. Some have gone so far as to find in Ezra and Nehemiah types of Christ; and their several and combined work has been made to prefigure the relations of Church and State for ever. It is easy to trace and condemn the error here. But we should be on our guard against the notion that the books contain only old history that has passed away. Devotion to the kingdom of God on the part of His servants, its grace and its dignity and its reward; opposition to that kingdom,

# EZRA AND NEHEMIAH.

its low endeavours, its futility, and its condemnation—these are lessons taught in every chapter. The everlasting distinction between the saints and the children of this world, and the importance of remembering this under all circumstances, is also taught. They who condemn the intolerance of Ezra and Nehemiah, and think the rigorous separation of the ancient people from their foreign wives a great mistake of these new legislators, altogether miss the lesson the books were intended to convey. The providence of God in the world, which is now the government of His Son the Head over all things to the Church, has no sublimer illustration than they present.—It may be added that the two writers, who are also the two main actors, are noble examples of the passive and active virtues of religion. Though their writings are not quoted in the New Testament, they contain a fair proportion of those precious apophthegms and watchwords of devotion that are the heritage of God's people in every age.

IX. It is of great importance to fix in the mind, before entering on the study of our two historians, a clear idea of the relation of the events they record to profane history and secular chronology. On one or two points opinions are divided; but the following dates may on the whole be relied on as most probably satisfying all demands:—

B.C. 558—529. Cyrus becomes king of the Medes and Persians, on the defeat of Astyages.
541. Belshazzar, vice-king of Babylon (Daniel's vision, chapter vii.).
538. Babylonian empire subverted, and Medo-Persian empire established by Cyrus. Darius the Mede made king of Babylon.
536. First year of Cyrus. Return under Zerubbabel (Ezra i.).
535. Second Temple founded (Ezra iii. 8).
529. Opposition of Samaritans (Ezra iv. 6). Cambyses (Ahasuerus of Ezra iv. 6).
522. Building of Temple stopped. Gomates or pseudo-Smerdis (Artaxerxes of Ezra iv. 7).
521—486. Darius I., son of Hystaspes, king of Persia, having slain Gomates (Ezra iv. 5—24, v. 5, vi. 1). Haggai and Zechariah begin their prophecies.
515. Second Temple completed (Ezra vi. 15).
486—465. Xerxes (Ahasuerus of Esther).
465—425. Artaxerxes Longimanus (Ezra vii. 1, Neh. ii. 1). Return of Jews under Ezra.
445. Nehemiah goes to Jerusalem (Neh. ii. 1, v. 14).
433. Nehemiah's return to Jerusalem (Neh. xiii. 6).
401—399. Malachi's last predictions. Death of Cyrus the Younger (also of Thucydides and Socrates).

X. The two books are the centre of what may be called the ESDRAS CYCLE of Biblical literature, the details of which are complicated, and must be studied in special works on the canon. The ancient Jews regarded the two canonical works as one, and in this they were followed by the early Fathers of the Christian Church. In the catalogues handed down to us they are distinguished as I. and II. Ezra or Esdras: so the Vulgate, Origen, and the Council of Laodicea. In the Alexandrine version, however, first comes our book of Ezra, with enlargements of various kinds; then, secondly, the genuine book itself; Nehemiah is there III. Esdras; and to these is added the later apocryphal IV. Esdras, containing certain final accretions to the Ezra literature. In the Vulgate the two added books, the enlarged translation and the apocryphal, are III. and IV. Ezra. At the close of the fourth century Jerome calls II. Ezra by the name of Nehemiah; and gradually its thoroughly independent character became generally recognised. For the character of the two apocryphal books—the latter of which has very little connection with the Biblical Ezra—works on the Apocrypha must be consulted. Suffice it to say here that what may be called—following the Greek style—I. Esdras is subordinately useful in some points of the textual criticism of our book of Ezra, especially where its numbers differ from those of Nehemiah.

# INTRODUCTION
## TO
# EZRA

I. All that is certainly known concerning Ezra is found in his own narrative as continued in Nehemiah. He was a priest, descended, through Seraiah, from Eleazar the son of Aaron; and also a scribe, devoted to the exposition of the Law of Moses. In the seventh year of Artaxerxes Longimanus, B.C. 458, he went from Babylon to Jerusalem at the head of a second company of the children of the Captivity, and with an ample commission for the restoration of the Temple and the reform of religion. After a rigorous inquisition into the abuses connected with mixed marriages, he is lost sight of, re-appearing afterwards in Nehemiah, with whom or under whom he takes part in the dedication of the wall and the conduct of religious service generally. He then finally disappears from the sacred history. Jewish tradition glorified his memory as second only to that of Moses. He is regarded as having been the first president of the "Great Synagogue," to which is attributed the settlement of the Jewish canon; to have instituted the synagogue service; to have been the organiser of much authoritative tradition traced down from Moses; to have introduced the present Hebrew type; and done other service to Jewish literature. Josephus says that he lived to a great age, and was buried in Jerusalem. Other traditions assign him a grave near Samara, after returning to Persia, and dying there aged 120.—There is no character in the Old Testament more perfect and complete than that of Ezra. We see him as a servant and as a master, as a student of the law and as its administrator, as supreme in authority and as subordinate, in public and private, uniformly and always the same devout, disinterested, patriotic lover of his people and friend of God.

II. The question of Ezra's authorship is closely connected with an analysis of the book. It contains two distinct records: one, of the first return from the Captivity under Zerubbabel, occupying six chapters; and the other, of the second detachment, under Ezra himself, occupying the remaining four. Between the two there is a chasm of fifty-seven years passed over in total silence. The former part, embracing a period of twenty-two years, from the memorable first year of Cyrus, B.C. 538, is mainly made up of extracts from archives which Ezra has woven into a narrative. Certain portions of this, as of the second part, are written in Chaldee: the documents, namely, are given in their original, and the writer, equally familiar with both forms of the Hebrew, does not quite limit himself to the documents themselves, the Chaldee overflowing here and there. Certainly the first six chapters may be regarded as Ezra's own compilation, and therefore as his own work. The second part gives the history of twelve months, being the record as it were of the discharge of a commission, narrating that in full and then abruptly breaking off. A close examination of the four chapters shows the same hand; the peculiar phrases—such as the "Lord God of Israel" and many others—are similar, with just those variations in uniformity which might be expected in one who had several languages at command. But there is one remarkable anomaly, that sometimes the first and sometimes the third person is used—an anomaly, however, that equally occurs in Daniel. It is to be explained at the outset by the humility of the writer, who introduces himself and his own character in the third person before he uses the direct style of narrative; and afterwards by the fact that public and great events are incorporated in the very style in which they were from time to time recorded. On the whole there is no reason to distrust the uniform tradition that has ascribed the whole book to Ezra.

# EZRA

**CHAPTER I.**—<sup>(1)</sup> Now in the first year of Cyrus king of Persia, that the word of the LORD <sup>a</sup> by the mouth of Jeremiah might be fulfilled, the LORD stirred up the spirit of Cyrus king of Persia, that he <sup>1</sup> made a proclamation throughout all his kingdom, and *put it* also in writing, saying,

<sup>(2)</sup> Thus saith Cyrus king of Persia, The LORD God of heaven hath given me all the kingdoms of the earth; and he hath <sup>b</sup> charged me to build him an house at Jerusalem, which *is* in Judah. <sup>(3)</sup> Who *is there* among you of all his people? his God be with him, and let him go up to Jerusalem, which *is* in Judah, and build the house of the LORD God of Israel, (he *is* the God,) which *is* in Jerusalem. <sup>(4)</sup> And whosoever remaineth in any place where he sojourneth, let the men of his place <sup>2</sup> help him with silver, and with gold, and with goods, and with beasts, beside the freewill offering for the house of God that *is* in Jerusalem.

<sup>(5)</sup> Then rose up the chief of the fathers of Judah and Benjamin, and the priests, and the Levites, with all *them* whose spirit God had raised, to go up to build the house of the LORD which *is* in Jerusalem. <sup>(6)</sup> And all they that *were* about them <sup>3</sup> strengthened their hands with vessels of silver, with gold, with goods,

*B.C. cir. 536.*

*a* 2 Chron. 36, 22; Jer. 25. 12; & 29. 10.

1 Heb., *caused a voice to pass.*

2 Heb., *lift him up.*

*b* Isa. 44. 28. & 45. 1, 13.

3 That is, *helped them.*

---

I. THE FIRST RETURN UNDER ZERUBBABEL.

(1–4) The decree of Cyrus: marking an epoch of very great importance, and therefore repeated almost word for word from the end of Chronicles.

<sup>(1)</sup> **The first year.**—Cyrus became king of Persia in B.C. 559. Twenty years afterwards he took Babylon from Belshazzar; and this first year of his rule in Babylon was his beginning as an agent in Jewish affairs and for the Kingdom of God.

**Stirred up.**—By a direct influence, probably through the instrumentality of Daniel. This prophet we may suppose Cyrus to have found in Babylon, and to have had his mind directed to the express prediction of Isa. xliv. 28, where his name is mentioned. But the writer, who again and again records the prophetic intervention of Haggai and Zechariah (chaps. v. 1, vi. 14), makes no allusion to the part that Daniel the earlier prophet had taken. He refers only to the Divine prediction by Jeremiah, which must be fulfilled: "And it shall come to pass, when seventy years are accomplished, that I will punish the king of Babylon" (Jer. xxv. 12); "For thus saith the Lord, that after seventy years be accomplished at Babylon, I will visit you, and perform my good word toward you, in causing you to return to this place" (Jer. xxix. 10).

<sup>(2)</sup> **Thus saith Cyrus king of Persia.**—In the interpretation of this decree two courses are open. We may suppose that "the spirit" of Cyrus was so effectually "stirred up" by the Spirit of God, through the prophecies of Isaiah, as to send out a written proclamation avowing his faith in Jehovah-Elohim, and thus publicly accepting the prediction: "He hath charged me to build." In this case the parenthesis of verse 3 (He is the God) may be compared with the confession of his father-in-law, Darius the Mede: "He is the living God" (Dan. vi. 26). Or we may assume that "Ormazd" in the original was reproduced in the Hebrew version that accompanied it by its equivalent, "Jehovah." The latter supposition avoids the difficulty involved in making Cyrus disavow the national faith in the presence of his empire. The decree itself runs much in the style of those found in the majority of Persian inscriptions, such as "By the grace of Ormazd is Darius king;" and the spirit of tolerance and piety in it is perfectly in harmony with all ancient testimonies to the character of Cyrus.

<sup>(4)</sup> **Whosoever remaineth.**—*As to all the Remnant in all places.* There is a singular correspondence between this and the beginning of Nehemiah; but there this familiar name for the survivors of the great national catastrophe is used of those who had returned to Jerusalem, while here it is used for the dispersion in all the provinces of the empire (Neh. i. 3).

**Where he sojourneth.**—Every individual Jew is thus significantly supposed to be only an exile.

**Let the men of his place help him.**—The heathen subjects of Cyrus are required to assist the departing sojourner, and expected also to send freewill offerings to the Temple. Note that in all these terms the spirit and phrase of the Hebrew people are used; and that there was more in the decree than is here given, as appears in the sequel. Cyrus was under strong influence, both human and Divine.

(5–11) Immediate result of the decree.

<sup>(5)</sup> **With all them whose spirit God had raised.**—Namely, *all* is the more exact rendering. The same influence that prompted the decree of Cyrus was necessary to overcome the inertness of the captives: many preferred to remain in Babylon.—The people were enumerated as tribes, families, and fathers' houses; the second and third orders of classification are not here distinguished from each other.

<sup>(6)</sup> **Precious things.**—The Hebrew equivalent is a rare word, which, when it occurs, is connected only with the precious metals.

and with beasts, and with precious things, beside all *that* was willingly offered.

⁽⁷⁾ Also Cyrus the king brought forth the vessels of the house of the LORD, ᵃ which Nebuchadnezzar had brought forth out of Jerusalem, and had put them in the house of his gods; ⁽⁸⁾ even those did Cyrus king of Persia bring forth by the hand of Mithredath the treasurer, and numbered them unto ᵇ Sheshbazzar, the prince of Judah. ⁽⁹⁾ And this *is* the number of them: thirty chargers of gold, a thousand chargers of silver, nine and twenty knives, ⁽¹⁰⁾ thirty basons of gold, silver basons of a second *sort* four hundred and ten, *and* other vessels a thousand. ⁽¹¹⁾ All the vessels of gold and of silver *were* five thousand and four hundred. All *these* did Sheshbazzar bring up with *them of* ¹ the captivity that were brought up from Babylon unto Jerusalem.

CHAPTER II.—⁽¹⁾ Now ᶜ these *are* the children of the province that went up out of the captivity, of those which had been carried away, whom Nebuchadnezzar the king of Babylon had carried away unto Babylon, and came again unto Jerusalem and Judah, every one unto his city; ⁽²⁾ which came with Zerubbabel: Jeshua, Nehemiah, ²Seraiah, Reelaiah, Mordecai, Bilshan, Mizpar, Bigvai, Rehum, Baanah. The number of the men of the people of Israel:

⁽³⁾ The children of Parosh, two thousand an hundred seventy and two. ⁽⁴⁾ The children of Shephatiah, three hundred seventy and two. ⁽⁵⁾ The children of Arah, seven hundred seventy and five. ⁽⁶⁾ The children of ᵈ Pahath-moab, of the children of Jeshua *and* Joab, two thousand eight hundred and twelve. ⁽⁷⁾ The children of Elam, a thousand two hundred fifty and four. ⁽⁸⁾ The children of Zattu, nine hundred forty and five. ⁽⁹⁾ The children of Zaccai, seven hundred and threescore. ⁽¹⁰⁾ The children of ³ Bani, six hundred forty and two. ⁽¹¹⁾ The children of Bebai, six hundred twenty and three. ⁽¹²⁾ The children of Azgad, a thousand two hundred twenty and two. ⁽¹³⁾ The chil-

*a* 2 Kings 24. 13; 2 Chron. 36. 7.

*b* See ch. 5. 14.

1 Heb., *the transportation.*

*c* Neh. 7. 6, &c.

2 Or, *Azariah,* Neh. 7. 7.

*d* Neh. 7. 11.

B.C. cir. 536.

3 Or, *Binnui,* Neh. 7. 15.

---

**Willingly offered.**—Although it is not so said, the people of Cyrus were "stirred up" like himself: how much he gave, and how much he valued the worship of the Temple, we shall hereafter see.

⁽⁷⁾ **His gods.**—Rather, *his god.* Merodach, to wit, whom he called "his lord" (Dan. i. 2). From 2 Kings xxv. 13—17 it appears that much had been taken away which Cyrus had not been able to find.

⁽⁸⁾ **Mithredath.**—"Dedicated to Mithra," the sun-god of the Persians, whose worship among the Vedic Indians had thus early reached Persia.

**Sheshbazzar.**—The Chaldee name of Zerubbabel, whose title, however, as Prince of Judah is given him from the Hebrew side. He was the legal heir of Jehoiachin, being the son of Pedaiah (1 Chron. iii. 19), who possibly married the widow of Salathiel or Shealtiel. And the title "Prince of Judah," or "Prince of the captivity," was specially given to him in common with a very few others.

⁽⁹⁾ **Chargers and knives.**—Rare words in the original, perhaps on the whole best rendered as here.

⁽¹⁰⁾ **Of a second sort.**—Of inferior quality.

⁽¹¹⁾ **Five thousand and four hundred.**—The total of the several sums should be in round numbers, such as are frequently used, two thousand and five hundred. Obviously, therefore, the writer, whom we must needs suppose to have his own previous numbers before him, here includes vessels not before enumerated as chargers and basons.

**Bring up.**—They were not, as sometimes said, the freewill offering of Cyrus. Sheshbazzar brought these rich vessels "with them of the captivity," and they were sent as already belonging to God, who vindicated by His judgment on Babylon their desecration at the feast of Belshazzar.

II.

⁽¹⁻⁷⁰⁾ Enumeration of the families and dedication of the substance of the company who returned.

⁽¹⁾ **The children of the province that went up out of the captivity.**—They came from "the captivity," which was now as it were a generic name—"Children of the captivity" in Babylon (Dan. ii. 2), in Judah (Ezra iv. 1)—and became "children of the province," the Judæan province of Persia.

**Every one unto his city.**—So far, that is, as his city was known. The various cities, or villages, are more distinctly enumerated in Nehemiah.

⁽²⁾ **Which came with Zerubbabel: Jeshua.**—The leaders of the people, perhaps the twelve tribes, are represented by twelve names, one of which, Nahamani, is here wanting; three others are given in slightly different forms.

⁽³⁾ **The children of Parosh . . .**—Then comes the enumeration of the family and local names. In the following instances we note when two of the three authorities agree. In verse 6, Ezra is confirmed by 1 Esdras as against Nehemiah's 2,818; in verse 8, against his 945; in verse 11, against his 628; in verse 15, against his 655; in verse 17, against his 324; in verse 33, against his 721. In verse 10, the children of Bani, or Binnui, are 642, but 1 Esdras agrees with Nehemiah in making them 648; in verse 14, the two latter correct 666 into 667.—In verse 20, heads of families become places; Nehemiah substitutes Gibeon for Gibbar. Verse 30 has no representative in Nehemiah. In verse 31, "the other Elam" has the same number as Elam in verse 7; and the Nebo of verse 29 is called in Nehemiah "the other Nebo," though the

*The Number of the Priests.* EZRA, II. *The Levites and the Nethinims.*

dren of Adonikam, six hundred sixty and six. <sup>(14)</sup> The children of Bigvai, two thousand fifty and six. <sup>(15)</sup> The children of Adin, four hundred fifty and four. <sup>(16)</sup> The children of Ater of Hezekiah, ninety and eight. <sup>(17)</sup> The children of Bezai, three hundred twenty and three. <sup>(18)</sup> The children of ¹Jorah, an hundred and twelve. <sup>(19)</sup> The children of Hashum, two hundred twenty and three. <sup>(20)</sup> The children of ²Gibbar, ninety and five. <sup>(21)</sup> The children of Beth-lehem, an hundred twenty and three. <sup>(22)</sup> The men of Netophah, fifty and six. <sup>(23)</sup> The men of Anathoth, an hundred twenty and eight. <sup>(24)</sup> The children of ³Azmaveth, forty and two. <sup>(25)</sup> The children of Kirjath-arim, Chephirah, and Beeroth, seven hundred and forty and three. <sup>(26)</sup> The children of Ramah and Gaba, six hundred twenty and one. <sup>(27)</sup> The men of Michmas, an hundred twenty and two. <sup>(28)</sup> The men of Beth-el and Ai, two hundred twenty and three. <sup>(29)</sup> The children of Nebo, fifty and two. <sup>(30)</sup> The children of Magbish, an hundred fifty and six. <sup>(31)</sup> The children of the other ᵃElam, a thousand two hundred fifty and four. <sup>(32)</sup> The children of Harim, three hundred and twenty. <sup>(33)</sup> The children of Lod, ⁴Hadid, and Ono, seven hundred twenty and five. <sup>(34)</sup> The children of Jericho, three hundred forty and five. <sup>(35)</sup> The children of Senaah, three thousand and six hundred and thirty.

<sup>(36)</sup> The priests: the children of ᵇJedaiah, of the house of Jeshua, nine hundred seventy and three. <sup>(37)</sup> The children of ᶜImmer, a thousand fifty and two. <sup>(38)</sup> The children of ᵈPashur, a thousand two hundred forty and seven. <sup>(39)</sup> The children of ᵉHarim, a thousand and seventeen.

<sup>(40)</sup> The Levites: the children of Jeshua and Kadmiel, of the children of ⁵Hodaviah, seventy and four. <sup>(41)</sup> The singers: the children of Asaph, an hundred twenty and eight. <sup>(42)</sup> The children of the porters: the children of Shallum, the children of Ater, the children of Talmon, the children of Akkub, the children of Hatita, the children of Shobai, in all an hundred thirty and nine.

<sup>(43)</sup> The Nethinims: the children of Ziha, the children of Hasupha, the children of Tabbaoth, <sup>(44)</sup> the children of Keros, the children of Siaha, the children of Padon, <sup>(45)</sup> the children of Lebanah, the children of Hagabah, the children of Akkub, <sup>(46)</sup> the children of Hagab, the children of ⁶Shalmai, the children of Hanan, <sup>(47)</sup> the children of Giddel, the children of Gahar, the children of Reaiah, <sup>(48)</sup> the children of Rezin, the children of Nekoda, the children of Gazzam, <sup>(49)</sup> the children of Uzza, the children of Paseah, the children of Besai, <sup>(50)</sup> the children of Asnah, the children of Mehunim, the children of Nephusim, <sup>(51)</sup> the children of Bakbuk, the children of Hakupha, the children of Harhur, <sup>(52)</sup> the children of ⁷Bazluth, the children of Mehida, the children of Harsha, <sup>(53)</sup> the children of Barkos, the children of Sisera, the children of Thamah, <sup>(54)</sup> the children of Neziah, the children of Hatipha.

<sup>(55)</sup> The children of Solomon's servants:

---

*Marginal notes:*
1 Or, *Hariph,* Neh. 7. 24.
2 Or, *Gibeon,* Neh. 7. 25.
3 Or, *Bethazmaveth,* Neh. 7. 28.
a See ver. 7.
4 Or, *Harid,* as it is in some copies.
b 1 Chron. 24. 7.
c 1 Chron. 24. 14.
d 1 Chron. 9. 12.
e 1 Chron. 24. 8.
5 Or, *Judah,* ch. 3. 9, called also *Hodevah,* Neh. 7. 43.
6 Or, *Shamlai.*
7 Or, *Bazlith,* Neh. 7. 54.

---

only one, as if the "other" had slipped in from what in Nehemiah is found in the next verse. In a few cases all the authorities differ, but the differences are not important.

<sup>(36)</sup> **The priests: the children of Jedaiah.**—The priests are then given by family names, their numbers being very large in proportion to each of the other classes. Three only of David's priestly courses are represented (1 Chron. xxiv. 7, 8, 14); Pashur, a name mentioned elsewhere as the name of a priestly race, not being among the twenty-four in the Chronicles.

**Of the house of Jeshua.**—A peculiar expression, seeming to indicate merely that the present high priest belonged to the race of Jedaiah, who, in that case, is not the same as the head of the second order in the Chronicles, unless indeed he sprang from the high-priestly family of Eleazar.

<sup>(40)</sup> **The Levites: the children of Jeshua.**—Then follow the Levitical families, not priests: that is, the Levites proper, the singers, the doorkeepers or porters. Of the first there were only two families, and these are both traced up to one, that of Hodaviah or Judah (ch. iii. 9) or Hodevah (Neh. vii. 43). The hereditary choristers are also few: of the families of Asaph, Heman, and Jeduthun the first alone is represented. Nehemiah makes their number twenty more; but 1 Esdras agrees with the text of Ezra.

<sup>(42)</sup> **The children of the porters.**—The porters, or gatekeepers, number six families, three of which appear in the old Jerusalem (1 Chron. ix. 17).

<sup>(43—58)</sup> **The Nethinims.**—By the etymology, *those given:* known by this name only in the later books. (See 1 Chron. ix. 2.) They were *hieroduli,* or temple-bondsmen: the lowest order of the ministry, performing the more laborious duties of the sanctuary. Their history runs through a long period. Moses apportioned them first, from the Midianite captives (Num. xxxi. 47); they were reinforced from the Gibeonites (Josh. ix. 23), and probably later by David (chap. viii. 20). Three

*Those who could not Shew their Pedigree.* EZRA, II. *The Number of the Whole Congregation.*

the children of Sotai, the children of Sophereth, the children of ¹Peruda, ⁽⁵⁶⁾ the children of Jaalah, the children of Darkon, the children of Giddel, ⁽⁵⁷⁾ the children of Shephatiah, the children of Hattil, the children of Pochereth of Zebaim, the children of ²Ami. ⁽⁵⁸⁾ All the ᵃNethinims, and the children of ᵇSolomon's servants, *were* three hundred ninety and two.

⁽⁵⁹⁾ And these *were* they which went up from Tel-melah, Tel-harsa, Cherub, Addan, *and* Immer: but they could not shew their father's house, and their ³seed, whether they *were* of Israel: ⁽⁶⁰⁾ the children of Delaiah, the children of Tobiah, the children of Nekoda, six hundred fifty and two. ⁽⁶¹⁾ And of the children of the priests: the children of Habaiah, the children of Koz, the children of ᶜBarzillai; which took a wife of the daughters of Barzillai the Gileadite, and was called after their name: ⁽⁶²⁾ these sought their register *among* those that were reckoned by genealogy, but they were not found: therefore ⁴were they, as polluted, put from the priesthood.

¹ Or, *Perida,* Neh. 7. 57.
² Or, *Anon,* Neh. 7. 56.
ᵃ Josh. 9. 21, 27, 1 Chron. 9. 2.
ᵇ 1 Kings 9. 21.
³ Or, *pedigree.*
ᶜ 2 Sam. 17. 27.
⁴ Heb., *they were polluted from the priesthood.*
⁵ Or, *governor.*
ᵈ Ex. 28. 30.
ᵉ 1 Chron. 26. 20.

⁽⁶³⁾ And the ⁵Tirshatha said unto them, that they should not eat of the most holy things till there stood up a priest with ᵈUrim and with Thummim.

⁽⁶⁴⁾ The whole congregation together *was* forty and two thousand three hundred *and* threescore, ⁽⁶⁵⁾ beside their servants and their maids, of whom *there were* seven thousand three hundred thirty and seven: and *there were* among them two hundred singing men and singing women. ⁽⁶⁶⁾ Their horses *were* seven hundred thirty and six; their mules, two hundred forty and five; ⁽⁶⁷⁾ their camels, four hundred thirty and five, *their* asses, six thousand seven hundred and twenty.

⁽⁶⁸⁾ And *some* of the chief of the fathers, when they came to the house of the LORD which *is* at Jerusalem, offered freely for the house of God to set it up in his place: ⁽⁶⁹⁾ they gave after their ability unto the ᵉtreasure of the work threescore and one thousand drams of gold, and five thousand pound of silver, and one hundred priests' garments.

---

names—Akkub, Hagab, and Asnah—have dropped from Nehemiah's list, which gives also some unimportant changes in the spelling of the names.

⁽⁵⁵⁾ **The children of Solomon's servants.**—These are mentioned in 1 Kings ix. as a servile class, formed of the residue of the Canaanites. They were probably inferior to the Nethinims, but are generally classed with them, as in the general enumeration here. Both these classes retained during their captivity their attachment to the service into which they had been received; and, the Levites being so few, their value in the reconstitution of the Temple gave them the special importance they assume in these books.

⁽⁵⁹⁻⁶³⁾ Finally, those who had lost the records of their lineage are mentioned. Of the people, the children of three families from Tel-melah, *Hill of salt*, Tel-harsa, *Hill of the wood*, and a few other places, are mentioned. Of the priests, there are also three families without their genealogy.

⁽⁶¹⁾ **Barzillai the Gileadite.**—See the well-known history in 2 Sam. xvii. 27.

**After their name.**—Rather, *after her name*, she having been probably an heiress.

⁽⁶²⁾ **Their register among those that were reckoned by genealogy.**—Better, *their record, or the record of the Enregistered.*

**Polluted.**—Levitically disqualified.

⁽⁶³⁾ **Tirshatha.**—Interchangeable with *Pechah*, or *governor*, as Zerubbabel is called in chapter v. 14 and always in Haggai. It is probably an old Persian term, signifying "The Feared."

**With Urim and with Thummim.**—See Exod. xxviii. 30. They were pronounced to be excluded from priestly functions. Without ark or temple, the people had not as yet that special presence of Jehovah before which the high priest could "inquire of the Lord by Urim and Thummim." Zerubbabel might hope that this privilege would return, and thought the official purity of the priestly line of sufficient importance such an inquiry. But the holy of holies in the new temple never had in it the ancient "tokens"; and by Urim and Thummim Jehovah was never again inquired of.

⁽⁶⁴⁾ This sum total is the same in Nehemiah; but the several sums in Ezra make 29,818, and in Nehemiah 31,089. The apocryphal Esdras agrees in the total, but makes in the particulars 33,950, adding that children below twelve were not reckoned. Many expedients of reconciliation have been adopted; but it is better to suppose that errors had crept into the original documents.

⁽⁶⁵⁾ The Rabbis accounted for these "ut lætior esset Israelitarum reditus," in order that the return of the Israelites might be more joyful; but they were hired for lamentation as well as joy; and here, possibly, to supply the defect of Levites. In Nehemiah (chap. vii. 67) there are 245: see for the probable reason of the mistranscription the 245 of the next verse in that chapter.

⁽⁶⁷⁾ The asses, as throughout earlier Hebrew history, are the chief and most numerous beasts of burden.

⁽⁶⁸⁾ They came to the site of the house not yet built, and offered for the building.

⁽⁶⁹⁾ The dram being a daric of a little more than our guinea, and the pound, or maneh, a little more than £4, the whole would be nearly £90,000, and not an exorbitant sum for a community far from poor. But Nehemiah's statement is smaller, and probably more correct.

**One hundred priests' garments.**—An almost necessary correction or supply in the defective text of

(70) So the priests, and the Levites, and some of the people, and the singers, and the porters, and the Nethinims, dwelt in their cities, and all Israel in their cities.

CHAPTER III.—(1) And when the seventh month was come, and the children of Israel *were* in the cities, the people gathered themselves together as one man to Jerusalem. (2) Then stood up ¹Jeshua the son of Jozadak, and his brethren the priests, and ²Zerubbabel the son of ᵃShealtiel, and his brethren, and builded the altar of the God of Israel, to offer burnt offerings thereon, as *it is* ᵇ written in the law of Moses the man of God. (3) And they set the altar upon his bases; for fear *was* upon them because of the people of those countries: and they offered burnt offerings thereon unto the LORD, *even* burnt offerings morning and evening. (4) They kept also the feast of tabernacles, ᶜas *it is* written, and ᵈ*offered* the daily burnt offerings by number, according to the custom, ³as the duty of every day required; (5) and afterward *offered* the continual burnt offering, both of the new moons, and of all the set feasts of the LORD that were consecrated, and of every one that willingly offered a freewill offering unto the LORD. (6) From the first day of the seventh month began they to offer burnt offerings unto the LORD. But ⁴the foundation of the temple of the LORD was not *yet* laid. (7) They gave money also unto the masons, and to the ⁵carpenters; and meat, and drink, and oil, unto them of Zidon, and to them of Tyre, to bring cedar trees from Lebanon to the sea of ᵉJoppa, according to the grant that they had of Cyrus king of Persia. (8) Now in the second year of their coming unto the house of God at Jerusalem, in the second month, began Zerubbabel the son of Shealtiel, and Jeshua the son of Jozadak, and the remnant of their brethren the priests and the Levites, and all they that were come out of the captivity unto Jerusalem; and appointed the Levites, from twenty

---

1 Or, *Joshua,* Hag. 1. 1.
2 Called *Zorobabel,* Matt. 1. 12; & Luke 3. 27.
ᵃ Matt. 1; 12 & Luke 3. 27, called *Salathiel.*
ᵇ Deut. 12. 5.
ᶜ Num. 29. 12.
ᵈ Ex. 23. 16.
3 Heb., *the matter of the day in his day.*
4 Heb., *the temple of the LORD was not yet founded.*
5 Or, *workmen.*
ᵉ Acts 9. 36.

---

Nehemiah (chap. vii. 70) makes his "four hundred and thirty priests' garments," as contributed by the Tirshatha, "five hundred pounds of silver and thirty priests' garments." This being so, the two accounts agree, always allowing that Ezra's 61,000 is a corruption of 41,000 in the gold, and his 5,000 pounds of silver and 100 priests' garments round numbers.

(70) **Some of the people.**—*Those of the people;* placed by Nehemiah after all the others.

**All Israel in their cities.**—The emphasis lies in the fact that, though Judah and Benjamin contributed the largest part, it was a national revival; and the constant repetition of "in their cities" has in it the same note of triumph.

III.

(1–13) *The altar set up, and the feasts established.*

(1) **The seventh month was come.**—Rather, *approached.* Tisri, answering to our September, was the most solemn month of the year, including the Day of Atonement and the Feast of Tabernacles, afterwards distinguished as "the feast" pre-eminently.

**As one man.**—Not all, but with one consent.

(2) **Builded the altar.**—Only as the beginning of their work. The Temple was, as it were, built around the altar, as the centre of all.

**Moses the man of God.**—Like David, Neh. xii. 24, 36.

(3) **Upon his bases.**—Upon its old site, or *its place,* discovered among the ruins. Thus was it signified that all the new was to be only a restoration of the old.

**For fear was upon them.**—Until their offerings went up they did not feel sure of the Divine protection. This was their first act of defiance in the presence of the nations around: near the altar they were strong.

(4) **According to the custom.**—It is necessary here to read Deut. xvi., Lev. xxiii., Num. xxix. The intention obviously is to lay stress on the provision made for an entire renewal of the Mosaic economy of service, as appears in the next verse.

(5) **Both of the new moons.**—*And of the new moons.* The whole verse is general and anticipatory. The new moons, the three feasts, and the constant presentation of freewill offerings, added to the daily sacrifice, made up the essentials of ritual; all being, like the arrangements in the Book of Leviticus, fixed before the Temple was built, and afterwards observed.

(6) **From the first day.**—The notes of time demand notice. The altar was raised before the month came; from the first until the fifteenth, when the Feast of Tabernacles began, the daily sacrifice was offered. The whole verse recapitulates, and its latter part is the transition to what follows.

(7) **They gave money.**—Their own workmen were paid in money; the Phœnicians, as in Solomon's days (1 Kings v.; 2 Chron. ii.), were paid in kind. This illustrates and is illustrated by Acts xii. 20.

**The sea of Joppa.**—The Jewish port to which the cedar-trees were sent by sea, and thence thirty-five miles inland to Jerusalem.

**The grant.**—The authority of Cyrus over Phœnicia seems not to have been doubtful.

(8) **In the second year.**—The second year of Cyrus, B.C. 537, was their second year in the holy place.

**In the second month.**—Zif, chosen apparently because it was the same month in which Solomon laid the first foundation (1 Kings vi.).

**Appointed the Levites, from twenty years.**—Their appointment to superintend, and their specified age, are in strict harmony with the original ordinances of David (1 Chron. xxiii.).

years old and upward, to set forward the work of the house of the LORD. ⁽⁹⁾ Then stood Jeshua *with* his sons and his brethren, Kadmiel and his sons, the sons of ¹Judah, ²together, to set forward the workmen in the house of God: the sons of Henadad, *with* their sons and their brethren the Levites. ⁽¹⁰⁾ And when the builders laid the foundation of the temple of the LORD, they set the priests in their apparel with trumpets, and the Levites the sons of Asaph with cymbals, to praise the LORD, after the ᵃordinance of David king of Israel. ⁽¹¹⁾ And they sang together by course in praising and giving thanks unto the LORD; because *he is* good, for his mercy *endureth* for ever toward Israel. And all the people shouted with a great shout, when they praised the LORD, because the foundation of the house of the LORD was laid. ⁽¹²⁾ But many of the priests and Levites and chief of the fathers, *who were* ancient men, that had seen the first house, when the foundation of this house was laid before their eyes, wept with a loud voice; and many shouted aloud for joy: ⁽¹³⁾ so that the people could not discern the noise of the shout of joy from the noise of the weeping of the people: for the people shouted with a loud shout, and the noise was heard afar off.

CHAPTER IV.—⁽¹⁾ Now when the adversaries of Judah and Benjamin heard that ³the children of the captivity builded the temple unto the LORD God of Israel; ⁽²⁾ then they came to Zerubbabel, and to the chief of the fathers, and said unto them, Let us build with you: for we seek your God, as ye *do*; and we do sacrifice unto him since the days of Esar-haddon king of Assur, which brought us up hither. ⁽³⁾ But Zerubbabel, and Jeshua, and the rest of the chief of the fathers of Israel, said unto them, Ye have nothing to do with us to build an house unto our God; but we ourselves together will build unto the LORD God of Israel, as king Cyrus the king of Persia hath commanded us. ⁽⁴⁾ Then the people of the land weakened the hands of the people of Judah, and troubled them in building,

1 Or, *Hodaviah*, ch. 2. 40.

B. C. 535.

2 Heb., *as one*.

B. C. cir. 678.

*a* 1 Chron. 6. 31, & 16. 7, & 25. 1.

3 Heb., *the sons of the transportation*.

---

⁽⁹⁾ **Together.**—*As one man.* Jeshua and Kadmiel, both of the stock of Judah, or Hodaviah (chap. ii. 40), or Hodevah (Neh. vii. 43), were the two heads of Levitical families; and their fewness is compensated by their unanimity and vigour. Henadad is not mentioned in chapter ii. 40, though it is a Levitical name in Nehemiah. Why omitted there, or why inserted here, it is not possible to determine.

⁽¹⁰⁾ **After the ordinance of David, king of Israel.**—All goes back to earlier times. As the first offerings on the altar were according to what was "written in the law of Moses, the man of God," so the musical ceremonial of this foundation is according to the precedent of David (see 1 Chron. vi., xvi. 25). The trumpets belonged to the priests, the cymbals to the Levites, in the ancient ordinances of worship.

⁽¹¹⁾ **They sang together.**—They answered each other in chorus, or antiphonally.

**Shouted.**—As afterwards in religious acclamation.

⁽¹²⁾ **But many of the priests and Levites . . . wept with a loud voice.** — This most affecting scene requires the comment of Hag. ii. and Zech. iv. The first house was destroyed in B.C. 588, fifty years before. The weeping of the ancients was not occasioned by any comparison as to size and grandeur, unless indeed they marked the smallness of their foundation stones. They thought chiefly of the great desolation as measured by the past; the younger people thought of the new future.

⁽¹³⁾ **The noise was heard afar off.**—The people also mingled in the weeping, which was with shrill cries. The rejoicing and the sorrow were blended, and the common sound was heard from far. All here has the stamp of truth.

IV.

⁽¹⁻²⁴⁾ The opposition of the Samaritans and its temporary success.

⁽¹⁾ **The adversaries.**—The Samaritans, so termed by Nehemiah (chap. iv. 11). These were a mixed race, the original Israelite element of which was nearly lost in the tribes imported into the northern part of the land by Sargon, Sennacherib, and Esar-haddon. (See 2 Kings xvii. 24—34.)

⁽²⁾ **As ye do.**—"They feared the Lord, and worshipped their own gods" (2 Kings xvii. 33): thus they came either in the spirit of hypocrites or with an intention to unite their own idolatries with the pure worship of Jehovah. In any case, they are counted enemies of the God of Israel.

**We do sacrifice unto Him since the days of Esar-haddon.**—He ended his reign B.C. 668, and therefore the Samaritans speak from a tradition extending backwards a century and a half.

**Which brought us up hither.**—Thus they entirely leave out of consideration what residue of Israel was yet to be found among them.

⁽³⁾ **Ye have nothing to do with us.** — The account in 2 Kings xvii. carefully studied will show that the stern refusal of the leaders was precisely in harmony with the will of God; there was nothing in it of that intolerant spirit which is sometimes imagined. The whole design of the Great Restoration would have been defeated by a concession at this point. The reference to the command of Cyrus is another and really subordinate kind of justification, pleaded as subjects of the King of Persia, whose decree was absolute and exclusive.

(5) and hired counsellors against them, to frustrate their purpose, all the days of Cyrus king of Persia, even until the reign of Darius king of Persia. (6) And in the reign of [1]Ahasuerus, in the beginning of his reign, wrote they *unto him* an accusation against the inhabitants of Judah and Jerusalem.

(7) And in the days of Artaxerxes wrote [2]Bishlam, Mithredath, Tabeel, and the rest of their [3]companions, unto Artaxerxes king of Persia; and the writing of the letter *was* written in the Syrian tongue, and interpreted in the Syrian tongue. (8) Rehum the chancellor, and Shimshai the [4]scribe, wrote a letter against Jerusalem to Artaxerxes the king in this sort: (9) then *wrote* Rehum the chancellor, and Shimshai the scribe, and the rest of their [5]companions; the Dinaites, the Apharsathchites, the Tarpelites, the Apharsites, the Archevites, the Babylonians, the Susanchites, the Dehavites, *and* the Elamites, (10) and the rest of the nations whom the great and noble Asnapper brought over, and set in the cities of Samaria, and the rest *that are* on this side the river, and [6]at such a time.

(11) This *is* the copy of the letter that they sent unto him, *even* unto Artaxerxes the king; Thy servants the men on this side the river, and at such a time. (12) Be it known unto the king, that the Jews which came up from thee to us are come unto Jerusalem, building the rebellious and the bad city, and have [7]set up the walls *thereof*, and [8]joined the foundations. (13) Be it known now unto the king, that, if this city be builded, and the walls set up *again*, *then* will they not [9]pay toll, tribute, and custom, and *so* thou shalt endamage the [10]revenue of the kings. (14) Now because [11]we have maintenance from *the king's* palace, and it was not meet for us to see the king's dishonour, therefore have we sent and certified the king; (15) that search may be made in the book of the records of thy fathers: so shalt thou

---

B.C. cir. 678.
B.C. 534.
[1] Heb., *Ahashverosh.*
B.C. 529.
B.C. 522.
[2] Or, *in peace.*
B.C. 522.
[3] Heb., *societies.*
[4] Or, *secretary.*
[5] Chald., *societies.*
[6] Chald., *Cheeneth.*
[7] Or, *finished.*
[8] Chald., *sewed together.*
[9] Chald., *give.*
[10] Or, *strength.*
[11] Chald., *we are salted with the salt of the palace.*

---

(5) **And hired counsellors against them.**—They adopted a systematic course of employing paid agents at the court: continued for eight years, till B.C. 529. Cambyses, his son, succeeded Cyrus; he died B.C. 522; then followed the pseudo-Smerdis, a usurper, whose short reign Darius did not reckon, but dated his own reign from B.C. 522. A comparison of dates shows that this was the first Darius, the son of Hystaspes.

(6) **In the beginning of his reign.**—This Ahasuerus, another name for Cambyses, reigned seven years; and his accession to the throne was the time seized by the Samaritans for their "accusation," of which we hear nothing more; suffice that the building languished.

(7) **In the days of Artaxerxes.**—This must be Gomates, the Magian priest who personated Smerdis, the dead son of Cyrus, and reigned only seven months: note that the expression used is "days," and not "reign" as in the previous verse. This Artaxerxes has been thought by many commentators to be the Longimanus of the sequel of this book and of Nehemiah, and they have identified the Ahasuerus of Ezra and Esther with Xerxes. This would explain the reference to "the walls" in verse 12; but in verses 23 and 24 the sequence of events is strict, and the word "ceased" links the parts of the narrative into unity. Moreover, the Persian princes had often more than one name. At the same time, there is nothing to make such an anticipatory and parenthetical insertion impossible.

**In the Syrian tongue.**—The characters and the words were Syrian or Aramaic; this explains the transition to another language at this point,

(8) **Rehum the chancellor.**—*The lord of judgment,* the counsellor of the Persian king, a conventional title of the civil governor.

**Shimshai the scribe.**—The royal secretary.

(9) **Then wrote . . .**—This verse and the following give the general superscription of the letter which the Persian officials wrote for the Samaritans: introduced, however, in a very peculiar manner, and to be followed by another introduction in verse 11. Of the names by which the Samaritans think fit to distinguish themselves the Apharsites and Dehavites are Persians; the Babylonians the original races of Babylon, Cuthah and Ava (2 Kings xvii. 24); the Susanchites are from Susa; the Apharsathchites, probably the Pharathiakites, a predatory people of Media; the Archevites, inhabitants of Erech (Gen. x. 10). The Dinaites and Tarpelites can be only conjecturally identified.

(10) **Asnapper** cannot be Esar-haddon, but was probably his chief officer.

**And at such a time.**—*And so forth.*

(11) **On this side the river.**—Literally, *beyond the river* Euphrates, as written for the Persian court.

**And at such a time.**—Rather, *and so forth;* meaning, "Thy servants, as aforesaid," alluding to the superscription.

(12) Virulence and craft and exaggeration are stamped on every sentence of the letter. It only says, however, that "they are preparing the walls thereof, and joining the foundations." Afterwards, however, the charge is modified in verses 13 and 16.

(13) **Toll, tribute, and custom.**—Toll for the highways; custom, a provision in kind; tribute, the money tax.

**The revenue.**—Rather, *at length;* literally *and at length damage will be done to the kings.*

(14) **Maintenance.**—more exactly, *we eat the salt of the palace.* This seems to be a general expression for dependence on the king, whose dishonour or loss they profess themselves unwilling to behold.

(15) **The book of the records of thy fathers.**—"The book of the records of the Chronicles" which in Esther vi. 1 is "read before the king."

find in the book of the records, and know that this city *is* a rebellious city, and hurtful unto kings and provinces, and that they have ¹moved sedition ²within the same of old time : for which cause was this city destroyed. (16) We certify the king that, if this city be builded *again*, and the walls thereof set up, by this means thou shalt have no portion on this side the river.

(17) *Then* sent the king an answer unto Rehum the chancellor, and *to* Shimshai the scribe, and *to* the rest of their ³companions that dwell in Samaria, and *unto* the rest beyond the river, Peace, and at such a time. (18) The letter which ye sent unto us hath been plainly read before me. (19) And ⁴I commanded, and search hath been made, and it is found that this city of old time hath ⁵made insurrection against kings, and *that* rebellion and sedition have been made therein. (20) There have been mighty kings also over Jerusalem, which have ruled over all *countries* beyond the river; and toll, tribute, and custom, was paid unto them. (21) ⁶Give ye now commandment to cause these men to cease, and that this city be not builded, until *another* commandment shall be given from me. (22) Take heed now that ye fail not to do this : why should damage grow to the hurt of the kings ?

(23) Now when the copy of king Artaxerxes' letter *was* read before Rehum, and Shimshai the scribe, and their companions, they went up in haste to Jerusalem unto the Jews, and made them to cease ⁷by force and power. (24) Then ceased the work of the house of God which *is* at Jerusalem. So it ceased unto the second year of the reign of Darius king of Persia.

CHAPTER V.—(1) Then the prophets, ᵃHaggai the prophet, and ᵇZechariah the son of Iddo, prophesied unto the Jews that *were* in Judah and Jerusalem in the name of the God of Israel, *even* unto them. (2) Then rose up Zerubbabel the son of Shealtiel, and Jeshua the son of Jozadak, and began to build the house of God which *is* at Jerusalem : and with them *were* the prophets of God helping them.

(3) At the same time came to them Tatnai, governor on this side the river, and Shethar-boznai, and their companions, and said thus unto them, Who

---

*Marginal notes:*
1 Chald., *made.*
2 Chald., *in the midst thereof.*
3 Chald., *societies.*
B.C. 420.
4 Chald., *by me a decree is set.*
B.C. 520.
5 Chald., *lifted up itself.*
6 Chald., *make a decree.*
7 Chald., *by arm and power.*
a Hag. 1. 1.
b Zech. 1. 1.

---

This extended beyond his own fathers back to the times of the predecessors of the Median dynasty.

**Of old time.**—From the days of eternity, or time immemorial. The spirit of exaggeration if not of falsehood appears in every word here.

(16) **No portion on this side the river.**—The same unscrupulous use of language : that is, if the river Euphrates is meant. In the days of Solomon, and once or twice subsequently, the Israelites had advanced towards the river, but it was not likely that they would ever do so again. The letter may, however, have been intended to suggest loosely that Jerusalem might become a centre of general disaffection.

(17) **Peace, and at such a time.**—*Salutation, and so forth.* The account of the reply and the beginning of it are strangely blended, as before.

(19) **Insurrection.**—Never against Persia; but such as are alluded to in 2 Kings xxiv.

(20) **Mighty kings.**—David and Solomon, and some few kings down to Josiah, had extended their sway and made nations tributary (2 Sam. viii.; 1 Kings x.). The earlier kings' names would perhaps be referred to historically, though not immediately connected with Persian annals.

(24) **The second year.**—The record here returns to verse 5, with more specific indication of time. The suspension of the general enterprise—called " the work of the house of God which is at Jerusalem "—lasted nearly two years. But it must be remembered that the altar was still the centre of a certain amount of worship.

V.

(1–2) Now occurs the intervention of the two prophets, Haggai and Zechariah, whose testimonies and predictions should at this point be read. They reveal a state of apathy which Ezra does not allude to; such a state of things, in fact, as would have thwarted the whole design of Providence had it not been changed. Hence the abrupt return of the spirit of prophecy, some of the last utterances of which provoked or " stirred up " —as Cyrus had been stirred up—the spirit of the two leaders and of the heads of the families.

(2) **Then rose up.**—This does not intimate that they had become indifferent. But the voice of prophecy inspirited them to go on without formal permission of Darius, who was known secretly to favour them already.

**The prophets of God helping them.**—In these two prophets we can read the invigorating sayings that encouraged the people almost from day to day and from stage to stage of their work.

(3–17) Tatnai's appeal to Darius.

(3) **Tatnai, governor on this side the river.**— Satrap, or Pechah, of the entire province of Syria and Phœnicia, and therefore with a jurisdiction over Judæa, and over Zerubbabel its Pechah or sub-Satrap. What Shimshai was to the Samaritan Pechah, Rehum, Shethar-boznai seems to be to Tatnai—his secretary.

**Who hath commanded you ?**—It is obvious that the overthrow of Smerdis, the Magian hater of

hath commanded you to build this house, and to make up this wall? ⁽⁴⁾ Then said we unto them after this manner, What are the names of the men ¹that make this building? ⁽⁵⁾ But the eye of their God was upon the elders of the Jews, that they could not cause them to cease, till the matter came to Darius: and then they returned answer by letter concerning this *matter*.

⁽⁶⁾ The copy of the letter that Tatnai, governor on this side the river, and Shethar-boznai, and his companions the Apharsachites, which *were* on this side the river, sent unto Darius the king: ⁽⁷⁾ they sent a letter unto him, ²wherein was written thus; Unto Darius the king, all peace. ⁽⁸⁾ Be it known unto the king, that we went into the province of Judea, to the house of the great God, which is builded with ³great stones, and timber is laid in the walls, and this work goeth fast on, and prospereth in their hands. ⁽⁹⁾ Then asked we those elders, *and* said unto them thus, Who commanded you to build this house, and to make up these walls? ⁽¹⁰⁾ We asked their names also, to certify thee, that we might write the names of the men that *were* the chief of them. ⁽¹¹⁾ And thus they returned us answer, saying, We are the servants of the God of heaven and earth, and build the house that was builded these many years ago, which a great king of Israel builded ᵃand set up. ⁽¹²⁾ But after that our fathers had provoked the God of heaven unto wrath, he gave them into the hand of ᵇNebuchadnezzar the king of Babylon, the Chaldean, who destroyed this house, and carried the people away into Babylon. ⁽¹³⁾ But in the first year of ᶜCyrus the king of Babylon *the same* king Cyrus made a decree to build this house of God. ⁽¹⁴⁾ And ᵈthe vessels also of gold and silver of the house of God, which Nebuchadnezzar took out of the temple that *was* in Jerusalem, and brought them into the temple of Babylon, those did Cyrus the king take out of the temple of Babylon, and they were delivered unto *one*, whose name *was* Sheshbazzar, whom he had made ⁴governor; ⁽¹⁵⁾ and said unto him, Take these vessels, go, carry them into the temple that *is* in Jerusalem, and let the house of God be builded in his place. ⁽¹⁶⁾ Then came the same Sheshbazzar, *and* laid the foundation of the house of God which *is* in Jerusalem:

*Marginal notes:*
1 Chald., *that build this building?*
2 Chald., *in the midst whereof.*
3 Chald., *stones of rolling.*
B.C. 519.
B.C. 536.
*a* 1 Kings 6. 1.
*b* 2 Kings 24. 2; & 25. 8.
*c* ch. 1. 1.
*d* ch. 1. 8; & 6. 5.
4 Or, *deputy.*

---

Zoroastrianism and destroyer of temples, had encouraged the builders to go on without fearing molestation from the Court of Darius. Moreover, the two prophets had made their duty too plain to be deferred. Still, the decree of the preceding chapter had never been expressly revoked.

⁽⁴⁾ **Then said we.**—The LXX. must here have read, "then said they." But there is no need to change the text; the sentence is not a question, but a statement: "we said to the effect, what the names were."

**What are the names of the men . . . ?**—It is clear that this graphic account is much compressed. We must understand (see verse 10) that the authorities demanded the names of the chief promoters of the building in order to make them responsible.

⁽⁵⁾ **And then they returned answer.**—*And* [*till*] *they should receive answer.* It is implied that "the eye of their God" was with special vigilance fixed on the work, and it will appear that His influence was upon the officials of Persia as well as upon the rulers of the Jews. The letter that follows shows this.

⁽⁶⁾ **The copy of the letter.**—This letter of Tatnai is introduced much in the same way as Rehum's; but its dispassionateness and good faith are in striking contrast with the latter.

**Apharsachites.**—Probably here the same as the Apharsites before, and suggesting some kind of Persian guard. But the reason of their introduction specifically here is obscure.

⁽⁸⁾ **To the house of the great God.** — A solemn tribute to the God of the Jews, which, however, the decree of Cyrus enables us to understand in this official document. Tatnai probably dwelt at Damascus, and when he went to Jerusalem was deeply impressed. But he only gives a statement of the progress which he observed in the Temple. "The walls" here are the walls within the Temple, not the city walls.

⁽¹¹⁾ **And thus they returned us answer.**—The elders of the Jews take the Syrian satrap into their confidence, and give in a few most pathetic words the record of their national honour, their national infidelity, and their national humiliation. Every word is true to the history, while the whole exhibits their deep humility and holy resolution.

⁽¹²⁾ **Gave them into the hand of Nebuchadnezzar the king of Babylon, the Chaldean.**—These words not only show that the people regarded themselves as punished by the sole hand of God, but also remind the overthrowers of the Chaldean power that they also themselves are no more than instruments of the same Divine will.

⁽¹⁵⁾ **Take these vessels, go, carry them . . . and let the house of God . . .**—The three imperatives in this verse, without a copula, followed by a fourth, vividly express the feeling of the suppliants in the remembrance of the decree: thus we have another note of historical truth.

⁽¹⁶⁾ **Since that time.**—No account is taken of the long interruption. Whether these words are part of the answer given to Tatnai by the Jewish leaders, or his own statement to Darius, it is evident that the unfinished building of a house decreed to be built by Cyrus is regarded as demanding investigation as to the nature and validity of the decree itself.

and since that time even until now hath it been in building, and *yet* it is not finished. ⁽¹⁷⁾ Now therefore, if *it seem* good to the king, let there be search made in the king's treasure house, which *is* there at Babylon, whether it be *so*, that a decree was made of Cyrus the king to build this house of God at Jerusalem, and let the king send his pleasure to us concerning this matter.

CHAPTER VI.—⁽¹⁾ Then Darius the king made a decree, and search was made in the house of the ¹rolls, where the treasures were ²laid up in Babylon. ⁽²⁾ And there was found at ³Achmetha, in the palace that *is* in the province of the Medes, a roll, and therein *was* a record thus written:

⁽³⁾ In the first year of Cyrus the king *the same* Cyrus the king made a decree *concerning* the house of God at Jerusalem, Let the house be builded, the place where they offered sacrifices, and let the foundations thereof be strongly laid; the height thereof threescore cubits, *and* the breadth thereof threescore cubits; ⁽⁴⁾ *with* three rows of great stones, and a row of new timber: and let the expences be given out of the king's house: ⁽⁵⁾ and also let the golden and silver vessels of the house of God,

¹ Chald., *books.*
² Chald., *made to descend.*
³ Or, *Ecbatana, or, in a coffer.*
B.C. 519.
⁴ Chald., *go.*
⁵ Chald., *their societies.*
⁶ Chald., *by me a decree is made.*
⁷ Chald., *made to cease.*
⁸ Chald., *of rest.*

which Nebuchadnezzar took forth out of the temple which *is* at Jerusalem, and brought unto Babylon, be restored, and ⁴brought again unto the temple which *is* at Jerusalem, *every one* to his place, and place *them* in the house of God.

⁽⁶⁾ Now *therefore*, Tatnai, governor beyond the river, Shethar-boznai, and ⁵your companions the Apharsachites, which *are* beyond the river, be ye far from thence: ⁽⁷⁾ let the work of this house of God alone; let the governor of the Jews and the elders of the Jews build this house of God in his place. ⁽⁸⁾ Moreover ⁶I make a decree what ye shall do to the elders of these Jews for the building of this house of God: that of the king's goods, *even* of the tribute beyond the river, forthwith expences be given unto these men, that they be not ⁷hindered. ⁽⁹⁾ And that which they have need of, both young bullocks, and rams, and lambs, for the burnt offerings of the God of heaven, wheat, salt, wine, and oil, according to the appointment of the priests which *are* at Jerusalem, let it be given them day by day without fail: ⁽¹⁰⁾ that they may offer sacrifices ⁸of sweet savours unto the God of heaven, and pray for the life of the king, and of his sons. ⁽¹¹⁾ Also I have made a decree, that whosoever shall

---

⁽¹⁷⁾ **Let there be search made.**—All depended on the original decree, which nothing done intermediately by the usurper could cancel. And the request of Tatnai seems to imply that it would be found: although the original was not found in Babylon, as was expected, a copy had been made.

### VI.

(1–15) The favourable decree of Darius, and its effect.

⁽¹⁾ **Made a decree.**—Rather, *gave an order.*

**Were laid up.**—In the original, *laid down*, in a chamber for the storing of documents and other treasures.

⁽²⁾ **At Achmetha.**—That is, Ecbatana, the Median capital of Cyrus. It is probable that the original roll of parchment had been destroyed at Babylon by Smerdis, but a copy of it was found here, probably in a Chaldean transcript.

⁽³⁾ **Strongly laid.**—"Thy foundation shall be laid" (Isa. xliv. 28). The decree adds a word that signifies "with sufficient support."

⁽⁵⁾ **And also let the golden and silver vessels . . . be restored.**—The desecration of these vessels by Belshazzar (Dan. v. 2, 3) was thus to be expiated. Every word, including the twice repeated "house of God," is most emphatic.

⁽⁶⁾ **Now therefore, Tatnai.**—Here there is an abrupt transition to the decree of Darius itself, the terms of which were either drawn up by Jewish help, or are freely rendered into the national phraseology by the historian.

**Be ye far from thence.**—That is, keep aloof from any kind of interference.

⁽⁸⁾ **Moreover.**—*I also make my decree.*

**Of the king's goods.**—From the tribute collected to be sent to Persia sums were previously to be deducted.

⁽⁹⁾ **Both young bullocks, and rams, and lambs.**—An accurate account of the provision required for the sacrifices and meat-offerings of the daily service of the Temple: how accurate will be seen by consulting Exod. xxix. and Lev. ii.

**Appointment** here is simply the word: that is, of direction.

⁽¹⁰⁾ **That they may offer sacrifices . . . and pray for the life of the king.**—Two ends are to be answered: the God of heaven is to be honoured, and the dynasty of Darius interceded for by the Jews. (Comp. Jer. xxix. 7.)

**Of sweet savours.**—The word occurs again only in Dan. ii. 46, and there is translated "sweet odours," meaning incense. The connection of this with the prayer following justifies the same translation here, and, moreover, indicates under what good instruction the decree was drawn up.

⁽¹¹⁾ **Alter this word** seems to mean "violate this command," since the alteration of a decree was a thing unheard of.

*The Temple is Finished.*      EZRA, VI.      *The Feast of the Dedication.*

alter this word, let timber be pulled down from his house, and being set up, ¹let him be hanged thereon; and let his house be made a dunghill for this. ⁽¹²⁾ And the God that hath caused his name to dwell there destroy all kings and people, that shall put to their hand to alter *and* to destroy this house of God which *is* at Jerusalem. I Darius have made a decree; let it be done with speed.

⁽¹³⁾ Then Tatnai, governor on this side the river, Shethar-boznai, and their companions, according to that which Darius the king had sent, so they did speedily. ⁽¹⁴⁾ And the elders of the Jews builded, and they prospered through the prophesying of Haggai the prophet and Zechariah the son of Iddo. And they builded, and finished *it*, according to the commandment of the God of Israel, and according to the ²commandment of Cyrus, and Darius, and Artaxerxes king of Persia. ⁽¹⁵⁾ And this house was finished on the third day of the month Adar, which was in the sixth year of the reign of Darius the king.

⁽¹⁶⁾ And the children of Israel, the priests, and the Levites, and the rest of ³the children of the captivity, kept the dedication of this house of God with joy, ⁽¹⁷⁾ and offered at the dedication of this house of God an hundred bullocks, two hundred rams, four hundred lambs; and for a sin offering for all Israel, twelve he goats, according to the number of the tribes of Israel. ⁽¹⁸⁾ And they set the priests in their divisions, and the Levites in their courses, for the service of God, which *is* at Jerusalem; ⁴ᵃ as it is written in the book of Moses.

⁽¹⁹⁾ And the children of the captivity kept the passover upon the fourteenth day of the first month. ⁽²⁰⁾ For the priests and the Levites were purified together, all of them *were* pure, and killed the passover for all the children of the captivity, and for their brethren the priests, and for themselves. ⁽²¹⁾ And the children of Israel, which were come again out of captivity, and all such as had separated themselves unto them from the filthiness of the heathen of the land, to seek the LORD God of Israel, did eat, ⁽²²⁾ and kept the feast of unleavened bread seven days with joy: for

*Marginal notes:* ¹ Chald., *let him be destroyed.*   ² Chald., *decree.*   ³ Chald., *the sons of the transportation.*   ⁴ Chald., *according to the writing.*   B.C. 515.   ᵃ Num. 3. 6; & 8. 9.

---

**Hanged** is literally *crucified*. Among the Persians crucifixion was generally the nailing of a body to a cross after decapitation; among the Assyrians it was transfixion or impalement. Here the "being set up" refers of course to the man, and not to the beam.

⁽¹⁴⁾ **Cyrus, and Darius, and Artaxerxes king of Persia.**—This verse includes all the agents in the great work with which the book deals: from Cyrus to Artaxerxes; the elders, that is, the heads of the Jews; the prophets (see chap. v. 1); but all is *from the God of Israel*, whose commandment Cyrus and all others fulfilled.

**Artaxerxes king of Persia.**—Evidently the Artaxerxes Longimanus of the sequel, whose contributions and help did so much toward the perfecting of the general design, though the "finishing" here mentioned took place fifty years before his reign. Observe that he alone is called "king of Persia," which shows that Ezra is writing in his time, and adds his name to the original record. Just as the later Artaxerxes is introduced, so the earlier Cyrus is, in this comprehensive review.

⁽¹⁵⁾ **The third day of the month Adar, which was in the sixth year.**—The event around which this part of the history revolves is dated with due care; it was on the third day of the last month of the ecclesiastical year, B.C. 516—515. Haggai (chap. i. 15) gives the exact date of the re-commencement: the time therefore was four years five months and ten days. But, dating from the first foundation (Ezra iii. 10), no less than twenty-one years had elapsed.

⁽¹⁶⁻²²⁾ The dedication of the second Temple.

⁽¹⁶⁾ **Children of the captivity.**—This designation is peculiarly appropriate here, as in verse 20. "All Israel" soon follows.

⁽¹⁷⁾ **Twelve he goats.**—The people are not now "Judah" or "Judah and Benjamin," but "all Israel." On the Day of Atonement, on the new moons, and on all the great feasts the kid was the sin-offering for the people. But only here is one offered for each tribe.

⁽¹⁸⁾ **In the book of Moses.**—The general arrangements only were given in the Pentateuch. The "courses" were of David's time; and their restoration must have been imperfect, as neither were the twenty-four courses of priests complete nor were the Levites in full force.

⁽¹⁹⁾ **Upon the fourteenth day of the first month.**—Recording the special celebration of the Passover—after the precedent of Hezekiah and Josiah —Ezra returns to the Hebrew language. The occasion was, as it were, a renewal of the redemption from Egypt, and another wilderness had been passed.

⁽²⁰⁾ **Purified together.**—This verse should be translated as follows, contrary to the present accentuation: "The priests were purified; and the Levites were purified as one man: all were pure; and killed." In this fact the present Levitical and official purity of both orders surpassed that of Hezekiah's celebration (2 Chron. xxix. 34, xxx. 3). It had come to be the practice that the Levites slaughtered all the paschal lambs.

⁽²¹⁾ **Separated themselves . . .**—Not proselytes from the heathen are intended, but the remnant of the Jews in the land who had consorted with the foreign populations introduced by the conquerors. Their intermarriages and other acts of conformity are constantly referred to throughout Ezra and Nehemiah.

⁽²²⁾ **And kept the feast.**—The Mazzoth, or week

the LORD had made them joyful, and turned the heart of the king of Assyria unto them, to strengthen their hands in the work of the house of God, the God of Israel.

CHAPTER VII.—<sup>(1)</sup> Now after these things, in the reign of Artaxerxes king of Persia, Ezra the son of Seraiah, the son of Azariah, the son of Hilkiah, <sup>(2)</sup> the son of Shallum, the son of Zadok, the son of Ahitub, <sup>(3)</sup> the son of Amariah, the son of Azariah, the son of Meraioth, <sup>(4)</sup> the son of Zerahiah, the son of Uzzi, the son of Bukki, <sup>(5)</sup> the son of Abishua, the son of Phinehas, the son of Eleazar, the son of Aaron the chief priest: <sup>(6)</sup> this Ezra went up from Babylon; and he *was* a ready scribe in the law of Moses, which the LORD God of Israel had given: and the king granted him all his request, according to the hand of the LORD his God upon him. <sup>(7)</sup> And there went up *some* of the children of Israel, and of the priests, and the Levites, and the singers, and the porters, and the Nethinims, unto Jerusalem, in the seventh year of Artaxerxes the king. <sup>(8)</sup> And he came to Jerusalem in the fifth month, which *was* in the seventh year of the king. <sup>(9)</sup> For upon the first *day* of the first month <sup>1</sup> began he to go up from Babylon, and on the first *day* of the fifth month came he to Jerusalem, according to the good hand of his God upon him. <sup>(10)</sup> For Ezra had prepared his heart to seek the law of the LORD, and to do *it*, and to teach in Israel statutes and judgments.

<sup>(11)</sup> Now this *is* the copy of the letter that the king Artaxerxes gave unto Ezra the priest, the scribe, *even* a scribe of the words of the commandments of the LORD, and of his statutes to Israel. <sup>(12)</sup> Artaxerxes, king of kings, <sup>2</sup> unto Ezra the priest, a scribe of the law of the God of heaven, perfect *peace*, and at such a time. <sup>(13)</sup> I make a decree, that all they of the people of Israel, and *of* his priests and Levites, in my realm, which are minded of their own freewill to go up to Jerusalem, go with thee.

B.C. 457

<sup>1</sup> Heb., *was the foundation of the going up.*

<sup>2</sup> Or, *to Ezra the priest, a perfect scribe of the law of the God of heaven, peace, &c.*

---

of unleavened bread, was the symbol of entire separation from evil, to the service of that God whom on the Passover they accepted as their God. The special joy of this feast was the feeling that the Lord had " turned the heart of the king of Assyria." The king of Persia is so called as a remembrancer of their oppression by his forerunners.

II.—THE SECOND RETURN UNDER EZRA.

VII.

(1—10) A general summary of Ezra's expedition under Divine guidance.

<sup>(1)</sup> **After these things.**—Fifty-seven years after: this special phrase is here alone used. During the interval we must place the events of the Book of Esther.

**Ezra the son of Seraiah.**—His lineage is given, as frequently in Scripture, compendiously, and according to the genealogical law which makes every ancestor a "father" and every descendant a "son." We know not the reason why certain names supplied in 1 Chron. vi. are here omitted; but Seraiah is claimed as the father of Ezra because he was the eminent high priest who last ministered in Solomon's Temple and was slain at Riblah (2 Kings xxv. 18). The links wanting in the lineage are easily supplied.

<sup>(6)</sup> **A ready scribe.**—The "ready writer" of Ps. xlv. 1. Ezra was a priest, and this title is rightly placed before that of scribe in what follows; but here at the outset, when he first appears in history, the title is used which expressed his pre-eminent function, that of guarding and interpreting the law (verse 10).

**All his request.**—This anticipates the letter of verse 11; a series of supplementary notes intervenes.

**According to the hand of the Lord his God upon him.**—The full formula for that special providence over God's servants which both Ezra and Nehemiah recognised.

<sup>(8)</sup> **In the seventh year.**—The repeated notes of time must be marked. The journey itself comes afterwards: it is here indicated as having occupied four months. Ezra's company also is summarised beforehand, according to the manner of this book.

<sup>(10)</sup> **For Ezra had prepared his heart.**—It must be remembered that the providence of God over him immediately precedes—not as the reward of his preparing his heart, but as the reason of it. First, he gave himself to study the law, then to practise it himself, and lastly to teach its positive statutes or ordinances and its moral judgments or precepts—a perfect description of a teacher in the congregation. There is nothing discordant in Ezra saying of himself that he had thus " set his heart."

(11—26) Credentials and commission of Ezra. After the general statement the particulars are given, beginning with the letter of authorisation, in which we discern throughout the hand of Ezra.

<sup>(11)</sup> **Even a scribe.**—In the case of Ezra the function of scribe was more important than that of priest. The word scribe originally meant the writer or copier of the law; but now it meant the expositor of its general moral commandments and of its special ceremonial statutes. It is with the latter more especially that the commission of Ezra had to do.

<sup>(12)</sup> **Artaxerxes, king of kings.**—Artachshatra in Persian, Artachshasta in Hebrew. The Persian monarchs inherited the title here given from the Babylonians (Dan. ii. 37). It is not used by the historian, only by the king himself.

*The Gracious Commission*        EZRA, VII.        *of Artaxerxes to Ezra.*

(14) Forasmuch as thou art sent [1] of the king, and of his *a* seven counsellors, to enquire concerning Judah and Jerusalem, according to the law of thy God which *is* in thine hand; (15) and to carry the silver and gold, which the king and his counsellors have freely offered unto the God of Israel, whose habitation *is* in Jerusalem, (16) *b* and all the silver and gold that thou canst find in all the province of Babylon, with the freewill offering of the people, and of the priests, offering willingly for the house of their God which *is* in Jerusalem: (17) that thou mayest buy speedily with this money bullocks, rams, lambs, with their meat offerings and their drink offerings, and offer them upon the altar of the house of your God which *is* in Jerusalem. (18) And whatsoever shall seem good to thee, and to thy brethren, to do with the rest of the silver and the gold, that do after the will of your God. (19) The vessels also that are given thee for the service of the house of thy God, *those* deliver thou before the God of Jerusalem. (20) And whatsoever more shall be needful for the house of thy God, which thou shalt have occasion to bestow, bestow *it* out of the king's treasure house. (21) And I, *even* I Artaxerxes the king, do make a decree to all the treasurers which *are* beyond the river, that whatsoever Ezra the priest, the scribe of the law of the God of heaven, shall require of you, it be done speedily, (22) unto an hundred talents of silver, and to an hundred [2] measures of wheat, and to an hundred baths of wine, and to an hundred baths of oil, and salt without prescribing *how much*. (23) [3] Whatsoever is commanded by the God of heaven, let it be diligently done for the house of the God of heaven: for why should there be wrath against the realm of the king and his sons? (24) Also we certify you, that touching any of the priests and Levites, singers, porters, Nethinims, or ministers of this house of God, it shall not be lawful to impose toll, tribute, or custom, upon them. (25) And thou, Ezra, after the wisdom of thy God, that *is* in thine hand, set magistrates and judges, which may judge all the people that *are* beyond the river, all such as know the laws of thy God; and teach ye them that know *them* not. (26) And whosoever will not do the law of thy God, and the law of the king, let judgment be executed speedily upon him,

1 Chald., *from before the king.*

*a* Esth. 1. 14.

B.C. cir. 457.

*b* ch. 8. 25.

2 Chald., *cors.*

3 Heb., *Whatsoever is of the decree.*

---

**Perfect peace, and at such a time.**—Literally, *perfect, and so forth.* The expression occurs only here, and is a difficult one. Our translation follows the apocryphal Esdras, and is on the whole to be accepted, a salutation being implied.

(14) **Seven counsellors.**—These are mentioned in Esther i. 14, and were probably the heads of those families who aided Darius Hystaspis against the pseudo-Smerdis, as mentioned by Herodotus.

**According to the law of thy God.**—Ezra's commission was first to enquire into the condition of the city and province, with regard to the relation of both to the Divine law.

(16) **Which is in Jerusalem.**—The repetition of this and similar phrases is after the manner of the literature of this period; but here, as in some other places, it implies deep reverence.

(17) **Buy speedily.**—Provide *first of all* for the sacrificial ceremonial. Every sacrifice had its own meat-offerings and drink-offerings (Num. xv.). These phrases in the commission of course Ezra dictated.

(18) **The rest . . .**—This clause of large latitude would be of great importance for the general beautifying of the Temple (verse 27).

(19) **The vessels.**—Offered (see chap. viii. 25) to be added to those sent up by Zerubbabel.

(20) **Out of the king's treasure house.**—Every satrap had his local treasury. The decree gives Ezra very large powers, but the following verses add a measure of qualification.

(22) **Unto an hundred talents of silver . . .**—A certain restriction is laid upon the amount, although the very restriction seems almost indefinite. The silver might reach £24,000 sterling. As to the rest, Palestine abounded in these productions, which were regularly remitted to the king's service. Salt especially was plentiful near the Dead Sea.

(23) **Whatsoever is commanded by the God of heaven.**—The last is the strongest ground for such an ample authorisation. In the solemn and devout firman the phrase " the God of heaven " occurs twice, and the Persian prince deprecates His wrath. In this seventh year of Artaxerxes, B.C. 458, the tide of success turned for Persia against the Athenians in Egypt.

**And his sons.**—Though Artaxerxes Longimanus was young at this time, he is said to have left eighteen sons.

(24) **We certify you.**—The exemption of so large a number as the entire ministry of the Temple from all kinds of taxation is emphatically introduced.

(25) **All such as know.**—The firman, or king's commission, returning directly to Ezra, makes him supreme in the province over the Jewish population.

**And teach ye them that know them not.**—That is, those Jews who had comparatively forsaken the law. Here he has absolute authority in religion.

(26) **Let judgment be executed speedily upon him.**—Hence civil authority is added to religious. All these powers were usually entrusted to the provincial administrators, with more or less of reservation, by the Persians. But it is obvious that their combination in the one person of this servant of Jehovah demanded express statement.

whether *it be* unto death, or ¹ to banishment, or to confiscation of goods, or to imprisonment. ⁽²⁷⁾ Blessed *be* the LORD God of our fathers, which hath put *such a thing* as this in the king's heart, to beautify the house of the LORD which *is* in Jerusalem: ⁽²⁸⁾ and hath extended mercy unto me before the king, and his counsellors, and before all the king's mighty princes. And I was strengthened as the hand of the LORD my God *was* upon me, and I gathered together out of Israel chief men to go up with me.

CHAPTER VIII.—⁽¹⁾ These *are* now the chief of their fathers, and *this is* the genealogy of them that went up with me from Babylon, in the reign of Artaxerxes the king. ⁽²⁾ Of the sons of Phinehas; Gershom: of the sons of Ithamar; Daniel: of the sons of David; Hattush. ⁽³⁾ Of the sons of Shechaniah, of the sons of Pharosh; Zechariah: and with him were reckoned by genealogy of the males an hundred and fifty. ⁽⁴⁾ Of the sons of Pahath-Moab; Elihoenai the son of Zerahiah, and with him two hundred males. ⁽⁵⁾ Of the sons of Shechaniah; the son of Jahaziel, and with him three hundred males. ⁽⁶⁾ Of the sons also of Adin; Ebed the son of Jonathan, and with him fifty males. ⁽⁷⁾ And of the sons of Elam; Jeshaiah the son of Athaliah, and with him seventy males. ⁽⁸⁾ And of the sons of Shephatiah; Zebadiah the son of Michael, and with him fourscore males. ⁽⁹⁾ Of the sons of Joab; Obadiah the son of Jehiel, and with him two hundred and eighteen males. ⁽¹⁰⁾ And of the sons of Shelomith; the son of Josiphiah, and with him an hundred and threescore males. ⁽¹¹⁾ And of the sons of Bebai; Zechariah the son of Bebai, and with him twenty and eight males. ⁽¹²⁾ And of the sons of Azgad; Johanan ² the son of Hakkatan, and with him an hundred and ten males. ⁽¹³⁾ And of the last sons of Adonikam, whose names *are* these, Eliphelet, Jeiel, and Shemaiah, and with them threescore males. ⁽¹⁴⁾ Of the sons also of Bigvai; Uthai, and ³ Zabbud, and with them seventy males.

⁽¹⁵⁾ And I gathered them together to the river that runneth to Ahava; and there ⁴ abode we in tents three days: and I viewed the people, and the priests, and found there none of the sons of Levi. ⁽¹⁶⁾ Then sent I for Eliezer, for Ariel, for Shemaiah, and for Elnathan, and for Jarib, and for Elnathan, and for Nathan, and for Zechariah, and for Meshullam, chief men; also for Joiarib, and for Elnathan, men of understanding. ⁽¹⁷⁾ And I sent them with commandment unto Iddo the chief at the

*Marginal notes:* ¹ Chald., *to rooting out.* ² Or, *the youngest son.* ³ Or, *Zaccur,* as some read. ⁴ Or, *pitched.*

*B.C. 457.*

---

**(27) Blessed be the Lord God.**—This is the solitary expression of Ezra's private devotion; and it is incorporated with his record in so artless a manner as to confirm the impression that the whole narrative is from his hand.

This sudden ejaculatory thanksgiving, in the midst of his narrative, reminds us of Nehemiah's habit.

**To beautify.**—A general term, signifying all that belonged to the restoration of the Temple.

**(28) And hath extended mercy unto me.**—The honour done to himself before the council of Persia he ascribes to the mercy of God. Once more we have an anticipation of the journey, with a parenthesis intervening.

### VIII.

(1—14) A list of the chief names, given by families, of those who accompanied Ezra.

**(1) This is the genealogy.**—The names of the heads of houses is followed generally by that of the wider families they belonged to. With this list is to be compared the register of those who went up with Zerubbabel (chap. ii. 2 *seq.*).

**(2, 3)** According to 1 Chron. iii. 22, Huttush was a descendant of David, and grandson of Shechaniah. The difficulty of the text therefore may probably be best solved by punctuating thus: "Of the sons of David, Hattush of the sons of Shechaniah. Of the sons of Pharosh, Zechariah."

**(5) The son of Jahaziel.**—Obviously a name is omitted. The LXX. have, "of the sons of Zattu, Shechaniah," before Jahaziel.

**(10)** Here also a name is wanting. The LXX. have, " of the sons of Bani, Shelomith, the son of Josiphiah."

**(13) And of the last sons.**—The younger branches, the elder being reported in chap. ii. 13.

(15—31) The journey through Ahava to Jerusalem.

**(15) Ahava.**—Both river and town. Nine days' journey brought them thither; and there is a place now called Hit, about eighty miles from Babylon, which has been identified with it.

**None of the sons of Levi.**—Only seventy-four had returned with Zerubbabel (chap. ii. 40); and here we have evidence that the disinclination continued. The importance of Levitcal service in the Temple accounts for the anxiety of Ezra.

**(16) Men of understanding.** — Teachers, and perhaps priests. These were joined with nine chief men as a deputation to Iddo.

**(17) The place Casiphia.** — Evidently near Ahavah, and a colony of Jews presided over by Iddo,

place Casiphia, and ¹ I told them what they should say unto Iddo, *and* to his brethren the Nethinims, at the place Casiphia, that they should bring unto us ministers for the house of our God. ⁽¹⁸⁾ And by the good hand of our God upon us they brought us a man of understanding, of the sons of Mahli, the son of Levi, the son of Israel; and Sherebiah, with his sons and his brethren, eighteen; ⁽¹⁹⁾ and Hashabiah, and with him Jeshaiah of the sons of Merari, his brethren and their sons, twenty; ⁽²⁰⁾ ᵃ also of the Nethinims, whom David and the princes had appointed for the service of the Levites, two hundred and twenty Nethinims: all of them were expressed by name.

⁽²¹⁾ Then I proclaimed a fast there, at the river of Ahava, that we might afflict ourselves before our God, to seek of him a right way for us, and for our little ones, and for all our substance. ⁽²²⁾ For I was ashamed to require of the king a band of soldiers and horsemen to help us against the enemy in the way: because we had spoken unto the king, saying, The hand of our God *is* upon all them for good that seek him; but his power and his wrath *is* against all them that forsake him. ⁽²³⁾ So we fasted and besought our God for this: and he was intreated of us.

⁽²⁴⁾ Then I separated twelve of the chief of the priests, Sherebiah, Hashabiah, and ten of their brethren with them, ⁽²⁵⁾ and weighed unto them the silver, and the gold, and the vessels, *even* the offering of the house of our God, which the king, and his counsellors, and his lords, and all Israel *there* present, had offered: ⁽²⁶⁾ I even weighed unto their hand six hundred and fifty talents of silver, and silver vessels an hundred talents, *and* of gold an hundred talents; ⁽²⁷⁾ also twenty basons of gold, of a thousand drams; and two vessels of ² fine copper, ³ precious as gold. ⁽²⁸⁾ And I said unto them, Ye *are* holy unto the LORD; the vessels *are* holy also; and the silver and the gold *are* a freewill offering unto the LORD God of your fathers. ⁽²⁹⁾ Watch ye, and keep *them*, until ye weigh *them* before the chief of the priests and the Levites, and chief of the fathers of Israel, at Jerusalem, in the chambers of the house of the LORD. ⁽³⁰⁾ So took the priests and the Levites the weight of the silver, and the gold, and the vessels, to bring *them* to Jerusalem unto the house of our God.

⁽³¹⁾ Then we departed from the river of Ahava on the twelfth *day* of the first month, to go unto Jerusalem: and the hand of our God was upon us, and he delivered us from the hand of the enemy, and of such as lay in wait by the

---

1 Heb., *I put words in their mouth.*

a See ch. 2. 43.

2 Heb., *yellow, or shining brass.*

3 Heb., *desirable.*

---

one of the humble race of the Nethinims, but at present chief under the Persians. Ezra was aware of their existence in these parts.

**Ministers.**—A term obviously including Levites and Nethinims.

⁽¹⁸⁾ **A man of understanding.** — Probably a proper name, *Ishsekel.* This is required by the "and" before "Sherebiah," who was a Levite, referred to by Nehemiah (chap. viii. 7).

⁽²⁰⁾ **The Nethinims.**—It is here alone recorded that David appointed these to aid the Levites.

**All of them were expressed by name.**—Not, as some think, that they were all famous, but that Iddo sent their names in a list not given. The relief of their coming is gratefully ascribed to the "good hand of our God upon us."

⁽²¹⁾ **To seek of him a right way for us.**— The wilderness was now before them, and an enemy, indefinitely referred to, was in the way: probably desert tribes, always lying in wait for unprotected caravans.

**Our little ones.**—An intimation that whole households went up.

**Our substance.**—Chiefly the treasures for the Temple, though the term signifies cattle and other goods, with an undertone of abundance.

⁽²²⁾ **Because we had spoken unto the king.** —The whole verse goes back to the past. Ezra had magnified God's providence before the king: His "hand" upon his own "for good"—the habitual tribute to Providence in this book and Nehemiah—and His power "against" His enemies "for evil" not being expressed. This sublime testimony made the "seeking" God a condition of safety. Hence the solemn fasting and prayer, following many precedents (Judges xx. 26; 1 Sam. vii. 6).

⁽²⁴⁾ **Sherebiah.**—Rather, *to Sherebiah*—that is, these two Levites, alone mentioned, with ten others, were associated with an equal number of priests in the charge of the Temple treasure.

⁽²⁵⁾ **And weighed.**—The gold and silver were in bars. According to the best computation, the silver would amount to a quarter of a million of our money, and the gold to about three-quarters of a million.

⁽²⁷⁾ **A thousand drams.**—*Darics,* and therefore the whole worth rather more than a thousand guineas.

**Fine copper.**—Probably the Roman Orichalcum, a metal very highly valued.

⁽²⁸⁾ **And I said unto them, Ye are holy unto the Lord.**—A unique verse in every respect. The treasures were consecrated, and they were committed to consecrated hands: a good account was to be given of them to the treasurers of the Temple.

⁽³¹⁾ **The hand of our God was upon us.**—This sums up the history of the journey.

*The Commission is Delivered.*     EZRA, IX.     *The Affinity of the People with Strangers.*

way. <sup>(32)</sup> And we came to Jerusalem, and abode there three days. <sup>(33)</sup> Now on the fourth day was the silver and the gold and the vessels weighed in the house of our God by the hand of Meremoth the son of Uriah the priest; and with him *was* Eleazar the son of Phinehas; and with them *was* Jozabad the son of Jeshua, and Noadiah the son of Binnui, Levites; <sup>(34)</sup> by number *and* by weight of every one: and all the weight was written at that time. <sup>(35)</sup> *Also* the children of those that had been carried away, which were come out of the captivity, offered burnt offerings unto the God of Israel, twelve bullocks for all Israel, ninety and six rams, seventy and seven lambs, twelve he goats *for* a sin offering: all *this was* a burnt offering unto the LORD. <sup>(36)</sup> And they delivered the king's commissions unto the king's lieutenants, and to the governors on this side the river: and they furthered the people, and the house of God.

B.C. 457.

CHAPTER IX.—<sup>(1)</sup> Now when these things were done, the princes came to me, saying, The people of Israel, and the priests, and the Levites, have not separated themselves from the people of the lands, *doing* according to their abominations, *even* of the Canaanites, the Hittites, the Perizzites, the Jebusites, the Ammonites, the Moabites, the Egyptians, and the Amorites. <sup>(2)</sup> For they have taken of their daughters for themselves, and for their sons: so that the holy seed have mingled themselves with the people of *those* lands: yea, the hand of the princes and rulers hath been chief in this trespass. <sup>(3)</sup> And when I heard this thing, I rent my garment and my mantle, and plucked off the hair of my head and of my beard, and sat down astonied. <sup>(4)</sup> Then were assembled unto me every one that trembled at the words of the God of Israel, because of the transgression of those that had been carried away; and I sat astonied until

---

(32—36) The arrival in Jerusalem, and first proceedings there.

(32) **Three days.**—Devoted, as in the similar case of Nehemiah, to rest and more private devotion.

(33) **Meremoth the son of Uriah . . .**—These names of priests and Levites, who had officially received the treasures, occur again in Nehemiah.

(34) **By number and by weight.**—The number of the vessels and the weight of the ingots were recorded and laid up for security.

(36) **And they delivered the king's commissions.**—First came sacrifices of burnt offering to God (verse 35); then, having rendered to God the things which were God's, they render to Cæsar the things of Cæsar. They delivered the king's commission, or firman, to the lieutenants or satraps in military authority, and to the governors, or pechahs, or pashas, in civil authority under them. The firman was of course accepted and acted upon: "they furthered the people."

IX.

<sup>(1)</sup> **Now when these things were done.**—The remainder of the book is occupied with the execution of Ezra's function as a moral reformer. One chief disorder is mentioned, that of the mixed marriages (verse 2), which the new lawgiver evidently regarded as fatal to the purity of the Divine service, and to the design of God in separating for a season this peculiar people.

(1—4) The report of the abuse of mixed marriages is formally brought before Ezra.

<sup>(1)</sup> **The princes.**—Heads of tribes, native rulers of Jerusalem, as distinguished from the satraps and governors. Zerubbabel's office had no successor; and the term princes expressed rather their eminence than their authority, which had been powerless to check the abuses they complain of.

**Doing according to their abominations.**—Rather, *as it regards their abominations*. They are not charged with abandonment to idolatry, but with that peculiar laxity which appears in the sequel.

**The Ammonites.**—It is remarkable that all the ancient proscribed races are mentioned, and not the specific nations by the names of which the Samaritans were known, as if to make the case as hateful as possible. At the same time, many of these races still lingered in the neighbourhood of Judæa.

<sup>(2)</sup> **The holy seed.**—The "holy nation" or "peculiar people" of Exod. xix. 6 is called the "holy seed" by Isaiah (chap. vi. 13), with reference to its being preserved and kept holy amidst judgments; and here the same term is used with reference to its desecration by being made common among the nations.

**The princes and rulers.**—The upper classes, whether priests and Levites or laymen.

**This trespass.**—There is no question as to the unlawfulness of these intermarriages, nor any palliation on account of necessity. The rulers report it, and Ezra receives the report as evidence that the whole purpose of God with regard to the people was, at the very outset of their new economy, in course of being defeated by the guilt of the heads of Israel. Their delinquency as such is admitted on all hands.

<sup>(3)</sup> **I rent my garment and my mantle.**—The actions of Ezra betoken his horror and grief. But both the rending of the outer and inner garment and the plucking the hair were symbolical acts, teaching their lesson to the people who witnessed, and, as we see, were deeply impressed.

<sup>(4)</sup> **Trembled.**—In fear of the Divine judgments.

**Transgression of those that had been carried away.**—The usual name of the people at this time. During their captivity, however, they had

the evening sacrifice. ⁽⁵⁾ And at the evening sacrifice I arose up from my ¹heaviness; and having rent my garment and my mantle, I fell upon my knees, and spread out my hands unto the LORD my God, ⁽⁶⁾ and said,

O my God, I am ashamed and blush to lift up my face to thee, my God: for our iniquities are increased over *our* head, and our ²trespass is grown up unto the heavens. ⁽⁷⁾ Since the days of our fathers *have* we *been* in a great trespass unto this day; and for our iniquities have we, our kings, *and* our priests, been delivered into the hand of the kings of the lands, to the sword, to captivity, and to a spoil, and to confusion of face, as *it is* this day. ⁽⁸⁾ And now for a ³little space grace hath been *shewed* from the LORD our God, to leave us a remnant to escape, and to give us ⁴ a nail in his holy place, that our God may lighten our eyes, and give us a little reviving in our bondage. ⁽⁹⁾ For we *were* bondmen; yet our God hath not forsaken us in our bondage, but hath extended mercy unto us in the sight of the kings of Persia, to give us a reviving, to set up the house of our God, and ⁵to repair the desolations thereof, and to give us a wall in Judah and in Jerusalem. ⁽¹⁰⁾ And now, O our God, what shall we say after this? for we have forsaken thy commandments, ⁽¹¹⁾ which thou hast commanded ⁶ by thy servants the prophets, saying, *ᵃ* The land unto which ye go to possess it, is an unclean land with the filthiness of the people of the lands, with their abominations, which have filled it ⁷ from one end to another with their uncleanness. ⁽¹²⁾ Now therefore give not your daughters unto their sons, neither take their daughters unto your sons, nor seek their peace or their wealth for ever: that ye may be strong, and eat the good of the land, and leave *it* for an inheritance to your children for ever. ⁽¹³⁾ And after all that is come upon us for our evil deeds, and for our great trespass, seeing that thou our God ⁸hast punished us less than our iniquities *deserve*, and hast given us *such* deliverance as this; ⁽¹⁴⁾ should we again break thy commandments, and join in affinity with the people of these abominations? wouldest not thou be angry with us till thou hadst consumed *us*, so that *there should be* no remnant nor escaping? ⁽¹⁵⁾ O LORD God of Israel, thou *art* righteous: for we remain yet escaped, as *it is* this day:

¹ Or, *affliction.*
² Or, *guiltiness.*
³ Heb., *moment.*
⁴ Or, *a pin:* that is, *a constant and sure abode.*
⁵ Heb., *to set up*
⁶ Heb., *by the hand of thy servants.*
ᵃ Ex. 23. 32; Deut. 7. 3.
⁷ Heb., *from mouth to mouth.*
⁸ Heb., *hast withheld beneath our iniquities.*

---

not been thus guilty. It was the aggravation of their guilt that they committed the trespass now.

(5—15) Ezra's prayer of confession and deprecation.

⁽⁵⁾ **And at the evening sacrifice I arose up.**—Until the afternoon Ezra had sat silent and in grief before the Temple, and in presence of the people. Then, amidst the solemnities of the sacrifice, he uttered the prayer which he had been meditating.

⁽⁶⁾ **And said, O my God.**—The confession begins with "O my God;" but Ezra is the representative of the people, and it proceeds "O our God" (verse 10), without once returning to the first person.

⁽⁷⁾ **Since the days of our fathers have we been in a great trespass.**—In these Common Prayers of Ezra, Nehemiah, and Daniel, the race of Israel is regarded as one, and national sins as one "great trespass." The repetition of "this day" at the beginning and at the end of the verse is to be observed: in the former place in reference to the sin; in the latter in reference to the punishment.

⁽⁸⁾ **A little space.**—The "little" here and at the close of the sentence are emphatic. All the present tokens of mercy are said at the conclusion of the prayer (verse 14) to be conditional in their continuance. The little space from the time of Cyrus was nearly two generations; but it was a moment only in relation to the past and the possible future. The idea is inverted in Isa. liv. 7: "For a small moment have I forsaken thee."

**Nail in his holy place.**—The Temple was itself the sure nail on which all their hopes hung.

**A little reviving.**—Literally, *make us a little life.* The present revival was but the beginning, and still by manifold tokens precarious.

⁽⁹⁾ **We were bondmen.**—Better, *we are bondmen.* In this lies the emphasis of the appeal.

**A wall.**—Like "the nail," a figurative expression for security. The literal wall was not yet rebuilt. This completes the description of Divine mercy: first, the people were a delivered remnant; the Temple was a sure nail for the future of religion; and their civil estate was made secure.

⁽¹⁰⁾ **After this.**—But all was a mercy for which there had been no adequate return.

⁽¹¹⁾ **Saying.**—In the later Old Testament Scriptures the quotation of the earlier is often of this character, giving the substance of many passages. The same style is observable in the New Testament.

⁽¹²⁾ **Give not your daughters.**—See Deut. vii. 3, the only place where the interdict includes both daughters and sons. It is observable that the giving of daughters in marriage to heathens is not mentioned either in Ezra or in Nehemiah.

**Nor seek their peace.**—An evident echo of that most stern injunction in Deut. xxiii. 6.

⁽¹⁵⁾ **O Lord God of Israel, thou art righteous.**—The solemn invocation shows that this is a summary of the whole prayer: God's righteousness is magnified, as accompanied by the grace which had preserved them, although as only a remnant; and as such covered with their trespasses; and especially with "this" the present trespass, the guilt of which underlies all.

behold, we *are* before thee in our trespasses: for we cannot stand before thee because of this.

CHAPTER X.—(1) Now when Ezra had prayed, and when he had confessed, weeping and casting himself down before the house of God, there assembled unto him out of Israel a very great congregation of men and women and children: for the people [1] wept very sore. (2) And Shechaniah the son of Jehiel, *one* of the sons of Elam, answered and said unto Ezra, We have trespassed against our God, and have taken strange wives of the people of the land: yet now there is hope in Israel concerning this thing. (3) Now therefore let us make a covenant with our God [2] to put away all the wives, and such as are born of them, according to the counsel of my lord, and of those that tremble at the commandment of our God; and let it be done according to the law. (4) Arise; for *this* matter *belongeth* unto thee: we also *will be* with thee: be of good courage, and do *it*.

(5) Then arose Ezra, and made the chief priests, the Levites, and all Israel, to swear that they should do according to this word. And they sware. (6) Then Ezra rose up from before the house of God, and went into the chamber of Johanan the son of Eliashib: and *when* he came thither, he did eat no bread, nor drink water: for he mourned because of the transgression of them that had been carried away. (7) And they made proclamation throughout Judah and Jerusalem unto all the children of the captivity, that they should gather themselves together unto Jerusalem; (8) and that whosoever would not come within three days, according to the counsel of the princes and the elders, all his substance should be [3] forfeited, and himself separated from the congregation of those that had been carried away.

(9) Then all the men of Judah and Benjamin gathered themselves together unto Jerusalem within three days. It *was* the ninth month, on the twentieth *day* of the month; and all the people sat in the street of the house of God, trembling because of *this* matter, and

[1] Heb., *wept a great weeping.*
[2] Heb., *to bring forth.*
[3] Heb., *devoted.*

---

## X.

(1—6) The covenant of repentance and amendment. Here the narrative assumes another form; and, in accordance with the solemnity of a great public transaction, Ezra adopts the third person.

(1) **Before the house of God.**—Prostrating himself towards the Temple in the court, where all the people saw him and marked his distress.

**Wept very sore.**—The evil penetrated domestic life, and the punishment, as was already foreseen by "the women bringing the children with them," brought special family distress.

(2) **Shechaniah.**—The son of one of the transgressors (verse 26), whose action as the representative of the people gives him an honourable memorial in Scripture.

**There is hope in Israel.**—A noble sentiment for a reformer even at the worst of times.

(3) Special covenants with God—general, as in 2 Kings xxiii. 3, and in regard to particular offences, as here, and in Jer. xxxiv. 8—were familiar in Jewish history. And at all times of critical sin or danger the voluntary intervention of individuals was held in honour. (Comp. Num. xxv. 12 *seq.*)

**According to the counsel of my lord.**—Better, *according to, or in, the counsel of the Lord.* Ezra would hardly be called "my lord," nor had he given any counsel.

**According to the law.**—Which in Deut. xxiv. prescribes the terms of divorce.

(4) **Arise; for this matter belongeth unto thee.**—The commission given to Ezra (chap. vii. 11 *seq.*) seems specially referred to, and the deep prostration of his spirit renders the encouragement here given very appropriate. It had its effect: as Ezra's grief had made the people sorrowful, so their vigour made him energetic.

(5) **According to this word.**—"According to" occurs three times, and each instance must be noted. First, it was "in the counsel of the Lord" as God's law, rightly interpreted, demanded this measure, however seemingly harsh; secondly, it was to be done "according to the law;" and, thirdly, according to the present covenant. which went beyond the law of Moses.

(6) **The chamber of Johanan the son of Eliashib.**—Ezra retired for fasting and prayer into one of the chambers opening on the court. It seems impossible to identify these names with the Eliashib of Nehemiah xii. 10 and his grandson. Both names were common.

(7—17) Conference of the people and commission to try individual cases.

(8) **Forfeited.**—This, as also what precedes and what follows, again recalls the express commission of chap. vii. But "according to the counsel" removes all appearance of arbitrariness on the part of Ezra.

(9) **Within three days.**—From the time of hearing the summons. No town was more than forty miles distant; and of course only those would come that were able, and who came within the scope of the proclamation, the precise terms of which are not given. They were not more than could assemble "in the street," or open court of the Temple. The minute specifications of date, and the two reasons for the trembling of the people, and the whole strain of the narrative, bear witness to the veracity of an eye-witness.

*They Promise Amendment.*     EZRA, X.     *Those who had Married Strange Wives.*

for ¹ the great rain. ⁽¹⁰⁾ And Ezra the priest stood up, and said unto them, Ye have transgressed, and ²have taken strange wives, to increase the trespass of Israel. ⁽¹¹⁾ Now therefore make confession unto the LORD God of your fathers, and do his pleasure: and separate yourselves from the people of the land, and from the strange wives.

⁽¹²⁾ Then all the congregation answered and said with a loud voice, As thou hast said, so must we do. ⁽¹³⁾ But the people *are* many, and *it is* a time of much rain, and we are not able to stand without, neither *is this* a work of one day or two: for ³we are many that have transgressed in this thing. ⁽¹⁴⁾ Let now our rulers of all the congregation stand, and let all them which have taken strange wives in our cities come at appointed times, and with them the elders of every city, and the judges thereof, until the fierce wrath of our God ⁴for this matter be turned from us.

⁽¹⁵⁾ Only Jonathan the son of Asahel and Jahaziah the son of Tikvah ⁵ were employed about this *matter*: and Meshullam and Shabbethai the Levite helped them. ⁽¹⁶⁾ And the children of the captivity did so.

And Ezra the priest, *with* certain chief of the fathers, after the house of their fathers, and all of them by *their* names, were separated, and sat down in the first day of the tenth month to examine the matter. ⁽¹⁷⁾ And they made an end with all the men that had taken strange wives by the first day of the first month.

⁽¹⁸⁾ And among the sons of the priests there were found that had taken strange wives: *namely*, of the sons of Jeshua the son of Jozadak, and his brethren; Maaseiah, and Eliezer, and Jarib, and Gedaliah. ⁽¹⁹⁾ And they gave their hands that they would put away their wives; and *being* guilty, *they offered* a ram of the flock for their trespass. ⁽²⁰⁾ And of the sons of Immer; Hanani, and Zebadiah. ⁽²¹⁾ And of the sons of Harim; Maaseiah, and Elijah, and Shemaiah, and Jehiel, and Uzziah. ⁽²²⁾ And of the sons of Pashur; Elioenai, Maaseiah, Ishmael, Nethaneel, Jozabad, and Elasah.

⁽²³⁾ Also of the Levites; Jozabad, and Shimei, and Kelaiah, (the same *is* Kelita,) Pethahiah, Judah, and Eliezer. ⁽²⁴⁾ Of the singers also; Eliashib: and of the porters; Shallum, and Telem, and Uri.

⁽²⁵⁾ Moreover of Israel: of the sons of Parosh; Ramiah, and Jeziah, and Malchiah, and Miamin, and Eleazar, and Malchijah, and Benaiah. ⁽²⁶⁾ And of the sons of Elam; Mattaniah, Zechariah, and Jehiel, and Abdi, and Jeremoth, and Eliah. ⁽²⁷⁾ And of the sons of

---

¹ Heb., *the showers.*

B.C. 456.

² Heb., *have caused to dwell,* or, *have brought back.*

³ Or, *we have greatly offended in this thing.*

⁴ Or, *till this matter be dispatched.*

⁵ Heb., *stood.*

---

It was the ninth month.—Chisleu, our December, the rainy month in Palestine.

⁽¹⁰⁾ **Ezra the priest.**—He stood up, not as the commissioner of Artaxerxes, not at this moment as the scribe, but as the representative of God.

⁽¹¹⁾ **Do his pleasure.**—This procedure, humanly severe, is connected with the Divine will.

**From the people of the land, and from the strange wives.**—The marriages were but a subordinate branch, though a very important one, of the wider sin: that of confederacy with idolators.

⁽¹³⁾ **We are many.**—Better, *we have greatly offended in this thing.* The greatness of the offence of course implied the number of the offenders.

⁽¹⁴⁾ **Stand.**—As a representative body in session.

**Until the fierce wrath of our God for this matter be turned from us.**—A difficult verse, owing to a slight peculiarity in the original. The meaning seems to be: *until the fierce wrath of our God—fierce while this matter lasts—be turned away from us.*

⁽¹⁵⁾ **Were employed about.**—Rather, *stood against.* Nothing is said as to the reason for opposition on the part of these and the two who abetted them. But the reason is obvious enough. Some modern expositors are of their mind, and regard the act of Ezra as remedying one sin by another still greater. They bring Malachi (chap. ii. 15) to their support; but nothing in his prediction about "the wife of thy youth," rightly understood, tends to condemn the conduct here described.

⁽¹⁶⁾ **By their names.**—As in chap. viii. 20, the names were before the writer, but are not given.

**And sat down.**—That is, *held a session.* This was ten days after the general assembly.

⁽¹⁷⁾ **And they made an end.**—Though the number of transgressors was only one hundred and thirteen, two months were occupied, which shows the care taken to do justice, especially to the claims of the women put away.

⁽¹⁸⁻⁴⁴⁾ List of the transgressors.

⁽¹⁹⁾ **They gave their hands.**—The four members of the high priest's family were peculiarly dealt with. They gave their distinct pledge, and offered each a special trespass offering. It is one among a multitude of similar tokens of authenticity in the history; an inventor would have given some reason for the peculiarity.

⁽²²⁾ **Pashur.**—Comparing chap. ii. 36—39, we find that all the priestly families that returned with Zerubbabel were implicated in the national offence.

⁽²⁵⁾ **Of Israel.**—Of the laity eighty-six are mentioned, belonging to ten races which returned with Zerubbabel.

Zattu; Elioenai, Eliashib, Mattaniah, and Jeremoth, and Zabad, and Aziza. <sup>(28)</sup> Of the sons also of Bebai; Jehohanan, Hananiah, Zabbai, *and* Athlai. <sup>(29)</sup> And of the sons of Bani; Meshullam, Malluch, and Adaiah, Jashub, and Sheal, and Ramoth. <sup>(30)</sup> And of the sons of Pahath-moab; Adna, and Chelal, Benaiah, Maaseiah, Mattaniah, Bezaleel, and Binnui, and Manasseh. <sup>(31)</sup> And *of* the sons of Harim; Eliezer, Ishijah, Malchiah, Shemaiah, Shimeon, <sup>(32)</sup> Benjamin, Malluch, *and* Shemariah. <sup>(33)</sup> Of the sons of Hashum; Mattenai, Mattathah, Zabad, Eliphelet, Jeremai, Manasseh, *and* Shimei. <sup>(34)</sup> Of the sons of Bani; Maadai, Amram, and Uel, <sup>(35)</sup> Benaiah, Bedeiah, Chelluh, <sup>(36)</sup> Vaniah, Meremoth, Eliashib, <sup>(37)</sup> Mattaniah, Mattenai, and Jaasau, <sup>(38)</sup> and Bani, and Binnui, Shimei, <sup>(39)</sup> and Shelemiah, and Nathan, and Adaiah, <sup>(40)</sup> <sup>1</sup>Machnadebai, Shashai, Sharai, <sup>(41)</sup> Azareel, and Shelemiah, Shemariah, <sup>(42)</sup> Shallum, Amariah, *and* Joseph. <sup>(43)</sup> Of the sons of Nebo; Jeiel, Mattithiah, Zabad, Zebina, Jadau, and Joel, Benaiah. <sup>(44)</sup> All these had taken strange wives: and *some* of them had wives by whom they had children.

<sup>1</sup> Or, *Mabnadebai*, according to some copies.

<sup>(34)</sup> **Bani.**—Probably this should be some other name, as Bani occurs before. The peculiarly large number of the representatives of his race suggests that there is some confusion in the present text.

<sup>(44)</sup> **All these had taken strange wives.**—Though the numbers are not summed up and distributed, it is evident that this closing sentence is emphatic. Ezra ends his history with a catalogue of the delinquents—strong testimony to the importance he attached to the reformation. The last words—literally, *and there were of them wives who had brought forth children*—tend in the same direction. Not even this pathetic fact restrained the thoroughness of the excision. But the Book of Nehemiah (chap. xiii. 23 *seq.*) will show that it was thorough only for a time.

# THE BOOK OF NEHEMIAH

# INTRODUCTION

## TO

# THE BOOK OF NEHEMIAH.

I. Of Nehemiah's personal history we know little beyond the few facts preserved in this book. He was of the tribe of Judah; and probably, like Zerubbabel his predecessor, of the royal stock. He was one of the "children of the captivity"; and, through circumstances of which we know nothing, rose to eminence in the Persian court. As cupbearer of Artaxerxes he was in a position of wealth and influence: the history shows how important both were in his vocation, and how nobly he used both in the service of his country. The events recorded furnish only a scanty memorial of Nehemiah's life; but they paint his character to perfection. He was a man of profound piety, connecting everything, great or small, with the will of God, in whose presence he lived and moved and had his being: this is attested by the interjectional prayers which habitually recur. His prudence was equally marked; and there is no better example of constant dependence on God united with practical forethought. He was disinterested and unselfish: his wealth was used for public ends, and there is not the slightest reference to self apart from the common good. This set the crown on his public administration, the energy, sagacity, and even severity of which were guided solely by the demands of his vocation. He always appeals to the judgment of a merciful God; and that appeal avails against much hard modern criticism which dwells on his alleged asperity, self-confidence and self-assertion. Ancient Jewish tradition gave his name a high place, not a whit below that of Ezra.

II. Passing from the book to the writer, we have the long-contested question as to the nature and extent of his authorship. It is generally admitted that the first seven chapters, as also the greater part of the last three, were Nehemiah's own composition. But a glance at the three intermediate chapters shows that he was not the author of these in the same sense; and this is confirmed by a minute comparison of the style and phraseology of the different portions. Those in which the writer appears in the first person, and which bear the peculiar stamp of his devotion, seem to have been extracts from his personal diary; while the others seem to have been incorporated from some public account authoritatively drawn up under the direction of Ezra and himself. But, though several hands contributed to the compilation of this middle section, it is easy to see that Nehemiah made the whole his own. For instance: the prayer in ch. ix. was probably Ezra's, but in the history surrounding the prayer there is no special mark of his style; and the remarkable transition to the "we" in ch. x., the sealing of the covenant, hardly allows either Nehemiah or Ezra to be the immediate author, but is rather like a free rendering of the very terms of the vow as written in a permanent document. The dedication of the wall is vividly described in the first person; and so is the energetic administration of reform after his return from Susa. But between these there are a few verses which seem to be derived from a national record. The six lists which are interwoven in this middle section were of course extracts from public archives. Those of ch. xi. fall appropriately into the narrative. The other lists have all the appearance of being inserted on account of their importance to the future commonwealth: one of them, that of the high priests from Jeshua to Jaddua, having been retouched at a later period. The interpolator probably added also verses 22 and 23 of the same chapter; as the notes will explain.

# THE BOOK OF NEHEMIAH

## CHAPTER I.

<sup>(1)</sup> The words of Nehemiah the son of Hachaliah.

And it came to pass in the month Chisleu, in the twentieth year, as I was in Shushan the palace, <sup>(2)</sup> that Hanani, one of my brethren, came, he and *certain* men of Judah; and I asked them concerning the Jews that had escaped, which were left of the captivity, and concerning Jerusalem. <sup>(3)</sup> And they said unto me, The remnant that are left of the captivity there in the province *are* in great affliction and reproach: the wall of Jerusalem also *<sup>a</sup>is* broken down, and the gates thereof are burned with fire.

<sup>(4)</sup> And it came to pass, when I heard these words, that I sat down and wept, and mourned *certain* days, and fasted, and prayed before the God of heaven, <sup>(5)</sup> and said, I beseech thee, *<sup>b</sup>*O LORD God of heaven, the great and terrible God, that keepeth covenant and mercy for them that love him and observe his commandments: <sup>(6)</sup> let thine ear now be attentive, and thine eyes open, that thou mayest hear the prayer of thy servant, which I pray before thee now, day and night, for the children of Israel thy servants, and confess the sins of the children of Israel, which we have sinned against thee: both I and my father's house have sinned. <sup>(7)</sup> We have dealt very corruptly against thee, and have not kept the commandments, nor the statutes, nor the judgments, which thou

B.C. cir. 446.

*a* 2 Kin. 25. 10.

*b* Dan. 9. 4.

---

<sup>(1)</sup> **The words of Nehemiah.**—Rather, *The narrative* or *record*. Both as referring to his affairs and as written by him.

(1—3) Introductory: tidings brought to Nehemiah concerning the sad estate of Jerusalem and the people.

<sup>(1)</sup> **In the month Chisleu.**—The names rather than the numbers of the months are generally employed after the captivity: Nisan, Iyar, Sivan, Tammuz, Av, Elul, Tishri, Marchesvan, Chisleu, Tebeth, Shevat, Adar; with an intercalary month, the second Adar. Chisleu answers nearly to our December.

**In the twentieth year.**—Of the reign of Artaxerxes Longimanus, which began B.C. 465 and ended B.C. 425.

**In Shushan the palace.**—Susa, the capital of Susiana; where, after the capture of the Babylonian empire, a great palace was built by Darius Hystaspis, the ruins of which are still seen. It was the principal and favourite residence of the Persian court, alternating with Persepolis, the older capital, and Babylon. Shushan was one of the most ancient cities in the world; and is associated with the visions of Daniel, and with the feast of Ahasuerus (Dan. viii. 2, Esther i. 3).

<sup>(2)</sup> **He and certain men of Judah.**—*From Judah*: Hanani was Nehemiah's own brother (ch. vii. 1). He and his companions came from "the province" of Judah (verse 3); nothing is said as to their motive in coming; and certainly there is no intimation that they had been sent to the Persian court on account of recent disturbances.

<sup>(3)</sup> **And they said.**—Nehemiah's question and his friends' answer refer first to the people and then to the city. As to the former the terms used have a deep pathos. Those who had returned to their country—now only *the province*—are, in the question, *the Jews that had escaped*; in the answer they are *the Remnant that are left*: both being *from the captivity*.

**In great affliction and reproach.**—In distress because of the contempt of the people around. All these expressions are familiar in the prophets; but they are united here in a peculiar and affecting combination. As to the city, the report is that the walls were still "broken down": lying prostrate, with partial exceptions, as Nebuchadnezzar left them a hundred and forty-two years before (2 Kings xxv. 10), and, moreover, what had not been recorded, "the gates thereof burned with fire." Though the Temple had been rebuilt, there is no valid reason for supposing that the walls of the city had been in part restored and again demolished.

(4—11) Nehemiah's appeal to God. The prayer is a perfect example of the private and individual devotion with which the later Hebrew Scriptures abound. It begins with formal and appropriate invocation (verse 5—8), flows into earnest confession (verses 6, 7), pleads the covenant promises (verses 8—10), and supplicates a present answer (verse 11). The extant Scriptures, freely used, are the foundation of all.

<sup>(4)</sup> **Fasted.**—Like Daniel, Esther, and Ezra, Nehemiah fasted: fasting appears in later Judaism a prominent part of individual devotion, as it is in the New Testament.

<sup>(6)</sup> **Both I and my father's house have sinned.**—The supplication was for the nation; and in such cases of personal intercession the individual assumes the sin of all the past.

commandest thy servant Moses. (8) Remember, I beseech thee, the word that thou commandest thy servant Moses, saying, *"If* ye transgress, I will scatter you abroad among the nations : (9) but *if* ye turn unto me, and keep my commandments, and do them; *though there were of you cast out unto the uttermost part of the heaven, *yet* will I gather them from thence, and will bring them unto the place that I have chosen to set my name there. (10) Now these *are* thy servants and thy people, whom thou hast redeemed by thy great power, and by thy strong hand. (11) O LORD, I beseech thee, let now thine ear be attentive to the prayer of thy servant, and to the prayer of thy servants, who desire to fear thy name : and prosper, I pray thee, thy servant this day, and grant him mercy in the sight of this man. For I was the king's cupbearer.

CHAPTER II.—(1) And it came to pass in the month Nisan, in the twentieth year of Artaxerxes the king, *that* wine *was* before him : and I took up the wine, and gave *it* unto the king. Now I had not been *beforetime* sad in his presence. (2) Wherefore the king said unto me, Why *is* thy countenance sad, seeing thou *art* not sick? this *is* nothing *else* but sorrow of heart. Then I was very sore afraid, (3) and said unto the king, Let the king live for ever : why should not my countenance be sad, when the city, the place of my fathers' sepulchres, *lieth* waste, and the gates thereof are consumed with fire?

(4) Then the king said unto me, For what dost thou make request? So I prayed to the God of heaven. (5) And I said unto the king, If it please the king, and if thy servant have found favour in thy sight, that thou wouldest send me unto Judah, unto the city of my fathers' sepulchres, that I may build it.

(6) And the king said unto me, (the ¹queen also sitting by him,) For how long shall thy journey be? and when wilt thou return? So it pleased the king to send me ; and I set him a time. (7) Moreover I said unto the king, If it please the king, let letters be given me to the governors beyond the river, that they may convey me over till I come into Judah ; (8) and a letter unto Asaph the keeper of the king's forest, that he may give me timber to make beams for the gates of the palace which *appertained* to the house, and for the wall of the city, and for the house that I shall enter into. And the king granted me, according to the good hand of my God upon me.

*a* Deut. 4. 25, &c.

*b* Deut. 30. 4.

¹ Heb. *wife.*

---

(8) **The spirit of many threatenings and promises is summed up, as in the prayer of ch. ix.
(11) This day . . . this man.**—During his "certain days" of mourning Nehemiah had fixed upon his plan, suggested by his God. "This day" is "this occasion": the appeal itself was deferred for some months. The king becomes "this man" in the presence of the "God of heaven."

**For I was the king's cupbearer.**—One of his cupbearers, therefore in high authority, having confidential access to him.

II.

(1—8) Nehemiah's appeal to the king.

(1) **Nisan.**—The old Abib, the first month of the Jewish year, following the vernal equinox. As we are still in the twentieth year of the king, the beginning of his reign must be dated before Chisleu. The record adopts Persian dates, and the two months fell in one year.

(2) **Then I was very sore afraid.**—Waiting on Providence, Nehemiah had discharged his duties for three months without being sad in the king's presence; but on this day his sorrow could not be repressed. His fear sprang from the king's abrupt inquiry. A sad countenance was never tolerated in the royal presence; and, though Artaxerxes was of a milder character than any other Persian monarch, the tone of his question showed that in this respect he was not an exception.

(3) **Nehemiah's family was of Jerusalem.** He does not as yet betray to the king the deepest desire of his heart, but simply refers to the desecration of his fathers' sepulchres, an appeal which had great force with the Persians, who respected the tomb.

(4) **So I prayed to the God of heaven.**—The first note of that habit of ejaculatory prayer which is a characteristic of this book.

(6) **The queen also sitting by him.**—Probably Damaspia, the one legitimate queen : *Shegal,* as in Ps. xlv. 13, where, however, she stands as in the presence of her Divine-human Lord. This was not a public feast, as in that case the queen would not be present (Esther i. 9—12).

**I set him a time.**—Whatever that was, circumstances afterwards prolonged it.

(7) **To the governors beyond the river.**—Between the Euphrates and Susa protection was not needed.

(8) **Keeper of the king's forest.**—Asaph, a Jew, was keeper of an artificial *park* or pleasure ground near Jerusalem : the Persian *pardes,* whence our "paradise." It was well planted with trees, as timber was to be supplied from it " for the gates of the palace," rather the *fortress,* which protected " the house," or temple, and was known in Roman times as Antonia; also for the city walls ; also " for the house that I shall enter into," that is, Nehemiah's own house, for his being appointed governor is pre-supposed.

(9) Then I came to the governors beyond the river, and gave them the king's letters. Now the king had sent captains of the army and horsemen with me. (10) When Sanballat the Horonite, and Tobiah the servant, the Ammonite, heard *of it*, it grieved them exceedingly that there was come a man to seek the welfare of the children of Israel.

(11) So I came to Jerusalem, and was there three days. (12) And I arose in the night, I and some few men with me; neither told I *any* man what my God had put in my heart to do at Jerusalem: neither *was there any* beast with me, save the beast that I rode upon. (13) And I went out by night by the gate of the valley, even before the dragon well, and to the dung port, and viewed the walls of Jerusalem, which were broken down, and the gates thereof were consumed with fire. (14) Then I went on to the gate of the fountain, and to the king's pool: but *there was* no place for the beast *that was* under me to pass. (15) Then went I up in the night by the brook, and viewed the wall, and turned back, and entered by the gate of the valley, and *so* returned. (16) And the rulers knew not whither I went, or what I did; neither had I as yet told *it* to the Jews, nor to the priests, nor to the nobles, nor to the rulers, nor to the rest that did the work. (17) Then said I unto them, Ye see the distress that we *are* in, how Jerusalem *lieth* waste, and the gates thereof are burned with fire: come, and let us build up the wall of Jerusalem, that we be no more a reproach. (18) Then I told them of the hand of my God which was good upon me; as also the king's words that he had spoken unto me. And they said, Let us rise up and build. So they strengthened their hands for *this* good *work*.

(19) But when Sanballat the Horonite, and Tobiah the servant, the Ammonite, and Geshem the Arabian, heard *it*, they laughed us to scorn, and despised us, and said, What *is* this thing that ye do? will ye rebel against the king? (20) Then answered I them, and said unto them, The God of heaven, he will prosper us; therefore we his servants will arise and build: but ye have no portion, nor right, nor memorial, in Jerusalem.

CHAPTER III.—(1) Then Eliashib the high priest rose up with his brethren the priests, and they builded the sheep

---

(9—11) His journey to Jerusalem, occupying some three months, and safe under good escort, is passed over in the narrative, as Ezra's had been. It is mentioned, however, that Sanballat, one of the "governors," was roused to hostility. After the laborious travelling Nehemiah rested three days, to review the past and prepare for the future.

(10) **Sanballat the Horonite.**—Satrap of Samaria under the Persians, whose secretary or minister was "Tobiah the servant, the Ammonite." Sanballat was from one of the Beth-horons, which had been in Ephraim, and were now in the kingdom of Samaria. His name is seemingly Babylonian, while that of Tobiah is Hebrew. The revival of Jerusalem would be a blow to the recent ascendency of Samaria.

(11) **Three days.**—For rest and devotion, after the example of Ezra.

(12—18) Nehemiah's cautious preliminaries.

(13) **The gate of the valley**, opening on Hinnom, to the south of the city. Nehemiah passed by "the dragon well," nowhere else mentioned, and not now to be traced, and surveyed the ruins from the "dung port," whence offal was taken to the valley of Hinnom.

(14) **The gate of the fountain** of Siloah (chapter iii. 15), called also "the king's pool."

(15) **By the gate of the valley, and so returned.**—The itineration seems to have completed the circuit of the walls.

(16) **The rest that did the work**, that is, afterwards. The caution of this procedure is justified by subsequent events: the city teemed with elements of danger. The nobles and rulers were possessed of no substantial repressive authority.

(17) **Then.**—There is no note of time. When his plans were matured, Nehemiah made an earnest appeal to their patriotism.

(18) **Then I told them.**—Nehemiah relates his providential call, with the king's commission, and the people were thoroughly enlisted in the good cause.

(19) **Geshem the Arabian.**—This name completes the triumvirate of the leaders of the opposition to the mission of Nehemiah. They were not independent chieftains: Tobiah was Sanballat's servant and counsellor, while Geshem was probably the leader of an Arabian company mostly in his service. The account of their contemptuous opposition is given in a few touches, as is the contempt with which it was met. They charged Nehemiah with rebellion, as afterwards, in chapter vi. 6.

(20) **He will prosper us.**—The reply is a defiance in the name of the God of heaven. The closing words imply that, as in the days of Zerubbabel, the Samaritan enemies desired really to have their share in the undertaking. Nehemiah makes Zerubbabel's answer, but strengthens it; they had nothing in common with Jerusalem, not even a place in its memorials, save one of shame.

III.

(1—32) The memorial of the builders: to succeeding generations of dwellers in Jerusalem a deeply interesting chapter. It contains also a very important topographical account of the ancient city, since repeatedly

*The Building of*          NEHEMIAH, III.          *the Gates of the City.*

gate; they sanctified it and set up the doors of it; even unto the town of Meah they sanctified it, unto the tower of "Hananeel. <sup>(2)</sup> And <sup>1</sup> next unto him builded the men of Jericho. And next to them builded Zaccur the son of Imri.

<sup>(3)</sup> But the fish gate did the sons of Hassenaah build, who *also* laid the beams thereof, and set up the doors thereof, the locks thereof, and the bars thereof. <sup>(4)</sup> And next unto them repaired Meremoth the son of Urijah, the son of Koz. And next unto them repaired Meshullam the son of Berechiah, the son of Meshezabeel. And next unto them repaired Zadok the son of Baana. <sup>(5)</sup> And next unto them the Tekoites repaired; but their nobles put not their necks to the work of their Lord.

<sup>(6)</sup> Moreover the old gate repaired Jehoiada the son of Paseah, and Meshullam the son of Besodeiah; they laid the beams thereof, and set up the doors thereof, and the locks thereof, and the bars thereof. <sup>(7)</sup> And next unto them

*B.C. cir. 445.*

*a* Jer. 31. 38.

<sup>1</sup> Heb., *at his hand.*

<sup>2</sup> Or, *left Jerusalem unto the broad wall.*

<sup>3</sup> Heb., *second measure.*

repaired Melatiah the Gibeonite, and Jadon the Meronothite, the men of Gibeon, and of Mizpah, unto the throne of the governor on this side the river. <sup>(8)</sup> Next unto him repaired Uzziel the son of Harhaiah, of the goldsmiths. Next unto him also repaired Hananiah the son of *one of* the apothecaries, and they <sup>2</sup>fortified Jerusalem unto the broad wall. <sup>(9)</sup> And next unto them repaired Rephaiah the son of Hur, the ruler of the half part of Jerusalem. <sup>(10)</sup> And next unto them repaired Jedaiah the son of Harumaph, even over against his house. And next unto him repaired Hattush the son of Hashabniah. <sup>(11)</sup> Malchijah the son of Harim, and Hashub the son of Pahath-moab, repaired the <sup>3</sup>other piece, and the tower of the furnaces. <sup>(12)</sup> And next unto him repaired Shallum the son of Halohesh, the ruler of the half part of Jerusalem, he and his daughters.

<sup>(13)</sup> The valley gate repaired Hanun, and the inhabitants of Zanoah; they

---

destroyed. But no amount of ingenuity will avail to remove every difficulty. The text is in some places defective. It must, further, be remembered that the record does not so much describe the process as sum up the result. Much of the work of the gates must have required time, but all is described here as if everything was finished at once.

<sup>(1)</sup> **Then Eliashib.**—The account begins with due honour to the high priest and the priesthood.

**The sheep gate** was in the neighbourhood of the priests' quarter. Through it the victims passed for sacrifice, first being washed in the neighbouring pool of Bethesda. This being built, "they sanctified it," as an earnest of the subsequent consecration of the entire wall. Their work and the sanctification of it extended to two towns near each other at the north-east corner.

<sup>(2)</sup> **Next unto him.**—*At his hand*, the customary phrase throughout the chapter, indicating the order of the building, which, however, involves some difficulty towards the close. The phrase, as first used, does honour to the high priest, who must be supposed to have presided only over the religious ceremonial.

**The men of Jericho.**—At the point, it will be observed, opposite their own city.

<sup>(3)</sup> **The fish gate.**—Through which fish entered from the Jordan and Galilee.

**The sons of Hassenaah.**—Contrary to custom, their names are not mentioned.

**The locks thereof, and the bars thereof.**—*The crossbars thereof, and the catches thereof,* the latter holding the former at the two ends. Similarly in several other verses.

<sup>(4)</sup> **Repaired.**—Literally, *strengthened;* as before it was *built.*

<sup>(5)</sup> **The Tekoites.**—This verse is remarkable, as introducing men of Tekoah, not mentioned among Zerubbabel's Returned, who furnish the solitary instance of internal opposition to the building; and as terming the common work "the work of the Lord." The ordinary people of the place, however, did double duty. (See verse 27.)

<sup>(6)</sup> **The old gate.**—Not mentioned elsewhere: probably that of Damascus; but (by a conjectural addition to the text,) it has been translated *the gate of the old wall*, as if distinguished from "the broad wall."

<sup>(7)</sup> **Unto the throne.**—*Unto the seat* of the pechah of the whole district this side the Euphrates: his residence when he came to Jerusalem.

<sup>(8)</sup> **And they fortified Jerusalem unto the broad wall.**—The word translated "fortified" means literally *left*, and this yields a good sense: *they left Jerusalem* untouched as far as a certain portion of the wall extended which needed no restoration. The gate of Ephraim was in this (see chapter xii. 38, 39); and it is significant that nothing is said about the rebuilding of this important gate.

<sup>(9)</sup> **The half part of Jerusalem.**—*Of the district* belonging to Jerusalem.

<sup>(11)</sup> **The other piece.**—This expression occurs a few times when the repairers have been mentioned as having repaired a first piece. But it occurs several times when there is no such mention; and in these cases, as here, must mean only what the margin indicates, *a second measure*, in relation to what had just been referred to.

<sup>(12)</sup> **He and his daughters.**—Shallum was governor of the second half-district around Jerusalem; and it has been thought that the "daughters" here are the villages of the district. But needlessly: the women of Jerusalem might do voluntarily what as females they were not pressed to do.

<sup>(13)</sup> **A thousand cubits.**—Not so much "built" as "strengthened." This comparatively large space—mentioned in round numbers—had probably suffered less damage, and therefore needed less repairing.

built it, and set up the doors thereof, the locks thereof, and the bars thereof, and a thousand cubits on the wall unto the dung gate.

(14) But the dung gate repaired Malchiah the son of Rechab, the ruler of part of Beth-haccerem; he built it, and set up the doors thereof, the locks thereof, and the bars thereof.

(15) But the gate of the fountain repaired Shallun the son of Col-hozeh, the ruler of part of Mizpah; he built it, and covered it, and set up the doors thereof, the locks thereof, and the bars thereof, and the wall of the pool of <sup>a</sup>Siloah by the king's garden, and unto the stairs that go down from the city of David. (16) After him repaired Nehemiah the son of Azbuk, the ruler of the half part of Beth-zur, unto *the place* over against the sepulchres of David, and to the <sup>b</sup>pool that was made, and unto the house of the mighty. (17) After him repaired the Levites, Rehum the son of Bani. Next unto him repaired Hashabiah, the ruler of the half part of Keilah, in his part. (18) After him repaired their brethren, Bavai the son of Henadad, the ruler of the half part of Keilah. (19) And next to him repaired Ezer the son of Jeshua, the ruler of Mizpah, another piece over against the going up to the armoury at the turning *of the wall*. (20) After him Baruch the son of <sup>1</sup>Zabbai earnestly repaired the other piece, from the turning *of the wall* unto the door of the house of Eliashib the high priest. (21) After him repaired Meremoth the son of Urijah the son of Koz another piece, from the door of the house of Eliashib even to the end of the house of Eliashib. (22) And after him repaired the priests, the men of the plain. (23) After him repaired Benjamin and Hashub over against their house. After him repaired Azariah the son of Maaseiah the son of Ananiah by his house. (24) After him repaired Binnui the son of Henadad another piece, from the house of Azariah unto the turning *of the wall*, even unto the corner. (25) Palal the son of Uzai, over against the turning *of the wall*, and the tower which lieth out from the king's high house, that *was* by the <sup>c</sup>court of the prison. After him Pedaiah the son of Parosh. (26) Moreover the Nethinims dwelt in <sup>d2</sup>Ophel, unto *the place* over against the water gate toward the east, and the tower that lieth out. (27) After them the Tekoites repaired another piece, over against the great tower that lieth out, even unto the wall of Ophel.

(28) From above the horse gate repaired the priests, every one over against his

*a* John 9. 7.
*b* 2 Kin. 20. 20.
1 Or, *Zaccai*.
*c* Jer. 32. 2.
*d* 2 Chron. 27. 3.
2 Or, *The tower*.

---

(14) **The son of Rechab.**—Not "a son," as if it meant that he was a Rechabite.

**Part of Beth-haccerem.**—The district around that place.

(15) **He covered it.**—Similar to *laid the beams* in verses 3, 6.

**The pool of Siloah.**—Called before "the king's pool," which received its water as "sent" through a long subterranean conduit, and supplied the king's gardens.

**The stairs.**—Down the steep sides of Ophel, of which traces are thought still to remain. From this point it is very hard to trace the exact course.

(16) **The sepulchres of David.**—Excavated on the western side of the Temple, and never yet traced.

**The pool that was made.**—This may have been the reservoir of Hezekiah (Isa. xxii. 11); and "the house of the mighty" may have been the barracks of David's elect troops (1 Chron. xi. 10).

(17) **The Levites.**—The circuit is coming round to the Temple.

**Rehum the son of Bani.**—The Levites were under him as a body.

**In his part.**—The other part of the Keilah district (now Kila) is in the next verse.

(19) **At the turning of the wall.**—Literally, *the armoury of the corner*: the north-west corner of the "city of David," with its special wall.

(20) **Earnestly repaired the other piece.**—The reason of this man's emulation in building near the high priest's house does not appear.

(21) **Another piece.**—Meremoth added to his other labour the repair of the wall under this house.

(22) **The men of the plain.**—Priests dwelling in the Jordan valley, the "Kikkar" of Scripture.

(24) **Unto the corner.**—The north-eastern angle of the "city of David."

(25) **The tower which lieth out from the king's high house.**—Better, *the high tower outlying from the king's palace.*

**That was by the court of the prison.**—The palace generally had its prison, and near this was the "prison-gate" of chap. xii. 39.

(26) **The Nethinims dwelt in Ophel.**—It has been proposed to insert "who" before dwelt (following the Syriac); but this is not necessary. Ophel was the long rounded spur running out south of the Temple, on the sides of which the ancient "temple servants" still dwelt, separated from others, on a tract of land reaching from the "water-gate toward the east" to the outlying tower of the king's citadel in the west. Nothing is said of their part in the general labour.

(27) **After them.**—Literally, *after him*, referring to Pedaiah of verse 25.

(28) **From above the horse gate.**—This gate was between the Temple and the palace, and the space from the wall of Ophel seems not to have needed repair.

house. (29) After them repaired Zadok the son of Immer over against his house. After him repaired also Shemaiah the son of Shechaniah, the keeper of the east gate. (30) After him repaired Hananiah the son of Shelemiah, and Hanun the sixth son of Zalaph, another piece. After him repaired Meshullam the son of Berechiah over against his chamber. (31) After him repaired Malchiah the goldsmith's son unto the place of the Nethinims, and of the merchants, over against the gate Miphkad, and to the [1]going up of the corner. (32) And between the going up of the corner unto the sheep gate repaired the goldsmiths and the merchants.

CHAPTER IV.—(1) But it came to pass, that when Sanballat heard that we builded the wall, he was wroth, and took great indignation, and mocked the Jews. (2) And he spake before his brethren and the army of Samaria, and said, What do these feeble Jews? will they [2]fortify themselves? will they sacrifice? will they make an end in a day? will they revive the stones out of the heaps of the rubbish which are burned? (3) Now Tobiah the Ammonite was by him, and he said, Even that which they build, if a fox go up, he shall even break down their stone wall. (4) Hear, O our God; for we are [3]despised: and turn their reproach upon their own head, and give them for a prey in the land of captivity: (5) and cover not their iniquity, and let not their sin be blotted out from before thee: for they have provoked thee to anger before the builders. (6) So built we the wall; and all the wall was joined together unto the half thereof: for the people had a mind to work.

(7) But it came to pass, that when Sanballat, and Tobiah, and the Arabians, and the Ammonites, and the Ashdodites, heard that the walls of Jerusalem [4]were made up, and that the breaches began to be stopped, then they were very wroth, (8) and conspired all of them together to come and to fight against Jerusalem, and [5]to hinder it. (9) Nevertheless we made our prayer unto our God, and set a watch against them day and night, because of them. (10) And Judah said, the strength of the bearers of burdens is decayed, and there is much rubbish; so that we are not able to build the wall. (11) And our adversaries said, They shall not know, neither see, till we come in the midst among them, and slay them, and cause the work to cease.

[1] Or, corner chamber.
[2] Heb., leave to themselves.
[3] Heb., despite.
[4] Heb., ascended.
[5] Heb., to make an error to it.

---

(29) **Shemaiah the son of Shechaniah.**—The name in 1 Chron. iii. 22 of a descendant of David.

(31) **The place of the Nethinims.**—Rather, the house.

**And of the merchants.**—Possibly there is some connection between the traders, who brought their doves and so forth for the worshippers, and the Nethinim to whose house or depôt they brought them. Near the sheep gate was the "going up of the corner," or an ascent to the gate Miphkad, about which nothing is known.

(32) **Unto the sheep gate.**—It appears that the "goldsmiths and the merchants" undertook the small space necessary to complete the circuit.

### IV.

(1—23) The opposition of the enemies, and Nehemiah's plans of defence.

(1) **Mocked the Jews.**—The mockery comes afterwards. Here, as often in Nehemiah, a general statement is made which is afterwards expanded.

(2) **His brethren and the army of Samaria.**—The counsellors and body-guard of Sanballat.

**Will they fortify themselves?**—Rather, will they leave them to themselves? The nations are referred to; but contempt is not scrupulous or precise.

**Will they sacrifice?**—This is the provocation of God mentioned in verse 5.

(4) **Hear, O our God.**—The habit of Nehemiah is to turn everything to devotion as he goes on. This prayer is full of an angry jealousy for the honour of a jealous God.

**They have provoked thee.**—The tone of its holy revenge pervades the Old Testament, and has not altogether departed in the New.

(6) **Unto the half.**—Up to half the height the wall was now continuous.

(7) **Were made up.**—Arose to the height before mentioned.

**Began to be stopped.**—The wall, they heard, was continuous. The tribes here enumerated were only small parties under the immediate influence of Sanballat: nothing beyond that would have been likely to occur among subjects in common of Persia.

(8) **And conspired.**—Not fearing the Persian authority, they resolved to attack the city; but it will be seen that they soon abandoned that project.

**To hinder it.**—Rather, to do it hurt.

(9) **Because of them.**—Rather, over against them: opposite to each point of their encampment. The setting watch was accompanied by solemn and united prayer.

(10) **And Judah said.**—As hereafter, in the case of the complaints of the people (chap. v.), the writer gives a summary of difficulties. The Jews, or "Judah"—a significant term—complained of their growing feebleness, especially as so many were diverted to the watches.

(11) **They shall not know.**—As to the adversaries, their plan was evidently to watch and surprise, instead of making the threatened attack.

(12) And it came to pass, that when the Jews which dwelt by them came, they said unto us ten times, ¹From all places whence ye shall return unto us *they will be upon you.* (13) Therefore set I ²in the lower places behind the wall, *and* on the higher places, I even set the people after their families with their swords, their spears, and their bows. (14) And I looked, and rose up, and said unto the nobles, and to the rulers, and to the rest of the people, Be not ye afraid of them: remember the Lord, *which is* great and terrible, and fight for your brethren, your sons, and your daughters, your wives, and your houses.

(15) And it came to pass, when our enemies heard that it was known unto us, and God had brought their counsel to nought, that we returned all of us to the wall, every one unto his work. (16) And it came to pass from that time forth, *that* the half of my servants wrought in the work, and the other half of them held both the spears, the shields, and the bows, and the habergeons; and the rulers *were* behind all the house of Judah. (17) They which builded on the wall, and they that bare burdens, with those that laded, *every one* with one of his hands wrought in the work, and with the other *hand* held a weapon. (18) For the builders, every one had his sword girded ³by his side, and *so* builded. And he that sounded the trumpet *was* by me. (19) And I said unto the nobles, and to the rulers, and to the rest of the people, The work *is* great and large, and we are separated upon the wall, one far from another. (20) In what place *therefore* ye hear the sound of the trumpet, resort ye thither unto us: our God shall fight for us.

(21) So we laboured in the work: and half of them held the spears from the rising of the morning till the stars appeared. (22) Likewise at the same time said I unto the people, Let every one with his servant lodge within Jerusalem, that in the night they may be a guard to us, and labour on the day. (23) So neither I, nor my brethren, nor my servants, nor the men of the guard which followed me, none of us put off our clothes, ⁴*saving that* every one put them off for washing.

CHAPTER V.—(1) And there was a great cry of the people and of their wives against their brethren the Jews. (2) For there were that said, We, our sons, and our daughters, *are* many: therefore we take up corn *for them*, that we may eat, and live. (3) *Some* also there were that said, We have mortgaged our lands, vineyards, and houses, that we might buy corn, because of the dearth. (4) There were also that said, We have borrowed

---

¹ Or, *That from all places ye must return to us.*

² Heb., *from the lower parts of the place, &c.*

³ Heb., *on his loins.*

⁴ Or, *every one went with his weapon for water.*

---

(12) **From all places.**—The neighbouring Jews in their terror said by repeated messages "from all places 'Ye shall return to us,'": that is, for our protection.

(13) **After their families.**—In allusion to the ambushes of verse 11, Nehemiah set families together—besides the appointed guards—"in the lower places," where the wall was not raised to the due height, that is, really, "on the higher places," or rather, *the bare places*, whence enemies might be better seen. The "lower" were the "bare" places.

(14) **And I looked.**—It appears that the energetic appeal now described was uttered on the actual approach of an attacking party.

(15) **We returned.**—This verse remarkably condenses the frustration of the attempt and the cessation of the special guard.

(16) **My servants.**—The building was resumed with special precautions, very minutely described. "Nehemiah's own servants" are distinguished from "all the house of Judah." The former were divided into two parties, one of which wrought on the work still unfinished and the other held their weapons.

**Habergeons** are coats of mail or corselets, thin plates of metal sewn upon leather.

**The rulers were behind.**—Ready to lead the defence, if necessary.

(17) **They which builded.**—Divided into masons and their burden-bearers. The latter held in one hand a weapon; the former built with both hands, and had their weapons at their side.

(21) **So we laboured.**—This is a general recapitulation, with additional note of the length of the day's work during this pressing season.

(23) **Saving that every one put them off for washing.**—This rendering is very improbable, as the words are simply: "every man his weapon water." Some interpret that "each man's weapon was his water": evidently too subtle a turn of thought. It is best, on the whole, to supply the ellipsis: "every man went with his weapon to the water."

V.

(1—13) Internal difficulties, springing from usury and oppression.

(1) **Their brethren the Jews.**—Nehemiah's other troubles had come from the enemies without: he begins this account by laying emphasis on the hard treatment of Jews by Jews.

(2) **We take up.**—*Let us receive.* This is a general appeal for the governor's help.

(3) **Because of the dearth.**—Not any particular famine, strictly speaking, but their present hunger. The past mortgages had straitened their resources.

(4) **We have borrowed money for the king's tribute.**—Literally, *we have made our fields and*

money for the king's tribute, *and that upon* our lands and vineyards. (5) Yet now our flesh *is* as the flesh of our brethren, our children as their children: and, lo, we bring into bondage our sons and our daughters to be servants, and *some* of our daughters are brought into bondage *already*: neither *is it* in our power *to redeem them;* for other men have our lands and vineyards.

(6) And I was very angry when I heard their cry and these words. (7) Then [1] I consulted with myself, and I rebuked the nobles, and the rulers, and said unto them, Ye exact usury, every one of his brother. And I set a great assembly against them. (8) And I said unto them, We after our ability have *redeemed our brethren the Jews, which were sold unto the heathen; and will ye even sell your brethren? or shall they be sold unto us? Then held they their peace, and found nothing *to answer*. (9) Also I said, it *is* not good that ye do: ought ye not to walk in the fear of our God because of the reproach of the heathen our enemies? (10) I likewise, *and* my brethren, and my servants, might exact of them money and corn: I pray you, let us leave off this usury. (11) Restore, I pray you, to them, even this day, their lands, their vineyards, their oliveyards, and their houses, also the hundredth *part* of the money, and of the corn, the wine, and the oil, that ye exact of them.

(12) Then said they, We will restore *them*, and will require nothing of them; so will we do as thou sayest. Then I called the priests, and took an oath of them, that they should do according to this promise. (13) Also I shook my lap, and said, So God shake out every man from his house, and from his labour, that performeth not this promise, even thus be he shaken out, and ²emptied. And all the congregation said, Amen, and praised the LORD. And the people did according to this promise.

(14) Moreover from the time that I was appointed to be their governor in the land of Judah, from the twentieth year even unto the two and thirtieth year of Artaxerxes the king, *that is*, twelve years, I and my brethren have not eaten the bread of the governor. (15) But the former governors that *had been* before

1 Heb. *my heart consulted in me.*

a Lev. 25. 48.

2 Heb., *empty*, or, *void*.

---

*vineyards answerable* for the payment of the Persian tribute. They had pledged the coming produce.

(5) **We bring into bondage.**—But the climax of the cry was the bondage of their children, especially of the daughters, whom they had been obliged to sell until the Jubile for money: children as precious to their parents as were the children of the rulers to them.

(6) **And I was very angry.**—Nehemiah, recently arrived, had not known this state of things. The common wailing and the three complaints in which it found expression are distinct.

(7) **I consulted.**—But he mastered himself, and studied his plan of operation. The matter was complicated, as the transgressors had violated rather the spirit than the letter of the law. Hence the rebuke, that they exacted usury each of his brother, failed in its object; and the governor called a general assembly, not "against them," but "concerning them."

(8) **Will ye even sell your brethren?**—The appeal is a strong one. Nehemiah and his friends had redeemed Jews from the heathen with money; these men had caused Jews to be sold to Jews.

**Nothing to answer.**—They might have replied had the letter of the law been urged; but this argument puts them to shame.

(9) **Because of the reproach.**—The text of another strong argument used in the assembly. We learn in chap. vi. how watchful the heathen were: all matters were reported to them, and every act of oppression would become a reproach against the God of the Jews.

(10) **Might exact.**—We *have lent them money and corn*. By his own example the governor pleads with them: not "let us leave off this usury," but let us all and together "remit the loans."

(11) **Also the hundredth part of the money.**—The monthly payment of one per cent. per month, twelve per cent. in the year, they were required to give up for the future.

(12) **We will restore.**—The promise was given to restore the mortgaged property and to require no more interest. But Nehemiah required an oath to give legal validity to the procedure, and the priests' presence gave it the highest religious sanction.

(13) **Shook my lap.**—This symbolical act imprecated on every man who broke this covenant an appropriate penalty: that he be emptied of all his possessions, even as the fold of Nehemiah's garment was emptied. And it is observable that the iniquity thus stopped is not referred to in the subsequent covenant (chap. x.), nor is it one of the offences which the governor found on his second return (chap. xiii.).

(14–19) Nehemiah's vindication of his own conduct.

(14) **I was appointed.**—*That he appointed me*, viz., Artaxerxes.

**Twelve years.**—The whole narrative, thus far, was written after his return from Jerusalem, and on a review of his governorship; hence, "their governor in the land of Judah." Of his second appointment the same thing might have been said: but that, at the time of writing, was in the future.

**I and my brethren have not eaten the bread of the governor.**—At the close of the twelve years' term, Nehemiah could say that he and his official attendants had not drawn the customary allowances from the people.

(15) **Besides forty shekels of silver.**—Either *in bread and wine over forty shekels*, or, *received in bread*

me were chargeable unto the people, and had taken of them bread and wine, beside forty shekels of silver; yea, even their servants bare rule over the people: but so did not I, because of the fear of God. (16) Yea, also I continued in the work of this wall, neither bought we any land: and all my servants *were* gathered thither unto the work. (17) Moreover *there were* at my table an hundred and fifty of the Jews and rulers, beside those that came unto us from among the heathen that *are* about us. (18) Now *that* which was prepared *for me* daily *was* one ox *and* six choice sheep; also fowls were prepared for me, and once in ten days store of all sorts of wine: yet for all this required not I the bread of the governor, because the bondage was heavy upon this people.

(19) *a* Think upon me, my God, for good, *according* to all that I have done for this people.

CHAPTER VI.—(1) Now it came to pass, when Sanballat, and Tobiah, and Geshem the Arabian, and the rest of our enemies, heard that I had builded the wall, and *that* there was no breach left therein; (though at that time I had not set up the doors upon the gates;) (2) that Sanballat and Geshem sent unto me, saying, Come, let us meet together in *some one of* the villages in the plain of Ono. But they thought to do me mischief. (3) And I sent messengers unto them, saying, I *am* doing a great work, so that I cannot come down: why should the work cease, whilst I leave it, and come down to you? (4) Yet they sent unto me four times after this sort; and I answered them after the same manner. (5) Then sent Sanballat his servant unto me in like manner the fifth time with an open letter in his hand; (6) Wherein *was* written, It is reported among the heathen, and ¹Gashmu saith *it, that* thou and the Jews think to rebel: for which cause thou buildest the wall, that thou mayest be their king, according to these words. (7) And thou hast also appointed prophets to preach of thee at Jerusalem, saying, *There is* a king in Judah: and now shall it be reported to the king according to these words. Come now

*a* ch. 13. 22.

1 Or, *Geshem*, ver. 2.

---

*and wine, and beyond that, forty shekels*. The latter, on the whole, is to be preferred; it would amount to about four pounds from the entire people daily.

**So did not I, because of the fear of God.**—Nehemiah contrasts his forbearance with the conduct of former governors; we cannot suppose him to mean Zerubbabel, but some of his successors. The practice he condemns was common among the satraps of the Persian princes. Note that usury and rigour were interdicted, in Lev. xxv. 36, 43, with the express sanction, "Fear thy God."

(16) **I continued.**—*I repaired*: that is, as superintendent. His servants and himself did not take advantage of the people's poverty to acquire their land by mortgage; they were, on the contrary, absorbed in the common work.

(17) **At my table.**—The charge on the governor's free hospitality was heavy: "of the Jews a hundred and fifty rulers, besides those that came" occasionally from the country.

**Because the bondage.**—Rather, *because the service of building* was heavy.

**The bondage.**—Rather, *the service* was heavy.

(19) **Think upon me, my God.**—Inserting the present prayer far from this people, Nehemiah humbly asks his recompense not from them, but from God. Nothing was more distant from his thoughts than the fame of his good deeds.

### VI.

(1—14) The enemies, whose wrath had been before much mingled with mockery, now resort to stratagem.

(1) **And the rest of our enemies.**—The Three always have the pre-eminence.

**The doors upon the gates.**—*Within the gates*. This parenthesis is a note of historical accuracy, and intimates that what had been before said as to the setting up of the doors (see chap. iii.) was by way of anticipation.

(2) **Sanballat and Geshem.**—In the original of verse 1, Tobiah is not distinguished from Sanballat by another preposition, as Geshem is; and here he is omitted, as not to appear in the conference otherwise than as Sanballat's secretary.

**In some one of the villages in the plain of Ono.**—Probably, *in Hahkiphirem*, the name of a village in the plain of Ono, which was on the borders of Philistia, more than twenty miles from Jerusalem.

(5) **The fifth time with an open letter in his hand.**—Four times they strive to induce Nehemiah to meet them, under various pretexts, with the intention of doing him personal harm. Each time his reply was to the effect that he was finishing his own work, not without a touch of irony. This answer has an universal application, which preachers have known how to use. In the fifth letter the tactics are changed: the silken bag containing the missive was not sealed, and it was hoped that Nehemiah would be alarmed by the thought that its contents had been read by the people.

(6) **It is reported among the heathen, and Gashmu saith it.**—Nehemiah can quote the very letter, with its dialectical change of Geshem into Gashmu. Sanballat sends Tobiah in his own name, and represents Geshem as circulating a report which, reaching the distant king, would be interpreted as rebellion. It is hinted that the heathen, or *the nations*, would take the part of the king. And the words of the prophets concerning the future King are referred to as likely to be attributed to Nehemiah's ambition.

therefore, and let us take counsel together. (8) Then I sent unto him, saying, There are no such things done as thou sayest, but thou feignest them out of thine own heart. (9) For they all made us afraid, saying, Their hands shall be weakened from the work, that it be not done. Now therefore, O God, strengthen my hands.

(10) Afterward I came unto the house of Shemaiah the son of Delaiah the son of Mehetabeel, who *was* shut up; and he said, Let us meet together in the house of God, within the temple, and let us shut the doors of the temple: for they will come to slay thee; yea, in the night will they come to slay thee. (11) And I said, Should such a man as I flee? and who *is there*, that, *being* as I *am*, would go into the temple to save his life? I will not go in. (12) And, lo, I perceived that God had not sent him; but that he pronounced this prophecy against me: for Tobiah and Sanballat had hired him. (13) Therefore *was* he hired, that I should be afraid, and do so, and sin, and *that* they might have *matter* for an evil report, that they might reproach me.

(14) My God, think thou upon Tobiah and Sanballat according to these their works, and on the prophetess Noadiah, and the rest of the prophets, that would have put me in fear.

(15) So the wall was finished in the twenty and fifth *day* of *the month* Elul, in fifty and two days. (16) And it came to pass, that when all our enemies heard *thereof*, and all the heathen that *were* about us saw *these things*, they were much cast down in their own eyes: for they perceived that this work was wrought of our God.

(17) Moreover in those days the nobles of Judah [1] sent many letters unto Tobiah, and *the letters* of Tobiah came unto them. (18) For *there were* many in Judah sworn unto him, because he *was* the son in law of Shechaniah the son of Arah; and his son Johanan had taken the daughter of Meshullam the son of Berechiah.

[1] Heb., *multiplied their letters passing to Tobiah.*

---

Finally, the letter suggests the desirableness of friendly counsel to avert the danger.

(9) **Now therefore, O God, strengthen my hands.**—The answer sent was that the thing was not true, and that the report itself did not exist. The reflection in Nehemiah's journal was that they sought to make him afraid. Quoting this, he adds the prayer that he recorded when he wrote it. It is one of those sudden, interjectional petitions which abound in the narrative, and is all the more remarkable from the absence of the words "O God," which are here inserted.

(10) **I came unto the house.**—As a specimen of another kind of attack, through false prophets, Shemaiah's plot is mentioned. This man—probably a priest—Nehemiah found shut up in his house; probably he sent for the governor, and represented himself as being in danger from the common enemy. He predicted that on the night ensuing an attempt would be made on Nehemiah's life, and proposed that they should meet "within the Temple"—that is, in the holy place, between the Holiest and the outer court—for security.

(11) **Should such a man as I flee?**—First, the expression of personal dignity. Then of fear: "Who, being as I am" (a layman), "would go into the Temple to save his life?" Rather, *and live?* (Numb. xviii. 7).

(13) **An evil report.**—Nehemiah perceived that not God, but Shemaiah himself, had uttered the prophecy "against me," and that he was hired to bring the governor into discredit as a violator of law.

(14) **Think thou upon Tobiah.**—This appeal to God is to be understood as an official prophetic prayer. Nehemiah puts God's own cause into God's own hands. The mention of the name of Noadiah, nowhere else referred to, shows the circumstantial nature of the narrative, and is an indirect evidence of its truth.

(15, 16) The finishing of the wall is recorded in the simplest manner: first, with a formal specification of the date and time; then in its effect upon the enemies, and as redounding to the glory of God.

(15) **In fifty and two days.**—The twenty-fifth day of Elul answers to about our September 15th; and, dating back, the wall began in the latter part of July, soon after Nehemiah's arrival. If we bear in mind that the wall was only partially overthrown, that the materials for restoration were at hand, and that the utmost skill had been shown in organising the bands of workmen, the time will not appear too short. There is no need to adopt the suggestion of Josephus, that the rebuilding occupied two years and four months.

**They perceived that this work was wrought of our God.**—Not miraculously, but under the Divine sanction and help. By this expression Nehemiah at once triumphs over his foes, and gives the glory where it was due. His own heroic part in the work is utterly forgotten.

(16) The enemies heard of it, and saw the result, and were ashamed.

(17—19) A supplementary account is here introduced, explaining the intrigues within Jerusalem to which reference has been made.

(17) **Many letters.**—There was a large correspondence between Tobiah and the nobles of Judah.

(18) **Sworn unto him.**—Shechaniah was of the family of Arah, which had come over with Zerubbabel (Ezra ii. 5). Tobiah had married his daughter, and Tobiah's son had married a daughter of Meshullam, one of the builders of the wall (chap. iii. 4, 30). This family connection led to a conspiracy by oath to thwart the governor. The names of Tobiah and his son are Hebrew; and it is probable that, though naturalised Ammonites, they were of Hebrew extraction. This renders it easier to understand the facility with which the affinity was contracted.

(19) Also they reported his good deeds before me, and uttered my ¹words to him. And Tobiah sent letters to put me in fear.

CHAPTER VII.—(1) Now it came to pass, when the wall was built, and I had set up the doors, and the porters and the singers and the Levites were appointed, (2) that I gave my brother Hanani, and Hananiah the ruler of the palace, charge over Jerusalem: for he *was* a faithful man, and feared God above many. (3) And I said unto them, Let not the gates of Jerusalem be opened until the sun be hot; and while they stand by, let them shut the doors, and bar *them*: and appoint watches of the inhabitants of Jerusalem, every one in his watch, and every one *to be* over against his house. (4) Now the city *was* ²large and great: but the people *were* few therein, and the houses *were* not built.

(5) And my God put into mine heart to gather together the nobles, and the rulers, and the people, that they might be reckoned by genealogy. And I found a register of the genealogy of them which came up at the first, and found written therein,

(6) ª These *are* the children of the province, that went up out of the captivity, of those that had been carried away, whom Nebuchadnezzar the king of Babylon had carried away, and came again to Jerusalem and to Judah, every one unto his city; (7) who came with Zerubbabel, Jeshua, Nehemiah, ³Azariah, Raamiah, Nahamani, Mordecai, Bilshan, Mispereth, Bigvai, Nehum, Baanah. The number, *I say*, of the men of the people of Israel *was this;*

(8) The children of Parosh, two thousand an hundred seventy and two. (9) The children of Shephatiah, three hundred seventy and two. (10) The children of Arah, six hundred fifty and two. (11) The children of Pahath-moab, of the children of Jeshua and Joab, two thousand and eight hundred *and* eighteen. (12) The children of Elam, a thousand two hundred fifty and four. (13) The children of Zattu, eight hundred forty and five. (14) The children of Zaccai, seven hundred and three score. (15) The children of ⁴Binnui, six hundred forty and eight. (16) The children of Bebai, six hundred twenty and eight. (17) The children of Azgad, two thousand three hundred twenty and two. (18) The children of Adonikam, six hundred three score and seven. (19) The children of Bigvai, two thousand three score and seven. (20) The children of Adin, six hundred fifty and five. (21) The children of Ater of Hezekiah, ninety and eight. (22) The children of Hashum, three hundred twenty and eight. (23) The children of Bezai, three hundred twenty and four. (24) The children of ⁵Hariph, an hundred

---

1 Or, *matters.*
2 Heb. *broad in spaces.*
a Ezra 2. 1, &c.
3 Or, *Seraiah.*
B.C. cir. 536.
4 Or, *Bani.*
5 Or, *Jora.*

---

(19) **Reported his good deeds.**—Besides the correspondence thus carried on, these nobles strove to exalt the character of Tobiah to the governor, while they made the enemy acquainted with all that went on. This intelligence enabled him to write the disquieting letters which Nehemiah says he was in the habit of receiving.

VII.

(1—4) Measures were taken for the security of the city, now made a complete fortress. The comparative thinness of the population taxed the governor's resources, and the result appears at a later stage.

(1) **Were appointed.**—*Placed in charge*, probably over all the walls. This was an extraordinary provision, to be explained by the fact that these organised bodies formed a large proportion of the inhabitants. The Levites had usually guarded only the Temple.

(2) **Hanani.**—Who probably had returned from Susa with his brother.

**Hananiah the ruler of the palace.**—*Commander of the fortress,* as in chap. ii. 8. He was in the immediate service of the Persian king, but his chief recommendation was his piety, which distinguished him from too many of the other rulers.

(3) **Until the sun be hot.**—General directions were given that the gates should not be thrown open so early as sunrise; they were to be opened and barred again while the guard was present; and the inhabitants were to be divided for night-watches, part on the walls and part before their own houses.

(4) **Large and great.**—Literally, *broad on both sides*, with large unoccupied spaces.

**The houses were not builded.**—In sufficient numbers to provide the requisite population for the city of God. The emphasis is on the fact that the people were few.

(5—73) The genealogical reckoning of the people, as the first step towards increasing the population of the metropolis, is determined on, not without express Divine suggestion; the allusion to this inspiration from God, is, as in chap. ii. 12, very emphatic. The original register of Zerubbabel is found and copied. The express language of both Ezra and Nehemiah makes it plain that this is no other than the list of those who came up with Zerubbabel and Joshua after the decree of Cyrus, in B.C. 538. Nehemiah's own census follows, in chap. xi. The exposition, especially as compared with Ezra ii., has been given on that chapter.

and twelve. ⁽²⁵⁾ The children of ¹Gibeon, ninety and five. ⁽²⁶⁾ The men of Bethlehem and Netophah, an hundred fourscore and eight. ⁽²⁷⁾ The men of Anathoth, an hundred twenty and eight. ⁽²⁸⁾ The men of ²Beth-azmaveth, forty and two. ⁽²⁹⁾ The men of ³Kirjath-jearim, Chephirah, and Beeroth, seven hundred forty and three. ⁽³⁰⁾ The men of Ramah and Gaba, six hundred twenty and one. ⁽³¹⁾ The men of Michmas, an hundred and twenty and two. ⁽³²⁾ The men of Beth-el and Ai, an hundred twenty and three. ⁽³³⁾ The men of the other Nebo, fifty and two. ⁽³⁴⁾ The children of the other *Elam, a thousand two hundred fifty and four. ⁽³⁵⁾ The children of Harim, three hundred and twenty. ⁽³⁶⁾ The children of Jericho, three hundred forty and five. ⁽³⁷⁾ The children of Lod, Hadid, and Ono, seven hundred twenty and one. ⁽³⁸⁾ The children of Senaah, three thousand nine hundred and thirty.

⁽³⁹⁾ The priests: the children of ᵇJedaiah, of the house of Jeshua, nine hundred seventy and three. ⁽⁴⁰⁾ The children of Immer, a thousand fifty and two. ⁽⁴¹⁾ The children of Pashur, a thousand two hundred forty and seven. ⁽⁴²⁾ The children of Harim, a thousand and seventeen.

⁽⁴³⁾ The Levites: the children of Jeshua, of Kadmiel, and of the children of ⁴Hodevah, seventy and four. ⁽⁴⁴⁾ The singers: the children of Asaph, an hundred forty and eight. ⁽⁴⁵⁾ The porters: the children of Shallum, the children of Ater, the children of Talmon, the children of Akkub, the children of Hatita, the children of Shobai, an hundred thirty and eight.

⁽⁴⁶⁾ The Nethinims: the children of Ziha, the children of Hashupha, the children of Tabbaoth, ⁽⁴⁷⁾ the children of Keros, the children of Sia, the children of Padon, ⁽⁴⁸⁾ the children of Lebana, the children of Hagaba, the children of Shalmai, ⁽⁴⁹⁾ the children of Hanan, the children of Giddel, the children of Gahar, ⁽⁵⁰⁾ the children of Reaiah, the children of Rezin, the children of Nekodah, ⁽⁵¹⁾ the children of Gazzam, the children of Uzza, the children of Phaseah, ⁽⁵²⁾ the children of Besai, the children of Meunim, the children of Nephishesim, ⁽⁵³⁾ the children of Bakbuk, the children of Hakupha, the children of Harhur, ⁽⁵⁴⁾ the children of Bazlith, the children of Mehida, the children of Harsha, ⁽⁵⁵⁾ the children of Barkos, the children of Sisera, the children of Tamah, ⁽⁵⁶⁾ the children of Neziah, the children of Hatipha.

⁽⁵⁷⁾ The children of Solomon's servants: the children of Sotai, the children of Sophereth, the children of Perida, ⁽⁵⁸⁾ the children of Jaala, the children of Darkon, the children of Giddel, ⁽⁵⁹⁾ the children of Shephatiah, the children of Hattil, the children of Pochereth of Zebaim, the children of ⁵Amon. ⁽⁶⁰⁾ All the Nethinims, and the children of Solomon's servants, were three hundred ninety and two.

⁽⁶¹⁾ ᶜAnd these were they which went up also from Tel-melah, Tel-haresha, Cherub, Addon, and Immer: but they could not shew their father's house, nor their ⁶seed, whether they were of Israel. ⁽⁶²⁾ The children of Delaiah, the children of Tobiah, the children of Nekoda, six hundred forty and two.

⁽⁶³⁾ And of the priests: the children of Habaiah, the children of Koz, the children of Barzillai, which took one of the daughters of Barzillai the Gileadite to wife, and was called after their name. ⁽⁶⁴⁾ These sought their register among those that were reckoned by genealogy, but it was not found: therefore were they, as polluted, put from the priesthood. ⁽⁶⁵⁾ And ⁷the Tirshatha said unto them, that they should not eat of the most holy things, till there stood up a priest with Urim and Thummim.

⁽⁶⁶⁾ The whole congregation together was forty and two thousand three hundred and threescore, ⁽⁶⁷⁾ beside their manservants and their maidservants, of whom there were seven thousand three hundred thirty and seven: and they had two hundred forty and five singing men and singing women. ⁽⁶⁸⁾ Their horses, seven hundred thirty and six: their mules, two hundred forty and five: ⁽⁶⁹⁾ their camels, four hundred thirty and five: six thousand seven hundred and twenty asses.

⁽⁷⁰⁾ And ⁸some of the chief of the fathers gave unto the work. The Tirshatha gave to the treasure a thousand drams of gold, fifty basons, five hundred and thirty priests' garments. ⁽⁷¹⁾ And some of the chief of the fathers gave to the treasure of the work twenty thousand drams of gold, and two thousand

---

1 Or, Gibbar.
2 Or, Azmaveth.
3 Or, Kirjath-arim.
a See ver. 12.
b 1 Chron. 24. 7.
4 Or, Hodaviah, Ezra 2. 40; or, Judah, Ezra 3. 9.
5 Or, Ami.
c Ezra 2. 59.
6 Or, pedigree.
7 Or, the governor.
8 Heb. part.

and two hundred pound of silver. ⁽⁷²⁾And *that* which the rest of the people gave *was* twenty thousand drams of gold, and two thousand pound of silver, and threescore and seven priests' garments.

⁽⁷³⁾ So the priests, and the Levites, and the porters, and the singers, and *some* of the people, and the Nethinims, and all Israel, dwelt in their cities; and when the seventh month came, the children of Israel *were* in their cities.

CHAPTER VIII.—⁽¹⁾ And all the people gathered themselves together as one man into the street that *was* before the water gate; ᵃand they spake unto Ezra the scribe to bring the book of the law of Moses, which the LORD had commanded to Israel. ⁽²⁾ And Ezra the priest brought the law before the congregation both of men and women, and all ¹that could hear with understanding, upon the first day of the seventh month. ⁽³⁾ And he read therein before the street that *was* before the water gate ²from the morning until midday, before the men and the women, and those that could understand; and the ears of all the people *were attentive* unto the book of the law. ⁽⁴⁾ And Ezra the scribe stood upon a ³pulpit of wood, which they had made for the purpose; and beside him stood Mattithiah, and Shema, and Anaiah, and Urijah, and Hilkiah,

B.C. cir. 445.

a Ezra 3. 1 & 7. 6.

1 Heb., *that understood in hearing.*

2 Heb., *from the light.*

3 Heb., *tower of wood.*

4 Heb., *eyes.*

5 Or, *the governor.*

and Maaseiah, on his right hand; and on his left hand, Pedaiah, and Mishael, and Malchiah, and Hashum, and Hashbadana, Zechariah, *and* Meshullam. ⁽⁵⁾And Ezra opened the book in the ⁴sight of all the people; (for he was above all the people;) and when he opened it all the people stood up: ⁽⁶⁾ and Ezra blessed the LORD, the great God. And all the people answered, Amen, Amen, with lifting up their hands: and they bowed their heads, and worshipped the LORD with *their* faces to the ground. ⁽⁷⁾ Also Jeshua, and Bani, and Sherebiah, Jamin, Akkub, Shabbethai, Hodijah, Maaseiah, Kelita, Azariah, Jozabad, Hanan, Pelaiah, and the Levites, caused the people to understand the law: and the people *stood* in their place. ⁽⁸⁾ So they read in the book in the law of God distinctly, and gave the sense, and caused *them* to understand the reading.

⁽⁹⁾ And Nehemiah, which *is* ⁵the Tirshatha, and Ezra the priest the scribe, and the Levites that taught the people, said unto all the people, This day *is* holy unto the LORD your God; mourn not, nor weep. For all the people wept, when they heard the words of the law. ⁽¹⁰⁾ Then he said unto them, Go your way, eat the fat, and drink the sweet, and send portions unto them for whom nothing is prepared: for *this* day *is* holy unto our Lord: neither be ye sorry; for

---

VIII.

Chap. vii. 73—chap. viii. 12.—**Ezra instructs the people in the law.**

Chap. vii. 73.—**And when the seventh month came.**—Here a new subject begins, as in Ezra, whom Nehemiah copies: adopting a sentence, just as Ezra adopted the last words of the Chronicles, and with similar slight changes.

⁽¹⁾ **As one man.**—The unanimity rather than the number is emphatic here.

**And they spake unto Ezra.**—Who appears in this book for the first time, having probably been at the court for twelve years.

⁽²⁾ **Both of men and women, and all that could hear with understanding.**—Men, women, and children who had reached years of discretion.

**Upon the first day of the seventh month.**—As the seventh was the most important month, in a religious sense, so the first day, the Feast of Trumpets, was the most important new moon (Lev. xxiii. 24).

⁽³⁾ **From the morning.**—*From daylight.* The Book of the Law must have been a comprehensive one. Out of it Ezra and his companions read hour after hour, selecting appropriate passages.

**And the ears of all the people . . . unto the book.**—A general statement; the detail now follows.

⁽⁴⁾ **Pulpit of wood.**—Literally, a *tower of wood.* Fourteen persons, however, were on what is afterwards called a platform, or stair, by his side.

⁽⁶⁾ **And Ezra blessed the Lord.**—The book was formally and solemnly opened in the sight of the people. At this request the multitude arose, and, after a doxology offered by Ezra, they all uttered a double Amen, "with lifting up of their hands," in token of their most fervent assent; and then "with faces bowed to the ground," in token of adoration.

**The great God** is Nehemiah's expression, not Ezra's; the sentence used is not reported.

⁽⁸⁾ **Gave the sense.**—They expounded obscurer passages, and in doing so naturally translated into the vernacular Aramaic dialect.

**Caused them to understand the reading.**—This simply explains the former: they *expounded as they read.*

⁽⁹⁾ **Mourn not, nor weep.**—The days of high festival were unsuitable for public and, as it were, objective sorrow. The Day of Atonement was coming for that; as also the special day of fasting and covenant, which was already in the plan of Nehemiah and Ezra.

⁽¹⁰⁾ **For the joy of the Lord is your strength.** This beautiful sentence is, literally, *delight in Jehovah*

the joy of the LORD is your strength. ⁽¹¹⁾ So the Levites stilled all the people, saying, Hold your peace, for the day *is* holy; neither be ye grieved. ⁽¹²⁾ And all the people went their way to eat, and to drink, and to send portions, and to make great mirth, because they had understood the words that were declared unto them.

⁽¹³⁾ And on the second day were gathered together the chief of the fathers of all the people, the priests, and the Levites, unto Ezra the scribe, even ¹to understand the words of the law. ⁽¹⁴⁾ And they found written in the law which the LORD had commanded ²by Moses, that the children of Israel should dwell in ᵃbooths in the feast of the seventh month: ⁽¹⁵⁾ and that they should publish and proclaim in all their cities, and in Jerusalem, saying, Go forth unto the mount, and fetch olive branches, and pine branches, and myrtle branches, and palm branches, and branches of thick trees, to make booths, as *it is* written. ⁽¹⁶⁾ So the people went forth, and brought *them*, and made themselves booths, every one upon the roof of his house, and in their courts, and in the courts of the house of God, and in the street of the water gate, and in the street of the gate of Ephraim. ⁽¹⁷⁾ And all the congregation of them that were come again out of the captivity made booths, and sat under the booths: for since the days of Jeshua the son of Nun unto that day had not the children of Israel done so. And there was very great gladness. ⁽¹⁸⁾ Also day by day, from the first day unto the last day, he read in the book of the law of God. And they kept the feast seven days; and on the eighth day *was* ³a solemn assembly, according unto the manner.

CHAPTER IX.—⁽¹⁾ Now in the twenty and fourth day of ᵇthis month the children of Israel were assembled with fasting, and with sackclothes, and earth upon them. ⁽²⁾ And the seed of Israel separated themselves from all ⁴strangers, and stood and confessed their sins, and the iniquities of their fathers. ⁽³⁾ And they stood up in their place, and read in the book of the law of the LORD their God *one* fourth part of the day; and *another* fourth part they confessed, and worshipped the LORD their God. ⁽⁴⁾ Then stood up upon the ⁵stairs, of the Levites, Jeshua, and Bani, Kadmiel, Shebaniah, Bunni, Sherebiah,

---

*Notes:*
1 Or, *that they might instruct in the words of the law*.
2 Heb., *by the hand of*.
a Lev. 23. 34; Deut. 16. 13.
3 Heb., *a restraint*.
b ch. 8. 2.
4 Heb., *strange children*.
5 Or, *scaffold*.

---

*is a strong refuge.* It is capable of unlimited application in preaching and devotion.

⁽¹¹⁾ **So the Levites.**—As before, what Ezra said was repeated to the people in various directions by the Levites. But there was evidently an almost irrepressible emotion.

⁽¹²⁾ **They had understood.**—They had caught the meaning of the command to rejoice.

(13—18) The Feast of Tabernacles.

⁽¹³⁾ **The chief of the fathers.**—Not the vast multitude now, as the great feast was not yet.

**Even to understand.**—*To consider*, or *give attention to*: that is, to learn the full meaning of the almost forgotten festival. The dwelling in booths had fallen into disuse.

⁽¹⁵⁾ **Saying.**—There is no such command in Leviticus; the Septuagint inserts, "And Ezra spake." But it is better to adopt Houbigant's slight emendation of the text, which thus runs: "And when they heard it, they proclaimed," &c. The command, then, is to go out to the Mount of Olives, and gather, not precisely the branches which the ancient law required, but such as circumstances allowed.

⁽¹⁶⁾ **And in their courts.**—Not only on the roofs, but in the internal courtyards.

**Of the house of God.**—The ministers of the Temple made these; and strangers to Jerusalem made them in the streets or open spaces near the gates.

⁽¹⁷⁾ **The children of the captivity.**—The pathos of this designation is evident here.

**Done so.**—Though the feast had been kept (1 Kings viii.; Ezra iii.), it had never thus been kept with universal dwelling in booths.

⁽¹⁸⁾ **According unto the manner.**—For the Azereth, or supplementary feast day, see Lev. xxiii. 36.

IX.

(1—38) The Fast, the Confession, and the Covenant.

⁽¹⁾ **In the twenty and fourth day.**—After one day of rest, the people assembled with all the tokens of sorrow, even to dust on the head (1 Sam. iv. 12): the external signs and the internal spirit were one.

⁽²⁾ **The seed of Israel separated themselves from all strangers.**—The change to "seed" has here a deep propriety. They carefully avoided the many aliens among them throughout this fast.

**And stood and confessed.**—It must be remembered that these verses give the programme of what is afterwards filled up: the very praise for which they "stood" was filled with confession.

⁽³⁾ **One fourth part.**—Both day and night were divided into four parts. All orders standing in their respective place, the reading occupied the morning and the worship the afternoon. It is the latter which is now made prominent, as the former had been prominent in the preceding chapter.

⁽⁴⁾ **Stairs, of the Levites.**—*The scaffold of the Levites,* without the comma: the steps of ascent to the pulpit of Ezra (chap. viii. 2).

Bani, and Chenani, and cried with a loud voice unto the LORD their God. (5) Then the Levites, Jeshua, and Kadmiel, Bani, Hashabniah, Sherebiah, Hodijah, Shebaniah, *and* Pethahiah, said,

Stand up *and* bless the LORD your God for ever and ever: and blessed be thy glorious name, which is exalted above all blessing and praise.

(6) Thou, *even* thou, *art* LORD alone; *a*thou hast made heaven, the heaven of heavens, with all their host, the earth, and all *things* that *are* therein, the seas, and all that *is* therein, and thou preservest them all; and the host of heaven worshippeth thee.

(7) Thou *art* the LORD the God, who didst choose *b*Abram, and broughtest him forth out of Ur of the Chaldees, and gavest him the name of Abraham; (8) and foundest his heart *c*faithful before thee, and madest a *d*covenant with him to give the land of the Canaanites, the Hittites, the Amorites, and the Perizzites, and the Jebusites, and the Girgashites, to give *it*, *I say*, to his seed, and hast performed thy words: for thou *art* righteous: (9) *e*and didst see the affliction of our fathers in Egypt, and heardest their cry by the Red sea; (10) and *f*shewedst signs and wonders upon Pharaoh, and on all his servants, and on all the people of his land: for thou knewest that they dealt proudly against them. So didst thou get thee a name, as *it is* this day. (11) *g*And thou didst divide the sea before them, so that they went through the midst of the sea on the dry land; and their persecutors thou threwest into the deeps, as a stone into the *h*mighty waters. (12) Moreover thou *i*leddest them in the day by a cloudy pillar; and in the night by a pillar of fire, to give them light in the way wherein they should go.

(13) *j*Thou camest down also upon mount Sinai, and spakest with them from heaven, and gavest them right judgments, and ¹true laws, good statutes and commandments: (14) and madest known unto them thy holy sabbath, and commandedst them precepts, statutes, and laws, by the hand of Moses thy servant: (15) and *k*gavest them bread from heaven for their hunger, and broughtest forth water for them out of the rock for their thirst, and promisedst them that they should *l*go in to possess the land ²which thou hadst sworn to give them.

(16) But they and our fathers dealt proudly, and hardened their necks, and hearkened not to thy commandments, (17) and refused to obey, neither were mindful of thy wonders that thou didst among them; but hardened their necks, and in their rebellion appointed *m*a captain to return to their bondage: but thou *art* ³a God ready to pardon, gracious and merciful, slow to anger, and of great kindness, and forsookest them not. (18) Yea, *n*when they had made

---

*a* Gen. 1. 1.
*b* Gen. 11. 31; & 12. 1; & 17. 5.
*c* Gen. 15. 6.
*d* Gen. 12. 7; & 15. 18; & 17. 7, 8.
*e* Ex. 3. 7 & 14. 10.
*f* Ex. 7, 8, 9, 10, 12, & 14, chapters.
*g* Ex. 14. 22.
*h* Ex. 15. 10.
*i* Ex. 13. 21.
*j* Ex. 19. 20 & 20. 1.
¹ Heb., *laws of truth.*
*k* Ex. 16. 15 & 17. 6; Num. 20. 9.
*l* Deut. 1. 8.
² Heb., *which thou hadst lift up thine hand to give them.*
*m* Num. 14. 4.
³ Heb., *a God of pardons.*
*n* Ex. 32. 4.

---

**Bani, and Chenani.**—Probably, *Binnui* and *Hanan* (chap. x. 9, 10).

**Their God.**—When the people are called upon (verse 5), it is "your God"; hence these eight Levites offered a prayer which is not inserted.

(5) **Hashabniah.**—Not found elsewhere. No reason is given why this company is somewhat different from the former; the LXX. arbitrarily omit all names after Kadmiel. Similarly, they insert "and Ezra said" before verse 6. The psalm was perhaps composed by Ezra, but uttered by the Levites in the name of the congregation.

**Stand up and bless . . . Blessed be.**—Or, *let them bless.*

**Thou, even thou, art Lord alone.**—The three phrases mark how the address to the people glides into direct adoration of God.

**Thy glorious name.**—Literally found again in Ps. lxxii. 19 alone.

(6) **Preservest them all.**—In this comprehensiveness reproduced only in Heb. i. 3.

**The host of heaven.**—First the stars, but here the angels (Ps. ciii. 21).

(8) The Hivites are for some reason omitted.

(11) **As a stone into the mighty waters.**—Compare the Song of Moses, and mark in the Hebrew both the identity and the variation.

(13) **Right judgements.**—Five of the names given to the law of God in Ps. cxix. are singled out and applied to the Sinaitic legislation first, and then to the subsequent ordinances of Moses generally. But the emphasis here is on the adjectives "right," "true," "good," as belonging rather to the eternal principles of the Decalogue.

(14) **Madest known unto them thy holy sabbath.**—Every word here, as well as the prominence given to this among the other "commandments," must be noted as illustrating the importance of this ordinance in the covenant of chapter x. and throughout the book.

(15) **Bread from heaven.**—A change of phrase, which our Lord consecrated for ever (John vi.).

(16) **Dealt proudly.**—Like the Egyptians themselves (verse 10). It is remarkable that the same word is used as in the Hebrew of Exod. xviii. 11 and Deut. i. 43.

(17) **In their rebellion.**—Rather, *appointed a captain to return to their bondage in Egypt.* This is the reading of some MSS., followed by the Septuagint,

them a molten calf, and said, This *is* thy God that brought thee up out of Egypt, and had wrought great provocations; (19) yet thou in thy manifold mercies forsookest them not in the wilderness: the *a*pillar of the cloud departed not from them by day, to lead them in the way; neither the pillar of fire by night, to shew them light, and the way wherein they should go.

(20) Thou gavest also thy *b*good spirit to instruct them, and withheldest not thy *c*manna from their mouth, and gavest them water for their thirst. (21) Yea, forty years didst thou sustain them in the wilderness, *so that* they lacked nothing; their *d*clothes waxed not old, and their feet swelled not. (22) Moreover thou gavest them kingdoms and nations, and didst divide them into corners: so they possessed the land of *e*Sihon, and the land of the king of Heshbon, and the land of Og king of Bashan. (23) Their children also multipliedst thou as the stars of heaven, and broughtest them into the land, concerning which thou hadst promised to their fathers, that they should go in to possess *it*. (24) So the children went in and possessed the land, and thou subduedst before them the inhabitants of the land, the Canaanites, and gavest them into their hands, with their kings, and the people of the land, that they might do with them ¹as they would. (25) And they took strong cities, and a fat land, and possessed houses full of all goods, ²wells digged, vineyards, and oliveyards, and ³fruit trees in abundance: so they did eat, and were filled, and became fat, and delighted themselves in thy great goodness.

(26) Nevertheless they were disobedient, and rebelled against thee, and cast thy law behind their backs, and slew thy *f*prophets which testified against them to turn them to thee, and they wrought great provocations. (27) Therefore thou deliveredst them into the hand of their enemies, who vexed them: and in the time of their trouble, when they cried unto thee, thou heardest *them* from heaven; and according to thy manifold mercies thou gavest them saviours, who saved them out of the hand of their enemies. (28) But after they had rest, ⁴they did evil again before thee: therefore leftest thou them in the hand of their enemies, so that they had the dominion over them: yet when they returned, and cried unto thee, thou heardest *them* from heaven; and many times didst thou deliver them according to thy mercies; (29) and testifiedst against them, that thou mightest bring them again unto thy law: yet they dealt proudly, and hearkened not unto thy commandments, but sinned against thy judgments, (which if a man do, he shall live in them;) and ⁵withdrew the shoulder, and hardened their neck, and would not hear. (30) Yet many years didst thou ⁶forbear them, and testifiedst *g*against them by thy spirit ⁷in thy prophets: yet would they not give ear: therefore gavest thou them into the hand of the people of the lands. (31) Nevertheless for thy great mercies' sake thou didst not utterly consume them, nor forsake them; for thou *art* a gracious and merciful God.

(32) Now therefore, our God, the great, the *h*mighty, and the terrible God, who keepest covenant and mercy, let not all the ⁸trouble seem little before thee, ⁹that hath come upon us, on our kings, on our princes, and on our priests, and on our prophets, and on our fathers, and on all thy people, since the time of the kings of Assyria unto this day. (33) Howbeit thou *art* just in all that is brought upon us; for thou hast done right, but we have done wickedly: (34) neither have

---

*a* Ex. 13. 22; Num. 14. 14; 1 Cor. 10. 1.
*b* Num. 11. 17.
*c* Ex. 16. 15 & 17. 6; Josh. 5. 12.
*d* Deut. 8. 4.
*e* Num. 21. 21, &c.
1 Heb., *according to their will.*
2 Or, *cisterns.*
3 Heb., *tree of food.*
*f* 1 Kings 19. 10.
4 Heb., *they returned to do evil.*
5 Heb., *they gave a withdrawing shoulder.*
6 Heb., *protract over them.*
*g* 2 Kings 17. 13; 2 Chr. 36. 15.
7 Heb., *in the hand of thy prophets.*
*h* Ex. 34. 6.
8 Heb., *weariness.*
9 Heb., *that hath found us.*

---

and is in harmony with Num. xiv. 4, though there the appointment is only proposed.

**A God ready to pardon.**—*A God of pardons:* only in Dan. ix. 9 and Ps. cxxx. 4.

(20) **Thy good spirit.**—Probably a reference to Num. xi. 17, 25. The epithet given to the Spirit is in Ps. cxliii. 10. But His teaching function occurs here only, and is a remarkable anticipation of the New Testament.

(22) **Divide them into corners.**—Strict usage of the term would require: *Thou didst divide unto them [these nations] in their boundaries.*

**And the land.**—There is a double reference to Sihon, king of Heshbon. This and Bashan were taken as the earnest of the possession of Canaan.

(27) **Their enemies who vexed them.**—The phraseology in this and the following verse shows that the Book of Judges is carefully remembered in the prayer.

(32) Here begins the prayer proper.

**Kings of Assyria.**—" The rod of God's anger" (Isa. x. 5). Pul, Tiglath-pileser, Shalmaneser, Sargon, Sennacherib, Esar-haddon, are traced in the sacred record as successive scourges.

(34) **Our kings.**—Note that the prophets are omitted in this enumeration.

our kings, our princes, our priests, nor our fathers, kept thy law, nor hearkened unto thy commandments and thy testimonies, wherewith thou didst testify against them. (35) For they have not served thee in their kingdom, and in thy great goodness that thou gavest them, and in the large and fat land which thou gavest before them, neither turned they from their wicked works. (36) Behold, we *are* servants this day, and *for* the land that thou gavest unto our fathers to eat the fruit thereof and the good thereof, behold, we *are* servants in it: (37) and it yieldeth much increase unto the kings whom thou hast set over us because of our sins: also they have dominion over our bodies, and over our cattle, at their pleasure, and we *are* in great distress. (38) And because of all this we make a sure *covenant*, and write *it*; and our princes, Levites, *and* priests, [1]seal unto it.

CHAPTER X.—(1) Now [2] those that sealed *were*, Nehemiah, [3] the Tirshatha, the son of Hachaliah, and Zidkijah, (2) Seraiah, Azariah, Jeremiah, (3) Pashur, Amariah, Malchijah, (4) Hattush, Shebaniah, Malluch, (5) Harim, Meremoth, Obadiah, (6) Daniel, Ginnethon, Baruch, (7) Meshullam, Abijah, Mijamin, (8) Maaziah, Bilgai, Shemaiah: these *were* the priests. (9) And the Levites: both Jeshua the son of Azaniah, Binnui of the sons of Henadad, Kadmiel; (10) and their brethren, Shebaniah, Hodijah, Kelita, Pelaiah, Hanan, (11) Micha, Rehob, Hashabiah, (12) Zaccur, Sherebiah, Shebaniah, (13) Hodijah, Bani, Beninu. (14) The chief of the people; Parosh, Pahathmoab, Elam, Zatthu, Bani, (15) Bunni, Azgad, Bebai, (16) Adonijah, Bigvai, Adin, (17) Ater, Hizkijah, Azzur, (18) Hodijah, Hashum, Bezai, (19) Hariph, Anathoth, Nebai, (20) Magpiash, Meshullam, Hezir, (21) Meshezabeel, Zadok, Jaddua, (22) Pelatiah, Hanan, Anaiah, (23) Hoshea, Hananiah, Hashub, (24) Hallohesh, Pileha, Shobek, (25) Rehum, Hashabnah, Maaseiah, (26) and Ahijah, Hanan, Anan, (27) Malluch, Harim, Baanah.

(28) *a*And the rest of the people, the priests, the Levites, the porters, the singers, the Nethinims, and all they that had separated themselves from the people of the lands unto the law of God, their wives, their sons, and their daughters, every one having knowledge, and having understanding; (29) they clave to their brethren, their nobles, and entered into a curse, and into an oath, to walk in God's law, which was given [4] by Moses the servant of God, and to observe and do all the commandments of the LORD our Lord, and his judgments and his

1 Heb., *are at the sealing*, or, *sealed*.
2 Heb., *at the sealings*.
3 Or, *the governor*.
*a* Ezra 2. 43.
4 Heb., *by the hand of*.

---

(37) **Yieldeth much increase.**—In money and kind a very large amount was sent by Syria to the Persian treasury.

**Over our bodies, and over our cattle.**—For military service; but the priests do not omit themselves.

**In great distress.**—Not so much under the Persian yoke as in the remembrance of God's judgments. The pathetic comparison between the Divine purpose in giving the land originally and their present bondage in it extends almost to every word.

(38) **Because of all this.**—On the ground of this confession, and to prove our sincerity.

**Seal unto it.**—*On the sealed* [*document*]. Each party impressed his seal on moist clay, which was then hardened. Sometimes these seals were attached to the document by separate strings. In chap. xi., "those who sealed" is, literally, *those on the sealed* [documents], in the plural.

X.

(1—28) The sealers of the covenant.

(1) **Zidkijah.**—Probably, *Zadok the scribe* (chap. xiii. 13), Nehemiah's secretary. (Comp. Ezra iv. 8.)

(2) **Seraiah.**—The family name of the high-priestly house to which Ezra and Eliashib belonged, one of whom—probably Ezra—affixed its seal.

(8) **These were the priests.**—That is, the names of the priestly families. (Comp. chap. xii. 1—6.)

(9) **And the Levites.**—Five of these family names are traceable (Ezra ii. 40, viii. 19; Neh. vii. 43).

(14) **The chief of the people.**—Some of the names are personal, some belong to families, some represent places, and some are independent. Comparing the list with Ezra ii., we find that years had added to the number of the houses.

(28—39) The points of the covenant.

(28) **All they that had separated themselves.** —If these meant proselytes from heathenism, this verse would be a perfect description of the constituents of the people. But we have no record as yet of a recognised body of such proselytes; and the word "separated" is the same as we find, with another meaning, in chap. ix. 2. Moreover, the following verses show that the covenant bears specially in mind the danger to God's law arising out of commerce with the heathen.

**Having understanding.**—Children who could intelligently take the oath were included.

(29) **They clave to their brethren.**—It was a union of the people as such, and sprang from a deep national conviction.

**Entered into a curse, and into an oath.**—The oath assumed the obligation; the curse imprecated the penalty of violation. (Comp. Deut. xxix. 12.)

*The points of*          NEHEMIAH, XI.          *the Covenant.*

statutes; (30) and that we would not give <sup>a</sup>our daughters unto the people of the land, nor take their daughters for our sons: (31) <sup>b</sup>and *if* the people of the land bring ware or any victuals on the sabbath day to sell, *that* we would not buy it of them on the sabbath, or on the holy day: and *that* we would leave the seventh year, and the <sup>c</sup>exaction of ¹every debt.

(32) Also we made ordinances for us, to charge ourselves yearly with the third part of a shekel for the service of the house of our God; (33) for the shewbread, and for the continual meat offering, and for the continual burnt offering, of the sabbaths, of the new moons, for the set feasts, and for the holy *things*, and for the sin offerings to make an atonement for Israel, and *for* all the work of the house of our God.

(34) And we cast the lots among the priests, the Levites, and the people, for the wood offering, to bring *it* into the house of our God, after the houses of our fathers, at times appointed year by year, to burn upon the altar of the Lord our God, as *it is* written in the <sup>d</sup>law: (35) and to bring the firstfruits of our ground, and the firstfruits of all fruit of all trees, year by year, unto the house of the Lord: (36) also the firstborn of our sons, and of our cattle, as *it is* written <sup>e</sup>in the law, and the firstlings of our herds and of our flocks, to bring to the house of our God, unto the priests that minister in the house of our God: (37) and *that* we should bring the firstfruits of our dough, and our offerings, and the fruit of all manner of trees, of wine and of oil, unto the priests, to the chambers of the house of our God; and the tithes of our ground unto the Levites, that the same Levites might have the tithes in all the cities of our tillage. (38) And the priest the son of Aaron shall be with the Levites, <sup>f</sup>when the Levites take tithes: and the Levites shall bring up the tithe of the tithes unto the house of our God, to the chambers, into the treasure house. (39) For the children of Israel and the children of Levi shall bring the offering of the corn, of the new wine, and the oil, unto the chambers, where *are* the vessels of the sanctuary, and the priests that minister, and the porters, and the singers: and we will not forsake the house of our God.

CHAPTER XI.—(1) And the rulers of the people dwelt at Jerusalem: the rest

*Marginal references:*
a Ex. 34. 16; Deut. 7. 3.
b Ex. 20. 10; Lev. 23. 3; Deut. 5. 12; ch. 13. 15, &c.
c Lev. 25. 4; Deut. 15. 2.
1 Heb., *every hand.*
d See Num. 28 & 29; Ex. 23. 19; Lev. 19. 23.
e Ex. 13. 2; Lev. 23. 17; Num. 15. 19 & 18. 12, &c.
f Num. 18. 26.

---

(31) **Or on the holy day.**—On the great festivals, equally with the Sabbath days of rest.

**Leave the seventh year.**—The Sabbatical year naturally follows; in it the ground should be left untilled.

**The exaction of every debt.**—The "Lord's release" of the seventh year (Deut. xv. 2).

(32) **Also we made ordinances for us.**—The covenant proceeds now to certain new regulations and resumption of neglected duties.

**To charge ourselves.**—Origin of that annual rate for the general service of the Temple which afterwards was raised to a half shekel (Matt. xvii. 24). The more ancient half shekel of the law was only an occasional tax (Exod. xxx. 13).

(34) **As it is written in the law.**—Lev. vi. 12 prescribes that the fire on the altar should be kept burning by wood. But here we have the origin of the "feast of the wood-offering"—a special day, subsequently substituted for the "times appointed year by year." The lot determined the order in which the various classes should supply the wood.

(35) **And to bring.**—Following "we made ordinances" (verse 32). The various firstfruits are specified according to the Mosaic law, which made this expression of natural piety an obligation; and the minuteness of the specification implies that neglect had crept in.

(36) **The firstborn of our sons, and of our cattle.**—Similarly collocated in Num. xvi. 15, 16; but there the cattle are defined as "unclean beasts," thus distinguished from "the firstlings of our herds and of our flocks." The latter were to be brought to "the priests that minister" for sacrifice; the former were, with the sons, to be redeemed by money, according to the priests' valuation.

(37) **To the chambers of the house of our God.**—To the store-chambers, minutely described as they were of old in 1 Kings vi., Hezekiah appears to have added formerly a treasure-house for the tithes, referred to in the next verse (2 Chron. xxxi. 11).

**In all the cities of our tillage.**—Agricultural towns, so called here with reference to the fruits of the earth, which were deposited first in certain selected places.

(38) **The son of Aaron.**—Consult Num. xviii. 22—26, which gives the reason for the distinction, here so marked, between the priest, the son of Aaron, and the Levites, the children of Levi. A priest was present when the tithes were gathered in the Levitical cities, to secure their own "tithe of the tithe," which then the Levites carried to Jerusalem.

(39) **Shall bring.**—The priests themselves were exempted from the care of gathering the tithes.

**We will not forsake the house of our God.**—Both the pledge and the violation of it in the sequel are explained by chap. xiii. 11—14.

### XI.

(1, 2) The history reverts to chap. vii. 5; lots are cast for the transfer of one-tenth of the people to the capital.

(1) **And the rulers.**—The narrative joins on to chap. vii. 4. The festival month had prevented the immediate carrying out of the governor's purpose.

of the people also cast lots, to bring one of ten to dwell in Jerusalem the holy city, and nine parts *to dwell* in *other* cities. ⁽²⁾ And the people blessed all the men, that willingly offered themselves to dwell at Jerusalem.

⁽³⁾ Now these *are* the chief of the province that dwelt in Jerusalem: but in the cities of Judah dwelt every one in his possession in their cities, *to wit*, Israel, the priests, and the Levites, and the Nethinims, and the children of Solomon's servants. ⁽⁴⁾ And at Jerusalem dwelt *certain* of the children of Judah, and of the children of Benjamin.

Of the children of Judah; Athaiah the son of Uzziah, the son of Zechariah, the son of Amariah, the son of Shephatiah, the son of Mahalaleel, of the children of Perez; ⁽⁵⁾ and Maaseiah the son of Baruch, the son of Col-hozeh, the son of Hazaiah, the son of Adaiah, the son of Joiarib, the son of Zechariah, the son of Shiloni. ⁽⁶⁾ All the sons of Perez that dwelt at Jerusalem *were* four hundred three score and eight valiant men.

⁽⁷⁾ And these *are* the sons of Benjamin; Sallu the son of Meshullam, the son of Joed, the son of Pedaiah, the son of Kolaiah, the son of Maaseiah, the son of Ithiel, the son of Jesaiah. ⁽⁸⁾ And after him Gabbai, Sallai, nine hundred twenty and eight. ⁽⁹⁾ And Joel the son of Zichri *was* their overseer: and Judah the son of Senuah *was* second over the city.

⁽¹⁰⁾ Of the priests: Jedaiah the son of Joiarib, Jachin. ⁽¹¹⁾ Seraiah the son of Hilkiah, the son of Meshullam, the son of Zadok, the son of Meraioth, the son of Ahitub, *was* the ruler of the house of God. ⁽¹²⁾ And their brethren that did the work of the house *were* eight hundred twenty and two: and Adaiah the son of Jeroham, the son of Pelaliah, the son of Amzi, the son of Zechariah, the son of Pashur, the son of Malchiah, ⁽¹³⁾ and his brethren, chief of the fathers, two hundred forty and two: and Amashai the son of Azareel, the son of Ahasai, the son of Meshillemoth, the son of Immer, ⁽¹⁴⁾ and their brethren, mighty men of valour, an hundred twenty and eight: and their overseer *was* Zabdiel, ¹the son of *one of* the great men.

⁽¹⁵⁾ Also of the Levites: Shemaiah the son of Hashub, the son of Azrikam, the son of Hashabiah, the son of Bunni; ⁽¹⁶⁾ and Shabbethai and Jozabad, of the chief of the Levites, ²*had* the oversight of the outward business of the house of God. ⁽¹⁷⁾ And Mattaniah the son of Micha, the son of Zabdi, the son of Asaph, *was* the principal to begin the thanksgiving in prayer: and Bakbukiah the second among his brethren, and Abda the son of Shammua, the son of Galal, the son of Jeduthun. ⁽¹⁸⁾ All the Levites in the holy city *were* two hun-

¹ Or, *the son of Haggedolim.*
² Heb., *were over.*

---

**The rest of the people.**—The rulers being already in the capital, Nehemiah ordered that one man in ten should be chosen by lot to transfer his family.

**Jerusalem the holy city.**—Remembering the "separation" that had taken place (chap. ix.), and the recent covenant (chap. x.), we see the solemnity of this epithet, now first used, and repeated in verse 18. "Then shall Jerusalem be holy, and no strangers shall pass through her any more" (Joel iii. 17). But the New Testament brings another comment on the phrase.

⁽²⁾ **The people blessed all the men that willingly offered themselves.**—We are not told that any compensation was made to them; and these words seem to indicate that the chosen ones freely submitted, their patriotism being applauded by all.—Jerusalem was the post of danger, and in any case it was a hardship to leave their country possessions (verse 3).

⁽³⁾ **Of the province.**—This betrays the hand of Nehemiah, who was still a Persian official as well as a governor of Judah; and it shows that here we have a general heading for the rest of the chapter. Both city and country are included in the rest of the verse.

**Israel.**—The two Israelitish tribes were represented, but, like Judah before, this has become a generic name.

⁽⁴⁻¹⁹⁾ The heads in Jerusalem: as compared with 1 Chron. ix., by no means complete. Judah and Benjamin are represented, with priests and Levites and porters.

⁽⁴⁾ **Perez.**—In 1 Chron. ix. the descendants of Perez (or Phares) are not given; but the descendants of Zerah, present there, are absent here. This may be a question of the right reading of the text.

⁽⁵⁾ **The son of Shiloni.**—Better, *the Shilonite*, or *descendants of Shelah*, youngest son of Judah.

⁽⁷⁾ The Benjamites were represented by two families, and gave the city two prefects (verse 9).

⁽¹⁰⁾ This should be read *Jedaiah, Joiarib, Jachin*, three priestly families (1 Chron. ix. 10).

⁽¹¹⁾ **Seraiah.**—The high-priestly family name. Eliashib was the present occupant.

⁽¹⁴⁾ **Of valour.**—Able for the service of God's house: *men of ability*, therefore.

**The son of one of the great men.**—Rather, *son of Haggedolim*.

⁽¹⁶⁾ **Outward business.**—This is a remarkable specification of the functions of the Levites, parallel with the "valour" of the priests just before. The preceding chapter explains the "outward business."

dred fourscore and four. (19) Moreover the porters, Akkub, Talmon, and their brethren that kept ¹the gates, were an hundred seventy and two.

(20) And the residue of Israel, of the priests, and the Levites, were in all the cities of Judah, every one in his inheritance. (21) ᵃBut the Nethinims dwelt in ²Ophel: and Ziha and Gispa were over the Nethinims.

(22) The overseer also of the Levites at Jerusalem was Uzzi the son of Bani, the son of Hashabiah, the son of Mattaniah, the son of Micha. Of the sons of Asaph, the singers were over the business of the house of God. (23) For it was the king's commandment concerning them, that ³a certain portion should be for the singers, due for every day.

(24) And Pethahiah the son of Meshezabeel, of the children of Zerah the son of Judah, was at the king's hand in all matters concerning the people.

(25) And for the villages, with their fields, some of the children of Judah dwelt at Kirjath-arba, and in the villages thereof, and at Dibon, and in the villages thereof, and at Jekabzeel, and in the villages thereof, (26) and at Jeshua, and at Moladah, and at Beth-phelet, (27) and at Hazar-shual, and at Beer-sheba, and in the villages thereof, (28) and at Ziklag, and at Mekonah, and in the villages thereof, (29) and at En-rimmon, and at Zareah, and at Jarmuth, (30) Zanoah, Adullam, and in their villages, at Lachish, and the fields thereof, at Azekah, and in the villages thereof. And they dwelt from Beer-sheba unto the valley of Hinnom.

(31) The children also of Benjamin ⁴from Geba dwelt ⁵at Michmash, and Aija, and Beth-el, and in their villages, (32) and at Anathoth, Nob, Ananiah, (33) Hazor, Ramah, Gittaim, (34) Hadid, Zeboim, Neballat, (35) Lod, and Ono, the valley of craftsmen.

(36) And of the Levites were divisions in Judah, and in Benjamin.

CHAPTER XII.—(1) Now these are the ᵇpriests and the Levites that went up with Zerubbabel the son of Shealtiel, and Jeshua: Seraiah, Jeremiah, Ezra, (2) Amariah, ⁶Malluch, Hattush, (3) ⁷Shechaniah, ⁸Rehum, ⁹Meremoth, (4) Iddo, ¹⁰Ginnetho, Abijah, (5) ¹¹Miamin, ¹²Maadiah, Bilgah, (6) Shemaiah, and Joiarib, Jedaiah, (7) ¹³Sallu, Amok, Hilkiah, Jedaiah. These were the chief of the priests and of their brethren in the days of Jeshua.

(8) Moreover the Levites: Jeshua, Binnui, Kadmiel, Sherebiah, Judah, and Mattaniah, which was over ¹⁴the thanksgiving, he and his brethren. (9) Also

1 Heb., at the gates.
ᵃ See ch. 3. 26.
2 Or, The tower.
3 Or, a sure ordinance.
4 Or, of Geba.
5 Or, to Michmash.
ᵇ Ezra 2. 1.
6 Or, Melicu, ver. 14.
7 Or, Shebaniah, ver. 14.
8 Or, Harim, ver. 15.
9 Or, Meraioth, ver. 15.
10 Or, 'Ginnethon, ver. 16.
11 Or, Miniamin, ver. 17.
12 Or, Moadiah, ver. 17.
13 Or, Sallai, ver. 20.
14 That is, the psalms of thanksgiving.

---

(19) **An hundred seventy and two.**—In 1 Chron. ix. the number is 212. The difference between the two accounts may partly be explained by the fact that in the Chronicles the list is confined to those who came with Zerubbabel, while here addition is made of those who came with Ezra. But see the commentary on 1 Chron. ix.

(20—36) The heads in the country.

(21) **Ophel.**—The Nethinims on the promontory of Ophel were either within or without the city, according as the one wall or the other was taken. Here they are regarded as outside.

(22) **The overseer.**—*Pakid,* or *visitor.*

**Of the sons of Asaph.**—It requires no disturbance of the original to read the whole of Uzzi's pedigree: "the son of Micha, of the sons of Asaph, the singers in the service of the house of God." Thus with the prayer of verse 17 there is a parallel.

(23) **The king's commandment.**—It seems that Artaxerxes had gone beyond the exemption of Ezra vii. 24, and given them a daily allowance, which it was the business of Uzzi to see to.

(24) **Of the children of Zerah.**—This makes the absence of Zerah in the beginning of the chapter very remarkable, and suggests some accidental omission.

**At the king's hand.**—Pethahiah was the king's agent in all the country matters of the "province."

(25) The children of Judah are now described very generally with respect to their distribution.

**Kirjath-arba.**—Hebron no longer, the ancient name being now recovered.

**In the villages thereof.**—Literally, *the daughters thereof;* being a different word from the "villages" at the beginning.

(30) **From Beer-sheba unto the valley of Hinnom.**—The men of Judah spread from the extreme south to the extreme north of Judah, an extent of some fifty miles.

(31) **From Geba.**—This verse should read: *the children also of Benjamin dwelt from Geba to Michmash.*

(36) **And of the Levites.**—The fewness of the Levites in the country warranted their summary notice in this way.

## XII.

(1—9) The priests and Levites of the First Return.

(1) **Seraiah, Jeremiah, Ezra.**—The first is the family name, represented by Jeshua. Of the two others we know nothing more than this record gives.

(6) **And Joiarib.**—The "and" begins the list of those who did not seal the covenant. See a like "and" in verse 19.

(7) **These were the chief.**—Genealogically, but not according to the courses, which are in none of the lists complete.

Bakbukiah and Unni, their brethren, were over against them in the watches.

(10) And Jeshua begat Joiakim, Joiakim also begat Eliashib, and Eliashib begat Joiada, (11) and Joiada begat Jonathan, and Jonathan begat Jaddua.

(12) And in the days of Joiakim were priests, the chief of the fathers: of Seraiah, Meraiah; of Jeremiah, Hananiah; (13) of Ezra, Meshullam; of Amariah, Jehohanan; (14) of Melicu, Jonathan; of Shebaniah, Joseph; (15) of Harim, Adna; of Meraioth, Helkai; (16) of Iddo, Zechariah; of Ginnethon, Meshullam; (17) of Abijah, Zichri; of Miniamin, of Moadiah, Piltai; (18) of Bilgah, Shammua; of Shemaiah, Jehonathan; (19) and of Joiarib, Mattenai; of Jedaiah, Uzzi; (20) of Sallai, Kallai; of Amok, Eber; (21) of Hilkiah, Hashabiah; of Jedaiah, Nethaneel.

(22) The Levites in the days of Eliashib, Joiada, and Johanan, and Jaddua, were recorded chief of the fathers: also the priests, to the reign of Darius the Persian. (23) The sons of Levi, the chief of the fathers, were written in the book of the <sup>a</sup>chronicles, even until the days of Johanan the son of Eliashib. (24) And the chief of the Levites; Hashabiah, Sherebiah, and Jeshua the son of Kadmiel, with their brethren over against them, to praise and to give thanks, according to the commandment of David the man of God, ward over against ward.

<sup>a</sup> 1 Chr. 9. 14, &c.

<sup>1</sup> Or, treasuries, or, assemblies.

(25) Mattaniah, and Bakbukiah, Obadiah, Meshullam, Talmon, Akkub, were porters keeping the ward at the <sup>1</sup>thresholds of the gates. (26) These were in the days of Joiakim the son of Jeshua, the son of Jozadak, and in the days of Nehemiah the governor, and of Ezra the priest, the scribe.

(27) And at the dedication of the wall of Jerusalem they sought the Levites out of all their places, to bring them to Jerusalem, to keep the dedication with gladness, both with thanksgivings, and with singing, with cymbals, psalteries, and with harps. (28) And the sons of the singers gathered themselves together, both out of the plain country round about Jerusalem, and from the villages of Netophathi; (29) also from the house of Gilgal, and out of the fields of Geba and Azmaveth: for the singers had builded them villages round about Jerusalem. (30) And the priests and the Levites purified themselves, and purified the people, and the gates, and the wall.

(31) Then I brought up the princes of Judah upon the wall, and appointed two great companies of them that gave thanks, whereof one went on the right hand upon the wall toward the dung gate: (32) and after them went Hoshaiah, and half of the princes of Judah, (33) and Azariah, Ezra, and Meshullam, (34) Judah, and Benjamin, and Shemaiah, and Jeremiah, (35) and certain of the priests' sons with

---

(10, 11) Pedigree of certain high priests, with supplement from a later hand. The six generations stretch over 200 years—from B.C. 536 to B.C. 332.

(11) **Jonathan.**—Should be Johanan (verse 22); and "Jaddua" is most probably the high priest who confronted Alexander the Great.

(12—26) List of representatives of Zerubbabel's priests in the days of Joiakim; to which is added an account of the Levites in his day. Between these there is an interpolation (verses 22, 23).

(14) **Melicu** is the "Malluch" of verse 2, and Hattush is omitted. Other anomalies of this kind may be noticed, of which no account can now be given.

(17) **Of Miniamin.**—Some name has dropped out.

(22, 23) **The Levites.**—Here is an evident interpolation. The writer says that the records of the heads of courses was continued down to Jaddua and Darius Codomannus.

(24) **And the chief.**—The account resumes with the Levites, and gives a list of the extant officers of the Temple, many names being the same as in earlier times.

(25) **At the thresholds.**—At the treasuries, or storechambers attached to the several gates of the Temple.

(27—43) The dedication of the wall. Henceforth Nehemiah speaks in his own person.

(27) **They sought the Levites.**—The dedication was to be processional and musical, as well as sacrificial: after the pattern of Solomon's dedication of the Temple.

(29) **The singers.**—As the Nethinim were settled in Ophel, so the class of Levitical singers were chiefly to be found in villages to the north of the city.

(30) **Purified themselves.**—Before consecration to God there must be purification from defilement. It is made emphatic that both priests and Levites purified themselves, that is, by offerings and ablutions (comp. 2 Chron. xxix. 15; Ezra vi. 20): the gates and the wall by being sprinkled.

(31) **The princes.**—The chiefs were assembled somewhere on the south-west wall, and then divided into two companies.

(32) **After them.**—These verses show that the clerical and the lay elements were mingled.

(33) **Ezra.**—Probably the same as the Azariah preceding.

(34) **Judah and Benjamin.**—A singular collocation: the laity of Judah and Benjamin, with priests before and after.

*The Offices of the Priests and Levites* NEHEMIAH, XIII. *appointed in the Temple.*

trumpets; *namely*, Zechariah the son of Jonathan, the son of Shemaiah, the son of Mattaniah, the son of Michaiah, the son of Zaccur, the son of Asaph: <sup>(36)</sup> and his brethren, Shemaiah, and Azarael, Milalai, Gilalai, Maai, Nethaneel, and Judah, Hanani, with the musical instruments of David the man of God, and Ezra the scribe before them. <sup>(37)</sup> And at the fountain gate, which was over against them, they went up by the stairs of the city of David, at the going up of the wall, above the house of David, even unto the water gate eastward.

<sup>(38)</sup> And the other *company of them that gave* thanks went over against *them*, and I after them, and the half of the people upon the wall, from beyond the tower of the furnaces even unto the broad wall; <sup>(39)</sup> and from above the gate of Ephraim, and above the old gate, and above the fish gate, and the tower of Hananeel, and the tower of Meah, even unto the sheep gate: and they stood still in the prison gate.

<sup>(40)</sup> So stood the two *companies of them that gave* thanks in the house of God, and I, and the half of the rulers with me: <sup>(41)</sup> and the priests; Eliakim, Maaseiah, Miniamin, Michaiah, Elioenai, Zechariah, *and* Hananiah, with trumpets; <sup>(42)</sup> and Maaseiah, and Shemaiah, and Eleazar, and Uzzi, and Jehohanan, and Malchijah, and Elam, and Ezer. And the singers <sup>1</sup>sang loud, with Jezrahiah *their* overseer. <sup>(43)</sup> Also that day they offered great sacrifices, and rejoiced: for God had made them rejoice with great joy: the wives also and the children rejoiced: so that the joy of Jerusalem was heard even afar off.

<sup>(44)</sup> And at that time were some appointed over the chambers for the treasures, for the offerings, for the firstfruits, and for the tithes, to gather into them out of the fields of the cities the portions <sup>2</sup>of the law for the priests and Levites: <sup>3</sup>for Judah rejoiced for the priests and for the Levites <sup>4</sup>that waited. <sup>(45)</sup> And both the singers and the porters kept the ward of their God, and the ward of the purification, <sup>a</sup>according to the commandment of David, *and* of Solomon his son. <sup>(46)</sup> For in the days of David <sup>b</sup>and Asaph of old *there were* chief of the singers, and songs of praise and thanksgiving unto God. <sup>(47)</sup> And all Israel in the days of Zerubbabel, and in the days of Nehemiah, gave the portions of the singers and the porters, every day his portion: and they <sup>5</sup>sanctified *holy things* unto the Levites; <sup>c</sup>and the Levites sanctified *them* unto the children of Aaron.

CHAPTER XIII.—<sup>(1)</sup> On that day <sup>6</sup>they read in the <sup>d</sup>book of Moses in the <sup>7</sup>audience of the people; and therein

---

1 Heb., *made their voice to be heard.*

2 That is, *appointed by the law.*

3 Heb., *for the joy of Judah.*

4 Heb., *that stood.*

*a* 1 Chron. 25 & 26.

*b* 1 Chron. 25. 1, &c.

5 That is, *set apart.*

*c* Num. 18. 26.

6 Heb., *there was read.*

*d* Num. 22. 5; Deut. 23. 3.

7 Heb., *ears.*

---

<sup>(36)</sup> **With the musical instruments of David the man of God.**—No part of the service deviated from sacred precedents (comp. verse 27).

**Ezra the scribe before them.**—Between the singers and the princes came he who was the greatest in dignity, though the second in office.

<sup>(38)</sup> **The other company.**—Comparing the order with chap. iii., the reader will have a clear view of the second company. They had the longer route, proceeding to the left, rounding the north "broad wall," passing the sheep-gate, and so meeting the priestly company near the prison-gate. The space where they met had the Temple straight in front, the prison-gate on the right, and the water-gate on the left.

<sup>(39)</sup> **The gate of Ephraim.**—Not mentioned in the process of repairing, as having remained comparatively intact with part of the " broad wall."

<sup>(40)</sup> **In the house of God.**—They stood first outside, but afterwards entered to present their offerings. But the main interest of the day was the professional worship under the open heavens.

<sup>(41)</sup> **And the priests.**—Like the names of the priests and Levites in verse 35, these are personal; not to be found in the former lists.

<sup>(43)</sup> **Rejoiced.**—This verse is full of joy; but before the rejoicing comes the abundant offering of sacrifices.

<sup>(44—47)</sup> Economical arrangements.

<sup>(44)</sup> **For Judah rejoiced.**—Not only was the Temple service restored to something like the completeness of the Davidical period, the people also everywhere took pleasure in the ministrations of the Temple, and provided amply for them. Hence the need of men to take charge of the treasuries of the firstfruits and tithes.

<sup>(45)</sup> **Kept the ward.**—This should be read differently. The priests and Levites *kept the ward of their God, and the ward of purification, and the singers and porters*, &c. To "keep the ward" is to observe the regular times and seasons of sacrifice and thanksgiving.

<sup>(46)</sup> **Of old.**—Always there is a reverence shown for the old precedents.

<sup>(47)</sup> **The Levites.**—Between the people and the priests came the Levites, who received the tithe and gave the priests their "tithe of the tithe" (Num. xviii. 26).

### XIII.

(1—3) Reform as to mixed marriages.

<sup>(1)</sup> **On that day.**—Probably the season of the Feast of Tabernacles, as before. But portions were selected to be read.

*Nehemiah reforms*          NEHEMIAH, XIII.          *various Abuses.*

was found written, that the Ammonite and the Moabite should not come into the congregation of God for ever; <sup>(2)</sup> <sup>a</sup>because they met not the children of Israel with bread and with water, but hired Balaam against them, that he should curse them: howbeit our God turned the curse into a blessing. <sup>(3)</sup> Now it came to pass, when they had heard the law, that they separated from Israel all the mixed multitude.

<sup>(4)</sup> And before this, Eliashib the priest, having the oversight of the chamber of the house of our God, *was* allied unto Tobiah <sup>(5)</sup> and he had prepared for him a great chamber, where aforetime they laid the meat offerings, the frankincense, and the vessels, and the tithes of the corn, the new wine, and the oil, <sup>2</sup>which was commanded *to be given* to the Levites, and the singers, and the porters; and the offerings of the priests. <sup>(6)</sup> But in all this *time* was not I at Jerusalem: for in the two and thirtieth year of Artaxerxes king of Babylon came I unto the king, and <sup>3</sup>after certain days <sup>4</sup>obtained I leave of the king: <sup>(7)</sup> and I came to Jerusalem, and understood of the evil that Eliashib did for Tobiah, in preparing him a chamber in the courts of the house of God. <sup>(8)</sup> And it grieved me sore: therefore I cast forth all the household stuff of Tobiah out of the chamber. <sup>(9)</sup> Then I commanded, and they cleansed the chambers: and thither brought I again the vessels of the house of God, with the meat offering and the frankincense.

<sup>(10)</sup> And I perceived that the portions of the Levites had not been given *them*: for the Levites and the singers, that did the work, were fled every one to his field. <sup>(11)</sup> Then contended I with the rulers, and said, Why is the house of God forsaken? And I gathered them together, and set them in their <sup>5</sup>place. <sup>(12)</sup> Then brought all Judah the tithe of the corn and the new wine and the oil unto the <sup>6</sup>treasuries. <sup>(13)</sup> And I made treasurers over the treasuries, Shelemiah the priest, and Zadok the scribe, and of the Levites, Pedaiah: and <sup>7</sup>next to them *was* Hanan the son of Zaccur, the son of

*a* Num. 22. 5; Josh. 24. 9.

<sup>1</sup> Heb., *being set over.*

<sup>2</sup> Heb., *the commandment of the Levites.*

<sup>3</sup> Heb., *at the end of days.*

<sup>4</sup> Or, *I earnestly requested.*

<sup>5</sup> Heb., *standing.*

<sup>6</sup> Or, *storehouses.*

<sup>7</sup> Heb., *at their hand.*

---

**They read in the book of Moses.**—"It was read" in the Pentateuch, and specially Deut. xxiii. This is introduced for the sake of the action taken, and the history is given in brief, with a striking and characteristic parenthesis of Nehemiah's own concerning the curse turned into a blessing.

**Therein was found written.**—What to the people generally was not known.

**For ever.**—No Ammonite or Ammonite family could have legal standing in the congregation, "even to their tenth generation;" and this interdict was to last "for ever." It virtually though not actually amounted to absolute exclusion.

<sup>(3)</sup> **The mixed multitude.**—For the "mixed multitude," or *Ereb*, which plays so prominent a part in Jewish history, see on Exod. xii. 38. The process here was that of shutting out heathens who were in the habit of mingling with the people in the services. In chap. ix. it was, as we saw, the people's separation from the practices and spirit of the heathen.

(4—9) The scandal of the high priest.

<sup>(4)</sup> **Eliashib the priest, having the oversight.** —Probably the high priest of chap. iii. 1, whose office alone would not have given him control over "the chamber:" that is, the series of chambers running round three walls of the Temple. He "was allied unto Tobiah," but in what way is not stated.

**Before this.**—That is, before the return of Nehemiah; indeed, there is a suspicious absence of Eliashib's name throughout the high religious festivities of the preceding chapters.

<sup>(5)</sup> **A great chamber.**—The sequel shows that many small chambers had been thrown into one.

<sup>(6)</sup> **Was not I at Jerusalem.**—Parenthetical explanation of this disorderly state of things.

**King of Babylon.**—Probably it was at Babylon that Nehemiah found the court, and therefore he does not say "King of Persia."

**After certain days.**—The time is left indefinite. But the "two and thirtieth year" shows that he had been in Jerusalem twelve years before his return to the king.

<sup>(8)</sup> **It grieved me sore.**—The second time we read of Nehemiah's deep emotion: first, because of the utter dissoluteness of which this was a token; and secondly, because it was a priestly desecration.

<sup>(9)</sup> **Cleansed.**—There was a formal purification. It is a note of minute accuracy that there is no mention of tithes being brought back as yet; the next verses show why.

(10—13) The provision for the Levites.

<sup>(10)</sup> **Fled every one to his field.**—They who performed the work of the Temple were obliged to seek their sustenance by cultivating the fields apportioned to them in the Levitical cities (Num. xxxv. 2).

<sup>(11)</sup> **Contended I with the rulers.**—See their express covenant in chap. x. 39. The rich men had taken advantage of Nehemiah's absence to indulge their covetousness.

**And I gathered them together.**—The Levites were summoned back from their fields.

<sup>(13)</sup> **And I made.**—The reform was made effectual by organisation. Eliashib had failed in his duty (verse 4); and the appointment of treasurers (chap. xii. 44) is now confirmed. One of the treasurers was a layman named Hanan (chap. x. 22); but they were all faithful men, and are mentioned in connection with the building of the wall. The majority being priests and Levites, they distributed "to their brethren." Zadok was pro-

Mattaniah: for they were counted faithful, and ¹their office *was* to distribute unto their brethren.

⁽¹⁴⁾ ᵃRemember me, O my God, concerning this, and wipe not out my ²good deeds that I have done for the house of my God, and for the ³offices thereof.

⁽¹⁵⁾ In those days saw I in Judah *some* treading wine presses on the sabbath, and bringing in sheaves, and lading asses; as also wine, grapes, and figs, and all *manner of* burdens, which they brought into Jerusalem on the sabbath day: and I testified *against them* in the day wherein they sold victuals. ⁽¹⁶⁾ There dwelt men of Tyre also therein, which brought fish, and all manner of ware, and sold on the sabbath unto the children of Judah, and in Jerusalem. ⁽¹⁷⁾ Then I contended with the nobles of Judah, and said unto them, What evil thing *is* this that ye do, and profane the sabbath day? ⁽¹⁸⁾ Did not your fathers thus, and did not our God bring all this evil upon us, and upon this city? yet ye bring more wrath upon Israel by profaning the sabbath.

⁽¹⁹⁾ And it came to pass, that when the gates of Jerusalem began to be dark before the sabbath, I commanded that the gates should be shut, and charged

---

1 Heb., *it was upon them.*

a ver. 22

2 Heb., *kindnesses.*

3 Or, *observations.*

4 Heb., *before the wall?*

5 Or, *multitude.*

6 Heb., *had made to dwell with them.*

B.C. cir. 434.

7 Heb., *they discerned not to speak.*

8 Heb., *of people and people.*

9 Or, *reviled them.*

---

that they should not be opened till after the sabbath: and *some* of my servants set I at the gates, *that* there should no burden be brought in on the sabbath day. ⁽²⁰⁾ So the merchants and sellers of all kind of ware lodged without Jerusalem once or twice. ⁽²¹⁾ Then I testified against them, and said unto them, Why lodge ye ⁴about the wall? if ye do *so* again, I will lay hands on you. From that time forth came they no *more* on the sabbath. ⁽²²⁾ And I commanded the Levites that they should cleanse themselves, and *that* they should come *and* keep the gates, to sanctify the sabbath day.

Remember me, O my God, *concerning* this also, and spare me according to the ⁵greatness of thy mercy.

⁽²³⁾ In those days also saw I Jews *that* ⁶had married wives of Ashdod, of Ammon, *and* of Moab: ⁽²⁴⁾ and their children spake half in the speech of Ashdod, and ⁷could not speak in the Jews' language, but according to the language ⁸of each people. ⁽²⁵⁾ And I contended with them, and ⁹cursed them, and smote certain of them, and plucked off their hair, and made them swear by God, *saying*, Ye shall not give your daughters unto their sons, nor take their daughters

---

bably the Zidkijah of chap. x. 1, and the secretary of Nehemiah.

⁽¹⁴⁾ **Remember me.**—Once more the faithful servant of God begs a merciful remembrance of what he had done for the honour of God in the "observances" of His Temple.

(15-22) Vindication of the Sabbath.

⁽¹⁵⁾ **Saw I in Judah.**—In the country Nehemiah marked the most determined profanation of the Sabbath; and this extended to Jerusalem, into which all kinds of burdens were on that day, as on others, carried.

⁽¹⁶⁾ **Men of Tyre.**—They brought timber for the building of the Temple, and received food in payment (Ezra iii. 7). Now they seem to have established themselves as a colony, and supplied fish, especially to the inhabitants. But their offence was the doing this "on the sabbath unto the children of Judah, and in Jerusalem." The verse closes emphatically.

⁽¹⁷⁾ **That ye do.**—The nobles, in the absence of Nehemiah, had been responsible, and the sin is charged upon them. The appeal supposes their familiarity with the express prediction of Jeremiah and its literal fulfilment (Jer. xvii. 27).

⁽¹⁹⁾ **Some of my servants.**—These are several times mentioned as employed in public duty. Here they are used provisionally, to keep out traffickers until the formal appointment of the Levitical guard (verse 22), after which they would be relieved.

⁽²⁰⁾ **Once or twice.**—For a time they lodged outside; the unseemliness of this, and the evidence it gave that they were only waiting to evade the law, made Nehemiah testify in word, and threaten forcible action. This effectually removed the evil.

⁽²²⁾ **Cleanse themselves.**—As for a sacred duty, not without reference to their past neglect, which required to be forgiven. This was a high tribute to the Sabbath ordinance, and as such in harmony with all the details of this episode.

**Remember me.**—In this prayer also Nehemiah commits his fidelity to the merciful estimate of God. But something in connection with the Sabbath, or with his retrospect of his own conduct, gives the passing prayer a peculiar pathos of humility.

(23-29) The mixed marriages again.

⁽²³⁾ **Saw I Jews.**—The punishment shows that these were exceptional cases; but the transgression was of the most flagrant kind (see verse 1).

⁽²⁴⁾ **Half in the speech of Ashdod.**—A mixture of Philistine and Aramaic.

⁽²⁵⁾ **Cursed them.**—Nehemiah simply echoed the covenant sanction on this very point (chap. x. 29, 30).

**Certain of them.**—Some were selected for special punishment and humiliation. Ezra, on a like occasion, humbled himself by plucking off the hair of his own head (Ezra ix. 3). Then they were obliged to repeat the oath of the covenant.

unto your sons, or for yourselves. <sup>(26)</sup> Did not Solomon king of Israel sin by these things? yet among many nations was there no king like him, who was beloved of his God, and God made him king over all Israel: <sup>a</sup>nevertheless even him did outlandish women cause to sin. <sup>(27)</sup> Shall we then hearken unto you to do all this great evil, to transgress against our God in marrying strange wives? <sup>(28)</sup> And *one* of the sons of Joiada, the son of Eliashib the high priest, *was* son in law to Sanballat the Horonite: therefore I chased him from me. <sup>(29)</sup> Remember them, O my God, <sup>1</sup>because they have defiled the priesthood, and the covenant of the priesthood, and of the Levites.

<sup>(30)</sup> Thus cleansed I them from all strangers, and appointed the wards of the priests and the Levites, every one in his business; <sup>(31)</sup> and for the wood offering, at times appointed, and for the firstfruits.

Remember me, O my God, for good.

*a* 1 Kings 11. 1, &c.

<sup>1</sup> Heb., *for the defilings.*

---

(26) **Did not Solomon . . .**—Here it is implied that the language of Scripture concerning Solomon was familiar both to Nehemiah and to these transgressors. It is a remarkable instance of the faithful application of their own chronicles.

(28) **I chased him from me.**—Eliashib himself was allied by marriage to Tobiah, and one of his grandsons was now brought into prominence as married to Sanballat. Him Nehemiah drove into exile.

(29) **Remember them.**—This priestly violation of law is committed to God alone for punishment.

**And of the Levites.**—God chose the tribe of Levi for Himself, specially the house of Aaron, and every priest was to be "holy to the Lord" (Lev. xxi. 6, 8). This was "the covenant of the priesthood;" though there may be an undertone of reference to the great covenant in chap. x.

(30, 31) Conclusion.

(30) This is a brief recapitulation of the special work of Nehemiah after his return.

**Thus cleansed I them.**—After the acts of discipline described above, there was doubtless some formal service of expiation.

(31) **Remember me, O my God, for good.**—With these words Nehemiah leaves the scene, committing himself and his discharge of duty to the Righteous Judge. His conscientious fidelity had brought him into collision not only with external enemies but with many of his own brethren. His rigorous reformation has been assailed by many moralists and commentators in every age. But in these words he commits all to God, as it were by anticipation.—It may be added that with these words end the annals of Old Testament history.

# THE BOOK OF ESTHER

# INTRODUCTION TO
# THE BOOK OF ESTHER

**I. Contents.**—The Book of Esther opens with the account of the feast given by King Ahasuerus at the end of the 180 days during which he had entertained the lords and princes of the kingdom at his palace in the city of Shushan. On the seventh day of the feast, the king, excited with wine, sends for his queen Vashti "to show the people and the princes her beauty;" with which unseemly request Vashti naturally refuses to comply. The enraged king takes counsel with his "wise men," and by a decree deposes Vashti from her place both as queen and wife, ordering that "all wives should give to their husbands honour," and that "every man should bear rule in his own house."

After this a number of maidens were selected, that from them Ahasuerus might choose the one who pleased him best. His choice fell upon Esther, a Jewish orphan girl, who had been brought up by her cousin Mordecai, at whose command she did not at first disclose her nationality to the king. About this time Mordecai was the means of frustrating an attempt made on the life of Ahasuerus; the plotters were hanged, but the discoverer of the plot was for the time forgotten.

A certain Haman now occupied the chief place in the king's favour, and Mordecai incurred his bitter enmity by his refusal to pay him the reverence yielded by others. Not content with the personal hatred, he sought the downfall of the whole Jewish race, and obtained from the king a decree, by virtue of which all the Jews throughout the empire were to be massacred. The terror such an edict would produce among the Jews can well be imagined, and the news at length reaches Esther in the palace, and she is bidden by her kinsman to use her influence with the king to obtain a reversal of the decree. To her objection that to venture uncalled into the king's presence is punishable with death, it is answered that, if her race are to perish, she must not think to purchase safety by a cowardly silence; "but," adds Mordecai, unwilling that his adopted child should lose so great an opportunity, "who knoweth whether thou art come to the kingdom for such a time as this?" The queen at last determines to make the effort, bidding her countrymen to join her in observing a three days' fast. The fast over, Esther, clad in her royal robes, but standing in the court as a suppliant, appeared before the king, who held out to her the golden sceptre in token that she had "obtained favour in his sight." She is bidden to proffer her request, but, evidently temporising, she merely asks that the king and Haman should come that day to the banquet which she had prepared. The repetition of the king's promise only leads to a fresh invitation to a second banquet on the following day, while Haman returns home proud at the honour done him, but with fresh exasperation against Mordecai, who remained sitting as he passed.

At home Haman discloses his grievance to his wife and his friends, and by their advice it is decided that a gallows of exceptional height should be made, and that on the morrow the king's leave should be got to hang Mordecai—far too unimportant a matter to be worth gainsaying. That very night God's providence interposes to save His people in an unlooked-for way. The king, unable to sleep, commands the book of the Chronicles of the kingdom to be read to him, and thus hears of the unrewarded service which Mordecai had done him, by the discovery of the plot. Thus in the morning he suddenly greets his minister with the question, "What shall be done unto the man whom the king delighteth to honour?" The favourite, unable to see the possibility of any one being intended save himself, suggests the bestowal of the most extravagant honours. How the answer he received must have seemed the precursor of the end, when he hears that it is for Mordecai that he has planned this triumph, and is bidden, as himself the chief noble in the realm, to see that the whole is carried into execution! The pageant is soon over; Mordecai returns to his station by the king's gate, and Haman to his home, to find how truly the dismal comments of his wife and friends echoed his own sad forebodings. The morrow comes and the second banquet; and Esther now feels that the need for temporising has passed, and prays for the life of herself and her people, and directly charges Haman with his nefarious scheme. Ahasuerus orders at once Haman's execution, which is done without delay, his property being given to the queen, and by her to Mordecai. But though the author of the decree had fallen, the decree itself still held good. It had been written in the king's name, and sealed with the king's seal, and no man might reverse it. In this dilemma, largely due to his own folly, the king issues another mandate empowering the Jews to stand on their defence, sparing no pains to spread this throughout the whole empire, thereby showing clearly how completely a change had taken place in the royal favour. The day of slaughter came, and not only did the Jews show themselves able to defend themselves, but they took a terrible vengeance on their enemies; five hundred men were slain by them in Shushan alone, including the ten sons of Haman. At Esther's further request, the king extended the time of massacre in that city over the next day also; and in the provinces 75,000 of the Jews' enemies perished. The two days following the great day of slaughter were made feast days for ever after, under the name of Purim. The book ends with "the declaration of the greatness of Mordecai," who has now risen to be "next unto the king, and great among the Jews."

**II. Date of the Events recorded.**—This simply resolves itself into the question, who is Ahasuerus? and there can be little doubt that we must identify him with the king known to the Greeks as Xerxes, and that for the following reasons:—

(1) The name Xerxes is a Greek reproduction of the Persian name *Khshayarsha* (meaning, according to

# ESTHER.

Canon Rawlinson, "the ruling eye"), and when Ahasuerus is transliterated more strictly according to the Hebrew spelling *Akhashverosh*, it will be seen that the essential elements of the word are almost exactly reproduced, the letter *aleph* being prefixed to facilitate the difficult pronunciation.

(2) The character of Ahasuerus as shown in this book presents a striking parallel with that of Xerxes. Ahasuerus is an ordinary specimen of an Eastern despot, who knows no law save the gratification of his own passions, and of the passing caprice of the moment. He sends for his queen in defiance of decency and courtesy, to grace a revel, and deposes her for a refusal simply indicative of self-respect; he is willing to order the destruction of a whole people throughout his empire, at the request of the favourite of the time; when the tide of favour turns, the favourite is not only disgraced, but he and all his family are ruthlessly destroyed, and Mordecai rises from a humble position to be the new vizier. Thus, though God shapes all this for good, the instrument is distinctly evil. How similar is the picture shown in the undying story of Herodotus, of the king who, reckless of the overthrow of his father's armies at Marathon ten short years before, will make a fresh attempt to crush the nation on whose success the freedom of the world was to hinge; who comes with a host so vast that, in the poet's hyperbole, they drink the rivers dry (Juv. x. 177); who has a throne erected to view the slaughter of Leonidas and his three hundred; who gazes from mount Ægaleos at the vast fleet in the bay of Salamis, soon to be routed and broken by Themistocles! The king, who a few weeks before has the Hellespont scourged because it presumes to be stormy and break his bridges, now flees away in panic, leaving his fleet to its fate. (See Herod. vii. 35; Æsch. *Pers.* 467, *seq.*; Juv. x. 174—187.)

(3) The extent of his empire. He rules "from India even unto Ethiopia" (chap. i. 1). India was not included in the empire of the early Persian kings, and therefore, though Cambyses, the son of Cyrus, is called Ahasuerus in Ezra iv. 6, he is excluded by the above consideration.

If then, as we can hardly doubt, Ahasuerus and Xerxes are the same, we can at once fix the date of the events recorded in the Book of Esther. Ahasuerus makes the great feast in the third year of his reign (chap. i. 3), Esther is taken into the royal palace in the seventh year (chap. ii. 16), they cast lots before Haman in the twelfth year (chap. iii. 7), and in the thirteenth year the plan of destruction is broached. Now the reign of Xerxes lasted from 485—464 B.C., therefore the events recorded in Esther range from 483—470 B.C.

## III. Author, and Date of Composition.

—A number of guesses, for they cannot be called anything more, have been put forward as to the author of this book, and of the best of these we can only say that it is possible. Some, as Clement of Alexandria, and Aben Ezra (*Comm. in Esther*, Int.), have assigned it to Mordecai; others, as Augustine (*de Civ. Dei.* l. xviii. c. 36), with much less show of probability, refer it to Ezra; the Talmud (*Tal. Babl., Baba Bathra*, f. 15*a*) gives the "men of the great synagogue;" and yet other theories are current.

In all this uncertainty we may as well at once confess our inability to settle who the author was, though we may perhaps obtain a fair notion of the conditions under which he wrote. It may probably be fairly inferred from such passages as chaps. ix. 32, x. 2, &c., that the writer had access to the documents to which he refers,

so that the book must have been written in Persia. This is further confirmed by traits that suggest that the writer is speaking as an eye-witness (see, for example, chaps. i. 6, viii. 10, 14, 15, &c.). Possibly too, even if Mordecai were not the author, matter directly derived from him may be seen in chap. ii. 5, 10, &c.

Again, it must be noticed that the name of God in every form is entirely absent from the book, that there is no allusion whatever to the Jewish nation as one exiled from the land of their fathers, to that land itself, or to the newly rebuilt Temple, or, in fact, to any Jewish institution whatsoever. Whether this reserve is to be explained by the writer's long residence in Persia having blunted the edge of his national feelings, or whether he may have thought it safer to keep his feelings and opinions in the background, it is impossible to say: very possibly both causes may have acted.

As regards the date, some of the foregoing considerations, if allowed, would weigh strongly in favour of a comparatively early date, inasmuch as they would make the writer more or less contemporaneous with the events he records—a view which the graphic style strongly supports. But it is obvious, from the way in which the book opens, that Ahasuerus or Xerxes was no longer king. Combining these two considerations, we should prefer to fix the composition of the book not long after the death of Xerxes (464 B.C.), say 450 B.C., a time when Athens was at the height of its power and fame, and Rome was merely a second-rate Italian commonwealth.

The above view, or something like it, is held by most sober critics, a common form of the view being to assign the book to the reign of the successor of Xerxes, Artaxerxes Longimanus (464—425 B.C.), and it may be noted that there can be little doubt that the Books of Ezra, Nehemiah, and Chronicles are to be assigned to that reign, and that the style of those books closely resembles that of Esther. Some have advocated a distinctly late date for Esther, assigning it to the period of the Greek *régime*, but the arguments brought forward seem to us of little weight.

## IV. Canonicity, and Place in Canon.

—In the Hebrew Bible, Esther stands as the last of the five *Megilloth*, or rolls, the others being Song of Songs, Ruth, Lamentations, and Ecclesiastes, and it is read through in the synagogues at the Feast of Purim. Among the Jews there can be no doubt that its canonicity was universally acknowledged, for in the earliest statement we have as to the contents of the Jewish Canon (Josephus, *contr. Apion.* i. 8), Esther is distinctly included by the mention of Artaxerxes. Here and there in early Christian lists of the books of the Old Testament Canon in its Palestinian form, as opposed to the longer Canon of the Alexandrian Jews, the Book of Esther is not mentioned. This is the case, for example, in the list given by Melito, Bishop of Sardis in the second century (Euseb. *Hist. Eccl.* iv. 26). Dr. Westcott (Smith's *Bible Dict.*, art. "Canon") suggests that this may be due to Esther having been viewed as a part of Ezra representing a general collection of post-captivity records. Whatever may be the true explanation, at any rate Esther is an integral part of the pure Hebrew Canon, and as such is mentioned by the Talmud; it was included, though with considerable addition, to which we refer below, in the Græco-Alexandrian Canon, and was received, while the Greek accretions were rejected, by Jerome into his Latin translation.

The position of Esther in the Hebrew Bible is an artificial one, clearly due to Liturgical reasons, the

# ESTHER.

*Megilloth* being read, each at one of the Feasts. In the LXX. and Vulgate, as well as in the English Bible, Esther comes at the end of the historical books. In the two former, Tobit and Judith intervene between Nehemiah and Esther; in the latter, those two books are relegated to the Apocrypha.

**V. Apocryphal Additions to Esther.**—In the text of Esther, as given by the LXX., we find large interpolations interspersed throughout the book. The chief of them are:—

(1) Mordecai's lineage, dream, and reward, forming a prelude to the whole book (chaps. xi. 2—xii. 6, English Version).

(2) A copy of the king's letters to destroy the Jews, inserted in chap. iii. (chap. xiii. 1—7, English Version).

(3) Prayers of Mordecai and Esther, in chap. iv. (chap. xiii. 8—xiv. 19, English Version).

(4) Amplification of Esther's visit to the king, in chap. v. (chap. xv., English Version).

(5) Edict of revocation, in chap. viii. (chap. **xvi.**, English Version).

(6) An exposition of Mordecai's dream; after which comes a statement, evidently intended to imply that the whole book was translated from the Hebrew (chaps. x. 4—13, **xi.** 1, English Version).

Thus in the LXX. the book with its additions makes a continuous narrative. But when Jerome set forth his new Latin Version based on the Hebrew, he naturally rejected those portions not found in the Hebrew, placing them at the end of the book, noting the cause of the rejection and the place of the insertion.

In the English Bible, however, while the position of the extracts is as it is in the Latin Vulgate, Jerome's notes are omitted, making the whole almost unintelligible. It is curious to note that chap. xi. 2 of the English Version forms the first verse in the Greek of Esther, and chap. xi. 1 the last verse.

# THE BOOK OF ESTHER

CHAPTER I.—<sup>(1)</sup> Now it came to pass in the days of Ahasuerus, (this *is* Ahasuerus which reigned, from India even unto Ethiopia, *over* an hundred and seven and twenty provinces:) <sup>(2)</sup> *that* in those days, when the king Ahasuerus sat on the throne of his kingdom, which *was* in Shushan the palace, <sup>(3)</sup> in the third year of his reign, he made a feast unto all his princes and his servants; the power of Persia and Media, the nobles and princes of the provinces, *being* before him: <sup>(4)</sup> when he shewed the riches of his glorious kingdom and the honour of his excellent majesty many days, *even* an hundred and fourscore days. <sup>(5)</sup> And when these days were expired, the king made a feast unto all the people that were [1] present in Shushan the palace, both unto great and small, seven days, in the court of the garden of the king's palace; <sup>(6)</sup> *where were* white, green, and [2] blue *hangings*, fastened with cords of fine linen and purple to silver rings and

B.C. cir. 521.

1 Heb., *found.*

B.C. cir. 519.

2 Or, *violet*

---

<sup>(1)</sup> **Ahasuerus.**—Three persons are called by this name in the Old Testament—(1) the Ahasuerus of Dan. ix. 1, the father of "Darius the Mede;" if, as is probable, this latter is the same with Astyages, Ahasuerus must be identified with Cyaxares: (2) the Ahasuerus of Ezra iv. 6, who is doubtless the same with Cambyses, the son of Cyrus; and (3) the one now before us, whom we have shown in the Introduction to be almost certainly Xerxes. For the history and character of this sovereign reference must be especially made to the contemporaneous writers, Herodotus (vii., viii. 1—90), and Æschylus in his play of *The Persians*. The spirited lines of Juvenal should also be read (*Sat.* x. 173—187). We find that Xerxes succeeded his father, Darius Hystaspes, in the year 485 B.C., five years after the momentous battle of Marathon. Undeterred by his father's failure, he resolves upon a fresh attack on Greece, and sets out in 481 B.C. from Susa for the West. He winters at Sardis, leaving it in the spring of the following year. The summer sees the fight of the pass of Thermopylæ, which has covered the name of Leonidas and his three hundred, though vanquished and slain, with undying glory; in the autumn Themistocles, by his victory over the Persians at Salamis, changes the history of the world, and the beginning thus made is carried on by the victories at Platæa and Mycale in 479 B.C. From the rout at Salamis, Xerxes had fled to Sardis, which he did not leave till the spring of 478 B.C. All that we know of the further course of the reign of Xerxes is but one unbroken tale of debauchery and bloodshed, which came to an end in 464 B.C., when he was murdered by two of his officers, Mithridates and Artabanus, and Artaxerxes Longimanus, his son (see Ezra vii.; Neh. ii.), reigned in his stead.

**This is Ahasuerus.**—This is added to make clear which particular sovereign we are here dealing with. We have seen that three of the name are mentioned in the Old Testament.

**Ethiopia.**—Herodotus tells us that Ethiopia paid tribute to Xerxes (iii. 97).

**An hundred and seven and twenty.**—In Dan. vi. 1. we find that Darius the Mede appointed a hundred and twenty satraps, but probably the similarity in numbers is quite accidental. There seem to have been a gradually increasing number of satrapies in the kingdom of Darius—20, 21, 23, 29 (Herod. iii. 89—94), and the nations in the empire of Xerxes are said to be sixty (*ib.* vii. 61—95). Thus the provinces here mentioned must include subdivisions of these.

<sup>(2)</sup> **Shushan.**—Susa. Mentioned also in Neh. i. 1. It was the general abode of the Persian kings. (See Herod. vii. 6.)

<sup>(3)</sup> **In the third year of his reign.**—Assuming, as we do, the identity of Ahasuerus and Xerxes, this will be 483 B.C., when Xerxes held a meeting at Susa of his princes to make arrangements for invading Greece. At so important a gathering, the feasting was a very obvious adjunct; and besides the coming campaign, a successful war had just been concluded in Egypt, and rejoicings for the past might have mingled with high hopes for the future, when the whole strength of the empire should be put forth to crush the presumptuous foe who had dared to measure swords with the "king of kings."

**Nobles.**—The word in the Hebrew, *partemim*, occurring here, in chap. vi. 9, and Dan. i. 3, is a Persian word, literally meaning "first." The Greek *protos* and Latin *primus* are evidently akin to it.

<sup>(4)</sup> **An hundred and fourscore days.**—As a period of mere feasting, this long time (half a year) is simply incredible, but we must understand it as a time during which troops were collected, and the plan of invasion settled.

<sup>(5)</sup> **All the people.**—So we find Cyrus feasting "all the Persians" (Herod. i. 126).

<sup>(6)</sup> **Where were white . . . .**—This should be [hangings of] "white cotton and blue." The word translated "cotton" (Heb., *carpas*) occurs only here. Canon Rawlinson remarks that "white and blue (or violet) were the royal colours of Persia."

**Linen.**—White linen; so the word is used, *e.g.*, in 2 Chron. v. 12.

**Marble.**—White marble, as in the last clause of the verse.

**Beds.**—That is, *the couches*. The gold is not to be referred simply to the gold-embroidered coverings, but to the framework of the couch.

*Vashti's Refusal to*      ESTHER, I.      *attend at the King's Feast.*

pillars of marble: the beds *were of* gold and silver, upon a pavement ¹of red, and blue, and white, and black, marble. ⁽⁷⁾ And they gave *them* drink in vessels of gold, (the vessels being diverse one from another,) and ²royal wine in abundance, ³according to the state of the king. ⁽⁸⁾ And the drinking *was* according to the law; none did compel: for so the king had appointed to all the officers of his house, that they should do according to every man's pleasure. ⁽⁹⁾ Also Vashti the queen made a feast for the women *in* the royal house which *belonged* to king Ahasuerus.

⁽¹⁰⁾ On the seventh day, when the heart of the king was merry with wine, he commanded Mehuman, Biztha, Harbona, Bigtha, and Abagtha, Zethar, and Carcas, the seven ⁴chamberlains that served in the presence of Ahasuerus the king, ⁽¹¹⁾ to bring Vashti the queen before the king with the crown royal, to show the people and the princes her beauty: for she *was* ⁵fair to look on. ⁽¹²⁾ But the queen Vashti refused to come at the king's commandment ⁶by *his* chamberlains: therefore was the king very wroth, and his anger burned in him.

⁽¹³⁾ Then the king said to the wise men, which knew the times, (for so *was* the king's manner toward all that knew law and judgment: ⁽¹⁴⁾ and the next unto him *was* Carshena, Shethar, Admatha, Tarshish, Meres, Marsena, *and* Memucan, the ᵃ seven princes of Persia and Media, which saw the king's face, *and* which sat the first in the kingdom;) ⁽¹⁵⁾ ⁷What shall we do unto the queen Vashti according to law, because she hath not performed the commandment of the king Ahasuerus by the chamberlains?

*Marginal notes:*
1 Or, *of porphyre, and marble, and alabaster, and stone of blue colour.*
2 Heb., *wine of the kingdom.*
3 Heb., *according to the hand of the king.*
4 Or, *eunuchs.*
5 Heb., *good of countenance.*
6 Heb., *which was by the hand of his eunuchs.*
a Ezra 7. 14.
7 Heb., *What to do.*

---

**Red and blue . . .**—These words are not names of colours, but of actual stones, although the meaning of most is doubtful enough. The first (*bahat*) is rendered by the LXX. as a stone of emerald colour, and may perhaps be malachite. The second (*shesh*) is white marble, the third (*dar*) is pearly, and the last (*sokhereth*) black.

(7) **In vessels of gold.**—This shows the immense treasures in the hand of the Persian king, when the whole population of Susa could be thus accommodated.

**Royal wine.**—Perhaps wine of Helbon (Ezek. xxvii. 18); the original seems to imply more than merely wine from the royal cellars: as the king was feasting his people, it could hardly have been otherwise.

**State.**—Literally, *hand*.

(8) **Law.**—Rather *ordinance* or *decree*, that is, specially put forth for this occasion. What this means is shown by what follows, namely, that the king had issued special orders to allow all to do as they pleased in the matter of drinking, instead of as usual compelling them to drink. This degrading habit is the more noticeable because the Persians were at first a nation of exceptionally temperate habits.

(9) **Vashti.**—According to Gesenius, the name Vashti means *beautiful*. Among the Persians it was customary that one wife of the sovereign should be supreme over the rest, and her we sometimes find exercising an authority which contrasts strangely with the degraded position of women generally. Such a one was Atossa, the mother of Xerxes. Vashti, too, before her deposition, was evidently *the* queen *par excellence*. We find, however, that the name given by the Greek writers to the queen of Xerxes was Amestris, of whose cruelty and dissolute life numerous details are given us by Herodotus and others. There seem good grounds for believing that she was the wife of Xerxes before he became king, which if established would of itself be sufficient to disprove the theory of some who would identify Esther and Amestris. Moreover, Herodotus tells us (vii. 61, 82) that Amestris was the cousin of Xerxes, the daughter of his father's brother; and although we cannot view Esther as of a specially high type of womanhood, still it would be most unjust to identify her with one whose character is presented to us in most unlovely guise. Bishop Wordsworth suggests that Amestris was a wife who had great influence with Xerxes between the fall of Vashti and the rise of Esther. If, however, Amestris was really the chief wife before Xerxes came to the throne, this could hardly be, and the time allowed seems much too scanty, seeing that in it falls the invasion of Greece. Or, lastly, we may with Canon Rawlinson say that Vashti is Amestris (the two names being different reproductions of the Persian, or Vashti being a sort of title) and that the deposition was a temporary one.

**The women.**—There should be no article.

(10) **Was merry with wine.**—The habit of the Persians to indulge in wine to excess may be inferred from verse 8.

**Chamberlains.**—Literally, *eunuchs*. The names of the men, whatever they may be, are apparently not Persian. The enumeration of all the seven names is suggestive of personal knowledge on the part of the writer.

(11) **To bring Vashti.**—It is evident from the way in which the incident is introduced that had Ahasuerus been sober he would not have asked such a thing. Vashti naturally sends a refusal.

**Crown royal.**—If this were like that worn by a king, it would be a tall cap decked with gems, and with a linen fillet of blue and white; this last was the *diadem*. (See Trench, *New Testament Synonyms*, § 23.)

(13) **Which knew the times.**—That is, who were skilled in precedents, and could advise accordingly.

**For so . . . .**—Translate, *for so was the king's business laid before . . .*

(14) **Marsena.**—It has been suggested that we may possibly recognise here Mardonius, the commander at Marathon; and in Admatha, Artabanus, the uncle of Xerxes.

**The seven princes.**—There were seven leading families in Persia, the heads of which were the king's chief advisers, the "seven counsellors" of Ezra vii. 14. Herodotus (iii. 84) speaks of the seven nobles who rose against the Pseudo-Smerdis as chief in the nation.

(16) And Memucan answered before the king and the princes, Vashti the queen hath not done wrong to the king only, but also to all the princes, and to all the people that *are* in all the provinces of the king Ahasuerus. (17) For *this* deed of the queen shall come abroad unto all women, so that they shall despise their husbands in their eyes, when it shall be reported, The king Ahasuerus commanded Vashti the queen to be brought in before him, but she came not. (18) *Likewise* shall the ladies of Persia and Media say this day unto all the king's princes, which have heard of the deed of the queen. Thus *shall there arise* too much contempt and wrath. (19) ¹ If it please the king, let there go a royal commandment ² from him, and let it be written among the laws of the Persians and the Medes, ³ that it be not altered, That Vashti come no more before king Ahasuerus; and let the king give her royal estate ⁴ unto another that is better than she. (20) And when the king's decree which he shall make shall be published throughout all his empire, (for it is great,) all the wives shall give to their husbands honour, both to great and small.

(21) And the saying ⁵ pleased the king and the princes; and the king did according to the word of Memucan: (22) for he sent letters into all the king's provinces, into every province according to the writing thereof, and to every people after their language, that every man should bear rule in his own house, and ⁶ that it should be published according to the language of every people.

CHAPTER II.—(1) After these things, when the wrath of king Ahasuerus was appeased, he remembered Vashti, and what she had done, and what was decreed against her. (2) Then said the king's servants that ministered unto him, Let there be fair young virgins sought for the king: (3) and let the king appoint officers in all the provinces of his kingdom, that they may gather together all the fair young virgins unto Shushan the palace, to the house of the women, ⁷ unto the custody of ⁸ Hege the king's chamberlain, keeper of the women; and let their things for purification be given *them*: (4) and let the maiden which pleaseth the king be queen instead of Vashti. And the thing pleased the king; and he did so.

(5) *Now* in Shushan the palace there

---

1 Heb., *If it be good with the king.*

2 Heb., *from before him.*

3 Heb., *that it pass not away.*

B.C. 518.

4 Heb., *unto her companion.*

5 Heb., *was good in the eyes of the king.*

6 Heb., *that one should publish it according to the language of his people.*

7 Heb., *unto the hand.*

8 Or, *Hegai*, ver. 8.

---

(16) **Answered before the king.**—Memucan, like a true courtier, gives palatable advice to his master, by counsel which is the true echo of the king's angry question.

**Done wrong.**—Literally, *dealt unfairly.*

(18) Translate, *and this day shall the princesses of Persia and Media, which heard the affair of the queen, say . . .*

**Contempt and wrath.**—Presumably, contemptuous defiance on the part of the wives, and anger on the part of the husbands.

(19) **That it be not altered.**—Literally, *that it pass not away.* The order having been committed to writing was, in theory at any rate, immutable. The best illustration is the well-known case of Daniel; see also below (chap. viii. 8). Probably a strong-willed monarch would interpret this inviolability rather freely.

(22) **He sent letters.**—The Persian Empire was the first to possess a postal system (see esp. Herod. vii. 98). The Greek word for "compel," in Matt. v. 41, xxvii. 32, is simply a corruption of the Persian word for the impressment of men and horses for the royal service.

**That every man should . . .**—The following words are, literally, *be ruling in his own house, and speaking according to the language of his own people.* The former clause may probably be taken as a proof of the existence of an undue amount of female influence generally in Persia; the second clause is more doubtful. The English Version does distinct violence to the Hebrew, perhaps because the literal rendering yielded a somewhat peculiar sense. Taking the words exactly as they stand, they can only mean that in a house where two or more languages are used, from the presence of foreign wives, the husband is to take care that his own language is not supplanted by any of theirs. This is intelligible enough, but is perhaps rather irrelevant to what goes before.

II.

(1) **After these things.**—We have seen that the great feast at Susa was in the year 483 B.C., and that in the spring of 481 B.C. Xerxes set out for Greece. At some unspecified time, then, between these limits the proposal now started is to be placed. The marriage of Esther, however (verse 16), did not come about till after the return from Greece, the king's long absence explaining the otherwise curious delay, and moreover, even in this interval, he was entangled in more than one illicit connection.

(3) **The house of the women.**—The harem, then as now, a prominent feature in the establishment of an Eastern king.

**Hege.**—Called Hegai in verse 8; a eunuch whose special charge seems to have been the virgins, while another, named Shaashgaz (verse 14), had the custody of the concubines. The whole verse shows, as conclusively as anything could do, in how degrading an aspect Eastern women were, as a whole, viewed. It was reserved for Christianity to indicate the true position of woman, not man's plaything, but the help meet for him, able to aid him in his spiritual and intellectual progress, yielding him intelligent obedience, not slavery.

(5) **Mordecai.**—Canon Rawlinson is disposed to identify Mordecai with Matacas, who was the most powerful of the eunuchs in the reign of Xerxes. It

was a certain Jew, whose name *was* Mordecai, the son of Jair, the son of Shimei, the son of Kish, a Benjamite; (6) "who had been carried away from Jerusalem with the captivity which had been carried away with Jeconiah king of Judah, whom Nebuchadnezzar the king of Babylon had carried away. (7) And he ¹brought up Hadassah, that *is*, Esther, his uncle's daughter: for she had neither father nor mother, and the maid *was* ²fair and beautiful; whom Mordecai, when her father and mother were dead, took for his own daughter. (8) So it came to pass, when the king's commandment and his decree was heard, and when many maidens were gathered together unto Shushan the palace, to the custody of Hegai, that Esther was brought also unto the king's house, to the custody of Hegai, keeper of the women. (9) And the maiden pleased him, and she obtained kindness of him; and he speedily gave her her things for purification, with ³such things as belonged to her, and seven maidens, *which were* meet to be given her, out of the king's house: and ⁴he preferred her and her maids unto the best *place* of the house of the women. (10) Esther had not shewed her people nor her kindred: for Mordecai had charged her that she should not shew it. (11) And Mordecai walked every day before the court of the women's house, ⁵to know how Esther did, and what should become of her.

(12) Now when every maid's turn was come to go in to king Ahasuerus, after that she had been twelve months, according to the manner of the women, (for so were the days of their purifications accomplished, *to wit*, six months with oil of myrrh, and six months with sweet odours, and with *other* things for the purifying of the women;) (13) then thus came *every* maiden unto the king; whatsoever she desired was given her to go with her out of the house of the women unto the king's house. (14) In the evening she went, and on the morrow she returned into the second house of the women, to the custody of Shaashgaz, the king's chamberlain, which kept the concubines: she came in unto the king no more, except the king delighted in her, and that she were called by name.

(15) Now when the turn of Esther, the daughter of Abihail the uncle of Mordecai, who had taken her for his daughter, was come to go in unto the king, she required nothing but what Hegai the king's chamberlain, the keeper of the women, appointed. And Esther obtained favour in the sight of all them that looked upon her. (16) So Esther was taken unto king Ahasuerus into his house royal in the

---

*a* 2 Kin. 24. 15; 2 Chron. 36. 10; Jer. 24. 1.

B.C. cir. 515.

1 Heb., *nourished.*

2 Heb., *fair of form, and good of countenance.*

3 Heb., *her portions.*

4 Heb., *he changed her.*

5 Heb., *to know the peace.*

---

may be assumed that Mordecai was a eunuch, by the way in which he was allowed access to the royal harem (verses 11, 22). The name Mordecai occurs in Ezra ii. 2; Neh. vii. 7, as one of those who returned to Judæa with Zerubbabel.

**The son of Jair.**—It is probable that the names here given are those of the actual father, grandfather, and great-grandfather of Mordecai; though some have thought that they are merely some of the more famous ancestors, Shimei being assumed to be the assailant of David, and Kish the father of Saul. The character of Mordecai strikes us at the outset as that of an ambitious, worldly man; who, though numbers of his tribe had returned to the land of their fathers, preferred to remain behind on the alien soil. The heroic lament of the exiles by Babel's streams, who would not sing the Lord's song in a strange land, who looked with horror at the thought that Jerusalem should be forgotten—such were not Mordecai's thoughts, far from it: why endure hardships, when there is a chance of his adopted daughter's beauty catching the eye of the sensual king, when through her he may vanquish his rival, and become that king's chief minister?

(6) **Who had been . . .**—The antecedent is obviously Kish, though as far as the mere grammar goes it might have been Mordecai.

**Jeconiah.**—That is, Jehoiachin. (See 2 Kings xxiv. 12—16.)

**Nebuchadnezzar . . . had carried away.**—This was in 598 B.C., 117 years before this time, so that the four generations are readily accounted for.

(7) **Hadassah.**—This is evidently formed from the Hebrew *hadas*, the myrtle: Esther is generally assumed to be a Persian name, meaning a star. Unless we assume that this latter name was given afterwards, and is here used by anticipation, we have here an early case of the common Jewish practice of using two names, a Hebrew and a Gentile one—*e.g.*, Saul, Paul; John, Mark; Joses, Justus, &c.

**Uncle.**—Abihail (see verse 15).

(9) **Obtained kindness of him.**—This is the same phrase as that which is rendered "obtained favour in his sight" in verse 17.

(10) **Esther had not shewed . . .**—From the hope on Mordecai's part that she might pass for a native Persian, and that her Jewish birth should be no hindrance to her advancement. The king does not learn his wife's nation till some time afterwards (chap. vii. 4).

(11) **Mordecai walked . . .**—Apparently he was one of the royal doorkeepers. (See chaps. ii. 21, v. 13.)

(12) **Manner.**—Translate, *law* or *ordinance*, as in chap. i. 8, 15.

(16) **The month Tebeth.**—This extended from the new moon in January to that in February; the name occurs only here. The fifth Egyptian month, lasting from December 20 to January 20, was called Tybi. The

tenth month, which *is* the month Tebeth, in the seventh year of his reign. (17) And the king loved Esther above all the women, and she obtained grace and ¹favour ²in his sight more than all the virgins; so that he set the royal crown upon her head, and made her queen instead of Vashti. (18) Then the king made a great feast unto all his princes and his servants, *even* Esther's feast; and he made a ³release to the provinces, and gave gifts, according to the state of the king.

(19) And when the virgins were gathered together the second time, then Mordecai sat in the king's gate. (20) Esther had not *yet* shewed her kindred nor her people; as Mordecai had charged her: for Esther did the commandment of Mordecai, like as when she was brought up with him.

(21) In those days, while Mordecai sat in the king's gate, two of the king's chamberlains, ⁴Bigthan and Teresh, of those which kept ⁵the door, were wroth, and sought to lay hand on the king Ahasuerus. (22) And the thing was known to Mordecai, who told *it* unto Esther the queen; and Esther certified the king *thereof* in Mordecai's name. (23) And when inquisition was made of the matter, it was found out; therefore they were both hanged on a tree: and it was written in the book of the chronicles before the king.

CHAPTER III.—(1) After these things did king Ahasuerus promote Haman the son of Hammedatha the Agagite, and advanced him, and set his seat above all the princes that *were* with him. (2) And all the king's servants, that *were* in the king's gate, bowed, and reverenced Haman: for the king had so commanded concerning him. But Mordecai bowed not, nor did *him* reverence. (3) Then the king's servants, which *were* in the king's gate, said unto Mordecai, Why trans-

---

1 Or, *kindness.*

2 Heb., *before him.*

B.C. cir. 514.

3 Heb., *rest.*

B.C. cir. 510.

4 Or, *Bigthana*, ch. ii. 2.

5 Heb., *the threshold.*

---

time referred to in the verse will be the January or February of the year 478 B.C., and must have been very shortly after Xerxes' return to Susa from the West. The long delay in replacing Vashti is simply to be explained by the long absence of Xerxes in Greece.

(18) **Release.**—Literally, *rest*. The word only occurs here: it may refer either to a release from tribute or from military service, probably the former. Either, however, would have been consistent with Persian usage. (See Herod. iii. 67, vi. 59.)

(19) **And when the virgins . . .**—Here begins a fresh incident in the history, whose date we cannot fix precisely, save that it falls between the marriage of Esther and the twelfth year of Ahasuerus (chap. iii. 7). The king "loved Esther above all the women," but how the word "love" is degraded in this connection is seen by the fact that after she had been his wife certainly less (possibly much less) than five years, there takes place a second gathering of virgins (there is no article in the Hebrew), like the one previously mentioned (chap. ii. 2). We should treat verse 20 as parenthetical, and join verse 21 closely to verse 19.

**Then Mordecai sat.**—Translate, *and Mordecai was sitting.*

(20) **Esther had not yet . . .**—Perhaps this verse is added to meet the supposition that the king wished to replace Esther through finding out her nation.

(21) **In those days.**—Here the thread of verse 19 is taken up, "then I say, in those days——"

**Bigthan.**—Called Bigtha in chap. i. 10; Bigthana in chap. vi. 2.

**Sought to lay hand on the king.**—It is noticeable that Xerxes was ultimately murdered by Artabanus, captain of the guard, and Mithridates, a *chamberlain.*

(22) **And Esther certified the king thereof.**—Doubtless by this means an increased influence was gained over the capricious mind of the king, an influence which before long served Esther in good stead.

(23) **Hanged on a tree.**—Were crucified; a common punishment among the Persians, especially on rebels (Herod. iii. 120, 125, 159, &c.). The dead body of Leonidas was crucified by Xerxes' orders after the desperate stand at Thermopylæ.

**Book of the chronicles.**—A sleepless night of Xerxes accidentally brought this matter, after it had been forgotten, before the king's mind. Herodotus often refers to these Persian Chronicles (vii. 100; viii. 85, 90).

III.

(1) **Haman . . . the Agagite.**—Nothing appears to be known of Haman save from this book. His name, as well as that of his father and his sons, is Persian; and it is thus difficult to see the meaning of the name *Agagite*, which has generally been assumed to imply descent from Agag, king of the Amalekites, with whom the name Agag *may* have been dynastic (Num. xxiv. 7; 1 Sam. xv. 8). Thus Josephus (*Ant.* xi. 6. 5) and the Chaldee Targum call him an Amalekite. But apart from the difficulty of the name being Persian, it is hard to see how, after the wholesale destruction of Amalek recorded in 1 Sam. xv., any members should have been left of the kingly family, maintaining a distinct tribal name for so many centuries. In one of the Greek Apocryphal additions to Esther (after chap. ix. 24) Haman is called a Macedonian.

(2) **Bowed not.**—Perhaps, rather, *did not prostrate himself*, for such was the ordinary Eastern practice (see Herod. iii. 86, vii. 134, 136, viii. 118). The objection on Mordecai's part was evidently mainly on religious grounds, as giving to a man Divine honours (Josephus *l.c.*), for it elicits from him the fact that he was a Jew (verse 4), to whom such an act of obeisance would be abhorrent. Whether Mordecai also rebelled against the ignominious character of the obeisance, we cannot say.

gressest thou the king's commandment? ⁽⁴⁾ Now it came to pass, when they spake daily unto him, and he hearkened not unto him, that they told Haman, to see whether Mordecai's matters would stand: for he had told them that he was a Jew. ⁽⁵⁾ And when Haman saw that Mordecai bowed not, nor did him reverence, then was Haman full of wrath. ⁽⁶⁾ And he thought scorn to lay hands on Mordecai alone; for they had shewed him the people of Mordecai: wherefore Haman sought to destroy all the Jews that were throughout the whole kingdom of Ahasuerus, even the people of Mordecai. ⁽⁷⁾ In the first month, that is, the month Nisan, in the twelfth year of king Ahasuerus, they cast Pur, that is, the lot, before Haman from day to day, and from month to month, to the twelfth month, that is, the month Adar. ⁽⁸⁾ And Haman said unto king Ahasuerus, There is a certain people scattered abroad and dispersed among the people in all the provinces of thy kingdom; and their laws are diverse from all people; neither keep they the king's laws: therefore it is not ¹for the king's profit to suffer them. ⁽⁹⁾ If it please the king, let it be written ²that they may be destroyed: and I will ³pay ten thousand talents of silver to the hands of those that have the charge of the business, to bring it into the king's treasuries. ⁽¹⁰⁾ And the king took his ring from his hand, and gave it unto Haman the son of Hammedatha the Agagite, the Jews' ⁴enemy. ⁽¹¹⁾ And the king said unto Haman, The silver is given to thee, the people also, to do with them as it seemeth good to thee.

⁽¹²⁾ Then were the king's ⁵scribes called on the thirteenth day of the first month, and there was written according to all that Haman had commanded unto the king's lieutenants, and to the governors that were over every province, and to the rulers of every people of every province according to the writing thereof, and to every people after their language; in the

*Marginal notes:* 1 Heb., meet, or, equal. 2 Heb., to destroy them. 3 Heb., weigh. B.C. 510. 4 Or, oppressor. 5 Or, secretaries.

---

**(4) Whether Mordecai's matters would stand.**—This should be, his *words*: whether his statement that he belonged to a nation who might only pay such reverence to God, would hold good.

(7) **In the first month . . . the twelfth year.**—In the March or April of 474 B.C.

**Nisan.**—The later name of the month, known in the Pentateuch as Abib. In this month the Passover had been first instituted, when God smote the Egyptians with a terrible visitation, the death of the first-born, and bade the destroying angel spare the houses with the blood-besprinkled door-posts. It was in the same month that the Passover received its final fulfilment, when "Christ our Passover was sacrificed for us," when no mere earthly Egypt was discomfited, but principalities and powers of evil.

**Pur.**—This is evidently a Persian word for "lot," for both here and in chap. ix. 24 the usual Hebrew word is added. It is doubtless connected with the Latin *pars, portio*, and the English *part*. The people who cast Pur were seeking for a lucky day, as indicated by the lots, for the purpose in hand. A lot was cast for each day of the month, and for each month in the year, and in some way or other one day and one month were indicated as the most favourable. The notion of lucky and unlucky days seems to have been prevalent in the East in early times, and indeed has, to a certain extent, found credence in the West.

**The twelfth month.**—The lucky month is thus indicated, but not the day. The LXX. adds a clause saying that it was on the fourteenth day, doubtless an interpolation on the strength of verse 13.

**Adar.**—The lunar month ending at the new moon in March. It was the twelfth month, so that nearly a year would intervene between the throwing of the lot and the carrying out of the scheme. Thus in God's providence ample time was allowed for redressing matters.

(8) **A certain people scattered abroad . . .**—A certain part of the nation had returned with Zerubbabel, but (Ezra ii. 64) these only amounted to 42,360, so that the great majority of the nation had preferred to stay comfortably where they were in the various districts of the Persian Empire.

**Neither keep they . . .**—The charge of disloyalty has been a favourite weapon in the hands of persecutors. Haman was not the first who had brought this charge against the Jews (see Ezra iv. 13, 16). Our Lord's accusers were those who knew no king but Cæsar. The early Christians found to their cost how deadly was the accusation of disloyalty to the Empire.

(9) **Ten thousand talents of silver.**—This would be about two and a half millions sterling, being indeed more than two-thirds of the whole annual revenue of the Empire (Herod. iii. 95). Haman may have been a man of excessive wealth (like the Pythius who offered Xerxes four millions of gold darics (Herod. vii. 28), or he probably may have hoped to draw the money from the spoils of the Jews.

(11) **And the king said . . .**—With indifference which seems incredible, but which is quite in accordance with what we otherwise know of Xerxes, the king simply hands over to his minister the whole nation and their possessions to do with as he will. The king perhaps was glad to throw the cares of government on his minister, and, too indolent to form an opinion for himself, was content to believe that the Jews were a worthless, disloyal people.

(12) **On the thirteenth day of the first month.**—From the next verse we see that the thirteenth of Adar was to be the lucky day for Haman's purpose, which may have suggested the thirteenth of Nisan as a suitable day for this preliminary step. Bishop Wordsworth reminds us that this day was the eve of the Passover, so that Haman's plot against the Jews strangely coincides in time with one five hundred

name of king Ahasuerus was it written, and sealed with the king's ring. (13) And the letters were sent by posts into all the king's provinces, to destroy, to kill, and to cause to perish, all Jews, both young and old, little children and women, in one day, *even* upon the thirteenth *day* of the twelfth month, which *is* the month Adar, and *to take* the spoil of them for a prey. (14) The copy of the writing for a commandment to be given in every province was published unto all people, that they should be ready against that day. (15) The posts went out, being hastened by the king's commandment, and the decree was given in Shushan the palace. And the king and Haman sat down to drink; but the city Shushan was perplexed.

CHAPTER IV.—(1) When Mordecai perceived all that was done, Mordecai rent his clothes, and put on sackcloth with ashes, and went out into the midst of the city, and cried with a loud and a bitter cry; (2) and came even before the king's gate: for none *might* enter into the king's gate clothed with sackcloth. (3) And in every province, whithersoever the king's commandment and his decree came, *there was* great mourning among the Jews, and fasting, and weeping, and wailing; and ¹many lay in sackcloth and ashes.

(4) So Esther's maids and her ²chamberlains came and told *it* her. Then was the queen exceedingly grieved; and she sent raiment to clothe Mordecai, and to take away his sackcloth from him: but he received *it* not. (5) Then called Esther for Hatach, *one* of the king's chamberlains, ³whom he had appointed to attend upon her, and gave him a commandment to Mordecai, to know what it *was*, and why it *was*. (6) So Hatach went forth to Mordecai unto the street of the city, which *was* before the king's gate. (7) And Mordecai told him of all that had happened unto him, and of the sum of the money that Haman had promised to pay to the king's treasuries for the Jews, to destroy them. (8) Also he gave him the copy of the writing of the decree that was given at Shushan to destroy them, to shew *it* unto Esther, and to declare *it* unto her, and to charge her that she should go in unto the king, to make supplication unto him, and to make request before him for her people. (9) And Hatach came and told Esther the words of Mordecai.

(10) Again Esther spake unto Hatach, and gave him commandment unto Mordecai; (11) All the king's servants, and

---

¹ Heb., *sackcloth and ashes were laid under many.*
² Heb., *eunuchs.*
B.C. cir. 510.
³ Heb., *whom he had set before her.*

---

years later, when the Jews themselves, aided by heathen hands and the powers of darkness, sought to vanquish the Saviour; and as the trembling Jews of Persia were delivered by God's goodness, so too by His goodness Satan himself was overthrown and the Lamb that was slain did triumph.

**Lieutenants.**—Literally, *satraps*. The Hebrew word here (*akhashdarpan*) is simply an attempt to transliterate the Persian *khshatrapa*, whence the Greek *satrapes*, and so the English word. The word occurs several times in this book and in Ezra and Daniel.

(13) **Posts.**—Literally, *the runners*. (See Note on chap. i. 22.)

(14) **Copy.**—Heb., *pathshegen*. A Persian word, only occurring here and in chaps. iv. 8, viii. 13.

(15) **Perplexed.**—The inhabitants of the capital were puzzled and alarmed, as well they might be, at so marvellously reckless an order. Their sympathies, too, were clearly with the Jews and against Haman. (See chap. viii. 15.)

IV.

(1) **Mordecai rent his clothes.**—This was a common sign of sorrow among Eastern nations generally. It will be noticed that the sorrow both of Mordecai and of the Jews generally (verse 3) is described by external manifestations solely. There is rending of garments, putting on of sackcloth and ashes, fasting and weeping and wailing: there is nothing said of prayer and entreaty to the God of Israel, and strong crying to Him who is able to save. Daniel and Ezra and Nehemiah are all Jews, who, like Mordecai and Esther, have to submit to the rule of the alien, though, unlike them, they, when the danger threatened, besought, and not in vain, the help of their God. (See Dan. vi. 10; Ezra viii. 23; Neh. i. 4, &c.)

(2) **None might enter . . .**—That nothing sad or ill-omened might meet the monarch's gaze, as though by shutting his eyes, as it were, to the presence of sorrow, or sickness, or death, he might suppose that he was successfully evading them.

(4) **So Esther's maids . . .**—It is perhaps fair to infer from this, that Esther's connection with Mordecai was known to those about her, though as yet not to the king.

(6) **Street.**—The square or wide open place. (Heb., *r'hob.*)

(10) **Again.**—There is nothing for this in the original, and it would be better to put *and*, as the statement of verse 10 is clearly continuous with verse 9.

(11) **There is one law of his . . .**—Literally, *one is his law*, that is, there is one unvarying rule for such. No one who had not been summoned might enter the king's presence under pain of death.

**The golden sceptre.**—We are told that in the representations of Persian kings at Persepolis, in every

the people of the king's provinces, do know, that whosoever, whether man or woman, shall come unto the king into the inner court, who is not called, *there is* one law of his to put *him* to death, except such to whom the king shall hold out the golden sceptre, that he may live: but I have not been called to come in unto the king these thirty days. (12) And they told to Mordecai Esther's words.

(13) Then Mordecai commanded to answer Esther, Think not with thyself that thou shalt escape in the king's house, more than all the Jews. (14) For if thou altogether holdest thy peace at this time, *then* shall there ¹enlargement and deliverance arise to the Jews from another place; but thou and thy father's house shall be destroyed: and who knoweth whether thou art come to the kingdom for *such* a time as this?

(15) Then Esther bade *them* return Mordecai *this answer*, (16) Go, gather together all the Jews that are ²present in Shushan, and fast ye for me, and neither eat nor drink three days, night or day: I also and my maidens will fast likewise; and so will I go in unto the king, which *is* not according to the law: and if I perish, I perish. (17) So Mordecai ³went his way, and did according to all that Esther had commanded him.

CHAPTER V.—(1) Now it came to pass on the third day, that Esther put on *her* royal *apparel*, and stood in the inner court of the king's house, over against the king's house: and the king sat upon his royal throne in the royal house, over against the gate of the house. (2) And it was so, when the king saw Esther the queen standing in the court, *that* she obtained favour in his sight: and the king held out to Esther the golden sceptre that *was* in his hand. So Esther drew near, and touched the top of the sceptre. (3) Then said the king unto her, What wilt thou, queen Esther? and what *is* thy request? it shall be even given thee to the half of the kingdom. (4) And Esther answered, If *it seem* good unto the king, let the king and Haman come this day unto the banquet that I have prepared for him. (5) Then the king said, Cause Haman to make haste, that he may do as Esther hath said. So the king and Haman came to the banquet that Esther had prepared.

1 Heb., *respiration.*

2 Heb., *found.*

3 Heb., *passed.*

---

case the monarch holds a long staff or sceptre in his right hand. How forcibly, after reading this verse, the contrast strikes us between the self-styled *king of kings*, to enter into whose presence even as a suppliant for help and protection was to risk death, and the King of Kings, who has Himself instructed man to say, "Let us go into His tabernacle and fall low on our knees before His footstool."

(14) **Enlargement.**—Literally, *a breathing-space.*

**From another place.**—Although he does not explain his meaning, and, indeed, seems to be speaking with studied reserve, still we may suppose that Mordecai here refers to Divine help, which he asserts will be vouchsafed in this extremity. It does not necessarily follow that we are to see in this declaration a proof of the earnestness of Mordecai's faith; probably had his faith been like that of many of his countrymen he would not have been in Persia at all, but with the struggling band in Judæa.

**Thou and thy father's house shall be destroyed.**—That is, by the hand of God, who having raised thee to this pitch of glory and power will require it from thee, if thou fail in that which it plainly devolves upon thee to do. It is clear there is a good deal of force in these last words of Mordecai. Esther's rise had been so marvellous that one might well see in it the hand of God, and if so there was clearly a very special object in view, which it must be her anxious care to work for. In the whole tone of the conversation, however, there seems a lack of higher and more noble feelings, an absence of any suggestion of turning for aid to God; and thus in return, when God carries out His purpose, and grants deliverance, it seems done indirectly, without the conferring of any special blessing on the human instruments.

V.

(1) **The third day.**—That is, of the fast. (See above, chap. iv. 16.)

**Royal apparel.**—Literally, *royalty.*

(3) **To the half of the kingdom.**—This tremendous offer occurs in further promises of Ahasuerus (chaps. v. 6, vii. 2). The same reckless promise is made by Herod Antipas to the daughter of Herodias (St. Mark vi. 23).

(4) **Let the king and Haman come this day unto the banquet.**—It was natural enough that, with so much depending on her request, the queen should show some hesitation: if anything took an untoward turn (for, in spite of the king's promise, she evidently felt uneasy) it might mean total ruin. She therefore temporises; she at any rate gains time, she secures a specially favourable opportunity for bringing forward the request, and the king clearly sees that she has kept her real petition in reserve, by himself again raising the question. It will be noticed that so long as Esther is working her way up to the due vantage-ground, the king is addressed in the third person, "let the king come," but when she makes the decisive appeal, in the second, "in thy sight, O king."

(6) And the king said unto Esther at the banquet of wine, What *is* thy petition? and it shall be granted thee: and what *is* thy request? even to the half of the kingdom it shall be performed. (7) Then answered Esther, and said, My petition and my request *is*; (8) if I have found favour in the sight of the king, and if it please the king to grant my petition, and ¹to perform my request, let the king and Haman come to the banquet that I shall prepare for them, and I will do to morrow as the king hath said. (9) Then went Haman forth that day joyful and with a glad heart: but when Haman saw Mordecai in the king's gate, that he stood not up, nor moved for him, he was full of indignation against Mordecai. (10) Nevertheless Haman refrained himself: and when he came home, he sent and ²called for his friends, and Zeresh his wife. (11) And Haman told them of the glory of his riches, and the multitude of his children, and all *the things* wherein the king had promoted him, and how he had advanced him above the princes and servants of the king. (12) Haman said moreover, Yea, Esther the queen did let no man come in with the king unto the banquet that she had prepared but myself; and to morrow am I invited unto her also with the king. (13) Yet all this availeth me nothing, so long as I see Mordecai the Jew sitting at the king's gate. (14) Then said Zeresh his wife and all his friends unto him, Let a ³gallows be made of fifty cubits high, and to morrow speak thou unto the king that Mordecai may be hanged thereon: then go thou in merrily with the king unto the banquet. And the thing pleased Haman; and he caused the gallows to be made.

CHAPTER VI.—(1) On that night ⁴could not the king sleep, and he commanded to bring the book of records of the chronicles; and they were read before the king. (2) And it was found written, that Mordecai had told of ⁵Bigthana and Teresh, two of the king's chamberlains, the keepers of the ⁶door, who sought to lay hand on the king Ahasuerus.

(3) And the king said, What honour

¹ Heb., *to do.*
² Heb., *caused to come.*
³ Heb., *tree.*
⁴ Heb., *the king's sleep fled away.*
⁵ Or, *Bigthan,* ch. 2. 21.
⁶ Heb., *threshold.*

---

(6) **The banquet of wine.**—The continuation of the banquet of verse 5: the dessert, so to speak.

(9) **He stood not up.**—In chap. iii. 2 we saw that Mordecai refused to bow or prostrate himself to Haman, here he refuses even the slightest sign of respect. The honourable independence of the former case here becomes indefensible rudeness.

(10) **Zeresh.**—A name probably derived from an old Persian word for "gold." According to the Targum she was the daughter of Tatnai, "the governour on this side the river," *i.e.,* of that part of the Persian Empire which lay beyond the Euphrates (Ezra v. 3).

(11) **Told them . . .**—As all this was of necessity sufficiently well known to his hearers, this was simply a piece of vain-glorious boasting, the pride that "goeth before destruction."

**The multitude of his children.**—He had ten sons (chap. ix. 10).

(13) **Availeth me nothing.**—Better, *suiteth, contenteth me not.*

(14) **Gallows.**—Literally, *tree;* the Hebrew word, as well as the corresponding Greek word used by the LXX., standing both for the living tree and the artificial structure. Doubtless the punishment intended for Mordecai was crucifixion, for hanging, in the common sense of the term, does not seem to have been in use among the Persians. The same Hebrew word occurring above (chap. ii. 23) is rendered *tree.* The Greek word employed is the same as that used in the New Testament for our Saviour's cross (Acts v. 30, x. 39, &c.). The Latin Vulgate here actually renders the word on its last occurrence by *crucem.*

**Fifty cubits high.**—That is, about seventy-five feet; the great height being to call as much attention as possible to the execution, that thereby Haman's glory might be proportionately increased.

VI.

(1) **Could not the king sleep.**—Literally, *the king's sleep fled away.* Here, in the most striking way in the whole book, the workings of God's providence on behalf of His people are shown. "God Himself is here, though His name be absent." The king's sleepless night falls after the day when Haman has resolved to ask on the morrow for Mordecai's execution, a foretaste of the richer vengeance he hopes to wreak on the whole nation of the Jews. It is by a mere chance, one would say, looking at the matter simply in its human aspect, that the king should call for the book of the royal chronicles, and not for music. It was by a mere chance too, it might seem, that the reader should happen to light upon the record of Mordecai's services; and yet when all these apparent accidents are wrought up into the coincidence they make, how completely is the providence visible, the power that will use men as the instruments of its work, whether they know it, or know it not, whether they be willing or unwilling, whether the glory of God is to be manifested in and by and through them, or manifested on them only.

**They were read before the king.**—Canon Rawlinson remarks that there is reason to think that the Persian kings were in most cases unable to read.

(2) **It was found written.**—See chap. ii. 21—23.

(3) **What honour and dignity hath been done.**—The names of those who were thought worthy of being accounted "royal benefactors" were enrolled on a special list, and they were supposed to be suitably rewarded, though not necessarily at the time. The reward

and dignity hath been done to Mordecai for this? Then said the king's servants that ministered unto him, There is nothing done for him. (4) And the king said, Who *is* in the court? Now Haman was come into the outward court of the king's house, to speak unto the king to hang Mordecai on the gallows that he had prepared for him. (5) And the king's servants said unto him, Behold, Haman standeth in the court. And the king said, Let him come in.

(6) So Haman came in. And the king said unto him, What shall be done unto the man [1] whom the king delighteth to honour? Now Haman thought in his heart, To whom would the king delight to do honour more than to myself? (7) And Haman answered the king, For the man [2] whom the king delighteth to honour, (8) [3] let the royal apparel be brought [4] which the king *useth* to wear, and the horse that the king rideth upon, and the crown royal which is set upon his head: (9) and let this apparel and horse be delivered to the hand of one of the king's most noble princes, that they may array the man *withal* whom the king delighteth to honour, and [5] bring him on horseback through the street of the city, and proclaim before him, Thus shall it be done to the man whom the king delighteth to honour.

(10) Then the king said to Haman, Make haste, *and* take the apparel and the horse, as thou hast said, and do even so to Mordecai the Jew, that sitteth at the king's gate: [6] let nothing fail of all that thou hast spoken. (11) Then took Haman the apparel and the horse, and arrayed Mordecai, and brought him on horseback through the street of the city, and proclaimed before him, Thus shall it be done unto the man whom the king delighteth to honour.

(12) And Mordecai came again to the king's gate. But Haman hasted to his house mourning, and having his head covered. (13) And Haman told Zeresh his wife and all his friends every *thing*

[1] Heb., *in whose honour the king delighteth?*

[2] Heb., *in whose honour the king delighteth.*

[3] Heb., *let them bring the royal apparel.*

[4] Heb., *wherewith the king clotheth himself.*

[5] Heb., *cause him to ride.*

[6] Heb., *suffer not a whit to fall.*

---

however was, in theory at any rate, a thing to which the "benefactor" had a distinct claim, and an almost legal right.

(4) **Haman was come.**—It being at length morning, Haman had come to the palace in due course, and was waiting in the outer court till the king should call for him. The king in the inner court ponders what recompense to bestow upon Mordecai, Haman in the outer court stands ready primed with a request that he may be hanged.

(6) **Whom the king delighteth . . .**—Literally, *in whose honour the king delighteth.*

(8) **Let the royal apparel be brought . . .**—These exceedingly great distinctions Haman suggests, thinking with unaccountable vanity (for nothing is said or implied as to any service rendered by him to the king) that the king must necessarily have been referring to him, and in a moment he is irretrievably committed. Whether Haman's character had at its best estate much discretion, or whether he rose to his high position, not by the qualities that should commend a statesman to a king, but, like many another Eastern Vizier, had by flattery and base arts gained the royal favour, we cannot say; here he shows the lack of the most ordinary discretion, his vanity is so inordinate that he cannot see the possibility of any one's merits save his own. The request which Haman made may be illustrated by the permission granted by Xerxes to his uncle Artabanus to put on the royal robes and sleep in the royal bed at Susa (Herod. vii. 15—17).

**The horse that the king rideth upon.**—Thus Pharaoh, desiring to honour Joseph, made him ride in his own chariot (Gen. xli. 43): David, wishing to show that Solomon had really become king in his father's lifetime, commands that he should ride on the king's mule (1 Kings i. 33, 44).

**And the crown royal which is set upon his head.**—If we take the Hebrew here quite literally, the meaning must be *and on whose* (i.e., the horse's) *head a royal crown is set.* The only objection to this view is, that there appears to be no evidence of such a custom among the Persians. Some render, *and that a* (or *the: the Hebrew is necessarily ambiguous in such a case*) *royal crown be set,* but this we consider does violence to the Hebrew. It must be noted that both the king in his reply, and the writer in describing what actually took place, make no mention of a crown as worn by Mordecai, nor does Haman in the following verse.

(9) **Noble.**—See above, chap. i. 3, Note.

**Street.**—See above, chap. iv. 6, Note.

(10) **The Jew.**—Mordecai's nationality would doubtless be given in the book of records. Thus Esther, in urging her petition by-and-by, has already on her side the king's good-will to one prominent member of the proscribed race.

(11) **Then took Haman . . .**—It would be a grim and curious study to analyse Haman's feelings at this juncture. Various thoughts were mingled there. Self-reproach, perhaps, that he had so thoughtlessly been the cause of the present display, bitter hatred of his rival now multiplied a thousandfold, and the evident knowledge that the game was played out, and that he was ruined. The more subtle the brain, the more truly must he have known this.

(12) **Mordecai came again to the king's gate.**—He had received his reward, and to the Eastern, who sees continually the Vizier and the poor man exchange places, there would be nothing startling in this resumption of the former humble post.

**His head covered.**—In token of mourning.

(13) **Told.**—The same word as on a former occasion, chap. v. 11. Then the tale was one of boastful pride in what he had, and no less boastful pride in what he hoped to be; now it is of bitter disappointment and bitter anticipation, not brightened by any of the thoughts which blunt the keenness of many a sorrow,

that had befallen him. Then said his wise men and Zeresh his wife unto him, If Mordecai *be* of the seed of the Jews, before whom thou hast begun to fall, thou shalt not prevail against him, but shalt surely fall before him. ⁽¹⁴⁾ And while they *were* yet talking with him, came the king's chamberlains, and hasted to bring Haman unto the banquet that Esther had prepared.

CHAPTER VII.—⁽¹⁾ So the king and Haman came ¹ to banquet with Esther the queen. ⁽²⁾ And the king said again unto Esther on the second day at the banquet of wine, What *is* thy petition, queen Esther? and it shall be granted thee: and what *is* thy request? and it shall be performed, *even* to the half of the kingdom. ⁽³⁾ Then Esther the queen answered and said, If I have found favour in thy sight, O king, and if it please the king, let my life be given me at my petition, and my people at my request: ⁽⁴⁾ for we are sold, I and my people, ² to be destroyed, to be slain, and to perish. But if we had been sold for bondmen and bondwomen, I had held my tongue, although the enemy could not countervail the king's damage. ⁽⁵⁾ Then the king Ahasuerus answered and said unto Esther the queen, Who is he, and where is he, ³ that durst presume in his heart to do so? ⁽⁶⁾ And Esther said, ⁴The adversary and enemy *is* this wicked Haman. Then Haman was afraid ⁵before the king and the queen.

⁽⁷⁾ And the king arising from the banquet of wine in his wrath *went* into the palace garden: and Haman stood up to make request for his life to Esther the queen; for he saw that there was evil determined against him by the king. ⁽⁸⁾ Then the king returned out of the palace garden into the place of the banquet of wine; and Haman was fallen upon the bed whereon Esther *was*. Then said the king, Will he force the queen also ⁶before me in the house? As the word went out of the king's mouth, they

1 Heb., *to drink.*
2 Heb., *that they should destroy, and kill, and cause to perish.*
3 Heb., *whose heart hath filled him.*
4 Heb., *The man adversary.*
5 Or, *at the presence of.*
6 Heb., *with me.*

---

as when men have nobly done their duty, though it is not God's will that their efforts should succeed for the time, and when the hope could be cherished that a brighter time must dawn before long. Nothing of this comfort could be Haman's. He had not failed in an honest discharge of his duty, but in a cruel and unjust scheme (not that the king can be called a whit better in this matter); he knew the usages of his country far too well to suppose for a moment that, after having made such an attempt, and having failed, he would be allowed to try a second time.

**If Mordecai . . . before whom thou hast begun . . .**—Poor comfort does the unfortunate schemer get from his household; he knew too well already that he had *begun* to fall, his heart must have told him all too truly that it was but the beginning: what then could he expect from this communication to his family? Had he been the representative of a fallen cause, fallen but not discredited, despairing even of his cause, yet not ashamed of the course that had resulted thus, he might have been helped with counsel and cheering and sympathy. Contrast Zeresh's perhaps last words to her husband with those, for example, of the wife of good John Rogers, or of Rowland Taylor, on their way to the stake, in the days of the Marian persecution.

### VII.

⁽²⁾ **What is thy petition?**—The king takes for granted that Esther's invitations to her banquets do not constitute her real request, but merely prepare the way for it.

⁽⁴⁾ **We are sold.**—See above, chap. iii. 9.

**To be destroyed . . . .**—Literally, *to destroy and to kill, and to cause to perish.* The identical words used in the king's proclamation for the destruction of the Jews. Herein Esther at once makes confession of her nationality, and relying on the king's still recent gratitude to one of the race, aided by his present cordiality to herself, she risks, as indeed she can no longer help doing, the fate of herself and her race on the momentary impulse of her fickle lord. Happily for her, God has willed that these, perhaps at any other time untrustworthy grounds of reliance, shall suffice. The "hearts of kings are in His rule and governance," and now the heart of one is "disposed and turned, as it seemeth best to His godly wisdom."

**Although the enemy . . . .**—The meaning of this clause is not quite clear. The literal translation is, *although* (or *because*) *the enemy is not equal to* (i.e., does not make up for) *the king's hurt.* This may mean (*a*) that Haman, *though* willing to pay a large sum into the royal treasury, cannot thereby make up for the loss which the king must incur by wholesale massacre being carried on in his realm; or (*b*) "were we merely to be sold into slavery, instead of being killed outright, I should have said nothing, because the enemy was not one worth the king's while to trouble himself about." We prefer the former view. The word "enemy" is that translated *adversary*, in verse 6, and properly means one who oppresses, afflicts, distresses. The word which is, literally, *equal to, comparable with*, has already occurred in chaps. iii. 8, v. 13.

⁽⁶⁾ **Was afraid . . . .**—Shrank back in terror before . . . See the use of the word in 1 Chron. xxi. 30; Dan. viii. 17.

⁽⁷⁾ **Evil.**—Heb., *the evil, the doom.*

⁽⁸⁾ **The bed**—*i.e.*, the couch on which she had been reclining at the banquet. This was the customary posture at meals, not only of the Persians, but also of the Greeks and Romans, and of the later Jews. The Last Supper was thus eaten. Haman had obviously thrown himself at the queen's feet to ask for mercy. The king on his return was evidently full of wrath against Haman, and though he was for the time God's instrument in averting Haman's wicked design, his own

covered Haman's face. (9) And Harbonah, one of the chamberlains, said before the king, Behold also, the ¹gallows fifty cubits high, which Haman had made for Mordecai, who had spoken good for the king, standeth in the house of Haman. Then the king said, Hang him thereon. (10) So they hanged Haman on the gallows that he had prepared for Mordecai. Then was the king's wrath pacified.

CHAPTER VIII.—(1) On that day did the king Ahasuerus give the house of Haman the Jews' enemy unto Esther the queen. And Mordecai came before the king; for Esther had told what he was unto her. (2) And the king took off his ring, which he had taken from Haman, and gave it unto Mordecai. And Esther set Mordecai over the house of Haman.

(3) And Esther spake yet again before the king, and fell down at his feet, ²and besought him with tears to put away the mischief of Haman the Agagite, and his device that he had devised against the Jews. (4) Then the king held out the golden sceptre toward Esther. So Esther arose, and stood before the king, (5) and said, If it please the king, and if I have found favour in his sight, and the thing *seem* right before the king, and I *be* pleasing in his eyes, let it be written to reverse ³the letters devised by Haman the son of Hammedatha the Agagite, ⁴which he wrote to destroy the Jews which *are* in all the king's provinces: (6) for how can I ⁵endure to see the evil that shall come unto my people? or how can I endure to see the destruction of my kindred?

(7) Then the king Ahasuerus said unto Esther the queen and to Mordecai the Jew, Behold, I have given Esther the house of Haman, and him they have hanged upon the gallows, because he laid his hand upon the Jews.

1 Heb., *tree*.
2 Heb., *and she wept and besought him*.
3 Heb., *the device*.
4 Or, *who wrote*.
5 Heb., *be able that I may see*.

---

base and worthless character is none the less conspicuous. The attempted massacre had been authorised with the full knowledge and consent of the king, who yet ignores utterly his own share of the responsibility. Great and noble ends are at times brought about by the instrumentality of unholy men, blind instruments in a purpose whose end they understand not. What greater blessing, for example, did God vouchsafe to England than the Reformation, whose foremost agent was a bloody and unholy king?

**Will he force** . . . .—Ahasuerus must have known perfectly well that Haman's position was that of a suppliant; his words do but indicate his utter anger, as the attendants clearly perceive, for they immediately covered Haman's face—he must not see the king's face again. (See above, chap. i. 13.)

(9) **Harbonah.**—See chap. i. 10.

**One of the chamberlains** . . . .—Translate, *one of the chamberlains* [*who stood, or served*] *before the king, said.*

**Hang him.**—In the LXX., *let him be crucified*. The climax of the story is now reached in the pithy words, "They hanged Haman upon the gallows that he had prepared for Mordecai." In his own house (verse 9), that is, probably, in some court or garden belonging to it, in the sight doubtless of his own children and his own servants, and the wife who had given him such cold comfort, did the unfortunate man meet his fate. Thus not only does God vouchsafe to deliver his people, but He brings on the enemy the very destruction he had devised for his adversary: "He hath fallen himself into the pit that he digged for other." Our Saviour has rescued us from our enemy who was too mighty for us, and has trodden down our foe, to be destroyed for ever in His own good time. So may we Christians see in the dangers threatening the Jews throughout this book a picture of our own, and in Haman's discomfiture a type of the victory of the Lamb over sin and Satan.

VIII.

(1) **Did . . . give the house of Haman.**—Confiscation of goods necessarily followed on a sentence of death in the East. So, with ourselves, a convicted felon's property is forfeited to the Crown.

(2) **Took off his ring . . . and gave it unto Mordecai.**—Constituting him thereby his Vizier, who would thus authenticate a royal decree, and by having, as it were, *carte blanche* given him for the time, would for that time save his master all further trouble. Mordecai's position had now become what Daniel's had been to Darius, that nobler servant to a worthier lord (see Dan. vi. 2, 38). He was the queen's cousin, and he had on one occasion been the means of saving the king's life, and therefore starts under distinctly favourable auspices.

(3) **Besought him . . . to put away the mischief.**—Esther's work was as yet only half done. She has seen the condemnation of the foe of her race, and the exaltation of her kinsman to his office. But the royal edict sent out against the Jews still remains valid, and being a written decree, sealed with the king's seal, is supposed to be beyond the possibility of alteration. It was not, therefore, a case where Mordecai's newly-acquired dignity would authorise him to interfere, and therefore Esther, who, now that the ice is once broken, becomes more courageous, makes a fresh appeal to the king to do what theoretically was beyond the king's power.

(4) **The king held out the golden sceptre.** —See Note on chap. iv. 11.

(5) **To reverse.**—Rather, *to bring back, to recall*. Esther shows considerable skill in wording her request. She avoids speaking of the *king's* letters, but calls them "the letters, the device of *Haman*, which *he* wrote." It is the king, however, to whom the injury is done— "to destroy the Jews which are in all the king's provinces."

*The Reversal of the Decree*     ESTHER, VIII.     *for the Massacre of the Jews.*

(8) Write ye also for the Jews, as it liketh you, in the king's name, and seal *it* with the king's ring: for the writing which is written in the king's name, and sealed with the king's ring, *a* may no man reverse.

(9) Then were the king's scribes called at that time in the third month, that *is*, the month Sivan, on the three and twentieth *day* thereof; and it was written according to all that Mordecai commanded unto the Jews, and to the lieutenants, and the deputies and rulers of the provinces which *are* from India unto Ethiopia, an hundred twenty and seven provinces, unto every province according to the writing thereof, and unto every people after their language, and to the Jews according to their writing, and according to their language. (10) And he wrote in the king Ahasuerus' name, and sealed *it* with the king's ring, and sent letters by posts on horseback, *and* riders on mules, camels, *and* young dromedaries: (11) wherein the king granted the Jews which *were* in every city to gather themselves together, and to stand for their life, to destroy, to slay, and to cause to perish, all the power of the people and province that would assault them, *both* little ones and women, and *to take* the spoil of them for a prey, (12) upon one day in all the provinces of king Ahasuerus, *namely*, upon the thirteenth *day* of the twelfth month, which *is* the month Adar. (13) The copy of the writing for a commandment to be given in every province *was* ¹published unto all people, and that the Jews should be ready against that day to avenge themselves on their enemies. (14) *So* the posts that rode upon mules *and* camels went out, being hastened and pressed on by the king's commandment. And the decree was given at Shushan the palace.

(15) And Mordecai went out from the presence of the king in royal apparel of ²blue and white, and with a great crown of gold, and with a garment of fine linen and purple: and the city of Shushan rejoiced and was glad. (16) The Jews had light, and gladness, and joy, and honour. (17) And in every province, and in every city, whithersoever the king's commandment and his decree came, the

*a* See ch. 1. 19.

¹ Heb., *revealed.*

² Or, *violet.*

---

(8) **Write ye . . . .**—Esther's device is seen through, and the king shrinks from taking so decisive a step as the revocation of a decree once issued. Such a writing "may no man reverse." Still he will do what he can. It may be possible to meet the difficulty, and save the Jews, without actual reversal of the decree. The king then refers to the proofs of his goodwill, as shown by hanging Haman for his scheme against the Jews, and giving his property to Esther, and bids Esther and Mordecai " write concerning the Jews according to what seems good in your eyes." Give, that is, any orders you please about them, short of repealing the former order. The result of this permission, whether the idea was suggested by the king, or occurred to Esther or Mordecai, was that authority was given to the Jews to defend themselves.

(9) **The month Sivan.**—This name also occurs in Baruch i. 8. Sivan began with the new moon in May. Rather more than two months had thus passed since the first edict had been sent out.

**Lieutenants.**—Satraps. (See Note on chap. iii. 12.)

(10) **Posts.**—*The* posts. Literally, *the runners.* (See Note on chap. i. 22.)

**Riders on mules.**—Rather, *on horses of great speed;* the "swift beast" of Micah i. 13.

**Camels, and young dromedaries.**—The words thus translated occur only here, and there is much doubt as to the meaning. It may suffice to mention two renderings :—(1) " Mules, the offspring of royal mares "—so Gesenius; or (2) we may connect the former word with the Persian word meaning *royal*—so Canon Rawlinson, who translates the whole clause, "riders upon coursers of the king's stud, offspring of high-bred steeds."

(11) **To stand for their life.**—It will be noticed that, so far at any rate as the edict authorises, the Jews are not permitted to take the initiative, but merely to stand on the defensive. As it was, it was risking civil war in all the cities of the empire, though the results were considerably lessened by numbers of people taking the hint obviously presented by the second edict. " Many of the people of the land became Jews, for the fear of the Jews came upon them."

**Take the spoil of them.**—We find that when the storm actually came the Jews declined to take advantage of this part of the edict.

(13) **To avenge themselves on their enemies.** —The Hebrew word used here " does not necessarily signify a violent emotion of a resentful spirit, but a steady resolve to defend the right; it is used of the Almighty Himself, rescuing the oppressed, defending the right, and punishing the assailant and the oppressor " (Wordsworth).

(14) **Mules and camels.**—See above on verse 10.

**Being hastened.**—Why this haste, seeing there yet remained nearly nine months (wanting ten days) before the first edict would come into play? There may probably have been fears lest the first edict, which indicated a distinct animus of the Court against the Jews, might have been interpreted freely, according to the spirit of it, and the date anticipated by eager partisans.

(15) **Blue and white.**—See Note on chap. i. 6.

**Crown.**—This is a different word from that previously used of a "royal crown" (chap. vi. 8).

**Garment.**—The inner robe or tunic. That of the king was of purple striped with white.

Jews had joy and gladness, a feast and a good day. And many of the people of the land became Jews; for the fear of the Jews fell upon them.

CHAPTER IX.— (1) Now in the twelfth month, that is, the month Adar, on the thirteenth day of the same, when the king's commandment and his decree drew near to be put in execution, in the day that the enemies of the Jews hoped to have power over them, (though it was turned to the contrary, that the Jews had rule over them that hated them;) (2) the Jews gathered themselves together in their cities throughout all the provinces of the king Ahasuerus, to lay hand on such as sought their hurt: and no man could withstand them; for the fear of them fell upon all people. (3) And all the rulers of the provinces, and the lieutenants, and the deputies, and [1] officers of the king, helped the Jews; because the fear of Mordecai fell upon them. (4) For Mordecai was great in the king's house, and his fame went out throughout all the provinces: for this man Mordecai waxed greater and greater.

(5) Thus the Jews smote all their enemies with the stroke of the sword, and slaughter, and destruction, and did [2] what they would unto those that hated them. (6) And in Shushan the palace the Jews slew and destroyed five hundred men. (7) And Parshandatha, and Dalphon, and Aspatha, (8) and Poratha, and Adalia, and Aridatha, (9) and Parmashta, and Arisai, and Aridai, and Vajezatha, (10) the ten sons of Haman the son of Hammedatha, the enemy of the Jews, slew they; but on the spoil laid they not their hand.

(11) On that day the number of those that were slain in Shushan the palace [3] was brought before the king. (12) And the king said unto Esther the queen, The Jews have slain and destroyed five hundred men in Shushan the palace, and the ten sons of Haman; what have they done in the rest of the king's provinces? now what is thy petition? and it shall be granted thee: or what is thy request further? and it shall be done. (13) Then said Esther, If it please the king, let it be granted to the Jews which are in Shushan to do to morrow also according unto this day's decree, and [4] let Haman's ten sons be hanged upon the gallows. (14) And the king commanded it so to be done: and the decree was given at Shushan; and they hanged

[1] Heb., those which did the business that belonged to the king.
[2] Heb., according to their will.
[3] Heb., came.
[4] Heb., let men hang.

B.C. cir. 509.

---

**Linen.**—White linen.

**The city of Shushan rejoiced.**—The tide of royal favour had changed, and the people of Shushan were evidently not very different from the mass of the populace of the present day, who shout with the winning side. Nothing succeeds like success, and the *mobile vulgus* of Susa cheered Mordecai as doubtless they would have hooted had they seen him led to execution. The crowds who welcomed our Lord into Jerusalem on His triumphal entry soon let their enthusiasm die away—"Hosanna!" now; to-morrow, "Crucify!"

(17) **Became Jews.**—That is, embraced their religion as proselytes.

IX.

(1) **Drew near.**—Arrived, came, as in chap. viii. 17.

(2) **To lay hand on such as sought their hurt.**—How far the Jews acted according to the strict letter of the edict, and "stood for their lives" only when attacked, is perhaps to be doubted. They had on their side all the executive of the empire (verse 3), and evidently to all intents and purposes the second edict was considered virtually to repeal the first. The Jews, therefore, being in favour at Court, and, as was not unnatural after their alarm, being now full of indignation and vengeance, were probably resolved to use their opportunities while they had the chance. If so, who could object so long as they did nothing against the authorities? and they, we have seen, were on their side.

That they did make a bloody use of their opportunity is shown clearly by verse 16.

(3) **Helped.**—Literally, *lifted up*. The same Hebrew verb is rendered *furthered* (Ezra viii. 36).

(6) **The palace.**—Doubtless the whole royal city, rather than the palace strictly so called. It is obvious that even Xerxes would hardly have allowed bloodshed, otherwise than by his direct orders, within the precincts of the palace.

(7—9) The names of the ten sons of Haman are, except Adalia, all readily traceable to old Persian roots. It may be noted that in a Hebrew Bible the ten names are written vertically, one under the other, in a column; and the Targum or Chaldee paraphrase says that the ten sons were hanged one above the other at fixed distances.

(10) **On the spoil laid they not their hand.**—This they might have done, according to the edict (chap. viii. 11).

(13) **Then said Esther . . .**—In the terse words of the heading, "Ahasuerus, at the request of Esther, granteth another day of slaughter, and Haman's sons to be hanged." It seems impossible here to acquit Esther of simple blood-thirstiness. Before the slaughter of the 13th of Adar was actually over, it is obvious that the Jews were no longer in any danger. It was known that the sympathies of the Court were entirely with the Jews, and the officers of the king consequently took their part. After one day's slaughter, in which in the capital alone 500 men were killed,

Haman's ten sons. ⁽¹⁵⁾ For the Jews that *were* in Shushan gathered themselves together on the fourteenth day also of the month Adar, and slew three hundred men at Shushan; but on the prey they laid not their hand.

⁽¹⁶⁾ But the other Jews that *were* in the king's provinces gathered themselves together, and stood for their lives, and had rest from their enemies, and slew of their foes seventy and five thousand, but they laid not their hands on the prey, ⁽¹⁷⁾ on the thirteenth day of the month Adar; and on the fourteenth day ¹of the same rested they, and made it a day of feasting and gladness. ⁽¹⁸⁾ But the Jews that *were* at Shushan assembled together on the thirteenth *day* thereof, and on the fourteenth thereof; and on the fifteenth *day* of the same they rested, and made it a day of feasting and gladness. ⁽¹⁹⁾ Therefore the Jews of the villages, that dwelt in the unwalled towns, made the fourteenth day of the month Adar, *a day of* gladness and feasting, and a good day, and of sending portions one to another.

⁽²⁰⁾ And Mordecai wrote these things, and sent letters unto all the Jews that *were* in all the provinces of the king Ahasuerus, *both* nigh and far. ⁽²¹⁾ To stablish *this* among them, that they should keep the fourteenth day of the month Adar, and the fifteenth day of the same, yearly, ⁽²²⁾ as the days wherein the Jews rested from their enemies, and the month which was turned unto them from sorrow to joy, and from mourning into a good day: that they should make them days of feasting and joy, and of sending portions one to another, and gifts to the poor. ⁽²³⁾ And the Jews undertook to do as they had begun, and as Mordecai had written unto them; ⁽²⁴⁾ because Haman the son of Hammedatha, the Agagite, the enemy of all the Jews, had devised against the Jews to destroy them, and had cast Pur, that *is*, the lot, to ²consume them, and to destroy them; ⁽²⁵⁾ but ³when *Esther* came before the king, he commanded by letters that his wicked device, which he devised against the Jews, should return upon his own head, and that he and his sons should be hanged on the gallows. ⁽²⁶⁾ Wherefore they called these days Purim after the name of ⁴Pur. Therefore for all the words of this letter, and *of that* which they had seen concerning this

1 Heb., *in it*.
2 Heb., *crush*.
B.C. 509.
B.C. cir. 509.
3 Heb., *when she came*.
4 That is, *Lot*.

---

we may be quite certain that the Jews were masters of the situation, and therefore we do not hesitate to call Esther's fresh action needless butchery. Were anything needed to bring out the matter in its true light, it might be seen in the request that the sons of Haman might be hanged. They had already been killed (verse 10), doubtless among the first, and Esther, therefore, asks for the dead bodies to be crucified, a gratuitous outrage on the dead. Because Esther was a person whom God made use of as an agent for a great purpose, we are not called upon to tone down and explain away the black spots in her history. To suggest that Esther had reason to fear "a renewal of the attacks of the enemies of the Jews" is out of the question, when the Jews had their feet on their necks. We must not, on the other hand, judge Esther according to the high Christian standard. It is true that the Old Testament taught "vengeance is Mine," but it needed the teaching of the New Testament to bring that truth home to men.

(15) **For the Jews . . .** —Translate, *And the Jews.*
(16) **Seventy and five thousand.**—The number as given in the LXX. is fifteen thousand, perhaps a more probable number. On the whole history, Bishop Wordsworth well remarks, "It shows the recklessness of human life, even of their own subjects, which then prevailed among the sovereigns of the most celebrated nations of the Eastern world; and it displays the ruinous consequences which would have resulted to human civilisation if Ahasuerus (Xerxes) had been victorious at Salamis. If Greece had not triumphed in that struggle with Asia, Oriental ruthlessness and Oriental polygamy might have become dominant in the West, and greater difficulties would have obstructed the progress of civilisation and Christianity. The Book of Esther reveals to us that the hand of God wrought for the deliverance of mankind at the Straits of Salamis, and on the banks of the Asopus at Platæa, as well as for the preservation of the Jews in the provinces of Persia."

(18) **On the fifteenth day . . . they rested.**—Both the fourteenth and fifteenth days are now kept as the festival of Purim, the former day being the chief.
(19) **The Jews of the villages . . . the unwalled towns.**—Virtually the same Hebrew word is used in both these cases (*perazim, perazoth*). The meaning is that of country towns, undefended by bulwarks, or, at any rate, not in the sense in which the capital would be. We find the word used in contrast with "fenced cities" in Deut. iii. 5.
(21) **And the fifteenth day of the same.**—The Jews in the provinces had already made the fourteenth day a day of gladness and feasting. Mordecai now bids that the fifteenth also be so kept.
(24) **Pur.**—See above on chap. iii. 7.
(25) **Esther.**—It will be seen that in the English Version this word is printed in italics. The Hebrew is literally, *and on her* (or *its*) *coming*. To make the pronoun refer to Esther seems harsh, seeing that she has not been mentioned for some time, and we therefore prefer to make it impersonal, "when *it* (*i.e.,* the matter) came."
(26) **Purim.**—As we have already stated, the festival of Purim is still observed by the Jews, on the 14th and 15th of Adar, the day preceding being kept as a fast. At Purim, the whole Book of Esther is read

matter, and which had come unto them, (27) the Jews ordained, and took upon them, and upon their seed, and upon all such as joined themselves unto them, so as it should not ¹fail, that they would keep these two days according to their writing, and according to their *appointed* time every year; (28) and *that* these days *should be* remembered and kept throughout every generation, every family, every province, and every city; and *that* these days of Purim should not ²fail from among the Jews, nor the memorial of them ³perish from their seed.

(29) Then Esther the queen, the daughter of Abihail, and Mordecai the Jew, wrote with ⁴all authority, to confirm this second letter of Purim. (30) And he sent the letters unto all the Jews, to the hundred twenty and seven provinces of the kingdom of Ahasuerus, *with* words of peace and truth, (31) to confirm these days of Purim in their times *appointed*, according as Mordecai the Jew and Esther the queen had enjoined them, and as they had decreed ⁵for themselves and for their seed, the matters of the fastings and their cry. (32) And the decree of Esther confirmed these matters of Purim; and it was written in the book.

CHAPTER X. — (1) And the king Ahasuerus laid a tribute upon the land, and *upon* the isles of the sea. (2) And all the acts of his power and of his might, and the declaration of the greatness of Mordecai, whereunto the king ⁶advanced him, *are* they not written in the book of the chronicles of the kings of Media and Persia? (3) For Mordecai the Jew *was* next unto king Ahasuerus, and great among the Jews, and accepted of the multitude of his brethren, seeking the wealth of his people, and speaking peace to all his seed.

1 Heb., *pass*.
2 Heb., *pass*.
3 Heb., *be ended*.
B.C. cir. 495.
4 Heb., *all strength*
5 Heb., *for their souls*.
6 Heb., *made him great*.

---

through in the service in the synagogues, a custom that can be traced back at any rate to the Christian era (2 Macc. xv. 36; Josephus, *Ant.* xi. 6. 13; Mishna, *Rosh ha-Shanah*, iii. 7).

(29) **This second letter.**—It seems to us that the first letter must be that extracted from the king by Esther (chap. viii. 8), and consequently this "second letter" is Mordecai's (chap. ix. 20), which is now confirmed in a more authoritative way.

(30) **The letters.**—Omit the article.

(31) **To confirm . . . enjoined . . . decreed.**—The same Hebrew verb stands for the three different English verbs; it is also the *stablish* of verse 21. To *fix* or *settle* represents the meaning.

**The matters of the fastings and their cry.**—These words come in rather awkwardly, and hence, and because they are passed over by the LXX., some have doubted their genuineness here. All Hebrew MSS., however, and all the other ancient versions, retain the words, and we must, therefore, suppose that the Jews throughout the empire had instituted fasts and lamentations, in addition to what Mordecai's letter had enjoined. Thus we may probably connect this with the fast now observed on Adar 13.

(32) **In the book.**—It is doubtful what "the book" here means. The Vulgate explains it of the Book of Esther itself, and so many modern scholars. Still "the book" hardly seems a natural Hebrew way of referring to a work on the part of its author as he writes it, and no similar case is adducible. Others think it must have been a book written at the time on the subject of the festival, which is, perhaps, possible. Canon Rawlinson identifies it with "the Book of the Chronicles of the Kings of Media and Persia," because such is the use of the word *book* elsewhere in Esther.

X.

(1) **Laid a tribute.**—The disastrous expedition to Greece must have taxed the resources of the empire to the utmost, and fresh tribute would therefore be requisite to fill the exhausted coffers. Besides this, a harassing war was still going on, even ten years after the battle of Salamis, on the coast of Asia Minor, and this would require fresh supplies.

**The isles of the sea.**—The chief island yet remaining to the Persian Empire was Cyprus. Those in the Ægean Sea were now free from Persian rule, but possibly, even after the loss, the old phrase may have been retained; just as in modern times we have Kings of "England, *France*, and Ireland," and of "the two Sicilies, and *Jerusalem*," &c.

(2) **Power.**—The same word as that translated *authority* in chap. ix. 29.

(3) **Mordecai the Jew was next unto king Ahasuerus.**—We have seen that the events recorded in this book carry us to the year 470 B.C., at which time Mordecai was at the zenith of his greatness. How long he kept it, whether death or disgrace brought it to a close, and if the latter, from what cause, we cannot say. All we know is, that near the end of Xerxes' reign his favourite and chief adviser was Artabanus, the captain of the guard, by whom he was murdered in B.C. 464. The last we hear of Mordecai, whatever was his after-fate, is that he was loyal to his people, and approved himself their benefactor, "seeking the wealth (*i.e.*, weal—literally, *good*), and speaking peace to all his seed," all of the stock of Israel.

www.ingramcontent.com/pod-product-compliance
Lightning Source LLC
Chambersburg PA
CBHW081143290426
44108CB00018B/2424